A HISTC

A HISTORY OF MILITARY THOUGHT

from the Enlightenment to the Cold War

AZAR GAT

UNIVERSITY PRESS

OXFORD
UNIVERSITY PRESS

Great Clarendon Street, Oxford OX2 6DP

Oxford University Press is a department of the University of Oxford.
It furthers the University's objective of excellence in research, scholarship,
and education by publishing worldwide in

Oxford New York

Auckland Cape Town Dar es Salaam Hong Kong Karachi
Kuala Lumpur Madrid Melbourne Mexico City Nairobi
New Delhi Shanghai Taipei Toronto

With offices in

Argentina Austria Brazil Chile Czech Republic France Greece
Guatemala Hungary Italy Japan South Korea Poland Portugal
Singapore Switzerland Thailand Turkey Ukraine Vietnam

Oxford is a registered trade mark of Oxford University Press
in the UK and in certain other countries

Published in the United States
by Oxford University Press Inc., New York

First published 2001

British Library Cataloguing in Publication Data
Data available

Library of Congress Cataloging in Publication Data
Data available

ISBN 978-0-19-924762-2

9 10

Typeset by Hope Services (Abingdon) Ltd
Printed in Great Britain
on acid-free paper by the
MPG Books Group, Bodmin and King's Lynn

To Ruthie

PREFACE

This book brings together in one volume my trilogy on the evolution of modern military thought (OUP 1989, 1992, 1998) set against its broader historical and intellectual background. It offers a panoramic but clearly-focused view of the wider conceptions of war, strategy, and military theory which have dominated Europe and the West from the eighteenth century to our 'post-modern' era.

Book I, From the Enlightenment to Clausewitz, traces the origins of the quest for a general theory of war to its origins in the cultural frameworks and historical and philosophical outlooks of the Enlightenment, on the one hand, and the movement which may best be described as the Counter-Enlightenment, the German Movement, or Romanticism, on the other. Broadly defined, these currents represent the two conflicting positions towards the study of man and human institutions which emerged in the wake of the scientific revolution of the seventeenth century. One of these looked to the exact and natural sciences as a model to be adopted and applied; the other, by contrast, maintained that the humanities were different in nature from the sciences and could never be studied by the same methods. On the whole, scholars have failed to grasp this culture-bound nature of military theory. Consequently, the origins, vision, and scope of eighteenth-century military thought in the context of the Enlightenment have not been recognized, nor has the background of Clausewitz's harsh polemics towards it, in the context of the general European reaction against the Enlightenment. Furthermore, the exact meaning of Clausewitz's own ideas has continuously baffled scholars, and the book sets out to resolve these endemic difficulties of interpretation, clearly explaining Clausewitz's development and what he meant to say.

Book II, The Nineteenth Century, traces the development of military thought from the aftermath of the Napoleonic era to the First World War. Among other themes, it lays out the strategic ideas of the Prussian-German military school, which greatly influenced the military in all the great powers; the factors that shaped the 'cult of the offensive' in the French Army before the First World War; and the competing strategic doctrines which dominated naval warfare during the ages of sail and steam.

Underlying Book III, Fascist and Liberal Visions of War, is the question of how the ascent of modern, industrial, and technological mass society affected military theory from the outset of the twentieth century. The book starts by examining the various theories of mechanized warfare which appeared from the beginning of the century throughout the developed world. It points out, and explains how it came about, that the earliest and most famous proponents of mechanized warfare were associated with proto-fascism and fascism. The book then combines a re-evaluation of B. H. Liddell Hart's contribution to strategic theory with an analysis of the rise in the post-First World War liberal West of a new conception of war which is still with us today. Developed in reaction against the nineteenth century's emphasis on all-out war and the nation-in-arms, this conception has revolved around the notions of containment, cold war, and limited war, and has relied heavily on economic coercion and high-tech forces. These strategic notions are usually associated with the advent of the nuclear age, but in fact they had already been tried out by the Western powers against the Axis in the 1930s as a complement and alternative to appeasement. They were revived against the Soviet Bloc even before Russia acquired nuclear capability. And they have become the advanced world's strategic norm in today's post-Cold War era, even against non-nuclear adversaries.

ACKNOWLEDGEMENTS

Over years of research I incurred many pleasant debts to people and institutions that lent me their help and support. First and foremost, I wish to thank Professor Sir Michael Howard, my supervisor and mentor during my doctoral studies at St Antony's College, Oxford, from which Book I of this volume emerged. I have been fortunate to continue to benefit from his penetrating criticism, thoughtful advice, and warm encouragement ever since. The late Professor Sir Isaiah Berlin not only provided much of the inspiration for my work but also took the trouble to secure the funds needed for supporting my stay at Oxford. Professors Wilhelm Deist at Militär-geschichtliches Forschungsamt, then in Freiburg i. Breisgau, Paul Kennedy and Geoffrey Parker at Yale, Robert O'Neill at Oxford, and Brian Bond and Lawrence Freedman at King's College, London, each helped in various ways, offering opinions, assistance, and friendship.

I am particularly grateful to the trusts and institutions that made possible my research stays in several countries. These include: the AVI Foundation, the British Council, and the Edward Boyle Memorial Trust; the Alexander von Humboldt Foundation; and the United States-Israel Foundation (Fulbright). Of the many libraries and archives consulted in the course of my work, I am most indebted to the staffs of the Bodleian Library, Oxford; the British Library, London; the Bundes Archiv-Militär Archiv, Freiburg; and the Liddell Hart Centre for Military Archives at King's College, London. The Trustees of the Liddell Hart Centre kindly gave me permission to cite from documents to which they hold copyright. Princeton University Press granted me permission to quote from their edition of Clausewitz's *On War*. I am thankful to *Journal of Strategic Studies*, *War in History*, *War and Society*, *Journal of Contemporary History*, *Political Studies*, and *Militärgeschichtliche Mitteilungen* for allowing me to incorporate material first published in these journals. Finally, I wish to thank the research authorities, and my colleagues, at Tel Aviv University for their support and for creating the atmosphere that made dedication to research possible.

CONTENTS

Book II: The Nineteenth Century

Book III: Fascist and Liberal Visions of War

Book I

From the Enlightenment to Clausewitz

1

Machiavelli and the Classical Notion of the Lessons of History in the Study of War

The idea that war could be studied systematically by historical observation, by the selection of successful forms of organization, and by the imitation of stratagems emerged in antiquity, and was powerfully revived—with a strong practical tendency—in the Renaissance. It was a counterpart to the tradition of classical political philosophy, the deductive conception of history, and the notion of a universal law of nature. Like them, it stemmed from historical experience in which fundamental change was hardly recognized and the basic features of human reality were perceived as enduring and recurring in numerous ways in differing periods and societies. Military theory was then simply a synthesis of the best military models of the known cultural past, whether in Greece or Rome. For Xenophon, in his *Hellenica* and *Anabasis*, the theory of war was comprised in the combat formation and drill of the phalanx, particularly the Spartan, while for Polybius in his *Histories* or for Vegetius in *De Re Militari* it consisted in the sophisticated organization and deployment of the Roman legion.

Roughly speaking, very little had changed from the classical era to Machiavelli's time in what can today be called the technological dimension of war, nor consequently in the character of war itself. The foot soldier, horse, armour, manual weapons, fortifications, and siege-machinery undeniably underwent considerable developments and transformations, and the importance of each fluctuated in a diversity of military establishments, the most prominent of which included the Persian, Greek, Macedonian, Gaul, Roman, Parthian, chivalrous, and Swiss models. Still, these weapon-systems remained remarkably similar, and the diversity of military models which were based upon them also revealed fundamental recurring characteristics. Historical experience thus offered an extensive testing ground of a relatively limited number of military systems, exposing their strong and weak points in multifarious circumstances.

In the Renaissance, Machiavelli attempted a synthesis of the whole of military experience from antiquity to the developments of the late Middle Ages. In this he brought the classical conception of the lessons of history to its pinnacle. His basic assumption was that despite historical change, man and society remained 'in essence' the same at all times and cultures because human nature was immutable: 'the world has always gone on in the same way,' he wrote; 'ancient kingdoms . . . differed from one another because of the difference in their customs, but the world remained the same'.[1] History could thus teach us lessons which were valid in every period. This conception, which dominated Machiavelli's political work, also guided his military thought.[2] But it was in the military sphere—rapidly and decisively influenced by technological change—that this outlook on history and theory faced an almost immediate breakdown.

The reason for Machiavelli's close attention to military affairs is obvious: he regarded the role of force as paramount both in domestic and foreign politics. Thus he discussed military affairs throughout his political works and later devoted to them a specialized study, *The Art of War* (1521). Here he sought to distil the lessons of military history and use them in devising a complete scheme for an army of his day.

The militia, the national army of citizens called to fight for their *patria*, was regarded by Machiavelli as the only proper form of military organization both from the social and the military points of view. This had been positively revealed in antiquity in the heyday of the Greek city-states and, more especially, of the Roman republic; in modern times this explained the extraordinary power of the small Swiss republic. The same lesson had been negatively demonstrated

[1] Niccolò Machiavelli, *The Discourses*, II, preface, in Allan Gilbert (ed.), *The Chief Works and Others* (Durham, 1965), i. 322.

[2] For the role of past lessons, among others in the military sphere, see e.g. *The Discourses*, I, pref., in *Chief Works*, i. For the widely discussed revival of the classical conception of history's purpose and lessons by the humanists and Machiavelli, see esp. Felix Gilbert, *Machiavelli and Guicciardini* (Princeton, 1965), chs. 4, 5; Denys Hay, *Annalists and Historians* (London, 1977), chs. 1, 5, 6, esp. pp. 93–4, and, for the case of Machiavelli, p. 113; Myron P. Gilmore, 'The Renaissance Conception of the Lessons of History', in his *Humanists and Jurists* (Cambridge Mass., 1963); Machiavelli is discussed on pp. 25–34.

in antiquity by the role played by mercenary armies in the decline of Greece and Rome. And in the modern period it was reaffirmed by the conduct of the disloyal, rapacious, treacherous, impudent, and cowardly *condottieri*, who were more dangerous to their employers than to the enemy, and who were responsible for the downfall in the international status of the once-proud Italian city-states. During his political career in the Chancellery of the Florentine republic and as the Secretary of the Office of Ten, Machiavelli witnessed the crippling effect of Florence's dependence on the *condottieri*, and was the driving force behind the attempt to re-establish the Florentine militia.[3]

As to the actual organization of the army, Machiavelli maintained that infantry armed with weapons for fighting at close quarters, protected by armour, and deployed in deep formation would break, under normal circumstances, the most vigorous cavalry charges. This lesson had been demonstrated numerous times by the Greeks and the Romans. With the decline of the Roman state and organized armies, it had been somewhat obscured; but it was strikingly redemonstrated—to the amazement of chivalrous Europe—with the revival of the classical formation of infantry by the Swiss on the battlefields of Burgundy and Italy. According to Machiavelli, infantry was therefore to be the backbone of a properly built army.[4]

Regarding the battle formation of the infantry itself, Machiavelli argued that, armed with sword and shield, and deployed in several flexible, manœuvrable, and mutually supporting squares, it would throw into disintegration and slay at close quarters enemy infantry armed with the pike and deployed in fewer, larger, and less manœuvrable squares. This had been demonstrated time and again in the great encounters of the Roman legion with the Macedonian and Seleucid phalanx—in Cynoscephalae, Magnesia, and Pydna—and had been analysed in depth by Polybius in a celebrated treatise in the *Histories* (XVIII, 28–32). The same lesson was corroborated—though perhaps less decisively—by the engagements between the

[3] See *The Prince*, ch. 12; and *The Art of War*, the principal theme of Bk. I. For the militia in Florentine and humanist tradition see C. C. Bayley's comprehensive *War and Society in Renaissance Florence: The* De Militia *of Leonardo Bruni* (Toronto, 1961); Machiavelli's involvement is described on pp. 240–315. For a much briefer summary of humanist attitudes see Quentin Skinner, *The Foundations of Modern Political Thought* (Cambridge, 1978) i. 76–7, 150–1, 173–5.

[4] *The Art of War*, II, in *Chief Works*, i. 602–4.

Spanish infantry armed with the sword and buckler, and the deep hedgehogs of the highly renowned Swiss infantry armed with the pike. Infantry, Machiavelli maintained, was therefore to be built by adopting the example of the Roman legion, though some of the features of the Macedonian and Swiss formations were also to be incorporated.[5]

As was the case in his political writings, Machiavelli freely adapted historical evidence to fit his argument. His hostility towards the *condottieri* made his account of their military conduct particularly tendentious. This has been exposed by modern research.[6] However, as pointed out by commentators, Machiavelli's aim was predominantly theoretical rather than historical.[7] Despite inaccuracies, he put forth a penetrating analysis of the principal military models of the past and achieved a remarkable synthesis of the legacy of classical military theory. Yet it took little time before his military views were struck by the full weight of an unprecedented historical change.

At the very time at which Machiavelli wrote and published *The Art of War*, the old forms of warfare were being revolutionized, predominantly because of the introduction of firearms. The Swiss formation could be regarded as a new Macedonian phalanx, while that of the Spaniards might have resembled in some respects the

[5] *The Art of War*, II and III, in *Chief Works*, vol. i, pp. 595–601 and 627–32 respectively.

[6] The reliability of Machiavelli's works as a source for the military events of his time was critically examined for the first time in Walter Hobohm's *Machiavellis Renaissance der Kriegskunst* (Berlin, 1913). For a concurrence with Hobohm and forceful defence of his work against criticism see Hans Delbrück, *History of the Art of War within the Framework of Political History*, (German original 1920; London 1985); iv. 101, 113; Delbrück's emphasis on understanding military affairs against their wider political background, and the legitimacy that he gave to limited strategy, 'the strategy of attrition', made him particularly aware of Machiavelli's bias against the *condottieri*. This bias has dominated the traditional historical view (for the interesting case of Clausewitz's attitude towards the *condottieri* as against his historicism, see below Ch. 7), and was still strongly expressed in Charles Oman, *The Art of War in the Middle Ages* (London, 1924), which reflected the 19th-cent. faith in the imperative of decision through battle; see esp. vol. ii, Bk. XII, ch. 2. But Machiavelli's account of *condottieri* warfare was convincingly criticized in Willibald Block, 'Die Condottieri: Studien über die sogenannten "unblutigen Schlachten"', *Historische Studien*, CX (1913); and recently the case for the *condottieri* was thoroughly made by Michael Mallett, *Mercenaries and their Masters: Warfare in Renaissance Italy* (London, 1974).

[7] See Delbrück, *History*, iv. 101, 113; and Felix Gilbert, 'Machiavelli: The Renaissance in the Art of War', in P. Paret (ed.), *Makers of Modern Strategy* (Princeton, 1986), 21–2.

Roman infantry. But the new arquebuses and guns could not be moulded into the old framework. The attempts to dismiss them as insignificant, or to adapt them into the paradigm of the classical battlefield as a 'new form' of archers and slingers,[8] were thwarted—the former in immediate failure, and the latter in decreasing achievements over a longer period of time—as their revolutionary effect on the battlefield grew ever stronger.

In the fictitious battle described in *The Art of War*, Machiavelli allowed the artillery to shoot only once and ineffectively before the armies closed. If commanders 'do rely on infantry and on the method aforesaid,' he wrote in *The Discourses*, 'artillery becomes wholly useless'.[9] Yet, while he was composing *The Discourses* and six years prior to the appearance of *The Art of War*, the guns of Francis I broke the dreadful Swiss infantry on the battlefield of Marignano (1515). And only a year after Machiavelli dismissed the significance of the new arquebuses, sarcastically remarking that they were useful mainly for terrorizing peasants,[10] the Spanish arquebusiers inflicted on the Swiss infantry its second great defeat at the Battle of Bicocca (1522).[11]

There have been some attempts to explain away and minimize Machiavelli's dismissal of firearms precisely when they were beginning to play an increasingly decisive role in the Italian wars of the late fifteenth and early sixteenth centuries. Felix Gilbert, for example, pointed out that Machiavelli's attitude to artillery in *The Discourses* (II, 17) was deliberately one-sided, having a polemic aim to restress the dominant role of valour.[12] Machiavelli's emphasis on moral forces is indeed undisputed, yet his attitude to firearms cannot be mainly understood as polemic tactics. This is certainly not the case with *The Art of War*, to which Gilbert does not refer in this

[8] *The Art of War*, II, in *Chief Works*, i. 597.

[9] Ibid. III, in *Chief Works*, i. 634; *The Discourses*, II, 17, in *Chief Works*, i. 371.

[10] *The Art of War*, II, in *Chief Works*, i. 625.

[11] For Renaissance warfare in the late 15th and early 16th cents. see Oman, *War in Middle Ages*; id., *The Art of War in the Sixteenth Century* (London, 1937); F. L. Taylor, *The Art of War in Italy 1494–1529* (Cambridge, 1921); Delbrück, *History*. For an updated narrative see J. R. Hale's chapters on military affairs in the *New Cambridge Modern History*, vols. i–iii (Cambridge, 1957, 1958, 1968). On attitudes to firearms see id., 'Gunpowder and the Renaissance', in his *Renaissance War Studies* (London, 1983); this comprehensive article surprisingly does not deal with Machiavelli. See also id., *War and Society in Renaissance Europe* (London, 1985).

[12] Gilbert, 'Machiavelli: The Renaissance in the Art of War', 14–15.

context. *The Art of War* is Machiavelli's positive and complete scheme for the building of armies, and reflects the full scope of his military outlook. His ideal army is totally of Roman and Macedonian-Swiss form, and though artillery is introduced, its significance and role in battle could not have been more belittled.[13]

Most commentators, however, have been critical of Machiavelli's military ideas. Oman, for example, wrote that Machiavelli, though very perceptive, was mistaken in all his major predictions of future military developments, particularly regarding firearms.[14] How then did the Florentine thinker, famous for his penetrating and sobering insights into the complexity of human relations, politics, and society, fail to recognize one of the most important milestones of military history? Clausewitz, otherwise an admirer of Machiavelli, pointed to the obvious reason in a letter to Fichte:

> So far as Machiavelli's book on the art of war itself is concerned, I recall missing the free, independent judgment that so strongly distinguishes his political writings. The art of war of the ancients attracted him too much, not only its spirit, but also in all of its forms.[15]

This line of explanation—independently arrived at by later commentators[16]—is undoubtedly true, but should be expanded. As mentioned above, the reasons for Machiavelli's great misjudgement go deeper. It can only be understood in the context of his conceptions of history and theory. His way of thinking in attempting to overcome the challenge of artillery is most revealing. He sought an analogy in antiquity:

> In approaching the enemy, infantry can with greater ease escape the discharge of artillery than in Antiquity they could escape the rush of elephants or of scythed chariots and of other strange weapons that the Roman infantry had to oppose. Against these they always found a remedy. And so much the more easily they would have found one against artillery.[17]

Machiavelli could not accept firearms as a significant military and political innovation because this would have undermined not only

[13] *The Art of War*, in *Chief Works*, i. 632.

[14] Oman, *War in Sixteenth Century*, pp. 93–4.

[15] Letter to Fichte, 11 Jan. 1809, in W. M. Schering (ed.), *Clausewitz, Geist und Tat* (Stuttgart, 1941), 76; P. Paret, *Clausewitz and the State* (Oxford, 1976), 176. See extensively below in the chapters on Clausewitz.

[16] Cf. Oman, *War in Middle Ages*, ii. 311.

[17] *The Discourses*, II. 17, in *Chief Works*, i. 371. For a similar reasoning see also *The Art of War*, III, in *Chief Works*, i. 637.

his model for military organization and virtues—the Roman army—but also the foundations of his historical and theoretical outlook. Such acceptance would have implied a historically unprecedented, fundamental change in the well-known recurring patterns of past warfare, invalidating the lessons offered by the historical perspective of two thousand years.[18]

The classical legacy continued to form the intellectual background and source of historical reference for military thinking—among other spheres of European culture—until the end of the eighteenth century. The works of the classical authors were widely studied and considered the best material for military instruction. These included the histories of Herodotus, Thucydides, Livy, Tacitus, Plutarch, and particularly of those historians who emphasized military aspects, such as Xenophon, Polybius, and Caesar. Equally popular were the military treatises of such authors as Arrian, Vegetius, Frontinus, Aelian, Polyaen, Vitruvius and the Byzantine emperors Maurice and Leo. They were published in numerous editions and continually elicited vivid attention and extensive commentary between the late fifteenth and late eighteenth centuries.[19]

Initially, the classical military models, when synthesized with modern firearms, were still of great relevance and influence. Machiavelli, and later the celebrated classical scholar and humanist philosopher, Justus Lipsius, in his *Politicorum libri sex* (1589) and *De militia Romana* (1596), propagated the organization, discipline, and flexible internal division of the Roman legion. These inspired the military reforms associated with Maurice of Orange and his Nassau cousins during the Dutch wars of independence, and the organization of the Swedish army under Eric and Gustavus Adolphus.[20] However, the old weapons and formations were gradually being abandoned. The pike, the last notable remnant of

[18] For a similar criticism of Machiavelli's political thought cf. H. Butterfield, *The Statecraft of Machiavelli* (London, 1955).

[19] For a comprehensive survey of the reprints of the military works of antiquity during this period see Max Jähns, *Geschichte der Kriegswissenschaften* (Munich and Leipzig, 1889), 244–8, 447–54, 869–75, 1142–3, 1461–3, 1823–37.

[20] See esp. W. Hahlweg, *Die Heeresreform der Oranier und die Antike* (Berlin, 1941); M. Roberts, *Gustavus Adolphus* (London, 1958), vol. ii, ch. III; G. Oestreich, *Neostoicism and the Early Modern State* (Cambridge, 1982), ch. 5, 'The Military Renascence'; and G. Rothenberg, 'The Seventeenth Century', in Paret (ed.), *Makers of Modern Strategy*, pp. 32–63.

ancient and medieval warfare, went out of use by the end of the seventeenth century when it was replaced by the bayonet fixed to the muzzle of the musket. This, together with the growing effectiveness of the musket and field-gun, led to a decrease in the depth of battle formation throughout the eighteenth century. The line won the day.[21] No longer did the classical military legacy represent a homogeneous historical experience or provide direct analogies and lessons for the present as Machiavelli had assumed in *The Art of War*.

Yet, the emergence of a strong opposition to the linear formation in the eighteenth century went hand in hand with a powerful revival in the reference to, and interest in, ancient warfare and military works. Folard advocated the restoration of the shock effect of the pike and the column in his *Histoire de Polybe* (1724–30), and in the 1770s his disciple Mesnil-Durand sparked the great doctrinal controversy between the *ordre profond* and the *ordre mince*. This led to a compromise and to the introduction of the famous column of the Wars of the Revolution and Napoleon as a formation for manœuvres and fighting.[22] As we shall see, de Saxe, Puységur, Guichard, Turpin, and Maizeroy relied on the ancient models and authorities almost as heavily as Machiavelli. There was almost no military thinker in the Enlightenment who did not refer to antiquity to some extent. Even the characteristic debate of the seventeenth and eighteenth centuries, as to whether the ancients or the moderns were culturally superior, was not lacking in the military sphere.

The notion of a fundamental historical change began to emerge with the Enlightenment, but a new attitude to the past, including military history, took shape only at the close of the eighteenth century. First, after the French Revolution, Tempelhoff, Bülow, and Clausewitz observed a new, 'modern' experience. In a direct reaction against the military thinkers of the French Enlightenment, Tempelhoff wrote that theory had to be based on contemporary experience rather than on the history of the Greeks and Romans.[23] Still more important was the emergence of historicism with its

[21] For the European armies in this period of transition see D. Chandler, *The Art of Warfare in the Age of Marlborough* (London, 1976).

[22] For a fuller account see below, ch. 3. For the doctrinal controversy see Jean L. A. Colin, *L'Infanterie au* XVIII*e* siècle (Paris, 1907); Robert S. Quimby, *The Background of Napoleonic Warfare* (New York, 1957).

[23] G. Tempelhoff, *History of the Seven Years War* (London, 1793), i. 84.

supreme sensitivity to the diversity of historical experience and the uniqueness of every period. Clausewitz, who introduced the historicist outlook into military thought, wrote:

> Wars that bear a considerable resemblance to those of the present day, especially with respect to armament, are primarily campaigns beginning with the War of the Austrian Succession. Even though many major and minor circumstances have changed considerably, these are close enough to modern warfare to be instructive . . . The further back you go, the less useful military history becomes . . . The history of Antiquity is without doubt the most useless . . . We are in no position . . . to apply [it] to the wholly different means we use today.[24]

The relative uniformity of historical experience as the basis for a theory of war which could be derived by direct observation, analysis, and critical analogy from the major military models of the past, and applied to the similar conditions of the present, was therefore gradually breaking down in the early modern period. Yet, this development was more than matched by the growth of a powerful, new theoretical ideal to subject all spheres of reality, including war, to the rule of reason. This ideal was greatly stimulated by the vision and achievements of the natural sciences which also put forward a new systematical model: to reveal the universal principles that dominate the diversity of phenomena. The overwhelming success of this enterprise, culminating in Newtonian science, was one of the principal driving forces of the Enlightenment and generated a corresponding awakening of military thought. But the proto-scientific outlook had already been influencing military theory in the seventeenth century.

[24] Carl von Clausewitz, *On War*, M. Howard and P. Paret (eds.) (Princeton, 1976), Bk II, ch. 6, p. 173.

Part One

THE MILITARY SCHOOL OF THE ENLIGHTENMENT

2
Montecuccoli

The Impact of Proto-Science on Military Theory

Known today only to a small circle of scholars, Raimondo Montecuccoli (1609–80) was regarded in the eighteenth century—much as Clausewitz has been in the last two centuries—as the most distinguished modern military thinker, whose widely cited and highly influential work was a classic that offered the foundations of a general theory of war.

What, then, was Montecuccoli's theoretical outlook, and, inseparably, what were its origins? While his life story and military career have had their normal share of historiographical attention, Montecuccoli's intellectual world—despite the evidence and despite his reputation as a 'military intellectual'—has not been explored nor connected to his military thought. The following chapter is therefore merely an introduction to a much-needed extensive study.

Deeply involved in the great intellectual fermentation in the first half of the seventeenth century, Montecuccoli gave expression to the ideas and attitudes of the late humanists, and was an enthusiastic student of the powerful tradition of research into the occult, alchemy, and natural magic. This was one of the major trends of the evolving scientific enterprise of the sixteenth and seventeenth centuries, and was widespread among the élite circles of the Habsburg empire.

Montecuccoli was born in 1609 to a noble family from the vicinity of Modena in northern Italy. Entering the Imperial army, he saw active service throughout the Thirty Years War, rising to the rank of general and distinguishing himself as a cavalry leader. After the war, he carried out diplomatic missions and commanded the Imperial forces in the Nordic war in Poland. In 1664 he defeated the invading Turkish army in his greatest battle at St Gotthard, and in 1673, during the Dutch war of Louis XIV, he conducted his most celebrated campaign against Turenne on the Rhine which was to be admired throughout the eighteenth century as a model of manœuvre. He again faced Turenne in the same theatre of operations in the campaign of 1675. Promoted to the rank of field marshal, Montecuccoli was appointed President of the Imperial War Council in 1668, and in this capacity he took the first steps in creating a professional standing army. Though awarded the titles Prince of the Empire and Duke of Melfi in 1679, his last years were clouded by power struggles and professional disputes with rivals both in court and within the army.[1]

We know very little about Montecuccoli's early education, but as a general he is described by a contemporary as a formidable intellectual figure with an extraordinary range of interests—well known as such even in the highly cultured environment of Vienna—and a patron of the sciences who possessed a huge library.[2] His intense intellectual preoccupations are clearly revealed in his major works, composed during three lulls in his military career.[3]

There has survived the varied list of sources—forty-five in all—that Montecuccoli used for the writing of his first major work, the *Treatise on War* (*Trattato della guerra*), composed while he spent four years in Swedish captivity in Stettin (1639–43).[4] The *Zibaldone*, Montecuccoli's extensive reference work, composed during the post-Westphalian period (1648–54), has also been preserved and includes sixty-nine bibliographical items.[5]

[1] The standard biographies of Montecuccoli are still Cesare Campori, *Raimondo Montecuccoli, la sua famiglia e i suoi tempi* (Florence, 1876); and Tommaso Sandonnini, *Il Generale Raimondo Montecuccoli e la sua famiglia* (Modena, 1914). Many articles and dissertations have been written in the last two centuries on Montecuccoli's military career; for a modern and comprehensive study of his greatest battle, see Georg Wagner, *Das Türkenjahr 1664, Raimund Montecuccoli, die Schlacht von St. Gotthard-Mogarsdorf*, issue 48 of *Burgenländische Forschungen* (1964). Two recent works are Hans Kaufmann, 'Raimondo Graf Montecuccoli 1609–1680', (doct. diss.; Berlin, 1972); and Thomas Barker, *The Military Intellectual and Battle: Montecuccoli and the Thirty Years War* (New York, 1975). For a concise overall account see Gunther Rothenberg, 'The Seventeenth Century' in Paret (ed.), *Makers of Modern Strategy*, pp. 55–63.

[2] The Italian tourist Abbé Pacichelli, cited by E. Vehse, *Memoirs of the Court and Aristocracy of Austria* (London, 1856), i. 432–4; Montecuccoli is depicted as cold, unsympathetic, and engaged in intrigue.

[3] Piero Pieri, 'La formazione dottrinale di Raimondo Montecuccoli', in *Revue internationale d'histoire militaire*, III (1951), 92–125.

[4] This list of sources has not been printed. The authors included are cited by Barker from the manuscript in Montecuccoli's family archive in Modena; see *Montecuccoli*, p. 227.

[5] This work has not been printed either; the authors and works are cited in A. Veltzé (ed.), *Ausgewählte Schriften des Raimund Fürsten Montecuccoli* (Vienna, 1899), vol. i, pp. cxiii–cxx.

Montecuccoli's central work from this period is *On the Art of War* (*Del arte militare*), a concise version of the *Treatise*, laying special emphasis on fortifications and siegecraft. The references in the last version, the celebrated *On the War against the Turks in Hungary* or *Aphorisms* (*Della guerra col Turco in Ungheria*; 1670)—a demonstration of Montecuccoli's military ideas through his campaign against the Turks—provide another insight into his intellectual background.[6]

These source lists, reference works, and military writings reveal a remarkable continuity in Montecuccoli's interests and ideas. They indicate that the thirty-two-year-old colonel and author of the *Treatise on War* had already consolidated his theoretical outlook and military conceptions, which underwent no further fundamental changes. Indeed, the *Treatise* is the largest of Montecuccoli's works, and since none of them were published during his lifetime, it is perhaps only accidental that the *Treatise* remained unpublished when his two later military discourses appeared at the beginning of the seventeenth century.

In the source list to his first work, Montecuccoli cites extensively the classical and the contemporary military authors whose full influence on his work has yet to be studied.[7] The conceptual framework of his work was undoubtedly influenced by systematic military treatises such as Giorgio Basta's *Il maestro di campo generale* (1606), Henri de Rohan's *Le Parfait Capitaine* (1631), Wallhausen's *Corpus militare* (1617), and perhaps also Mario Savorgnano's *Arte militare terrestre e maritima* (1599; not cited by Montecuccoli). However, it is mostly in the scope of general works and non-military authors cited by Montecuccoli that the clue to his outstanding theoretical outlook and endeavour is to be sought.

[6] Montecuccoli's extensive writings have been compiled from the Vienna War Archives in Veltzé's four vol. edn. The first and second vols. contain Montecuccoli's military works, the third his historical writings, and the fourth correspondence and miscellaneous works. The *Treatise on War* has not been published elsewhere. *On The Art of War* and esp. *The War against the Turks in Hungary* were published in all the major European languages with the exception of English. Only one of Montecuccoli's smaller works, *On Battle* (*Della battaglie*), appeared in English in Barker, *Montecuccoli*.

[7] A short account of these authors, based on Jähns, is given by Barker, *Montecuccoli*, pp. 55–8, 227, who also cites the intellectual authorities with little understanding and some factual errors.

These authorities fall into two major categories, the first being political authors and essayists. Montecuccoli cites Machiavelli's writings, Campanella's *Monarchia Hispania*, Bacon's *Essays*, and many other then very popular and now almost forgotten works such as those of the French man of letters, J. L. Guez de Balzac (1597–1654), particularly his *Le Prince*.[8] Yet the dominant influence on his work was that of the late humanist tradition as propounded by Justus Lipsius (1547–1606).

Lipsius's intellectual influence throughout Europe and in the Habsburg Empire in the late sixteenth and early seventeenth centuries was outstanding.[9] It was equally unparalleled in the military field, where Lipsius was the major proponent of Roman military values and practices, and influenced Maurice of Nassau's military reforms.[10] His principal influence on Montecuccoli's military works was, however, quite different. In Lipsius's celebrated *Six Books of Politics* (1589), which reflected the increasing dominance of the centralized state, Montecuccoli found a comprehensive and systematic presentation of war within a political framework, derived from political motives and directed towards political aims. As we shall see, Book I of the *Treatise on War*, Montecuccoli's earliest theoretical work, directly refers to, and closely follows Lipsius's conceptions.[11]

Similar attitudes to war were offered by Aristotle and by the Roman stoics—the school most popular among the humanists—particularly Cicero and Seneca. And they were also central to the jurist tradition. Cicero and Grotius are cited in this connection in the opening of *On the War against the Turks in Hungary*.[12]

[8] Machiavelli is cited as no. 13 in the *Zibaldone*, in which the first twenty items are, broadly speaking, political. *Monarchia Hispania* by Campanella, one of Montecuccoli's favourite authors who had also appeared in the earlier source list, is no. 17. Bacon's *Essays* comprise no. 2; Balzac's works are cited as nos. 5 and 18.

[9] See Oestreich's excellent *Neostoicism and the Early Modern State*; J. L. Saunders, *Justus Lipsius, The Philosophy of Renaissance Stoicism* (New York, 1955); and for Lipsius's popularity and influence in the Habsburg empire, R. J. W. Evans's highly comprehensive studies: *Rudolf II and his World, A Study in Intellectual History 1576–1612* (Oxford, 1973), esp. pp. 95–6, and, in the context of humanist culture, 116–61; id., *The Making of the Habsburg Monarchy 1550–1700* (Oxford, 1979), esp. pp. 25, 113.

[10] See ch. 1, n. 20 above.

[11] Oestreich, *Neostoicism*, pp. 80–1; unaware of Montecuccoli's scientific interests, Oestreich is mistaken, however, in attributing Montecuccoli's conception of science to Lipsius; see Montecuccoli's list of sources to the *Treatise*, and nos. 3 and 4 of the *Zibaldone*.

[12] For references to Aristotle, Cicero, and Seneca see mainly the introds. to *On the Art of War*, and *The War against the Turks* and, for Aristotle, see also *Zibaldone*, no. 6.

The second and even more extensive category of authors and works cited by Montecuccoli is truly remarkable. More than half of the *Zibaldone*, comprising about forty works, is a compendium of the great authorities of the occult and magical natural philosophy, covering Paracelsian alchemy and medicine, and Hermetic, cabbalistic, and Rosicrucian wisdom and visions. Indeed, some of these authorities were previously included in the source list to the *Treatise*.

One of those cited in the *Treatise* is the English Hermetic, cabbalistic, and Paracelsian natural philosopher, Robert Fludd (1574–1637), famous throughout Europe for his works on mathematical mystery and magic which he defended in a celebrated debate against Kepler. According to a contemporary, Montecuccoli 'was able to recite [his works] word for word'.[13] Another occultist cited in the source list is Johann Faulhaber, the author of *Magia arcana Coelestis sive Cabalisticus* (1613).[14] Johann Amos Comenius (1592–1670), the influential Czech bishop and philosopher of education, whose pacific, universal, and humanist ideas were deeply embedded in the mystical tradition, is also included.[15] Finally, the appearance in the source list of the works of Georgius Agricola (1494–1555), one of the pioneers of modern geology and mineralogy, also attest to Montecuccoli's keen interest in the scientific thought of the time.[16]

This interest is fully revealed in the *Zibaldone*. Tommaso Campanella (1568–1639), the celebrated mystical and millenarian natural philosopher and political thinker mentioned earlier in the political section, is represented by an additional seventeen works, covering the full range of his metaphysical thought (nos. 22–38). Another prominent representative of the Italian occultist natural philosophy is Gianbattista Porta, whose popular *Magia Naturalis*

[13] Cited by Vehse, *Memoirs*, i. 434; Evans, *Habsburg Monarchy*, pp. 347–8. For Fludd, see Allen G. Debus, *The Chemical Philosophy, Paracelsian Science and Medicine in the Sixteenth and Seventeenth Centuries* (New York, 1977), i. 205–93; and F. A. Yates, *Giordano Bruno and the Hermetic Tradition* (London, 1964), ch. XXII; id., *The Art of Memory* (London, 1966), ch. XV, and *Theatre of the World* (London, 1969), chs. III–IV.

[14] See Evans, *Habsburg Monarchy*, p. 397.

[15] Ibid., esp. pp. 395, 399; and Evans, *Rudolf II*, esp. pp. 82, 276–7, 283–5, 290.

[16] Frank D. Adams, *The Birth and Development of the Geological Sciences* (London, 1938), ch. VI.

is cited (no. 40; 1644 edn.).[17] Among the founders of the Hermetic tradition, the famous Raymon Lull (1236–*c*.1316), the first to introduce the secret calculations of Jewish cabbala into European thought, is represented by his equally famous *Secreti di Natura*, translated together with St Albertus Magnus's *Delle cose minerali e metalliche* (no. 62; 1557 edn.).[18]

Extensive reference is made to the most important physicists and chemist-alchemists of the period, including Valerianus Magnus (1585–1661), the student of the vacuum (no. 39); Johann Rudolph Glauber (1603/4–1668/70), chemist and physicist (nos. 41–2); Andreas Libavius, the anti-Paracelsian chemist (no. 51; many works are cited); Zacharias Brendel (1592–1638), MD chemist and alchemist (no. 53); Johann Hartmann (1568–1631), the first professor of chemistry in Europe, holding a chair in Marburg (no. 55); and Oswald Croll, Paracelsian chemist and physician, who wandered through Europe finding an audience for his secret teaching in the Habsburg provinces and court, and whose *Basilica Chymica*, cited by Montecuccoli (no. 57), was published in eighteen editions between 1609–58.[19]

This group is inseparable from the corpus of medical works listed in the *Zibaldone*, most of which are by Paracelsian authors, including Johann Schröder (1600–64), author of the widely read *Pharmacopoeia Medico-chymica* (no. 45); Pierre Jean Fabre (d. 1650), graduate of Montpellier and author of the equally popular *Palladium Spagyrica* (no. 48); Lazar Riverius, another representative of and well-known professor at Montpellier (no. 58); J. B. van Helmont (1579–1644), a medical doctor of European renown (no. 50); and Jean Béguin, author of the pharmacological *Tyrocinium*

[17] See D. P. Walker, *Spiritual and Demonic Magic from Ficino to Campanella* (London, 1958); and for the Italian nature philosophers, J. H. Randall Jun., *The Career of Philosophy from the Middle Ages to the Enlightenment* (New York, 1962), 197–220.

[18] For Lull and Lullism, see J. N. Hillgarth, *Raymon Lull and Lullism* (Oxford, 1971); and F. A. Yates, *The Occult Philosophy in the Elizabethan Age* (London, 1979), ch. I.

[19] For Magnus's science and mysticism, see Evans, *Habsburg Monarchy*, esp. pp. 330, 337, 342, and for Glauber's influence in the Viennese court pp. 361 and 365. For Libavius see B. Easlea, *Witch-hunting, Magic and the New Philosophy* (Sussex, 1980), 107, and Debus, *Chemical Philosophy*, i. 169–73. For Hartmann and Croll, see ibid., pp. 125 and 117–24 respectively. For all the authorities cited, see also vols. vii and viii of L. Thorndike's *magnum opus*, *A History of Magic and Experimental Science* (New York, 1923–58).

Chymicum which appeared in no less than forty-one editions between 1610 and 1690 (no. 52; 1640 edn. is cited).[20]

Finally, still very closely related, is the popular literature of the various secret and traditional prescriptions. An example of this is the *Secreti* (1561) of Signora Isabella Cortese (no. 61; 1603 edn. is cited).[21]

Not all of the authors and works cited above were Paracelsian. Some, notably Libavius, were even opponents of the magical tradition. So also was Francis Bacon whose *Essays* are cited twice in the *Zibaldone*, both in the philosophical and the scientific sections.[22] While he rejected the mechanical-mathematical philosophy, and was a true child of the experimental enterprise attempting to control nature by discovering its secrets, Bacon was also one of the well-known critics of natural magic. Yet, the overwhelming majority of the natural philosophers cited both in the source list to the *Treatise on War* and in *Zibaldone* are Paracelsian, and they leave little doubt where Montecuccoli's interests lay.

Where it was noticed, this fact caused some concern among Montecuccoli's interpreters about the 'scientific' nature of his outlook.[23] This concern is obviously somewhat anachronistic and tends to assume a standard concept of science, as perceived by the men of the eighteenth century. Indeed, with the triumph of the mechanical-mathematical interpretation of nature, the occult tradition of natural philosophy was expelled from the domain of science as superstition. However, until the late seventeenth century, the struggle between the contending currents of natural philosophy still raged, and Newton's secret research into the occult was the last remarkable example of this. Montecuccoli's interests reflected the enormous, sometimes passionate interest of the educated social and political élite throughout the Habsburg empire in all spheres of the occult and natural magic. His title as the Protector of the *Leopoldinische Akademie der Naturforscher des heiligen Römischen*

[20] For Schröder, see Thorndike, *Magic and Experimental Science*, viii. 88–92. For Fabre and Béguin, see Debus, *Chemical Philosophy*, pp. 261 and 167–8 respectively. For Helmont and his Paracelsianism, ibid. 295–343, and W. Pagel, *Joan Baptista van Helmont* (Cambridge, 1982). For Riverius see the latter, pp. 37–62.

[21] Thorndike, *Magic and Experimental Science*, vi. 218.

[22] Nos. 2 and 40; the first Latin edn. of the *Essays* is cited, 'Sermones fideles', Lugd. Batav. 1641; see R. W. Gibson, *Bacon: A Bibliography of his Works and Baconiana to the Year 1750* (Oxford, 1950).

[23] Barker, *Montecuccoli*, pp. 5, 58.

Reiches (which was later to move to Halle) was typical of the patronage that the court and magnates bestowed upon the great proponents of these arts.[24]

It was thus from within this highly involved intellectual environment, in the context of the scholarly tradition of the late Renaissance and the extensive proto-scientific awakening, that Montecuccoli set out to undertake a scientific study of war.

In the opening of his earliest work Montecuccoli wrote:

> Many ancients and moderns have written on war. Most of them, however, have not crossed the boundaries of theory. When some, such as Basta, Melzi, Rohan, la Noue, etc. have combined theory with its application, they have either undertaken to cultivate only one part of this vast field, or have restricted themselves to generalities, without getting down to the details of the supporting sciences . . . which make the perfect military general. It is impossible to understand the whole fully, if one is not familiar with its constitutive parts.[25]

Thus, he wrote in his second, more concise work, 'I have thought, in a limited framework, to summarize methodically the exceedingly vast territory of this science' which deals with an art of the utmost political importance.[26]

Like all sciences, the science of war aims to reduce experience to universal and fundamental rules.[27] These can then be applied to particular times and circumstances by means of skilful judgement, which is necessary in order to put the individual examples in a general perspective.[28]

In his celebrated *On the War against the Turks in Hungary*, written late in life, Montecuccoli offered a sophisticated epistemological account of this process, directly referring to, and closely following, Aristotle's analysis in the *Metaphysics* (A.I.):

> The innate force of reason, while comprehending the objects, also turns them into concepts which it stores in the memory. From several combined

[24] For Montecuccoli and the Academy, see Veltzé (ed.), *Ausgewählte Schriften (AS)*, vol. i, pp. cxxx. For the occult culture in the Habsburg empire and court, including the contents of many libraries and reading lists which are very similar to Montecuccoli's, see again Evans, *Rudolf II*, esp. ch. 6, and id., *Habsburg Monarchy*, esp. ch. 10.

[25] 'An den Leser', *Abhandlung über den Krieg*, in Veltzé (ed.), *AS* i. 5–6.

[26] Introd. to *Von der Kriegskunst*, *AS* ii. 29; Cicero is cited on the importance of the art of war.

[27] Ibid.; see also *Abhandlung über den Krieg*, *AS* i. 7.

[28] *Abhandlung über den Krieg*, *AS* i. 7–8; citing the 'physicist' as an illustration.

recollections, experience emerges, and from many experiences there springs general understanding, which is the beginning of all sciences and arts.[29]

Hence the intimate relationship and interdependence between the theory of general rules and practice. While theory is derived from reality, it then serves to guide and judge action. Each is essential to the other.[30] Thus 'as the mathematician uses to do', the first part of Montecuccoli's book offers the principles of the art of war, while the second applies them—'like derivatives'—to the war against the Turks in Hungary.[31]

The universal rules of war encompass 'the whole of world history from the beginning of things'. There is 'no remarkable military deed . . . [that] cannot be reduced to these instructions'.[32] 'Disregarding the invention of artillery, which has somewhat changed the forms of war, the rest of the rules remain correct and valid.'[33]

Book I of the *Treatise on War* is an extensive study of the nature and political context of war, based on Lipsius's discussion in Books 5–6 of the *Six Books of Politics* to which constant reference is made. Wars are divided into internal and external, and their causes are elaborated under the headings of either remote or immediate. The prerequisites of just wars are discussed. The political preparations for war, particularly the striking of alliances, are described, as well as the preparations of military means, divided into provisions, arms, and money. Lastly, the army itself is examined, including the hierarchy of command, and—reflecting neo-classical notions—recruitment methods; native soldiers are declared to be greatly superior to foreign troops. Book II deals with the conduct of war, and the final Book III with the conclusion of war and the attainment of a favourable peace, which was the purpose of the war.[34]

[29] *Vom Kriege mit den Türken*, *AS* ii. 199.

[30] Ibid.

[31] Ibid. 200.

[32] *Von der Kriegskunst*, *AS* ii. 29.

[33] *Vom Kriege mit den Türken*, *AS* ii. 200.

[34] For the three stages of war, see J. Lipsius, *Sixe Books of Politickes* (London, 1594), Bk. V, ch. 3; for the two types and the causes of war, ibid. and VI, 2–3, Montecuccoli, *Abhandlung*, *AS* i. 21–4; on just war, Lipsius, V, 4, Montecuccoli, i. 24–5; on the three types of military means, Lipsius, V, 6, Montecuccoli, i. 75–6; on military command, Lipsius, V, 14–17, Montecuccoli, i. 81–92; on recruitment, in the footsteps of Vegetius and Machiavelli, Lipsius, V, 9–12, Montecuccoli, i. 95; and on the favourable peace as the aim of war, Lipsius, V, 18–20. See also Oestreich, *Neostoicism*, pp. 80–1.

In Montecuccoli's later works these themes are repeated in a much more concise form, some of which are compressed into aphorisms and tables. Referring to Grotius's citation of Cicero's definition of war as 'a conflict with the use of violence', Montecuccoli wrote: 'War is an activity to inflict damage in every way; its aim is victory.'[35] The art of war is defined as 'the study of the good manner to conduct war'.[36] Wars are divided according to location, whether on land or at sea; type, whether defensive or offensive; and circumstance, whether civil or internal, just or unjust.[37]

Montecuccoli's extensive and systematic treatment of military organization and the conduct of war, encompassing training, discipline, supply, intelligence, fortifications, marching, encamping, and fighting, clearly reveals the tension between historical change on the one hand and Montecuccoli's theoretical ideals and historical notions on the other. His universal science of war was obviously simply a reflection of the warfare of his day, between the campaigns of Gustavus Adolphus and the early wars of Louis XIV.

At the political and social level, this was primarily linked with the rise of the centralized state, the monetary economy, and the growing professional armies. Montecuccoli's activity as head of the Austrian army and his writings, particularly the *War against the Turks in Hungary* composed at the same period, strikingly reflect these trends.

Among the developments resulting were both increasing supply problems and more elaborate logistic arrangements which, together with the cumbersome combination of pike and musket, and the effectiveness of field and permanent fortifications, made a strategic and tactical decision difficult to reach. Montecuccoli's campaign against Turenne won him his reputation as a master of manœuvre warfare. In his writings, he elaborated on supply considerations and warned against risking the country's army and fortune in battle, unless conditions were promising.[38]

[35] *Vom Kriege mit den Türken*, Bk. I, ch. I, Aphorism 1, *AS* ii. 206.

[36] *Von der Kriegskunst*, *AS* ii. 31.

[37] Ibid., and *Vom Kriege mit den Türken*, *AS* ii. 206. Also compare these with the works of Basta, Wallhausen, and Savorgnino cited above.

[38] *Abhandlung*, II. 3; *Vom Kriege mit den Türken*, I. 6, III. 6. Rothenberg, 'The Seventeenth Century' in Paret (ed.), *Makers of Modern Strategy*; G. Perjés, 'Army Provisioning, Logistics and Strategy in the Second Half of the 17th Century', *Acta Historicae Hungaricae*, XVI 1–2 (1970), 1–51; M. Roberts, 'The Military Revolution 1560–1660' in his *Essays in Swedish History* (London, 1967); G. Parker, 'The "Military Revolution 1560–1660"—a Myth?', *Journal of Modern History*, 48 (1976), 195–214; M. van Creveld, *Supplying War* (Cambridge, 1977), ch. 1.

The field of fortifications is of particular interest. Since the Italian wars in the late fifteenth and early sixteenth centuries and the rise of the new art of fortifications, developed to counter gunfire and based on the geometrical maximization of congruent fields of fire, the study of mathematics was widely regarded as fundamental for the study of war.[39] Lorini, the most distinguished Italian fortifications expert at the close of the sixteenth century, cited in Montecuccoli's source list, stated that fortifications were a science which, like medicine, was based on rules and mathematical considerations.[40] Indeed, corresponding to the *esprit géométrique* of the seventeenth century, the study of military geometry was a popular pastime at European courts.[41]

In *On the Art of War*, following an intellectual and educational pattern established by a whole series of military authors from the second half of the sixteenth century, Montecuccoli presented decimal arithmetic, the calculation of spaces, and trigonometry as necessary knowledge for the art of war, and devoted the first three chapters of the work to their systematic teaching.[42]

Montecuccoli's writings, probably regarded as a state secret and only circulated internally, were never published during his lifetime. However, when *On the War against the Turks in Hungary* or *Aphorisms*—as well as *On the Art of War*—appeared at the beginning of the eighteenth century, it was universally read. It was translated into all the major European languages (apart from English), and was published, within about a hundred years, in seven Italian, two Latin, two Spanish, six French, one Russian, and three German editions.[43]

The military thinkers of the Enlightenment were not that interested in Montecuccoli's military conceptions. On the contrary, with the

[39] For the emergence of geometrical fortifications, see C. Duffy, *Siege Warfare: The Fortress in the Early Modern World 1494–1660* (London, 1979). For the role of mathematics in the mind of military thinkers in the 16th cent. in connection with the new art of fortifications, see Hale, *Renaissance War Studies*, ch. 7, 'The argument of Some Title Pages of the Renaissance'.

[40] Jähns, *Geschichte der Kreigswissenschaften*, pp. 845–6.

[41] For the Austrian case, see Evans, *Habsburg Monarchy*, p. 334.

[42] For the literary pattern, see Hale in *New Cambridge Modern History*, iii. 178–9. For a comparison with Vauban's slightly later, epoch-making system, see Kaufmann, *Montecuccoli*, ch. 5.

[43] Rothenberg, 'The Seventeenth Century' in Paret (ed.), *Makers of Modern Strategy*, p. 60.

military developments of the eighteenth century these became quite outdated and, as we shall see, the military thinkers of the Enlightenment with their universal outlook found this somewhat disturbing. It was Montecuccoli's theoretical vision and conceptual framework that were widely admired and adopted. The men of the Enlightenment were, fortunately, not aware of the exact nature of Montecuccoli's scientific interests which probably would have horrified them. But his intellectual assumptions appeared familiar enough. It was not his particular form of science but the scientific outlook itself that counted. Montecuccoli worked out a sophisticated formulation of a new theoretical paradigm in the study of war, expressing a new, emerging world-view. Following the introduction of firearms, historical change was, to a limited degree, recognized; but it was overshadowed by the notion of universal rules and principles which was inspired by the sciences and reflected a new intellectual enterprise to subject all spheres of life to the domination of reason.

3
The Quest for a General Theory of War

The Military Thinkers of the French Enlightenment

Reflecting the Outlook of the Enlightenment

In the middle of the eighteenth century a sharp upsurge in the volume of military literature—reflecting an intense and unique intellectual activity—took place in Europe, spreading from France to the rest of the continent. Indeed, it may be instructive to start with some quantitative data. According to Pöhler's bibliographical survey of military works, more than seventy items were published, in an almost even distribution throughout the seventeenth century, in the 'art of war' category, which encompasses the more general and comprehensive theoretical works. A similar rate of publications was maintained in the first half of the eighteenth century with more than thirty items appearing in the years 1700–48. Then, between 1748–56, twenty-five items were published in a dramatic fourfold increase, and this rate was maintained in the period between the Seven Years War and the French Revolution (1756–89) with the publication of more than one hundred works. No substantial change in the number of publications occurred in the Napoleonic period or throughout the nineteenth century. The middle of the eighteenth century, therefore, marked a revolutionary growth in military publications.[1]

While this quantitative analysis shows the scope of the literary tide, it cannot reveal its origins and nature. In trying to explain these in

[1] J. Pöhler, *Bibliotheca historico-militaris* (Leipzig, 1887–97), iii. 583–610; the bibliographical items include new editions, which, like original publications, are indicative of the increasing literary activity. Such a quantitative analysis of an essentially qualitative matter is obviously crude, particularly as the distinction between works on the art of war, military history, tactics, and the various arms is fundamentally arbitrary, and the concepts themselves underwent considerable change in meaning. A similar trend is noticeable, however, in all the above-mentioned categories.

his monumental compendium of military literature, Jähns looked for answers from within the military sphere itself. The wars of Frederick the Great, he suggested, stimulated the awakening of military thinking and writing.[2]

This is hardly a satisfactory explanation. The upsurge in literary activity had taken place before the Seven Years War in which Frederick the Great earned his military reputation. Furthermore, the rate of military publications was hardly affected by any military event, be it the Thirty Years War, the wars of Louis XIV, or those of the Revolution and Napoleon. The flourishing of military literature from the middle of the eighteenth century and the ideas peculiar to it cannot be explained on military grounds.

Jähns's interpretation is merely indicative of the curious fate of one of the most influential schools of military thought, which dominated the eighteenth century, and whose legacy has since shaped the theoretical outlook on war.[3] The very existence of this school, not to mention its profound origins, collective ideas, and scope of influence, has hardly been recognized by modern scholars. Stemming from the all-encompassing ideas of the Enlightenment, which dominated all spheres of European thought and culture (including Frederick the Great's world-view), it closely followed the fortunes of the Enlightenment from its heyday to its eclipse.

This intellectual milieu can only be very roughly outlined here. On the accumulated strata of the doctrine of natural law, the neo-classical search for rules and principles in the arts, and Cartesianism, which together had dominated Louis XIV's France, stressing that reality was subject to universal order and to the mastery of reason, the gospel of Newtonian science was added. This gospel had conquered French culture by the 1730s largely owing to the support of Voltaire, its most influential propagator, and the far-reaching intellectual prospects that it appeared to have opened up affected

[2] Jähns, *Geschichte der Kriegswissenschaften*, p. 1451.

[3] Jähns's work with its invaluable, exhaustive account of primary sources is an astonishing example of 19th cent. German historical scholarship. However, following in Moltke's footsteps and in accordance with contemporary views, Jähns's conception of military *Wissenschaft* as organized, systematic knowledge based on clear concepts is modest (ibid., pp. v–vi). Coupled with the fact that Jähns is unaware of the general intellectual context of military thought (or indeed of any social or political context), this conception, imposed as it is on Jähns's subject-matter, is an unhistorical instrument, insensitive to the actual nature of the theoretical outlook of any particular period, especially the Enlightenment.

all sciences and arts. Most of the thinkers of the Enlightenment were not interested in physics as such and did not delve into the mathematical subtleties of science. Newtonian science was for them a symbol of the ability of the human mind to master reality, and they sought to extend its astonishing achievements to include the whole intellectual world. The scientific model was perceived by them as a general method for the foundation of all human knowledge and activity on an enduring basis of critical empiricism and reason.[4]

This common ideal overshadowed the many differences of opinion between the *philosophes*, who were mostly divided between deists and atheists, dualists and materialists, exponents of natural law and advocates of utility, believers in progress and primitivists, supporters of enlightened absolutism, aristocracy, and democracy—to mention the most notable differences. It was responsible for a remarkable degree of cohesion that encompassed all spheres of culture, and it was shared by a large educated community whose social élite mingled in the salons. This community embraced the ideal of universal knowledge, believed man could understand everything, and encouraged and approached with enthusiasm any new attempt to reveal the universal foundations of each discipline.[5]

Following in Locke's footsteps, Condillac developed associationist psychology in his *Essai sur l'origine des connaissances humaines* (1746), *Traité des systèmes* (1749), and *Traité des sensations* (1754). And Helvétius carried it in an hedonist direction and towards utilitarian ethics in his *De l'esprit* (1758). Society and politics were governed by principles that arose from the nature of things; Montesquieu's *De l'esprit des lois* (1748) expounded this in a manner that drew general admiration throughout Europe. Political economy was formed as a science in the 1750s with the activity of the physiocrats headed by Gournay, Quesnay, and Turgot. La Mettrie's *L'Homme machine* (1747) and Holbach's *Système de la nature* (1770) offered a materialist explanation of man and nature. Rousseau wrote his prize-winning essay *Discours sur les sciences et les arts* for the

[4] From the plethora of scholarly literature on the Enlightenment, recent and most extensive works are Peter Gay, *The Enlightenment: an Interpretation* (2 vols.; London, 1967–9), and Ira O. Wade, *The Structure and Form of the French Enlightenment* (2 vols.; Princeton, 1977); see also Paul Hazard, *European Thought in the Eighteenth Century* (London, 1954).

[5] For the ambivalent role of the salons and the social environment, see K. Martin, *French Liberal Thought in the Eighteenth Century* (London, 1954), 103–16.

Academy of Dijon in 1749–50, his *Du contrat social* appeared in 1762, and his *Émile* (1762) opened an era of educational theory. The *Encyclopédie* edited by Diderot and D'Alembert first came out in 1751, symbolizing the period; all spheres of human culture and all natural phenomena were to be subjugated to intellectual domination, and war was no exception.

Under the entry 'Guerre', Le Blond, a well-known fortifications expert, described the theory of war as being based on rules and principles derived from the experience of various generations. Military theory was founded by the classical authors and further developed by modern military thinkers, notably Montecuccoli and a series of more recent authors, most of whom were French.[6]

One of these was Antoine Manassès de Pas, Marquis de Feuquières (1648–1711), a lieutenant-general in the French army, whose widely read *Mémoires* (1711), translated into English and German, offered a set of military maxims in all branches of the conduct of war. These maxims were freely demonstrated by a perceptive analysis of cases taken from the wars of Louis XIV. Another author was the famous Jean Charles, Chevalier de Folard (1669–1752), whose works, particularly his *Histoire de Polybe* (1724–30) and related studies, calling for the revival of shock tactics, provoked interest throughout Europe.

As mentioned above, however, it was from the late 1740s that a new theoretical enterprise, unprecedented in scope and sense of vocation—emerged in a whole series of military works. At the height of the French Enlightenment, military thinkers incorporated the all-encompassing outlook of the period into the military field. War, they complained, was ruled by 'arbitrary traditions', 'blind prejudices', 'disorder and confusion'. All these had to be replaced by critical analyses and systematic schemes which the men of the period understood in definitive and universal terms, largely overriding circumstantial differences and historical change. The organization of armies and conduct of war would thus become an orderly discipline with clear theoretical tenets.

The ideal of Newtonian science excited the military thinkers of the Enlightenment and gave rise to an ever-present yearning to infuse the study of war with the maximum mathematical precision and certainty possible. However, the model that dominated their work

[6] Diderot and D'Alembert (edd.), *Encyclopédie*, vii (Paris, 1757), 823–6.

was less rigorous, and stemmed from the highly influential legacy of seventeenth-century neo-classicism in the arts.

The neo-classicists believed that they had found in Aristotle's *Poetics* a set of rules and principles for the construction and critique of artistic creation, among which the doctrine of the three unities and the rigid framework of genres were particularly influential. These rules and principles were embodied, according to the neo-classicists, in the works of the geniuses of the classical period on the one hand and of the age of Louis XIV on the other, which provided a universal standard of measurement to which all creative activity had to conform. From the beginning of the eighteenth century, this conceptual framework was being increasingly infused throughout Europe with a more liberating spirit, placing growing emphasis on the role of the creative imagination and the free operation of genius. This legacy dominated the arts in France until the late eighteenth century; and the arts dominated the Enlightenment, including its military facet.[7]

Indeed, the military thinkers of the Enlightenment maintained that the art of war was also susceptible to systematic formulation, based on rules and principles of universal validity which had been revealed in the campaigns of the great military leaders of history. At the same time, it escaped formalization in part, while the rules and principles themselves always required circumstantial application by the creative genius of the general.

De Saxe

Maurice de Saxe (1696–1750) was one of the many illegitimate sons of Frederick Augustus ('the Strong') of Saxony, later King of Poland. Early in his life, de Saxe became a soldier of fortune, and acquired his first military experience in the War of the Spanish Succession and, under Eugène of Savoy, in the war against the Turks. In 1720, he joined the French army, where he made a name for himself not only in the field but also in court and social circles. His continual efforts to procure an independent principality met with failure. But his victories at Fontenoy (1745), Raucoux (1746), and Laffeld (1747),

[7] For a general survey, see C. H. C. Wright, *French Classicism* (Cambridge Mass., 1920). Also see E. Cassirer's classical account in *The Philosophy of the Enlightenment* (Princeton, 1951), pt. VII; and R. Wellek, *A History of Modern Criticism* (London, 1955), vol. i.

as commander of the French invasion of Flanders during the latter part of the War of the Austrian Succession, gained him the rank of Marshal General of All the Armies of France and European renown as one of the greatest generals of the period.[8] His *Reveries on the Art of War* was widely circulated and aroused great interest. It is discussed here first despite a chronological ambiguity: though written in 1732, the book was only published posthumously in 1756 and was preceded by several other major expressions of the new quest for a general theory of war.

De Saxe's famous description of the state of military theory was transmitted through Jomini to the nineteenth century. It is an archetypal expression of the world-view of the Enlightenment: 'War is a science covered with shadows in whose obscurity one cannot move with an assured step. Routine and prejudice, the natural result of ignorance, are its foundation and support. All sciences have principles and rules; war has none.'[9]

Much as he regrets this situation, it may appear that de Saxe does not presume to change it. He seems openly to declare this at the beginning of his book: 'This work was not born from a desire to establish a new system [*système*] of the art of war; I composed it to amuse and instruct myself.'[10] Furthermore, the author himself appears to suggest that his book should not be taken too seriously. In a note to the readers he states: 'I wrote this book in thirteen nights. I was sick; thus it very probably shows the fever I had. This should supply my excuses for the irregularity of the arrangement, as well as for the inelegance of the style. I wrote militarily and to dissipate my boredom.'[11] What more can be said to belittle the significance

[8] De Saxe's life story and colourful love affairs, which did not lag behind his father's, have attracted some two dozen popular biographies, but a modern scholarly study is still missing. His campaigns up to 1746 were studied exhaustively by the Historical Branch of the French General Staff: see J. Colin, *Les Campagnes du Maréchal de Saxe*, (3 vols., Paris, 1901–6), followed by a fourth volume, *La Campagne du Maréchal de Saxe 1745–6*, by Henry Pichat (Paris, 1909). For his ideas on battle formation and deployment, see Quimby, *The Background of Napoleonic Warfare*, pp. 41–61.

[9] Since both English translations of the time (London, 1757, and Edinburgh, 1759) are unreliable, reference is made to the modern, albeit abridged translation of de Saxe's *Mes Rêveries* in T. Phillips (ed.), *Roots of Strategy* (Harrisburg, 1940); here, see p. 189. Wherever I deviate from this version, the French original (Amsterdam and Leipzig, 1757) is quoted in brackets.

[10] *Reveries*, p. 189.

[11] Ibid., p. 300.

of one's own work? The readers of the nineteenth and twentieth centuries who were removed from the values, literary forms and stylistic norms of the early modern period, could have received, with Jomini's courteous assistance, no other impression.

In fact, before the emergence of new attitudes during the Enlightenment, it was customary for authors to present themselves as casual scribblers and amateurs who wrote only incidently to 'amuse themselves' and 'ease their boredom'. The chivalrous ethos still dominated social values, and authors recoiled at the idea of being regarded as scholars. Thus, if we were to take their own account of themselves seriously, Montaigne, the brilliant essayist, scribbled with no attention to style, merely for himself and for the amusement of his family and friends; Montecuccoli wrote for himself, to clarify his own concepts; Feuquières wrote out of a fatherly devotion to his son's education; and de Saxe composed a work of some three hundred printed pages during thirteen nights of fever.[12] These accepted literary gestures should not be taken at face value.

It was convenient for Jomini to cite de Saxe's gloomy account of the state of military theory as evidence of the insignificance of all preceding theoretical work. Having done this, he now turned, for the same reason, to crush de Saxe's own work:

> The good Marshal Saxe, instead of piercing those obscurities of which he complained with so much justice, contented himself with writing systems for clothing soldiers in woolen blouses, for forming them upon four ranks, two of which to be armed with pikes; finally for proposing small field pieces which he named 'amusettes' and which truly merited that title.[13]

Ironically, in his treatment of his predecessors, Jomini only reiterated the characteristic attitude of almost all the military thinkers of the Enlightenment, including de Saxe. Since military theory was required to be definitive and universal, and since all past attempts were obviously not, they could only be perceived as failures. De Saxe himself dismissed all earlier theoretical work, though in a much subtler manner than Jomini. The great generals, he wrote, left no

[12] For this literary custom, its roots in the chivalrous system of values, and the case of Montaigne, see Peter Burke, *Montaigne* (Oxford, 1981), 3–4. For Montecuccoli see his *Ausgewählte Schriften*, i. 5; for Feuquières, see his *Memoirs Historical and Political* (London, 1736), vol. i, p. xxxii. For the change in the social ideal during the Enlightenment from the 'gentleman' to the 'bourgeois' and the 'philosophe', see P. Hazard, *The European Mind 1680–1715* (London, 1953), 319–34.

[13] Jomini, *Summary of the Art of War* (New York, 1854), 10.

instructive principles, and historians wrote on war from their imagination. Gustavus Adolphus established a military method in the organization of his army and was followed by many disciples. His contemporary Montecuccoli was the only one to examine the military profession in some detail. However, since the time of Gustavus Adolphus,

> there has been a gradual decline amongst us, which must be imputed to our having learned only his forms, without regard to principles . . . Thus there remains nothing but customs, the principles of which are unknown to us. Chevalier Folard had been the only one who has dared to pass the bounds of these prejudices,

but in the final analysis he too has been wrong.[14] Rather than shunning the theoretical challenge and indulging in trivialities, as Jomini implied, de Saxe was preparing the ground for his own military system.

In describing de Saxe's ideas, Jomini obviously selected the most marginal examples and those which appeared particularly peculiar in the 1830s. However, his scorn also throws light on de Saxe's conception of theory, which was similar to that of Montecuccoli and all the early military thinkers of the Enlightenment. A definitive military system was to encompass and determine all aspects of war down to the smallest details. Clausewitz described this as the first stage in the development of military theory:

> Formerly, the terms 'art of war' or 'science of war' were used to designate only the total body of knowledge and skill that was concerned with material factors. The design, production and use of weapons, the construction of fortifications and entrenchments, the internal organization of the army, and the mechanism of its movements constituted the substance of this knowledge and skill. All contributed to the establishment of an effective fighting force.[15]

This was precisely the nature of de Saxe's theoretical effort. 'The courage of the troops', he wrote, adapting the conceptual framework of neo-classicism, 'is so variable . . . that the true skill of a general consists in knowing how to guarantee it by his dispositions, his positions and those traits of genius that characterize great captains.' However, 'before enlarging too much upon the elevated [*elevées*] parts of war, it will be necessary to treat of the lesser, by which I mean

[14] *Reveries*, pp. 189–90.

[15] Clausewitz, *On War*, II, 2, p. 133.

the principles [*principes*] of the art'. As in architecture for example, the knowledge of the fundamental principles is a prerequisite to the operation of genius.[16] Accordingly, the first part of the *Reveries* deals with the 'details' of army organization, battle formation, armament, and so on, whereas the second part is concerned with the 'sublime parts' of war: all forms of warfare—in the open field, on mountains and rough terrain, during a seige, and against field fortifications—dominated by the general's genius.

De Saxe's work is a comprehensive treatise on war. He puts forward his ideal military model, his 'legion', and taking issue with the views and practices of his age, he advances many original ideas. However, rather than discussing his military doctrines, the aim of this book is to elucidate the intellectual premises that dominated his mind: he saw a need to subject military affairs to reasoned criticism and intellectual treatment, and the ensuing military doctrines were perceived as forming a definitive system.

The *Reveries* attracted much attention when it appeared in 1756. The author's fame contributed to this, and his ideas were widely discussed throughout Europe. The book was reprinted three times in 1757 alone, and again in 1761 and 1763. It was almost as widely circulated in German (1757, 1767) and English (1757, 1759, 1776) editions. A collection of miscellaneous military studies written by de Saxe shortly before his death, was published in 1762 under the title *Esprit des lois de la tactique*. The influence of Montesquieu is apparent both in the book's title and references. In one of the essays, 'Memoire militaire sur les Tartares et les Chinois', de Saxe responded to the emerging global view of the world and to the fashionable interest, stimulated by Voltaire, in the vast, remote, and ancient Chinese civilization.[17] In another essay, he discussed Marquis de Puységur's new book on military theory published in 1748.

Puységur

Jacques-François de Chastenet, Marquis de Puységur (1655–1743) began his long military career in the wars of Louis XIV during which

[16] *Reveries*, pp. 190–2.

[17] See esp. Basil Guy, 'The French Image of China before and after Voltaire', *Studies on Voltaire and the Eighteenth Century*, xxi (1963); J. H. Brumfitt, *Voltaire—Historian* (Oxford, 1958), esp. ch. II, pp. 76–84; Cassirer, *Philosophy of Enlightenment*, pp. 197–233.

he became Marshal Luxemburg's quartermaster-general (chief of staff), and finished it in the 1730s, in the War of the Polish Succession, as Marshal of France. His widely read *Art of War by Principles and Rules*, published posthumously in 1748 (reprinted 1749), was the first to propound the new ideal of a general theory of war, and was translated into German and Italian (1753).

Echoing Montecuccoli, Puységur wrote that war was the most important of sciences and arts, and yet lacked a systematic theoretical study, with people relying on tradition and personal experience. In his search for a theory of war, he reviewed the military works of antiquity, Turenne's memoirs, and Montecuccoli's writings, but found no satisfactory, comprehensive theory. In the *Art of War by Principles and Rules* he attempted to correct this state of affairs.[18]

The universal theory of war was to be derived from historical observation. Again using an argument of Montecuccoli's, Puységur dismissed the challenge of historical change. The introduction of firearms, he wrote, led some to believe that modern war was a new type of war for which the military theory of the ancients was no longer relevant. There could be no greater mistake. Despite all changes in armament, the science and art of war remained the same at all times. Expressing neo-classical conceptions, Puységur emphasized that the successes of all the great generals throughout history had been the result of adherence to the universal rules of war.[19]

The full scope of historical experience was therefore to be the source of military theory. Puységur's main interest lay in developing a system for the movements and deployment of armies, and for this the practices of antiquity were indeed still of considerable value. The works of Homer, Herodotus, Socrates, Xenophon, Thucydides, Polybius, Arrian, Plutarch, and Vegetius are cited in his *Art of War by Principles and Rules* together with those of Turenne and Montecuccoli.[20] Turenne's campaigns are compared to Caesar's.[21] Finally Puységur's own scheme is presented and then demonstrated

[18] Puységur, *Art de la guerre par principes et par régles* (Paris, 1748), *avant-propos*.

[19] Ibid., *avant-propos*.

[20] Ibid., pt. 1, chs. I and II.

[21] Ibid., pt. 2, chs. IV, VI, IX–XI.

in a fictitious campaign geographically set between the Seine and the Loire rivers.[22]

Alongside this fundamentally historical approach, Puységur also gave expression to a much more ambitious theoretical ideal. The perfection of the systematic siege warfare by Marshal Vauban, Louis the XIV's famous master of siegecraft, fascinated the military thinkers of the Enlightenment, for it exemplified the seemingly enormous potential of the *esprit géométrique* in the military field.

Vauban's highly renowned *De l'attaque et de la defense des places*, published in numerous editions, was the standard work for students of fortifications and siegecraft until the second half of the nineteenth century when these subjects were transformed by mechanization and developments in metallurgy and ballistics. Vauban perfected the geometrical system of fortifications and also developed a highly effective method of attacking fortresses. The besieging army with its sappers and guns approached the enemy fortifications through a system of earthworks, advancing in zigzag trenches and deploying in successive 'parallel' ones, thus being protected from the defender's fire. This was a systematic and uniform procedure that achieved an almost certain breakthrough with little bloodshed.[23]

As Clausewitz wrote in his account of the development of military theory: 'Siege warfare gave the first glimpse of the conduct of operations, of intellectual effort.'[24] Indeed, the military thinkers of the Enlightenment regarded it as an ideal to be expanded. Once conceived, the methods of fortifications and siegecraft provided a clear and exact—almost fully geometrical—guide for action, requiring only mechanical application. And if siege warfare was subject to a priori and precise reasoning, why could not the same be achieved in all branches of war?

This was the reasoning propounded by Puységur. Field warfare had to be made as scientific as siegecraft had been by Vauban. For

[22] For Puységur's ideas on marching and deployment, see Quimby, *The Background of Napoleonic Warfare*, pp. 16–25.

[23] Vauban, *Traité de l'attaque et de la defense des places* (2 vols., La Hare, 1737). For Vauban's life and military career, see Paul Lazard, *Vauban* (Paris, 1934) and Reginald Blomfield, *Sebastin Le Prestre de Vauban 1633–1707* (London, 1938). A good, concise account is Henry Guerlac's 'Vauban: The Impact of Science on War' in Earle (ed.), *Makers of Modern Strategy*. Also see C. Duffy, *Siege Warfare, 1494–1660*; id., *Fire and Stone, the Science of Fortress Warfare 1660–1860* (London, 1975); and id., *The Fortress in the Age of Vauban and Frederick the Great 1660–1789* (London, 1985).

[24] Clausewitz, *On War*, II, 2, p. 133.

this, emphasis had to be put on the study of geometry and geography and on their application to the art of war.[25] Armies operated in space, and while geography offered concrete knowledge of this space, geometry was to provide a precise instrument for analysing and regulating the movements of armies within it. This ideal attracted all the military thinkers of the Enlightenment, but was not pursued rigorously until Bülow.

Turpin de Crisse

Count Turpin de Crisse, a hussar officer and later a lieutenant-general, contributed extensively to the growth of military literature from the late 1740s. His many works included commentaries on Caesar (1769, 1785, and 1787), Montecuccoli (1769 and 1770), and Vegetius (1775, 1779, and 1783). His comprehensive *Essai sur l'art de la guerre* (1754 and 1757)—like the works of all the major military thinkers of the French Enlightenment—was well known throughout Europe and translated into German (1756 and 1785), English (1761), and Russian (1758).

In his theoretical outlook, Turpin was somewhat less radical than most of his contemporaries. Rather than blaming the rule of tradition and prejudice alone for the lack of systematic military theory, he pointed out the problems inherent in the subject-matter itself. In war, rules and principles were difficult to determine and hard to apply:

> Of most other sciences the principles are fixed . . . Philosophy, mathematics, architecture and many others are all founded upon invariable combinations. Every man, even of a narrow understanding, may remember rules [and] apply them properly . . . but the study of war is of another kind . . . nothing but a mind enlightened by a diligent study can make a due application of rules to circumstances.

Both genius and study are required.[26]

Though less precise and determinant than in other sciences and arts, the rules and principles of war were still absolutely and universally valid. 'The principles of war among all nations and in all times have been the same, but the little experience of the early ages of the world

[25] Puységur, *Art de la guerre*, p. 2.

[26] L. de Turpin de Crisse, *The Art of the War* (London, 1761), vol. i, pp. i–ii.

would not permit those principles to unfold themselves.'[27] The fundamental universalism of the military thinkers of the Enlightenment allowed no change in the essentials of the art of war or of military theory.

In his *Essai sur l'art de la guerre*, Turpin discusses extensively all branches of war very much after the manner of Montecuccoli. One of the last chapters of the treatise, entitled 'A Principle on which the Plan of Campaign May Be Established', is however of particular interest, being one of the earliest attempts to systematize the conduct of operations. Puységur posed the challenge of expanding the achievement of systematic siegecraft to field warfare. Turpin proposes a direct application of Vauban's celebrated technique. Indeed, he writes,

> Why could there not be some general method established which, being accommodated to the circumstances of time and place, would render the event of the operations more certain and their success less dubious? Art is now brought to that perfection, and there is almost a certainty of carrying a place when the siege of it is properly formed . . . it seems probable that the principles which serve for the conducting of a siege, may become rules for forming the plan . . . of campaign.[28]

A general must choose his objective and advance towards it until he meets with resistance. Then he should build a system of fortifications and depots across the front—the equivalent of the 'first parallel'. Having established that, he may resume his advance, zigzagging and forcing the enemy to withdraw. He should then establish a second system of fortifications and depots—the 'second parallel'. From there, he may again zigzag forward to a 'third parallel' which would already bring his objective within reach.[29] 'The success of campaign . . . based upon this maxim', wrote Turpin, 'seems to be almost certain.'[30] Furthermore, 'a general who proposes succeeding by such a method will find prudence more necessary than bravery.'[31]

Maizeroy

The poor performance of the French army in the Seven Years War stimulated intense intellectual activity within the French military

[27] Ibid. 183. [28] Ibid. 99, 106. [29] Ibid. 99–103.
[30] Ibid. 103. [31] Ibid. 99.

up until the Revolution. The deep sense of inferiority in military organization and doctrine generated a willingness to carry out extensive experiments and reforms. These made the French army the most progressive in Europe, and forged many of the military instruments that were to be employed by the armies of the Revolution and Napoleon.[32]

The Seven Years War had established the Prussian army as the best in Europe. The generalship of Frederick the Great was universally admired, and its role in bringing about the Prussian successes was obvious. But genius was regarded as an intangible quality which could hardly be studied, and it was therefore the organization and doctrines of the Prussian army that attracted all the attention. It was believed that the Prussians had won their brilliant victories by perfecting almost mechanically the firing and manœuvring potential of the linear formation operating in close order. Consequently it was universally assumed that what the French army needed was a battle formation that would equal and even surpass the Prussian model. In the 1760s and particularly the 1770s, the efforts of the military thinkers of the French Enlightenment were thus totally concentrated on developing such a formation.

All agreed on one point: the French could not and ought not to compete with the automatic, almost inhuman perfection of the Prussian drill and battle order. From Folard to du Picq, Foch, and Grandmaison, French military thinkers held to the opinion that the French people were too volatile and 'had too much imagination' to be subjected to the iron discipline of the 'phlegmatic' Prussians, or to equal their perseverance. On the other hand, French enthusiasm, initiative, aggressiveness, and quarrelsome nature allowed for freer and more flexible doctrines.

In the 1720s, Folard revived the idea of the deep formation and shock tactics as a reaction against the triumph of linear formation and firepower. De Saxe too advocated more reliance on the *arme blanche*. And in the 1750s Folard's ideas were propagated by his disciple Mesnil-Durand in *Projet d'un ordre françois en tactique* (1755). Although these ideas were received with interest, they became

[32] The pioneering and admirable study of this development is J. L. A. Colin, *L'Infanterie au XVIIIe siècle* (Paris, 1907), see esp. ch. II, pp. 73–134. Also see Quimby, *The Background of Napoleonic Warfare*; Albert Latreille, *L'Armée et la nation à la fin de l'ancien régime* (Paris, 1914); and Émile G. Léonard, *L'armée et ses problèmes au XVIIIe siècle* (Paris, 1958), esp. chs. X and XII.

the focus of attention only after the Seven Years War when they sparked the great doctrinal controversy over the *ordre profond* and the *ordre mince*.

The French Enlightenment swarmed with definitive systems intended to regulate this or that sphere of human life, and, characteristically, all the participants in the intense military controversy believed that it was to produce a system of a definitive and absolute nature. As Clausewitz wrote in his outline of the development of military theory: 'tactics attempted to convert the structure of its component parts into a general system.'[33]

Paul Gideon Joly de Maizeroy (1719–1780) was a lieutenant-colonel in the French army when the first two volumes of his *Cours de tactique, théoretique, pratique et historique* appeared in 1766. These were followed by two complementary volumes (1767 and 1773) and by the *Theorie de la guerre* (1777). The *Cours* was reprinted twice (1776 and 1785) and translated into German (1767 and 1773) and English (1781). A well-known student of classical warfare, Maizeroy became a member of the French Royal Academy of Inscriptions and *belles-lettres*.

Unlike many of his contemporaries, Maizeroy did not declare himself the founder of military science, which he already regarded as an established fact. It was true, he wrote, that the art of war in France had 'followed a blind and lazy routine',[34] but fortunately, 'in an enlightened and learned age in which so many men's eyes are employed in discovering the numerous abuses which prevail in every department of science and art, that of war has had its observers like the rest'.[35] Folard had been the first to work out and set down a military system,[36] developed by Mesnil-Durand. And Puységur, Turpin, and de Saxe had propounded their own systems. Maizeroy too had one to offer.

Historical study was the basis of military theory. Together with Guichard, Maizeroy was the most important expert of his time on the art of war in antiquity. He wrote several specialized works on

[33] Clausewitz, *On War*, II, 2, p. 133.

[34] P. G. Joly de Maizeroy, *A System of Tactics* (London, 1781), i, 357. This is a trans. of the first two vols. of the *Cours de tactique, théoretique, pratique et historique* (Paris, 1785).

[35] Ibid. ii. 179.

[36] Ibid. i. 357.

that subject, and devoted the first part of the *Cours* to a scholarly study of Greek and Roman warfare, which he compared with, and brought to bear on, modern warfare. Maizeroy also published the first French translation of *Tactica* (1770), the military treatise written in the ninth century by the Byzantine Emperor Leo on the basis of Emperor Maurice's sixth-century *Strategica*. Finally, reflecting the broadening of the historical and geographical scope beyond the boundaries of Europe, Maizeroy also examined, in the third part of the *Cours*, the warfare of the Turks and Asians.

Throughout history, Maizeroy believed, war conveyed clear lessons, provided it was seriously studied. 'The theory of the Greeks was fixed, certain and uniform, because it was treasured up in methodical treatises.'[37] No change could affect the universal fundamentals of the art of war:

> Though the invention of powder and of new arms have occasioned various changes in the mechanism of war, we are not to believe that it has had any great influence on the fundamental part of that science, nor on the great manœuvres. The art of directing the great operations is still the same.[38]

Adapting neo-classical conceptions, de Saxe had distinguished between the fundamental part of war, governed by rules and principles, and the sublime part; and Turpin had stated that war, while based on rules and principles, required a great deal of creative application. Maizeroy elaborated on this intellectual framework. One part of war, the

> merely mechanical, which comprehends the composing and ordering of troops, with the manner of encamping, marching, manœuvring and fighting . . . may be deduced from principles and taught by rules; the other [is] quite sublime and residing solely in the head of the general, as depending on time, place and other circumstances, which are eternally varying, so as never to be twice the same in all respects.[39]

The construction of armies and their combat doctrines constitutes the sphere of 'tactics'. The meaning of this concept in the eighteenth century has often been unclear to later readers. Deriving from the Greeks the concept was rarely used until the eighteenth century. With the revival of interest in classical warfare, stimulated by Folard,

[37] Maizeroy, *Cours de tactique*, i. 361.
[38] Ibid., p. viii. [39] Ibid. ii. 353.

the concept became popular with the military thinkers of the Enlightenment, and has since been a central military technical term, though changing slightly in meaning. The military thinkers of the Enlightenment used it in the Greek original sense to mean a system of army organization and battle formation. However, in the 1760s and particularly in the 1770s, as they became engrossed in this field and regarded it as the core of military theory, they also used 'tactics' as a general term for the art of war as a whole. Furthermore, since they tended to look upon the conduct of armies on the battlefield predominantly as a product of their battle formation and related doctrines, 'tactics' also implied the conduct of battle itself.[40] Only at the end of the century, with Bülow, did the emphasis in the concept change and assume its current meaning as the art of conducting battle.

The search for the perfect system of tactics is therefore the principal theme in Maizeroy's writings. In the controversy over the column and the line, Maizeroy held a moderate position in favour of the *ordre profond*. He regarded his position to be a direct conclusion from the universal nature of military theory; any doctrine had to be based on the experience of the Greeks and Romans as well as on contemporary conditions. Those who maintained that the invention of firearms rendered deep formation obsolete, implied that war was a craft rather than a science, because they disregarded a universal principle—the importance of depth for cohesion and morale.[41]

Furthermore, the principles of tactics were not only universally valid but also based upon the rigorous and precise rationale of mathematics. Explicitly referring to the Pythagorean philosophy that numbers underlay all phenomena, Maizeroy maintained that military formation had to be based on the correct choice of the universal numbers that insured flexible internal division and manœuvre. Odd numbers, for instance, prevented the subdivision into two equal parts.[42]

The conduct of operations was the second branch of the art of war. Maizeroy gave this branch a new technical term, 'strategy', whose

[40] Compare Le Blond's article 'Tactique', in the *Encyclopédie*, xv (Paris, 1765), 823–6.

[41] Maizeroy, *Cours de tactique*, iv. 13.

[42] Ibid. iv. 21–4.

origins in modern military theory also seem to have been lost. Maizeroy, who translated the Byzantine military classics into French, was the one who introduced the concept that derived from the Greek word for general and was used by Emperor Maurice as the title for his military treatise *Strategicon*. Maizeroy employed it for the first time in 1777 in his later work *Theorie de la guerre*. The concept was slow in penetrating French military jargon and was still almost unknown in Britain at the beginning of the nineteenth century. In Germany, however, where Maizeroy was widely read, and where a German translation of Leo's was published in 1781, the term was rapidly accepted and already incorporated into the military literature of the 1780s. Bülow divided the conduct of operations between strategy and tactics in the sense which is known today, and through his works and German military literature this usage was accepted throughout Europe during the nineteenth century.[43]

To what extent then can strategy be reduced to precise and universal rules and principles? In 1777 Maizeroy expounded upon his positions of 1766, which had already been implied by de Saxe and Turpin. Strategy belongs

> to the most sublime faculty of mind, to reason. Tactics is easily reduced to firm rules because it is entirely geometrical like fortifications. Strategy appears to be much less susceptible to this, since it is dependent upon innumerable circumstances—physical, political, and moral—which are never the same and which are entirely the domain of genius. Nevertheless, there exist some general rules which can be determined safely and regarded as immutable.[44]

These rules of strategy (also called the 'military dialectic' by Maizeroy) are:

> not to do what one's enemy appears to desire; to identify the enemy's principal objective in order not to be misled by his diversions; always to be ready to disrupt his initiatives without being dominated by them; to maintain a general freedom of movement for foreseen plans and for those to which circumstances may give rise; to engage one's adversary in his daring enterprises and critical moments without compromising one's own position; to be always in control of the engagement by choosing the right time and place.

[43] Bülow, *The Spirit of the Modern System of War* (London, 1806), 86–7. The translator's note (p. 34) indicates that the term strategy was still virtually unknown in Britain.

[44] Maizeroy, *Théorie de la guerre* (Nancy, 1777), pp. lxxxv–lxxxvi.

To these are also added: 'not to deviate from one's main objective . . . [and] to secure one's communications'.[45] Maizeroy demonstrates these principles through an analysis of several campaigns of great French generals.

Maizeroy's principles of strategy—remarkably similar to the twentieth-century abstract notion of the principles of war—were quite an isolated theoretical structure. At the end of the eighteenth century when interest was to focus on discovering the rationale of operations, the search was to be for much more concrete and meaningful principles. And Maizeroy's own period of writing in the 1770s was totally dominated by the quest for a definitive system of tactics.

Guibert

The intensive doctrinal fermentation in the French army following the Seven Years War reached its climax in the 1770s with the great controversy over the *ordre profond* and *ordre mince*. Guibert's *Essai général de tactique* appeared at the beginning of that decade and won the admiration of the salons. Mesnil-Durand launched a fierce counter-attack in his *Fragments de tactique* (1774), once again propounding the superiority of the column and shock action. An extensive testing of his system was conducted in the camp of Vaussieux (1778) under the supervision of Marshal Broglie, the foremost soldier in France. And one year later Guibert published his *Defense du système de guerre moderne* (1779). The *philosophes'* attention was attracted to military theory as a result of this controversy, and especially owing to the work and personality of Guibert.

Jacques Antoine Hippolyte Comte de Guibert (1743–90) embodied the remarkable integration of military theory with its intellectual environment. He was a child of the Enlightenment through and through, embedded in its cultural achievements, sharing its characteristic ideas, and stimulated by its particular code of values and standards of excellence. At the age of twenty-six he had already composed a tragedy in verse, *Le Connétable de Bourbon* (1769), but he achieved his meteoric renown in his own professional field a year later when he published his military treatise, the *Essai général de tactique*.

[45] Ibid. 304–5.

Guibert grew up under the strong influence of his father's military career. The elder Guibert was Marshal Broglie's right-hand man in the Seven Years War, and assisted him in carrying out his famous military reforms, including the introduction of a proto-divisional system. After the war, he was responsible for developing combat formations and drills in the War Office. The young Guibert joined the army as a small boy. He participated in the campaigns of the Seven Years War, and later in the war in Corsica (1768), and rose to the rank of colonel by the age of twenty-six. Receiving his military education personally from his father, and serving with his staff in the latter part of the Seven Years War, Guibert became deeply involved in his father's interests and preoccupations. Closely familiar with official French military thinking and planning, he appeared on the scene of military theory.[46]

The *Essai général de tactique* was obviously first and foremost a contemporary military work, and it was Guibert's brilliant propositions in the military sphere that aroused great interest in professional circles and made his book one of the most influential military treatises of the eighteenth century. But it was Guibert's belief—characteristic of the period—that his work offered a definitive system of tactics, finally creating a science of war, and it was the comprehensive expression that he gave to the ideas of the Enlightenment, that made his book a success with the *philosophes* and the talk of the salons. Guibert wrote the *Essai* with a pronounced and conscious intention to create an immortal masterpiece; this is apparent in every line of his work. His intellectual environment clearly determined not only the nature and strength of this desire but also the attitudes and themes required for its realization. The ambitious and enthusiastic young man appeared to have incorporated into his military treatise as many ideas of the Enlightenment as possible and touched upon most of its major concerns.

[46] No comprehensive biography of Guibert has yet been written. See F. E. Toulongeon's introd. to Guibert's *Journal d'un voyage en Allemagne 1773*, in Guibert's *Œuvres* (Paris, 1803), published by his widow; Flavien D'Aldéguier, *Discours sur la vie et les écrits de Guibert* (Paris, 1855); R. R. Palmer, 'Frederick the Great, Guibert, Bülow', in Earle (ed.) *Makers of Modern Strategy*, repr. in Paret (ed.), *Makers of Modern Strategy*; and Lucien Poirier, *Les Voix de la stratégie—Guibert* (Paris, 1977). For the most interesting testimonies on Guibert's period of glory, see below.

The introduction of the *Essai* opens in defence of the *philosophes* against the accusation that they threaten the foundations of society and particularly that they undermine patriotism.[47] A 'Preliminary Discourse' beginning with 'A Review of Modern Politics' was mainly responsible for the success of the *Essai* in the salons. Firstly, modern political and social institutions are compared with those of antiquity, and Guibert takes sides with the ancients in the famous controversy that spanned the seventeenth and eighteenth centuries in France.[48] In a well-known passage—later to be regarded as prophetic—he asserts that the best political and military constitution and an enormous potential of power are embodied in the vital institutions of the republic of the masses, drawn in the image of the ideal, simple, and vigorous republics of antiquity.[49]

Unfortunately, modern Europe appears to be too corrupt and degenerate to rise to this model. Indeed, 'what . . . do the politics of Europe present to a philosophic mind disposed to contemplate them? Tyrannical ignorance or weak administrations.'[50] Like most of the *philosophes*, Guibert therefore places his hopes on enlightened absolutism:[51] 'some moral and philosophical truths which gradually filter through error, will by degrees unfold themselves; at last one day or other reach a sovereign . . . and render posterity more happy.'[52] Frederick the Great, the friend and hope of the *philosophes*,[53] is Guibert's natural hero. Prussia's political and military institutions as well as the personality of its king are highly praised, both in the *Essai* and in later works.[54]

47 J. A. H. Guibert, *A General Essay on Tactics* (London, 1781), vol. i, p. vi.

48 For a general account of the controversy between the 'Ancients' and the 'Moderns', see J. B. Bury, *The Idea of Progress* (New York, 1932), ch. 4; and O. A. Oldridge, 'Ancients and Moderns in the Eighteenth Century', in P. Wiener (ed.), *Dictionary of the History of Ideas, Studies of Selective Pivotal Ideas* (New York, 1968), i. 76–87.

49 Guibert, *Essay*, p. viii.

50 Ibid., p. iv.

51 For the *philosophes'* attitude toward enlightened despotism that changed from hope to disappointment, see esp. Martin, *French Liberal Thought*, pp. 132–42; Hazard, *European Thought*, pp. 325–34; and Gay, *The Enlightenment*, i. 483–97.

52 *Essay*, p. 4.

53 See n. 51 above, and for the particular case of Voltaire see P. Gay, *Voltaire's Politics* (Princeton, 1959), pp. 144–70.

54 See esp. Guibert's *Observations on the Military Establishment and Discipline of the King of Prussia* (Berlin, 1777; English trans., London, 1780); and *Éloge du Roi de Prusse* (London, 1787).

Montesquieu revealed to the men of the Enlightenment a new depth of connection between all the elements of the socio-political fabric. Guibert responds to the challenge:

Politics is naturally divided into two parts, *interior* and *exterior* politics. The first is the basis for the second. All which belongs to the happiness and strength of a people springs from their sources, laws, manners, customs, prejudice, national spirit, justice, police, population, agriculture, trade, revenues of the nation, expenses of government, duties [and] application of their produce.[55]

A comprehensive scientific study of the politico-military sphere must, therefore, analyse all these factors in depth. Guibert explains that he has not yet carried this out in the *Essai général de tactique*, and this is why he calls it 'general'. But he does intend to take upon himself the writing of this extensive work, which is to be called 'A Complete Course of Tactics'. He even presents the full outline of this work (which he was never to write). It is to open with an analysis of the political constitutions of all the European countries (thirty-four in all). The domestic politics of each of these countries is to be examined in view of all the above-mentioned factors, while their foreign policy is to be studied in relation to each other. Only then will all the elements of military science itself be discussed: 'Elementary Tactics' deals with the various arms, and 'Great Tactics' deals with marching, combat deployment, and encamping.[56]

From the political background Guibert proceeds to discuss war itself. First, 'A Review of the Art of War Since the Beginning of the World' extends the new universal view of history to the military sphere.[57] Then the main problem is presented: the state of the science of war. The ambitious young man acknowledges no predecessors. As usual, all competitors are brushed aside with a thoroughness only to be equalled by Jomini. Guibert alleges that the great generals of history left no principles. Works in military history are inaccurate and, in particular, do not provide guidance; they do not point out 'causes and effects'. There are also some didactic works such as those of Caesar, Rohan, Montecuccoli, Marshal de Saxe, and the King of Prussia, but they too are deficient; they are not detailed and explicit enough. Finally, there are modern writers, but

[55] *Essay*, p. xxi.
[56] Ibid., pp. lxxviii ff.
[57] Ibid., p. xvi.

who can be recommended? Folard? Puységur, who is full of errors? Guichard, who dealt mostly with antiquity? De Saxe? As to the writers who are still alive, Guibert's attitude is somewhat different; here one must be more generous or, perhaps, cautious. He declares that he has, of course, no intention of offending Turpin, Mesnil-Durand, or Maizeroy; he has learnt a great deal from them.[58]

Something fundamental is very wrong in the science of war:

Almost all sciences have certain or fixed elements, which succeeding ages have only extended and developed, but the tactics, till now wavering and uncertain, confined to time, arms, customs, all the physical and moral qualities of a people, have of course been obliged to vary without end and for a space of a century to leave behind them nothing else but principles disavowed and unpracticed, which have ever been cancelled and destroyed by the following age.[59]

The tension between historical change and circumstantial differences on the one hand and the dominating universal view inspired by the scientific ideal on the other, was inherent in the minds of the military thinkers of the Enlightenment.

Military science, Guibert asserts, must adopt the methods that brought success in other sciences. The works of Newton, Leibnitz, and D'Alembert are the models to be followed.[60] Guibert is not satisfied with anything less than the top of mathematical science. Incorrect methodology, he maintains, rather than the nature of the subject-matter itself, has been responsible for the failure of military theory:

Let us suppose that the first mathematical truths are taught to a people inhabiting the two extremes of the globe . . . they must evidently in time arrive at the same result of principles. But has there been in the tactics any clear truth demonstrated? Are the fundamental principles of this science established? Has one age ever agreed on this point with its preceding one? But why was there no such work, which could have laid a firm foundation for its principles? It is for this reason that the military have for a long time been ignorant how to analyse the subject . . . and unacquainted with the method of explaining and arranging their ideas.[61]

[58] Ibid., pp. xlvi–xlviii.
[59] Ibid. 1.
[60] Ibid., p. xxvii.
[61] Ibid. 2–3.

Guibert's system of tactics is to solve the confusion and lay down definitive principles of universal validity. Then,

> the tactics . . . would constitute a science at every period of time, in every place, and among every species of arms; that is to say, if ever by some revolution among the nature of our arms which it is not possible to foresee, the order of depth should be again adapted, there would be no necessity in putting the same in practice to change either manœuvre or constitution.[62]

Guibert's system of tactics will thus settle all theoretical differences and establish a clear guide for action. The radical and ambitious young man finds the great works of the Enlightenment somewhat deficient in this respect; they leave the reader with no definite solution to the question of how to proceed. Montesquieu's masterpiece is one example; Helvétius's and the *Grande Encyclopédie* are another.[63] Science should be advanced to encompass everything:

> It would be very interesting to see military science improve . . . in this manner . . . I have already remarked how the same revolution be made in politics. This maxim would likewise take place in almost all the sciences, provided their theory was divested of all those errors . . of false methods . . . Then the encyclopedia of human understanding, now becoming the repository of truth, would assume her reign and affirm herself amidst the various alterations of ages.[64]

It is hardly surprising that Guibert's book was received warmly by the *philosophes* and in the salons.

The intellectual circles in which Guibert's work was highly acclaimed were neither particularly interested in, nor knowledgeable about, military affairs. But its military worth was in any case recognized widely, and it was its general intellectual connotations that impressed the laymen. Guibert's contemporaries were accustomed to the publication of masterpieces that laid the foundation of one sphere or another of human life and thought. The *Essai général de tactique* was accepted as one of these works. 'M. de Guibert', wrote the celebrated literary critic Sainte-Beuve more than a century later,

> was a young colonel for whom society . . . roused itself to a pitch of enthusiasm. He . . . published an 'Essay on Tactics' preceded by a survey

[62] *Essay*, p. 99. [63] Ibid., p. lxviii. [64] Ibid., p. lviii.

of the state of political and military science in Europe . . . He competed at the Academy on subjects of patriotic eulogy; he had tragedies in his desk on national subjects. 'He aimed at nothing less', said La Harpe, 'than replacing Turenne, Corneille and Bossuet'. [He was] a man whom every one, beginning with Voltaire, considered at his dawn as vowed to glory and grandeur . . . you will not find a writer of his day who does not use the word [genius] in relation to him.[65]

Guibert's success in the Parisian intellectual circles was indeed spectacular. Mlle de Lespinasse, who hosted one of the most important salons in the capital and was a close friend of D'Alembert, fell in love with Guibert. The hundreds of letters she wrote to him between 1773 and 1776 when she died of a 'broken heart' after he married another woman, vividly evoke the Parisian intellectual environment and Guibert's success, aspirations, and connections with the *philosophes*.[66] Another great mistress of the salons and intimate of Guibert, Mme de Staël, wrote *Éloge de Monsieur de Guibert* after his death, in which she attempted to explain his failure to fulfil the hopes placed upon him in his youth.[67] The poem *La Tactique*, written by Voltaire after the publication of the *Essai*, is another vivid testimony to the social success of the work and to the impression left by the personality of its author, particularly in view of Voltaire's ambivalent attitudes to the subject of the work itself.

The patriarch of the Enlightenment was throughout his life a bitter enemy of war. Frederick the Great's unscrupulous use of military means was one of the major factors that cooled relations between Voltaire and the philosopher-king. In a series of works of which *Candide* was only the most famous, Voltaire never tired of denouncing war, blaming it on the cynical ambition of rulers and the folly of peoples.[68] He may also have made the theory of war a target for his irony by saying that 'the art of war is like that of

[65] Introd. to Mlle J. de Lespinasse, *Letters* (London, 1902), 8–9.

[66] Ibid. The letters were published by Guibert's widow in 1809; a complete edn., including some of Guibert's own letters, was published by a descendant of Guibert in 1906, and translated into English in 1929.

[67] Madame la Baronne de Staël, *Œuvres complètes* (Paris, 1821), xvii, 275–317, ed. by her son.

[68] For Voltaire's views on war, see ch. XI of Léonard's excellent *L'Armée au XVIIIe siècle*, which includes a great deal of material on the *philosophes'* attitude to war. Also see Gay, *Voltaire's Politics*, pp. 160–1; and Martin, *French Liberal Thought*, pp. 265–7.

medicine, murderous and conjectural'.[69] But when the *Essai général de tactique* was published, Voltaire did not doubt that this was indeed a general theory of war, and a new achievement of the Age of Reason.

The poem *La Tactique* (1774) opens with a bookseller showing Voltaire the new work:

> Tactics, says I, I do declare, till now
> Not half their worth and value did I know.
> 'The name' he answered 'came from Greece to France;'
>
> . . .
>
> I therefore shut the door and read it through,
> Intent to gain by heart, with instant labour,
> The Art, my friends—to kill my neighbour.
>
> . . .
>
> Strangely surprised at this so boasted Art,
> Back I returned to CAILLE [the bookseller] with
> wounded heart,
> And throwing him his book, in warmth, I said,
> 'Go, thou by Satan for his uses made,
> The Tactics give to the Chevalier de Tot
>
> . . .
>
> But first to FREDERIC bestow
> your skill,
> And be assured he knows its meaning well;
>
> . . .
>
> A greater murderer than the great Eugene,
> Or great Gustavus
>
> . . .
>
> Thus I express'd myself—while, listening nigh,
> A youth had mark'd me with a curious eye;
> His uniform two epaulets did grace,
> Which his profession, and his rank express;
> His mien was steady, tranquil, and serene,
> His talents, not his courage, there were seen;

[69] I could not locate this quotation, cited without reference in J. Fuller, *The Foundations of the Science of War* (London, 1925), 19.

In short, it was the Author of the book,
He thus accosted me, with modest look:
'I can perceive' says he 'you disapprove;
you are an old Philosopher, and love
Mankind entire—This Art is not humane,
But needful to the earth, I say't with pain,
Where many an ABEL has a brother CAIN'.

In the poem Guibert goes on to pose the question how history would have looked had the civilized nations from Rome to France not defended themselves against the barbarians, and what the fate of culture and of the fatherland would have been.[70]

I made not a reply—the truth I saw,
And felt the force of reason's sovereign law.
I look'd on War the first of human Arts;
On him . . .
Who made the science, in his numbers, swell
Fit to command, in what he knew so well,

Yet, in my breast, I own, there rose a sigh,
I wish'd the Art, from want of use, might die;
That equity, on earth might bring to bear
Th'ideal peace, o'the Abbé de la Saint-Pierre.[71]

The *Essai* went through four editions in five years (1770, 1772, 1773, 1775), and was translated into German (1774) and English (1781). In a journey to Germany in 1773, Guibert met Frederick the Great and Joseph II.[72] In 1785 he was elected member of the

[70] For Voltaire's general attitude that regarded wars in defence of one's country and of civilization as a necessary evil, see Gay, *Voltaire's Politics*, pp. 160–1.

[71] 'Tactics', in Voltaire, *Works*, trans. T. Smollett (London, 1779–81), Misc., i. 126–30.

[72] Frederick casually referred to the *Essai* and to Guibert, his admirer, in his correspondence with D'Alembert and Voltaire. In a letter to Voltaire in which he complained about the intellectual poverty of the generation, Frederick humorously described the books sent for him by his literary agents from Paris: 'a book has been published on the art of shaving dedicated to Louis XV . . . essays on tactics are written by young officers who know not how to spell Vegetius' (The King to Voltaire, 16 Jan. 1773, in Frederick, *Posthumous Works*, trans. T. Holcroft (London, 1789), viii. 249–50). This remark is, however, perhaps too incidental to be indicative of the king's attitude; it may be an example of his famous cynicism. For a neutral and even more incidental reference to Guibert, see: The King to D'Alembert, 17 Sept. 1772, ibid. xi. 318.

French Royal Society of Sciences. He continued his military career and military, political, historical, and dramatic writings until his death during the early stages of the Revolution.

'It would be very easy at this date, but not very just, to make a caricature of M. de Guibert.'[73] When Sainte-Beuve wrote these words at the end of the nineteenth century, Guibert's reputation was at its lowest ebb, and he was mostly remembered as a short-lived celebrity and the lover of Mlle de Lespinasse. However, Sainte-Beuve's words were soon to become much more meaningful than he himself intended. Indeed, Guibert's theoretical aspirations may now appear boundless and his burning ambition amusing. But such a view would ignore the intellectual context in which he operated—the world-view, vision, and ideals of the men of the French Enlightenment. Moreover, at the beginning of the twentieth century, Colin's classical studies of the origins of French warfare under the Revolution and Napolean revealed the full influence of Guibert's military ideas which can only be touched upon here.

Perhaps Guibert did not create the one definitive general military system, but he wrote a superb doctrinal work which greatly influenced the development of future warfare. He propounded revolutionary ideas: mobility, rapidity, and boldness in the conduct of operations; the solving of logistical problems by a massive reliance on the countryside; movement in independent formations, similar to the proto-divisional system introduced by Marshal Broglie; and flexible manœuvring in open columns before deploying into the firing-line, instead of the highly complex and rigid manœuvring of the linear formation that had been employed and perfected by the Prussians. These ideas flowed into the melting-pot of the dynamic French military thinking of the last years of the *ancien régime*, and moulded the doctrines of the French army on the eve of the Revolution. Guibert's ideas were practically the basis of the official Ordinance of 1791 with which the armies of the Revolution went to war, and the *Essai* played a major role in the military education of Napoleon.[74]

[73] Introd. to Mlle de Lespinasse, *Letters*, pp. 8–9.

[74] In addition to the works cited in n. 32 above, see J. Colin, *La Tactique et la discipline dans les armées de la Révolution* (Paris, 1902); and id., *L'Éducation militaire de Napoléon* (Paris, 1901).

After the wars of the Revolution and during the Napoleonic period, when military thinkers began to analyse new experiences and challenges, they did so—despite the overwhelming revolution in military reality and perceptions—in the light of the dominant theoretical ideal that had been spread throughout Europe by the major military thinkers of the French Enlightenment. In Germany this ideal was carried forward by the military thinkers of the *Aufklärung*, who were initially only a provincial group heavily influenced by the ideas from France, the centre of culture, but who later applied these ideas in new and revolutionary directions.

4

From Military Education to a Science of Operations:

The Military Thinkers of the German Aufklärung

The development of military thought in Germany during the last third of the eighteenth century fits remarkably well into the general pattern that characterized the career of the Enlightenment in Europe. Initially, the military school of the German *Aufklärung* was overshadowed by its senior French counterpart. It emerged as a significant movement only in the 1770s, a generation after the theoretical developments in France. And although it originated independently, from a cultural environment similar to the French, and bore distinctive intellectual characteristics, the German school was influenced decisively by the major military thinkers of the French Enlightenment. However, after a period of growth during the 1780s, the intellectual enterprise of the military *Aufklärer*s took off towards the end of the century in novel, if not radical directions, winning attention throughout Europe. Finally, it contributed dialectically to the emergence of new, formidable theoretical trends that, in the context of a general reaction against the ideas of the Enlightenment, rejected the intellectual premises that had guided the military thinkers of that period, but nevertheless continued, though in a redefined form, to follow their dominant ideal—the search for a general theory of war.

I THE MILITARY *AUFKLÄRERS*

The full impact of the Enlightenment on the military field—which still deserves to be studied—transcends the scope and aims of this work. Because of the relatively provincial character of the military school of the *Aufklärung* during its formative period, confined as it was to the linguistic boundaries of Germany, an exhaustive survey of the many military writers who operated in the 1770s and 1780s will not be attempted here either.[1] This chapter only outlines some of the major expressions of the influence of the Enlightenment on the military field, and focuses on the most notable exponents of its ideas and on their distinctive message. Scharnhorst's life story and intellectual notions—an excellent case-study which will be treated in the second part of this book for reasons of later historical developments—provide an additional insight into the period.

The subtle differences between the character and intellectual trends of the German Enlightenment and its French counterpart also found expression in the military sphere. Whereas the building of systems was the driving force behind the military thinkers of the French Enlightenment, the early military thinkers of the *Aufklärung* were motivated by a more humanistic vision with a strong educational emphasis. In France the creation of a military science was at the centre of the intellectual inquiry, and the quest was for a general and definitive formula. In Germany the scientific ideal was at first less rigorous—perceived as a systematic broadening of military knowledge—and most of the attention was concentrated on disseminating that knowledge throughout the wider circles of the

[1] A gold-mine of information on this subject is contained in the third vol. of Jähns's *Geschichte der Kriegswissenschaften*. The limitations of Jähns's treatment of this material, particularly his total unawareness of the intellectual background of the developments that he describes, have, however, already been mentioned. A rich variety of primary sources is also incorporated in Reinhard Höhn's *Revolution, Heer, Kriegsbild* (Darmstadt, 1944), which deals with the intellectual transformation involved in the transition from the warfare of the *ancien régime* to the wars of Revolution, and discusses extensively some of the trends described in this chapter. This is a very valuable work despite some difficult problems (see P. Paret, *Yorck and the Era of the Prussian Reform* (Princeton, 1966), 283–4), particularly Höhn's selective and sometimes inaccurate use of the sources, often harnessed to support a stereotyped argument. Various themes are also discussed in W. O. Shanahan, 'Enlightenment and War: Austro-Prussian Military Practice 1760–1790', in G. Rothenberg, B. Király, and P. F. Sugar (edd.), *War and Society in East Central Europe*, ii (New York, 1982), 82–111.

officer corps. This is mainly characteristic of the ideas and activities of the first military *Aufklärers* in the 1770s, but also has a bearing on the theoretical outlook of Frederick the Great, the pre-eminent representative of the Enlightenment in Germany.

The image of Frederick the Great in relation to the Enlightenment was somewhat ambivalent and underwent considerable transformation not only in the public's view but also in the military sphere. On the one hand, he was the hero of the military thinkers of the Enlightenment. While in philosophy, the sciences, and the arts, the philosopher-king sought the company of Voltaire, D'Alembert, La Mettrie, and Maupertuis, in the military field it was he who was the most important authority in Europe, admired as the foremost genius of the period and as the creator of a highly renowned military system. His military works and regulations and the institutions that he developed and established for the instruction of his officers also reflected the ideas of the Enlightenment.

Yet, on the other hand, Frederick's attitude to the rank and file, whom he regarded as fodder for his war machine and upon whom he imposed machine-like conduct and brutal discipline, appalled Voltaire, and aroused disapproval among some of the military even during the king's reign.[2] After the wars of the Revolution and the appearance of France's national conscripts who were motivated by patriotic and ideological sentiments, this limited disapproval turned into a deluge of criticism against the Frederickian military system. And following the defeat of 1806, with the activities of the reformists in the Prussian army, Frederick's system became synonymous with all that was outdated and inadequate in the *ancien régime*.

A similar development occurred in the field of military education. The king's activities in this field fell short of the programmes envisaged by the military *Aufklärers* who, from the 1770s, were calling for an improvement in officers' education, and for its extension into the ranks. As a result of these changing perspectives, Frederick has been portrayed as a military reactionary more than as an exponent of the world-view of the Enlightenment.

[2] For a very early example see the anonymous 'Versuch von der Kriegeszucht' in *Krieges Bibliothek*, I (Breslau, 1755); this periodical was edited by Georg Dietrich v. Gröben who was also perhaps the author of the essay; cited by Paret, *Yorck*, p. 18.

Frederick's military writings were composed when the intellectual enterprise of the military thinkers of the French Enlightenment was still in its infancy. His *Principes généraux de la guerre* or *Military Instruction for his Generals* had already been written in 1746 after the War of the Austrian Succession, while the *Elements de castramétrie et de tactique*, his most comprehensive military work, was composed in 1770 before Guibert—his admirer and the most forceful exponent of the theoretical ideas from France—created a sensation with his *Essai*. Unlike the histories, verse, philosophical and political essays, and aesthetical and dramatical critiques which the 'philosopher of *sans-souci*', as the king called himself, wrote and published for his pleasure, Frederick's military works were written with a clear practical aim and safeguarded like any other state paper. Only his *Instructions for his Generals*, which fell into the hands of the Austrians in 1760, was published immediately in German and French (1761), English, Spanish, and Swedish (1762).[3]

Still, Frederick's military writings were just as clear an expression of the ideas of the Enlightenment as the works of the French military thinkers or his own unofficial writings. They reflected the belief that the art of war, like all arts, required a professional education and considerable knowledge, and could be treated theoretically on the basis of rules and principles that relied on historical evidence, could be used as a partial substitute for direct experience, and should be applied to particular cases through critical judgement.

At the opening of his *Eléments de castramétrie et de tactique* the king wrote:

> Those who are persuaded that valour alone suffices for the general officer, deceive themselves greatly; it is an essential quality, no doubt, but it must be matched with much other knowledge . . . [The general] must use judgment in everything and how can he do this if he lacks knowledge?[4]

The officer must have 'perfect knowledge of tactics or the art of manœuvre, of attacks, defences, retreats, marches, crossing rivers, convoys [and] forages . . . He must posses full knowledge of the

[3] Frederick's military writings were published in vols. 28–30 of the *Œuvres de Frédéric le grand* (Berlin, 1856). The German trans., vol. vi of *Die Werke Friedrichs des Grossen* (Berlin, 1913) also includes the *Militärische Testament* not authorized for publication in the original edn. There is also an earlier German trans. of the *Militärische Schriften* (Berlin, 1882).

[4] *Œuvres*, 29. 4.

county . . . field fortifications . . terrain . . . [and] defence and attack of fortresses.[5]

Frederick listed these branches of knowledge in his introduction to de Quincy's *Histoire militaire du règne de Louis XIV*, which was only one of the military classics that he ordered to be translated and distributed among his officers. Other works included Feuquières's *Memoires* and extracts from Folard's *Histoire de Polybe*. In his introduction to the latter, Frederick gave expression to the characteristic sentiment of the period: 'The art of war, which certainly deserves to be studied and investigated as much as any of the other arts, still lacks classic works.' He alleged that Caesar's works taught very little, and nothing of value was left from the late Roman empire. The art of war had been reborn only in the modern period with Maurice of Orange.[6]

Every art has its rules and maxims; they must be studied. Theory facilitates practice. The lifetime of one man is not sufficiently long to enable him to acquire perfect knowledge and experience; theory helps to supplement it; it provides a youth with early experience and makes him skilful also through the mistakes of others. In the profession of war the rules of the art are never transgressed without punishment from the enemy.[7]

The neo-classical conceptual framework is apparent: 'it is only after repeated examination of what one has done that the artists succeed in understanding principles . . . Such research is the product of the applied mind.'[8] The king himself repeatedly synthesized his political and military experience for the benefit of his successors. 'I have seen enough', he wrote in his *Military Testament*, 'to offer general rules which are of special application in Prussia.'[9]

Applied thinking is always required because experience never repeats itself in exactly the same manner. In the introduction to his *History of the Seven Years War*, Frederick wrote:

It is not probable that any similar chain of causes should, in a short time, produce the same circumstances as those under which we were . . . generals are never placed in exactly similar situations . . . past facts are good to store

[5] *Œuvres*, 29. 58, *avant-propos* (1771).
[6] Ibid. 28. 112, *avant-propos* (1753).
[7] Ibid. 29. 58–9.
[8] Ibid. 28. 169, 'Reflexions sur la tactique et sur quelques parties de la guerre' (1758).
[9] *Werke*, vi. 246.

in the imagination and the memory; they furnish a repository of ideas whence a supply of materials may be obtained, but which ought to be purified by passing through the strainer of judgment.[10]

In addition to the works of instruction that he circulated among his officers, and the seminars that he conducted for them, Frederick expanded and reorganized the cadet corps and established the *Académie militaire*, an officer academy with a broad general programme of studies which he sent to D'Alembert for his assessment.[11] These educational enterprises coincided with the appearance of military schools throughout Europe—one of the major indications of the influence of the Enlightenment.

The proliferation of military schools is undoubtedly connected to the rise of the absolutist state and the growth of central administration, but its roots go much deeper. The dominance of the absolutist state and the expansion of the standing professional armies predated the appearance of military schools. What was at work here was the emergence of the new idea that the military profession could be studied theoretically, and therefore required academic instruction; furthermore, that a broad general education was also essential for developing the officer's personality.

The most notable expression of this idea was the establishment of academies for officers alongside earlier and expanded cadet corps. The *École royal militaire* in France and the *Militär-Akademie* in the Austrian Empire were founded in 1752. The *Académie militaire* also known as the *Académie des nobles*, was created by Frederick in 1765. In Württemberg the military academy which had been formed in the early 1770s was incorporated into the new *Karls hohe Schule*. A *Militär-Akademie* was also founded in Bavaria (1789). Finally, Britain followed suit with the Royal Military College (1799), later at Sandhurst (1812), and the United States founded West Point in 1802. Because of Germany's political fragmentation and the flourishing of the German universities in the eighteenth century,[12]

[10] *The History of the Seven Years War*, *Posthumous Works*, vol. ii, pp. ix, xi, xii.

[11] The King to D'Alembert, 24 Mar. 1765, ibid. xi. 23.

[12] For this relative vitality and proliferation (nearly 50 in number), compared with the decline of the universities in France (22) and England (2), see T. C. W. Blanning, *Reform and Revolution in Mainz 1743–1803* (Cambridge, 1974), 11–12. For an extensive study and critical view see Charles E. McClelland, *State, Society and University in Germany, 1700–1914* (Cambridge, 1980), pt. I.

the academic idea was particularly in evidence in Germany. Even small German states such as Hessen-Hanau (1771) and Münster (1767) established military academies. Perhaps the most interesting case was in the tiny principality of Schaumberg-Lippe where Count Wilhelm, a general, man of the Enlightenment, and military *Aufklärer*, founded a military academy in 1766, where the cadet Scharnhorst received his earliest military education.[13]

Alongside the various types of officer schools there also appeared professional schools for the various arms, particularly for officers and NCOs of artillery and military engineering. These professions were universally regarded as scientific and the need for systematic theoretical training for them was recognized far more than for any other form of military education. Schools of engineering and artillery were founded or centralized in France (1749 and 1756 respectively), Austria (1717, reorganized 1755; 1786), Britain—the Woolwich Academy—(1741), Prussia (1788 and 1791), Saxony (1743 and 1766), Bavaria (1752 and 1786), and Hanover (1782 and 1786). The affiliation of West Point to the United States' corps of engineers is well known. Tempelhoff commanded the artillery school in Prussia, and the young Scharnhorst became an instructor at the newly formed artillery school in Hanover.[14]

These new military schools, however, still trained only part of the officer corps in Germany, and many officers continued to enter service without any regular training. Thus, perhaps the most interesting development was the spontaneous mushrooming of regimental military schools throughout Germany from the late 1770s. They were a product of both the proliferation of the state academies and the military literature of the Enlightenment discussed below. By and large, they were founded on the independent initiative of regiment commanders, exponents of the military *Aufklärung*, many of whom were graduates of the official academies. Usually the instructors in the school who taught the junior officers and often the NCOs were the senior officers of the regiment. With his transfer

[13] This outline is based upon K. von Poten's *Geschichte des Militär-Erziehungs und Bildungswesens in den Landen deutscher Zunge*, vols. 10, 11, 15, 17, and 18 of C. Kehrbach (ed.), *Monumenta Germaniae Pedagogica* (Berlin, 1889–97); and Jähns, *Kriegswissenschaften*, pp. 2447–92. For an 18th-cent. account by one of the military *Aufklärers* see F. Miller, *Reine Taktik* (Stuttgart 1787–8), i. 79–100. Also see Le Blonde, 'Études militaires' in the *Encyclopédie*, vi (1756), 94–6.

[14] See n. 13 above.

to the Hanoverian service in 1778, Scharnhorst, the graduate of Count Wilhelm's military academy, became an instructor in the military school established by the regiment commander, Colonel von Estorff, a notable representative of the growing circle of military *Aufklärers*. During his period in the Neuruppin garrison, the young Clausewitz may have participated in the activities of the school created in 1799 for the NCOs of his regiment by Colonel von Tschammer, a strong believer in the importance of education, and administrated by Major von Sydow, himself one of the first graduates of the *Académie militaire*.[15]

There was therefore a close interplay between the proliferation of military academies and schools and the emergence and expansion of a community of officers, who were advocates of the idea of military science and education, and who maintained intensive intellectual intercourse through extensive military literature that flourished in Germany from the late 1770s, cutting across its internal boundaries. The pioneering works of Ferdinand Friedrich von Nicolai and Friedrich Willhelm von Zanthier which appeared towards the middle of the 1770s, became the intellectual platform of this community.

The emphasis on education—typical of the Enlightenment belief in the ability to transform man and society and in the value of knowledge—was particularly popular during the German *Aufklärung*, which centred on the universities and which was highly influenced by pietism, more humanist and less political than its French counterpart.[16] While disciples of Rousseau such as Basedow, Salzmann, Rochow, Richter, and Pestalozzi were writing about, and experimenting with, the naturalistic approach to the education of children, military writers were stressing the necessity of military study and developing programmes for the education (*Bildung*) of officers.

Ferdinand Friedrich von Nicolai (1730–1806; not to be confused with the more famous exponent of the Enlightenment) was a colonel and staff officer in the Württembergian army. In 1769, on the request of Duke Carl Eugen and in collaboration with the University of Tübingen, he developed an educational programme for the planned

[15] Paret, *Clausewitz*, pp. 52–3; for the emergence in Prussia of regimental schools for the general education of the soldier's children, see ibid. 46–51.

[16] The best concise treatment of the differences between the French Enlightenment and the German *Aufklärung* is perhaps Blanning's 'The German Problem in the Eighteenth Century', pt. I of his *Reform and Revolution*.

military academy.[17] His ideas and experience were later offered to the public in the widely read *An Attempt at an Outline for the Education of Officers* (1773 and 1775).

The prevailing view, Nicolai wrote at the opening of his book, regards war as an art bestowed by nature on men of special talent. If war was a science of principles with mathematical foundations requiring theoretical study, the arguement goes, how could we explain Condé's victory at Rocroi when he was only twenty-two years, and had no previous military education? This view, Nicolai believed, characteristic of the Enlightenment, was the product of prejudice, ignorance, and the rule of tradition.[18] The ancients had a clear and fixed military science. And though war has changed owing to the invention of gunpowder, Maurice of Nassau and Gustavus Adolphus succeeded in their studies, and Montecuccoli re-established the science of war which was further developed by later thinkers.[19]

These opening theoretical statements are followed by the main subject of the work—a comprehensive programme for the education of officers. Military education alone is not sufficient; it must be preceded by a broad general curriculum to educate the man within the officer. Firstly, basic education is to be provided, including religion, languages, art, and the classics, followed by the advanced studies that include pure and applied sciences as well as history, geography, statistics, logic, ethics, and the laws of nature, nations, and war. For each of these disciplines Nicolai proposes a detailed programme of study and extensive bibliography. Finally, the military sciences themselves may be studied including: (*a*) equipment, organization, and armament; (*b*) military architecture; and (*c*) tactics, the science of warfare. Among these, the art of fortifications has achieved the highest scientific and mathematical status; Nicolai himself wrote a book on the subject, *Essai d'architecture militaire* (1755). The recommended reading material for the military sciences encompasses ancient and modern military classics as well as the works of all the major military thinkers of the French Enlightenment.

At about the same period, the characteristic themes of the new scientific-educational vision were also being propounded in Friedrich

[17] Poten, *Militär-Erziehungs*, 18. 316; for the academy see text above.

[18] F. Nicolai, *Versuch eines Grundrisses zur Bildung des Offiziers* (Ulm, 1775), 1–2.

[19] Ibid. 10–11.

Wilhelm von Zanthier's *An Attempt to Study the Art of War* (1775). All sciences, Zanthier writes, echoing Montecuccoli, de Saxe, and Guibert, have their textbooks and scholars, but the science of war has none. There are some works, but a general system is lacking. If war is to be studied as a science rather than a craft, theory above all must bring order into this labyrinth by clearly defining its various branches. Accordingly, Zanthier suggests the themes to be studied—battle deployment, marching, operational planning, camping, crossing rivers, and establishing winter quarters—and points out the principles of each.[20]

The works of Nicolai and Zanthier pioneered a wave of similar works that, from the late 1770s, stressed the scientific nature of war, the need for systematizing its study, and the necessity of military education.[21] Perhaps the military *Aufklärers* did not comprise a majority in the officer corps, but they were obviously the officers who expressed their ideas in writing. It might therefore be more interesting to note a rare literary reaction against their increasingly influential views, which articulated traditional feelings and attitudes. The message of Leopold Schönberg von Brenckenhoff's little book, *Paradoxa, gröstentheils militärischen Inhalts*, which was published in several editions (1780, 1783, 1798), may be briefly summarized. Firstly, Brenckenhoff asserted that war was a craft to be experienced, hence all the difficulties in treating it theoretically. Second, and perhaps even more thought-provoking, was his claim that rather than advancing the military profession, education was probably harmful to military virtues. 'Philosophy clarifies our mind and makes us better human beings, but worse soldiers.'[22] Given a choice between an

[20] F. Zanthier, *Versuch über die Kunst den Krieg zu studiren* (n.p., 1775), 3–4 ff.; also see his later *Versuch über die Märsche der Armeen, die Läger, Schlachten und der Operations Plan* (Dresden, 1778).

[21] For a survey of works and authors, see: Jähns, *Kriegswissenschaften* pp. 2439–45; Höhn, *Revolution, Heer, Kriegsbild*, pp. 90–103. One characteristic work is Col. J. von Scholten's *Was muss ein Offizier wissen?* (Dessau and Leipzig, 1782), an address to the Society of the Friends of the Sciences and Good Taste. But the most interesting example is perhaps F. Nockhern von Schorn's *Versuch über ein allgemeines System aller militairischen Kentnisse* (Nuremberg, 1785; French edn., 1783). Nockhern von Schorn, a colonel in the Dutch army and an amazingly pretentious man, was clearly influenced by Kant's philosophy and fame, and ventured to generate a philosophical revolution in the study of war. His theoretical gospel, definitions, and educational programme deeply impressed Jähns, as they corresponded to his own conception of military science; Jähns, *Kriegswissenschaften*, pp. 1775–9.

[22] L. Brenckenhoff, *Paradoxa, grösentheils militärischen Inhalts* (n.p., 1783), 11.

army of savages and an army of educated troops whose officers are experts in the sciences and philosophy, Brenckenhoff stated that he would prefer the former.[23]

Brenckenhoff's doubts were not shared by the growing circle of officers who advocated the idea of military science and education, and whose activities throughout Germany became quite distinct by the late 1770s. The principal mouthpiece of this circle was the literary organ which it pioneered and popularized—the military periodical. As noted by Jähns, if France was the leader in all spheres of military thought, the emergence and flourishing of the military periodical was almost unique to Germany.[24] These publications reflected the general proliferation of periodicals in the Germany of the *Aufklärung*, which was related to a sharp increase in book production and the rapid expansion of the reading public.[25] Against the background of total political fragmentation, the military periodicals functioned as a means of intellectual communication for officers of similar interests beyond the restricted frameworks of the particular armies in which they served.

Gröben's *Kriegsbibliothek*, appearing from 1755, was the first military periodical in Europe. Twenty-three issues were published with a short intermission and several changes of title until 1784. Johann Georg Estor's *Sammlung militärischer Abhandlungen* appeared in Frankfurt am Main in 1763. Military periodicals did not truly flourish, however, until the late 1770s. The *Kriegerisches Wochenblatt* was published in Berlin in 1778. *Der Soldat* appeared in Hamburg in 1779/80, and the *Militärische Taschenbuch* was published in Leipzig in 1780. Andreas Böhnn, professor of mathematics in the University of Giessen and a disciple of the famous philosopher Christian Wolff, published a professional military periodical for officers of engineering and artillery, *Magazin für Ingenieurs und Artilleristen* (twelve issues in 1777–89). The young Scharnhorst, one of the most notable military *Aufklärers*, edited some of the principal periodicals of the time. The four issues of his *Militär*

[23] Brenckenhoff, *Paradoxa*, pp. 11–12.

[24] Jähns, *Kriegswissenschaften*, p. 1812.

[25] The number of both published books and writers practically doubled itself every decade in the last third of the 1770s; Albert Ward, *Book Production, Fiction and the German Reading Public, 1740–1800* (Oxford, 1974), esp. pp. 64, 167–8; Jonathan B. Knudsen, *Justus Möser and the German Enlightenment* (Cambridge, 1986), 145.

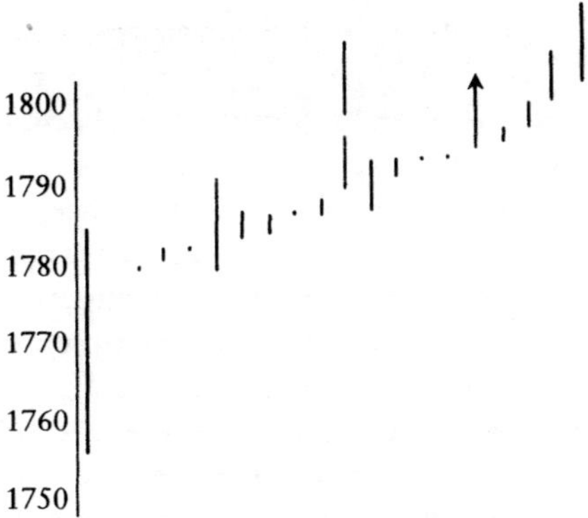

Fig. 1 Military Periodicals in the German *Aufklärung*: Spread and Duration of Publication

Bibliothek appeared in 1782–4, followed in 1785 by four issues of the *Bibliothek für Offiziere*. His *Neues Militärisches Journal* appeared between 1788 and 1793, resuming publication after the wars of the Revolution (1797–1805).

During the 1780s and 1790s there appeared Walter's *Bellona* (Dresden, 1781–5); de Stamford's and Massenbach's *Militärische Monatsschfrift* (Berlin, 1785–7); Oesfeld's *Genealogischer militärischer Kalender* (Berlin, 1784–90); Schleicher's *Neue militärische Bibliothek* (Marburg, 1789–90); *Neue militärische Briefe und Aufsätze* (Breslau, 1790); Schwerin's *Soldatenwesen* (Berlin, 1789); *Kleine militärische Bibliothek* (Breslau, 1790); *Archiv für Aufklärung über das Soldatenwesen* (Berlin 1792–3); *Der Österreichische Militär-Almanach* (Vienna, 1791); Küster's *Offizier-Lesebuch* (Berlin, 1793–7); *Berliner militär Kalender* (Berlin 1797–1803); and Hoyer's *Neue militärische Magazin* (1798–1808) (see Figure 1).[26]

A comparison with France, where only three short-lived military journals were published during the same period, highlights the volume of military literature in Germany.[27] The subscription lists, for example, which appear at the opening of Scharnhorst's periodicals, and which include hundreds of officers from all

[26] Jähns, *Kriegswissenschaften*, pp. 1812–23.
[27] Ibid. 1823.

over Germany, also attest to the scope and character of the reading public.[28]

During the 1780s the military periodicals reflected the relatively tranquil times. The professional and technical articles corresponded to the moderate conception of military science, aiming at the expansion of knowledge, and the discussion mainly reflected the great doctrinal controversies in France. This picture was transformed radically in the 1790s. The wars of the Revolution and the appearance of the French Revolutionary armies threw military thought in Germany into fierce debate between the guardians of the warfare of the *ancien régime* and the Frederickian military system on the one hand, and the advocates of the new military practices of the Revolution on the other.

Even prior to these developments, the controversial publication in Germany of the works of Lloyd, another disciple of the military thinkers of the French Enlightenment, stimulated renewed interest in the campaigns of the Seven Years War. The new focus on the conduct of operations led German military thinking in new, and even radical, theoretical directions. Until the 1790s, the military literature of the *Aufklärung* had been by and large confined to Germany's linguistic boundaries, and overshadowed by its French counterpart. Now the works of Lloyd, Tempelhoff, and Bülow attracted attention throughout Europe, and were translated into all the major languages of the continent.

[28] This subject still deserves to be studied; for Scharnhorst's periodicals, see below, ch. 7. I.

II LLOYD: HIS INTERNATIONAL CAREER, INTELLECTUAL SCOPE, AND THE CAMPAIGNS OF THE SEVEN YEARS WAR

The almost legendary life story of Henry Humphrey Evans Lloyd (*c.* 1718–83) has many facets. As a soldier of fortune, he served most of the political causes of Europe both on the battlefield and in clandestine operations. Deeply rooted in the Enlightenment and influenced by its great thinkers, he wrote extensively on his many interests. He adapted the theoretical teaching of the French military school to a German theme, and became the only British military thinker (if indeed he can be called one) until Fuller and Liddell Hart to influence the development of European military thought. Yet, he has received relatively little attention in his own country, and the full details of his life still remain unknown.[1]

Lloyd was born to a clergyman in a small village in north Wales and was educated at Jesus College, Oxford. Attracted to the military profession but unable financially to purchase a commission, he entered the clergy. In 1744, he went to France where, in a Jesuit college, he privately tutored officers in geography and field engineering, subjects on which he was already considered an expert. A year later, he took the first opportunity to leave the church and join the French army, in whose ranks he took part in the Battle of Fontenoy. His excellent drawings and ground survey of the battlefield attracted the attention of the army's chief engineer who awarded him a junior commission in the engineering corps. When the 'Young Pretender' prepared for his invasion of Scotland, Lloyd joined the expedition as a third engineer with a rank of captain. However, after the landing in Scotland, he was despatched to Wales carrying letters

[1] John Drummond, the son of a Scottish family that supported the Stewarts, and a friend of Lloyd in France between 1744 and 1756, wrote a short account of his life for the fifth edn. of Lloyd's *A Political and Military Rhapsody on the Invasion and Defence of Great Britain and Ireland* (London, 1798); see pp. ix–xii (this publication constitutes a later edn. of *A Rhapsody of the Present System of French Politics, of the Projected Invasion, and the means to Defeat It* (London, 1779)). Lloyd's son, the philologist and translator Hannibal Evans Lloyd, wrote a similar, though naturally somewhat biased, introd. to an even later edn. of this work (1842). The entry in *The Dictionary of National Biography (DNB)*, 1301–2 is mostly based on these two sources. Much new and exciting information and hitherto unknown works of Lloyd himself have been introduced by Franco Venturi in his excellent 'Le avventure del generale Henry Lloyd', *Rivista Storia Italiana (RSI)*, xci (1979), 369–433; for Lloyd's probable date of birth, see p. 369.

from the 'Pretender' to his supporters. This mission was the beginning of his international espionage career. Disguised as a clergyman, he left Wales and conducted a survey of England's southern sea-shores, preparing the groundwork for a French invasion. His activities aroused suspicion and he was arrested and transported to London. Fortunately for him, his participation in the expedition to Scotland was not discovered, and in 1747 he was released and returned to France.[2]

Promoted to the rank of major, Lloyd distinguished himself as an engineering officer at the siege of Bergen-op-Zoom. After the peace of 1748, he sought his fortune in the Prussian army, but fell back with the French in 1754 when new plans for the invasion of Britain were being drawn up, and again offered his services to the French Minister of War, Marshal Belle-Isle. He crossed the channel in 1756, and, this time disguised as a merchant, carried out his second extensive reconnaissance of British shores. However, as the plan to invade was abandoned, he sought military action elsewhere, joined the Austrian army, and was posted in Marshal Lacy's staff. Promoted to the rank of lieutenant-colonel, he participated in the first campaigns of the Seven Years War, and in 1760 commanded a reconnaissance force that followed the movements of the Prussian army.

During this period he met Pietro Verri (1728–97), the famous Milanese exponent of the Enlightenment, political economist, and man of letters, who served at that time (1759) as a captain in the Imperial army. The two men became friends, conducting long conversations and patrolling together. Verri was deeply impressed by Lloyd's intellectual breadth, varied interests, talents, and military expertise, and, according to Venturi, his works clearly reveal the influence of Lloyd.[3] In 1760, personal differences made Lloyd switch sides and join the service of the Duke of Brunswick. When the war in Germany ended, he attempted to join Count Wilhelm Schaumberg-Lippe who was defending Britain's ally Portugal against a French-supported Spanish invasion. He corresponded with the Count, sending him a political and military 'Memoir on the present state of Portugal'.[4]

[2] He probably travelled under an assumed name because no record of his imprisonment exists; *DNB* xi. 1301.

[3] Venturi, *RSI* xci. 374–5. Lloyd again met Verri in 1768–70 during his mission in Italy: ibid. 394–400.

[4] Ibid. 376–81. For Count Wilhelm, see pp. 159–60 below.

However, the hostilities in Portugal ended, and Lloyd resettled in England and embarked on an extensive literary career which was interrupted several times. In 1768 he went to Italy on a secret mission, this time serving the British government in an attempt to organize supplies for the defenders of Corsica against the French invasion.[5] In 1773–4 he accepted a Russian invitation to command a division against the Turks, and was promoted to the rank of major-general. In 1779, during the American War of Independence he composed his widely read *Rhapsody of the Present System of French Politics, of the Projected Invasion and the Means to Defeat It*, this time intending to point out ways to prevent a French invasion. Although the government paid his heirs not to publish further editions of this work, it was nevertheless published under a slightly different title during the invasion scare of 1794 and appeared in several later editions during subsequent invasion scares. According to his son, in 1782 Lloyd was intended to assume command in North America, but this claim seems doubtful.[6] He died in The Hague in 1783 and British agents are said to have conducted a search of his house and removed certain papers.[7]

The first volume of Lloyd's *The History of the Late War in Germany between the King of Prussia and the Empress of Germany and her Allies* appeared in London in 1766 with an extensive theoretical and programmatic introduction. His 'Reflections on the Principles of the Art of War' also known as 'Political and Military Memoirs' was published as a continuation of this volume in the second edition of the *History* (1781). The second volume of the *History*, compiled from Lloyd's papers, appeared posthumously in 1784. All these works were translated extensively in many different forms. The first volume appeared in at least three German and three French translations.[8] The *Memoirs* were brought out in no less than five

[5] According to the *DNB*, xi. 1302, there is no record of Lloyd's alleged governmental pension that was mentioned by Drummond (p. xiii of Lloyd's *Rhapsody on the Invasion and Defence of GB*), and it may have been Secret Service money.

[6] Hannibal E. Lloyd, introd. to Lloyd's *Political and Military Rhapsody* (1842 edn.), 9.

[7] *DNB* xi. 1302.

[8] Frankfurt and Leipzig 1777, Brunswick 1777 and 1779; London and Brussels 1784 and 1803, Lausanne 1784.

German and three French editions.[9] And Lloyd's complete work was translated into German by Tempelhoff (1783–94). This may still be an incomplete account.

Most elements of Lloyd's theoretical conception reflected the ideas propounded by the French military school, but since that school has fallen into oblivion, this fact has not been recognized by modern readers. These much rehashed themes will therefore be recounted here briefly, simply to show Lloyd's clear affinity to his predecessors, particularly to de Saxe. In his introduction to the *History* (1766), Lloyd writes that works on war, both historical and didactic, are unsatisfactory. The former are inaccurate and not elaborate enough, and the latter are too abstract. His own work combines the two forms.[10] Though very difficult to study, war, like all sciences and arts, is based upon fixed and invariable rules and principles. These comprise the mechanical part of the art and largely lend themselves to mathematical formulation. However, they require application to changing circumstances: this is the sublime part of the art which cannot be studied, and falls totally in the province of creative genius. As in poetry and rhetoric, principles are useless without divine fire.[11]

Lloyd's principles relate to the organization of armies. The first deals, for example, with the clothing of the troops, the second with shooting, the third with marching and deploying.[12] As mentioned, many of the principles of war are susceptible to mathematical formulation; Lloyd had distinguished himself as a military engineer from his youth. Fortifications are 'purely geometrical . . . and may therefore be learnt by anyone'.[13] This is also the case with artillery, which 'is nothing but geometry', and with the art of encamping.[14] Mathematical principles are also essential for calculating marches, which are based on considerations of time and space. They are even necessary for determining battle formations since 'the impulse that bodies, animate or inanimate, make on each other . . . is in proportion to mass and velocity'.[15]

[9] Frankfurt and Leipzig 1783, Münster 1783, Vienna 1785, Leipzig 1789 and 1802; London 1784, Basle 1798, Paris 1801.

[10] *History of the Late War between the King of Prussia and the Empress of Germany and her Allies* (London, 1781), vol. i introd., i–iv.

[11] Ibid., pp. vi–viii.

[12] Ibid., pp. viii ff.

[13] Ibid., pp. xxi–xxii.

[14] Ibid., pp. xxiii, xxi.

[15] Ibid., pp. xx–xxi.

This far-reaching mechanistic position is not coincidental. Lloyd, who often described the army as a great machine, strongly adhered to the mechanistic and materialistic interpretation of the world. 'The modern philosophy,' he wrote, 'though for the most part founded on mathematical principles, has not in the course of a century been able to expel entirely the dreams and visions of Plato and Aristotle.'[16]

Lloyd's mechanistic outlook is fully revealed in his more extensive theoretical essay, 'Reflections on the Principles of the Art of War', or 'Memoirs' (1781). After the customary comparison between the ancients and the moderns, leading to the conclusion that shock-arms and the *ordre profond* should be incorporated more widely, Lloyd moves on to one of his major theoretical contributions to the military school of the Enlightenment. He is the first to develop his predecessors' notions regarding the moral qualities of the troops into a systematic study by applying the mechanistic-hedonistic psychology of the Enlightenment to the military field.

Thanks to Venturi's recent discoveries, we know that in the late 1760s, after writing the first volume of his *History*, Lloyd wrote a substantial manuscript, 'Essai philosophique sur les gouvernements', which he probably intended to expand into a larger work 'on the different governments established among mankind'.[17] He apparently referred to this work when he told Piero Verri in 1768 that he intended to write a book which would be inspired by Helvétius and Montesquieu.[18] The influence of the former dominates chapters 2 and 3 of the 'Essai philosophique'—'Des sensations' and 'Des passions'—and it is again manifest in Lloyd's psychological discussion in the 'Memoirs', entitled 'The Philosophy of War'.

In the footsteps of Hobbes's *Leviathan* (1651), La Mettrie's *L'Homme machine* (1747), and Helvétius's *De l'esprit* (1758), Lloyd writes: 'Fear of, and an aversion to pain, and the desire for pleasure, are the spring and cause of all actions, both in man and other species of animals . . . Pain and pleasure arise from interior and mechanical causes.'[19] He discusses at length the emotions motivating generals and troops,

[16] Ibid. 12.

[17] The manuscript is deposited at the Fitzwilliam Museum in Cambridge; Venturi, *RSI* xci. 383. For the intended expansion see Lloyd's anonymous *An Essay on the English Constitution* (London, 1770), preface.

[18] Venturi, *RSI* xci. 383.

[19] Ibid. 80–1.

listing pride, envy, glory, honour and shame, riches, religion, women, music, and so on.[20]

His enquiry into their causes and effects has a clear practical purpose: by using the right approach, the general can control and manipulate the human material at his disposal. By 'offering such motives to the troops as naturally tend to raise their courage when depressed and check it when violent or insolent . . . he becomes entirely master of their inclinations and disposes of their forces with unlimited authority'.[21] Echoing de Saxe, Lloyd calls this 'the most difficult and sublime part of this, or of any other profession'.[22]

Montesquieu was the chief inspiration behind another of Lloyd's contributions to the military school of the Enlightenment. Like Guibert, but independently, Lloyd applied Montesquieu's major legacy to the military field. Already in the introduction to the first volume of his *History* (1766), he had emphasized the significance of 'natural history' and 'political law' in determining the face of war. Population, climate, production, soil, government, and similar factors were responsible for the varying national character of the European armies, each of which was briefly discussed by Lloyd.[23] As mentioned above, the 'Essai philosophique sur les gouvernements' was also inspired by Montesquieu, and so were two later works of Lloyd, which were published anonymously and which were presented as parts of the planned treatise 'on the different governments'.

In *An Essay on the English Constitution* (1770), a political pamphlet, Lloyd elaborated on the balance of power in England between monarchy, aristocracy, and democracy. He also proposed a pioneering economic and demographic analysis of military power according to which the size of the population plus the volume of revenues provided a measurement for the 'constant power', the infrastructure of a state.[24] This was a product of his interest in political economy. In *An Essay on the Theory of Money* (1771), in which he advocated the extensive use of paper money, Lloyd

[20] Venturi, *RSI* xci. 69–96.

[21] Ibid. 70.

[22] Ibid. 70.

[23] *History*, vol. i, pp. xxxi ff.

[24] Lloyd, *English Constitution*, ch. IX. Also see id., *An Essay on the Theory of Money* (London, 1771), ch. V; and id., *Rhapsody of the Present System of French Politics* (London, 1779), ch. II.

elaborated on the relationship between the quantity of money in the economy and a series of social measurements.

Simultaneously, Guibert attempted his own application of Montesquieu's legacy to the military field in his *Essai*, which was praised by Lloyd.[25] And in his 'Principles' (1781) Lloyd returned to the same subject in a chapter entitled the 'Connection between the Different Species of Government and Military Operations'. Explicitly relying on Montesquieu, he analysed the military characteristics, institutions, and virtues of despotic, monarchic, republican, and aristocratic regimes.[26]

Interestingly enough, Lloyd's influence on the development of military thought was to transcend his own theoretical intentions and conscious contributions. His history of the Seven Years War was to be instrumental in shifting the interest of military theorists from the organization of armies to the conduct of operations. This field had already been Puységur's main concern and received some attention from all the military thinkers of the French Enlightenment, though they tended to classify it as belonging to the sublime, indeterminant part of the art of war. However, the great successes of the Prussian army were predominantly interpreted in a characteristic structural approach which concentrated on the Prussian military system. Attention thus focused on devising a system of 'tactics' for the French army, and this preoccupation was reinforced even further by the ideas of Folard and Mesnil-Durand that incited the great controversy over the line and the column. Now, Lloyd wrote a widely read campaign history of the greatest war of the period. His controversial account of Frederick the Great's generalship provoked much interest. Attention was beginning to turn from the systems of organization to the conduct of operations.

Puységur wrote that a science of operations had to be based on the study of geography and geometry. From his youth, when he had privately taught geography to officers, Lloyd had earned a reputation for being an expert in this field. His comprehensive survey of British

[25] *History*, vol. i, pt. 2, p. 131.

[26] Ibid. 97–125; the reference to Montesquieu is on p. 98. For an earlier version see the *Rhapsody* (1779), ch. III.

shores from the point of view of a possible invasion was later published in his *Rhapsody*. The *History of the Late War in Germany* (1766) also opened with an extensive geographical survey of the participating states and the theatres of operations. This included a detailed analysis of distances, directions, mountain ranges, river lines, sea-shores, fertility of soil, and density and concentration of population.

This geographical analysis was associated with the growing military use of more accurate maps, made available by the developments in cartography. The advance in this field, stimulated by the great geographical discoveries of the sixteenth century and made possible by the introduction of accurate methods of measurement during the seventeenth century, was enhanced in the eighteenth century by military demands and government involvement. Frederick the Great was still poorly equipped with maps,[27] but, by the second half of the century, most of western and central Europe was covered by an extensive, quite accurate network of maps.

César François Cassini de Thury's thorough topographical survey of France, subsidized by the French government, had begun in the 1730s and was completed in 1789. A fairly accurate topographical atlas of Germany was published in 1750 by the geographical publishing house of J. B. Homann. F. W. Schettan's extensive topographical atlas of Prussia and her neighbours was completed in 1780, but disappeared immediately into the Prussian archives. J. G. A. Jäger's *Grand atlas d'Allemagne* appeared in 1789. The Ordnance Survey was founded in Britain in 1791, concentrating at first on the cartography of the southern counties for military purposes.[28]

Maps not only provided and displayed accurate information on the theatre of operations, but also became increasingly more dominant as the medium of operational planning and staff work. As a result, strategic planning was now commonly thought of in

[27] Christopher Duffy, *The Army of Frederick the Great* (London, 1974), 146–7.

[28] R. V. Tooley and C. Bricker, *A History of Cartography* (London, 1968), 42, 64, 40. Apart from the previous reference and a few words in Colin's *L'Education militaire de Napoléon*, pp. 99–103, there appears to be no study of the development of the military use of maps. What seems to be a very important contribution, Josef Konintz's *Cartography in France 1660–1848* (Chicago, 1987), appeared too late to be consulted in this book.

graphical terms. The movements of armies in space were represented by a whole new range of graphic images. Lloyd introduced one of the first and most useful of these images, the *line of operations*, which represented the communications of the army in the field with its bases of supply, and which expressed one of the dominant features of eighteenth-century warfare.

The ever-increasing size of European armies throughout the modern period, supported by the growing political and financial power of the absolutist state, no longer enabled field-armies to sustain themselves totally on local requisitions of food supplies.[29] On the other hand, the resources of the state also made possible an auxiliary system of supply based on depots and convoys, first organized by Le Tellier and Louvois for the expanding armies of Louis XIV.[30] Coupled with the relative and much stereotyped reluctance of the generals of the *ancien régime* to risk their hard-to-replace troops and political fortunes in a decisive battle, these supply arrangements led to what post-Napoleonic commentators were to call 'wars of manœuvre'. The campaigns of Montecuccoli against the French on the Rhine were among the early examples of this strategic pattern which was dominated by the attempt to threaten the enemy's communications while securing one's own. These practices were therefore already more than a century old when Lloyd introduced the concept of the line of operations in 1781. Old practices were now represented by the new images derived from map planning, and the resulting concepts were to gain dominance because they were perceived as a key for applying the theoretical ideal of the Enlightenment to a new focus of interest, the conduct of operations.

Lloyd introduced the concept of the line of operations only in his theoretical work of 1781 and merely as one among many other themes. He apparently used a concept which was already gaining some currency rather than inventing it himself.[31] He explained that this line, which linked the army in the field to its depots, resulted from the dependence of contemporary European armies on their organized system of supply. The Tartars, for example, who lived

[29] See ch. 2, n. 38 above.

[30] Van Creveld, *Supplying War*, ch. 1.

[31] In his *History*, i. 134, Lloyd writes that 'the line . . . is called The Line of Operations', rather than '*I call* this line . . .'

exclusively off the countryside, were independent of supply lines, and could thus operate with equal freedom in all directions.[32] But this was not the case with modern European armies. The security of their supply line was a central consideration in their operational planning.

From the nature of these lines of operations and supply, several major implications arise. As far as circumstances allow, the shortest and most convenient line must be chosen. It must be directed so as not to be exposed to flank attacks. If extended too far, it might be cut off, leaving the army in the field without supplies in the midst of hostile territory. Thus in order to shorten his lines, the attacker must try to advance his bases as far as possible. On the other side, the defender should manœuvre to threaten the enemy's line of operations, thus forcing him to retreat without even being defeated in battle. The fate of the entire war is therefore dependent on the choice of the line of operations. Other conditions being equal, he who possesses the shorter and more secure lines of operations has the advantage.[33]

Lloyd's *History*, which was very critical of Frederick the Great's generalship in the Seven Years War, provoked in turn much criticism in Germany and Prussia, partly on national grounds, but chiefly for more substantial reasons. Lloyd was clearly biased toward the Austrian cause, and his criticism was often superficial and unsubstantiated. In his Prussian 'counter-history', *Geschichte des siebenjährigen Krieges* (6 vols.; 1785–1801), Colonel, later General, Tempelhoff made this point.

However, while taking issue with Lloyd's interpretation of the war, Tempelhoff, one of the principal military *Aufklärer*s shared his fundamental outlook on military theory and also accepted his reasoning concerning the line of operations. Theory, he explained, was the counterpart of experience in the study of war. Rather than being pedantic, as many regarded it to be, its principles were derived from, and directed towards, action. Without it, everything appeared coincidental, and no analysis was possible in so important and complex a science. In the light of theory, prejudices, errors, and old habits could be rejected.[34] As for the line of operations, armies indeed

[32] Lloyd, *History*, i. 133.

[33] Ibid. 134–43.

[34] Georg Friedrich von Tempelhoff, *History of the Seven Years War* (London, 1793), i. 81–2; since the German original was not available to me, references are made to this abridged English edn.

marched on their stomachs; if the need of supplies was not satisfied there could be no operations. In the Thirty Years War it had still been possible to march in any direction, but the larger armies of later times had to rely on magazines, supply convoys, and lines of operations. These lines had to be as short and straight as possible. The success of a campaign was totally dependent upon their security.[35] Now if Lloyd's principles were correct, his application of them had to be wrong; his criticism of Frederick the Great's conduct of operations, written in 1766, was contradicted by his observations on the line of operations developed in 1781.[36]

Lloyd's concept of the line of operations and its broader implications which may be called the 'rationale of operations', were extremely fertile theoretical devices that gave conceptual representation to fundamental features of contemporary and later warfare, and, as such, were to have a long career. This fact has been somewhat obscured by the double-edged revolution in military thinking that was to take place at the turn of the eighteenth century, and whose implications and legacy were extremely hostile towards Lloyd's military ideas.

First, there was the emergence of all-out war, the product of the moral energies and material resources introduced by Revolutionary France. In his rationale of operations based on the logic of supplies, Lloyd reflected the Austrian attitudes to warfare during and after the Seven Years War. This was by far the most extreme example of the alleged reluctance of the generals of the *ancien régime* to risk a decisive battle. To those who experienced Revolutionary and Napoleonic warfare, these traditional attitudes appeared as a gross, absurd error. Indeed, 'absurdity' was the verdict of Napoleon himself on Lloyd's approach to warfare.[37]

The new military outlook was shared by Clausewitz, who, as we shall see, as part of a general reaction against the Enlightenment, also led an intellectual revolution against the traditional conception of military theory. His criticism was fuelled by the tendency, headed by Tempelhoff, to perfect the logic of supply into a more complete and precise rationale of operations, leading to increasingly artificial forms.[38]

[35] Ibid. 61–74. [36] Ibid. 74–81.

[37] Napoleon I, *Notes inédites de L'Empereur Napoléon Ier sur les mémoires militaires du géneral Lloyd* (Bordeaux, 1901).

[38] See e.g. Tempelhoff, *History*, i. 63–74, and his essay on convoys in *History*, ii. 215–36. For Scharnhorst's criticism see p. 166 below; and for Clausewitz's attitude, Clausewitz, *On War*, II, 2, p. 135. For a modern criticism of Tempelhoff's largely artificial portrayal of the contemporary supply system, see van Creveld, *Supplying War*, p. 29.

No one reflected the diversity of ideas and the many conflicts created by this double-edged revolution in military thought more strikingly and extremely than Adam Heinrich Dietrich von Bülow with his extraordinary mixture of old and new. Bülow also completed the shift of interest within the military school of the Enlightenment from the construction of armies to the conduct of operations. Whereas the concept of the line of operations had been only one of the themes in Lloyd's theoretical work, and not even the principal one, Bülow now transformed it into the centrepiece of a new science of operations.

III BÜLOW: BETWEEN A GEOMETRICAL SCIENCE OF STRATEGY AND THE REVOLUTION IN WAR

Renowned as an extremely arrogant and provocative man and working at a time when warfare was revolutionized, Adam Heinrich Dietrich von Bülow (1757–1807) gave the most sensational and controversial expression to each of the changing and often conflicting themes that he propounded during the seven years of his short career as a military theorist. While offering a thoroughly geometrical science of strategy and pushing some of the theoretical notions of the military thinkers of the Enlightenment to the extreme, he was also the most radical advocate both of the old 'war of manœuvre' and the tactical innovations and social resources introduced into war by the Revolution and Napoleon.

Bülow was born in 1757 and joined the Prussian army at the age of fifteen, serving first in the infantry and later in the cavalry. In 1790 he left the Prussian service as a lieutenant and began travelling, trying his luck in unsuccessful commercial enterprises, journalism, and writing. He lived in France, the Netherlands, and England, visited the United States, and wrote his first book on the new American republic (1797). More than a dozen books, primarily on military subjects, followed in less than ten years.[1] In his second book, *Geist des neuern Kriegssystems* (1799), he developed his well-known conception of operations which aroused both positive and negative responses.

Bülow's rationale of operations derived directly from the theoretical and historical reasoning propounded by Lloyd and Tempelhoff.[2] The modern conduct of war, he argued, was based on lines of operations, themselves a product of the greatest revolution in the history of war, the introduction of firearms. Firearms raised

[1] Edward Bülow, a son-in-law of Bülow's brother, General Bülow-Dennewitz who distinguished himself in the Napoleonic Wars, wrote a biographical introduction to a selection from Bülow's writings that he edited in collaboration with Wilhelm Rüstow: *Militärische und vermischte Schriften* (Leipzig, 1853), 3–48. Also see Jähns, *Kriegswissenschaften*, pp. 2133–45.

[2] Bülow himself ignored Lloyd's pioneering role in introducing the concept of the line of operations, and attributed it to his rival, Tempelhoff: see Bülow, *The Spirit of the Modern System of War* (London, 1806), 245. Bülow apparently intended to flatter Tempelhoff who was still alive, active, and close by, and who indeed praised his work.

the need for a regular supply of ammunition. Furthermore, the volume of fire took the place of individual valour as the decisive factor in battle, and consequently the number of troops that a state could throw into war became the determinant factor of military might. According to Bülow's interpretation of the 'military revolution', this, in turn, drove the European powers continually to expand their military forces, thus creating the need for an elaborate supply system—the 'base' of magazines and the 'line of operations' for the movement of convoys to the army in the field.[3] From the campaigns of Montecuccoli against Turenne, and those of Louis XIV, particularly the War of the Spanish Succession, the new supply system became the rationale behind the conduct of operations. The manœuvres of the field-armies and the complex systems of fortresses became the principal means of threatening the enemy's lines of operations while securing one's own, and replaced battle as the centre of warfare.[4]

However, Lloyd's and Tempelhoff's rationale of supply and operations appeared to suggest a wider and more sophisticated theoretical treatment. Could not the armies' movements in space in relation to each other's location and bases be represented geometrically? Puységur had suggested that geometrical study was needed in order to establish the conduct of operations on solid theoretical grounds; and in Turpin's idea to adapt Vauban's siege-system to field warfare there had also been implicit a clear geometrical element.[5] On the whole, Bülow's attempt corresponded to some of the deepest, yet never pursued notions of the military thinkers of the Enlightenment.

An attacking army advancing into enemy territory and towards its objective, the 'object', creates in its movement a sort of imaginary triangle in whose vertex it stands. It draws its supplies from a system of magazines in its rear, at the base of the triangle (the 'base'), and its supply routes form a segment whose boundaries are the sides of the triangle. The defender's field-armies or forces situated in fortresses may penetrate from these sides toward the rear of the attacking army,

[3] *System*, pp. 1–5.

[4] Ibid., and also p. 236.

[5] It is interesting to note that by 1805, Bülow was aware of Turpin's earlier attempt to systematize the conduct of operations. He concluded his *Lehrsätze* by extensively quoting from Turpin's fifty-year-old work: *Lehrsätze des neuern Krieges, oder reine und angewandte Strategie* (Berlin, 1805), 253–74, esp. 261–4.

threaten to cut off the lines of supply, and force the enemy to retreat. Surely, the defender's ability to approach the attacker's rear without being cut off himself depends on the depth of the attacker's advance and the width of his supply lines; or, in other words, on the shape of the imaginary triangle. The deeper the advance of the attacking army and the narrower his supply base, the shorter the distance that the defender, penetrating from the flank, has to cover in order to cut off the attacker, and the safer his own supply lines. In geometrical terms, the narrower the base of the triangle and the longer the perpendicular to it (that is, the narrower the 'object angle'), the easier it is for the defender to cut off the attacker without being cut off himself (see Figure 2).

Could the point from which the attacker's advance becomes, logistically speaking, insecure, be accurately fixed? Bülow claimed that he succeeded in determining it with geometrical precision and certainty. Having examined a series of lines of operations he concluded that an 'object angle' of 90 degrees was the critical point. An angle narrower than 90 degrees did not allow adequate cover for the attacker's lines of operations; and the narrower it became, the more insecure his advance. On the other side, an angle wider than 90 degrees guaranteed the security of the attacker's lines, for by trying to cut them off, the defender exposed his own

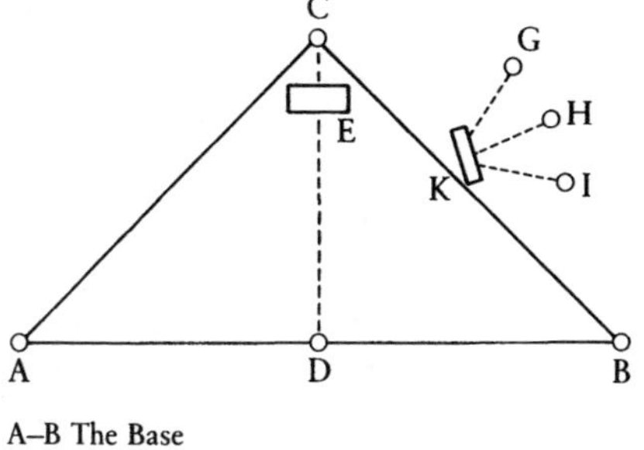

A–B The Base
C The Object
D–C The Attacker's Line of Operations
E The Attacking Army
G, H, I, K The Defender's Fortresses and Field Forces

Fig. 2 A Figure from Bülow's *Spirit of the Modern System of War*

lines; and the wider the angle, the more secure the attacker's advance became.[6]

If indeed this was the case, then Bülow had discovered the mathematical secret of strategy, and established it as a science. From now on, according to Bülow, there was no need for crude considerations and the hazardous trial of battle in order to plan and decide the fate of a campaign. If the attacker relied on an unsound base, the defender could force him to retreat without resorting to battle.[7] Battle was made unnecessary by the scientific perfection of strategy. 'War will be no longer called an art, but a science . . . every one will be then capable of understanding and application; the art itself will be a science, or be lost in it.'[8] The military thinkers of the Enlightenment always left room, alongside the 'scientific' part of war, for that which could not be reduced to rules and principles and was governed by creative genius. Now, 'the sphere of military genius will at last be so narrowed, that a man of talents will no longer be willing to devote himself to this ungrateful trade'.[9]

Indeed, not only the artistic part of war but war itself was to disappear. In the second part of *The Spirit of the Modern System of War*, Bülow analysed the implications of the new military science on the European international system, and reached the conclusion that Europe would be divided into several large states between which perpetual peace would prevail. This was to be the result of the equilibrium inherent in the principle of the base. On the one hand, modern war gave the advantage to large states with mass armies and long borders which provided a wide base. Small states would therefore be swallowed up by the larger ones.[10] There would remain only Spain, France, Italy, Switzerland, the Austrian Empire, Prussia with northern Germany, Denmark, Sweden, Russia, the British Isles, and European Turkey.[11] On the other hand, according to the principle of the base, the strength of the attacker decreased with the increase of distance between himself and his depots. Bülow had already offered a geometrical measurement for the rate of this decrease; now he suggested an arithmetical one, derived directly from Newtonian mechanics. Military force was subjected to the law of gravitation:

[6] Bülow, *System*, 36–68.
[7] Ibid. 34–5.
[8] Ibid. 228–9.
[9] Ibid. 228.
[10] Ibid. 187–97.
[11] Ibid. 277–86.

> The agency of military energies, like the other effects of nature, becomes weaker . . . in an inverse ratio of the square of the distance; that is to say, in this particular, of the length of the line of operations. Why should not this law, which governs all natural effects, be applicable to war, which now consists in little more than the impulsion and repulsion of physical masses? If, which I do not doubt, it is admissible in the theory of lines of operations, we may in future easily calculate the utmost extent to which military success may be carried.[12]

From a certain point the principle of the base therefore works to the advantage of the defender.[13] 'Every power, then, must ultimately be circumscribed within a certain sphere of military activity, beyond which it must take care not to go.'[14] With the division of Europe between eleven large states, none would be capable of further territorial expansion. War would become pointless. The perpetual peace of the philosophers, propounded shortly before in Kant's *Zum ewigen Frieden* (1795), would be the final result of the principle of the base.[15]

Bülow thus offered not only a geometrical science of strategy but also a mathematical science of politics. Indeed in the twentieth century, he was to be proclaimed a forerunner by the advocates of a geopolitical science.[16]

When Bülow put forward his science of operations in 1799, military practice and theory were already undergoing a far-reaching transformation brought about by the wars of the Revolution and Napoleon. From the late 1790s, a lively debate regarding the significance and scope of this transformation was taking place in professional circles in Germany and raging in the military periodicals

[12] Ibid. 198–9.
[13] Ibid. 213–21.
[14] Ibid. 199.
[15] Ibid. 222–9.
[16] Robert Strausz-Hupé, *Geopolitics: The Struggle for Space and Power* (New York, 1942), 14–21; cited by R. R. Palmer, 'Frederick the Great, Guibert, Bülow' in Earle (ed.), *Makers of Modern Strategy*, p. 69. It is also interesting to note that the surprising similarity of the map of Europe after the unification of Italy and the Austro-Prussian war of 1866 to Bülow's predictions (setting aside the relevance of his analysis) led in 1867 to a republication in Britain of the political part of the *System* as *Pacatus Orbis* (London, 1867).

and literature. Taking the form of a confrontation between the guardians of the old Frederickian system and the supporters of the military as well as social innovations introduced by the Revolution, this debate centred on two main issues: (*a*) the flexible tactics of the French Revolutionary armies, particularly the extensive use of *tirailleurs*, skirmishers in open formation, as opposed to the Frederickian rigid linear tactics; (*b*) the French armies of mass conscription motivated by patriotic and ideological sentiments, as opposed to the professional standing armies of the *ancien régime*, held together by a combination of brutal discipline and *esprit de corps*.[17]

Bülow was fast becoming one of the major advocates of the new Revolutionary warfare and the most provocative critic of the Frederickian system. In *The Spirit of the New System of War* he made the case for the *tirailleurs*, which he elaborated and presented even more forcefully in his later *Neue Taktik der Neuern, wie sie seyn sollte* (1805).[18] This development in tactics had no bearing on his system, but other principal features of the new warfare certainly had. This fact was already becoming manifest in Bülow's own analysis of the campaign of 1800.

In his introduction to *The Campaign of 1800*, Bülow reiterated his claim to be the founder of military science, reasserted the system of the base and the angle of 90 degrees, and made an effort to present them as the rationale behind the French success.[19] However, in the book itself, he hardly resorted to his system. Instead, his analysis concentrated on the social and political infrastructure of Revolutionary France as the major reason for her victory over the Austrian Empire. *Militarily and Politically Considered* was the subtitle of the book. The campaign could only be understood by looking at the nature of the nations involved. The Revolution had abolished feudalism and provided France with mass armies, many times larger than those her enemies could raise, and these were animated by a new

[17] For French Revolutionary tactics see John A. Lynn's new study, *The Bayonets of the Republic* (Chicago, 1984). For the military debate in Germany see: Paret, *Yorck*; Höhn, *Revolution, Heer, Kriegsbild*; W. Shanahan, *Prussian Military Reforms 1786–1813* (New York, 1945), ch. III; and the chs. on Berenhorst and Scharnhorst below.

[18] Bülow, *System*, esp. pp. 174–86.

[19] Bülow, *Der Feldzug von 1800, militärisch-politisch betrachtet* (Berlin, 1801), esp. pp. ix and xiv.

spirit.[20] Money motivated the armies of the *ancien régime*, whereas the Revolution promoted moral forces.[21] Human masses and moral energies were at the root of French power.

The primacy of the social and political infrastructure did not necessarily conflict with Bülow's rationale of operations, but it certainly revealed its very narrow nature which could hardly support his military and political sciences. Furthermore, the rationale itself also suffered devastating blows. Firstly, the foundation of Bülow's system, the logic of supply, artificial as it may have been, was now completely undermined. As he himself, among many others, was quick to note, the armies of the Revolution were living at the expense of the enemy, both financially and logistically.[22] Napoleon's wide-ranging, lightning campaign at the head of the Army of the Reserve, across the Alps, into the Po valley, and towards the Austrian rear, could not be reconciled with Bülow's logistical assumptions, and even less with the 90 degree angle.

Secondly, and even more damaging for Bülow's system, was the fact that Napoleon, who enjoyed new, vast resources and a more flexible military instrument, placed the decisive battle at the centre of warfare. The destruction of the enemy field-army was the goal on which operations focused with a massive and rapid concentration of maximum forces. Once his armies were destroyed, the enemy had to sue for peace. The decisiveness of Napoleon's campaigns struck Europe, adding to the overall picture of the collapse of eighteenth-century warfare. Soon after the appearance of Bülow's system, one of its principal features was thus being theoretically discredited as a result of the revolution in warfare. The following ideas from *The Spirit of the Modern System of War* now stood in stark contrast to the spirit of Napoleon's modern system of war: 'Lines of operations are always directed . . . against the enemy's country . . . and not against the enemy himself; for, the object of war at present should much rather be those places which contain the means of an adversary military power, than men.'[23] And in an even more embarrassing formulation: 'It is more conformable to the genius of war and the latest mode of carrying it out, that a general should make his own magazines and the safety of his lines of convoy, the principal object of his operations, rather than the army of the enemy itself.'[24] Indeed, 'it is always possible to avoid a battle'.[25]

[20] Ibid. 4–8. [21] Ibid. 5. [22] Ibid. 5.
[23] *System*, p. 18. [24] Ibid. 81. [25] Ibid. 184.

Bülow therefore needed considerable intellectual twists and turns in order to maintain the appearance that his system of operations was perfectly compatible with Napoleonic warfare. He could find support in the fact that the manœuvre against the enemy rear, the *manœuvre sur les derrières*, was the most decisive pattern of Napoleonic warfare, the one used in the campaign of 1800 in Italy.[26] It could be argued that Marengo was merely the inevitable outcome of the envelopment of the Austrian army; the great strategic manœuvre, not the battle which Napoleon nearly lost, decided the fate of the campaign. Indeed, this was the point that Bülow was now to emphasize. His system, he said, placed the manœuvre against the enemy's flanks and rear at the centre of the art of war. This manœuvre aimed at achieving such a strategic advantage that victory would be assured before, or even without, battle.[27] He argued that in *The Spirit of the Modern System of War* he had already stressed the dominant significance of movement and warned against passivity.[28] 'It is a universal law that movement multiplies force.'[29]

The tensions between Bülow's ideas in *The Spirit of the Modern System of War* and *The Campaign of 1800* resurfaced even more forcefully in his two later major works. In his *Lehrsätze des neuern Krieges, oder reine und angewandte Strategie aus dem Geist des neuern Kriegssystems*, published in 1805 but written before the campaign of that year, Bülow again presented his system of 1799, and attempted to demonstrate it, using examples taken chiefly from the campaign of 1800. Some changes were introduced into this new version of the *System*. Firstly, Bülow's geopolitical system, which had hardly progressed towards realization between 1799 and 1805, was excluded from the book. Secondly, the formal certainty of geometry was offered not only for the rationale of operations itself but also for the presentation of the system as a whole. The book was based on three premises from which the entire system was deduced as theorems.[30] However, with the great French

[26] See H. Camon's classical analysis: *La Guerre Napoléonienne*, 2 (Paris, 1907), 9–139.

[27] Bülow, *Der Feldzug von 1800*, p. xii.

[28] Ibid., p. xi.

[29] Ibid. 10–11, 18.

[30] In adopting this Spinozist form, Bülow may have been influenced by J. G. J. Venturini's *Lehrbuch der angewandten Taktik, oder eigentlichen Kriegswissenschaft* (Schleswig, 1800), which was also built in a deductive, semi-geometrical form, though with quite conventional contents. See the following paragraph for Bülow's joint venture with Venturini.

victories of 1805, Bülow returned to the forms of analysis that he had used in 1800–1, being now even more radical, both militarily and politically.

After the successes of his first books, Bülow hoped to obtain a suitable appointment in the Prussian service, but no such appointment was offered to him. He therefore worked as a journalist in London and Paris, where he wrote a book on Napoleon, *Über Napoleon Kaiser der Franzosen* (1804).[31] Later, in 1806, in Berlin, he co-edited a military journal entitled *Annales des Krieges*.[32] The other editors included Venturini, J. Voss, and another celebrated military thinker, Georg Heinrich von Berenhorst, the most respected critic of the Frederickian system, who greatly influenced Bülow in this respect, despite the paradigmatical gulf between their conceptions of military theory.[33] Bülow's criticism of his country, blended with personal frustration, extreme self-esteem, and a provocative style, became bitingly sarcastic in response to the collapse of the powers of the *ancien régime* in the campaign of 1805.

Within three months, a gigantic campaign and two decisive military encounters brought about the military destruction and virtual occupation of the Austrian Empire, which was supported by the armies of Russia. Such a fate had befallen no major European power in the modern period. The traditional European balance of power broke down, and Prussia found herself exposed and in an extremely dangerous diplomatic and military position. At this moment of crisis, Bülow wrote *The Campaign of 1805, Militarily and Politically Considered*, which was published, because of its radical ideas, at the author's own expense. Heterogeneous in composition, the book combined a description of the campaign with a political and military programme for the transformation of the Prussian state. It censured the Prussian system in the name of the new political and social order of Revolutionary France.

A comparison between the states of Germany and France revealed the former's inferiority in terms of the socio-political infrastructure. Bülow alleged that in order to survive, the Prussian state must undergo comprehensive reforms. She must give priority to talent over birth, and make full use of social potential by introducing general conscription and opening her administration and officer corps to the

[31] Jähns, *Kreigswissenschaften*, p. 2133.

[32] Bülow and Rüstow (edd.), *Schriften*, p. 24.

[33] See Ch. 6. II below.

able. The system of social rewards must support this aim by promoting utility to the state. Imitating the model of the French Legion of Honour, Bülow proposed an elaborate scheme for three orders of merit.[34]

In the strictly military field, Bülow faced his old dilemma. He had to reconcile Napoleonic warfare with the conceptions on which his reputation rested. At Ulm Napoleon brought the strategic manœuvre against the enemy's rear to its pinnacle. Mack's army, more than 70,000 men strong, capitulated without battle after being placed in a hopeless strategical position. The *Grande Armèe* that marched from its long and enveloping lines along the Rhine and the Main, cut it off from Austria in a sweeping movement.[35] Ulm, like Marengo, could therefore be presented as consistent with Bülow's system of operations of 1799; again, the strategic manœuvre overshadowed, and even eliminated, the need for battle. However, it was difficult to explain Austerlitz in this manner. Furthermore, as in the campaign of 1800 in Italy, the encirclement was achieved not on the basis of the system's calculations. Bülow's own account clearly expressed the real secret of the Napoleonic conduct of operations: the emperor 'uses his capital'.[36] A revolutionary exploitation of initiative, mobility, and concentration of force is responsible for his success. He executes the doctrines of Guibert.[37]

Bülow's writings were more than the Prussian government was prepared to tolerate. When Prussia faced her gravest trial, Bülow described Austerlitz as the modern Actium and predicted a French hegemony over Europe.[38] He was arrested, declared insane, and detained first in Berlin, and later, with the fall of the city and the French advance, in Colberg and Riga under Russian custody. In 1807 he died in prison, according to his relatives, due to ill-treatment.[39]

Bülow's novel, sensational, and controversial works attracted wide attention, and made his name known throughout Europe. The *System* was republished in 1805 (and again in 1835), and was translated into French (1802, reprinted 1814) and English (1806, reprinted 1814, 1825). *The Campaign of 1800* was translated into

[34] Bülow, *Der Feldzug von 1805, militärisch-politisch betrachtet* (n.p., 1806), vol. ii, pp. xviii–xxxiii, 108, 132 ff.

[35] Ibid., vol. i, pp. lxiii and lix.

[36] Ibid., vol. ii, p. 109.

[37] Ibid., vol. i, p. lix.

[38] Ibid., vol. ii, 158.

[39] Bülow and Rustow (edd.), *Schriften*, pp. 37 ff.

French in 1804.[40] Reactions were numerous and polarized. Bülow referred extensively to them in his works and even included large sections from his critics' comments on various subjects in his *New Tactics of the Moderns as They Should Be*.[41]

Regarding Bülow's system, several characteristic approaches can be discerned. Tempelhoff, who in the last years of the century headed a tendency to analyse the conduct of operations according to an increasingly formal rationale of supplies, praised Bülow's work which could be seen as the logical conclusion of his own.[42] Likewise, General Binzer, the Chief of Staff of the Danish army wrote a short and very complimentary book on Bülow's work.[43]

However, it is important to understand that while Bülow attempted to realize some of the deep-rooted but remote theoretical ideals of the military thinkers of the Enlightenment, he, *ipso facto*, violated the tenets of their traditional, well-established theoretical outlook. In his introduction to the English translation of the *System* (1806), Malorti de Martemont expressed this clearly. The art of war, he wrote, would never become totally scientific as Bülow suggested. While in part it could be reduced to rules and principles, another part, influenced by the diversity of political, moral, and physical conditions, was perpetually wavering, and required application by creative genius.[44] Scharnhorst, one of the most distinguished military *Aufklärers*, who rejected the new theoretical trends, criticized Bülow's career in his book review 'H. v. Bülow nach seiner Hypergenialität und seinen Abenteurn geschildert'.[45] Finally, under Scharnhorst's influence at the Institute for Young Officers in Berlin, the young Clausewitz developed a new theoretical outlook in a double-edged reaction against the theoretical legacy of the Enlightenment and the war of manœuvre.

[40] An edn. with Napoleon's notes written at St Helena appeared in 1831; a later edn. was published in 1841.

[41] Bülow, *Neue Taktik der Neuern, wie Sie seyn sollte* (Leipzig, 1805), 175–300.

[42] Jähns, *Kriegswissenschaften*, 2142.

[43] J. L. J. Binzer, *Über die militärischen Werke des Herrn von Bülow* (Kiel, 1803; repr. 1831).

[44] *System*, pp. iii–vii.

[45] Published in the *Göttinger gelehrten* (Berlin, 1807), Jähns, *Kriegswissenschaften*, p. 2142; for Scharnhorst's theoretical position, see Ch. 7. I below.

Clausewitz's critique of Bülow's *Lehrsätze des neuern Krieges* was published anonymously in 1805 in the military periodical *Neue Bellona* under the title 'Remarks on the Pure and Applied Strategy of Mr von Bülow'. The twenty-five-year-old officer, who admitted that in his youth he had been attracted by Bülow's vision, now sharply criticized his theoretical outlook and system.[46] First, from Clausewitz's point of view, determined by his particular interpretation of Napoleonic warfare, Bülow's promotion of the strategic manœuvre and rejection of battle amounted to a totally false conception of the nature of war. Bülow refused to understand what the whole world had already learnt to accept—that tactics was about fighting and centred on the engagement.[47] Bülow's geometrical system was equally false and artificial, and therefore constantly conflicted with reality. The tension that emerged in Bülow's own works did not escape Clausewitz; Bülow's own examples refuted his principles.[48] All this was the unavoidable result of the attempt to force a priori mathematical categories on the diversity of historical experience; Bülow lacked a critical historical approach.[49] Not only was history adapted by Bülow to fit his theory but everything that was not consistent with his desire to systematize was ignored. He focused on the geographical factors because they lent themselves to quantitative analysis, but disregarded the nature of the people involved, the moral forces that animate war, and the enemy against whom the war was directed. War was a map-game for him.[50] A true study of war must take into account the full diversity and complexity of the conditions involved.[51] Bülow's system was but one abstraction on top of the other; a single concept was generalized to create a false science.[52]

In *On War*, Clausewitz repeated his early criticism:

One ingenious mind sought to condense a whole array of factors, some of which did indeed stand in intellectual relation to one another, into a single concept, that of the *base* . . . He started by substituting this concept for all these individual factors; next substituting the area or extent of this base for the concept itself, and ended up by substituting for this area the angle which the fighting forces created with their base line. All this led to a

[46] Clausewitz, 'Bemerkungen über die reine und angewandte Strategie des Herrn von Bülow', *Neue Bellona*, IX 3 (1805); repr. in *Verstreute kleine Schriften*, W. Hahlweg (ed.), (Osnabrück, 1979); see p. 87.

[47] Ibid. 70, 78–9.

[48] Ibid. 75–6, 84–7.

[49] Ibid. 87.

[50] Ibid. 73, 79, 81.

[51] Ibid. 82.

[52] Ibid. 87.

purely geometrical result, which is completely useless. This uselessness is actually inevitable in view of the fact that none of these substitutions could be made without doing violence to the facts and without dropping part of the content of the original idea. The concept of a base is a necessary tool in strategy and the author deserves credit for having discovered it; but it is completely inadmissible to use in the manner described.[53]

In the criticism of Bülow's theoretical outlook one point has remained unnoticed: the geometrical basis of the system itself was simply wrong. Bülow's rationale of operations is based on the fact that the attacker's lines of supply in the midst of hostile territory rely on a much narrower base than that of the defender who operates in his own territory. In a geometrical formulation: the attacker draws his supplies from a narrow, triangular segment of space smaller than 180 degrees, whereas the defender can draw his from all the rest of the space's circumference (see Fig. 3). This situation gives the defender a clear advantage in a contest of manœuvre whose aim is to cut off the enemy's lines while preserving one's own.

Let us examine the situation described by Bülow.[54] In order to place himself at the attacker's rear, the defender (D) has to cover a shorter distance than the one that the attacker (A) must cross in attempting a counter-move (Fig. 4). Therefore in the event of such a move, the defender can withdraw to cover his own lines and still retain his threatening position at the attacker's rear. Now, his advantage is decreasing in proportion to the segment of space on which the attacker relies; the distance that he must cross in order to place himself at the attacker's rear increases and the attacker's prospects of carrying out a counter-manœuvre improve.

However, the 90 degree angle is not, as Bülow suggests, a turning-point from which the attacker's route becomes shorter. Even when the 'objective angle' becomes obtuse, the attacker still has a longer distance to cover in his counter-manœuvre, because he moves on the longest side of a triangle (Fig. 5). Thus, though the defender's advantage decreases with the increase in the attacker's angle, it does not disappear until both parties rely on a similar segment of space, that is until the attacker's salient disappears. Then,

[53] Clausewitz, *On War*, II, 2, p. 135.

[54] *System*, pp. 38–9.

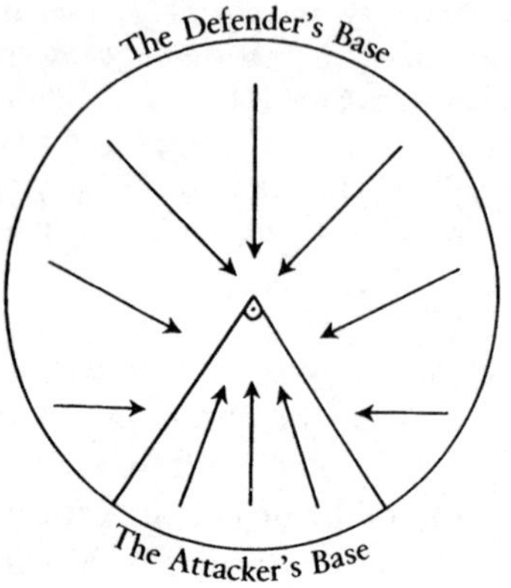

The Defender's Base

The Attacker's Base

Fig. 3

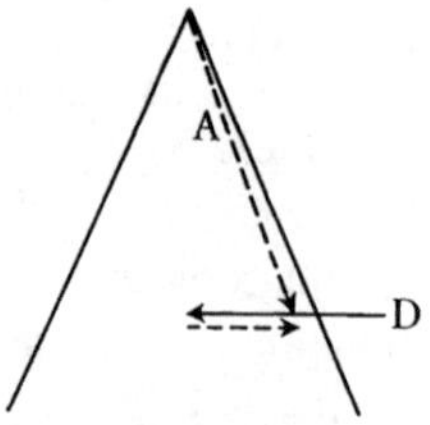

A

D

The Attacker's Base of Operations

Fig. 4

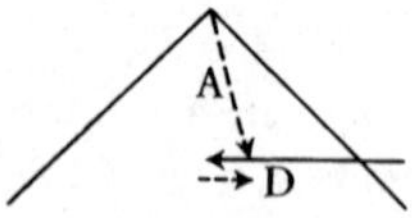

A

D

The Attacker's Base of Operations

Fig. 5a

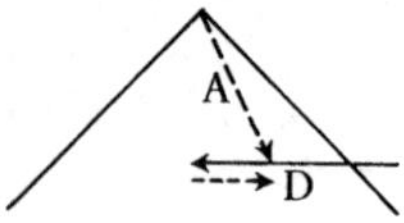

A

D

The Attacker's Base of Operations

Fig. 5b

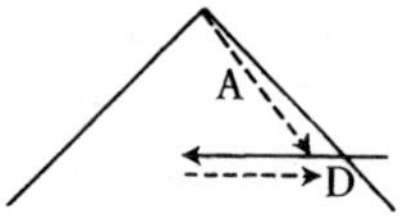

A

D

The Attacker's Base of Operations

Fig. 5c

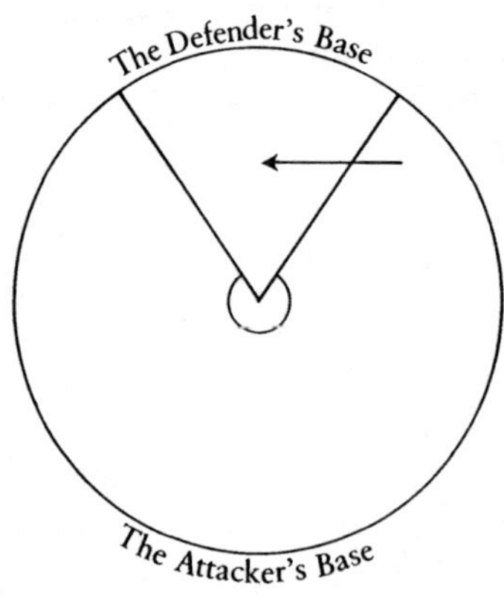

Fig. 6

Figs. 3–6 The Geometrical Rationale of Bülow's System

if the attacker operates from a base larger than 180 degrees, he himself enjoys, as Bülow points out, the advantage of a wider base (Fig. 6).[55]

All the exciting conclusions drawn from the 90 degree angle were therefore without foundation. The rationale of supplies and manœuvre amounts to no more than the obvious: that salients are exposed to being cut off.

The error in the geometrical core of Bülow's system of operations is, of course, no more than a curiosity. It simply demonstrates that even here Bülow's thinking was sloppy and superficial. Unfortunately, Bülow's sensational geometrical system, coupled with the obscurity into which the military school of the Enlightenment has sunk in historical consciousness, have led to a remarkably vague and stereotyped image of Clausewitz's predecessors. This consisted of the largely mythical post-Napoleonic trio of the eighteenth-century geometrical school, the war of manœuvre, and military conservatism.

Firstly, there was no real 'geometrical military school' in the eighteenth century. As we have seen, there were certainly deep-rooted geometrical notions and a remote ideal. Linear tactics also encouraged the extensive use of graphic schematizations but, apart from rare exceptions, they were hardly more than illustrations.[56] Finally, there was the search for the rationale of operations which emerged towards the end of the century, and which only Bülow developed into a geometrical system of operations. What can be described as a geometrical school of operations existed, in fact, to some degree only in the Napoleonic period, when military writers such as August Wagner and, more importantly, Archduke Charles, who were influenced by Bülow, based their analysis of operations on geometrical forms and considerations, though without Bülow's claims to mathematical precision and rigour.

In any case, the geometrical attempt was by no means inseparably linked with the idea of the rationale of operations. Bülow's fantastic system must not obscure this. Bülow's work attracted lively interest

[55] *System*, p. 65. Indeed the 90 degree angle leads to a paradox; the attacker is supposed to have the advantage when he relies on more than a 90 degree angle; but at the same time, and until the attacker relies on one of more than 270 degrees, the defender too relies on more than 90 degrees and should have the advantage himself.

[56] For F. Miller's *Reine Taktik* (Stuttgart, 1787–8), see also p. 166 below.

because it corresponded to a widely held feeling that the relative movement of contemporary armies in the theatre of operations, in relation to each other's position, communications, and objectives, was susceptible to a fruitful schematization in terms of time and space. This was by no means an unsound view. Lloyd had already proffered a quite penetrating analysis of the war of manœuvre which, since the Seven Years War, was gaining favour among the Austrian high command. But the military thinkers of the Enlightenment were far from being universally identified with the war of manœuvre, and it is enough to cite Guibert in this context. Indeed, now, the rationale of operations required a new formulation in terms of Napoleonic warfare.

The many different intellectual, military, and political transformations at the turn of the nineteenth century were therefore reflected in a variety of individual expressions. Bülow combined an extreme statement of some of the theoretical notions of the Enlightenment with the strategy of manœuvre, and military and political radicalism. Archduke Charles combined the theoretical outlook of the Enlightenment with a conservative adaptation of the strategy of manœuvre and the military and political institutions of the *ancien régime* to the Napoleonic era. Jomini synthesized the theoretical legacy of the Enlightenment with Napoleonic warfare, developing an updated, credible, and highly successful rationale of operations. Berenhorst expressed a Counter-Enlightenment point of view and harsh criticism of the Frederickian political and military system. Scharnhorst fused the classical views of the *Aufklärung* with reformist political and military positions. And Clausewitz combined his political and military reformism with the intellectual outlook of the German Movement and the Napoleonic war of destruction.

5

The Napoleonic Age: Archduke Charles, Jomini, and the Revolution in War

I ARCHDUKE CHARLES AND THE AUSTRIAN MILITARY SCHOOL

The image of the eighteenth century as an era of limited political aims and cautious strategy of manœuvre—an image created by the men of the post-Napoleonic period and highlighted by the German military school of the nineteenth century—is somewhat stereotyped. It is true that compared with the age of the wars of religion or the age of national wars, the wars between 1648 and 1789 were indeed relatively limited in their scope and aims. As has been progressively recognized since the days of Delbrück, the lack of ideological fervour, coupled with the *Realpolitik*, the restrictive social structure, and the professional armies of the *ancien régime* were all responsible for this. However, politically, the successive coalition wars against Louis XIV, Maria Theresa, and Frederick the Great involved not only a heavy strain on the resources of the countries of those monarchs, but also (particularly in the latter cases) the prospect of grim political consequences in the event of defeat. As to the military aspect, the campaigns of Marlborough or Frederick, which between them dominated eighteenth-century warfare, were hardly characterized by an unwillingness to fight. Nor did the French or the Austrians (the latter, at least in the first half of the century) shrink from major battles.[1]

If the eighteenth century came to be so strongly identified as the era of manœuvre warfare, it was predominantly because of tendencies which had become increasingly prominent late in the century, first in Austria and then in Prussia, and which were violently challenged with the coming of the Revolution and Napoleon. After the traumatic experience of the War of the Austrian Succession, and in the face of the superior qualities of the Prussian army and the military genius

[1] See C. Duffy, 'The Seven Years War as a Limited War', in Rothenberg *et al.* (edd.), *War and Society*, pp. 67–74.

of Frederick, the Austrians adopted a cautious strategy. Like the Dutch military school in the protracted wars against Spain and France from the late sixteenth to the early eighteenth centuries, the Austrian armies made extensive use of strong defensive positions, field-works, and fortresses, and fully exploited the leverage of supply and communications, rather than risk an open battle. Indeed, shaken by his own ordeal in the Seven Years War, alarmed by the increasing human cost incurred in order to drive the Austrian armies out of their positions, and concerned by the growing number of fortresses, Frederick himself in the last decades of his reign moved away from the lightning strategy of his great wars, which he no longer considered feasible. He made this clear in his *Militärische Testament* (1768), and conducted a campaign of positions in the diplomatic and bloodless War of the Bavarian Succession (1778–9). These attitudes, fully reflected in the theoretical works of Lloyd and Tempelhoff, thus became prevalent in the Austrian and Prussian armies when they encountered Revolutionary France.

After participating half-heartedy in the early campaigns of the first coalition (1792–5), Prussia did not return to the war against France until 1806, when her army was destroyed by Napoleon's mass armies and crushing strategy. On the brink of destruction, Prussia had to adapt to the new character of war, embarking on inseparable political and military reforms, laying the foundations for a national army, and adopting an active, battle-oriented strategy. Events were different, however, in Austria. Though forced to reform her military organization during her long and intermittent struggle with Revolutionary France and Napoleon, Austria was far less susceptible of change than even the Prussia of the *ancien régime*. The heterogeneous character of her political structure and particularly her deep ethnic fragmentation, placed Austria in a state of fundamental disadvantage in the age of national war.[2]

Hence the closely linked themes in the distinctive approach of the Austrian school to war. The mobilization of mass armies and popular energies were in conflict with the empire's very *raison d'être*. Limited

[2] See esp. K. Peball, 'Zum Kriegsbild der österreichischen Armee und seiner geschichtlichen Bedeutung in den Kriegen gegen die Französische Revolution und Napoleon I', in W. v. Groote and K. J. Müller (edd.), *Napoleon I und das Militärwesen seiner Zeit* (Freiburg, 1968), 129–82; and G. E. Rothenberg, *Napoleon's Great Adversaries, The Archduke Charles and the Austrian Army, 1792–1814* (London, 1982).

conscription, modelled on the Prussian 'canton system', was introduced in 1771, but attempts to form a second-line militia before the war of 1809 were treated with distrust by Archduke Charles and the Austrian high command, and never took off. In the struggle against the superior Napoleonic power, Austria was therefore totally dependent on her standing army which was large, but expensive and difficult to replace. Safeguarding this army and ensuring that it was not rushed into major battle under less than favourable conditions were thus paramount considerations for both Daun and Charles, even to the point of letting many potentially decisive opportunities slip away. Indeed, despite fierce personal and political rivalry, and considerable differences in temperament and style of generalship between such men as Daun, Lacy, and Loudon in the Seven Years War, or Archduke Charles and Schwarzenberg in the Napoleonic Wars, these general notions and attitudes underlay the Austrian conduct of war.

The widely respected theoretical works of Archduke Charles stand out in the comparatively meagre output of military literature in Austria of the Enlightenment.[3] Like Charles's active but less-than-bold generalship, and comprehensive but pronouncedly limited military reforms, these works are a striking expression of Austria's fundamental condition during the transition from old to new.

Archduke Charles (1771–1847), the son of Emperor Leopold II and the younger brother of Francis I, first experienced war against Revolutionary France in the campaigns of 1793–4 in Flanders. In 1796, he defeated Jourdan and Moreau in an excellent campaign in southern Germany, and although beaten by Napoleon in the Tyrol a year later, he again fought successfully against Jourdan in the German theatre of operations in 1799.

Acknowledged as the best general of the Habsburg monarchy, Charles was called on to reorganize the Austrian army after the defeat of 1800. He was appointed field marshal, president of the *Kriegshofart*, and head of a newly formed ministry of war, thus securing a considerable degree of control over the deeply factional Austrian high command. His brother the emperor, in accordance

[3] See the very sketchy treatment of Manfried Rauchensteiner, 'The Development of War Theories in Austria at the End of the Eighteenth Century', in G. Rothenberg *et al.* (edd.), *War and Society*, 75–82.

with what one historian has called the 'Wallenstein complex' of the Habsburg monarchy, took, however, special care that he did not have a free hand in the army or a say in political matters.[4] The endemic friction with the crown and court, and Charles's lack of sufficient personal authority in the army itself, became more pronounced before the renewed outbreak of hostilities in 1805. Objecting as he did to the war against France, Charles was stripped of some of his authority, but was none the less given command in Italy, the anticipated main theatre of operations. This time, however, Napoleon chose the Danube valley for his main thrust, and Charles was too slow to influence the course of events which culminated at Austerlitz.

After that defeat, Charles regained control over the Austrian army with the rank of generalissimo. Though opposed to the new war with France in 1809, he led the Austrian army to victory at the Battle of Aspern-Essling over the French army headed by Napoleon, who had entered Vienna and was attempting to cross the Danube to the north. The war was decided in favour of the French only six weeks later at the heavy and drawn-out battle of Wagram. After signing an unauthorized armistice with Napoleon, Charles was relieved of all duties. Regarded as too uncontrollable by the emperor and Metternich, he was not recalled during the last campaigns against Napoleon in 1813–15, and never again saw active service.[5]

This fact did not, however, diminish Charles's universal reputation as the best general in continental Europe east of the Rhine, nor the widely held respect for his personality and military record. His historical and theoretical works were therefore received with much interest, particularly his accounts of the campaigns of 1796 and 1799, and his *Principles of Strategy*, which appeared for public distribution

[4] G. Craig, 'Command and Staff Problems in the Austrian Army, 1740–1866', in M. Howard (ed.), *The Theory and Practice of War* (London, 1965), 45–67.

[5] Excluding some half a dozen popular biographies and numerous accounts of his major campaigns, the most comprehensive (official and semi-official) studies of Charles's life, incorporating a great deal of primary material, appeared in the late 19th cent., at the same time as the publication of Charles's collected works. These multi-vol. biographies include: H. R. v. Zeissberg, *Erzherzog Carl von Oesterreich* (Vienna and Leipzig, 1895); M. E. v. Angeli, *Erzherzog Carl von Oesterreich als Feldherr und Heersorganisator* (Vienna and Leipzig, 1896); and O. Criste, *Erzherzog Carl von Oesterreich* (Vienna and Leipzig, 1912). For a modern work in English, see Rothenberg, *Napoleon's Great Adversaries*.

in 1814 and was quickly translated into French (1817) and Italian (1819).[6]

Charles's work follows three well-established theoretical paths: the theoretical outlook of the Enlightenment; the rationale of communications as devised by Lloyd and Tempelhoff and only mildly adapted to Napoleonic strategy; and the geometrical analysis introduced by Bülow, though without his wilder pretensions to scientific and mathematical rigour.

Charles's first major theoretical treatise, *Principles of the Higher Art of War* (1806), was written in collaboration with his military mentor, Colonel Lindenau, once an adjutant of Frederick's and an author on tactics, and with General Mayer, his chief of staff and a close supporter.[7] It was distributed among the generals of the Austrian army as part of a comprehensive vitalization of instruction material. The book concludes:

> The principles of the science of war are few and unchanging. Only their application is never the same and can never be the same. Every change in the conditions of armies: in their arms, strength and position, every new invention, involves a different application of these rules.[8]

Thus, while 'the principles of war are founded on mathematical, evident truths', judgement, trained by historical study and military education, presides over their application. Both the science of principles and historical study must reinforce genius and experience in the making of generals.[9]

In his early work 'On the War with the New Franks' (1795), an analysis of the Austrian conduct of war in the first campaigns against the armies of Revolutionary France who were still ill-organized, Charles was critical of his country's military strategy. He argued that, in view of their enemy's relative weakness, the Austrians were much too defensive, were excessively concerned over the safety of their

[6] Archduke Charles [Carl von Oesterreich], *Ausgewählte Schriften* (*AS*), F. X. Malcher (ed.) (Vienna and Leipzig, 1893–4), include six vols. and an atlas. A concise edn. of his major theoretical works, *Ausgewählte militärische Schriften* (Berlin, 1882), appeared in the *Militärische Klassiker* series.

[7] Rothenberg, *Napoleon's Great Adversaries*, p.106. Karl Freidrich von Lindenau's major work, *Über die höhere preussische Taktik* (Leipzig, 1790), is a programmatic scheme of evolutions in linear formation.

[8] *Grundsätze der höheren Kriegskunst*, *AS* i. 50.

[9] Ibid. 49–51; the same ideas are expressed in Charles's later *Grundsätze der Strategie*, *AS* i. 231–3.

magazines and communications, and dispersed their forces too widely in the strategic deployment devised by Lacy and known as the 'cordon system', thus ending up inferior everywhere.[10]

However, a decade later, when he commanded Austria's war effort against the full might of Napoleonic power, Charles's views no longer diverged from his country's traditional attitudes. Though stressing the principle of the concentration of force at the decisive point—probably under Jomini's influence—[11] he was far from advocating bold action. Dispassionately he wrote that a 'mathematical truth teaches us that a decisive result cannot be achieved when totally equal forces operate against one another'.[12] All the more so, as Austria was not even equal to France, despite the considerable expansion of her standing army. The underlying link between Austria's strategic position and Charles's theoretical conceptions is clear:

> Only when the last object, which is essential for the survival of the state is about to fall into the hands of the enemy, when no other means of relief is left open, may the general risk a battle even with inferior forces; then he may depart from every rule . . . It is a battle of despair, the loss of which one does not survive.[13]

Indeed, for Charles, the focal point of war lay not in battle but elsewhere: 'A principal rule in offensive as well as in defensive war is never to choose with one's main force a line of operations or position in which the enemy is close to our lines of communications and magazines.'[14] The attacker should seek to penetrate into his enemy's country in order to cut him off from the means that support his war effort, whereas the defender must cover his communications and play for time.[15]

The affinity between Charles's cautious political premises and his characteristic strategic outlook is again revealed in *Principles of Strategy*:

> The events of war have such decisive results that it is the general's first duty to secure the outcome as far as he possibly can. But this can only be achieved if the means required for the conduct of war are available . . . Every

[10] 'Über den Krieg mit den Neufranken', *AS* v. 5–15, esp. 6–7.

[11] *Grunsätze der höheren Kriegskunst*, *AS* i. 3–4; Jomini's probable influence was pointed out by H. Ommen, 'Die Kriegsführung des Erzherzogs Carl', *Historische Studien*, XVI (1900), 109.

[12] *Grundsätze der höheren Kriegskunst*, *AS* i. 50.

[13] *Grundsätze der Strategie*, *AS* i. 330.

[14] *Grundsätze der höheren Kriegskunst*, *AS* i. 6.

[15] Ibid. 7–8.

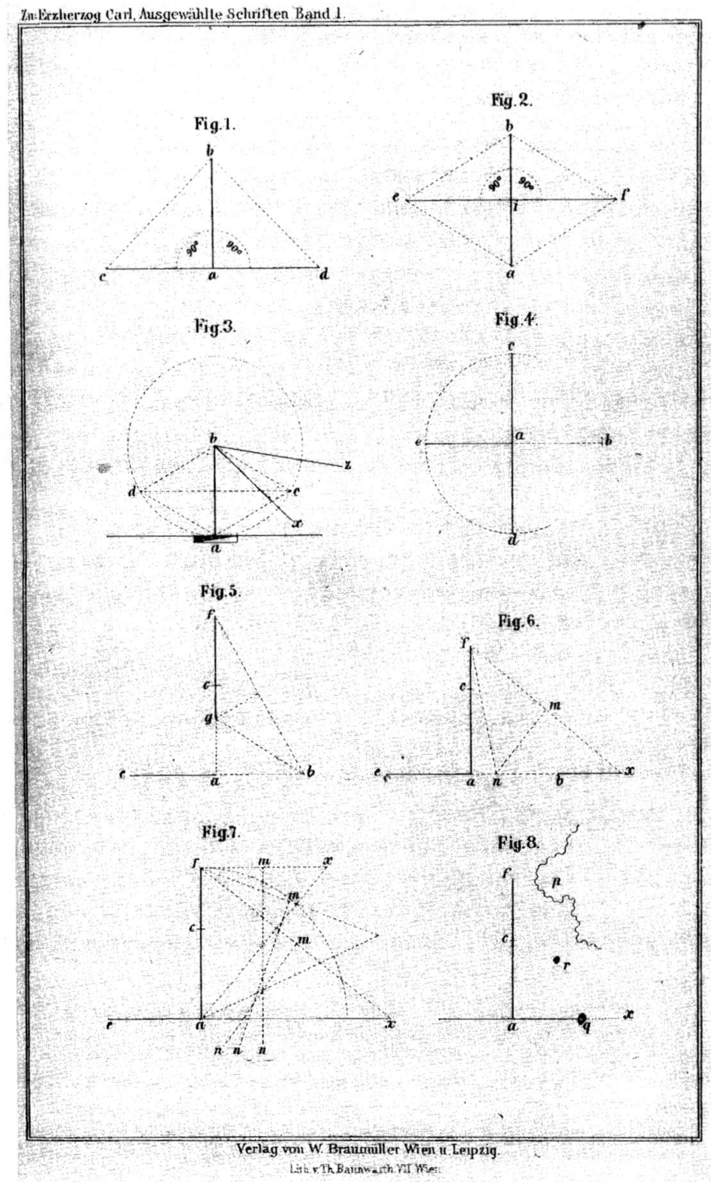

Fig. 7 Geometrical Figures from Archduke Charles's *Principles of Strategy*

deployment and movement must therefore provide full security for the key to the country behind, for the *base of operations* where supplies are accumulated, for the communications with these supplies, and for the *line of operations* chosen by the army for his advance from its base to the *objective of operations.*[16]

Indeed, Charles adopted not only Bülow's general theoretical scheme, but also the geometrical analysis of operations, though without the mathematical centre-piece of Bülow's system—the 90 degrees angle and its exciting implications (see Fig. 7). Thus, while Charles's conclusions regarding the ability of armies to cover their base and line of operations are not as sensational as Bülow's, they do tend to appear somewhat trivial as well as unnecessary.[17] 'On the one hand', wrote Caemmerer, 'they prove in a very roundabout way things quite obvious; and . . . on the other hand, the results remain highly debatable, since in war not only distance has to be considered, but also direction, number and conditions of the road.'[18]

Charles's main contribution to the rationale of operations is the concept of strategic key-points which dominate the base, communications, and objective. Situated at the most vital junctions and channels of movement, these geographical strongholds—particularly in closed regions—constitute the 'key to the country' and to the conduct of a campaign. Their identification and seizure ought therefore to be the general's first consideration in operational planning.[19]

The appearance of Charles's *Principles of Strategy* (1814) and the favourable reception it enjoyed, which could not, naturally, be dissociated from the author's royal status and military prestige, evidently alarmed Jomini, since it threatened to overshadow his own work and undermine his claim to be the founder of military science.

[16] *Grundsätze der Strategie*, *AS* i. 237; my emphases. While Ommen ('Kriegsführung', p. 121) is quite right in pointing out that Charles had already used the concept of the base, related to the system of fortresses and depots, as early as 1795 (*AS* v. 9), Charles's debt to the systematical conceptual framework formulated by Bülow is obvious.

[17] For the geometrical analysis see *Grundsätze der Strategie*, *AS* i. 237–40 and tables.

[18] R. v. Caemmerer, *The Development of Strategical Science during the 19th Century* (London, 1905), 58.

[19] *Grundsätze der Strategie*, *AS* i. 240–3.

However, for obvious reasons, Charles could not be dismissed in the typical Jominian fashion like the scores of military writers mentioned in the *Treatise* and later *Summary*. A more diplomatic approach was called for here. Charles was therefore the only military author to whom Jomini gave, literally, a 'royal treatment', and with whom he was even prepared to 'share' the leadership of military theory, not, however, without stressing his own pioneering position.[20] On Charles's request, he also agreed to take upon himself the translation of *Strategie* into French. As we shall see, Charles's work was partly responsible for Jomini's decision to write the *Summary*, and also left its mark on the character of that book.

Given the nature of Charles's ideas, Clausewitz's treatment of Charles is conspicuously inconspicuous, lacking Clausewitz's usual zeal in dealing with other, less eminent military thinkers whose ideas paralleled those of Charles. In *On War*, referring to Charles as 'a sound historian, a shrewd critic and, what counts even more, a good general', he criticized neither Charles's military outlook nor his geometrical theories which he would normally have treated with hail and thunder.[21] His strongest criticism of Charles's military outlook appears in his work on the campaigns of 1799 in Italy and Switzerland.

> Firstly, he [Charles] lacks an enterprising spirit and the hunger for victory. Secondly . . . while his judgement is generally good, he has fundamentally a completely erroneous view of strategy. In war all should be done in order to destroy the enemy's forces, but this destruction does not exist as a separate aim in his conceptual outlook. . . . For him success is merely the occupation of certain positions and areas.[22]

What Clausewitz wrote when Archduke Charles was at the height of his reputation as the best general of a respected European power, became the prevailing view when Austria declined into a second-rate power, and the German military school, expressing the might of a united Germany, dominated military theory, naming Clausewitz as its forefather, and promoting crushing decision in battle. Caemmerer's review of Charles's theoretical works is characteristic:

[20] Jomini, *Treatise on Grand Military Operations* (New York, 1865; based on the 3rd edn. (1818) of the *Traité*), p. xxi; id., *Summary of the Art of War*, pp. 13–14.

[21] Clausewitz, *On War*, VI, 16. p. 123.

[22] *Die Feldzüge von 1799 in Italien und in der Schweiz*, in Clausewitz, *Hinterlassene Werke*, (Berlin, 1832–7), v. 152.

How strange these [Charles's] words sound if we consider that at the time they were written the man [Napoleon] who so impressively had taught the world the importance of tactical success, was at the zenith of power and glory. In all this [Charles's works] we cannot find a trace of cheerful confidence in one's strength and ability.[23]

Charles's erroneous strategic outlook, wrote Caemmerer, stemmed from, and in turn reinforced, military tendencies which proved catastrophic for the destiny of the Austrian empire. The origins of this outlook were to be found in Field Marshal Daun's headquarters in the Seven Years War, and its influence could be discerned in the extreme caution and peculiar manœuvres of the Austrian army under Schwarzenberg in the campaign of 1814 in France, and again in the wars of 1859 and 1866. Instead of seeking battle, the Austrian generals looked for 'key-points'.[24]

While the Austrian military school certainly tended towards theoretical artificiality and 'strategic mannerism', Caemmerer's judgement is typical of the refusal of the German military school to acknowledge the deeper historical and strategic roots of any military outlook different from its own. This is revealed remarkably by Caemmerer's own conclusion written in 1904:

At the present moment we live in an age where an extraordinary progress in the technics of firearms exposes us to the danger of over-estimating the value of defensive positions, and where such theories of the importance of ground in strategy as advanced by the Archduke Charles might again become that serious danger for weak minds. . . . It was therefore necessary to leave no doubt about their failure in history.[25]

Ironically, within ten years, in encountering new historical conditions, it was the military outlook of the German military school that was shattered and called into question, while 'the value of defensive positions' and 'the importance of ground' became paramount.

[23] Caemmerer, *Strategical Science*, p. 61.

[24] Ibid. 61, 69; for an even more nationalistic example of the German school's attitude, which contrasts Charles and his milieu with the new German spirit from Clausewitz to Bismarck, Nietzsche, and Treitschke, see R. Lorenz, 'Erzherzog Carl als Denker', in A. Faust (ed.), *Das Bild des Krieges im deutschen Denken* (Stuttgart and Berlin, 1941), 235–76.

[25] Caemmerer, *Strategical Science*, p. 70.

Because of the situation in which Austria found herself in fighting with the superior Napoleonic power there was no reason to look for 'cheerful confidence in one's own strength and ability' in Charles's work. This in itself is a sufficient reason why his writings could never have achieved the same popularity as those of Jomini or Clausewitz. The centre of military thought has normally tended to follow the centre of military power. Thus, during France's period of greatness, it was Jomini's interpretation of Napoleon's bold strategy that was studied throughout the Western world. And when Germany became the major power in Europe with a supreme military orientation, a German military school presenting Clausewitz as its forerunner dominated military thought and the interpretation of military history.

II JOMINI: SYNTHESIZING THE LEGACY OF THE ENLIGHTENMENT WITH NAPOLEONIC WARFARE

Background and Early Development

Antoine Henri Jomini (1779–1869) synthesized the theoretical ideal of the Enlightenment with Napoleonic warfare, producing a penetrating and fertile rationale of the new type of operations. Hence both the enormous success and influence of his work in the nineteenth century and its decline in the twentieth.

Unfortunately, since the work of the military thinkers of the eighteenth century lost most of its relevancy in post-Napoleonic warfare and fell into oblivion, the origins of Jomini's theoretical outlook have become totally obscure. Though Jomini gave one of the most comprehensive descriptions of contemporary military literature in the introduction to his *Summary of the Art of War* and made several references to his predecessors in other works, modern readers have usually been unfamiliar with the thinkers cited and particularly with their characteristic theoretical outlook. Moreover, by doing his utmost to emphasize his originality, Jomini did not make the work of historians easier. Consequently, one study called Jomini the 'Adam Smith' of military thought, and in attempting to trace his intellectual origins which clearly pointed to the Enlightenment, searched for his mentor among the most eminent philosophers of that age, and tended to find him in Montesquieu.[1] Another deemed to have discovered the source of his conception of theory in Lloyd.[2]

In fact, the intensely philosophical age of the Enlightenment was over, and Jomini, representing a new type of professional soldier, had little philosophical background or interest. He simply continued to follow the theoretical vision and conceptual framework established by all the military thinkers of the Enlightenment. He claimed no originality for his conception of theory but merely argued that he had finally filled an old theoretical ideal with real content.

[1] C. Brinton, G. Craig, and F. Gilbert, 'Jomini', in Earle (ed.), *Makers of Modern Strategy*, 79–80, 91.

[2] John Shy, 'Jomini', in Paret (ed.), *Makers of Modern Strategy*, esp. pp. 148–9.

Jomini was born in 1779 to a respected family in the town of Payerne, Canton Vaud, in French-speaking Switzerland.[3] Excited by the political and military events of the period, he left a banking and commercial career in Paris, and in 1798, using personal connections, he became secretary to the Minister of War of the Helvetic Republic, the French satellite, and rose to the rank of *chef de bataillon*. In 1801, he returned to his commercial and financial occupations in Paris, but his attention was now totally drawn to the military field.

In 1802 Jomini began reading extensively the works of the major military thinkers of the French Enlightenment 'commencing with Puységur, finishing with . . . Guibert'.[4] A year later he wrote his first work, composed of a set of maxims. He managed to bring it to the attention of Marshal Ney, who was impressed by the young Swiss and invited him to join his staff at the camp of Boulogne, though with no official appointment. At that time Jomini discovered the French translation of Lloyd, and Bülow's 'system', and decided to put his early work in the fire and write a new one in its place. This was the celebrated *Treatise* on the campaigns of Frederick the Great and the wars of the Revolution. The first two volumes of the *Treatise* were published in 1804–5 and three others followed until the completion of the first edition in 1809–10.[5]

As an unofficial member of Ney's staff, Jomini took part in the campaign of 1805. After Austerlitz and with Ney's assistance, he succeeded in passing the first volumes of the *Treatise* to Napoleon. The emperor's favourable impression of the work brought Jomini

[3] No scientific biography of Jomini has yet been written. From the three existing biographies, the earliest, written by Jomini's disciple and friend, the Swiss Colonel Lecomte, during Jomini's lifetime and, apparently, from his own mouth, is naturally, uncritical. However it constitutes the almost sole source of all subsequent biographies: Ferdinand Lecomte, *Le Général Jomini, sa vie et ses écrits* (Paris and Lausanne, 1860). The biography written by the celebrated French literary critic C. Sainte-Beuve, *Le Général Jomini, étude* (Paris, 1869), adds significant documents from the correspondence of Napoleon and Berthier. The latest biography, Xavier de Courville's *Jomini ou le devin de Napoléon* (Paris, 1935), written by a descendant of Jomini, adds virtually nothing to its two predecessors. On Jomini's family and youth see Jean-Pierre Chuad, 'Les Années d'enfance et de jeunesse d'Antoine Henri Jomini' in *Le Général Antoine Henri Jomini* (Lausanne, 1969), 11–24.

[4] Jomini, *Summary*, pp. 11–12; all references are made to the American trans. of the *Précis: Summary of the Art of War* (Philadelphia, 1862); However, references to the bibliographical introd. which is not included in this edn., are made to a previous trans. (New York, 1854).

[5] Ibid. 12–13; see n. 15 below for the *Traité*'s development and changes of title.

an official appointment in Ney's staff and a rank of colonel.[6] With Ney's corps he participated in the campaigns of 1806–7 in Prussia and Poland, rising after the Battle of Friedland to the position of chief of staff. In this capacity he took part in the campaign of 1808 in Spain. In December 1810, he was appointed brigadier-general, and in the Russian campaign of 1812–13 he became military governor first of Vilna, and later of Smolensk. The campaign of 1813 in Germany saw him back in his old position as chief of staff to Ney, with whom he fought the Battle of Bautzen. However, the rejection of Ney's recommendation to appoint him major-general, the famous hostility of Berthier, Napoleon's chief of staff, and alleged unjust treatment from the Emperor himself brought him to desert to the Allies, a course taken by several of Napoleon's generals during his years of decline. Jomini had already been offered an appointment in the Russian army in 1810, and now, in 1813, he became attached to Tsar Alexander's headquarters.

After the war, as a Russian general, Jomini's major works included the fifteen volumes of the *Histoire critique et militaire des guerres de la révolution* (Paris, 1820–4), the four volumes of the *Vie politique et militaire de Napoléon* (Paris, 1827), and the successive versions of his *Summary of the Art of War*, which marked the pinnacle of his growing reputation as the most important military theoretician of the era.

The early stages in the development of Jomini's ideas have remained largely obscure. Their study involves certain difficulties since the sole evidence is Jomini's own account which is highly tendentious and at times contradictory.

As mentioned, in 1802 Jomini began an extensive perusal of the works of the military thinkers of the French Enlightenment, 'commencing with Puységur, finishing with Mesnil-Durand and Guibert'. He found 'everywhere but systems more or less complete of the tactics of battles, which could give but an imperfect idea of war, because they all contradicted each other in a deplorable manner'.[7] This inevitable dismissal of all previous theoretical work, intending to prepare the ground for presenting the author himself as the founder of military science, is familiar enough already. It does include, however, a new theme. The preoccupation of the military

[6] See below: 'Jomini and Napoleon'.

[7] *Summary*, p. 12; see also p. 9.

thinkers of the Enlightenment with battle formation and deployment seemed now—with the shift of interest to the conduct of operations—most unsatisfactory. For this very reason, Jomini's discovery of Lloyd and Bülow appears to have left a deep impression on him which even his later attempts to minimize could hardly conceal. Indeed, according to his own account, his discovery of Lloyd and Bülow led to his decision to burn his early work and write another one in its place.

It is true that Jomini tried to explain this decision mainly on literary and technical grounds, confining his debt to Lloyd and Bülow merely to the inspiration of substituting a more vivid historical demonstration of his principles for an abstract presentation.[8] The forced nature of this argument is particularly patent in relation to Bülow's abstract work. Attempting to fix the consolidation of his ideas as early as possible and thus magnify his claims to originality, Jomini even wrote in the introduction to the third edition of the *Treatise* (1818) that the writing of this book had begun in 1802, ignoring the early attempt of 1802–3 of which we know, as mentioned above, only from his later and more confident account in the *Summary*.[9]

Throughout his life, Jomini never passed up an opportunity to belittle the stature of other military authors. When writing the *Treatise* in his twenties, struggling to consolidate his own identity against that of his predecessors, he was highly sardonic towards Lloyd and Bülow. Thirty years later, in 1837, when he was the most celebrated military theoretician of the period, he permitted himself, in the introduction to the *Summary*, little more generosity. Lloyd, he wrote,

> raised in his interesting memoirs important questions of strategy which he unfortunately left buried in a labyrinth of minute details on the tactics of formation and upon the philosophy of war. But . . . it is necessary to render him the justice to say that he first pointed out the good route. However, his narrative of the Seven Years War . . . was more instructive (for me at least) than all he had written dogmatically.[10]

Jomini's diplomatic treatment of Archduke Charles's work appears, however, to betray a more balanced and genuine appreciation of the significance of Lloyd's and Bülow's writings and of their

[8] Ibid. 12–13.
[9] Jomini, *Treatise on Grand Military Operations* (New York, 1865), p. xxi.
[10] *Summary*, pp. 10–11.

influence on the development of his own ideas. Charles's work, he wrote, 'put the complement to the basis of the strategic science, of which Lloyd and Bülow had first raised the veil, and of which I had indicated the first principles in 1805 in a chapter upon lines of operations'.[11] The concept of *lines of operations* Jomini did not invent; he inherited it. Lloyd's and Bülow's treatment of the conduct of operations gave his own theoretical work a decisive turn.

If a reconstruction of the early stages of Jomini's development is therefore attempted, it may be assumed that the early, abstract work from 1802–3, which was written after the study of the military thinkers of the French Enlightenment and which impressed Ney, was built around a set of maxims that, like the military works of the Enlightenment, were intended to cover all aspects of the treated field, which was now, apparently, the conduct of operations. The traces of this early theoretical stage can perhaps be identified in the many minor maxims scattered throughout the *Treatise* of 1804–5 alongside the major principles of operations, but diminishing in significance with Jomini's later development. These maxims deal, for example, with the defence of villages and their incorporation into the line of battle, the employment of cavalry along the edge of woods and on rugged terrain, the conduct of a besieging army which comes under attack, the securing of heights, and so on.[12]

However, the core of Jomini's early work seems to have been an embryonic formulation of a principle for the conduct of operations, applicable to both levels of battle and campaign. Describing the beginning of his intellectual development he wrote:

> Already had the narrative of Frederick the Great commenced to initiate me in the secret which had caused him to gain the miraculous victory of Leuthen. I perceived that this secret consisted in the very simple manœuvre of carrying the bulk of his forces upon a single wing of the hostile army; and Lloyd soon came to fortify me in this conviction. I found again, afterwards, the same cause in the first successes of Napoleon in Italy, which gave me the idea that by applying, through strategy, to the whole chess table of war, this principle which Frederick had applied to battle, we should have the key to all the science of war.[13]

Jomini's retrospective account is confirmed also by his earliest-known work, the *Treatise* of 1804–5: 'the conduct of the king at Leuthen',

[11] *Summary*, p. 13.
[12] *Treatise*, pp. 158, 162, 165–6, 422–3.
[13] *Summary*, p. 12.

he wrote, 'includes, in our opinion, the principle of all combinations in war'.[14]

With this principle Jomini gave theoretical expression to the new military reality and ideal raised to prominence by Napoleonic warfare: concentration of force. However, only the discovery of Lloyd's line and rationale of operations, turned by Bülow into the foundation of a new, albeit fantastic, science of operations, paved the way for Jomini's mature theoretical work. The fusion of the principle of the concentration of force with the rationale of operations gave him the key to the analysis of the Napoleonic art of operations, and this was precisely the synthesis achieved in the *Treatise* that Jomini began to write and publish in 1804–5.

The Conception of Theory and the Principles of Operations

After the period of consolidation (1802–4), Jomini's work reveals a remarkable continuity and consistency. The young man had completed most of his intellectual development by his late twenties, between 1804–9 when he wrote the *Treatise*, or in fact, by 1806–7 after experiencing the peak of Napoleonic warfare in the campaigns of 1805–7, and writing the summary of his principles which later became the concluding chapter of the *Treatise*.[15] Little was added

[14] *Treatise*, ch. VII, p. 252; see also p. 255.

[15] The confusion surrounding the exact development of the *Traité*, complicated by changing titles and differing eds. which Lecomte had failed to put in order (Lecomte, *Jomini*, pp. 321–2), was clarified by J. I. Alger's *Antoine Henri Jomini: A Bibliographical Survey* (West Point, 1975). The first two vols. on the first campaigns of the Seven Years War appeared in 1804–5 (see Alger, *Survey*, p. 2 for the divergence in dates) under the following title: *Traité de grand tactique, ou relation de la guerre de sept ans, extraite de Tempelhoff commentée et comparée aux opérations des dernières guerres, avec un recueil des maximes les plus importantes de l'art militaire*. The first vol. promised a seven vol. work: five vols. on the Seven Years War, a sixth on the campaigns of 1792–1800, and a seventh, a theoretical one. However, this plan was abandoned. On the publisher's request, the vol. on the first wars of the Revolution, to be the fifth vol. of the second edn., was next to appear: *Traité de grand tactique, relation critique des campagnes des Français contre des coalisés* (1806). The third and fourth vols., on the last campaigns of the Seven Years War, appeared in 1807 and 1809 respectively, under the new main title *Traité des grandes opérations militaires*. The article that summarized the principles, and was to become the concluding chapter of the *Traité*, was written in December 1806 when Jomini was stationed at Glogau in Silesia, and was published separately in 1807 as well as in Ruhle von Lilienstern's journal, *Pallas* (1808). The second edn. of the *Traité des grandes opérations militaires* included three additional vols. on the campaigns of the Revolution. The first six vols. of this edn. appeared in 1811, and the last two, delayed by the censure, were only published in 1816. From the third edn. of 1818, the campaigns of the Revolution were transferred to the *Histoire critique et militaire des guerres de la Révolution*.

or changed between the ideas of the twenty-eight-year-old colonel and those of the fifty-eight-year-old general and celebrated military thinker who published his *Summary of the Art of War* in 1837.[16]

As mentioned above, Jomini's conception of military theory was ready-made for him:

> The fundamental principles upon which rest all good combinations of war have always existed . . . These principles are unchangeable; they are independent of the nature of the arms employed, of times and places . . . For thirty centuries there have lived generals who have been more or less happy in their application . . . the battles of Wagram, Pharsalia and Cannae were gained from the same original cause.[17]

> Genius has a great deal to do with success, since it presides over the application of recognized rules, and seizes, as it were, all the subtle shades of which their application is susceptible. But in any case, the man of genius does not act contrary to these rules.[18]

Unfortunately, according to Jomini, his predecessors in the search for a universal theory of war had erred in looking for complete systems, some to the point of ridicule, thus inviting scepticism regarding fixed principles.[19] The need therefore arose for a 'demonstration of immutable principles and . . . [for] establishing a common standard from opinions which had differed so widely. It has been my fortune', wrote Jomini, 'to undertake this difficult task.'[20]

The same theoretical outlook was reiterated in the *Summary* of 1837:

> There exists a small number of fundamental principles of war, and if they are found sometimes modified according to circumstances, they can nevertheless serve in general as a compass to the chief of an army . . . Natural genius will doubtless know how, by happy inspirations, to apply principles as well as the best studied theory could do it; but a simple theory . . . without giving absolute systems . . . will often supply genius and will even serve to extend its development.[21]

On one central point, however, Jomini's theoretical outlook fundamentally differed from that of his predecessors. This divergence

[16] The *Introduction à l'étude des grandes combinaisons de la stratégie et de la tactique* (Paris, 1829) constituted an early version of the *Summary*. A more developed version, *Tableau analytique des principales combinaisons de la guerre, et de leur rapports avec la politique des états*, appeared a year later.

[17] *Treatise*, the concluding ch., p. 445.

[18] Ibid., ch. 7, pp. 253–4.

[19] Ibid., the concluding ch., pp. 446–7.

[20] Ibid. 447.

[21] Ibid. 18.

was related to the shift in emphasis from tactics to strategy, but the explanation for it lies deeper. The military thinkers of the Enlightenment maintained that the details of military organization and deployment were fundamentally mechanical and could be fixed in a definitive system, whereas the conduct of operations was almost entirely in flux, and therefore fell chiefly in the realm of the general's ingenious inspiration. This conception can still be found in the *Summary*, for instance, in the statement that 'the most minute . . . the most accessory points of tactics [are] the only part of war, perhaps, which it is possible to subject to fixed rules'.[22] However, a new approach clearly dominated this work, an approach which was to characterize military thought in the nineteenth and twentieth centuries and in which strategy could be reduced to universal principles while tactics were difficult to regulate and were exposed to constant transformations.

The interplay of moral forces which could hardly be foreseen was described by Jomini as one factor that prevented a general theoretical determination of tactics.[23] The main reason for the reversal of opinions was, however, the increasing awareness by the men of the period of the significance of techno-tactical developments that had been virtually ignored by the military thinkers of the Enlightenment with their universal frame of mind. During his career, Jomini witnessed changes in tactics which made battle formation more flexible and which rendered the military theory of the eighteenth century clearly outdated. Tactics could no longer be reduced to rigid patterns, he wrote in the *Summary*.[24] Napoleon had the same idea in mind when he remarked that tactics had to change every ten years. By the end of his long life, Jomini saw revolutionary technological innovations whose potential effect on the field of tactics was far-reaching. Some of the developments in armament, such as the Congreve rocket, the howitzer firing shrapnel shell, Perkins's steam-gun, and the improved musket, had already attracted his attention in the *Summary* of 1837.[25] Only strategy appeared to escape change:

> The new inventions of the last twenty years seem to threaten a great revolution in army organization, armament and tactics. Strategy alone will remain unaltered, with its principles the same as under the Scipios and Caesars,

[22] Ibid. 9.
[23] Ibid. 321.
[24] Ibid. 195.
[25] Ibid. 48, 299.

Frederick and Napoleon, since they are independent of the nature of the arms and the organization of the troops.[26]

Tactics can still be studied theoretically by rules and principles; but 'strategy particularly may be regulated by fixed laws resembling those of the positive sciences'.[27]

The growing impact of the industrial revolution did not however stop with tactics. At the end of his life, faced with new challenges to the whole of his theoretical outlook, Jomini argued that the growing military use of railways could not change his universal principles of strategy.[28]

There was therefore some justification for Jomini's claim to be the founder of 'real' military science. The conduct of operations, he maintained, had to be the focus of the theoretical effort.[29] The attempt to reveal its principles was his central aim, and again shows remarkable continuity from the first volumes of the *Treatise* in 1805–7 to the *Summary* of 1837.

The *Traité de grand tactique* or, in its later title *Traité des grandes opérations militaires*, was based on Lloyd's and Tempelhoff's accounts of the Seven Years War, and took issue with their contending interpretations. The core of the work was, however, a set of principles for the conduct of operations, which had at first been derived from some dominant features of Frederickian warfare, but which were soon adapted to reflect the Napoleonic rationale of operations. These principles were scattered throughout the *Treatise* but were also concentrated in several summarizing chapters, whose differing dates of publication help to trace the final stages in the development of Jomini's ideas. In the first two volumes of the

[26] *Treatise*, p. 48, see also p. 9. Archduke Charles developed a similar conception at roughly the same time. In contrast to the military thinkers of the French Enlightenment, he too wrote that 'strategy is the science of war' whereas 'tactics is the art of war' and applies the principles of strategy to changing circumstances and new inventions: Archduke Charles, *Grundsätze der Strategie*, *AS* i. 235; *Grundsätze der höheren Kriegskunst*, *AS* i. 50.

[27] *Summary*, p. 321.

[28] Lecomte, *Jomini* (3rd edn. 1894); cited by Alger, *Survey*, p. 19.

[29] Jomini fully adopted the concept of 'strategy' and the distinction between 'strategy' and 'tactics' along the lines introduced by Bülow only in the *Summary*, after they had been accepted in German military literature and used both by Archduke Charles and Clausewitz. When writing the *Treatise*, he still employed the traditional concepts of 'grand tactics' or 'operations' for the whole conduct of operations. He also lent his principles equal validity in the conduct of both battle and campaign.

Treatise, published in 1804–5, chapter 7 provided an initial summary of the principles of operations, further developed in chapter 14, 'Upon Lines of Operations'. These were the chapters that impressed Napoleon after Austerlitz.[30] In December 1806, having experienced Napoleon's great campaigns, Jomini reformulated his principles with minor additions in an essay which was to become the concluding chapter of the *Treatise*.

The essence of Jomini's work lay in revising Lloyd's rationale of operations in terms of the new Napoleonic warfare, and in reformulating Bülow's vision of strategic science into a more moderate and common-sensical form. We have seen that Bülow had already had to contend with the collapse of the traditional conduct of operations when confronted by Napoleonic strategy. Jomini, who was not tied by past prestige to old conceptions, could make these adjustments without any inhibitions.

Firstly, the premises of the rationale of operations itself had to be revised. The lines of operations, wrote Jomini, 'have been considered merely in their material relations. Lloyd and Bülow have only attached to them the importance which pertains to the magazines and depots of an army.'[31] This conception had, obviously, been exaggerated even in relation to eighteenth-century warfare; and now, with the heavy reliance on the countryside and the new emphasis on decision, it became totally inadequate. This, however, did not imply that the lines of operations lost their importance. 'The greatest secret of war consists in becoming master of the communications of the enemy'; Jomini attributed this statement to Napoleon himself.[32] Only the function of these lines changed with the new type of warfare. Now, they were not perceived merely as lines of supply, but also, or perhaps chiefly, as lines of retreat and communications with friendly forces. The seizure of the enemy's communications could lead not only to his starvation and withdrawal but also to his destruction.

The destruction of the enemy's field armies was the new military aim, necessitating a second adjustment in Lloyd's and Bülow's rationale of operations. In 1804–5 when the two first volumes of the *Treatise* were published, Jomini's position was still relatively conservative: one has 'to give battle only when great advantages are to be derived, or the position of the army makes

[30] See below 'Jomini and Napoleon'.

[31] *Treatise*, ch. 14, p. 12.

[32] Ibid., ch. 15, p. 59.

it necessary'.[33] However, after the great decisive campaigns of 1805–7 his position became bolder. 'The art of war', he wrote, rejecting the positions of Lloyd and Bülow, 'does not consist in running races upon the communications of our enemy, but in the securing of them, and marching thereon, for the purpose of bringing him to battle.[34] Furthermore, 'after the victory, the vanquished should be allowed no time to rally, but should be pursued without relaxation'.[35] For all that, Jomini never considered battle to be the almost exclusive means of war as Clausewitz did. 'Battles have been stated by some writers to be the chief and deciding features of war,' he wrote in the *Summary* in direct reaction to Clausewitz's ideas; 'This assertion is not strictly true, as armies have been destroyed by strategic operations without the occurrence of pitched battles.'[36]

Finally, the rest of the new military values were stressed. Initiative was placed by Jomini at the head of his principles in 1804–5 and again in 1806–7.[37] Mobility and movement were other fundamental features of Napoleonic strategy: 'the system of rapid and continuous marches multiplies the effect of an army'; indeed, a 'march of thirty miles a day' was presented by Napoleon in his famous dictum as one of the three components of his art of operations.[38] Most important of all was the concentration of force, Jomini's earliest principle. 'The employment of masses upon the decisive points', he wrote, 'constitutes alone good combinations, and . . . it should be independent of all positions'.[39]

These, then, were the changes and revisions that the body and spirit of the old rationale of operations had to undergo in order to be accommodated to the Napoleonic form of operations. This was the basis for Jomini's new synthesis. The secret of operations, in the conduct of both battle and campaign, lay in the concentration of maximum force to achieve local superiority at the decisive point. Initiative and forced marches were means to this end;[40] but the real secret of the operational formula lay in the skilful use of the lines of operations:

[33] *Treatise*, ch. 13, p. 443.

[34] Ibid., ch. 27, p. 323.

[35] Ibid., ch. 13, p. 443.

[36] *Summary*, p. 178. For Clausewitz's views on this matter see Ch. 8 of this book.

[37] *Treatise*, ch. 5, principle 1, p. 201; the concluding ch. principle 1, pp. 448–9.

[38] *Summary*, pp. 176, 137.

[39] *Treatise*, ch. 3, p. 149; see also ibid., ch. 7, p. 252, and *Summary*, 'The Fundamental Principles of War', p. 71.

[40] *Treatise*, ch. 7, p. 252; *Summary*, pp. 72–3, and p. 176, principle 6.

If the art of war consists in bringing into action upon the decisive point of the theatre of operations the greatest possible force, the choice of the line of operations (as the primary means of attaining this end) may be regarded as fundamental in devising a good plan for a campaign.[41]

The choice of the most advantageous line of operations was therefore the centre of Jomini's work, and already in 1804–5 he had put forward two main patterns to which he remained loyal throughout his life:

It would generally be better to direct the line of operations upon one extremity, whence we can at will reach the rear of the enemy's line of defence. The direction upon the centre is best only when the adversary's line is very long, and the different corps which guard it separated by long intervals.[42]

Thus, when two armies confront each other, both on the battlefield and in the theatre of operations, operations should usually be directed against one of the extremities of the enemy's front and towards his communications with his rear. Jomini's initial idea, patterned on the model of Leuthen, may have been focused on the battlefield and the destruction of the enemy's wing.[43] However, with his discovery of Lloyd and Bülow, and Napoleon's Marengo campaign of 1800, he seems to have switched the emphasis to the strategic scale and the manoeuvre around the enemy's flank, in an attempt to seize his communications, cut him off, and destroy him. 'The combinations of the campaign of 1800', he wrote in 1804–5, 'have clearly demonstrated the truth of this maxim.'[44] And Napoleon's great campaigns of 1805–7 strikingly reinforced it: the manœuvre towards the enemy's rear and against his communications—*la manœuvre sur les derrières* in Camon's classic typology, influenced by Jomini's conceptions—led to the capitulation of Mack's army at Ulm (1805) and to the destruction of the Prussian army at Jena-Auerstädt (1806). Both in 1800 and 1806 the fate of the war was decided in a single, all-embracing blow. Following Jena, Jomini began to stress the advantages of manœuvring the enemy against impassable obstacles; attacked from his flank and rear, he faced total destruction.[45]

[41] *Summary*, p. 113; and p. 176, principle 6.

[42] *Treatise*, ch. 5, principle 3, pp. 201–2; see also ch. 14, principle 4, pp. 42–3, and in the concluding ch., principle 2, pp. 449–50.

[43] *Treatise*, ch. 7, p. 252, and Jomini's later account in the *Summary*, p. 12.

[44] *Treatise*, ch. 14, p. 43; and *Summary*, p. 12.

[45] For the example of 1806 and its abstract expression, see mainly the *Summary*, p. 115.

The manœuvre against the enemy's rear was one of the most impressive, and certainly the most decisive, forms of Napoleonic strategy.

Yet, when the enemy's front, both on the battlefield and in the theatre of operations, was over-extended or even composed of several separate corps, a single, great outflanking movement was ruled out. In this case another course of action became available which, although it did not threaten the enemy's communications and consequently was not as destructive as manœuvring against the enemy's rear, still used the particular pattern of these communications to achieve a decisive superiority at the point of engagement. The attacker could break through the enemy's front, or, if the enemy was deployed in several separate corps, penetrate between them. He was, then, concentrated (that is, he 'used a single line of operations') in a 'central position', and operated on 'interior lines' against a divided enemy operating on 'several exterior lines'. Each of the enemy's corps could then be defeated separately.

That was Frederick's natural position in the Seven Years War and the secret of his celebrated manœuvres which aimed to crush each of the armies of the coalition in succession. That was also the position in which Napoleon strove to place himself—with brilliant success—in his first campaign of 1796, when he penetrated between the armies of Piedmont and Austria in the Ligurian Alps, beating the former and driving her out of the war, and then turning against and defeating the latter. He again operated in interior lines when he marched to crush the Austrian armies which descended separately from the passes of the Alps to raise the siege from the fortress of Mantua (1796–7).

Jomini developed his conceptions of the central position and interior lines as one of the most important lessons of his study of the Seven Years War, which was confirmed by Napoleon's strategy. He thus regarded these forms of warfare as having a decisive advantage, and his great fame became chiefly associated with them. 'An army whose lines are interior and nearer than those of an enemy,' he wrote in 1804–5, 'can by a strategic movement, overwhelm those of the enemy successively . . . It follows from this that a double line of operations . . . would always be dangerous and fatal,' whereas 'single interior lines of operations are always the most sure.'[46] These were also the conclusions of Jomini's famous summary of his principles in 1806–7.

[46] *Treatise*, ch. 7, principles 2, 4, 6, pp. 249–50; See also ch. 14, principles 2 and 3, p. 42; and p. 39.

Jomini restated his double conception of operations in the *Summary*:

It may be laid down as a general principle that the decisive points of manœuvre are on that flank of the enemy upon which, if his opponent operates, he can more easily cut him off from his base and supporting forces without being exposed to the same danger . . . If the enemy's forces are in detachments or are too much extended, the decisive point is his centre, for by piercing that, his forces will be more divided, their weakness increased, and the fractions crushed separately.[47]

The former course of action 'led to the success of Napoleon in 1800, 1805 and 1806; the latter was successful in 1796, 1809 and 1814'.[48] Jomini's conception of operations was in essence, then, a formal presentation of the Napoleonic art of war at its heyday; that was the source of its power but also of its limitations.

Challenges and Criticism

Jomini claimed to have revealed the principles of Napoleonic warfare which were at the same time *also* the universal principles of the art of war. This double status was based on the belief that Napoleon's genius actually embodied the universal principles of war. There was a latent tension here which was only revealed when the Napoleonic system of war was shown to be less than perfect. As with the categories of neo-classicism, the universal validity of Jomini's principles, particularly his doctrine of the central position and interior lines, was thrown into question when significant exceptions could be presented against them. These were provided by Napoleon's last campaigns in the years 1813–15, and particularly by the great autumn campaign of 1813.

In 1814 Napoleon operated against the Allied armies that invaded France, with a virtuosity and speed displayed in his best campaigns. He attacked them successively, conducting forced marches between Schwarzenberg's Austrian army in the east, Blücher's Prusso-Russian army in the north-east, and the Prussian, Russian, and Swedish forces of the Army of the North. This, however, did not save him from defeat which was indeed almost unavoidable in view of the absolute numerical superiority of the Allies.

[47] *Summary*, p. 88; see also pp. 90, 114, 175–6.
[48] Ibid., 'Summary of the Principles of Strategy', p. 6.

In 1815 Napoleon attempted his classic penetration strategy, breaking through the centre of the Allies' line between the British and the Prussians in order to push them back in opposite directions and crush them separately. He almost succeeded in this when he defeated the Prussians at Ligny and turned to crush the British at Waterloo. The poor co-ordination of the French army was partly responsible for Napoleon's failure, but the counter-strategy of the Allies was no less influential. Unlike their conduct in Napoleon's early campaigns, the divided enemy armies, after their initial surprise, did not leave the initiative to the French. The Allies' attempt to achieve a forward concentration of forces had failed, but after the defeat at Ligny, the Prussians avoided the expected north-eastern retreat which would have moved them away from the British. In a determined action, Blücher succeeded in reuniting with Wellington on the battlefield of Waterloo, destroying Napoleon's campaign plan.

In 1814, although Napoleon operated with a clearly inferior force, he nevertheless achieved impressive successes; and in 1815 his subordinates, Grouchy and Ney, could be blamed for the failure. This, however, could not be said about the gigantic autumn campaign of 1813 in Germany. The French army and the armies of the Coalition were almost equal in size, but Napoleon, who kept his forces united, failed to crush his enemies separately. The powers of Europe, who for seventeen years had experienced the destructiveness of the Napoleonic art of war, prepared their homework very carefully. As an antidote to Napoleon's strategy of interior lines they refused to be exposed to his main thrust, and took counter-initiatives. The army against which Napoleon concentrated his forces, refused battle, withdrew, and drew the enemy after it. Napoleon's blow, therefore, struck thin air. Simultaneously, the rest of the Allied armies moved against the French rear, exerting superior pressure on the delaying corps left by Napoleon to screen his movements, and forcing his main thrust to halt and withdraw in order to confront the threat. Not only did Napoleon exhaust his forces in vain attempts to defeat the Allied armies separately, but he also failed to prevent their concentration on the battlefield at Leipzig. Furthermore, the new technique highlighted some inherent advantages of the exterior lines and a certain paradox in Jomini's thought. The side operating in exterior lines surrounded his opponent from several directions. He was, therefore, in a much better position to envelop his opponent and threaten his communications. The campaign of 1813 thus aroused extensive debate regarding the validity of one of Jomini's principal ideas.

Jomini was forced on the defensive. While he did not retract the statements attributing the advantage to interior lines, he did reformulate them more cautiously and claimed that he had never rejected operations on exterior lines under certain circumstances.[49] He argued that exceptional conditions prevailed in Napoleon's last campaigns: that Napoleon was numerically inferior, and that both sides used huge armies which, on the one hand, made it difficult for Napoleon to achieve rapid concentration of force, and on the other, increased the ability of each Allied army to resist independently. In principle, he argued that a few exceptions were not sufficient to invalidate a rule based on the main body of military experience.[50] What then should be regarded as the main body of military experience and what are unusual circumstances? What was the rule and what were the exceptions?

Once again the challenge of a new historical experience, rather than theoretical reasoning, undermined Jomini's conception of the central position and interior lines. In the great German wars of unification, both against Austria and against France, the Prussian army deployed several armies by rail in exterior and enveloping lines of operations and with decisive results. New means of communication, such as the telegraph, facilitated the co-ordination of the separate armies. A new controversy therefore broke out in Germany as to whether the Moltkean strategy, the new military model, introduced a new rationale of operations, completely different from the Napoleonic one and based on the superiority of exterior lines.[51] Which part of the historical experience was the 'correct one'?

What then was the problem with Jomini's theoretical work? The problem was that he regarded his conceptions, which were a penetrating schematization of the Napoleonic form of operations, to be a universal military theory. Jomini's great achievement was that he provided his contemporaries, who were striving to grasp the nature of the new type of warfare, with the clearest, most instructive conceptual framework for this task. His conceptions have since stood

[49] *Summary*, pp. 113, 126–7. [50] Ibid. 123–8.

[51] For a summary of the controversy, see Caemmerer, *Strategical Science*, pref. and ch. VIII.

behind every major interpretation of the Napoleonic art of operations, and proved highly valuable for soldiers as long as the major features of this form of warfare continued to prevail.[52] However, as a highly successful reflection of a particular period, Jomini's conceptions were far from being universally valid. Despite Bülow's boundless theoretical claims, he regarded his system as a product of the particular conditions of the modern period—the reliance on a system of supply. Conversely, Jomini, a true child of the Enlightenment, limited his principles by leaving room for creative application, circumstances, chance, and the like, but regarded them as valid in every time and place.

The result was an encapsulation of all the problems for which the famous 'unhistorical approach' of the Enlightenment was blamed.[53] Jomini claimed that all military history from 'Scipio and Caesar to Napoleon' had been guided by the principles that he extracted from Napoleonic warfare, and referred to all periods of history that clearly contradicted this claim as undeveloped or degenerate. For instance, he did not perceive the complicated supply system of the eighteenth century as the product of the particular conditions of that period, but rather viewed it as an error caused by inadequate thinking and 'prejudice' that even Frederick the Great was unable to shake off.[54] The same line of reasoning applied to strategy. Rather than understanding Frederick's strategy against the background of the political and military conditions of his time, Jomini maintained that Frederick had not operated according to Napoleonic principles because military thought had not yet developed enough to recognize these principles. 'Until Frederick's time but little was known except concerning' tactics, and 'the fact is, that the art of war made but little progress' even under Frederick. Frederick 'entirely misunderstood' the principles of operations.[55]

The vast majority of Jomini's contemporaries shared the fundamentals of his theoretical outlook as established by the military thinkers of the Enlightenment. Criticism of his ideas, particularly

[52] The two major interpretations of the Napoleonic art of war, that of Camon in France and York von Wartenburg in Germany, owed much to Jomini's categories of analysis. See York von Wartenburg, *Napoleon as a General* (London, 1902), i. 276–7, 299 for praises for Jomini.

[53] See Chs. 6.I and 7.II of this work.

[54] *Treatise*, ch. 1, p. 93; ch. 3, p. 164.

[55] Ibid., ch. 26, p. 278.

that of interior lines after the campaign of 1813, was limited to the details (albeit important ones) rather than the essence of his theoretical work. However, with Clausewitz who rejected the entire military tradition of the Enlightenment, the very legitimacy of Jomini's theoretical approach was denied. It was not that Clausewitz thought that 'Jomini said something which was utterly wrong'; indeed, compared with Bülow, 'it cannot be denied that he thinks and argues in an extremely more solid manner'.[56] Furthermore, until 1813, Clausewitz shared Jomini's belief in the primacy of the central position and interior lines.[57] However, Clausewitz was interested not so much in the certain practical value of Jomini's ideas but in their presentation as a general science of war which he regarded as absurd. Jomini's abstract principles, he argued, ignored the living reality of war, the operation of moral forces, and the unique conditions of every particular case. Jomini's criticism of Frederick the Great, for example, was totally unhistorical and superficial. The complicated options facing Frederick in highly complex situations could not be reduced to, or judged by, a couple of abstract principles.[58]

Clausewitz's early notes on strategy were not published until 1937, but his major works which appeared in 1832–7, expressed the same ideas and made them public. In *On War* he again argued that principles like those of Jomini which were abstracted from the real conditions of particular cases could never be universally valid, and that Jomini's criticism of other periods for not acting according to the Napoleonic system of warfare was strictly forbidden.[59] In a more direct reference to Jomini's work, Clausewitz's judgement was short and harsh:

> As a reaction to that fallacy [Bülow's] another geometrical principle was then exalted: that of the so-called interior lines. Even though this tenet rests on a solid ground—on the fact that the engagement is the only effective means in war—its purely geometrical character still makes it another lopsided principle that could never govern a real situation.[60]

That the conduct of war could not be reduced to universal principles was the general message of *On War*. War was affected by innumerable

[56] Clausewitz, 'Strategie', the important addition of 1808, in Hahlweg (ed.), *Verstreute kleine Schriften* pp. 48 and 47.

[57] See pp. 205 and 208 of this work.

[58] 'Strategie' (1808), pp. 47–9.

[59] Clausewitz, *On War*, VI, 30, p. 516.

[60] Ibid. II, 2, pp. 135–6.

factors, dominant among which were political conditions and moral forces; it was saturated with the unknown and incalculable, and was changing throughout history.

It is not hard to imagine that the publication of Clausewitz's works was an unpleasant surprise for Jomini. Completely unexpected, a huge and most impressive work, whose theoretical sophistication was indisputable, appeared on the scene, threatening Jomini's growing domination over military theory and challenging the accepted tenets of the study of war. It is apparent that Clausewitz's clear sense of superiority and the short, dismissive nature of his criticism wounded Jomini very deeply, even more than the general arguments of his work. Jomini's references to Clausewitz throughout the *Summary* imply as much. In his survey of military literature at the beginning of the *Summary*, Jomini made an effort to check his anger, and his treatment of Clausewitz was more elaborate and cautious than his customary treatment of any other military writer with the exception of Archduke Charles. However, his aim was to fight back and he neglected no opportunity or subtlety to belittle the value of his rival's work. In 1831, he wrote,

> the Prussian General Clausewitz died, leaving to his widow the care of publishing his posthumous works which were presented as unfinished sketches. This work made a great sensation in Germany . . . One cannot deny to General Clausewitz great learning and a facile pen; but this pen, at times a little vagrant, is above all too pretentious for a didactic discussion, the simplicity and clearness of which ought to be its first merit. Besides that, the author shows himself by far too skeptical in point of military science . . . As for myself, I own that I have been able to find in this learned labyrinth but a small number of luminous ideas and remarkable articles; and far from having shared the skepticism of the author, no work would have contributed more than his to make me feel the necessity and utility of good theories.[61]

Clausewitz's remarks about the many inaccuracies in Jomini's historical studies annoyed Jomini very much. He wrote bitterly that Clausewitz

> has been an unscrupulous plagiarist, pillaging his predecessors, copying their reflections, and saying evil afterwards of their works after having travestied them under other forms. Those who shall have read my campaign of 1799, published ten years before his, will not deny my assertions, for there is not one of my reflections which he has not repeated.[62]

[61] *Summary*, pp. 14–15. [62] Ibid. 21.

In addition, throughout the *Summary*, Jomini took issue with Clausewitz on a series of points, unleashing his wounded pride. Regarding mountain warfare he wrote about 'General Clausewitz, whose logic is frequently defective'. Concerning the importance of manœuvre in battle, he wrote that 'Clausewitz commits a grave error'.[63] Yet, Jomini's full response to the challenge of Clausewitz, as well as to that of Archduke Charles, is revealed mainly indirectly in the *Summary*.

Jomini's Response and Later Development

Clausewitz as a rival and Archduke Charles both as an ally and contender played an important role in Jomini's decision to write the *Summary*. Jomini himself wrote that the publication of Charles's *Grundsätze der Strategie* (1814) convinced him of the need to supplement his historical *Treatise* with an abstract theoretical work. This led to the first early version of the *Summary*, the *Introduction à l'étude des grandes combinaisons de la stratégie et la tactique* (1829).[64] When yet another impressive and comprehensive theoretical work such as *On War* was published, Jomini could hardly fall behind. His aim in writing the *Summary* was, therefore, to produce a comprehensive theoretical work of his own which would include and surpass what he regarded as Charles's main achievements, and repel the challenge posed by Clausewitz.

Although the *Treatise* was mostly historical and full of references to many aspects of war, it was dominated by Jomini's principles of operations, the source of his great reputation as the interpreter of the Napoleonic art of war. As the *Summary* was intended to involve a more comprehensive and rounded treatment of war, it was more heterogeneous in nature. The principal theoretical additions were the first two chapters, 'The Relation of Diplomacy to War' and 'Military Policy'. The former 'included those considerations from which a statesman concludes whether a war is proper, opportune, or indispensable, and determines the various operations necessary to attain the object of the war'.[65] A typology of aims in war follows (rights, economic interests, balance of power, ideology, territories, and mania for conquest), together with a classification of the various types of war. The second chapter, 'Military Policy',

[63] Ibid. 166, 178. [64] Ibid. 14. [65] Ibid.

embraces the political considerations relating to the operation of armies . . . the passions of the people to be fought, their military system, their immediate means and reserves, their financial resources, the attachment they bear to their government or their institutions . . . finally, the resources and obstacles of every kind likely to be met.[66]

Contrary to what might be assumed, these chapters were not written under Clausewitz's influence. They had appeared for the first time in the second early version of the *Summary*, the *Tableau analytique des principales combinaisons de la guerre, et de leur rapports avec la politique des états* (1830), written before the publication of *On War*. In fact, the theoretical framework developed in 1830 had already been outlined in the third edition of the *Treatise* in 1818. At the end of the concluding chapter of principles Jomini wrote:

It is not necessary to remind our readers that we have here merely treated of those principles which relate . . . to the purely military part of the art of war; other combinations no less important . . . pertain more to the government of empires than the commanding of armies. To succeed in great enterprises it is . . . necessary . . . to take into consideration the resources . . . internal condition . . . the relative situation of their neighbors . . . the passions of the people . . . their peculiar institutions and the strength of their attachment to them . . . In a word, it is absolutely necessary to know that science which consists of a mixture of politics, administration and war, the basis of which has been so well laid by Montesquieu.[67]

Like Guibert and Lloyd, and even perhaps under their influence, Jomini applied the theoretical legacy of Montesquieu to the military field.

Some additions were also built around the rationale of operations itself, mainly under the influence of Archduke Charles. Jomini's principles of operations in the *Treatise* were renowned for being remarkably simple, clear, and concise in formulation. Yet, because of his effort to match and even surpass Charles's system of strategic points, they became in the *Summary* much more elaborate, less sharp in presentation, and entangled in complex definitions and jargon. Jomini had tended always to identify definitions with the scientific approach. In the *Treatise* he had already defined single, double, interior, exterior, extended, deep, concentric, eccentric, secondary, and accidental lines.[68] Charles's work only reinforced this tendency

[66] *Summary*, p. 38. [67] *Treatise*, the concluding ch., pp. 460–1.
[68] *Treatise*, ch. 14, pp 11–12.

in Jomini. He was not prepared to fall behind Charles in what he regarded to be one of the fundamentals of the science of war—a systematic approach in characterizing the theatre of operations. In the *Summary* he therefore identified and defined fixed and accidental-intermediate bases of operations; objective, strategic-manœuvre, decisive-strategic, geographic-strategic, and refuge points; operational and strategic fronts, and strategic positions, zones, and lines of operations; and temporary, strategic, and communication lines.[69] All this jargon originated late, and, as noted by a modern commentator, only obscured Jomini's central teaching.[70] Moreover, it strengthened the criticism that his work was pedantic and geometric.

Jomini responded to the criticism that his approach was mechanistic and geometric with somewhat justified astonishment and bitterness. He believed that he was accused of opinions he had never held:

> My principles have been badly comprehended by several writers . . . some have made the most erroneous application of them . . . others have drawn from them exaggerated consequences which have never been able to enter my head; for a general officer, after having assisted in a dozen campaigns, ought to know that war is a great drama, in which a thousand physical or moral causes operate more or less powerfully, and which cannot be reduced to mathematical calculations . . . I hope that after these avowals, I could not be accused of wishing to make of this art a mechanism of determined wheel-work, nor of pretending, on the contrary, that the reading of a single chapter of principles is able to give, all at once, the talent of conducting an army.[71]

It is important to understand Jomini's reaction to the criticism against him. His theoretical outlook was based totally on the intellectual legacy of the military thinkers of the Enlightenment, accepted for a century as self-evident. In view of this, the criticism against him which expressed new intellectual trends was unintelligible to him. Military views, as such, were not so much the issue, but rather differing perspectives regarding the question as to which theoretical approach was at all legitimate and worth pursuing.

[69] *Summary*, pp. 74–132.

[70] Michael Howard, 'Jomini and the Classical Tradition in Military Thought', in Howard (ed.), *The Theory and Practice of War*, pp. 16–17.

[71] *Summary*, pp. 17–18.

Like all the military thinkers of the Enlightenment, Jomini was always aware of the importance of moral and immeasurable factors but regarded them as belonging to the 'sublime' part of war which was not susceptible to scientific treatment and comprised the 'art' component in the conduct of war. It is true that Lloyd studied the psychological motives of troops with a practical purpose in mind, but on the whole the military thinkers of the Enlightenment saw no use in elaborating upon the moral, incalculable, and unforeseen which could hardly produce practical results.

The same applied to the criticism of the alleged geometrical nature of Jomini's work, expressed in particularly harsh words in Clausewitz's *On War*. Here too, Jomini's claim that he was unfairly treated, can be understood. Since the writing of the *Treatise*, Jomini always stressed that he did not believe in a military 'system', certainly not in a complete geometrical system such as that of Bülow. Instead, he believed in 'principles', or, in other words, in a much more flexible and less pretentious theoretical framework. This was not merely empty rhetoric or intellectual hair-splitting. Jomini's principles of operations were simple, relatively undogmatic, and faithfully expressed the spirit of contemporary warfare. His comment on the conceptions associated chiefly with Bülow and Charles was in this respect characteristic: 'They want war too methodical, too measured,' he wrote; 'I would make it brisk, bold, impetuous, perhaps sometimes even audacious . . . to reduce war to geometry would be to impose fetters on the genius of the greatest captains and to submit to the yoke of an exaggerated pedantry.'[72]

Indeed, Jomini never based his work on geometrical considerations in the full sense of the term. Unlike Bülow and Charles, he was far from forming his principles on calculations of angles and distances, and he repeatedly emphasized that the sketches in his works should be regarded as no more than illustrations.

To clarify this important point it might be worthwhile to distinguish between 'geometrical' and 'spatial' military theory. Since the shift of interest to the conduct of operations, the attention of military thinkers had been focused on the relationship between the movements of armies in space. As we have seen, this line of thought led to the formulation of several rationales of operations which were sometimes very fruitful. Lloyd schematized the rationale of the war

[72] *Summary*, p. 135.

of manœuvre, and Jomini developed an even more successful schematization of the Napoleonic art of operations. However, one had to be aware that the 'spatial' approach was but an abstraction and was therefore limited in validity. This was particularly important since the approach invited dangerous temptations. First and foremost, there was the tendency to give the spatial relationships a geometrical expression, thus realizing a quest that was deeply rooted in the Enlightenment, and making the rationale of operations precise and strictly scientific. This tendency found its most extreme manifestation with Bülow, but hardly touched Jomini. While he certainly expressed the universal tendency of the Enlightenment, Jomini was absolutely free from geometrical dogmatism.

If one may say so, Jomini's death in 1869 came at the most suitable time from the point of view of his international reputation. In old age, during the last decades of his long life, he was able to enjoy his position as the most celebrated and influential military thinker of his times. Archduke Charles had died twenty-two years earlier, and, in any case, his works were never so influential throughout Europe as those of Jomini. Clausewitz's works, whose sensational publication in Germany had alarmed Jomini in the 1830s, seemed to have fallen into respectful oblivion. The many eminent persons of the Napoleonic era with whom Jomini was on bad personal terms were also all dead. And new generations of officers, educated at military academies on Jomini's theoretical works and monumental histories, treated him with the admiration reserved for classic authors. Willisen and Rüstow in Germany, Napier and Hamley in Britain, and Mahan in the United States are only some of his most notable and declared disciples in the nineteenth century.[73]

Yet, immediately after Jomini's death, the picture began to change. Following the crushing victories of the Prussian armies under the orchestration of one who declared himself to be Clausewitz's disciple, the centre of military power and thought passed to Germany. A new, active, and powerful German military school influenced military thought throughout Europe, presenting Clausewitz as its mentor and projecting a particular interpretation of his ideas. Consequently,

[73] Jomini's wide-ranging influence in the 19th cent. still deserves to be studied; for an outline see Howard, 'Jomini', in Howard (ed.), *The Theory and Practice of War*, p. 14; and Shy, 'Jomini', in Paret (ed.), *Makers of Modern Strategy*, pp. 177–9.

Jomini's star was in eclipse. He gained a dubious image in Germany which absorbed and assimilated Clausewitz's criticism of universal doctrines of operations, criticism that was reinforced by Moltke's attitude. Jomini's reputation was also clearly declining in France which had previously been the military centre of Europe, and where, after the French defeat, the army was eager to learn the secrets of German military proficiency. In the peripheral countries, however, like the United States and Britain which were less sensitive and slower in reacting to the changes in the military centre of gravity, Jomini's dominance remained unchallenged. On the eve of the First World War in a course of lectures presented before the students of Oxford, Spenser Wilkinson, the University's first professor of military history, declared that the science of war had advanced very little since Jomini; Jomini had formulated the principles used in the study of military operations.[74]

The First World War was the second and more crucial turning-point in Jomini's decline, because in many ways it ended the Napoleonic model of warfare. In the Napoleonic-Jominian paradigm, still sufficiently relevant throughout the nineteenth century, armies manœuvred against one another in a relatively open space. In contrast, those who took part in the fighting on the Western front, when searching for an analogy in previous experience, could only describe it as a gigantic siege. The growing armies with their increasing fire-power filled space from one end to the other, blocking all movement with long and continuous front lines. The revival of the war of movement in the Second World War brought back some relevancy to the Jominian categories of manœuvre. But warfare was now conducted with mechanized armies and air forces, supported by huge industrial and technological infrastructures. A work that reflected the Napoleonic pattern of operations could hardly retain its former practical value in the new age. Since the First World War Jomini has therefore been known only to students of military history, and their attitude to him, influenced by the legacy of the German military school and by the decline of his influence, has by and large been unfavourable.

Ironically, this attitude largely reflects the legacy of Jomini's own theoretical outlook which was derived from the military thinkers of the Enlightenment. His work has been judged not so much from the

[74] Spenser Wilkinson, *The French Army Before Napoleon*, (Oxford, 1915), 15.

point of view of its success in analysing the warfare of its time but rather for its claim to be a universal theory of war. It has been unfavourably compared with Clausewitz's work, the main themes of which are widely believed to have remained as valid as ever.

Jomini and Napoleon

Jomini's great reputation in the nineteenth century rested partly on the belief that he had revealed the principles of Napoleonic warfare. And Jomini himself was anxious to show that he had not only succeeded in interpreting Napoleon's campaigns but that he was also able to foresee their development in the midst of events, and that his work and talents had been acknowledged by Napoleon, the warlord himself.

Those who came across the question of the personal and theoretical relationship between Napoleon and Jomini encountered the same historiographical problem; the source of almost all the direct evidence was Jomini himself, who was obviously biased. Furthermore, suspiciously enough, this evidence was produced only in the biography written in 1860 by his friend Lecomte when the persons involved, who did not share Jomini's fortune of an extremely long life, were long dead. Much of the biography even appears to be inconsistent with Jomini's own account related throughout his extensive works.

Lecomte's biography alleges, for example, that in 1800 the twenty-one-year-old Jomini, while conversing with friends on the future course of the war, anticipated Napoleon's Italian campaign and manœuvre against the Austrian rear.[75] If this was so, then one must believe that Jomini had predicted Napoleon's plan of campaign and developed his concept of the manœuvre against the enemy's rear even before he began his theoretical studies in 1802–3; and even more improbable, that he, who never failed to emphasize his successes, refrained from mentioning this theoretical achievement in the *Treatise* and *Summary*.

Lecomte's biography also describes Napoleon's impression of the first volumes of the *Treatise* in 1805. After fifty-five years, we are supposed to believe that Napoleon exclaimed (and someone wrote down) the following:

[75] Lecomte, *Jomini*, p. 10.

And people say that the times are not progressing. Here is a young chief of battalion [Jomini's Swiss rank], and of all men a Swiss, who teaches us things that many of my teachers never told me, and that only few generals understand. How did Fouché allow the publication of such a book?! It betrays to the enemy the whole of my system of war![76]

Here too, it is very much out of character for Jomini to have failed to cite much earlier this first-rate praise from Napoleon himself.

On 15 September 1806, on the eve of Napoleon's invasion of Prussia, Jomini prepared a memorandum, cited in his biography, in which he suggested a plan similar to the one actually carried out by the emperor in the Jena campaign.[77] The biography also describes a dialogue which is purported to have taken place between Napoleon and Jomini at the end of a staff meeting. Jomini asked Napoleon if he could join him four days later at Bamberg, implying that he had already deciphered the emperor's secret intentions. The surprised Napoleon asked Jomini who had told him that he was going to Bamberg, and Jomini replied: 'the map of Germany, Your Highness, and your campaigns of Marengo and Ulm'.[78] Although Jomini, closely familiar with Napoleon's previous campaigns, may have anticipated that the emperor would again resort to the manœuvre against the enemy's rear, the story of his conversation with Napoleon raises all the doubts mentioned before. As to his memorandum, Caemmerer has already pointed out that Jomini was well acquainted with the general deployment of the French corps and that by 15 September he probably also had the preliminary marching orders of, at least, his own corps. It was therefore not difficult for him to put two and two together.[79]

Despite what appears almost certainly to be, at the very least, exaggeration on the part of a celebrated military theorist, who in old age, when no one was left to challenge his words, tried to magnify his reputation, there exists a hard core of facts which cannot be ignored regarding his relationship with Napoleon. Jomini, an anonymous foreigner, received from Napoleon in 1805 the rank of colonel and a senior staff position. Even in the socially highly mobile French army this was not common, and the only explanation is that the emperor was genuinely impressed with Jomini's theoretical work. Even if Jomini did not play as decisive a role in Ney's staff as Lecomte's

[76] Lecomte, *Jomini*, p. 29. [77] Ibid. 33–4. [78] Ibid. 47.
[79] Caemmerer, *Strategical Science*, p. 38.

biography would have us believe, it is still very plausible that the talented young man, whose skill for military analysis was undisputed and who had just made a penetrating study of the Napoleonic art of operations, did play a dominant role as chief of staff to Ney (who, as has been repeatedly said, was not particularly known for his intellectual abilities), and was in a position to keep in close touch with Napoleon's operational planning at the time of the events themselves.

Some clues on Napoleon's attitude to Jomini may also be inferred from Napoleon's own remarks and theoretical positions. At St Helena he praised Jomini's account in the *Treatise* of the Italian campaign of 1796–7, and exonerated him from the accusation that he revealed the French war plans to the Allies after his desertion.[80] In one of his talks, reflecting on the benefits that could have been gained from the teaching of Frederick's campaigns in the French military schools, Napoleon said:

> Jomini would have been a good man for that purpose. Such teaching would have put excellent ideas into the heads of young pupils. It is true that Jomini always argues for fixed principles. Genius works by inspiration. What is good in certain circumstances may be bad in others; but one ought to consider principles as an axis which holds certain relations to a curve. It may be good to recognize that on this or that occasion one has swerved from fixed principles of war.[81]

This statement is particularly instructive despite the fact that here Napoleon appears to be in his more sceptical mood. Indeed, his distinction between the role of principles in war and the effect of changing circumstances which are mastered by ingenious inspiration, reveals that Napoleon's theoretical outlook, like Jomini's, was the product of his intellectual background.

That Napoleon, the person who came to symbolize the advent of the nineteenth century, was deeply rooted in the eighteenth century is now widely accepted. Colin had uncovered the influence of contemporary military thinkers on the formation of the military ideas of the young Napoleon, and Napoleon's categories of thought were no exception. After all, Montecuccoli, Feuquières, Folard, de Saxe, Frederick the Great, Guibert, and Lloyd were among the military

[80] C. Montholon (ed.), *Mémoires pour servir à l'histoire de France sous Napoléon, écrits à Sainte Hélène* (Paris, 1823), i. 1.
[81] G. Gourgaud (ed.), *Talks of Napoleon at St. Helena* (London, 1904), 215.

thinkers of the Enlightenment whose works he read in the course of his military education.[82]

Though Napoleon left no theoretical military work and his sporadic dictums were mostly compiled from his dictations to his adjutants during his exile at St Helena, his theoretical outlook is clear enough. The following words could have been written by any of the above-mentioned thinkers as well as by Jomini:

> All great captains have done great things *only* by conforming to the rules and natural principles of the art; that is to say, by the wisdom of their combinations . . . They have succeeded only by thus *conforming*, whatever may have been the audacity of their enterprises and the extent of their success. They have never ceased to make war a *veritable science*. It is only under this title that they are our great models, and it is only in *imitating* them that one can hope to approach them.[83]

The following passage could also have been taken from Jomini's own works:

> Gustavus Adolphus, Turenne and Frederick, as also Alexander, Hannibal and Caesar have all acted on the same principles. To keep your forces united, to be vulnerable at no point, to bear down with rapidity upon important points—these are the principles which insure victory.[84]

This passage indicates that the remarkable similarity in outlook between Napoleon and Jomini encompassed not only their theoretical and historical premises, but also their military conceptions, a fact already pointed out by Caemmerer.[85] 'An army should have but a single line of operations,' wrote Napoleon; 'to operate upon lines remote from each other and without communications between them, is a fault . . . It ought then to be adopted as a principle that the columns of an army should be always kept united, so that the enemy cannot thrust himself between them.' That is because 'by concentrating his forces he may not only prevent their junction but also defeat them one by one'.[86]

Napoleon' maxims, despite their sporadic nature, show clearly that Jomini not only formulated a very penetrating conceptualization of the Napoleonic art of war, but also that he did so in terms very akin

[82] Colin, *L'Éducation militaire de Napoléon*, see esp. ch. I.

[83] My emphases; Napoleon, *Military Maxims* in T. Phillips (ed.), *Roots of Strategy*, maxim no. 112; see also no. 5.

[84] Ibid., no. 77.

[85] Caemmerer, *Strategical Science*, p. 37.

[86] Napoleon, *Military Maxims*, nos. 12, 11, 4.

to those used by Napoleon. Indeed, it is even possible that Napoleon adopted in his dicta some of Jomini's formulations. This affinity is particularly interesting not merely because it supports Jomini's claims. It also indicates that while new intellectual trends devised a new theoretical outlook in which the general's genius, modelled on Napoleon, was given the major role, Napoleon himself—like Jomini and most of his contemporaries—viewed and interpreted war and his own activities as a general through a single conceptual framework, the one propounded by the military thinkers of the Enlightenment.

Part Two

THE GERMAN MOVEMENT CLAUSEWITZ AND THE ORIGINS OF THE GERMAN MILITARY SCHOOL

6

The Reaction against the Enlightenment

New Perspectives on Military Theory

I THE EMERGENCE OF A NEW CLIMATE OF IDEAS

One of the most striking impressions in reading the works of the military thinkers of the Enlightenment is the all-embracing uniformity of their theoretical outlook. They differed, to be sure, in many other respects; for example, their spheres of interest varied and underwent considerable change, and, above all, they were deeply divided on their actual military outlook and ideas. However, they did not differ in the fundamentals of their guiding objective—the search for a general theory of war—which derived from their intellectual environment. Here too there were, of course, varying interpretations and emphases, but the central themes of this objective were both clear and indisputable. War, like all fields of nature and human activity, was susceptible to a comprehensive and systematic theoretical study. In part, it could be reduced to rules and principles of universal validity and possibly even mathematical certainty, for which Newtonian mechanics set the example. However, like the arts, it was also partly in flux, constantly changing, dependent on circumstances, affected by the unforseen and incalculable, and therefore always requiring application through the general's creative genius.

A conspicuous and highly significant fact is that for at least fifty years, from the appearance of Puységur's *Art de la guerre par principes et par règles* in 1748 until the end of the 1790s, virtually no theoretical challenge compromised the domination of this outlook. Nothing is more indicative of its power and close affinity to the highly influential intellectual environment from which it emerged.

This remarkable intellectual coherence came to an end with the appearance of Berenhorst's *Reflections on the Art of War* in 1796–9.

This is not to say that the ideas of the Enlightenment then lost their influence. On the contrary, as we have seen, at the beginning of the nineteenth century, Bülow, Charles, and Jomini developed these ideas in new and highly influential directions; and the overwhelming majority of contemporary military thinkers continued to view war through the perspectives set by the military school of the Enlightenment. However, the absolute hegemony that this school had maintained over military theory was irreversibly broken. Within a few years, Clausewitz began to formulate the most comprehensive and sophsticated expression of new ideas in the field of military thought, thus laying the intellectual foundations for what was to be a new German military school.

The breach in the hegemony of the military school of the Enlightenment, like its fifty years of domination, can only be understood against the background of the general intellectual developments in Europe in the late eighteenth and early nineteenth centuries. It can even be said that only a small minority of the principal themes propounded by Berenhorst and Clausewitz originated within the military field itself. Most were extracted from, and set in motion by, the ideas and ideals of new and powerful cultural trends.

These trends, it must be stressed, were far from forming a single intellectual framework. They expressed a wide variety of views and beliefs which derived from very different and remote sources, represented diverse human groups and inclinations, and aimed at different, if not entirely opposite goals. They were far more heterogeneous than the intellectual framework of the Enlightenment against which they reacted in varying degrees. Indeed, some of these trends were closer to the Enlightenment than to each other.

The diversity is already apparent in the fact that there is no comprehensive name to describe all these trends as a single movement. Irrationalism, historicism, critical philosophy, religious revivalism, vitalism and wholism, idealism, romanticism, conservatism, nationalism, and reactionaryism, were major themes in the new intellectual climate, but none of them could represent the whole. Two accepted terms appear, however, to describe in the most suitable fashion both the general and military points of view. The first is the 'Counter-Enlightenment'. Here too, however, the name must not obscure the fact that the various trends in this cultural movement differed in their antagonism to, and reaction against, the Enlightenment, and, also that most of them were, in fact, heavily in its debt. Furthermore, the emphasis on the negative aspect of the movement may overshadow its clear positive messages. Another accepted term, the 'German Movement', focuses on the country where these trends broke out in the most powerful, diverse, and fertile manner, and had the most profound and wide-ranging influence. It particularly fits the military sphere where the new trends appeared almost exclusively in Germany.

The diversity of the trends in the new intellectual climate was also manifest in the field of military thought, which influenced Berenhorst and Clausewitz in very different ways. On the whole, Berenhorst is a classical exponent of the 'Counter-Enlightenment', whereas Clausewitz may best be understood in the framework of the 'German Movement'. In view of this diversity of ideas and influences, it may be better, perhaps, first to delineate briefly those themes and trends in the new intellectual paradigm whose role in the emergence of the German military school was particularly dominant. This survey is, necessarily, somewhat superficial, and focuses on Germany, on the trends that were critical of the Enlightenment, and the themes that were particularly relevant to the development of military thought. The theoretical outlook of the military exponents of these new trends, Clausewitz in particular, will then be examined separately, in a more extensive, concrete, and distinctive form.

The new cultural trends emerged in Germany in two major waves. The first emerged in the 1770s at the zenith of the Enlightenment in Germany. It was oppositional in nature, associated with a group that operated, to a large extent, outside and against the cultural establishment, and whose most notable members included Hamann, Herder, the young Goethe and the writers and dramatists of the 'Storm and Stress' movement, Lavater and Möser. The second wave emerged throughout Europe at the turn of the century and was accelerated by the threat posed by the French Revolution and the Napoleonic Empire. Sweeping in influence, it embraced the major trends of romanticism, nationalism, and idealism. In addition, in the midst of the German cultural community and inside the fortress of the Enlightenment, Kant exerted an all-encompassing influence, and his decisive role in creating the new intellectual climate was both unique and ambivalent. While he stood, from the point of view of his intellectual development, personality, and self-consciousness, at the pinnacle of the German *Aufklärung*, and was appalled by many of the ideas of the Counter-Enlightenment, he also undermined some of the central doctrines and beliefs of the Enlightenment in his critical philosophy.

The new German Movement challenged the fundamentals of the Enlightenment's world-view, which may be considered under four major headings: the conceptions of knowledge and reality, man, art, and history. Its opposition to the French intellectual and political imperialism went hand in hand with the awakening of the German national sentiments which developed in a highly political direction, placing a strong emphasis on the role of the state.

(*a*) Behind the intellectual world of the Enlightenment there stood the tradition of natural law, the legacies of both Cartesian rationalism and British empiricism, the neo-classical conceptions in the arts, and the model of Newtonian science. The conception of knowledge consolidated from these sources by the men of the Enlightenment implied that, essentially, the complex world of experience was governed by relatively few principles which were at once simple, fundamental, universal, and tending to precision. Newton's three laws of mechanics exemplified all these qualities most remarkably.

By contrast, the thinkers of the Counter-Enlightenment regarded this conception of knowledge and reality to be fundamentally false or, at least, highly exaggerated. The world was for them not basically simple but, on the contrary, highly complex, composed of innumerable and unique elements and events, and always in a state of flux. Hence their much cooler attitude to the scientific ideal embodied in Newtonian science.

Hamann (1730–87), Kant's rebellious disciple and the spiritual mentor of the men of the 'Storm and Stress' period, scorned the Enlightenment's blindness to, and loss of touch with, rich and vital reality on which it arrogantly attempted to force artificial, crude, and superficial principles and conceptual frameworks. Genuine knowledge was always the knowledge of singular and unique cases. The sciences, which Hamann treated with contempt and in which he was hardly interested, could, at best, serve as crude approximations in resolving certain practical, fundamentally mechanical problems.[1]

[1] For Hamann's life, world-view, and influence see W. M. Alexander, *Johann Georg Hamann, Philosophy and Faith* (The Hague, 1966). For a penetrating, concise outline see Isaiah Berlin's marvellous articles, esp. 'Hume and the Sources of German Anti-Rationalism' in his *Against the Current: Essays in the History of Ideas* (Oxford, 1981), pp. 165–70; and also 'The Counter-Enlightenment', ibid. 6–9, to which this chapter owes a great deal.

Hamann's friends among the men of the 'Storm and Stress' period shared his criticism of the Enlightenment for its totally erroneous attempt to force the categories which had proved successful in physics on reality as a whole. Despite his admiration for the achievements of the natural sciences, Herder (1744–1803) believed that their conceptions, while suitable for the inanimate and simple bodies of mechanics, were totally unsuitable for understanding other spheres of a rich and complex world, in particular for the understanding of man and society.[2]

Goethe, who was enthusiastically interested and actively involved in the scientific developments of his time, believed that the analytic and classifying method did not even suit the natural sciences. Already in the Enlightenment, the biological and vitalistic theories of Maupertuis and Buffon had aroused much interest in Diderot, who looked upon the domination of mechanics over his period with some apprehension.[3] The discoveries in the fields of electricity and the chemistry of gases, during the last third of the eighteenth century, further reinforced the tendency to view nature through organic and vitalistic conceptions. Goethe pointed out that the classifications of biology and mineralogy were imposing human conceptual frameworks on a nature whose diversity of forms and changes was infinite. The long list of 'intermediate cases' and 'exceptions' created by these classifications revealed their artificiality all too clearly. In his diatribe against Newton's optics, Goethe argued that any attempt to base the diversity of the spectrum of colours on the crushing of the white colour was to be totally rejected.[4]

Paradoxically, Kant's all-embracing influence also worked to restrict the belief in the power of reason and to weaken the domination of the model of Newtonian science. Though one of the declared aims of the *Critique of Pure Reason* (1781) was to rescue the achievements of the natural sciences from the threat of scepticism, it only achieved this by excluding whole sections of reality from the

[2] For Herder's attitude to science, see H. B. Nisbet, *Herder and the Philosophy and History of Science* (Cambridge, 1970).

[3] On the latent tension within the Enlightenment between the domination of the mechanistic explanation and the organic-vitalistic view, see Colin Kiernan, 'Science and the Enlightenment in Eighteenth Century France', in T. Besterman (ed.), *Studies on Voltaire and the Eighteenth Century*, LIX (1968).

[4] On Goethe and contemporary science, see George A. Wells, *Goethe and the Development of Science* (The Netherlands, 1978).

domain and capacity of reason. Moreover, the aim of the *Critique of Practical Reason* (1788) was to establish the autonomy of the human soul from the regularity which dominated nature.

These developments also found expression in the works of the early Romantics at the turn of the century, and were philosophically formulated in Schelling's *Naturphilosophie*. Nature embraced an endless diversity of forms, was motivated by vitalistic forces, and maintained a dynamic relationship with man.[5] Attempting to remedy what they regarded as ruptures created by Kant's philosophy between the various faculties of man and between man and reality, the idealists Fichte, Schelling, and particularly Hegel, developed to the utmost the holistic and integrative notions inherent in the German Movement. All elements of reality were but aspects and manifestations of a single whole.

These new perspectives had particular bearing on the study of man, the real interest of the men of the German Movement.

(*b*) The attitude of the men of the German Movement to the legacy of the British empiricists in human psychology was ambivalent. On the one hand, they admired the achievements of empiricism in describing the construction of human consciousness from the materials of experience, and the primacy they gave to the study of man in understanding the world. On the other hand, following Leibnitz and Kant, they rejected the empiricist claim that man was a *tabula rasa*, and the dissection of the human mind into atomistic impressions and sensations. This conception, they felt, missed the essence of man as an active, creative, and imaginative unity which integrated the impressions of experience. The deep and multifaceted human experience, as intuitively and intimately known to every individual, was diametrically opposed to the crude, mechanistic, and skeletal system portrayed both by associative psychology and the materialists. Goethe expressed the attitude he shared with his friends when he called Holbach's work 'ghostly' and 'corpse-like'.[6]

The men of the Counter-Enlightenment were interested in direct and concrete human experience. This orientation was deeply rooted in, among others, the pietist stream of Lutheranism whose influence

[5] See esp. Alexander Gode von Aesch, *Natural Science in German Romanticism* (New York, 1941).

[6] Goethe, *Dichtung und Wahrheit*, Bk. II, in *Werke*, x. 537–9 (Zurich, 1949–52); cited by Roy Pascal, *The German Sturm und Drang* (London, 1953), 131.

from the end of the seventeenth century, particularly in East Prussia, was considerable. The works of Hamann, Lavater, Herder, Jacobi, and even Kant were deeply embedded in this powerful spiritualist tradition. The pietist emphasis on personal experience and its suspicion of all dogma had at first, paradoxically, helped to pave the way for the Enlightenment in Germany, but were later directed against the Enlightenment, against the tyranny of its ideas, and both its atheism and rationalist natural religion.[7]

Hamann, the major exponent of spiritualism, argued that only imaginative, empathic insights, rather than abstract and universal principles, could penetrate into the wealth and uniqueness of human reality. Man was a complete creature, whose whole personality, rather than narrow aspects of it, were expressed in all spheres of his activity. Goethe summarized Hamann's teaching in saying: 'Everything that man undertakes, whether it be produced in action or word or anything else, must spring from his whole united powers; all separation of powers is to be repudiated.'[8] He and other 'Storm and Stress' writers, like Merck, Lenz, and Klinger, highlighted man's vitality, activity, and power of feelings in their plays. The men of the movement enthusiastically accepted Rousseau's human sensitivity and, as we shall see, the emphasis that the British aesthetic school, which originated with Shaftesbury, had put on the creative imagination.[9]

At the turn of the century all these themes were raised to prominence in the works of the early Romantics—the brothers Schlegel, Tieck, and Novalis. Their friend, the celebrated and influential preacher and religious thinker Schleiermacher, also stressed the uniqueness and potential of feelings, sensations, and thoughts revealed in every individual. He gave these ideas systematic expression in his *Monologen* (1800). The Romantics' philosophical patron Fichte, in his *Science of Knowledge* (1794) and *Theory of Knowledge* (1797), made man the creator of reality through his free spiritual activity. And the Romantics adapted this to promote the

[7] For this well-known relationship, see e.g. K. S. Pinson, *Pietism as a Factor in the Rise of German Nationalism* (New York, 1968).

[8] Goethe, *Dichtung und Wahrheit*, XII, in *Werke*, x. 563; cited by Pascal, *Sturm und Drang*, pp. 9–10.

[9] For the intellectual world of the men of the 'Storm and Stress' period, see Pascal's learned *Sturm und Drang*.

omnipotence of the creative imagination and force of feelings in the arts.[10]

(*c*) The emphasis on the creative, unique, and imaginative character of the individual, which could not be reduced to abstract and mechanical principles, was closely associated with a growing reaction against the legacy of seventeenth-century neo-classicism in the arts. In Britain, the country least influenced by neo-classicism, a line of writers and critics had been following in Shaftesbury's footsteps from the beginning of the eighteenth century. Leibnitz introduced Shaftesbury's influence to the continent, and particularly to Germany. There, the tenets of neo-classicism were directly challenged in the Gottsched affair, while Diderot represented moderate criticism of neo-classicism in France. All these people promoted the ideas of the originality of genius and the force of creative imagination and used them to counter the conceptual frameworks of neo-classicism. In his *Critique of Judgement* (1790) Kant consolidated the transformation in the eighteenth-century outlook on artistic creation, and the Romantics gave the last great push to the decline of neo-classicism.[11]

The reaction against neo-classicism went hand in hand with a powerful wave of interest in and admiration for forms of art hitherto considered by the men of the Enlightenment to be barbarous, lacking in taste or aesthetic knowledge, and produced by uncivilized or semi-civilized societies. The enthusiasm for Homer; for the poetry, folk-tales, and myths of the ancient Hebrews, Celts, and Germans, and of primitive people in general; for the spirit and art of the Middle Ages; and for the expressive genius of Shakespeare, whom the neo-classicists considered with horror to be a barbarous and demonic writer who disregarded all genres and

[10] For a general and critical survey of German Romanticism, see Ralph Tymms, *German Romantic Literature* (London, 1955); and for the Romantics' world-view see H. G. Schenk, *The Mind of the European Romantics* (London, 1966).

[11] In addition to the works cited in Ch. 2 n. 7 see esp. James Engell's highly comprehensive *The Creative Imagination, Enlightenment to Romanticism* (Cambridge Mass., 1981); see also L. W. Beck, *Early German Philosophy, Kant and His Predecessors* (Cambridge Mass., 1969), 278–88; and, for a defence of neo-classicism against stereotyped criticism, see E. B. O. Borgerhoff, *The Freedom of French Classicism* (Princeton, 1950). 17th-cent. neo-classicism as a conception of art is obviously not to be confused with late 18th-cent. German *Klassizismus* as an artistic style and view of life, mainly associated with the Weimar poets. The concept has been used in different ways for different periods.

conventions, were all closely linked to a profound transformation in viewing the past.

(*d*) In the second half of the eighteenth century a new historical outlook, later to be known as historicism, began to take shape. Criticism was levelled against the tendency of the men of the Enlightenment to view other societies and historical periods through the perspectives and values of their own time, which were thus perceived as a universal standard of measurement for the interpretation, criticism, and rejection of complete historical eras.

The beginnings of this transformation are to be traced, however, to the Enlightenment itself, particularly to the influence of Montesquieu, who introduced his contemporaries to a new depth of analysis of the relationships between the environmental, economic, religious, political, and constitutional factors which moulded the diversity of societies and cultures. Rousseau's yearning for primitive man, reflecting a growing alienation from modern society, was also highly important. These influences were reinforced, as mentioned above, by a wave of interest, particularly in Britain and Germany, in the ancient Greeks, biblical Hebrews, archaic peoples of the North, and Gothic architecture. All this influenced, and culminated in, the work of Herder.[12]

Herder argued in his works, particularly *Auch eine Philosophie der Geschichte* (1774) and *Ideen zur Philosophie der Geschichte der Menschheit* (1784–91), that every culture was a unique historical entity that stemmed from the particular circumstances and experience of its time and place and, in turn, expressed them in the totality of its values, ways of life and thought, institutions, and creative art. A dogmatic examination according to so-called universal standards precluded any real understanding, which could only be achieved by sympathetic and imaginative insights into the concrete conditions of a bygone reality and consciousness, aiming to reconstruct them in their own particular terms. Rather than superficial abstractions, a close and detailed study of the diverse forms of specific historical

[12] For the diversity of sources which influenced the genesis of historicism, see particularly the study of one of the most distinguished exponents of the movement: Friedrich Meinecke, *Historicism, the Rise of a New Historical Outlook* (London, 1972); for a more critical approach see G. Iggers, *The German Conception of History* (Middletown Con., 1968). A recent comprehensive study is P. H. Reil's *The German Enlightenment and the Rise of Historicism* (Berkeley, 1975).

situations was needed.[13] As an example of such a study, the men of the 'Storm and Stress' period were delighted with Justus Möser's close, penetrating, and vivid records of the ways of life, customs, and affairs of his fellow townsmen and peasants in the small principality of Osnabrück, and with his research into their medieval past.[14]

In Strasburg, Herder revealed to the young Goethe the beauty of the city's medieval cathedral, built in the Gothic style that was despised by the men of the Enlightenment. The writers of the 'Storm and Stress' movement felt an affinity to the past, and the Romantics enthusiastically embraced its diversity. Folk-songs and folk-tales, regarded as a vulgar subculture by the men of the Enlightenment, were elevated by Herder to the status of creative, authentic, and revealing indications of past ways of life. The Romantics followed in his footsteps not only in their literary themes but also in compiling folk-songs and legends. Clemens Brentano and Achim von Arnim published in Heidelberg an anthology of German folk-songs, *Des Knaben Wunderhorn, Alte Deutsche Lieder* (1805–8). The Grimm brothers followed suit with their celebrated collection of folk-tales, *Kinder und Hausmärchen* (1812).

These were the beginnings of historicism whose influence on the sciences of man was revolutionary and all-embracing. Human reality, according to the historicist message, was moulded by history, and changed with time and place, thus undermining any universal generalization. It could genuinely be understood only in a particular historical context. Directed against French Revolutionary ideas, this message, bolstered by Burke's highly influential *Reflections on the Revolution in France* (1790), was widely voiced by political theorists. Adam Müller in *Die Elemente der Staatskunst* (1809) lay the foundation of the historical school of economics. The principles that the political economists of the eighteenth century (headed by Adam Smith) had formulated and regarded as the universal rules of economics were considered by this school to be a reflection of the

[13] For Herder's conception of history see, in addition to the works cited in the previous note, A. O. Lovejoy, 'Herder and the Enlightenment Philosophy of History', in his *Essays in the History of Ideas* (Baltimore, 1948), 166–82; G. A. Wells, 'Herder's Two Philosophies of History', in the *Journal of the History of Ideas*, XXI (1960), 527–37; and I. Berlin, 'Herder' in id., *Vico and Herder* (London, 1976).

[14] See Knudsen, *Justus Möser and the German Enlightenment*; for a good concise account see Klaus Epstein, *The Genesis of German Conservatism* (Princeton, 1966), ch. 6.

particular conditions and interests prevailing in the capitalist, proto-industrial Britain of the time. Friedrich Karl Savigny launched the historical school of jurisprudence in his celebrated *Vom Beruf unserer Zeit für Gesetzgebung und Rechtswissenschaft* (1814). Law was not, and could not be, determined according to universal and abstract principles, argued Savigny; it developed out of the particular historical conditions of every society. Schleiermacher presented the dogmas, conventions, and institutions of religion as changing throughout history. And Hegel bonded the human mind and philosophy to history which reflected the various stages in the development of consciousness. Finally, in the more strictly historical field, there emerged the great historical school of the nineteenth century, associated with the name of Ranke.

These were some of the major themes in the German reaction to the dominating ideas of the French Enlightenment.[15] From being a provincial and somewhat backward culture which Möser—to the delight of his friends—defended in his *Über die deutsche Sprache und Literatur* (1781) against the scorn of the French-oriented Frederick the Great, German culture in the last decades of the eighteenth century became the centre of stimulating intellectual activity. Its growth was therefore linked with an anti-French tendency and awakening national sentiments. A German cultural self-awareness emerged in reaction against French intellectual imperialism, and developed, in response to Napoleonic political imperialism, in a clear political direction with a strong emphasis on the primacy of the state.

[15] For the social and economic aspects of the transition, see Henri Brunschwig, *Enlightenment and Romanticism in Eighteenth Century Prussia* (Chicago, 1974). A very critical assessment of the origins of German cultural identity in the 18th cent. is to be found in chs. 4 and 6 of Arnold Hauser's breath-taking *The Social History of Art*, ii (London, 1951).

II BERENHORST: COUNTER-ENLIGHTENMENT AND THE CRITICISM OF THE FREDERICKIAN SYSTEM

As pointed out by Berlin, the fierce and wide-ranging opposition to the ideas of the Enlightenment was as old as the Enlightenment itself. This opposition came, however, from traditionalist and conservative elements outside the intellectual circles with whom they had no common ground for genuine communication. This situation changed with the Counter-Enlightenment. The opposition now came from within the intellectual élite, had developed from the legacy of the Enlightenment itself, and challenged its ideas in its own language.[1]

This picture holds equally true in the military field. As mentioned earlier, many soldiers were probably alien to the 'military Enlightenment', and perhaps still more were simply indifferent to it. But naturally, very few, such as Brenckenhoff in his *Paradoxa*, gave their thoughts or feelings systematic intellectual and literary expression, and thus the absolute domination of the ideas of the Enlightenment over the field of military theory was hardly compromised. This changed with the work of Georg Heinrich von Berenhorst (1733–1814). Typical of the men of the Counter-Enlightenment, such as Hamann, he was a child of the Enlightenment who underwent a profound intellectual and psychological transformation. Experiencing the religious-spiritualist revival and influenced by Kant's critical philosophy, he adapted the new intellectual trends to the military field in a sophisticated, sometimes sardonic, sometimes aphoristic manner.

Berenhorst was the illegitimate son of Prince Leopold I of Anhalt-Dessau, the famous *Alte Dessaur*, one of the architects of the Prussian army and young Frederick's right-hand man. At the age of fifteen he joined an infantry regiment, and as a member of Prince Heinrich's staff and, from 1759, in Frederick's own headquarters, he took part in the great campaigns of the Seven Years War. He then entered the diplomatic service of his native

[1] Berlin, 'The Counter-Enlightenment', in *Against the Current*, p. 1.

principality, and after retirement in 1790, embarked upon his literary career.[2]

It is, however, Berenhorst's intellectual and psychological development, more than the biographical outline sketched above, that is of particular interest. Berenhorst himself left us an autobiographical essay which has not received the attention it deserves. He entitled it 'Selbstbekenntnisse', 'Confessions', in direct reference to the celebrated work of Rousseau, the hero of the new appeal to emotions and the inner world.[3]

In his youth, wrote Berenhorst, he was close to religion, but as he grew up his attitude changed. He read Helvétius's *De l'esprit*, lost his faith, and became a materialist. He accepted the explanation of man as a machine, and his religion was 'pantheism without morality'. He went on to read Lucretius, the exponent of atomism and materialism in antiquity, and the writings of Montaigne, Bayle, and Voltaire, who promoted scepticism, the critical spirit, and religious toleration. He was deeply influenced by the works of Nicolas Fréret, the leading figure in the French Academy of Inscriptions in the first half of the eighteenth century, who laid the foundations for the historical criticism of Christianity.[4]

Then, in his late thirties and forties, came the great spiritual transformation. He read the works of authors such as N. S. Bergier, one of the devout participants in the *Encyclopédie*, J. F. W. Jerusalem, one of the neologians, A. von Haller, the celebrated scientist and poet, and Lessing, who all strove to eliminate the conflicts between revealed religion and reason.[5] However, he was primarily influenced by the major exponents of the great pietist, spiritualist revival. He watched with interest Lavater's onslaught on Mendelssohn (1769), and the famous controversy between the latter and Jacobi regarding the nature of Lessing's religious faith (1785). He came to reject both natural law and natural religion, and to

[2] A concise biography of Berenhorst and an account of his works is contained in Edward Bülow's introd. to a collection from Berenhorst's literary remains: *Aus dem Nachlasse* (2 vols.; Dessau, 1845 and 1847). Many other items from Berenhorst's family archives are cited in Rudolf Bahn's *Georg Heinrich von Berenhorst* (doct. diss.; Halle, 1911). Eberhard Kessel's 'Georg Heinrich von Berenhorst', in *Sachsen und Anhalt*, IX (1933), 161–98, is a perceptive analysis of Berenhorst's work. Also see E. Hagemann, *Die deutsche Lehre vom Kriege; von Berenhorst zu Clausewitz* (Berlin, 1940), 6–20.

[3] See Berenhorst, 'Selbstbekenntnisse', in E. von Bülow (ed.), *Aus dem Nachlasse*, ii. 3 for the title's reference to Rousseau.

[4] Ibid. 4–5.

[5] Ibid. 6–7.

promote inner life, intuition, emotions, and free will.[6] It is no coincidence that his literary remains include several critiques of plays of the 'Storm and Stress' dramatists, particularly the 'great Goethe'.[7]

Kant's influence was equally decisive. In her perceptive portrayal of German culture, *De l'Allemagne* (1813), IV, 112, Mme de Staël described the all-embracing effect of his work: 'the *Critique* [of Pure Reason] created such a sensation in Germany that almost everything achieved since then, in literature as well as philosophy, derives from the impetus given by this work'. The military field was no exception. In his 'Confessions' Berenhorst wrote that he laboured much to understand Kant's works and succeeded in gaining access to his speculative philosophy. Kant saved free will and set the boundaries of human knowledge. Berenhorst regarded his own work to be, to some extent, a Kantian critique of military theory.[8]

The first volume of Berenhorst's *Reflections on the Art of War, its Progress, Contradictions, and Certainty* appeared in 1796, while the second, together with a revised edition of the first, appeared in 1798, and the third in 1799. According to a contemporary, at that time 'no book was as widely read as *Reflections*'.[9]

Berenhorst's historical account of the development of the science and art of war (that is, the intellectual treatment of war as embodied in military institutions and military organization) clearly reveals his heavy debt to the Enlightenment. As a face-to-face encounter, classical warfare, he wrote, was based on courage and physical strength. Yet the ancients also brought the science of war to a pinnacle of perfection which had not been achieved since. 'The ancients', he stated, 'I mean the Greeks and Romans, were, compared with the moderns, how should one put this?—more artistic.'[10] The Middle Ages were in this respect very different, and there was very

[6] 'Selbstbekenntnisse', *Aus dem Nachlasse*, ii. 6–14. Berenhorst's attitude to natural religion is also revealed in several references in his major military works; see e.g. *Betrachtungen über die Kriegskunst, über ihre Fortschritte, ihre Widersprüche und ihre Zuverlässigkeit* (3rd edn., Leipzig, 1827), 170.

[7] *Aus dem Nachlasse*, ii. 131 ff.

[8] 'Selbstbekenntnisse', *Aus dem Nachlasse*, ii. 14–16; again, in a typical aside, see e.g. Berenhorst's discussion of the distinction between *Vernuft* and *Verstand*: *Aphorismen* in *Betrachtungen*, pp 539–40.

[9] Cited in Jähns, *Geschichte der Kriegswissenschaften*, p. 2128.

[10] Berenhorst, *Betrachtungen*, pp. 40–1; for war in the classical period and a comparison between the ancients and the moderns, see chs. I and V.

little to be said about them. As they constituted an era of backwardness resembling the dawn of warfare before the classical period, 'courage and physical force alone' decided the fate of wars.[11] The art and science of war resumed development with the military reforms and innovations of the Dutch during their wars of independence, and of Gustavus Adolphus.[12] Louvois's military organization under Louis XIV gave the French hegemony in the science of war for a hundred years,[13] while a new level of achievement was reached by Frederick's Prussia.

Yet military science and art, which were the intellectual parts of war, were different in nature from what they had been assumed to be by the military thinkers of the Enlightenment. Indeed, other factors may have been of far greater importance in war. In a note entitled 'The Main Idea of the Whole Work' written when he was composing the *Reflections*, Berenhorst stated that the art of war, like the rest of the sciences and the arts, advanced knowledge and supported innate talent. However, it was not based on immutable laws but was rather associated with the unknown and uncontrollable modifications of the human spirit, and operated in an environment saturated with will-power and emotions.[14] In connection with the attacks launched by the Prussian army against all odds in the battles of the Seven Years War, contradicting 'all the rules of the art', Berenhorst wrote that 'if at that moment someone, such as, perhaps, Puységur, had flown above the belligerents in a balloon, he would have said: "I judge according to the principles—the Prussians must be beaten and defeated". But fate was different.' The spirit of the army and blind chance carried the day. 'The Prussians won in spite of the art.'[15]

According to Berenhorst, the moral forces that animate the troops are therefore a major factor in the conduct of war. Far from being automata, the troops could be inspired with a fierce fighting spirit, particularly when motivated by patriotic enthusiasm. Indeed, Berenhorst was the most respected critic of the Frederickian system in the great military debate in Germany over French Revolutionary warfare. His criticism derived, however, from much deeper roots, reflecting an older and more comprehensive opposition. It was typical of the men of the Counter-Enlightenment who detested the 'King

[11] Ibid., p. 9. [12] Ibid., ch. III. [13] Ibid., ch. IV.
[14] *Aus dem Nachlasse*, i. 3. [15] *Betrachtungen*, pp. 66–7.

of Prussia' with his bureaucratic, lifeless, 'machine-like' state, and French rationalistic orientation. Frederick was severely criticized by Berenhorst for lacking national consciousness, and assimilation into a foreign culture.[16] It was not surprising that the king, who could barely speak German, and whose people were but subjects to him, regarded his troops as no more than soulless material for his war-machine, and had no appreciation for the military potential of patriotic sentiments. All the interrelated elements of the Prussian military system—its mercenary troops, ruthless discipline, mechanical drill, and linear tactics—suppressed rather than enhanced moral forces. Armies should reintroduce the pike, as de Saxe recommended, and rely on shock tactics to achieve decision in battle.

A critique of Berenhorst's theoretical views and a defence of the Frederickian system, *Betrachtungen über einige Unrichtigkeiten in den Betrachtungen über die Kriegskunst* (1802) was written by the military scholar and *Aufklärer* Colonel Massenbach, who was a contributor to Nicolai's *Allgemeine deutsche Bibliothek*, the literary bastion of the Berlin Enlightenment, and whose career was later ruined by the defeat of 1806. Berenhorst replied in the same year with a polemic work which stressed the message of the *Reflections* even more, and he reasserted his ideas in *Aphorisms* (1805).

War, he wrote, unlike mathematics and astronomy, could not be formulated as an a priori science.[17] He emphasized his affinity to and belief in the sciences, but requested his critics to bear in mind the numerous examples in military history in which armies with natural courage, ignorant of the art of war, had carried the day, and the many others in which principles had been revealed as useless or inadequate. 'What then is left of the certainty, let alone usefulness, of science?'[18] Rules and principles tend to be artificial, dogmatic, and uncircumstantial; principles, abstracted from experience, are indiscriminately applied to an altered situation. 'What is the use of rules when one is covered up to one's ears with exceptions?'[19] The emphasis on the science and art of war corresponds to the old illusion of the philosophers about the intellectual essence of man.[20] In fact, the real power of armies rests in the moral and physical force of the troops rather than in all the sciences of the officers.[21] The qualities

[16] See e.g. *Betrachtungen*, p. 170. [17] *Randglossen* in *Betrachtungen*, p. 477.
[18] Ibid. 472–3. [19] Ibid. 499–500. [20] Ibid. 477. [21] Ibid. 449–50.

and characteristics of a general are mainly innate which the sciences can develop only slightly, though they provide him with ideas—particularly the study of military history and the art of war—and they improve him as a human being.[22]

Berenhorst's writings in 1802–5 indicate a growing shift from a critical approach to pronounced theoretical scepticism. The developments in both his military and intellectual environment undoubtedly contributed to this. In the wake of Prussia's defeat by Napoleon in 1806, Berenhorst played bitterly with several variations on the ironic pun: 'the French and Prussian generals divided the art of war between them; the Prussians took the former and the French the latter'.[23]

In relation to Jomini's principles which he regarded as fundamentally sound, Berenhorst in 1809 employed the argument he had already used in *Reflections* concerning the art of war of antiquity. Though the Greeks and Romans had subjected war to the highest level of intellectual control, he wrote then, their science of war had played to their advantage only as long as they confronted barbarous peoples; when they fought each other science had been neutralized, and courage and talent had again decided the issue. Now, the same applied to Jomini's principles. As long as Napoleon was the only one to exercise them, he could achieve success, but once everyone employed his system, it would cancel itself out, and numerical superiority, courage, and the general's fortunes would again reign supreme.[24] Theoretical argument aside, this was a penetrating anticipation of the events of 1813–15.

Responding to a letter in which Valentini had told him that Clausewitz did not believe in a general art of planning operations, Berenhorst wrote in 1812: 'I tend to agree with him . . . the [plans] are rendered absurd in one way or another by unforeseen circumstances . . . Then should we proceed without any plan just into the blue? I wish I could reply "yes", but fear of the gentlemen who think in formulae holds me back.'[25] Paradoxically, Berenhorst's affinity to the Enlightenment is strikingly revealed here. He could only see an alternative between a science of principles and anarchy, and despite his theoretical scepticism he could not embrace the latter.

[22] *Aphorismen* in *Betrachtungen*, p. 542. [23] *Aus dem Nachlasse*, i. 192–3.

[24] For the argument in relation to antiquity see *Betachtungen*, p. 2; and for its application to Napoleonic warfare and Jomini's principles see *Aus dem Nachlasse*, ii. 295–6.

[25] *Aus dem Nachlasse*, ii. 333, 353–4; cited by Paret, *Clausewitz*, p. 206.

7
Clausewitz

Demolishing and Rebuilding the Theoretical Ideal

I SCHARNHORST'S PLACE AND LEGACY

Scharnhorst discovered Clausewitz, acted as a second father to him, guided his development, and paved the way for him to reach the upper levels of the Prussian army and state and to be at the centre of the military and political events of the period. Furthermore, Scharnhorst made what was perhaps the most decisive contribution to the formation of Clausewitz's military outlook and theoretical conceptions. This is the view shared by all students of Clausewitz. Clausewitz called him 'the father and friend of my spirit'.[1]

What then was Scharnhorst's outlook on military theory, and what exactly did he bequeath to Clausewitz? These questions have received only cursory treatment. In his political and military views as well as in his work in reforming the Prussian army, Scharnhorst is said to have rejected radicalism from both the right and the left, and to have striven to harmonize the achievements of the *ancien régime* with the innovations and requirements raised by the Revolution.[2] However, this characteristic of his life's work and world-view has not been fully recognized in his approach to military theory. He has been largely portrayed as one who rejected and opposed the theoretical conception spread by the military thinkers of the Enlightenment.[3]

[1] A letter to his fiancée, 28 Jan. 1807; K. Linnebach (ed.), *Karl und Marie von Clausewitz. Ein Lebensbild in Briefen und Tagebuchblättern* (Berlin, 1916), 85.

[2] A picture established by Max Lehmann, *Scharnhorst* (2 vols., Leipzig, 1886–7).

[3] Apart from the studies about Clausewitz, see esp. Höhn's valuable *Revolution, Heer, Kriegsbild*, esp. pp. 467–514, and his more concise *Scharnhorst's Vermächtnis* (Bonn, 1952); see also Hansjürgen Usczeck, *Scharnhorst. Theoretiker, Reformer, Patriot* (East Berlin, 1979), which largely follows in Höhn's footsteps with a Marxist twist and much contemporary rhetoric.

There are two main reasons for this image. Firstly, the general unawareness of the distinctive ideas and form of the military school of the Enlightenment explains why Scharnhorst's extensive literary activity and theoretical conceptions from the 1780s, though not unknown, have mostly been studied from a political and military point of view, while their intellectual context has largely remained obscure. Scharnhorst's link with the intellectual world and with the prominent authors of the eighteenth century as outlined by Stadelmann has thus not been fully appreciated either.[4] Secondly, views about Scharnhorst's theoretical approach have naturally been influenced by what is known about Clausewitz's theoretical outlook. This tendency was reinforced by Clausewitz himself, whose close relationship with Scharnhorst occurred at the beginning of the nineteenth century when the latter was emphasizing a particular aspect of his ideas. Clausewitz too strengthened the impression that, fundamentally, Scharnhorst rejected the traditional conceptions of military theory.

In truth, Scharnhorst was from his youth one of the best-known active military *Aufklärer*s. Throughout his life he on the one hand defended the theoretical vision of the Enlightenment against its opponents, while on the other he rejected the radical interpretations of this vision, particularly when they took a new revolutionary direction at the turn of the eighteenth century.

Gerhard Johann David Scharnhorst was born in 1755 to a retired non-commissioned officer of the Hanoverian army and to a daughter and heiress of an affluent free farmer.[5] In 1773, he entered the military academy founded by Count Wilhelm zu Schaumburg-Lippe-Bückeburg in his tiny state near Hanover, an event that was to mould his entire career and intellectual development.

Count Wilhelm (1724–76), an international soldier and exponent of the Enlightenment, was brought up in England and France and showed a lively intellectual interest in many fields, especially in mathematics and history. He gained his military experience in the

[4] Rudolf Stadelmann, *Scharnhorst. Schicksal und geistige Welt, ein Fragment* (Wiesbaden, 1952).

[5] For Scharnhorst's life story see the monumental biographies of Georg Heinrich Klippel, *Das Leben des Generals von Scharnhorst* (3 vols.; Leipzig, 1869–71), and Max Lehmann, *Scharnhorst*. For a concise account in English, see ch. 4 of P. Paret's *Clausewitz and the State*.

War of the Austrian Succession in Holland and Italy, and in the Seven Years War he commanded the defence of Portugal, Britain's ally, against a Spanish invasion. Among the acquaintances with whom he corresponded and conversed were Mendelssohn, Goethe, Möser, and Herder. Influenced by the writings of Thomas Abbt, who called for the revival of Roman patriotism, he experimented with a citizen militia in his tiny state. The military reforms that he introduced, the book that he wrote, *Mémoires pour servir à l'art militaire défensif* (1775), and the military academy that he established, all reflected the military ideas and ideals of the Enlightenment.[6] The academy's broad curriculum, drawn up by the count himself, who was also the chief instructor, was typical of the military academies and educational programmes of the period. The cadets were taught pure and applied mathematics, civil architecture, physics, natural history, economics, geography, history and military history, and the military sciences of tactics, artillery, and fortifications.[7]

After Count Wilhelm's death, Scharnhorst in 1778 transferred to the Hanoverian service. His interest in military education was now further developed as he collaborated with other officers of similar persuasions in a series of pioneering projects. The commander of the cavalry regiment in which he entered, von Estorff (himself a notable military *Aufklärer* and author of a book, *Fragmente militairischer Betrachtungen über die Einrichtung des Kriegswesens in mittlern Staaten* (1780)), founded a regimental school for the officers and NCOs where mathematics and military studies were taught. Scharnhorst was an instructor in this school and used the experience for further expanding his military studies and developing his educational ideas. The writings of Nicolai, whom Scharnhorst considered to be the foremost military scholar in Germany, were a major source of influence.[8] In 1782 Scharnhorst was appointed instructor in the newly formed artillery academy in Hanover whose syllabus was again comprised of geometry, pure and applied mathematics, fortifications, artillery, and tactics.[9] In those years he also began his extensive literary activities which soon rendered him one of the best-known figures in the community of the military *Aufklärers*.

[6] Klippel, *Leben*, i. 38–60; Lehmann, *Scharnhorst*, i. 12–29. For his period in Portugal, see C. Harraschik-Ehl, *Scharnhorsts Lehrer: Graf Wilhelm von Schaumburg-Lippe in Portugal* (Osnabrück, 1974).

[7] Klippel, *Leben*, i. 51.

[8] Ibid. 70–3.

[9] Ibid. 84–90.

As mentioned above, from 1782, when he was twenty-seven years old, Scharnhorst initiated and edited a series of military periodicals which soon became among the most widely read of their kind in Germany, with hundreds of subscribers. The *Militair Bibliothek* (four issues; 1782–4) and *Bibliothek für Offiziere* (four issues; 1785) mostly contained translated selections from the latest military literature in Europe, but also included an increasing number of articles and critiques. The *Neues Militärisches Journal* appeared in thirteen volumes from 1788 to 1805, with a lull between 1793 and 1797, when Scharnhorst took part in the wars of the Revolution.[10]

Scharnhorst was also the author of two widely circulated military works. The *Handbook for Officers on the Applied Parts of the Sciences of War* was a mine of information on the various branches of war, and included extensive technical and statistical data on the organization and equipment of contemporary European armies—impressive evidence of the scope of Scharnhorst's military knowledge.[11] The more concise *Military Pocket-book for Use in the Field* was a general manual on the conduct of war, with instructions for marches, camps, and reconnaissance; for warfare in the open field, against field fortifications, and during a siege; and for the use of cavalry, infantry, artillery, and engineering: it was a typical product of the military literature of the *Aufklärung*.[12] The book gained much popularity, went through several further editions (1793, 1794, and 1815), and was translated into English (1811). A study of Scharnhorst's extensive writings in these periodicals and books and in other unpublished works elucidates the nature and context of his theoretical outlook.[13]

The young Scharnhorst opened his introduction to the *Militair Bibliothek* (1782) with the proclamation, typical of the military

[10] The six vols. which appeared after 1797 were subtitled *Militärische Denkwürdigkeiten unserer Zeiten* and numbered separately.

[11] Lieut. G. Scharnhorst, *Handbuch für Offiziere in den angewandten Theilen der Krieges Wissenschaften* (3 vols., Hanover, 1787–90); about 170 subscribers are listed at the beginning of the first vol.

[12] Capt. G. Scharnhorst, *Militairisches Taschenbuch zum Gebrauch im Felde* (Hanover, 1792).

[13] No complete edition of Scharnhorst's works exists. Many unpublished works, some of which are now lost, were printed, however, by his biographers, and large extracts from his major published works were reprinted in C. von de Goltz (ed.), *Militärische Schriften von Scharnhorst* (Berlin, 1881). A new collection is U. von Gersdoff (ed.), *Ausgewählte Schriften*, (Osnabrück, 1983).

Aufklärers, of the importance and value of military knowledge, which were allegedly recognized and expressed by the great generals of history. Passages from several authorities, from Folard to Maizeroy and Frederick the Great, are cited to drive this point home. The introduction also contains a survey of military literature recommended for the study of the various branches of war. As a basis, Scharnhorst suggests the works of Nicolai and Zanthier. Then, detailed bibliographies are offered for the necessary auxiliary disciplines and the war sciences themselves. In the spheres of tactics, operational activity, and strategy (the new concept is borrowed from Maizeroy; see *Handbuch*, iii. 1–2), the central place is occupied by the works of Maizeroy, Guibert, Turpin, Puységur, Feuquières, Montecuccoli, Folard, de Saxe, Santa-Cruze, and Frederick the Great.[14]

The emphasis on the necessity and usefulness of military theory is also the theme of a work written around 1790, reflecting the developments in military education in Germany and entitled 'On the Utility and Establishment of Military Schools for Young Officers'. Echoing Nicolai, Scharnhorst wrote that a sound theory based on rules and principles explained the successes of Frederick the Great, Gustavus Adolphus, Condé, Caesar, and Alexander. If years of service were sufficient training, old corporals would make generals.[15]

What then is the nature of military theory, and what exactly does it teach? Scharnhorst began to address himself to this question in his early works, reaching his final conclusion by the end of the 1780s. It can be summarized as follows: through conceptualization, military theory makes possible the intellectual treatment of the factors active in war. In his introduction to the *Militair Bibliothek* in 1782, the young Scharnhorst formulated this into a characteristic theoretical framework that accompanied him throughout his life: military theory provided 'correct concepts' (*richtige Begriffe*). These concepts, he wrote three years later in his introduction to the *Bibliothek für Offiziere*, had to be grounded in 'the nature of things or in experience'.

This line of thought is developed in the *Handbuch für Offiziere* in 1787. An inherent interdependence exists between theory and

[14] *Militair Bibliothek* i. 1–38; for a similar survey and a list of the periodical's subscribers, see the introduction to the 2nd issue (1783).

[15] 'Ueber den Nutzen und die Etablirung einer Militär-Schule für die jüngern Offiziere', quoted in Lehmann, *Scharnhorst*, i. 43.

reality. First, one needs clear concepts and principles which clarify the links between the parts of war and the whole; these concepts and principles are necessarily based on the nature of things, and there is no knowledge without them. Then one must understand the actual operation of these concepts and principles in action, for reason alone is not sufficient for developing reality. The application of the concepts and principles to reality requires judgement, which is in turn sharpened only by experience and constant exercise, the major means of which is historical study. Thus, the proper method for educating young officers is, first, to provide them with 'correct theory' and encourage them to think independently and 'clarify their concepts'. This would create a sound basis for analysing experience.[16]

While quite in harmony with the theoretical outlook of the Enlightenment, this theoretical framework reveals a distinctive note and points to several intellectual influences. Firstly, the unique focus on the role of conceptualization in the creation of theory, the relationship between theory and reality, and the link between the parts of war and the whole, is strikingly similar to Montecuccoli's intellectual structure in the introduction to his celebrated *War against the Turks in Hungary*. Indeed Scharnhorst's close affinity to Montecuccoli has been pointed out by Stadelmann. In a letter to a friend written in 1810, Scharnhorst recommended Montecuccoli's work, calling it *Lebensbuch*, and asserted that it had been his constant companion, accompanying him through good and bad times.[17]

Scharnhorst's insistence on the insufficiency of reason alone for developing reality also suggests that this theoretical structure and his theoretical interests may have been reinforced by Kant's theory of knowledge and emphasis on the interpretive role of concepts and interdependence of mind and experience. Though no direct evidence for his familiarity with Kant's work is known, the fact that Scharnhorst's early works appeared in 1782–7 makes such an influence very plausible.[18]

Finally, from the 1780s and throughout his life, Scharnhorst saw theory as 'necessarily' grounded not only in 'experience' but also in

[16] *Handbuch für Offiziere*, vol. i, pp. v–vii and 1–4.

[17] Letter of 30 Aug. 1810, in K. Linnebach (ed.), *Scharnhorsts Briefe* (Munich and Leipzig 1914), 404–5; Stadelmann, *Scharnhorst*, pp. 92–9.

[18] Following a general remark by Lehmann, Willhelm Wagner argued for a Kantian influence on Scharnhorst over the issue of the standing armies: W. Wagner, *Die preussischen Reformer und die zeitgenössische Philosophie* (Cologne, 1956), 127–8; in view of the extensive debate on that issue, this argument, like some of Wagner's other conclusions, appears to be rather hasty.

the 'nature of things'. This was the characteristic conception which he bequeathed to Clausewitz. Unaware of the part Scharnhorst played in its transference, Raymond Aron, in his treatment of Clausewitz, was the first to call attention to the striking affinity of this conception to Montesquieu.[19] It clearly resembles Montesquieu's famous conception of laws, defined at the opening of the *Spirit of the Laws*, as the 'necessary relations arising from the nature of things'. Indeed, it was revealed by Stadelmann that Scharnhorst ordered the *Spirit of the Laws* from his bookseller in the mid-1790s, which does not exclude an earlier acquaintance with it.[20]

Montesquieu's influence and those of other authors with whom we know Scharnhorst was familiar[21] may also have had much to do with another major feature of Scharnhorst's theoretical approach. As pointed out by Stadelmann, Scharnhorst operated in the midst of a transformation in historical outlook which went hand in hand with a growing sensitivity to the many facets of reality and the interdependence between its component parts.[22] All the military thinkers of the Enlightenment emphasized the paramount value of historical experience. Scharnhorst's works were characterized, however, by a distinctive tendency towards a detailed, concrete, and comprehensive reconstruction of the historical cases in point. Military historians, Clausewitz wrote in his booklet of instructions for the Prussian crown prince,

> invent history instead of writing it . . . The detailed knowledge of a few individual engagements is more useful than the general knowledge of a great many campaigns . . . An example of such an account, which cannot be surpassed, is the description of the defense of Menin in 1794, in the memoirs of General von Scharnhorst. This narrative . . . gives Your Royal Highness an example of how to write military history.[23]

[19] R. Aron, *Clausewitz, den Krieg denken* (Frankfurt am Main, 1980), esp. pp. 163, 308, 331–5.

[20] Stadelmann, *Scharnhorst*, pp. 105–8.

[21] Voltaire's *Siècle de Louis XIV*, Helvétius's *De l'esprit* and *De l'homme*, Rousseau's *Du contrat social*, the writings of Ferguson, Gibbon, and apparently also Möser and Herder were familiar to Scharnhorst: see Stadelmann, *Scharnhorst*, pp. 102–17; some of this was already known from the biographies of Klippel and Lehmann and from Scharnhorst's letters.

[22] Stadelmann, *Scharnhorst*, p. 119.

[23] Carl von Clausewitz, *Principles of War*, (Harrisburg, 1942), 68–9; see also id., *On War*, II, 6, p. 170. *Die Verteidigung der Stadt Menin* appeared in the *Neues Militärisches Journal*, XI (1803), and in book form in Hanover the same year; reprinted in Goltz (ed.), *Schriften*, pp. 1–58.

Only a detailed historical account can come close to reconstructing the living reality of war, thus achieving some of the value of firsthand experience and conveying the complexity of factors and forces active in war, which may never be explained by a single factor or principle alone.

The 'Development of the General Reasons for the French Success in the Wars of the Revolution', written in 1797 by Scharnhorst and his friend Friedrich von der Decker, provides another analytical example of the same approach. The argument that the French success cannot be reduced to a single factor is the theme of the first chapter, followed by twelve chapters in which the variety of conditions that affected the struggle between the French Revolutionary armies and those of the Allies are traced and presented. These include the political background of the war, the strategic situation of the belligerents, their positions and geographical location, numerical strength and sources of reinforcement and supply, the military organization and methods of warfare, the power of motives, and last but not least, the difference in social infrastructure between the powers of the *ancien régime* and Revolutionary France.[24]

The concrete and comprehensive theoretical approach that characterized Scharnhorst's work from the outset also found typical expression in the definition of the aims of the *Militärische Gesellschaft* that he founded in Berlin in 1801–2. The discussions of the society, according to the first article of regulations, would try to avoid 'one-sidedness' and 'would put theory and practice in proper relationship'.[25]

What then, was Scharnhorst's exact place in relation to the military school of the Enlightenment, and what was his attitude towards it? As mentioned earlier, several factors have contributed to a misrepresentation of Scharnhorst's position on these matters. Scharnhorst was one of the most notable and best-known military *Aufklärers*. Together with his contemporaries, he believed that war was susceptible to intellectual study, theoretical and historical, based upon clear concepts and principles derived from experience. Some branches of war, such as artillery, fortifications, and siegecraft were even

[24] Scharnhorst, 'Entwicklung der allgemeinen Ursachen des Glücks der Franzosen in dem Revolutionskriege', *Neues Militärisches Journal*, VIII (1797); reprinted in Goltz (ed.), *Schriften*, pp. 192–242.

[25] The regulations are cited in Klippel, *Leben* ii. 255–62.

susceptible to a geometrical-mathematical formulation. Hence the supreme importance of the officers' military education and the effort to develop suitable programmes and institutions for this purpose.

Now, as we have seen, within the military school of the Enlightenment there were already gleams of more radical ideas and aspiration, which were unacceptable to Scharnhorst. In his critique in the *Neues Militärisches Journal*, I (1788), of Franz Miller's *Reine Taktik der Infanterie, Cavallerie und Artillerie* (1787–8), Scharnhorst rejected Miller's geometrical and even trigonometrical considerations for battle formation and deployment. Though he believed in the paramount importance of mathematics in the field of fortifications and artillery, as well as in training the officer's mind for logical thinking, he maintained that mathematics could not be applied to the conduct of operations.[26]

The 1790s saw the publication of the works of Lloyd and Tempelhoff and the advent of new trends. Much as Scharnhorst regarded Tempelhoff as a first-rate artillery expert and military historian,[27] he rejected his artificial constructions for the conduct of operations. In a later work which was written in 1811, but which undoubtedly expressed his earlier attitudes, and which clearly betrays the origins of Clausewitz's ideas, he recalled:

> Tempelhoff wrote an essay in which—starting from an arbitrary number of bread and supply wagons—he catalogued all movements that in his opinion an army could undertake. He took supply as the centripetal and operations as the centrifugal force; they balanced at a radius of fifteen miles. This pretty equation made people forget a thousand contradictory experiences. The disease was so catching that the soundest heads were affected.[28]

The novel trends, developing within the legacy of the Enlightenment and relating to the new interest in the conduct of operations, were indeed becoming increasingly influential. Simultaneously, Berenhorst represented a comprehensive reaction against the theoretical tenets of the Enlightenment. Thus, Scharnhorst was now fighting on two fronts. In a critique in the *Neues Militärisches Journal* of Berenhorst's *Nothwendige Randglossen*, Scharnhorst emphasized the advantages of the standing army against Berenhorst's attacks, and also rejected his ironic challenge to the classical conceptions of the military

[26] Also see *Handbuch für Offiziere*, vol. iii, p. v.

[27] See e.g. ibid. i. 4.

[28] Scharnhorst, 'On Infantry Tactics', printed in Paret, *Yorck*, app., 259.

thinkers of the Enlightenment. Where Berenhorst wrote that 'the Prussians won in spite of the art' (*Die Preussen siegten der Kunst zum Hohn*), Scharnhorst replied that 'They won to the honour of the art' (*Sie siegten der Kunst zu Ehren*). While admitting that in the situation they were in, theoretical considerations appeared to be against the Prussians, Scharnhorst argued that, on the other hand, they only won because of their superior organization, discipline, and tactics. Against Berenhorst's undermining criticism, Scharnhorst restated the classical conceptual framework of the Enlightenment: the art of war, like painting and the rest of the arts, has two parts: the one is mechanical and susceptible to theoretical study, the other circumstantial and dominated by creative genius and experience.[29]

Unfortunately for the understanding of Scharnhorst's position in relation to the legacy of the Enlightenment, the last and best-known period of his life, at the outset of the nineteenth century, was also marked by the flourishing of systems for the conduct of operations. These were regarded by him as artificial and one-sided, and stood in contrast to his traditional understanding of the theoretical ideal of the Enlightenment. Against them Scharnhorst directed the main thrust of his criticism in the years in which Clausewitz became acquainted with him and absorbed the fundamentals of his theoretical approach. Clausewitz therefore presented and praised him as an opponent and critic of contemporary military theory, represented by the systems and principles of Bülow, Mathieu Dumas (a well-known historian of the wars of the Revolution who emphasized the key role of high, commanding positions), and Jomini.[30]

To remove any doubt that Scharnhorst did not, in the last period of his life, move away from the position he had held since his youth in the 1780s, but rather that it was the theoretical legacy of the Enlightenment that, so to speak, moved away from him, it is enough to examine his essay 'The Use of Military History, the Causes of its Deficiencies', written in 1806. Here all the themes we have already met are repeated, and the exact scope of Scharnhorst's objection to the new theoretical trends may be seen. The great generals of history, writes

[29] *Neues Militärisches Journal*, XII (1804), 344 ff. For a full reiteration of Scharnhorst's theoretical outlook, made in the same year, see the opening chs. of *Handbuch der Artillerie* (Hanover, 1804), reprinted in *Ausgewählte Schriften*, pp. 153–62.

[30] Clausewitz, 'Über das Leben und den Charakter von Scharnhorst', in L. von Ranke (ed.), *Historisch-Politische Zeitschrift*, I (1832), 197–8.

Scharnhorst—Hannibal, Scipio, Caesar, Turenne, Montecuccoli, and Frederick—studied the principles of the art of war. Some branches of this art are even susceptible to mathematical formulation, but others are dependent on circumstances and cannot be mechanically studied. That is why study alone without genius will never make a great general. One of the branches that has remained without a systematic theory is the conduct of war. In modern times some men, especially the French, have attempted to formulate universal principles for this field, but these have been invalidated by reality and changing experience. Instead, it would be better to concentrate on the study of history. In the education of young officers it leads back to the fundamental rules and principles, and guarantees that the theory of war in all its parts is based on the 'nature of things' and 'experience'.[31]

Far from being the opponent of the traditional conception of military theory, Scharnhorst, in accordance with his general world-view and position throughout his career, was therefore one of the most prominent exponents of the enlightened school of military thought, defending it against reactionary tendencies on the one hand, and against later radical trends which were taking control over it on the other.

Scharnhorst's influence on the young Clausewitz, his pupil and closest protégé, cannot be exaggerated. His role in moulding Clausewitz's political, social, and military views, not to mention the course of his life, was decisive, and his theoretical notions became the basis for Clausewitz's own developing theoretical outlook.

The changing theoretical background against which the two operated, should, however, be stressed first. The generation that separated them gave a totally different starting-point to their thought and theoretical work. The young Clausewitz began his theoretical involvement at the beginning of the nineteenth century, when the theoretical outlook of the Enlightenment was already established and new developments within it created sensation and controversy. To this were added the emergence of a new cultural paradigm and the Napoleonic revolution in warfare. Synthesizing all these trends, Clausewitz emerged as an opponent of what by now had become traditional military theory.

[31] Scharnhorst, 'Nutzen der militärischen Geschichte, Ursach ihres Mangels' (1806), printed in *Ausgewählte Schriften*, pp. 199–207.

Returning to Scharnhorst's legacy; in his youth Clausewitz was attracted, as he was to admit later, by the seductive promise of Bülow's system.[32] These very early notions disappeared entirely when he entered the Berlin Institute for Young Officers. Under Scharnhorst's influence, he—like other disciples of Scharnhorst—rejected the new systems for the conduct of operations as one-sided abstractions which created an intolerable gulf between theory and reality. Instead, he learnt from Scharnhorst that theory had to be concrete and circumstantial, encompass the complexity of political, human, and military conditions that formed reality, and be closely linked to historical experience. Such theory would form free, undogmatic principles, such as Scharnhorst had formulated in his *Handbuch für Offiziere*, and would deal with 'actual war' as Scharnhorst had taught in the Berlin Institute, in contrast to the popular abstractions of the time.[33]

In addition to all this, Scharnhorst also bequeathed to Clausewitz another key conception: theory had to reflect the relationship between the parts of war and the whole, and be 'necessarily grounded in the nature of things'. In essence, there was implicit here a far-reaching theoretical ideal, which was to play a decisive role in Clausewitz's thought.

After the Napoleonic Wars when Clausewitz began to immerse himself in his great theoretical work, he had to clarify for himself, develop, and elaborate the crude, half-intuitive theoretical framework which he had inherited from Scharnhorst, and which he himself had started to work on in his youth.

32 Clausewitz, 'Bülow', in Hahlweg (ed.), *Verstreute kleine Schriften*, p. 87.
33 Clausewitz, 'Leben und Charakter von Scharnhorst', pp. 198, 177.

II REFORMULATING MILITARY THEORY IN TERMS OF A NEW INTELLECTUAL PARADIGM

In turning from the military thinkers of the Enlightenment to the study of Clausewitz, a marked difference in the scope, depth, and nature of the treatment accorded to these subjects is clearly noticeable. The military thinkers of the Enlightenment have largely been neglected, their background and collective ideal have not been recognized, and their ideas have been subjected to the polemic and stereotyped criticism which reflect Clausewitz's point of view and the legacy of the German military school of the nineteenth century. Conversely, the domination of this school over the field of military theory secured the 'canonization' of Clausewitz in the late nineteenth and early twentieth centuries, albeit with a somewhat popular and selective interpretation of his thought.

Unfortunately, this imbalance has only been exacerbated in our times. As mentioned earlier, the practical military value of Jomini's work, which had kept the theoretical conceptions of the Enlightenment very much alive, declined sharply after the First World War. By contrast, the interest in Clausewitz, after an eclipse between the two World Wars (except in Germany), was revived in the 1950s, predominantly owing to the significance that his treatment of the relationship between policy and war and of limited war bore on the political and military problems of the nuclear age. A 'Clausewitz renaissance' has developed in strategic and political literature, perhaps no less popularized and selective in nature than the attitudes to Clausewitz in the nineteenth century, though, ironically, with opposing emphases.

The rapidly growing involvement of academic historical research has not altered these tendencies either, but, on the contrary, has reinforced them. The main problem has been that the cultural context of Clausewitz's ideas—the transition from the Enlightenment to the German Movement that was hostile to it—has not on the whole been recognized. Indeed, this may already be seen in the confusion that prevails regarding the philosophical influences on his work. The liberation of modern historical study—heralded by Cassirer—from the polemical attitudes that, in the nineteenth century, characterized the campaign of the German Movement against the ideas of the Enlightenment which were labelled as superficial, artificial, and unhistorical, has not reached the military field. In the study of the Enlightenment as a whole, it has been widely recognized that though the accusations of the men of the German Movement had some validity, their hostile fervour drove them into committing against the Enlightenment the very offence with which they had charged it: unsympathetic interpretations that were alien to the values, views, interests, and aims of the period itself. Yet, in the military field, historians and commentators have unwittingly continued to express what was in fact Counter-Enlightenment rhetoric.

For all that, our knowledge and understanding of Clausewitz have been vastly increased since the systematic and academic study of his work began. The works of Hans Rothfels in the 1920s, Herbert Rosinski, Eberhard Kessel, and Walter Malmsten Schering in the three subsequent decades, and Werner Hahlweg from the 1950s, brought to light many of Clausewitz's early writings which are of vital importance to the understanding of his development. To these should be added the critical editions of *On War* published by Hahlweg since 1952. The stages in the development of Clausewitz's work, his military and theoretical ideas, and his political outlook have all received scholarly attention.[1] From the 1950s, the Clausewitz renaissance in strategic and political literature has been matched by an increase in historical studies of Clausewitz, expanding beyond the frontiers of Germany and culminating in the works of Peter Paret and Raymond Aron, both published in 1976.

A few opening remarks on these two books will help to clarify the guide-lines of this work in the study of Clausewitz. Paret's biography *Clausewitz and the State* is the best of its kind, combining extensive research, a remarkable reconstruction of Clausewitz's historical environment, and a sympathetic psychological portrait. Paret also devotes much attention to Clausewitz's intellectual background, and brings together a great deal of relevant material to which the present study is greatly in debt. However, it is the contention of this work that Paret does not fully succeed in placing Clausewitz in his actual intellectual context, nor in identifying some of the major influences on his work. He also fails to recognize Clausewitz's theoretical development, particularly the crucial significance and scope of the transformation that took place in 1827

[1] For the authors and works, see throughout my discussion of Clausewitz's ideas. I have taken the same liberty of postponing documentation all through these introductory remarks.

in his way of thinking. As this is coupled with a subtle, unintentional projection of today's attitudes on Clausewitz's thought, Paret also totally misinterprets the essence of Clausewitz's military teaching throughout his life.

Aron's attraction to Clausewitz is especially of interest. Already in the 1950s, he had discovered in Clausewitz a thinker whose ideas closely corresponded to his own regarding the nature of theory in the study of international relations—a problem that had pre-occupied him ever since the outbreak in the early 1950s of the great methodological debate in that field. The far-reaching affinity in their views is revealed in Aron's fundamental political 'realism'; in his rejection of the wider aspirations of the 'scientific school' in the study of international relations; in his rejection of any theory based on a single isolated factor, rendering it artificial and one-sided; in his emphasis on the primacy of historical experience in shaping theory; and last but not least, in his belief that, for all that, the concept of 'theory' can still be given much meaning and possess great value.[2]

From this unique viewpoint Aron offers the most comprehensive and elaborate analysis of Clausewitz's work and theoretical conceptions. The scope of his study is remarkable, and much of his interpretation is penetrating.[3] However, his special affinity to Clausewitz is overshadowed by a serious handicap. Like many of his predecessors, Aron is hardly aware of the cultural context in which Clausewitz worked, nor of the intellectual trends to which he gave expression. 'Professing' to a positivist method of interpretation,[4] Aron's theoretical *naïveté* is astonishing. This problem cannot but contribute to the fact that Aron (following in Schering's footsteps, though to a much lesser extent) is inclined to read into Clausewitz's work intellectual patterns and categories which are totally artificial and which obscure even further a subject which is already obscure enough.

All this explains the shift in emphasis and aims in the second part of this study. As mentioned above, the paucity and the largely

[2] For R. Aron's well-known views on these matters, see esp. his *Peace and War, A Theory of International Relations* (New York, 1967), and 'What is a Theory of International Relations?', *Journal of International Affairs*, XXI (1967), 185–206. Also see id., *Clausewitz*, pp. 17–20; since the English edition is substantially abridged, all references are made to the German version.

[3] All references in this work are limited to Aron's first vol. which deals with Clausewitz himself, rather than with his influence in the 19th and 20th cents., which is the subject of Aron's second vol.

[4] Aron, *Clausewitz*, p. 23.

polemic and stereotyped nature of the research on the military thinkers of the eighteenth century has made it necessary to present, in as sympathetic a manner as possible, a general picture of their world-view in the context of their intellectual environment. However, the relative abundance of research on Clausewitz, the prevailing tendencies in viewing his ideas, and, indeed, the intellectual complexity of the subject itself, necessitate a more focused and critical approach from now on. The formation of Clausewitz's conception of theory and criticism of the military thinkers of the Enlightenment will be presented against the background of the new cultural paradigm which emerged in Germany at the turn of the nineteenth century. Then, the development of Clausewitz's efforts to create an adequate military theory of his own will be traced and close attention will be given to the fundamental problems he encountered in the process, which wreaked havoc on his lifelong theoretical outlook and forced him to adopt new ideas and theoretical devices.

Carl Philip Gottlieb von Clausewitz was born in 1780 to a family whose claim to nobility was dubious. His father, who joined the Prussian army when it was in desperate need for men during the Seven Years War, rose to the rank of lieutenant only to be discharged after the war when Frederick purged the Prussian officer corps of middle-class elements. After Frederick's death, he succeeded, however, in securing appointments as NCOs for three of his sons. The twelve-year-old Carl began his military service in an infantry regiment in 1792, and in 1793–5 he took part in the campaigns of the First Coalition against Revolutionary France. The following six years of peace were spent by the young lieutenant in the provincial garrison town of Neuruppin. He left it only in 1801 when he was admitted into the Institute for Young Officers in Berlin, which had been revived, enlarged, and thoroughly reformed by Scharnhorst, who had shortly before entered the Prussian service. This was a turning-point in Clausewitz's life. During his three years of study at the Institute he made the acquaintance of Scharnhorst, absorbed the foundations of his military outlook, and became his closest protégé. His education was broadened dramatically, and new intellectual horizons were opened. After finishing first in his class, he was on the road leading to the centre of the political and military events in the Prussia of the Napoleonic Wars, of reform, and of the Restoration.

In 1804 Clausewitz was appointed adjutant to Prince August, cousin of Frederick Wilhelm III King of Prussia. In this capacity and as a brevet captain, he took part in the Battle of Auerstädt (1806), and after Prussia's catastrophic defeat, he and the Prince fell into French captivity. At the end of 1807 the two returned from their imprisonment in France, and at the beginning of 1809 Clausewitz was co-opted by Scharnhorst as his assistant in the *Allgemeine Kriegsdepartement*, the nucleus of a new ministry of war. As head of the department, Scharnhorst orchestrated the military reforms of Prussia, championed and carried out by a group of young officers. Among the reformers, Clausewitz made the acquaintance of Gneisenau, Scharnhorst's major ally, who became an intimate friend. During this period he also married Countess Marie von Brühl, who had been his fiancée for five years. Their uniquely close attachment is revealed in their correspondence, which constitutes the principal source for Clausewitz's biography. It was Marie who published Clausewitz's posthumous works.

Clausewitz's military career was continuously matched by intensive intellectual activity. His strong interest in military theory dates at least from his days at the Institute. His early writings refer, among others, to Montecuccoli, Feuquières, Santa-Cruz, Folard, de Saxe, Puységur, Turpin, Guibert, Frederick, Lloyd, Tempelhoff, Berenhorst, Bülow, Dumas, Venturini, Massenbach, and Jomini.[5] And in a series of works written during his twenties and early thirties, he formulated the theoretical conceptions which were to find their final place in his major work, *On War*.

In 1810 Clausewitz was appointed major in the General Staff, instructor in the new Officers' Academy, and military tutor to the Prussian crown prince. His work during the reform era, motivated by the desire to see Prussia liberated through the destruction of the Napoleonic Empire, culminated in 1812. With the French invasion of Russia, Clausewitz, like some of his comrades, left Prussia and joined the Russian army, acting against the instructions and policy of his king. In Russia he was promoted to colonel, served in various staff posts, and took part in the Battle of Borodino.

After Napoleon's retreat and despite the fact that Prussia joined the war against France, Frederick William III refused to accept

[5] Hans Rothfels, *Carl von Clausewitz, Politik und Krieg* (Berlin, 1920), 29–30; Paret, *Clausewitz*, p. 81.

Clausewitz back into the Prussian service. His friends, however, arranged for him to be attached to Blücher's headquarters as a Russian liaison officer, and again working together with Scharnhorst, Clausewitz played an important role in the Prussian command at the battles of Bautzen and Lützen (Scharnhorst was mortally wounded during the latter). Since all efforts to obtain the king's pardon failed, Clausewitz was compelled to serve in the German Legion of volunteers and in secondary theatres of operations for the duration of the campaigns of autumn 1813 and of 1814. Only after Napoleon's defeat was he accepted back into the Prussian service. In the campaign of 1815 he served as the chief of staff to the corps which contained Grouchy at Wavre, while the main body of the Prussian army marched to join Wellington at Waterloo.

After the war, Clausewitz was appointed chief of staff to the force stationed in Prussia's newly acquired territories along the Rhine, and he remained at Koblenz in that capacity until 1818. He was then promoted to general and appointed head of the Military Academy at Berlin, largely an administrative function. The end of the era of war and the beginning of a long period of peace paralleled the triumph of the Restoration in Prussia. The disappearance of the external challenge of his youth and the king's suspicious attitude towards his radical reputation, which clouded his military career, made Clausewitz concentrate on the intellectual interests which had hitherto been overshadowed by his military activities. During his time at Koblenz, Clausewitz made the first attempt to write a general theoretical work on war, and this was followed by a continuous period of work while serving in Berlin. In 1830, the course of the work was interrupted by Clausewitz's appointment as commander of one of the artillery divisions of the Prussian army. A short time later, with the outbreak of the revolutions of 1830, he was appointed chief of staff to the army raised under Gneisenau in anticipation of possible Prussian intervention in Poland. In 1831, both men fell victim to the great cholera epidemic which swept across the continent.[6]

[6] This biographical sketch is merely intended to provide a framework for the study of Clausewitz's intellectual development. The first biography of Clausewitz, incorporating his letters and some of his unpublished works, was written by Karl Schwartz, *Leben des Generals von Clausewitz und der Frau Marie von Clausewitz* (2 vols.; Berlin 1878); amendments and supplements, particularly regarding Clausewitz's family and childhood, were introduced by Eberhard Kessel, 'Carl von Clausewitz: Herkunft und Persönlichkeit', *Wissen und Wehr*, XVIII (1937); for the recent and by far the best biography, see Paret, *Clausewitz*.

In his early twenties Clausewitz absorbed Scharnhorst's criticism of the new systems of operations as one-sided abstractions, divorced from reality. Simultaneously, Clausewitz's intellectual environment powerfully projected the message that the world-view of the French Enlightenment, on which the old theory of war was based, was fundamentally false. Since the 'Storm and Stress' period, the ideas of the French Enlightenment had been labelled artificial, superficial, and pretentious. And this became the prevailing cultural and political outlook in Germany at the advent of the nineteenth century, following the disillusion with the French Revolution and the fierce reaction against Napoleonic imperialism.

A classic example of the outlook and sentiment of the time can be found in the comparison Clausewitz drew in late 1807, on his return from French captivity, between the national characteristics of the French and the Germans. French feelings and thinking, he wrote, were active, excited, and quick, but also shallow and always prepared to sacrifice content for form and appearance. By contrast, German feelings and thinking were calm, deep, and penetrating, and they strove toward comprehensive expression and understanding.[7] That Clausewitz was here expressing prevailing ideas propounded for example by Möser, Wilhelm von Humboldt, the Romantics, and Fichte, has already been noted by some of Clausewitz's interpreters.[8] In another, later, classical example of contemporary attitudes in Germany, Clausewitz criticizes the views of 'philosophers who are right about everything by means of universal concepts', being 'strongly influenced by Parisian philosophy and politics'.[9]

Clausewitz's cultural environment was not only critical of the legacy of the Enlightenment but also provided him with an alternative conception of reality, to be used as a basis for a reformulation of military theory. Berenhorst had already given expression to some of the most distinctive themes of the new climate of ideas. The young Clausewitz now developed a different, more comprehensive, and sophisticated synthesis of the new intellectual themes, stressing the diversity and living nature of human reality and centring on the conceptions of rules, genius, moral forces, factors of uncertainty, and history.

[7] 'Die Deutschen und die Franzosen', in Hans Rothfels (ed.), *Carl von Clausewitz, Politische Schriften und Briefe* (Munich, 1922), esp. pp. 37–45.

[8] Rothfels, *Clausewitz, Politik und Krieg*, pp. 113–16; Paret, *Clausewitz*, pp. 133–4.

[9] 'Umtriebe', in Rothfels (ed.), *Schriften*, p. 166.

We have seen that the military thinkers of the Enlightenment drew their conception of theory, based on the twin concepts of rules and genius, from the legacy and development in the Enlightenment of the seventeenth-century neo-classical theory of art. Into this theory there were injected, throughout the eighteenth century, increasing emphases on the role of free, creative genius, a development which was also reflected in the works of the military thinkers of the Enlightenment. With Kant the transformation in the eighteenth-century outlook on the theory of art was completed, and the emphases were finally reversed. Genius did not embody the rules as had been believed by the neo-classicists. Nor was it an essential, creative, and imaginative force, as important as the rules themselves. Genius was rather the exclusive source of all artistic creation which could not be adequately formalized in any set of rules. It was the measurement of all rules which were only justified as crude means for capturing, by way of concepts, something of its creative force. 'Genius', wrote Kant in his *Critique of Judgement*, 'is the talent (natural endowment) which gives the rule to art . . . [it] is a talent for producing that for which no definite rule can be given.' The genius's example can merely provide 'a methodical instruction according to rules, collected, so far as the circumstances admit.'[10]

The fact that Clausewitz's conception of military theory was rooted in Kant's theory of art was for the first time and most clearly pointed out in 1883 by Kant's student, the philosopher Hermann Cohen, and has since been repeated by all of Clausewitz's major interpreters (in contrast to much uninformed comment chiefly by non-German authors).[11] Although no direct evidence as to Clausewitz's familiarity

[10] Immanuel Kant, *The Critique of Judgement* (Oxford, 1961), esp. articles 46–50; the quotations are from pp. 168, 181.

[11] See esp. Hermann Cohen, *Von Kants Einfluss auf die deutsche Kultur* (Berlin, 1883), 31–2; Rothfels, *Clausewitz, Politik und Krieg*, pp. 23–5; Walter Malmsten Schering, *Die Kriegsphilosophie von Clausewitz* (Hamburg, 1935), 105–11, and id., *Wehrphilosophie* (Leipzig, 1939), 343–4; Erich Weniger, 'Philosophie und Bildung im Denken von Clausewitz', in W. Hubatsch (ed.), *Schicksalswege Deutscher Vergangenheit* (Düsseldorf, 1950), 123–43; Paret, *Clausewitz*, esp. pp. 160–3; and Werner Hahlweg, esp. 'Philosophie und Theorie bei Clausewitz', in Clausewitz Gesellschaft (ed.), *Freiheit ohne Krieg* (Bonn, 1980), 325–32. Schering was the first to argue that Clausewitz may have also been influenced by 18th-cent. German aesthetical thinkers, such as Sulzer and Lessing, who paved the way for Kant (*Wehrphilosophie*, p. 343). While this may obviously be true and applies to the whole break from Gottsched's neo-classicism pioneered by Bodmer and Breitinger, Clausewitz's conceptions are clearly Kantian and whether he was familiar with Kant's predecessors is purely conjectural.

with Kant's works exists, we know that Clausewitz was introduced to them through the lectures of Kiesewetter, one of Kant's best-known popularizers and one of the pillars of the Institute for Young Officers where he was the instructor of mathematics and logic.[12]

Like the military thinkers of the Enlightenment, and even more consciously than them, Clausewitz found in the theory of art a highly suggestive model for the theory of the 'art' of war. Both dealt with the theory of action; in both, given means were employed to achieve a required effect through a creative process which involved principles of an operational nature. From his earliest works to *On War*, Clausewitz adapted Kant's theory of art to criticize the work of the military thinkers of the Enlightenment, and to develop his own conception of the theory of war.

Already in 1805, Clausewitz had employed the new conceptual framework in his criticism of Bülow. Bülow's definitions of strategy and tactics, he argued, were invalid, because Bülow did not state their purpose. Stating the purpose is essential to the definition of art which is 'the use of given means to achieve a higher end'.[13] Furthermore, Clausewitz objected to Bülow's opinion that, if need be, the general ought to follow his genius above and contrary to the rules:

> one *never* rises above the rules, and thus when one appears to go *against* a rule, one is either *wrong*, or *the case does not fall under the rule any more* . . . he who possesses genius ought to make use of it, *this is completely according to the rule!*[14]

Any division or conflict between genius and rules was now inadmissable. In a fragment written in 1808 or 1809 Clausewitz reasserted this: 'genius, dear sirs, never acts contrary to the rules'.[15]

In an essay 'On Art and Theory of Art'—written at an unknown time, perhaps after Clausewitz's period of study in the Institute but possibly only in the late 1810s or early 1820s as a preparatory work for the writing of *On War*—the conception of theory is elaborated upon as Clausewitz strives to clarify his ideas. Like Kant, he distinguishes between science, whose aim is knowledge through

[12] Some of Clausewitz's notes, taken in one of Kiesewetter's lectures on mathematics, were found by Schering in Clausewitz's family archive (now lost); Schering, *Kriegsphilosophie*, pp. 105 ff.

[13] 'Bülow', in Hahlweg (ed.), *Verstreute kleine Schriften*, pp. 67–8.

[14] Ibid. 80–1.

[15] The fragment, 'Tactische Rhapsodien' was never printed and appears to have been lost. The quotation is from Rothfels, *Clausewitz, Politik und Krieg*, p. 156.

conceptualization, and art, whose essence is the attainment of a certain aim through the creative ability of combining given means. Between the two concepts there exists, Clausewitz points out, a certain overlapping, and art is assisted by knowledge. Thus, 'the theory of art teaches this combination [of means to an end] as far as concepts can . . . Theory is the representation of art by way of concepts.'[16] However, this representation is fundamentally very limited and varying. In his notes on strategy (1809), Clausewitz wrote for example, following Scharnhorst, that 'the part of strategy that deals with the combination of battles must always remain in the sphere of free (unsystematic) reasoning'.[17]

All these themes receive comprehensive treatment in Book II of *On War*, 'On the Theory of War'. Clausewitz again presents the distinction between a science of concepts and an art of creative capability. War fits much more into the model of art, while the title science is better kept for fields such as mathematics and astronomy. However, Clausewitz also makes it clear that these are no more than analogies. The major difference between the nature of creative activity in the arts and in war is that in war the object reacts. From this point of view, as well as from that of its subject-matter, war belongs much more to the field of social intercourse, being close to commerce and above all to politics.[18]

The various systems for the conduct of operations are again accused of being abstracted from reality and separating genius from rules:

> Anything that could not be reached by the meagre wisdom of such one-sided points of view was held to be beyond scientific control: it lay in the realm of genius which *rises above all rules*. Pity the soldier who is supposed to crawl among these scraps of rules, not good enough for genius, which genius can ignore, or laugh at. No; what genius does is the best rule and theory can do no better than show how and why this should be the case.[19]

[16] The fragment: 'Über Kunst and Kunsttheorie' was printed by W. M. Schering (ed.), *Clausewitz, Geist und Tat* (Stuttgart, 1941); see esp. pp. 154–5, 159. For Kant's distinction between science and art, see his *Critique of Judgement*, article 43, pp. 162–4. Three other fragments on the theory of art were also printed by Schering in *Geist und Tat*.

[17] 'Strategie' (1809), in Hahlweg (ed.), *Verstreute kleine Schriften*, p. 61.

[18] *On War*, II, 3, pp. 148–50.

[19] Ibid. II, 2, p. 136.

Appealing to the genius who is supposed to stand above the rules 'amounts to admitting that rules are not only made for idiots, but are idiotic in themselves.'[20]

The relationship between rules and genius is therefore clearly concluded in terms of the new paradigm in the theory of art:

> It is simply not possible to construct a model for the art of war that can serve as a scaffolding on which the commander can rely for support at any time . . . no matter how versatile the code, the situation will always lead to the consequences we have already alluded to: *talent and genius operate outside the rules, and theory conflicts with practice.*[21]

The emphasis with Clausewitz, therefore, shifts from the rules to the freely creating genius. Genius, however, is not a new sort of abstraction. It is a quality belonging to living men whose activity is dependent on their particular psychological profile, motivations, and aims, as well as on the conditions of their environment. Rejecting dead abstractions for real life and acting personalities was a dominant theme in German cultural outlook and artistic creation since the 'Storm and Stress' period. It remained at the centre of Goethe's and Schiller's outlook in their mature works. And its importance for the Romantics cannot of course be exaggerated. Here too, Clausewitz gave expression to a new world-view whose domination over Germany, when he started his intellectual and literary activities in the first years of the nineteenth century, was already secure.[22] An interesting fact, pointed out by Paret, is that Schiller, the author of historical dramas based on charismatic personalities (*The Maiden of Orleans*, *William Tell*, *Mary Stuart*, and *Wallenstein*) is the author most frequently mentioned in Clausewitz's letters.[23] Schiller is also known as the most philosophically inclined among the great German artists of the late eighteenth century, as Kant's disciple, and as the author of aesthetical works in which he stressed the free operation of genius.[24]

[20] *On War*, III, 3, p. 184.

[21] Ibid. II, 2, p. 140.

[22] Oestreich's suggestion that Clausewitz's conception of genius owed something to the neo-stoical tradition in the early modern period as reflected in the German *Klassizismus* might be, broadly speaking, true, though Oestreich relies on Rothfels's and Schering's very incomplete interpretation of Clausewitz's immediate and dominant intellectual background; Oestreich, *Neostoicism and the Early Modern State*, p. 88.

[23] Paret, *Clausewitz*, p. 84.

[24] For Schiller's aesthetic conceptions and Kant's philosophy, see e.g. R. D. Miller, *Schiller and the Ideal of Freedom, A Study of Schiller's Philosophical Works with Chapters on Kant* (Oxford, 1970).

It is, therefore, not surprising that Clausewitz's emphasis on the role of the creative personality constitutes, as Paret notes here too, one of the striking differences between his outlook and that of Scharnhorst.[25] The explanation for that goes, however, further than Paret's suggestion of variations in interests or aims between the two. This difference offers, in fact, a classic demonstration of the paradigmatic change between the teacher and his pupil. Scharnhorst was a typical representative of the military school of the Enlightenment, which was institutionally and structurally oriented. Characteristically, the military thinkers of the Enlightenment interpreted Frederick's victories chiefly as a product of the Prussian battle deployment. And the legacy of the Enlightenment, adapted by Jomini, continued its reign, interpreting Napoleon's sensational successes in utterly impersonal terms. Neither Frederick nor even Napoleon drew Clausewitz's attention to the role of the great personality; a new world-view was needed for that, and again, it may be traced to his earliest works.

In his notes on strategy of 1804, Clausewitz wrote that a strategic plan 'is a pure expression of [the general's] manner of thinking and feeling, and almost never a course chosen by free consideration'.[26] In this provocative argument he expanded Machiavelli's well-known point and also cited the example the latter used: Fabius *cunctator* 'did not delay operations against the Carthaginians because this type of war so suited circumstances, but rather because it was his nature to delay'.[27]

This point of view, which elevates the general's personality above any abstract strategic considerations, is also strikingly manifest in Clausewitz's interpretation of the operations of Gustavus Adolphus and Frederick the Great. In 'Gustavus Adolphus's Campaigns of 1630–1632', apparently written during the Napoleonic period,[28] Clausewitz presents the personality and motivations of the king and his adversaries as the key to the events of the war—clearly a conscious antithesis to the military thinkers of the Enlightenment.[29] Schiller's famous trilogy *Wallenstein*, published

[25] Paret, *Clausewitz*, p. 166.

[26] 'Strategie' (1804), in Hahlweg (ed.) *Verstreute kleine Schriften*, p. 10.

[27] Ibid.

[28] 'Gustav Adolphs Feldzüge von 1630–1632', *Hinterlassene Werke* (Berlin, 1832–7), vol. ix; for the date of composition see the editor's introd., p. vi.

[29] This was first pointed out by Rothfels, *Clausewitz, Politik und Krieg*, pp. 61–9; touched upon in Kessel's introd. to the first edn. of *Strategie* (Hamburg, 1937), p. 24; and developed in Paret, *Clausewitz*, pp. 85–8.

in 1800, and one of Clausewitz's favourite works, may very well have influenced both Clausewitz's choice of subject and manner of treatment.[30]

Historical study, writes Clausewitz, dwells on 'the mathematical level of physical forces' and ignores the subjective forces in war; yet, it is precisely these forces which are the most decisive.[31] To understand the events of the war, one should understand the particular psychological profile of the operating individuals in the context of their particular milieu. 'Is it not wiser to pay less attention to what the enemy *can* do and pay more attention to what he *will* do? . . . here lies a more fruitful field for strategy than the degrees of angles of operations.'[32]

The idea stressed in 'Gustavus Adolphus' is again sharply expressed in Clausewitz's note on strategy of 1808, directed against Jomini's analysis of the campaigns of Frederick the Great. As we have already noted in the chapter on Jomini, Clausewitz rejected the substitution of abstract, lifeless principles for Frederick's complex and concrete reality and particular psychology:

> To appreciate the value of his [Jomini's] abstractions, one must ask if one wants to give up all of Frederick II's practical life as a general for these couple of general maxims which are so easy to grasp? . . . did Frederick violate these maxims out of ignorance? . . . It is impossible to hang [the diversity of Frederick's generalship] . . . on a couple of meagre ideas . . . What is the conclusion of all this? That the general's temper greatly influences his actions . . . that one must not judge generals by mere reason alone.[33]

Not only was the abstract intellectual interpretation of the activities of great generals deemed to be fundamentally artificial, but so was

[30] Schiller's reputation and career as a historian, which culminated in his appointment as professor of history at Jena, is overshadowed by his dramatic and philosophical achievements. *Wallenstein* was preceded by a widely read *Geschichte des Dreissigjährigen Krieges* (1791–3) in which he was already trying to uncover the proper relation between the great personality and the conditions of his time. Also see: W. M. Simon, *Friedrich Schiller, the Poet as Historian* (Keele, 1966); and Lesley Sharpe, *Schiller and the Historical Character* (Oxford, 1982). For Clausewitz's reference to Yorck's inquiry of the troops' mood at the decisive meeting in Tauroggen when he made up his mind to take his corps out of the Napoleonic army, as recalling Schiller's *Wallenstein*, see Clausewitz, *The Campaign of 1812 in Russia* (London, 1843), 239 (*Hinterlassene Werke*, vol. vii); Paret, *Clausewitz*, p. 230.

[31] 'Gustav Adolph', *Hinterlassene Werke*, ix. 8.

[32] Ibid. 46.

[33] 'Strategie' (1808), Hahlweg (ed.), *Verstreute kleine Schriften* pp. 47–9.

the excessive emphasis on intellectual faculties and necessary knowledge. In his notes on strategy of 1804, Clausewitz lists the disciplines that the military thinkers of the Enlightenment carefully compiled for their educational programmes for officers: mathematics, map drawing, geography, artillery, fortifications, siegecraft, entrenchments, tactics, and strategy. Regarding each subject, he concludes that the general only requires a broad but sound, rather than a detailed, knowledge. He has no need for 'professorial' or 'pedantic' knowledge, and can manage with a 'few abstract truths'. What he predominantly requires is sound judgement and a strong character: 'a strong, ambitious spirit'.[34]

Clausewitz's clearly ironic attitude towards the Enlightenment ideal of knowledge is again manifest in his *Principles of War for the Crown Prince* (1812):

> Extensive knowledge and deeper learning are by no means necessary [for the general], nor are extraordinary intellectual faculties . . . For a long time the contrary has been maintained . . . because of the vanity of the authors who have written about it . . . As recently as the Revolutionary War we find many men who proved themselves able military leaders, yes, even military leaders of the first order, without having had any military education. In the case of Condé, Wallenstein, Suvorov, and a multitude of others it is very doubtful whether or not they had the advantage of such education.[35]

The last sentence in particular, which is a straightforward rejection of one of the major doctrines of the Enlightenment, once again demonstrates the paradigmatic shift between Clausewitz and his mentor. It was clearly at variance with Scharnhorst's lifelong beliefs and statements.

Clausewitz discusses the qualities that a general requires in his treatment of military genius in *On War*, which will not be elaborated upon here. The important point is again that character and spirit are more essential than cognitive faculties; fundamentally, war is an activity more than an intellectual discipline. Even the required cognitive qualities are of the empirical and applied sort.[36] It is true that Clausewitz twice repeats Napoleon's dictum that the complexity of the problems involved in war is of the order of mathematical problems that would require a Newton. However what distinguishes

[34] 'Strategie' (1804), Hahlweg (ed.), *Verstreute kleine Schriften*, pp. 6–8.
[35] *Principles of War*, p. 60.
[36] See esp. *On War*, I, 3, 'On Military Genius'.

military knowledge is its relation to life. 'Experience, with its wealth of lessons, will never produce a *Newton* or an *Euler*, but it may well bring forth the higher calculations of a *Condé* or a *Frederick*.'[37]

Clausewitz's emphasis on the general's personality, emotions, and motivations went hand in hand with his emphasis on the decisive role of the moral forces that animate armies. Here too, as we have seen in Jomini's case, the understanding of the change in the intellectual paradigm is essential. The military thinkers of the Enlightenment were far from ignoring the importance of moral forces, and Lloyd even offered an extensive study on the subject, adapting the conceptions and views of the contemporary psychology of desires. However, on the whole, they regarded moral forces as too elusive and belonging to the sublime part of war. And since they were interested in intellectual control, they saw no point in discussing moral forces at length. The intellectual transformation generated by the men of the 'Storm and Stress' period and the Romantics, which placed man's inner world at the centre of human experience, involved a radical change in the interpretation of, and regard for, the ideal of knowledge. The new perspective was largely rooted in anti-rationalistic trends, and thus the focusing on uncontrollable elements was for many of its exponents a special point to be made rather than a sacrifice. The Enlightenment ideal of understanding and control was substituted by a comprehensive and vitalistic one, and consequently the standards for what was considered significant and worth discussing also changed.

Without attempting an impossible summary of the comprehensive intellectual environment and its influences on Clausewitz, it is nevertheless worth noting the following points: that Clausewitz shared with his wife the universal admiration for Goethe and Schiller and in fact, as was probably common with courting couples, *Werther* was a subject of conversation during one of their first meetings;[38] that upon their return from captivity in 1807, Clausewitz and Prince August were the guests of Madame de Staël in her famous place of exile at Coppet in Switzerland for two months, where Clausewitz made the acquaintance of August Wilhelm Schlegel, with whom he

[37] *On War*, II, 2, p. 146; I, 3, p. 112; VII, 3, p. 586.

[38] See Marie's description of her acquaintance with her husband in Schwartz, *Leben*, i. 185.

was impressed despite the fact that he was far from accepting his world-view as a whole;[39] and that prominent Romantic poets and dramatists such as Achim von Arnim, Clemens Brentano, Heinrich von Kleist, and Friedrich, Baron de la Motte Fouqué, as well as Fichte and Schleiermacher, moved in the same social circle in Berlin as the Clausewitzes.[40]

If the origins of Clausewitz's conception of moral forces are wide and varied, its nature is easier to define. Firstly, it is clear that he rejected both idealism and mysticism. 'I recognize', he wrote, 'no pure spiritual thing apart from thoughts; all notions, even all sensations with no exceptions, are a mixture of spiritual and material nature.'[41] Clausewitz's relation to the various themes in Romanticism is strikingly summarized by Peter Paret:

> He benefited enormously from the liberating emphasis that the early Romantics placed on the psychological qualities of the individual; but he did not follow such writers as Novalis or the Schlegel brothers in their surrender to emotion. The religious wave of Romanticism did not touch him; nor did its mysticism, nostalgia, and its sham-medieval, patriarchal view of the state. In feeling and manner he was far closer to the men who had passed through the anti-rationalist revolt of the 'Sturm und Drang' to seek internal and external harmony, and who gave expression to their belief in the unity of all phenomena.[42]

The emphasis on moral elements is already very distinctive in the notes on strategy of 1804, and, as we have seen, it is given systematic expression in the criticism of Bülow and the legacy of the Enlightenment. According to Clausewitz, emotional forces were indeed difficult to determine and control, but they were essential not only for a true, comprehensive, and living conception of war, but also for understanding the nature and boundaries of its theory. In his quest for precision, Bülow concentrates on the material elements which are susceptible to mathematical calculations, and ignores the moral forces that animate war. He thus misrepresents the real nature of war, and creates a mechanistic and one-sided theory.[43]

[39] Clausewitz's letter to his fianceé, 5 Oct. 1807: Schwartz, *Leben*, i. 299.

[40] Hagemann, *Von Berenhorst zu Clausewitz*, p. 69; Paret, *Clausewitz*, p. 212.

[41] From a fragment written in 1807–8, 'Historisch-Politische Aufzeichnungen', in Rothfels (ed.), *Schriften*, p. 59; the metaphysical conception expressed in the passage is, incidentally, clearly Kantian.

[42] Paret, *Clausewitz*, p. 149.

[43] 'Bülow', in *Verstreute kleine Schriften*, pp. 79, 81.

Several statements that Clausewitz made during the reform era reflect the new cultural paradigm in a particularly classical manner. Immediately after rejecting the fantasies of the new mystical sects, Clausewitz goes on to write that they nevertheless express a genuine need of the time, 'the need to return from the tendency to rationalize to the neglected wealth of feeling and fantasy'.[44] On 11 January 1809, in response to an article that Fichte wrote on Machiavelli, Clausewitz sent a letter to the famous philosopher, in which he criticized 'the tendency, particularly in the eighteenth century [to] form the whole into an artificial machine, in which the moral forces were subordinated to the mechanical'. Conversely, he wrote, the 'true spirit of war seems to me to lie in mobilizing the energies of every individual in the army to the greatest possible extent, and in infusing him with bellicose feelings, so that the fire of war spreads to all elements of the army'. That would be the end of the old attitudes, 'for in every art the natural enemy of mannerism is the *spirit*'.[45]

In three separate discussions in *On War*, Clausewitz outlines the moral forces that motivate war, expanding the ideas presented in the critique of Bülow written in 1805.[46] The problem with military thinkers is that 'they direct their inquiry exclusively towards physical quantities, whereas all military action is intertwined with psychological forces and effects'. Thus, 'it is paltry philosophy if in the old fashioned way one lays down rules and principles in total disregard of moral values'.[47]

The one-sided nature of the old theory stems from a genuine difficulty:

> Theory becomes infinitely more difficult as soon as it touches the realm of moral values. Architects and painters know precisely what they are about as long as they deal with material phenomena . . . but when they come to the aesthetics of their work . . . the rules dissolve into nothing but vague ideas.[48]

Moral forces do not evade theoretical treatment altogether. A series of patterns 'in the sphere of mind and spirit have been proved by

[44] Rothfels (ed.), *Schriften*, p. 59.

[45] Schering (ed.), *Geist und Tat*, pp. 77, 78, 80; Paret, *Clausewitz*, pp. 176–7. Compare with W. von Humboldt, p. 245 below.

[46] *On War*, I, 4–5; II, 2, pp. 137–9; III, 3–7.

[47] Ibid. II, 2, p. 136; III, 3, p. 184.

[48] Ibid. II, 2, pp. 136–7.

experience: they recur constantly, and are therefore entitled to receive their due as objective factors'. Yet, in general, moral forces 'will not yield to academic wisdom. They cannot be classified or counted. They have to be seen or felt.'[49]

The effect of moral forces as well as the bilateral nature of war are among the main factors which turn war into a field saturated with the unknown and unforeseen, and create a gulf between planning and the actual course of war. Here too the gap between the military thinkers of the Enlightenment and Clausewitz fits the pattern we have already met. The Enlightenment thinkers were quite aware of the factors of uncertainty but focused on what they considered to be suitable for intellectual formulation. Clausewitz regarded their attitude as dogmatic and divorced from reality, and demanded an all-encompassing theory. 'They aim at fixed values; but in war everything is uncertain, and calculations have to be made with variable quantities.'[50]

It is illuminating to compare this with the works of the Prussian general Friedrich Constantin von Lossau (1767–1848), a participant in Scharnhorst's *Militärische Gesellschaft* and one of the reformers, whose book *War* (1815) elaborated many of the ideas later to become famous in Clausewitz's *On War*. Because of the great progress which had been made in the sciences and the arts in the last centuries, wrote Lossau, people sought similar achievements in the study of war. They forgot, however, the decisive influence of the human personality and of chance in war, to which Berenhorst was the first to call attention.[51]

Clausewitz again expressed the attitudes of his intellectual environment but this time a suitable concept was less at hand. Thus, though he had emphasized the uncertainties involved in war from his early works, he only adopted the concept of 'friction' at a later stage, initially in the *Principles of War for the Crown Prince* of 1812.[52] 'The

[49] Ibid. III, 3, 184. [50] Ibid. II, 2, p. 136.

[51] F. von Lossau, *Der Krieg* (Leipzig, 1815), 284–8; the book deals extensively with the warrior's intellectual and moral faculties, presenting war as a clash of wills motivated by patriotic and other psychological energies. On Lossau see Hagemann, *Von Berenhorst zu Clausewitz*, pp. 44–55.

[52] The relatively late appearance of the concept of friction has been pointed out by Kessel, 'Zur Genesis der modernen Kriegslehre', *Wehrwissenschaftliche Rundschau*, III/9 (1953), p. 408. Rothfels (*Clausewitz, Politik und Krieg*, p. 90) has called attention to a very similar formulation in *The Spirit of the Laws*, Bk. XVII, ch. 8, where Montesquieu wrote that, like in mechanics, frictions often change the implications of theory. However, the popularity of this mechanistic image in the 18th cent. makes any direct inference pointless.

conduct of war', he wrote, 'resembles the working of an intricate machine with tremendous friction, so that combinations which are easily planned on paper can be executed only with great effort.'[53]

This idea is reiterated in *On War*. The gulf between planning and reality is mainly rooted in the enormous complexity of factors involved, whose effects are difficult to foresee. This is all the more so since war is characterized by the 'uncertainty of all information' which means that 'all action takes place, so to speak, in a kind of twilight'.[54]

Clausewitz's demand for a theory which fully expresses the diversity of reality is closely related to the emergence of a new outlook on history that he introduced into the study of war. His place in the rise of historicism, pointed out by some of his interpreters,[55] is of paramount importance to the understanding of his theoretical outlook and the tensions inherent in it.

As shown by Paret, Clausewitz's early works already contain references to Machiavelli, Montaigne, Montesquieu, Robertson, Johannes von Müller: the historian of the Swiss confederation, Ancillon: the Prussian conservative anti-Enlightenment and anti-Revolutionary historian and statesman, and Gentz: the arch-conservative and disciple of Burke. Evidence for Clausewitz's familiarity with the works of Herder and Möser exists only at later stages of his life but he probably read them much earlier. This historical reading blended with the dominant influence of Scharnhorst's concrete, particularist, and circumstantial approach to the past.[56]

Again one should look at the German intellectual environment in which Clausewitz operated. Moving in the same social circle in Berlin as the Clausewitzes were Adam Müller, Savigny, and Schleiermacher.[57] The first was the most prominent spokesman of

[53] *Principles of War*, pp. 61–8; the quotation is from p. 61.

[54] *On War* I, 7; II, 2, p. 140.

[55] This was well treated by Rothfels, *Clausewitz, Politik und Krieg*, pp. 61–9; noted by Kessel (following the appearance of Meinecke's *Historismus* in 1936) in his introd. to the first edn. of *Strategie*, p. 11; and was lately discussed at length by Paret, *Clausewitz*.

[56] Paret, *Clausewitz*, pp. 81–2. See ibid. 312 for Clausewitz's note to the library in 1820 requesting, among others, a collection of Herder's essays and anthology of Greek lyrics and epigrams, *Herders Zerstreute Blätter*. For a reference to Möser see 'Umtriebe', which is much in affinity with Möser's views, Rothfels (ed.), *Schriften*, p. 164.

[57] Hagemann, *Von Berenhorst zu Clausewitz*, p. 69; Paret, *Clausewitz*, pp. 212, 316.

the historical approach to politics and economics; the second, the founder of the 'historical school' of jurisprudence; and the third, the one who offered a historically conscious explanation for the diversity of religious faith. Rejection of the universal abstractions of the Enlightenment in favour of the belief in historical diversity and the complexity of the forms of society and politics was one of the dominant themes of the Counter-Enlightenment, and characterized the disillusion with the ideas of the French Revolution. Clausewitz's criticism of the philosophers in Germany who were influenced by Parisian philosophy and politics and 'who have minds which are too distinguished to value local and historical particularities', is again a classic expression of these attitudes. It could have literally been written by Möser, Burke, Adam Müller, or Gentz.[58]

Once more Clausewitz's historical outlook is already revealed in his early writings. As pointed out by Rothfels, it dominated his two works on the Thirty Years War: 'Gustavus Adolphus' and an apparently lost manuscript, 'Views on the History of the Thirty Years War'. Clausewitz consciously chose to deal with a war whose total and devastating nature had terrified the men of the eighteenth century and was regarded by them to be 'inhumane and barbarous'.[59] He interpreted the events in a highly sympathetic manner, revealing the utmost sensitivity to the particular conditions of the period and the concrete challenges that the personalities involved had faced. In contrast to the universal standards employed by the men of the Enlightenment, Clausewitz asserted that the nature of each war depended on the state of the countries and peoples involved, on their customs, political situation, spirit, culture, and so on.[60] Indeed, 'The various great wars constitute many different eras in the history of the art.'[61]

This classic statement of the historicist position was reiterated by Clausewitz on several later occasions. The claim to perfection, he wrote in the essay 'On the State of the Theory of War' is 'one of those boasts with which every period now and again seeks to ornament the events of its day'.[62] Against Bülow's and Jomini's

[58] 'Umtriebe' in Rothfels (ed.), *Schriften*, p. 166. For Clausewitz's political views, see the last section of Ch. 8. II.

[59] 'Gustav Adolph', *Werke*, ix. 19; Rothfels, *Politik und Krieg*, pp. 61–2.

[60] See n. 59 above.

[61] 'Ansichten aus der Geschichte des Dreissigjährigen Krieges'; cited by Rothfels, *Clausewitz, Politik und Krieg*, pp. 61–2.

[62] 'Über den Zustand der Theorie der Kriegskunst', in Schering (ed.), *Geist und Tat*, pp. 52.

universal principles and standards of measurement, he wrote in *On War*:

> It is plain that circumstances exert an influence that cuts across all general principles . . . a critic has no right to rank the various styles and methods that emerge as if they were stages of excellence, subordinating one to the other. They exist side by side, and their use must be judged on its merits in each individual case.[63]

Following in Scharnhorst's footsteps, Clausewitz therefore emphasized the absolute dependence of theory on concrete historical experience. Historical experience is the source of all knowledge, and, in view of the artificial nature of contemporary military theory, it is by far superior to any other study. He concluded his *Principles of War for the Crown Prince* by stressing precisely this point.

Clausewitz's conception of the nature of historical experience and study is most fully presented in *On War*, Book II, chs. 5 and 6. Though this constitutes one of his most interesting analyses, only some of its main points can be cited here. Most historical writing, he maintained, bore witness to an arrogant, dogmatic, and superficial study and judgement of the past. The subjugation of the past to the rule of one-sided systems and principles involved rising above the conditions and individuals peculiar to each particular case, and harnessing a wide, but tendentious, uncircumstantial, and uncritical variety of examples to support abstract conceptions. The purpose of historical study is not to provide doctrines but to train judgement through indirect experience of a profession in which direct experience of sufficient scope is often unattainable. This can only be achieved by intimate familiarity with the conditions of the events studied, even at the expense of concentrating on a selective few historical cases. Furthermore, since the practical purpose of the study of military history is geared to the present, it should focus on modern history. The closer the period is to the present, the more conditions are likely to be similar to it.

It is, therefore, not surprising that Clausewitz's historical works constitute the bulk of his remaining literary works. Seven of the ten volumes of his *Werke* are composed of studies of the great campaigns of modern Europe since the Thirty Years War, particularly the wars of the Revolution and Napoleon. His theoretical work too is

[63] *On War*, VI, 30, p. 516.

characterized not only by many historical analyses and references but also by a strong historical spirit. The most striking example is to be found in *On War*, VIII, 6B. In a few pages Clausewitz offers a most penetrating outline of the transformation of war throughout history as a result of

> the nature of states and societies as they are determined by their times and prevailing conditions . . . The semi-barbarous Tartars, the republics of antiquity, the feudal lords and trading cities of the Middle Ages, eighteenth-century kings and the rulers and peoples of the nineteenth century—all conducted war in their own particular way, using different methods and pursuing different aims.[64]

The perceptive analysis that follows—much richer than implied in the opening passage—will not be cited here. More important is the conception behind it which concludes the narrative:

> Our purpose was not to assign, in passing, a handful of principles of warfare to each period. We wanted to show how every age had its own kind of war, its own limiting conditions and its own peculiar preconceptions. Each period, therefore, would have held to its own theory of war, even if the urge had always and universally existed to work things out on scientific principles.[65]

The last sentences represent the culmination of Clausewitz's historicist conception. Their implications for the possibility of a universal theory of war, as opposed to a theoretical formulation of the conditions peculiar to each time and place, is strikingly Pyrrhonic and destructive. They present, however, only one aspect of Clausewitz's thought. The core of his theoretical work and the major difficulties he encountered in its development were how to formulate a universal theory of war which would be valid despite and within the great diversity of historical experience.

[64] *On War*, VIII, 6B, p. 586. [65] Ibid. 593.

III HOW TO FORM A UNIVERSAL THEORY OF WAR?

Clausewitz's reformulation of the concept of military theory, which was directed against the theoretical outlook of the Enlightenment, was bound up with his effort to devise an adequate military theory of his own. His ideas evolved from general notions during the reform era into a comprehensive and systematic treatise on war written during the period of peace.

In his first works, when he was mainly concerned with developing his attack which aimed at the destruction of the strategic systems, Clausewitz's ideas regarding the possibility of formulating a positive theory of war appear mainly in a negative form. In his critique of Bülow in 1805, Clausewitz was almost unwilling to commit himself on this point. If he were to be asked, he wrote, in the light of the demands that he set for a theory of strategy, whether such strategic theory was at all possible, his reply would be 'that we have neither committed ourselves to write one, nor to prove its possibility, and that we were less inclined to object to the confession: "I do not believe in the art [of war]"' [Berenhorst's], than to the 'Babylonic confusion of language which prevails in military ideas'.[1]

During the reform era a developing shift in Clausewitz's emphases can be traced. Although he was still much concerned with the criticism of contemporary military thinkers, his thoughts were moving forward to more positive problems. In the essay 'On the State of the Theory of War', Clausewitz opposed contemporary military thinkers not because their theory was unhistorical, but because most of them found it difficult to think theoretically, and therefore resorted to examples and eclectic historical discussions. This problem was less severe than might be thought because, according to Clausewitz, history was the basis of theory, and in the absence of adequate theory, historical study was the only possible form of military education. 'However', Clausewitz wrote in the conclusion of the essay, 'none of this keeps us from confessing that we expect great advantage from an intelligent development of theory, partly for the training of young students, and even more for the development of the art itself.' As pointed out by Paret, the programmatic note here is unmistakable.[2]

[1] 'Bülow', in Hahlweg (ed.), *Verstreute kleine Schriften*, p. 82.

[2] 'Über den Zustand der Theorie der Kriegskunst', in Schering (ed.), *Geist und Tat*, pp. 59–60; Paret, *Clausewitz*, p. 156.

Indeed, in the years 1807–9, Clausewitz laid the foundations for his theory of war by developing an intellectual structure that would integrate the diversity of historical experience with a universal approach. In his note 'On Abstract Principles of Strategy' (1808), he briefly surveyed the transformations of the face of war since the Thirty Years War. The result of these transformations was that military theories, which have actually simply reflected changing 'manners' of warfare, have always been invalidated by new historical experience. These changes had been so rapid and far-reaching that 'the books on war have always come out late and in all times they have described dead manners'.[3]

If this is the case, is a universal theory of war possible at all? It is possible, according to Clausewitz, because beyond the diversity of historical experience and the changing 'manners' of each period there exists a universal, constant element, which is the true object of theory. Theory should aim at the 'lasting spirit of war', a concept which already figures prominently in Clausewitz's notes of 1804. The various forms of the art of war decline in time, but the spirit of war escapes change, and must not be 'lost sight of'.[4]

The same conceptual framework is repeated in Clausewitz's letter to Fichte in January 1809, in which Clausewitz criticizes Machiavelli and, implicitly, also Fichte himself for trying to revive the warfare of the ancients. Rather than obsolete 'manners' and 'forms' it is the 'lasting spirit of war' that should be restored.[5]

This conception that suggests an integration of the historical with the universal was deeply rooted in Clausewitz's intellectual environment. Paret pointed out its clear affinity to Schleiermacher's celebrated conception of religion, which attracted much attention during Clausewitz's formative years. Positive religions and ethical systems, wrote Schleiermacher in his famous *Reden über die Religion* (1799) and *Monologen* (1800) appeared in history in a rich variety of forms; they rise and decline but their spirit remains one and universal. Shortly before composing the note on strategy of 1808, Clausewitz wrote to his fiancée:

[3] 'Strategie' (1808), in Hahlweg (ed.), *Verstreute kleine Schriften*, p. 47.

[4] Ibid. 46–7. The similarity to Lossau's ideas is amazing: a systematic theory of war is impossible, and 'thus there can be no lasting textbook for war'. 'War always appears as new; only the spirit of war remains the same.' Lossau, *Der Krieg* p. 35.

[5] Letter to Fichte, Schering (ed.), *Geist und Tat*, esp. p. 77.

Religious feeling in its elemental purity will eternally exist in men's hearts, but no positive religion can last forever. Virtue will eternally exert its beneficial influence on society; but the universality of this global spirit cannot be expressed in the restrictive form of a code of laws, and form itself will shatter sooner or later when the stream of time has washed away or reshaped the surrounding contours.[6]

Schleiermacher's influence here is all too apparent. As we shall see, Clausewitz's conception of the compatibility of the historical and the universal also derived from several other sources and was quite common during the genesis of historicism.

What is the nature of the universal in war? Clausewitz's notes on strategy of 1808–9 reveal the problem that was to figure prominently in his attempts to formulate a theory. The theory of strategy 'allows the setting up of few or no abstract propositions'. One cannot escape the multitude of minor circumstances. 'All the authors that in modern times have sought to treat this part of theory abstractly and philosophically provide a clear indication of this; they are either simply trivial, or they get rid of triviality through one-sidedness.' Venturini belongs to the former category; Bülow and Dumas to the latter.[7] Contemporary military thinkers are criticized, but the theoretical problem preoccupies Clausewitz's own mind. One can either offer clearcut doctrines by ignoring all exceptional conditions, or try to cover all possibilities and provide no positive advice. A priori abstractions always fall between the Scylla of partial validity and the Charybdis of the commonplace.

In the note of 1809, Clausewitz elaborated on this problem:

Formula [is] abstraction. When by the abstraction nothing which belongs to the thing gets lost—as is the case in mathematics—the abstraction fully achieves its purpose. But when it must omit the living matter in order to hold to the dead form, which is of course the easiest to abstract, it would

[6] Letter to Marie, 5 Oct. 1807, Linnebach (ed.), *Briefen*, pp. 142–3, cited by Paret, *Clausewitz*, p. 167. Clausewitz's affinity to Schleiermacher's ideas was briefly pointed out by Weniger, 'Philosophie und Bildung im Denken von Clausewitz', in Hubatsch (ed.), *Schicksalwege*, p. 143, and repeated by Paret. In 1808 Schleiermacher became the professor of theology in the newly founded University of Berlin and one of the major exponents of the awakening Prussian national spirit. As shown by Paret, Clausewitz almost certainly knew him personally at that period. For Schleiermacher's ideas in this connection, see his speeches *On Religion* (London, 1893), esp. speeches 1, 2, 5. Schleiermacher's emphasis on emotion as the constitutive element of religion was, of course, in step with Clausewitz's general affinity with the message of Romanticism.

[7] 'Strategie' (1808), in Hahlweg (ed.), *Verstreute kleine Schriften*, p. 46.

be in the end a dry skeleton of dull truths squeezed into a doctrine. It is really astonishing to find people who waste their time on such efforts, when one bears in mind that precisely that which is the most important in war and strategy, namely the great particularity, peculiarity, and local circumstances, escape these abstractions and scientific systems.[8]

Clausewitz's period of service between 1810 and 1812 as instructor at the military academy and military tutor to the Prussian crown prince undoubtedly stimulated his interest in formulating an adequate positive theory of war. For the first time, he was engaged in teaching, and had to give his views on war a didactic form which culminated in his *Principles of War for the Crown Prince*. However, the beginning of the period of peace was, in this respect, the crucial turning-point in Clausewitz's career. His intellectual activity now became his major preoccupation, focusing on the writing of a comprehensive theoretical work on war. During his period in Koblenz (1816–18), Clausewitz wrote a concise theoretical treatise, the first attempt in a process which was to lead to the writing of *On War*. This early treatise has not survived, but what appears to be its preface and an additional comment that Clausewitz wrote on the treatise's character and composition were included in the posthumous publication of his works. In the preface and comment Clausewitz again put forward the theoretical structure that had emerged in 1807–9.

The 'scientific character' of his work, Clausewitz wrote,

> consists in an attempt to investigate the essence of the phenomena of war and to indicate the links between these phenomena and the nature of their component parts . . . the propositions of this book therefore base their inner necessity [*innere Notwendigkeit*] on the secure foundation either of experience or of the concept [*Begriff*] of war as such.[9]

While its surface is in flux, war has an immutable core: its 'spirit', 'essence', 'nature' or 'concept'.

We have already seen the affinity of this conception to that of Schleiermacher. Its formulation in 1816–18 also clearly reveals

[8] 'Strategie' (1809), in Hahlweg (ed.), *Verstreute kleine Schriften*, pp. 60–1.

[9] 'Author's Preface', *On War*, p. 61; whenever I hereafter deviate from the Princeton edition of *On War*, the German original is cited in square brackets. Again compare this with Lossau, another disciple of Scharnhorst whose book had appeared only a few years before: theory aims at 'correct concepts' on the 'nature of war', which 'appear when one develops the concept of war.' Lossau, *Der Krieg*, pp. 2, 6.

Clausewitz's profound debt to Scharnhorst. Theory aimed at correct concepts, had to be grounded in experience or in the nature of war, and pointed out the necessary relations between the parts and the whole; this was the intellectual framework that Scharnhorst had formulated in the 1780s and reiterated throughout his life. As mentioned earlier, Aron was the first to call attention to the striking similarity of this formula to Montesquieu's celebrated definition of laws as 'the necessary relation arising from the nature of things'. Indeed, Clausewitz too, appears to have drawn not solely from Scharnhorst but also from Montesquieu himself. In his comment on the treatise of 1816–18, Clausewitz presents Montesquieu's work as the model that was in his mind when writing his own work.[10] While this reference focuses on structure rather than on content, Clausewitz's conception of the nature of theory and his reference to Montesquieu at the very moment when this conception is elaborated upon and put into practice betray a much deeper affinity. Clausewitz was familiar with, and referred to, Montesquieu's work as a young man, and now, when he turned to write his theoretical treatise, Montesquieu's integration of the historical and empirical on the one hand with the universal on the other appears to have emerged as a model. This affinity should certainly not be exaggerated; to use Clausewitz's words in a wider sense, 'the manner in which Montesquieu dealt with his subject was vaguely in my mind'.[11]

The blending of a high degree of sensitivity to the diversity of historical experience with a belief in certain universal elements is typical of the early period of historicism. Meinecke argued that this blend reflected the legacy of the old tradition of natural law within the historicist outlook which reacted against this tradition.[12] Indeed, the tension inherent in this blend has been pointed out especially in relation to its most classic manifestation in Montesquieu's *Spirit of the Laws*.[13] Returning to Clausewitz, would the notion of a universal

[10] 'Comment', *On War*, p. 63. [11] Ibid.

[12] In this connection see Herder's highly interesting statement: 'The art of war may change with the changes in weapons, times, and state of the world; but the spirit of man—which invents, deceives, conceals its purposes, goes to the attack, defends itself or retreats, discovers the weaknesses of its enemy, and in one way or another uses or misuses them for its advantage—remains at all times the same.' Herder, *Ideen zur Philosophie der Geschichte der Menschheit* (1784–91) XIII, 6; cited by Rothfels, *Clausewitz*, p. 63. Whether Clausewitz was actually aware of this passage is unknown.

[13] See Meinecke, *Historicism*, ch. 3; and Berlin, 'Montesquieu', *Against the Current*, pp. 130–61. For the general inherent tension here see, Reil, *The German Enlightenment and the Rise of Historicism*, ch. VIII, and esp. p. 162.

essence withstand the threat of historical relativity? Would the belief in the 'nature of things' not conflict with the test of 'experience'? In 1816–18 Clausewitz believed that his solution rose to the challenge.

He was still preoccupied, however, with the tendency of universal propositions to lead towards empty formalism, triviality, and truisms. In the preface of 1816–18, he quoted extensively from a work by the famous G. C. Lichtenberg (1742–99), the Göttingen science professor who grew highly sceptical about human knowledge and outlook on the world, and whose aphorisms, published posthumously, were widely read. According to Clausewitz, Lichtenberg's 'Extract from Fire Regulations', satirizing the meticulous, dead formalism of system builders, strikingly fitted the existing military theories.[14] Curiously enough, as we have seen in the note on strategy of 1808, Clausewitz argued the precise opposite against the systems of Dumas, Bülow, and Jomini, his major opponents. They formulated principles which were packed full of content but which were one-sided. In fact, the whole issue reflects a recurring theme in Clausewitz's own mind which also reappears in the comment on the work of 1816–18 and is stated in more personal terms: 'I wanted at all costs to avoid every commonplace, everything obvious.'[15]

Clausewitz approached the writing of *On War* with fairly consolidated ideas on the nature and boundaries of military theory. Like his contemporaries, he believed that the conduct of operations was the true subject of theory, not yet discovered by the early military thinkers of the Enlightenment.[16] However, Scharnhorst's influence and the legacy of Kant's theory of art convinced him that doctrines of absolute applicability for the conduct of war were impossible. The historicist outlook and Schleiermacher's formulation of the traditional message of pietism and Moravianism, which rejected all religious dogmas, positive doctrines, and any other attempt to capture the variety of universal religious feeling in rigid intellectual structures, reinforced this conviction. No rule or principle could cover the diversity of reality, nor the different requirements of action. The point made in 1808 is reiterated: 'all the principles, rules, and methods

[14] 'Author's Preface', *On War*, pp. 61–2. For Lichtenberg see J. P. Stern, *Lichtenberg, A Doctrine of Scattered Occasions* (Indiana, 1959).

[15] 'Comment', *On War*, p. 63.

[16] See esp. *On War*, II, 2, pp. 133–4.

will increasingly lack universality and absolute truth the closer they come to being positive doctrine'.[17]

Rules and principles for action are by no means illegitimate in themselves as long as their value and limits are understood correctly. As in Kant's theory of art, their justification is that they provide a way to give the officer some guidance for conduct in war by conceptual means. Hierarchically, they include the very general, such as law—which is too comprehensive and strict a conception to be applicable to anything in war—and progress to principles and rules, directions, regulations, and methods which deal with minute details.[18]

The availability and usefulness of these rules of action diminishes the higher the level of the conduct of war. At the lower levels, in the sphere of tactics, rules of action are easier to formulate because they deal with more physical, material, and technical factors. They are also essential because the enormous number of activities and people involved in these levels require rules, directives, and methods to regulate and unify their operations, render general training possible, and direct rapid and determined action under conditions of shortage of information and time, without the need for rethinking the situation in each individual case. By contrast, at the higher levels of war, in strategy, activity is imbued with subjective factors and conscious decisions, and the issues in point are major and crucial. Here, the commander's free considerations play the decisive part.[19] In any case, all rules for action require circumstantial and critical application involving judgement, and can never be used to criticize opposing decisions and courses of action taken in individual cases and under specific conditions.[20]

In itself, this conception of rules and principles is therefore not very different from that of Clausewitz's predecessors, particularly if one does not accept Clausewitz's caricature of them. However, for Clausewitz, these practical rules and principles could never be considered as the theory of war itself. For that, one had to look elsewhere. The rules and principles merely provided one of the

[17] *On War*, II, 5, pp. 157–8; see again the section, 'A Positive Doctrine is Unattainable', ibid. II, 2, p. 140.

[18] *On War*, II, 4, pp. 151–2.

[19] Ibid. II, 2, pp. 140–1, 147; II, 4, pp. 152–3.

[20] Ibid. II, 4, pp. 151–2, see also II, 5, p. 158; and 'Über Kunst und Kunsttheorie', in Schering (ed.), *Geist und Tat*, pp. 161–2.

bridges—and the crudest one at that—between the need for concrete action and the real theory of war. 'Theory should be study, not doctrine'; it is not a 'manual for action'.[21] The entire military school of the Enlightenment with its rules and principles simply missed the main point: the universal nature of war, its lasting spirit.

What then is the theory of war? The conception that emerged in 1808–9 and 1816–18 reappears. Theory is to be 'used to analyse the constitutive elements of war'.[22] It is 'the field of universal truth that cannot be inferred merely from the individual instances under study'. But it also belongs to the empirical sciences in the sense that 'while, for the most part, it is derived from the nature of things, this very nature is usually revealed to us only by experience'.[23]

Again, if one shrinks from one-sided doctrines, one is in danger of falling into empty formalism. 'When we contemplate all this, we are overcome by the fear that we shall be irresistibly dragged down to a state of dreary pedantry, and grub around in the underworld of ponderous concepts.' Fortunately, in the broad sense, theory is far from being divorced from concrete action. 'Theory cannot equip the mind with formulas for solving problems . . . but it can give the mind insight into the great mass of phenomena and of their relationships, then leave it free to rise into the higher realms of action.'[24] Ultimately, theory is to become capability through critical analysis and practical rules and principles.[25]

This is therefore Clausewitz's conception of theory and his guiding ideal. Above historical study and crude rules there exists a universal theory which reflects the lasting nature of war, transcends the diversity and transformations of past experience, and is both generally valid and instructive. Indeed, it is time to turn to the application of this conception.

In an undated note, written sometime during an advanced stage of the composition of *On War* and describing the state of his work, Clausewitz argued for the feasibility of a universal theory of war, citing a long list of propositions which summarized themes from the

[21] *On War*, II, 2, p. 141. [22] Ibid.; see also VIII, 1, pp. 577–8.

[23] Ibid. II, 5, p. 157; II, 6, p. 170.

[24] Ibid. VIII, 1, p. 578; compare this with the preface to the work of 1816–18 where Clausewitz wrote that instead of presenting ready-made doctrinal structures (*fertige Lehrgebäudes*), his work offered material for them; 'Author's Preface', ibid. p. 61.

[25] See esp. *On War*, II, 2, pp. 141 and 147; II, 5, p. 156; VIII, 1, p. 578.

manuscript. Though obviously schematic and ill-organized, this list is highly significant. It is rarely referred to, one dares suggest, because commentators have been somewhat uneasy about its content.

It is a very difficult task to construct a philosophical [*philosophische*] theory for the art of war, and so many attempts have failed that most people say it is impossible, since it deals with matters that no permanent law can provide for. One would agree, and abandon the attempts, were it not for the obvious fact that a whole range of propositions can be demonstrated without difficulty: that defence is the stronger form of fighting with the negative purpose, attack the weaker form with the positive purpose; that major successes help bring about minor ones, so that strategic results can be traced back to certain turning points; that a demonstration is a weaker use of force than real attack, and that it must therefore be clearly justified; that victory consists not only in the occupation of the battlefield, but in the destruction of the enemy's physical and psychological forces, which is usually not attainable until the enemy is pursued after a victorious battle; that success is always greater at the point where the victory was gained, and that consequently changing from one line of operations, one direction, to another can at best be regarded as a necessary evil; that a turning movement can only be justified by general superiority or by having better lines of communication or retreat than the enemy's; that flank positions are governed by the same consideration; that every attack loses impetus as it progresses.[26]

How universal are these propositions and how successful are they in escaping the dilemma of one-sidedness and triviality? This is perhaps better left to the reader's own consideration. Rather than discussing these propositions eclectically, the following chapter will attempt to trace the development of Clausewitz's central line of thought on the nature of war.

[26] 'Undated Note', *On War*, p. 71.

7

Clausewitz

The Nature of War

I MILITARY DECISIVENESS AND POLITICAL GREATNESS: THE NAPOLEONIC MODEL

The nature of war is fighting; hence all the characteristics of its 'lasting spirit': the primacy of the engagement and of the major battle, aided by a massive concentration of forces and aggressive conduct, and aiming at the total overthrow of the enemy. Throughout his life, this conception was the centre-piece of Clausewitz's military outlook. It reflected the overwhelming impact of the Napoleonic experience, was the source of Clausewitz's attacks on the war of manœuvre in all periods and particularly in the eighteenth century, and formed the basis for his belief in a universal theory of war.

Ironically, in 1827, this whole military outlook fell into a deep crisis. In the middle of composing *On War*, Clausewitz's line of thought underwent a drastic change of direction, the only revolutionary transformation in the otherwise steady evolution of his ideas. In a note on the state of his work dated 10 July of that year, Clausewitz announced his intention to revise *On War* on the basis of two guiding ideas: firstly, that there are two types of war: all-out war and limited war; and secondly that war is the continuation of policy by other means.

The crisis of his conception of the nature of war was equally destructive for Clausewitz's lifelong conception of theory. In his efforts to resolve this comprehensive crisis, he transformed but *did not* abandon his old military outlook, and resorted to completely new theoretical devices. He was preoccupied with this during his last three working years.

Unfortunately, the origins and nature of Clausewitz's new theoretical framework have remained a mystery, and consequently, the exact nature of the transformation in his thought has not been entirely clear either. This explains why Clausewitz's ideas could be interpreted so differently by successive generations. Whereas the men of the nineteenth century emphasized the place of the major battle and the element of destruction in Clausewitz's thought, modern readers, contending with the problem of limited war and seeking out the full complexity of the link between political and military activity, have stressed themes in his later thought. As this has been coupled by a strong reaction, particularly in Germany, against the military and political legacy of the German Reich, a new, 'good' Clausewitz has had to be created, set apart from his 'bad' successors. While blaming their discredited predecessors for being tendentious and one-sided, modern interpreters have therefore themselves failed to recognize that the imperative of destruction was the basis of Clausewitz's conception of war. As we shall see, some have even denied that he held such an idea at all. The obscurity of Clausewitz's text has continually left room for conflicting and unhistorical interpretations.

Clausewitz's conception of the nature of war stemmed from both his military and political outlook, and was incorporated into his definition of war. In the military sphere this conception reflected the earth-shattering collapse of the warfare of the *ancien régime* when confronted by the Revolutionary and Napoleonic art of war. With the emperor's great triumphs of 1805–7 this process was completed. For the first time in the history of modern Europe a single state had inflicted a crushing defeat over all the other powers of the continent. Eighteenth-century warfare, which, because of the political and social structure of the *ancien régime*, had been relatively limited in aims and scope was now increasingly discredited and perceived as inadequate, if not absurd.

This upheaval was not, of course, expressed solely by Clausewitz but underlay almost the whole of military thought at the turn of the nineteenth century. We have already seen it reflected in varying degrees in the transition from Bülow and Archduke Charles to Jomini. The total mobilization of forces, initiative, aggressiveness, and rapid decision in battle now dominated warfare. Yet, nowhere was the reaction against the past and the embracing of the new spirit of war as powerful as in the defeated Prussia. And of all of Clausewitz's contemporaries no one gave the new trends more far-reaching expression—a fact which, until our own times, was obvious to everyone.

Closely linked to Clausewitz's military outlook were his political attitudes. Again interpreters have not paid them sufficient attention and failed to appreciate their interrelation with Clausewitz's theoretical work, ignoring his actual historical background and intellectual career. Clausewitz saw the face and map of Europe radically altered by determined and powerful political and military actions and witnessed his country, which dabbled in diplomatic manœuvres and military half-measures, lose its independence and status as a great power in a single powerful blow. To these experiences were added the dynamic and vitalistic effect of Romanticism and the fervent energy and feeling generated by rising nationalism. Clausewitz urged the state to pursue great objectives, to be determined in its actions, and to put the utmost power behind them. It is not surprising that these notions, as well as Clausewitz's military views found support and reinforcement in Machiavelli's works.

Paret points out the major themes behind Clausewitz's enthusiastic interest in and warm appreciation of Machiavelli, which is well documented in Clausewitz's early works:[1] the emphasis on the moral energies that animate nations and armies, and the comprehensive and penetrating presentation of politics, in the centre of which stands the role and skilful use of force.[2] To understand the full scope of Clausewitz's attraction to Machiavelli it is necessary, however, to note the fascinating parallels in their historical and psychological position, both in the military and the political spheres. There is a surprising similarity in the developments they witnessed and in their reactions to them.

In the military sphere Machiavelli saw the weakness of the mercenary armies, the *condottieri*, with their cautious tactics, fully exposed by the emergence of the new vigorous national armies of Switzerland, France and Spain, and he called for the creation of a civic militia, motivated by national sentiments. Clausewitz witnessed the collapse of the professional armies of the *ancien régime* when

[1] 'Strategie' (1804) in Hahlweg (ed.), *Verstreute kleine Schriften*, p. 9, presenting Machiavelli as having 'a very sound judgement in military affairs'; Rothfels (ed.) *Schriften*, p. 63: 'no book in the world is as essential for the politician as Machiavelli's'. For other references see 'Strategie' (1804), articles 4, 5, 6; 'Historisch-politische Aufzeichnungen' (1805) and 'Bei Gelegenheit der russichen Manifeste nach dem Tilsiter Frieden', in Rothfels (ed.), *Schriften*, pp. 4 and 62 respectively; and Clausewitz's letter to Fichte, in Schering (ed.), *Geist und Tat*, p. 77.

[2] Paret, *Clausewitz*, pp. 169–79.

confronted by the aggressive armies of mass conscription raised by Revolutionary France, and he too demanded the creation of an army of general conscription supported by a national militia. Throughout his life, Clausewitz, following in Machiavelli's footsteps, denounced the era of the *condottieri*, as well as the warfare of the *ancien régime*, as a degeneration of the art of war.[3]

In the political sphere, Machiavelli witnessed the eclipse of the once-proud Italian city-states and the impotence of their diplomacy in contrast to the real political and military might of the new powers. He stressed the dominance of force in politics and called for a dynamic political and patriotic revival. Clausewitz, as mentioned earlier, saw the diplomatic manœuvres of the mediocre heirs of Frederick the Great stripped of all their efficacy by Napoleonic power. After the disaster, he stood out, even in the reform circle, in his call for a bold and determined policy, and in his relentless search for every opportunity—the Spanish guerrilla warfare, the Austrian war of 1809, the French invasion of Russia—to launch a total war of independence, even if it might lead to destruction. His bitter and fierce criticism of his country during this period is clearly marked by Machiavellian themes: contempt for half-measures, indecisiveness, and inactivity which, in the end, are bound to lose all worlds. In his defence of Machiavelli, Clausewitz wrote: 'Chapter 21 in Machiavelli's "Prince" [warning against neutrality and calling for rallying with one of the sides] is the code for all diplomacy, and woe to those who distance themselves from it!'[4] Activity, vitality, and power in the political as well as in the military spheres were the essence of Clausewitz's outlook.

This outlook was incorporated into Clausewitz's conception of the nature of war: 'Essentially war is fighting, for fighting is the only effective principle in the manyfold activities generally designated as war.' The developments in weapons 'brought about great changes in the forms of fighting. Still no matter how it is constituted, the concept of fighting remains unchanged.'[5]

[3] See e.g. *On War*, II, 6, p. 174; VIII, 3, p. 587.

[4] Rothfels (ed.), *Schriften*, p. 64. For Clausewitz's national fervour, plans of insurrection against the French, and criticism of his country's policies, see esp. Paret, *Clausewitz*, chs. 8.I, 8.IV.

[5] *On War*, II, 1, p. 127. Compare Schleiermacher's speeches *On Religion*, for example: 'everything called by this name [religion] has a common content', religious feeling (p. 13); 'The essential oneness of religiousness spreads itself out in a great variety' (p. 50).

We have finally reached the actual content of Clausewitz's theoretical conception, which was unveiled in his letter on religion, note on strategy, and letter to Fichte. Whereas the 'forms' of war are diverse and changing, its 'spirit' is universal. Like religious feeling in religion, fighting is the constitutive element of war, which allows us to regard the many different wars as part of a single phenomenon. This, however, is not merely a statement defining the common denominator of all wars; military theory which is blind to, or evades, the imperative of fighting—as the thinkers of the eighteenth century allegedly did—creates a false picture of war, which is bound to lead to disaster. The dominance of fighting determines the whole character of war. From his earliest works Clausewitz stressed this point.

In the notes on strategy of 1804, the full scope of Clausewitz's military outlook, inextricably linked to his political state of mind, is unfolded for the first time. Firstly, Clausewitz rejects the limited warfare of the eighteenth century and denounces the central role of fortresses, the division of armies, and Fabian strategy.[6] The correct conduct of war is diametrically opposed 'I would not like to print this, but I cannot hide from myself that a general cannot be too bold in his plans, provided that he is in full command of his senses, and only sets himself aims that he himself is convinced he can achieve.'[7] In a nutshell, 'the art of war tells us: *go for the greatest, most decisive purpose you can achieve; choose the shorest way to it that you dare to go*'.[8] '*War should be conducted with the utmost necessary or possible degree of effort.*'[9] One should achieve the utmost concentration of force, and strike the enemy with the maximum power. Defence ought to be adopted only if one is too weak to attack. The enveloping strategic manœuvre against the enemy's rear, recommended by Bülow with the approval of Venturini, Dumas, and Massenbach, has indeed the advantage of threatening the enemy's communications; but its success is dubious, and direct action from a central position is more effective. Frederick the Great's conduct in the Seven Years War, Napoleon's Italian campaign of 1796, and many other examples from the history of war attest to this. Clausewitz worked out a strikingly similar conception to the one that Jomini developed that very same year but had not yet published.[10]

[6] 'Strategie' (1804), s. 9, in Hahlweg (ed.), *Verstreute kleine Schriften*, pp. 14–16.
[7] Ibid., s. 12, pp. 19–20.
[8] Ibid., s. 12, p. 19.
[9] Ibid., s. 13, p. 21.
[10] Ibid., s. 22, pp. 35–6; s. 13, pp. 24–5; s. 15, pp. 27–9; s. 19, p. 33.

All this derived from the main point: 'It can be absolutely universally said: all that demands the use of military forces has the idea of the engagement at its base.' Engagement is the centre of war, toward which all efforts are directed. The belief of Bülow and his fellow-thinkers that victory could be won by means of a brilliant strategic manœuvre, without resorting to battle, was an absurd illusion. Manœuvres are, of course, necessary, but only to achieve favourable conditions for the engagement. Even when the engagement itself does not take place, its expected outcome regulates the conduct of the belligerents like the effect of 'cash on credit in commerce'. 'Strategy works with no materials other than the engagement.' Thus, whereas tactics is defined as the 'use of military forces in the engagement', strategy is but the 'use of individual engagements to achieve the aim of the war'.[11]

This military outlook went hand in hand with *corresponding* attitudes to the political aims of war, and the relationship between policy and war. War is fought for the attainment of a political purpose, 'the purpose of war'. And in 1804 this purpose was also formulated in radical and aggressive terms: either to destroy the enemy's state or to dictate the terms of peace.[12] Among Clausewitz's interpreters who looked upon these alternatives through the prism of the intellectual revolution of 1827, Aron was the only one to note that in 1804 the choice was *not* between total and limited war. Dictated peace terms implied bringing the enemy to his knees. Indeed, *both* options are cited explicitly in 1827 under the single aim of completely overthrowing the enemy.[13] This crushing political purpose is matched by the objective of the military operations, 'the purpose in war', which is 'to paralyse the enemy forces'. 'The destruction of the enemy's armed forces is the immediate purpose of war, and the most direct way to it always constitutes the rule for the art. This destruction can be achieved by occupying his country or annihilating his war provisions or his army.'[14] In considering the 'purpose of operations' one should 'always choose the most difficult, *for this is the one most closely related to the spirit of the art of war*'.[15]

[11] 'Strategie' (1804), s. 20, p. 33; s. 21, p. 35.

[12] Ibid., s. 13, p. 20.

[13] Aron, *Clausewitz*, pp. 88–9. The term 'two types' (*doppelte Art*) which is repeated in 1827, added to this confusion.

[14] 'Strategie' (1804), s. 13, pp. 20–1.

[15] Ibid., s. 12, p. 20.

It is therefore misleading to assume that in 1804 Clausewitz had already been aware of the range of political aims and objectives, and that in 1827 he simply elaborated on it or became fully aware of its implications for the conduct of war. There was a perfect harmony in 1804 between Clausewitz's political and military convictions; *both* were formulated in radical terms. Total concentration of force, the imperative of fighting for decision—these were Clausewitz's conceptions of the nature of war within the context of his general political outlook which called for determined action and great objectives.

This military outlook and political state of mind are again fully revealed in Clausewitz's next comprehensive work, *Principles of War for the Crown Prince* (1812). Clausewitz sent the work to the prince when he left Prussia to join the Russian army, and in it he made a special effort to impress upon the young prince in that critical hour the fervour of his outlook on politics and war. In the programmatic passage that concluded the work he wrote to the prince: 'A powerful emotion must stimulate the great ability of a military leader . . . Open your heart to such emotion. Be audacious and cunning in your plans, firm and persevering in their execution, determined to find a glorious end.'[16]

The work itself reiterates all the themes raised in 1804:

> We always have the choice between the most audacious and the most careful solution. Some people think that the theory of war always advises the latter. That assumption is false. If the theory does advise anything, it is the *nature of war* to advise the most decisive, that is, the most audacious.[17]

The aims in the conduct of war are (*a*) to conquer and destroy the armed forces of the enemy; (*b*) to take possession of the resources of his army; and (*c*) to win public opinion.[18] These aims, it must be noted, are *not* alternative but complementary; they are intended to secure the complete defeat of the enemy.

The first principle of the art of war is the concentration of force, supported by dynamic and determined conduct which avoids half-measures.[19] A defensive position should only be adopted as a means

[16] *Principles*, p. 69.
[17] Ibid. 13–14; my emphasis.
[18] Ibid. 45.
[19] Ibid. 12, 17–19, 21, 46.

for attacking the enemy from a position of advantage.[20] The engagement is the focal point of war, much more important than the skilful combination of engagements (that is strategy).[21] Thus, in war, direct, crushing operations from a central position are superior to concentric enveloping manœuvres; Jomini was right about this while Bülow indulged in illusions. Clausewitz even goes so far as to make the fantastic statement (after Marengo, Ulm, and Jena, to name only the most important examples) that 'Napoleon never engaged in strategic envelopment'.[22]

All this is enough to show that Clausewitz's conceptions were clearly a particular reflection of Napoleonic warfare as perceived in its peak years. This was precisely how Berenhorst saw them when he read Clausewitz's *Principles*:

> The most significant parts of his wisdom, he abstracted from the wisdom, the actions, and the maxims of Napoleon. Indeed, his relationship to Carnot's and Napoleon's method or system of war, today's art of war, is like the relationship of Reinhold, Kiesewetter, and Berg to the philosophy of Hume and Kant [that is, they interpret and populize it] . . . He certainly has the merit of explaining the new art of war very well and intelligently, and he should be recognized as the first to have done so.[23]

Characteristically, Berenhorst regarded Clausewitz's ideas simply as a penetrating interpretation of the particular form of warfare that then prevailed.

Finally, the same themes and view of war are expressed in the early and unrevised parts of *On War*, Books II–VII. They will be briefly noted again, if only to establish the clear continuity in Clausewitz's outlook:

> The very concept of war will permit us to make the following unequivocal statements: 1) Destruction of the enemy forces is the overriding principle of war . . . 2) Such destruction of forces can *usually* be accomplished only by fighting. 3) Only major engagements involving all forces lead to major success. 4) The greatest successes are obtained where all engagements coalesce into one great battle.[24]

[20] *Principles*, p. 17.
[21] Ibid. 15.
[22] Ibid. 48–9.
[23] Berenhorst to Valentini, 1 Nov. 1812, Bulow (ed.), *Nachlasse*, ii. 353. Rather than revealing an affinity with Clausewitz's way of thinking (as suggested by Paret, *Clausewitz*, p. 205), these words stood, in fact, in stark contrast to it; Clausewitz did not regard his ideas as a mere expression of a particular form of warfare.
[24] *On War*, IV, 11, p. 258.

Destruction should be the aim in each individual engagement.[25] Defence is indeed stronger than attack and thus it is the weapon of the weak; but once the defender gains the advantage, he must revert to the attack. The second part of this formula and Clausewitz's full meaning have been missed by most modern commentators who characteristically contrasted his wisdom with his successors' mania for the attack.[26] Again, to stress the link between Clausewitz's military and political outlook: the 'very destruction of the enemy's forces is also part of the final purpose [of war]. That purpose itself is only a slight modification of that destructive aim.' Ignoring this point was at the root of all the false military theories before the Napoleonic Wars.[27]

Even when the engagement does not take place, the very threat of it regulates the conduct of the belligerents. Any other military objective—the occupation of provinces, cities, fortresses, roads, and bridges, the seizure of ammunition, and so on—must merely be seen as an intermediate means intended to achieve a greater advantage for the engagement.[28] The same applies to strategic manœuvres. First, it is interesting to see that as the campaigns of 1813 and 1814 cast doubt on the conception of interior lines, Clausewitz withdrew from his own unequivocal position of 1804 and 1812. In principle, he writes, no a priori advantage can be attributed to either interior or exterior lines; the choice between them is dependent upon the type of warfare and upon circumstances.[29] In either case, he maintains as before, that the strategic manœuvre is secondary in importance to the engagement, and must be subservient to it:

Admittedly, an engagement at one point may be worth more than at another. Admittedly, there is a skillful ordering of priority of engagements in strategy . . . We do claim, however, that direct annihilation of the enemy's forces must always be the *dominant consideration*. We simply want to establish this dominance of the destructive principle . . . one should not swing wider than latitude allows . . . rather than try to outbid the enemy

[25] Ibid. IV, 3, p. 229.

[26] For a fuller analysis of the real nature of this highly interesting relationship, the subject of Bks. VI and VII, see my article 'Clausewitz on Defence and Attack', *Journal of Strategic Studies*, X (March, 1988).

[27] *On War*, IV, 3, esp. p. 228.

[28] Ibid. III, 1, pp. 181–2.

[29] Ibid. VII, 13, pp. 541–2.

with complicated schemes, one should, on the contrary, try to outdo him in simplicity.[30]

Ulm was an exceptional event; the decisive battle is the dominant feature of war.[31]

This outlook encompasses not only the manœuvre, but also every other military means other than the engagement itself. Once Clausewitz's starting point is understood, all his military ideas become crystal clear. For all the significance of surprise, Clausewitz maintains that 'by its very nature [it] can rarely be *outstandingly* successful. It would be a mistake, therefore, to regard surprise as a key element of success in war.'[32] The same applies to cunning. For all its importance and 'however much one longs to see opposing generals vie with one another in craft, cleverness, and cunning, the fact remains that these qualities do not figure prominently in the history of war . . . The reason for this is obvious . . . strategy is exclusively concerned with engagements.'[33] The truly important factors are superiority of numbers and concentration of force at the decisive point.[34]

Hence also Clausewitz's exclusion of all preparatory activities (as well as the supporting services such as maintenance, administration, and supply) from the theory of war proper, which has occasionally surprised commentators. Theory only takes these activities into account as influencing conditions, because, strictly, it 'deals with the engagement, with fighting itself'. Marches, camps, and billets only narrowly escape the same fate, because 'in one respect [they] are still part of combat'.[35]

All these notions lead to Clausewitz's surprisingly dull description of contemporary battle. No manœuvres or stratagems are portrayed. The only image conveyed is of a direct, grey clash of physical and moral masses.[36]

The men of the nineteenth century, the heyday of the idea of all-out war, elevated Clausewitz to the pantheon of classics for his outlook on war described above. But for the present-day reader, after the collapse of the dogma of destruction in the First World War and

[30] *On War*, IV, 3, pp. 228–9.
[31] Ibid. IV, 11, p. 260.
[32] Ibid. III, 9, p. 198.
[33] Ibid. III, 10, p. 202.
[34] Ibid. III, 11, p. 204.
[35] Ibid. II, 1; for the citations, see pp. 132, 129.
[36] Ibid. IV, 2, p. 226.

the renaissance of limited war in the nuclear age, this outlook should have raised questions had its real nature not been obscured by Clausewitz's later development and the difficulties of interpreting it.

However, already at the beginning of the twentieth century when the conception of all-out war still reigned, Camon, one of the most important interpreters of the Napoleonic art of war, argued that Clausewitz misunderstood the essence of Napoleonic strategy, particularly the key manœuvre against the enemy's rear, *la manœuvre sur les derrières*.[37] Jomini's analysis of the Napoleonic art of operations, as opposed to the full context of Napoleonic warfare, was perhaps more concrete and realistic. Indeed, Clausewitz's conception of the Napoleonic art of war was largely a myth, born out of Prussia's traumatic experience and reflecting the prevailing emphasis on moral energies. To draw an otherwise most unlikely parallel, Clausewitz was in a way the theoretical counterpart of the action-hungry Field Marshal Blücher.

Hans Delbrück, the well-known military historian, raised the theoretical problem itself in the late nineteenth and early twentieth centuries when he questioned the universal validity of all-out war, paradoxically relying on Clausewitz's later conceptions. He advocated the legitimacy of the strategy of attrition, and started a celebrated but hardly successful debate in which he was attacked by Theodor and Friedrich von Bernhardi and by Colmar von der Goltz who represented the established strategic convictions of the time. Limited strategy, Delbrück maintained, such as that of the eighteenth century, had to be understood as the natural outgrowth of the particular conditions of the period.[38]

The deep crisis of the idea of all-out war and the direct attack on Clausewitz did not, however, take place until after the traumatic experience of the First World War. Liddell Hart, the most renowned and influential leader of the reaction against the military tradition of the nineteenth century, rehabilitated the discredited warfare of the eighteenth century and very sharply criticized (albeit somewhat superficially and tendentiously) Clausewitz and his legacy.[39] In

[37] H. Camon, *Clausewitz* (Paris, 1911); this work provides a close scrutiny of Clausewitz's histories of Napoleon's campaigns.

[38] For a summary of the debate see Delbrück, *History*, iv. 378–82.

[39] See esp. B. H. Liddell Hart, *The Ghost of Napoleon* (New Haven, 1934).

opposition to Bülow, Clausewitz had said that the aim of strategy was merely to achieve the most favourable conditions of time and place for the battle, and to make use of its results. One could argue, he wrote, that the perfection of strategy was therefore to achieve such favourable conditions as to render battle unnecessary. But, in fact, in reality it was usually advisable to count on fighting. If a general could not rely on the determination of his troops to fight, he would find himself continuously inferior.[40] Completely unaware of this argument, Liddell Hart again reversed the outlook on war; 'even if a decisive battle be the goal,' he wrote, 'the aim of strategy must be to bring about this battle under the most advantageous circumstances . . . The perfection of strategy would be, therefore, to produce a decision without any serious fighting.'[41] Clausewitz and Liddell Hart each interpreted the same logic in terms of the warfare of their times and arrived at diametrically opposed conclusions. Military reality and theory completed a full circle between Bülow and Liddell Hart.[42]

The main problem raised by Clausewitz's military outlook, and most of the reactions described here, have been well presented by Aron: 'Did Clausewitz's antidogmatism degenerate into a new dogmatism?'[43]

Having seen in the previous chapters his conception of theory and criticism of his predecessors, the full irony of Clausewitz's conception of war should be clear. He, who passionately believed that his predecessors' theoretical approach and view of war were totally false, was convinced that he had the key to the true nature of war. The paradoxical result of this conviction was that some of his principal arguments against his predecessors boomeranged. His outlook on war was, in its own way, no less one-sided, dogmatic, prescriptive, and unhistorical.

This puzzling discrepancy can only be understood against the background of the dominant role that Napoleon's crushing warfare played in the period's consciousness and in the discrediting of the

[40] 'Bülow', in *Hahlweg* (ed.), *Verstreute kleine Schriften*, pp. 78–9.

[41] B. H. Liddell Hart, *Strategy, the Indirect Approach* (London, 1954), 338.

[42] That the validity of Clausewitz's criticism of Bülow's attitude to manœuvre and battle is not as obvious as maintained by the German military school was also cautiously pointed out by E. A. Nohn, 'Der unzeitgemässe Clausewitz', *Wehrwissenschaftliche Rundschau*, V (1956).

[43] Aron, *Clausewitz*, p. 85.

old conduct of war, particularly in Prussia.[44] Clausewitz who was one of the major exponents of the new trends gave them logical expression with his definition of war as fighting, interpreted in an expansive and imperative manner. In Clausewitz's eyes this was not one-sidedness and dogmatism but at last the true universal nature of war and consequently the key to its proper conduct.

From this conviction derives also the prescriptive aspect of theory. Much has been written to the effect that Clausewitz totally rejected prescriptive theory, and as we have seen, this interpretation does have roots in Clausewitz's conception of theory. However, this is only a partial understanding of his approach as a whole. He maintained that the theory of war was not prescriptive only in the sense that any doctrine derived from it would always be partial and require judgment in application. But he did believe that the true theory of war provided lessons which the general had to bear in mind. Theory was by no means divorced from praxis; on the contrary, it had to be translated into praxis. Now we have also seen what concrete ideas he had in mind: to aim for great objectives, to achieve the utmost concentration of force, to act as aggressively as possible in order to annihilate the enemy army in a major decisive battle, and to destroy the ability of the enemy state to resist. He believed that 'unnecessary' manœuvres, preference for indirect military means, and evading decision in battle contradicted the spirit of war, were bound to lead to failure, and thus had to be avoided. These ideas are highly imperative; Clausewitz had no interest in empty truths.[45]

These strong convictions regarding the fundamental and universal nature of war also overshadow Clausewitz's historical sensitivity.

[44] See the remarkable similarity of Clausewitz's ideas to those of yet another pupil of Scharnhorst and a fellow-student of Clausewitz in the Institute, Rühle von Lilienstern, a man of vast intellectual interests, an intimate of Adam Müller and Heinrich von Kleist, and a friend of Goethe, Gentz, and the Schlegels. Rühle opened his *Handbuch für den Offizier*, a rev. ed. of Scharnhorst's work (Berlin, 1817), with the following statements: 'The engagement is the principal element of war . . . war is fighting' (p. 1); war is battles chained together or one great battle with intermissions (pp. 1, 435). Rühle, whose military career paralleled that of Clausewitz, also stressed the dominance of moral forces and the need for a theory of war which is rooted in reality and the nature of war (esp. pp. 438–44). For Rühle, see Hagemann, *Von Berenhorst zu Clausewitz*, pp. 55–66; Louis Sauzin's introd. to *Rühle von Lilienstern et son apologie de la guerre* (Paris, 1937); and Paret, *Clausewitz*, pp. 272, 314.

[45] Here too compare with Lossau's *Der Krieg*, p. 2: 'From these concepts [of the nature of war] there must emerge clearly what war is, what the warrior must want, and how one should study war in time of peace.'

In opposition to Jomini in particular, Clausewitz stressed the diversity of historical experience, and asserted that the theoretician must not elevate himself above the times by the force of standards of measurement which he regarded to be universal. Every period's particular form of warfare stemmed from its unique political, social, cultural, and personal conditions. As we have seen, he concluded his historical description of the transformations of the art of war in the context of the particular conditions of each period as follows: 'Each period, therefore, would have held to its own theory of war.' Indeed, this was the pinnacle of Clausewitz's historicism yet also its boundary; the next sentences limit the relativism implicit in this historical view:

> But the conduct of war [*Kriegführung*], though conditioned by the particular characteristics of states and their armed forces, must contain some more general—indeed, a universal—element with which every theorist ought above all to be concerned. The age in which this postulate, this universally valid element was at its strongest was the most recent one.[46]

The wars of the Revolution and Napoleon revealed the nature of war as fighting and a clash of forces, and dispelled the false conceptions which prevailed in various periods in the past.[47] Here too, as throughout his life, Clausewitz treats the warfare of the *condottieri* and that of the *ancien régime* not as genuine expressions of the conditions peculiar to their times, but as a grotesque distortion of the nature of war, necessarily leading to collapse. For all his criticism of Jomini, Clausewitz himself turned the warfare of his own period into a universal yardstick and employed it to dismiss the warfare of complete historical periods, disregarding their internal, circumstantial logic.

All this can only be understood in the spirit of Jomini's bitter complaint that Clausewitz's 'first volume [Books I–IV of *On War*; Jomini clearly referred mainly to Book II] is but a declamation against all theory of war, whilst the two succeeding volumes [the rest of *On War*], full of theoretic maxims, proves that the author believes in the efficacy of his own doctrines, if he does not believe in those of others'.[48] Clausewitz was convinced that in contrast to his predecessors' arbitrary and misleading systems, he himself had

[46] *On War*, VIII, 3B, p. 593.
[47] Ibid.
[48] Jomini, *Summary*, p. 15.

discerned the true nature of war, manifested in the genius of Napoleon, 'the God of War'.[49]

It was nevertheless Clausewitz's sensitivity to the diversity of historical experience that, in 1827, when most of *On War* was already drafted, finally led to the crisis in his outlook on war and conception of theory. The first realization of a problem emerges toward the end of Book VI, 'Defence'.[50] This is no coincidence. Since the aim of defence is to preserve the status quo, the defender may choose to delay operations, withdraw, and avoid confrontation in the hope of wearing the enemy down. This may lead to what Clausewitz called a 'war of observation': a prolonged, indecisive struggle which lacks energy and involves almost no fighting. In truth, the attacker too, sometimes appears to 'ignore the strict logical necessity of pressing on to the goal'.[51] This realization leads to a wider one:

> There is no denying that a great majority of wars and campaigns are more a state of observation than a struggle for life and death—a struggle, that is, in which at least one of the parties is determined to gain a decision. A theory based on this idea could be applied only to the wars of the nineteenth century.[52]

Indeed, 'To be of any practical use', theory must take into account that, apart from 'the kind of war that is completely governed and saturated by the urge for a decision—of true war', there exists a second kind of war.[53] Moreover, 'the history of war, in every age and country, shows not only that most campaigns are of this type, but that the majority is so overwhelming as to make all other campaigns seem more like exceptions to the rule'.[54]

Clausewitz's view of the nature of war as all-out fighting, centring on the engagement, fell into crisis. The note that Clausewitz wrote on 10 July 1827 heralded the celebrated transformation in his thought with which he was to struggle in the writing of Book VIII and revision of Book I of *On War*, and which will be described in the next section.

[49] *On War*, VIII, 3B, p. 593.
[50] Michael Howard, *Clausewitz* (Oxford, 1983), 47, 58.
[51] *On War*, VI, 30, p. 501.
[52] Ibid. VI, 28, pp. 488.
[53] Ibid. VI, 28, pp. 488–9.
[54] Ibid. VI, 30, p. 501.

The devastating effect of this crisis on Clausewitz's conception of theory must first, however, be elucidated:

> One might wonder whether there is any truth at all in our concept of the absolute character of war were it not for the fact that with our own eyes we have seen warfare achieve this state of absolute perfection. After the short prelude of the French Revolution, Bonaparte brought it swiftly and ruthlessly to that point . . . Surely it is both natural and inescapable that this phenomenon should cause us to turn again to the original [*ursprüngliche*] concept of war with all its rigorous implications. Are we then to take this as the standard, and judge all wars by it, however much they may diverge? Should we deduce all the *demands* [*Forderungen*] of theory from it? . . . [Then] our theory will everywhere approximate to logical necessity, and will tend to be clear and unambiguous. But in that case, what are we to say about all the wars that have been fought since the days of Alexander—excepting certain Roman campaigns—down to Bonaparte? . . . We would be bound to say . . . that our theory, though strictly logical, would not apply to reality.[55]

This dilemma shatters Clausewitz's lifelong conception of theory. 'Is one war of the same nature as another?', he asked in a note in which he wrote down the new problems in an attempt to clarify his thoughts.[56] 'All *imperatives* inherent in the concept of war seem to dissolve, and its foundations are threatened.'[57]

Having seen in the previous chapter the development of Clausewitz's conception of theory, the crisis into which this conception fell ought now to be clear: theory conflicted with reality; the 'concept of war' did not withstand the 'test of experience'; the universal contradicted the historical; the unity of the phenomenon of war, based on a 'lasting spirit' that encompassed the diversity of 'forms', disintegrated; and the practical imperatives derived from this 'spirit'—the significant content of theory—lost their validity.

[55] *On War*, VIII, 2, p. 580; the emphasis on the prescriptive aspect of theory is mine.

[56] Schering (ed.), *Geist und Tat*, p. 309; Aron, *Clausewitz*, p. 101.

[57] *On War*, VIII, 6A, p. 604; the emphasis on the prescriptive aspect of theory is mine.

II POLITICS AND WAR: THE AMBIGUOUS TRANSFORMATION CLARIFIED

The relationship between politics and war dominated Clausewitz's thought during his last years, generated a revision in his theory of war, and has attracted most of the attention in our time. This subject was presented by Clausewitz—for reasons which will be dealt with—as a single whole, all the elements of which were closely bound together. However, three major ideas can be discerned here, whose origins, development, and content, though not unrelated, were separate and distinct: (*a*) war as an extension of its social milieu, an idea that reflected the historicist message; (*b*) the diverging scope of political aims and military operations; (*c*) the state as the highest and unifying expression of human life and the guardian of political and moral ends, logically governing the military body; this idea reflected the Prussian traditional *raison d'état* and the formative stage of what was to be known as the German conception of the state.

War and the Social Milieu: Applying the Historicist Message

War is an integral part of comprehensive social and political reality which shapes its particular characteristics in any given period; out of all of Clausewitz's ideas on politics and war this was the one that played a dominant role in his thought from his youth. He absorbed it from the rising conceptions of historicism and directly from Scharnhorst. In fact, in the modern sense, this idea is concerned with the relationship of war to society rather than to politics. Most of the following themes have already been discussed throughout this work, particularly in relation to Scharnhorst's and Clausewitz's historical outlook, and will therefore be only briefly reviewed here.

As we have seen, Montesquieu's *Spirit of the Laws* revealed to the men of the eighteenth century a new depth of affinity between the array of elements and circumstances which made up any given historical fabric. Geographical and economical conditions, social structure, legal and political systems, religious faith and institutions, and cultural forms were intertwined in a diversity of particular manifestations. This highly influential idea left its mark on the military thinkers of the Enlightenment, and was extensively applied to the field of war by Guibert and Lloyd as well as by Jomini in his later works. However, its impact was restricted by the pronounced universalism of the military thinkers of the Enlightenment. Only when this idea was developed as one of the foundations of historicism by Herder, Möser, and the exponents of cultural and political pluralism and evolution, and propagated as a form of resistance to French ideas and imperialism, were its implications more fully absorbed in the military field.

With the great debates over French Revolutionary warfare, this idea came to the forefront of German military thought. It figured prominently in Scharnhorst's 'General Reasons for the French Success in the Wars of the Revolution' (1797), as well as in the works of Berenhorst and Bülow. Both the intellectual and the military environment of the young Clausewitz expounded this same idea.

Throughout his life, from his early studies of the Thirty Years War, this view of war within the context of its particular social and political reality was fundamental to Clausewitz's historical and theoretical outlook. It is also clearly revealed in his analysis of the great events of the wars of the Revolution and Napoleon, in which he followed in Scharnhorst's footsteps. Under Scharnhorst, he was one of the exponents of the military reforms which were closely linked to a comprehensive reform of Prussian society and politics, and which were based on a clear appreciation of the social and political sources of French power. In his review 'Prussia in her Great Catastrophe' written in the 1820s, Clausewitz elaborately expressed the assumptions that guided the reformers. In 1806 the army and administration were a product of the Frederickian absolutist state. While in the eighteenth century they had been perfected within the conditions and limitations of the *ancien régime*, they now became hopelessly inadequate in post-Revolutionary Europe.[1]

In *On War* Clausewitz outlined the transformation of warfare and the way it had been perceived:

> In the last decade of the eighteenth century, when that remarkable change in the art of war took place, when the best armies saw part of their doctrine become ineffective and military victories occurred on a scale that up to then had been inconceivable, it seemed that all mistakes had been military mistakes . . . [but] clearly the tremendous effects of the French Revolution abroad were caused not so much by new military methods and concepts as by radical

[1] 'Nachrichten über Preussen in seiner grossen Katastrophe', ch. 1, in Rothfels (ed.), *Schriften*, pp. 202–17.

changes in policies and administration, by the new character of government, altered conditions of the French people, and the like . . . Not until statesmen had at last perceived the nature of the forces that had emerged in France, and had grasped that new political conditions now obtained in Europe, could they foresee the broad effect all this would have on war.[2]

Not only military institutions and methods of warfare but also political aims and the conduct of operations are dependent upon the array of cultural, social, and personal circumstances. The growing realization of this was central to the transformation of 1827.

The Nature of War versus Policy: What were the Origins and Nature of Clausewitz's Dialectic?

As we might expect, a full understanding of the transformation in Clausewitz's thought in 1827, which resulted in the inclusion of the concept of limited war in military theory, cannot be gained without viewing the changes that occurred in his political perspectives. We saw that during the heroic period of the Napoleonic Wars and Prussia's struggle for independence, he tended to have in mind great and far-reaching political aims. This was the state of mind which guided his activities and harsh criticism of his country's policies, and which found clear theoretical expression in 1804 and 1812, when he twice outlined his outlook on war. This was also the state of mind wich favoured his conception of military decision.

However, with the end of the heroic period and with the return of the politics of European equilibrium, Clausewitz's concern shifted to the limited and complex considerations that these politics entailed. The problem that now claimed his attention was how to secure Prussia's status, strength, and stability within the European concert of powers against the dangers posed by both external and internal forces. This is what Paret calls the shift in Clausewitz's political outlook from an idealistic strain to an emphasis on *Ordnung*.[3] This perspective dominated his writings from that period on Prussia's foreign policy, and culminated in his works on European politics written in the last year of his life.

While it was not the direct cause of his conceptual change of course in 1827, the shift in Clausewitz's political state of mind provided a receptive background against which this change took root, and

[2] *On War*, VIII, 6B, p. 609. [3] Paret, *Clausewitz*, p. 421.

in the process became itself conscious and pronounced. Here too, Clausewitz's political perspectives and military conceptions went hand in hand and complemented each other.

This twofold nature of the transformation in Clausewitz's thought, political and military, explains why in July 1827 he put forward two ideas as guide-lines for the revision of his work. The new idea that war can be of two types, aiming either at completely overthrowing the enemy or at a limited objective, appears first. This idea is explained by another: the character and scale of military operations are closely linked to the character and scope of the political objectives; consequently, great significance is now attached to the conception that war is but a continuation of policy by other means.[4] This conception might have been integral to Clausewitz's thought throughout his life; but when both policy and war had been viewed in expansive terms, it could not have had much significance.

As the depth of the crisis that Clausewitz's outlook on war and conception of theory underwent in 1827 has not been realized fully, the exact nature of his intellectual development during his last years has also remained somewhat vague. This has been particularly so since, in his attempt to resolve the crisis, Clausewitz borrowed from his cultural environment new intellectual devices whose origins and nature have also remained a mystery. For the sake of clarity, these developments will be treated separately. First, the nature of the transformation in Clausewitz's thought will be examined. Then, the new intellectual devices which he employed and which made possible his particular solution to the problem he faced will be traced and explained.

In brief, the late development of Clausewitz's thought can only be understood within the context of his attempt to bridge the gulf in his theory of war by reconciling his old conceptions of the nature of war which he did not abandon, with his new awareness of the diversity of wars in reality. As largely noticed by Aron, the revision in Clausewitz's thought took shape in two main stages. Beginning at the end of Book VI and continuing in Book VIII, the last book of *On War*, it was further developed in Book I, the only one that Clausewitz succeeded in addressing in his plan to revise the whole of the work.

[4] 'Note of 10 July 1827', *On War*, p. 69; see App.

At the end of Book VI Clausewitz realizes that the war of destruction is not the exclusive form of war, and that by ignoring that which does not conform to it, theory becomes cut off from historical reality. We have seen the devastating threat that this growing realization posed to his conception of the nature of war, which was dominated by the Napoleonic experience. What was now to become of this conception? Initially, Clausewitz was unprepared to abandon it. It was therefore necessary for him to devise an intellectual structure which would accommodate it together with his new ideas. He therefore recognizes the existence of two types of war, *but* claims that the war of destruction expresses the nature of war and thus takes priority; against half-hearted war, an all-out one would always gain the upper hand. A new concept now becomes necessary: 'the urge for decision' is 'true war, or *absolute war* if we may call it that'.[5] Limited wars are not a genuine form of war but the results of various factors which exercise counter-influences on the real, absolute nature of war and modify it.[6]

In Book VIII Clausewitz examines the problem extensively and compromises with the same solution:

> What exactly is this nonconducting medium, this barrier that prevents a full discharge? Why is it that the philosophical conception is not sufficient? [*der philosophischen Vorstellungsweise nicht Genüge?*] The barrier in question is the vast array of factors, forces and conditions in national affairs that are affected by war . . . Logic comes to a stop in this labyrinth . . . This inconsistency . . . is the reason why war turns into something quite different from what it should be according to its concept [*Begriff*]—turns into something incoherent and incomplete.[7]

However, since theory cannot ignore reality, one must leave

> room for every sort of extraneous matter. We must allow for natural inertia, for all the friction of its parts, for all the inconsistency, imprecision, and timidity of man; and finally we must face the fact that war and its forms result from ideas, emotions, and conditions prevailing at the time . . . Theory must concede all this; but it has the duty to give priority to the absolute form of war.[8]

Various factors which are *alien* to the nature of war therefore prevent it from fully realizing its true character. These factors are of two kinds.

[5] *On War*, VI, 28, pp. 488–9; my italics.
[6] Ibid. VI, 30, p. 501.
[7] Ibid. VIII, 2, pp. 579–80.
[8] Ibid. pp. 580–1.

First, within war itself factors of friction and uncertainty operate; and man himself, the actual agent of war, is a creature whose timidity and limited comprehension prevent him from fully carrying out the demands imposed by the nature of war on those who want to succeed. Clausewitz had already developed this conception in a work which was probably written during his period at Koblenz. 'On Progress and Stagnation in Military Activity'. Since the constitutive element of war was fighting, it was necessary to explain how there could be lulls or periods of low activity in war at all.[9] Now Clausewitz expands this explanation to include not only periods of limited activity within war but whole limited wars. And he adds a new component by claiming that apart from the internal interfering factors, war is also constrained by external forces. It does not exist in isolation, but is affected by the historical conditions out of which it arises. In most cases, war is not the dominant activity in the life of nations. A variety of other values, goals, and considerations guide nations and prevent a maximization of the conduct of war. All these factors, interior and exterior, are alien to the nature of war, but limit its intensity in practice. Limited wars, which include most of the wars in history, are therefore the result.

Hence the relationship between war and politics, which encompasses most of the exterior factors mentioned above. In Book VIII, 'War Plans', Clausewitz expounds upon the full implications of his new ideas, asserting that the scale, character, and objectives of the military operations result largely from an interplay with the scope and nature of the political aims. The explication of this point in particular was an original contribution of Clausewitz, to be further developed only with the modern study of international relations. The influence of the political aim on the objective of operations, he wrote, 'will set its [the war's] course, prescribe the scale of means and effort which is required, and make its influence felt throughout down to the smallest operational detail'.[10] He elaborates on this point in the chapter on the 'Scale of the Military Objective and the Effort to be Made'. Both, he claims, are governed by 'the scale of political demands on either side', as well as by the characteristics of the belligerents and by their reciprocal actions which lead to the escalation

[9] 'Über das Fortschreiten und den Stillstand der Kriegerischen Begebenheiten', in *Zeitschrift für Preussische Geschichte und Landeskunde*, XV (1878), 233–40. The main ideas of this work appear in the early part of *On War* as ch. 16 of Bk. III.

[10] *On War*, VIII, 2, 579.

of the conflict.[11] This is also the theme of the chapter on 'The Effect of the Political Aim on the Military Objective'. He concludes that 'once this influence of the political objective on war is admitted, as it must be, there is no stopping it; consequently we must also be willing to wage such minimal wars which consist in *merely threatening the enemy*, with *negotiations held in reserve*'.[12] Finally, in the celebrated chapter entitled 'War Is an Instrument of Policy' Clausewitz fully elaborates the idea that war cannot be understood outside the political context:

War is only a branch of political activity . . . it is in no sense autonomous . . . The main lines along which military events progress, and to which they are restricted, are political lines that continue throughout the war into the subsequent peace . . . All the factors that go to make up war and determine its salient features—the strength and allies of each antagonist, the character of the people and their governments, and so forth . . . are these not all political?[13]

However, these widely quoted passages form only half of the picture. While all the characteristics of war are decisively influenced by politics, this influence is by no means part of the nature of war; on the contrary, the influence of politics is an *external* force which works *against* the true essence of war, harnesses it to its needs, and in the process modifies the imperatives which it imposes. 'In making use of war, policy evades all rigorous conclusions proceeding from the nature of war . . . [It] converts the overwhelmingly destructive element of war into a mere instrument.'[14]

The historical survey of the development of the art of war—to which we have already referred several times—was in fact far from being a detached, disinterested, historicist study.[15] We are now in a position to see its actual purpose. The survey was part of the process by which Clausewitz laboured to clarify his thoughts and aimed to examine concretely (*a*) the array of conditions which had prevented the realization of the true, absolute nature of war in most periods of history; (*b*) the circumstances in which this nature had appeared under the Romans, Alexander the Great and, obviously, the French Revolutionaries and Napoleon; and (*c*) the resulting theoretical conclusions.

11 Ibid. VIII, 3B, p. 585

12 Ibid. VIII, 6A, pp. 603–4.

13 Ibid. VIII, 6B, pp. 605–6.

14 Ibid.

15 As claimed by Paret, *Clausewitz*, pp. 348–9.

Under the *condottieri*, 'war lost many of its risks; its character was wholly changed, and no deduction from its proper nature was still applicable'. War was also limited during the *ancien régime*. 'All Europe rejoiced at this development. It was seen as a logical outcome of Enlightenment. This was a misconception. Enlightenment can never lead to inconsistency . . . [Indeed] so long as this was the general style of warfare with its violence limited in such strict and obvious ways, no one saw any inconsistency in it.' But the Revolution and Napoleon unleashed the forces contained in society, and war then 'took on an entirely different character, or rather closely approached its true character, its absolute perfection . . . untrammelled by any conventional restraints, [it] had broken loose in all its elemental fury'. What does the future hold? Will limited wars reappear? This, Clausewitz wrote, was difficult to answer, yet limited wars were not very likely in the future: 'once barriers—which in a sense consist only in man's ignorance of what is possible—are torn down, they are not so easily set up again.'[16]

What is the theoretical conclusion of all this?

> We can thus only say that the aims a belligerent adopts, and the resources he employs, must be governed by the particular characteristics of his own position; but they will also conform to the spirit of the age and to its general character. Finally, they *must also be drawn from the nature of war*.[17]

The compromise that Clausewitz worked out between his lifelong view of war and his new awareness that the conduct of war takes many forms and that this is so primarily because of changing political conditions, led him, therefore to develop a new theory which recognized two types of war, but regarded the one, absolute war, to be the genuine expression of the nature of war, and superior to the other. Yet, as he continued to probe his new ideas, this theory became insufficient. The chapter 'War is an Instrument of Policy' marked a further shift. If the understanding of war was dominated by its political function, the primacy given to absolute war lost much of its point. In the dilemma between his lifelong view of war on the one hand, and the diversity of political aims and military operations in historical reality on the other, Clausewitz was moving a further step towards the latter. Nevertheless, he did not altogether abandon

[16] *On War*, VIII, 3B, pp. 587, 591, 593.
[17] Ibid. VIII, 3, p. 594; Clausewitz's emphasis.

the core of his old conception, that the constitutive element of war, fighting, dominates the nature of war. Nor did he relinquish his belief in the superiority of the engagement and the clash of forces over all other military means. This was the basis for the amended compromise of Book I, which Clausewitz revised, as he had planned in July 1827, after he completed Book VIII, the last book of *On War*.[18]

In Book I, the essence of war is also presented as an eruption of force and violence: 'The impulse to destroy the enemy . . . is central to the very concept [*Begriff*] of war . . . war is an act of force, and there is no . . . limit to the application of that force.'[19] However, the unlimited nature of violence in war no longer relies directly on the notion that all-out war is clearly superior; Napoleonic warfare is no longer perceived as the only correct form of war. Violence in war is now presented in connection with tendencies towards escalation which are inherent in the interplay between the belligerents' aims and efforts.

Clausewitz's extensive argumentation can be summarized as follows: the nature of war implies that the aim of the belligerents must be the total destruction of the enemy's ability to fight, because otherwise his complete surrender will never be secured. In addition, since each side attempts to surpass the other's efforts, escalation and a tendency to maximize the mobilization of forces is also created.[20] Thus, 'were it a complete, untrammelled, absolute manifestation of violence (as the pure concept would require) war would of its own independent will . . . rule by the laws of its own nature, very much like a mine that can explode only in the manner or direction predetermined by the setting.'[21]

Why then, if war is 'pulsation of violence', does it not discharge itself in a single explosion? Why is it divided into several engagements, and why does it last for long periods of time, occasionally lacking energy and determination, and even falling into inactivity?[22] Clausewitz's reply in Book I elaborates the argument put forward in Book VIII (itself, as mentioned, an expansion of an early work) with one significant change; the lulls in military activity are no longer seen in a negative light, and the factors which explain

[18] See App.
[19] *On War*, I, 1, s.3, pp. 76–7.
[20] Ibid. I, 1, s. 3–5, p. 77.
[21] Ibid. I, 1, s.23, p. 87.
[22] Ibid. I, 1, pp. 79–80; s.12–19, pp. 81–5; the quotation is from s.23, p. 87.

them no longer include man's imperfection and timidity. War is not discharged in a single explosion due to the activity of various factors within war which are summarized for the most part by the concept of friction, and owing to influences, mainly political, which are exterior to war.

It is again important to understand that the influences of politics on war do not belong to the nature of war, but, on the contrary, contradict it. The political influences 'are the forces that give rise to war; the same forces circumscribe and moderate it. They themselves, however, are not part of war . . . To introduce the principle of moderation into the theory of war itself would always lead to . . . absurdity.'[23] Politics thus places itself above war and modifies it to suit its needs.

The modifications of the nature of war by the actual context in which war takes place, therefore completely change its character. At this point Clausewitz announces the opening of an entirely new discussion concentrating on the characteristics of war in reality.[24] The aims and means of war are no longer dictated by the maximal imperative inherent in the nature of war, but vary according to each particular case. The aim of war is shifted from the total overthrow of the enemy to the aim put forward by politics. Consequently, war is no longer conducted on a total scale but according to the requirements of the political aim. Clausewitz again discusses in depth the interaction between the scope of the political aim, its importance to the parties involved, and the scale of the effort required to achieve it.[25]

As indicated in the opening passage of Book I, chapter 2, Clausewitz's revision of his military theory is now applied to a closer examination of the purpose and means in war. This explication is highly significant because it clearly reveals how far Clausewitz had retracted from his belief in all-out decision. It can be summarized as follows: he now gives an equal status to a variety of war aims and operational objectives, or, to use the terminology of 1804, purposes of war and purposes in war. But he still regards the clash of forces as the dominant means for the attainment of any purpose, and treats with suspicion any means to evade it.

Following the arguments of chapter 1,

[23] *On War*, I, 1, s.3, p. 76.
[24] Ibid. I, 1, s.6, p. 78.
[25] Ibid. I, 1, s.10–11, pp. 80–1.

we can now see that in war many roads lead to success, and that they do not all involve the opponent's outright defeat. They range from *the destruction of the enemy's forces, the conquest of his territory, to a temporary occupation or invasion, to projects with an immediate political purpose, and finally to passively awaiting the enemy's attacks.*[26]

However, this plurality does not extend to the military means. Already in chapter 1, echoing his criticism of Bülow in 1805, Clausewitz had written: 'Kind-hearted people might of course think there was some ingenious way to disarm or defeat an enemy without too much bloodshed, and might imagine this is the true goal of the art of war. Pleasant as it sounds, it is a fallacy that must be exposed.'[27] Now, in chapter 2, Clausewitz wrote on the means in conducting war, reiterating his positions from 1804: 'There is only one: *combat*. However many forms combat takes . . . it is inherent in the very concept of war.'[28] The decisive clash of forces may be supported by other means. It may not even take place at all but still exert decisive influence merely by its probability and expected outcome. Yet, in any case, the 'destruction of the enemy forces is always the superior, more effective means, with which others cannot compete'.[29]

To conclude,

> our discussion has shown that while in war many different roads can lead to the goal, to the attainment of the political object, fighting is the only possible means. Everything is governed by a supreme law, *the decision by force of arms* . . . A commander who prefers another strategy must first be sure that his opponent . . . will not appeal to that supreme tribunal . . . If the political aims are small, the motives slight and tensions low, a prudent general may look for any way to avoid major crises and decisive actions . . . and finally reach a peaceful settlement. If his assumptions are sound and promise success we are not entitled to criticize him. But he must never forget that he is moving on devious paths where the god of war may catch him unaware.[30]

The men of the nineteenth century, criticized for tendentious interpretation, were therefore perfectly justified here in regarding Clausewitz's writings as the classic formulation of their belief in the dominance of the great battle. On this point Clausewitz held effectively the same position throughout his life. Indeed here too,

[26] Ibid. I, 2, p. 94.
[27] Ibid. I, 1, s.3, p. 75.
[28] Ibid. I, 2, p. 95.
[29] Ibid. p. 97.
[30] Ibid. p. 99.

it is in our period that Clausewitz's position has tended to be interpreted in terms that conveniently correspond to contemporary views of war.[31] This endemic misinterpretation of Clausewitz's ideas has been mainly due to the failure to grasp fully the origins and nature of the transformation of his thought and, particularly of the new intellectual forms in which this transformation was expressed.

It is not surprising that since publication, *On War* has had the reputation of being a very difficult and complicated philosophical work. The interested reader wishing to read the treatise which, from the time of the German wars of unification and the domination of the German military school was considered to be the masterpiece of military thought, encounters in the first and basic chapter of the book a highly complex intellectual structure, which hardly reveals a 'commonsense' understanding of war. He reads about 'absolute war' that was first defined in maximal and dramatic terms but was then totally overturned and assumed completely different expressions in reality as an instrument of policy. He has no means of understanding the nature and origins of this structure which was supported by an equally puzzling argument that explained why any limitation was alien to the nature of war, and elaborated the reasons for the lull in military activities and for their duration over substantial periods of time. Since its appearance, *On War* was therefore known for being much quoted but little read.

Ironically, this situation may have even enhanced Clausewitz's reputation. The men of the nineteenth century, in any case, emphasized most of the same points as Clausewitz's, and the obscure and elaborate reasoning of Books I and VIII only added to Clausewitz's image of profundity, as they were regarded as demonstrating the 'philosophical' manner of expression that was only to be expected of a philosophical masterpiece on war. It was generally

[31] Paret, for instance, writes: 'Clausewitz's supposed preference for the major, decisive battle, in particular, is an erroneous assumption, based on the very inability to follow his dialectic that he had predicted.' (Paret, *Clausewitz*, p. 369.) As evidence, Paret cites the passage on the variety of roads leading to success in war, but fails to cite Clausewitz's further emphasis that the pluralism of objectives is not matched by a pluralism of means. 'Clausewitz's dialectic' and the inability to follow it are discussed below. Here it is merely necessary to clarify that Clausewitz, of course, did not mention dialectic or anything to that effect when expressing apprehension that his work would be misunderstood (indeed, he did not mention dialectic anywhere).

assumed that this manner of reasoning was somehow related to the highly influential German idealistic philosophy (famous, or infamous, for the difficulties in understanding it) and especially to Hegel. Shortly after the publication of *On War* one critic, alluding precisely to this view, wrote:

> The streams whose crystal floods pour over nuggets of pure gold do not flow in any flat and accessible river bed but in a narrow rocky valley surrounded by gigantic Ideas, and over its entrance the mighty Spirit stands guard like a cherub with his sword, turning back all who expect to be admitted at the usual price for a play of ideas.[32]

Camon conveyed the same impression though from a point of view which was much less favourable than that of most of his contemporaries. In a much quoted passage he described Clausewitz as: 'The most German of Germans . . . In reading him one constantly has the feeling of being in a metaphysical fog.'[33] This was the closest one could get to admitting a failure to understand what Clausewitz actually had in mind.

Unfortunately, Clausewitz's modern interpreters too have been puzzled by his late intellectual formulations. We now have the advantage of possessing a sequence of Clausewitz's early works which provide an almost continuous picture of the development of his thought from 1804. Equally helpful is the fact that Clausewitz did not live to finish the revision of *On War*, and that the book we possess is therefore a draft that provides a history of the course of the work, almost linearly documenting the development of his thought, the problems he encountered, and his attempts to resolve them. Yet, the objective difficulties of the subject and biased approaches to it have reinforced each other in obscuring the nature and development of Clausewitz's ideas.

The interpretations of chapter 1 of Book I, which represent hardly more than an attempt to paraphrase Clausewitz's own words, have reflected this chronic confusion. In the struggle to understand his ideas it has often proved difficult to see the wood for the trees. Aron,

[32] *Preussische Militair-Literatur Zeitung*, 1832, quoted by Howard, 'The Influence of Clausewitz', in *On War*, p. 27.

[33] Camon, *Clausewitz*, p. viii. Bernard Brodie, one of the chief contributors to the 'Clausewitz renaissance', dismissed this complaint with the words: 'This is simply nonsense'. This remark is, however, an unfortunate reflection on Brodie's own 'high-spirited' commentary to *On War*: 'The Continuing Relevance of *On War*' and 'A Guide to the Reading of *On War*', in *On War*, the quotation is from p. 18.

whose interpretation of Clausewitz's major theses is the most comprehensive and penetrating, has unfortunately only perfected this tendency by attempting to place Clausewitz's formulations in chapter 1 in some meaningful general context. According to Aron, Clausewitz first uses an 'abstract model' which exists only in 'the world of concepts and ideals', and then shows how this model operates in reality.[34] Now firstly, Clausewitz never believed in a 'world of concepts and ideals'.[35] But, apart from that, why did Clausewitz need this kind of 'abstract model' at all? According to Aron, chapter 1 is simply the culmination of 'Clausewitz's system', which has always first distinguished sharply between concepts by way of 'antithesis' and then examined their actual appearance in reality.[36] Following in Schering's footsteps Aron, therefore, interprets the whole of Clausewitz's thought on the basis of the 'dialectic' between ends and means, moral and physical, defence and attack, and even number and morale, boldness and caution, and ambition and risk.[37]

The passage cited by Aron as revealing 'Clausewitz's method throughout his life' is taken from Clausewitz's critique of Bülow written in 1805. There, Clausewitz criticizes Bülow's definitions of strategy and tactics for not being clear and for overlapping each other. To define distinct concepts, Clausewitz writes, their boundaries must be delineated precisely. For this, the nature of the concept in question should be traced until it reveals a change at its extreme limit. This point is the concept's boundary.

A certain similarity in sound has led Aron to interpret an entirely different matter in the spirit of 1827–30.[38] The passage of 1805 is a lesson in clear and distinct definitions which looks like a typical product of the logic lessons that Clausewitz had just attended at the Institute, and which very probably reflected the influence of Kant, the great distinction-maker, through the medium of Kiesewetter.[39]

[34] Aron, *Clausewitz*, pp. 106, 114.

[35] In this respect a trans. of Clausewitz's *Abstraction* and *Wirklichbkeit* (*On War*, I, 1, p. 6), or *wirkliche Welt* and *blosse Beggriff* (*On War*, I, 1, p. 8) as 'real world' and 'abstract world' may be misleading. Clausewitz never speaks of an abstract world or a world of ideas.

[36] Aron, *Clausewitz*, pp. 104, 111.

[37] Ibid. 322, 325.

[38] 'Bülow', in Hahliveg (ed.), *Verstreute kleine Schriften*, p. 68. It must be noted that the word 'extreme' (*extrem*) used in 1805, does not appear at all in Bk. I, ch. 1. Again the English trans. might be misleading here. In describing the tendency of war to magnify, Clausewitz consistently uses the term *Äusserst*.

[39] As suggested by Gallie; see below, n. 42.

It is by no means said there that the nature of the concept lies at its extreme; on the contrary, the concept's extreme boundaries are revealed by the very fact that henceforth, by definition, the essence of the concept ceases to be in force. Throughout his life Clausewitz defined his subject-matter clearly and distinctively and never saw the essence of a phenomenon in its most extreme expression. That fighting, the constitutive element of war, should be interpreted in expansive terms stems, as we have seen, not from Clausewitz's 'logical method' but from his lifelong outlook on war based on the dominating experience of his age. In his attempt to gain a coherent understanding of the mystery of Clausewitz's later formulations, Aron has created a myth of 'Clausewitz's lifelong method'.

The myth is in fact revealed by Aron's own argument. 'All his life,' he wrote, 'Clausewitz practised the method put forward in 1805, or rather half of this method; namely he chose, as the point of departure, extremes or complete antitheses. There is hardly a trace of the search for boundaries in the Treatise [*On War*].'[40] Indeed, there is no search for boundaries in *On War*, but this is precisely the issue in 1805; there may be antitheses in the latter parts of *On War*, but there are none in 1805! As an example of the 'system of antitheses' which is supposed to have characterized Clausewitz's writing throughout his life, Aron turns to the end of Book VI of *On War* (written in 1826–7).[41] This is no coincidence; no earlier example exists. In all his works prior to *On War* and in most of *On War* itself, nothing in Clausewitz's writing, generally characterized by its clarity and realistic approach, comes close to the formulations of his last years which gave his work the reputation of being covered by 'metaphysical fog'. This should have been obvious. Though largely aware of the transformation of Clausewitz's military outlook, Aron failed to realize its scope and implications for Clausewitz's theoretical approach. While he noted the late appearance of the concept of 'absolute war' and its close link to Clausewitz's late development, he sought to explain it by referring to an early 'method'. Instead of clarifying Clausewitz's late ideas, he obscured his earlier ones as well.

The fact that something was very wrong with Clausewitz's reasoning in Books VIII and I, and consequently also in the way it was usually interpreted was finally noticed by W. B. Gallie. Clausewitz's interpreters, he wrote, struggled in vain to explain his

[40] Aron, *Clausewitz*, p. 79. [41] Ibid.

intellectual structure, mistakenly assuming that this structure was coherent. Not being a specialist on Clausewitz, Gallie himself failed to reveal the historical and intellectual origins of Clausewitz's problematic formulations. He was not aware of the development of Clausewitz's ideas, accepted Aron's conception of 'Clausewitz's lifelong method' and merely sought to correct its 'logic'. Yet, Gallie at last exposed the fact that had embarrassed Clausewitz's interpreters: Clausewitz's conceptions, he maintained, were the result of a tension which could not be reconciled between his definition of war itself and his notion that war was a political means.[42]

A full understanding of the theoretical formulations that have created so much confusion can only be achieved by realizing the interaction between the theoretical crisis in which Clausewitz found himself in 1827 and the intellectual devices that his cultural environment offered him at that same time. The preservation of the core of his old conceptions within his new ones, despite their contradictory nature, was made possible, and even perceived by Clausewitz as an achievement, by borrowing from the most ambitious intellectual attempt at an all-encompassing and integrative explanation of all the contrasts and contradictions of reality; namely, the German idealistic philosophy which was elevated by Hegel at precisely that time to a zenith of power, and whose influence on Clausewitz has always been the subject of wonder and speculation.

In a cautious attempt to delineate the affinity of Clausewitz's thought to German idealism, Paret stressed in particular that from the intellectual climate of the period, Clausewitz absorbed the emphasis of idealism on the integrative interrelation of all phenomena as well as a tendency to a dialectic discussion in terms of theses and antitheses, contradictions, polarity, activity and passivity, positive and negative.[43] In fact, Paret too projected the image of Clausewitz's late work on his earlier writings. From his youth until the final stages of his work on *On War*, Clausewitz shows no substantial affinity to the distinctive doctrines of idealism; but he does reveal the decisive influence of these doctrines during his last years.

First, the fact that has somehow been lost sight of must be stressed again; in all of Clausewitz's extensive writings until the last stage of

[42] W. B. Gallie, 'Clausewitz On the Nature of War', *Philosophers of Peace and War, Kant, Clausewitz, Marx, Engels and Tolstoy* (Cambridge, 1978), esp. pp. 48–65.

[43] Paret, *Clausewitz*, esp. pp. 5, 85, 150–1.

his life, there are no theses and antitheses, no polarity or dialectic (unless of course one reads them into ordinary reasoning and simple contrasts and reciprocal relations) nor, indeed, any mention of 'absolute war'. Nor do they appear in the early or unrevised books of *On War*, which continue Clausewitz's lifelong train of thought. As for the quest for an all-encompassing and comprehensive explanation of reality, this had been one of the principal themes of the German Movement as a whole from the days of the 'Storm and Stress'. While Clausewitz continued this quest throughout his life, only in the last phase of his work did it assume the totally integrative character unique to idealism.

Clausewitz's world-view and intellectual affinities should also be understood from another perspective and from a psychological point of view. As pointed out by Paret, Clausewitz was not a professional philosopher but a typical educated representative of his period who absorbed attitudes and scraps of ideas, not necessarily at first hand, from his cultural environment.[44] To this, however, it should be added that unlike any typically educated person of his period, Clausewitz was throughout his life motivated by the desire to work out a comprehensive view of war, and naturally he was highly sensitive to anything in his cultural environment which could have had a bearing on the realization of this aim. This kind of involvement and interest partly explains the fact that Clausewitz drew mainly on what had already been considered classic literature: Machiavelli, Montesquieu, the great figures of the 'Storm and Stress' movement and German *Klassizismus*, Kant, and so on. By contrast, Fichte's or Schelling's idealism (as, for that matter, Romanticism) was in the first decade of the nineteenth century a radical trend, albeit of wide-ranging reputation. As we have seen, Clausewitz shared many of the ideas of the Romantics but was far from agreeing with their overall outlook. The same applied to idealism. In a letter to his fiancée on 15 April 1808, Clausewitz refers to one of Fichte's political works: 'he has a manner of reasoning that pleases me very much, and I felt that all my tendency to speculative reasoning was awakened and stimulated again'.[45] Later, following Fichte's article on Machiavelli, Clausewitz even wrote directly to the famous philosopher. However, there is no sign that he was effectively influenced by Fichte's philosophy or dialectic. On the contrary, while sharing Fichte's

[44] Ibid. 151.

[45] Schwartz, *Leben*, i. 305.

patriotic sentiments and emphases on moral forces and creativity, Clausewitz, as noted by Paret, was clearly a 'realist' and rejected purely spiritual entities, any form of 'mysticism' and teleological conceptions of history.[46] In short, he shared no affinity with idealistic metaphysics. He aimed at a realistic military theory, firmly grounded in historical experience and in the nature of war.

However, by 1826–7 both Clausewitz's theoretical expectations and the status and power of the idealistic philosophy had changed drastically and their paths had crossed. It became clear to Clausewitz that there was a serious discrepancy between his conception of the universal nature of war and the test of historical experience. While regarding both to be indispensable, he was forced to reject one of them. Fortunately, in the same years in Berlin, Clausewitz's city of residence, Hegel's idealism was reaching a climax of influence, unequalled in Germany since the days of Kant. And one of the chief lessons of this philosophy was that all the contrasts and contradictions of reality were actually but differing aspects of a single unity. In this, the 'identity' ideal of all phenomena inherent in the German Movement was brought to its pinnacle. Clausewitz was, therefore, not compelled to resolve the contradiction created in his mind by abandoning one of the two conceptions that he regarded as essential; on the contrary, resolving this contradiction, while keeping its components by viewing them from a higher standpoint, was now perceived as an achievement and an indication that his theory of war was on the right systematical road.

Was Clausewitz then a disciple of Hegel, and if so, how was he influenced? This question has been the cause of much speculation since the publication of *On War*, repeatedly expressed by as different and remote commentators as the above-mentioned Prussian military critic of 1832 and Lenin.[47] The first attempt to tackle it was made in 1911 by Lieutenant-Colonel Paul Creuzinger in *Hegel's Influence on Clausewitz*.[48] If we are to believe Creuzinger, there is not a single idea in *On War*, from tactical conceptions to strategical outlook, that is not shaped by Hegel's influence. Creuzinger knew that in all probability Clausewitz could only have been influenced

[46] Paret, *Clausewitz*, pp. 151, 350; and p. 185 of this work.

[47] V. I. Lenin, 'The Collapse of the Second International', *Collected Works* (Moscow, 1964), 21. p. 219.

[48] Paul Creuzinger, *Hegels Einfluss auf Clausewitz* (Berlin, 1911). Lenin possibly relied on this work in his explicit presentation of Clausewitz as Hegel's disciple.

by Hegel from the 1820s, for prior to that, Hegel had been relatively unknown. But as Creuzinger was only familiar with *On War*, he was unaware of the fact that most of the conceptions that he attributed to Hegel's influence had already been outlined by Clausewitz in his early works.

Unfortunately, Creuzinger's work placed the whole argument on a totally misleading course. In reaction to Creuzinger, Schering laboured to show that Clausewitz's supposed dialectic was not exactly similar to Hegel's.[49] In Schering's footsteps went both Paret, who added that Clausewitz's dialectic could have been influenced by many others apart from Hegel,[50] and Aron, to whom Schering's argument appeared particularly valid in view of the abundance of 'antitheses' and dialectic relationships he found in Clausewitz's work. Aron also went to great lengths to show that Clausewitz's conceptions had no affinity to Hegel's metaphysics.[51] While Schering, Paret, and Aron did not totally rule out the possibility that Hegel might have somewhat influenced Clausewitz, they dismissed this possibility almost completely and conferred upon it (in view of Creuzinger's assertions, justifiably) a dubious image.

What, then, do we know about Clausewitz's affinity to Hegel? In contrast to Fichte's case, we have no reference to Hegel in Clausewitz's writings. Yet this does not mean much; in Clausewitz's letters to Marie, the main source for his biography, there is a large gap in the 1820s when they lived together in Berlin; and these were precisely the years when Hegel served as rector of the University of Berlin and his reputation achieved unprecedented heights. Indeed, we do possess contemporary evidence, revealed by Paret, which almost certainly proves that Clausewitz was acquainted with Hegel in the salons of Berlin.[52]

As for the influence of Hegel's ideas, we do not know whether, and how much, Clausewitz read Hegel or indeed understood him, or, alternatively, whether he absorbed some of Hegel's ideas from the intellectual environment in Berlin. However, all that we do know of Clausewitz's intellectual interests and involvement makes it highly improbable that the philosophy which achieved such widespread

[49] Schering, *Kriegsphilosophie*, pp. 111–19.

[50] Paret, *Clausewitz*, pp. 84, 150.

[51] Aron, *Clausewitz*, pp. 321–31.

[52] H. Hoffman von Fallersleben, *Mein Leben* (Hanover, 1868) i. 311–12; cited by Paret, *Clausewitz*, p. 316.

influence failed to attract his attention. And, above all, we have the highly distinctive, new intellectual patterns in his late work to support this.

Indeed, this work does not reveal any affinity to Hegel's metaphysics, idealism, or conception of history. But it does reveal what appears to be a direct influence of Hegel's political and social ideas, which will be discussed in the next section. Furthermore, it reveals a new and vigorous use of dialectic tools, along with a much stronger comprehensive and integrative ideal. The question as to whether this new dialectic was exactly like Hegel's, or the argument that from his youth Clausewitz had come in contact with the dialectics of Fichte, Schleiermacher and, perhaps, Schelling, and the all-embracing 'identity' quest of the German Movement, miss the point. Clausewitz adapted scraps of ideas to his needs, and his distinctive use of dialectic tools together with a new forceful emphasis on the totally integrative nature of theory only made an appearance in the later stages of his work, during the period in which idealism and Hegel's influence surged to a peak.

The integrative quest of the period is forcefully revealed in Clausewitz's early treatise on war in 1816–18, where he betrays a certain fear that his work, intelligent as it might be, lacks the real internal, unifying logic to be *the* desired 'Theory of War'. 'Perhaps a greater mind,' he wrote, 'will soon appear to replace these individual nuggets with a single whole cast of solid metal, free from all impurity.'[53] In this respect the transition from Book VI, 'Defence', to Book VII, 'The Attack', marked a turning-point, apparently brought about by two discussions in which Clausewitz was then engaged. The first was the interesting interrelationship between defence and attack, already vaguely emerging in the *Principles of War for the Crown Prince* (1812), but extensively developed in Book VI.[54] Elaborating on this, Clausewitz appears to have come to the view that this interrelationship could perhaps be given a tighter theoretical expression. Precisely then, at the end of Book VI, the problem of the two types of war and the discrepancy between the nature of war and historical experience was added. Both issues now invited the employment of a new and highly acclaimed intellectual device: dialectic reconciliation.

[53] 'Author's Preface', *On War*, pp. 61–2. [54] See p. 207, n. 26.

In Book VII, on attack, Clausewitz's attraction to this new device is still only alluded to, but unmistakably so. The book opens with a chapter on the relationship between attack and defence:

Where two concepts [*Begriffe*] form true logical contrasts [*Gegensätze*],[55] each complementary to the other, then fundamentally each is implied in the other. The limitation of our mind may not allow us to comprehend both simultaneously, and to discover by contrast the totality [*Totalität*] of one in the totality of the other. Nevertheless each will shed enough reciprocal light to clarify many of the details.[56]

This distinctive formulation, hitherto unprecedented in his writings, strikingly shows that the dialectical reasoning which was becoming dominant in Clausewitz's intellectual environment by the mid-1820s, influenced his own thought decisively. While apart from this opening statement Clausewitz hardly employed dialectic in Book VII, he used it with increasing skill and in a highly significant role in Book VIII and in the revision of Book I.

In the famous chapter 'War Is an Instrument of Policy', Clausewitz finally resolves the contradiction in his mind between war as the all-out use of force and the varying degrees of limited war revealed in historical experience, without relinquishing either of these ideas. War as a political and multi-faceted phenomenon is the unity that fuses the pure nature of war, which constitutes merely a partial understanding of reality, with the political conditions and requirements:

Up to now, we have considered the difference that distinguishes the nature of war [*Natur des Krieges*] from every other human interest, individual or social . . . We have examined this incompatibility from various angles so that none of its conflicting elements should be missed. Now we must seek out the unity into which these contradictory elements combine in real life, which they do by partly neutralizing one another . . . Being incomplete and self-contradictory it [war] cannot follow its own laws, but has to be treated as a part of some other whole; the name of which is policy . . . Thus the contradictions in which war involves . . . man, are resolved . . . Only if war is looked at in this way does its unity reappear; only then can we see that all wars are things of the same nature.[57]

[55] Since here, as well as in Bks. VIII and I, Clausewitz never used the concept *Idee*, it would perhaps be preferable not to translate *Begriff* and *Gegensätze* as idea and antithesis which tend to assume the required.

[56] *On War*, VII, 1, p. 523.

[57] Ibid. VIII, 6B, pp. 605–6.

The unity of the phenomenon of war, that is, the constitutive element common to all wars, is salvaged. The 'primordial violence, hatred, and enmity' of the nature of war are directed by the 'commander's creative spirit' through the 'play of chance and probability' to achieve the political aim. This is the 'remarkable trinity' which is presented by Clausewitz at the end of the first chapter of Book I, and which makes war 'more than a true chameleon that slightly adapts its characteristics to the given case'.[58]

Indeed, in the first chapters of Book I, Clausewitz's dialectic reaches its peak, and his conception of the nature of war finds its place in the actual diversity of war which previously threatened to invalidate it. Clausewitz has not become an idealist nor does he believe in any 'world of ideas'. He considered the concept of absolute war as an analysis of the actual forces which in his view comprise the nature of war. It was possible for him to maintain this view by claiming that this nature never existed in isolation, but always interacted with the other forces and influences of reality, chiefly politics, which modified and governed its original tendencies. A new intellectual tool assisted him in devising what he regarded as an adequate solution to the crisis into which his universal theory of war had fallen in 1827.

Political and Ethical World-View

The idea that the military command had to be subordinated to the political leadership was regarded by Clausewitz as a direct implication of the close link between the conduct of war and political aims. This idea stemmed, however, from much deeper historical and intellectual origins, and reflected Clausewitz's political and ethical outlook.

The accepted view that Clausewitz refrained from dealing with the ethical aspects of war, and that he confined himself to the study of war 'as it is',[59] requires careful historical scrutiny, though based on an apparently unequivocal statement by Clausewitz himself. After describing the advantages of guerrilla warfare he wrote: 'the question only remains whether mankind at large will gain by this further expansion of the element of war; a question to which the answer should be the same as to the question of war itself. We shall leave

[58] *On War*, I, 1, 28, p. 89.

[59] See e.g. Werner Hahlweg, *Carl von Clausewitz* (Göttingen, 1957), 62; cited with approval by Paret, *Clausewitz*, p. 352; see also pp. 348–9.

both to the philosophers.'[60] This statement also corresponds with Clausewitz's general tendency to avoid too direct a reference to philosophical questions about which he did not feel professionally qualified, and which might expose his work to criticism outside the military sphere.

However, to deduce from this that Clausewitz had no views on ethics in the framework of his general world-view, or that his outlook on war was divorced from this world-view seems inconceivable, particularly as we are dealing with a man for whom a comprehensive understanding of reality was a genuine need and the object of continuous efforts, who had an acute historical sense, and whose life was marked by a deep political commitment expressed in highly charged statements. Paret emphasizes that Clausewitz's historicist approach rendered his historical outlook almost totally free from value-judgements which assume universal, supra historical standards of measurements. This is reinforced, according to Paret, by Clausewitz's special point of view; he avoided ideological positions because his concern was with 'the diplomatic and military efficiency of any political community', expressed in 'results, which are judged in terms of energy and force'.[61] Though Paret's work is the most extensive study of Clausewitz's affinity to the state, this interpretation in fact totally obscures the real context of that affinity and its implications for the understanding of Clausewitz's world-view as a whole. 'Which Side was Clausewitz On?' asked C. B. A. Behrens in a concise and penetrating review of Paret's book, undermining the almost liberal image that Clausewitz has acquired in the West of today.[62] Indeed, 'military and political efficiency of political communities judged in terms of energy and force' is not a valueless standard of measurement; rather, it is a striking expression of Clausewitz's political and ethical outlook, deeply embedded in his intellectual milieu.

Here too, Clausewitz was a true child of his time. He operated during the fateful transition of German national consciousness from its Enlightenment, eighteenth-century forms, as expressed either in the humanitarian, cosmopolitan, and cultural orientation of, for example, Kant, Herder, Möser, and Schiller, or in the strict and limited framework of the absolutist state. These forms were transformed radically with the French imperialist threat, the

[60] *On War*, VI, 26, p. 479.

[61] Paret, *Clausewitz*, pp. 348, 352.

[62] C. B. A. Behrens, 'Which Side was Clausewitz On?' in *The New York Review of Books*, 14 Oct. 1976.

humiliating defeats at the hands of Napoleon, and the political settlements that he imposed on Germany. The fervent awakening of the German national movement which resulted, swept throughout society in a highly political form and with a strong emphasis on the dominant role of the state. These trends found expression in the deeds and the legend of the German war of independence of 1813, and were formulated into what was to be called the German conception of the state. This conception was carried on by the German historical school, strengthened by the failure of the liberal vision in 1848, and sanctified after the establishment of the German Reich by Bismarck's ingenious *Realpolitik*.[63]

The intention here is obviously not to understand Clausewitz in Treitschke's terms, or against the background of the height of militarism and social Darwinism in Wilhelmine Germany. However, Clausewitz's political and ethical outlook, and thus also his view of war, cannot be understood without realizing his position during the crisis of Prussian absolutism and at the formative period of a famous and highly influential intellectual tradition that gave Germany its unique place, separate from the political philosophy of the liberal West.

'German thought' wrote Troeltsch, 'whether in politics or in history or in ethics, is based on the ideas of the Romantic Counter-Revolution.'[64] Clausewitz operated in the historical and intellectual environment that, among others, gave rise to Fichte, Adam Müller, Savigny, and Hegel, all of whom, incidently, he probably knew personally. And a few years after his death, Ranke's influence started to shape the perspectives of German historical scholarship. With all these men Clausewitz shared certain broad assumptions that were

[63] See esp. R. L. F. Meinecke's celebrated works: *Cosmopolitanism and the National State* (Munich & Berlin, 1907; Princeton, 1970), at once an account of the process outlined above, and the most prominent explication of the German historical position by one of its greatest representatives; the same twofold significance belongs to his *Machiavellism, the Doctrine of raison d'etat and its Place in Modern History* (Munich, 1924; London, 1957), an expansion of the theme of the previous work, interpreting the political thought of the modern period, and written in a less optimistic mood after the First World War. Similarly illuminating and representative is E. Troeltsch, 'The Idea of Natural Law and Humanity in World Politics', App. to O. Gierke, *Natural Law and the Theory of Society 1500–1800* (Cambridge, 1934), 201–22. From the sea of literature written on the 'German Problem', see L. Krieger, *The German Idea of Freedom, History of a Political Tradition* (Boston, 1957); and G. G. Iggers, *The German Conception of History, the German Tradition of Historical Thought from Herder to the Present* (Middletown, Conn., 1968), a penetrating account and critique of the intellectual assumptions of the German historical school.

[64] Troeltsch, 'The Idea of Natural Law' in Gierke, *Natural Law*, p. 203.

to be common to the German conception of the state. In general terms these basic assumptions were: by and large, the state was the framework in which civilized communities developed; internally, the state was the higher and unifying expression of communal life; externally, owing to the natural dynamics in a society of sovereign entities, the interaction between states was governed by considerations of *raison d'état* or *Realpolitik*; within such a framework of relations, war had an integral part.

To do justice to Clausewitz's political and ethical outlook, which is mostly indirectly stated in his works, wider space than this volume can offer is obviously required. In the following discussion, therefore, only the principal themes of this outlook are mentioned in their relation to Clausewitz's view of war, and the first is war within the framework of political and international reality.

Clausewitz's concern with Machiavelli was part of a general revival of interest in Machiavelli in Germany, promoted most significantly by Fichte. This was one of the striking expressions of the new political attitudes that Clausewitz shared with the generation who witnessed the Napoleonic wars and the awakening of German national sentiment.[65] We have already noted some aspects of his affinity to Machiavelli, especially the importance placed on the vitality and dynamism of the political community, the call for great policies, and the rejection of half-measures. Clausewitz and Fichte, like most of their contemporaries, applied the darker side of Machiavelli's teaching to foreign affairs.[66] As noted by Paret, they both believed that Machiavelli's ideas on the relationship between the prince and his subjects mainly reflected his own political conditions of the Italian Renaissance, and no longer suited the enlightened societies of their own time. However, they thought that in the relations between states, where no law was in force, Machiavelli's conceptions were penetrating. 'Those who affect disgust for his [Machiavelli's] principles', wrote Clausewitz in 1807–8, 'are a kind of humanistic "petit-maîtres". What he says about the princes' policies toward their subjects is certainly largely outdated, because the condition of states have very much changed since his times . . . But this author is

[65] See esp. A. Elkan, 'Die Entdeckung Machiavellis in Deutschland zu Beginn des 19 Jahrhunderts', *Historische Zeitschrift*, CXIX (1919), 427–58.

[66] For a comprehensive discussion of Clausewitz, Fichte, and Machiavelli see again: Paret, *Clausewitz*, pp. 169–79.

especially instructive in regard to foreign relations.'[67] These are governed by considerations of *raison d'état*, and are dominated by the direct and implied use of force. Enlightened people, Fichte maintained, must face this reality.[68]

This view, which combined fundamental attitudes with an evaluation of the international reality in Europe, also found consistent expression in Clausewitz's analyses of contemporary political questions. In 'Umtriebe' written in the early 1820s, Clausewitz criticized the Romantic and liberal demands for the national unification of Germany. In a remarkable anticipation of the events of 1848 and 1866–70, he wrote:

> Germany can reach political unity in *one* way only, through the sword, when one state subdues all others. The time has not arrived for such subjugation, and if it should ever come it is impossible to predict at present which of the German states will become master of the others.[69]

Two works written by Clausewitz in the last year of his life, 'The Conditions in Europe Since the Polish Partitions' and 'Reducing the Many Political Questions that Preoccupy Germany, to the Question of Our Existence', are classic examples of what Meinecke described with satisfaction as the growing recognition in Germany of the primacy of *raison d'état* in political reality, as opposed to the old conceptions of cosmopolitan liberalism. In these works, Clausewitz discussed the questions preoccupying educated public opinion in Germany during the revolutions of 1830–1, in particular the Polish, Belgian, and Italian demands for unification and national independence which had been received with sympathy. His historical and political analysis focused exclusively on the *Realpolitik* considerations of Prussia and Germany, with total disregard not only for humanitarian concerns but also for any political considerations other than those derived from *raison d'état*, such as the domestic and social implications with which the events of 1830–1 were obviously imbued. According to Clausewitz, it was necessary for the

[67] Rothfels (ed.), *Schriften*, p. 63. For a similar way of thinking in the case of Fichte, see Paret, *Clausewitz*, p. 175.

[68] It is only too instructive that Meinecke describes Machiavelli as the first to reveal the true nature of the relation between states (*The Doctrine of raison d'état*, esp. ch. 1), and points to his revival in Germany with Fichte as marking a sobering process in German political thought, from 18th-cent. conceptions to a correct view of the state's true role (*Cosmopolitanism*, esp. ch. 6).

[69] 'Umtriebe' in Rothfels (ed.), *Schriften*, p. 171.

German people to oppose the independence of Poland, Belgium, and Italy because of those countries' natural allegiance to France. Their independence would severely impair the traditional German interest in preventing French hegemony in Europe.[70]

That these works were clearly directed against the prevailing views of liberal public opinion, was revealed by Clausewitz himself:

I sought to make it clear to the good people that something besides *cosmopolitanism* should determine our position on the Belgian, Polish and other questions, that German independence was in the gravest danger, and that it was time to think about ourselves.[71]

This approach, which Clausewitz regarded as exposing reality as it actually was, as against liberal illusions, in fact incorporated a strong political preference for, and to a large extent was itself an unconscious expression of, a particular ideological point of view peculiar to the new attitudes in Germany.[72] The analysis in terms of *raison d'état* indeed called attention to certain characteristics of international relations, but also both explicitly and implicitly advocated political aims that focused on the power and stability of the state. This was the essence of Clausewitz's political outlook both on domestic affairs, which will be discussed later, and on foreign relations.

The new attitudes towards the essence and role of the state found their classic philosophical formulation in Hegel's *The Philosophy of Right*, one of the most influential works of political philosophy in the nineteenth century, published in Berlin in 1821. The affinity of Clausewitz's ideas to this famous work has, unfortunately, fallen victim to the general confusion concerning Hegel's influence on Clausewitz. Clausewitz was not a Hegelian, but some of the opinions which he had held from his youth and which had dominated his intellectual milieu appear to have received a definitive and distinctive conceptualization under the influence of Hegel's ideas.

According to Hegel, social ethics are the result of the general and unifying point of view achieved within the framework of the state.

[70] 'Die Verhältnisse Europas seit der Teilung Polens' and 'Zurückführung der vielen politischen Fragen, welche Deutschland beschäftigen, auf die unserer Gesamtexistenz' in Rothfels (ed.), *Schriften*, pp. 222–38. For a full discussion see Paret, *Clausewitz*, pp. 406–9.

[71] 21 Feb. 1831, in Schwartz, *Leben*, ii. 313; cited by Paret, *Clausewitz*, p. 406; my emphasis.

[72] This point was forcefully made in relation to the whole of the German tradition by Iggers, *The German Conception of History*, esp. p. 17.

Since in international society there exists no supreme authority which could enforce such norms of behaviour, so-called international law can only be a pale copy of the intra-state system, and is dependent on the good will of the states involved.[73] 'Attached to force', wrote Clausewitz at the opening of *On War*, 'are certain self-imposed, imperceptible limitations hardly worth mentioning, known as international law and custom, but they scarcely weaken it . . . moral force has no existence save as expressed in the state and the law.'[74]

From this view of the international system and the limits of moral order stems also the role and moral status of war. As mentioned above, the belief that this question finds no expression in Clausewitz's work, does not take into account the full scope and context of his world-view. Since in the international arena the rule of law does not exist and the prevailing behaviour is of almost unrestrained individualism, war is inherent in the system. 'People in our contemporary states must naturally love peace and hate war,' wrote Lossau; but states have interests that generate conflicts, 'and since no tribunal can resolve their conflicts, they seek justice by themselves. *Wars are therefore the exterior means of states to achieve by violence what they cannot achieve by peaceful means.*'[75] So long as this is the case, judging war by moral standards of measurement, derived from the intra-state reality of the civilized nations, would be pointless and wishful thinking and cannot be harmonized with reality. It was characteristic of the German Movement to reject any unsubstantiated attempt to shut out major parts of reality with kind-hearted ideals and standards of measurement of universal pretension.[76] In his *Apologie de la guerre* (1813), directed against Kant and the ideas of the eighteenth century, Rühle von Lilienstern, influenced by his friend Adam Müller, justified war by the realities of human behaviour and political life.[77] Furthermore, the idea that war also had a positive role to play in the development of civilization, and that it might even

[73] G. W. F. Hegel, *The Philosophy of Right* (Oxford, 1942), 'International Law', articles 330–40, pp. 212–16.

[74] *On War*, I, i, s.2, p. 75.

[75] Lossau, *Der Krieg*, p. 3; for the famous dictum see also p. 4.

[76] 'War', wrote Hegel, 'is not to be regarded as an absolute evil and as a purely external accident, which itself therefore has some accidental cause, be it injustices, the passions of nations or the holders of power, etc., or in short, something or other which ought not to be. It is to what is by nature accidental that accidents happen.' Thus, 'wars occur when the necessity of the case requires'. Hegel, *The Philosophy of Right*, article 324, p. 209; addition, p. 296.

[77] See above, Ch. 8. I, n. 44.

have an essential role in strengthening the social body, was also characteristic of the German Movement.[78] This too implied that the evaluation of war according to the categories of accepted social morals was narrow-sighted and inadequate.

This widely held view found a striking expression even with a prominent humanist such as Wilhelm von Humboldt, one of the chief reformers and a personal acquaintance of Clausewitz. In his *Limits of the State* (1791), Humboldt writes that war is 'one of the most wholesome manifestations that plays a role in the education of the human race'. War 'alone gives to the total structure the strength and the diversity without which facility would be weakness and unity would be void'. Anticipating the reformers, he wrote that professional armies should be replaced by a national army in order to 'inspire the citizen with a spirit of true war'.[79] In a memorandum concerning the army's budget in 1817, Humboldt, then Prussia's minister of education, listed the 'influence on the character of the nation' among the contributions of a strong army.[80]

'In times of peace', wrote Hegel, 'the particular spheres and functions pursue the path of satisfying their particular aims and minding their own business . . . In a situation of exigency, however, whether in home or foreign affairs, the organism of which these particular spheres are members fuses into [one].' Thus, 'war is the state of affairs which deals in earnest with the vanity of temporal goods and concerns . . . Corruption in nations would be the product of prolonged, let alone "perpetual", peace.'[81] Clausewitz expressed this *Zeitgeist* in almost identical terms. In *On War* he wrote the following passages, which are hardly ever cited:

Today practically no means other than war will educate a people in this spirit of boldness . . . Nothing else will counteract the softness and the desire

[78] See even Kant, 'Idea for a Universal History from a Cosmopolitan Point of View', and 'Perpetual Peace', in *Kant On History* (Indianapolis, 1963), 15–16, 19, 110–11; cited by Iggers, *The German Conception of History*, p. 47.

[79] Wilhelm von Humboldt, 'Ideen zu einem Versuch die Grenzen der Wirksamkeit des Staats zu bestimmen' in *Gesammelte Schriften* (Berlin, 1903–36), i. 137; cited by Iggers, *The German Conception of History*, p. 97. The book was published in full only in 1851, but parts of it, including the ch. on war appeared immediately after being written; Iggers, p. 297 n. 30. Cf. Humboldt with Clausewitz's letter to Fichte, p. 186 of this work.

[80] Humboldt, *Gesammelte Schriften*, xii. 170; cited by Iggers, *The German Conception of History*, p. 54.

[81] Hegel, *The Philosophy of Right*, article 278, p. 180–1; article 324, p. 210, and addition, p. 295.

for ease which debase the people in times of growing prosperity and increasing trade. A people and nation can hope for a strong position in the world only if national character and familiarity with war fortify each other by continual interaction.[82]

In his attitude towards the place of war within the human reality, Clausewitz was also, therefore, a true child of his times, and reflected the transformation of German national and political consciousness at the turn of the nineteenth century. Since his youth he had firmly believed—though he did not formulate this systematically—that the international arena was dominated by the behaviour of sovereign states guided by considerations of *raison d'état* in which power played the major role. In this reality, war was an immanent phenomenon, and perhaps also one which was not lacking in advantages; judging it by ethical categories taken from the social context was therefore pointless.

This outlook, which regards the state as the central organ of political reality, and which reflects the patriotic ideal that guided Clausewitz throughout his life, is also manifest in his views on the internal politics and structure of the state.

As mentioned earlier, the subordination of the military command to the political leadership was regarded by Clausewitz as a direct implication of the close link he discerned between political aims and military operations. In what was in fact largely a reaction against his own previous positions, he argued that it was erroneous to assume that once war was declared, the political leadership had to give the army command a free hand and all available means for purely military planning. There was no such thing as purely military planning; military planning was derived from the political aims of the war.[83] The relationship between political aims and military means was, of course, not one-sided. The means had to suit the ends, but the ends too could not be divorced from the available means; 'the political aim is [not] a tyrant', and the politician should not 'issue orders that defeat the purpose they are meant to serve'.[84] A continuous interplay exists between the aims and the means.[85]

[82] *On War*, III, 6, p. 192.

[83] Ibid. VIII, 6B, p. 607.

[84] Ibid. I, 1, s. 23, p. 87; VIII, 6B, p. 608. This point was also stressed in a famous letter which Clausewitz wrote in 1827 to the then chief of staff General Müffling, and which was to be cited by Moltke during his clash with Bismarck; for the letter see *Two Letters on Strategy*, ed. and trans. by P. Paret and D. Morgan (Carlisle, 1984).

[85] For an elaboration of this relationship, see *On War*, VIII, 6B, pp. 607–8; ibid. I, 1, s. 23–4, p. 87.

Yet, this discussion also provides us with a further insight into Clausewitz's political outlook and conception of the state. The summary of the relationship between political leadership and military command in purely instrumental terms is characteristic. 'No conflict', he wrote, 'need arise any longer between political and military interests—not from the nature of the case at any rate—and should it arise it will show no more than a lack of understanding.'[86] The fact that political and military establishments consist of people who in real life may differ and even clash, not only over the matching of aims and means but also over the desired political values, objectives, and directions of action themselves, seemingly does not occur to Clausewitz.

The ideal that guided Clausewitz throughout his life—the vitality, stability, and power of the community in its political framework—was a characteristic product, historically and ideologically, of the continuous rise of the centralized state throughout the early modern period and its triumph over all other social focuses of power. As a result of this, all independent armed forces were also incorporated into a central army with a purely instrumental role. This historical development and corresponding ethos had particular significance in Prussia, where, since the time of the Great Elector, they had been responsible for the transformation of the Hohenzollern state from a poor principality into a major European power. Both the development and ethos reached their peak with the perfection of absolutism under Frederick the Great; and were transformed by the resistance to French political ideas and occupation, reappearing in an updated and more comprehensive form, with an emphasis on the corporative nature of the nation and state.

Clausewitz's political position when the French Revolution shattered the *ancien régime*, and when the question of social and political constitutions was at the centre of the European agenda, must be borne in mind. What in fact was his exact ideological attitude to the major social and political currents of his period? This point remained somewhat unclear, and was thus addressed by Behrens in 'Which Side was Clausewitz On?'.[87] For themselves, Clausewitz did not share the aspirations of the Third Estate nor the defensive

[86] Ibid. VIII, 6B, p. 607.

[87] Behrens's principal point was largely accepted by Paret, who expanded it in 'Die politischen Ansichten von Clausewitz', in Clausewitz Gesellschaft (ed.), *Freiheit ohne Krieg*, pp. 332–48.

position of the old ruling classes; he held neither a republican, constitutional, nor absolutist position. He was guided by a passionate political vision derived from the traditional Prussian political ethos and reinforced by the new organic and evolutionary view of society and the nation: this political vision aimed at the greatness and well-being of the people and state as defined in terms of stability, vitality, and power.

Like Scharnhorst he was one of the exponents of the Prussian reform movement because he thought that the *ancien régime* no longer suited the conditions and needs of the period, and believed that the expansion of the social basis of the Prussian state was essential for its continued survival, independence, and status of power in the post-Revolutionary era.[88] For these reasons he relentlessly defended the *Landwehr* during the political struggles of the Restoration which culminated in W. von Humboldt's resignation in 1819, and even at one time proposed a form of parliamentary institution.[89] Yet, only a short while later and for the very same reasons, he came out strongly against the nationalist and liberal unrest and even opposed the demands for a constitution and parliament, which he regarded in the early 1820s as divorced from Prussia's present reality and dangerous for her stability and well-being.[90]

Parliament was for Clausewitz predominantly a means for social cohesion through the expansion of the government's base of support. Similarly, in his arguments for the *Landwehr*, the main target for the attacks of the forces of reaction, he attempted to show that its necessity for the defence and international position of Prussia far outweighed, and even made irrelevant, any particular social or class argument for, or especially against, it. This was not merely a clever way to evade what was actually the core of the problem, as Paret appears to imply.[91] Nor was the criterion that Clausewitz used an

[88] See Krieger, *The German Idea of Freedom*, pp. 196–202, which is better on Gneisenau than on Clausewitz.

[89] 'Über die politischen Vortheile und Nachteile der Preussischen Landwehr', written at the end of 1819; in Schwartz, *Leben*, ii. 288–93; for the idea of parliament, to expand the government's base of support, see ibid. 291. The argument for the *Landwehr* is further elaborated on in 'Unsere Kriegsverfassung' written at the same period; Rothfels (ed.), *Schriften*, pp. 142–53.

[90] See 'Umtriebe' in Rothfels, (ed.) *Schriften*, pp. 153–95, called by Paret—in view of what appears as a change of political positions by Clausewitz—'the most puzzling of all of Clausewitz's works'; Paret, *Clausewitz*, p. 299.

[91] Ibid. 295.

objective standard of measurement. Rather this approach reflected his particular political attitudes which subordinated any social and political ideal or objective to what he regarded as the true interest of the state and people. As pointed out by Behrens and followed up by Paret, Clausewitz basically maintained the eighteenth-century, Frederickian, paternalist view of politics. And this was reinforced by the new corporate conception of society. As he put forward in 'Umtriebe', the welfare of the people had to be the government's main concern; furthermore, the new conditions required a closer involvement of the people in government than had been the case in Frederick's time, as a means of social cohesion. However, the actual conduct of politics was not a matter for particular interests but was to be firmly held in the hands of the government which had to be guided by what Clausewitz regarded as the general great interests of society as a whole.[92]

In the very years in which Clausewitz wrote 'Umtriebe', Hegel gave the prevailing view of the state its supreme philosophical expression in *The Philosophy of Right* (1821). According to Hegel, the various groups and interests contending in civil society, the sphere of the war of all against all, find their ethical and rational solution in the state. The leadership of the state remains above the struggle of the particular forces. It embodies unity, disinterest, the supreme expression of society as a whole. The similarity of this conception to Clausewitz's trend of thought is obvious. Unfortunately we only know that 'Umtriebe' was written sometime in the early 1820s, but whether before or after 1821 is unclear. Consequently it is very difficult to determine whether Clausewitz's own ideas were indeed reinforced and influenced by Hegel's celebrated conceptions or simply expressed, independently, very similar intellectual trends, common to the German movement.

Be that as it may, Clausewitz again alluded to his own political outlook in Books VIII and I of *On War*, written in the late 1820s. As we have seen, at that time it is highly improbable that he was not familiar with *The Philosophy of Right*, and indeed there appear to be some distinct features that suggest its influence. In explaining the supremacy of the political over the military, Clausewitz wrote:

It can be taken as agreed that the aim of policy is to unify and reconcile all aspects of internal administration as well as of spiritual values, and

[92] In 'Umtriebe' see esp. pp. 176–7. Also see Behrens, '*Which Side*' and Paret, 'Die politischen Ansichten von Clausewitz', pp. 340–2.

whatever else the *moral philosopher may care to add*. Policy, of course, is nothing in itself; it is simply the trustee for all these interests against the outside world. That it can err, subserve the ambitions, private interests, and vanity of those in power, is neither here nor there . . . here we can only treat policy as representative of all interests of the community.[93]

Later, in describing the 'remarkable trinity', Clausewitz actually refers to policy as 'reason' governing the passions of the people and the activity of the army.[94]

In the last stages of the writing of *On War*, Clausewitz's attitudes to politics and the state were therefore more formally conceptualized. These attitudes reflected deep-rooted traditions embedded both in the Prussian historical context and in the distinctive character of the German political philosophy. They were very probably influenced in the last decade of Clausewitz's life by Hegel's highly renowned ideas. Controversies over state policy were regarded by Clausewitz as a problem of interpreting a rational common political interest (providing, of course, they did not 'subserve ambitions, private interests, and vanity'), rather than as a struggle between contending political visions and objectives within the state. As Gerhard Ritter points out, Clausewitz did not acknowledge the possibility of an existential gap between different aims in society.[95] The rejection of the atomistic view of society for an organic and rational harmony of interests was central to the ideas of the German movement. In this context the relationship between political leadership and military command was also understood in purely instrumental terms.

Yet, Clausewitz's own life story not only sets this conception into its historical context but also places it in an ironic light. Throughout the great events of his period, the struggle for independence against Napoleon and the reform of the Prussian state, Clausewitz, the military man, bitterly opposed the political aims and even the declared policy of his king. He and his fellow reformers in the army, who comprised a 'purely military body', took part not merely in discussions on the adjustment of aims and means, but in a formidable

[93] *On War*, VIII, 6B, pp. 606–7; my italics. These ideas undoubtedly formalized earlier notions. Compare with Lossau, *Der Krieg*, p. 7: 'Politics operates for the existence and external prosperity of states. It safeguards the individual interests equally; it determines the fundamental idea, the direction, and the aim that the state should advance.'

[94] *On War*, I, 1, s .28, p. 89.

[95] Gerhard Ritter, *The Sword and The Scepter* (Miami, 1969, IV), i. 67.

power struggle within the Prussian leadership, which stemmed from conflicting class interests and contending social and political visions, and which centred on no less than the reshaping of Prussia's social structure and foreign policy. At a time of crisis, Clausewitz left for Russia to fight Napoleon, acting against government policy and his king's orders. The fundamental controversies in reality encompassed a much wider scope than could be resolved by *raisons d'état*, and cut across the institutional lines of political leadership and military command.

This irony has escaped those who today have raised to prominence Clausewitz's conception of the relationship between political leadership and military command. They have had in mind the controversies between Bismarck and Moltke, and Truman and MacArthur, where a rejection of the particular positions held by the military command was happily in union with our contemporary political outlook that postulates the supremacy of the political leadership.

Indeed, the significance of Clausewitz's conceptions of the relationship between political leadership and military command largely derives from the role these conceptions have played in supporting the political outlook of today.

During the Franco-Prussian War, in his famous clash with Bismarck, Moltke formulated the general staff's claim to a shared authority with the *Kanzler* in the leadership of the state, under the king's supreme authority. In this he gave expression to the relationship between political and military leadership that was embedded in the political structure and ethos of the Second Reich. In the 1930s Ludendorff expressed the natural point of view of a militarist value-system when he declared Clausewitz obsolete, and made the political leadership an instrument of the military command for the harnessing of civilian life to the needs of war.[96]

National self-examination after the Second World War led the German historians to Clausewitz, whose conception of the relationship between political leadership and military command could be integrated into the new liberal-democratic ideal. This conception, divorced from its actual historical and intellectual context, and sharply contrasted with the legacy of the Second Reich, became

[96] E. Ludendorff, *The Total War* (London, n.d.).

one of the major reasons for Clausewitz's revival. In the United States, the complex problems of controlling the military machinery in a superpower democracy led to a similar trend.[97]

A certain compatibility in viewing the relationship between political leadership and military command was thus responsible for the fact that the conceptions of a Prussian thinker, whose political thought centred on adapting the tradition of Prussian *étatisme* to the conditions of nationalist post-Revolutionary Europe, were enlisted to serve the political and ideological code of the liberal Western democracies.

[97] The most notable example for the renaissance of Clausewitz's ideas in this context is Bernard Brodie's *War and Politics* (New York, 1973).

CONCLUSION

This book really requires two conclusions, to match the two major arguments raised in it. The first is concerned strictly with the interpretation of the core of Clausewitz's military thought, his conception of the nature of war. The second deals with the wider intellectual framework of military thought, as presented in relation to the two periods described, and the implications of this presentation for the understanding of military theory in general. About this second topic in particular, there is much more to be said than I can possibly hope to discuss here. A few words of conclusion will have to suffice.

From the outset, there was a latent tension in Clausewitz's thought between his historicist sense and particularist notions on the one hand, and his universalist quest on the other. This tension surfaced in 1827, calling into question some of Clausewitz's ideas regarding defence and attack, and rapidly expanding to threaten his conception of the nature of war. Henceforth, his thinking underwent a process of continuous transformation which was terminated only by his death. Had it been carried further, this process had the *potential* to demolish most of the surviving components of Clausewitz's lifelong conception of war. Indeed, this is why Delbrück was able to rely on Clausewitz's ideas in rehabilitating eighteenth-century warfare, and why modern interpreters could often disregard Clausewitz's emphasis on the clash of forces in combat. In both cases, however, Clausewitz himself never went so far.

In the event, his intellectual development in his final years introduced a great deal of 'mystification', and it is very doubtful whether he would have retreated from this direction. This appears to be so because, apart from its success in incorporating his old ideas with his new ones, his later intellectual structure had the great appeal of satisfying his deep psychological need to give his work the form expected from a 'truly philosophical' treatment of war.

The tensions in Clausewitz's own work resulted in corresponding interpretative antinomies. Thus, for example, his work was regarded both as an analysis of contemporary Napoleonic warfare and, at the same time, as a universal theory of war. Closely linked is the preposterous idea that Clausewitz was concerned with the nature of war, as distinct and remote from any normative approach to the actual conduct of war. Nothing could be further removed from Clausewitz's own motives and work throughout his life. Another example, mentioned before, is to be found in Clausewitz's attitude to eighteenth-century warfare. Since this warfare has been rehabilitated in both historical and strategic thinking, and since Clausewitz was not to be accused of harbouring an unhistorical approach, his attitude had to be presented merely as a criticism of the *excesses* of the war of manœuvre.

The endemic difficulties in interpreting Clausewitz have stemmed largely from the fact that *On War* is a classic case where the text cannot be understood without its context; not only the military and intellectual context but also that provided by the evolution of Clausewitz's own thought. The opening part of *On War* reflects in effect the latest stage in his development, while the middle reflects the earliest, and the last the intermediate, each incorporating fundamentally contrasting ideas. In short, reading *On War* as it stands, without the necessary preliminary knowledge, is bound to result in misunderstanding.

Although aware of the unfinished state of the work, and to some degree cognizant of its internal development, many of Clausewitz's interpreters have still attempted to explain *On War* as a coherent whole. When coupled with our contemporary attitudes and sensitivities, this has often led to a harmonizing interpretation and partisan approach, with the real Clausewitz sterilized and almost disappearing behind mountains of scholarly talk.

Conversely, it is clear that the men of the nineteenth century (and for that matter also Liddell Hart) were not so ridiculously mistaken in their understanding of Clausewitz as it has become the fashion to believe. While being perhaps slightly more nationalist and militarist than him, they were organically—both historically and intellectually—far closer to him than the men of our era ever could be.

Much of Clausewitz's reputation as a profound thinker has therefore resulted from the confusion among his interpreters. In a sense, Clausewitz could never have been wrong or less than profound because no one could be quite sure that he understood the true meaning of Clausewitz's ideas. Yet, Clausewitz's real intellectual greatness and one reason for the living interest in his work stems from a unique achievement that has never been equalled. He offered a most sophisticated formulation of the theory of war, based on a highly stimulating intellectual paradigm, and brought the conception of military theory into line with the forefront of the general theoretical outlook of his time.

Delineating the subsequent career of the two intellectual traditions described in this book would require another volume. One tradition, in close affinity to the scientific enterprise, went through positivism to logical positivism and its descendants in the social sciences. The other tradition, stressing the gulf between the sciences and the humanities and the dominance of history and man's inner world over the latter, was similarly carried forward by the German Movement of the nineteenth century to our contemporary contentions. These underlying historical trends have received too little attention.

In this book in any case, the primary aim is not to strike a new balance between the two theoretical traditions that have dominated modern military thought, though in many respects such a balance may certainly be implied. Nor is it to bring the one into, or remove the other from, the scene of contemporary strategic thinking, though the striking resemblance of their arguments to the modern debate between the 'traditional' and 'scientific' schools in the social sciences makes their intellectual legacy appear remarkably relevant. While the ideas of the military thinkers of the Enlightenment in particular were poorly understood and caricatured, and while it has been stressed in this work that human thinking takes a variety of forms, a historical approach does not imply an equal acceptance of all ideas. It should, however, make the strange familiar and comprehensible.

A great deal of progress has been made in understanding war in its wider contexts, particularly the social one. Yet, this development has barely touched the intellectual sphere, with unfortunate consequences for the study of military thought. Hence the main point of this book, at once historical and theoretical; in it an attempt has been made to reject the 'naïve' approach to military thought.

Historically, Clausewitz's ideas did not appear out of thin air, nor were his predecessors curious eccentrics with peculiar ideas, as the German military school would have us believe. Historians have been largely unaware of the historical traditions that have predetermined their view of the period. Our story is in fact merely one aspect of an old and well-known story: the conflict between the Enlightenment and the German Movement. Both the works of the military thinkers of the Enlightenment and those of Clausewitz were strikingly comprehensive expressions of the general manner in which the intellectual élites of Western civilization in two successive periods understood and interpreted their world.

The theoretical point is closely related: that *what* people think cannot be separated from the question of *how* they think, or from the circumstances in which they operate and to which they react. Military theory is not a general body of knowledge to be discovered and elaborated, but is comprised of changing conceptual frameworks which are developed in response to varying challenges, and which always involve interpretation, reflecting particular human perspectives, attitudes, and emphases. Consequently there is no such thing as a 'theoretical', 'positivist' understanding of past military theories 'as they are', nor is there much sense in discussing them 'abstractly' or judging their value without keeping in mind the historical and intellectual circumstances in which they were formed. The theoretical premises of every conception of military theory cannot but depend on some overall (albeit unconscious) picture of the world.

APPENDIX

Clausewitz's Final Notes Revisited

Among his literary remains, Clausewitz left us two notes written at an advanced stage of his work on *On War* which describe the state of the treatise and his plans for its future development. These notes are highly important for the understanding of Clausewitz's intellectual career, particularly because of the comprehensive revision of his work which he undertook, but did not complete, in the last years of his life. Unfortunately, only one of these notes, albeit the most important one, announcing the planned revision, is dated: 10 July 1827. The other bears no date.

Clausewitz's wife, Marie, who, with the assistance of her brother and Major O'Etzel, published Clausewitz's posthumous works, made no attempt to date this note or to connect it to any specific event.[1] However, apparently she tended to believe—though was careful not to determine—that it was written subsequent to the note of July 1827, and placed it after this note at the opening of Clausewitz's *Collected Works*. She wrote that it 'appears to belong to a very late date'[2].

A century later, Clausewitz's interpreters were much bolder. Endorsing the prevailing view, they decided that the undated note must have been composed in 1830 when we know from Marie that Clausewitz, who had been transferred from his post as the Director of the War School in Berlin to field service in the artillery, had been obliged to stop his work on *On War* and had packed and sealed his papers until time allowed him to resume writing. This date has had

[1] E.g. she was much more prepared to commit herself in the case of a considerably older note. She attributed it (and apparently rightly so) to Clausewitz's period in Koblenz in 1816–18 when he wrote the early concise work which was to lead to the composition of *On War*; see *Hinterlassene Werke*, vol. i, p. viii.

[2] Ibid., p. xix.

much appeal not least because it created the somewhat romantic picture of a fateful moment when Clausewitz, upon leaving his work to which he was never to return, left a final record of his intentions. From the 1930s there has therefore been a consensus among Clausewitz's interpreters regarding the dating of this note.[3]

What I would like to argue here is that this dating is highly improbable, that it created some difficult problems that scholars have failed to resolve, and, even more importantly, that it is conspicuously divorced from all that we know about Clausewitz's later development. I will suggest that the undated note was written in fact shortly *prior* to the note of July 1827, possibly only a few months before.

In the note of July 1827, Clausewitz assesses the far-reaching implications on his work of his new discovery that there are two types of war, absolute and limited, and that war is the continuation of policy by other means. With most of *On War* already written, he now must 'regard the first six books which are already in a clean copy merely as a rather formless mass that must be thoroughly reworked once more'.[4] He therefore states his intention to work in the light of his new guidelines on Books VII and VIII, in both of which he has only sketched or outlined several chapters ('*entworfen*' '*Skizzen*' for Book VII, and '*entworfen*' for Book VIII). Then, after finishing the original plan of the work, he will return to revise the first six books.[5]

Now, the undated note was allegedly written in 1830. Yet it reveals no progress on the state of affairs described in July 1827. In fact, if it were not for the basic assumption, I would suggest that one would have had to admit that the undated note represents a slight *regression* on the note of July 1827. Let us examine the texts. In the note of July 1827, Book VI is undistinguished among the first six completed, though unrevised books of *On War*. By contrast, in the undated note, Clausewitz while appearing to single out Book VI

[3] The date and circumstances were suggested in the first rigorous treatment of the issue in Herbert Rosinski's 'Die Entwicklung von Clausewitz Werk "Vom Kriege" im Lichte seiner "Vorreden" und "Nachrichten"', *Historische Zeitschrift* CLI (1935), 278–93. Despite other differences of opinion, this was accepted by Eberhard Kessel in 'Zur Entstehungsgeschichte von Clausewitz Werk "Vom Kriege"', *Historische Zeitshcrift*, CLII (1935), 97–100, and reiterated by all of Clausewitz's later interpreters.

[4] 'Note of 10 July 1827', *On War*, p. 69.

[5] Ibid., pp. 69–70.

for especially harsh treatment, describes it as a mere attempt or sketch (*blosser Versuch*).[6] This is particularly puzzling since Book VI, as we know it, comprises more than a fourth of the whole work, and is 2.5 to 3.5 times as large as any of the other books of *On War*. Regarding Books VII and VIII, whereas in the note of July 1827 Clausewitz states that in both he has sketched or drafted several chapters, in the undated note he writes similar things only about Book VII (*die Gegenstände flüchtig hingeworfen*). About Book VIII he speaks only in the future tense, presenting its planned subject and nature. There is no sign in the text that any of this Book actually exists.[7]

Indeed, Clausewitz's modern interpreters have found the final notes somewhat problematic. Since they have assumed that the undated note was written in 1830, they have all agreed that for some reason or another, after three years, Clausewitz seems to have made very little progress. Furthermore, it appeared that Clausewitz had almost completely disregarded his working plan of July 1827. He did not, or barely (there are slightly different opinions here) work on Books VII and VIII which are, at best, described in both notes in fairly similar terms. Instead, we are told, he went directly to the revision of his first books, where he did some work on Book I and perhaps also on a few others. In his work on *On War*, this is all that he achieved between 1827 and 1830.

Let us begin with Books VII and VIII as we know them. Marie believed that they were indeed unfinished and in a state of rough sketches.[8] We have an important clue as to why. From Clausewitz's note of July 1827 we know that he produced clean copies of the first six books of *On War* which he previously regarded as more or less complete, possibly after finishing each of them. However, once he started the process of clarifying his new ideas, there was no point in doing that. Whatever work he did on Books VII and VIII, he apparently did not produce clean copies of them. Thus for Marie, the state of the manuscript, the evidence of the undated note, and her assumption about the note's 'very late' composition must have reinforced each other.

Now, Books VII and VIII were not copied into a clean version, but, in the state in which we know them, should they be described as

[6] Ibid., p. 70. [7] Ibid., pp. 69, 70.

[8] *Hinterlassene Werke*, vol. iii, p. v.

sketched in outline form? All of Clausewitz's interpreters have been obliged by their dating of the undated note to reply in the affirmative. But there are no real grounds for such a statement. If size is considered, then Book VII is very average, while Book VIII is the third largest in *On War*.[9] Content-wise, Book VII 'The Attack' appears quite complete, particularly as Clausewitz specifically states that it is only a supplement to Book VI 'Defence'.[10] Chapter 16 even deals with limited objectives and falls in step with his new guidelines. As for Book VIII, this is where Clausewitz elaborates his new ideas most fully and extensively.

Why then would Clausewitz in 1830 particularly describe the last three books of *On War* as sketches (if, indeed, he says even that about Book VIII)? Moreover, if after July 1827 he did not work on Books VII and VIII, how is it that they express his new ideas? Alternatively, if he did work on these books, why does the undated note reflect absolutely no progress on the note of July 1827? These contradictions have remained unresolved.

There is one crucial reason why all of Clausewitz's interpreters have believed that the undated note was written in 1830 and recorded the progress of his work-plan put forward three years earlier. In the undated note, Clausewitz wrote: 'The first chapter of Book One alone I regard as finished. It will at least serve the whole by indicating the direction I meant to follow everywhere.'[11] Since we know that the beginning of Book I indeed represents the latest stage in the development of Clausewitz's ideas, this statement has been perceived as the latest account of the revision of his work.

This brings us to the core of the argument. Interpreters who have had the note of July 1827 in mind, have overlooked something very fundamental. In the undated note, Clausewitz does not mention any revision nor does he even allude to the ideas of policy and war, or absolute, limited, and real wars. In short, he does not refer to what was in 1830 the focus of his work and his major concern for the future, to what is universally supposed to have been the whole purpose of the note. Indeed, assuming this purpose, Clausewitz's account appears strangely obscure. He fails to enlighten us about the things that were the most important to him. Instead he presents

[9] Book VII is larger than Books I, II, and III, roughly as large as Book IV, and smaller than Books VI, V, and VIII. Book VIII is only smaller than Books VI and V.

[10] *On War* VII, 1, p. 523.

[11] Ibid., p. 70.

a very long list of propositions which are intended to prove the possibility of a general theory of war, and which summarize major themes from *On War*. Curiously enough, the ideas of policy and war, and absolute, limited, or real war do not appear here either. The undated note could not have been written in 1830.

If this is so then how are we to understand Clausewitz's reference to the first chapter of Book I as the only one he regarded as finished? I would suggest that a remarkable coincidence was responsible here for the misinterpretation, but this is better explained from the beginning.

The undated note appears to have been composed shortly before the note of July 1827, possibly early in the same year. It was written when, and because, Clausewitz discovered that there was a problem in regarding all-out war as the only type of war and the sole foundation of theory. We know this happened while he was writing Book VI, or perhaps when he was already copying it. The whole of his intellectual enterprise now appeared in jeopardy.

Hence a dominant characteristic of the note, its melancholic tone. Apart from the fact that Clausewitz declares that most of his work is unsatisfactory and should be regarded merely as 'working material', he devotes the larger part of the note to the assessment of the question whether a theory of war, despite its 'extraordinary difficulties', is possible at all. Although his tone appears to be unusually subdued, he answers in the affirmative, relying on the list of propositions which he regards as universal and which are taken from the first books of *On War*.

This brings us to another dominant characteristic of the note: in Clausewitz's intellectual development it is patently archaic.[12] As mentioned above, there is no trace of his new ideas. The exciting and fundamental arguments of Book VIII cannot be found in the list of propositions. Interestingly enough, the opening theme in the list is the relationship between defence and attack, the subject of Book VI. Indeed, let us return to Clausewitz's account of his work in the note and examine it in the light of our new date.

Clausewitz describes Book VI as a mere attempt or sketch (*blosser Versuch*) and states that he will rewrite it entirely and look for

[12] This can already be seen in the clearly archaic title which Clausewitz uses for his manuscript: 'on the conduct of great wars' [*über die Führung des grossen Krieges*].

another 'way out' (*Ausweg*). Assuming as he did that the note was written in 1830, Aron believed that Clausewitz deemed it necessary to revise his views on defence and attack in the light of his new ideas on policy and war.[13] While this might be true, it still does not explain why Book VI is singled out. Surely the same revision was needed for all of Clausewitz's early books, particularly Book III dealing with strategy. However, once we redate the note, all this becomes much clearer.

When he was writing Book VI, Clausewitz encountered a major problem—the possibility of a defence with a limited aim. Not only did he now become dissatisfied with Book VI but he sensed that the problem might have a bearing on all his previous work. While there were now question marks on all his work, Clausewitz had not yet clarified to himself the exact nature and full implications of the problem, and still believed that at least the fundamentals of his work remained unaffected whatever the adaptations and additions he would have to make. In case of an early death, he wanted the world to know both sides of the coin. He therefore stated that the first chapter of Book I—which, as one would expect, in the early phase of *On War* also dealt with the question 'What is War?' and encapsulated Clausewitz's fundamental view on the subject—was the only one that he regarded as finished, and that it indicated the direction he wanted to follow everywhere.[14]

In the last two books of *On War*, only the main topics of Book VII were roughly sketched. In Book VIII there was the main idea but apparently nothing substantial written.[15]

Now, whereas Clausewitz wrote the undated note when he sensed that he had encountered a difficult problem, he composed the note of July 1827 when he began to clarify to himself the nature and implications of this problem and work out a solution for it. This proximity of time and subject is responsible for the remarkable similarity between the two notes which in many respects are almost a mirror image of one another. The sequence of events may have been as follows. Firstly, Clausewitz devised the idea of the two types of war, absolute and limited. Putting this idea into practice, he wrote the last three chapters of Book VI, thus finding—as he had stated he would do—another way out (*Ausweg*). He could then finish

[13] Aron, *Clausewitz*, pp. 239–50.
[14] 'Undated Note', *On War*, p. 70. [15] Ibid.

copying the book. His new idea led him to develop the idea of the relationship between policy and war. In the note of July 1827 he tells us what he did next. He foresaw that 'the main application of this point will not be made until Book Eight'. He therefore 'drafted several chapters' of this new book, 'done with the idea that the labour itself would show what the real problems were'. Indeed, 'that in fact is what happened', and having clarified his mind to a large extent and having decided what needed to be done, he then wrote the note of July 1827.[16]

In this note he presented his two new ideas and their implications on his work. The first six books which were already in a clean copy would now have to be revised. However, he would first work on and finish the last two books. Book VII 'On Attack', which apparently remained in the state it had been when the earlier note had been written, would be revised and completed. After finishing this book, he would 'go at once and work out Book VIII in full'. This book, 'War Plans', is where his new ideas would really be elaborated.[17] This process would be of crucial importance:

> If the working out of Book Eight results in clearing my own mind and in really establishing the main features of war, it will be all the easier for me to apply the same criteria to the first six books . . . *Only when I have reached that point therefore*, shall I take the revision of the first six books in hand.[18]

How did this work-plan materialize between 1827 and 1830 when Clausewitz had to stop his work? As mentioned above, when the undated note was given the date 1830, all had to agree that Clausewitz appeared neither to have made substantial progress nor to follow his planned programme. Now we have no 'Final Note', yet the course of Clausewitz's work during his last three creative years becomes quite clear and consistent with the *On War* that we know. As he had stated he would do, he first worked on and completed Book VII 'On Attack', inserting his new idea of the two types of war in chapters 15 and 16. He then went on to write and finish the large Book VIII 'War Plans', the natural place and the real testing ground of the new ideas. Only after developing these ideas extensively and clarifying his thoughts in writing this book, did he undertake the revision of the first six books.

[16] Ibid., p. 69. [17] Ibid., pp. 69–70.
[18] Ibid., p. 70; my italics.

How much progress did he make in the revision of these first books? Schering, famous for his unsubstantiated speculations and tendentious fantasies, 'discovered', for example, in his latest work *Clausewitz, Geist und Tat* (1941) a new intellectual transformation centring on Book II. Rothfels believed that Clausewitz revised 'parts at least of Book I (probably chapters 1–3) and of Book II (certainly chapter 2)'.[19] Most interpreters hold more or less the same opinion. Yet, there is absolutely no evidence for this expansive hypothesis. There is nothing new in chapter 2 of Book II, and certainly not a trace of the ideas of the different types of war and policy and war. Moreover, their opinion is clearly contradicted by one of the solid pieces of evidence that we do possess and that has also been curiously overlooked.

In her introduction, Marie tells us specifically that in preparing Clausewitz's literary works for publication, her brother 'found the beginnings of the revision that my beloved husband mentions as a future project in the note of 1827 . . . The revisions have been inserted in those places [*Stellen*] of Book I for which they were intended (*they did not go further*).'[20] When we remember that the first books of *On War* were in clean copy, Marie's testimony becomes even clearer. In going back to revise these books Clausewitz apparently did not literally rewrite them completely. He merely rewrote, amended, and added sections (some of which were obviously quite extensive) to be incorporated into the existing text.

All this fits in perfectly with another piece of evidence. We know from Marie that in November 1831, after concluding his mission on the Polish frontier and shortly before his death, Clausewitz hoped to finish his work during the course of that winter.[21] If it is assumed, by dating the undated note 1830, that between 1827 and 1830 he made very little progress in writing Books VII and VIII and that these books remained but sketches, this hope appears peculiarly optimistic. However, once that basic assumption is abandoned, Clausewitz's hope is revealed in a new light. He wrote the now-extensive Books VII and VIII, and revised Book I which he had naturally anticipated—as we know from the note of 1827—to be the most affected by the revision and the application of his new ideas.[22] In the winter of 1831 he therefore believed that he was

[19] Hans Rothfels, 'Clausewitz', in Earle (ed.), *Makers of Modern Strategy*, p. 108.
[20] *On War*, p. 67; my italics. [21] Ibid., p. 66. [22] Ibid., p. 69.

mainly left with the incorporation of these ideas into the rest of the text of *On War*—surely no small task, but far smaller than the one interpreters have assumed.

If indeed we no longer possess a 'Final Note' with Clausewitz's own testimony, then which parts of *On War* did he regard as truly finished before his death? This question appears to me to be somewhat misleading, because after the intellectual transformation of July 1827, Clausewitz's ideas were undergoing continuous development. The idea of limited war which appeared at the end of Book VI and which was later incorporated into Book VII, was supplemented in the note of July 1827 by the idea of the relationship between policy and war. Both ideas were then worked out in Book VIII where Clausewitz continued to elaborate his thoughts. Chapters 1 and 2 of Book I reveal a further development where Clausewitz no longer regards absolute war as superior to real war. There is no evidence that the revision went any further in Book I and there was indeed no reason why any of the other chapters of this book should have been affected by Clausewitz's new ideas. As it is, Books II–V of *On War* were completely unrevised but the revision was probably needed most badly in Book III on strategy. In the more advanced part of *On War*, it is doubtful whether Clausewitz deemed further considerable revision of Books VI and VII necessary, but he probably wanted to bring Book VIII into line with the latest developments of Book I. Whether Clausewitz would have developed his new ideas further and in new directions, thus generating new changes throughout his work, no one can tell.

Book II

The Nineteenth Century

1

Positivism, Romanticism, and Military Theory 1815–1870

MODERN views on the nature of military theory originated from the most intensely philosophical period in European history. They were formed in response to the all-pervasive, epoch-making, and bitterly conflicting intellectual climates of the Enlightenment on the one hand, and the Counter-Enlightenment or Romanticism on the other.

The very idea that something called military theory existed—or rather was very much lacking—was the product of the intellectual gospel of the Enlightenment. Stimulated by the spectacular successes of the natural sciences, the men of the Enlightenment sought to bring everything under the domination of reason by creating orderly sciences and disciplines in all spheres of human endeavour. Dominating Europe from the middle of the eighteenth century, the military school of the Enlightenment was burning with an overriding sense of vocation to form a universal theory of war, based on immutable rules and principles, systematically taught, and applied to changing circumstances by the general's creative genius.

By the turn of the century, however, a new sweeping intellectual movement, largely hostile to the ideas of the Enlightenment, was emerging throughout Europe. Particularly active in Germany, the Romantics stressed the complexity and diversity of human reality, which could not be reduced to abstract formulas and which was dominated by emotions, creativity, and the historical conditions of each period. It was in this framework that a new outlook on the nature of military theory was formed, in the works of writers such as Berenhorst and, above all, Clausewitz, breaching the hitherto absolute hegemony of the military school of the Enlightenment.

At the beginning of the nineteenth century, therefore, the transforming experience of Napoleonic warfare, made possible by the social energies unleashed by the French Revolution, was subjected to theoretical formulation in terms of two conflicting intellectual paradigms. The theoretical legacy of the Enlightenment, which in the eighteenth century had been applied mostly to the relatively limited and cautious warfare of the *ancien régime*, was now adapted to reflect the new crushing mode of warfare. To be sure, the older, battle-shy theories of Lloyd and Bülow were also carried into the Napoleonic age by military thinkers such as August Wagner and, most notably, Archduke Charles of Austria. Under the immediate impact of Napoleon's downfall, these theories were even reinforced for a while in some minds by misgivings regarding the adventurous nature of the emperor's strategy, which was blamed for the loss of whole armies in the Russian and Saxon campaigns of 1812 and 1813.[1] But for most of the generation which had undergone the shattering trial of Napoleonic warfare, eighteenth-century strategy was totally discredited, while Napoleon was the 'god of war'. And it was Jomini who won fame by updating the theoretical outlook of the Enlightenment to produce a striking schematization of Napoleon's aggressive rationale of operations. He emphasized the overthrowing of the enemy's army in rapid manœuvring to cut its communications or to penetrate between and overwhelm each of its fractions separately. At the same time, in Prussia—the focal point of the fierce reaction against the world-view of the Enlightenment—Clausewitz combined another interpretation of the Napoleonic war of destruction with a completely new formulation of the concept of military theory, constructed from the materials of Romanticism.[2]

Thus it is important to realize that, in general, there was little difference in military outlook *per se* between Clausewitz and Jomini; both reflected the spirit and outline of Napoleonic strategy. Clausewitz's highly polemic rhetoric against the military theory of his day and against Jomini (which recent commentators have surpassed each other in paraphrasing) can only be understood in its cultural context, namely the all-out attack of the new German Movement on the world-view of the Enlightenment, which

[1] See Baron Rogniat, *Considérations sur l'art de la guerre* (Paris, 1816). The book aroused a public sensation and sparked a literary skirmish with the exiled emperor himself; Napoleon's counter-attack from St Helena in Montholon's *Mémoires* (Paris, 1823) provoked Rogniat's *Réponse aux notes critiques de Napoléon* (Paris, 1823). For one favourable reaction in Germany see Carl von Decker, *Ansichten über die Kriegführung im Geist der Zeit* (Berlin, 1817).

[2] See Book I.

rendered his predecessors' intellectual assumptions totally unacceptable to Clausewitz. Hence also the background for the subsequent development of military theory. The conventional picture of a struggle between Jominian and Clausewitzian ideas and influences is oblivious to the wider context. The shift in the centre of military power from France to Germany after 1870–1 marked a decisive change in the fortunes of the two contending conceptions of military theory; but, both before and after this, their fortunes were equally tied up with the fortunes of the cultural traditions from which they had emerged. They could only take root and flourish where they found the climate of ideas favourable. Their spread and influence matched remarkably the contours of the intellectual map of Europe, shaped by those currents of thought which had their origins in the Enlightenment and Romanticism and which formed people's outlook on the world in the nineteenth century.

Although Romanticism had indigenous expressions everywhere in Europe, it was the wealth and depth of German literature and philosophy that attracted the minds of the élite in all countries from the late 1810s to the 1830s, exerting a profound and lasting influence even on the intellectual opponents of the movement. By the 1840s, however, the tide of Romanticism was ebbing throughout Europe, and it was the descendants of the Enlightenment who dominated the mid-century. Favoured by a remarkable scientific and technological advance which spread the culture of science, positivism, in its broadest sense, became the prevalent *état d'esprit*. The progressive application of the scientific methods of observation and induction to the more complex sciences of man and society would elevate these disciplines too from their state of infancy; this was the mood most characteristically articulated in France by Auguste Comte, whose doctrines found equally receptive ground on both sides of the Channel. Needless to say, this climate of ideas was favourable to the theoretical legacy of the military school of the Enlightenment.

It was not that soldiers in the nineteenth century were either very interested in, or knowledgeable about, the major intellectual currents that dominated their times, although most military thinkers—by nature people of intellectual inclination—were remarkably conscious of them. The all-encompassing philosophical ideal of the eighteenth century was a thing of the past, and with it had gone much of the enthusiastic sense of vocation to lay the foundations of military theory, the discipline which during the Enlightenment had always been there to be discovered. All the same, the intellectual frameworks remained, and military outlook was in some important respects almost predetermined by the prevailing cultural perspectives.

There were, of course, many other important factors at work. No great war took place in Europe between the fall of Napoleon and the German Wars of Unification. The predominance of domestic politics and social developments resulted in a long period of reduced international and military tensions, as the autocratic regimes of the Restoration struggled with the rising middle classes, with nationalism, and with the effects of the expanding Industrial Revolution and urbanization. Governments were therefore more concerned to employ their armies as a weapon in internal affairs, and indeed to crush the seeds of revolution within the armies themselves, than to use them in war against allied governments with similar interests. While the guns were silent, however, the products of industrialization, such as the rifle and the breach-loader, the steam engine and the electric telegraph, were quietly transforming war, with military theory following in their wake.

In the previous book, I traced the emergence of the two dominating conceptions of military theory within their centres of origin up to the late 1830s. This introductory chapter will therefore begin by widening the angle of vision to two countries of the periphery—Britain and the United States—before again picking up the threads of development in France and Germany.

It is well known that the British army of the Napoleonic era was fundamentally an eighteenth-century institution. Being the least-affected of all European forces by the military innovations which Revolutionary France had introduced and which all her continental rivals had had to adopt to a greater or lesser degree, it remained a professional force which drew its officers from the privileged, and its rank and file from the lowest classes of society. With the coming of peace, in a rapidly changing society and gradually reformed political system which had traditionally regarded the army as a potential danger and as alien to British values, the neglected army was to become increasingly anachronistic.[3] This, however, was

[3] See Gwyn Harries-Jenkins, *The Army in Victorian Society* (London, 1977); Edward M. Spiers, *The Army and Society 1815–1914* (London, 1980); Hew

hardly the reality for the proud veterans of the Peninsula and of Waterloo in the generation after 1815. Nor was the philistine image which later became associated with the British officer-corps applicable to them. Indeed, when certain of those gentlemen turned their attention to military writing, they produced some fascinating expressions of the major trends vying with each other in British society in the early nineteenth century.

The prevailing approach to military theory—in Britain as everywhere else—had been derived since the eighteenth century from the ideas of the Enlightenment. Jomini synthesized the intellectual legacy of the military school of the Enlightenment with the characteristics of Napoleonic warfare, and outside France—where the vain Swiss was not very popular among his former comrades-in-arms—his pre-eminence was readily acknowledged. A disciple of Jomini and the best-known military author in Britain was Sir William Napier (1785–1860), famous for his masterful, voluminous *History of the War in the Peninsula*. At the age of fourteen, Napier followed his two elder brothers into the army and, under Moore and Wellington, he actively participated in the Peninsula campaigns from 1808 to 1814, rising to the rank of lieutenant-colonel. Retiring from the army on half pay in 1819, he first looked for an outlet for his considerable artistic talents in painting and sculpture, and finally found his vocation in the research and writing of his great work.

Napier's attitudes in politics, philosophy, and military theory all converge in one central core of beliefs; his upbringing made him a radical Whig, sympathetic to France, and an intellectual child of the Enlightenment. His father had always condemned the war against Revolutionary France, and the son was equally critical of Tory war-policy in his *History*. Throughout his life he was an enthusiastic and unreserved admirer of Napoleon, whom he regarded not only as the greatest military genius there had ever been but also as an enlightened ruler.[4] Domestically, by 1805 he strongly favoured the

Strachan, *Wellington's Legacy: The Reform of the British Army* (Manchester, 1984). John W. Fortescue, *A History of the British Army* (London, 1930), vols. xi–xiii is still the only comprehensive narrative. Two brief accounts are Michael Howard, 'Wellington and the British Army', in his *Studies in War and Peace* (London, 1970), 50–64; and Geoffrey Best, *War and Society in Revolutionary Europe* (Leicester, 1982), 231–43.

[4] See H. A. Bruce (ed.), *Life of General Sir William Napier* (London, 1864), i. 29; the author was General Sir Patrick MacDougall who, like Bruce, was Napier's

radical efforts to democratize the British political system and to protect the poor against the growing effects of the Industrial Revolution. He married the niece of the radical Whig leader Charles Fox. Later, like most of the radicals, he became increasingly alienated from Whig politics and, after the Reform Bill of 1832, he denounced the party for betraying the popular cause by denying the franchise to the masses.[5] The writings of William Cobbett, which he read in his youth, made him a life-long critic of commercial circles and of *laissez-faire* economists. Employing his pen with his usual zeal, he fiercely objected to the Poor Law Amendment in the 1830s and to the repeal of the Corn Laws in the 1840s.[6]

Napier's Whig starting-point was closely associated with the development of British thought from the seventeenth century on. He was thoroughly familiar with the 'writings of the English philosophers . . . from Lord Bacon down to Adam Smith and Dugald Stewart'.[7] Not surprisingly, when he turned his attention to military theory, he found the main themes familiar enough.

His earliest work was the first review of Jomini's *Treatise on Grand Military Operations* to be published in Britain. It appeared in 1821 in the *Edinburgh Review*, the leading liberal journal in the country. Whereas in conquered Germany, where people had been eager to grasp the secret of Napoleonic warfare, the young Jomini had already been a celebrity by 1808, it took longer for him to penetrate the parochial British scene.[8] Napier's review was un-

son-in-law. Two brief accounts are T. R. E. Holmes, 'Sir William Napier', in his *Four Famous Soldiers* (London, 1889), 227–59; and J. Fortescue, 'Napier's "Peninsular War" ', in his *Historical and Military Essays* (London, 1928), 219–35. Finally, an excellent work to which this section is greatly indebted is Jay Luvaas, *The Education of an Army: British Military Thought, 1815–1940* (London, 1965); for Napier see 7–38.

5 Bruce, *Napier*, i. 346–8; Holmes, *Four Famous Soldiers*, 249–50. For Napier's close association with the radical MPs John Arthur Roebuck and Joseph Parkes (which in 1832 involved his name in talks of radical revolution) see William Thomas, *The Philosophic Radicals* (Oxford, 1979), 234, 239, 257, 295.

6 Bruce, *Napier*, i. 346–8; also see Napier's *Observations on the Corn Laws* (London, 1841), an excellent piece of political and economic pamphleteering against the Cobdenites.

7 Bruce, *Napier*, i. 26; for a reference to Locke's epistemology, see Napier's 'Essay on Education of the Deaf and Dumb', ibid., ii. 523.

8 In Britain, as everywhere else in Europe, the *Traité* was read (when it was read) in the original French, widely understood by the educated classes. But it was even better-known through numerous comments, reviews, abstracts, and second-hand references. After all, the principal ideas of the work could be summarized on the back of a postcard. Large extracts from the historical parts of the *Traité* were

reservedly admiring, presenting the *Treatise* as 'one of the most profound, original, and interesting [works] that has appeared in our day'.[9] He reproduced fully the theoretical outlook developed by the military thinkers of the Enlightenment and faithfully accepted Jomini's view of himself as the one who finally succeeded in supplying his predecessors' confused ideas with true content. Indeed, for the men of the post-Napoleonic period, eighteenth-century warfare (and hence military theory) appeared not as the outgrowth of eighteenth-century society and politics but as an erroneous system put right by Napoleon.

According to Napier, the art of war was advancing: 'Till the middle of the last century the greatest and most distinguished leaders had seldom been able to free themselves from the shackles of the wretched system of warfare which they found established.'[10] They had depended totally on magazines and had dispersed their forces to defend their frontiers, rather than keeping them united. A brilliant exception, wrote Napier, had been Marlborough, and the truth regarding the proper way of conducting operations had been gradually revealed since the time of Frederick the Great. However, Frederick's genius had been predominantly tactical and had fallen short of a true grasp of strategy. It was Napoleon who had brought the art of war to the pinnacle of perfection, by crushing the tyranny of the magazines, concentrating his forces, moving them on interior lines, and substituting battle for manœuvre.[11] 'This last', wrote Napier, 'was the period in which the principles of the military art were brought to all the perfection of which they appear to be capable . . . Napoleon incontestably surpassed all who preceded him and left nothing in which he could himself be surpassed.'[12]

According to Napier, the true principles of the art of war, as practised by Napoleon, had been unveiled by Jomini. The advancement of the art had thus been matched by the advancement of military theory. While historical works had traditionally contained only tiresome memoirs and unprofitable details, wrote Napier, Lloyd had begun to discover the principles of the art in the

published in *The History of the Seven Years War* (London, 1808?); the theoretical parts were abstracted in J. A. Gilbert, *An Exposition of the First Principles of Grand Military Combinations and Movements, Compiled from the Treatise upon Great Military Operations* (London, 1825).

[9] Napier, 'Traité des grandes opérations militaires', *The Edinburgh Review*, 35 (1821), 377.
[10] Ibid. 378.
[11] Ibid. 378, 380, 383–4, 387–91.
[12] Ibid. 380.

philosophical manner. Tempelhoff had followed suit, and Guibert, whose books Bonaparte is said to have carried with him to the field, had produced many illuminating ideas which, if they had not established the art, were at least free from the prejudices of their day. 'Jomini however', says Napier, 'has been the first to give a complete exposition of the principles of war. His powerful and original mind enabled him to far outstrip the authors who had preceded him.'[13] His principles 'do not depend upon the particular institutions of any country or age, but . . . in great part are applicable to all times and places'. Starting from a broad survey of the military events of the last 70 years, Jomini 'elicits by a sort of *induction* the true causes of their failure and success'.[14]

Napier met Jomini in Paris in 1824 whilst he was carrying out the extensive preparatory research for his *History*.[15] The great work that made him famous appeared in six volumes and took twelve years to publish (1828–40). The theoretical outlook of the Enlightenment and Jomini's principles of the art of war underlie the book, which masterfully reveals those principles at work in the conduct of the great military geniuses Napoleon and Wellington. Napier's theoretical outlook is again strikingly manifested in a letter which he wrote in 1847 and in which he rejected the idea of composing a work on 'The Philosophy of War'. The following lines could equally well have been written (in fact had been) by Guibert, Lloyd, or Jomini:

> Such a work involves a preliminary investigation of the human mind as to why men engage in warfare at all. Then would come the distinction between religious wars, civil wars, wars of aggression and aggrandisement, wars of defence, wars of folly, and wars of necessity. Then the progress of the art! its varying phases in different degrees of civilisation, how far it can be carried on by barbarous nations, how far it depends upon civil institutions and the progress of the sciences; how much it depends on such extraneous matters, and how much upon original genius in general. And all reasoning on this point must, to carry weight, be supported by illustrations taken from history and experience . . . I believe the greatest genius would shrink from it, as beyond the power of man to treat with accuracy and authority. Bacon, who has considered all things belonging to philosophy, has not touched upon it.[16]

[13] Napier, 377–8.

[14] Ibid. 379; my italics.

[15] Bruce, *Napier*, i. 240–3; to his wife he wrote that Jomini reminded him of Tom Paine.

[16] Ibid., ii. 277–8.

A typical exponent of the Whig interpretation of history, Napier crusaded for the truth as he saw it, and was categorical, almost hysterical, in his judgement of people.[17] Commanding a brilliant, seemingly effortless style, he engaged in endless literary battles with the victims of his *History*, against political targets, and on many other issues. The bitter personal skirmishes around the *History* alone produced a forest of pamphlets. One of those with whom he crossed swords was another veteran of the Napoleonic wars, Major John Mitchell, who, like Napier, reached the rank of major-general while on the reserve list. Their open dispute concerned mostly matters of tactics, but they also had a deeper symbolic significance. Mitchell was, to my knowledge, the only non-German military author in pre-1871 Europe to be decisively influenced by the new winds which had been blowing from the German cultural scene from the late eighteenth and early nineteenth centuries.

Romanticism was an all-European movement. It was most notably represented in Britain by the Lake Poets—Wordsworth, Coleridge, and Southey; and its religious aspects found characteristic expression in the Oxford Movement and the Roman Catholic revival. But nowhere were its intellectual manifestations in the spheres of philosophy, history, politics, and the arts so comprehensive, profound, and stimulating as in Germany. All the leading ideas of the day, wrote Hippolyte Taine in the middle of the nineteenth century, were produced in Germany between 1780 and 1830.[18] From the 1810s, German ideas were imported everywhere in Europe, to extremely fertile effect. Madame de Staël's *De l'Allemagne* (1813) introduced them into France, and in Britain it was mainly Coleridge and Carlyle who in the 1820s and 1830s brought German philosophy and literature before the dazzled educated public. The Romantics emphasized emotions and inner life and rejected any reduction of the wealth and totality of experience to dead abstractions and principles. Striking as they did at the foundations of the accepted tenets of the Enlightenment, these ideas profoundly impressed the young John Stuart Mill, at the centre of the enemy camp. As he recalled in his *Autobiography*, they showed him the way out of a severe mental crisis and marked a turning-point in his relationship with his towering father and with Benthamite doctrines, rooted in the eighteenth century. In the

[17] See Luvaas, *The Education of an Army*, 16, 42.

[18] Cited by John Dewey, *German Philosophy and Politics* (New York, 1915), 14.

military field in Britain, these ideas hardly had any effect at all, but where they did appear, the story could not have been more characteristic. John Mitchell (1785–1859) brought them from Germany and found his main forum in the Tory *Frazer's Magazine*, dominated by Coleridge, in the company of such authors as Carlyle himself.[19]

In 1797 Mitchell accompanied his father on a four-year diplomatic mission to Berlin. During this period, he attended the Ritterakademie at Lüneburg. At sixteen, he tells us, he read Klopstock to his first love, and she read Goethe's *Werther* to him.[20] He returned to Britain in 1801, but his German period determined his intellectual career for life. He joined the British army in 1803 and during the war served in the West Indies, Spain, and the Low Countries. Before and after Napoleon's final defeat, he was often used by Wellington as an interpreter in the negotiations with Austria, Prussia, and the smaller German states. Retiring on half pay in 1826, he too turned to historical and journalistic writing.[21] Under the pseudonyms 'Captain Orlando Sabertash' and 'Bombardino', he wrote in *Frazer's Magazine* several series of light, humoristic, and perceptive pieces on military affairs, on social news from the European salons—in which he was a welcome and frequent visitor—and on many of the great men he met there. The latter pieces mainly comprised admiring portraits of Romantic artists and conservative politicians: Heine, Hugo, Berryer, Guizot, David, Thiers, Lamartine, and Chateaubriand.[22] He wrote two large military biographies of Wallenstein and Napoleon and several smaller ones. His *Thoughts on Tactics* presented in a systematic manner the ideas he had expressed in numerous articles on military affairs, mostly published in the *United Service Journal*. Like Napier's writings, all these were united by a common intellectual

[19] On *Frazer's Magazine* see Miriam Thrall, *Rebellious Frazer's. No. 1 Yorke's Magazine in the Days of Maginn, Thackeray and Carlyle* (New York, 1934); Mitchell is mentioned on 27–8, 30.

[20] *Frazer's Town and Country Magazine*, 26 (1842), 347.

[21] The principal source on Mitchell's life is Leonhard Schmitz's introductory memoir to Mitchell, *Biographies of Eminent Soldiers of the Last Four Centuries* (London, 1865), pp. vi–xviii; based on this is the sketch in *DNB*, xii. 519–20. The only comprehensive study is to be found in Luvaas, *The Education of an Army*, 39–64.

[22] 'Reminiscences of Men and Things', *Frazer's Magazine*, 26 (1842), 733–6, 740–2; 27 (1843), 99–106, 145–151, 298–301, 454–64, 687–704. Mitchell writes that he loves David despite his being a republican: ibid. 27, 151.

framework, evident in Mitchell's politics, cultural orientation, and military theory. They were all strikingly dominated by a German point of view.

Mitchell's Napoleon is the infamous tyrant portrayed by the German nationalists. The story of his fall is dominated by the rising of the peoples, particularly the awakening of the German national spirit which culminated in the German War of Liberation of 1813. This was a very unusual perspective in early nineteenth-century Britain.[23] Mitchell's France was the detested power that subjugated other nations in the name of so-called universal doctrines of reason. In his highly sympathetic essay on Metternich, containing barely veiled criticism of contemporary Whig attitudes, Mitchell denounced the

> multiplied attacks made [in the last fifty years] by what are falsely called liberal goverments upon the rights, liberties and independence of peoples and states. . . . To the conservative principle [many European countries] . . . are indebted for all the national institutions they continue to possess. . . . If the people of a country love the unity and strength of an absolute monarchy, they are much oppressed by having what is termed among us a liberal and constitutional monarchy forced upon them.[24]

This was no mere reaction. Mitchell's view reflected the intellectual position that had developed in Germany since the days of Herder and Möser in response to the threatening ideas of the French Enlightenment, and which had turned into a form of national resistance against French imperialism after 1806. Every society, it was argued, bore the source of its happiness within itself. The delicate fabric of its peculiar institutions, woven by long historical evolution, could not simply be torn down and replaced by some ingenious scheme based on abstract principles.

The influence of the German Movement determined every aspect of Mitchell's military thought. If Napier's theoretical outlook was totally derived from Jomini, Mitchell's military writings were from beginning to end no more than an English transplantation of Berenhorst's *Reflections on the Art of War* (1796–9). For Mitchell, Jomini added nothing to military theory, although, for a Frenchman, he was 'a pretty fair relater of events'. The French military authors were, he claimed, much inferior to the German.[25] It was 'Berenhorst

[23] J. Mitchell, *The Fall of Napoleon* (3 vols.; London, 1845).
[24] *Frazer's Magazine*, 29 (1844), 333.
[25] Id., *Thoughts on Tactics and Military Organization* (London, 1838), 121.

of whom the present writer avows himself a humble follower'.[26] And to Berenhorst, Mitchell added a bright new star when, in the late 1830s, he became familiar with Clausewitz's collected works.[27]

From Berenhorst's *Reflections*—a characteristic product of the 'Storm and Stress' period in German culture—Mitchell drew both his reliance on the military thinkers of the Enlightenment and a light-hearted, sardonic attitude towards their theoretical efforts. Military theory, he wrote, had made very little progress from its glorious origins with the Greeks through the darkness of the Middle Ages to the various achievements of the modern era. Despite all the talk about the advance of military science and art, no general principles had been established.[28] Why this was so, 'the late General Clausewitz tells us in a very able, though lengthy, and often obscure book on War': unlike any other science or art, in war the object reacts.[29]

The two main tactical points forcefully championed by Mitchell derived from the same source. Regarding cavalry he believed—against recent experience and accepted opinion—that it could and should be trained to charge and break infantry formations. Here too he was strictly expressing the opinions of Berenhorst and those of Bismark, the Württembergian cavalry specialist.[30] Regarding infantry he argued, provoking a lively and ultimately very unpleasant exchange with a brilliantly polemic Napier, that the bayonet was an absolutely useless weapon. To create a real shock-effect, half of the soldiers ought instead to be armed with the pike, abandoned more than a century earlier. This, of course, was a late episode in the famous controversy of the eighteenth century over the

[26] *Thoughts on Tactics and Military Organization*, 12.

[27] For the very few but respectful references to Clausewitz in Britain upon the publication of his works, see H. Strachan, *From Waterloo to Balaclava: Tactics, Technology and the British Army, 1815–1854* (Cambridge, 1985), 8–10.

[28] See mainly *Thoughts on Tactics*, 1–7, 111–21. Cf. Berenhorst, *Betrachtungen*; for Berenhorst's intellectual background and ideas, see above Book I, 152–7.

[29] *Thoughts on Tactics*, 8; a footnote explains that Clausewitz was 'a general in the Prussian service lately deceased. His posthumous work, "Vom Kriege", was published in Berlin in 1832.' In 1840, in the course of his literary debate with a sarcastic Napier, Mitchell compared Napier unfavourably with 'General Clausewitz whose writings have since attracted so much notice in Germany'; Clausewitz's masterly history of the wars in Europe since 1792 'shows us at last how military history should be written': *United Service Journal* (1840), 264. For further, increasingly admiring comments by Mitchell, see Strachan, *From Waterloo to Balaclava*, 8–10.

[30] See esp. *Thoughts on Tactics*, 73–110, 177–212. Bismark was translated into English: *Lectures on the Tactics of Cavalry*. (London, 1827, 2nd. edn. 1855).

ordre profond and the *ordre mince*, and again Mitchell was strongly adhering to the ideas advocated by Berenhorst, in the footsteps of Folard and de Saxe.[31]

These tactical points assumed their fuller significance in the context of Berenhorst's comprehensive criticism of the Frederickian system. Voicing the Counter-Enlightenment's intellectual opposition to Frederick's bureaucratic, machine-like state, Berenhorst totally rejected the principles of the Prussian military system, which was based on brutal discipline, inhuman drill, and automatic performance on the battlefield. Instead of suppressing individuality, argued Berenhorst, the army's main aim must be to inflame the soldiers with an unbeatable fighting-spirit. This required, of course, a complete reversal of attitude towards the soldier. Rather than being regarded as cannon-fodder, he had to be treated as a human being. After the military successes of the French Revolutionary armies, Berenhorst became the leading figure in the growing intellectual ferment in Prussia. His most notable ally was the controversial military thinker A. H. D. von Bülow, who criticized the class basis of the Prussian army and state and urged that the Frederickian system be abolished and that advancement be determined according to merit. Indeed, following the disaster of 1806, these were the ideas that were to find their consummation in the Prussian reform movement.[32]

The criticism which had been levelled against the Prussian army of the *ancien régime* remained perfectly applicable to the only army that retained its eighteenth-century form well into the nineteenth century. More than thirty years after the Prussian reformers, Mitchell was fiercely campaigning on the very same battlegrounds against the distinct social characteristics of the British army. He called for a humane attitude towards the soldier, for the abolition of corporal punishment, and for the improvement of the troops' appalling living-conditions. He was the principal public opponent of the purchase system of officer commissions, which he denounced as hindering talent and military proficiency.[33] Like the Prussian

[31] *Thoughts on Tactics*, 25–72, 123–76; for his exchange with Napier on this matter see *United Service Journal*, 3 (1839), 103–6, 531–36; 1 (1840), 262–8.

[32] For Bülow see above Book I, 79–94; for Mitchell's acknowledged debt to Bülow see, for example, *Thoughts on Tactics*, 12.

[33] Again Mitchell's arguments in the *United Service Journal* from the mid-1830s are recapitulated in *Thoughts on Tactics*, esp. pp. v–viii, 239–90.

reform movement itself, this demonstrates that, contrary to their reactionary image, the German Movement and Romanticism, on account of their fundamental evolutionist approach, could be either reformist or conservative, depending on the circumstances and the opponent. Indeed, when from the 1840s the political and public urges for reform finally reached the army, it was the radical Napier who, with his customary zeal, opposed any talk of reform.[34] His position derived not only from a sense of pride in the British army of the Peninsula, symbolized by the towering figure of the Duke of Wellington, but also from deeper intellectual sources. If, as Napier maintained, 'this last was the period in which the principles of the military art were brought to all the perfection of which they appear to be capable', could any change be a change for the better? Like Jomini, Napier was not very receptive to change. It is no coincidence, for example, that for both men the introduction, in the middle of the century of the rifle as the standard infantry-weapon came as unwelcome news; it posed a threat to a universalist conception of war.[35]

Mitchell's intellectual origins made him a highly interesting exception, but an exception he was. British officers may have had little time to consider their profession, and even less to reflect on military theory, but inasmuch as they were exposed to any such speculation, it was derived entirely from the military thinkers of the Enlightenment. This exposure increased after the Crimean débâcle, when the neglected army suddenly found itself at the centre of public interest and facing calls for a comprehensive overhaul. When, in response to this demand, Napier's son-in-law, Lieutenant-Colonel—later Major-General—Sir Patrick MacDougall, composed *The Theory of War, Illustrated by Numerous Examples from Military History* for the education of his fellow officers, he humbly stated that he was merely digesting Jomini, Archduke Charles, and

[34] See esp. Napier's pamphlet *Six Letters in Vindication of the British Army, Exposing the Calumnies of the Liverpool Financial Reform Association* (London, 1849); this is Napier at his best in an exchange with Gladstone, the association's secretary.

[35] After the devastating use of the rifle in the Crimea, Jomini in the new edn. of the *Précis de l'art de la guerre* (1855), 2nd. app., still denied that tactics could ever radically change. For an exchange between Jomini and a French critic on this matter, see 'General Jomini and the "Spectateur Militaire" ', *United Service Journal* (1856), 201–5. The railway was, of course, an even greater challenge. For the attitude of Charles and William Napier toward the Minié rifle see Luvaas, *The Education of an Army*, 34–5.

Napier.[36] The book went through three editions within six years. It made MacDougall the natural choice for the post of first commandant of the staff college which was founded in 1858.[37]

Similar in character to the *Theory of War* but of much wider influence was the famous *The Operations of War* (1866). It was composed by Sir Edward Bruce Hamley (1824–93), the first professor of military history at the staff college and, in the 1870s, its fourth commandant.[38] Hamley had one foot in the world of literature and contributed regularly to *Blackwood's Magazine*, one of the most popular periodicals in the country. He was a man of the London salons, a member of the Athenaeum, the famous scientific and literary club, and a friend of the circle of philosophers who made the club their centre, Herbert Spencer being the most famous of them.[39] His mastery of style and exposition made the *Operations of War* one of the most successful military textbooks ever. Based entirely on Jomini's rationale of operations and Archduke Charles's geographical analysis, the book demonstrated the principles of strategy in the clearest and most didactic manner through descriptions of a variety of modern military campaigns. It soon became the official textbook both at Camberley and at West Point and went through five editions in Hamley's own lifetime alone.

However, as mentioned before with respect to all Jominian military literature which turned the characteristics of Napoleonic warfare into the universal principles of war, Hamley's writings were difficult to adapt to the sweeping changes brought about by

[36] P. L. MacDougall, *The Theory of War, Illustrated by Numerous Examples from Military History* (London, 1856); see esp. v–vii. For another, condensed exposition of Jominian principles with an introductory congratulating letter by Napier, see Edward Yates, *Elementary Treatise on Strategy* (London, 1852); the author was a fellow of St John's College, Cambridge. Also see his *Elementary Treatise on Tactics*. (London, 1853).

[37] For MacDougall see the sketch in *DNB* Supplement, 993–4; Luvaas, *The Education of an Army*, 101–29; and Brian Bond, *The Victorian Army and the Staff College 1854–1914* (London, 1972), 83–4.

[38] See Alexander Innes Shand, *The Life of General Sir Edward Bruce Hamley* (2 vols.; London, 1895); E. M. Lloyd in *DNB* Supplement, xxii. 807–10; Luvaas, *The Education of an Army*, 130–68; Bond, *The Staff College*, 84–8, 131–3; A. R. Godwin-Austin, *The Staff and the Staff College* (London, 1927), esp. 112–14, 133–4.

[39] Shand, *Sir Edward Bruce Hamley*, esp. i. 23, 43–8, 181. An interesting picture of Hamley's attitudes, despite his Toryism, is given in his sharp critique *Thomas Carlyle: Mirage Philosophy* (London, 1881) and, on the other side, his highly sympathetic biography *Voltaire* (London, 1877).

steam and advanced metallurgy.[40] Not surprisingly, the fortunes of Jomini and Hamley were closely linked. Despite being formulated in a period of revolutionary change, Hamley's tactics, like Jomini's, never departed from the Napoleonic model, and in the sixth edition of the *Operations of War* (1907), published after Hamley's death, the original part on tactics was therefore omitted altogether. The First World War, with its long, continuous fronts, made the Napoleonic strategic model largely irrelevant and marked the final eclipse of both Jomini and Hamley. In 1923 the *Operations of War* was reprinted for the last time.

It has been observed, however, that a reaction against the book had already been setting in during the 1890s, though the reason for this has never been properly explained. In 1894 the book lost its monopoly as the set text in military history for the staff college entrance-examination. In 1898 it was subjected to comprehensive criticism by Lieutenant-Colonel G. F. R. Henderson, then the professor of military history at Camberley.[41] In criticizing Hamley for being schematic and for ignoring the spirit of war, the commander's intentions, and moral forces, Henderson was voicing the classical themes of the German military school. His criticism reflected a decisive shift in the direction in which the world now looked for military theory.[42]

The intellectual world of the founding fathers of the American republic was grounded in the ideas of the British and French Enlightenment. In the military field this meant strong aversion to the institution of standing armies, mistrusted as a potentially dangerous instrument of despotism and selfish interests and as alien to the values of civil society. The natural preference—reflecting both the prevalent sentiment among the *philosophes* as well as existing American institutions—was for a militia of free citizens, called up in time of danger to defend their country. All the same,

[40] See Luvaas, *The Education of an Army*, 141–50.

[41] Ibid. 150–1; Bond, *The Staff College*, 87–8.

[42] As was the custom with many of the military thinkers of the Enlightenment, Hamley stressed the importance of moral forces but excused himself from discussing them. In the introduction to later editions of *The Operations of War*, he named Clausewitz as their most notable student. With the Prussian army beginning to attract universal attention after 1866, Hamley sent a copy of his book to Moltke. But Moltke's reply was polite and formal rather than complimentary as it is sometimes presented, and indeed could not have been different: Shand, *Sir Edward Bruce Hamley*, i. 183–4.

when the War of Independence, and later the defence needs of the young republic, almost forced the creation of a small regular army, it was again Europe and European organization, tactics, and military thought that constituted the formative influence, bringing the military outlook and literature of the Enlightenment with them.[43]

The most notable manifestation of this was the founding of the United States Military Academy at West Point. The origins of the Academy, the ideas behind it, and its curriculum reflected and paralleled the story of the military academies pioneered all over Europe in the second half of the eighteenth century in response to the Enlightenment ideal of military education. Early discussions about an academy had been prompted by the War of Independence, and they continued thereafter, largely under the influence of French and German officers. As in Europe, the military schools for the professions of artillery and engineering were the first to appear, established by Washington at West Point in 1794 to remedy the acute lack of technical expertise in the young army. In 1799 the prolific Hamilton submitted to Secretary of War McHenry a complete scheme for the establishment of five military schools: one Fundamental School and four Schools of Application for engineering and artillery, cavalry, infantry, and the navy. Secretary McHenry presented the scheme to Congress with only minor modifications. 'The art of war', he told Congress, 'is subjected to mechanical, geometrical, moral and physical rules; it calls for profound study; its theory is immense; the details infinite, and its principles are rendered useful only by a happy adaptation of them to the circumstances of place and ground.' As evidence of the importance of military professionalism and science, he cited the military authors of Antiquity as well as Machiavelli and Marshal de Puységur, who had left, he wrote, an 'excellent treatise on war'.[44]

Nothing came of the proposal. But, significantly, it was none other than President Jefferson—the arch-enemy of state machinery

[43] For the militia vs. standing army and for the general view of war, see Russell F. Weigley, *History of the United States Army* (Bloomington, Ind., 1967), 29–94; Marcus Cunliffe, *Soldiers and Civilians: The Martial Spirit in America 1775–1865* (London, 1969); Reginald Stuart, *War and American Thought from the Revolution to the Monroe Doctrine* (Kent, Oh., 1982).

[44] Hamilton to McHenry, 23 Nov. 1799, in Henry Cabot Lodge (ed.), *The Works of Alexander Hamilton* (New York, 1886), vi. 265–72; Documents 39, 40, 14 Jan. and 13 Feb. 1800, in *American State Papers, Military Affairs* (Washington, DC, 1832), i. 133–5, 142–4.

and military professionalism—who took action to open the Military Academy in 1802.[45] Historians who found this puzzling forgot that he was also one of the greatest exponents of the American Enlightenment.[46] The man he chose to organize the institution was Jonathan Williams, a civilian and grandnephew of Benjamin Franklin. Williams was a man of wide scholarly pursuits who had collaborated with his famous relative in several scientific projects and was himself a member of the American Philosophical Society and a contributor to its *Transactions*. Having long been an enthusiast for fortification and military science, he was commissioned by Jefferson as a major in the artillery in 1801. It is characteristic of the age and the man that one of Williams's first initiatives was to found the United States Military Philosophical Society—with Jefferson himself as its first patron—to discuss and 'promote military science'.[47]

Like the Woolwich Academy, West Point emphasized the technical professions, an approach which was also in line with the desire to integrate the army into society. From 1817, following the war of 1812, the academy was thoroughly reorganized under the command of Captain Sylvanus Thayer with a view to making it the seedbed of an increasingly professional, though miniature, army. Thayer, who made an extensive tour of study in France and brought with him some thousand books on the military art, looked to the French military schools, especially the École polytechnique, and to French military teaching as a model. Again, it was the legacy of the Enlightenment that lay behind American military education.

From 1818 the academy's standard text for the study of the

[45] See R. E. Dupuy, *The Story of West Point: 1802–1943* (Washington, DC, 1943), 27–31; Sidney Forman, *West Point* (New York, 1950), 16–19; Weigley, *History of the United States Army*, 105–6. For the wider intellectual and institutional context see above Book I esp. 61–65.

[46] See for example Weigley, in Paret (ed.), *Makers of Modern Strategy from Machiavelli to the Nuclear Age* (Princeton, NJ, 1986), 412–3. Theodore J. Crackel in 'The Founding of West Point: Jefferson and the Politics of Security', *Armed Forces and Society*, 7 (1981), 529–43, dismisses the Enlightenment background without bothering with either evidence or argument (p. 532). Also see Reginald C. Stuart, *The Half-Way Pacifist: Thomas Jefferson's View of War* (Toronto, 1978), which does not refer, however, to the creation of West Point.

[47] For Williams and the Military Philosophical Society and its proceedings see esp. Forman, *West Point* 23–31; also Dupuy, *The Story of West Point*, 27–31; M. E. Lombard, 'Jonathan Williams', *Dictionary of American Biography*, xx. 280–2. Scharnhorst's *Militärische Gesellschaft*, springing from the same intellectual sources and strikingly similar in orientation, was also founded in 1802.

science and art of war was Captain J. M. O'Connor's translation of Gay de Vernon's *Traité élémentaire d'art militaire et de fortification* (1805). The French original, composed by an engineering officer and professor of fortifications at the École polytechnique for the students of that school, concentrated on the technical services, but the translator added an extensive summary of

> the best principles and maxims of such writers as Guibert, Lloyd, Tempelhoff and Jomini, particularly of the latter, whose work [the *Treatise*] is considered a masterpiece and as the highest authority. Indeed no man should pretend to be capable of commanding any considerable body of troops unless he has studied and meditated on the principles laid down by Jomini.[48]

From the 1830s Vernon's book was replaced by the widely circulated notes of Denis Hart Mahan (WP 1824). As Thayer's protégé, Mahan was sent to study in France. In his capacity as the professor of civil and military engineering and of the art of war and later as chairman of the Academic Board, he became the leading figure in the academy for four decades. He also wrote a little book, *An Elementary Treatise on Advanced Guard, Out-Posts and Detachment Service of Troops . . . with a Historical Sketch on the Rise and Progress of Tactics* (1847), which was typical of the Enlightenment genre of military literature.[49] But the first major American treatise on the conduct of operations was written by one of Mahan's closest pupils, Lieutenant Henry Wagner Halleck (WP 1839). It was entitled *Elements of Military Art and Science, or Course of Instruction in Strategy, Fortifications, Tactics of Battles etc.* (1846). Halleck was a widely read military writer, and his vast knowledge found full expression in his comprehensive book. In the fields of strategy and tactics the book was totally dominated by Jomini, as well as by the work of August Wagner and Archduke Charles.[50]

[48] S. F. Gay de Vernon, *A Treatise on the Science of War and Fortifications . . . to which is Added a Summary of the Principles and Maxims of Grand Tactics and Operations* (2 vols.; New York, 1817); the summary of Jomini's work appears in ii. 385–490; the quotation is from i. v.

[49] On Mahan see Dupuy, *The Story of West Point*, 133–47, 165–72, 195–204; Forman, *West Point*, 58, 82, 87.

[50] For the strategic teaching see esp. *Elements of Military Art and Science* (New York, 1846), 35–54; the recommended bibliography for the strategic section alone includes the theories and histories of Jomini, Charles, Wagner, Rocquancourt, Jacquinot de Presle, Gay de Vernon, Lloyd, Tempelhoff, Grimoard, Fuché, Saint-Cyr, Laverne, Beauvais, Kausler, Gourgaud, Montholon, Napoleon, Foy, Dumas,

In the Napoleonic Club, founded at West Point in 1848, officers met under Mahan's chairmanship to discuss Napoleon's campaigns, largely through the medium of Jomini. One of the most notable participants was George B. McClellan (WP 1846) who thought Jomini was 'the ablest of military writers and the first author in any age who gathered from the campaigns of the great generals the true principles of war'.[51] Another occasional participant may have been Robert E. Lee. His class at West Point (1825) had studied Gay de Vernon as the text for the subject of Grand Tactics, one of the five military subjects taught at the academy. When he became the superintendent of the academy in 1852, his small private library included Jomini's *Précis de l'art de la guerre* in the original French.[52] Halleck, McClellan, and possibly also Thomas J. (Stonewall) Jackson visited Jomini in Europe.[53] E. T. Hitchcock and P. G. T. Beauregard were his disciples. William T. Sherman said in 1862 that 'should any officer . . . be ignorant of his tactics, regulations or even the principles of the art of war (Mahan and Jomini), it would be a lasting disgrace'.[54] All the translations of Jomini's major works into English were done in America. Indeed, and this has not been fully recognized, in no other country was Jomini translated so extensively. The *Précis* was translated (badly) in 1854. It served as the official text of a new course, the 'Theory and Practice of Strategy and Grand Tactics', introduced into West Point in 1860.[55] The Civil War produced not only a new, better translation of the *Précis* but also full translations of Jomini's multi-volume *Traité des grandes opérations militaires* (the only one

Ségur, Pelet, Koch, Clausewitz, Guibert, Thiers, and Napier (p. 58–60); compare with the bibliographical introduction to Jomini, *Summary of the Art of War* (New York, 1854), 14–21.

[51] McClellan, 'Jomini', in *The Galaxy*, 7 (1869), 874–88, cited in David Donald, 'Refighting the Civil War', in his *Lincoln Reconsidered* (New York, 1956), 89, 194.

[52] For the curriculum and for Lee's private library and borrowing-list from the academy's library, see Douglas S. Freeman's thoroughly documented *R. E. Lee* (4 vols.; New York, 1934), i. 76–7, 352–3, 358. Freeman is right in pointing out that 'Grand Tactics' included what has later been called strategy; this was still the French usage in the early nineteenth century, before the term 'strategy' was fully accepted from the German (see above Book I, 40–2, 114). The currently accepted opinion that no 'strategy' at all was taught in the academy is, therefore, based on a misunderstanding. Also see Eben Swift, 'The Military Education of Robert E. Lee', *Virginia Magazine of History and Biography*, 35 (1927), 97–108; Donald, 'Refighting the Civil War', 88–9.

[53] Swift, 'The Military Education of Robert E. Lee', 151.

[54] Donald, 'Refighting the Civil War', 90.

[55] Ibid. 89.

existing in any language) and of *Vie politique et militaire de Napoléon*, the latter done by Halleck himself, the Union's general in chief.[56]

All this is known well enough because of the climatic events that followed. The Civil War was conducted by West Pointers, and it has justly been said that generals on both sides went into the war with a sword in one hand and Jomini's *Summary of the Art of War* in the other.[57] Opinion regarding the exact nature of both Jomini's teaching and influence had undergone some noticeable changes, however. Strangely enough, while early commentators had a good grasp of what Jomini stood for and a balanced picture of his influence, later ones seemed no longer to have either. The reason for this is not difficult to trace; as Clausewitz was reconquering the West from the 1950s, interpretations reflected Jomini's deteriorating image.

To understand what Jomini's teaching was, it must not be forgotten that he won fame by successfully schematizing Frederickian and Napoleonic warfare. He emphasized initiative, aggressive conduct, mobility, and concentration of force, and regarded the destruction of the enemy army as the principal aim of military operations. This was to be achieved either by manœuvring against his rear and cutting off his lines of operations and retreat or, if the enemy divided his forces, by operating from a central position and crushing each of these fractions separately. Excellent studies regarding Jomini's influence in America perceived this clearly.[58] However, from the late 1950s a new note crept in. Since it was known that Clausewitz opposed Jomini, military historians could no longer regard Jomini as an adequate interpreter of Napoleon. It was not enough that he was regarded as too deeply rooted in the eighteenth century and thus too moderate and remote from the idea of the nation-in-arms; the tendency to distinguish clearly (and unfavourably) between Clausewitz and Jomini has now somehow

[56] Jomini, *Summary of the Art of War* (New York, 1854), trans. by Maj. O. F. Winship and Lieut. E. E. McLean; *The Art of War* (Philadelphia, 1862), trans. by Captain G. W. Mendell and Lieutenant W. P. Craighill; *Treatise on Grand Military Operations* (2 vols.; New York, 1865), trans. by Col. S. B. Holabird; *Life of Napoleon* (4 vols.; New York, 1864), trans. by Major-General H. W. Halleck.

[57] J. D. Hittle's introduction to *Jomini and his Summary of the Art of War* (Harrisburg, Pa., 1947), 2.

[58] Swift, 'The Military Education of Robert E. Lee', esp. 150–4; Donald, 'Refighting the Civil War'.

given rise to the erroneous notion that the latter even failed to grasp the essence of Napoleonic strategy and regarded the occupation of territory rather than the enemy army as the object of military operations.[59] Clausewitz's own writings make clear that this was totally untrue. What ever shortcomings he found in Jomini, Clausewitz thought his great merit was that, in contrast to his predecessors in the eighteenth century (Lloyd, Bülow, Archduke Charles, etc.), he maintained that 'the engagement is the only effective means in war'.[60] Indeed, from the early 1970s, a much-called-for correction finally redressed the picture.[61]

The same tendency also found expression in the assessments of Jomini's influence on the conduct of the Civil War generals, an influence which everyone agrees existed. Early interpreters were aware of the different aspects of the matter, inherent in the nature of Jomini's theories. They noted the Jominian leading theme behind the classical campaigns of central position and interior lines masterminded by Lee in 1862; one was brilliantly carried out by Stonewall Jackson in the Shenandoah Valley, and another was conducted by Lee himself against the armies of McClellan and Pope, culminating in the great enveloping battle of the Second Manassas.[62] On the other hand, the shortcomings of Jomini's teaching were also clearly pointed out. Changing circumstances were everywhere rendering parts of what Jomini had regarded as a universal theory of war obsolete. The rifle was transforming tactics,

[59] A series of military historians seem to have followed in each other's footsteps here; see esp. T. Harry Williams, 'The Military Leadership of North and South', in D. Donald (ed.), *Why the North Won the Civil War* (Baton Rouge, La., 1960), 28–47, esp. 30; Stephen E. Ambrose, *Halleck: Lincoln's Chief of Staff* (Baton Rouge, La., 1962), esp. 5–7; John R. Elting, 'Jomini: Disciple of Napoleon', *Military Affairs*, 28 (1964), 17–26, which is otherwise the best biographical study of Jomini in English; Weigley, *The American Way of War: A History of United States Military Strategy and Policy* (London, 1973), 82–3, 84, 88.

[60] Carl von Clausewitz, *On War*, trans. Michael Howard and Peter Paret, (Princeton, NJ, 1976), ii. 2, 136.

[61] The turning-point was Archer Jones, 'Jomini and the Strategy of the American Civil War: A Reinterpretation', *Military Affairs*, 34 (1970), 127–31; further elaborated in Jones and Thomas L. Connelly, *The Politics of Command, Factions and Ideas in Confederate Strategy* (Baton Rouge, La., 1973), esp. 6–30; and Jones and Herman Hattaway, *How the North Won* (London, 1983), esp. 12–14, 21–4. Also see Joseph L. Harsh, 'Battlesword and Rapier: Clausewitz, Jomini and the American Civil War', *Military Affairs*, 38 (1974), 133–8. T. H. Williams in effect admitted the mistake in 'The Return to Jomini: Some Thoughts on Recent Civil War Writing', ibid. 39 (1975), 204–6.

[62] Swift, 'The Military Education of Robert E. Lee'; Donald, 'Refighting the Civil War', 91–5.

and, more fatal to Jomini, the ability to transport troops quickly by railway over vast distances was calling into question the advantage of the interior lines in strategy.[63] Moltke's campaigns of 1866 and 1870–1 were later to prove this decisively, but the new developments were still difficult for Jomini's disciples in North America to grasp. Lincoln, no professional soldier, intuitively reproduced the Allies' strategy against Napoleon in 1813, suggesting that the North could best deny the initiative to the enemy and make effective use of its own numerical superiority by launching a closely co-ordinated concentric attack on the whole periphery of the South. But Halleck was dismissive: 'To operate on exterior lines against an enemy occupying a central position will fail, as it has always failed, in ninety-nine cases out of a hundred. It is condemned by every military authority I have ever read.'[64]

Indeed, later commentators tended to associate Halleck's and McClellan's indecisiveness with Jominian pedantry. At the same time, since Jomini had now come to be seen as moderate and as one who had regarded the occupation of territories rather than the destruction of the enemy army as the object of operations, his reputation as the inspiration behind the crushing campaigns of the brilliant generals of the Confederacy became problematic. As a result, several historians tied themselves in some curious knots. One stated that Jomini had regarded the occupation of territory as the object of operations, but later argued that the South won its initial successes through the application of Jominian doctrines, which led to a decisive battle.[65] Another historian purged Jomini altogether of responsibility for Confederate strategy, leaving him to share indirect responsibility only for the Union's blunders. While arguing that Civil War generals on all sides, and especially Lee, were obsessed with the climactic battle, he attributed this to the Napoleonic model, forgetting that he himself maintained that it had been predominantly through the medium of Jomini that these generals had studied Napoleon.[66]

In truth, Jomini's was a striking interpretation of Napoleonic

[63] Donald, 'Refighting the Civil War', 96–7.

[64] *The Collected Works of Abraham Lincoln*, ed. Roy P. Basler (New Brunswick, 1953), v. 98–9; *The War of the Rebellion: A Compilation of the Official Records of the Union and Confederate Armies* (Washington, DC, 1880–1901), Series One, xi, pt. 2, 497; cited by Weigley, *The American Way of War*, 493.

[65] Williams, 'The Military Leadership of North and South', 30, 38.

[66] Weigley, *The American Way of War*, 82–3, 92–127.

generalship, and without attributing to the Civil War generals excessive bookishness or theoretical preoccupation, one can say that, on both sides, they could only operate—for better or for worse—on the basis of the strategic concepts which they had acquired in the course of their common education. Significantly, the only notable exception was the very mediocre student at West Point (1843) who had resigned from the army in 1854. When asked by a young officer about Jomini after he had become famous, Grant answered that he had never paid him much attention. 'The art of war', he said, 'is simple enough; find out where your enemy is, get at him as soon as you can, strike at him as hard as you can, and keep moving on.'[67]

In their handling of the French army, the returning Bourbons faced their usual dilemma. They had to uproot the legacy of the Revolution and Empire in one of the most typical and glorious institutions of those regimes, while accommodating some of their achievements and avoiding an all-out confrontation with their wide circles of sympathizers and beneficiaries. Here too, the result was an uneasy compromise which brought together Napoleonic veterans and returning *émigrés*, and incorporated limited conscription, and (until 1824) a reserve, with long-service army. Codified in the Saint-Cyr Law of 1818, these were the institutional principles of the French army from the Restoration throughout the period of the July Monarchy and Second Empire.

Reaffirmed by the Soult Law of 1832, these principles now reflected the satisfaction of the middle classes with the professional army, which enabled them to exempt their sons from military service by finding replacements, and whose base was limited enough to prevent it from becoming an instrument of popular revolution. Correspondingly, the prevailing mood in the army itself changed from widely held Bonapartist sympathies to detached conservatism. When called upon to do so, it could be relied on to crush radical disturbances, from the ominous silk-weavers insurrection in Lyons in 1831 to the great June 1848 uprising in Paris. The army too came to prefer long-term service as a remedy for the notoriously undisciplined character of the French conscript.[68]

[67] Louis A. Coolidge, *Ulysses S. Grant* (Boston, 1922), 54.

[68] See J. Monteilhet, *Les Institutions militaires de la France (1814–1924)* (Paris, 1926), ch. 1; Raoul Girardet, *La Société militaire dans la France contemporaine,*

These principles of organization also matched the limited scope of the army's military tasks. During the Restoration the army was employed in the two semi-political interventions in Spain (1823) and Greece (1827), and began the long conquest and pacification of Algeria (1830). Despite some sabre-rattling over the Eastern Question in 1840, Louis-Philippe recoiled from any military confrontation with a highly suspicious Europe. Only Napoleon III's revisionist and opportunist politics resulted – apart from world-wide colonial adventures – in two large-scale, but strictly contained wars, in Crimea (1854–1856) and Lombardy (1859), against major European powers.

Thus there was little in the military experience of post-Revolutionary France to match its glorious past. Nor did the poor living-conditions, dull routine, and social as well as cultural isolation of the French officer-corps, many members of which came from a very humble background, provide much intellectual stimulation.[69] During the Restoration, Napoleon's retired marshals and generals satisfied the public's nostalgic thirst for an account of the nation's and their own glorious days in the most popular literary genre of the Romantic period—history. Their memoirs and such theoretical works as Marshal Marmont's *De l'esprit des institutions militaires* (1846) reflected the prevailing synthesis of the Enlightenment's conception of military theory and Napoleonic strategy.[70] There was, however, very little that was original and significant in French military thinking during the July Monarchy and Second Empire. Colonial experience could produce anti-guerilla doctrines, such as those of Marshal Bugeaud, the veteran of

1815–1939 (Paris, 1953), pt. one; Pierre Chalmin, *L'Officier français de 1815 à 1870* (Paris, 1957); Douglas Porch, *Army and Revolution: France 1815–1848* (London, 1974). For a brief account see Best, *War and Society in Revolutionary Europe*, 215–222.

[69] See previous note and William Serman, *Les Origines des officiers français 1848–1870* (Paris, 1979).

[70] For a characteristic popular example see Gouvion Saint-Cyr, *Mémoires pour servir à l'histoire militaire sous le directoire, le consulat et l'empire* (4 vols.; Paris, 1831), esp. the foreword and the introductory essay: 'Pensée sur la guerre'. Marmont, *De l'esprit des institutions militaires* (Paris, 1846), discusses the '*positivist* principles of war' (my italics) and their application; as mentioned, Jomini is often deliberately ignored. For an overview of authors and works see P. G. Griffith, *Military Thought in the French Army, 1815–1851* (Manchester, 1989), 57–62; E. Guillon, *Nos écrivains militaires* (2 vols.; Paris, 1898), ii. 142–236; and E. Carrias, *La Pensée militaire française* (Paris, 1960), 226–62.

the Peninsula and conquerer of Algeria.[71] The conduct of operations in relatively small and isolated forces in a hostile environment reinforced the tendency of the French army to promote cohesion and morale as the paramount military qualities.[72] But the use of light, independent, mobile units against irregulars was scarcely relevant—indeed was probably downright alien—to the needs of a large-scale European war.

Thus, when the army under the Second Empire regained some of its former glory and cultivated a professional reputation and heroic mystique—built up outside the fortifications of Sebastopol and on the battlefields of Magenta and Solferino—it did so with much bravery, panache, and *esprit de corps*. But equally characteristic was the administrative and logistic chaos, influenced by long experience of improvisation and leading to an almost ideological spirit of contempt for orderly staff-work, as well as a lack of training in it. Only the emergence of a major challenge to French military supremacy in Europe introduced a new sense of alarm and apprehension into the military establishment and generated considerable intellectual ferment.

Prussia was the only one of Napoleon's rivals to adopt the principle of the nation-in-arms after her defeat in 1806 and to retain it after 1815. It was the revival of this principle later on that made possible the decisive victory of her mass armies over the Austrians in 1866. In the early 1860s the King of Prussia transformed the main legacy of this experiment, the independent Landwehr militia, which had been both politically and militarily unreliable, into a mere second-line reserve of a large army of short-term universal conscription. In a remarkable reversal of political fronts between king and parliament, the autocratic ruler thus created a well-trained and disciplined national army of unprecedented size. After the Prussian victory of 1866, the newly created North German Confederation possessed about one and a half times as many front-line troops and double the overall number of men in arms as the considerably more populous France. This was the fundamental problem that the French army had to confront.

In late 1866 Napoleon III, concerned by these developments, set

[71] H. D'Ideville, *Memoirs of Marshal Bugeaud, From his Private Correspondence and Original Documents* (2 vols.; London, 1884); A. T. Sullivan, *Thomas-Robert Bugeaud* (Hamden, Conn., 1983).

[72] See Griffith, *Military Thought in the French Army*, 117–22.

a one-million-man target for the French army, in order to match the estimated strength of the Prussians. However, the idea of adopting the Prussian military system was rejected by most of the emperor's advisers on both military and political grounds. The army had got used to believing that universal short-term conscription with a large reserve could only create half-trained mobs. Civilians objected to universal conscription as disruptive of their way of life and socially dangerous. In early 1868 a compromise measure was carried through the Corps Législatif by Marshal Niel, Napoleon's newly appointed Minister of War. It maintained the principle of a long-service regular army based on limited conscription, but established a first-line reserve and a second-line militia (the Garde Mobile) which, unlike their German counterparts, were mostly composed of those exempted from conscription and were therefore almost totally untrained. Thus, although the basis of the regular army itself was expanded and the target of one million men in arms was secured on paper, the new reserve and militia were militarily useless. Both military and civil authorities regarded them with contempt and made sure they would never materialize.

The public controversy over the problem of defence was fuelled by General Trochu's best-selling book *L'Armée française en 1867*, based on the confidential recommendations of a military commission set up by the emperor, of which the author was a member. Trochu was blunt about the army's mystique, sacred traditions, and practices. He argued that in order to meet the new challenge, the army had to expand along the lines put forward by Niel, and reform thoroughly its administration, military education, system of promotion, and tactics.[73]

The debate over the two conflicting forms of military-social institutions was complicated by a tactical element. From the middle of the century, the paramount military question preoccupying soldiers all over Europe was the tactical significance of the new, accurate, long-range rifle. Replacing the smooth-bore musket and widely used for the first time in the Crimean War, the rifle threatened to revolutionize tactics by calling into question the feasibility of mass charges, carried out by dense infantry- and

[73] Trochu, *L'Armée francaise en 1867* (20th edn., Paris 1870); Michael E. Howard, *The Franco-Prussian War* (London, 1961), ch. 1; also see Lynn M. Case, *French Opinion On War and Diplomacy during the Second Empire* (Philadelphia, 1954).

cavalry-formations. The war of 1866 introduced a new factor into the problem and, in this respect too, was the cause of much excitement in France. The Prussians employed a breech-loader, the 'needle-gun', which was given much of the credit for their success. The French responded quickly by adopting an even more advanced breech-loader, the *chassepot*.

Great military literature has always been produced in response to great challenges and stimuli, whether military, intellectual, or other. The acute challenge to the tradition and ethos of French professionalism, the controversies surrounding the proposed reform of the French military system, and the problem of the modern battlefield created a more than adequate stimulus. They drove a rather obscure but highly perceptive colonel, who as a junior officer had distinguished himself under Trochu in the Crimea, to explore the essence of fighting-performance. The result was *Battle Studies*, one of the most fascinating and original works on military affairs ever to be written, and widely acclaimed as a classic. As it happens, however, the book has received remarkably little serious scholarly attention and attracted no full-length study. Much about its origins and influence has thus remained either unrecognized or shrouded in myth, and deserves closer scrutiny.

The little we know about the man Charles-Jean-Jacques-Joseph Ardant du Picq is derived from army records and from a short biographical letter that his brother was requested to write for the second edition of his works. Ardant du Picq was born in 1821 and graduated from Saint-Cyr in 1844. He fought in the Crimea, where he was taken prisoner while storming the central bastion at Sebastopol. He then took part in the campaigns in Syria (1860–1) and Algeria (1864–6), rising steadily in rank and receiving the customary decorations and medals. He was likeable and was respected as an honest man of independent mind. He was mortally wounded while leading his regiment near Metz in the opening stage of the Franco-Prussian War.[74]

The man's writings are more enlightening than this sketch of a rather undistinguished life-story. Versed in modern, predominantly French, military literature, du Picq cites Montecuccoli, Folard, de Saxe, Guibert, Napoleon, Jomini, Saint-Cyr, Bismark (the military

[74] Introductory material to Ardant du Picq, *Battle Studies* (Harrisburg, Pa., 1947; 1st edn. New York, 1921; based on the 2nd edn. of *Études sur le combat*, ed. Ernest Judet), 25–31.

writer), Decker, Thiers, and Bugeaud. Like all proponents of the current of military thought that had its roots in the Enlightenment, he sought to advance military science. However, both his mode of thinking and his concerns were quite different and novel. He did not share the traditional preoccupation with the conduct of grand operations. Finding military theory too mechanistic, materialistic, and dominated by mathematical reasoning,[75] he quoted Marshal de Saxe's famous saying that the human heart was the starting-point of all matters pertaining to war.[76] Fighting-performance, he believed, was rooted in the most elementary instincts of man's individual and group psychology.

The human heart is the constant element in war: 'Centuries have not changed human nature . . . at bottom there is always found the same man.'[77] After the Romantic onslaught on the philosophers of the eighteenth century, du Picq needs no reminder of the varied particular manifestations of human nature, to which he is ever attentive; and in the age of progress he is fully aware of historical change:

> The art of war is subjected to many modifications by industrial and scientific progress. But one thing does not change, the heart of man.[78]

> I have heard philosophers reproached for studying too exclusively man in general and neglecting the race, the country, the era, so that their studies of him offer little of real social or political value. [However] the opposite criticism can be made of military men of all countries. . . . They fail to consider as a factor in the problem man confronted by danger.[79]

It was du Picq's belief that military theorists not only missed the vital element in war but also neglected the really important data in their preoccupation with grand strategies. 'The smallest detail, taken from an actual incident in war,' he wrote, 'is more instructive for me, a soldier, than all the Thiers and Jominis in the world'; more instructive than 'the plans and general conduct of the campaign of the greatest captain'.[80] Indeed, he believed that ground-level information about actual fighting constituted the basis for a truly scientific study of war.

Commentators have noted but never dwelt on du Picq's

[75] *Battle Studies*, 40, 50, 192.
[76] Ibid. 39.
[77] Ibid. 39–40.
[78] Ibid. 109.
[79] Ibid.
[80] Ibid. 5, 7.

scientism.[81] Yet it constitutes a major source of his inspiration. His was not the enthusiastic but loose theoretical ideal of the eighteenth century but the rigorous programme and research-method of positivism, the dominating intellectual current during the Second Empire.[82] According to du Picq, military science was to be produced through a careful analysis of the vast data of experience, systematically gathered:

> From a series of true accounts there should emanate an ensemble of characteristic details which in themselves are very apt to show in a striking, irrefutable way what was necessarily and forcibly taking place at such and such a moment of an action in war. Take the estimate of the soldier obtained in this manner to serve as a base for what might possibly be a rational method of fighting. It will put us on guard against *a priori* school methods.[83]

Du Picq insisted that copious evidence regarding the soldier's real behaviour in the past is the key to his conduct in the future.[84] This would produce 'prescribed tactics', which, while not being too dogmatic, would lay down with mathematical logic 'some clearly defined rules, established by experience' to serve as a guiding doctrine.[85] Against the notorious gulf between theory and practice in war which existed in his day, he wrote, 'let us gather carefully the lessons of . . . experience, remembering *Bacon's* saying, "Experience excels science".'[86]

In his search for primary data on the fundamental characteristics of fighting man, du Picq first went to Antiquity, where 'battle was simple and clear', and where, in the case-studies of Cannae and Parasalus, he believed he could trust 'the clear presentation of Polybius, who obtained his information from the fugitives of Cannae', and 'the impassive clearness of Caesar in describing the art of war'.[87] The result was the pamphlet *Étude du combat d'après*

[81] See almost the only scholarly article on du Picq, Stefan Possony's half of 'Du Picq and Foch: The French School', in E. Earle (ed.), *Makers of Modern Strategy* (Princeton, NJ, 1943), 208.

[82] Throughout this chapter the term positivism is used in its broadest sense—almost interchangeably with scientism—rather than in the stricter one as the teaching of Auguste Comte. Two good works in English are: D. G. Charlton, *Positivist Thought in France during the Second Empire 1852–1870* (Oxford, 1959); and W. M. Simon, *European Positivism in the Nineteenth Century* (New York, 1963).

[83] *Battle Studies*, 7–8.

[84] Ibid. 103–4.

[85] ibid. 138–40.

[86] Ibid. 260; my italics.

[87] Ibid. 39, 55.

l'antique, 'Ancient Battle', completed in 1868 and distributed privately. He then addressed himself to modern battle, in a study which he did not live to finish. Here he had no intention of relying on 'the accounts of historians alone'. In all but a very few cases, he wrote, historians 'show the action of troop units only in a general way. Action in detail and the individual action of the soldier remain enveloped in a cloud of dust, in narratives as in reality.'[88] Historians tend to impose order upon the chaos of war, and their heroic rhetoric is often misleading as to man's true behaviour in battle. Fortunately, argued du Picq, for modern battle we possess another source of information, incomparable in wealth—the first-hand experience of soldiers. For the man who advocated Baconian methods—which had been canonized in D'Alembert's famous introduction to the *Grande encyclopédie* and had ever since been the archetypal model for positivist thought—the problem was how to get to this source, pose the right questions, and have the findings gathered and assessed on a grand scale.

In 1868 du Picq composed a highly detailed questionnaire and had it distributed among his fellow officers of all ranks. This striking example of positivist behavioural research—which ended with the above-quoted warning against a priori school methods—is worth quoting at some length. In a copy intended for the commanding general at Limoges, one reads:

> Concerning a regiment, a battalion, a company, a squad, it is interesting to know: The disposition taken to meet the enemy or the order of the march towards them. What becomes of this disposition or this march order under the isolated or combined influences of accidents of the terrain and the approach of danger?
>
> Is this order changed or is it continued in force when approaching the enemy?
>
> What becomes of it upon arriving within the range of the guns, within the range of bullets?
>
> At what distance is a voluntary or an ordered disposition taken before starting operations for commencing fire, for charging, or both?
>
> How did the fight start? How about the firing? How did the men adapt themselves? (This may be learned from the results: So many bullets fired, so many men shot down—when such data are available.) How was the charge made? At what distance did the enemy flee before it? At what distance did the charge fall back before the fire or the good order or good dispositions

[88] Ibid. 103.

of the enemy, or before such and such a movement of the enemy? What did it cost? What can be said about all these with reference to the enemy?
The behaviour, i.e. the order, the disorder, the shouts, the silence, the confusion, the calmness of the officers and men whether with us or with the enemy, before, during, or after the combat?
How has the soldier been controlled and directed during the action? At what instance has he had a tendency to quit the line in order to remain behind or to rush ahead?
At what moment, if the control were escaping from the leader's hands, has it no longer been possible to exercise it?
At what instant has this control escaped from the battalion commander? When from the captain, the section leader, the squad leader? At what time, in short, if such a thing did take place, was there but a disordered impulse, whether to the front or to the rear carrying along pell-mell with it both the leaders and men?
Where and when did the halt take place?
Where and when were the leaders able to resume command of the men?
At what moments before, during, or after the day, was the battalion roll-call made? The results of these roll-calls?
How many dead, how many wounded on the one side and on the other; the kind of wounds of the officers, non commissioned officers, corporals, privates, etc. etc.[89]

Replies were slow in coming, but this, as du Picq's brother remarks, was due to indifference rather than to ill will. However, from mid-1868 to early 1869, du Picq did receive a few of the accounts he was seeking. These were based on personal experience on the battlefields of the Second Empire and some of them proved to be of considerable interest.[90] He continued to seek out first-hand information among his comrades-in-arms, but it would be an exaggeration to say that this was absolutely essential for him. Positivist notions aside, his mind had, in fact, long been made up. Until the outbreak of the war of 1870, he immersed himself in the writing of a 'Study on Battle', compiled posthumously under the title 'Modern Battle'. Together with 'Ancient Battle', it comprises a unity of supreme stylistic beauty, perceptive power and originality.

[89] *Battle Studies*, 5–7.

[90] Introductory material to *Battle Studies*, pp. xvi–xvii, 28; for extracts from some of the most detailed and interesting accounts, including du Picq's re-questioning, which were kept by du Picq's family, see ibid. 263–273. Of course du Picq composed the questionnaire for the study of modern battle in 1868, after finishing 'Ancient Battle', and not the other way around, as Possony's confused chronology seems to suggest: 'Du Picq and Foch', in Earle (ed.), *Makers of Modern Strategy*, 209.

'Man does not enter battle to fight but for victory. He does everything that he can to avoid the first and obtain the second.'[91] This is du Picq's main thesis. Man is dominated by the instinct of self-preservation, whose agent is fear. Therefore, he may be induced or forced to fight for something, but fighting itself is unnatural to him.

Primitive man almost never fights face to face. He ambushes in order to kill his enemy in a moment of surprise. If attacked, he flees. The Arabs in Algeria provide a clear example of this.[92] It is only civilized societies that produce long-drawn-out battles. They do so by imposing collective duty and cohesive organization on human nature. This is the function of discipline and tactics. They can never overcome human nature, and mass formations are always liable to flee in panic; but the better conceived they are, the better are the results.[93]

The Greeks achieved considerable results in this respect, but in Antiquity it was the Romans who excelled all others. They showed profound understanding of morale, combining rigorous discipline with masterly tactics. The Greek phalanx was a mass formation in deep order, based on the notion that the rear ranks would push the front ones into battle and replace the casualties. Yet the truth of the matter was that, placed so close to the sounds and sights of battle, the rear ranks were all-too-exposed to the terrible psychological exhaustion of the face-to-face clash, which man can stand only to a very limited extent. Thus, if something went wrong, they were the first to fall back. Conversely, the Romans protected their reserves against the tremendous moral fatigue of the front line by placing them at a sufficient distance from the turmoil of battle. The legion was formed in three separate lines, with the veteran troops waiting calmly in the rear. Detached in this way, they were able to counter any adverse development in the front rather than be engulfed in it themselves.[94]

Fighting in a disciplined formation was the secret of the Greek and Roman victories over the Asiatic hordes and of the Romans' victories over the fearful Gauls and Germans, far more warlike than themselves and greatly superior in number. Living before the development of the critical study of ancient military sources that

[91] *Battle Studies*, 43, 94.
[92] Ibid. 43.
[93] Ibid. 47–9.
[94] Ibid. 50–4.

was to be rigorously undertaken by Delbrück—du Picq was unaware of the often wildly inaccurate and partisan nature of the numbers given by the ancient accounts, even though he was remarkably sceptical of the modern ones.[95] Thus he was convinced that ancient battle strikingly demonstrated that collective cohesion by far outweighed not only individual valour but also great numerical superiority. The Romans won because in a disciplined formation man's natural aversion to fighting was counterbalanced by the fact that he was both physically and morally protected by his fellows.

Hence the nature of ancient battle. In the clash, says du Picq, the soldiers took great care not to get separated from their friends. The front lines therefore very rarely mixed, and casualties at this stage were not heavy. Only a moral collapse could really cause an orderly formation to fall apart. This was why a surprise attack, especially against the flank or rear of an army, had always been such a decisive act, regardless of its actual strength. It created terror and, therefore, disintegration. The encircled Romans in Cannae, almost double the number of their Punic enemies, put down their weapons only for that reason.[96] There are, says du Picq, many examples of armies who swore to conquer or perish, but very few of them kept their oath. Leonidas' three hundred at Thermopylae were immortalized for a good reason. There is a moment when horror prevails, discipline and collective unity break down, and the army dissolves into a terrified mob running for its life.[97] It is only at that stage, when the army disintegrates and during the pursuit, that the real killing occurs. This was why in ancient battles the vanquished suffered casualties much greater than the victor, whose losses were usually light. In turn, this was one of the reasons for the unbeatable fighting-spirit of troops with long experience of triumph; they knew they were not only invincible but also practically invulnerable.[98]

[95] *Battle Studies*, 134.

[96] Ibid. 81–5.

[97] Ibid. 94–5.

[98] Ibid. 99, 113. Du Picq's analysis remarkably anticipated Victor D. Hanson's insightful *The Western Way of Warfare: Infantry Tactics in Classical Greece* (Oxford, 1990); indeed, his approach anticipated the whole modern school of writers who, like S. L. A. Marshall and John Keegan, concentrated on the experience of battle and on individual and group psychology. See Roger J. Spiller, 'S. L. A. Marshall and the Ratio of Fire', *RUSI Journal* (1988), 63–71; incidentally, this article demonstrates that in Marshall's case too his ideas predated his famous researches, whose scientific character and whose conclusions he to a large extent fabricated.

The lessons of ancient battle supported the dominating legacy of the African school in the French army, which believed it beat off hordes of savages by force of superior cohesion, discipline, and tactics.[99] Indeed, for du Picq, ancient battle was only a means to reveal man's nature and the root causes that made him fight in spite of it. The purpose of the work was to illuminate the study of modern tactics, although modern battle was considerably different from the ancient type; the introduction and perfection of firearms had brought some fundamental changes. Du Picq called attention to the highly conspicuous fact that, although firearms were much deadlier than the weapons of Antiquity, casualties had, proportionately, diminished. Since 'man is capable of standing only before a certain amount of terror', he kept himself at a distance. Battle was now waged from afar. According to du Picq, firearms had actually given man a choice to act in accordance with his nature and avoid a face-to-face encounter as far as he possibly could.[100] Furthermore, since the bullet was blind to bravery, the victors now also suffered heavily and had lost what was previously one of the major stimuli of their moral strength. At the same time, with the increased distance between the opposing forces, breaking contact and retreating had become easier and a greater temptation.[101] Enforcing discipline, keeping the dispersed men under control, and making them fight had become more difficult than ever.

The urgent problem now was to discover what tactics were needed in the era of the accurate and long-range rifled breech-loaders such as the Prussian 'needle gun' and the French *chassepot*. It was du Picq's contention that the days of the dense formation were over. Taking up the great doctrinal controversy of the eighteenth century regarding the *ordre profond* and the *ordre mince*, du Picq maintained that the belief in the shock power of the column had always been mythical and mechanistic. Physical shock, claimed du Picq, was only a word, since real contact and the glorified bayonet-charge to the end almost never happened. The effect of a charging column was predominantly moral and was successful only against a wavering enemy who disintegrated because he could not bear face-to-face fighting. When the defenders kept calm and steady, as the British did in the Peninsula, it was the

99 Griffith, *Military Thought in the French Army*, 117–22.
100 *Battle Studies*, 112–14.
101 Ibid. 99–100, 113.

attackers' turn to waver and retreat before actual contact was made.[102] With the modern rifled breech-loader, claimed du Picq, the employment of the deep formation was finally doomed. So also was the prevailing two-men-deep line, using the inherently inaccurate fire-by-command. In its place, the French army ought to adopt an open formation. Most of the soldiers ought to disperse and operate in a single loose line of skirmishers, leaving large intervals between them, taking advantage of the terrain, and using aimed fire at will. Strong reserves ought to be kept concentrated behind, and the easy-to-control column should be used only for manœuvring.[103] Rapid-firing arms had given the advantage to the *defensive* and rendered an advance under fire almost impossible: 'This is so evident that only a madman could dispute it.' (So much for Foch's alleged mentor.) For the attack, the army should look for the right opportunity and try to outflank the enemy or manœuvre him out of his position.[104] These highly perceptive insights were very similar both to Moltke's trend of thought from the late 1850s and to the actual tactics employed by the Prussians after their initial costly attacks on French defensive positions in the early battles of the war of 1870–1.

The great enigma that remained was whether men, when faced with the horrors of the modern battlefield and dispersed out of effective control, would be willing or could be made to fight at all. According to du Picq, many were in effect already hiding inside the battlefield. What was the value of an army 200,000 strong, if only half that number were fighting and the other half disappeared in a hundred ways? It was better to have 100,000 men who could be counted upon. Gideon, wrote du Picq, preferred the three hundred he knew would fight to the thirty thousand he sent home. It was Napoleon who had created the false theory of the 'big battalions', and he was the one responsible for the modern preoccupation with numbers. In modern battle, more than ever before, one needs morally reliable troops, and these, said du Picq, were created only by discipline, training, and *esprit de corps*, welded by experience.[105]

[102] *Battle Studies*, 143–55.

[103] Ibid. 115, 160–75.

[104] Ibid. 155, 162, 180. Du Picq failed, however, to appreciate the significance of the challenge facing cavalry. He thought that its problem was no bigger than the one facing infantry. Like almost everyone in Europe, he did not believe that the American experience of long-range cavalry-raids was applicable to Europe: ibid. 179–204.

[105] Ibid. 106, 111, 121, 131–3.

As mentioned before, all this was a direct response to the challenge of the Prussian mass armies and to Marshal Niel's controversial reforms. There is no doubt where du Picq's sympathies lay. When finishing 'Ancient Battle', which was based on a largely erroneous evaluation of numbers in Antiquity, he wondered if a small cohesive army might not even in his day gain the upper hand against a larger one.[106] Yet later he effectively became resigned to the idea that France had no choice but to create a large army.[107] The problem was that Niel's compromise reforms were not going to provide her with one. That was what complicated matters in the pre-1870 debate in France. Du Picq shared the almost universal scepticism in the army about the proposed reforms. 'Our projected organization', he wrote, 'will give us four hundred thousand good soldiers. But all our reserves will be without cohesion if they are thrown into this or that organization on the eve of battle.'[108] The 'second portion' of the recruits, serving only for five months before passing over to the reserve, were of dubious military value, while the Garde Mobile was practically useless. Neither was at all comparable with the Prussian reserve and Landwehr, and du Picq was quick to point this out. King William's military reforms in Prussia were sound. 'The Prussians conquered at Sadowa with made soldiers, united, accustomed to discipline. Such soldiers can be made in three or four years now.'[109] The Prussian army was a far cry from a shapeless mass. 'An army is not really strong unless it is developed from a social institution.'[110]

From the time of the Enlightenment, every military thinker in France knew that military institutions were very much the product of racial differences and social institutions. In stressing such national characteristics as French enthusiasm and restlessness, British calmness and perseverance, and German flock-like discipline and order, du Picq was reiterating views that were a century old and were prevalent not only in France but all over Europe.[111] His ideas about contemporary developments in European society and politics and their relationship to war were also highly characteristic

[106] Ibid. 105–6.

[107] See, for example, ibid. 230.

[108] Ibid. 131; compare, for example, with Marshal Randon, the Minister of War: 'It [the proposed organization] will only give us recruits. What we need is soldiers,' quoted in Howard, *The Franco-Prussian War*, 32.

[109] *Battle Studies*, 217, 131; also 123.

[110] Ibid. 222.

[111] See, for example, ibid. 40, 129, 223.

of the time. Like the proponents of all trends of thought that traced their origins to the Enlightenment, he believed that traditional societies admired military virtues and that aristocracies were by nature bellicose and acted as a spur to war. 'Peace spells death to a nobility,' he wrote. 'Consequently nobles do not desire it, and stir up rivalries among peoples, rivalries which alone can justify their existence as leaders in war, and consequently as leaders in peace.'[112] Like Renan in *La Réforme intellectuelle et morale de la France* (1871), du Picq argued that, with the advance of society and of democratic values, the military spirit was waning: 'This is why the military spirit is dead in France.' Militarily, however, this posed a problem. Surrounded as she was by the still-aristocratic societies of Prussia, Austria, and Russia, France was at a disadvantage.[113] Like many post-Revolutionary Europeans, at whatever end of the political spectrum, du Picq was convinced that the historic trend towards democracy was universal and unstoppable. But unlike Tocqueville or Thiers, he did not look upon it with apprehension; the cause of democracy was in line with French interests. With Revolutionary France defeated,

> democracy takes up her work in all European countries. . . . This work is slower but surer than the rapid work of war which, exalting rivalries, halts for a moment the work of democracy within the nations themselves. . . . Thus we are closer to the triumph of democracy than if we had been victors.[114]

It was only a matter of time 'until the Russian, Austrian and Prussian states became democratic societies, like ours'.[115]

In the meantime, the ruling classes struggle to maintain their supremacy. Du Picq's analysis of the decade's events in Prussia is highly perceptive, even if it is not entirely original. 'The King of Prussia and the Prussian nobility, threatened by democracy,' he writes, 'have had to change the passion for equality in their people into a passion for domination over foreign nations. . . . They have succeeded. They are forced to continue with their system.' Using Machiavellian doctrines, they arouse German jingoism.[116] Another great menace is that arch-enemy of the French and of progressive forces all over Europe—tsarism, which had only recently created a

112 *Battle Studies*, 216–17.
113 Ibid. 217–21.
114 Ibid. 218.
115 Ibid. 221.
116 Ibid. 217, 221–2.

wave of indignation in the West by ruthlessly suppressing the Polish revolt of 1863; tsarism 'calls for a crusade to drive back Russia and the uncultured Slav race'.[117]

'French democracy rightfully desires to live', writes du Picq.[118] And since France can no longer depend on the military spirit of a social warrior-class, she must constitute her army on the only basis that counts in a commercial society. 'Good pay establishes position in a democracy . . . M. Guizot says "Get rich".' Existing conditions must be changed and the officers and NCOs must be paid well.[119] In addition, the officers must not be troubled with too much study or work. Leisure in peacetime is one of the main attractions of the military profession. While voices in France were urging the emulation of Prussian excellence, du Picq was equally hostile to the idea of intensive military education and to the armchair scholars of the general staff.[120]

The shattering defeat in the war of 1870–1 (in which Ardant du Picq was killed) caused much intellectual ferment among the French military and led to a marked intellectual revival. Contrary to popular belief, however, du Picq's work had no influence on this development. 'Ancient Battle' and 'Modern Battle' were published posthumously in two succesive issues of the *Bulletin de la Réunion des officiers* (1876–7), followed by the first edition in book form of *Études sur le combat* in 1880. However, these obscure publications had no apparent impact. One modern commentator, expecting to find evidence for an opinion everyone takes for granted, has recently noted this with surprise.[121] The simple fact is that du Picq and his work are cited by none of the major exponents of the new French military school which emerged from the mid-1880s around the École supérieure de guerre: Maillard, Cardot, Gilbert, Bonnal, Langlois, and the young Foch. Nor are they mentioned in E. Guillon's extensive survey of French military literature, published in 1898.[122] Reviews of the second edition of *Battle Studies* (1903)

[117] Ibid. 222.

[118] Ibid. 218.

[119] Ibid. 218; this was the common argument in the army; cf. Griffith, *Military Thought in the French Army*, 15.

[120] *Battle Studies*, 219, 212. Howard, *The Franco-Prussian War*, 38. On the French staff-corps, its isolation from, and tense relationship with, the officers of the line see Griffith, *Military Thought in the French Army.*

[121] Joseph Arnold, 'French Tactical Doctrine', 62.

[122] Guillon, *Écrivains militaires.*

leave the unmistakable impression that the work was, for all practical purposes, new.[123] Indeed, du Picq's work became so popular after the publication of the second edition precisely because its emphasis on moral forces could then be enlisted to support the already established and powerful trends which had developed independently over the previous decade and a half.

The reasons for du Picq's sudden success after 1903 will be elaborated in Chapter 3. It is a fact, however, that the second edition of *Battle Studies* had an immediate impact and turned it into a much-admired classic. The book sold five more editions before the outbreak of the First World War. It was cited by everybody from both the older and younger generations of French military authors. Although du Picq had believed that the strength of the defence had been growing, had rejected close formations and bayonet charges, and had never advocated the *offensive à outrance*, his psychological and moral teaching none the less served as one of the main sources of inspiration for the 'Young Turks' in the French general staff, who advocated the offensive in the decade before the war.

However, later commentators and historians—who anyway tended to confuse the views of the 'Young Turks' and the offensive school with their predecessors' Clausewitzian and Napoleonic teachings—erroneously projected du Picq's influence further back to the first, obscure, publication of his work. In 1912 a survey of military literature indicated that the ideas which Cardot had begun to teach at the École de guerre in 1885 had first been mooted by du Picq. No claim for historical links between the two was made, however.[124] All the same, relying on this work, Irvine's pioneering study in English of French military ideas (1942), already strongly associated the appearance of the first edition of *Battle Studies* in 1880 with the emergence of the new wave in French military thinking in the mid-1880s.[125] This notion has been widely accepted ever since, even though no evidence has ever been produced. It is easy to understand why it grew and took hold. Both the

[123] See, for example, Pierre Lehautcourt, 'Le Colonel Ardant du Picq', *La Revue de Paris* (May–June 1904), 347–66.

[124] Jean Dany, 'La Littérature militaire d'aujourd'hui', ibid. (Mar.–Apr. 1912), 612.

[125] Dallas Irvine, 'The French Discovery of Clausewitz and Napoleon', *Journal of the American Military Institute*, 4 (1942), 151.

chronological proximity and the obvious similarity between Clausewitz's and du Picq's emphasis on morale made the mistake almost natural.

The 'du Picq connection' became particularly significant and interesting in relation to Ferdinand Foch. As we shall see, Foch's military thinking was formed during his professorship at the École de guerre (1894–1900) and was composed totally of the exciting ideas his older and more senior colleagues had developed in the school in the decade before his arrival. However, Foch was the only member of that remarkable group of professors not to have reached retirement age yet when the First World War broke out. Thus, because of his subsequent career, his pre-1914 role was blown out of proportion and became the subject of great interest. It was the naïve and enthusiastic translators and editors of the American edition of *Battle Studies* (1921) who presented du Picq as the spiritual mentor of the new French school headed by Marshal Foch, who had just led the Allies to victory in the Great War. They solicited an introductory congratulatory letter from Foch, which was in fact very brief and formal and, furthermore, mentioned absolutely no debt to du Picq.[126] Still, the image they created was accepted—and received a scholarly stamp, from E. M. Earle's authoritative and widely read *Makers of Modern Strategy* (1943), which carelessly, though with more restraint, coupled du Picq and Foch together as the 'French school'.[127] The false impression was again created mainly by means of strong insinuations, because no evidence existed. But there was also the casual remark by du Picq's American editors, anxious to stress his importance, that his book was referred to in such works as Foch's famous *The Principles of War*, translated into English the year before. In fact no such reference exists. Foch, the great name-dropper, cites everyone except du Picq.[128] His book, published in 1903, comprised the lectures he had delivered at the École de guerre a few years earlier, when practically no one knew of du Picq.

Indeed, the origins of the French school, including Foch's

[126] Frank Simonds, Colonel John Greely, and Major Robert Cotton in the introductory material to *Battle Studies*, pp. v–xii.

[127] Stefan Possony and Étienne Mantoux, 'Du Picq and Foch: The French School', in Earle (ed.), *Makers of Modern Strategy*, esp. 218.

[128] Introductory material to *Battle Studies*, p. xiii.

teaching, lay elsewhere. Fifteen years after the defeat of 1870–1, the main influence came from across the German border. It introduced an entirely new military outlook, which replaced the traditional concepts and the positivist notions that such military authors as Lewal, Berthaut, Jung, Derrécagaix, and Pierron had continued to propound after 1871.

Only in Germany was the reaction against the Enlightenment so profound and all-encompassing as to influence military theory decisively and produce a new conception of its nature. Berenhorst and, later, such pupils of Scharnhorst's as Rühle von Lilienstern, Lossau, and, above all, Clausewitz, who in their formative years went through the Romantic revolution, fiercely rejected what they regarded as Enlightenment abstractions. They called for a comprehensive theory of war which would reflect the diversity of human reality, and emphasized creative genius, moral forces, and the factors of uncertainty and chance. Even here, however, the new conception of military theory no more than compromised the dominance of the military school of the Enlightenment. The general intellectual struggle in Germany between the legacy of the Enlightenment and what was increasingly becoming a distinctive German Movement was as yet far from conclusive in its results. Moreover, in the military field in particular, the theoretical legacy of the Enlightenment was closely tied up with one of the few useful analytical tools in the profession—the rationale of operations, especially in its updated Napoleonic-Jominian formulation.

Thus, even during the height of Romanticism, some of Clausewitz's associates in Prussia, such as Decker and Valentini, were paraphrasing the theories of Bülow, Wagner, and Archduke Charles.[129] This was certainly the case in the smaller German states, which were much less touched by the emotional wave that so deeply affected large sections of the Prussian intellectual and political élite

[129] Decker, *Kriegführung* and *Grundzüge der praktischen Strategie* (2nd edn., Berlin, 1841). Decker was instructor in the *Allgemeine Kriegsschule* when Clausewitz was the director; on their attitude towards each other see Peter Paret, *Clausewitz and the State* (Oxford, 1976), 313–14. Georg Wilhelm von Valentini, *Die Lehre vom Krieg* (2nd edn., Berlin, 1833); there was a mutual antipathy between Valentini and the reformers, including Clausewitz: Paret, *Clausewitz and the State*, 192. Both Valentini and Decker were prolific and successful authors, best known for their works on the 'little war'.

at the beginning of the nineteenth century.[130] By the 1840s, as Jomini was outliving his contemporaries' resentments and criticisms and consolidating his early meteoric success into a European pre-eminence with the publication of his *Summary of the Art of War* (1837), it was his bold, Napoleonic theories that dominated the scene. After a characteristically German conceptual analysis, these were compactly summarized by Wilhelm von Willisen (b. 1790) in his *Theory of Great War* (1840): 'apply strength against weakness, front against flank, masses against a stretched front, superior against inferior force.' Napopleon himself had indicated how this was to be achieved: 'the secret of victory lies in the secret of communications'.[131]

Willisen's career came under a shadow when, in 1850, he failed to defend Schleswig-Holstein on behalf of the German Confederation against the Danish army. But his book, based on his lectures at the Kriegsschule, was an accepted text both in Prussia and abroad. In 1866, commenting on the development of the campaign in Bohemia, he hardly concealed his indignation at Moltke's dispersed strategy, which broke the Jominian golden rule. 'All that can be said of the movements now being executed', he wrote, 'is that they repair the worst fault that could have been committed—dissemination of forces in two widely separated groups'.[132]

A disciple was Wilhelm Rüstow (1821–78), the most prolific and diverse military scholar in Europe after 1850 and a man of unusual biography, whose significance transcended the military sphere. Rüstow was a lieutenant of engineers in the Prussian army when the revolution of 1848 broke out. Like Heinrich von Bülow during an earlier great revolutionary crisis, he was a committed and vocal enemy of Prussia's political and social system.[133] A staunch republican, he was one of the very few Prussian officers who openly

[130] See for example J. von Theobald, *Die Kunst der großen Kriegs operationen nach den besten Quellen frey bearbeitet* (Stuttgart, 1820).

[131] Karl Wilhelm von Willisen, *Theorie des großen Krieges* (Berlin, 1840), 81, 76, and also 105. On Willisen see R. von Caemmerer, *The Development of Strategical Science during the 19th Century* (London, 1905), 131–56.

[132] Quoted by F. E. Whitton, *Moltke* (London, 1921), 119. Willisen also opposed the adoption of the 'needle gun' by the Prussian army: Dennis Showalter, *Railroads and Rifles: Soldiers, Technology and the Unification of Germany* (Hamden, Conn., 1975), 90, 97–8.

[133] Rüstow was co-editor of Bülow's *Militärische und vermischte Schriften* (Leipzig, 1853).

sided with the revolution, speaking and writing in favour of the replacement of the regular army—the instrument of absolutism and mirror of the class system—with a true popular army.[134]

When the army finally put an end to the revolution, Rüstow had to resign and leave Prussia. He settled in Switzerland and became a freelance military writer, publishing more than two dozen books on all aspects of the military profession. He wrote some scholarly military histories, scientific studies of ancient warfare (in collaboration with H. Köchly, a professor of Classics in Zurich), campaign histories of all the wars of his day, and highly technical works on fortification. In 1860 he joined Garibaldi and acted as his chief of staff with the effective rank of major-general in the famous campaign of liberation through the Kingdom of the Two Sicilies.[135] After returning to Switzerland, he was accepted into the Swiss general staff with the rank of colonel and taught military history for a short while at the University of Zurich.[136]

Rüstow had a profound understanding of the way war was shaped throughout history by political and social conditions. This should not be attributed too narrowly to an intellectual bequest from either Clausewitz or Willisen and Jomini, although Rüstow was influenced by the writings of both in this regard.[137] All expressed nineteenth-century historicism, which dominated this age of social transformation and revolutionary change. A deeply

[134] Wilhelm Rüstow, *Der deutsche Militärstaat, vor und während der Revolution* (Königsberg, 1850), repr. with a brief biographical introduction by G. Oestreich, (Osnabrück, 1971). During the constitutional crisis of the early 1860s Rüstow was again intensely involved in the campaign against the subjugation of the Landwehr, the people's army, to the Junkers' regular army. He wrote several pamphlets on this subject in 1862–3.

[135] See Rüstow's account from the field of battle, 'Die Brigade Milano', in Ludwig Walesrode (ed.), *Demokratische Studien* (Hamburg, 1860), in the company of some of the most famous names of German and European radicalism. Visiting in Garibaldi's headquarters were, among others, Lassalle and the revolutionary poet Georges Herwegh. Incidentally, Rüstow was later instrumental in causing Lasselle's death, when, for romantic reasons, he pushed him into the duel in which he was killed: Shlomo Na'aman, *Lassalle* (Hanover, 1970), 763–84.

[136] For Rüstow see also the preface to the English edition of his book *The War for the Rhine Frontier 1870* (3 vols.; London, 1871); Marcel Herwegh's *Guillaume Rustow: Un grand soldat, un grand caractère* (Paris 1935); see also two unpublished doctoral dissertations: R. von Steiger, 'Der Rüstow Prozeß 1848–1850' (Berne, 1937); P. Wiede, 'Wilhelm Rüstow' (Munich, 1958).

[137] See Rüstow, *Der Krieg und seine Mittel* (Leipzig, 1857), bk. 1, 13–124; and esp. *Die Feldherrkunst des neunzehnten Jahrhunderts* (2 vols.; Zurich, 1857), i. 5–43, 505–66. Here (p. 506) he made his famous remark that 'Clauzewitz is much quoted but little read'. He himself had a reserved respect for Clausewitz.

historical approach characterizes Rüstow's excellent *Generalship in the Nineteenth Century* (1857), which traces the development of military practice and theory from the age of absolutism through the Revolution up to the Restoration. That the book never received the attention it deserved must have been due to Rüstow's position as an outsider in both the military and the academic world. It was his *History of Infantry* (1857) that first kindled Delbrück's interest in military history and led to the latter's great life-work, which integrated military history into German historical scholarship.[138]

Yet his universalist outlook, set limits on Rüstow's historical approach. As we have seen, by the middle of the nineteenth century, disciples of Jomini everywhere were facing the same problem, as the rifle and the railway threatened to revolutionize both tactics and strategy. Writing in 1857, Rüstow maintained that the principles of the art of war were eternal, varying only in the forms they took, and that the rifle would make no fundamental change in tactics and certainly not in strategy, where Napoleonic principles could not be superseded. By 1872, in his treatment of the German Wars of Unification, the argument was unchanged but the position was defensive. The breech-loader and Moltke's concentric strategy overtaxed the flexibility of the theoretical framework.[139]

In the consultations which took place during the preliminary stages of the war of 1866, Moltke had to overcome the opposition of the Adjutant-General, von Alvensleben, and of Colonel Düring of the general staff to his proposed deployment and advance on exterior lines.[140] But the campaigns in Bohemia and France established his military pre-eminence. They also marked the ascent of a formidable Prussian-German military school, with a highly distinctive and dominating theoretical outlook, to match the new German Reich, with its acute political and cultural self-awareness.

138 Rüstow, *Geschichte der Infanterie* (Gotha, 1857).

139 Rüstow, *Die Feldherrkunst*, i. 2; *Strategie und Taktik der neuesten Zeit* (3 vols.; Zurich, 1872–4), i. pp. vii, 109. His problem was well pointed-out by Caemmerer, *Strategical Science*, 220–1.

140 Walter Goerlitz, *The German General Staff* (London, 1953), 85; Showalter, *Railroads and Rifles*, 62.

2

The German Military School: Its World-View and Conception of War 1815–1914

THE German Wars of Unification transformed the political and military map of Europe. For two centuries, since the days of Louis XIV, France had been, despite some reversals, the predominant power on the Continent; henceforth this position was taken by the new German Empire. Prussia accomplished this in a remarkable feat of military proficiency, and it was to her that the world now looked in military affairs. All armies remodelled themselves on her system of conscription and reserve, general staff and military education, organization and tactics. But behind German might they also discovered a formidable and cohesive military school, possessing a highly distinctive view of war. Flowing from Germany, this view of war decisively influenced people's approach to military theory, doctrine, and history from the late nineteenth century; in many respects it still does. Indeed, the military approach of the Prussian-German military school did not merely consist of a body of operational doctrines; these took their place in a much wider outlook on politics, history, and human nature which dominated German thought from the turn of the nineteenth century.

The characteristic ideas of the Prussian-German military school were shaped by the meeting of two revolutions: one intellectual, the other military. 'German thought', wrote Ernst Troeltsch, 'whether in politics or in history or in ethics is based on the ideas of the Romantic Counter-Revolution' against the ideas of the Enlightenment;[1] and military thought was no exception. In the first place, the new intellectual currents introduced a new understanding of the role of war in human reality. In response to the acute threat of

[1] Ernst Troeltsch, 'The Idea of Natural Law and Humanity in World Politics', app. to O. Gierke, *Natural Law and the Theory of Society 1500–1800* (Cambridge, 1934), 203.

French Revolutionary ideas and political imperialism, the cosmopolitan, cultural humanitarianism of eighteenth-century Germany gave way to a general awakening of nationalism in a highly political form. Fichte and Adam Müller, Schleiermacher and Hegel only articulated and further disseminated sentiments and ideas which had developed and become prevalent among large sections of the Prussian élite during the patriotic struggle against Napoleon. Old Prussian *étatisme* and the new Romantic emphasis on the organic unity of the *Volk* now merged into a highly influential set of beliefs: the state is the dominating agent in human development, enforcing law and morality at home but subjected to no higher authority in its relations with other states; consequently, in the international arena, war is not accidental or abnormal but an unavoidable and natural means of arbitration, not to be judged by the moral standards derived from intra-state reality; furthermore, war actually plays an important positive role in countering corruption and softness within nations and in strengthening the social fabric. This new outlook, which gradually gained currency, was also reflected in the private and public writings of many of the military reformers, among them the still-almost-anonymous Clausewitz.[2]

The Romantic world-view also produced a new conception of the nature of military theory, in stark opposition to the theoretical outlook of the Enlightenment. To recapitulate: military writers in Germany held that, like all spheres of human activity, war was not susceptible to the methods which had proved so successful in the natural sciences; war was the sphere of clashing wills, rising emotions, uncertainty, and confusion; no universal rules and principles could in any real sense reflect its diverse complexity and endless contingencies; these could only be mastered by the general's practical genius and iron will.

Finally, the effects of Romanticism blended well with the overwhelming impact of the French and Napoleonic revolution in the military field. Even before the catastrophic defeat of 1806, but

[2] For all this, including Clausewitz's view on the moral status of war, which was far from being non-existent as modern commentators have assumed, see above Book I, 238–52 and the authorities cited. See also the first and best volume of Gerhard Ritter's monumental study *The Sword and the Scepter* (4 vols.; Miami, Fla., 1969; German original 1954), the ideas in which closely parallel my own, both here and regarding Moltke. I was not sufficiently aware of this at the time I wrote Book I.

much more strongly after it, a new conception of war was emerging in shattered Prussia. The German cultural scene, which since the late eighteenth century had been highly sensitive to the interdependence of all elements of the social fabric, provided military observers with a unique insight into the social origins of the revolution in war. Critics of the Frederickian military system at the turn of the century and, later, the reformers, traced the sources of French power to the total mobilization of patriotic energies and popular masses, which made possible the pursuit of great objectives by means of bold and crushing strategy. Prussia's grave condition, which made the struggle against Napoleon one of national survival, called for a similar commitment. The relatively limited warfare of the *ancien régime* was totally discredited. The reformers' work and plans for a general insurrection, come what may, envisioned all-out war. This became the characteristic mark of the Prussian military around the symbolic figure of Blücher, 'Marshal Vorwärts', and Gneisenau, his chief of staff, during the campaigns that brought down Napoleon in 1813–15. Prussian headquarters became the major advocate of aggressive strategy and the most vocal and insistent force pushing for a total overthrow of French power. These were the attitudes which received their most striking theoretical formulation from Clausewitz. He believed that they expressed the true and lasting nature of war, and that one could not depart from them with impunity—a belief which he began to qualify only during the last years of his life.

This view of war, conception of military theory, and approach to the conduct of operations became the intellectual creed of the Prussian-German military school because they were intertwined with the major trends which dominated German thought in the nineteenth century. Here too lies the key to the understanding of 'Clausewitz's influence'. Ideas do not just appear out of thin air; nor do individual thinkers get hold of people's minds single-handedly by sheer abstract appeal. Clausewitz had given expression to the ideas and attitudes that had dominated his intellectual environment; and his work was canonized by later generations in Germany, who named him as their classic authority, because they could find in his writings a sophisticated formulation in the military field of the way they themselves saw their world. After the Second World War, with the start of German national self-examination and ideological reorientation, historians inside, and then outside,

Germany sharply contrasted a 'good' and largely sterilized Clausewitz with his 'bad' successors. But in truth, while developing in a more aggressively nationalist and militarist direction, the Prussian-German military school was both historically and intellectually far closer to him than our period could ever be.[3]

Thus, as its title indicates, this chapter adopts a particularly wide point of view, more so than any other chapter of the book. It attempts to outline the German 'military mind' and place it in the context of the German 'public mind', or *Weltanschauung*, as a whole. No aspect of the former, it is suggested, can be properly understood without reference to the latter. Inevitably, this involves a broader survey of German history in the period concerned than would normally be regarded necessary in a work of this nature. All the more so since the distinctive German tradition which had its most powerful and creative period in the nineteenth century was far from being monolithic or unaffected by the passage of time. The cosmopolitan, non-political age of Goethe gave way, after the reform era, to the awakening of German national consciousness. The liberal struggle against the Restoration was disappointed in the revolutions of 1848 and shattered after the Prussian constitutional struggle of the 1860s, when Germany was united from above by Prussia's most conservative forces. The creation of the German Empire by Bismarck in 1871 turned Germany into the strongest power on the Continent and was followed by rapid industrial and demographic growth, economic expansion, and urbanization. However, with these came the shadows and anxieties of grave domestic and foreign threats and challenges, amplified by growing secularism and materialism. All these shifts in conditions and concerns, experiences and perspectives found expression in the military field too. Indeed, spanning almost the entire century, no life-story reflected this more strikingly, or was more closely associated with determining the course of events, than that of Helmuth Carl Bernard von Moltke (1800–91).

MOLTKE AND THE ERA OF GERMAN UNIFICATION

From the time of the earliest historical appraisals of Moltke it has been widely agreed that he personified the transformation of the

[3] See above Book I, 170–256.

German public mind during the nineteenth century.[4] The posthumous publication of his youthful writings and letters not only provided further evidence of his outstanding intellectual faculties and moral integrity; they also revealed a wealth and liveliness of personality which added new dimensions to the Olympian remoteness and silent austerity which characterized his public image in old age. Indicating the diversity and breadth of his interests, these early writings also revealed an outlook and attitude to life which had been free from bias, humanist, cosmopolitan, undogmatic and tolerant in regard to religion, and almost entirely non-political. While Moltke had emerged from anonymity to world fame only in his sixties, there now appeared a new and quite unexpected 'young Moltke'. Indeed, the change went deeper than variations in temperament between young and old age and transcended the mere personal level.

Moltke's father was an impoverished former lieutenant of the Prussian army, who found employment in Denmark. The young Moltke was sent to the Royal Danish Academy for Cadets in Copenhagen, where he graduated in 1818 as first in his class. In 1822, armed with excellent recommendations, he transferred to the Prussian service. His achievements during his studies at the Prussian War School (1823–6) under the directorship of Clausewitz (who had little contact with the students) were also considerable.[5] In 1828 he was assigned to the topographical branch of the general staff, of which he became a member in 1832, and in which he was to remain.[6] At the same time, however, his extra-military activities played at least as important a part in his life. He was born into the later phase of that great age which gave Germany its reputation as 'the nation of poets and thinkers'.

During the 1820s and early 1830s, Moltke, poverty-stricken, shy, and socially withdrawn, occupied himself with a variety of intellectual pursuits. When he left the Kriegsschule, he already

[4] See the nationalist historian Dietrich Schäfer on the tenth anniversary of Moltke's death: *Zu Moltkes Gedächtnis. Rede* (Jena, 1901).

[5] For his record in both services see *Moltke, His Life and Character, Sketched in Journals, Letters, Memoirs, a Novel and Autobiographical Notes* (New York, 1892; vol. i. of *Gesammelte Schriften und Denkwürdigkeiten des General Feldmarschalls Grafen Helmuth von Moltke*, Berlin, 1892), 28–36.

[6] The standard biography is Eberhard Kessel, *Moltke* (Stuttgart, 1957); earlier ones include those by Max Jähns (1894–1900), Wilhelm Bigge (1901), Fritz von der Goltz (1903), Wilhelm von Blume (1907), and, in English, Spenser Wilkinson (1913) and F. E. Whitton (1921).

spoke German, Danish, and French. He then taught himself English and took lessons in Russian and Italian. In his later travels he also picked up Turkish. In 1832 he was competent enough in English to undertake the translation of Gibbon's monumental *Decline and Fall of the Roman Empire*, on which he worked after duty for two years in an attempt to supplement his income. In the course of their long years of correspondence, he and his brother Ludwig often discussed their translations of English poets, as well as German poetry and their own poetic efforts. Helmuth loved music, had a considerable talent for drawing, read extensively, and wrote as much. In 1828 he wrote a short novel, *The Two Friends*, in the style of German classicism. The revolutions of 1830–1 stimulated two small historical studies, which were both published in book form: *Holland and Belgium in their Mutual Relations from their Separation under Philip II* (1831), and *The Internal State of Affairs and the Social Condition of Poland* (1832).[7]

In 1836 Moltke took six months' leave to travel to Vienna, Constantinople, Athens, and Naples. At the request of the Turkish government he stayed in the Ottoman Empire for three years as a military instructor. The trip produced a volume of letters, some of which were published in book form; a collection of his surveys of the Dardanelles, Constantinople, and the Bosphorus; a book on the Russo-Turkish campaign of 1829; and various articles.[8] Tours of the interior of Asia Minor and the Mesopotamian desert produced further cartographical works and some valuable geographical information. These were sent to Professor Karl Ritter, the pioneer of the discipline of natural and historical geography and Moltke's former teacher at the Kriegsschule.[9] After marrying and working several years on the staff of the IV Army Corps, Moltke spent

[7] For the novel see *Life and Character*, 37–91. The two historical works were reprinted in *Essays, Speeches and Memoirs of Field-Marshal Count Helmuth von Moltke*, i (New York, 1893; vol. ii of *Gesammelte Schriften*), 1–163.

[8] *Briefe über Zustände und Begebenheiten in der Türkei 1835–39* (1841, 4th edn., Berlin, 1882), with an introduction by Karl Ritter; Norbert Fischer (ed.), *Moltke als Topograph* (Berlin, 1944); *The Russians in Bulgaria and Rumelia in 1828 and 1829* (London, 1854); 'Essays upon the Eastern Question (1841–1844)', repr. in *Essays, Speeches and Memoirs*, i. 267–308. Also see Jehuda L. Wallach, *Anatomie einer Militärhilfe: Die preußisch-deutschen Militärmissionen in der Türkei 1835–1919* (Düsseldorf, 1976), 17–29.

[9] 'Autobiography', in *Life and Character*, 20–3; Ernst Curtius, 'Memorial Speech at the Royal Academy of Sciences at Berlin', 2 July 1891, in *Essays, Speeches and Memoirs*, ii. (New York, 1893; vol. vii of *Gesammelte Schriften*), 221–31; Mutschke, *Moltke als Geograph* (Freiburg, 1935).

another year abroad as aide-de-camp to Prince Henry of Prussia, during which time he lived in Rome (1845–6). This year produced a number of geographical and historical notes, strongly influenced by Niebuhr's *Römische Geschichte*, the seminal work of modern critical historiography, which Moltke admired deeply. A topographical map of the environs of Rome, surveyed and drawn by Moltke, was published (1852, 1859) and led to an exchange of letters with Alexander von Humboldt.[10] Moltke also took great interest in the development of the railway, at first primarily as a great instrument of economic development and for private financial reasons. Between 1841 and 1844 he sat on the board of the company constructing the Hamburg–Berlin line. His 'Considerations on the Choice of Railway Routes' (1843) is impressive both in its command of the economic and technical details and in its mastery of exposition.[11]

All of Moltke's works make splendid reading. The beauty of his narrative is matched by keen powers of observation, strong judgement, and a comprehensive view of his subject-matter. The author's sympathetic character also shines through, and his intellectual approach was clearly equally sympathetic.

Both Moltke's religion and his politics were typical of the age of Goethe. Throughout his life he was permeated with a deep sense of cosmic religiosity which recognized no strict form or dogma and gave almost equal status to all historical religions as different expressions of the same spiritual and moral truth.[12] His treatment of political issues was similarly unbiased. His work on Holland and Belgium and his study of Polish history, society, and politics offer excellent proof of this. Both works were written against the turbulent background of the revolutions of 1830–1, and in both cases Prussia's vital interests were deeply involved. Yet not only was Moltke's point of view unaffected by the political tensions and concerns of his day; it was also remarkably devoid of national

[10] See previous note and *Life and Character*, 144–78; *Letters to Mother and Brothers* (vol. iv of *Gesammelte Schriften*), 263, 276.

[11] The article was reprinted in *Essays, Speeches and memoirs*, ii. 223–63; also see *Letters to Mother and Brothers*, 249; Showalter, *Railroads and Rifles*, 29–30.

[12] See Moltke, 'Thoughts on this Life and Trust in a Future Life', *Life and Character*, 325–32; see also his repudiation of any established church: *Field-Marshal Count Helmuth von Moltke as a Correspondent* (New York, 1893; vol. v of *Gesammelte Schriften*), 257–8; and an interest in Strauss's famous *Life of Jesus*, the controversial critical study of the Scriptures: ibid. 174.

chauvinism. Clausewitz's articles from these very same years, dealing with the problem of Belgian and Polish independence in the light of German and Prussian interests and European position, were typical of the new attitudes and concerns of the German nationalists and provide a remarkable contrast to Moltke's works.[13] Quite apart from being openly hostile to Polish political aspirations, Clausewitz was full of contempt for the Poles, 'a people that had remained half-Tartar in the midst of civilized European states'. Even more strongly did he despise and detest the Jews in Poland, those 'dirty German Jews, swarming like vermin in the dirt and misery'.[14] By contrast, Moltke's treatment of the Poles and the Polish Jews was highly sympathetic, trying to convey the inner feeling and form of their social and communal life with a kind of anthropological delight more in keeping with an earlier generation of German cultural and cosmopolitan nationalism than with the new political one.[15] Rather than being personal, the differences here—which reverse the roles into which Clausewitz and Moltke have been typecast in recent historiography—are symptomatic of the changing intellectual climate in Germany.

Nowhere is this and Moltke's early outlook more strikingly expressed than in one of his articles on the Eastern Question (1841):

> We candidly confess our belief in the idea, on which so much ridicule has been cast, of a general European peace. Not that long and bloody wars are to cease from henceforth, our armies be disbanded, and our cannons recast into nails; that is too much to expect; but is not the whole course of the world's history an approximation to such a peace? . . . Wars will become rarer and rarer because they are growing expensive beyond measure; positively because of the actual cost, negatively because of the necessary neglect of work. Has not the population of Prussia, under a good and wise administration, increased by a fourth in twenty-five years of peace? And

[13] Clausewitz, 'Die Verhältnisse Europas seit der Teilung Polens' and 'Zurückführung der vielen politischen Fragen, welche Deutschland beschäftigen, auf die unserer Gesamtexistenz', in *Carl von Clausewitz, Politische Schriften und Briefe*, ed. Hans Rothfels (Munich, 1922), 222–38. Also see Peter Paret, *Clausewitz and the State* (Oxford, 1976), 406–9, 419–20.

[14] Cited by Paret, *Clausewitz and the State*, 420, 212. The rising national chauvinism was by no means shared by the majority of the reformers; compare with Boyen's observations on the Poles and Galician Jews: ibid. 212.

[15] See Frederick Hertz, *The German Public Mind in the Nineteenth Century* (London, 1975), 228.

> are not her fifteen millions of inhabitants better fed, clothed and instructed today than her eleven millions used to be? Are not such results equal to a victorious campaign or to the conquest of a province, with this great difference, that they were not gained at the expense of other nations, nor with the sacrifice of the enormous number of victims that a war demands? . . . When we consider the milliards which Europe has to spend every year on her military budget, the millions of men in the prime of life who are called away from their business in order to be trained for a possible war, it is not hard to see how these immense powers might be utilized and made more and more productive.[16]

In view of things to come, this was an astounding profession of political faith.

Indeed, the 1840s saw clouds gathering on both the foreign and the domestic horizon. The system of Vienna was beginning to waver. New threats and anxieties were growing everywhere. Political attitudes were changing. In 1840 Thiers's demand for the annexation of the left bank of the Rhine to France shook Europe and aroused German public opinion to a pitch of national fervour. A new note crept into Moltke's writings. The calm and scholarly objectivity of his works on Holland, Belgium, and Poland gave way to passionate nationalist polemic.[17] The cataclysmic events of 1848–50 generated crises of unprecedented gravity. Moltke's letters to his brothers, which had been totally apolitical in spirit, were now suddenly charged with politics as both Prussia's character as a state, Germany's fate, and his own personal future became the subject of uncertainty and concern. Previously, he had held a moderate reformist position, respecting both historical roots and the necessity for further development.[18] In the early 1840s he believed that Prussia stood in the forefront of reform and reasoned liberty.[19] The situation in 1848, however, was revolutionary, not reformist. Like members of the propertied classes everywhere,

[16] Moltke, 'Germany and Palestine', *Essays, Speeches and Memoirs*, i. 276–7.

[17] Moltke, 'The Western Boundary' (1841), ibid. 165–220. While French pamphleteers evoked the image of Romanic civilization, recovering lost territories from the Germanic world, Moltke contrasted the ancient traditions of Romano-French despotism with German freedom, and unfolded the story of the French violations of the territorial integrity of the German Reich since the fifteenth century.

[18] See Moltke's notes on the Hungarian nobility (1835), perceptively indicating both its glorious historical role and its patent anachronism in 'the epoch of steamships, militia, spinning and printing machines, constitutions and reform': 'Journal Written on his Way to Constantinopole', *Life and Character*, 103.

[19] Cited by Goerlitz, *The German General Staff* (London, 1950), 71.

Moltke was fearful that the liberal revolution would be taken over by a democratic 'red republic' led by skilful demagogues, in a general rebellion 'of those who own nothing against those who own something'.[20] After the autumn of 1848, when the Austrian and Prussian governments had recovered their nerve, Moltke regarded the reaction which was setting in as inevitable.[21]

For the 'shriekers in Frankfurt', the professors and lawyers of the National Assembly with their presumptuous schemes and empty gestures, Moltke had little respect.[22] But their principal aim, German unity, and the emotions and forces they set in motion were the very things that he himself grew to cherish most.[23] While the king of Prussia rejected the imperial crown when it was offered to him by the Frankfurt assembly, Prussia moved on her own initiative to create a German union under her leadership. Moltke was thrilled.[24] From mid-1850 Prussia and Austria faced each other in arms. Moltke's corps was mobilized for twenty-four weeks. Then Prussia backed down in the humiliating settlement of Olmütz, and Moltke exploded with indignation. 'The worst government cannot ruin this nation,' he concluded bitterly; 'Prussia will stand yet at the head of Germany.'[25]

The experience of 1848–50 marked a turning-point in modern German history. The public mood and perceptions were transformed, and so were Moltke's. The disillusion with the impotent liberal leadership and liberal ideals, which had crumbled before real power both at home and abroad, turned into contempt and a new emphasis on the role of power and determined action in politics. 'There will be an age of heroes after the age of shouters and writers,' wrote Moltke at the end of 1849.[26] He had changed and was aware of it.[27] His letters were now dominated by politics. Calm and sympathetic understanding gave way to passionate conviction and cold determination. The moderate reformist turned into a staunch conservative. From his position of responsibility—he

[20] The quotations are from 17 Feb. 1850, 17 Nov. and 9 July 1848, *Letters to Mother and Brothers*, 135, 125, 115.

[21] 9 Sep. and 17 Nov. 1848, 27 Sept. 1849, 29 May 1850, ibid. 120, 125, 268, 141.

[22] The quotation is from 9 July 1848, ibid. 115; also see, for example, 21 Sept. 1848, ibid. 122.

[23] 27 Sept. 1849 and 21 Mar. 1850, ibid. 268, 138.

[24] As early as Sept. 1848 this had become his guiding ideal; ibid. 123.

[25] 25 Feb. 1851, ibid. 145.

[26] 27 Sept. 1849, ibid. 268.

[27] 15 Jan. 1850, ibid. 269.

became chief of staff of an army corps in August 1848—he viewed an increasingly destabilized European system: an adventurous emperor in a revisionist France; an arrogant Austria, determined to keep Prussia down and block the unification of Germany; and a Denmark who exploited German disunity to change the status quo in Schleswig-Holstein. His point of view was completely transformed. Now it was totally Prussian- and German-oriented, imbued with a sense of self-righteousness and a distaste for Prussia's adversaries. Reflecting the change of course in German historical scholarship as a whole, Ranke's older universal historicism was supplemented among Moltke's favourite readings with the new nationalist perspective and preoccupation of Droysen and his successors in the influential Prussian historical school. These boiled down to the doctrine that from her origins it had been Prussia's historical mission to unite Germany, and her cause was therefore the true and moral cause of Germany.[28] The man who a decade before had professed his belief in a general European peace, now repeatedly saw war on the cards, both before the German Wars of Unification and in the subsequent two decades until his death.

From the mid-1850s he was beginning to rise to positions of national significance, and then, thanks entirely to his outstanding personal qualities and remarkable achievements, he shot to national and international prominence. In 1855 he was appointed senior aide-de-camp to Prince Frederick William of Prussia, and a year later he was promoted to major-general. In 1857 he became acting chief of the Great General Staff and in the following year chief of staff. His great creative and analytical powers and mastery of exposition were now channelled into his own professional sphere, producing a massive output of operational plans, staff studies, and memoranda. His successful role in the Danish war of 1864, and especially his masterminding of the Bohemian campaign of 1866, won him the confidence of the king. They transformed the general staff from a mere planning-bureau of little authority into

[28] For Moltke's admiration for Ranke, see ibid. 276, and *Moltke as a Correspondent*, 263. It was with Ranke's solicitation that Moltke was accepted in 1860 as an honorary member of the Prussian Royal Academy of Sciences: *Essays, Speeches and Memoirs*, ii. 233. For Moltke's recommendation of Droysen's *History of Prussian Politics* right after its publication, see *Letters to Mother and Brothers*, 16 Mar. 1856, 280–1. For the Prussian historical school and Droysen in particular, see Georg Iggers, *The German Conception of History* (Middletown, Conn., 1968), 90–123 and 104–15 respectively.

the effective high command of the army in time of war, and promoted its chief from a position of secondary significance to the role of war-lord. In 1867 Moltke was elected as a Conservative member both to the Prussian Upper House and to the Reichstag of the newly created North German Confederation; this latter position was to be replaced after 1871 and until his death by a seat in the Reichstag of the German Empire. He now saw only one solution to the German problem: 'For fifty years German unity has been extolled in prose, in verse, in song, and in toasts.' These years 'have shown that union can never be achieved by means of peaceful understanding . . . It is God's will that Prussia should solve the problem' with her sword.[29] A full circle had been closed with the early enthusiasts for the ideal of German unification among the Prussian reformers. It had been around 1820 that Clausewitz had written: 'Germany can reach political unity in *one* way only, through the sword, when one state subdues all the others.'[30]

Germany was united by the sword. The formative experience of 1848 was reinforced by the collective lessons of the era of unification. The story is familiar enough. The liberals' defeat had been completed in the Prussian constitutional crisis of the 1860s, when they had opposed the government on the very reforms of the army that made the victories of 1866 and 1870–1 possible. The German Reich was created in war by force of arms and state power. Not only did this determine the political and social structure of the new empire; it also shaped the dominating outlook shared by its political, social and intellectual establishment. It reinforced older intellectual trends which had been building up the distinctive German tradition since the Romantic revolt and the political and ideological struggle against the 'ideas of 1789'. Moltke's world-view, crystallized after the creation of the empire into a hard core of convictions, typified this comprehensive outlook.

First, there was the nature of international relations and the role of war. United Germany was the strongest power in Europe and, under Bismarck, during the first two decades of her existence, she was also a power of the status quo. Yet from his post at the general

[29] There are two virtually identical formulations of this idea in early 1868; the quotations are from 'Drafts of Undelivered Speeches in the Parliament of the Customs Union', *Essays, Speeches and Memoirs*, ii. 18, 14; also see 26 May 1866 and 24 Jan. 1868, *Letters to Mother and Brothers*, 178, 184–5.

[30] 'Umtriebe', in Rothfels (ed.), *Clausewitz, Politische Schriften*, 171.

staff, Moltke saw no reason for complacency. Called to defend the government's military budgets in the periodical highly contentious parliamentary debates on these, he repeatedly declared Germany's peaceful intentions, based on her satisfaction with the existing European order, and candidly professed that she had no interest in further territorial expansion that would compromise her ethnic integrity.[31] However, the apprehensions of Germany's neighbours were only natural and, owing to her special geopolitical position, Germany, in her turn, had an endemic security problem. 'We are placed right in the midst of all the Great Powers,' Moltke told the Reichstag; 'Our Eastern and Western neighbours have only to form front in one direction, we in all directions.'[32] From 1859 he had repeatedly expressed his concern at the possibility of a gigantic clash between the great European races: a Germanic centre caught in the middle between an 'alliance of the Slavic East and the Romance West'. After 1871 this became a leading theme in his plans for war.[33] On the western border lay a humiliated and revanchist France, whose remarkable recovery and rapid rearmament caused much alarm across the Rhine. On the eastern border lay the Russian Empire, lured by Bismarck's masterful diplomacy, but always bound to be alienated by her conflicts in the Balkans with Germany's other ally, the Habsburg monarchy. Were France and Russia to co-operate, Germany would find it extremely difficult to win a war. Before 1870 Moltke had continuously pressed for an immediate war against France, before her army had had time to reform. The intended purpose of war at that time had been to change the status quo and bring about the unification of Germany. Now, in every major international crisis—with France in 1875 and 1887 and especially with Russia in 1887–8—Moltke and the general staff urged a preventive war, although the political motive of such a war was fundamentally defensive.[34] How the temporary weakening of the defeated enemy was to be maintained without

[31] Sitting of the Reichstag on the Imperial Military Bill, 16 Feb. 1874, *Essays, Speeches and Memoirs*, ii. 114–15; Debate on the Imperial Budget, 24 Apr. 1877, ibid. 120.

[32] Debate on the Imperial Military Law, 1 Mar. 1880, ibid. 124–5.

[33] See the many references in Ferdinand von Schmerfeld (ed.), *Die deutschen Aufmarschpläne 1871–1890* (Berlin, 1929), cited by Ritter, *Sword and Scepter*, 229; 313, n. 59.

[34] Walter Kloster, *Der deutsche Generalstab und der Präventivkrieg-Gedanke* (Stuttgart, 1932), 6–33; Ritter, *Sword and Scepter*, 227–38; Rudolph Stadelmann, *Moltke und der Staat* (Krefeld, 1950), 279–334.

periodic wars is a question to which Moltke appeared to have no real answer.[35] In fact, what he most probably had in mind was the imposition of peace terms that would set permanent restrictions on the enemy's armed forces, and indeed on its independence.

The lessons of the era of unification and the problems of European power-politics reinforced the legacy of German culture since its reaction against Enlightenment liberalism and cosmopolitanism. Travelling the same intellectual road himself, Moltke now arrived at exactly the same view of war which had been developed by Adam Müller and Rühle von Lilienstern, Hegel and Clausewitz. 'What sensible man would not wish that it were possible to apply to peaceful objects the enormous expenditure incurred by Europe for military purposes?' he asked the Reichstag in 1868; yet 'war is, in reality, but the carrying on of diplomacy by different means'.[36] The phenomenon of war is embedded in the nature of the international system. While 'within a country, the law protects the rights and liberty of the individuals, without as between state and state might is the only right'. No tribunal of international arbitration exists, and were it to exist, it 'would lack the power of executing its decrees'.[37] The only practical guarantee against war is not an international agreement but a strong and peaceful Germany which would impose peace on her neighbours.[38]

These remarks before the Reichstag were more fully elaborated in the famous replies that Moltke wrote in 1880–1 to two activists campaigning in favour of international law and peace who had approaced him for his opinion and support. It was as if his ideas from forty years before regarding a general European peace had been written by another man. He now believed not only that war was natural and necessary, and thus impossible to eliminate by kind-hearted visionaries, but that it also had a positive, and even a sublime, role to play in human life:

> Permanent peace is a dream and not even a beautiful one, and war is a law of God's order in the world, by which the noblest virtues of man, courage and self-denial, loyalty and self-sacrifice, even to the point of death, are developed. Without war the world would deteriorate into materialism.[39]

[35] Ritter, *Sword and Scepter*, 227–8.
[36] 15 June 1868, *Essays, Speeches and Memoirs*, ii. 50.
[37] 16 Feb. 1874, ibid. 105.
[38] Ibid. 50, 115.
[39] Moltke to Prof. Dr. Bluntschli, 11 Dec. 1880, *Moltke as a Correspondent*, 272.

Rising social-Darwinist notions found their place in the framework of Lutheran political realism and spiritual non-worldliness:

> Is not the life of man, his whole nature, a battle of that which is to be with that which is? And so it is in the life of nations. . . . Who is able to escape misfortune in this world, or who can even run away from the burdens of life? Are not both by God's providence conditions of our earthly existence?[40]

In most of this, Moltke practically saw eye to eye with a man whom he befriended in the Reichstag, Heinrich von Treitschke.[41] A Berlin history professor, editor of the *Preußische Jahrbücher* and the most vigorous public spokesman for the new merger of Prussianism and German nationalism, Treitschke became the most notable and influential representative of the German school of political philosophy in Imperial Germany. The competition and struggle between states, the higher agents of human development, was for Treitschke the very stuff of which history was made:

> The features of history are virile, unsuited to sentimental or feminine natures. Brave people alone have an existence, an evolution or a future; the weak and cowardly perish, and perish justly. The grandeur of history lies in the perpetual conflict of nations, and it is simply foolish to desire the suppression of their rivalry.[42]

> War, therefore, will endure to the end of history as long as there is multiplicity of states. The laws of human thought and of human nature forbid any alternative, neither is one to be wished for. . . . War is the one remedy for an ailing nation. Social selfishness and party hatreds must be dumb before the call of state when its existence is at stake.[43]

Treitschke's *History of Germany in the Nineteenth Century* took its place on the short-list of Moltke's favourite readings. Composed in 1890 for the *Revue des Revues*, this list reflects Moltke's—and Germany's—intellectual evolution: the Bible, Homer, Shakespeare, Schiller, and Goethe appear side by side with Clausewitz, Ranke, Carlyle, and the nationalist historians Sybel and Treitschke.[44]

The publication in the newspapers of Moltke's replies regarding

[40] Moltke to M. Goubareff, 4 Feb. 1881, *Moltke as a Correspondent*, 279–80.

[41] Stadelmann, *Moltke und der Staat*, 366–8.

[42] Treitschke, *Politics* (2 vols.; London, 1916), i. 21. The book was compiled after the author's death, from the notes of lectures he had delivered in the early 1880s.

[43] Ibid., i. 65–6; also see ii. 395–6.

[44] *Moltke as a Correspondent*, 262–3; also see *Life and Character*, 228.

perpetual peace incited attacks in the Berlin press accusing the field-marshal of militarism.[45] The German Empire had been the creation of Prussia, shaped in the image of her authoritarian political system and dominated by her old ruling classes. But the political and social structure of the Reich, as well as its ruling ethos, was widely opposed. In the Reichstag, in order to push the government's legislation through, Bismarck was manœuvring opportunistically but with increasing difficulty between the conservative parties, the National Liberals, and even the Catholic Centre Party. While the Reichstag had been given very limited authority in the German constitution, and virtually none at all in foreign and military affairs, it still voted the Imperial budget. The government fixed the term of the military budget at seven years and usually got its way, but Moltke was not alone in finding the endemic political and ideological haggling with the parliamentary opposition depressing. Here again was the rule of empty talk, challenging the integrity and stability of the Reich at home, and inspired by irresponsible and dangerous illusions in treating the Reich's military needs. Delegates had to be reminded: that the milliards that Napoleon I had extracted from defeated Prussia were a permanent lesson to a country which tried to economize on its vital defence-expenditure; that universal military service was the school of the nation, implanting a sense of duty and obedience in its citizens; that the alternative to the regular army, the militia, promoted by the Left against Prussian militarism, had never succeeded and could never succeed.[46]

The most distressing political development, however, was the rise of the Social Democratic Party. For Moltke, this was an old mortal enemy. During the campaign of 1870–1, he had been constantly preoccupied with the spectre of radical and socialist revolution and sought to make the defeat of the popular armies raised by Gambetta for the defence of the French republic a lesson for the whole of Europe.[47] The horrors of the civil war in France confirmed his worst fears. During his long membership of the Reichstag, the only occasion on which he rose to speak on other

[45] *Moltke as a Correspondent*, 285–6.

[46] These were recurring themes in Moltke's parliamentary polemics. See *Essays, Speeches and Memoirs*, ii. 106, 138 for Napoleon's milliards; p. 14 for universal military service; pp. 111–12 for the militia.

[47] 1 Feb. 1871, ibid. 254; 21 Sept., 27 Oct., 23 Nov. 1870, and 1 Mar. 1871, *Letters to Mother and Brothers*, 193, 200, 203, 213.

than military issues was when the government introduced the Socialist Bill in 1878, a measure which marked the start of twelve years of struggle to suppress the Social Democratic Party by legal means. Against the socialist idea, he directed arguments which were very akin to the ones he used a little later against the idea of a permanent peace. Want, misery, and privation were inseparable conditions of human existence. Although they might slowly improve in time, their abolition was both unattainable and undesirable for the development of the human race.[48]

This striking similarity was significant. The idea both of permanent peace and of socialism conflicted with the very concept of the state which had been developed in Prussia from the turn of the nineteenth century and which was consecrated with the establishment of the German Reich: the definition of the state as power (*Macht*) without, and law and justice (*Recht*) within.[49] Those who threatened either, whether foreign rivals or domestic political forces like Catholicism or socialism, were proclaimed enemies of the state (*Reichsfeinde*).[50]

Indeed, for Moltke, the government was the rock of stability both in domestic and foreign affairs. In contrast to the liberal and socialist ideas that wars were incited by governments in the interest of the old ruling classes, Moltke maintained throughout his life that in the age of the masses, the passions of the people were a far greater stimulus for the outbreak of wars and were directly responsible for the out-and-out character they had assumed. 'In these days', he wrote to his mother as early as 1831, 'war and peace and the relations of nations are no longer cabinet questions; in many countries the people themselves govern the cabinet, and thus an element is introduced into politics on which it is impossible to reckon.'[51] After the out-and-out struggle with French national resistance in 1871, and in his polemic with the Left on matters of peace and war, this became a recurring theme: 'Strong governments are a pledge of peace. But the passions of the populace, the

[48] *Essays, Speeches and Memoirs*, ii. 76–7. Also see on the similarity between war and social deprivation: Mar. 1879, 18 Feb. 1878, 10 Feb. 1881, *Moltke as a Correspondent*, 270, 269, 279, 292.

[49] Cf. Treitschke, *Politics*, i. 19.

[50] See Wolfgang Petter, ' "Enemies" and "Reich Enemies": An Analysis of Threat Perceptions and Political Strategy in Imperial Germany, 1871–1914', in Wilhelm Deist (ed.), *The German Military in the Age of Total War* (Worcester, 1985), 22–39.

[51] 1831 Feb. 13, *Letters to Mother and Brothers*, 47.

ambition of party leaders, and public opinion led astray both in speeches and by the press—all these, gentlemen, are elements which may prove stronger than the will of those who rule.'[52] In 1890, rising to defend the expansion of the German army in one of his last appearances before the Reichstag, Moltke saw equally bleak consequences at home and abroad from the rising of the masses: '. . . these elements take the form of national and racial aspirations, and, above all, dissatisfaction with the existing state of affairs'. 'The days of the cabinet wars are past,' he told the Reichstag, 'now we have only the people's war.'[53] His famous vision of the resulting character of war was prophetic:

> If war breaks out, one cannot foresee how long it will last or how it will end. It is the great powers of Europe which, armed as they never were before, are now entering the arena against each other. There is not one of these that can be so completely overcome in one or even in two campaigns that it will be forced to declare itself vanquished or to conclude an onerous peace; not one that will be unable to rise again, even if only after a year, to renew the struggle. Gentlemen, it may be the Seven Years War, it may be the Thirty Years War; and woe to him who sets Europe in flames, who first casts the match into the powder-barrel.[54]

Indeed, views on the nature of international relations and on the place of war within human reality were closely related to the outlook on the conduct of war itself. Moltke's remarkable insight into the future foresaw the ultimate military consequences of the politicization of the masses, brought about by the combined effects of nationalism, urbanization, mass education, and mass communications. But the process had begun exactly a century before; people's wars had been taking the place of cabinet wars since the French Revolution and the emergence of the modern nation-state. By centralizing power and establishing the principle of popular sovereignty, France had been able to mobilize and throw into war social resources and human masses on an unprecedented scale and had managed to generate immense moral energies. These in turn had found their strategic corollary expressed in Danton's famous formula: 'L'audace, et encore de l'audace, et toujours l'audace.' Developed and refined by Napoleon, the new system of war had

[52] 11 Jan. 1887, *Essays, Speeches and memoirs*, ii. 133; also see, for example: Mar. 1879 and 10 Feb. 1881, *Moltke as a Correspondent*, 270, 280.

[53] *Essays, Speeches and Memoirs*, ii. 136.

[54] Ibid. 137.

consisted of a massive concentration of force and crushing strategy, aiming at the enemy's total overthrow. After Prussia's catastrophic defeat, both these new sources of power and the resulting mode of war had been highlighted and celebrated by the Prussian reformers. Whereas the reformers had been thrown out of power after Napoleon's downfall, both their institutional and their doctrinal legacy remained. With her Landwehr militia, Prussia remained the only power in Europe of the Restoration to base her military system on the mobilization of her people. This system was later turned by King Wilhelm I and his Minister of War, von Roon, into an effective nation-in-arms. Similarly, the reformers' new, uniquely aggressive operational conception, modelled on Napoleonic strategy and emphasizing determined action and the destruction of the enemy army in battle, had found expression in the tremendous zeal of the Prussian army in the campaigns of 1813–15 and persisted thereafter. When the reorganization of the 1860s gave the Prussian army the numerical superiority over its rivals formerly enjoyed by the armies of Revolutionary France, the crushing strategic concepts had again found their natural counterpart.

The belief that no rigorous system of military theory was possible was fundamental to the new currents of military thought in Prussia. Ever since the Romantic revolt against the ideas of the Enlightenment, the doctrine of universal natural law had been rejected in each and every department of German culture. No sphere of human activity, conditioned as it was by its historical setting and dominated by a multitude of acts of volition, could ever be compressed into a formal system of rules and principles; this cultural premiss, introduced into the military field by Clausewitz, was widely disseminated by Moltke: little could be said about war theoretically. After Moltke's death, in publishing his extensive military memoranda, correspondence, and staff studies in the multi-volume *Militärische Werke*, the general staff took the liberty of piecing together under systematic headings passages which had been written in different circumstances, often even without referring to their source. But Moltke himself only summarized his strategic teaching in a brief essay composed for direct practical purposes between his two great wars: 'Instructions for Superior Commanders of Troops' (1869), supplemented after the war in France by the even briefer 'On Strategy' (1871). 'The doctrines of strategy', he wrote, 'hardly go beyond the first propositions of common sense; one can hardly call them a science; their value lies almost entirely in their concrete application.'[55] From the beginning of operations, only the general's will and force of action can prevail over the moral and physical complexity of war, 'Strategy is [but] a system of expediences.'[56] For example, 'one reads much in theoretical books about the advantages of "operating on the interior lines". Yet one will have to ask oneself in each particular case what at the moment will be the most advantageous thing to do.'[57]

Indeed, the celebrated principle of the interior lines is a case in point. Moltke faced unanimous criticism when in 1866 he chose to disregard what was widely accepted as the advantage of interior lines, deploying his armies on a front extending from Saxony to Silesia. Military commentators all over Europe disapproved and, until the campaign of 1870–1 silenced them for good, they attributed Prussian success to poor Austrian generalship.[58] The high priest at Jomini's altar, his friend and biographer Lecomte, did not mince words:

> Since war was first waged seldom have such masses been placed in a more ghastly situation. The historical blunder of the Austrian commanders advancing in 1796 to the relief of Mantua in three columns—a blunder so thoroughly punished by Bonaparte—was at any rate a strategic masterpiece compared with the Prussian plan of 1866.[59]

Moltke also had his critics in the Prussian army itself, but here his innovative strategies could at least be explained by appealing to prevailing intellectual notions. First, the particular circumstances of each case always take priority over any established rule: *individuum est ineffabile*. In 1866 the extended deployment was dictated by the special circumstances of the earlier Austrian mobilization, which imposed a defensive position on the Prussians at the initial stage of the campaign, and which had to be countered by rapid mobilization and deployment, using all available railway-lines. However, Moltke's case went far beyond the claim of special circumstances. It is no

[55] 'Verordnungen für die höheren Truppenführer' (1869), in *Militärische Werke*, II, ii (1900), 172.

[56] 'Über Strategie' (1871), ibid. 219–3.

[57] 'Taktische Aufgaben', Nr. 58 (1878), ibid., II, i. (1892), 133.

[58] For a selection of commentaries see Gordon Craig, *The Battle of Königgrätz* (London, 1964), 176–7.

[59] Quoted by Whitton, *Moltke* (London, 1921), 118–19.

accident that, while disciples of Jomini everywhere found the strategic as well as the tactical effects of the railway, the electric telegraph, and the rifle indigestible, it was in Prussia that their revolutionary significance was more readily accepted. Its deep historicist roots made military thought in Germany inherently more conscious of, and receptive to, historical change. Compared with the military theories of Jomini and his fellow thinkers, wrote Rudolph Caemmerer, the enormous advantage of the German conception of military theory 'lies in its *capacity for further development*'.[60]

It is this quality that accounts for Moltke's theoretical flexibility. The 'progress of technology,' he wrote, 'easier communications, new weapons, in short completely altered conditions, make it appear that the means by which victory was gained formerly, and even the rules laid down by the greatest generals, are frequently inapplicable to the present'.[61] If massed together from the opening of a campaign, the huge new armies would choke communications, and prove difficult to operate and impossible to supply. But by initially deploying over vast spaces, they could make full use of existing railway-heads for rapid mobilization and supply, and march on converging routes to achieve massive concentration on the field of battle.[62] 'March divided, strike united' was the new dictum. From the time of his appointment as chief of the general staff, Moltke advanced far-reaching proposals for the systematic preplanned use of the railway.[63] Prussia's exposed geographical position and system of reserves provided the most favourable ground for the acceptance of such ideas. The electric telegraph greatly facilitated the co-ordination of the entire process of mobilization and deployment, and the largely increased fire-capability of the rifle, by enhancing the power of defence, made it considerably more difficult for the enemy to overwhelm each of the army corps separately, before effective support could arrive.

Even before, but especially after, the Italian campaign of 1859, Moltke keenly observed the far-reaching effects of the rifle on tactics and strategy. Though not directly the responsibility of the

[60] Caemmerer, *The Development of Strategical Science during the 19th Century* (London, 1905), 54; italics in the original.

[61] 'Verordnungen', *Militärische Werke*, II, ii, 172.

[62] Ibid. 173.

[63] Dennis Showalter, *Railroads and Rifles: Soldiers, Technology and the Unification of Germany* (Hamden, Conn., 1975), 39–43.

general staff, this subject was at the top of the European military agenda and was intensely discussed in the Prussian army. Moltke produced a series of memoranda which constituted perhaps the most accurate and comprehensive assessment written at the time. He clearly foresaw that the ability of cavalry to operate against infantry was considerably weakened, and that mass infantry bayonet-charges were a thing of the past. Attacking infantry would have to advance in small columns, thickly protected by skirmishers, take full advantage of the ground, and always seek to avoid frontal engagements by turning the enemy's flank.[64] The remarkable strengthening of fire-power from defensive positions, claimed Moltke, rendered the strategic offence which made maximum use of tactical defence the most advantageous form of war at that time.[65] Upholding circumstantial analysis against all formal assertions, Moltke consciously disregarded Clausewitz's insistence that defence was intrinsically stronger than attack. No general answer existed to the question of which of them was stronger, he wrote in his 'Instructions' of 1869. While the attack enjoyed the advantage of initiative, defence could make better use of the cover of ground. The individual case must always decide.[66] Similarly, it was more than just his utter humility that prevented Moltke from crowning his operations on exterior lines as a new 'strategic system'. The debate on the differences between Napoleon's and his own systems of war was one that was conducted by others at a later stage.[67]

Significantly, on both sides of this debate a consensus prevailed that, while the forms (*Formen*) of war may change with time, its spirit (*Geist*), or essence (*Wesen*), remains unchanged.[68] Indeed, the rejection of any formal system and the strong awareness of circumstantial differences and historical change must not mislead;

[64] 'Taktisch-strategische Aufsätze', 12 July 1858, 5 Jan. 1860, Apr. and May 1861, 1865, ibid., esp. 7–9, 19–24, 27–41, 49–65. See also Showalter, *Railroads and Rifles*, 110–13.

[65] Ibid., esp. 7, 31, 56, 65.

[66] Ibid., 208.

[67] See Colmar von der Goltz, *The Conduct of War* (London, 1899, first publ. in German 1895), 135–44; Hugo Baron von Freytag-Loringhoven, *Die Heerführung Napoleons und Moltkes* (Berlin, 1897); S. W. L. von Schlichting, *Taktische und strategische Grundsätze der Gegenwart* (3 vols.; Berlin, 1897–9); id. *Moltke und Benedek* (Berlin, 1900); id. *Moltkes Vermächtnis* (Munich, 1901); Alfred Krauss, *Moltke, Benedek und Napoleon* (Vienna, 1901); Carl Bleibtreu, *Napoleon'sche und Moltke'sche Strategie* (Vienna, 1901); Fritz von der Goltz, *Moltke* (Berlin, 1903), 182–95; Caemmerer, *Strategical Science*, pref. and ch. 8.

[68] For each side of the argument, see most strikingly: Krauss, foreword; F. von der Goltz, 182–6.

in the tradition of nineteenth-century German idealism these notions were always matched by a strong claim to capture the inner essence of reality.[69] The Prussian-German military school had an overriding and highly prescriptive conception of the conduct of war. While Clausewitz and his friends had argued that the dominating Napoleonic mode of warfare could not be reduced to rules and principles, they had still believed that it represented the universal nature of war and exhibited the true implications from its concept (*Begriff*); this is an ambivalence which nowadays has been the cause of much misunderstanding. The essence of war was fighting, which implied the destruction of the enemy forces in battle. In the 'Instructions' Moltke presented this conception of war, and his own innovative contributions, with his customary brevity and comprehensiveness:

> The victory in the decision by arms is the most important moment in war. Only victory breaks the enemy will and compels him to submit to our own. Neither the occupation of territory nor the capturing of fortified places, but only the destruction of the enemy fighting-power will, as a rule, decide. This is thus the primary object of operations.[70]

Acting boldly and aggressively, the army must seize the initiative and seek the enemy army wherever it may be found. Since the uncertainty and confusion of war, the severe shortage of information, and enemy activities work against all operational planning, there is no point in devising detailed schemes beyond the deployment (*Aufmarsch*) phase. Only the aim and the general line of advance are to be clearly stated. During the course of the campaign, effective co-operation between the separate units must depend on the initiative of local commanders and on their having been trained to leave everything and rush towards the sound of the guns. For the battle itself, one cannot be too strong. Once the enemy is located and engaged, all forces converge to achieve overwhelming superiority, strategic envelopment, and tactical encirclement. A decisive battle of destruction would be the desirable result. 'The operations against France', stated Moltke's memorandum of 6 May 1870 to the general staff,

> will simply consist in our advancing in as close a formation as possible for a few marches on French soil, till we meet the French army and then fight a

[69] See, for example, Iggers, *The German Conception of History*, esp. 111.
[70] 'Verordnungen', *Militärische Werke*, II. ii. 173.

battle. The direction of this advance is in general towards Paris, because in that direction we are most certain to hit the mark we are aiming at, the enemy's army.[71]

Carried out with considerable numerical advantage and with greatly superior railway, mobilization, and staff systems, this operational conception produced absolutely decisive results. In 1866 the Prussian First, Second, and Elbe Armies managed to unite on the battlefield of Königgrätz, and while the Austrian army under Benedek did succeed in escaping their pincer movement—and total annihilation—it was no longer capable of effective resistance. In 1870, after some confused and bloody clashes on the frontier, one half of the French army was shut up in the fortress of Metz and the other pushed against the Belgian border near Sedan. The two capitulations that ensued sent virtually the entire French regular army, some 300,000 men in all, as prisoners of war to Germany.

However, while Königgrätz, Metz, and Sedan destroyed the Austrian and French armies, both wars still had to be brought to an end. This is where the famous disputes between Bismarck and the military broke out. In 1866 the king and his military advisers wanted to give the Austrian army no time to rally, occupy Vienna, and dictate peace terms which would include war indemnities and the annexation of Austrian Silesia, the Sudeten, and the Kingdom of Saxony to Prussia. Bismarck, however, was mostly concerned about the prospects of French intervention. Having achieved what he regarded as Prussia's principal aim, which was the exclusion of Austria from German affairs, as well as extensive annexations and the creation of a Prussian-led confederation in north Germany, he virtually forced a moderate peace on his enraged sovereign. In 1870–1, the picture was even more complicated. After the destruction of the French regular armies, war went on. The republican government prepared the capital for siege and, raising the banner of 1792, began to mobilize huge armies in the provinces, while *francs tireurs* harassed the advancing Prussian columns and lines of communication. On the other side, Bismarck was again primarily concerned about possible intervention by the other powers, and was manœuvring to find a suitable French partner and the means by which pressure could be exerted on him to negotiate a favourable peace. This required careful control over the direction

[71] *Militärische Werke*, I. iii. 131–2.

and aims of military operations. Tensions between Bismarck and the military began to mount over the fate of Bazaine's besieged army in Metz, which Bismarck thought he might use to reinstitute a Bonapartist ruler in Paris. These tensions developed into a head-on confrontation with Moltke and the general staff concerning the occupation of Paris, which Bismarck regarded as nothing more than a political bargaining-card for the attainment of peace. The army strongly resented any political interference in its business, while Bismarck acted with customary ruthlessness to impose his will.

This conflict has been dissected by historians ever since.[72] It has been presented as the first instance of a bid by the general staff for autonomy from, and equal status with, civil authority in the German Reich—one that was destined to have far-reaching influence on German history. With the army free from parliamentary control and responsible only to the person of the king, its claim was deeply rooted in the Prussian, and later German, political structure and ethos. 'Up till now', wrote Moltke to the King after being called to order, 'I have considered that the Chief of the General Staff (especially in war) and the Federal Chancellor are two equally warranted and mutually independent agencies under the direct command of Your Royal Majesty.'[73]

The positions of the military both in 1866 and 1870–1 have been presented as totally divorced from political considerations and have been widely attributed to a narrow military point of view, only to be expected of generals. This explanation, however, hardly gets to the bottom of the matter, as some leading historians have noted.[74] Contrary to popular belief, soldiers as such are no more naturally disposed to radical military measures than other parts of the political community. To understand their attitudes, one has to examine the political and cultural environment in which they operate. The Prussian military had a highly distinctive conception

[72] For the latest and most comprehensive accounts see Stadelmann, *Moltke*, 212–64; Ritter, *Sword and Scepter*, i. 219–25; Gordon Craig, *The Politics of the Prussian Army* (Oxford, 1955), 196–216; Michael E. Howard, *The Franco-Prussian War* (London, 1961), 271, 352–7, 436–43.

[73] 29 Jan. 1871, Craig, *The Politics of the Prussian Army*, 214; Stadelmann, *Moltke*, 437, where the full document is printed.

[74] See Ritter, *Sword and Scepter*, i. 193–4; his acute analysis goes partly against the general drift of his own work, which blames Germany's later historical course on the improper place of the military. For Stadelmann see below.

of war, at once military and political, developed during the great struggle against Napoleon: crushing strategy was to bring the enemy to his knees in the pursuit of great political objectives. The similarity between the attitudes of the reformers in 1814–15 and the positions of the military and the King (himself a veteran of 1815) in 1866 and 1870–1 is striking. Stein and the Prussian headquarters of Blücher and Gneisenau, in almost open defiance of Frederick William III, had been passionately demanding extensive territorial annexations to Prussia, including the whole Kingdom of Saxony, and had been willing to go to war with Austria, supported by the other European powers, if their demands were not met. Similarly, both in 1814 and 1815, they forcefully pressed for a total overthrow of French power, for the occupation of Paris and France, and for a punitive peace, treating with open hostility, and trying by all means at their disposal to pre-empt and frustrate, the alternative, subtle political schemes that Metternich had been entertaining.[75] When the tsar had expressed the opinion that the king of Prussia might need help against his Jacobine army, he had hit the nail right on the head. The conflict in 1814–15, as in 1866–71, was not so much between political and military points of view. Stein allied with Blücher and Gneisenau; Schwarzenberg with Metternich. The conflict was more between the old cabinet conception of politics and war and the one emerging in the age of nationalism and all-out strategy. As pointed out by Stadelmann, it was Metternich's world in collision with Clausewitz's. While Bismarck was a classical representative of *raison d'état* and the five-power order, Moltke developed into an exponent of state nationalism and national war.[76]

In 1870–1 Moltke was adamant that French resistance must be crushed. He recommended that the activities of the *francs tireurs* be suppressed by the most severe reprisals and regarded the fall of Paris mainly as a means to free the German armies to deal with the French popular forces. In the heat of his debate with Bismarck the Prussian crown prince observed that 'Count Bismarck desired peace, but General Count Moltke a war of extermination.'[77] Moltke's conversation with the crown prince concerning the future

[75] See Ritter's excellent analysis in ch. 4 of *Sword and Scepter*, i.

[76] Stadelmann, *Moltke*, 176 and foreword respectively.

[77] 13 Jan. 1871, *The War Diary of the Emperor Frederick III, 1870–1871*, 258.

course of the war after the fall of Paris puts Moltke's plans squarely in the context of his overall conception of strategy's means and ends:

> MOLTKE: We shall push forward into the south of France in order finally to break the enemy's power.
>
> THE CROWN PRINCE: But what will happen when our own strength is exhausted, when we can no longer win battles?
>
> MOLTKE: We must always win battles. We must throw France completely to the ground.
>
> THE CROWN PRINCE: And what then?
>
> MOLTKE: Then we can dictate the kind of peace we want.[78]

Moltke always stressed that war was but a political means.[79] His insistence that politics must not interfere with the aim and conduct of strategy cannot, therefore, simply be dismissed as a soldier's effort at a clear demarcation of his professional sphere. His attitude was the outgrowth of an expansive and sweeping conception of the nature of war and strategy, which could never be violated with impunity. After his experience in 1870–1 he worked out the following formula:

> Diplomacy avails itself to war to attain its ends, crucially influencing the beginning of war and its end. It does the latter by reserving to itself the privilege of raising or lowering its demands in the course of the war. In the presence of such uncertainty, strategy has no choice but to strive for the highest goal attainable with the means given.[80]

Since this position is often contrasted with Clausewitz's, it must be made clear that it is almost identical with Clausewitz's own formulations in his notes on strategy of 1804 and in the period until 1827, when he began to undergo the intellectual transformation which was terminated by his death.[81] Both expressed a new and highly pronounced conception of war and strategy which had been developed in Prussia in the era of national war.

Indeed, the experience of French popular resistance in 1870–1 demonstrated the scale of resources mobilized when two great

[78] 8 Jan. 1871, quoted by Goerlitz, *The German General Staff*, 92, from H. Uncken (ed.), *Großherzog Friedrich I von Baden und deutsche Politik von 1854–1871, Briefwechsel, Denkschriften, Tagebücher* (Berlin and Leipzig, 1927), 300–1.

[79] See, for example, 'Verordnungen' (1869), *Militärische Werke*, II. ii. 206

[80] 'Über Strategie', ibid. 291; Ritter, *Sword and Scepter*, i. 194–5.

[81] Book I above, 205–7.

modern nations were locked in a life-and-death struggle. The destruction of the enemy's armies was no longer sufficient. In his letter to Professor Bluntschli, in which he denounced the idea of a permanent peace, Moltke made this clear: 'I cannot at all agree with the "Déclaration de St. Pétersbourg" that the "weakening of the hostile fighting power" is the only right proceeding in a war. No; all the resources of the hostile government must be affected, her finance, railways, victuals, even her prestige.'[82] This type of war, he told the Reichstag in 1890, might take seven or even thirty years. National war and all-out strategy in a modern industrial setting and on a modern industrial scale were breeding total war.

'WORLD-POWER OR DECLINE'

In rapid succession between 1888 and 1890, Kaiser Wilhelm I, Bismarck, and Moltke—the three men with whose names the era of unification and the establishment of the German Reich were most intimately connected—either died or departed from public life. This was a coincidence which corresponded only too aptly to deeper trends that were transforming both German society and the international system in the late nineteenth century. A younger generation, which had grown up in a formidable German Empire with a sense of Prussia's great triumphs, now faced two fundamental and largely parallel developments. Internally, from the mid-1890s, German industrialization, hand in hand with urbanization and demographic growth, which had begun seriously in the 1850s and had taken off after the unification, entered a continuous period of outstandingly rapid expansion. Far outstripping the other great powers of Europe in her growth-rate, Germany now emerged from a position of rough equality in population and production to assume a marked and consistently widening superiority over all her major potential rivals. In the process, the country was transformed from a predominantly rural to a predominantly urban one, while her traditional social and political order was here struggling to keep its own and here forced to recede before modern capitalist mass society. Externally, Germany's fast-growing dependence on, and interest in, foreign trade and markets coincided with the general

[82] *Moltke as a Correspondent*, 274.

expansion of the Western industrial powers over the undeveloped world. The partitioning of Asia and Africa injected great instability, fierce competition, and tremendous new tensions into the old European power-system. In the age of imperialism, the European power-struggle was assuming global dimensions.

It is the interweaving of Germany's political, social, and intellectual traditions with these new conditions and challenges that accounts for all aspects of her development, including that of the military. This has been argued and demonstrated in the vast volume of works which have flowed, since the 1960s, from the Fischer controversy and from the reorientation of the German historical approach to Imperial Germany in the era before the world wars. Of this most contentious and massively documented period, the following passages can present only an overview.

It is customary to begin from the economic and demographic data, and with good reason. Between 1870 and 1914 German population grew 66 per cent, from 41 to 68 million. By comparison, France, Germany's major military rival, grew only 11 per cent, from 36 to 40 million. Thus German advantage grew from 13 per cent to 70 per cent. Moreover, when production figures are considered, Germany's advantage over France in 1910–13 was sixfold in coal production, more than threefold in pig-iron production, and fourfold in steel production. Overall, her manufacturing production was two and a half times that of France.

Between 1870 and 1913 German coal production increased by a factor of 6 and pig-iron production by a factor of 9.36. By comparison, in Britain, Germany's major economic contender, figures increased by only 2.25 and 1.5 times respectively. Whereas in 1870, Germany's industrial production was only a fraction of Britain's, by 1900 she had almost caught up with her in absolute terms, and by 1913 she had overtaken her, narrowing the gap in per capita production. In 1913, while being 10 per cent inferior to Britain in coal production, Germany was more than 50 per cent superior in pig-iron production and 134 per cent superior in steel production. Her overall manufacturing production was some 9 per cent greater.

In Europe, only the Russian growth-rate compared with the German, but starting from total backwardness, Russia was still very far behind Germany in 1913 by all indicators except population. Although Germany was less than half as populous as

Russia, her coal production was more than eight times as great and her pig-iron and steel production almost four times as great. Her overall manufacturing production was twice as great as Russia's. Yet her vast resources and fast growth-rate made Russia Germany's major potential rival.[83]

All in all, Germany was becoming at least as strong as France and Russia put together, and more powerful than Britain. On a global level, only the colossal United States was greatly superior to Germany by all indicators and potentially was already becoming the greatest power.[84]

All sections of Germany's ruling élite and of public opinion at large were highly conscious of these underlying trends. Not only was the balance of European power tilting in Germany's favour; the shift coincided with the dawn of a new era in world history. In a new global industrial and commercial system, Western expansion indicated that the future lay with world empires—politically, economically, and militarily. The opening-up and shrinking of the world were dwarfing the old continent of Europe. One could either take the step forward to the status of a world power in a new international system or be relegated to insignificance and decline. The new generation seemed to be facing a historic mission which was as demanding and magnificent as their fathers', and was in many ways similar to it. Then, the need had been to unite Germany and make her a great European power despite enormous domestic obstacles and against the opposition of some of the long-established great powers. Now, she had to be made a world power and expand to new continents already largely possessed by older colonial empires. Whereas under Bismarck, during the first decades of her

[83] Carlo M. Cipolla (ed.), *The Fontana Economic History of Europe* (Glasgow, 1973), iv. 747, 770–5; A. J. P. Taylor, *The Struggle for Mastery in Europe* (Oxford, 1954), pp. xxv–xxxi; H. J. Habakkuk and M. Postan (ed.), *The Cambridge Economic History of Europe* (*CEH*) (Cambridge, 1966), vi. 25; Paul Kennedy, *The Rise and Fall of the Great Powers* (London, 1988), 199–203. The figures vary slightly between these sources.

[84] Estimates of European state power on the basis of economic and demographic data in L. L. Farrar's stimulating *Arrogance and Anxiety: The Ambivalence of German Power, 1848–1914* (Iowa City, 1981), 10–39, are found crude in comparison with Kennedy's sophisticated set of measurements. If share of world manufacturing production is taken as a rough measure of state power in the industrial period, the percentages for 1913 are: Germany 14.8; Britain 13.6; Russia 8.2; France 6.1; Austro-Hungary 4.4; the USA 32.0: Kennedy, *The Rise and Fall of the Great Powers*, 202. The figures in *CEH* are slightly different, esp. regarding Russian production, estimated at 5.5 per cent.

existence, the German Empire had been a power of the status quo, she was now set against it, as Prussia under Bismarck had been before unification. Once again she seemed to need those qualities and resources that were held responsible for her glorious past ventures: great ambition and determination, boldness, and a spirit of dedication and self-sacrifice. Once again no great changes could be affected without the necessary modicum of ruthlessness and—as the other powers were unlikely to give way willingly—without the risk, indeed almost the inevitability, of war.

About all this a fundamental consensus prevailed almost across the board in German public life. The ethos of the old ruling class in the ministerial, administrative, and military establishment was matched, if not surpassed, by the enthusiasm of the bourgeoisie. The upper echelons of the bourgeoisie—the new magnates of business and industry and the political parties which spoke for them—in effect already shared in the leadership of Germany and could not be more aware of the prospects that lay ahead. The left-wing liberals may have opposed the grip of the old ruling class on the Reich's political, social, and military system, but many of them regarded precisely the creation of a German world-empire as a means of mobilizing the great popular energies of modern mass society, thus bridging the fearful divide between the working classes and the rest of society. The most distinguished university professors articulated this vision. By the eve of the Great War, even the Social Democratic Party, ideologically a mortal enemy of imperialism and military might alike, was beginning to feel the pressure for a more patriotic stand both within its rank and file and among its voters. Nobody personified the various trends, forces, and hopes that characterized Germany more forcefully than the man who aptly gave the period its name. This was the young and brilliant, but erratic and complex, Kaiser Wilhelm II, who by the turn of the century had led his country off on the two complementary courses of *Welt-* and *Flottenpolitik*.[85] On the whole, it would be fair to say that, within the prevailing consensus regarding Germany's future, differences, as important as they may have been, were mostly a matter of degree and were concerned with means.

This consensus also accounts for the views in the army. The latter, and especially the legendary Prussian Great General Staff,

[85] See the lively contributions to John Röhl and Nicolaus Sombart (eds.), *Kaiser Wilhelm II: New Interpretations* (Cambridge, 1982).

was regarded and feared by contemporaries as the bastion of German militarism and as the evil spirit of international politics. A more sophisticated version of this view influenced early historical works both inside and outside Germany, which sought to find in the peculiar position of the army within the state much of the reason for Germany's history and fate in modern times.[86] However, with the historical reappraisal of the trends and mood which dominated German policy and public opinion in the Wilhelmine era, a new picture emerged. While the army certainly had an important and largely independent position within the Reich's political and administrative structure, and, like each of the other bodies in this structure, certainly possessed its own characteristic professional and social point of view, this point of view was on the whole indistinguishable from the prevailing consensus.[87] Nor was it, of course, monolithic within this consensus. In this respect, opinions in the army, and the army's military orientation, mirrored the attitudes ruling the Reich and the general direction of German policy almost theme by theme.

In comparison with any of the other great powers, the dominating intellectual traditions in Germany needed remarkably little adaptation to the age of imperialism. The ideas which had found their most famous expression with Treitschke and Moltke were commonplace. In the military field, one could find them stated at the opening of almost each and every treatise. They were intended to provide the necessary foundation for any realistic appreciation of the essence of war and of its function in the relations between states.[88] Moltke's views were echoed by such disciples as Colonel, later General of Infantry, Wilhelm von Blume, whose book *Strategie* (1882) was based on a course of lectures delivered at the *Kriegsakademie*. The state, wrote Blume, was the highest form of organization in humanity's course of self-education towards ethical, intellectual, and material elevation. As such, each state constitutes a distinct cultural entity, whose interests may sometimes conflict with those of other states. Although civilized nations try to settle their differences peacefully, war, despite its horrors, is often

[86] See esp. Ritter, *Sword and Scepter*; Craig, *The Politics of the Prussian Army*.

[87] See esp. L. L. Farrar, *The Short-War Illusion* (Oxford, 1973), 20; id. *Arrogance and Anxiety*, 146–8, 176, 198–9.

[88] See Detlef Bald, 'Zum Kriegsbild der militärischen Führung im Kaiserreich', in J. Dülffer and K. Holl (eds.), *Bereit zum Krieg: Kriegsmentalität im wilhelminischen Deutschland, 1890–1914* (Göttingen, 1986), 150–3.

the unavoidable result. No state can forget this without risking destruction.[89] The prolific military author Lieutenant-General Albrecht von Boguslawski reiterated Moltke's opinions to the letter in his book *War in Its True Significance to the State and People.* War, he wrote, was the law of nature, while perpetual peace, advocated by the philosophers of the eighteenth century, was a dream, and not even a beautiful one.[90] It is therefore not surprising that, in comparison with its counterparts in the other European countries, the German peace-movement never gained any public stature. Its ideal went against the national ethos and was widely seen as naïve, undesirable, and dangerous.[91] Its activists, together with all other sorts of pacifists, were regarded with a mixture of contempt and despair by broad-minded men of the world, who saw them as 'political children'.[92] When the Hague Conferences convened in 1899 and 1907, they were regarded with cynicism, scepticism, and suspicion by all powers. But in Germany they were regarded with almost open hostility as a plot to tie the country's hands.[93]

In his international best seller *The Nation in Arms* (German orig. 1883), which in Germany alone ran through five editions by 1898, Major, later Field-Marshal, Colmar von der Goltz propounded the accepted ideas with greater zest: 'Wars are the fate of mankind, the inevitable destiny of nations.'[94] The various nations confront each other like individuals in the state of nature. No tribunal or arbitration has the power to curb their selfish interests and impose peace upon them. Individual good will notwithstanding, the

[89] Wilhelm von Blume, *Strategie. Eine Studie* (Berlin, 1882), 1–9; a 2nd edn. was published in 1886, and a 3rd, rev. one in 1912.

[90] Albrecht von Boguslawski, *Der Krieg in seiner wahren Bedeutung für Staat und Volk* (Berlin, 1892). For practically identical ideas see Wilhelm Balck, *Modern German Tactics* (London, 1899; first publ. in German 1892), 1–5; and Freytag-Loringhoven, *Krieg und Politik in der Neuzeit* (Berlin, 1911), esp. 268–80. During the war, as deputy chief of the general staff, Freytag-Loringhoven found the time to issue a collection from Treitschke's works: *Heinrich von Treitschke: Auswahl für das Feld* (Leipzig, 1917).

[91] For this and other opinions on the role of war, see Roger Chickering, *Imperial Germany and a World Without War: The Peace Movement and German Society 1892–1914* (Princeton, NJ 1975), esp. 183, 392–6.

[92] The quotation is from A. Boguslawski, *Betrachtungen über Heerwesen und Kriegführung* (Berlin, 1897), 89–90.

[93] A recent study is Jost Dülffer, *Regeln gegen den Krieg? Die Haager Friedenskonferenzen von 1899 und 1907* (Frankfurt a.M., 1981).

[94] Colmar von der Goltz, *The Nation in Arms* (London, 1906), 470.

dynamics of their position allows them no relaxation in their military efforts.[95] This is particularly true in the age of national war. The experience of French popular resistance in 1870–1, about which von der Goltz wrote his first book, is ominous:

> The advent of future war is regarded with anxious expectation. Everyone seems to feel that it will be waged with a destructive force such as has hitherto never been displayed. War is now an exodus of nations and no longer a mere conflict between armies. All moral energies will be gathered for a life-and-death struggle; the whole sum of the intelligence residing in either people will be employed for their mutual destruction. . . . If obstinacy and persistency were displayed equally by both sides, the end of the struggle would only be conceivable after general devastation and pauperisation had completely exhausted the physical, and long suffering the moral, forces . . . it may be necessary to literally flood a country with troops and to exert extreme pressure upon the population for years on end.[96]

Behind this picture of war lay an overpowering perception of human history: 'a nation, like an individual, has to fulfil a certain mission in the time given it. The discharge of the duties of civilisation brings nations into conflict.'[97] Nineteenth-century historicism, an acute sense of unified human development and cultural growth, and intense nationalism came together with German idealism in the idea, most famously formulated by Hegel, that great historical nations dominated and personified the various stages of humanity's development. In the age of imperialism, hardly any other view in Germany was as influential in shaping popular perception of humanity's past, present, and future. 'The destiny of nations is like that of men,' wrote von der Goltz, 'nations rise, they grow, they bloom, they decay, and cease to be.' Germany, exploding with vigour, was now destined to take the place of older, decaying empires; her hour had come and she must rise to the challenge. 'The star of the young Empire has only just risen on the horizon; its full course lies still before it.'[98]

Predominance, of course, is never surrendered; it always has to be won. By the turn of the century, political realities and historical perspectives were everywhere receiving a timely reinforcement from the teaching of biology and the all-pervasive cultural impact of the Darwinian revolution. Human evolution was the scene of a

[95] Ibid. 10–11.
[96] Ibid. 463–5.
[97] Ibid. 463.
[98] Ibid. 474.

perpetual life-and-death struggle between races, peoples, and nations over space, resources, and power; only the fittest survived, while the others were doomed to extinction, disintegration, or subjugation.[99] Side by side with scientific racism, a very powerful culture of popular racism developed, which in Germany ran from the Kaiser himself downwards. The theories of the French Count Gobineau were transmitted and popularized by Wagner and developed by his son-in-law, Houston Stewart Chamberlain, in his widely read *Foundations of the Nineteenth Century* (1899). The book presented the racial struggle as the motive power of history and postulated the superiority of the Germanic peoples, and the Germans in particular, over all other races.[100] Representatives of the scholarly community cautioned that there was no scientific basis for biological demarcations between the various ethnic groups within the white race, and pointed out that all modern European nations, the Germans not excepting, were ethnically mixed.[101] Yet it was precisely here that much of the popular attraction of racism lay. By 1897 Boguslawski, while acknowledging the limited applicability of racial distinctions to Europe, went on to delineate the combination of racial and national qualities that characterized each of the major European armies.[102]

By the first decade of the twentieth century, the popular perception was that the Germanic race was gaining the ascendancy, while the inferior Latin and Celtic nations, particularly France, were declining. Things were more disturbing on Germany's eastern frontier. This was the scene of the historic and gigantic clash 'between Germandom and Slavdom' led by Russia, which so troubled Helmuth von Moltke the younger, nephew of the great Moltke and chief of the general staff from 1906 to 1914.[103] In his

[99] For the overall cultural impact, see Alfred Kelly, *The Descent of Darwin: The Popularization of Darwinism in Germany, 1860–1914* (Chapel Hill, NC, 1981).

[100] Two standard works are Léon Poliakov, *The Aryan Myth: A History of Racist and Nationalist Ideas in Europe* (London, 1974); and George L. Mosse, *Toward the Final Solution: A History of European Racism* (London, 1978). A good brief account for Germany is Roger Chickering, *We Men Who Feel Most German: A Cultural Study of the Pan-German League* (Boston, 1984), 237–45.

[101] See, for example, Max Weber, *Economy and Society* (New York, 1968), i. 385–98; Hans Delbrück, *Government and the Will of the People* (New York, 1923; first publ. in German 1914), 3–4. See also Fritz Fischer, *War of Illusions* (London, 1975), 255–7.

[102] Boguslawski, *Heerwesen und Kriegführung*, 21–35.

[103] The quotation is from a letter to the Austrian chief of staff, 10 Feb. 1913, in Conrad von Hötzendorf, *Aus meiner Dienstzeit, 1906–1918* (5 vols.; Berlin, 1921–5), iii. 146–7.

worried mind, the strong racial overtones which had always overlain his predecessors' preoccupations with the strategic problem of war with Russia, now assumed the more modern character of a racial life-and-death struggle for survival and world leadership. From 1912, with the rising tensions in the Balkans, the slogan of the coming 'racial war between the Teutons and the Slavs' was on everyone's lips, both in government and amongst the public.[104] Japan's spectacular defeat of Russia in 1904–5—the first victory of a modernized oriental nation over a great Western power—gave much food for thought. There was universal admiration for the young, vigorous race of warrior spirit, with whom the Germans felt a special affinity. 'How did the racial character of the Japanese bear up under the pressure of war against superior numbers?', ran the topic of one year's final essay in the Kriegsakademie.[105] Yet admiration was mixed with phobias concerning the growth of the 'Yellow Peril' that threatened white racial and political supremacy.[106] Blacks, of course, were regarded as subhuman and did not count at all. In 1904 the revolt of the Herrero nation in South West Africa was answered with a systematic policy and strategy of extermination, exceptional even by colonial standards. Anti-Semitism was increasingly prevalent from the 1870s and assumed a racial character.

National pride, rapid economic growth, the sight of a new world being opened up, a sense of historical and cultural mission amplified by racial overtones, and considerations of domestic politics—all these helped bring about the formation of German *Weltpolitik* by the turn of the twentieth century. Admittedly, in the long-drawn-out argument over the 'German problem' in modern European history, it has long been contended that in all these respects Germany was far from unique. As we shall see, similar views and ambitions prevailed throughout the Western world and motivated all the great powers in the age of imperialism.[107]

[104] For a rich selection of such comments see Fischer, *War of Illusions*, 190–5.

[105] Cited by Arden Bucholtz, *Hans Delbrück and the German Military Establishment: War Images in Conflict* (Iowa, 1985), 58.

[106] See, for example, Fritz von der Goltz, *Die gelbe Gefahr im Licht der Geschichte (The Yellow Peril in the Light of History)* (Leipzig, 1907). Fritz was Colmar's son and himself a general staff officer and military adviser to the Argentinan army.

[107] The most notable ideological defence is that by Ritter, *The German Problem* (Columbus, Oh., 1965). Outside Germany an authority like A. J. P. Taylor doubted in the wake of the Fischer controversy, that German power-politics was fundamentally

Yet it has also been pointed out that, because of her great strength and aspirations, Germany was the only great power whose aims and view of the future ultimately involved the destruction of the European balance of power and the virtual domination of Europe. Furthermore, German history and national ethos had been shaped in sharp and conscious rejection of the traditions of Enlightenment liberalism which in the West at least tempered the practices of *Realpolitik*. This gave German ambitions and conduct a particularly ruthless and menacing quality and appearance.

The Naval Laws of 1898 and 1900, which inaugurated the massive build-up of the German battle-fleet—soon to become the second most powerful in the world and a challenge to British naval supremacy—signalled the German intent to break out of the continent of Europe. While formerly measuring herself by continental standards mainly against France and Russia, Germany now measured herself by world standards against England, Russia, and the United States. Given Germany's new economic and global orientation, and with French power declining, England was assuming the position of Germany's arch-rival in the eyes of German decision-makers and the public at large. The prospect of a preventive continental war against France and Russia, which had dominated German military thought in the 1880s, was now overshadowed (at least in perception) by the prospect of war against England.

The realignment of the international system to face the growing German challenge took Germany completely by surprise. In 1904, having tried and failed to reach an agreement with Germany, England overcame her deep traditional rivalry with France and came to a settlement with her over their colonial differences. In another surprising move for Germany, the Anglo-French Entente was expanded and consolidated when, in 1907, England resolved the historical disputes in which she had been engaged with the Russian Empire, France's ally, in central Asia. Germany found herself isolated, with only Austria-Hungary on her side. Her attempt to undermine the Entente by forcing a show-down over Morocco in 1905–6, when Russia was paralysed by defeat and revolution, only brought England and France closer together. A second crisis over Morocco, in 1911, and successive Balkan crises

different or unique. See also David Calleo, *The German Problem Reconsidered* (New York, 1978), introduction and 49–53.

in 1908 and 1912–13, raised tensions in Europe to unprecedented levels and further strengthened the coalition against Germany. In turn, Germany felt politically contained and militarily encircled by what she perceived as a concerted effort to block her development into a world power. Enthusiastic expansionism now blended with deep anxieties over German security and survival. It was widely felt among the German ruling élite that what it regarded as Germany's necessary and legitimate growth was being gravely threatened: the hostility directed at her, and the formidable odds ranged against her, were jeopardizing her fundamental security. The impressive revival of Russian power in the years preceding the First World War, manifest in continuous economic expansion, massive military build-up and rapid railway-construction, seemed to be tipping the scale irrevocably against Germany in a matter of a few years.[108] The growing Russian strength made both Chancellor Bethmann-Hollweg and Chief of Staff Moltke profoundly pessimistic about Germany's future. It played a dominant role in steering German policy in the direction of pre-emptive or early war, an idea that was first mooted in the war council of December 1912 and figured prominently in German thinking until the July crisis of 1914.[109] Indeed, following the great debate over Germany's motives and aims on the eve of the First World War, it has been argued that neither expansionism and aggression nor insecurity and desperation were sufficient to explain German behaviour; only the highly dangerous combination of both could do this.[110]

The open confrontation between Germany and the Entente powers, which created an atmosphere of perpetual world-crisis in the decade preceding the Great War, charged German ambitions with intense public emotion and magnified the country's sense of being faced with decisions of fateful historical significance. No book expressed the views, unspoken assumptions, and hopes that prevailed in Germany more bluntly, or shocked foreign public opinion more deeply, than Friedrich von Bernhardi's famous *Germany and the Next War* (German orig. 1912), written in the wake of the second Moroccan crisis. The book won its author, a recently retired general of cavalry and one of Germany's foremost

[108] See Norman Stone, *The Eastern Front, 1914–1917* (London, 1975), chs. 1–2.

[109] See Fischer, *War of Illusions*, 161–4, 370–88.

[110] See esp. Farrar, *The Short-War Illusion*, pp. xvi, 33–7; id. *Arrogance and Anxiety*.

military writers, international renown. His even more shocking *Our Future* (1912), written after the Second Balkan War, further enhanced his reputation. In the Entente's war-propaganda he was to occupy an especially notorious place—together with Treitschke and Nietzsche—as the epitome of the German spirit and as one of its most influential representatives.[111]

The titles of the first five chapters of *Germany and the Next War* speak for themselves: 'The Right to Make War', 'The Duty to Make War', 'A Brief Survey of Germany's Historical Development', 'Germany's Historical Mission', and 'World Power or Downfall'.

> . . . nations do not form a single society . . . all real progress is founded upon the struggle for existence and the struggle for power prevailing among them. That struggle eliminates the weak and used-up nations and allows strong nations possessed of sturdy civilisation to maintain themselves and to obtain a position of predominant power until they too have fulfilled the civilising task and have to go down before young and rising nations.[112]

Thus 'war is a biological necessity'. Darwin and modern science corroborate Heraclitus' dictum that 'war is the father of all things'.[113]

Relying extensively on Fichte and Treitschke, Bernhardi exalted the cultural role and historical function of the state.[114] Its existence, he wrote, like that of the individual, 'is valuable only when it is consciously and actively employed for the attainment of great ends'.[115] Celebrating the glorious past of the German people as the exponent of reasoned liberty, Bernhardi rallied his countrymen to their future mission.[116]

In the new partitioning of the world, says Bernhardi, Germany started off belatedly and badly. A nation of 65 million people cannot be treated as inferior to a France of 40 million and an

[111] See J. A. Cramb, *Germany and England* (London, 1914); Charles S. Terry, *Treitschke, Bernhardi and Some Theologians* (Glasgow, 1915); Anon., *Bernhardi Converted* (London, 1915); James Crichton-Browne, *Bernhardi and Creation* (Glasgow, 1916).

[112] Friedrich von Bernhardi, *Britain as Germany's Vassal* (London, 1914; trans. of *Unsere Zukunft*), 27–8.

[113] Bernhardi, *Germany and the Next War* (New York, 1914), 18; also see *Britain as Germany's Vassal*, 106–7, 111–12.

[114] *Germany and the Next War*, 24–5, 45.

[115] Ibid. 56–7.

[116] Ibid. 58–65; *Britain as Germany's Vassal*, 30–46.

England of 45 million, of whom only part are of Germanic origin. In the coming realignment of the world, France must agree to, or be forced to acknowledge, German hegemony in Europe. Germany will consolidate her already massive economic control over Central Europe and the Balkans into an economic union and political alliance of Mitteleuropa, led by herself and through her sister-empire and proxy, Austria-Hungary. This union will extend to form a wider sphere of influence in the Ottoman Empire and the Near East. The major effort, however, should be made in the colonial sphere. Here, the first target is the formation of a huge German Mittelafrica, created by welding Germany's existing colonies to Portugal's old colonies and to the Belgian Congo, both ready for re-partition. England may either agree to the direction of German policy and form an alliance with her against the United States, the Slavs, and the Yellow Peril, who are the true future rivals of the European powers, or come to a collision with Germany.[117]

The main contribution of the massively documented works of Fritz Fischer was to show that Bernhardi's ideas and views of Germany's political aims were not shared only by the political Right but in fact reflected the wider consensus growing among Germany's ruling élite. While government circles and the liberal press denounced Bernhardi's book as irresponsible and harmful to Germany's foreign relations, the political vision to which he gave expression was actually the one which was to guide Germany during the Great War.[118] Helmuth von Moltke the younger, the chief of the general staff whose perception of Germany's position made him one of the major 'hawks' in the years preceding the war, delivered this characteristic statement in late 1914:

> The Latin peoples have passed the zenith of their development, they can no longer introduce new fertilising elements into the development of the world as a whole. The Slav peoples, Russia in particular, are still too backward culturally to be able to take over the leadership of mankind. Under the rule of knout Europe would be led back to the state of spiritual barbarism. Britain pursues only material objectives. Germany alone . . . can at present take over the leadership of mankind into higher goals. . . . This war will

[117] *Germany and the Next War*, 132–55, 207–8; *Britain as Germany's Vassal*, 94–5, 104–7.

[118] Fischer, *Germany's Aims in the First World War* (New York, 1967; first publ. in German 1961), 34–5. See also, for various segments of German society, the essays compiled in Dülffer and Holl (eds.), *Bereit zum Krieg*.

lead to a new development in world history and . . . determine the direction in which the whole world will move for the next centuries . . .[119]

The German outlook on the future was mainly dynamic and optimistic. Equally, however, Bernhardi's famous slogan, 'world power or decline', captured the grave doubts and pessimistic thoughts which were depressing and tormenting the minds of Germany's ruling élite. 'Mighty deeds raised Germany from political disruptions and feebleness,' wrote Bernhardi; but was Germany still capable of living up to her present and future challenges?[120]

The rapid modernization of Germany, while doubling and redoubling her power and wealth, also bred a deeply felt cultural malaise. The disintegration of traditional society and of community life brought about massive social dislocation and urban alienation. Secularization, together with capitalist commercialism and materialism, eroded the old system of values and beliefs. To be sure, the development was European-wide. By the turn of the nineteenth century it gave rise throughout the Continent to the second of the great waves of anti-modernism which, since the late eighteenth century and in remarkably regular centennial intervals, have followed periods of great modernist enthusiasm. But in Germany in particular, where modernization was exceptionally rapid, this wave coincided with the major themes of the country's cultural tradition, which formed its distinct self-identity after the Romantic revolt.

Side by side with overflowing optimism regarding Germany's future, and great enthusiasm for technological advances, there was widespread unease at the present and nostalgic yearning for the qualities of a lost past.[121] The meteoric rise to fame experienced by Nietzsche's works in the late 1890s was symptomatic of an age which tried to escape from the uniformity, conformity, and mechanization of mass society by appealing to individual creativity, elementary forces of life, and aesthetic experience. In Germany in particular, these feelings blended well with the tendency to equate the ailings of modernity with Western liberalism, false rationalism, and the Judaeo-Roman tradition of Christian morality, all regarded as alien to the natural free spirit of ancient and historic Germandom.

[119] Helmuth von Moltke (the younger), *Betrachtungen und Erinnerungen* (Hamburg, 1914), 11; quoted by Fischer, *War of Illusions*, 549.

[120] Bernhardi, *Germany and the Next War*, 9.

[121] See the excellent introduction in Fritz Stern, *The Politics of Cultural Despair* (Berkeley, Calif., 1961).

Works—like those of popular authors such as Paul de Lagarde and Julius Langbehn—which propounded these ideas were enormously successful from the 1890s.[122] In addition, there were widespread fears that, historically, prosperity eroded organic unity and public virtue and spelt decadence and disintegration for great civilizations. Spengler's *Decline of the West* was published at the end of the Great War but conceived before it.[123] Was Germany losing her edge?—that was the disturbing question. During the second Moroccan crisis the younger Moltke—the spiritualist, cultural pessimist, and admirer of Paul de Lagarde—[124]wrote to his wife:

> If we again creep out of this affair with our tail between our legs, if we cannot be aroused to an energetic demand which we are prepared to enforce by the sword, then I am doubtful about the future of the German Empire. Then I shall resign. But before, I will propose that we abolish the army and place ourselves under the protectorate of Japan. Then we will be able to make money without disturbance and make fools of ourselves.[125]

In the military field, no one expressed the prevailing mood and concerns more forcefully than Field-Marshal von der Goltz. His works reveal great attention to, and an acute grasp of, the rapid technological advances that were transforming war. But at the same time he was anxious that modernity should not lose the Germans their simple ancient warrior vigour. The cycle of civilization was obvious:

> Victory brings might, might riches, but prosperity luxury. . . . The more civilized, the more wealthy a nation becomes, the greater the capacity for pleasure and indulgence. It shrinks from effort and comes gradually to estimate property and ease more highly than the brutal pursuit of war.[126]

122 Felix Dahn's *Moltke als Erzieher* (Breslau, 1892) emulated Langbehn's famous *Rembrandt als Erzieher* (1890) which opposed an imaginary Rembrandt, personifying the true German spirit, with present-day philistinism. Dahn, a history professor and popular novelist who exalted pagan and medieval Germandom, also made Moltke the hero of a play (1890) modelled on Schiller's *Wallenstein*, and participated in the editing of Moltke's *Gesammelte Schriften*: George Mosse, *The Crisis of German Ideology* (London, 1966), 69–70; *Moltke as a Correspondent*, 307–8.

123 H. Stuart Hughes, *Consciousness and Society: The Reorientation of European Social Thought 1890–1930* (London, 1959), 378.

124 For a good brief portrait of Moltke, see Isabel Hull, *The Entourage of Kaiser Wilhelm II* (Cambridge, 1982), 239–42.

125 Moltke, *Betrachtungen und Erinnerungen*, 19 Aug. 1911, 362.

126 Colmar von der Goltz, *Jena to Eylau* (London, 1913), 74; see also *The Nation in Arms*, 8.

> Germany . . . has become rich, and her riches increase daily. She grows in culture, but this growth in culture is unfavourable to the warlike development of her people. . . . Present-day philosophy teaches free development of personality. Everything which stands in its way should be put aside . . . Involuntarily the question arises; will the spoilt multitudes . . . be willing to respond to the stern call to sacrifice life and property in defence of the Fatherland?[127]

In his historical journey to the great scene of Prussia's downfall and regeneration, von der Goltz found a remarkable degree of analogy with the conditions and problems of his own age, with a clear warning attached. The reformers had traced Prussia's collapse before Napoleon predominantly to the inadequacy of her old political, social, and military system in the Revolutionary age of popular participation, and this line of explanation was re-emphasized in the great biographical histories of the military reformers written after the unification by Max Lehmann, Georg Heinrich Pertz, Hans Delbrück, and Friedrich Meinecke. However, for von der Goltz, the radical implications of this conclusion for his own time were unacceptable. He set out to rehabilitate the old army and state.[128] The main problem, he argued, was not a social one; the difficulty lay rather in a false conception of the nature of both politics and war, also pointed out by the reformers. Prussia had fallen victim to 'cosmopolitanism, the love of peace, humanitarian twaddle, and the deteriorated pre-Jena methods of warfare'.[129] False intellectual doctrines, generated during the Enlightenment, spoiled the natural moral strength of the army.[130] Now as then, one must guard against

> half-heartedness in our military effort, the hidden working of heresies which hypnotize our common sense by a parade of pseudo-scientific arguments, against any adulteration or dilution of the warlike spirit and of warlike passion, against diplomatic generals, against the interference of political considerations with strategical and tactical decisions, and above all against the tendency to value more highly the art of war and perfection of technical training than the soldierly virtues.[131]

[127] *Jena to Eylau*, 70–3.

[128] Ibid. v–viii; *Von Rosbach bis Jena* (Berlin, 1906; earlier version, *Rosbach und Jena*, 1883). For Delbrück's criticism of the party-political and present-oriented character of von der Goltz's analysis see his *Historische und politische Aufsätze* (Berlin, 1886), iii. 113–30.

[129] Colmar von der Goltz, *Jena to Eylau*, 329.

[130] *The Nation in Arms*, 17–19.

[131] *Jena to Eylau*, 76.

Absorbed by the idea of an impending war with England for world position, von der Goltz worked with governmental support to foster traditional values among the younger generation.[132]

Another widespread cause for concern in Germany was domestic politics. The rapid transformation of the country from a traditional agrarian society into an industrial and urban mass-society was becoming increasingly more difficult to accommodate to the Reich's authoritarian and semi-feudal regime. The Wilhelmine era was thus characterized by the chronic and worsening problem of securing a stable Reichstag majority for the government, as well as by an ever growing divide between the propertied classes and a continually expanding working class.[133] In the army, people looked upon the domestic situation no differently from their peers in the rest of the Reich's political community. General Waldersee, Moltke's deptuty between 1882 and 1888 and chief of the general staff until 1891, was politically active and was widely talked of as the best appointee if the Reichstag became totally ungovernable and a royal *coup d'état* took place.[134] But otherwise, soldiers, even in higher ranks, were rarely more than involved spectators.[135] Like Moltke, they shared the widespread disgust with the parliamentary haggling and the 'rule of talk', and were concerned at the government's difficulties and at the 'irresponsible attitude' of the Reichstag, which compromised national unity and interests.

As before, in the periodical parliamentary debates on the military budget, the Reichstag was repeatedly reminded of the animosity, threats, and military build-up of the other great powers, and of the need for responsible defence-preparations. A war scare was exploited by Bismarck in 1887 to push through an increase in the

[132] Von der Goltz became chairman of the semi-military Young German League, which registered 750,000 members in 1914. See Mosse, *The Crisis of German Ideology*, 171–89; and for von der Goltz's outlook and concern his *Denkwürdigkeiten* (Berlin, 1929), 325–39; the testimony of his Turkish friend, Pertev Demirhan, *General-Feldmarschall Colmar von der Goltz* (Göttingen, 1960), esp. 90–1; Hermann Teske, *Colmar Freiherr von der Goltz* (Göttingen, 1957), 68–70; Bernhardi, *Britain as Germany's Vassal*, 245; Martin Kitchen, *The German Officer Corps 1890–1914* (Oxford, 1968), 103, 139–42.

[133] See esp. Hans-Ulrich Wehler, *The German Empire* (Leamington Spa, 1985; first publ. in German 1973).

[134] See Alfred von Waldersee, *Denkwürdigkeiten*, ed. H. O. Meisner (3 vols.; Berlin, 1923); Goerlitz, *The German General Staff*, 103–26; Kitchen, *The German Officer Corps*, 64–95.

[135] For the politics of Wilhelm's inner military circle see Hull, *The Entourage of Wilhelm II*, 208–35.

army's strength. In 1892–3, Chancellor Caprivi, a former general himself, agreed to a reform of the army in return for Reichstag approval for its expansion. The term of active military service for the infantry was reduced from three to two years, allowing for a larger annual intake of men and, thus, for a considerable expansion of the army reserve.[136] Despite the indignant rhetoric, however, the truth of the matter was that, on the whole, the government got more or less what it wanted. The army was expanded with every successive Army Law, in line with German demographic growth and the increases in French armament (see Table 1). The standing army was kept at slightly over 1 per cent of the population during most of the Reich's lifetime. During Bismarck's time, this was regarded as sufficient. However, from the 1890s, with the formation of the Franco-Russian alliance and the growing certainty that Germany would have to fight on two fronts, the military odds

TABLE 1. *Strength of the German Army, 1874–1914*[137]

Year	Population (millions)	Active Corps	Reserve Formations	Manpower (Active)
1874	43	18		425,000
1880	45	18	18 div.	454,000
1887	48	18	18 div.	496,000
1890	49	20	20 div.	514,000
1893	52	20	20 div.	588,000
1900	56	23 + 5 sup.	20 div. (5 corps)	610,000
1911	65	23 + 2 sup.	14 1/2 corps	634,000
1912	66	25	14 1/2 corps	665,000
1913	67	25	14 1/2 corps	760,000
1914	68	25	14 1/2 corps	830,000

[136] J. Alden Nichols, *Germany after Bismarck: The Caprivi Era* (Cambridge, Mass, 1958) 192–64; Stig Förster, *Der doppelte Militarismus. Die deutsche Heeresrüstungspolitik zwischen Status-quo-Sicherung und Aggression 1890–1913* (Stuttgart, 1985), 36–74.

[137] Data on strength and organization can be found in Reichsarchiv, *Der Weltkrieg 1914–1918, Kriegsrüstung und Kriegswirtschaft* (Berlin, 1930), i. supp., 357–534. Also based on the Reich's archieves and useful are Ludwig Rüdt von Collenberg, *Die deutsche Armee von 1871 bis 1914* (Berlin, 1914); Kurt Jany, *Die königlich-preußische Armee und das deutsche Reichsheer, 1807 bis 1914*, iv (Berlin, 1933), 214–338.

changed drastically for the worse. Chief of Staff Waldersee and Minister of War Verdy du Vernois tried to push for the enforcement of universal military service for all eligible men, which existed only in law.[138] Only a fixed quota from the age-group due for conscription was actually being called for active service each year, leaving a considerable portion untrained. Waldersee's successor, Schlieffen, continued to press for the expansion of the army to meet the growing threat. However, the War Ministry and the government itself flatly rejected his requests.[139] In the first decade of the twentieth century, when German policy was becoming more aggressive, when the international tensions were mounting and the Reichstag was becoming more responsive, the German army's growth-rate was declining in relative terms. There were two main reasons for this apparent paradox. First, and most important, as German attention was shifting from the continent of Europe to the world scene, the army requests were overshadowed by the grandiose naval build-up.[140] Secondly, the army's growth was kept in check by social considerations which served partly as an excuse to avoid the financial problem, but were none the less real enough.

The social transformation of Germany worried the army deeply, affecting as it did the composition of both the officer corps and the rank and file. Reluctantly, the expanding army had to open itself to officers from the growing and prospering middle class. There were simply not enough candidates from the nobility.[141] Middle-class

[138] For Verdy's proposed reforms see Förster, *Der doppelte Militarismus*, 28–36; and for the army and parliament Manfred Messerschmidt, 'Die politische Geschichte der preußisch-deutschen Armee', in Militärgeschichtliches Forschungsamt (ed.), *Handbuch zur deutschen Militärgeschichte 1648–1939*, (Munich, 1979), ii. 232–48; Wiegand Schmidt-Richberg, 'Die Regierungszeit Wilhelms II', ibid., iii. 116–22. Also see Wilhelm Deist, 'Die Armee in Staat und Gesellschaft 1890–1914', in M. Stürmer (ed.), *Das kaiserliche Deutschland. Politik und Gesellschaft 1870–1918* (Düsseldorf, 1970), 312–39.

[139] Alfred von Schlieffen, *Briefe.*, ed. E. Kessel, (Göttingen, 1958), 13 Nov. 1892, 297; Reichsarchiv, *Der Weltkrieg*, i. supp., 57–72, 77–9, 84–7; Ritter, *Sword and Scepter*, ii. 206–16; Förster, *Der doppelte Militarismus*, 112–16, 129–34; Kitchen, *The German Officer Corps*, 31–3.

[140] By 1902 the naval estimates already amounted to 30 per cent of the army's. By 1911 they were half their size: Reichsarchiv, *Der Weltkrieg*, i, supp., 530. After 1905 the size of the regular army dropped below 1 per cent for the first time: H. von Kuhl, *Der deutsche Generalstab in Vorbereitung und Durchführung des Weltkrieges* (Berlin, 1920), 110.

[141] In 1860 the ratio of aristocrat to middle-class officers in the Prussian army was 2 to 1 in favour of the nobility. By 1913 this ratio had been reversed. In the same years, the ratio in the highest ranks of general and colonel changed from 86 per cent

officers were anxious to adopt the ruling ethos of their society and profession, and therefore totally assimilated their values and outlook. Yet army authorities feared that the traditional spirit of the officer corps would be eroded by democratization, liberalism, and penetration by bourgeois mentality.[142]

A much more threatening product of industrialization and urbanization came, however, from further below. In 1871 the ratio of rural to urban population in Germany was 2 to 1; by 1914 this had almost been reversed, with parity being reached in the mid-1890s.[143] The creation of huge concentrations of workers in the large cities was reflected in the steady rise in the power of the Social Democratic Party. From the military point of view, the most serious problem was the prospect of socialist ideas penetrating the rank and file. This would have compromised the loyalty and reliability of the army as the ultimate weapon of the government and of the existing order against domestic threats, as well as undermining its discipline, patriotism, and fighting-spirit as a military instrument. The army indoctrinated its members heavily against social democracy and suppressed any sign of socialist subversion, but it could hardly have expected to counter the social and political realities.[144]

The only remedy lay in the army's conscription-policy, which

and 14 per cent in favour of the nobility to parity. Karl Demeter, *The German Officer-Corps in Society and State 1650–1945* (London, 1965), 28–9, 267; Kitchen, *The German Officer Corps*, 24–5; W. Deist, 'Zur Geschichte des preußischen Offizierkorps, *1888–1918', in H. H. Hofmann (ed.), Das deutsche Offizierkorps, 1860–1960* (Boppard am Rhein, 1980), 47–50.

[142] Like most ideas regarding the social and economic development of Imperial Germany, all this was suggested in the late 1920s by Eckart Kehr in his seminal articles on German armament; see esp. 'Class Struggle and Armament Policy in Imperial Germany' and 'The Genesis of the Royal Prussian Reserve Officer' in Kehr, *Economic Interest, Militarism and Foreign Policy: Essays*, ed. G. Craig (Berkeley, Calif., 1977), 63–74, 97–108. Also see Hartmut John, *Das Reserveoffizierkorps im Deutschen Kaiserreich 1890–1914* (Frankfurt a.M., 1981); Kitchen, *The Germany Officer Corps*, 22–36, 120–3.

[143] Koppel Pinson, *Modern Germany* (New York, 1966), 221.

[144] For attacks on social democracy, following closely in Moltke's footsteps, see e.g. A. Boguslawski, *Volkskamp—nicht Scheinkampf: Ein Wort zur politischen Lage im Innern* (Berlin, 1895); and id. *Der Krieg in seiner wahren Bedeutung*. See also Reinhard Höhn, *Sozialismus und Heer* (Berlin, 1959), ii; Messerschmidt, 'Politische Geschichte', in Militärgeschichtliches Forschungsamt (ed.), *Handbuch zur deutschen Mitilärgeschichte*, ii. 248–74; Schmidt-Richberg, 'Regierungszeit Wilhelm II', ibid., iii. 111-16; Kitchen, *The German Officer Corps*, 143–86; Bernd-Felix Schulte, *Die deutsche Armee 1900–1914: Zwischen Beharren und Verändern* (Düsseldorf, 1977), 258–90, 535–47.

favoured the rural and country population and discriminated against the city proletariat.[145] However, when, in 1905, France passed the Two Years Service Law and rigorously abolished all exemptions from conscription, this remedy started to look most unsatisfactory. Whereas France was calling up 82 per cent of those liable for service, in Germany the figure was only 53 per cent.[146] In 1909, whilst urging the expansion of the army to meet the demands of a two-front war, Schlieffen pointed out that France, with a population of 40 million, was taking into her army 220,000 men annually and was keeping them with the colours for 25 years, thus creating a wartime establishment of 5.6 million; at the same time, Germany, with a population of 62 million, was calling up an annual contingent of 250,000 men and was keeping them with the colours for 19 years, thus possessing a wartime establishment of only 4.75 million.[147]

Especially for people like von der Goltz and Bernhardi, who called for the total mobilization of national resources for the eventuality, indeed the inevitability, of war, this was an agonizing and intolerable waste and it called for radical measures.[148] However, while denouncing the neglect of universal military service, upon which Germany's greatness had been built, both von der Goltz and Bernhardi were very ambivalent about mass armies, raising doubts as to their actual necessity and military effectiveness.[149] Less aristocratic minds were needed to draw the full conclusions from

[145] In 1911 64.15 per cent of the conscripts came from rural areas which, according to the census of 1905, comprised only 42.5 per cent of the population. Small and country towns, which comprised 25.5 per cent of the population, added another 22.34 per cent of the conscripts. The medium-sized towns, comprising 12.9 per cent of the population, provided only 7.37 per cent of the conscripts. From the large cities, the strongholds of social democracy, which comprised 19.1 per cent of the population, merely 6.14 per cent of the conscripts were drafted: Bernhardi, *Germany and the Next War*, 243–4.

[146] Reichsarchiv, *Der Weltkrieg*, i. supp., 168–9.

[147] 'Der Krieg in der Gegenwart', in Schlieffen, *Gessammelte Schriften*, i. 14. Of course, Schlieffen was, at least partly, fixing the figures; he counted the French territorial reserve but left out the equivalent German Landsturm. In both countries people served 2 years in the active army, 10 or 11 years in the first-line reserve (reserve and the Landwehr First Portion in Germany, reserve in France), and 12 or 13 years in the second and third-line reserve (territorials and territorial reserve in France, the Landwehr Second Portion and Landsturm in German).

[148] Ibid. 68–71; *Britain as Germany's Vassal*, 64, 169–70.

[149] Colmar von der Goltz, *The Nation in Arms*, 5; Bernhardi, *Britain as Germany's Vassal*, 169; id., *On War of To-Day*, i. 11, 79–101, ii. 438–56.

the character of modern war and from Germany's political and military aims, and to disregard class problems.[150]

Indeed, the initiative for a massive expansion of the army, which would make Germany a real nation-in-arms, came from the middle-class head of the deployment section in the general staff, Lieutenant-Colonel, later Colonel, Erich Ludendorff. He began pressing in this direction from 1910. In highly characteristic memoranda composed for the chief of the general staff, the younger Moltke, and sent to the Minister of War, he wrote:

> Every state fighting with every fiber for survival must strain its every resources to live up to its highest obligations.[151]

> Our enemies are so numerous that it may in certain circumstances become our inescapable duty to oppose them with our entire able-bodied manpower.[152]

> We must again become the nation in arms great men in great times once made us. Germany must ever advance, never retreat.[153]

The political atmosphere after the Second Moroccan Crisis and during the Balkan Wars awoke new urgency in his superior, and also made the Ministry of War and the chancellor much more attentive. Disillusionment with the naval race again tipped the balance in the army's favour. In December 1912 the general staff asked for the addition of some 150,000 conscripts to the army's annual intake (an increase in the regular army of 300,000 men or about 50 per cent over two years of service). This would effectively have established universal military service. In addition to the raising of three new active army corps, more regular cadres were to be provided for the creation of more, better organized and better-equipped reserve divisions and corps. Supplementing the large numbers of reservists who brought the active corps to war-strength, these reserve formations were greatly to increase the number of reservists intended for front-line action. An effort was also made to create more effective formations for the multitude of largely untrained reservists, who had not been called for active service but had been massed together in replacement (*Ersatz*) units.

The enormity of the request startled the War Minister, von

[150] Fischer, *War of Illusions*, 105–6.

[151] 20 Aug. 1910, *Der Weltkrieg*, i, supp. 124; Ritter, *Sword and Scepter*, ii. 221.

[152] 1 July 1910, ibid. 119; Ritter, ii. 221.

[153] 25 Nov. 1912, ibid. 147; Ritter, ii. 223.

Heeringen, and the Chancellor, Bethmann-Hollweg, especially as the army had been expanded twice in the two preceding years. In the end, however, a compromise bill was brought before the Reichstag.[154] The deliberations in the Reichstag were accompanied by the massive propaganda campaign, led by the new Army League (Wehrverein), which had been founded in 1912 by another middle-class officer, Major-General August Keim. Like the many other patriotic associations which flourished in Wilhelmine Germany, the league appealed to middle-class patriotism and urged massive armament-measures in preparation for an inevitable world war, which would establish Germany's world position.[155] The Army Act of 1913 was approved by the Reichstag at a tremendous cost. No new active corps were added to the existing twenty-five, but the army was expanded by 136,000 men, and the organization of the reserves was much improved. Ludendorff was transferred to a field command.

The plan with which Germany went to war was the famous Schlieffen Plan. It aimed at winning all-out victory in a two-front war by concentrating almost all available forces for a gigantic lightning campaign of encirclement and annihilation against France, sweeping through neutral Belgium. The eastern front, where the Russian army was slow to mobilize owing to the backwardness of the Russian railway-system, was left virtually unprotected until a decision had been reached in the west. Even more than for its strategic boldness, the plan won fame because it underwent radically different interpretations with every major shift in the view of Germany's past. It mirrors the changing attitudes to Germany's motivation, aims, and achievements before and during the First World War.

154 For the general staff's request, see Moltke to Bethmann-Hollweg (drafted by Ludendorff), 21 Dec. 1912, ibid., i, supp. 158–73. The naval estimates which had been half as large as the army's in 1911, dropped to 43 per cent in 1912 and to 30 per cent in 1913, as the army estimates soared 75 per cent, from 931,600,000 to 1,629,600,000 RM: ibid. 530. The regular army was expanded to an all-time high of 1.2 per cent of the population: Kuhl, *Der deutsche Generalstab*, 110. Also see Hans Herzfeld, *Die deutsche Rüstungpolitik vor dem Weltkrieg*; Förster, *Der doppelte Militarismus*, 208–96.

155 By late 1912, the Army League claimed 40,000 individual members and 100,000 corporate ones. Half a year later the numbers rose to 78,000 and 200,000 respectively. Fischer, *War of Illusions*, 107; Chickering, *We Men Who Feel Most German*, 267–77. On the patriotic associations, see Geoff Eley, *Reshaping the German Right: Radical Nationalism and Political Change after Bismarck* (London, 1980).

For most of the German military after the painful defeat, the plan became the haven of lost opportunities, the ingenious recipe for victory watered down and mishandled by Schlieffen's successor in the general staff, the younger Moltke.[156] However, with Germany's collapse in the Second World War, the old dreams of power were dashed. It was in this atmosphere that the doyen of the post-war generation of German historians, Gerhard Ritter, undertook a critical study of the plan, drawing on the original drafts which were fully disclosed only at that time. He argued persuasively that, rather than an assured recipe for victory, the plan had in fact been a reckless gamble which risked everything on one card in a desperate attempt to come up with a decisive military result in a situation in which no such result was possible. At the same time, Ritter stuck to the traditional line of the German historians who, ever since the 'war guilt' debate, had persistently denied that their country had been particularly or inherently aggressive in either her outlook or policies. For Ritter, the problem of German militarism was rooted mainly in the evolution of the German military into a position of virtual independence from the responsible civilian government of the Reich. The Schlieffen Plan reflected this problem in that it was a 'purely military' scheme, devised, in typical fashion, by a 'military technician', in total disregard of political considerations, in which he had little interest.[157] Only with the growth of a younger generation of historians in the liberal post-war years, and with the revelations coming out of the Fischer controversy, did a different view of German history in the Wilhelmine era emerge. With it the ground was prepared for yet another shift in the assessment of the Schlieffen Plan.

On the whole, despite institutional biases and personal differences, a broad political consensus prevailed throughout the history of the German Reich among its ruling élite, including its military section. Under Bismarck, Germany was a power of the status quo. Correspondingly, Moltke's plans in the event of a two-front war

[156] See esp. W. Groener, *Das Testament des Grafen Schlieffen* (Berlin, 1927); id., *Der Feldherr wider Willen* (Berlin, 1930); and also W. Foerster, *Graf Schlieffen und der Weltkrieg* (2nd. edn.; Berlin, 1925); id., *Aus der Gedankenwerkstatt des deutschen Generalstabs* (Berlin, 1931); Jehuda L. Wallach, *Das Dogma der Vernichtungsschlacht* (Frankfurt a.M., 1967), 305–16.

[157] Ritter, *The Schlieffen Plan* (London, 1958; first publ. in German 1956); id. *Sword and Scepter*, ii, 193–226; also see Wallach, *Das Dogma der Vernichtungschlacht*, 58–64 *et passim*.

were fundamentally defensive. He did not believe that a quick, decisive victory was possible in this eventuality. He therefore planned to split the German army equally between the Russian and French fronts and, while opting for limited offensive operations in the east, hoped to achieve no more than a favourable negotiated peace.[158] Even the warmonger Waldersee, his deputy and successor, did not deviate from either the political or the military aspects of this assessment. The 'preventive war' which he urged was fundamentally a defensive measure. However, in the Wilhelmine era, with the growth of German power and appetites, Germany embarked on an expansionist and revisionist *Weltpolitik*. The Schlieffen Plan, aiming at an out-and-out victory, became in effect the military equivalent of this policy.[159] Initially reflecting the traditional concerns of the general staff over a two-front war, it became Germany's only hope of achieving a decisive military result. A mere military draw could no longer be accepted as sufficient.[160] This is why the plan could not have been abandoned even after its author had long gone and its chances of success had grown very slim indeed.

It is true that the German general staff enjoyed almost absolute autonomy in its war-planning and devised the plan independently without any consultation with the civilian authorities.[161] Thus the main features of the plan paralleled German policy in the decade before the war, rather than being shaped by, and co-ordinated with, it. It is also true that the Schlieffen Plan harboured grave political implications and assumed a momentum of its own during the weeks of crisis that resulted in the outbreak of the First World War. By preparing an offensive two-front war in which Germany had to take the initiative, the plan in effect made such a war an inevitability, and by allowing for the violation of Belgian neutrality,

158 See again Schmerfeld (ed.), *Die deutschen Aufmarschpläne*.

159 According to the older view this congruence could only be interpreted as 'coincidental'; see, for example, Andreas Hillgruber, *Germany and the Two World Wars* (London, 1981; first publ. in German 1967), 6–8.

160 Even Ritter unwittingly comes to the same conclusion: *The Schlieffen Plan*, 21. However, for the new interpretation see esp. Farrar, *Arrogance and Anxiety*, 23–4, 146–8, 198–9; and also Hull, *The Entourage of Wilhelm II*, 255–6.

161 See Jack Snyder's objections in 'Civil-Military Relations and the Cult of the Offensive 1914 and 1984', in S. E. Miller (ed.), *Military Strategy and the Origins of the First World War* (Princeton, NJ, 1985), 125–9. Snyder himself admits, however, that on the whole the Schlieffen Plan's promise of quick decisive results suited the politicians very well.

it made British participation equally inevitable. However, to put the blame on Schlieffen's 'apolitical mind' is greatly misleading. For some fifteen years, all of Germany's leading statesmen knew and approved of the Schlieffen Plan and of its political implications. Schlieffen maintained close relations with Baron von Holstein, the leading personality in the Foreign Ministry, with whom he collaborated particularly closely during the Moroccan crisis of 1905.

Schlieffen's professional preoccupation and avoidance of any political involvement are indisputable. This, however, is quite different from military isolation. A historian of the older generation was already disputing the 'strictly military' view of Schlieffen, pointing out that his conservatism, royalism, devoutness, and anti-revolutionism clearly reflected his political world.[162] Indeed, Schlieffen's political outlook was typical of his milieu. In his famous essay 'War of the Present' (1909), he outlined Germany's international situation: France, the old enemy, was driven by her desire for revenge; England, the new enemy, was motivated by fierce competition with Germany's massively expanding economy; Russian hostility was inspired by the 'inherited antipathy of the Slavs for the Germans', as well as by modern economic factors. An economic integration of Mitteleuropa was essential to combat Germany's superior enemies.[163]

Like Germany's foreign policy as a whole, the Schlieffen Plan was an almost desperate attempt to reconcile Germany's great strength and ambitions with her relative inferiority *vis-à-vis* the Entente coalition and her perception of threat and insecurity. If the plan was overstretching the limits of German power, so was German policy.[164] Both politicians and soldiers attributed their predecessors' achievements to great resolution and determination. In fact, the diplomatic isolation of the enemy, ensuring numerical military advantage, had been by far the more important cause of Prussia's successes during the unification struggle.[165] With the massive

[162] See Kessel's introduction to Schlieffen, *Briefe*, 49–51.

[163] Schlieffen, 'Der Krieg in der Gegenwart', *Gesammelte Schriften*, i. 20, *et passim*.

[164] For a similar argument in the naval sphere, where another 'apolitical technician', Tirpitz, was also blamed by German historians of the older generation for Germany's misfortune, see Jonathan Steinberg, *Yesterday's Deterrent: Tirpitz and the Birth of the German Battle Fleet* (London, 1965), 22–5.

[165] See note 160 above.

expansion of the Russian army and railway system in the years preceding the war, one of the most crucial assumptions and prerequisites of the Schlieffen Plan—the slow rate of Russian mobilization—had been rapidly eroded.[166] Yet, despite Moltke's growing doubts, there was no alternative to the plan if Germany was to win a decisive victory.

Of course, the German conception of the conduct of war was much more in tune with aggressive foreign policy. There was always concern among the German military that policy should not impose restrictions on war which would thwart its natural tendency to use unlimited force to destroy the enemy. Despite some reservations about his claim that defence was stronger than attack, there was unanimity with Clausewitz in regarding the offensive as the sole legitimate form of war, and defence as a temporary expedient, to be employed only when one was not strong enough to attack.[167] Only the offensive, culminating in the great battle, can bring about the destruction of the enemy's armed forces and the breaking of his will to resist, which are the sole legitimate means and end in war. This kernel of ideas, consecrated by the authority of Clausewitz and Moltke, was universally agreed.[168] For Schlieffen, the political necessity and the military ideal happily coincided. Furthermore, as Moltke had pointed out, in the age of global industrial and commercial economy the need for a quick decision

[166] During the 1890s and 1900s, Russian mobilization in the west could take place at the rate of less than 200 trains per day; by 1910 the number rose to 250 and by 1914 to 360. By 1917 the rate would have risen to 560 trains, with mobilization completed by the eighteenth day, only 3 days after the German and French mobilizations: Stone, *The Eastern Front*, 40–1. The German general staff and government were painfully aware of this development, as well as of Russian military growth. In 1912 the Germans estimated that by 1915 the war establishment of the Russian field-army in Europe would increase by more than 50 per cent, from numerical parity with the German army to a superiority of more than 30 per cent: Kuhl, *Der deutsche Generalstab*, 109.

[167] For Clausewitz's positions, which postulated the offensive whenever possible and which have been mellowed by recent interpreters, see Azar Gat, 'Clausewitz on Defence and Attack', *Journal of Strategic Studies*, 10 (1988), 20–6. For criticism of Clausewitz's definition of defence as stronger than attack, see Colmar von der Goltz, *The nation in Arms*, 254–75; Bernhardi, *On War of To-Day*, ii. 1–32. For a concurrence with Clausewitz's position see Caemmerer, *Strategical Science*, 94–109.

[168] For this all-pervasive axiom see, for example, Blume, *Strategie*, 112, 151; Colmar von der Goltz, *The Nation in Arms*, 331, 468; id., *The Conduct of War*, 5–21; Scherff, *Von der Kriegführung* (Berlin, 1883), 85 *et passim*; *Die Lehre vom Kriege* (Berlin, 1897), 3; Prince Kraft zu Hohenlohe-Ingelfingen, *Letters on Strategy* (London, 1898; first publ. in German 1887), 9–10; Balck, *Modern German Tactics*, 5; Bernhardi, *On War of To-Day*, ii. 209–12, 336–8, 353.

had only been strengthened. The idea that war had to be cut short to avoid economic collapse—which, with the coming of the twentieth century, was widely talked of as ruling out a general war in modern conditions—played a significant role in Schlieffen's mind.[169]

The fundamental conception of the nature of war and military theory clearly set the framework within which every military question, past or present, was approached and judged. On the one hand, all dogma was rejected, and allowance was made for great theoretical flexibility. On the other, a whole cluster of ideas was regarded as embedded in the very nature of the phenomenon of war, which was unaffected by change. 'Lasting nature' and 'changing forms' cohabited. This was not merely the bequest of Clausewitz and Moltke; it expressed the all-pervasive and fundamental tenets of German culture.

Whereas in the West positivism ruled supreme during the second half of the nineteenth century, in Germany it hardly gained any ground at all. There the intellectual legacy of the Romantic period, with its sharp distinction between *Geistwissenschaften* and *Naturwissenschaften* held sway, revived and elaborated philosophically by the work of Wilhelm Diltey and the Marburg school. This distinction implied that the methods employed and the laws formulated in the natural sciences did not apply in human affairs. Man and human phenomena are ever shaped by history and dominated by the faculties of feeling, imagination, and volition. Since Ranke, the singularity of historical events had been the first article of faith for German historians. The principles of classical British political economy were rejected by the German historical school of economy from Adam Müller, through Friedrich List and Wilhelm Roscher, to Gustav Schmoller and Werner Sombart. The doctrine of universal natural law was rejected by German political philosophers and jurists. Similarly, German military authors never tired of repudiating all formal systems of principles for military theory, and persistently stressed the overriding importance of free circumstantial study, historical change, and moral forces.[170]

[169] See Kehr's provocative *Economic Interest*, 53–5. Also see, for example, Moltke, 'Verordnungen' (1869), *Militärische Werke*, II. ii. 173; Ritter, *The Schlieffen Plan*, 47–8.

[170] Blume, *Strategie*, 33–5; Kraft zu Hohenlohe-Ingelfingen, *Letters on Strategy*, 4, 10–11; Schlichting, *Moltkes Vermächtnis*, 6; Verdy du Vernois, *Studien über den*

Hence the considerable opposition in the higher ranks of the army to Schlieffen's growing dogmatism. In the general staff, Schlieffen was greatly admired, almost worshipped, by his subordinates, especially the younger generation of officers. But some of the army's most distinguished and conscientious officers objected to what they regarded as crude violations of the army's most fundamental theoretical tenets. In his obsession with his great plan of war against France, Schlieffen directed the historical section of the general staff to undertake a trans-historic study of the causes of victory in history, aimed at proving that all great victories had been won purely by encirclement.[171] He constantly impressed this doctrine on his subordinates during manœuvres, staff rides, and war games.[172] Finally, after his retirement, he pursued the same line in his historical 'Cannae Studies' and the essay 'War of the Present'.[173] His most outspoken critic in this matter was Bernhardi, who left his position as head of the historical section because of disagreements with Schlieffen. He publicly and thoroughly criticized Schlieffen's anonymous 'War of the Present' (1909), arguing principally, on various grounds, that the doctrine of encirclement could not be elevated to the status of sole recipe for victory. The conduct of operations, he argued, was ever flexible, depending on the circumstances as judged by the commander in the field. A break through the enemy's front, totally repudiated by Schlieffen, had its advantages and its opportune moments.[174] This view was shared, for example, by General Karl von Bülow, the army's quartermaster-general, who was to command the Second Army of the Germans' enveloping right wing in 1914.[175]

Krieg (4 vols.; Berlin, 1891–1909), pt. iii. (1902), 1–60; Freytag-Loringhoven, *Die Macht der Persönlichkeit im Kriege: Studien nach Clausewitz* (Berlin, 1905); Bernhardi, *War of To-Day, i. 1–2, 30–60.*

171 *Generalstab (ed.), Der Schlachterfolg, mit welchen Mitteln wurde er erstrebt?* (1903); Freytag-Loringhoven, *Generalfeldmarschall Graf von Schlieffen* (Leipzig, 1920), 58.

172 See Ritter, *The Schlieffen Plan*, 50.

173 The 'Cannae-Studien' are printed in Schlieffen, *Gesammelte Schriften*, i. 25–266.

174 Bernhardi, *On War of To-Day*, ii. 40–51, 90–8, 154–81, 286; id. *Denkwürdigkeiten aus meinem Leben* (Berlin, 1927), 223–4.

175 Friedrich von Boetticher, 'Der Lehrmeister des neuzeitlichen Krieges', in F. von Cochenhausen (ed.), *Von Scharnhorst zu Schlieffen 1806–1906: Hundert Jahre preußisch-deutscher Generalstab* (Berlin, 1933), 317.

The intense timetable essential to the success of the Schlieffen Plan necessitated meticulous day-to-day planning of the whole course of the campaign and strict adherence to the plan by the commanding generals. This went against the army's most fundamental beliefs, bequeathed from Clausewitz and Moltke, that friction would frustrate all pre-conceived plans and that consequently only general directives should be issued beyond the deployment (*Aufmarsch*) stage, while the subordinate commanders should be given wide freedom of action and room for individual initiative during the course of the campaign. General Sigismund von Schlichting, one of the most respected officers in the army, expressed these feelings most forcefully by contrasting the practices of his day with *Moltke's Legacy* (1901).[176] Similarly, in his audience with the Kaiser, in which he was offered the position of chief of the general staff, the younger Moltke criticized the general staff's war games, telling the Kaiser he did not believe that mass armies of millions could be controlled centrally. He doubted that modern wars could be won rapidly, at a single stroke. Modern war, he said, was likely to be a 'long, hard struggle with a country which will not let itself be subdued until its whole national power is broken'.[177] The growing unease in the army made Schlieffen state more than once that he did not believe in fixed formulas for victory.

As mentioned before, the other side of the theoretical coin was the canon of ideas and doctrines which were believed to express the true nature of war. There was an obvious historical and intellectual link between the conception of war which postulated out-and-out effort to destroy the enemy, and the professional canon of the German historians and political philosophers which postulated the predominance of the state and the nation and the primacy of foreign policy. Both were perceived by their exponents not as theoretical and ideological dogmas but as a correct and realistic *Weltanschauung*, on which the Germans prided themselves in comparison with the liberal West. In both cases there was almost total commitment within the professional communities to the fundamental theoretical premisses. In both cases challenges came mostly from outside and remained well on the fringes, while, at the same time, attracting a sharp, almost unanimous, negative response

[176] Schlichting, *Moltkes Vermächtniss*; Freiherr von Gayl, *General von Schlichting* (Berlin, 1913), 342–50; Caemmerer, *Strategical Science*, ch. 10.

[177] Moltke (the younger), *Erinnerungen*, 29 Jan. 1905, 308.

and stirring great excitement. In the Wilhelmine era, the ideas of Karl Lamprecht had this effect on the historical profession,[178] while those of Hans Delbrück and Ivan Bloch had the same effect on the military profession. In their very different ways and propounding totally different ideas, they all had one thing in common: they were heretical in relation to the prevailing outlook. Hence the more general significance of their interesting cases. Here lay the reason why, despite the sensation they created, they had almost no practical influence and are of interest only to historians of ideas. They serve to hightlight the boundaries of established opinion.

It was 1879 and Hans Delbrück had just left his post as tutor to one of the sons of the German crown prince and was about to begin his career as a young historian at the University of Berlin, when his great controversy with military opinion broke out. It was to last intermittently for fifty years in Delbrück's lifetime alone, and it continued for another decade thereafter. Only when Germany's collapse in the Second World War precipitated the eclipse of her traditional conception of war did it finally die out.

Delbrück was deeply and actively involved in German public life. He was well-connected in Court circles and in the corridors of government, sat for the Free Conservative Party in the Prussian Landtag (1882–5) and the German Reichstag (1884–90), and was Treitschke's successor as editor of the *Preußische Jahrbücher*. Because of his scholarly pre-eminence, social sensibilities, rejection of the vulgar forms of political extremism, conciliatory positions from the later stage of the First World War, and rivalry with Ludendorff and Tirpitz after that war, historians after the Second World War cast him in a 'good guy' role. Thus, while thoroughly documenting his affinity with the existing order, his belief in the political primacy and cultural role of the state, and his anti-parliamentarianism, a post-war study in Germany chose to label him as a critic of the Wilhelmine period.[179] Similarly, in two high-quality American studies of his military work, the fact that he was

[178] See Iggers, *The German Conception of History*, 197–200; Fritz K. Ringer, *The Decline of the German Mandarins: The German Academic Community 1890–1933* (Cambridge, Mass., 1969), 302–4; Felix Gilbert's introduction to *The Historical Essays of Otto Hintze* (New York, 1975).

[179] Annelise Thimme, *Hans Delbrück als Kritiker der Wilhelminischen Epoche* (Düsseldorf, 1955).

one of the most important and forceful public spokesmen of German imperialism and navalism is simply not mentioned.[180]

In truth, Delbrück was in every sense a true upholder of the Reich's ethos in its progressive brand.[181] He was typical of the intellectuals and politicians who shared Max Weber's analysis of the necessity of imperialist expansion in the age of modern, commercial mass-society.[182] Whereas mercantilistic considerations of raw materials and markets were uppermost in everyone's mind, by 1912 Delbrück was prepared to accept the Manchester school's claim that colonies did not pay. However, viewing the expanding global sphere of the English-speaking nations and countries as an enviable model, he saw colonialism predominantly as a means of propagating German civilization and at the same time finding an outlet for Germany's demographic growth.[183] With sophisticated wit he found the opportunity to remind his British audience in 1913 that the decline and fall of the Roman Empire provided 'the strongest empirical proof that peace is not the highest good of humanity'.[184] Like most Germans, he was thrilled when war came in 1914.[185]

[180] Bucholtz, *Hans Delbrück and the German Military Establishment*; Gordon Craig, 'Delbrück: The Military Historian', in P. Paret (ed.), *Makers of Modern Strategy from Machiavelli to the Nuclear Age* (Princeton, NJ, 1986), 326–53. An older, and in this respect more balanced, essay is Reinhard Bauer, 'Hans Delbrück', in B. Schmitt (ed.), *Some Historians of Modern Europe* (Chicago, 1941), 100–29.

[181] Like Max Weber, he regarded parliamentarism as nothing more than a means of securing popular legitimacy for the state in modern mass-society. Both men mocked the Western ideas of popular sovereignty and democracy: Wolfgang J. Mommsen, *Max Weber and German Politics 1890–1920* (London, 1984); Ilse Dronberger, *The Political Thought of Max Weber* (New York, 1971); Delbrück, *Government and the Will of the People*. The similarity with the ideas of Clausewitz and his fellow reformers—the progressive wing of the German Movement a century before—is striking: cf. Book I above, 246–9.

[182] Emile Daniels, 'Delbrück als Politiker', in id. (ed.), *Am Webstuhl der Zeit* (Berlin, 1928), esp. 8–10. Also see F. J. Schmidt, K. Molinski, S. Mette, *Hans Delbrück. Der Historiker und Politiker* (Berlin, 1928), 137–89. A brief, balanced introduction is Andreas Hillgruber, 'Hans Delbrück', in H.-U. Wehler (ed.), *Deutsche Historiker* (Göttingen, 1972), iv. 40–52. Specifically on his programme to harness the German working-class to the patriotic and imperial cause, see Delbrück, Schmoller, and Wagner, *Über die Stumm'sche Herrenhaus-Rede gegen die Kathedersozialisten* (Berlin, 1897), 5–7.

[183] See the third collection of Delbrück's essays, *Vor und nach dem Weltkrieg, politische und historische Aufsätze 1902–1925* (Berlin, 1926), esp. 362–6 (Mar. 1912).

[184] Delbrück, *Numbers in History* (London, 1914), 55.

[185] See his patriotic and enthusiastic pamphlet *Über den kriegerischen Charakter des deutschen Volkes* (Berlin, 1914). In *Bismarcks Erbe* (Berlin, 1915), while advocating restraint in Germany's European ambitions, he restated her need of

Delbrück's controversy with some of Germany's leading military authorities, therefore, sprang from a different source. It was in fact inherent in his great life-work, which despite the suspicion from both academic and military quarters—a suspicion he never fully overcame[186]—subjected the previously neglected field of military history to the methods and standards of German historical scholarship. This included the critical study of sources, which exposed the partisan and largely fictitious nature of past accounts, especially the greatly inflated figures for enemy strength quoted for the most famous wars of Antiquity and the Middle Ages.[187] It also included the fundamental historicist tenet that every age should be understood in its own particular terms or, conversely, that all human institutions and practices—including the military—are in a deeper sense the necessary outgrowth and expression of the conditions prevailing in their times. This was the basis on which Delbrück's monumental *History of the Art of War within the Framework of Political History* (1900–20) was founded.

In Clausewitz's case, the historicist notions which had always been present in his mind surfaced in 1827 to undermine his life-long conception of the nature of war, based on the Napoleonic model. Not without pain, he then came to recognize that, apart from all-out or 'absolute' war (as he now called it), there also existed in history a second type of war, limited in its objectives and scale, which could not just be dismissed as an aberration or perversion of the true nature of war. In trying to explain this divergence, he turned primarily to the differences in the political conditions and the aims which gave rise to war. However, the planned revision of his work was terminated by his death, and his disciples in Germany tended to interpret the confusing mixture of his old and new ideas found in *On War* as a philosophical manner of expression. They stuck to his fundamental conception of war as an out-and-out effort to destroy the enemy, which reflected the dominating experience of the age, and which they themselves shared whole-heartedly.

world policies and aims, reminding his readers that 'every great nation is a colonizing nation'; ibid. 171–2.

[186] See Delbrück's preface to the fourth and last vol. of *History of the Art of War within the Framework of Political History* (London, 1985; first publ. in German 1920), x–xi.

[187] For a brief presentation of his method and results see Delbrück's brilliant *Numbers in History*.

Delbrück came to a similar conclusion as Clausewitz, but much earlier in his life, when he was only just beginning his research into military history. While working on his biography of Gneisenau, he was struck by the fundamental difference which he found between the old, eighteenth-century mode of warfare and that of the Napoleonic era. He explained this difference by referring to the radical change which had occurred in European politics and society in the transition from the restricting conditions prevailing under the *ancien régime* to the post-Revolutionary situation, in which popular resources and energies had been mobilized. This explanation fitted well into the general historical outlook; both military institutions and the conduct of war expressed the particular conditions prevailing in their age. Relying for support on Clausewitz's later ideas, Delbrück argued that varying historical conditions gave rise to two different types of strategy—the strategy of annihilation (*Niederwerfung*) and the strategy of attrition or exhaustion (*Ermattung*). Some of the great generals of history, from Pericles to Frederick the Great, were, in his opinion, exponents of the latter.[188]

The debate which developed, and in which von der Goltz, Theodor and Friedrich von Bernhardi, Caemmerer, Jähns and Boguslawski played the leading role on the military side, raged on two related battlegrounds. First, had Frederick the Great, who had previously been regarded as a precursor of Napoleon, really sought to wear the enemy down rather than destroy him in battle? Second, what had been the exact nature of the transformation in Clausewitz's ideas? On both issues Delbrück scored only part of the points. He could easily prove that Frederick's limited resources had set very definite limits to his ambitions. Frederick, argued Delbrück, never hoped to crush or occupy the Austrian Empire completely, as Napoleon would do, but only sought to gain limited territorial advantages. In the Seven Years War, when he was pressed by a greatly superior coalition, his only aim was to survive until his enemies gave up the fight. There was also little doubt, that after his ordeal, and having suffered very heavy casualties in attacking ever stronger Austrian defences, he had grown increasingly reluctant to risk his hard-to-replace troops in costly battles. His last campaign, in the War of the Bavarian Succession, was conducted as a pure campaign of manœuvre. All these were very significant points.

[188] The thesis was fully elaborated in Delbrück, *Die Strategie des Perikles erläutert durch die Strategie Friedrichs des Großen* (Berlin, 1890).

However, Delbrück's opponents, who raged over the slander of the great king's name, also had a point. Could Frederick's lightning campaigns and offensive battles be appropriately termed a strategy of exhaustion? Was there really no fundamental difference between the king's strategy and that of his arch-rival, the Austrian Field-Marshal Daun? Indeed, was not Delbrück's dichotomy crude and over-simplifying?[189]

Much of the same applied to the problem of Clausewitz's development. There was no escaping the fact that in 1827 he had admitted limited war into the theory of war and had intended to revise his whole work along this line. The argument that this revision had been oriented towards the past and had had no theoretical bearing on the present or future, was easily dismissed by Delbrück, who pointed out that Clausewitz had looked for the concept of war as such, which claimed universal validity. However, Delbrück's opponents rightly contended that, unlike Delbrück, Clausewitz had been talking about limited war, not limited strategy. They argued that what Clausewitz had come to recognize had been only limited political aims, and that, at the same time, he had continued to regard the destruction of the enemy forces, and particularly the clash of forces, as the only legitimate means in war.[190] Indeed, since Clausewitz's intellectual transformation had not been completed, on account of his death, in some of these points he remained half-way between his old and his new ideas.[191] For example, unlike Delbrück, he never came to rehabilitate eighteenth-century warfare, which he had always regarded as the most preposterous and disastrous distortion of the true nature of war. When other academic historians took up the debate in the 1920s and 1930s, they all had their reservations about the accuracy of Delbrück's observations.[192]

However, the reason why Delbrück found it so difficult to convince anybody was hardly because of these almost scholastic,

[189] For a summary of the debate and a list of the major contributions see Delbrück, *History of the Art of War*, vi, 378–82.

[190] Ibid.

[191] Book I above, 225–8.

[192] Otto Hintze, 'Delbrück, Clausewitz and die Strategie Friedrichs des Großen', *Forschungen zur Brandenburgischen und Preußischen Geschichte*, 33 (1920), 131–77; Eberhard Kessel, 'Doppelpolige Strategie: Eine Studie zu Clausewitz, Delbrück und Friedrich dem Großen', *Wissen und Wehr*, 12 (1931), 623–31; reprinted in Johannes Kunisch (ed.), *Militärgeschichte und Kriegstheorie in neuerer Zeit* (Berlin, 1987).

albeit important, points. The sheer scale of the storm his opinions created indicates that he touched on some very deep nerve. He undermined the all-powerful conception of war and its conduct which postulated as the sole legitimate form of war out-and-out effort to achieve the total overthrow of the enemy by means of a gigantic clash of forces. As his critics put it, he violated the fundamental distinction between the 'fluctuating forms' (*Erscheinungsformen*) of war and its lasting 'inner essence' (*innere Wesensbedingungen*).[193] His ideas entailed an entirely new interpretation of the past, and especially of eighteenth-century warfare, in the fierce reaction against which the nineteenth century's conception of war had been formed. Furthermore, his ideas implied disturbing, and possibly even dangerous, conclusions for the present and future. Delbrück's problem is strikingly revealed in the solemn words of one of the younger historians who joined the debate and who never belonged to the military establishment. Even from his US exile in the late 1930s Herbert Rosinski wrote with enthusiasm:

> The great tradition of decisive mobile strategy, from Scharnhorst onwards throughout the century, [was] not any infallible receipt, not a method or a system, but the very spirit of strategy—the adaptation of the changing forms and means of war to its ultimate object, the complete overthrow of the enemy's power of resistance.[194]

By contrast, when the First World War, which he regarded as defensive and imposed on Germany, persisted, Delbrück's old theoretical notions and basic political realism merged. His old controversy with military opinion now assumed a totally new practical significance. By 1916, when the desired lightning victory had failed to materialize and a war of positions and attrition set in, he was maintaining that Germany could not hope to overwhelm her strong enemies totally but should rather seek to wear them down in order to win a favourable negotiated peace. For that, she had to renounce all ambitions in regard to territorial annexation in the West (but not in the East or in Africa). Delbrück thus became the principal public opponent of the grandiose schemes of territorial expansion in Europe which grew to dominate both German policy

[193] Friedrich von Bernhardi, *Delbrück, Friedrich der Große und Clausewitz* (Berlin, 1892), cited in Bucholtz, *Hans Delbrück*, 38.

[194] Herbert Rosinski, *The German Army* (London, 1939), 138–9.

and public opinion during the war. In the later stage of the war, these were ruthlessly pursued by Ludendorff, who, from his position in the army supreme command, exercised a 'silent dictatorship' over Germany, in a bid for total victory in a total war. In his war-memoirs Ludendorff defined his purpose in unmistakable terms: 'concentrating all our resources and using them to the utmost in order to achieve peace on the battle-field, *as the very nature of war demands*'.[195] After the war, Delbrück became the most outspoken public critic of Ludendorff's direction of the war, both in the Reichstag committee which investigated the reasons for Germany's defeat, and in a long-drawn-out literary skirmish with Ludendorff himself, who made the imperative of total war his flag.[196]

Yet, as already mentioned, although Delbrück challenged one, albeit fundamental, aspect of the German conception of war, he wholeheartedly shared the wider premisses of this conception. In terms of theory, this consisted in the historic indispensability and even desirability of war in relations between states. Practically, it meant calm acceptance of the fact that Germany's growth into a position of world power might very well involve war with other powers who would not forfeit their position willingly. Indeed, when Ivan Bloch denied the very feasibility of war in modern conditions, with clear theoretical and practical implications, Delbrück was quick to join the ranks as one of his most devastating critics.[197]

In the age in which war is being continually revolutionized by rapid technological changes, there has been little to match Bloch's remarkably prescient *War of the Future* (1898). Accurately delineating the features of what was to be the most curious and unexpected of all wars, it was composed—and perhaps this was no accident—by a complete amateur. Bloch was a well-connected Russian banker and railway magnate of Jewish-Polish origin, who after retirement immersed himself in the study of modern war. Eight years of work produced six mammoth quarto volumes, packed with fancy pictures, diagrams and tables, economic data,

[195] Erich Ludendorff, *My War Memories 1914–1918* (London, 1919), 5; my italics. This is the whole drift of his *Kriegführung und Politik* (Berlin, 1922).

[196] Delbrück, *Ludendorff, Tirpitz, Falkenhayn* (Berlin, 1920); id. *Ludendorffs Selbstporträt* (Berlin, 1922).

[197] Delbrück, 'Zukunftskrieg und Zukunftsfriede', *Preußische Jahrbücher*, 96 (1899), reprinted in *Erinnerungen, Aufsätze und Reden* (Berlin, 1902), 498–525.

and technical surveys:[198] 'He brought to the study of war an entirely new sort of mind, one in which the analytical skills of the engineer, the economist, and the sociologist were all combined. His book was in fact the first work of modern operational analysis.'[199] Analysing both the structure of world economy and the trend of modern weapons-technology, and drawing extensively on contemporary military literature and the experience of recent wars, he came out with unequivocal conclusions: war had become militarily impossible to decide and therefore also economically and socially suicidal.

In the military field, the meteoric increase in fire-power, set in motion by the Industrial Revolution towards the middle of the nineteenth century, went on after the German Wars of Unification. By the 1880s magazine-fed rifles had been adopted by all armies. In the mid-1880s, smokeless powder cleared the battlefield for both rifles and guns. The introduction of recoil-breakers produced the rapid-firing guns in the late 1890s. Finally, from the mid-1880s, the machine-gun began to make its appearance. All these doubled and trebled fire-rates, ranges, and accuracy, which had already begun to soar by 1870–1. For Bloch the implications were clear. They had been strikingly demonstrated in the first war in which magazine rifles had been used, the Russo-Turkish War of 1877–8. There, in their fortified camp at Plevna, entrenched and protected behind parapets, the Turks had repulsed three Russian assaults, with heavy losses; and since then the power of defence had been further magnified. In future war, argued Bloch, the entire front would freeze, leaving a desert of fire between the opposing armies:

> At first there will be increased slaughter on so terrible a scale as to render it impossible to get troops to push the battle to a decisive issue. . . . Then, instead of a war fought on to the bitter end in a series of decisive battles, we shall have as a substitute a long period of continually increasing strain upon the resources of the combatants.[200]

[198] The complete work appeared in Russian (1898), French (1898), and German (1899) editions. For those confounded by this labyrinth, the English concise one-volume edition *Is War Now Impossible?* (London, 1899), is sufficient, if not better. By the same standard Bloch's interview with W. T. Stead, originally published in the *Review of Reviews*, is exquisite: *Has War Become Impossible?* (London, 1899).

[199] Michael E. Howard, 'Men Againt Fire, Expectations of War in 1914', in Miller (ed.) *Military Strategy and the Origins of the First World War*, 41. If the language is no problem, there is a new biography in Polish: Ryszard Kolodziejczyk, *Jan Bloch (1836–1902)* (Warsaw, 1983).

[200] Bloch, *Has War Become Impossible?*, 6–7.

> Everybody will be entrenched in the next war. It will be a great war of entrenchments. The spade will be as indispensable to the soldier as his rifle. . . . Battles will last for days, and in the end it is very doubtful whether any decisive victory can be gained.[201]

Once a stalemate is created, says Bloch, and the war turns into a struggle of attrition, the economic factor comes in. The modern industrial economies are totally interdependent because of an elaborate global division of labour and a highly developed system of trade. The disruption of war would be ruinous for them. Under these conditions, war is perhaps not impossible but is certainly suicidal. A general European war would mean 'a frightful series of catastrophes which would probably result in the overturn of all civilized and ordered government'. It would bring, 'even upon the victorious power, the destruction of its resources and the break-up of society'.[202]

In appreciating this astounding piece of prophecy and the sensation it created, one thing must be made absolutely clear: all armies and military men throughout Europe were highly aware of, and deeply concerned about, the sharp rise in fire-power and its detrimental effect on the offensive. In fact, all discussions of tactics for more than half a century had been dominated by this awareness and concern. In almost the same way, the economic consequences of a prolonged general war were widely talked about in the generation preceding the war, and the prospect of great domestic upheavals which would destroy the old political and social system was on everybody's mind. Bloch, however, won fame by drawing such radical conclusions from these common concerns.

It was not only that Bloch's conclusions were too radical to be believed on the existing evidence. His work aroused widespread objections because its implications were politically and militarily unacceptable. 'War,' wrote Bloch, 'once being regarded as unavoidable, the rulers shut their eyes to its consequences.'[203] Of course, he too had his point of view; he was a pacifist. Only he happened to be right. The objections of the military all stemmed from one source. In both detail and spirit they went back to the central conception of war. Bloch, it was argued, projected technical and tactical weapon-performance on to the picture of war as a whole; to use a later phrase, he 'succumbed to the technological imperative'. He over-emphasized the mechanical aspect of war and disregarded the

[201] Ibid. 17–18. [202] Ibid. 21. [203] Ibid. 37.

paramount role of moral forces. Thus he failed to see the advantages of initiative and morale inherent in the offensive.[204] Above all, his rejection of war could not be accepted. As already mentioned, this was the crux of the matter. Bloch threatened a whole philosophy of life, and such philosophies are rarely susceptible to change. As one anonymous critic put it:

> As long as in . . . civilized states two 'modern' men still fight with one another for any reason . . . war between states will not be in the realm of the impossible, in spite of all the social and economic dangers and in spite of all the calculations of this ignorant theoretician.[205]

Indeed, the experience of the two subsequent major conflicts, the Boer War and, especially, the more regular Russo-Japanese War, seemed to confirm that the news about the death of war had been premature.[206] All armies noted that the strength of defence had grown enormously. Yet they also observed that victory had been gained, and that it had been gained through offensive spirit, superior morale, unwavering resolution, and the capacity to accept and sustain very heavy losses.[207] This was exactly in line with their all-powerful conception of war—past, present, and future. Writing in 1904, Lieutenant General Caemmerer, a sober and prudent soldier and a forceful exponent of the German conception of war, warned against a regression to the errors and misconceptions of the eighteenth century regarding the fundamental nature of war:

> At the present moment we live in an age when an extraordinary progress in the technics of firearms exposes us to the danger of over-estimating the value of defensive positions, and where such theories of the importance of ground in strategy . . . might again become [a] serious danger for weak

[204] A good account of the Bloch debate in Germany can be found in Chickering, *Imperial Germany*, 388–92.

[205] Ibid. 391–2.

[206] Howard, 'The Doctrine of the Offensive in 1914', in Paret (ed.), *Makers of Modern Strategy*, 518. For Bloch's lectures during the South African War and for the British lessons, see T. H. E. Travers, 'Technology, Tactics and Morale: Jean de Bloch, the Boer War, and British Military Theory, 1900–1914', *Journal of Modern History*, 51 (1979), 264–86.

[207] See, for example, Schlieffen's close subordinate and chief of the historical section of the general staff, Freytag-Loringhoven, *Der Infantrie-Angriff in den neuesten Kriegen: Ein Beitrag zur Klärung der Angriffsfrage* (Berlin, 1905). On the responses in Germany to the South African and Russo-Japanese wars, see Schulte, *Die deutsche Armee*, 173–191, 199–233, which contains harsh criticism of the outdatedness of German tactics.

minds . . . It was therefore necessary to leave no doubts about their failure in history.[208]

To sum up, the German army possessed a close-knit conception of war, developed in the age of national war. This conception had been evolved on the basis of the Napoleonic model during the Romantic period and the era of Prussian reform, and had been fortified by Prussia's great triumphs in the era of unification. Its operational aspect postulated the complete overthrow of the enemy's power of resistance through the destruction of his field-army in great battles of annihilation. This in turn implied rapid concentration of forces, mobile strategy, and aggressive and offensive conduct. It was with this overriding view of war that the German army went to war in 1914, when it found that, with all nations armed to their teeth, in a new industrial setting, and with technology favouring the defence, the character of war had altered considerably. War as envisaged in the fundamental conception failed to materialize. No decision could be reached. A static total war of resources and attrition set in. Throughout the war, Germany struggled to win the desired decisive victory in a war which was perceived from the traditional intellectual perspective as, in a sense, nothing more than a very difficult case. For the German military, the war remained an all-out struggle of nations for survival and power in which material strength and moral greatness would be the deciding factors.[209] Indeed, the new face of war was equally surprising for all armies, who for almost half a century had taken their cue in military affairs from Germany, studying her great military authorities and assimilating at least the leading tenets of her operational concept.

[208] Caemmerer, *Strategical Science*, 70.

[209] And so it remained for conservative circles after the war. For some of the leading figures mentioned in this chapter, see Bernhardi, *Vom Kriege der Zukunft* (Berlin, 1920); August Keim, *Graf Schlieffen* (Berlin, 1921); Ludendorff, *Der totale Krieg* (Munich, 1935).

3

The Cult of the Offensive: The Sources of French Military Doctrine 1871–1914

THE story of French military doctrine on the eve and at the outbreak of the First World War is puzzling and has remained so despite all attempts at explanation. Rarely if ever in history had such a stark contrast developed between military doctrine, preached with an almost fanatic conviction, and the realities of war. The growth of fire-power and, correspondingly, the increasing preponderance of field-works and growing efficacy of tactical defence had been progressively demonstrated in the half century which elapsed between the American Civil War and the wars in South Africa and Manchuria. But the French army, alone of all armies, developed and went to war with the unique doctrine of unconditional offensive. Determining French war-planning in 1914, this doctrine came very close to submitting France to German invasion and was largely responsible for the terrifying human cost incurred by the French in their futile attacks on German positions during the early phase of the war. Within five months, France had suffered almost one million casualties, and almost another million and a half men were lost in 1915.[1] The predominance of the trench, the machine-gun, and the barbed-wire entanglement came as a surprise to all the belligerents; but, from the point of view of doctrine, it was the French army which suffered the rudest shock.

How is such a curious and gross blunder to be explained? Four independent lines of interpretation have been offered since the inter-war period. First, military historians have traced the origins of post-1871 French military theory to the French discovery of German military ideas in the mid-1880s. Coming as a revelation to

[1] The figures went down to 900,000 in 1916, 546,000 in 1917, and 1,095,000 in 1918; Paul-Marie de la Gorce, *The French Army: A Military-Political History* (London, 1963), 103.

a group of leading figures in the new staff college, the École de guerre, this discovery prompted an intellectual renaissance of great magnitude and influence. The doctrine of the offensive, it has been argued, was a further outgrowth of this formative development.[2]

Secondly, another school of historians has attributed the army's doctrines to its political leanings and sociological traits. Proceeding in the tradition of the Left's sweeping campaign in the 1900s to republicanize the army after the Dreyfus Affair and expressing the deep antagonism which prevailed between Left and Right in France in the 1920s and 1930s, these historians have viewed the army as one of the last strongholds of conservatism and anti-republicanism. They have argued that the army struggled desperately to maintain its distinctive spirit and character as a closed professional body against all efforts to turn it into an army of reservists, a real nation-in-arms. The cultivation of the offensive doctrine, arguably fit only for highly trained and cohesive professionals, is often regarded by these historians as one of the principal ideological products of this struggle.[3]

Thirdly, the fanaticism and divorce from reality which characterized the advocates of the offensive and which appear to have bordered on the abnormal, if not the pathological, called for a deeper psychological insight. The French army, it has been argued, suffered from a deep-seated inferiority complex *vis-à-vis* its German counterpart. While German power was growing steadily and the disparity between the two armies was widening to hopeless proportions, the doctrine of the offensive became the means by which the French army escaped from the desperate reality of material odds into a world of fantasy and spiritual wishful thinking.[4]

[2] B. H. Liddell Hart, *Foch, The Man of Orleans* (London, 1931), 21–30; id., 'French Military Ideas before the First World War', in M. Gilbert (ed.), *A Century of Conflict 1850–1950* (London, 1966), 135–48; Dallas D. Irvine, 'The French Discovery of Clausewitz and Napoleon', *Journal of the American Military Institute*, 4 (1942), 143–61; Stefan Possony and Étienne Mantoux, 'Du Picq and Foch', in E. M. Earle (ed.), *Makers of Modern Strategy from Machiavelli to Hitler* (Princeton, NJ, 1943), 218.

[3] Monteilhet, *Les Institutions militaires de la France (1814–1924)*; Georges Michon, *La Préparation à la guerre: La Loi de trois ans (1910–1914)* (Paris, 1935); see also R. Girardet, *La Société militaire dans la France contemporaine, 1815–1939* (Paris, 1953), 193–278; Richard Challener, *The French Theory of the Nation in Arms* (New York, 1955).

[4] John Bowditch, 'The Concept of Élan Vital: A Rationalization of Weakness', in E. M. Earle (ed.), *Modern France* (Princeton, NJ, 1951), 32–43.

Fourthly, an affinity has long been discerned between the doctrine of the offensive and the French intellectual climate at the outset of the twentieth century. This intellectual climate was dominated by vitalistic notions customarily associated with Bergson's philosophy but in fact prevalent in French culture generally. It was also characterized by the yearning for spiritual and moral regeneration.[5]

Some of these lines of interpretation—almost self-contained from their beginning—have recently been restated even more vigorously, to the virtual exclusion of all other explanations.[6] Consequently, provided with remarkably coherent but mutually exclusive interpretations, historians seem to be facing a most unfortunate situation, in which it appears that the more we know the less we understand. The present chapter therefore attempts to bring together in a meaningful historical synthesis some fairly well-known materials. It will be argued that all the above-mentioned interpretations possess long lineage and appear perfectly plausible because all four are indeed well-founded. None of them, however, can stand alone. Like all historical phenomena, the doctrine of the offensive evolved from the joining-up and interweaving of several historical threads originating from separate and diverse sources.

THE FRENCH DISCOVERY OF CLAUSEWITZ AND NAPOLEON

The humiliating defeat of 1870–1 was traumatic for France. She was forced to accede to harsh peace-terms, topped by the handing-over to Germany of Alsace-Lorraine and by the payment of a huge war-indemnity, designed to cripple her finances and delay her military recovery for a generation. Furthermore, both politically and militarily, she had lost her traditional position as the predominant power in Europe. From being the terror of her

[5] E.g. ibid.; and, in his footsteps, Barbara Tuchman, *The Guns of August* (New York, 1962), 48; M. E. Howard, 'The Influence of Clausewitz', in Clausewitz, *On War* (Princeton, NJ, 1976), 37.

[6] For the second line of interpretation see J. Snyder, *The Ideology of the Offensive* (Ithaca, NY, 1984), 41–106; for the third, Douglas Porch, *The March to the Marne: The French Army, 1871–1914* (Cambridge, 1981), 213–31; id., 'Clausewitz and the French, 1871–1914', in M. Handel (ed.), *Clausewitz and Modern Strategy* (London, 1986), 287–301.

neighbours, she was now herself placed in a condition of inferiority *vis-à-vis* a powerful and arrogant Germany.

The war had been a crushing demonstration of German military superiority, but the reasons for this painful fact were not entirely clear, and explanations diverged. For Adolphe Thiers, for example, the problem amounted to no more than the criminally bad politics of Napoleon III and the related state of French military unpreparedness. Others were far more pessimistic. There was widespread gloom, and deeper concern that hierarchic and disciplined German society, respecting authority, duty, order, and hard work, was fundamentally superior to morally degenerate and politically and socially divided France.[7] On the more practical level, however, German military preponderance was widely attributed to the greatly superior Prussian reserve, mobilization, and staff systems, which enabled Prussia and her allies to deploy, supply, and control in the field, with astonishing effectiveness, vast armies that enjoyed overwhelming numerical advantage. However distasteful this fact was, the Prussian military model set the agenda for military reform in France after 1871. Considered from organizational and institutional points of view by a whole host of military pamphleteers and by the responsible governmental and army authorities, the Prussian model dictated, and generated, a sweeping restructuring of the French army during the 1870s.

The adoption of the Prussian system of short, universal military service was favoured by most generals and politicians in the wake of the defeat. It was mainly the personal position and high-handed interference of Thiers, the Republic's formidable president, that prevented it from being accepted more or less in its entirety. Adhering to the old liberal principles of the Orlean monarchy, he both feared the arming of the people and objected to the compulsory conscription of the sons of the bourgeoisie. Flaunting his authority as the foremost historian of the First Empire, he argued that the strength of the Napoleonic armies had lain in their hard core of veterans. He saw no serious fault in the old long-service professional army, which he wanted to keep as a reliable political instrument. Threatening at one point to resign, he effectively forced a compromise on the National Assembly. Thus the Law of 1872 enacted the principle of universal military service

[7] Ernest Renan, *La Réforme intellectuelle et morale de la France* (Paris, 1871); also see Trochu in Porch, *The March to the Marne*, 36.

and abolished paid substitution but stipulated two different lengths of service. While part of the recruits, determined by lot, were to serve for a period of five years, the rest were to serve for only six months to one year before passing to the reserve. On the model of the German one-year volunteers, high-school graduates enrolling in the universities and providing for their own uniform and maintenance served for one year only and were released to the reserve as second lieutenants. Young men training to be teachers or priests were totally exempted, and there were many other exemptions on family and social grounds.[8] In practice, however, successive ministers of war soon circumvented the law by administrative means. Regarding the shorter period of service as militarily unsound, they introduced a more egalitarian system by reducing the number of one-year conscripts and keeping them with the colours for longer periods of time. At the same time, they increased the number of long-term conscripts, while releasing them before the end of their legal term.[9] The law itself was changed only in 1889.

The army, which before 1870 had had no permanent organization above the regimental level, adopted the Prussian brigade, division, and corps structure. Like the German army, it was formed (in metropolitan France) into eighteen army corps.[10] In a great effort of construction, the railway network leading to the German border was vastly expanded, and the difference in speed between German and French mobilization was considerably reduced.[11] A new general staff was created in the Ministry of War in 1871 and reformed in 1874 to replace the old and inadequate Dépôt de guerre. Although providing a badly needed permanent and central organ of operational planning, it was still far inferior to its German counterpart. The supreme command remained with the responsible political and military authorities—the president and the minister of war—and was later entrusted to a generalissimo, a post created in

[8] Monteilhet, *Les Institutions militaires*, 109–153; David Ralston, *The Army of the Republic: The Place of the Military in the Political Evolution of France 1871–1914* (Cambridge, Mass., 1967), 35–48; Allan Mitchell, *Victors and Vanquished: The German Influence on Army and Church in France after 1870* (London, 1984), 20–30.

[9] Of an average annual contingent of almost 300,000, about half were fully exempted on various grounds. Of those recruited, the ratio of short- to long-term conscripts was, on average, more than 1 : 2 until 1877, and then fell to about 1 : 4 by 1880: Porch, *The March to the Marne*, 29.

[10] Ralston, *The Army of the Republic*, 49–52; Mitchell, *Victors and Vanquished*, 32–48.

[11] Mitchell, *Victors and Vanquished*, 60–4.

time of war only. Thus, as in the original Prussian command-structure before the extraordinary shifts of power in the Moltke era, the new French general staff was no more than a planning-bureau. It was officially designated the General Staff of the Minister of War to underline its subordinate role and was headed by a relatively junior general.

The staff corps was also reformed on the Prussian model. The closed staff-corps system, whose members had seen no active service with the troops and had therefore been out of touch with the rest of the army, was abolished. The Prussian system of rotating general-staff officers between staff- and field-posts was adopted in its place.[12] The old staff college was closed and a new one, emulating the Prussian Kriegsakademie, was created in 1876–8 to train the army's future command-echelon. The École militaire supérieure or École supérieure de guerre, as it was renamed in 1880, accepted officers with several years of regimental service after a competitive entrance-examination and offered a two-year course, as against three years in its German counterpart.

While the massive fortification of the eastern border carried out from 1874 by General Séré de Rivières shielded France from a swift German attack,[13] the French army was again becoming a force to be reckoned with. Although Gambetta returned from his tour in Germany in 1876 convinced that the French army was no match for the German,[14] Moltke was much impressed and alarmed by the speed and scale of the French recovery. The French, he told the Reichstag in 1874, were adopting the German military institutions under French names.[15] From the late 1870s, he assumed a defensive posture for the German army in the west in the case of a two-front war.

The instititional reforms in the French army were matched by strong intellectual ferment. The old Imperial army had been famous not only for its panache and its exaltation of the manly and martial virtues but also for its disdain of, and aversion to, all forms of

[12] Ralston, *The Army of the Republic*, 141–161, 89–94; Porch, *The March to the Marne*, 82–7.

[13] A. Marchand, *Plans de concentration de 1871 à 1914* (Paris, 1926), 4–9; Mitchell, *Victors and Vanquished*, 53–60.

[14] Herbert Tint, *The Decline of French Patriotism, 1870–1940* (London, 1964), 23.

[15] Moltke, *Essays, Speeches and Memoirs of Field-Marshal Count Helmuth von Moltke* (2 vols.; New York, 1893), ii. 109.

intellectualism and bookishness. Marshal MacMahon had reputedly stated that he would eliminate from the promotion list any officer whose name he had seen on the cover of a book.[16] The generals of the Empire had been baffled by the map-exercises and *Kriegspiele* on the Prussian model, which Napoleon III had tried to introduce before 1870.[17] Furthermore, in the tradition of the Revolutionary armies, the great majority of the French officers had been promoted directly from the ranks and had humble social origins, many of them barely knowing how to read or write. The contrast with their German peers in the campaign of 1870–1 was striking.[18] It was to the intellectual and professional qualities of the German officer-corps—no less than to the excellence of the German system of elementary education, shaping the rank and file—that the outcome of Metz and Sedan was generally credited. The reform of French military education, ranging from the establishment of NCO schools through the reform of the cadet academies to the creation of the École de guerre, was an acknowledgement that the French were lacking in the fundamentals of the military profession.[19] 'Before the war none of us knew anything,' admitted General Galliffet, one of the heroes of the old army.[20] New professional military journals like the *Revue militaire des armées étrangères* (1872) and the *Revue d'artillerie* (1873) were founded to promote military knowledge. Military literature proliferated.

The process of reform was accompanied in the early 1870s by the publication of a great many works devising and debating schemes for, and methods of, conscription and mobilization, staff organization, and military education. The most distinguished of the new military authors was Colonel, later General, Jules-Lewis Lewal. Chief of the historical-statistical bureau of the Dépôt de la guerre before 1870, he won renown after the war as one of the most outspoken critics of the old army and the author of the most comprehensive scheme of reform, *La Réforme de l'armée* (1871). He later became the founding father of the École de guerre (1877–80) and Minister of War (1885). In a series of books which

[16] Gorce, *The French Army*, 9. For more examples of the same attitude, see Irvine, 'The French Discovery of Clausewitz and Napoleon', 146–8.

[17] Porch, *The March to the Marne*, 41.

[18] Howard, *The Franco-Prussian War*, 16; Porch, *The March to the Marne*, 37–8.

[19] Porch, *The March to the Marne*, 39–41.

[20] Ralston, *The Army of the Republic*, 87.

appeared under the common title *Études de guerre* (1873–90), he gradually gravitated from questions of military organization and education towards the topic of the conduct of armies in the field. Hesitantly, French military authors were again stepping into the long-neglected field of operational doctrine. They came equipped with the concepts of positivism and scientism, which dominated their intellectual environment, as well as with the classical heritage of military theory since the age of the Enlightenment.

As noted by recent historians, Lewal's positivism was intertwined with a thoroughgoing determination to infuse the French army with a true spirit of professionalism. He believed that the scientific and systematic study and conduct of war were the secret of the success of the German education and staff system and accounted for its superiority. 'War is today a positivist science,' he preached to his readers.[21] Military organization, he maintained, was based on a number of positive principles and axioms.[22] In his *Introduction to the Positive Part of Strategy* (1892), he quoted Marmont, following in the tradition of the Enlightenment, to the effect that war had two parts: one speculative and moral, the other positive and based on principles.[23] In strategy, the latter consisted fundamentally of the Napoleonic-Jominian rationale of operations.[24]

Other military authors wrote in the same vein, presenting the classical rationale of operations in the context of modern concerns and practices in the fields of mobilization, transportation, and deployment. So did General Jean-Auguste Berthaut, Minister of War from 1876 to 1877; Colonel, later General, Victor Derrécagaix, captain in the old general staff and, in the mid-1880s, deputy chief of the École de guerre; and General Édouard Pierron.[25] Positivism, however, was most remarkably represented in the works of General Théodore Jung, who certainly deserves a separate study. His *War and Society* (1889) is a unique catalogue of positivist thought and an astonishing testimony to the author's extensive philosophical and scientific interests. He cites every prominent name in European

[21] Mitchell, *Victors and Vanquished*, 87.

[22] J. L. Lewal, *La Réforme de l'armée* (Paris, 1871), 3.

[23] Id., *Introduction à La Partie positive de la stratégie* (Paris, 1892), 36–7.

[24] Ibid. 49–53.

[25] J. A. Berthaut, *Principes de stratégie, étude sur la conduite des armées* (Paris, 1881); V. D. Derrécagaix, *La Guerre moderne* (Paris, 1885; trans, as *Modern War*, Washington, DC, 1888); Édouard Pierron, *Stratégie et grande tactique, d'après l'expérience des dernières guerres* (Paris, 1887).

science and positivist thought to support his main thesis:[26] that the study of war is part of that growing science of society which takes its example from the older and more established exact and natural sciences. Like mathematics, physics, and biology, it searches for uniform patterns of cause and effect and formulates them into simple, necessary, and universal laws.[27]

From the mid-1880s, however, a new note crept in. By 1892, in *The Positive Part of Strategy*, Lewal was giving Clausewitz a prominent place alongside the previously accepted authorities—de Saxe, Guibert, Archduke Charles, Jomini, Marmont, and Rüstow. By 1895 he was stressing the role of will-power, *la volonté*, in war and suggesting that 'it would appear exaggerated to argue with Jomini that, since Napoleon, strategy is fixed and incapable of further perfection'.[28] Derrécagaix was changing even more swiftly and decisively. As early as 1885 he was already presenting Clausewitz's conception of war and quoting von der Goltz and Blume. By 1901 he was totally converted.[29] Pierron wrote the introduction to the new translation of Clausewitz's *On War*. New influences were at work, and a new, vigorous group of intellectual activists was forming and taking the lead.

It took some time before the French acquired any idea at all of German military theory. As mentioned before, after their defeat and throughout the 1870s, they interpreted German superiority and success—not without good reason—almost purely in organizational and institutional terms. In regard to command, they deemed the source of German military proficiency to be in the legendary Prussian staff-corps, renowned for being meticulously recruited, methodically and scientifically trained to inhuman exactness and

[26] The precursors of social science—Bacon, Vico, Herder, Diderot, Condorcet, Comte, Blainville, Spencer, and Buckle—are followed in France by Coste, Littré, Taine, Laugel, Fouillée, Laffitte, Bourdeau, Moroeau, and Binet (to name only some of those cited); in England by Bagehot, Bain, Huxley, Flint, etc.; and in Germany by Hartmann, Lotze, Moleschott, Virchow, Wundt, Heckel, Buchner, Helmholtz, and others; Théodore Jung, *La Guerre et la société* (Paris, 1889), 1–3, 84. The book is dedicated to the famous Dr Charcot, Freud's teacher. See also E. Guillon, *Nos écrivains militaires* (2 vols.; Paris, 1898), 382–8.

[27] Jung, *La Guerre et la société*, esp. 1, 5, 119, 122. See also his *Stratégie, tactique et politique* (Paris, 1890).

[28] Lewal, *Stratégie de combat*, i (Paris, 1895), 6 ff.

[29] Derrécagaix, *Modern War*, 25–7 *et passim.*; id. *La Guerre et l'armée* (Paris, 1901), 5–8 *et passim.* Also see Pierron, *La Stratégie et la tactique allemande au début du XX*e *siècle* (Paris, 1900).

co-ordination, and functioning with automatic technical perfection. Crowning this image was the grim Moltke, regarded by the French as no great general but as the technocratic and autocratic chief of a bureaucratic machine.[30] Only gradually did closer study provide more intimate knowledge and insight. After 1871 German won the status of being the sole obligatory foreign language taught at the cadet schools and the École de guerre. The *Revue militaire de l'étranger* (from 1901 *Revue militaire des armées étrangères*), which provided French officers with translated selections from foreign military publications, naturally focused on Germany. However, the most decisive change in this respect occurred only in the 1880s. Moltke remained his silent self for the French and as unpopular as ever.[31] But, with the appearance of Blume's *Strategie* (1882; trans. 1884), Hohenlohe's *Letters on Strategy* (1887; trans. 1887) and, above all, von der Goltz's *The Nation in Arms* (1883; trans. 1884), the German conception of war and its conduct was revealed for the first time with a striking clarity and impressive cohesiveness. From these books the French learned that the German military traced their lineage to a great master, Clausewitz. *On War* was translated into French in 1886–7.[32] German military authors were becoming household names. Review articles and translations abounded. The so-called 'French discovery of Clausewitz and Napoleon' got under way.[33]

In 1884 Lucien Cardot, major in the intelligence bureau of the French general staff, discovered Clausewitz, and a year later he delivered three brilliant lectures on Prussian military thought at the École de guerre.[34] In 1887, following the translation into French of

30 Most characteristic is Lewal's obituary, *Le Maréchal de Moltke, organisateur et stratège* (Paris, 1891); and Caemmerer's both exacerbated and amused response in *Strategical Science*, 229. Also see E. Carrias, *La Pensée militaire française* (Paris, 1960), 281.

31 See the citations from Bonnal, Gilbert and Foch in Witold Zaniewicki, 'L'Impact de 1870 sur la pensée militaire française', *Revue de Défense Nationale*, 26 (1970), 1331–41.

32 Clausewitz, *Théorie de la grande guerre* (3 vols.; Paris, 1886–7). An older French translation (Paris, 1849–52) was out of print.

33 Irvine, 'The French discovery of Clausewitz and Napoleon', though often didactic, is the only rigorous study; see 152–7. Curiously, Mitchell's *Victors and Vanquished*, whose special theme is the German influence on the French army, does not even mention the influence of German military ideas.

34 H. Camon, *Clausewitz* (Paris, 1911), 1; J. Dany, 'La Littérature militaire d'aujourd'hui', *La Revue de Paris* (Mar.–Apr. 1912), 612; Irvine, 'The French Discovery of Clausewitz and Napoleon', 154–7.

Clausewitz's *On War*, an extensive review of the book was published in *La Nouvelle Revue* by France's leading military commentator, Captain Georges Gilbert (1851–1901). The author was an artillery officer who had distinguished himself in the first course of the École de guerre in 1876–7. He came under the patronage of General Miribel, the army's foremost strategic mind, but had to retire from the army in 1877 on account of poor health.[35]. His review was both favourable and perceptive.

Clausewitz, explained Gilbert, had expressed the spirit of Napoleonic warfare and had inspired Moltke. His work must be understood in connection with the transformation of war which had taken place between the eighteenth and nineteenth centuries. Eighteenth-century warfare, shaped by the character of the absolutist state and cabinet politics, had been indecisive and dominated by sieges, manœuvres, and finances. By contrast, the mass armies which had been introduced by the Revolution and had been infused with patriotism had enabled Napoleon to achieve decisive results against the whole of Europe. After Prussia's defeat and under Scharnhorst, Clausewitz had participated in the creation of the Prussian reserve-system which later won the day at Sadowa and Sedan. He had also rejected the old and erroneous theory of war, which had been preoccupied with geometric and geographic considerations. His philosophical volumes, said Gilbert, reveal the relation of war to society, the economy, and politics.[36] Clausewitz's theory of war consists in the ruthless subjugation of everything to one aim: the destruction of the enemy's main army in the major, Napoleonic battle, followed by a relentless pursuit. According to Clausewitz, one ought to act with all forces concentrated and strike swiftly without relaxation, while resolving all logistic problems by living off the countryside.[37] This, wrote Gilbert, was a 'simple, sound and virile' conception of war, though it was perhaps a little exaggerated in its reaction against geometry, was too direct, and was inappreciative of the significance of the lines of operations.[38]

Here already were all the elements of the French discovery of

[35] See Charles Malo's preface to Georges Gilbert's posthumous *Guerre sud-africaine* (Paris, 1902), ix–xix; Juliette Adam, *Le Capitaine Georges Gilbert* (Paris, 1924).

[36] Georges Gilbert, 'Étude sur Clausewitz', *La Nouvelle Revue*, (47), 1 and 15 Aug. 1887, 540–6; reprinted in id., *Essais de critique militaire* (2nd edn., Paris, 1890).

[37] Ibid. 547–55.

[38] Ibid. 554, 558. See also Carrias, *La Pensée militaire française*, 280–1.

Clausewitz and Napoleon, a discovery which soon acquired a powerful momentum. The French recognized that the Germans possessed a very distinctive conception of war, most vigorous, direct, and aggressive in character. The German victories and French defeat in 1870–1 were now largely attributed to this conception of war. However, it was also noted that this conception of war had been developed in Prussia after 1806, at the time of her great catastrophe, in imitation of French Revolutionary innovations and Napoleonic strategy. It therefore appeared that France had been defeated by the use of her own methods, which she herself had neglected after 1815. Hence the growth of the 'Napoleonic renaissance' in France, whose scholarly intensity has not been equalled before or since. This in turn was quickly followed by a realization that the Clausewitzian conception was in fact a simplistic, if not crude, model of Napoleonic strategy. Thus, while finding the German conception of war an astounding and influential revelation, the French could none the less recover some of their independent identity and national self-esteem.

The reason for the French attraction to the Prussian conception of warfare is obvious. Here was a clear and impressive theoretical edifice and doctrine of a kind that was lacking on their own side, and it rested on the two towering military models of the century—Napoleonic warfare and the Prussian campaigns of 1866 and 1870. It offered the French a new and invigorating sense of direction and seemed to revive their own best traditions. It called for the qualities of initiative and aggressiveness, which the French had always regarded as their peculiar national traits. Their response was overwhelming.

The focus of the new movement was, not surprisingly, the École de guerre. There was now an exciting theory to teach. The professor of infantry tactics from 1882, Major, later Lieutenant-Colonel, Maillard, propagated the new doctrine. '*The destruction of the enemy* is the aim; *the offensive* is the means', stated his *Elements of War* (1891), published upon his departure from the school.[39] The book offered a penetrating analysis of the Napoleonic manœuvre. It highlighted Napoleon's clear determination of the

[39] L. Maillard, *Éléments de la guerre* (Paris, 1891), p. v. The text of the lectures exists in the *École de guerre's* library. Also see Dany, 'La Littérature militaire', 614; Carrias, *La Pensée militaire* française, 278–9.

decisive point and line of advance, resolute and carefully co-ordinated marches in dispersed order, and rapid concentration of all forces to overwhelm the enemy.[40] Examining the nuts and bolts of the Napoleonic operational formation, Maillard showed how every column, and the army as a whole, had been covered by an advance guard and a rearguard which secured their freedom of operation in all directions. Moltke is often cited, but only as a disciple of the great Corsican. In his stimulating comparison of Jena and Sedan, Georges Gilbert, Maillard's friend, showed how the victor of 1870 in effect only duplicated the strategic pattern employed in 1806.[41] For the French the Prussians became merely a vehicle on their way back to Napoleon.

Maillard left the École de guerre in 1890 (he died as a general in 1901), but at the school his friends and colleagues were propounding the same ideas. The most distinguished of these was Henri Bonnal, who dominated the school and French strategic thinking for two decades. He arrived at the Écoles de guerre as a major in 1885 and rose to become the professor of military history, strategy and applied tactics (1892–6) and, in the first years of the twentieth century, the commanding general. Bonnal was a formidable military historian and thinker. The lectures which he delivered at the school in the 1890s grew into a series of monumental studies: *Sadowa* (Fr. orig. 1901), *De Rosbach à Ulm* (1903), *La Manœuvre d'Iéna 1806* (1904), *La Manœuvre de Landshut 1808–1809* (1905), *La Manœuvre de Vilna 1811–1812* (1905), and *La Manœuvre de Saint-Privat* (3 vols., 1904–1912). Based on exhaustive research in the French archives, which was characteristic of the new Napoleonic scholarship, these studies made him a leading authority on Napoleonic and Prussian strategy.

The explosion of Napoleonic research in France from the late 1880s laid bare the origins and structure of Napoleonic strategy. Pierron's pioneering essay *How Was Napoleon's Military Genius Formed?* (1889) anticipated Major Colin's classic study *The Military Education of Napoleon* (1900) in exploring the origins of Napoleon's early operational schemes.[42] At the same time,

[40] Maillard, *Éléments de la guerre*, pp. x–xv, 3.

[41] Georges Gilbert, 'Septembre et octobre 1806—juillet et août 1870', in *Critique militaire*, 59–378; Irvine, 'The French Discovery of Clausewitz and Napoleon', 158.

[42] Édouard Pierron, *Comment s'est formé le génie militaire de Napoléon I*[er]? (Paris, 1889); Jean Colin, *L'Éducation militaire de Napoléon* (Paris, 1900); see also Irvine, 'The French Discovery of Clausewitz and Napoleon', 159.

Napoleon's campaigns and systems of operations were dissected by Bonnal, Camon, and Grouard. Like Maillard, Bonnal emphasized the flexibility of the emperor's operational formation, the so-called *bataillon carré*, screened as it had been by an advance guard and a rearguard and ready to turn and strike in all directions. More than anyone else before him, he also brought to light the imaginative qualities of Napoleon's genius: his mastery of deception, feints, and diversions to create surprise, disorientation, and miscalculation on the enemy's part.

Thus it is not surprising that Bonnal and his friends found Clausewitz's perception of Napoleonic strategy curiously crude and, in some fundamental respects, totally inadequate. Historians who tended to dismiss this affront to the great philosopher of war as nothing more than an expression of French chauvinism and wounded national pride, missed the main point here. Viewing Napoleon's strategy from distant and defeated Prussia, Clausewitz had been primarily impressed by its immense energy, boldness, and decisiveness. Fiercely reacting against the old 'strategy of manœuvre', he had portrayed Napoleonic strategy as extremely direct and vigorously simple and had missed a great deal of its subtlety of conception and manœuvre. Gilbert sensed this immediately in his seminal review of 1887, and Bonnal was as perceptive and accurate in assessing both the strength and the weaknesses of the Clausewitzian interpretation. He pointed out that, while Napoleon had always sought the great battle, he had never been as direct as Clausewitz had imagined in going about it.[43] The translation into French between 1899 and 1908 of Clausewitz's major histories of the campaigns of 1796, 1799, 1812, 1813, 1814, and 1815 made the shortcomings of the Clausewitzian interpretation even more obvious. Bonnal and Camon were astonished by Clausewitz's assertion that 'Napoleon never engaged in strategic envelopment'.[44] Both cited the many instances of Napoleon's *manœuvre sur les derrières*, the manœuvre against the enemy's rear, one of the most fundamental patterns of Napoleonic strategy. They failed to understand how Clausewitz could so misinterpret the

[43] L. Rousset (ed.), *Les Maîtres de la guerre Frédérick II, Napoléon, Moltke, d'après des travaux inédits de M. le général Bonnal* (Paris, 1899), 226–7 (the text of Bonnal's lectures exists in the *École de guerre*'s library); Bonnal, *De la méthode dans les hautes études militaires en Allemagne et en France* (Paris, 1902), 10–11.

[44] Clausewitz, *Principles of War* (Harrisburg, Pa., 1942), 49.

Marengo, Ulm, and Jena campaigns, to name only the most famous examples.[45]

It has been justly pointed out, however, that the problem of the French army was not Napoleonic strategy but how to fight the next war.[46] Bonnal and his friends were stepping on to less firm ground when they turned from history to evaluate Prussian strategy and consider operational doctrine. Bonnal had many sensible, and even brilliant, things to say when he extended his criticism of Clausewitz to the Prussian conception of warfare as a whole. At the same time, however, his picture of Prussian strategy was open to the same charges of oversimplification which he himself levelled against Clausewitz's interpretation of Napeolonic strategy.

In his learned study *Sadowa* (manuscript form 1894; printed 1901) Bonnal argued that the Prussian army, while emulating Napoleonic warfare, understood little of its subtleties, wagering everything on the rapid concentration of forces for battle.[47] This accounted both for its strength and for its weaknesses:

> Its sword play is pre-eminently plain, and absolutely innocent of feints. Its strategic and tactical phrases consist of a few words which never vary—that is, its art is rudimentary. But it makes good of the poverty of its combinations. It is its tenacity, its energy, its attention to detail, and its unity of thought which render it so formidable an adversary.[48]

> Even on the defensive, the Prussians attack everywhere and always. This gives them a moral advantage over a timorous or weak opponent, but when . . . it becomes a sealed pattern, it is highly dangerous, and over and above this it negates superior control. . . . An unbridled offensive is extremely dangerous when the adversary can manœuvre and can count . . . on the certainty that the assailants will rush upon the first bait they see.[49]

Herein Bonnal saw the opportunities for French strategy: it ought to take the form of flexible defence in a truly Napoleonic fashion, keeping all forces united and operating in full co-ordination to defeat the enemy's thrusts. The French field-commanders at all levels were not expected to act on their own initiative or exhibit the

[45] Bonnal, *Hautes études militaires*, 10–11; Camon, *Clausewitz*; J. Colin, *The Transformation of War* (London, 1912), 298–300. See also book I above, 208–11.

[46] Michael E. Howard, 'The Influence of Clausewitz', in Clausewitz, *On War* (Princeton, NJ. 1976), 36.

[47] Bonnal, *Sadowa: A Study* (London, 1907), 48.

[48] Ibid. 49.

[49] Ibid. 243–4.

same degree of independence which had become necessary for the Prussians on account of their dispersed mode of operations. According to Bonnal, the Prussians had erred gravely when they had split their forces in 1866, and their loose method of command and control bordered on the effective abnegation of central war-planning.[50] A vigorous French army, acting swiftly in a well-calculated and carefully controlled strategy, would not leave then unpunished.

Thus in the 1890s, at least in partial disregard of the new conditions prevailing in the age of mass armies and railways, the French army revived the more concentrated, Napoleonic order of battle, supposedly possessing superior qualities of unity and central control. With some theoreticians this sometimes assumed absurd proportions. Caemmerer could hardly believe his eyes at Lewal's scheme to deploy and manœuvre in close order an army of one quarter of a million men, which he planned to squeeze on a front of only 16 miles. To the four French field-armies, altogether over one million men, Lewal allocated no more than 68 miles.[51] On a more practical level, however, French war-planning and official doctrine were also changing in conformity with the new military ideas.

The French war-plans conceived between 1875 and 1886 (Plans 1–7) were defensive in character. The French armies were spread along the German frontier, and their line of assembly was moved progressively forward from the rear, as the French railway- and fortress-systems were building up and the fear of an earlier German attack diminished.[52] After 1886, however, the Eastern crisis suggested the possibility of co-operation with Russia. Thus Plans 8 and 9 (1887 and 1888), while changing little in the deployment scheme, adopted the offensive.[53] At the same time, the French discovery of Clausewitz and Napoleon was changing attitudes at a

[50] Ibid. 52–3, 243. Foch reiterated these ideas in his staff-college lectures: *De la conduite de la guerre* (2nd edn.; Paris, 1909), see also *Marshal Foch: His own Words on Many Things*, ed. Raymond Recouly (London, 1929), 130. Colin was an exception in pointing out the changes in the road network since Napoleon, which accounted for Moltke's strategy: *The Transformation of War*, 304–6.

[51] Lewal, *Stratégie de marche* (Paris, 1893); id., *Stratégie de combat* (2 vols., Paris, 1895–6); Caemmerer, *Strategical Science*, 230–8.

[52] Marchand, *Plans de concentration*, 13–72; État-Major de l'Armée, *Les Armées françaises dans la grande guerre* (Paris, 1936), I, i. 3–12.

[53] Marchand, 73–91; État-Major, *Les Armées françaises dans la grande guerre*, 12–18.

deeper level. Serving in 1890–1 in the third (operations) bureau of General Miribel's general staff, Captain Ferdinand Foch later remembered what he regarded as defensive mentality and excessive reliance on terrain on the French part.[54] But generations and ideas were swiftly changing. Major Grouard was typical in denouncing reliance on fortified places, past and present, as 'the greatest military mistake of our epoch'. Reviewing the war of 1870–1, he argued that rather than lock himself and his army up in Metz, Bazaine should have withdrawn deep into the interior of the country and forced the Prussians to follow and overextend themselves. Prevailing doctrines, warned Grouard, were potentially as disastrous. Primaily associated with the name of the great Belgian fortress–builder Brialmont, they promoted fortresses as 'strategic pivots' for the field armies. While Grouard maintained that field fortifications might prove beneficial to a numerically inferior army, he emphasized that they never ought to rule strategy and become a substitute for active and aggressive conduct.[55]

By the 1890s (Plans 10–13, 1889–95), the French army was moving towards a more active form of defence—the so-called defensive-offensive strategy.[56] This trend reached its height when Bonnal was entrusted with the drafting of Plan 14 (1898), whose principles remained in force also in Plans 15 and 16 (1903 and 1909). A 'Napoleonic' order in depth reinforced the shallower, 'cordon-like', formation adopted, on the German example, after 1871. A whole army—incorporating the new 20th Corps posted at the exposed position of Nancy—formed the *couverture*. This was the screening and delaying force whose primary role was to protect the process of mobilization. A powerful army was deployed behind the four front-line armies, to act as a new 'mass of manœuvre'. Giving flexibility to the whole system of defence, it was ready to counter-attack in any direction at the opportune moment, at the command of the general-in-chief.[57]

[54] Ferdinand Foch, *The Memoirs of Marshal Foch* (New York, 1931), p. xxxix.

[55] A. Grouard, *La Perte des états et les camps retranchés: réplique au général Brialmont* (Paris, 1889); id. *Faillait-il quitter Metz en 1870?* (Paris, 1893); id. *Comment quitter Metz en 1870? Avec une note sure le rôle de la fortification* (Paris, 1901).

[56] Marchand, *Plans de concentration*, 92–127; État-Major, *Les Armées françaises dans la grande guerre*, I, i. 18–26.

[57] *Les Armées françaises dans la grande guerre*, 26–33; Henri Contamine, *La Revanche* (Paris, 1957), 77–9; Samuel Williamson, *The Politics of Grand Strategy: Britain and France Prepare for War, 1904–1914* (Cambridge, Mass., 1969), 117.

Official doctrine, as codified in the field regulations, followed a similar route. The Infantry Regulations of 1875 reflected the experience of 1870–1, when modern breach-loaders took a murderous toll on frontally attacking infantry. The regulations stressed the importance of fire-power and the careful use of ground for cover. A dispersed order of battle was recommended for the attack. Soon the lessons of Plevna (1877) corroborated and reinforced those of 1870–1.[58] However, with the army regaining some of its confidence and with the coming of new ideas, care was taken that the offensive spirit should not be lost in the face of stronger fire-power. The Infantry Field Regulations which were issued in 1884 stressed 'the principle of the decisive attack, head held high, with no attention to losses'. They called for energetic and vigorous advance even under heavy fire and against well-defended trenches.[59] Finally, issued in 1895, the Field Service Regulations were inspired by Bonnal and rightly considered by him as the consummation of the French military renaissance which centred on the École de guerre. Philosophically, they proudly proclaimed unity of doctrine, while denying dogmatic systems and principles. Strategically, they postulated the breaking of the enemy's will to resist, the indispensability of offensive action for the attainment of decisive results, and the total rejection of passive defence. They prescribed that the commander ought to maintain freedom of operation, hold the enemy at bay with a strong advance-guard, and choose the right moment to concentrate all forces rapidly for the decisive event. Clausewitz and Napoleon ruled supreme.[60]

The second half of the 1890s therefore marked the high point in the creativity and influence of the intellectual activists at the École de guerre. Colonel Hippolyte Langlois, the artillery professor from the mid-1880s and the commanding general between 1895 and 1902, was one of the chief proponents of the active and aggressive doctrine.[61] Major Cherfils, the cavalry professor, who stressed the

[58] Émile Mayer, *Autour de la guerre actuelle* (Paris, 1917), 106–7; E. Carrias, *La Pensée militaire française*, 275; Contamine, *La Revanche*, 44.

[59] Mayer, *Autour de la guerre actuelle*, 107–9; Carrias, *La Pensée militaire française*, p. 276.

[60] Bonnal, *Hautes études militaires*, 17–20; Carrias, *La Pensée militaire française*, 283–4; Irvine, 'The French Discovery of Clausewitz and Napoleon', 160–1.

[61] Hippolyte Langlois, *L'Artillerie de campagne en liaison avec les autres armes* (2 vols.; Paris, 1892); Dany, 'La Littérature militaire', 614–15; Irvine, 'The French Discovery of Clausewitz and Napoleon', 160.

use of the *arme blanche* and the cavalry charge, and Major Niox, the professor of military geography, were other leading activists in the new school.[62] Indeed, the group of instructors at the École de guerre earned recognition as 'the new French military school' for possessing a whole set of characteristics more accessible perhaps to sociologists of intellectual communities. Its members were concentrated around a single institution. They preached a fairly unified doctrine. And they were imbued with that fresh, pioneering sense of intellectual enthusiasm which is almost inseparable from any great enterprise. They were a church with a gospel, and soon they were bringing up a second generation. Gilbert, their friend and ally outside the army, proudly presented the team of the leading institution: Maillard, Bonnal, Langlois, Cherfils, and Niox were being followed by their pupils—Foch, Leblond, Lanrezac, and Ruffey, almost all familiar names from the Great War.[63]

Foch entered the École de guerre as a student in 1885, when the new wave in French military thinking was beginning to gather momentum. Not before 1882–3, he was later to write, was war taught in France on a rational and practical basis.[64] The school was, in his words, 'an absolute revelation' to him. The 'remarkable body of instructors' included 'Cardot, Maillard, Millet, Langlois and Cherfils'.[65] In 1895 he returned to the École de guerre as the assistant professor of military history, strategy, and applied tactics. A year later, with some understandable misgivings, he accepted the professorship itself, made vacant by Bonnal's departure.

As mentioned in the first chapter, all assessments of Foch's teaching and influence before 1914 have been influenced by the central role he was subsequently to play in the First World War. Nominated in 1918 to the supreme command of the allied armies in France, Marshal Foch became a figure of world fame and the focus of popular interest. Hence the somewhat distorted perspective dominating the scholarly literature. Retrospectively, Foch has been blown up out of his natural place in the new French military school.

[62] Maxime Cherfils, *Cavalerie en campagne* (2nd edn.; Paris, 1893); Dany 'La Littérature militaire', 614–5; Irvine, 'The French Discovery of Clausewitz and Napoleon', 160.

[63] Georges Gilbert, *La Guerre sud-africaine*, 534. Similarly see H. Langlois, *Lessons from Two Recent Wars, The Russo-Turkish and South African War* (London, 1909), p. vii; Mayer, *Autour de la guerre actuelle*, 109.

[64] Foch, *The Principles of War* (London, 1920; first publ. in French 1903), 2.

[65] Foch, *Memoirs*, p. xxxvii.

His teachers—the true innovators—had all retired before the Great War and thus remained rather forgotten staff-college professors. Had the war not come in 1914 and had Foch retired peacefully at sixty-four a year later, he would have ranked far behind Bonnal (and Langlois) in both intellectual and operational influence.

Foch was not a formidable military historian and critic like his predecessor. Upon being nominated professor at the École de guerre, he had to start virtually from scratch. 'What forced me to work at my profession', he was later to confess, 'was having to teach it.'[66] His course of study and teaching, however, was ready-made for him at the school. Firstly, it was shaped by German military literature, in which von der Goltz held the most influential place and, in turn, led back to Clausewitz. The German-influenced message was that war, and modern war in particular, was a life-and-death struggle between armed nations, which could only end in the breaking of the enemy's will to resist. The decisive battle, aiming at the destruction of the enemy's army, was the only legitimate means, and aggressive conduct the only legitimate mode of action. Secondly, on the operational level, Foch inherited the neo-Napoleonic teachings of Maillard and Bonnal. These emphasized freedom of operation as well as the manœuvre, secured by a strong reconnoitring advance-guard—the famous *sûreté*—and leading to a rapid concentration of forces for the decisive blow. Foch's *Des principes de la guerre* (1903), consisting of his lectures at the École de guerre (the text in the school library), blended these themes with examples taken from the wars of Napoleon and the Wars of German Unification. Nothing here was new. Both in content and form the book was fairly loosely put together. Nowhere did it approach the scholarly power and subtlety of exposition which had characterized the work of some of Foch's older associates.

But then Foch's main strength lay elsewhere. It has long been observed that he was, above all, a man of character. 'I am certain', Keynes was to write years later, 'that Foch's mind and character are of an extreme simplicity—of an almost medieval simplicity. He is honest, fearless and tenacious.'[67] It was his inner strength, inexhaustible springs of energy, conviction, devotion, integrity, and

[66] C. Bugnet (ed.), *Foch Talks* (London, 1929), 69.

[67] J. M. Keynes, *Two Memoirs* (London, 1949), 15; quoted in W. J. Fossati, 'Educational Influences in the Career of Marshal Ferdinand Foch of France' (unpub. doc. diss., University of Kansas, 1976), 70.

congenial manner that made him a source of inspiration both before and after 1914. As Liddell Hart has put it, he was a man of faith; 'he was convincing because he was passionately convinced'.[68] When he taught, it was the sublime concepts and phrases and the exaltation of moral forces and will-power that attracted him most. These were also the elements that most appealed to him in Clausewitz's work. A devout Catholic, he quoted de Maistre: 'A battle lost is a battle one thinks one has lost, for a battle cannot be lost physically.'[69] One contemporary eye-witness reports that his solemn lectures impressed his students but were not always entirely clear to them.[70] A secret report, drafted by the police before Foch's nomination to command the École de guerre in 1908, alleged that, 'during his professorship at the École de guerre, [he] taught metaphysics—and metaphysics so abstruse that it made idiots of a number of his pupils'.[71]

All the same, when Foch was forced to leave the École de guerre in 1901, it was for different reasons. If the second half of the 1890s marked the high point in the activity of the new French military school, the twentieth century brought in its wake grave crises. While the army as a whole was torn apart in the aftermath of the Dreyfus Affair, the teachings of the new school were seriously questioned following the experiences of South Africa and Manchuria. They were coming under heavy fire from different quarters.

MILITARY INFERIORITY, DOMESTIC PRESSURES, AND THE PHILOSOPHY OF *ÉLAN VITAL*

The professional debate over the probable effect of the magazine rifle, smokeless powder, the rapid-firing gun, and the machine-gun intensified in the 1890s, culminating in the controversy surrounding Bloch's sensational work (1898). For example, in the series of articles written between 1888 and 1891, Captain, later Major, Émile Mayer, Foch's old school-mate at the École polytechnique,

[68] Liddell Hart, *Foch*, 458 *et passim*. Liddell Hart was the first to strip off the hagiographic mystique surrounding Foch. But, as history, his book is marred by didactic rhetoric and by Liddell Hart's tendency to confuse past occurrences with his own intellectual battles in the 1920s and 1930s.

[69] Foch, *Principles of War*, 286.

[70] George Aston, *The Biography of the Late Marshal Foch* (London, 1929), 73.

[71] Quoted in Liddell Hart, *Foch*, 42–3.

argued that the growth of fire-power would render war immobile and favour the defence.[72] These concerns receded, however, from before the walls of the École de guerre. There, in the late 1890s, Foch was 'proving mathematically' that the much-talked-about improvements in firearms were, in fact, favourable to the offence.[73] Mayer was later to complain that, with the new ideas and aggressive doctrines coming out of the École de guerre (which he himself never attended), his opinions, when noted, had only provoked anger and disfavour. In the end, his articles were rejected by French journals and published only in Switzerland. With the outbreak of the South African war, however, both weapons and tactics were put to the test of war, and the results—most disquieting from the point of view of the prevailing doctrine—could not be ignored.

In 1902 Mayer, who had retired from the army and was working as a military writer, drew his own conclusions from the war. Paraphrasing Bloch, he argued that fighting would freeze along continuous and impregnable human walls. War would terminate only in total human and financial exhaustion.[74] By now, however, people in the highest ranks of the army, much more influential than an outsider like Mayer, were advancing similar ideas. The most important of them was François de Négrier, one of the leading and

[72] Mayer won his place in the historical literature because of his revealing war-time and post-war works, in which he settled accounts with pre-war doctrine in general and with Foch in particular. See esp. Mayer, *Comment on pouvait prévoir l'immobilisation des fronts dans la guerre moderne* (Paris, 1916), presenting articles he had written 25 years earlier; id., *Autour de la guerre actuelle*, 164–5; id, *La Psychologie du commandement, avec plusieurs lettres inédites du Maréchal Foch* (Paris, 1924), 5–10; id., *Trois maréchaux: Joffre, Galliéni, Foch* (Paris, 1928), 120–227 and, specifically about his articles, 127–33.

[73] Foch, *Principles of War*, 32; this was even then an extraordinary argument and has justly earned notoriety. After the war, Foch was embarrassed by Mayer's revelations and only reluctantly granted him permission to publish the old correspondence between them (Foch to Mayer, 21 Oct. 1921, in Mayer, *La Psychologie du commandement*, 6.) His brief account of his *École de guerre* period in his memoirs is a shameless forgery. By association, he tries to create the impression that he taught there the preponderance of fire-power: Foch, *Memoirs*, pp. xxxvii–xxxviii, xxxix. Later in the book, he criticizes the doctrine of the offensive and the excessive emphasis on morale and the decisive victory, without even hinting that he was one of the chief proponents of these approaches: ibid., pp. lvi–lxi.

[74] Mayer argues, perhaps correctly, that it was Bloch who was influenced by his article 'L'Évolution de la tactique', which had been published in *Bibliothèque universelle* in Feb. 1891; Mayer, *L'Immobilisation des fronts*, 74.

most outspoken generals in the army. In a series of anonymous but stirring articles in the *Revue de deux mondes*, he argued that the South African war demonstrated that front lines had become almost inviolable. The days of attacks in deep order were over. Infantry advance could only be carried out in thin lines and small groups. Cavalry could no longer charge and had to dismount to fight. The extension of the front to envelop the enemy's position was the only feasible method of attack. Observing German manœuvres, Négrier came to the conclusion that the Germans were extending each army's front to fifty kilometres, far beyond the width advocated by the French neo-Napoleonics. He blamed the professors of the staff college, saying that, in reintroducing dense order of battle and concentrations in mass, they had substituted the principles of Napoleonic strategy for the needs of modern tactics. He argued that the regulations of 1875, emphasizing fire-power, had been far more realistic.[75]

Similar ideas regarding the nature of modern tactics were expressed by General Kessler in his book *Tactique des trois armes* (1903).[76] In lectures delivered in 1902, Colonel Berot, chief of the operations bureau in the general staff (a predecessor of Grandmaison's), suggested that the army ought to combine the advantages of the tactical defence and of the strategic offence.[77] In late 1901, General Lamiraux, ex-vice-president of the Conseil superieur de la guerre, confessed about the prevailing confusion:

> No one, or almost no one, can agree with his neighbour on tactical questions. Some say: firepower is all important . . . Others tell you: Attack! Always attack! . . . How does one create a method from such dissimilar ideas? We cannot do it. We take a bit of one, add a pinch of the other and hope that any errors . . . will sort themselves out in combat.[78]

Soon, however, the change of opinion found official expression in the new Infantry Field Regulations issued in 1904. Disperse order was adopted, and the use of terrain for cover emphasized.[79] At the École de guerre itself, the professor of infantry tactics in the mid-1900s, Colonel de Maud'huy, taught that modern firearms vastly

[75] Carrias, *La Pensée militaire française*, 288–9.

[76] Joffre, *The Memoirs of Marshal Joffre* (2 vols.; London, 1932), i. 27.

[77] Stephen Ryan, *Pétain the Soldier* (London, 1969), 28–9.

[78] 29 Nov. 1901, *France militaire*; quoted by Porch, *The March to the Marne*, 221.

[79] Carrias, *La Pensée militaire française*, 290.

increased the power of local defence. He argued that in order to succeed, the attacker would have to assemble massive concentrations of artillery and infantry in his chosen zone of attack.[80]

The members of the new military school were thrown on the defensive. Both Langlois and Bonnal responded at length to the charges levelled against them by Négrier and to the ideas he, Kessler, and others had advanced. Examining the battle of Plevna, Langlois came to the conclusion that an adequately planned and executed attack would have carried the place.[81] In concurrence with Gilbert's posthumous work, *La Guerre sud-africaine* (1902), he argued that the special conditions which prevailed in South Africa were hardly applicable to Europe.[82] He admitted that the rapidly improving firearms employed by entrenched infantry had made frontal attack increasingly difficult and costly. Yet he reminded his readers that beyond any contingent changes in armaments stood the eternal principles of war, the first of which was the imperative of inflicting a powerful blow on the enemy in order to force him to admit defeat.[83] He expressed concern that heavy artillery and field howitzers—whose adoption was urged to combat entrenched infantry—might become a means to escape from the main challenge, which was ultimately the need to assault and overthrow the enemy.[84] He conceded that better means and methods of attack must certainly be employed to deal with the new conditions.[85] But he argued that the writings of Négrier and Kessler were positively dangerous because, by influencing and confusing the minds of many young officers, they not only undermined trust in leaders and regulations but also killed the offensive spirit, which was essential for victory.[86] If anything, he argued, modern war would require even greater moral energies. Following the publication of the second edition of *Battle Studies* the same year, Langlois cited Ardant du Picq to this effect for the first time.[87]

Herein lay the core of the matter. When one ponders over the seemingly inexplicable blindness of the leading pre-1914 French

[80] Contamine, *La Revanche*, 168–9; Ronald H. Cole, ' "Forward with the Bayonet! ": The French Army Prepares for Offensive Warfare, 1911–1914' (unpub. diss., University of Maryland, 1975), 265–7.

[81] Langlois, *Lessons from Two Recent Wars*, 35–7.

[82] Ibid. 89.

[83] Ibid. 85, 124–5.

[84] Ibid. 85.

[85] Ibid. 125–39.

[86] Ibid. 111–12. For Bonnal's milder responses, see his *La Récente Guerre sud-africaine* (Paris, 1903); id., *L'Art nouveau en tactique* (Paris, 1904).

[87] Ibid. 124, 140.

military theoreticians to the effect of modern firearms, one ought to understand that their problem was least of all tactics itself. Mayer recounts his arguments with Niox and Foch, in which the latter stated that the impregnability of fronts is a problem recognized by all. However, he added, everyone also recognized that a decisive result would have to be achieved.[88] Pre-1914 military theoreticians, not only in France but everywhere in Europe, did not suffer from stupidity, as is often suggested. Quite the opposite. They were handicapped, so to speak, by an overdeveloped sense of history and too erudite a conception of warfare—one with which, paradoxically, many of the proponents of fire-power were not burdened.[89] Their minds were dominated by the Napoleonic and Prussian models, which had been endlessly studied and long hammered-out into the most powerful theory of war. If they tended to resist the changes in tactics and, like Langlois, defend the bayonet and the cavalry charge and doubt the ability of heavy field-artillery to crush entrenched infantry, it was mainly as a means to an end.[90] Their picture of war was principally strategic and moral. What they objected to was not so much the notion that the battlefield had become a murderous place, but the implication that grand, aggressive, and decisive strategy was no longer feasible. They feared that excessive emphasis on fire-power, cover, and the advantages of defence would lead back to the proverbial errors of the eighteenth century and the passivity of which the French were allegedly guilty in 1870, and destroy the moral willingness to advance and fight.[91] If there was anything that the accumulated wisdom of history taught them, it was that weakness was always quick to raise its head under any pretext, and that nothing important had ever been achieved without great valour and sacrifice.

As mentioned in the previous chapter, this was precisely why the Russo-Japanese War, while again demonstrating the protracted and immobile character of modern war and the strength of fire-power,

[88] Mayer, *Trois maréchaux*, 135.

[89] It is a point of interest that long before the events told here, the intellectual calibre of the vigorous Négrier, then the youngest corps commander in the French army, was called into question. See Charles W. Dilke, 'The French Armies', *The Fortnightly Review*, 1 Nov. 1891, 609: 'he is probably a general of armies of the future, but his knowledge of the science of modern war is disputed by the men of books' (referring then to Derrécagaix, Fay, and their generation).

[90] Langlois, *Lessons from two Recent Wars*, 35, 100–1, 119–20.

[91] See for example Foch, *Principles of War*, 31–33.

if anything only reinforced the dominating view of warfare. Despite everything, in a war between two regular, European-style armies, it was the attacker, vigorous and willing to make great sacrifices, who ultimately conquered.[92] Négrier repeated the highly perceptive observations which he had made after the previous war, but he added that only offensive tactics could bring victory, and he rejected passive 'positionism' as the 'heresy' responsible for the Russian defeat.[93] However, Joffre remembered the war as a 'shining confirmation' of Langlois's views.[94] Foch though the same about the Napoelonic principles and his own work: 'In strategy as well as in tactics one attacks.' No revolution in industry has altered the fundamental principles of war.[95] 'Firepower does not weaken the offensive,' wrote General Bazaine-Hayter, commander of the 13th Corps in 1906. 'Never forget that a defensive battle will seldom bring victory. However powerful weapons become, the victory will go to the offensive which stimulates moral forces, disconcerts the enemy and deprives him of his freedom of action.'[96] Indeed, the war in Manchuria was soon followed by an entirely new reaction and line of interpretation.[97] If in the first half of the 1900s, the challenge to the prevailing doctrine was coming from the proponents of fire-power, in the second half of the decade, this was overshadowed by the growth of an even greater challenge from the other end of the spectrum. Coinciding with Bonnal's retirement from the army, the operational and strategic teachings of which he was the chief author were beginning to come under attack as equivocal and, in practice, defensive-minded.

Even in its heyday Bonnal's scheme of active and aggressive defence changing into the counter-offensive—the so-called defensive-offensive—did not win universal approval from his friends and colleagues. Georges Gilbert, for one, had called from the 1880s for the revival of the *furia française*, in line with his more comprehensive vision of French national regeneration. Much more critical was Lucian Cardot. At the same time as he revealed Clausewitz to the French, he propagated the ideas of the Russian general Mikhail

[92] See Snyder, *The Ideology of the Offensive*, 79–81.

[93] F. de Négrier, *Lessons of the Russo-Japanese War* (London, 1906; first publ. in the *Revue des deux mondes*, 15 Jan. 1906), esp. 71, 54–5.

[94] Joffre, *Memoirs*, 28.

[95] Foch, *De la conduite de la guerre* (2nd. edn.; Paris, 1909), ix–x.

[96] Cited by Porch, *The Road to the Marne*, 226.

[97] Snyder, *The Ideology of the Offensive*, 80–1.

Ivanovich Dragomirov, also an admirer of Clausewitz and very popular with the French from the mid-1880s.[98] One of the few Russian military theoreticians with a European reputation and one-time head of the Russian general-staff academy, Dragomirov was the leader of the so-called nationalist school of strategists in Russia. In the tradition of Suvorov, he advocated mass bayonet-charges in deep column, which would fully bring out the sweep of superior morale which carried all before it.[99] In the guise of an imaginary Russian officer, Loukiane Carlovitch, 'the Cossack from Kouban', Cardot satirized contemporary French military thinking. He criticized the 'antithesis in vogue: the defensive-offensive' as absurd, illusive, and chimeric, attractive in theory but impossible in practice.[100] He argued that the initial defensive posture was most harmful to morale and left the initiative to the enemy and to the tyranny of circumstances. It evoked the shadow of 1870.[101] He mocked the fuss around the new firearms and, as a retired general after the wars in South Africa and Manchuria, swore allegiance to Dragomirov and scorned the new, 'modern style', school of battle tactics.[102]

The publication of the second edition of Ardant du Picq's *Battle Studies* (1903) could not have come at a more opportune moment. The army and the country were then preoccupied by the very same problems that had preoccupied du Picq in the late 1860s. His acute studies of troop psychology, especially on a fire-ridden and highly lethal battlefield, again became very relevant, and his emphasis on group cohesion and morale excited interest and exercised great appeal. Bonnal and Langlois quoted him in support of their own long-held opinions concerning the paramount importance of morale.[103] More importantly, brilliant middle-rank officers who

[98] See M. I. Dragomirov, *Manuel pour la préparation des troupes au combat* (3 vols.; Paris, 1886–8); id., *Principes essentiels pour la conduite de la guerre: Clausewitz interprété par le Général Dragomiroff* (Paris, 1889).

[99] See Walter Pinter, 'Russian Military Thought: The Western Model and the shadow of Suvorov', in Paret (ed.), *Makers of Modern Strategy from Machiavelli to the Nuclear Age* (Princetown, NJ, 1986), 367. Dragomirov's rival in Russia was his successor as director of the general staff's academy, G. Antonowitsch Leer, a representative of the classical school: ibid. 367–8; H. A. Leer, *Positive Strategie* (Vienna, 1871), and the various other versions of this book.

[100] Loukiane Carlovitch [Cardot], *Éducation et instruction des troupes* (3 vols.; Paris, 1896–7), 144–7.

[101] Ibid. 147–8.

[102] Cardot, *Hérésies et apostasies militaires de notre temps* (Paris, 1908), *passim*.

[103] Bonnal, *Hautes études militaires*, 15; Langlois, *Lessons from Two Recent Wars*, 124, 140.

later became the 'Young Turks' in the French general staff, like Captain Frédéric Culmann and the famous Major de Grandmaison, were much impressed by him.[104] Like his, their interest was mainly moral and tactical, rather than strategic. As mentioned in the first chapter, although du Picq had had no offensive bias, the problems he addressed and his psychological teaching still served as one of the main sources of inspiration for their offensive doctrine.

Thus preference for the out-and-out offensive, previously held by men like Gilbert and Cardot, was now taken up by younger minds. This was reflected in two books written after the wars in South Africa and Manchuria by the prolific military writer Captain Frédéric Culmann of the French general staff. Culmann argued that, in view of the devastating effect of modern firearms, the greatest moral forces would be needed to make soldiers rise and advance to the attack. Only a doctrine of *offensive à outrance* was capable of instilling the necessary attitude in them. The defensive-offensive, he maintained, was inherently inhibiting and bound to end in pure defence.[105]

Major François-Jules-Louis Loyzeau de Grandmaison, one of Foch's favourite pupils during his professorship at the École de guerre,[106] came to similar conclusions. In a subtlely written book on infantry training (1906), prefaced by Langlois, his logic was the one we have already encountered. Starting from an assessment of the new developments in tactics, he recognized that the attacker would now have to make use of a variety of new measures. He would have to make full use of the ground for cover, would have to attack at night, advance in open formation and small groups, and rely on close artillery support.[107] In the end, however, and especially against a resolute and well-armed enemy, there was no escaping from the final head-on assault: 'This can only be done brutally, without concern for losses, without economy.'[108] In du Picq's spirit but with an offensive point, Grandmaison argued that

[104] For Frédéric Culmann, see, for example, *Tactique d'artillerie; Le Canon de tir rapide dans la bataille* (Paris, 1906), 6, 17, 21, 37, *et passim.*; Grandmaison cites no one in his *Dressage de l'infanterie en vue du combat offensif* (Paris, 1906), but du Picq's influence is very apparent.

[105] Culmann, *Deux tactiques en présence* (Paris, 1904), 23–8; for his *offensive à outrance*, a phrase more commonly used in post-, rather than pre-war works, see ibid. 291; also see id., *Étude sur les caractères généraux de la guerre d'extrême-orient* (Paris, 1909), cited by Snyder, *The Ideology of the Offensive*, 79–80.

[106] *Foch Talks*, 199.

[107] Grandmaison, *Dressage de l'infanterie*, 10–29.

[108] Ibid. 30–1.

all victorious armies, including the French at the beginning of the nineteenth century and the German in 1870, had always possessed this in common: 'the spirit of all-out offensive and *sans arrière-pensée*, animating equally both chiefs and soldiers'.[109] 'To win victory, it is necessary to instil fear in the enemy; when one is afraid one is defeated. The only means to instil fear in the enemy is to *attack* him resolutely without worrying who is the stronger.'[110] According to Grandmaison, following in du Picq's footsteps, the instinct of self-preservation and the feelings of danger and fatigue dominate troops' behaviour. In modern conditions, everyone is more or less left to himself in the terrible environment of the battlefield, and the result is demoralizing. Hence the paramount importance of leadership, group cohesion, and individual initiative, fostered in common training.[111] The essence of tactical training, argued Grandmaison, lies in familiarizing the spirit with the unbearable by continually repeating the same exercises.[112]

Similar ideas were gaining ground with the younger generation of French officers after Manchuria. According to the evidence of one general, Grandmaison told him as early as 1907: 'We are a group of young officers convinced of the justice of our ideas, of the superiority of our theories and our methods, and are resolved to make them prevail despite all opposition.'[113] In 1908 Grandmaison became the chief of the third (operations) bureau of the French general staff. He was a man of 'high intelligence, ardent temperament, generous character . . . a power of considerable proportions'.[114] The strong impression he left on people was most memorably exemplified in the two famous lectures he delivered in 1911 at the Centre of High Military Education. Opened that year, the centre was intended to supplement the École de guerre by providing a third-year training for the army's best staff-officers. In those lectures, Grandmaison criticized the prevailing defensive-offensive doctrine and its emphasis on security, advance action, and reconnaissance. He argued that the regulations of 1895 carried a double message, which, in practice, allowed for a defensive and

109 *Dressage de l'infanterie*, 68.

110 Ibid. 89.

111 Ibid. 33–4, 38–47.

112 Ibid. 59; also 123.

113 Cited by Cole, ' "Forward with the Bayonet" ', 222.

114 M.-E. Debeney, *La Guerre et les hommes* (Paris, 1937), 281; Joel A. Setzen, 'The Doctrine of the Offensive in the French Army on the Eve of World War I' (unpub. diss., University of Chicago, 1972), 81; also 81–108 for a good treatment of Grandmaison.

passive interpretation by commanders anxious to play safe.[115] Against the arguments of the proponents of fire-power, he posed a series of shrewd questions: Once contact was made, could an advancing force really extend its front to avoid a frontal attack and envelop its enemy? Furthermore, assuming that both sides were extending their fronts, where would this end? Finally, would not such an extension involve the risk of the enemy's counter-attacking to pierce through one's overstretched front, in a strategic Austerlitz-like manner?[116] Victory in war, he argued, depends on superior morale and brutal aggressiveness. The enemy must be attacked immediately, with all forces united. Reconnaissance forces, flank detachments, and reserves must be reduced to the essential and must not remain idle and out of action. The attacker imposes his will on the enemy and paralyses his forces. Hit suddenly from all directions, the defender thinks only of parrying the blows. Therefore, on the offensive, imprudence is the best security.[117]

French military thought was taking a decisive turn. From the mid-1880s, it had differed little from the mainstream of European military ideas, originating from Germany. Based on a similar reading of history and dominated by a similar view of the fundamentals of war and strategy, its ethos and concept of operation had been active and aggressive but only preferably offensive, depending mainly on the relative strengths of the opposing armies. The reaction of French military thinkers to the challenge of South Africa and Manchuria was also, on the whole, indistinguishable from the standard reaction in all European armies. It was only from the late 1900s that French military thought took a distinctively independent course of its own. Henceforth, we are dealing with a peculiarly French phenomenon.

One reason for this unique development was undoubtedly the growing realization in France that the country was hopelessly losing out in her material race with Germany.[118] After 1870 French hopes of revival and *revanche* had hinged on the hope, albeit remote, of building up French power and armed forces to something like parity with Germany. For years, approximate numerical

[115] Grandmaison, *Deux conférences, faites aux officiers de l'état-major de l'armée (février, 1911): La Notion de sûreté et l'engagement des grandes unités* (Paris, 1911), 2, 14–25. [116] Ibid. 3–5.

[117] See esp. ibid. 3, 11, 27–8, 36, 76.

[118] See the references in notes 4 and 6 above.

equality had in fact been maintained. From the mid-1870s and throughout the 1880s, both regular armies had reached the half-million mark, with the French slightly in the lead during much of that time. However, from the 1890s, Germany expanding population and army reform were giving her an unassailable advantage. During the 1890s, this adverse development was more than compensated, both materially and morally, by the Russo-French alliance. But after 1904 Russia was devastated, and on the Continent France stood alone against an increasingly menacing and powerful Germany. After the second Moroccan crisis, Germany's renewed attention to her army and intensified mobilization of manpower pushed the German figures to 760,000 in 1913 and 830,000 in 1914. Against this, already exhausting the full potential of her stagnant population, French numbers remained static.[119] As mentioned in the previous chapter, while in 1871 the German population had totalled 41 million in comparison with France's 36 million, it grew to 60 million in 1905 and to 68 million by 1914, as against France's 39–40 million.

Financially, the French position was only a little better. Owing to France's heavy defence-expenditure—the highest among all the Great Powers—her military estimates had slightly surpassed Germany's until well into the 1890s. However, by the coming of the twentieth century, it was Germany who was taking the lead, notwithstanding her simultaneously gigantic naval programme.[120] By virtue of her considerable financial strength France could for a time keep up the race, but German industry, growing at a colossal rate, was increasingly making it an unequal one. By 1914 Germany had 6,000 field guns to France's 3,800, and 4,500 machine-guns to the French 2,500. In heavy field-artillery she possessed an almost total monopoly. Furthermore, each German gun had 2,000 rounds, as opposed to 1,390 on the French side.[121] The emergence of the doctrine of the offensive after 1905 and its adoption by the army

[119] See Contamine, *La Revanche*, 39, 54, 62, 64, 81, 94, 108, 136, 142; J. Revol, *Histoire de l'armée française* (Paris, 1929), 203.

[120] A. J. P. Taylor, *The Struggle for Mastery in Europe* (Oxford, 1954), pp. xxvi–xxviii; Reichsarchiv, *Der Weltkrieg, 1914–1918: Kriegsrüstung und Kriegswirtschaft*, i. supp. 530. The contemporary French estimates of German military expenditure, cited by Porch, *The March to the Marne*, 227, are grossly inflated but still serve as an indication of French anxieties.

[121] Charles de Gaulle, *France and Her Army* (London, 1945), 89. See also Cole, ' "Forward with the Bayonet" ' 118–19, 129.

after 1911 closely paralleled the growing awareness in France of that country's material weakness *vis-à-vis* Germany.[122] The French flight to moral strength was only natural. Here again du Picq's emphasis on quality, as opposed to numbers, came at the right moment and was very readily accepted.

> We cannot . . . fight Germany nowadays with equal numbers [wrote Langlois in 1903]. Are we therefore to think that our cause is irremediably the weaker for this reason? I do not agree with this. The belief in the all power of numbers is demoralising, it has always been wrong, and it is more so now than ever. Individual training, military education and above all morale are the dominant factor in the fight.[123]

In 1907, after retiring from the army and being elected as senator of the Republic and member of the Academie française, Langlois continued to argue in the same vein. Having assessed the German material advantage, he proceeded on a happier note: 'But if we compare the value of the personnel, the individual values, we have an incontestable advantage over our neighbours'; 'Germany will always have the advantage of us in numbers . . . but we can compensate for that advantage by utilizing the precious qualities of race that are peculiar to us.'[124] Parliamentary deputy and ex-serviceman Adolphe Messimy expressed a similar opinion in 1908: 'We want an army which compensates numerical weakness with military quality.'[125] Serving as Minister of War during two crucial periods, in 1911 and 1914, he had ample opportunity to advance his views. 'Neither numbers nor miraculous machines will determine victory,' he wrote in 1913; 'this will go to soldiers with valour and "quality"—and by this I mean superior physical and moral endurance, offensive strength.'[126]

The army was losing out not only against the foreign threat but also on the domestic scene. At the outset of the twentieth century it was subjected to a devastating political onslaught. The morale of the officer corps plummeted. On the eve of the First World War, when it was trying to rebuild its shaken morale, the vitalizing doctrine of the offensive appeared as a useful tool.

[122] For a thorough analysis and comparison of the ominous demographic and economic trends, see, for example, Culmann, *Deux tactiques*, 297–328.

[123] Langlois, *Lessons from Two Recent Wars*, 141–2.

[124] Langlois, 'Notre situation militaire', *Revue des deux mondes*, (15 Oct. 1907), 780, 793; quoted by Bowditch, 'Rationalization of Weakness', in Earle (ed.), *Modern France*, 39.

[125] Quoted by Porch, *The March to the Marne*, 227.

[126] Ibid.

Perhaps more than any other country in Europe, France was divided by politics, indeed, over the very character of the regime itself. Born with the collapse of the Second Empire and the confusion of defeat, it took some time before it became clear that the Third Republic had come to stay. The so-called Moderate Republicans who had come to power in 1879 took action to make the republic truly and irreversibly republican. They thoroughly purged the administrative, judicial, and educational systems of conservative and clerical presence and influences. However, until the occurrence of the Dreyfus Affair in the mid-1890s, relations between the republic and the army were co-operative and correct, even if not entirely free from ambiguity. Attracting many sons of the families of nobles and notables, whose traditional careers in the civil service had been blocked, the officer corps in general may have inclined toward the Right. But the army as a body remained strictly aloof from politics, whereas the republic, in turn, left the army untouched as the focus and symbol of the nation's patriotic consensus.

The one point where party politics and army affairs touched each other was on the issue of conscription. Equal service for all and opposition to the law of 1872 had long been central to the Republican programme. In 1889, after a long process of legislation, a law on three-year service was finally approved by the National Assembly. In practice, it made no radical change. For budgetary reasons the soldiers of the first portion had already been serving for only four years or less, a period which had been further interrupted by long furloughs. In addition, budgetary constraints forced the deputies to swallow the retention of the second portion of conscripts, for the army could not use three full annual classes without being considerably expanded. Social and educational exemptions were also retained in somewhat amended forms. The purpose and significance of the law was thus principally political and declarative. Yet it was precisely for this reason that the attitude of the army towards it tended to be negative. As in Germany, the military objections were compounded by deep aversion and distrust of what was viewed by the soldiers as irresponsible party-political meddling in a vital business of defence.[127]

[127] For the law of 1889 see esp. Monteilhet, *Les Institutions militaires*, 220–35; Ralston, *The Army of the Republic*, 96–115.

All this, however, did little to interrupt the cordial relations between the republic and the army, whose golden age came to an end only with the eruption of the Dreyfus Affair. The army tried to block the efforts to clear the name of the Jewish general-staff officer, whose conviction for espionage for Germany turned out to be based on forged material. This fuelled the worst political crisis in the history of the Third Republic. In the name of justice as against the honour of the army, the differences in French politics between Left and Right surfaced and divided French society into two antagonistic camps. The polarization of the political scene resulted in a shift in government from centre to centre-left. From 1898 the Moderate Republicans relied for support on a left-wing block. From 1902 the government became dominated by the so-called Radical Democrats. The Radicals' political aim was to smash for good what they considered the anti-republican camp, exposed in the Dreyfus Affair. The army, which had previously been spared political persecution but which was now identified with the forces of reaction, was to be thoroughly and forcibly republicanized.

The Radicals' campaign rested on the assumption that the problem with the army was socially and politically rooted. They believed that the influx of aristocrats into the army after 1871 had changed the traditionally rather humble composition of the French officer-corps, and that the network of Jesuit high schools contributed out of all proportion to the entrance lists of the most prestigious officer-schools.[128] Nothing less than root treatment was therefore deemed necessary, and General Louis André, Minister of War from 1900 to 1904 and a zealous republican, attempted such treatment in the most thorough and ruthless manner. The army promotion-committees were abolished, and authority over promotions was transferred to the ministry. The minister and his assistants drew up the promotion lists, paying special attention to the candidates' political opinions and religious persuasions. Officers possessing republican sympathies were rapidly promoted. Officers known for right-wing or Catholic opinions or backgrounds were removed

[128] The validity of this picture is debated and the figures are open to conflicting interpretations. The accepted view is best summarized in Girardet, *La Société militaire*, esp. 186, 195–6; François Bédarida, 'L'Armée et la république: Les Opinions des officiers français en 1876–78', *Revue Historique* (1964), 119–64. That view has been challenged as exaggerated in all respects by Porch, *The March to the Marne*, 17–22.

from positions of importance and their advancement was delayed. To obtain the neccessary information, the ministry did not hesitate to employ not only the provincial prefects but also the network of Masonic lodges. The military schools were purged and liberalized. Candidates could now enrol in the cadet schools only after having served first for one year in the ranks. More officers were commissioned directly from among the NCOs. Caste practices and privileges among the officer corps were abolished. The army high command was lowered in stature and placed in closer subordination to the ministry.[129]

The effect of the political onslaught on the morale of the officer corps was devastating. The army was already losing much of the popularity it had enjoyed in the decades after the war of 1870–1. The memory of defeat, and desire for revenge were fading. Middle-class individualism and socialist pacifism and anti-militarism combined from the mid-1890s in mutual distaste for the army and army life.[130] The employment of the army in the suppression of ecclesiastical establishments and workers' strikes contributed to the collapse of morale.[131] The results were not slow to appear. The number of applicants to Saint-Cyr dropped from 1,920 in 1897 to 982 in 1907. Almost half of the artillery officers who graduated from the Ecole polytechnique between 1905 and 1907 had resigned from the army by 1910.[132] Standards, as recorded especially in the professional arms and at the École de guerre, were falling sharply.[133]

The political persecution of the army coincided with, and accelerated, the parliamentary initiative to enact a law introducing a two-year service. The shortening in Germany in 1893 of the term of service for infantry to two years gave full legitimacy to French republican and egalitarian aspirations and made a similar development in France only a matter of time. Public debate started in the mid-1890s, and legislation was completed in 1905. All social and educational exemptions were abolished. Under the law of 1889 more than a third of each annual class had escaped conscription

[129] See Ralston, *The Army of the Republic*, 260–301; and, in a critical vein, Porch, *The March to the Marne*, 73–104.

[130] Girardet, *La Société militaire*, 213–35.

[131] See Ralston, *The Army of the Republic*, 280–6; Porch, *The March to the Marne*, 105–33.

[132] Girardet, *La Société militaire*, 274.

[133] Porch, *The March to the Marne*, 84–5.

altogether and only three-fifths had served the full three years.[134] Under the new law all young Frenchmen were made to serve the equal term of two years. From 1905 France put under the colours no less than 83 per cent of each annual class, leaving only the physically unfit out of the army. As in 1889, the motivation for the law was predominantly political, but this time the practical consequences were none the less considerable. More exhaustive conscription for a shorter term of active service implied that, while the size of the regular army was slightly reduced, France was going to have many more trained men in case of war. It also followed that the regular army was now regarded less as a professional fighting-force of seasoned soldiers and more as a training-school for the reserves.

Harassed as it was during and after the Dreyfus Affair, the army could only see the Two Years Law as a further blow in the political campaign launched against it. Already in 1895, when the idea of the change was first brought before the Conseil supérieur de la guerre, it was totally rejected by the council. Furthermore, this time, the law found virtually no support in the army as a whole.[135] The arguments had not changed much from the 1870s and 1880s. Again, the opponents of the law argued that the short period of service did not suffice to make soldiers out of civilians. What was perhaps possible with the docile German conscript living in a hierarchic society was impossible with the indisciplined and egalitarian French. Again, they pointed out that the shorter period of service would worsen the army's already acute problem of persuading a sufficient number of old-timers to re-enlist as NCOs. Furthermore, while pressure was put on the army to rely more heavily on the reserves, many officers were convinced that the terrible effect of modern firearms would require even higher morale, tactical proficiency, and cohesion in the next war. Their attitude was somewhat reminiscent of the response of Louis Napoleon's officers to the ill-organized reserve-programme imposed on them before 1870. Langlois cited Ardant du Picq in praising the superior qualities of the smaller and highly trained army.[136]

Indeed, here as well du Picq's work suddenly became most

[134] Ralston, *The Army of the Republic*, 302–3.

[135] Ibid. 391. See, for example, Derrécagaix, *La Guerre et l'armée*; and, in support of the law, Émile Manceau (Mayer), *Nos institutions militaires* (Paris, 1901).

[136] Langlois, *Lessons from Two Recent Wars*, 140–1.

relevant. It is certainly no coincidence that the editor of the new comprehensive edition of *Battle Studies* (1903), who wrote the exalting introduction and solicited the biographical details from du Picq's family, was none other than Ernest Judet, the anti-Dreyfusite journalist and editor of the popular and aggressive right-wing *Le Petit Journal*. While the army came under heavy pressure to open up to society, and while the government was forcing it to accept the reduction of military service to two years, men like Judet were delighted by du Picq's profound scepticism of armed hordes, and by his assertion that the officer corps had to be by nature aristocratic.[137] The Two Years Law and the new intense political involvement radicalized positions and brought the question down to fundamentals: where did the main weight of French defence lie, with the regular army or with the whole nation-in-arms?

In the aftermath of the Dreyfus Affair and up until the 1920s and 1930s, this question became overcharged with politics and emerged as one of the main points of contention between Right and Left in France. Spilling over from the political scene, it also grew to dominate the historical profession itself; in fact, historians of French military affairs have written about little else. Their perspectives and attitudes reflected and echoed the political overtones and rhetoric, particularly those of the Left, to which many of these historians belonged. The army's preference for the regulars and its distrust of the reservists have been explained principally in non-military terms as a function of its political and social conservatism.[138] Furthermore, in the critical post-war years, the army's distrust of the reserves was added to the catalogue of blunders and examples of military thick-headedness that occurred in the First World War. In the process, however, the essence and complexity of the military problem itself, as seen at the time, was all but ignored.[139] Since the growth of the doctrine of the offensive has been linked to the French army's preference for the regulars, this

[137] *Battle Studies*, 22–3.

[138] See esp. the left-wing historians Monteilhet (1926) and Michon (1935), and also Girardet (1953), Challener (1955) and Ralston (1967). Snyder (1984) argues an organizational rather than political and social bias on the part of the army. Porch (1981) provides an important, if at times over-zealous, corrective to the historians of the nation-in-arms school.

[139] The exceptions are Porch, *The March to the Marne*, which goes a long way in this direction, and Jean-Charles Jauffret, 'L'Organisation de la réserve à l'époque de la revanche, 1871–1914', *Revue Historique des Armées* (1989), 27–37.

problem is worth looking into at some length. Armies struggled with the parameters of this problem not only in France but all over Europe, including in Germany itself.

The problem of the reserves was predominantly one of effective organization and cadres. As professional soldiers in all countries often pointed out, multitudes of trained reservists did not in themselves constitute a fighting force. In 1870–1 the Prussian solution had been simple. The active units had been kept on half strength in peacetime and, on mobilization, had been swollen with reservists, who doubled the strength of each company. This, however, had been possible only as long as the regulars and the reservists encompassed roughly the same number of annual classes—three in active service and four in the reserve. The Landwehr, encompassing five more annual classes, had been formed in separate units and assigned to second-line duties. By the late 1870s, however, the number of reservists grew beyond the capacity of the active units to absorb them, especially as the term of service in the reserve was extended to four and a half years. The active units still absorbed about two-thirds of the reservists, but a new form of organization had to be found for the excess, and none could be as satisfactory as the old system. The German solution was the creation of separate reserve divisions in the ratio of one reserve division to each active corps. But this was only the beginning of the process.

From 1893 the term of active service for infantry in Germany was cut to two years, while the number of classes serving in the reserve was correspondingly raised to five. The active units could now absorb only a minority of the reservists. In order to economize on costly overheads, the German army avoided the creation of more reserve formations and tried a different approach. It created a fourth, cadre, demi-battalion in each active regiment. This was considered unsatisfactory, however, and in 1898 the army retracted and incorporated the reservists from the fourth battalion in new, separate reserve-divisions. As their number grew, the reserve divisions were later formed into reserve corps. None the less, because of the heavy expenditure on armaments and professional cadres which would have been required in order to bring these formations up to full combat-effectiveness, they remained far inferior to their active counterparts and were intended primarily for secondary missions. As we saw in the previous chapter, only the pressure of Germany's international and strategic position in the decade before the war induced Schlieffen and his successors to assign the reserve formations to first-line duties. Even more importantly, Schlieffen's paper schemes could only materialize when the Reichstag was moved to vote the huge sums needed for the expansion and upgrading of the reserve formations.[140]

The French army experienced the same problems and experimented with similar solutions. Contrary to the popular impression, however, it went ahead of its German rival in using reservists for active field-service during much of the period concerned. The manpower trauma of 1870–1 had its effect. The army laws of the 1870s copied the various German reserve-categories in a slightly modified form. All reservists up to the age of 30 (33 from 1892) were assigned to the reserve, which was the equivalent of the German reserve plus Landwehr. As in Germany, large numbers of reservists were absorbed into the active units, doubling the size of the regular army on mobilization. However, since the mean active term of service of slightly over three years was matched, on average, by six classes of reservists, many reservists had to be directed to special fourth battalions created in each active regiment by the cadre law of 1875. Furthermore, the older classes of reservists between the ages of 30 and 35 were also used and formed into separate territorial divisions. They were thus assigned a much more active role than their comparable German Landsturm, which was not intended for field service. The French Plan 3 (1882), for example, deployed two territorial armies at the rear of the five line-armies, which were composed of the regular troops and their reserves.[141] Later plans during the 1880s went even further in joining the territorial divisions and troops more closely to the active corps.[142] The French were in fact using fourteen annual classes for active field-service, as against the German's twelve.

In 1888, when the Germans created the Landwehr's second portion, thus assigning their own older classes of reservists a somewhat more active role, the French went a step further. Actively encouraged by the able civilian Minister of War Freycinet, the

[140] See, against the general drift of his argument, Snyder, *The Ideology of the Offensive*, 228, n. 109.

[141] Marchand, *Plans de concentration*, 28; État-Major de l'Armeé, *Les Armées françaises*, I, i. 6–7.

[142] Marchand, *Plans de concentration*, 53, 61, 83, 204–5; État-Major de l'Armée; *Les Armées françaises*, 8–18.

architect of the armies of national defence in 1870–1, the Conseil supérieur de la guerre adopted a grandiose scheme whereby sixteen reserve corps, composed of mixed regiments of reservists and territorials, were to be formed to supplement the twenty active corps.[143] The scheme, however, was probably too ambitious to be realized. The chorus of historians who have denounced the army's conservatism in abandoning the scheme have lost sight of the general European perspective and have taken all too lightly the enormity of the project. It is worth remembering that the German army reached something like the above-mentioned strength and composition only on the eve of the war and after huge investments. The arguments of the generals that the reserve formations would be worthless without adequate cadres and artillery and that such cadres and artillery were simply not available, should not be dismissed as mere excuses. The proposed scheme was soon abandoned for more practical arrangements. Between 1890 and 1895 the number of reserve corps was reduced to five, while each active corps received a third reserve-division.[144] In 1897 the army retreated from the system of grand reserve-formations and reverted to the fourth battalion in each active regiment, in addition to separate reserve-divisions.[145] These reserve divisions were concentrated in reserve groups and placed in the second line, close to the front.

Scepticism regarding the combat-worth of the reserve units (as opposed to the reservists incorporated in, and doubling the strength of, the active units—a distinction that is often forgotten) was particularly notable among the proponents of morale and active and aggressive conduct in the late 1880s and 1890s. They doubted that the reserve formations were adapted to this mode of warfare. Georges Gilbert, for example, argued that, lacking artillery and cohesion, Freycinet's reserve-formations would be of little value.[146] In 1893 the army attempted to stiffen the reserve units by creating a small cadre of regular officers in each regiment. However, critics argued that these posts were filled with the army's less-than-best officers and that the nature of the job allowed them to spend their

[143] État Major de l'Armée, *Les Armées françaises*, 18–19.

[144] Ibid. 20, 25.

[145] Ibid. 27; Marchand, *Plans de concentration*, 296–7.

[146] See Georges Gilbert's collection of essays, *Lois et institutions militaires* (Paris, 1895), 173–448; Contamine, *La Revanche*, 71–2.

time in total idleness.[147] Starting from the Bonnal-inspired Plan 14 (1898), the reserve units were returned primarily to second-line or garrison duties, which was still no different from the role envisaged by the Germans for their own comparable reserve and Landwehr formations. Only in the decade before the war, and only to any great extent after 1911, did the basic features of this picture change. While the Germans were moving towards assigning their reserve formations to a more active role, the Two Years Law and subsequent political contentions were radicalizing positions in France regarding the French reserves.

The Two Years Law created a multitude of trained reservists and coincided with the mounting pressure on the army to open up to civil society. The army was expected to rely more heavily on the reservists and invest greater efforts in their training. However, left-wing critics accused the army of sabotaging the law. For example, it was argued that, even after the enactment of the law, the army, which had been claiming that two years was too short a period for the training of conscripts, was in fact wasting an alarming part of conscripts' time on various non-combat jobs. Many of these jobs took the form of traditional personal services for the officers, which the army did nothing to abolish.[148] The reservists' training also left much to be desired.[149] The seemingly vicious circle of the army's distrust and neglect and the reservists' poor performance could probably not be reduced to either component. The fact remains, however, that many reservists avoided training, and that during training discipline was often poor and performance unimpressive.[150] Whereas Germany, where the army enjoyed the highest social esteem, had no difficulty in creating a large and proud body of reserve officers, in France reserve officers were in acutely short supply because of unwillingness to volunteer.[151] Indeed, returning to the fundamental problem of cadres, a comparison with Germany

[147] Monteilhet, *Les Institutions militaires*, 238; Porch, *The March to the Marne*, 26.

[148] Monteilhet, *Les Institutions militaires*, 315; Ralston, *The Army of the Republic*, 313; Porch, *The March to the Marne*, 195; Gerd Krumeich, *Armament and Politics in France on the Eve of the First World War: The Introduction of the Three Years Conscription* (London, 1984), 105–6.

[149] Monteilhet, *Les Institutions militaires*, 253; Porch, *The March to the Marne*, 204–5; Gorce, *The French Army*, 56–7.

[150] In 1907, for example, 36 per cent of the reservists called for training did not respond to the call; Jauffret, 'L'Organisation de la réserve', 35.

[151] Ibid., 33; Porch, *The March to the Marne*, 204–6.

speaks for itself. In 1902 Germany possessed some 75,000 to 80,000 NCOs to France's 22,000.[152] The extensive German army laws of 1911, 1912, and 1913 gave the German army 112,000 NCOs, as against 48,000 in its French rival. There were 215 career NCOs in a German infantry regiment as opposed to only 95 in its French counterpart.[153]

There was nothing in these deficiencies that several weeks or months of war-experience could not remedy. While some French reserve units may have performed poorly in the opening days of the First World War,[154] they quickly played a decisive role and, with the prolonging of the war, all distinctions between regulars and reservists disappeared completely. Yet the French army, like all armies, expected a short and decisive war, in which only battle-ready troops could participate effectively. It has been too easily forgotten that reserve formations had never been employed in the first line before the First World War, not even in 1870–1, as is widely assumed. They were a novelty and a great unknown factor. Nobody knew or could know exactly if and how they would perform. None other than Michel, whose famous plan for the amalgamation of reserve and regular units is discussed below, asked in 1911: 'These Reserve divisions exist on paper only, but who can guarantee their solidity?'[155] Michel, it is worth bearing in mind, had been the Inspector of Reserve Regiments in 1907–8 and one of their most ardent supporters. His own answer to his question was negative, and his scheme in fact called for the suppression of all reserve formations.[156] This fact has been ignored by modern historians. Only after two protracted total world wars could the army's pre-war distrust of the reserve units be dispelled and the short-war illusion ridiculed.

From 1905 intelligence regarding German intentions was changing French planning, while the effect of the Two Years Law was

[152] French parliamentary deliberations, cited in Ralston, *The Army of the Republic*, 301; cf. Reichsarchiv, *Der Weltkrieg*, i. supp. 485.

[153] Cited in Porch, *The March to the Marne*, 194; figures in the German sources are similar except that the 215 career NCOs were about 80 per cent and not all of the NCOs in a German infantry regiment: Reichsarchiv, *Der Weltkrieg*, 509, 512. See Porch, *The March to the Marne*, 196–200, for a thorough analysis of the French NCOs problem; also Setzen 'The Doctrine of the Offensive', 54–6.

[154] Porch, *The March to the Marne*, 211.

[155] État-Major de l'Armée, *Les Armées françaises*, I. i, ann., pp. 11, 8, 13; see Porch, *The March to the Marne*, 211, for basically the same argument as mine.

[156] État-Major de l'Armée, *Les Armées françaises*, I. i. ann., pp. 8, 12–13.

changing their reserves' organization. In 1904 French intelligence got hold of accurate information suggesting that the Germans planned a very strong outflanking movement through Belgium and Luxemburg, using reserve formations in an active role. Further intelligence reports supported this information but neither made clear that the German move would extend beyond the Meuse and Sambre in a deep north-westerly sweep, nor ruled out a German attack in Lorraine. In response, the French forces' centre of gravity was moved northward in a series of gradual adjustments. Plan 15 *bis* (1907) created a new army to the north of Verdun. Plan 16 (1909) supported this army by positioning behind it a new strategic 'army of manœuvre' as well as two, instead of one, groups of reserve divisions. All were ready to counter-attack in the direction of the Ardennes.[157] Plan 16 also incorporated the increasing number of reservists made available by the law of 1905. The fourth battalions were removed and concentrated in reserve brigades, which were created in most corps. The number of reserve divisions was increased by the creation of a reserve division in each corps-region. The plan thus raised the number of reserve battalions deployed from 320 to 463, in addition to the 108 battalions in the nine territorial divisions.[158]

More indications regarding the direction and scale of the German attack continued to accumulate.[159] By 1911 General Wilson, director of military operations in the British War Office, was reported to have estimated that the German offensive in the west would make extensive use of reserve divisions and extend as far as Lille.[160] On the basis of a similar assessment, General Michel, the new vice-president of the Conseil supérieur de la guerre and

[157] Marchand, *Plans de concentration*, 156–81; *Les Armées françaises*, 31–7; Williamson, *The Politics of Grand Strategy*, 53–5, 117–24; Jan Karl Tanenbaum, 'French Estimates of Germany's Operational War Plans', in Ernest R. May (ed.), *Knowing One's Enemies: Intelligence Assessment before the Two World Wars* (Princeton, NJ, 1984), 150–171; Cole, ' "Forward with the Bayonet" ', 296–300; Snyder, *The Ideology of the Offensive*, 81–90.

[158] État-Major de l'Armée, *Les Armées françaises*, I, i. 34–5; Contamine, *La Revanche*, 116–17.

[159] See Tanenbaum, 'French Estimates', in May (ed.), *Knowing One's Enemy*, 156–170; Snyder, *The Ideology of the Offensive*, 87–90.

[160] Tanenbaum, 'French Estimates', in May (ed.), *Knowing One's Enemy*, 159; Snyder, *The Ideology of the Offensive*, 88; État-Major de l'Armée, *Les Armées françaises*, 37. Gamelin's claim in 1954 that Foch held the same opinion as Wilson, his close friend, finds no support in any other source, not even in Foch's own memoirs; Gamelin, *Manœuvre et victoire de la Marne*, 42.

generalissimo designate in the event of war, felt that Plan 16 was inadequate. He worked out a radically new war-plan, which stretched the French forces from the Swiss border to the North Sea and shifted the main French effort to the Belgian sector. The French forces on the Franco-German frontier were to be reduced to no more than three corps, with a further three arriving in a second wave. No less than eleven corps were to be deployed along the Belgian frontier, while another three concentrated in reserve around Paris. The forces covering the German frontier and the Ardennes were to adopt a defensive stance. The main French effort was to take place on the extreme left and counter-attack the right flank of the German main thrust on the Belgian plains. As with the Germans, the doubling of the French front length necessitated the massive incorporation of reserve units in the first line. To accomplish this, Michel proposed another radical scheme, whereby the active and reserve units were to be totally amalgamated. All active and reserve regiments were to be coupled in new demi-brigades. Thus the strength of each corps was to be almost doubled, to forty-eight battalions.[161]

It is well known that Michel's strategic scheme anticipated to a remarkable extent the form that the French deployment ultimately assumed, after great upheavals, in the opening campaign of 1914. But both his schemes were radical enough to be received with distrust by his colleagues. Many practical objections were raised. There were serious question-marks regarding the soundness of his scheme for the reserves. The amalgamation of the active and reserve troops would also mean French mobilization would lag three days behind that of the Germans. Finally, what if the Germans did not cross the Meuse and Sambre, or carried out their main offensive in Lorraine after all? Especially in the latter case, most of the French army would have been deployed out of reach. The benefit of hindsight on 1914 must not mislead; any French plan had to provide for both contingencies.[162] However, the factor that tipped

[161] État-Major de l'Armée, *Les Armées françaises*, I, i. 38; and ann., pp. 7–17; Percin, *Les Erreurs du haut commandement*, 39–49.

[162] See previous note and also the general-staff study, cited in Tanenbaum, 'French Estimates', in May (ed.), *Knowing One's Enemy*, 161–2, and Snyder, *The Ideology of the Offensive*, 93–4. Joffre's claim in his *Memoirs*, 17–18, that Michel's plan would have exposed France completely if the German attack were to come from Lorraine, was far less apologetic than it has usually been presented as being. Also see his considerations regarding Plan 17, ibid. 78–9.

the scale against Michel's schemes and brought his downfall was not military but political and related to a deeper change in the French national mood. Michel was one of the republican generals promoted rapidly under the Radical government. He had little authority over his colleagues. Unfortunately for him, by 1911 the Radical agenda had exhausted itself and new concerns were emerging. In the wake of the Agadir crisis, the growing German threat prompted the so-called 'nationalist revival' in France. French politics reverted from the centre-left to the centre-right. The government was determined to bolster national defence by working more closely with the army. In effect, Michel was forced to go by the new Minister of War, Messimy, even before his scheme was totally rejected by his colleagues in the Conseil supérieur de la guerre.[163]

After two decades of preoccupation with domestic issues, the nationalist revival marked a shift in French public concerns. The international tensions which had been building up in the successive crises after 1905 focused attention on the foreign threat and the prospect of war. Nationalist feelings surged. Patriotism was back in fashion.[164] Ministers of War Messimy and Millerand revoked many of the steps taken by André.[165] The high command was reorganized and a new post created, Chief of the Army General Staff, which combined the previously separate positions of generalissimo and chief of staff. In 1912 a new cadre law for the infantry strengthened the regular staff- and command-element in the reserve regiments.[166] The most controversial measure, however, came in response to the German army laws of 1911, 1912, and 1913, which gave the German regular army a two-to-one superiority over its French rival. To counter this huge increase, the French government in 1913 saw no choice but to lengthen again the term of active service to three years.

In the fierce parliamentary debate which developed over the measure, delegates from the Left pointed out its dubious value, and historians followed in indicating the ulterior motives of both the

[163] For the famous incident, see also Adolphe-Marie Messimy, *Mes souvenirs* (Paris, 1937), 74–6.

[164] The standard work is Eugen Weber, *The Nationalist Revival in France, 1905–1914* (Berkeley, Calif., 1959).

[165] See Porch, *The March to the Marne*, 169–90.

[166] Ibid. 191–2.

ruling middle-class parties and the army.[167] However, while the army never liked the Two Years Law, there is little reason to doubt that the measure was a natural and genuine, if desperate, response to the growing German preponderance.[168] The law raised the strength of the standing army by keeping a third annual class with the colours. It could not, however, raise France's total war-establishment to the level achieved by the now-extensive exploitation of the much larger German age-classes. The army defended the logic of the law by inflating the danger of a German *attaque brusquée*, which would be carried out by the German regular army before mobilization and would overrun the inferior French frontier forces. In truth, however, it was much more concerned with ensuring its own ability to take up offensive operations as early as possible.[169] Left-wing critics argued that the law was a point-blank attempt to reassert the position of the regulars and the professional army at the expense of the reservists and the idea of the nation-in-arms. But a more sympathetic assessment concludes that the authors of the law believed it would strengthen the whole military system, of both regulars and reserves.[170] Adopted in 1913, Plan 17 incorporated 401 reserve battalions, somewhat less than Plan 16, but they were better staffed and better organized.[171]

The Left's charges assume their full significance only in the context of the socialists' fundamental position regarding the problem of national defence, not only in France but everywhere in Europe. From the middle of the nineteenth century, this consisted in the total rejection of both the institution of standing armies and of aggressive wars. For the socialists, the citizen militia on the Swiss model, intended for pure national defence, was the only legitimate form of military establishment. The great socialist leader Jean

[167] Monteilhet, *Les Institutions militaires*, 267–302; Michon, *La Préparation à la guerre, passim*. A good summary and refutation of the domestic interpretations based on ulterior motives, can be found in Krumeich's meticulous *Armament and Politics in France*, 5–20, which concludes that the principal motive for the law was after all military.

[168] Ralston, *The Army of the Republic*, pp. 353–6.

[169] Krumeich, *Armament and Politics in France* 17 *et passim*.

[170] See Porch, *The March to the Marne*, 191 *et passim*.; also Joffre, *Memoirs*, ii. app. 1, pp. 592–5.

[171] Instead of 22 reserve divisions, each consisting of 18 battalions, there were now 25 divisions of 12 battalions each. The six-battalion strong reserve brigades in the active corps were replaced by 2 regiments of 2 battalions each: État-Major de l'Armée, *Armées françaises*, 47–8, 55; Contamine, *La Revanche*, 141.

Jaurès was only elaborating on these ideas when, in the course of the parliamentary debate, he presented the comprehensive and systematic scheme he had developed in his book, *L'Armée nouvelle* (first publ. 1910). Taking issue with the teachings of Gilbert, Langlois, and Bonnal, he reminded the professors of the staff college that Clausewitz had argued that the defence was stronger than the attack, and pointed out that the popular nature of the Revolutionary armies was the true source of Napoleon's successes. His critics, who replied that Frenchmen did not quite resemble the Swiss and that France was not a little mountain-fortress but a Great Power, who needed an army comparable to that of the Germans to back up her European and global interests,[172] only demonstrated the fundamental nature of the dispute. The argument was not technical. What Jaurès had in mind was a different sort of France and a different sort of international system.

The nationalist revival worked to enhance the army's morale in both a direct and an indirect way. In the first place, the desire for moral and spiritual regeneration was one of its most characteristic features. Secondly, by resuming positive political co-operation with the army, it helped the army recover from the blows which it had suffered since the Dreyfus Affair and which had brought its morale to the lowest depth. The connection between this recovery and the acceptance of the doctrine of the offensive after 1911 has been indicated by historians. Joffre, the new head of the French army, consciously encouraged the young enthusiasts for the offensive and the force of morale in the general staff, as a means to restore the army's badly shaken sense of purpose and self-confidence.[173]

By alleviating the external pressures on the army, the nationalist revival also helped the army ward off what it regarded as unsound and dangerous pressures to incorporate reserve units in a full first-line role. Here again the doctrine of the offensive intervened favourably. The army's distrust of the reserves was reinforced by the doctrine of the offensive, while the doctrine of the offensive also possessed the merit of helping to ward off the pressures concerning the reserves. The reserves were simply not up to that type of warfare which allegedly necessitated great tactical skill and

[172] Porch, *The March to the Marne*, 210; Ralston, *The Army of the Republic*, 348–9, 352.

[173] Porch, *The March to the Marne*, 217–18, 223–4; Cole, ' "Forward with the Bayonet" ', 55, 225–6, 235; Snyder, *The Ideology of the Offensive*, 95.

cohesion. Indeed, the army's persistent scepticism in regard to indications that the Germans were planning a deep sweep through Belgium using reserve formations in the front line has also been explained by the emergence of a closed entrenched bias, rooted in political or organizational preference. Had evidence of a massive German attack on the Belgian plains been believed, this would have required the extension of the French front and the use of reserve formations in the first line.[174]

There is undoubtedly some truth in this explanation for French thinking and behaviour. It ought not be pushed too far, however. The correlation in the army between either political conservativism or organizational resistance to change on the one hand and enthusiasm for the offensive on the other is far from being clear-cut. Politically, it has long been pointed out that good republican generals like Galliéni and Joffre himself were distrustful of the reserves and, together with the republican Sarrail, advocated the offensive. At the same time, a right-winger like Négrier emphasized the strength of modern defence and was one of the few who in 1904 took the possibility of a German invasion through Belgium very seriously. Another right-winger like Grouard advocated both the defence and the incorporation of the reserve units in the first line.[175] Organizational traditionalism fares no better. As it happened, Négrier was the most outspoken opponent of the reserves at the time of the deliberations on the Two Years Law, and so also was General Kessler.[176] Furthermore, the emphasis on morale and the

[174] See Monteilhet, *Les Institutions militaires*, 331–2, arguing for the existence of a politically rooted bias in the army; and Snyder, *The Ideology of the Offensive*, arguing for an organizational one.

[175] Contamine, *La Revanche*, 87; and also Porch, *The March to the Marne*, 249–50. On Sarrail, see J. K. Tanenbaum, *General Maurice Sarrail, 1856–1929* (Chapel Hill, NC, 1974), 28; and on Négrier in 1904, id., 'French Estimates', in May (ed.), *Knowing One's Enemy*, 155.

[176] On Kessler, see in Snyder himself, *The Ideology of the Offensive*, 75. Snyder's lucidly argued and skilfully documented thesis aims to explain everything by the army's 'organizationally motivated bias'. His book, however, seems to be guilty of its own 'professionally motivated bias' as a political scientist. It is one thing to suggest a syndrome within reality and quite another to explain the totality and complexity of this reality by it. To leave many lesser points aside, Snyder is dealing, by his own definition, with a pan-European phenomenon. Yet he finds no pan-European reasons for it. Such factors as the formative experiences of 1866 and 1870 and social Darwinism are mentioned only to be quickly dismissed: ibid. 29, 39–40, 199. On the other hand, while he attributes the spirit of the offensive in France, Germany, and Russia to different particular causes in each country, these causes are

spirit of the offensive went far beyond the military. Otherwise it would never have been accepted and encouraged by the civilians. Messimy is only one example. In 1912 Fallières, the President of the Republic, addressed the Conseil supérieur de la guerre in the following words: 'We are determined to march straight against the enemy without hesitation. The offensive alone is suited to the temperament of our soldiers, and it ought to assure us victory, provided we are willing to consecrate to the effort all our forces without exception.'[177] The nationalist revival was undoubtedly behind this attitude of encouragement and support. But the nationalist revival itself drew much of its driving force and spirit from a wider intellectual mood prevailing in France. With the advent of the twentieth century, that intellectual mood profoundly influenced feelings about, and perceptions of, the essentials of being and of human life. The military were playing a familiar and appealing tune.

As mentioned in the previous chapter, the yearning for moral and spiritual regeneration and for a rediscovery of the elementary forces of life was a cross-European sentiment that gathered momentum with the coming of the new century. Like its namesake a century before, so-called neo-Romanticism was characterized by a revolt against excessive and alienating rationalism and by the celebration of intuition, spontaneous action, and self-expression. In *fin de siècle* France, people associated the prevailing social and cultural *malaise* with the atomism and lack of a communal sense of purpose, belonging, and common binding values that are characteristic of modern society. The Dreyfus Affair, while dividing Frenchmen most deeply, provided a great rallying-point for the intellectuals and an outlet for their moral and idealistic energy. But in the aftermath of the affair, the years of Radical rule, the persecution of the church, and the growing strife in industrial relations with organized labour and socialism brought about disillusionment and disgust with republican petty politics. Discontent with materialism and with what was perceived as the triviality, mediocrity, and

somehow all revealed to be of an organizational nature. Armies are not 'naturally inclined towards the offensive'; for historical reasons, however, they tended to be so in the nineteenth century. The same criticism applies to Stephen van Evera, 'The Cult of the Offensive and the Origins of the First World War', in Miller (ed.), *Military Strategy and the Origins of the First World War* (Princeton, NJ, 1985), 58–107.

[177] Joffre, *Memoirs*, 30.

spiritual dullness of bourgeois society prompted the search for old and new unifying ideals, mystique, and sources of vitality.

For the second time in the space of a century, the first signs of the cultural change were revealed in the arts, where impressionism, primitivism, symbolism, and cubism replaced the classical naturalism which had ruled France until the 1870s. As in Germany, a cult of Nietzsche developed from the late 1890s. Admiring novelists like André Gide, Marcel Proust, and Alain Fournier concentrated on the psychological and the subconscious at the same time as Freud was independently developing psychoanalysis in Vienna. However, the cultural hero of the pre-war decade in France was Henri Bergson, professor of philosophy at the Collège de France from 1905 and author of *Creative Evolution* (1907). His mesmerizing Friday-afternoon lectures became public events, attended by statesmen, intellectuals, and celebrities of all sorts. Bergson led the philosophical attack against the mechanistic outlook of positivism. Since the late nineteenth century, this outlook had already been eroded by the developments in science, especially in the sphere of electromagnetics and the theory of fields, which were soon crowned by Einstein's theory of relativity (1905). Bergson argued that human analytic faculties artificially dissected reality into separate static units, thus fundamentally distorting its living and dynamic quality. Only the force of intuition could come to grips with the very essence of being, which was perpetual creative evolution in the flux of time, the so-called *élan vital.*

'Bergsonism' was enormously successful because it corresponded and appealed to the prevailing sentiments of the time, providing support, inspiration, and stimulus for many diverse and remote intellectual concerns. For example, one regular participant in Bergson's lectures was Georges Sorel. His *Reflections on Violence* (1908), celebrating the inspiring myth and the vitalizing force of direct action as the moving forces of history, influenced revolutionary syndicalism and was later looked upon sympathetically by both Fascism and Bolshevism. His companion to the lectures was the young poet and moralist, Charles Péguy, who called for his country's spiritual and moral regeneration and purification and who looked for a unifying mystique for all Frenchmen. Like many others at that time, he found his way to the Church, which, profiting from the general quest for faith, experienced a sudden and rather unforeseen revival. On the right, Charles Maurras and Action française called for revolutionary means to replace the decadent Republic with a monarchic France, based on integral nationalism and racial solidity. His friend, the novelist Maurice Barrès, also exalted nationalism and the unifying bonds of common ancestry, history, and culture. Finally, the acute foreign threat and shadow of war in the decade before 1914 enhanced the sense of common destiny, the feeling of moral seriousness and the willingness to act vigorously, especially among the educated young.[178] In his impressionist book *Les Jeunes gens d'aujourd'hui* (1913), Agathon contrasted the 'generation of 1912' with the generation of their fathers in the 1890s. He characterized his young contemporaries as 'eager to act in the world [and] just as eager for a set of beliefs that would sustain them in their activity and give it direction'.[179] 'Life', wrote one student, 'is neither intellectual nor critical, but vigorous.' Other youths declared that 'France needed heroism to live', and saw 'in war an aesthetic ideal of energy and force'.[180] In this context, it is again not difficult to understand the popularity enjoyed by du Picq's work when it was republished in 1903. Readers admired his elevation of the human spirit above mechanistic considerations, which they found in harmony with their own critique of modern 'mechanistic' mass society.[181]

It is only against this background that one can assess the revolt of the so-called 'Young Turks' in the general staff against the generation of the 1890s and the answers they offered to French material inferiority and the hazards of both the modern battlefield and the international arena. Returning to command the École de guerre in 1908–11, after having been ostracized from his professorial chair in 1901 at the height of André's purges, Foch was now assuming an elevated, inspiring posture that was after his own heart. Apparently even more than before, he was emphasizing moral energy, action, and will-power. However, there is no reason to suppose that either his lofty mystique or the École de guerre as an

[178] The literature on this subject is extensive. See especially: Alexander Sedgwick, *The Third French Republic, 1870–1914* (New York, 1968), 120–9; H. Stuart Hughes, *Consciousness and Society, The Reorientation of European Social Thought, 1890–1930* (London, 1959), esp. 337–44; Ronald Stromberg, *Redemption by War: The Intellectuals and 1914* (Lawrence, Kan., 1982), *passim*.

[179] Cited in Paul Mazgaj, *The Action Française and Revolutionary Syndicalism* (Chapel Hill, 1979), 34; Agathon was a pseudonym for Henri Massis and Alfred de Tarde. Robert Wohl, *The Generation of 1914* (Cambridge, Mass., 1979), 5–18.

[180] Cited from Agathon by Gorce, *French Army*, 91–2.

[181] See Barbey d'Aureville in *Battle Studies*, 11–13.

institution played any significant role at that time in the development of the doctrine of offensive. In contrast to the accepted view, it has been pointed out that at the École de guerre there was great plurality in tactical matters in the years preceding the war.[182] Many of the professors there, especially those of infantry tactics, opposed the extremities of Grandmaison and his friends. To this category belonged the assistant professor, and later professor, of infantry tactics (1902–3, 1904–6, and 1908–11) Major, later Lieutenant-Colonel, Pétain. Like his predecessor Maud'huy, he taught the lessons of Manchuria and emphasized the strength of modern fire-power. So did his own successor, Debeney.[183] The belief that Pétain's advancement was delayed on that account is totally unfounded. His career had always been pedestrian. The new offensive doctrine was advanced by a committed avant-garde of young middle-ranking officers of the general staff, who were supported by some representatives of the older generation like generals Pau and Castelnau.[184] The doctrine was successful because it was adopted by Joffre, who admired the young group for its energy and promise, who was no strategist himself, and who regarded it as one of his primary missions to rid the army of its confusion and lack of confidence by providing it with a clear, unified, and inspiring doctrine.[185]

In the space of one year Joffre's general staff altered French doctrine and war-planning. The new Complementary Regulations

[182] Debeney, *La Guerre et les hommes*, 12, 277–8; cited and developed by Porch, *The March to the Marne*, 219. Porch is right in making this point but seems to be unaware of the decisive role the *École de guerre* had in fact played during the later part of the nineteenth century. He does not deal with the revival of French military thought and with the Clausewitzian and Napoleonic school of that period, nor does he distinguish between that school and the new offensive one. Consequently, he is right in arguing that the change in the intellectual climate could not be the reason for the adoption of Clausewitz by the French in the 1880s, because the intellectual change came only two decades later; yet he is wrong in extending his argument to the doctrine of the offensive, which developed precisely then; Porch, 'Clausewitz and the French', 291–2.

[183] See previous note and also Contamine, *La Revanche*, 164, 170, 183–4; Ryan, *Pétain*, 24–36; Herbert R. Lottman, *Pétain: Hero or Traitor?* (New York, 1985), 34, 38–9; Cole, ' "Forward with the Bayonet" ', 256–7, 262–4, 265–7; the texts of the lectures exist in the École de guerre's library.

[184] For a selection of articles favourable to the offensive, written between 1911 and 1914 mostly by young officers, see Cole, ' "Forward with the Bayonet" ', 218–21.

[185] Joffre's evidence in his *Memoirs*, 26, 29–30, is abundantly clear. Also see n. 173 above.

for the Conduct of Large Formations (issued 28 October 1913), Field Service Regulations (2 December 1913), and Infantry Field Regulations (20 April 1914) codified the doctrine of the offensive in unmistaken terms.[186] The first of these documents was drawn up by a committee headed by General Pau. Its General Remarks proclaimed:

The conduct of war is dominated by the necessity of giving to the operations the spirit of a vigorous offensive.

Of all the nations, France is the one whose military history offers the most striking examples of the great results to which the offensive in war leads, as well as of the disasters entailed by the passive defence . . . The lessons of the past have borne their fruit, the French army, returning to its traditions, admits henceforth no law in the conduct of operations other than that of the offensive . . .[187]

Chapter 1 proceeded in the same vein:

Military operations aim at the destruction of the organized forces of the enemy. The decisive battle followed by an energetic pursuit involving the destruction of his armies is the sole method of breaking down the will of the adversary . . . The offensive alone leads to positive results . . . From the very outset of operations he [the commander] will impress on the operations such a stamp of violence and tenacity that the enemy, shaken in his *morale* and paralysed in his action, will be forced to remain on the defensive . . . *Battles are beyond everything else moral struggles.*[188]

The continuity with, and divergence from, the regulations of 1895 are both obvious, and the latter is even specifically stated.[189] In operational terms, the new regulations rejected even the expediency of defence and thus also the defensive-offensive. Hence also the major difference between Plan 17, the new French war-plan drawn up under Joffre, and Plans 14–16, its predecessors during the previous fifteen years.

Approved in outline by the Conseil supérieur de la guerre on 18 April 1913 and taking force from 15 April 1914, Plan 17 strengthened the French concentration against Germany by assuming the friendly or neutral attitude of Britain and Italy. More

[186] Joffre, *Memoirs*, 33–5.

[187] *Conduite des grandes unités*, English trans. by the General Staff, War Office, *The Operations of Large Formations* (London, 1914), 7–8; italics in the original.

[188] Ibid. 20–1. For the regulations see also Cole, ' "Forward with the Bayonet" ', 227–34, 280–8; Carrias, *La Pensée militarie française*, 296–8.

[189] *Large Formations*, 8.

important, it continued the tilting and extension of the French deployment in a north-westerly direction, to counter a German sweep through Belgium. Joffre had already adjusted Plan 16 along these lines, before devising his own new plan. Plan 17 deployed a strong army, the Fifth, along the Belgian Ardennes and assigned it five corps, two reserve divisions, and one cavalry division. In close support were placed the cavalry corps and a group of reserve divisions, each three divisions strong. With the British Expeditionary Force to its left and the 'army of manœuvre', the Fourth, brought forward to its right, the Fifth Army was to move into Belgium, if the 'Belgian hypothesis' in the Plan materialized. Although this hypothesis was regarded as almost certain, available information still left room for doubt as to whether it would constitute the sole German offensive effort, extend beyond the Meuse and Sambre, or incorporate a large number of reserve units in the front line.[190] This ambiguity has generally been dismissed all too easily by historians. The truly distinguishing feature of the Plan was, however, its offensive nature. The possibility of a pre-emptive French offensive in Belgium had been ruled out by the politicians for obvious reasons in the preliminary stage of the planning. Yet, animated by the offensive imperative and encouraged by Russians pledges for early offensives in Poland in support of their allies, the authors of Plan 17 were determined not to lose the initiative to the Germans and to dictate the course of operations by opening the war with an immediate all-out attack in Lorraine.[191] 'Whatever the circumstances,' read the Plan's opening lines, 'the intention of the commander-in-chief is to advance with all forces united to the attack on the German armies.'[192]

Herein lay the decisive strategic flaw of the Plan. Neither the issue of the reserves nor the Belgian problem, while being themselves mutually connected and inextricably influenced by the

[190] For the conflicting indications and considerations here, see Joffre, *Memoirs*, 61–4, 145. Also see Tanenbaum, 'French Estimates', in May (ed.), *Knowing One's Enemy*, 165–7.

[191] The text of the plan is printed in État-Major de l'Armèe, *Les Armées françaises*, I, i. ann., pp. 21–35; for its history and the considerations behind it see ibid., I, i. 44–61, 75–91; Joffre, *Memoirs*, 36–112. For the Entente's Belgian problem, see Krause, 'Anglo-French Military Planning, 1905–1914', 234–54, 333–5. Krause's assertion that the Russian factor was the major reason for the offensive emphasis adopted in Plan 17 is unsubstantiated and is greatly oversimplifying: ibid. 183–5, 377.

[192] Ibid., I. i. ann., p. 21.

offensive spirit, were as crucial to the events of 1914 as they have been claimed to be in retrospect. It is true that, before the war, the French high command had been playing down indications that the Germans might use reserve units in a full front-line role, a practice which the French themselves ruled out. Furthermore, many French reservists were left out of any combat-formation and were amassed in rear depots for later use as replacements.[193] However in 1914 the French high command fed its available reserve-units into battle very quickly, even before the German practice was fully recognized. The two new armies of Alsace and Lorraine, which were formed during the early stages of the Battle of the Frontiers to support the French offensive, were composed mainly of reserve divisions, which even previously had been deployed very close to the front. As the overwhelming strength of the German right wing was recognized, these armies were disbanded and their forces transported to join the two reserve divisions from Paris to form the French Sixth Army on the allies' far left.

This brings us to the Belgian problem. Although the strength of the forces assigned by Plan 17 to the Belgian sector was certainly inadequate, this inadequacy was not as grave as it appears in hindsight. As mentioned, the French had to prepare for various strategic options. This is justly pointed out by Joffre.[194] Before they could complete their deployment, they had to be certain of the actual direction of the Germans' major offensive efforts. However, there was no symmetry here between the various possible threats. From the first day of the operations the French had to be ready for a strong German offensive in Lorraine. However, if the attack came through Belgium, they would have had ample time to adjust. They could rely on their railway system to redeploy, once the German armies marched into Belgium. In this respect, the French deployment according to Plan 17 allowed for great flexibility. The French merely had to keep an open mind and maintain their freedom of operation. Only they did not. Rather than wait, as in previous French war-plans, until the German intentions were clarified, they committed themselves to a major offensive in Lorraine. Before this was called off, they had not merely suffered heavy losses but had surrendered the north of France to the Germans and risked total

[193] See Percin, *1914: Les Erreurs du haut commandement* (Paris, 1920), 10, 56, which is perhaps a little exaggerated.

[194] Joffre, *Memoirs*, 63–4, 68, 78–9.

defeat. The problem thus lay primarily in the doctrine of unlimited offensive, and indeed it was on this aspect that most contemporary critics of Plan 17 focused.

General Galliéni, the commander of the Fifth Army, resigned his command when Joffre rejected his request that his army be reinforced from five to nine corps. While being offensive-minded himself, he was not as extreme as the 'Young Turks' in the general staff. In view of the many uncertainties involved, he preferred more restraint during the opening stage of the campaign, until the German intentions were clarified.[195] General Lanrezac, Galliéni's successor as commander of the Fifth Army, expressed similar misgivings. Tactically, like many of the army's senior generals, he did not take the *offensive à outrance* too seriously. 'Bah!' he told a fellow officer, 'new ideas must not be resisted too much. Time, I hope, will take it upon itself to calm the ardour of these young men.'[196] Strategically, he feared the exposure of the Belgian sector and the commitment to attack in Lorraine, where he anyhow saw little prospect of success.[197] General Pierre Ruffey, the commander of the Third Army, was among the very few who anticipated that the main German effort would take place beyond the Meuse. He too advocated a counter-offensive strategy, with the main allied effort being developed in Belgium.[198] Galliéni, Lanrezac, and Ruffey all independently submitted memoranda presenting their points of view. Even General Castelnau, Joffre's deputy in the general staff and one of the authors of Plan 17, began to have something like second thoughts after being nominated to command the Second Army in Lorraine. He wondered if it was not advisable after all to delay the decisive battle in that theatre and adopt a 'counter-offensive' strategy until the Russians had time to intervene in force.[199]

Indeed, while the tactical aspect of the doctrine of unlimited

[195] Tanenbaum, 'French Estimates', in May (ed.). *Knowing One's Enemy*, 170; Cole, ' "Forward with the Bayonet" ', 264–5 for Galliéni's views of tactics, and 339–40 for his criticism of Plan 17; Snyder, *The Ideology of the Offensive*, 95–6, 103, 231–2; Gaëtan Galliéni, *Les Carnets de Galliéni* (Paris, 1932), 17–18.

[196] Cited in Cole, ' "Forward with the Bayonet" ', 258; also see 259.

[197] Charles L. M. Lanrezac, *Le Plan de campagne française et le premier mois de la guerre* (Paris, 1929), 30–43; cited by Cole, ' "Forward with the Bayonet" ', 343–4; Snyder, *The Ideology of the Offensive*, 103.

[198] See his memoranda, cited in Cole, ' "Forward with the Bayonet" ', 345–6.

[199] Private memoir cited in ibid. 337–8; Snyder, *The Ideology of the Offensive*, 43–4.

offensive, as codified in the new field regulations, was opposed by the proponents of fire-power and qualified by many others, its operational and strategic aspects, embodied in Plan 17, were criticized in principle by the exponents of the old defensive-offensive school of the 1890s. Bonnal, whose teaching and legacy became the target of Grandmaison's criticism, responded luke-warmly.[200] The main public spokesman of the neo-Napoleonic school in this regard was another of its representatives who, despite his importance, had always remained somewhat of an outsider.

Lieutenant-Colonel Auguste A. Grouard was one of the two men (the other being Mayer) to whom Liddell Hart gave his favourite part in his history of French military thought. It was the role—cast in Liddell Hart's own image—of the honest and far-sighted student of military affairs, who saw the truth and used his pen to warn his country but, ironically, was boycotted precisely for that by a blind and hostile establishment.[201] Later historians adopted this picture, but Grouard's real story was neither as dramatic and didactic nor as simple. Liddell Hart missed out parts of it and misrepresented or passed in silence over others. In fact, from the 1880s Grouard was one of the principal contributors to the Napoleonic revival, coupled as it was with a critical evaluation of the events of 1870–1. Like the other neo-Napoleonics, he denounced past passivity and reliance on fortresses and called for an energetic, aggressive, and crushing French strategy.[202] Like the others, he produced extensive studies of Napoleon's campaigns and elucidated the emperor's system of operations in a strongly Jominian vein.[203] He differed from the others only in that he did not go through the École de guerre, which seriously hampered his career, despite the favour shown to him by General de Miribel. He retired from the army with the rank of lieutenant-colonel in 1900 and earned a living as a military writer. Grouard was far from being opposed to traditional French military theory, and it was only after 1911, when it moved to what he regarded as curious and dangerous extremes, that he grew alarmed.

[200] Bonnal, 'Considérations sur la tactique actuelle', *Journal des sciences militaires*, 5 (15 Oct. 1912), 380–1; cited by Williamson, *Politics of Grand Strategy*, 219–20.

[201] Liddell Hart, *Foch*, 49–50; and esp. id. 'French Military Ideas', 144–7.

[202] See above n. 55 and related text.

[203] See esp. Grouard, *La Campagne d'automne de 1813 et les lignes intérieures* (Paris, 1897); id., *Maximes de Guerre de Napoléon Ier* (Paris, 1898); id., *La Critique de la campagne de 1815* (Paris, 1904).

Traditional and long-accepted ideas were echoed in his strategic assessment, *France and Germany, the Possible War* (1913).

Grouard's main argument was that France's only possible strategy was the defensive-offensive. Politically, she could not begin a war with an offensive, because she had to leave the first move to the Germans in order to secure the backing of her allies, Britain and Russia. Militarily, she was simply weaker than Germany and took slightly longer to mobilize.[204] In this Grouard merely restated the French strategic logic that had prevailed since the 1890s. French strategic options had not changed either. For Grouard, defensive posture by no means implied passivity. On the contrary, French defence had to be bold and active.[205] Citing Bonnal, Grouard pointed out that the Germans operated with widely dispersed armies, looking to envelop their adversary.[206] The effective Napoleonic-Jominian antidote to that strategy was, said Grouard, to keep the French forces united, make use of the French central position, and operate on interior lines to strike the enemy's armies separately as they exposed themselves.[207] The only updating required in the schemes of the defensive-offensive school from the 1890s resulted from the seriousness of the Belgian option in the present. Contrary to the later myth, however, Grouard did not differ one bit here either from his fellow military writers or from the planners in the general staff. Like both these groups, he regarded the probability of a German attack through Belgium as almost certain, but thought it would aim at outflanking the French army north of Verdun and would not extend beyond the Meuse.[208] This was the prevailing assumption in France, widely discussed in other popular books of the period like Colonel Boucher's *L'Offensive contre l'Allemagne* (1911) and *La Belgique à jamais indépendante* (1913), and Captain Sorb's *La Doctrine de défense nationale* (1912).[209] Against a German invasion through the Ardennes, Grouard suggested a French counter-offensive from the wedge formed by the junction of the Meuse and Sambre, which he believed, like Joffre, would turn the German right wing. This was exactly the course of action taken by the French Fifth Army in 1914. Grouard differed from the authors of Plan 17 in one thing only, though it was not a small one. He argued that the French must

[204] Id., *France et Allemagne; La Guerre éventuelle* (Paris, 1913; periodical publication from 1911), 198.
[205] Ibid. 4, 69 ff.
[206] Ibid. 85–95.
[207] Ibid. 153–70.
[208] Ibid. 98–110, 185.
[209] Ibid. 98.

not commit themselves to an early offensive but must maintain their freedom of operations until the German intentions became known. Then the bulk of the French forces should redeploy by rail to strike the decisive blow.

Returning to our original framing of the problem of French military doctrine, a brief summary is in order. Many different factors and influences interacted in producing the doctrine of the offensive on the eve of the First World War. From the mid-1880s the French discovery of German military ideas and return to Napoleon led to a marked intellectual revival. A new, prolific military school, centred around the École de guerre, emphasized active and aggressive conduct, aiming at the destruction of the enemy's main forces in battle. However, with the coming of the twentieth century, the army's newly gained confidence was badly shaken by military, domestic, and international events. The wars in South Africa and Manchuria demonstrated the strength of modern defence. The Radical campaign to republicanize the army isolated the army from the nation and diminished its popularity. Material imparity with Germany was widening steadily, while the German threat was growing alarmingly. When, after 1911, the national revival again changed the political setting, forces and ideas which had matured in the previous half-decade suggested themselves as possible solutions to the army's problems. Young middle-ranking officers in the general staff advanced the notions of superior morale and out-and-out offensive as the answer both to the problems of modern firearms and to German material superiority. In this they were expressing, and in turn were supported by, the quest for moral regeneration and by the vitalistic philosophies engulfing French culture and society. Newly appointed to high command, Joffre perceived the ideas of the 'Young Turks' as an excellent means to revitalize the army, boost its morale, and provide it with a unifying doctrine. The official adoption of the doctrine of the offensive and Plan 17 were the result.

4

From Sail to Steam: Naval Theory and the Military Parallel 1882–1914

IMPERIALISM lay at the root of the great naval build-up of the late nineteenth and early twentieth centuries, kindled public enthusiasm for naval affairs, and stimulated a remarkable growth of naval literature and ideas. While this was taking place, naval warfare itself was being transformed by the process of mechanization which had been going on from the middle of the nineteenth century. The age of sail, which had begun three centuries earlier with the defeat of the Spanish Armada, was coming to a close. Navies were grappling with new conditions and with the uncertainties created by rapid technological changes.

All aspects of these naval developments have been admirably researched by historians. These include: the shifting global balance of power at sea and the naval growth and maritime policies of each of the Great Powers, with special reference to the two mighty rivals—Britain and Germany; the interrelationships between domestic politics, economics, colonial ambitions, and the new navalism; the influence of the technological advances on naval architecture, strategy, and tactics; and the nature and context of the new naval theories, especially those of Mahan. If this chapter ventures to add anything at all about the naval thinking of the period, it will only be within the context of the general themes developed by this book as a whole. A striking similarity existed between naval and military ideas in the nineteenth century, and not only because Mahan, Corbett, and other naval thinkers were deeply influenced by the leading military theorists of their age. This sort of influence was possible only because, for many centuries, the major features of both military and naval warfare had been, and continued to be, grounded in, and determined by, a common set of technological, socio-political and economic conditions.

Furthermore, by a remarkable coincidence, both military and naval thought shared surprisingly similar strategic models: the one being French Revolutionary and Imperial might, incarnated in Napoleon; the other, no less dominating, was British naval supremacy, personified by Lord Nelson.

MAHAN AND THE SWEEP OF HISTORY

From the mid-1880s, having previously attracted very little official or public attention, naval affairs were moving centre stage in all the major countries. The prolonged dispute which erupted after 1882 over the British occupation of Egypt poisoned Anglo-French relations. For the first time in the space of a century, naval circles in France, and especially the famous Jeune école, were again looking for ways of challenging British naval supremacy. Being obliged to reckon with the threat of war against a Franco-Russian naval combination, Britain was driven on the waves of public concern to overhaul the slumbering Royal Navy and re-examine her naval policy. The Naval Act of 1889 crowned these efforts. In the following decade, the new industrial powers—the United States, Germany, and Japan—prompted by interests of world trade as well as by the pursuit of dominance, prestige, and destiny, also entered the naval arena. In all these naval powers, both old and new, the new concerns, opening horizons, and rapid growth called for, and generated, much intellectual ferment—naval visions, naval propaganda, and naval theories. It was mere coincidence that by far the most successful and influential product of this intellectual activity came from America.

The career of Alfred Thayer Mahan (1840–1914) and, inseparable from it, the circle of the 'New Navy' activists in which he operated, as well as the wider context of emerging American navalism, have all been more than thoroughly investigated.[1] In

[1] On Mahan himself, see in order of appearance as well as of excellence and criticism—ranging from the historically naïve to the exhaustive and from the admiring to the unsympathetic: Charles C. Taylor, *The Life of Admiral Mahan* (New York, 1920); William D. Puleston, *Mahan: The Life and Work of Captain Alfred Thayer Mahan* (New Haven, Conn., 1939); William E. Livezey, *Mahan on Sea Power* (Norman, Okla., 1947); Robert Seager II, *Alfred Thayer Mahan: The Man and His Letters* (Annapolis, Md., 1977). Robert Seager II and Doris D. Maguire ed. *Letters and Papers of Alfred Thayer Mahan* (Annapolis, Md., 1975);

1884 Commodore Stephen B. Luce, the creator and first president of the new Naval War College, then being established at Newport, Rhode Island, offered Commander Mahan, then on duty in the Pacific station in South American waters, the chair of naval history and tactics at the college. After almost thirty years of less-than-satisfying service in the US Navy, Mahan accepted. Although he was the son of the great Dennis Mahan and was himself the author of the volume *The Navy in the Civil War, The Gulf and Inland Waters* (first publ. 1883), published as part of a series of books on the navy during the Civil War, he was scarcely qualified and little prepared for his new post. He was Luce's third choice for the job. But he was a man of intellectual bent, and he was encouraged and guided by Luce.

The self-taught and intellectually alert Luce (1827–1917) was one of the most professionally conscious and educationally minded officers in the navy. The establishment of the Naval War College was largely his own personal doing, the fruit of years of diligent campaigning. In retrospect, he viewed his Civil War experience with General Sherman as a milestone in the development of his ideas. 'You naval fellows', the general told him, 'have been hammering away at Charleston for the past three years. But . . . I will cut her communications and Charleston will fall into your hands like a ripe pear.'

> After hearing General Sherman's clear exposition of the military situation [wrote Luce] the scales seemed to fall from my eyes. 'Here', I said to myself, 'is a soldier who knows his business!' It dawned upon me that there were certain fundamental principles underlying military operations which it were well to look into; principles of general application, whether the operations were conducted on land or at sea.[2]

Luce's assignment to the Artillery School at Fort Monroe and his association with Emory Upton, the champion of higher professional education in the theory of war at the US Army's military schools,

Mahan's autobiographical book is *From Sail to Steam: Recollections of Naval Life* (London and New York, 1907). Two brief essays by Margaret T. Sprout and Philip A. Crowl respectively can be found in Earle's and Paret's editions of *Makers of Modern Strategy*.

[2] Stephen B. Luce, 'Naval Administration III', *United States Naval Institute Proceedings* (Dec. 1903), 820; also cited by A. T. Mahan, *Naval Strategy, Compared and Contrasted with the Principles and Practice of Military Operations On Land* (London, 1911), 15.

crystallized in his mind the project which he was thereafter to pursue. In 1877 he wrote a letter to the Secretary of the Navy, raising for the first time the idea of establishing a naval war college. In the letter he explained:

As the principles of strategy are always the same and apply equally to the army on land and the army afloat—the Navy—it strikes me that our officers should be taught the Art of War very much in the same manner that our army officers are taught that branch . . . the rules of the Art should be applied to naval operations and . . . the course should be combined with the study of naval history.[3]

By 1884 Luce's relentless efforts in the Navy Department and among his fellow officers had been crowned with success. The establishment of a Naval War College was ordered and, while retaining his command of the North Atlantic Squadron, he was named its first president.[4] He had a very clear notion, reiterated both in his speeches and in his writings, of what he expected of the college. This notion derived from the positivist culture of science which had pervaded both scientific and popular consciousness in the English-speaking world from the middle of the nineteenth century.[5] Like Ardant du Picq (with whose works he was obviously unfamiliar), he sought to apply the scientific method to the infant science of maritime warfare; like Théodore Jung (with whose work he was equally unfamiliar), he offered his ideas in what amounted to a truly remarkable positivist statement. He studied his subject, albeit in a lay manner, and enlisted a heavy battery of authorities in his support. The ultimate expression of this was his lecture 'On the Study of Naval Warfare as a Science', which he twice delivered at the Naval War College—in 1885 and as the inaugural lecture of 1886:

Science is contributing so liberally to every department of knowledge and has already done so much towards developing a truer understanding of the various arts, including that of the mariner, that it seems only natural and

[3] Luce to R. W. Thompson, Secretary of the Navy, Aug. 1877, in Albert Gleaves, *Life and Letters of Rear Admiral Stephen B. Luce, U.S. Navy, Founder of the Naval War College* (New York, 1925), 169; Upton to Luce, ibid., p. 170; see also Luce, 'War Schools', *United States Naval Institute Proceedings*, 1883, 633–57; Roland Spector, *Professors of War: The Naval War College and the Development of the Naval Profession* (Newport, RI, 1977), 16–17.

[4] Gleaves, *Luce*, 168 ff; Spector, *Professors of War*, 20–6.

[5] See Spector, *Professors of War*, 17–20.

reasonable that we should call science to our aid to lead us to a truer comprehension of naval warfare, as naval warfare is to be practiced in the future.[6]

Quoting William Hamilton, Francis Lieber, and above all Henry Thomas Buckle for their definitions of science, which he interpreted in a strongly positivist vein,[7] Luce set out to show how the universal scientific method and standards could be applied to his chosen subject:

The grouping together of a number of important facts gathered from the accounts of naval battles will enable the naval student who has acquired the habit of generalization to lay down principles for his own guidance in war.[8]

Naval history abounds in materials whereon to erect a science, as science has been defined and illustrated, and it is our present purpose to build up with these materials the science of naval warfare. We are far from saying that the various problems of war may be treated as rigorously as those of the physical sciences; but there is no question that the naval battles of the past furnish a mass of facts amply sufficient for the formulation of laws or principles which, once established, would raise maritime war to the level of a science. Having established our principles by the inductive process, we may then resort to the deductive method of applying those principles to such a changed condition of the art of war as may be imposed by later inventions.[9]

According to Luce, it was this method of observation, accumulation, induction, generalization, and in turn deduction, which accounted for the advances in all of the sciences achieved by such great figures as Lavoisier in chemistry, Cuvier in geology, and especially Kepler and Newton in astronomy, standing on the shoulders of Hipparchus, Ptolemy, Copernicus, Brahe, and Galileo.[10] The comparative approach, argued Luce, was another scientific device of paramount importance, enriching the study of one field with the discoveries drawn from neighbouring ones by way of

[6] Luce, 'On the Study of Naval Warfare as a Science', *United States Naval Institute Proceedings* (1886), 527–46; reprinted in *The Writings of Stephen B. Luce*, ed. John D. Hayes and John B. Hattendorff (Newport, RI, 1975); here p. 50.

[7] Ibid. 51; the editors have provided an excellent service in compiling a brief presentation-note for each of the many authorities cited by Luce.

[8] Ibid. 54; also see Luce, 'On the Study of Naval History (Grand Tactics)', *United States Naval Institute Proceedings* (1887), 175–201; reprinted ibid.; here p. 75.

[9] Luce, 'Naval Warfare as a Science', *Writings*, 53.

[10] Ibid. 51–2.

analogy. Using the comparative approach, Dalton, Matteucci, Brown-Séquard and Velpeau, Bidder and Schmidt, and Harvey achieved major breakthroughs in physiology. Max Müller advocated it in philology.[11]

> Hence, we have not only comparative anatomy and comparative physiology, but comparative philology, comparative grammar, comparative religion, comparative literature, and why not we ask . . . comparative war, or a comparative study of military operations of a sea army and a land army.[12]

In history, suggested Luce, the role of naval and military commander was often filled by the same person: Cimon and Lysander, Pompey and Agrippa, Don John of Austria and Lord Howard of Effingham, Raleigh and Blake, Rupert and Monk.[13] As the two fields are intimately related, military theory can be drawn upon in developing the infant science of naval warfare:

> Having no authoritative treatise on the art of naval warfare under steam . . . we must, perforce, resort to the well known rules of the military art . . . It is by this means alone that we can raise naval warfare from the empirical stage to the dignity of a science.[14]

Relying on history, which is 'philosophy teaching by example',

> and knowing ourselves to be on the road that leads to the establishment of the science of naval warfare by steam, let us confidently look for that master mind who will lay the foundations of that science, and do for it what Jomini has done for the military science.[15]

Years later Luce would add: 'He appeared in the person of Captain A. T. Mahan, U.S.N.'[16]

At the age of forty-five, Mahan, as he put it, 'was drifting on the lines of simple respectability as aimlessly as one very well could'.[17] Luce's offer was to revolutionize his life and make him a world celebrity. Previously, he had shown no marked interest in the subject he was invited to teach, and he would later describe the state of his knowledge at that time as 'profound ignorance'.[18]

[11] Luce, 'Naval Warfare as a Science', *Writings*, 54–5.

[12] Ibid. 57.

[13] Ibid. 57–8; 'Naval History', ibid. 76–77.

[14] 'Naval Warfare as a Science', ibid. 55–6.

[15] Ibid. 68; 'Naval History', ibid. 74–5.

[16] 'Naval Warfare as a Science', ibid. 68, citing Luce's handwritten comment in the Naval War College, 26 July 1899; similarly, see in a letter soliciting a publisher for Mahan's *Influence* I, 5 Aug. 1889, and in a letter to Mahan 15 July 1907; Gleaves, *Life and Letters of Luce*, 268, 296.

[17] Mahan, *From Sail to Steam*, 274.

[18] Ibid. 278.

While the thought of his heredity, which he mentioned in his letter of acceptance to Luce, helped him overcome his hesitations, he was almost totally unfamiliar with his father's work.[19] He had to begin virtually from scratch, reading everything he could lay his hands on. At the English Club in Lima he came across Mommsen's *History of Rome* and was struck by the author's comments about the significance of the part played by Roman naval preponderance in determining the course and outcome of Hannibal's war.[20] Delayed at sea for almost a year and having missed the first course of the Naval War College (September 1885), he received permission to remain in New York until the following August, so that he could use the city's libraries as he worked on the preparation of his lectures.

Luce had asked him to run two lecture-courses: one dealing with naval tactics, which was mainly contemporary, and another on naval history. Mahan thought he could handle the former more easily, even though his crude ideas about naval manœuvre under steam, embodied in his manuscript 'Fleet Battle Tactics', proved to be less than satisfactory.[21] Little more than speculation and bewilderment existed regarding this subject in all navies during the 1880s. He was more worried about the course in naval history, which called for much greater scholarship. He spent his first months of study in New York in concentrated reading of both general history and the standard eighteenth- and nineteenth-century British and French naval histories, biographies, and treatises.[22] This set the historical boundaries of his work: the great age of sail and the struggle between England, Holland, and France for naval mastery from the middle of the seventeenth century to 1815.[23] By then he had also defined the main theme which was to run through his lectures. It was to be the significance of control of the sea or sea power (Mahan coined the phrase to command attention) in the history of nations, and its interdependence with other historical factors and national characteristics. He discovered fairly rapidly that this subject had never been systematically

[19] Mahan to Luce, 4 Sept. 1884, *Letters and Papers*, i. 577–8; *From Sail to Steam*, 273.

[20] Mahan to Luce, 16 May 1885, *Letters and Papers*, i. 606; *From Sail to Steam*, 277.

[21] Seager, *Alfred Thayer Mahan*, 166.

[22] For the authors and works, see Mahan to Luce, 3, 14, and 19 Nov. 1885, 18 Jan, 1886, *Letters and Papers*, i. 617–19, 621–2; *From Sail to Steam*, 278–81.

[23] Mahan to Luce, 22 Jan. 1886, *Letters and Papers*, i. 622–4.

approached from such a comprehensive perspective and that it therefore offered much scope for work.[24] The question which remained unresolved and which he deliberately postponed to the end was the one Luce had impressed upon him from the beginning: what generally applicable sense could be made of all this?—'What use is the knowledge of these bygone days?'[25]

At Luce's urging, he turned to an obvious source of inspiration, military theory, which he discovered with a sense of revelation. A few years earlier, he later wrote, 'I had read carefully Napier's *Peninsular War*, and had found myself in a new world of thought, keenly interested and appreciative, less of the military narrative . . . than of the military sequence of cause and effect.'[26] In early 1886, having finished the bulk of his history reading, and having been constantly encouraged by Luce, who had sent him his paper 'On the Study of Naval History as a Science', he reported to Luce that he was finally planning to turn to the most demanding subject of naval theory. 'I will keep the analogy between land and naval warfare before my eyes,' he promised, 'I expect to begin with Jomini, etc. . . . and with an admirable system of one kind of war before me, to contribute something to the development of a systematic study of war in another field.'[27] Reading Jomini and Hamley, he found what he was looking for:

> The authority of Jomini chiefly set me to study in this fashion [didactic and generalizing] the many naval histories before me. From him I learnt the few, very few, leading considerations in military combination; and in these I found the key by which . . . I could elicit, from the naval history upon which I had looked despondingly, instruction still pertinent.[28]

In September 1886, by the beginning of the second academic year at the Naval War College, the course of lectures which would become *The Influence of Sea Power Upon History* was complete.

[24] Ibid.; *From Sail to Steam*, 276.

[25] Mahan to Luce, 22 Jan. 1886, *Letters and Papers*, 623.

[26] Mahan, *From Sail to Steam*, 273.

[27] Mahan to Luce, 6 and 22 Jan 1886 in Gleaves, *Life and Letters of Luce*, 312, Mahan, *Letters and Papers*, i. 622–4. Also see Luce's reminding Mahan of his development and of Luce's share therein, especially the idea of the 'comparative method', suggested in his article of 1886: 15 July 1907, Gleaves, *Life and Letters of Luce*, 296.

[28] Mahan, *From Sail to Steam*, 282; also 278, and *Naval Strategy, Compared and Contrasted with the Principles and Practice of Military Operations on Land*, 17.

By the time Mahan (promoted to captain) arrived in Newport in the summer of 1886, Luce had been ordered to sea, and Mahan found himself the new president of the college. He served in this capacity from 1886 to 1889 and again from 1892 to 1893, supervising the minuscule faculty and classes, but mostly struggling to keep the college afloat in the face of a desperate shortage of funds, poor facilities, and a less-than-appreciative Navy Department. Between 1889 and 1892, when the college was suspended, Mahan used the time to prepare his lectures for publication. *The Influence of Sea Power upon History, 1660–1783* appeared in 1890, and was followed two years later by *The Influence of Sea Power upon the French Revolution and Empire* in two volumes. Success was immediate on both sides of the Atlantic, and especially in Britain. In 1893, profoundly against his wishes and despite his friends' efforts to pull strings on his behalf, Mahan was ordered to sea aboard the USS *Chicago*. As it turned out, this was a blessing in disguise. The *Chicago*'s visits of good will to English ports during 1893 and 1894 became the occasions for enthusiastic public receptions for Mahan. Dinners, formal invitations, and weekends in the country were showered upon him. The most distinguished invitations came from Queen Victoria and her guests, including Kaiser Wilhelm II; the Prince of Wales; the Prime Minister, Lord Rosebery; the leader of the Conservative party, Lord Salisbury; Lord Balfour; the First Lord of the Admiralty; and the Lord Mayor of London. Gladstone called Mahan's second *Influence* book 'the book of the age'. The press-coverage included similar superlatives. Mahan became the first foreigner received as a guest of honour at the meeting of the Royal Navy Club. The universities of Oxford and Cambridge awarded him honorary doctoral degrees in the same week.[29] These were followed in America by degrees from Harvard, Yale, Columbia, McGill, and Dartmouth College. All in all, it was his success in Britain which impressed America most and made him a famous man at home as well.

His new literary pursuits and fame opened up new prospects for Mahan. In 1896 he retired from the navy and thereafter occupied himself solely with writing. His major intellectual contribution had already been made, but he continued to publish books: *The Life of*

[29] Mahan, *From Sail to Steam*, 313–16; id., *Letters and Papers*, ii. esp. 105, 128–36, 203, 296–300, 312.

Nelson (first publ. 1897); *Sea Power in its Relation to the War of 1812* (1905); *Naval Strategy* (1911)—a compilation of his lectures at the Naval College; and several lesser historical and biographical works. His magazine articles on current affairs were much in demand, earned him hundreds of dollars apiece, and were later compiled and republished in book form. In these articles Mahan dealt with naval and strategic themes and called for greater American awareness of, and involvement in, world affairs, particularly in areas where the USA had major interests—the Caribbeans and Central America, China and the Far East. Official recognition was not lacking. Upon the outbreak of the Spanish–American War in 1898, Mahan was summoned to the Naval War Board, established to advise the secretary of the navy and the president. A year later he was appointed to advise the American delegation to the first Hague Peace Conference, where he was received as a world authority whose opinions carried great weight. Recognition came also from the American Historical Association which in 1902 elected him its president.

The major themes of Mahan's teaching have been noted often enough. Firstly, there was his 'philosophy of sea power' and his role as 'the evangelist of sea power'. These were grounded in his reading of naval history, in its interrelationship with modern European history. As the imperialist contest grew hotter, both philosophy and role were aimed at promoting naval expansion. Secondly, on the more strictly strategic level, there were the tenets of his theory of naval warfare.

Highlighting the historical role and significance of sea power was Mahan's most original achievement, and it won him the admiration of his contemporaries. Since his work first appeared, it has often been said that this particular notion was not novel but had been expressed centuries before by a succession of writers from Walter Raleigh and Francis Bacon onward. However, as Mahan himself put it, there is a difference between the scattered aphorisms previously issued regarding the blessings bestowed by the command of the sea and his own systematic exposition of the subject.[30] He was certainly the first to present naval history—previously written on a purely technical and operational basis—against the background of the wide sweep of historical events, interwoven and interacting with political and economic factors.

[30] Mahan, *From Sail to Steam*, 276.

Mahan's masterly history was not written, as he put it, 'after the high modern pattern'. His historical judgement was strong and balanced and he was careful to have his facts right, but the facts in themselves meant little to him. As many critics were quick to point out, both then and later, and as he himself admitted: 'Original research was not within my scope, nor was it necessary to the scheme . . . outlined'.[31] Confessing his faults as a historian in his presidential address to the American Historical Association, he went over to a brilliant attack on historical positivism, represented by the formidable figure of Lord Acton. Facts were only 'the bricks and mortar of the historian', he told his listeners. Clarity of structure and content and accessibility to readers were essential. What mattered most was historical meaning and significance.[32] Indeed, it so happened that, while Mahan's historical craftsmanship and the depth of his research improved considerably with every book he wrote, the value of his later books bore no relation to that of his earlier ones. Both the scope of his historical scene and his overriding message had been exhausted in his first two *Influence* books. It was for its historical interpretation and major thesis that his work attracted both fame and criticism.

His cardinal message was simple and compelling. Reviewing the great struggle for naval predominance between the major mercantilist powers in the age of commercial capitalism, Mahan came up with the following conclusions. It had been her naval supremacy that had given England not only security but also a commanding global position, commercial wealth, and, because of these, preponderance in Europe. Naval supremacy had given England a growing monopoly over trade, colonies, and industry. The denial of these assets to her major enemy, France, the stranglehold which England could apply to France's sea ports, and the large subsidies by which she bought and sustained European allies, ultimately destroyed the bids for European hegemony made both by Louis XIV and by Napoleon. The role which sea power played in shaping modern Europe and the modern world could thus hardly be exaggerated.

It is to Mahan's great credit that his treatment of the subject, whatever its shortcomings and omissions, is well-rounded and far from the superficially argumentative. Yet pointed criticisms both of

[31] Ibid. 277–8.

[32] Mahan, 'Subordination in Historical Treatment' (1902), in *Naval Administration and Warfare* (Boston, 1908), 245–72.

the detail and of the wider context provided by this picture have been made, rarely in Mahan's own time but to an increasing extent later on. Specifically, it has been argued that his analysis of the reasons for Britain's success did not take sufficient account of the major role played by British military forces on the Continent, from the days of Elizabeth I and Marlborough to those of the Elder Pitt and Wellington. Their role had been vital to the consolidation of successful coalitions against Britain's enemies, without which no military or political decision in Britain's favour could have been reached. Mahan, it is said, greatly exaggerated the ability of the British navy to 'strangle' single-handedly a large, rich, and fertile continental power like France, whose dependence on foreign sea-trade was far less critical than he believed.

On a more general level, it has been argued that Mahan's analysis and general conclusions were dominated by the particular characteristics of the great period which he investigated and which had, in fact, been unique in many ways. This was the so-called Columbian, Vasco da Gama, or Oceanic era, in which the coastal European nations, having mastered the technological skills for long-distance sea-voyages, acquired great wealth and power by their virtual monopoly of the world's main commercial highway. The significance of the sea, however, had not been nearly as great before the era of the sail, the compass, and the quadrant. Nor was it to remain so in the industrial age—a fact which was even more problematic for Mahan's thesis. This was argued by a number of Mahan's contemporaries: the American lawyer and historian Brooks Adams expressed these ideas in his *America's Economic Supremacy*, (1900), and they were stated even more clearly by the British geographer Sir Halford Mackinder in his lecture 'The Geographical Pivot of History' (1904). Both men pointed out that steam locomotion was opening up the vast continental masses of the Americas and Asia, previously remote and sparsely populated.[33] For the first time in history, land transportation, up till then dependent solely on human and animal muscle, was able to challenge the incontestable advantage which sea and river transportation had possessed in moving vast quantities of goods over great distances at low cost. Additionally, in the new age of industrial

[33] Brooks Adams, *America's Economic Supremacy* (New York, 1900), esp. 38–43; Halford J. Mackinder, 'The Geographical Pivot of History', *Geographical Journal*, 23 (1904), 421–37.

capitalism, domestic industrial capacity largely overshadowed overseas commerce and colonies as the main source of national wealth and naval power. If this was so, the lessons Mahan was drawing from the age of the sail and of commercial mercantilism were much less applicable to the present than he assumed.[34]

This was a significant point because it touched both upon Mahan's innermost motivation for writing his history and upon the manner in which it was received. By taking up his professorship at the new Naval College, whose future was far from secure, and by serving in a minuscule and obsolete navy which was only beginning to experience growth, Mahan was enlisted to the ranks of the gathering campaign for naval expansion. As he himself stated, the aim of his work was 'to imbue his hearers with an exalted sense of the mission of their calling, and . . . contribute to give the service and the country a more definite impression of the necessity to provide a fleet adequate to great undertakings'.[35] In this campaign, Mahan was by no means alone, nor was he even a pioneer or particularly prominent. He was typical of the 'New Navy' circle in which he moved and which, consisting as it did of young officers of middle rank, had been promulgating the creation of a strong and modern American navy since the early 1880s.[36] Only after the success of his first two *Influence* books did Mahan become one of the major and most influential figures in American navalism.

Indeed, while some early, naïve commentators tended to associate almost every expression of the new navalism with Mahan's influence, later ones took a more critical view. The facts are known well enough. The first *Influence* book had appeared in fifteen editions by 1900 and in twenty-four by 1914. The second did almost as well, being published in eleven editions by 1900 and in

[34] Gerald S. Graham's brilliant observations in *The Politics of Naval Supremacy: Studies in British Maritime Ascendancy* (Cambridge, 1965), 1–30, esp. 28–9, 124, have been developed by Paul Kennedy, *The Rise and Fall of British Naval Mastery* (London, 1976), *passim.*; see also Herbert Rosinski, 'Mahan and World War II' (1941), in his *Development of Naval Thought*, ed. B. M. Simpson (Newport, RI, 1977), 27–8; Bernard Semmel, *Liberlism and Naval Strategy; Ideology, Interest and Sea Power during the Pax Britannica* (London, 1986), 3–4. Earlier criticisms are summarized by William L. Langer, *The Diplomacy of Imperialsim* (New York, 1951), 418.

[35] Mahan, *Influence* II, vol. i, p. iv.

[36] See esp. Peter Karsten, *The Naval Aristocracy: The Golden Age of Annapolis and the Emergence of Modern American Navalism* (New York, 1972), 306–17, 326, *et passim*, for an excellent study of the naval mind and for pre-Mahan 'Mahanities'.

fourteen by 1914.[37] In America, the Assistant Secretary of the Navy and later President of the USA, Theodore Roosevelt, became an enthusiastic admirer and close friend of Mahan; Senator Henry Cabot Lodge amplified his views; Secretary of the Navy Tracy sought his advice;[38] Tracy's successor, Herbert, abandoned his previously hostile position and became converted to navalism upon reading Mahan's second *Influence* book; from the mid-1890s, Mahan's name and authority ranked high in Congressional deliberations over naval affairs. All the same, it is also clear that most of the people referred to above had become ardent navalists long before they had heard of Mahan. American navalism as a broad political and cultural movement had been expanding hand in hand with the country's industrial and commercial growth, was being boosted by the pressures of European colonialism, and was gathering momentum virtually independently of the work or activity of any single person. Mahan's 'philosophy of sea power' was enthusiastically received by all navalists because it defined, focused, and gave clear direction to, the ideas and notions already held by many of them. It provided them with a magnificent, magisterial demonstration of their case. Indeed, in this it also added considerable weight to their argument.[39]

Mahan's philosophy of sea power had a similar effect abroad. His works were soon translated into German, French, Japanese, Russian, Italian, Spanish, and Swedish. They were published precisely at the time when Britain was beginning to rearm in the face of the new Franco-Russian challenge to her previously undisputed maritime supremacy. As public opinion became agitated and as the government became increasingly aware of the country's relative naval decline, ancient traditions were evoked to rally support and enhance morale. Mahan's history and analysis of the

[37] *A Bibliography of the Works of Alfred Thayer Mahan*, ed. John B. Hattendorf and Lynn C. Hattendorf (Newport, RI, 1986). See also Langer, *The Diplomacy of Imperialism*, 418.

[38] Mahan made the contact by sending copies of his book to the last two names immediately upon its publication; 10 and 19 May 1890, *Letters and Papers*, ii. 10–11.

[39] A good updated summary is Crowl, 'Mahan', in Paret (ed.), *Makers of Modern Strategy*, 470–2. Harold and Margaret Sprout, *The Rise of American Naval Power, 1776–1918* (Princeton, NJ, 1966), 205–22, is probably still the most useful survey of the political scene; the authors of this pioneering study, originally published in 1939, renounced their strongly Mahanite views in their introduction to the second edition.

rise of British naval power were a major contribution in this regard and helped to set the naval build-up in an appealing historical and strategic framework.[40]

In Germany, traditionally a continental power, Mahan's role in this respect may have been even greater. In May 1894, less than a year after he had dined with Mahan at Queen Victoria's table, Kaiser Wilhelm II wrote to Poultney Bigelow of the *New York Herald*: 'I am just now not reading but devouring Captain Mahan's book and am trying to learn it by heart. It is a first-class book and classical in all points. It is on board all my ships and constantly quoted by my captains and officers.'[41] Germany's new naval orientation was the almost inevitable result of the stupendous growth of her industry and power, as well as of the mounting imperialist contest. Yet it is hardly disputed that the scale, direction, and persistence of her naval build-up were most decisively influenced by the personal interest, not to say obsession, of the Kaiser. Tirpitz, the other leading figure behind the German naval build-up, apparently needed no Mahan to crystallize his ideas regarding German naval policy. As early as 1888 and 1891, but especially in his Memorandum IX of 1894 (all composed before he read Mahan), he had already advocated the formation of a navy of battleships, to be concentrated in home waters. Still, in their campaign to create a large German navy and for the acquisition of colonies, Tirpitz and the Reich's Naval Office, in collaboration with the Colonial Society and later the Naval League, found Mahan's inspiring works an excellent weapon of propaganda. In 1898, working on the preparation of the first Naval Law, Tirpitz initiated the pubication of Mahan's first *Influence* book (already translated in a periodical series two years earlier). Of the 8,000 copies printed, 2,000 were to be distributed directly by the Naval Office itself. The second *Influence* book was also translated in 1898. Naval College professors, like Vice-Admiral von Maltzahn in *Naval Warfare* (1908), and academic propagandists, like Ernst von Halle in *Sea Power in German History* (1907), transplanted Mahan into German soil.[42]

As Mahan himself noted, his works were most widely translated

[40] See briefly in Langer, *The Diplomacy of Imperialism*, 422–3.

[41] C. C. Taylor, *The Life of Admiral Mahan*, 131.

[42] See esp. Tirpitz, *My Memoirs* (2 vols.; London, 1919), i. 55, 112; Volker Berghahn, *Der Tirpitz-Plan* (Düsseldorf, 1971), 145, 179–80, 424.

into Japanese, the first translation being initiated by the Club of Naval Officers in 1896. In the island empire as well, which was embarking on an imperialist and navalist course, his works provided a political and strategic rationale for policy and painted the road to destiny in vivid colours. They were placed in the libraries of middle and high schools in Japan and served as texts in all naval schools.[43]

Mahan's social Darwinist, racist, and imperialist opinions harmonized with his naval theories in much the same way that similar ideas in Germany correlated with German military ideas. In fact, his views were indistinguishable from, say, Moltke's, and indeed in both cases Christian sentiments played an important part. Close similarities suggest that Mahan was familiar with Moltke's opinions; the latter's works were published in New York in 1892–3. Moreover, it is a measure of the age in which they both lived that Mahan, like Moltke, underwent intellectual transformation; until the mid-1880s he was an anti-imperialist.[44] However, with the onset of the age of imperialism and upon taking up his research of the great sea empires, he changed completely. Here too his views were no different from those prevailing among his contemporaries in the navy.[45] Only that his opinions received world-wide circulation.

In justifying the partition of Asia, Mahan explained that 'growth is a property of healthful life'.[46] One state does not interfere in the affairs of another unless 'its stage of political development corresponds to that of childhood or decay':[47]

> The claim of the indigenous population to retain indefinitely control of territory depends not upon natural right but upon political fitness . . . in such a manner to insure the natural right of the world at large that resources should not be left idle, but be utilized for the general good.[48]

'The onward movement of the world has to be accepted as a fact.'[49] Virile states compete in a process of natural evolution which inevitably breeds struggle and suffering.[50]

[43] Mahan, *From Sail to Steam*, 303; C. C. Taylor, *The Life of Admiral Mahan*, 114–15.

[44] Mahan, *From Sail to Steam*, 274.

[45] See Karsten's excellent *Naval Aristocracy*, esp. 205–31; Spector, *Professors of War*, 83.

[46] Mahan, *The Problem of Asia and Its Effects upon International Policies* (London, 1900), 29–30.

[47] Ibid. 32.

[48] Ibid. 98.

[49] Ibid. 61, 16.

[50] Ibid. 15, 46.

In the late 1890s, when Russian pressure in the Far East made the partition of China appear imminent, Mahan advocated co-operation between the three Teutonic sea-powers—Germany, Britain, and the USA—to contain Slavic Russia.[51] Analysing the differences between the two races, he regarded some as environmental and cultural and others as 'fundamental, deep seated in the racial constitution'.[52] The French, a Latino-Gallic mixture, were weaker, and there was, therefore, no third genius race competing.[53] Later, following the growth in German naval power, Mahan advocated co-operation between the two Anglo-Saxon nations against the German threat.[54]

During the two Hague Conferences, Mahan appeared as a bastion of realism. He stood fast against any limitations on war, armament, and the freedom of action at sea. From a Christian and moral point of view, he argued, war in some circumstances is righteous and even mandatory. States, like individuals, must exercise judgement and assume responsibility for their actions.[55] Furthermore, 'power, force, is a faculty of national life; one of the talents committed to nations by God'.[56] Fighting-spirit is rooted in the 'nobler qualities of bravery, courage, loyalty, patriotism', which must not be thrown out with the bath water.[57] Arbitration and an international code of law cannot always take the place,

> either practically or beneficially, of the processes and results obtained by the free play of natural forces. Of those forces national efficiency is a chief element; and armament, being the representative of the national strength, is the exponent . . . It is of the first importance that the European family of states retain in full the power of national self-assertion, of which the sentiment of nationality is the spirit and armament the embodiment.[58]

Like Delbrück, whom he cited often in his last years, Mahan warned his readers that 'the consolidated Roman Empire with its Pax Romana is not a wholly happy augury for a future of peace

[51] Ibid. 104. [52] Ibid. 114–15. [53] Ibid. 105–6.

[54] Mahan, *The Interest of America in International Conditions* (London, 1910), 71–124.

[55] Mahan, 'The Power that Makes for Peace', *Some Neglected Aspects of War* (London, 1907), 97–114, esp. 100.

[56] Mahan, 'The Peace Conference and the Moral Aspect of War', *Lessons of the War with Spain and Other Articles* (Boston, 1899), 232.

[57] Mahan, 'The Power that Makes for Peace', *Neglected Aspects of War*, 8–9.

[58] Mahan, *Armaments and Arbitration, or the Place of Force in the International Relations of States* (London, 1912), 10.

dependent upon a central court and general disarmament'.[59] He became involved in a sharp literary exchange with Norman Angel, whose popular book *The Great Illusion* (1910) rejected war on the grounds that it no longer paid. He argued that, while of course being wasteful in itself, war could create the conditions for future greatness, as the British and German cases demonstrated.[60]

The second major theme in Mahan's work was his doctrine of naval warfare. Like his philosophy of sea power, this is easily summarized: one can gain command of the sea and all the benefits it entails only by destroying the enemy's main battle fleet in battle or, if the enemy shrinks from direct confrontation, by bottling up his navy in its harbours. 'Jomini's dictum that the organized forces of the enemy are ever the chief objective, pierced like a two-edged sword to the joints and marrow of many specious propositions,' he wrote.[61] 'Postponement of immediate action to "ulterior motives" ', such as attacking the enemy's commerce, never succeeded in the past and can never succeed in the future. Hence the paramount importance of battleships or ships-of-the-line in the navy. For all their importance, cruisers, or, as they were formerly called, frigates, cannot win a war. Strategic concentration of force and tactical boldness are the leading principles of naval operations.

That this was 'Jomini turned to sea' has been pointed out often enough, not least—and on many occasions—by Mahan himself. The structure of his work—as a strategic commentary on the historical narrative, developing and illustrating principles—was also derived from Jomini's *Treatise on Grand Military Operations*.[62] However, this smooth adaptation could never have been contemplated, much less carried out, if it had not been for the remarkable similarity which existed between military and naval developments in the period covered by both the *Influence* books and the *Treatise*. Deeper reasons made nineteenth-century military and naval pictures of the past, strategic models, and doctrines analogous. To demonstrate this, a brief journey through the centuries is called for, excused only by the sweep of Mahan's own *tour de force*.

That regular, state-sponsored and state-organized armies and navies appeared at much the same time is understandable enough.

[59] Mahan. 13.
[60] Ibid. 121–54; Seager, *Alfred Thayer Mahan*, 586–91.
[61] Mahan, *From Sail to Steam*, 283. [62] Ibid.

The growth of the modern, centralized state and of a money economy from the early sixteenth century was responsible for that. The *tercios* and the *armada* which together terrorized Europe were part of the same 'Military Revolution'. So were the armies and fleets formed by the United Provinces. From the middle of the seventeenth century, all warlike activity was virtually monopolized by the state. State bureaucracy under Louvois and Le Tellier created the large regular armies of Louis XIV's France, while under Colbert it provided her with a formidable, modern, and efficient navy. During roughly the same period, a modern army and a strong regular navy were created in the England of the Lord Protector.

The similarity was no less striking in regard to weapons and battle tactics. Although introduced both on land and at sea at the outset of the sixteenth century, it took time before firearms came to dominate warfare. This was due partly to problems of technical efficiency and partly—especially in regard to artillery—to the cost and the number of pieces available. Mediterranean naval warfare throughout the sixteenth century was still carried out by fleets of galleys, which added artillery and arquebus fire to the traditional tactics of ramming and boarding.[63] In much the same way, sixteenth-century land-warfare was carried out by the old deep squares of pikemen, except that they were now supported, or more often immobilized, by the new firearms. As late as the middle of the seventeenth century, the pike still held its own on land, while the fleets of sail which dominated naval warfare in the North Sea and the Atlantic still used boarding and fire-ships as widely as they used artillery fire; in fact, boarding and the use of fire-ships were the favourite tactics of the Dutch. The deep order and the *mêlée* were the prevailing form of combat at sea. Only at the end of the seventeenth century, at the same time as the pikemen were returning their weapons for all time, did the artillery duel become the predominant form of naval warfare. The far-reaching tactical results of these parallel developments were remarkably similar.

By the late seventeenth century at sea and the early eighteenth century on land, the need to maximize fire-power led to the universal adoption of the same order of battle, the line, by all armies and navies in Europe. The complexity of manœuvring this

[63] See the fine work by John Francis Guilmartin jun., *Gunpowder and Galleys: Changing Technology and Mediterranean Warfare at Sea in the Sixteenth Century*, (Cambridge, 1974).

long, thin, and fragile formation, sometimes stretching for kilometres and dozens of kilometres both on land and at sea, proved baffling. In both cases, it called for endless drill, strict central command, clearer subdivision, and an intricate system of communication. At sea, during the Second Dutch War, the first official signal-book was introduced into the Royal Navy by the Duke of York (later King James II), and a permanent system of squadrons and flag-officers soon followed. The line also proved problematic in the offensive. The approach to the attack was made enormously cumbersome by the need to maintain formation and to refrain from exposing the leading units to devastating fire from the enemy's line. When contact was made, the shock-effect of the thin line was minor, and the chances of achieving major breakthroughs in the enemy's line were very slim indeed. At sea, in two famous incidents in 1744 and 1756, Admirals Matthews and Byng found themselves in situations which ran counter to the accepted practices, as prescribed by the Admiralty's regulations. They failed to align their fleets parallel to the French before attacking. Approaching the enemy line at an obtuse angle, their van came under heavy fire, while the rest of the British line was still too far away and unable to intervene. Matthews, who chose to proceed with the attack, suffered heavy losses and was court-martialled for misconduct. Twelve years later, Byng, who had sat as a judge at Matthews's court-marshal, failed to support his van, and then allowed the French to take Minorca. He was court-martialled and sentenced to death.

The difficulties of the attacker were compounded by the reluctance of the defender to accept battle. On land, often anxious not to waste their hard-to-replace regulars in the hazardous trial of arms, armies resorted to strongly fortified positions, from which it was extremely difficult to oust them. Similarly, the French navy in the eighteenth century was under strict orders to try as much as possible to avoid the loss of ships. With her resources divided between land and sea, France could not afford an out-and-out naval contest with Britain, and French tactics reflected this policy. Normally, while the British navy sought the attack, the French remained on the defence. They either took position to windward and thus kept out of reach; or they placed themselves to leeward, waiting to blunt the British attack during the vulnerable approach, when the British men-of-war, turning their bows to the enemy, were unable to use their broadsides effectively. The French could then receive them with full broadsides, before tacking to the rear and reforming in line, ready for another round. Their artillery fire, aimed at the sails and rigging of the British ships, served the same purpose by incapacitating them and neutralizing the attack.

The tactical impasse was complemented at the strategic level to create the famous syndrome known as the 'indecisiveness' of eighteenth-century warfare. On land, while tending not to rush into battle, generals employed a variety of other means to obtain an advantage over their rivals. First among these was the operation against the enemy's communications, which gave rise to the the so-called 'war of manœuvre'. Things were not very different at sea. Shrinking from a head-on collision with the stronger British navy, the French looked for other ways of waging naval war. The principal one was the attack on British naval communications. At sea this meant not so much military communications as seashore traffic and worldwide trade-routes. Britain's wealth was largely derived from her overseas commerce. If this could be seriously disrupted, Britain would have to accept defeat. For a century and a half, from the days of Vauban and the legendary Jean Bart to the days of Napoleon and his no less gallant raiders, French frigates and privateers, operating from Brest and Toulon as well as from Dunkirk, St Malo, Dieppe, and a host of other small ports, raided and harassed British trade. The British responded by blockading the French ports and by concentrating their merchant ships in well-protected convoys. The contest had its ups and downs. At times it became very close indeed.

The indecisiveness of eighteenth-century warfare created concern and prompted a search for radical new solutions among specialists in both the military and naval fields. In both fields, there was dissatisfaction with, and growing reaction against, the accepted linear tactics. The ideas of the famous Chevalier de Folard regarding the superior flexibility and greater shock-effect of the column were taken up in France after the humiliating failures of the French armies in the Seven Years War. Intensive debate and extensive experimentation resulted in the development of new tactics, largely associated with the teachings of Count de Guibert. These tactics relied heavily on the column, both for manœuvring and for attacking, and were to find their consummation in the Revolutionary and Napoleonic armies. France was also the centre of systematic naval theory. The creation of naval academies, the

Enlightenment spirit of enquiry and systematization, and the prestige, honours, and rewards bestowed on authors by French society and by state academies for the advancement of learning were all responsible for that. In 1697 Paul Hoste, professor of mathematics at the Royal Naval College in Toulon, wrote the first systematic treatise on sailing ships' manœuvres. Captain de Morogues, Bourde de Villehuet, and Viscount Grenier—all working under the auspices of the French Royal Academy of Sciences—elaborated on the same theme and were widely read throughout Europe.[64] Characteristically, the English, though being the greatest naval nation, shared none of the French bent for theorizing. Characteristically too, if there was any serious theorizing to be done in Britain in the Age of the Enlightenment, it was left to the Scots. During the dark days of the American War of Independence, John Clerk of Eldin, a gifted amateur and life-long enthusiast for naval affairs, was anxiously recording the successes of French evasive tactics and the repeated failures of the British in the previous fifty years to pin down the French and break through their line. In 1782, in a privately circulated essay which was later (1790) expanded and published as a book entitled *An Essay on Naval Tactics, Systematical and Historical*, Eldin acutely analyzed the tactical impasse and put forward new methods of attack.

Eldin proposed that, rather than ensuring that the two opposing fleets sailed parallel before attacking, as Admiralty regulations prescribed, the British ought to open the attack once their van had passed the enemy's rear. In that way, the approaching ships would not be exposed to the devastating fire of the whole French line. Cutting through the middle of the enemy line, they would achieve overwhelming concentration against only part of his fleet, leaving his van with the awkward alternative of either escaping and abandoning the rear to its fate or turning back to fight at a disadvantage. This was what the unfortunate Matthews had tried to do in 1744, but he had failed, owing to lack of co-ordination between his squadrons, and had thus brought about a disastrous new stiffening in naval practices. Instead of sailing in the rigid line,

[64] Paul Hoste, *L'Art des armées navales* (Lyon, 1697), English trans., 1762, 1834; S. F. V. B. de Morogues, *Tactique navale*, (Paris, 1763), English trans. 1767, note the academy's report in the preface; Bourde de Villehuet, *Le Manœuvrier, ou essai sur la théorie et la pratique des mouvements du navire et des évolutions navales* (Paris, 1765), English trans., 1788; Vicomte J. R. de Grenier, *L'Art de la guerre sur mer, ou tactique navale* (Paris, 1787).

suggested Eldin, the British fleet ought to be divided into separate short columns or divisions, which would be easier to handle and more flexible to manœuvre.

At the same time the French armies, at the end of the *ancien régime*, were implementing very similar ideas on land, things were also changing in the British navy. In 1782, the same year in which Eldin wrote his essay, Admiral Rodney chanced on a similar manœuvre in the course of his battle with de Grasse off the coast of Dominica (the Battle of the Saints). His fleet, still in line, cut through the French centre from leeward. Eldin later tried to suggest that Rodney had been influenced by his work, but this has been proved untrue.[65] The tactical predicament simply produced similar solutions in different minds. On the French side too, the dashing Suffren in his brilliant East Indies campaign attacked the British rear from windward off Madras two months before Rodney's manœuvre. And in 1787, observing the new developments, Grenier called for the substitution of the line by a flexible formation in short columns.

Still, the nascent revolution in tactics was able to develop as dramatically as it did only in consequence of the new conditions created by the French Revolution. This was true of both land- and sea-warfare, though in curiously opposite ways. As is well known, it was the patriotic and revolutionary *élan*, as well as the inexperience of the French troops, which made column shock-tactics so effective and so suitable for them. Yet these qualities, urged by the Revolutionary authorities and later by Napoleon, proved no substitute for technical skills and proficiency when it came to the sea. They only aggravated the condition of the French navy, already shaken by the emigration, persecution, and purges of its aristocratic officer-corps. The French navy was much weakened by the Revolution, becoming a mere shadow of its former self. If the successes of Nelson's shock-tactics, from St Vincent and the Nile to Trafalgar, are to be properly understood, this factor must be borne in mind. In 1794, at the Battle of the Glorious First of June, Lord Howe had already broken the French line in several places. In 1797 Admiral Duncan had attacked the weaker Dutch fleet in the Battle

[65] John Clerk of Eldin, *An Essay on Naval Tactics, Systematical and Historical* (2nd edn.; Edinburgh, 1804), xiv; persuasively refuted by the son of Rodney's flag-captain, Major-General Sir Howard Douglas, *Naval Evolutions: A Memoir* (London, 1832).

of Camperdown, breaking through the enemy line in two columns. At Trafalgar, Nelson employed similar tactics, attacking almost perpendicularly in two columns. During the approach, the head of the British columns suffered severe damage, but would have sustained even heavier losses had the French been up to their old standards. In that case, the British columns attacking the Franco-Spanish line in Iberian waters might have suffered the fate of the French columns attacking the British-Spanish line on the Iberian mainland. In another curious mirror-image of the developments on land, the attacker enjoyed a significant advantage in artillery. While reformed and improved artillery was one of the factors that contributed to the successes of the French Revolutionary and Napoleonic armies, the British cannonade, devastating at close range, was highly effective in the mêlée which was the ultimate result of the new naval tactics. In short, similar developments and conditions made possible the spectacular new battles of destruction which established French preponderance on land and British mastery at sea.

This similarity of conditions and developments also produced the remarkable resemblance which existed in the nineteenth century between military and naval theory and picture of the past. Mahan's historical interpretation, which reflected the accepted view among naval historians, was barely distinguishable from that of the military historians and theoreticians of the century. First and foremost, the Napoleonic and Nelsonian examples cast eighteenth-century warfare in an unfavourable light. Post-Napoleonic military writers rejected linear tactics and regarded the eighteenth-century 'war of manœuvre' a gross historical aberration, swept aside by Bonaparte's genius and vigour. The views of post-Nelsonian naval writers were similarily crystallized by Mahan. The cause of all mischief, he wrote, was 'the effete system to which the middle eighteenth century had degraded the erroneous but comparatively hearty tradition received by it from the seventeenth'.[66] A military theoretician like Jomini viewed Frederick the Great as a forerunner of Napoleon, but one who had none the less been unable to free himself from the methods of his time. In the same way, naval

[66] Mahan, *Types of Naval Officers Drawn from the History of the British Navy* (London, 1902), 56 *et passim*; *Influence I*, *passim*; and on many other occasions, e.g. *The Major Operations of the Navies in the War of American Independence* (London, 1913), 93; *Armaments and Arbitration* (London, 1912), 204.

writers regarded a whole line of great admirals in the glorious British naval tradition—Hawke, Rodney, Howe, and Jervis—as having 'anticipated' Nelson. Here too however, Mahan maintained that Rodney, for example, 'despite his brilliant personal courage and professional skill, which . . . was far in advance of his contemporaries . . . belongs rather to the wary, cautious school of the French tacticians than to the impetuous eagerness of Nelson'.[67]

For Mahan, French naval policy, which, owing to inferior resources, prescribed tactical and strategic restraint, was the worst of all naval mistakes. These 'unhappy prejudices' and 'false system' ensured France's ultimate defeat.[68] In avoiding battle, the French resigned the struggle for naval mastery. Just as the Austrians under Daun and Archduke Charles were reputed to have done on land, the French 'subordinated the control of the sea by the destruction of the enemy's fleets, of his organized naval forces, to the success of particular operations, the retention of particular points, the carrying out of particular ulterior strategic ends'.[69] As a single ray of light, wrote Mahan, Suffren's 'great and transcendent merit lay in the clearness with which he recognized in the English fleet, the exponent of the British sea power, the proper enemy of the French fleet'. He 'saw plainly that the way to assure those [ulterior] objects [the French were pursuing] was not by economizing his own ships, but by destroying those of the enemy. Attack, not defence, was the road to sea power in his eyes.'[70]

The *guerre de course*, resorted to by the French, was anathema to Mahan. In his view, the belief that Britain's might could be bypassed and her vulnerable lifelines attacked was an illusion and a violation of the most fundamental principle of naval warfare. This was clearly proved by the outcome of the Anglo-French conflict, in which the French were justly defeated. That the defeat basically reflected the balance of power between the two opposing navies and would probably have occurred whatever strategy the French employed, mattered little to Mahan.[71] In his opinion, rather than resort to commerce-destroying, the weaker navy should have

[67] Mahan, *Influence I*, 377–8.
[68] Ibid. 79–80.
[69] Ibid. 339.
[70] Ibid. 425.
[71] For the underlying French inferiority in money, manpower and war materials, see James Pritchard, *Louis XV's Navy 1748–1762: A Study of Organization and Administration* (Montreal, 1987). More specifically on the French lack of timber and its effect on their strategy, see Paul Walden Bamford, *Forests and French Sea Power 1660–1789* (Toronto, 1956).

waited for its opportunity, or better still, should have initiated a situation in which the enemy's navy would be divided and could be attacked in detail in a Jominian fashion.[72] Mahan, the historian who gave special attention to trade statistics, recorded the impressive numbers of British merchant ships captured by the French. British losses in each of the great wars against France—the War of the League of Augsburg, the War of the Spanish Succession, the War of the Austrian Succession, the Seven Years War, and the Revolutionary Wars—amounted to thousands, with hundreds of ships being captured each year.[73] Not unnaturally, French commerce-destroying was particularly effective during the zeniths of French power under Louis XIV and during the Revolution and Empire. During the latter period, British losses exceeded 10,000 ships. Britain's expanding and ultimately huge trade-carrying capacity enabled her to take the punishment, but Mahan was fully aware of how close Britain came to defeat in the final years before Napoleon's collapse.[74] Furthermore, in his study of the Anglo-American war of 1812, he in effect endorsed the American naval strategy of commerce-raiding as the only possible one for the weaker side and as quite effective as such.[75] Still, for him the ultimate result of Anglo-French contest was merely the confirmation of a principle. Which came first logically, the principle or the particular historical experience, was a meaningless question for him. In the tradition of the Enlightenment, which in his particular case was mixed with a deep religious faith in a divine cosmic order,[76] he believed that the universal principle is revealed in, and validated by, experience.

[72] Mahan, *Influence II*, 179–80.

[73] Mahan, *From Sail to Steam*, 282; *Influence I*, 317–19; *Influence II*, ii. 221–2; Kennedy, *The Rise and Fall of British Naval Mastery*, 53, 72, 79, 85, 93, 110, 131. Also see the pointed criticism of the gap which exists here between Mahan the historian and Mahan the dogmatic Jominian strategist in Geoffrey Sympox's excellent *The Crisis of French Sea Power 1688–1697, From the* guerre d'escadre *to the* guerre de course (The Hague, 1974), esp. 227–9.

[74] Mahan, *Influence II*, ii. 199–271.

[75] Mahan, *Sea Power in Its Relations to the War of 1812* (2 vols.; London, 1905), i. 285–9.

[76] This theme, which earlier historians had noted, was elaborated by Seager. The religious philosophy of Mahan's uncle, Milo, a distinguished ecclesiastical historian and thinker and an important influence on the young Alfred Mahan, advanced the idea that a mathematical, Pythagorian-like, divine design manifested itself in the world; Seager, *Alfred Thayer Mahan*, 4–5, 10, 445–8. Also see Mahan's own book, *The Harvest Within: Thoughts on the Life of the Christian* (London, 1909).

Finally, true application of fundamental truths was strikingly demonstrated by Nelson, whose genius embodied the principles of naval warfare in the same way that Bonaparte's embodied those of war on land. Indeed, as anyone familiar with the Napoleonic conduct of operations would not fail to recognize, the nature of both those sets of principles was almost indistinguishable. According to Mahan, Nelson possessed 'the eye of a seaman *determined on attack*'. His motto was 'first secure the victory, then make the most of it'. In May 1805 his first plan of attack in the Trafalgar campaign opened with the following words: 'The business of the English Commander-in-Chief being first to bring the Enemy's Fleet to Battle, on the most advantageous terms to himself . . . and secondly, to continue . . . until the business is decided'. He was looking for 'a close and decisive Battle . . . If the two Fleets are both willing to fight, but little manœuvring is necessary'.[77]

Given this outstanding similarity between the military and naval pictures of the past and strategic theories, it is hardly surprising that Mahan's theories experienced the very same problems which Jomini's had met in confronting changing historical conditions and technological transformation, indeed, they failed at the very same points. On land, improved firearms were transforming tactics, and steam locomotion was revolutionizing strategy. While Jomini and his disciples, steeped in the Napoleonic era and committed to immutable principles, found it hard enough to swallow the former, they could never accept the latter. At sea, steam ironclads, steel guns and armour, the torpedo, the mine, and, finally, the internal combustion engine were revolutionizing naval warfare in much the same way.[78] Yet, holding to the axiom that the details of tactics might change but that the principles of strategy were universal, and nostalgically attached to the great age of sail, Mahan was at pains to ward off anything that might threaten the foundations of his theories of sea power and naval warfare. The case of the railroad has already been mentioned. Jomini had continued to deny that it could change the eternal principles of strategy as demonstrated by Napoleon—until he was proved wrong by the Prussians. Mahan was equally insistent that the railroad could not overshadow sea-

[77] Mahan, *The Life of Nelson, The Embodiment of the Sea Power of Great Britain* (London, 1899), 294, 490, 694–5.

[78] By far the best study of these developments and of their overall significance is Marder, *The Anatomy of British Sea Power* (London, 1940); see also Bernard Brodie, *Sea Power in the Machine Age* (Princeton, NJ, 1941).

and river-transportation and thus the supremacy of naval power, because the latter would always remain cheaper. 'These distinctions', he wrote, 'are not accidental or temporary; they are of the nature of things and permanent.'[79]

Mahan had little to say about steam locomotion at sea. In any case, steam locomotion did not seem to make much difference to the principles of naval warfare, especially the dominance of the great naval battle and the supremacy of the battleship. Even here, however, when, in 1906, the British revolutionized battleship architecture with the introduction of the huge, controversial, all-big-gun HMS *Dreadnought*, Mahan opposed the new trend outright. He feared an escalating contest over size, to which no definite end could be foreseen. He thought there was no point in building ships larger than 10,000 tons (compared with the *Dreadnought*'s 18,000), the equivalents of the seventy-four-gun ship-of-the-line which had become the standard in the age of sail.[80] An escalating contest over size did develop and was not to stop before the battleship itself, more than three times larger than the original *Dreadnought* was taken out of use after the Second World War. Yet the race itself was, technically speaking, inevitable, given the fact that, in contrast to the situation with wooden sailing-ships, there was no natural limit to the size of steel hulls, or to the size of the steam or diesel engines constructed for these increasingly powerful monsters. Mahan also opposed the introduction of the single, large-calibre battery which, with the *Dreadnought*, became the standard weapon of battleships. He favoured the mixed battery which had formed the armament of battleships since the days of sail. He was not sufficiently familiar with the new developments in long-range gunnery and fire-control which had made the all-big-gun ship possible. He apprehended the very idea of long-range artillery duels as a retreat from the dashing Nelsonian tradition of hand-to-hand combat to the older, now-discarded, linear tactics. When William S. Sims, then a lieutenant-commander, answered Mahan's arguments publicly on the pages of *U.S. Naval Institute Proceedings*, it became clear, not least to Mahan himself, that the ageing authority was out of touch.[81]

[79] Mahan, *The Problem of Asia*, 37–8.

[80] Mahan, *Lessons of the War with Spain*, 41, 264–6; id., *Naval Administration and Warfare*, 141–3.

[81] Mahan, 'Reflections, Historic and Other, Suggested by the Battle of the Japan Sea', *United States Navy Institute Proceedings* (June 1906), 447–71; W. S. Sims,

However, the really serious challenges to the precepts and principles of classical naval warfare came from elsewhere. The torpedo was the most extraordinary and potent new naval weapon in the 1880s. In France, the Jeune école made it the centre-piece of its programme, envisioning swarms of small, fast torpedo-boats, which would raid and destroy mammoth but helpless British battle-fleets.[82] Whether the big battleship was doomed was a question no one ventured to answer definitely in the 1880s, not even the British Admiralty. In 1886 the parliamentary secretary to the Admiralty confessed that he might be approaching Parliament for new battleships for the last time.[83] Upon entering the Naval War College, Mahan automatically enlisted in the struggle of the 'New Navy' circle for a navy of battleships which would be able to command American waters. The old policy, which had been based on monitors and cruisers for coastal defence and commerce-raiding and which prevailed for as long as the USA was too weak to challenge the command of the seas, was now totally rejected.[84] The torpedo had many enthusiasts in the navy, but Mahan's verdict was typically belittling. In his War College lectures on tactics, he dismissed the torpedo-boat on the grounds that 'in the days of the sailing ships, which have made nearly all naval history so far', the fire-ship had proven unsuccessful, and 'there is little reason to doubt that the experience we have yet to gain in this will be like the experience the world has always had heretofore'.[85]

'The Inherent Tactical Qualities of the All-Big-Gun, One Caliber Battleship of High Speed, Large Displacement and Gun Power', ibid. (Sep. 1906), 1337–66; Mahan, *Letters and Papers*, iii. 170–1, 177–80, 193, 204; *Fear God and Dread Nought: The Correspondence of Admiral of the Fleet Lord Fisher of Kilverstone*, ed. Arthur Marder (3 vols.; London, 1956), ii. 96–7.

[82] The most complete exposition of the *Jeune école's* programme and vision, written by one of its major exponents, is Gabriel Charmes, *Naval Reform* (London, 1887); the best study is Theodore Ropp, *The Development of a Modern Navy: French Naval Policy 1871–1904* (Annapolis, Md., 1987), esp. 19–22, 155–80, 254–80; also see John Raymond Walser, 'France's Search for a Battlefleet: French Naval Policy 1898–1914' (unpub. doc. diss., University of North California, 1976), 49–50.

[83] Marder, *The Anatomy of British Sea Power*, 125; the whole chapter (pp. 119–143) is excellent on the confusion of tactical ideas in the 1880s. Also see Admiral Sir George Elliot's popular but instructive *A Treatise on Future Naval Battles and How to Fight them* (London, 1885), esp. 1–38.

[84] See the developing tendency and many statements to that effect, preceding, and unrelated to, Mahan, in Spector, *Professors of War*, 47–9; also Mahan, *Lessons of the War with Spain*, 264–80.

[85] Mahan, 'Fleet Battle Tactics', 1886, unpub. lectures, quoted in Spector, *Professors of War*, 45. Also see, more lukewarmly, *Influence I*, 110–11, 113–14.

To its French enthusiasts, the torpedo and the mine held the promise of breaking one of the most effective devices in the traditional British system of war—the blockade. Slipping out of harbour under cover of night, torpedo-boats would imperil any ship which remained within range, dozens of miles away. As the British navy discovered to its alarm during the extensive manœuvres which it conducted in 1888 to examine the problem, a close blockade to seal off the French harbours had become virtually impossible.[86] Whether this really was so, and what the consequences would be for the future of British naval mastery, were some of the most troubling questions with which naval circles in Britain grappled from the 1880s. Mahan had no doubts over the matter. The tactics which had served Hawke, Jervis, and Nelson so effectively would remain in force for as long as ships were ships and harbours were harbours. However, when war came in 1914, a close blockading of the German harbours was totally out of the question. A blockade of Germany could be imposed only by virtue of Germany's great geographical disadvantage; her routes to the open sea, unlike those of France, could be bottled up hundreds of miles away from her shores, at the two narrow entrances to the North Sea, through the Channel and the Shetlands, both of which were under British control.

When, after almost three-quarters of a century of peaceful relations, France's old rivalry with Britain was reignited by the British occupation of Egypt, the French resorted to their old strategy of commerce-destroying. They regarded it as a means of striking at Britain's oceanic lifelines, while avoiding direct confrontation with her stronger navy. The successful operations of the Confederate's commerce-raiders, notably the *Alabama*, during the American Civil War were another source of inspiration for the French. Dominating France's naval policy in the mid-1880s, the Jeune école calculated that in the late nineteenth century, when Britain was dependent as never before on imported foodstuffs to feed her populations, the revived *guerre de course* might have a deadly effect. With the price of naval insurance rocketing and with French gunboats bombarding British coastal towns, Britain might be severely shaken.

The influence of the Jeune école ebbed in the 1890s. The great

[86] Marder, *The Anatomy of British Sea Power*, 107–9.

British naval revival that followed the passage of the Naval Act of 1889—a revival which contrasted sharply with the badly conceived French construction-schemes—damaged French morale. Enthusiasm for the torpedo subsided with the introduction of the destroyer, designed to protect battle-fleets from marauding torpedo-boats. Naval analysts everywhere were on the whole agreed that in modern times commerce-destroying would be less rather than more effective than in the age of sail. Telegraph communications, which linked all the major stations of the British navy, would make it much easier to track down French raiders. The need for coaling would severely restrict their range and freedom of action. From the late 1890s, all navies were again concentrating on building battleships and preparing for major naval battles. Britain, Tirpitz's Germany, America, and Japan were taking the lead. The *guerre de course*, which had kindled imagination in the 1880s, was falling into disrepute, and Mahan's teaching, again while not creating the trend, influenced it considerably by the firmness and authoritativeness of its conclusions. Commerce-destroying, he argued, had never been, and could never become, a substitute for the command of the sea, no matter what technical means were used. This was a universal truth, repeatedly revealed in history and unaffected by changes in one detail or another.

Once again, however, the introduction of a new weapon-system, the submarine, which had been made possible by the invention of the internal combustion engine at the end of the nineteenth century, was to prove a technological change which would undermine Mahan's universal principles. That Mahan regarded the submarine as nothing more than a submerged, coast-defence torpedo-boat, possibly particularly effective and troublesome because of its peculiar quality, was nothing special; practically nobody thought otherwise before 1914, not even that progressive-minded reformer and ardent supporter of the submarine, Admiral John Fisher.[87] Mahan's theories, however, ruled out a priori the idea of a naval campaign launched by submarines.[88] And yet, in two world wars, despite having unprecedented naval superiority over its continental rival, Britain was to come closer than ever before to being defeated at sea. She was driven to that point by an enemy who used the new and deadly weapon in a large-scale, ferocious *guerre de course*.

[87] Ibid. 363, 367–8, 495.

[88] E.g. Mahan, *Naval Strategy*, 3–4.

That Britain did not in the end lose the war at sea was not due to any inherent limitations of commerce-destroying. It was due above all to the fact that at the time of crisis she was joined—in both world wars—by a gigantic ally, the USA, whose massive resources made the struggle against Germany, at sea and otherwise, an unequal one and almost inevitable in its ultimate results. To balance the record, however, it might be noted that, while less dogmatic minds in Britain thought that the days of the wasteful and cumbersome convoy-system to protect commerce were over, Mahan held fast to the opinion that such a system was as necessary as it had been in the age of sail. Indeed, by 1917 the convoy system had been reintroduced as the most effective defence against the submarine.

When the First World War came, naval circles found themselves in a remarkably similar predicament to the one with which their army counterparts were struggling on land. While most of the new weapons and tactical developments were known, and their significance was at least partially recognized, warfare as a whole assumed an unexpected, strange, and, as it were, unsatisfactory character. Rather than leading quickly to a major battle of destruction in the North Sea, in which the fate of the naval operations would be decided in Nelsonian fashion and command of the sea established, the war turned out to be a protracted struggle of attrition. Hundreds of miles of artificial obstacles, as well as patrolling submarines, hindered movement almost as severely as on the Western front. The navy could no longer regard the enemy's shores as its front line or sail wherever it pleased in the same way that armies no longer travelled relatively open spaces in their theatres of operations. Both on land and at sea, the war became one of position. In the deadlock which emerged in the new technological environment, both the Napoleonic and Nelsonian models and the strategic theories based upon them and claiming universal validity failed to materialize.

CORBETT'S REVISIONISM FROM DRAKE TO JUTLAND

As the foremost historian of British sea-power in the late nineteenth and early twentieth centuries has noted, public interest in the navy, which was later to become such a distinctive part of British identity, barely existed before the 1880s.[89] In the age of Pax Britannica after 1815, when Britain truly ruled the waves unchallenged, the British public took the Royal Navy's policing of the world's oceans for granted. For the Victorians it was inseparable from, and as solid as, Britain's innate superiority and benevolent influence over the rest of the world.[90] Their confidence was only rarely shaken. One such occasion came in 1859, when the French launched the first ironclad, *La Gloire*, and created panic over the possibility that 'steam had bridged the English Channel'. Another came in 1866–71, when Prussia overturned the European balance of power with impressive demonstrations of military proficiency.

While industrialization and ever increasing world-trade were revolutionizing the British economy, and steam was transforming naval warfare, there was in Britain only one man who publicly gave serious consideration to the implications inherent in the new conditions for the defence of the British Isles and the Empire. Captain (later Sir) John Colomb (1838–1909) of the Royal Marines had retired from military service in 1866–7 to start a career in politics, initially in Irish local government and later in Parliament. Possibly the first strategic analyst Britain had known, his pamphlets, articles, and lectures called for a comprehensive and coherent approach to the problem of the defence of the Empire, taken as a whole. He fully appreciated the close relationship which existed between strategy and the emerging world economy, and excelled in analyzing trade statistics and in demonstrating their significance in relation to the problem of imperial defence. Many of his acute observations, the manner in which he framed the questions, and the phrases he coined gained universal currency later in the century, when naval affairs moved to the forefront of public attention. Cruelly, however, little credit was awarded John Colomb for his pioneering work over the previous decades. There was something in the man which made people regard him as a bore.[91]

While the Prussian military successes in 1866 and 1871 aroused

[89] Marder, *The Anatomy of British Sea Power*, 44–5.

[90] For British attitudes during the age of Pax Britannica, see Semmel, *Liberalism and Naval Strategy*, *passim*.

[91] The man and his work are presented in Howard d'Egville, *Imperial Defence and Closer Union: A Short Record of the Life Work of Sir John Colomb and of the Movement Toward Imperial Organization* (London, 1913); D. M. Schurman, *The Education of a Navy: The Development of British Naval Strategic Thought 1867–1914* (London, 1965), 16–35.

public concern over defence and generated the Cardwell reforms in the British army, John Colomb reminded his readers that the question of defence did not begin with the qualities of the needle-gun but with the overall organization and allocation of national forces to meet national goals. Britain's defence problems were entirely different from those of a continental power.[92] Britain was a colonial empire which had to contend with, and reconcile, the different but interrelated defence-requirements of the island-state itself, of the empire's sea-communications, and of the colonies, particularly India. According to Colomb, the public's agitation over the defence of Britain against invasion and over the schemes for military reform was characterized by a tendency to consider only one aspect of the problem in isolation. 'Supposing we had the most perfect military system the world has ever seen—every man a trained soldier, every hill-top crowned with batteries, every road swept by mitrailleuse[s], what would it avail us?' he asked.[93] Colomb was the first to point out a fact which later became the cornerstone of the argument of the so-called 'blue-water school', namely, the prospect of a major invasion presupposed that the British navy would be so overwhelmed as to lose control over Britain's home waters; however, in that eventuality no invasion would be necessary. By the late nineteenth century, Britain was becoming increasingly dependent on imported foodstuffs, whicn formed more than half her total consumption by the 1880s. Her problem was thus not invasion but investment;[94] or as Fisher who had little patience for the Colombs later put it: 'It is not *invasion* we have to fear if our navy is beaten, IT'S STARVATION!'[95] Impressed by the Prussians, the public focused its attention on the army and neglected the navy. Yet, no matter now strong the army was to become, its strength would in effect prove irrelevant to the protection of the British islands.

John Colomb, however, was no naval fanatic like some later 'blue water' enthusiasts. In his admirably systematic analysis of the

[92] John Colomb, *The Protection of Our Commerce and Distribution of Our Naval Forces Considered* (London, 1867); id., *Imperial Defence* (London, 1871), 5–6. For the background see Schurman, *Education of a Navy*, 17–19.

[93] Colomb, *Imperial Defence*, 7.

[94] See progressively in Colomb's works: *Imperial Defence*, 6–7; *Colonial Defence*, (London, 1877), 3 *et passim*; and, admirably documented with trade statistics and data on food imports, *Naval Intelligence and Protection of Commerce in War* (London, 1881), 7 *et passim*.

[95] Quoted in Marder, *The Anatomy of British Sea Power*, 65.

Empire's strategic situation, he stressed that national defence had never been the problem of the navy alone, and never would be.[96] A combined package of naval and military means was necessary to meet the Empire's varied defence-needs. While the navy blockaded the enemy's ports, protected commerce, and defended the British islands against invasion and investment, and the colonies against sea-borne expeditions, it was not able to provide full protection against naval and military raids on ports and coastal towns. For those purposes and for those only, argued Colomb, Britain needed coast-defence vessels and fortifications, garrisons and militia. Thus the work of the 'brick-and-mortar school', which had dominated during the invasion scare of 1859, may have been misguided and overdone but was not entirely misplaced. The navy, added Colomb, was insufficient to the task also in that it was unable to defend the colonies against land invasions by continental powers like Russia or the United States, and was unable to carry the war into the enemy's own territory. This, according to Colomb, was where the army ought to come in, working in close co-operation and co-ordination with the navy.[97] In retrospect, after a century of strategic debate, the wisdom of his balanced programme is vindicated by most commentators, even if its pioneering advocate has never received the credit he deserves.

Better-known and operating in an environment which was becoming increasingly concerned about naval affairs was John Colomb's elder brother, Philip (1831–99). During his long service in the navy, Philip Colomb developed a system of light-signals which the navy adopted, wrote a lively account of his period of duty in the Indian Ocean, and in 1878 won the Naval Essay Prize of the Royal United Services Institution for his paper *Great Britain's Maritime Power: How Best Developed*. He retired from the navy in 1886 and was subsequently promoted to Rear-Admiral (1887) and Vice-Admiral (1892). Only then, when he became instructor of naval strategy and tactics at the Royal Naval College at Greenwich, at almost the same time as Mahan was appointed to Newport, did the period of his scholarly and literary productivity begin.[98]

[96] Colomb, *Imperial Defence*, 8.

[97] See esp. Colomb, *Protection and Distribution*, 10–12; *Imperial Defence*, 8, 14–18, *et passim*; *Colonial Defence*, *passim*.

[98] The only study is the chapter in Schurman's excellent *Education of a Navy*, 36–56.

Philip Colomb's prize essay of 1877 was heavily influenced by his brother's opinions, whose contribution he fully acknowledged. The essay stressed the need for a comprehensive view of the empire's defence-requirements and addressed itself to Britain's new food-problem and its strategic consequences. Under the new conditions, he argued, the island's main worry was enemy blockade, not invasion.[99] He differed from his brother on one point only. He did not accept the latter's subtle analysis of the complex modality of the navy's mission. For Philip Colomb that mission amounted to the much simpler formula of blockading the enemy in its ports and protecting Britain's commercial and maritime communications.[100] This was a difference which, when developed a decade later, was to make him one of the earliest exponents and the foremost theoretician of the 'blue-water school'.

Philip Colomb's essays on Britain's strategic naval problems, written mostly in the late 1880s, appeared in book form in 1893 under the title *Essays on Naval Defence*. His theoretical-historical studies, first issued as a magazine serial, were then compiled and republished as *Naval Warfare, Its Ruling Principles and Practice, Historically Treated* (1891). Both books advance similar ideas. As British supremacy at sea was being challenged for the first time since Trafalgar, and the prospect of a naval war against a Franco-Russian coalition was looming large, Colomb returned to the great naval struggles of the past to evoke the image of Britain as an oceanic empire and mistress of the seas. In those days, Britain had been defended purely by the navy. The sea was her domain. Its communications resembled a country's inland roads. The enemy's shores were her frontiers. (This was another catch-phrase which Fisher was to make his own.)[101]

In two lectures delivered in 1888 and 1889 at the Royal United Service Institution, Colomb amazed his audience of both services, particularly the army officers, by denying the value of anything but a high-seas navy for Britain's defence. In the previous chapter we saw that, in the name of a true and shining conception of warfare, which they discovered in a more distant and glorious past, French

[99] Philip Colomb, *Great Britain's Maritime Power: How Best Developed* (London, 1878), 3–7; the essay was reprinted in id., *Essays on Naval Defence* (London, 1893), 31–128. [100] Ibid. 10.

[101] Philip Colomb, *Essays on Naval Defence*, 20–3, 129–30. For Fisher see Marder, *The Anatomy of British Sea Power*, 68.

military theorists of the period were rebelling against the fixed fortifications which had been constructed in France in the previous decade. In the same way, Colomb argued that coastal defences, garrisons, and gun-boats, inherited from the panic of 1859, were virtually useless. He maintained that careful historical study showed that whenever naval supremacy had been achieved, fortifications were never put to the test; on the other hand, he argued, once naval supremacy had been lost, no fortifications were able to save major bases like Minorca or Gibraltar from a resolute enemy attack.[102] The sole aim of naval war, he argued, was command of the sea. Once this was achieved, everything else would follow.[103] Since now as before, the enemy's fleet was unlikely to challenge the Royal Navy in the open, the blockade, in its close or more distant forms, would remain the basis of British strategy even under the altered conditions of the present. While the action of commerce-raiders was now limited by coaling, and while the wasteful convoy-system might have lost its usefulness, the *guerre de course* would none the less remain the main threat.[104]

That Britain needed no Mahan to formulate the principles of naval supremacy and to articulate the ethos of her great past is evident. Yet it is equally evident that Mahan became almost at once an international celebrity, while Colomb won only modest reputation, mainly in professional circles. One reason for this was that Colomb, as one historian has put it, was 'scooped'.[105] *Naval Warfare*, which had been conceived simultaneously with Mahan's work, was published in book form only a year later. More important still, however, was the fact that Mahan's *Influence* book was more suited to the general public, more historical and less technical. It was enlightening and delighting, almost sublime. Mahan had no equal in interweaving naval history into the wider picture of general history, and, in the preface to his book, Colomb modestly bowed to the 'abler pen and deeper thinker' whose work had been published before his book left the press.[106] Having said this, however, as naval theory *per se*, Colomb's book is probably the more impressive. The main themes are the same as Mahan's

[102] Colomb, *Essays on Naval Defence*, 11–13, 149–51, 160–93.
[103] Ibid. 190, 210.
[104] Ibid. 154–9, 194–257.
[105] Schurman, *Education of a Navy*, 53.
[106] Philip Colomb, *Naval Warfare, Its Ruling Principles and Practice, Historically Treated* (London, 1891), p. viii.

but, as a systematic treatise, *Naval Warfare* is much more neatly organized.

In synthesizing the theoretical out of the historical, Colomb skilfully let every period in the chronological sequence of British naval ascendancy present a different naval theme. The struggle against Spain serves as the first, introductory chapter of the book, which deals with the nature of naval warfare. Unlike Mahan, Colomb distinguished clearly between war at sea before and during the age of sail. Before, there were naval battles, naval (or, more accurately, sea-borne) expeditions, and naval (sea-borne) raids, but no naval warfare in the later sense. This appeared only when the advent of sail produced sea-keeping ships which could remain at sea for very long periods and thus claim and maintain command over that 'vast common land'.[107] This was the reality which emerged during the Elizabethan age. It was grasped by Monson and Raleigh, who discovered the true principles of the naval art, centring on the acquisition of command of the sea.[108]

The Anglo-Dutch naval wars, says Colomb, demonstrated this new rationale. Command of the sea was the means; the destruction and protection of trade the end. The English won because of their greater naval strength and superior geographical position. The chapters in *Naval Warfare* dealing with the Anglo-French struggle examine the problem of the invasion of the British islands, which for more than a century was the main aim of French strategic planning. In Colomb's opinion, the French failed because of erroneous principles. Unless one expects strong support in the invaded country (Jacobite), no invasion can be attempted without first securing command over the water-crossings. The French tried to make do without the only means which could have led them to success—the concentration of superior naval forces in the Channel. Their ulterior purpose distracted them from the fundamental imperatives of war at sea.

Finally, in one case-study after another, Colomb examined the subject of sea-borne expeditions and came up with some significant observations. He discerned a major reason for failures in such expeditions in a duality of purpose, when a naval campaign distracted attention from the land operation. He emphasized the necessity of an adequate military force to accompany the fleet. The

[107] Colomb, *Naval Warfare*, 1–6; cf. Guilmartin, *Gunpowder and Galleys*, 2–3, 16, 18 *et passim*.

[108] Colomb, *Naval Warfare*, 10–24.

navy could not be expected to perform the military mission. He argued that once naval control over a local theatre of operations had been achieved, fortifications could only delay the fall of remote colonial and strategic outposts and bases.[109]

Naval Warfare was an admirably coherent and systematic exposition, clearly oriented to the present and of great didactic value. At the same time, however, it is obvious that like Mahan's *Influence* books, Colomb's book suffered from the characteristic flaws of the 'blue water' argument. In emphasizing the war at sea and the navy, it tended to downgrade, at least by omission, the role of continental operations and the army. Exalting as it did the potency of the navy, it overlooked its limitations. Bewitched by the 'Nelsonian model', it reduced the diversity of naval warfare and the complexity of historical conditions to one standard method. Like the military theories of its time, its apparently deep commitment to the past was in fact tendentious. To a large degree, both were cultivating a historical myth, nourished from the springs of national tradition at times of wavering confidence.

In the naval, as in the field of military history and theory, opposition, limited as it was, to the prevailing picture of the past and to the ruling strategic precepts drew largely on the methods and standards of modern historical scholarship. This was what Mahan respectfully called history 'after the high modern pattern', but actually regarded as somewhat pedantic and as something which he himself did not need. The growth of modern naval historical scholarship is connected with the name of Sir John Laughton (1830–1915), a Cambridge graduate in mathematics who became head of the department of meteorology and marine surveying at Greenwich when the Royal Naval College was opened there in 1873. In 1876 he started teaching naval history at the college. In 1885 he retired from the navy to become professor of modern history at King's College, London.[110]

Laughton wrote extensively in two diverging genres: popular history on the one hand, and meticulously researched chronicles on the other, particularly the hundreds of items he wrote for the *Dictionary of National Biography*. On the whole, reading him is disappointing. Although, in a seminal RUSI lecture delivered in 1874, he called for the scientific study of naval history, he in fact

[109] Ibid., esp. 203, 278, 375, 430.

[110] See again Schurman, *Education of a Navy*, 83–109.

propagated the historical and strategic outlook, which Mahan and Colomb were later to make their own and develop into a magnificent edifice.[111] His main contribution, however, lay elsewhere. From 1879 he had access to the Public Record Office, which later (1887) opened its gates to all scholars. In 1893 he founded the Navy Record Society, whose first secretary he became. Well-connected and eminent among all those concerned with naval affairs, Laughton initiated and presided over the vast compilation and publication of primary archival material from the navy's records.[112] One whom he persuaded to take part in this enterprise was Sir Julian Corbett.

Corbett (1854–1922) came to naval history in mid-life and from a civilian background. He took a first in law at Cambridge but, never liking the legal profession and being a man of independent means, he retired from active practice altogether in 1882. He travelled extensively, sought a literary career, and wrote a few, marginally successful novels. The popular biographies he wrote of Monk and Drake led him to join the Navy Record Society when that was founded in 1893. In 1896 he accepted Laughton's request to edit a volume of documents on the Spanish war, 1585–7. Thus began a career which was to dominate the rest of his life.[113]

Corbett's historical writings can be divided into two categories: the volumes he edited for the Navy Record Society on the development of British fighting-instructions and signals, and his histories of selected periods in British naval warfare. Both involved radically new interpretations of the past; the one of naval tactics, the other of naval strategy. In line with these came a new understanding of the present. All these themes were interrelated but, for clarity's sake, they will be treated here in succession.

In *Fighting Instructions, 1530–1816*, Corbett compiled and commented upon all printed British naval regulations which had survived and had been discovered from the earliest times. Although

[111] See esp. John K. Laughton, 'The Scientific Study of History', *Journal of the Royal United Services Institution*, 18, 1875, 508–27; id., *Essays on Naval Tactics* (London, 1874), 3–17; id., *Studies in Naval History* (London, 1887), *passim.*

[112] See Julian S. Corbett, 'The Revival of Naval History', 4 Oct. 1916, *Corbett Papers*, Box 4.

[113] Schurman, *Julian S. Corbett, 1854–1922* (London, 1981), cannot be bettered. See also id., *Education of a Navy*, 147–84; Peter M. Stamford, 'The Work of Sir Julian Corbett in the Dreadnought Era', *United States Naval Institute Proceedings*, 77 (1951), 61–71; and Eric J. Grove's fine Introduction to Corbett, *Some Principles of Maritime Strategy* (Annapolis, Md., 1988), pp. xi–xlv.

the book's title went back to the Elizabethan age, material predating the Anglo-Dutch wars was not found, and possibly had not existed in the first place. In respect of the middle of the seventeenth century onwards, however, the *Instructions*, fragmented and incomplete as they were, provided the main primary source on the development of British, and foreign, naval tactics. Confronted with the bare evidence of the past, undisguised by later traditions and interpretations, Corbett's strong historical sense gradually came to detect a story different from the accepted one.

Tracing the succession of fighting-instructions which, since 1653, had been establishing the line as the ruling battle-formation, Corbett doubted that these instructions had been foolishly pedantic or had led to a degeneration of naval warfare in the eighteenth century. At almost the same time, in Germany, Delbrück was appealing to the relativity and inner logic of historical situations in rehabilitating eighteenth-century land-warfare, which had been discredited by the men of his own century. In a rather similar way, Corbett argued that the new discipline of the instructions and the new linear tactics had evolved over a long period of time, in response to the existing historical conditions. Increasing fire-power had necessitated a regulated system of control and manœuvre, even at the cost of individual initiative. The breaking of the enemy's line had been becoming rarer and rarer simply because increasing fire-power had been making it too dangerous a manœuvre.[114] Thus, argued Corbett, 'the manœuvre of breaking the line was abandoned by the tacticians of that era, not from ignorance nor from lack of enterprise, but from a deliberate tactical conviction gained by the experience of war'.[115]

If *Fighting Instructions* provided a historically sympathetic view of the origins and function of linear tactics, newly discovered documents, which Corbett compiled under the title *Signals and Instructions, 1776–1794* (1908), offered a fresh look over the period in which linear tactics were reformed. During the very same years that Corbett was working on the *Instructions*, Colin, researching in the French archives, was discovering that Revolutionary column-tactics had been rooted in an evolutionary process which had been gathering momentum during the last decades of the *ancien régime*. Studying British records, Corbett was independently

[114] Julian Corbett, *Fighting Instructions, 1530–1816* (London, 1905), 134–5, 176, 178, 183.

[115] Ibid. 184.

arriving at similar conclusions regarding naval warfare. He found out that the change from linear to column shock-tactics had not occurred in one revolutionary step, and were not an ingenious creation of people like Eldin, Rodney, Howe, or Nelson. He showed that signals for the breaking of the enemy's line had been issued by individual admirals at least as early as the 1770s, even before Rodney's famous manœuvre. These signals had been devised under the influence of the French authorities Morogues and Villehuet, whose treatises on naval tactics, composed in the 1760s, had been read by virtually everybody. Corbett suggested that Eldin's ideas provoked little attention in 1790 because reform was already in full swing within the Admiralty. In any case, he argued, the dramatic successes brought about by the new tactics were due solely to the degeneration of the French navy. Had it not been for that, Nelson's perpendicular attack at Trafalgar would have been an act of madness. Indeed, tactical instructions after Nelson recognized no dramatic change and remained in essence conservative and linear as before.[116]

Corbett's successive and voluminous studies of British naval operations from Drake to Nelson undermined the prevailing picture of the past and the accepted tenets of naval theory in an even more radical fashion than did his works on the records of British naval tactics. The similarity with Delbrück's work is striking and, in view of the resemblance which existed between the military and naval traditions that both men grew to challenge, is not really surprising. Like Delbrück, Corbett came out with a thorough revision of strategic outlook, whose implications for the present were far-reaching. For all the differences between the German academic and the Anglo-Saxon's more cavalier attitude to scholarly apparatus, in both cases their revisions stemmed from a deeply historical approach. In the process, both men profited enormously from Clausewitz's distinction between absolute and limited war and from his emphasis on the relationship between the military means and the political aim. Finally, in both cases the new ideas met with resistance and became the centre of controversy.

[116] Corbett (ed.), *Signals and Instructions, 1776–1794* (London, 1908), *passim*; id., *Fighting Instructions*, 313–60; id., *The Campaign of Trafalgar* (London, 1910), 347–59. On the whole, Corbett's conclusions are borne out by modern historical scholarship; see esp. John Creswell's highly knowledgeable and even more demythologizing *British Admirals of the Eighteenth Century* (London, 1972).

In *Drake and the Tudor Navy* (2 vols; 1898), Corbett's first serious historical work, questions of naval doctrine are rarely discussed and strategic judgement is rarely passed. The book is above all a historical one, and is a sound one as such, despite the author's evident admiration for his hero. In the book, however, Corbett still holds as self-evident that command of the sea is the proper aim of naval war. He began to diverge from accepted 'blue water' assumptions only with his second book, *The Successors of Drake* (1900).

In that book, Corbett dealt with the period 1596–1603, generally regarded as an anticlimax to the victory over the Armada. The victory had not led to the total destruction of Spanish naval power, or to a blockade of the Spanish ports aimed at cutting off the flow of bullion from America, as people like Drake, Hawkins, and Raleigh had recommended. The continuation of the war had seen the revival of the Spanish navy and, on the English part, the war had seemed to degenerate into mostly unsuccessful raids. For navalists both then and later, the blame for this development fell mainly on the queen's over-cautious attitude and on her continental strategy, which wasted resources and diverted attention from the naval campaign. But for Corbett the matter was far from clear-cut. He pointed out, as later historians of the period would do, that Elizabethan England had still been a relatively poor and weak country, bearing no comparison with the mighty and wealthy Spanish Empire. It had probably been beyond her power and would have been too risky a policy on her part to aim at overthrowing Spain. He also pointed out that the queen had given her naval commanders many opportunities to carry out their plans. Most of these plans had failed, however, principally because the navy had not carried sufficient troops on board its ships to support its actions. Here was a lesson which Britain still had not learned. People forget that what Nelson started, Wellington ended. While talking much about sea power, they forget that its real effect is in determining the extent to which armies can be transported freely by sea.[117]

Corbett's *England in the Mediterranean 1603–1713* (2 vols.;

[117] Corbett, *The Successors of Drake* (London, 1900), esp. 1, 407–10. Also see Schurman, *Education of a Navy*, 152; R. B. Wernham, 'Elizabethan War Aims and Strategy', in S. T. Bindoff, J. Hurstfield, and C. H. Williams (eds.), *Elizabethan Government and Society* (London, 1961), 340–68; G. Mattingly, *The Defeat of the Spanish Armada* (London, 1959); Kennedy, *The Rise and Fall of British Naval Mastery*, 27–30.

1904), based on lectures he delivered in Greenwich and repeated as the Ford Lectures at Oxford, did not carry much in the way of a theoretical message. But then came Corbett's discovery of Clausewitz, which, feeding Corbett's own train of thought, proved to be enormously stimulating for him. His next historical work, *England in the Seven Years War: A Study in Combined Strategy* (2 vols.; 1907), became a case-study for a thorough-going revision of naval theory.

The main thrust of Corbett's argument was directed against what he called the narrowing of the concept of naval warfare to the winning of battles and the gaining of command of the sea. This concept he considered misleading and educationally dangerous. He maintained that command of the sea was certainly the main aim of war at sea but not the only one. An opportunity to fight a battle does not always exist, nor is battle always necessary. For example, he argued, in the Mediterranean theatre during the Spanish War of Succession, the English won without beating the enemy's fleet; their naval supremacy being recognized, they could still reap most of the advantages.[118] Hence,

> we require for the guidance of our naval policy and naval action something of wider vision than the current conception of naval strategy, something that will keep before our eyes not merely the enemy's fleets or the great routes of commerce, or the command of the sea, but also the relations of naval policy and action to the whole area of diplomatic and military effort.[119]

This, he maintained, was particularly important in view of the naval myth which had grown to govern official and public opinion alike:

> Of late years the world has become so deeply impressed with the efficacy of sea power that we are inclined to forget how impotent it is of itself to decide a war against great Continental states, how tedious is the pressure of naval action unless it be nicely coordinated with military and diplomatic pressure.[120]

The war with Spain came to an end only fifteen years after the defeat of the Armada; the war with Napoleon's France only ten years after Trafalgar. Truly great powers, argued Corbett, cannot

[118] Corbett, *England in the Seven Years War: A Study in Combined Strategy* (2 vols.; London, 1907), i. 3–5. [119] Ibid. 5. [120] Ibid.

be defeated solely at sea.[121] In concluding his study of *The Campaign of Trafalgar*, Corbett rejected the Mahanite view of the struggle against Imperial France. The naval victory, he argued, secured the British command of the seas and safeguarded the empire but left Napoleon as the dictator of Europe. Sea power had done all that sea power could possibly do, but for Europe, whose fate was decided at Austerlitz, not Trafalgar, this was a failure.[122]

> Here then we get a formula widely different from the current definitions of naval strategy . . . We begin to distinguish more clearly between the means and the end of naval policy . . . the historical method reveals that the command of the sea is only a means to an end. It never has been and never can be the end itself.[123]

Clausewitz postulated in theory what the Elder Pitt had demonstrated in practice, that war was a continuation and means of state policy and, consequently, could take different forms, either unlimited or limited.[124] This, argued Corbett, applied equally to the French, whose defensive naval strategy during the Seven Years War proved adapted to their position. Their strategy must not be dismissed only because in that particular case France lost the war.[125]

Past and present were intimately linked in Corbett's thinking. His revision of naval theory and history was stimulated by, and in turn affected, his growing role as the navy's leading intellectual. From 1901 he was writing regularly on naval affairs for the liberal journal *The Monthly Review*. Lending support to the major reforms by which Fisher, Second and later First Sea Lord, was overhauling the navy, he became one of the principal members of Fisher's circle.[126] From 1902 he was lecturing on naval history in the new war course opened at the Naval War College in 1900. From 1905 he began to lecture on naval strategy. At the same time, he became the Admiralty's chief unofficial strategic adviser.

In the war course, Corbett was trying to convey to the attending flag-officers something very different from the accepted precepts of

[121] Ibid. 5, 7.
[122] Corbett, *Trafalgar*, 408, 423–4.
[123] Corbett, *England in the Seven Years War*, i. 6.
[124] Ibid. i. 24, 28, 190, 336.
[125] Ibid. ii. 373–4.
[126] For their extensive correspondence see *Corbett Papers*, Box 12, only partly printed in Fisher, *Fear God and Dread Nought*.

navalism. His arguments were nothing as inspiring as the teachings of Mahan, that great pamphleteer and populizer of naval history and theory, as Corbett—sometimes admiringly, sometimes critically—referred to him.[127] Unlike Delbrück, who debated with relish against the advocates of all-out war, Corbett was operating within, and trying to influence, the naval establishment. He had to filter his ideas through, often in a roundabout way. This may have been psychologically more palatable to his audience but it also left them more bemused. They suspected his logic was leading him astray, especially as he was a civilian theoretician rather than a practical seaman. In 1906, in order to provide a clear frame of reference for his students, Corbett, in collaboration with the director of the War College, Captain Edmond J. W. Slade, issued a slim booklet entitled *Strategic Terms and Definitions used in Lectures on Naval History*, and better known as the 'Green Pamphlet'. A second, revised version of the pamphlet, *Notes on Strategy*, was issued in 1909. Corbett's book *Some Principles of Maritime Strategy* (1911) put flesh on the bare bones of the pamphlet and offered his ideas to the general public.[128]

While being in essence an *étude* on Clausewitz, Corbett's work, notwithstanding its various modest titles, was a thoroughgoing and most original revision of the accepted tenets of naval theory and indeed, more implicitly, of strategic theory as a whole. It was free of the idiosyncrasies and lingering dogmas which characterized Clausewitz's work on account of its peculiar development. At the same time, it synthesized Clausewitz's teachings and the special features of war at sea in a way which ultimately transcended even Clausewitz's later formulas, or else took them to their radical conclusions. Although for didactic reasons Corbett's arguments are often fairly involved, the work has few, if any, equals in clarity of mind, subtelty, and undogmatic thinking.

Corbett's work both tightened and loosened the connection between naval and land warfare. From the outset, he emphasized

[127] See e.g. Corbett, 'The Revival of Naval History' (1916), 2, *Corbett Papers*, Box 4; id., 'The Teaching of Naval and Military History' (1916), 17–18, ibid., Box 6; Grove, Introduction to Corbett, *Principles of Maritime Strategy*, p. xxx. Mahan treated Corbett with respect, and Corbett on his part refrained from criticizing Mahan's work publicly and directly, at least during the latter's lifetime.

[128] The two editions of the 'Green Pamphlet' (*Corbett Papers*, Box 6) are appended to the 1988 edn., of *Principles of Maritime Strategy*, 305–45.

that war at sea was only one branch of the phenomenon of war as a whole, to be understood in the same conceptual framework developed for land warfare by the great military thinkers of the early nineteenth century—Clausewitz and Jomini. Its proper designation was maritime rather than naval war because, both in means and ends, it extended beyond the action of navies and stood in close relationship to the development of land operations. Indeed, on the whole, war at sea took second place to war on land. While navalists everywhere exalted the marvels of commanding the seas, Corbett pointed out that 'men live upon land and not upon the sea'.[129]

It was from this simple fact, according to Corbett, that most of the crucial differences between land- and sea-warfare stemmed. Naval war, he suggested, tended to be much less decisive. While it could inflict heavy damage on some enemies, it usually lacked the means to hurt them decisively and overthrow them. Thus,

> it is almost impossible that a war can be decided by naval action alone. Unaided, naval pressure can only work by a process of exhaustion. Its effects must always be slow, and so galling both to our own commercial community and to neutrals, that the tendency is always to accept terms of peace that are far from conclusive. For a firm decision a quicker and more drastic form of pressure is required. Since men live upon the land and not upon the sea, great issues between nations at war have always been decided—except in the rarest cases—either by what your army can do against your enemy's territory and national life or else by the fear of what the fleet makes it possible for your army to do.[130]

Even in regard to land strategy, argued Corbett, military writers had gone too far in emphasizing the need to overthrow the enemy totally. Corbett's interpretation of the growth of nineteenth-century military theory and of Clausewitz's development is outstanding even by today's standards. He pointed out that the conditions created by the French Revolution (which the English had in fact anticipated in their own Puritan Revolution) had brought about mass popular mobilization. It was under these conditions that military effort has been directed towards the destruction of the enemy's main forces and the complete overthrow of his powers of resistance. This mode of war had been consecrated by military

[129] Corbett, *Principles of Maritime Strategy*, 15–16. [130] Ibid.

theorists who had taken the accidental and transient for the essential and universal and had condemned any other form of strategy as heresy. It has taken some time for Clausewitz to realize his own error and devise the concept of limited war.[131]

According to Corbett, what was true of land warfare was even truer at sea, where conditions made limited wars very much the rule. On the Continent, even the limited wars which Clausewitz described between neighbouring countries over disputed provinces tended to engulf all of the belligerents' forces and resources. By contrast, in commanding the sea, the British could, for example, effectively isolate the various theatres of war and thus conduct truly limited operations in locations of their own choosing.[132] Britain could opt for a limited involvement in a total continental war.[133] This was the principle apprehended by Francis Bacon: 'He that commands the sea is at great liberty and may take as little of the war as he will, whereas those that be strongest by land are many times nevertheless in great straits.'[134] Hence the historical divergence which existed between the continental doctrines of war and British naval doctrines.[135]

From here Corbett proceeded to reverse completely all accepted military tenets. First, he highlighted the advantages of defence, although he carefully refrained from subscribing fully to Clausewitz's formula that defence was inherently, and thus universally, stronger than attack.[136] Picking up one of Clausewitz explanations for the strength of the defence, he pointed out, for instance, that strategic defence made it possible for Britain to endure a war even in the extreme eventuality of her losing command of the sea. Losing command did not yet imply that command had passed to the enemy. In fact, disputed command, when none of the belligerents is in control of the sea, is the more common condition in naval warfare. When command is disputed—as happened, for example, during the American War of Independence—enduring is sufficient for survival.[137] Taking another instance, Corbett picked up Moltke's proposition that under existing conditions of modern firearms, the strategic offensive combined with tactical defence was the most effective form of war. Britain could, for example, utilize

[131] Corbett, 19–27.
[132] Ibid. 52–9.
[133] Ibid. 60–71.
[134] Ibid. 58.
[135] Ibid. 41, 51.
[136] Ibid. 72–3.
[137] Ibid. 91–2.

her superior sea-power to seize an isolated territorial object, which she could then defend easily against enemy counter-offensives.[138]

The implication was obvious:

> it is a direct negation of the current doctrine that in war there can be but one legitimate object, the overthrow of the enemy's means of resistance, and that the primary objective must always be his armed forces. It raises in fact the whole question as to whether it is not sometimes legitimate and even correct to aim directly at the ulterior object of the war.[139]

Corbett was openly contradicting von der Goltz and Prince Kraft von Hohenlohe,[140] and silently turning Mahan on his head.

Corbett was diplomatic enough to emphasize that he did not advocate a return to the old and discredited war of manœuvre, and did not depreciate the importance of fighting and of the major battle in war.[141] At the same time, however, he was subtly warning his readers of the fallacy 'that war consists entirely of battles between armies and fleets'. This fallacy, he maintained, 'ignores the fundamental fact that battles are only the means of enabling you to do that which really brings wars to an end—that is to exert pressure on the citizens and their collective life'.[142] If battle were only a means to an end, he argued, other means might sometimes prove no less effective. Furthermore, while on land one could normally force the enemy's army to fight, at sea the enemy's fleet often hid in port, and other means for defeating it became indispensable.[143]

Finally, Corbett called into question concentration of force, the fundamental precept which completed the nineteenth-century conception of war. Concentration, he wrote, had become 'a kind of shibboleth . . . Critics have come to lose sight of the old war experience, that without division no strategical combinations are possible.'[144] In the past, he argued, 'the riper and fresher our experience and the surer our grip of war, the looser were our combinations . . . victories have not only to be won, but worked for. They must be worked for by bold strategic combinations, which as a rule entail at least apparent dispersal.'[145] When one's forces are kept flexibly dispersed, the enemy is left in the dark

138 Ibid. 72–4.
139 Ibid. 74.
140 Ibid. 74–5.
141 Ibid. 76, 86.
142 Ibid. 97.
143 Ibid. 155–6.
144 Ibid. 134.
145 Ibid.

regarding one's intentions and strength and is more easily lured into destruction.[146] The weaker French also often dispersed for sporadic action. For Corbett, this was no sign of 'constitutional ineptitude', as it had usually been regarded, but a shrewd strategy which embarrassed the stronger British navy, forced it to disperse, and gave the French the hope of winning at least minor successes.[147]

All this was revolutionary, even when expressed in Corbett's low-key manner. Thus, although *Some Principles of Maritime Strategy* was favourably accepted on both sides of the Atlantic, there was no lack of critics.[148] The anonymous 'Captain R.N.' called *Some Principles* 'the crowning mistake of Mr Corbett's career':

> For some years Mr Corbett in the process of lecturing in the R.N. War College, permitted himself the indulgence of offering his audience his own views on the correctness or otherwise of the strategy adopted by naval officers in the past. His audience had usually treated his amateur excursions into the subject goodnaturedly; nevertheless his presumption has been resented, and he has apparently been deaf to the polite hints thrown out to him.[149]

More scholarly criticism came from one of Britain's leading military commentators and foremost authority on Napoleonic and Prussian strategy, the first Chichele Professor of Military History at Oxford, Spenser Wilkinson. His most unsympathetic reviews were not merely academic. His friends—Admirals Beresford, Custance, and Bridge—formed the relentless opposition to Fisher's innovations and direction of the navy. However, although that opposition was not devoid of personal and political motives, the battle was largely drawn along principled lines. Staunchly Mahanite as it was, the group attacked Fisher and his circle on almost predictable grounds in regard to battleship construction, tactics, and strategy: they fiercely objected to the *Dreadnought*; they rejected long-range gunnery, which would undermine Nelsonian tactical boldness; they regarded the offensive alone as the proper strategy, leading to decisive results, in the best British tradition. The debate which developed between Fisher's supporters and opponents was later known as the argument

[146] Corbett, 152. [147] Ibid. 138.

[148] See *Corbett Papers*, Box 5 for the huge number of reactions; also Grove, Introduction, *Principles of Maritime Strategy*, pp. xxxvi–xxxix.

[149] Captain R.N., *Naval and Military Record* (1911), 821, in the *Corbett Papers*, Box 5; also Grove, Introduction, *Principles of Maritime Strategy*, pp. xxxix–xl.

between the 'historical' and the 'technological' schools. While the former appealed to the immutable lessons of history, the latter held that new technological developments and innovations had altered those lessons considerably.[150]

In three different critiques, Wilkinson denounced the harmful effect of Corbett's work. If his book were read by officers, he warned, it

> must have a disastrous effect upon the Navy, for it cannot but leave their minds in doubt upon every one of the principles which the strategists of four great navies of the modern world are agreed in regarding as fundamental . . . He seems to me to assume that the teaching of the strategists . . . I have just mentioned is to be regarded as doubtful.

Taking issue with Corbett's main thesis, Wilkinson argued that 'naval warfare . . . tends to be more decisive than land warfare and approximates more to the absolute form towards which all warfare is drawn as soon as it becomes national'. He promised his readers that the German fleet was designed for a decisive battle; 'it means to take the greatest risks for the highest stakes'.[151]

However, when war came, the German High Seas Fleet did not go out to look for the expected major battle with the superior British Grand Fleet. A stalemate prevailed in the North Sea. As was happening with Delbrück's opinions, Corbett's peacetime historical teaching, which in his case had always carried a moral for the present, was suddenly becoming highly relevant. Admittedly, before the war, he had judged—like most experts—that in the age of steam and the wireless both commerce-destroying and the convoy system were becoming less effective than ever.[152] He had failed to appreciate the impact the submarine would have in this regard.[153] At the same time, however, many of the other things he had said now came true. The British navy avoided the hazardous attack on the German fleet in its home waters. But, by blockading Germany and

[150] A thorough study of the controversy can be found in Semmel, *Liberalism and Naval Strategy*, 134–51. For Fisher's endorsements of Mahan's doctrines so long as they were not enlisted to block (his) reform ('history is a record of exploded ideas'), see e.g. Ruddock F. Mackay, *Fisher of Kilverstone* (Oxford, 1973), 263–6.

[151] Spenser Wilkinson, 'Stragegy at Sea', *Morning Post*, 19 Feb. 1912; also 3 Aug. 1909, and *The Star, Johannesburg*, 9 Mar. 1912: *Corbett Papers*, Box 5; Grove, Introduction, *Principles of Maritime Strategy*, pp. xxxviii–xxxix.

[152] Corbett, *Principles of Maritime Strategy*, 266–71, 279.

[153] Ibid. 231–2.

completely cutting off her maritime communications, it was still fulfilling its war function. He was also right in arguing that the effects of such a blockade on a major European power would take a very long time to make themselves felt, and that this would lead to a protracted war of attrition. Only a military effort on the Continent could deliver something in the form of a decisive result.

Be that as it may, in the aftermath of Jutland, both official circles and the public at large, which had been led to expect that the British navy would swiftly dominate the North Sea in Nelsonian fashion, could only regard the British naval performance since the beginning of the war as bitterly disappointing. In reply to this criticism, in an article he wrote after Jutland, Winston Churchill drew arguments from Corbett to defend the navy and the naval policy which Fisher and himself had adopted at the beginning of the war. He reassured his readers that, by dominating German communications, the navy possessed all the advantages it could have gained from a victorious battle. By holding to its strong position, it compelled the Germans to come out and fight at a disadvantage, if they wished to break the British strategic stranglehold. Churchill did not name Corbett, who during the war was strategic adviser and official historian at the Admiralty, but others recognized the source of the doctrine he espoused. Responding to Churchill's article in a letter to *The Times*, the intellectual admiral, Reginald Custance (also without naming Corbett) pointed to the disastrous doctrine which he alleged had grown to dominate the navy in the previous ten years, as the direct cause of the dispirited British strategy.[154] In another letter to *The Times* a day later, and then in the House of Lords, the veteran imperial administrator and naval activist George Clarke, Lord Sydenham of Combe, followed up Custance. With disbelief, he quoted from Churchill's article and from the 'Green Pamphlet'.

> The first duty of the navy [he said] is to capture or destroy the enemy's armed ships whenever and wherever they are accessible. Clearly in these days submarines and mines have imposed some new restrictions upon naval action, but that great principle of naval war is eternal. It applies just as much to the Battle of Salamis as to the Battle of Jutland.[155]

The controversy over British naval performance dragged on and

[154] Custance, Letter to *The Times*, 9 Oct. 1916, *Corbett Papers*, Box 7.

[155] 15 Nov. 1916, *Parliamentary Debates, Lords* (1916), 510–11. Also see correspondence with Corbett, 30 Nov. and 1 Dec. 1916, *Corbett Papers*, Box 7.

did not terminate with the end of the war. Corbett's official history of the war at sea had difficulties in being approved by the Admiralty. Particularly problematic was the third volume, covering Jutland, which was completed at the height of the Beatty–Jellicoe controversy. The Admiralty Board approved publication but inserted the following statement by way of preface: 'Their lordships find that some of the principles advocated in this book, especially the tendency to minimize the importance of seeking battle and forcing it to a conclusion, are directly in conflict with their views.'[156] Corbett was spared the anguish of witnessing those reservations in print. He died in September 1922, some two weeks after having submitted his manuscript.

Churchill's *World Crisis* (1923–31) rekindled the controversy. The book prompted criticism by some of Britain's leading military and naval authorities.[157] In 1931 Lord Sydenham, who, after the war, had grown increasingly critical and pessimistic regarding Britain's performance and future, again blamed Corbett's 'sea heresies' for Britain's having failed to gain any spectacular naval success during the war. Corbett was in good company; the eighty-three-year-old Sydenham compared his theories to those of Einstein, which, as he put it, also 'fog the vision'. He went on to confess that he had always been repelled by Clausewitz and 'the psycho-analysis to which he subjected himself' [*sic*!].[158] As occurred in respect of the Delbrück controversy in Germany, the argument faded away only when the Second World War finally put an end to a previous tradition of supremacy—a British one at sea and a German one on land. At almost the same time, the advent of nuclear weapons closed the curtain on the nineteenth-century Napoleonic-Nelsonian conception of unlimited war.

[156] Quoted in Grove, Introduction, *Principles of Maritime Strategy*, p. xliv.

[157] Lord Sydenham of Combe, Admiral Sir R. Bacon, General Sir W. D. Bird and Sir Charles Oman, *The World Crisis by Winston Churchill: A Criticism* (London, 1927).

[158] Lord Sydenham, 'Sea Heresies', *The Naval Review* (May 1931), 233.

5

Marxism, Clausewitz, and Military Theory 1848 to the Nuclear Age

THE affinity between Marxist thinking on war and military theory and Clausewitz's teachings is well known. Marx and Engels, busy as they were with their manifold occupations, reportedly exchanged brief admiring comments about his work. Engels in particular, the military expert of the two, was allegedly considerably influenced by Clausewitz's writings, both during the course of his military self-education and after. Lenin studied *On War* carefully and approvingly, used it repeatedly in his political pamphlets, and recommended it to party functionaries. Both Trotsky and Stalin referred to Clausewitz's work, and a host of Soviet writers on strategy followed them in this course in the nuclear age. When the Cold War began, observers in the United States did not fail to point out this Marxist 'Clausewitz connection'. Simultaneously, interest was awakened in Germany, and for reasons which in some respects did not differ much between East and West; while Clausewitz was given a new image in post-war Germany and dissociated from the Prussian and German militarist tradition, his Marxist connection helped to demonstrate the wider scope of his influence and highlighted his universal appeal. Between all these sources, over the last few decades, the relevant material from the writings of the fathers of Marxism has been diligently collected, repeatedly cited, and endlessly rehashed.

Rather than recount a familiar story, this chapter aims to do two things. First, it seeks to correct some misconceptions, especially concerning the relationship of Engels and Marx to Clausewitz. It will be argued that neither had any special interest in, or appreciation of, Clausewitz's work, and that Engels was not influenced by it to any considerable extent. Commentators have been prejudiced in their treatment of the evidence by their knowledge of Clausewitz's later successes with Marxists, especially with Lenin,[1] and by his present-day popularity. The second, more general objective of this chapter, seemingly in conflict with the previous one, is to get to the roots of the Marxist affinity with Clausewitz's work. Curiously, this primary question has, on the whole, escaped notice. The similarity between the Marxist outlook and some of Clausewitz's ideas—notably his view of war as the continuation of policy—has been widely and appropriately cited as the reason for Clausewitz's popularity with the Marxists. But this similarity itself has never been regarded as much more than an interesting coincidence. After all, what could be the point of connection between the Prussian general and the international revolutionaries?

As this chapter suggests, Clausewitz's ideas and Marxist thinking were linked by threads which ran deep into a common intellectual matrix. Both Clausewitz's thinking and Marxism, as a radical development of left-wing Hegelianism, had their roots in the great achievements of German thought in the late eighteenth and early nineteenth centuries. Prominent within that stimulating cultural environment were a pronounced historicist outlook and a powerful urge—which reached its pinnacle in the German idealist philosophy—to embrace and comprehend the nature of reality in its totality. To be sure, these notions were developed in many diverse and even conflicting directions by different currents of thought. This explains, with remarkable consistency, both the Marxists' affinity to Clausewitz's ideas and the points of criticism which qualified their basic agreement.

Engels's distinguished career as a military writer, while being one of his least familiar sides, has none the less attracted considerable scholarly attention.[2] He took up military studies very seriously in

[1] This prejudice goes at least as far back as the various editions, in different languages, of *Selected Correspondence, Karl Marx and Friedrich Engels* (London, 1934). A note by the editors of the Marx-Engels-Lenin Institute in Moscow (p. 100 of the English edition) already combined a brief quotation from Engels with Lenin's later endorsement of Clausewitz.

[2] See esp. Gerhard Zirke, *Der General: Friedrich Engels, der erste Militärtheoretiker der Arbeiterklassen* (Leipzig, 1957); Jehuda L. Wallach, *Die Kriegslehre von Friedrich Engels* (Frankfurt, a. M., 1968); Martin Berger, *Engels, Armies, and Revolution: The Revolutionary Tactics of Classical Marxism* (Hamden, Conn., 1977).

1851, with a view to acquiring the foundations of the discipline which, as the events of 1848–9 had demonstrated, was essential to the success of any future revolutionary action. Within a short period during which he engaged in intensive reading, he turned himself into an expert and soon became one of the most acute military observers in Europe. It has long been noted that his military writings constituted by far the greatest part of his literary output. No wonder he was nicknamed 'The General' by his friends. Throughout the 1850s, on Marx's behalf and under Marx's name, he wrote numerous articles on military affairs for the *New York Daily Tribune*, of which Marx was the London correspondent. For *The New American Cyclopaedia* (1858), published by the *Tribune*, Marx himself wrote on the marshals of the Napoleonic wars, while Engels added substantial pieces on more technical military matters.[3] In the early 1860s, again on Marx's behalf, Engels wrote on the military aspects of the American Civil War for the Viennese journal *Die Presse*.[4] To the volunteers' bulletin, the *Volunteer Journal of Lancashire and Cheshire*, he contributed ten articles on various subjects. For obvious reasons, he took interest in that militia, created after the invasion-scare of 1859. Finally, for the *Manchester Guardian* and the *Pall-Mall Gazette* respectively, he reviewed both the Austro-Prussian War of 1866 and the Franco-Prussian War 1870–1.[5]

In tracing Engels's career as a military writer, many commentators have assigned to Clausewitz a place of honour. They have based that impression primarily on two casual but much-quoted remarks which appeared in the Marx–Engels correspondence of January 1858 and which have been widely interpreted as a clear indication that Marx and Engels had a special attitude to Clausewitz's work. Those casual remarks, however, have been singled out from the fairly extensive evidence we possess regarding Engels's attitude to

[3] All newspaper and *Cyclopaedia* articles can be found in the complete English edition: Karl Marx and Friedrich Engels, *Collected Works* (London, 1975–), xii–xviii. Engels's military writings appeared in Russian and German, the latter version being entitled, *Ausgewählte militärische Schriften* (2 vols.; Berlin, 1958, 1964).

[4] Marx and Engels, *Works*, xviii–xix; id., *On America and the Civil War* (New York, 1972).

[5] Marx and Engels, *Works*, xviii; xx. 164–82; xxii. 9–258; *Engels As Military Critic: Articles by Friedrich Engels, Reprinted from the Volunteer Journal and the Manchester Guardian of the 1860s*, ed. Chaloner and W. O. Henderson (Manchester, 1959).

contemporary military writers, thus creating a huge distortion by omission. Furthermore, these remarks have been treated superficially and have often been magnified by prejudiced translation.

The course of Engels's military education and much other relevant material are well documented in his vast correspondence. For help in compiling a comprehensive reading-list, he approached Joseph Weydemeyer, a former Prussian officer turned revolutionary and a close friend and disciple of Marx and Engels. Explaining at some length his motivation for taking up military studies, he systematically detailed the scope of his interest, namely achieving a good overall technical command of the basics of the profession of war. He told Weydemeyer that he already possessed old Montecuccoli's works and that he had found Napier's history of the Peninsular War 'by far the best work of military history I have seen up till now'. He inquired about German stuff, naming Willisen and Clausewitz, and asked Weydemeyer what he thought about them. Finally, he inquired about Jomini. None of these authorities had he yet read. He also asked for good specialized maps for the study of modern campaigns from 1792 up to 1849.[6] After receiving Weydemeyer's reply, he added some follow-up questions and reported that he had already acquired Decker (which Marx mislaid).[7]

By April 1853 Engels had informed Weydemeyer about the substantial progress he had made in his military studies, both technical and historical. 'Prussian military literature is positively the worst there is,' he complained; after 1822, he says, it is characterized by 'repulsively pretentious pedantry . . . a bogus omniscience which is the very devil'.[8] Admittedly, in this criticism Engels probably had mainly Willisen and other smaller luminaries in mind. In this, and in other, even earlier, letters to Marx, he repeatedly expressed his amusement at, and contempt for, Willisen's proverbial pedantry and mock military philosophy.[9] It appears that

[6] Engels to Weydemeyer, 19 June 1851, *Works*, xxxviii. 370–2.

[7] Engels to Weydemeyer, 7 Aug. 1851, ibid. 405–6.

[8] Engels to Weydemeyer, 12 Apr. 1853, ibid., xxxix. 305. Presumably, in citing the date 1822, Engels was referring to C. Decker's book, *Der kleine Krieg* (Berlin, 1822), which he had mentioned in his previous letter and which had possibly been recommended to him by Weydemeyer.

[9] Ibid. 310; Engels to Marx, 7 May 1852, ibid. 103–4: 'Willisen's book should really be called the *Philosophy* of great wars. This in itself would indicate that it contains more philosophizing than military science, that the most self-evident things

he had then not yet read Clausewitz's *On War*. However, proceeding to describe his studies of the Napoleonic campaigns, Engels added the following assessments (which are somehow never cited) of the various histories of these campaigns: '*au bout du compte* [in the final analysis] Jomini gives the best account of them; despite many fine things, I can't really bring myself to like that natural genius, Clausewitz.'[10] Jomini is by far the most cited military authority in Engels's correspondence, while Rüstow, Jomini's disciple, takes second place. But here too no mention of this inconvenient fact is to be found in the extensive literature which informs us about Engels's admiration for Clausewitz.

Even in their treatment of the famous Marx–Engels exchange of letters upon which everything rests, commentators have silently passed over the opening scene. The first letter (never cited) came from Marx. Going over their many pressing obligations for the *Tribune* and *Cyclopaedia*, he wrote to Engels: 'I sent the chaps about 8 sheets under the heading "Blücher", the same being subtitled "The Silesian Army in the Campaigns etc.". As I had to spend so much time reading Clausewitz, Müffling, etc., some degree of compensation was called for.'[11] Engels's much-quoted comments came in reply to this, at the end of the business letter to Marx in which he discusses his progress and problems with the *Cyclopaedia* articles:

> I am reading, *inter alia*, Clausewitz's *Vom Krieg*. An odd way of philosophising, but *per se* very good. On the question as to whether one should speak of the art of the science of war, he says that, more than anything else, war resembles commerce. Combat is to war what cash payment is to commerce; however seldom it need happen in reality,

are constructed a priori with the most profound and exhaustive thoroughness and that, sandwiched between these, are the most methodical discourses on simplicity and multiplicity and such like opposites. What can one say about military science which begins with the concept of art *en général*, then goes on to demonstrate that the art of cookery is also an art, expatiates on the relationship of art to science and finally subsumes all the rules, relationships, potentialities, etc., etc., of the art of war under the one absolute axiom: the stronger always overcomes the weaker.' Also see Engels to Marx, 9 May 1854, ibid. 451–2.

[10] Engels to Weydemeyer, 12 Apr. 1853, *Works*, xxxix. 305; the German original is: 'Jomini ist *au bout du compte* doch der beste Darsteller davon, das Naturgenie Clausewitz will mir trotz mancher hübschen Sachen nicht recht zusagen.'; *Marx-Engels Gesamtausgabe* (Berlin, 1975–), xxviii. 577.

[11] Marx to Engels, 31 Oct. 1857, *Works*, xl. 198; the German is '*Schadenersatz*'—compensation, indemnification.

everything is directed towards it and ultimately it is bound to occur and prove decisive.[12]

Obviously, while complimenting Clausewitz's book and indicating that he did not grasp the meaning and purpose of his obscure intellectual acrobatics any more than other readers of *On War*, both before and after, Engels picked for his friend a piece of picantry in a field which could be of interest to Marx. Marx enjoyed the cleverness of the idea. 'I hunted through Clausewitz, more or less, when doing Blücher,' he replied, 'The fellow possesses a common sense bordering on wit [*Witz*]'.[13]

Commentators who have seized upon these lines are in general guilty of two vices. The German '*Witz*' carries various meanings and some ambivalence, almost equally conveyed by the English 'wit'. While some commentators offered this most natural English equivalent, others, concerned that Marx's comment might appear as having been made in something less than absolute seriousness, chose to leave the reader no option. The recent complete edition of the Marx–Engels works has rendered '*Witz*' as 'ingenious'; another authority has 'brilliance'—both lexically possible but prejudiced interpretations.[14] Moreover, commentators have universally assumed that Marx's compliment was made in reference to Clausewitz's work in general, which he supposedly 'hunted through' when writing 'Blücher'. In fact, his comment was merely a direct response to the clever idea which Engels had cited to him from Clausewitz's *On War*. Marx himself never read *On War*. For his article on Blücher, he consulted only Clausewitz's relevant histories of the campaigns of 1812–15.[15] For all their value, there was surely nothing in those histories that was capable of prompting

[12] Engels to Marx, 7 Jan. 1858, ibid. 241–2.

[13] Marx to Engels, 11 Jan. 1858, ibid., xl. 247; where deviating from the translation of the standard English edition, I have inserted the German original in brackets; see next paragraph and note.

[14] 'Ingenious', ibid.; 'brilliance' in Bernard Semmel (ed.), *Marxism and the Science of War*, (Oxford, 1981), 66. By contrast, while confusing the order of the Marx-Engels letter exchange so that Engels's 'very good' comes more convincingly as a reply to Marx's 'common sense', Hahlweg uses the more natural translation ['wittiness']: 'Clausewitz, Lenin, and Communist Military Attitudes Today', *Journal of the Royal United Services Institute*, 105 (1960), 221; 'wit' is used by Michael E. Howard, 'The Influence of Clausewitz', in Clausewitz, *On War* (2nd. edn., Princeton, NJ, 1984), 44.

[15] See the manuscript evidence: Marx and Engels, *Works*, xl. 198, 247; Hahlweg, 'Sozialismus und Militärwissenschaft bei Friedrich Engels', in H. Pelger (ed.), *Friedrich Engels 1820–1970* (Hanover, 1971), 66.

his remark that Clausewitz was a fellow who possessed 'a common sense bordering on wit'. How much Marx really enjoyed them was already apparent to us from his letter of 31 October 1857.

But enough of this textual criticism of the Marxist holy scriptures and back to the wider picture. Commentators have long noted the rather surprising fact that most of Engels's military works were 'strictly professional' in character and virtually devoid of Marxist interpretations.[16] The course of his military education was no different. He was set upon acquiring the foundations of a profession, and he studied these systematically, along the most conventional lines, as if preparing himself for the 'ensign and lieutenant examination'.[17] Accordingly, he engaged in extensive reading of the military authorities that were accepted in his time. Among these, Clausewitz certainly held a place of honour, but outside the mainstream, while Jomini and his disciples reigned supreme. As mentioned previously, the references in Engels's writings indicate that his own hierarchy of authorities was no different.

Engels's review of the Austro-Prussian War of 1866 is a classical case in point. His intelligent articles in the *Manchester Guardian* are deservedly regarded with esteem. Yet the fact remains that he misjudged the situation in exactly the same manner as the rest of the military observers: he backed the wrong horse completely, believing in the superiority of the Austrians; he regarded the Prussian reserves as poorly motivated and inexperienced; finally, during mobilization, and especially when hostilities began, he was shocked and perplexed by the Prussian violation of the most sacred Napoleonic–Jominian principle:

> Suppose a young Prussian ensign or cornet, under examination for a lieutenancy, to be asked what would be the safest plan for a Prussian army to invade Bohemia? Suppose our young officer were to answer your best way will be to divide your troops into two almost equal bodies, to send one around by the east of the Riesengebirge, the other by the west, and affect their junction in Gitschin. What would the examining officer say to this? He would inform the young gentleman that this plan sinned against the two very first laws of strategy: Firstly, never to divide your troops so that

[16] W. B. Gallie, *Philosophers of Peace and War, Kant, Clausewitz, Marx, Engels and Tolstoy* (Cambridge, 1978), 73; Semmel, *Marxism and the Science of War*, 8, 45–6 *et passim*; also see Trotsky, *Military Writings* (New York, 1969), 135.

[17] Engels to Weydemeyer, 7 Aug. 1851, *Works*, xxxviii. 405.

they cannot support each other, but to keep them well together; and, secondly, in case of an advance on different roads, to effect the junction at the point which is not within reach of the enemy; that, therefore, the plan prepared was the very worst of all . . . Yet this is the very plan which the wise and learned staff of the Prussian army have adopted. It is almost incredible; but it is so.[18]

Three days later, like all other experts educated on the legacy of Napoleon and Jomini, he was forced to eat his words; 'The campaign which the Prussians opened with a signal strategy blunder', he wrote, 'has been since carried on by them with such a terrible tactical energy that it was brought to a victorious close in exactly eight days.'[19]

Later in his life, in the course of his comprehensive polemic *Anti-Dühring* (1876–8), Engels devoted a few pages to outlining a Marxist view of the historical nature of war. He set out to show that war changed and assumed a new character with every change in material and, by implication, economic conditions:

At the beginning of the fourteenth century, gunpowder came from the Arabs to Western Europe, and . . . completely revolutionized methods of warfare. . . . From the outset . . . firearms were the weapons of the towns and of the rising monarchy, drawing its support from the towns . . . With the armour-clad cavalry of the feudal lords, the feudal lords' supremacy was also broken; with the development of the bourgeoisie, infantry and guns became more and more the decisive types of weapons. . . . It was not until the early part of the eighteenth century that the flint-lock musket with a bayonet finally displaced the pike in the equipment of the infantry. The foot soldiers of that period were the mercenaries of princes; they consisted of the most demoralized elements of society . . . and only held together by the whip . . . The only type of fighting in which these soldiers could apply the new weapons was the tactics of the line. . . . Like the American, the French Revolution could oppose to the trained mercenary armies of the coalition only poorly trained but great masses of soldiers, the levy of the whole nation. . . . a form had to be invented for use by large bodies of troops, and this form was found in the *column*. . . . The revolutionary system of arming the whole people was soon restricted to compulsory

[18] 3 July 1866, *Works*, xx. 176–7; for a similar criticism before the beginning of operations see 20 June 1866, ibid. 165–6; in *Engels as Military Critic*, the page numbers are 133–4, 123 respectively. Engels had already referred to Jomini's 'interior lines' in 1859 in analysing the strategic situation in north Italy; *Works*, xvi. 226.

[19] 6 July 1866, *Works*, 179; *Engels as Military Critic*, 136–7.

conscription . . . and in this form it was adopted by most of the large states on the continent. [With the progress of this process in the future,] the armies of princes become transformed into armies of the people.[20]

Reading *On War*, one can find remarkably similar passages, which may raise questions regarding Engels's possible sources of inspiration. The character of war, writes Clausewitz, depends on

> The nature of states and societies as they are determined by their times and prevailing conditions. . . . The semi-barbarous Tartars, the republics of antiquity, the feudal lords and trading cities of the Middle Ages, eighteenth century kings and the rulers and peoples of the nineteenth century—all conducted war in their own peculiar way, using different methods and pursuing different aims.[21]

However, Engels's outline, as well as his similar review of naval developments in *Anti-Dühring*, were no more influenced by Clausewitz than had been the famous historical outline in *The Communist Manifesto* (1848). In fact, in the military passages of *Anti-Dühring*, Engels merely developed ideas which he had already articulated in his brilliant but less widely known manuscript, 'Conditions and Prospects of a War of the Holy Alliance against France in 1852' (April 1851).[22] This had been written long before he read even one line from Clausewitz—indeed even before he undertook his extensive course of reading in military literature. In the same way, it appears that Engels's historical analysis was equally uninfluenced to any significant extent by Rüstow, a fellow radical whose works Engels consulted much more than Clausewitz's. Nor, for that matter, did Engels's own work influence Delbrück's great historical enterprise, begun shortly after the publication of

[20] Engels, *Herr Eugen Dühring's Revolution in Science* (London, n.d.), 190–4.

[21] Clausewitz, *On War*, viii. 6B, 586; this is followed by an elaborate historical survey, 586–93.

[22] 'Conditions and Prospects', in Marx and Engels, *Works*, x. 556. In this work Engels also anticipated the further growth and increasing mobility of the armies of the future, beyond their bourgeois-Napoleonic stage of development. These would be made possible, he said, by growing productivity, by the improved communications offered by the railroad and the electric telegraph, and by the higher level of education enjoyed by both the officer corps and the rank and file. He wrongly believed, however, as Moltke's armies demonstrated, that all these new conditions would be able to develop only within the framework of a socialist society: ibid., 550–6. Semmel, in his useful anthology, *Marxism and the Science of War*, 8–12, 45–6, *et passim*, was evidently unaware of this early work when he argued that Engels had never offered a Marxist interpretation of military affairs before *Anti-Dühring*.

Anti-Dühring and stimulated in part by Rüstow's work. All the above-mentioned people thus expressed similar ideas in rather similar language, not because of any line of influence running between them, but primarily because of the all-pervasive effect of German historicism which stimulated them all. War, like all phenomena, had little in the way of a permanent nature. Like all phenomena, it was in a process of continuous change, affected by, and interacting with, other fields of human life. This fundamental historicist notion was the common source of Clausewitz's philosophy of war, Hegel's dialectic, together with its materialist and socialist descendants, and the great stream of nineteenth-century German historical scholarship.[23]

For Engels himself, these fundamental affinities and similarities were of little importance. The whole of German culture was permeated with various applications of the historicist idea, most of which were designated as ideological enemies of Marxism.[24] In Germany and Europe in the middle of the nineteenth century, the number of quasi-Hegelian systems alone, against which Marx and Engels directed some of their most pointed polemics, amounted to dozens at least. Engels had even less patience for military 'philosophizing', as his attitude towards Willisen and, indeed, the distinction he made in his compliment for Clausewitz, demonstrate. For Marx and Engels, philosophizing was *the* German disease. For later Marxists, however things were not quite the same. For example, by the time Lenin—never a military expert himself—was prompted by the outbreak of the First World War to study Clausewitz's *On War*, Clausewitz had already become the undisputed master of military theory in all the most important military states. At the same time, for Lenin and the public he addressed, instances of German historicism were not as commonplace as they had been for Marx and Engels two and three generations earlier. Given also Lenin's particular political preoccupations during the war years, his special interest in Clausewitz was natural. It was now left for Lenin and other leading Marxists to bring out the various themes which connected Clausewitz's theory of war and the Marxist outlook.

Lenin's contribution has been more than adequately documented.

23 For the historicist idea and Clausewitz's thought and development see above, Book I, 149–51, 188–191 *et passim*.

24 For an overview see above, Ch. 2, p. 368.

Principally, it consisted in popularizing Clausewitz's formula regarding the relationship between politics and war and in giving Clausewitz the official stamp of Marxist legitimacy. The facts need not be repeated at length. During late 1914 or early 1915, while in exile in Switzerland, Lenin borrowed the first edition of Clausewitz's *On War* from the public library in Berne.[25] He was evidently much impressed by the book. As was his habit, he copied long extracts from the German text into a special notebook, underlining words, passages, and ideas of particular importance and adding numerous annotations in Russian. Apart from a few passing comments on other matters, he concentrated overwhelmingly on two themes. One was the dialectic of defence and attack; the other—far more extensive, and encompassing about two-thirds of his notebook—was the function of war as a political instrument, its overall dependence on political and social conditions, and, consequently, its continuous transformation through history. His many favourable comments on Clausewitz's formulas regarding the relationship between politics and war are much quoted. But he also seized with enthusiasm on all the passages in which Clausewitz demonstrated the historical nature of war (*On War*, i, 1, 27; vii. 30; viii. 3 and 6B). 'To each epoch—its own wars', he wrote in the margins.[26]

Lenin read Clausewitz for a purpose and put him to immediate use. With the outbreak of the First World War and the collapse of socialist solidarity, he directed all his efforts to denouncing the leaders of the Second International who, in the cause of national self-defence, had forsaken their previous commitment against war. In his pamphlets he argued that the war was nothing but a capitalist war, waged by the capitalist states and ruling classes for the advancement of their interests, and he repeatedly used Clausewitz's famous dictum as a sharp weapon. He instructed his readers that, rather than representing a break from earlier interests and political

[25] The assumption made by some historians that Lenin must have become acquainted with Clausewitz through Engels's papers, is not supported by evidence but merely deduced from the false premiss regarding Engels and Clausewitz. In his many references to Clausewitz, Lenin himself consistently connected the former's teaching with Marx and Engels only indirectly.

[26] Lenin's notebook (item no. 18674 in the archive of the Lenin Institute in Moscow) was published in Lenin's collected works: *Leninskii Sbornik* (Moscow, 1930), xii. 387–452. I have used the French translation: *Les Fondements théoriques de la guerre et de la paix en U.R.S.S.—suivi du Cahier de Lénine sur Clausewitz*, ed. B. C. Friedl (Paris, 1945), 47–78; a German edition has also been issued: *Clausewitz Werk 'Vom Kriege', Auszüge und Randglossen* (Berlin, 1957).

relations, 'War is simply the continuation of politics by other [i.e. violent] means'.[27] He again found citations from Clausewitz useful in explaining the Bolshevik position against the continuation of the war in 1917 and in advocating a strategy of deep withdrawal into the interiors of Russia in early 1918.[28] Later, he even recommended to party functionaries that they study Clausewitz.[29]

Although Lenin's appreciation of Clausewitz's work was undoubtedly genuine, the prominent supporting role he assigned to Clausewitz in his own political campaign obviously helped determine the eminently respectful way he presented Clausewitz and his ideas to his readers. Bearing this in mind, Lenin's silent amendments and extensions of Clausewitz's theses, as well as other subtle points, are as important to an understanding of the Marxist attitude to Clausewitz as were his oft-quoted praises for the 'famous', 'one of the greatest' and 'profoundest' writers 'on the history and philosophy of war'. From a Marxist point of view, Lenin's description of Clausewitz as a writer 'whose thinking was stimulated by Hegel', was at once a mark of distinction and a point of reservation.[30] On the one hand, it legitimized Clausewitz by establishing his kinship with Marxism, whose roots in Hegelian philosophy were well known. Clausewitz's work and Marxism were thus presented as distant cousins. In this context, Lenin also noted instances where Clausewitz had used dialectic.[31] On the other hand, the fact that Marxism had developed in reaction against Hegelian 'Idealism' was equally well known. Of particular importance to our case was Marx's early *Critique of Hegel's Philosophy of Right* (1843), which overturned Hegel's famous work in political philosophy (1821).

Marx rejected Hegel's central idea that the state took an impartial position, above the struggle of the particular interests in society. He argued instead that, more accurately, the state reflected and represented in the political sphere the power and interests of

[27] Lenin, 'The Collapse of the Second International' (May–June 1915), *Collected Works* (London, 1960–1970), vol. xxi. 219–20; id. 'Socialism and War' (July–Aug. 1915), ibid. 304.

[28] Lenin, 'War and Revolution' (May 1917), ibid., xxiv. 399; id., ' "Left-Wing" Childishness and the Petty Bourgeois Mentality' (Feb. 1918), ibid. xxvii. 332.

[29] V. Sorin, in *Pravda*, no. 111 (1923); cited in *Leninskii Sbornik*, xii. 390.

[30] Lenin, 'Collapse of the Second International', *Works*, xxi. 219.

[31] For the sources and nature of Clausewitz's dialectic see above, Book I, 232–8.

the social ruling classes. Indeed, this idea became one of the most important articles of Marxist theory. Now Clausewitz's view (and exaltation) of the state was clearly Hegelian, which Lenin did not fail to see.[32] In his marginal annotations to the relevant passages in *On War* (viii 6B), he heavily underlined Clausewitz's position, which he cited as follows: 'politics = the representation of all interests of society as a whole'. However, Lenin's aim at that moment was not to argue with Clausewitz but rather to use Clausewitz's more general idea in his argument with Kautsky, Plechanov, and other leaders of the Second International. He therefore corrected Clausewitz silently but consistently. In all his citations of Clausewitz's dictum, he went on to explain that war continued the politics of states *and* of classes within these states.[33] On other occasions, he repeatedly stated that war was always caused by, and waged in favour of, the interests of the ruling classes in society.[34]

Where Lenin opted for low-key amendments, modern Soviet military scholars, annoyed by Western portrayals of Lenin as Clausewitz's disciple, took a direct approach. In a series of official texts on military theory, they uniformly pointed out where Clausewitz's views and Marxism diverged. While accepting his famous formula regarding the relationship between politics and war, they added that Clausewitz was an idealist who interpreted politics idealistically as the 'intelligence of the personified state' and 'representative of the interests of all of society'; he understood politics primarily as foreign relations, disregarding their domestic and economic roots.[35] Western commentators who have tended to treat these statements with amusement, as nothing but examples of

[32] Book I above, 238–52.

[33] See the references in notes 27 and 28 above.

[34] See e.g. Lenin, 'Speech on the War before the First All-Russia Congress of Soviets', *Works*, xxv. 29–42, esp. 32–3. Also see Hahlweg, 'Lenin und Clausewitz', *Archiv für Kulturgeschichte*, 36 (1954), 382–4; id. 'Clausewitz, Lenin and Communist Military Attitudes', 222.

[35] There are several, almost identical statements of this position in works composed since the late 1950s and translated into English in the early 1970s: T. R. Kondratkov's contribution to A. S. Milovidov (ed.), *The Philosophical Heritage of V. I. Lenin and the Problems of Contemporary War* (Moscow, 1972), 39–40; presumably by the same author in B. Byely, G. Fyodorov, V. Kulakov (eds.), *Marxism-Leninism on War and Army* (Moscow, 1972), 7–8; Ye. Savkin, *The Basic Principles of Operational Art* (Moscow, 1972), 23. See also Col.-Gen. M. V. Gareev, *M. V. Frunze, Military Theorist* (Suffolk, 1988), 86.

Soviet doctrinarism, harsh rhetoric, and xenophobia, have missed the point here. The motivation behind the Soviet military writers' criticism of Clausewitz is no more important than Lenin's motivation for adopting him. In both cases, when the motivation is recognized and accounted for, the substance of the Marxist 'Clausewitz connection' remains. Both the Marxists' agreement and their differences with Clausewitz's ideas are fundamental in nature and have their roots in a common intellectual seed-bed in early nineteenth-century Germany.

Indeed, although Lenin's famous citations from Clausewitz focused attention on the relationship between politics and war, the depth of the intellectual undercurrents connecting Marxism and Clausewitz's theory of war are revealed in an even more intriguing manner in other, less noted, areas. We have seen that Lenin discovered and adopted Clausewitz as a weapon that could be used in his polemic against the leaders of the Second International. In the same way, Trotsky, Lenin's second in the revolutionary hierarchy and a leading Marxist theoretician, resorted to Clausewitz when he too found himself immersed in a controversy, albeit of a totally different nature. During the early 1920s, the young Red generals who had distinguished themselves in the Civil War—notably Frunze, in collaboration with Gusev, Tukhachevsky, and others—called for the creation of a 'Unified Military Doctrine' for the Red Army, which would reflect and express its Marxist, revolutionary, and proletarian character. At the Tenth and Eleventh Congresses of the Communist Party (1921 and 1922) and in a battle of articles which raged in the interim between those events, Trotsky, the commissar of war, opposed their idea outright. The proposals of the revolutionary generals and the details of the controversy are none of our concern here.[36] But Trotsky's articulation of the Marxist position regarding the nature of military theory has no equal and is of great interest. He rejected the notion that there was a science of war, based on eternal principles, and ridiculed the idea that Marxism prescribed or was able to offer a set of doctrines for any particular art or trade, military or otherwise. These, he

[36] The controversy is adequately summarized in Walter D. Jacobs's inadequately entitled book, *Frunze: The Soviet Clausewitz, 1885–1925* (The Hague, 1969), 24–88. A briefer summary can be found in Condoleezza Rice, 'The Making of Soviet Strategy', P. Paret (ed.), *Makers of Modern Strategy from Machiavelli to the Nuclear Age* (Princeton, NJ, 1986), 653–8.

maintained, were practical occupations, whose major traits were ever determined by the historical conditions prevailing in any particular period.

'There is not and there never has been a military "science",' argued Trotsky, 'What is commonly called the theory of war or military science represents not a totality of scientific laws explaining objective events but an aggregate of practical usages, methods of adaptation and proficiencies.'[37] Reviewing the so-called principles of war advanced by writers like Foch, he ridiculed them as mere trivia, both contradictory and too general to be of any practical use.[38] The dubious nature of the attempt to erect military systems based on fundamental principles, he wrote,

> was very well understood by old Clausewitz who said: 'It is not impossible perhaps to write a systematic theory of war, both logical and wide in scope. But our theory, up to the present, is far from being either. Not to mention their unscientific spirit in the attempt to make their systems consistent and complete, many such works are stuffed with commonplaces and idle chatter of every kind . . .'[39]

According to Trotsky, to attempt to turn practical military usages into a science with the aid of Marxism, which is nothing more than 'a method that analyzes the development of historical man', is 'scholastic and hopeless'.[40]

> This is the same thing as trying to construct a theory of architecture or a text book on veterinary medicine with the aid of the Marxist method. A history of war, like a history of architecture, can be written from the Marxist viewpoint, because history is a science. But the so-called theory of war, i.e., practical [military] leadership is something else again.[41]

> A scientific history of warfare explains why in a given epoch, with a given social organization, men waged war in a certain way and not differently. . . . But it is quite self-evident that a scientific history of war

[37] Trotsky, 'Our Current Basic Military Tasks' (1 Apr. 1922), *Military Writings*, 73.

[38] Trotsky, 'Marxism and Military Knowledge' (8 May 1922), ibid. 122–30.

[39] Trotsky, 'Military Doctrine or Pseudo-Military Doctrinairism' (5 Dec. 1921), ibid. 43. The motto of this article is also a quotation from Clausewitz: 'In the practical arts the theoretical must not be allowed to grow too high, but must be kept close to experience, their proper soil'; ibid. 31.

[40] Trotsky, 'Marxism and Military Knowledge', 8 May 1922, ibid. 110; id. 'Basic Military Tasks', ibid. 75.

[41] Trotsky, 'Basic Military Tasks', ibid. 74.

aims by its very nature to explain that which undergoes change and the reasons for these changes but not to establish eternal truths.[42]

This was the crux of the matter. Because of the historical nature of war, argued Trotsky,

All military theoreticians cannot escape from the following contradiction: In order to demonstrate the eternal character of the principles of military art they have to throw out the entire 'ballast' of living historical experience and reduce them to pleonasms, commonplaces, Euclidian postulates, logical axioms, etc. On the other hand, in order to demonstrate the importance of these principles in military affairs, they have to stuff these principles with the content of a specific epoch, a specific stage in the development of an army or in the development of military affairs.[43]

In this respect military affairs are exactly the same as political economy, the Marxist science *par excellence*:

Marxist political economy . . . is not a science of how to manage a business . . . It is the science of how in a certain epoch certain economic relations (capitalist) took shape . . . Economic laws established by Marx . . . are not eternal principles as is represented by the bourgeois Manchester school, according to which private ownership of the means of production, buying and selling, competition and the rest are eternal principles of economy . . . Doctrinaires in military affairs behave in exactly the same way with regard to military truths. . . . The army of *Landsknechts*, the regular armies of the seventeenth and eighteenth centuries, the national army called to life by the Great French Revolution—all these correspond to definite epochs of economic and political development, and they all rest upon certain technology . . . But what does military philosophy do? As a rule it looks upon the methods and usages of a preceding epoch as eternal truths, at last

[42] Trotsky, 'Marxism and Military Knowledge', ibid. 119.

[43] Ibid. 129. This is amazingly similar to Clausewitz's comments in his private notes on strategy written in 1808 and 1809, with which Trotsky could not have been familiar (the notes were published for the first time only in 1937): 'All the authors that in modern times have sought to treat this part of theory [strategy] abstractly and philosophically . . . are either simply trivial, or they get rid of triviality through one sidedness.' 'When [abstraction] must omit the living matter in order to hold to the dead form, which is of course the easier to abstract, it would be in the end a dry skeleton of dry truths squeezed into a doctrine. It is really astonishing to find people who waste their time on such efforts, when one bears in mind that precisely that which is the most important in war and strategy, namely the great particularity, peculiarity, and local circumstances, escape these abstractions and scientific systems'. Clausewitz, 'Strategy', in *Verstreute kleine Schriften*, ed. W. Hahlweg (Osnabrück, 1979), 46, 60–1; also see above, Book I, 176–80 189–200; the citations are from 194–5.

discovered by mankind and destined to retain their meaning for all times and all peoples.[44]

Clausewitz, Trotsky pointed out, warned very correctly against the tendency to generalize from limited experience.

He [Clausewitz] wrote: 'What is more natural than that the revolutionary war (of France) had its own way of doing things? and what theory could have included that peculiar method? The trouble is that such a manner, originating from a special case, easily outlives its day, because it continues *unchanged*, while circumstances imperceptibly undergo complete *change* . . .'[45]

To grasp fully what Trotsky had no difficulty in perceiving, a deeper understanding of the similarity which existed between Clausewitz's and the Marxist position is again called for. This similarity was not merely coincidental. It reflected the fundamental message of German historicism, which both Clausewitz and the Marxists expressed and developed in their respective fields. Emerging as it did in the late eighteenth and early nineteenth centuries, German historicism denied that the systems and principles propounded in the eighteenth century in every branch of knowledge by the men of the Enlightenment possessed anything like the universal validity claimed for them. At best, argued historicist thinkers, these so-called universal systems and principles were only abstractions, more or less successful, of the conditions prevailing in one particular period, most commonly that of the system-builders themselves. Hence the remarkable analogy, noted by Trotsky, between the criticisms which both Marx and Clausewitz made against their respective predecessors. Marx thought that the classical political economists from Adam Smith onward, that is, the economic school of the Enlightenment, had excelled in analysing the structures, relationships, and modes of operation which had prevailed in the emerging capitalist economy, as it had begun to take shape in early modern Britain. He argued, however, that they had characteristically erred in elevating these historically conditioned features to the status of abstract, universal principles of economic science—past, present, and future. Clausewitz, for his part, argued that the military thinkers of the Enlightenment had merely reflected in their systems and principles—pretentiously regarded by them as

[44] Trotsky, 'Marxism and Military Knowledge', *Military Writings*, 119–20.
[45] Trotsky, 'Pseudo-Military Doctrinairism', ibid. 56–7.

universal—one of the many different forms that war had taken through the ages.

To be sure, Clausewitz himself was occupied during most of his life in an attempt to generalize from the limited Napoleonic experience, a mistake which he realized and began to retract only during the last years of his life. It also goes without saying that his seminal historicist notions came nowhere near the comprehensiveness and sophistication of Marx's fully developed historicism. Yet Marxists could not fail to recognize the familiarity of Clausewitz's position. Lenin himself noted this familiarity with obvious satisfaction, jotting down in his notebook on Clausewitz: 'The truth is not "in the systems".'[46] He did not dwell on the matter, however, because, as already mentioned, his main use for Clausewitz's work lay elsewhere.

The fundamental nature of the correlation which existed between Clausewitz's and the Marxist position in this regard is attested by the fact that later Marxists returned to it in exactly the same manner as Trotsky. This is significant because, whereas it can be argued that Lenin's authority secured the Marxist adoption of Clausewitz's formula regarding the relationship between politics and war, Trotsky and his works have been proclaimed as heretical by the Marxist community. All the same, basic Cold War Soviet military texts proclaim:

> Many bourgeois military theoreticians maintain that the laws of military science are eternal and immutable. Military history proves them wrong, for it shows that these laws are historically conditioned, which can be seen from the fact that some laws emerge while others stop operating.[47]

> Clausewitz, whose ideas, in Lenin's words, 'were fertilized by Hegel', viewed the phenomena of war and military art in their development and movement, speaking out against 'eternal principles' of military art.[48]

[46] Lenin, *Fondements théoriques de la guerre et de la paix en U.R.S.S.*, 65.

[47] Byely *et al.* (ed.), *Marxism-Leninism on War*, 315. Also see almost identically in Savkin, *Operational Art*, 2–3 and 5; p. 5 reads: 'The principles of military art bear a historical character . . . a change in objective reality . . . leads inevitably to a change in the principles.'

[48] Savkin, *Operational Art*, 23. In Soviet military literature there are many references to the 'objective laws of war' which constitute the 'science of war'. These 'laws', however, merely express and classify relationships and hierarchies which exist within war itself and, according to Marxist theory, between war and economic, social, and political reality and historical development. Soviet concepts in this regard are compiled and discussed from a rather positivist point of view in Julian Lider, *The Political and Military Laws of War: An Analysis of Marxist-Leninist Concepts* (Guildford, 1979).

Further light is shed on the common historical roots of this striking intellectual agreement by the following, outwardly unlikely, comparison: 'The most important feature of Marxist–Leninist philosophy', states a Soviet military text, 'is its *capacity of unlimited creative development and improvement.*'[49] More than half a century earlier, in Wilhelmine Germany, a leading military writer on the Prussian general staff had contrasted Jomini's principles with the German conception of military theory which had first been elaborated by Clausewitz. The enormous advantage of the German conception, he had written, 'lies in its *capacity for further development*'.[50] It would thus appear that both Prussian 'reactionary militarism' and Soviet 'proletarian revolutionism' in effect shared a common intellectual source in early nineteenth-century German historicism.

Soviet commentators could not feel entirely at ease with their strange bedfellows. In a letter he wrote in 1946, shortly after the end of the Soviet Union's desperate struggle against Nazi Germany, Stalin informed the Soviet military historian, Colonel Razin, that 'we are obliged to criticize not only Clausewitz but also Moltke, Schlieffen, Ludendorff, Keitel, and other bearers of military ideology in Germany'. He went on to dismiss the relevancy of Clausewitz's military teaching to the present, but he did that in a quite revealing manner; he argued that history had rendered that teaching increasingly irrelevant for practical purposes, in the same way that it had rendered large parts of Marx's theory itself irrelevant. Stalin, too, was employing the historicist idea:

> What must be noted in particular about Clausewitz is that he is, of course, obsolete as a military authority. Strictly speaking, Clausewitz was the representative of the hand-tool period of warfare. But we are now in the *machine* age of warfare. The machine age undoubtedly demands new military ideologists. It is ridiculous to take lessons from Clausewitz now . . . We do not regard Marx's theory as something completed and untouchable; we are convinced, on the contrary, that it had merely laid the cornerstone of that science, which Socialists *must* move further in all directions, unless they want to be left behind by life . . .[51]

[49] Byely *et al.* (ed.), *Marxism-Leninism on War*, 293; italics in the original.

[50] Caemmerer, *Strategical Science*, 54; italics in the original.

[51] Stalin's letter was published in Feb. 1947 in the magazine *Bolshevik*, and is cited in B. Dexter, 'Clausewitz and Soviet Strategy', *Foreign Affairs*, 29 (1950), 44–5; see also R. Garthoff, *Soviet Military Doctrine* (London, 1953), 55–6.

A later Soviet military authority referred to the same problem with greater refinement:

> As the dialectic of Hegel was one of the sources for the forming Marxist philosophy, so the military works of Clausewitz, regardless of their class limitations, were one of the sources for the development of bourgeois military theory . . . as in the philosophy of Hegel, the strongest aspect of the works by Clausewitz was the dialectical approach to the phenomena of objective reality and the viewing of a number of complex phenomena in war and military art in their relationship and development. For this reason, it is inadmissible, along with the reactionary elements, to disregard the progressive features in the works of Clausewitz merely because he was the military ideologist of the manufacturing period of the conduct of war, just as we do not completely discard the philosophy of Hegel and Feuerbach.[52]

In conclusion, the main point of all the above is worth emphasizing. When all due allowances have been made, one may say that the West, and the English-speaking countries in particular, have been dominated, in their ethos and their conception of knowledge, primarily by the legacy of the Enlightenment and by its positivist descendants in the nineteenth and twentieth centuries. Thus, although in the nuclear age the West has embraced Clausewitz and almost made him its own, its actual insight into, and affinity with, his intellectual world are, in effect, fairly superficial. Quite the opposite is true, however, of both Marxism and the Prussian-German military school of the nineteenth century. Needless to say, there are great differences in this regard between the two. The Prussian military school shared Clausewitz's admiration for the state and, with the change in Germany's position, progressed from the brand of patriotism which had characterized his generation to more aggressive forms of nationalism. Marxists, for their part, could only regard Clausewitz's devotion to the state and to his country as either naïvely idealist or downright chauvinist. At the same time, however, both the Germans and the Marxists could not fail to respond with special awareness to Clausewitz's historicist notions, comprehensive approach to the phenomenon of war, and rejection of all systems. In the Prussian-German case, this response reflected a clear recognition and enthusiastic reaffirmation of key elements embedded in German national culture. In the Marxist case too, different as it may be,

[52] Gareev, *Frunze*, 86.

there has been recognition that, going back to the formative period of the early nineteenth century, Clausewitz's ideas had derived from the very same currents of thought which a little later stimulated the development of Marxism. Hence, even if not intimate, these historical and intellectual family-ties are nevertheless still detectable in the genetic code of Marxist theory.

Conclusion

WITHIN the time-span dealt with in this book, the nineteenth century may be viewed as an age of epigoni. By and large, after the great theoretical statements made by military writers like Jomini and Clausewitz in the aftermath of the Napoleonic wars, nothing fundamental seems to have changed in the way people in the Western world in the nineteenth century viewed war and military theory. Works like du Picq's *Battle Studies* and Bloch's *La Guerre future* stand out for their originality among military writings of that century, but none of them became epoch-making in their influence, as had the works of Jomini and Clausewitz.

How is this conspicuous fact to be explained? If we disregard the naïve notion that geniuses and great theories appear at certain times and places just by accident, then the historical preconditions which account for their development must be sought out. New ideas emerge during periods of revolutionary change or at times of crisis, in response to great historical challenges. They express human effort to come to grips with new developments and integrate them within meaningful intellectual frameworks. The edifices thus created then dominate until they themselves are rendered inadequate by new paradigmatic changes.

The stimulating cultural activity of the Enlightenment and the Romantic period expressed precisely these kinds of formative developments. During those periods, men attempted to work out the implications of the scientific revolution for the study of human-related subjects, war included. The two fundamental positions which grew out of this intellectual process underlie the modern outlook and still vie for supremacy to this day in the humanities and social sciences. Similarly, the advent of national, all-out war, which first emerged in all its fury during the wars of the Revolution and Empire, also marked a historical junction. Men's efforts to come to terms with the new phenomenon during, and in the wake of, the Napoleonic era produced the military theories which were to dominate the nineteenth century. Almost anything written about war later that century followed the paradigmatic notions worked out by the generation which had lived through the cataclysmic change. Mahan, to name one of the century's few great successes, won fame for responding to the challenge raised by the imperialist contest and by the ensuing naval race. But in terms of theory he merely applied long-established intellectual and strategic categories to a previously neglected subject.

It was none the less in the naval sphere that the ruling strategic precepts of the nineteenth century were challenged. Corbett argued that the fundamental features of naval warfare were in many ways different from those of land warfare. Furthermore, he suggested that the parameters of British policy had been historically different from those which the leading continental powers such as France and Prussia-Germany had used, and upon which the prevailing theory of war had been based. From this starting-point, he proceeded to turn nineteenth-century military theory on its head, reversing almost each and every one of its sacred tenets and articles of faith.

Indeed, it is no coincidence that Britain was the country which provided the background for the emergence of a new strategic outlook, once new historical preconditions developed. The strategic paradigm which had dominated the nineteenth century fell into crisis when the First World War failed to produce a quick and decisive result and, assuming a Moloch-like character, left both victors and vanquished almost equally exhausted. After the war, reflecting the general change of opinion about international relations and war, and building on distinctively British cultural and political traditions, people like Liddell Hart were to apply Corbett's revolutionary theses to produce a comprehensive reformulation of military theory. This involved a total rejection of both all-out war and the strategic theory which went with it. In inter-war Britain, new challenges and new cultural perspectives were again to give rise to new grand theories.

Book III

Fascist and Liberal Visions of War

Part I

Fascist Modernism and Visionaries of Machine Warfare

I

Introduction: *'The Janus Face' of Fascism*

This part suggests that a close affinity existed between the radical visions of machine warfare—inspiring and debated by soldiers and civilians during the first decades of the twentieth century—and the cultural and intellectual currents partaking of the proto-fascist and fascist outlook, or 'mood'. The mechanization of warfare was of course rooted in the general developments of the age, and was dependent upon tangible and material factors such as industrial capacity, technological advance, and geostrategic position. All the same, visions of machine warfare largely belonged to the domain of ideas and the imagination, flowering most vividly where their cultural and intellectual subsoil proved particularly fertile. Almost as a rule, they drew heavily from the modernist notions and visions, celebration of the machine, and ideals of action, vigour, and speed prominent within proto-fascism.

This proposition will probably not be foreign to historians of fascist ideas and imagery or to students of fascist-modernist artistic culture, as it might be to military historians. The role of the machine and the concept of a futurist machine-dominated society in the proto-fascist climate of ideas has become a well-recognized theme. Increasingly since the 1960s, indeed, fascism as a political and cultural phenomenon has been receiving far more serious scholarly attention than it had before. Two major revisions of earlier views have emerged. First, scholars have argued that although fascism became a potent political force in the wake of the political, social, and cultural dislocation brought about by the First World War—and in reaction against the spectre of Bolshevism—its growth dates from well before the interwar period, from as far back as the late nineteenth century. Second, rather than being a 'revolution of nihilism', led and carried out by gangs of thugs who were driven solely by a lust for power, fascism has been recognized as a comprehensive cultural 'mood', outlook, creed, or even ideology. It enjoyed strong appeal among intellectuals as a third way to modernity, an alternative to both liberalism and socialism.[1]

To be sure, as a generic term fascism is notoriously ambiguous. Italian Fascism and German National-Socialism differed from each other in some of their principal features; and these two central models were again different from the French, British, and other fascist variants which rose in industrialized Europe, to say nothing of the authoritarian-conservative regimes and right-wing radical movements in the predominantly agrarian countries of Eastern Europe, the Iberian peninsula, and Latin America, which from the 1930s adopted many features of fascist political culture. Concerned that ideological, chronological, and local diversity might render the concept itself dubious and unusable, some scholars have suggested a 'fascist minimum', of which the following is my own rough synthesis. Inevitably in view of our particular subject, it is tilted towards the intellectuals' outlook rather than towards the fascist rank and file or the practices of fascist regimes.

Fascism emerged on the heels of industrialization, urbanization, and the growth of mass society. Those who shared in the proto-fascist and fascist 'mood' rebelled against bourgeois culture, with its 'decadent' materialism, commercialism, atomistic and alienating individualism, and liberal-humanitarian values. They dreaded the further advance of plebeianism, mediocrity, and triviality expected with growing democratization. Espousing idealism and exalting youth, elementary dynamism, and vitalism, they called for comprehensive spiritual and cultural rejuvenation and the creation of a new man within a radically reconstructed society. They sought to overcome divisive parliamentarism, capitalism, and socialism through the application of communal solutions which would mobilize the energies and loyalty of the masses around unifying national traditions, myths, and ideals. At the same time, they held that government should firmly remain in the hands of a worthy élite, the creator and leader of the New Order.[2]

[1] References in these introductory remarks are necessarily sparing. See esp. G. Mosse, *The Crisis of German Ideology* (New York, 1964); *The Nationalization of the Masses* (New York, 1975); *Nazism* (Oxford, 1978); J. Weiss, *The Fascist Tradition* (New York, 1967); J. Gregor, *The Ideology of Fascism* (New York, 1969); A. Hamilton, *The Appeal of Fascism*, (London, 1971); Z. Sternhell, *Neither Right nor Left* (Berkeley, Calif., 1986); D. Carrol, *French Literary Fascism* (Princeton, NJ, 1995).

[2] In addition to the references in the previous note, two pioneering works are E. Nolte, *Three Faces of Fascism* (New York, 1969), and E. Weber, *Varieties of Fascism* (Princeton, NJ, 1964); most usefully, see: H. R. Trevor-Roper, 'The Phenomenon of Fascism', in S. J. Woolf (ed.), *European Fascism* (New York, 1969); A. Greil, 'The Modernization of

Fascist attitude towards the modern is a particularly ambivalent issue. The question of whether fascism was reactionary or radical and forward-looking is much debated. Here, most significantly, the considerable differences existing between the various movements and intellectual currents which partook of the fascist 'mood' are discernible. German National-Socialism remarkably demonstrated the 'Janus face' of fascism: hostile to Western rationalist tradition, deeply nostalgic, and steeped in *völkisch* and agrarian mythology, while also projecting a futuristic utopia, in which a vigorous German race would rule the vast territories of the new Reich and compete for global mastery, riding the most technologically advanced machines. On the other hand, the Italian Fascists, although also recalling the glories of ancient Rome, saw themselves as the modern movement *par excellence*—the true heirs of the 1789 revolutionary tradition, nineteenth-century Garibaldian republicanism, and the positivist vision of progress. From the turn of the century the poet Gabriele d'Annunzio, a precursor of the movement and its future artistic figurehead, celebrated the machine and modern technology, clothed in classical and mythological imagery, as a liberating and sublime aesthetic, moral, and spiritual vehicle of the new age. In a similar vein, one of the main sources of Italian Fascism was the Futurist movement in the arts, led by Filippo Tommaso Marinetti. The Futurists fiercely rejected any nostalgic yearnings for the past, aestheticized and worshipped the products of modern technology, and marvelled at the qualities of a modernist, machine-dominated society. For the Italian Fascists fascism was the order of the future, superseding obsolete parliamentary democracy in the new age of modern, industrial mass society. These notions were even more central to the Franco-Belgian fascist variety of Plannism, numbering among its theorists and adherents people like Henry de Man, Marcel Déat, Jacques Doriot, and the leading figure of Modernism in architecture, Le Corbusier. Equally, the followers of Sir Oswald Mosley in the British Union of Fascists claimed modernity as their own. For these movements fascism was predominantly the modern response to the needs of the modern era,

Consciousness and the Appeal of Fascism', *Comparative Political Studies*, 10 (1977), 213–38; A. J. Gregor, 'Fascism and the "Countermodernization of Consciousness"', ibid. 239–58; G. Mosse's Introduction to Mosse (ed.), *International Fascism*, (London, 1979), 1–41; S. T. Larsen, B. Hagtvet, and J. P. Myklebust (eds.), *Who Were the Fascists?* (Bergen, 1980); S. Payne, *Fascism: Comparison and Definition* (Madison, Wis., 1980); *A History of Fascism, 1914–1945* (Madison, Wis., 1995), esp. 3–19, 462–70, 487–95; R. Griffin, *The Nature of Fascism* (London, 1991).

transcending both capitalism and socialism. It would create a fully organized and efficient society, ruled by a meritocratic, managerial government of experts, both made necessary by the complexities of the new technological age.[3]

It is these modernist currents and aspects of proto-fascism and fascism that will concern us here. The futuristic aesthetization of the machine and of technological society (which has been amply highlighted by scholars) and the fascist-modernist view of the shape of the modern world (which has not) were both powerful cultural forces. Machine warfare visionaries may simply be thought to have identified with the fascist cult of violence, militarism, and quest for armament and for strong armed forces—and some of them certainly did. Yet these fascist attributes primarily hold true for the defeated and humiliated Germany of the 1920s and 1930s, and to a lesser degree for Fascist Italy. French fascism was mostly pacifist, and Mosley and his movement shared the general British reaction against the experience of the First World War. They genuinely regarded themselves as the 'party of peace', even before the prospect of war with Nazi Germany and Fascist Italy arose in the 1930s. Machine warfare visionaries were attracted to fascism for much broader reasons. Invariably, and almost by definition, they were people of strong intellectual bent. They were driven by, or were searching for, a comprehensive outlook, interpretation of history and the direction it was taking, and view of the current state of humanity, in which to anchor and from within which to develop their own specialized vision. More often than not, it was towards the modernist strands of proto-fascism and fascism that they gravitated.

Prelude: Positivism, Technology, and Future Society; Jules Verne and H. G. Wells

It is generally recognized that the late nineteenth century was characterized by a widespread so-called 'neo-Romantic revolt' against positi-

[3] Again, only briefly at this point: R. de Felice, *Fascism* (New Brunswick, NJ, 1977), 55, 103, 106; A. Cassels, 'Janus: The Two Faces of Fascism', and H. Turner Jr., 'Fascism and Modernization', in Turner (ed.), *Reappraisals of Fascism* (New York, 1975), 69–92 and 117–39 respectively; A. J. Gregor, 'Fascism and Modernization', *World Politics*, 26 (1974), 370–84; A. J. Joes, 'On the Modernity of Fascism', *Comparative Political Studies*, 10 (1977), 259–68; Sternhell, *Neither Right nor Left*, 141–212, on Plannism; J. Herf, *Reactionary Modernism* (Cambridge, 1984); Payne, *History of Fascism*, esp. 471–86; Griffin, *Fascism*, 47–8; A. Hewitt, *Fascist Modernism: Aesthetics, Politics, and the Avant-Garde* (Stanford, Calif., 1993). References to the much-debated National Socialist case are reserved for the relevant chapter below.

vism. This is taken to signify growing doubts regarding the mid-nineteenth-century optimistic belief in a comprehensive, continuous, and accelerating progress, fuelled by the rapid advance of science, technology, and education, and leading to steady moral improvement and growing economic and social well-being. The revolt involved a rejection of the materialistic–mechanistic conception of reason, focusing instead on the elementary forces of life, the irrational springs of individual and communal psyche, and a cult of action and creativity. For all that, in some important respects the label 'revolt against positivism' is not altogether satisfactory and needs to be used with discrimination. Positivism may be loosely employed to denote the prevailing outlook of the progressive educated public in the West during the mid-nineteenth century, but more technically it consisted of the various and often widely varying doctrines of such thinkers as Saint-Simon, Fourier, Auguste Comte, Herbert Spencer, and their disciples. With them the element of the irrational, cyclical conceptions of history, and authoritarianism were as prevalent as secular materialism, linear optimism, and individualistic liberalism. The most diverse persuasions could draw from the positivist tradition, and did. The ideas of Jules Verne and H. G. Wells, the two most famous popular visionaries of the machine in the pre-fascist era, demonstrate this point.

The high tide of optimistic democratic-liberalism is exemplified by the inventor of the scientific novel and 'child of Second Empire positivism', Jules Verne (1828–1905). His internationally successful books shared and built upon the general enthusiasm for the remarkable feats of science, technology, and engineering, whose rapid advance was conspicuously changing daily life and firing the public's imagination during the second half of the nineteenth century. In an age of explorations the *Voyages extraordinaires* took his readers to the stretches of an unfolding globe and beyond, and dazzled them with the products and transforming effects of future technology, which Verne suggested lay not very far over the horizon. What he offered was not just spacecraft and aircraft, automobiles and submarines, gigantic cannons, huge projectiles, and gas shells, but also social visions. Verne was an 1848 liberal for his entire life, who would actively support the republic in 1870 and later run for the municipal council of Amiens on the republican-left ticket (while also being an anti-Dreyfusite). In his novels he stood for anti-authoritarian, humanitarian individualism, freedom for oppressed peoples, and international brotherhood, qualified only by strong, sometimes chauvinist, French patriotism. In his characteristically Saint-Simonian and

Fourierist utopian garden communities rational planning, enlightened social organization, electricity, and advanced sanitation brought about general welfare and happiness. For all that, even this progressive optimist succumbed to fits of anxiety and pessimism. We now know they had already marked one of his earliest, most prophetic but unpublished novels, *Paris au xx siècle* (completed in 1863), and they increased as he grew older and mid-century enthusiasm gave way to *fin-de-siècle* gloom. As the social, cultural, and environmental costs of industrialization and commercialism became more apparent, Verne's social and humanitarian utopias were repeatedly overshadowed by evil or alienating technology, whose sombre potential ran amok, threatening doom to both nature and humanity.[4]

Expressing the turn-of-the-century mood of both boundless belief in progress and deep anxiety was the most famous prophet of technology of his time and the practitioner of social futurology, H. G. Wells (1866–1946). Far more than Verne, whose British counterpart he was often regarded to be, Wells was a highly committed popular social philosopher as well as a novelist. A scientist by education, he was a student of the celebrated Thomas Huxley, Charles Darwin's champion in the great public debates that followed the publication of *The Origin of Species* (1859) and *The Descent of Man* (1871). An evolutionist like the rest of his generation, Wells none the less shared Huxley's objections to the social Darwinists' application of the categories of biology to the understanding of man's social life. Like Huxley, he held that the spectacular growth of human civilization once man's biological potential had evolved was primarily a cultural and historical process. This process was now entering a new stage. From his remarkable *Anticipation of the Reaction of Mechanical and Scientific Progress upon Human Life and Thought* (1902) onward, Wells sought to predict the shape of, and prepare humanity for, the industrial–commercial, urban, global, and scientific–technological civilization which was in the making. He believed that it would require radically new forms of human organization.

A friend of G. B. Shaw and the Webbs, and for a time a member of

[4] See esp. J. Chesneaux, *The Political and Social Ideas of Jules Verne* (London, 1972) (for his connections with the Saint-Simonians, see pp. 82–6); J. Noiray, *Le Romancier et la machine: l'image de la machine dans le roman français (1850–1900)*, ii (Paris, 1982) (a citation by Verne from Comte is printed on p. 220); J. Jules-Verne, *Jules Verne* (New York, 1976); A. Martin, *The Mask of the Prophet: The Extraordinary Fictions of Jules Verne* (Oxford, 1990), 130, 183.

the Fabian Society (which he failed to convert into a radical political order), Wells shared the Edwardian progressive–liberal–socialist quest for planned social reform. This was integrated, however, within his wider view of the course human history was taking, which he crystallized early on in his career and which became his lifelong panacea. He believed that the developments of the modern age, particularly the emergence of a global economy and the revolution in communications (he predicted the proliferation of the automobile and the coming of air flight), were leading towards a world state. In this new global community a culture of science and technology, education, freedom, and enlightened humanitarianism would prevail. Yet, like the French positivists of the previous century—Saint-Simon, Fourier, and Comte, who had advanced a remarkably similar views of the direction and ultimate destination of human development—and unlike Spencer, whom he criticized on that account, Wells thought modern society and the new world state would be neither democratic nor characterized by individualistic, unregulated *laissez-faire*. He shared the educated class's growing suspicions of the rationality of the masses, expressed for example by Wells's close friend, the famous social psychologist Graham Wallace, and by Gustave le Bon, whose highly influential works Wells often cited. Wells's élitism, while of a heroic and individualistic character, was of a different sort from that of a Carlyle, a Nietzsche, or a Shaw. For him, democracy was only a historical phase, mainly because the evolving highly advanced scientific, technological, and industrial society would require sophisticated coordination and planning, which could only be carried out by a government of experts, a Platonic meritocratic élite of managers and scientists.[5]

Wells held that a world state was becoming an overriding necessity because the enormous potential destructiveness of modern technology threatened to bring about the end of civilization if the existing antagonistic state system continued. Most of Wells's technological novels dealt with war. His early success, *The War of the Worlds* (1898), with its extraterrestrial instruments of war, was still innocent 'scare' science

[5] A good study of Wells's political and social outlook is W. Wagar, *H. G. Wells and the World State* (New York, 1961); see also H. G. Wells, *Experiment in Autobiography* (New York, 1934). Two excellent studies of some relevant aspects of the intellectual background of the time are G. R. Searle, *The Quest for National Efficiency* (Oxford, 1971), and P. Crook, *Darwinism, War, and History* (Cambridge, 1994). For Wells's military ideas, see T. H. E. Travers, 'Future Warfare: H. G. Wells and British Military Theory, 1895–1916', in B. Bond and I. Roy (eds.), *War and Society* (London, n.d.), 67–87.

fiction. But Wells was dead serious in his later works. In *Anticipations* he cited Ivan Bloch's analysis of the shape of future war, predicting that the rapid rise of firepower would create a tactical and strategic stalemate which in turn would bring about the collapse of the closely knit world economy, famine, and breakdown of the warring societies. To Bloch's analysis Wells added a great struggle for the conquest of the air by aircraft, whose appearance at around 1950 or 2000 he had been anticipating since the mid-1890s (the mistaken prediction of the date was shared at that time even by Wilbur Wright). The air fleets would then proceed to attack land targets. After great upheavals, the general calamity would lead to the creation of a world state.

Indeed, Wells's analysis of modern war went further than Bloch's. In *Anticipations* he considered that a progressively mechanized war would bring forth a new type of highly trained professional army, the product of the new technological and scientific age. The old mass armies of amateurs and recruits were doomed. The modern trend was to link the new type of soldier 'with the engineer and doctor and all the continually developing mass of scientifically educated men that the advance of science and mechanism is producing'. In the public debate in Britain in the years preceding the First World War, Wells would reject the idea of a conscript army in favour of an élite force.[6] In 'The Land Ironclads', published in *The Strand Magazine* in 1903, he prophesied mechanized land warfare, with land ships manned by soldier-engineers.[7] It was, however, aircraft that figured most prominently in his work. They became the subject of his novel *The War in the Air* (1908), a stark warning issued against the background of mounting international tensions. In this novel the airships and aircraft of the great powers crossed oceans and continents in a truly global world war. They sank fleets of dreadnoughts (whose days, Wells believed, were coming to a close because of the torpedo boat, submarine, and aircraft)[8] and attacked the enemy's heartland, his centres of population and industry. This was again followed by a collapse of modern advanced civilization, and opened decades of anarchy and endemic strife. Wells's novel *The World Set Free* (1914), published before the war, starts with a positivist history of man's ascent from his ancient origins up to his present-day wealth-

[6] Travers, 'Wells', 68–9.

[7] Ibid. 69, 72–3; also H. G. Wells, *Italy, France and Britain at War* (New York, 1917), 153.

[8] Travers, 'Wells', 79; A. J. A. Morris, *The Scaremongers: The Advocacy of War and Rearmament, 1896–1914* (London, 1984), 346–7.

creating and emancipating, science- and technology-based civilization.[9] It then describes the invention of an atomic bomb (*sic*) in 1933 and of atomic power stations (*sic*) for civilian use in 1953. (This is not as startling as it may sound: Wells took his inspiration from the recent advances in nuclear physics made by Ramsay, Rutherford, and Soddy.)[10] A short time later in the mid-century, an atomic war between the great powers, which were governed by mediocracies, racked civilization. This disaster led to the emergence of a new world republic in which atomic weapons and other armament were banned.

By the end of the First World War Wells was campaigning for the creation of a League of Nations, and during the interwar period he dedicated all his energy to popularizing the ideas of a world state and élite government. By the 1930s he ceased to concern himself with anything else. His *The Shape of Things to Come* (1933), filmed by Alexander Korda in 1936, merely repeated his by now constant theme: the rise of modern civilization; its collapse in destructive wars leading to mass epidemics and medieval anarchy; its tortuous regeneration; and the establishment of a world state. The new civilization would possess a regulated economy, would be led by a class of managers, experts, and aviators, would exercise far-reaching control of the environment, including bio-molecular engineering of plants, and would organize society and education with the view of promoting general happiness. The Second World War, which seemed to confirm Wells's worst fears, broke his heart.

In some important respects, in which he echoed the French positivists of the first half of the nineteenth century, Wells's cast of mind made him a typical potential recruit for fascism. He thought democracy mediocre and unsuitable for the modern world. He rejected economic liberalism in favour of communalism and social planning, while also rejecting Marxism. He called for the creation of a new type of élite government, which in *Modern Utopia* (1905), for example, he even suggested should engage in breeding on eugenic principles. He believed the modern world would bring about new forms of social ethics and secular religions. In his more pessimistic moods he thought that civilization was in a structural crisis and that present culture was sick. Even his doctrine of free love (which again echoed Saint Simon and Fourier) was reminiscent of a characteristic streak within the proto-fascist mood.

[9] This would be fully developed in Wells's brilliant positivist work *The Outline of History* (London, 1920).

[10] H. G. Wells, *The World Set Free* (London, 1927), 25.

On the other hand, Wells's differences with the fascist cast of mind were also of a fundamental nature, and explain why he never came within the fascist orbit. He was anti-authoritarian, humanistic, pacifist, and cosmopolitan. On the whole he rejected social Darwinism, racism, and flights into the mystical—all typical, though individually not necessarily indispensable, components of the fascist mix. Other intellectuals, from both left and right, who shared many of Wells's views but were a generation younger, hovered much closer to fascism.

2

J. F. C. Fuller and Future Warfare

John Frederick Charles Fuller's (1878–1966) intellectual intensity, wide-ranging interests, and literary scope have been fully documented in his own vast output and autobiography, and by his biographers.[1] None the less, for students of military affairs they still appear as an interesting, piquant, but largely unconnected addendum to his military work. In particular his involvement in Oswald Mosley's British Union of Fascists during the 1930s has been viewed as an unfortunate accident in his career, to be mainly attributed to his famously eccentric personality or to the fascist emphasis on order and all things military.[2] By contrast, this study aims to advance the following propositions, some of which have long been known: Fuller developed as an intellectual well before he became a military thinker; the nature of this development made him a characteristic participant in the proto-fascist mood; his interest in and major contributions to his own military profession evolved distinctively out of his general intellectual development; his vision of future mechanized armies in particular drew its inspiration, breadth, and vigour from his general outlook and interests; thus his formal fascist phase was only the logical conclusion of a lifelong intellectual bent.

The Forming of a Proto-Fascist Intellectual

The undistinguished child of an Anglican clergyman, Fuller was sent into an army career by his family. Upon entering Sandhurst in 1897, he

[1] J. F. C. Fuller, *Memoirs of an Unconventional Soldier* (London, 1936); and two excellent intellectual biographies: A. J. Trythall, *'Boney' Fuller: The Intellectual General* (London, 1977); B. H. Reid, *J. F. C. Fuller: Military Thinker* (London, 1987).

[2] Even Reid, *Fuller*, 176–7, seems to espouse this view, even though it goes against the drift of his book; but see Trythall, *Fuller*, 181–3; also J. Luvaas, 'Major General J. F. C. Fuller', in *The Education of an Army* (London, 1965), 364–5.

was little interested either in his profession or in the customary social pursuits of regimental life in the light infantry. But, a loner and introvert, he found the army's dull routine convenient for the satisfaction of a newly developed hunger for books, mostly of a philosophical nature. He became, and would ever remain, an intense autodidact. His reading first made him agnostic and anti-religious: 'this pronounced mental change coincided with the last lap of the great theologico-Darwinian controversy, and in consequence I soon became immersed in Huxley, Lecky, Samuel Laing and other rationalist writers.'[3] Brian Holden Reid has admirably analysed Fuller's extensive reading lists during 1898–1901, the years of the Boer War in which he participated:

> During these years something approaching 200 volumes found their way into his hands. . . . An interest in Carlyle was already evident before Fuller left for South Africa, as he read *Sartor Resartus* in 1898, followed a year later by *Heroes and Hero Worship* and the *History of Frederick the Great* in 1902. He also devoured Laing's *Problems of the Future* and *Human Origins*, Darwin's *Descent of Man* and Freeman's *History of the Norman Conquest*. . . . From 1899 onward religious books held his attention. These included Laing's *A Modern Zoroastrianism*, Allen's *Evolution of the Idea of God*, Arnold's *Death and Afterwards* and *Science and the Christian Tradition*, Wiedemann's *The Ancient Egyptian Doctrine of the Soul*, and 'Saladin', *Why am I an Agnostic?* . . . Fuller continued to read widely in philosophy. He read Paul Carus's *A Primer of Philosophy* and Kant's *Dreams of a Spirit Seer*. An interest in science is noteworthy and titles like Laing's *Modern Science and Modern Thought* are found in his notebooks. . . . Fuller reflected seriously on what he had read. After reading Carlyle's *History of the French Revolution* . . . he speculated that man is but a 'veneered brute' and once the veneer wore off, man's latent savagery 'springs forth' in all its ghastly ferocity. This view of man's inherent animalism was fortified some months later when Fuller thought he had discovered the full implications of Darwin's Theory of Evolution. 'I am a great believer in Darwin and Evolution[,] the whole theory is so grand, so beautiful and true.' He then turned to Wall's *Darwinism and Race Progress* and made some jottings on the universal application of the theory. Further grist to his Darwinist mill was provided by his study of two books by the Social Darwinian, Benjamin Kidd, *The Control of the Tropics* and *Social Evolution*.[4]

[3] Fuller, *Memoirs*, 458–9.

[4] Reid, *Fuller*, 11–12; the reading lists are in Fuller's material deposited at the Liddell Hart Centre of Military Archives, King's College, London (hereafter King's), IV/4/1. They range widely over history, art history, and literature.

Among the earliest books Fuller read during that period was *The First Greek Philosophers*, containing the surviving fragments of Heraclitus. Heraclitus' dialectics and celebration of war, 'the father of all things', made him popular among social-Darwinists of all countries during that time.[5] As Fuller's biographer has aptly concluded: 'Thus at [from] the beginning of his career Fuller identified himself with a major intellectual current, and one that owed little to the democratic, empirical English tradition.'[6]

Apart from evolutionism, several other intellectual traits which the young Fuller exhibited and which he maintained for life connected unmistakably with ideas and sentiments which, although enjoying a much wider currency, were all feeding the evolving proto-fascist mood. One of these traits was anti-socialism and élitism. Fuller wrote to his brother in 1906:

> That the masses are socialistic is not very grave danger; for socialism is but the scum on the democratic cauldron. Socialism is anti-progressive, tending to level the higher to the lower, true democracy is diametrically the reserve it raises: the former is but a passing phase bubbling to the surface, a cleansing, a semi-education, the latter a step in the evolutionary ladder.[7]

As Reid again points out, Fuller 'absorbed the ideas of Benjamin Kidd and Karl Pearson as to the need for order, efficiency and discipline in the administration of all departments of state. This Edwardian vision of a technocratic élite of functional men was widely popularized in the years immediately before the First World War.'[8]

A second and even more fundamental trait was anti-materialism, about which Fuller wrote to his mother while still a young subaltern: 'the generality of people are cold, unfeeling, unloveable. And why? simply because Mammon bosses the show.'[9] Again, this widespread sentiment in turn-of-the-century Europe was expressed, for example, by the social-Darwinist and popular writer Benjamin Kidd, whom Fuller avidly read. Even more than Huxley, Kidd 'wanted a massive shift of human consciousness away from the dominating values of Mammon, ego, agnostic science, appealing to the 'emotion of the ideal', to man's capacity for self-transcendence and higher spirituality'.[10]

[5] Reid, *Fuller*, 9–10; Fuller, *Memoirs*, 7.
[6] Reid, *Fuller*, 10.
[7] King's, IV/3/139b, quoted by Trythall, *Fuller*, 20–1.
[8] Reid, *Fuller*, 19; see also G. R. Searle, *The Quest for National Efficiency*.
[9] King's, IV/3/4, quoted in Reid, *Fuller*, 9.
[10] P. Crook, *Darwinism, War, and History* (Cambridge, 1994) 70.

Indeed, third and closely linked to anti-materialism came the search for a new spirituality, which in turn led Fuller to mysticism. During the years 1903–6 he was stationed in India. Breaking away from religious conventions and accepted social mores, he was at that time preoccupied with sexual morality, reading extensively and embracing the doctrine of free love.[11] During that period he also immersed himself in the study of Indian culture. 'I studied the *Vedas* and the *Upanishads*—in translations, of course—and took a deep interest in the Yoga philosophy.' He then read George Berkeley's idealist philosophy and Spencer's *First Principles*, about which he wrote:

> this noted book brought me into contact with his idea of the Unknowable. I then began to realize that, though conventional religion might be nauseating, crudely it stood for something which was neither rational nor irrational, but wonderful; a something which was beyond all things. . . . the only true course of reform lay in replacing an old worn-out spirituality by a new.

Spencer himself was an atheist and the most rationalist of the positivist major figures, but in his concept of the Unknowable he demarcated the limits of scientific knowledge, beyond which religion and metaphysics reigned. He also echoed his French predecessors, who had held that religion was not merely superstition but *inter alia* an archaic mode for expressing ideas about the world and the nature of being. In describing his own intellectual transformation from critical agnosticism to new spirituality, Fuller used the positivist terminology from Saint-Simon onward regarding the constant rotation of cultural epochs from the 'iconoclastic' to the 'synthetic', or from the 'destructive' to the 'constructive'.[12] Believing that their era called for a new 'synthetic' religious revival, Saint-Simon, Comte, and their disciples had turned with great zeal to creating a new positivist Religion of Humanity or of the 'Great Being', and to establishing its church and elaborate cult.

In 1905 Fuller's first two published articles appeared in the *Agnostic Journal*, but by then he was moving beyond his anti-religious phase. It was to the search for the hidden meaning and unity behind the appearance of phenomena, and for illuminating secret wisdom, that he had now turned.[13] In 1905 he made contact with Aleister Crowley, who

[11] Reid, *Fuller*, 13. Fuller read Lecky, *History of European Morals*, Ellis, *Studies in the Psychology of Sex*, Huston, *A Plea for Polygamy*, Rosenbaum, *The Plague of Lust, The Blight of Respectability*, and Westermark, *The History of Human Marriage.*

[12] All citations are from Fuller, *Memoirs*, 17, 459–60.

[13] Ibid.; Trythall, *Fuller*, 20.

would become known as 'the most notorious magician of the century . . . the best-equipped magician to emerge since the seventeenth century'.[14] The long tradition of occultism enjoyed a great revival throughout the West at the turn of the century as part of the neo-Romantic wave. It drew on an extensive series of magical and mysterious texts, actually or supposedly derived from a variety of ancient sources: Egyptian Hermetism and cults, Greek myths and Pythagorean and Platonic teaching, Jewish Cabbala, Christian Rosicrucianism, Far Eastern wisdom, and so on. It sought to decipher and to unite with the cosmic forces operating behind reality by interpreting the secret meanings within mysterious symbols, words, and numbers, through the use of ecstasy, and through liturgy. Crowley began his involvement with the occult as a member of the magical order of the Golden Dawn, where he soon quarrelled with the founder of the order and with other members, such as the poet W. B. Yeats, another would-be fascist sympathizer. He then started his own independent career. Whereas the Golden Dawn mainly emphasized texts and liturgy, the tempestuous, domineering, and brilliant Crowley would increasingly use drugs and sexual ecstasies. He claimed to have had a series of encounters with ancient demons, and wrote a number of books in which he proclaimed himself the founder of a new religion which would replace Christianity and transcend its boundaries of good and evil.[15]

Towards the end of his stay in India, Fuller responded to an advertisement by Crowley promising a £100 prize for the winning writer of a book on Crowley's teaching. Fuller entered as the sole competitor and won the prize (which Crowley never paid). The book he wrote, his first, *The Star in the West* (1907), was full of the enthusiasm of the convert, announcing to the world the new gospel in an archaic, mystical, and elevated style. According to Fuller, Crowley's new religion synthesized the wisdoms of East and West and reconciled all conflicting philosophical positions.[16] Returning to Britain in 1906, Fuller became Crowley's closest disciple, wholly absorbed in the activities of his group, and co-editor and contributor to his journal, *The Equinox*. He had

[14] R. Cavendish, *A History of Magic* (London, 1977), 147–8; on Fuller, see p. 148.

[15] See E. Howe, *The Magicians of the Golden Dawn: A Documentary History of a Magical Order, 1887–1923* (London, 1972); J. Symonds, *The Great Beast: The Life and Magic of Aleister Crowley* (London, 1971); R. Cavendish, *The Magical Arts* (London, 1984).

[16] In Fuller's view, Crowley synthesized Plato, Aristotle, Bacon, Descartes, Spinoza, Malebranche, Berkeley, Hume, Kant, Fichte, Schelling, Hegel, Comte, Spencer, and Huxley, as well as Cabbala, Buddhism, Yoga, and agnosticism.

several mystical experiences but, faithfully married from 1907, he left his doctrine of free love behind him.[17]

All this is not an irrelevant curiosity. As Reid has rightly pointed out in respect to the mystics of that period: 'Before 1939 these groups were largely right wing in political complexion.'[18] Recent research has revealed the spread of occult sects in the West at the turn of the century, with which Crowley and his followers maintained close contact. It highlighted the mystical influences on the young Adolf Hitler, on other Nazi leaders such as Heinrich Himmler, Alfred Rosenberg, and Rudolf Hess, and on Nazi ideology, which cannot be fully understood without these influences. In Germany and the German-speaking parts of the Habsburg empire these sects mixed occultism with Wagnerian *völkisch* nationalism and racism. They depicted a mythological past in which a bright Aryan order of priests ruled inferior dark races. That archaic order was disrupted by the destructive and chaotic Jews, spreading Christianity as one of their poisonous weapons, and carrying out an eternal Manichaean struggle against the Aryans. Here is an element that is discernible not only in the Nazis' racism and murderous demonization of the Jews but in their apocalyptic fantasies, utopian millenarianism, and vision of the SS as a semi-religious warrior order.[19] All over the West, leading modernist poets and novelists who were attracted to proto-fascism and fascism (and were virulent anti-semites), like Ezra Pound, T. S. Eliot, W. B. Yeats, Wyndham Lewis, and, more ambivalently, D. H. Lawrence, were also deeply involved with the occult.[20]

[17] Capt. J. F. C. Fuller, *The Star in the West: A Critical Essay upon the Works of Aleister Crowley* (London, 1907); Symonds, *The Great Beast*, esp. 96–7, 121; Trythall, *Fuller*, 20–1, 24–6; Reid, *Fuller*, 14–16. Most of Fuller's occult library is at Rutgers University. Galley proofs of mystical books published in 1908, which Fuller apparently helped to proof read, are in Box XI.

[18] Reid, *Fuller*, 14.

[19] The most comprehensive and impressive study is J. Webb, *The Occult Establishment* (La Salle, Ill., 1976); for the fascist connection in Britain, see pp. 125–36, and for Germany and the Nazis, pp. 275–344, esp. pp. 299–330; also N. Goodrick-Clarke, *The Occult Roots of Nazism* (New York, 1985); and E. Howe, *Astrology and the Third Reich* (Wellingborough, Northants, 1984). The whole theme was pioneered and developed by G. Mosse, *The Crisis of German Ideology* (New York, 1964), 313–14; *The Nationalization of the Masses* (New York, 1975), 197–9; *Nazism* (Oxford, 1978), 59–61; 'Introduction' to G. Mosse (ed.), *International Fascism* (London, 1970), 7–10; and, most fully, 'The Mystical Origins of National Socialism', in his *Masses and Man: Nationalist and Fascist Perception of Reality* (Detroit, 1987), 197–213.

[20] Of the considerable literature on this subject, see most recently: L. Surette, *The Birth of Modernism: Ezra Pound, T. S. Eliot, W. B. Yeats, and the Occult* (London, 1993); G. M. Harper (ed.), *Yeats and the Occult* (Canada, 1975); G. Hough, *The Mystery Religion of W. B. Yeats* (Brighton, Sussex, 1984); W. Chace, *The Political Identities of Ezra Pound and T. J. S. Eliot* (Stanford, Calif., 1973).

While Fuller was never a 'hard' biological racist, his anti-Semitic article 'The Cancer of Europe', published in the first issue of *The Fascist Quarterly* (1935), blamed the Jews, portrayed as a meta-historical force, for a thousand years' Manichaean struggle to destroy Christian civilization. Quoting from the Cabbalist book *The Zohar* and from the prophets, Fuller claimed that the Jews were materialists and anti-spiritualists, successively using magic, money, and psychoanalysis to further their cause.[21]

Although he quarrelled with Crowley in 1911, and the two parted ways, Fuller retained for life his mystical bent. Among his many books were one on Yoga and one on Cabbala.[22] He carried forward from his preoccupation with the occult to his other interests, including the military, a holistic and dialectical outlook, a search for the fundamental that underlay the appearance of reality, and an emphasis on the moral and on the exercise of conflicting wills.[23]

In 1907–12 Fuller served as the adjutant of a Volunteer, and later Territorial, battalion, where he proved to be a successful leader and trainer. In 1912 he returned to his regular regiment as a company commander. He also acted as rail transport officer to the Aldershot command and as brigade machine-gun officer—all valuable experiences in view of the nature of the approaching war. In 1911, after his break with Crowley, he suddenly decided to enter the Staff College. Failing the examination in 1912, he got in the next year. For the first time his mind focused on his own military profession, bringing to it the same intellectual absorption which had characterized his earlier activities and the intellectual equipment he had acquired in them: 'during the years in which I attacked conventional religion, subconsciously I was forging a piece of mental machinery wherewith I could thresh the grist from the chaff of the conventional theories of war . . . '[24] Fuller possessed the strong, independent mind of the autodidact, sharpened by more than a decade of critical contemplation, some experience in writing, and, above all, the knowledge and conceptual frameworks he had absorbed from his

[21] 'The Cancer of Europe', *Fascist Quarterly*, 1 (1935), 66–81; the occult nature of his anti-Semitism has been noted by Webb, *The Occult Establishment*, 127, 220.

[22] Fuller, 'The Black Arts', *Occult Review* (Apr. 1923); *Yoga: A Study of the Mystical Philosophy of the Brahmins and Buddhists* (London, 1925; 2nd edn 1933); *The Secret Wisdom of the Qabalah: A Study of Jewish Mystical Thought* (London, 1936). Two manuscripts, 'The Hidden Wisdom of the Illuminati' (1926) and 'Four Dimensional Man' (1930), can be found at King's, IV/14 and IV/16. Fuller's story of his involvement and break with Crowley is at Rutgers, V/5.

[23] See Reid, *Fuller*, 19–20.

[24] *Memoirs*, 459–60.

extensive, if haphazard, reading. Inevitably, his work would always swing between brilliant originality and dilettantism, and in his early literary efforts the latter was often more conspicuous.

Fuller's literary remains held at Rutgers University include what appears to be his first substantial military work, a typescript of a book, 'The Foundation of an Imperial Army', composed in 1910–11. Written in a vague, semi-mystical, and somewhat tiresome style, it was never published and has remained unknown. It is a good catalogue of Fuller's intellectual makeup and roots. It advocated imperial unity, national efficiency, and a mass conscript army and reserve on the European pattern in addition to the professional colonial army. It called for a unity of 'body, mind and spirit', and for the cultivation of 'a vigorous and virile race' in a revived Empire. It put forward elaborate schemes for national regeneration and for the regimentation of society, the economy, and professional training. Fuller suggested, for example, that from the age of 4 all boys and girls should start to receive semi-military and patriotic education. All these themes were common enough among right-wingers in Edwardian Britain, and so were even the more radical ideas expressed by Fuller. He wrote that 'capitalists and paupers are the offsprings of a degenerate race', while rejecting socialism as a levelling doctrine. Specifically citing Wells's *Anticipations*, he wished to 'destroy ultimately and for ever the cancer of party-politics'. Wells's influence was clearly also responsible for a glaring inconsistency in Fuller's work and anticipated his later ideas: while advocating the creation of a British conscript army, Fuller claimed that the German mass army reflected early nineteenth-century democracy, whereas now the world was moving into the scientific-commercial epoch.[25]

Positivism and the Science of War

Fuller's published career as a military writer started with several humbler but more useful technical articles and booklets on training and organization, which stemmed from his experience with the volunteers,

[25] Fuller, 'The Foundation of an Imperial Army', (Rutgers), quotations from pp. 32, 41, 51–2. Tim Travers in his 'Future Warfare: H. G. Wells and British Military Theory, 1895–1916, in B. Bond and I. Roy (eds.), *War and Society* (London, n.d.), 81–2 and n. 90, has commented on the striking similarity of ideas between Wells and Fuller, expressing surprise that there was no evidence of recognition between the two. Fuller's typescript now leaves no doubt that he borrowed heavily from Wells.

Territorials, and Regulars.[26] This also led him to study Sir John Moore's innovative, flexible, and humane system of training during the wars of the French Revolution.[27] Soon, however, these interests developed deeper, into battlefield psychology and tactics. Here Fuller found two major themes from his intellectual background readily applicable: one of these was the positivist tenet that 'the physical and social sciences were governed by identical forces and could be treated in the same way';[28] the other was the then fashionable interest in crowd psychology. Fuller's *Training Soldiers for War* (1914), composed before but published after the outbreak of the war, opened with the statement that the training of soldiers was a science as much as an art, based on the psychology of individuals and of crowds. The booklet was wholly derived from two interrelated sources. As the author frankly admitted: 'I consider it preferable to base this work on the clear reasonings of such men as de Maud'huy, de Grandmaison and Langlois, and the many other French writers, who are too little known or studied in this country.'[29] And influencing the French school itself was the highly popular psychology of the crowd, especially that of Gustave le Bon, whom Fuller again cited extensively.[30]

Le Bon's *La Psychologie des foules* (1895), translated into English as *The Crowd* (1896), went through forty-five editions in France alone, and was translated into sixteen languages. A positivist in his approach to science, fiercely anti-socialist, and dreading the entrance of the masses into politics, Le Bon described the collective behaviour of the crowd as impulsive, driven by primal instincts, irrational, and open to manipulation. As such it was dangerous but also left an opportunity for skilful control by a small leading élite, which, according to Le Bon, had always been the sole agent of progress in any society. Highly popular, a biological racist, vulgar, and suspect in academic circles, Le Bon was read with great interest by Mussolini and by Hitler, who borrowed

[26] Capt. Fuller, 'The Mobilization of a Territorial Infantry Battalion', *Army Review*, 5 (1913), 1–32; *Hints on Training Territorial Infantry* (London, 1913); 'The Three Flag System of Instructing Infantry Fire Tactics', *Army Review*, 6 (1914), 119–22; 'Notes on the Entrainment of Troops to and from Manoeuvres', *Army Review*, 7 (1914), 184–213.

[27] Taken up before the war, this study was worked into an article, 'The Training of the New Armies, 1803–1805', *Journal of the Royal United Services Institution*, 61 (1916), 779–90, and then expanded into 2 volumes, *Sir John Moore's System of Training* (London, 1924), and *British Light Infantry in the Eighteenth Century* (London, 1925).

[28] Reid, *Fuller*, 19.

[29] *Training Soldiers for War* (London, 1914), p. vii and *passim*.

[30] Le Bon is cited e.g. ibid. 10, 21, 23. As chief instructor at the Staff College in 1923–5, Fuller would place Le Bon's *The Crowd* on the required reading list: Trythall, *Fuller*, 103.

much from him in *Mein Kampf.* Le Bon was also in close touch with some of the leading professors at the École de Guerre, like Henri Bonnal and Louis de Maud'huy, whom he influenced by his educational and psychological theories. By the mid-1900s courses in military psychology were established in the French military schools. Within a sweeping cultural wave of vitalism and Bergsonianism in France in the decade before the war, Le Bon's teaching provided much of the psychological basis for the doctrines of the younger French offensive school grouped around Grandmaison.[31]

For Fuller, Le Bon's teaching probably coincided with the instinct theories of the founders of functional psychology, the American William James, whom Fuller is known to have read, and the British William MacDougal, author of *Introduction to Social Psychology* (1908). They were also in tune with the writings of Karl Pearson, the positivist, social-Darwinist Galton Professor of Eugenics at the University of London, and another of Fuller's favourites. In 'The Foundation of an Imperial Army' Fuller had already written about the necessity of turning the 'mob' into a 'dynamic crowd', and it was on these psychological foundations that he now based his work on training and tactics. Though highly complex, he argued, human nature was based on the same principles which underlay every living organism. Sensations, memories, and emotions form the mind, and are processed by imagination and reason. Constant repetition creates instinctive behaviour, stamped into the species through natural selection during evolution. Like Grandmaison, whose *Dressage de l'infanterie en vue de combat offensif* (1906) he followed closely, Fuller maintained that it was the function of drill to turn an unformed crowd into disciplined soldiers. Repeated training would create battlefield-conditioned reflexes, counter the natural instincts of fear and self-preservation, and habituate the soldiers to closing with the enemy. Like Langlois, Fuller suggested that the increase in firepower brought about by the quick-firing gun and the machine-gun might favour the offensive by overwhelming the defender in the chosen sector of attack. Thus, to the disdain of his commanders

[31] G. Le Bon, *The Crowd: A Study of the Popular Mind* (London, 1896); also *The Psychology of Peoples* (London, 1899). R. A. Nye, *The Origins of Crowd Psychology: Gustave Le Bon and the Crisis of Mass Democracy in the Third Republic* (London, 1975), provides ample evidence for Le Bon's influence on the French military (pp. 123–53; Fuller is mentioned on p. 144); I was unfamiliar with this source when writing Book II, ch. 3. See also Mosse, *Nazism*, 58; R. de Felice, *Fascism* (New Brunswick, NJ, 1977), 74; M. Billig, *Fascists* (New York, 1978), 20–3.

at the Staff College, he advocated penetration rather than envelopment as the preferable method of attack. In his memoirs Fuller presented this as an example of foresight about the nature of the First World War, barely mentioning the unrealistic reasoning behind his views and passing in silence over their sources in the by then discredited French offensive school.[32]

During these years Fuller's military thinking was also developing in another, related direction. Preparing himself for the Staff College, he read in the beginning of the *Field Service Regulation*: 'The fundamental principles of war are neither very numerous nor in themselves very abstruse, but the application of them is difficult, and cannot be made subject to rules.'[33] Naturally, the conception of principles of war awoke his deepest interest. Descending from the military thinkers of the Enlightenment, it was engraved in military textbooks during the nineteenth century, especially in those countries most influenced by positivism, the Enlightenment's direct heir and Fuller's own creed. The positivist view that the methods which had been crowned with success in the sciences should now be applied to achieve comparable results in the human sciences was clearly expressed by Fuller in a letter to his father in 1916. He thought it

> an extraordinary thing [that] whilst every science is run on a few definite principles, war today should be run on the dice-box of luck. . . . We can predict certain events in war as surely as Darwin could in life directly he grasped the fundamental principles of evolution. However we have no military Darwin as yet, let us hope the Germans will not discover one.[34]

This was practically a verbatim restatement of the views of the military thinkers of the Enlightenment, only with Darwin substituted for Newton. However, as Fuller complained, he had found no principles stated after the promising start of the *Field Service Regulations*, and his instructors at the Staff College had proved no help in this respect either. Surprisingly, he mentioned neither Jomini's celebrated set of principles, which had been studied throughout Europe and in the United States during the nineteenth century, nor Edward Hamley's

[32] Fuller, *Training Soldiers*; also, both from before the war and specifically citing Grandmaison, 'The Procedure of the Infantry Attack: A Synthesis from a Psychological Standpoint', *JRUSI*, 58 (1914), 63–8; 'The Tactical Penetration', ibid. 59 (1914), 378–89; in addition, *Memoirs*, 23–6; Trythall, *Fuller*, 26–31; Reid, *Fuller*, 22–7, 31, 138–9; Crook, *Darwinism, War, and History*, 132–6.

[33] Fuller, *Memoirs*, 28.

[34] King's, IV/3/190; quoted by Trythall, *Fuller*, 38.

widely circulated *Operations of War*, which neatly and elegantly presented Jomini's principles to generations of British Staff College students. By the coming of the twentieth century both had suffered a decline in popularity, caused both by the spread of the anti-positivist Prussian-German military theory and by the transformation of war itself. The principles that Jomini had abstracted from the Napoleonic system of operations but considered universally applicable had largely been rendered irrelevant by rapidly changing conditions.[35] In any event, Fuller started afresh, returning to Napoleon for inspiration but moving on to a higher level of abstraction. He had read Napoleon's *Maxims* back in 1901, and had been led to study the history of Napoleon's campaigns and his voluminous *Correspondence* by the Edwardian scholar-soldier, Lt. Col. F. M. Maude, to whom he had been introduced by Crowley in 1909. A child of the Enlightenment, Napoleon had repeatedly expressed in his writings the belief in military science based on a few immutable principles. And Maude, himself interested in military science, an evolutionist, and apparently a mystic, was an important source of influence on Fuller.[36]

By the outbreak of the First World War Fuller had crystallized the following list of six principles:

> The principle of the Objective—the true objective being that point at which the enemy may be most decisively defeated; generally this point is to be found along the line of least resistance. The principle of Mass—that is, concentration of strength and effort at the decisive point. The principle of the Offensive; the principles of Security, Surprise and Movement (i.e. rapidity).[37]

As Reid has shown, in developing the principles of war Fuller consciously borrowed from Spencer's *First Principles*, as for example the latter's assertion that 'motion follows the line of least resistance or the line of greatest traction or the result of the two'.[38] At the Staff College, during the war, and for a decade later, Fuller worked on his principles, repeatedly rearranging them to make them truly primary and comprehensive. In the early 1920s his list of principles was incorporated into the British *Field Service Regulations*, became standard, and was copied

35 See above Book I and Book II, esp. ch 1.

36 King's, IV/12/35; Trythall, Fuller, 25; Reid, Fuller, 20–2; 89–90; Book I above, 135–7.

37 *Memoirs*, 28; *Training Soldiers*, 42.

38 Reid, *Fuller*, 35, 93.

with slight variations by the Americans and by many other armies.[39] The heuristic and pedagogic value of these principles of war remains a matter of debate. In comparison to those of Jomini, for example, they claim greater universality—which was achieved, however, at the price of greater abstraction from any concrete reality.

The principles of war represented 'the tip of an iceberg in his [Fuller's] thinking, an iceberg labelled Science of War'.[40] In his writings during and after the First World War, culminating in *The Foundations of the Science of War* (1926), Fuller continuously worked towards the crystallization of such a science. He rediscovered the military thinkers of the Enlightenment, such as Maurice de Saxe, Henry Evans Lloyd, J. A. H. Guibert, and Robert Jackson, whose pleas for the formation of a universal theory of war he repeatedly cited and used (as they themselves had done in respect to each other) to prepare the ground for the coming of his own theory of war:[41]

> In a small way I am trying to do for war what Copernicus did for astronomy, Newton for physics, and Darwin for natural history. My book, I believe, is the first in which a writer has attempted to apply the method of science to the study of war; for Lloyd, Jackson, Clausewitz, Jomini, and Foch did not do this.[42]

Informing his readers that he had read extensively in philosophy and science in his youth, Fuller cited Spencer, Huxley, Pearson, and a variety of popular scientific writers for their definitions of science and of the scientific method. He blamed the lack of a scientific approach to the study of war for the dismal failure of prewar military thinking (with the exception of Ivan Bloch) to predict the nature of the First World War. As Bacon, Descartes, and Locke had taught the modern world, he wrote, authority must give way to scientific study, based on an observation of historical experience, description, classification, critical thought, and generalization. War must pass from the alchemical to the

[39] Fuller, 'The Principles of War, with Reference to the Campaigns of 1914–15', *JRUSI*, 61 (1916), 1–40; 'Gold Medal (Military) Prize Essay for 1919: "The Application of Recent Developments in Mechanics and Other Scientific Knowledge to Preparation and Training for Future War on Land"', ibid. 65 (1920), 244; *Memoirs*, 28, 54, 388–9; *The Foundations of the Science of War* (London, 1926), 13–15; Trythall, *Fuller*, 108–9; Reid, *Fuller*, 94–5.

[40] Trythall, *Fuller*, 35.

[41] See e.g. Fuller, *The Reformation of War* (London, 1923), 24, 76; *The Foundations of the Science of War*, 18–25; Jomini, Clausewitz, and Foch are also cited; 'The Discipline of Robert Jackson', *Army Quarterly*, 10 (1925), 98–109; 'Major General Henry Lloyd: Adventurer and Military Philosopher', ibid. 12 (1926), 300–14; and repeatedly after in Fuller's later work.

[42] *The Foundations of the Science of War*, 18.

scientific stage, from which it could then be applied to concrete problems through art.[43]

As had been the case with the military thinkers of the Enlightenment, the actual fruits of Fuller's programmatic rhetoric regarding the science of war were, at best, mixed. Apart from his principles, there were several other components to his proposed military science. These included interesting evolutionary theories—mainly derived from James, Kidd, and Pearson, and written in a social-Darwinist vein—regarding the biological and anthropological origins of war and its fundamental cultural–historical role in relations between and within societies.[44] There was a scholastic and cumbersome exposition of the 'elements' of war: men, movement, weapons and protection, each having negative and positive spheres of action, and all effected by 'conditions', such as time, space, ground, weather, numbers, morale, communications, supply, armament, and the like. In *The Foundations of the Science of War* Fuller even attempted a comprehensive speculative system, according to which war, like reality in general, was governed by what he called 'the Threefold Order', in which everything was divided into threes that came together in higher entities.[45] The system was embarrassingly artificial, the worst example of amateur metaphysics, and it was rightly received with perplexity and ridicule by readers of the book. It had its source in the dialectical and holistic ideas that Fuller had shared with Crowley and other turn-of-the-century mystics, which in turn had been vaguely inspired by German idealism. As Reid rightly points out, it was reminiscent, for example, of the system and ideas of the mystical social thinkers G. I. Gurdjieff and his disciple P. D. Ouspensky, who enjoyed great vogue in Western salons during the 1920s and 1930s and whom we shall repeatedly encounter on the following pages.[46] Finally, Fuller's book incorporated elaborate, sometimes useful but mostly clumsy and immature schemes for reorganizing and making efficient all the departments of the defence establishment. As mentioned before, the advancement of schemes for a sweeping overhaul of state apparatus had been characteristic of the movement for national efficiency before the First World War, and it would later

[43] Fuller 17, 20–47; cf. Fuller, *Tanks in the Great War, 1914–1918* (London, 1920), 297–9.

[44] See esp. Fuller, *The Reformation of War*, 6–23, 56–74.

[45] Fuller, 'Prize Essay', 240–4; 'The Foundations of the Science of War', *Army Quarterly*, 1 (1920), 90–111; *The Reformation of War*, 24–55; *The Foundations of the Science of War*, 48–62 and *passim*.

[46] Reid, *Fuller*, 12, 15, 17.

become a prominent feature of fascist programmes.[47] Soon Fuller was to advocate the systematic use of scientific management and scientific production techniques—Taylorism and Fordism—whose gospel was powerfully spreading from America during the 1920s.[48] The pervasive and intricate relation of Taylorist and Fordist ideology to fascist ideas will be discussed more fully later on.

But, of course, it was mainly for the way Fuller applied his positivist view of history and his *Kulturkritik* to form a comprehensive vision of the potential of a new mechanical invention—the tank—that he acquired his intellectual pre-eminence and worldwide reputation as Britain's leading military theorist. Within his sweeping interpretation of modern developments both machine armies and fascism were perceived as the trends of the future, the products of the machine age and of machine-dominated societies.

Machine Age Armies

Fuller was nominated GSO2 and then GSO1 to the newly created Heavy Branch of the Machine Gun Corps, later the Tank Corps, at the end of 1916. He had played no role in the invention and early evolution of the tank, in which Ernest Swinton, Winston Churchill, and Maurice Hankey had figured most prominently on the British side. He soon established himself indisputably as the brain of the new corps, developing its tactical doctrine and devising its operational schemes during the years 1917–18, as the corps grew from infancy to become a crucial weapon for the *Entente*. In general, however, his ideas were not altogether unique.

The first question that preoccupied people's minds both inside and outside the tank corps was how this completely new, untried, and fragile instrument was to be integrated most effectively in the battle against the German fortified line on the Western Front. Tactical methods, the details of cooperation with infantry, artillery, and aircraft, and the elaborate procedures of supply and communication had all to be worked out from scratch and continuously developed with experience. Fuller played a leading role in performing this task, but unknown to him, many of the ideas he developed in a series of staff papers and helped implement in practice had already been advanced by Swinton in his

47 'Prize Essay', 257–61; *The Reformation of War*, 229–55; *The Foundations of the Science of War*, 78–92; Searle, *The Quest for National Efficiency*.

48 Fuller, *The Generalship of Ulysses S. Grant* (London, 1929), 15.

prophetic memoranda during 1915 and 1916. Both men recommended that the tank be employed offensively, in large numbers, with the aid of surprise, on suitable dry land, on a wide enough front of attack, and in cooperation with the other arms. Both believed its mobility, armour, and firepower could carry it through as far as the German second and third lines of defence, several miles deep. It would protect the infantry advance, create and threaten exposed enemy flanks, and prevent the attack from losing momentum as it moved out of the range of its artillery support. Hopefully, the tactical impasse of the war would thus be broken.[49]

From the summer of 1917 Fuller's staff papers on the employment of tanks reveal a clear progression towards a more ambitious conception. As the original heavy tanks were supplemented by medium models, he increasingly considered that the breaking of the enemy's trench lines should be followed by a pursuit and deeper exploitation of success by medium tanks, armoured cars, cavalry, and tractor-drawn artillery. In the summer of 1917 he proposed only raids and limited battles until greater superiority over the Germans could be built, and a decisive offensive in 1918, later postponed to 1919. His raid concept foreshadowed the Battle of Cambrai in November 1917, the tank's first major success. For the later, decisive offensive Fuller gradually developed an operational scheme, of which the famous so-called 'Plan 1919' of May 1918 was only the ultimate version. The scheme was based on a 1000-strong tank army, divided into three. In the final version, 'Plan 1919', one force was intended for a conventional all-arms attack on the enemy defensive lines, while another was to be deployed in a direct breakthrough against the enemy's command system deep in his rear to create paralysis, panic, and complete breakdown of control. In Fuller's characteristic imagery, this was described as a shot at the enemy's brain and nervous system. Large-scale strategic pursuit by a third mechanized force would then turn the enemy's defeat into total collapse.

As Fuller himself admitted, many of these ideas were, again, not exclusively his own. Medium tanks, including the advanced Medium D,

[49] Ernest Swinton's papers, 'The Necessity for Machine-Gun Destroyers' (1 June 1915) and 'Notes on the Employment of Tanks' (Feb. 1916), are both cited in his *Eyewitness* (London, 1932), 129–34, 198–214. For Fuller, see 'Training Note No. 16' (Feb. 1917) and 'Projected Bases for the Tactical Employment of Tanks in 1918' (11 June 1917), in the bound volume of Tank Corps documents entitled 'Tank Strategy and Tactics 1916–1918', King's, TS TCO I/6 and I/16; this and the other volumes contain some of the most important source material on the development of Tank Corps tactics; also Fuller, *Memoirs*, 96–8, 122–30.

on which 'Plan 1919' was based, had been developed specifically for follow-up operations. The *Entente* powers were producing tanks by the thousand and at an accelerating rate during the last phase of the war. Ideas for a massive tank offensive in 1919 were entertained by the spring of 1918 by Field Marshals Henry Wilson and Ferdinand Foch, and by several of those concerned with tanks at the staffs of the *Entente* powers. These ideas developed simultaneously, though Fuller certainly played a significant role in advancing the concept.[50]

Finally, 'Plan 1919' already contained the germs of an even more advanced vision of war, that of a fully mechanized and highly mobile army. Originally, this vision had not been conceived by Fuller either, but by his subordinate, the GSO3 Captain Giffard Le Q. Martel. As early as November 1916 Martel wrote a paper entitled 'A Tank Army', in which he suggested that in the future great powers' armies would take the form of armoured forces whose characteristics would much resemble those of navies. Unhindered by geographical obstacles, they would be capable of operating freely across the land (and across water obstacles), supplied and defended in fortified bases, behind trenches and minefields. For the various functions Martel envisioned a variety of armoured vehicles which he labelled 'torpedo-tank', 'destroyer-tank', and 'battle-tank', as well as specialist and supply tanks. When he showed this paper to Fuller in March 1917, the latter at first objected on the grounds that the tank was merely an auxiliary to the infantry.[51] Gradually, however, Fuller took up the idea in its entirety and anchored it within a wider philosophy of history.

Indeed, that precisely was the point which made Fuller the leading prophet of the new epoch of warfare. More than single-mindedness, an obsessive streak of character, unorthodox personality, and presence at the right time and place were needed for the part. Swinton moved on to other tasks at the Committee of Imperial Defence after launching the

[50] Fuller, 'Projected Bases for the Tactical Employment of Tanks in 1918', 'Tank Operations Decisive and Preparatory, 1918–1919' (Jan. 1918), King's, TS TCO I/40, envisioning the employment of more than 10,000-tanks, and 'The Tactics of the Attack as Affected by the Speed and Circuit of the Medium 'D' Tank' (May-June 1918), King's, TS TCO I/50; 'Tank Raids' (6 Aug. 1917), in the bound volume of documents 'The Battle of Cambrai 1917', King's, I/BC I/2/2; *Memoirs*, 126–7, 172–5, 234–7, 318–41. See also most recently J. P. Harris, *Men, Ideas and Tanks: British Military Thought and Armoured Forces, 1903–1939* (Manchester, 1995), 47–172.

[51] G. Le Q. Martel, 'A Tank Army' (Nov. 1916), King's, TS TCO I/9; *In the Wake of the Tank* (London, 1931), 15–16; *An Outspoken Soldier* (London, 1949), 14; Fuller, *Memoirs*, 111–12, 318.

tank, and would later become Chichele Professor of Military History at Oxford. Martel was an engineer, and his main interest after the war would be tank design. But Fuller was a positivist student of war, and, like Wells, it was through this perspective that he would interpret the wider significance of the tank as one aspect of a comprehensive historical development.

Less than three months after Martel had shown him his tank army paper, Fuller wrote in his tactical memorandum:

> The one thing to realise is, that mechanical warfare is going to supersede muscular warfare. That is to say, more and more is war going to depend on the engine than on man's legs. In the administrative services this war has already largely replaced horse traction by motor traction. Except for the armoured car, the tank is the first application of this means of movement to the fighting units. The tank to-day carries forward the riflemen of the future. These riflemen, or machine gunners, must be supported by tank artillery and tank bayonet-men, so as to occupy and make good what the tank riflemen render possible. If this is sound reasoning, then we should forthwith prepare to raise the mechanical army we shall require.[52]

Six months later Fuller suggested that the new epoch opening in land warfare was bringing forward developments which had already taken place not only at sea but in the whole sphere of economic production: 'the application of petrol to land warfare will prove as great a step in tactics as that of steam in naval warfare. . . . the application of machinery to land warfare is as great a saver of man-power as its application to manufacture.'[53] Man-carried and horse-drawn rifle and cannon armies were rapidly declining into obsolescence, to be wholly superseded in the end by mechanical armies and mechanical warfare.[54] As 'Plan 1919' stated, the old and the new could not be harmonized, as the tactics of the First World War had attempted to do, because mechanical armies represented an entirely new level of capabilities. Old arms, such as infantry and artillery, would become mechanical, and the former in particular would be reduced in size and importance. Cavalry would disappear. Aircraft would closely cooperate with the mechanical land armies.[55]

These were the ideas that Fuller continued to develop in a series of

[52] 'Projected Bases for the Tactical Employment of Tanks in 1918' *Memoirs*, 129–30.

[53] 29 Dec. 1917, quoted in *Memoirs*, 228.

[54] 'Tank Operations Decisive and Preparatory, 1918–1919' *Memoirs*, 235–6.

[55] 'The Tactics of the Attack as Affected by the Speed and Circuit of the Medium "D" Tank'; *Memoirs*, esp. 322–4, 330–3.

lectures and articles in the aftermath of the war. From August 1918 he headed a new branch in the War Office responsible for the organization and establishments of the Tank Corps, and he soon won himself a reputation as an intellectual maverick and propagandist of futurist mechanized warfare. In August 1919 he submitted to his superiors a memorandum entitled 'A New Model Army'. This became the core of an essay, 'The Application of Recent Developments in Mechanics and Other Scientific Knowledge to Preparation and Training for Future War on Land', which won the gold medal at a special competition announced by the Royal United Services Institute for Defence Studies. The development of war, Fuller stated, followed the general development of civilization as a whole. This had been profoundly affected by recent advances in the sciences, especially in the fields of electricity, chemistry, and mechanics. Their application to war produced the two leading land inventions of the First World War: poison gas and the petrol-engined tank. A new epoch in military history had opened in which manpower would be replaced by machine-power. The slow and vulnerable manual mass armies would give way to mechanical armies relying on scientific and industrial infrastructure at home. Fuller outlined a programme for an evolutionary transformation of the old-style army, according to which its transport and fighting echelons were to be gradually mechanized, and the traditional arms reduced in size. In the last stage the army would become fully mechanized. He borrowed the analogy Martel had drawn with naval warfare, where mechanization had already taken place, to project fleets of armoured vehicles possessing naval designations.[56] In his later works he would further pursue this analogy, suggesting that the armoured fleets would freely travel the face of the earth, barely hindered by either geography or logistics. Fuller even invaded the naval sphere itself, entering and outrageously winning the Naval Prize Essay competition for 1920. Then and throughout the interwar period he predicted the decline of the Dreadnought before the aircraft, the aircraft carrier, and the submarine.[57]

Fuller continued with his historical interpretation of the rise of the tank. To get the proper perspective on the confounding development of warfare during the First World War, he wrote in 1920, one should ask

[56] 'Prize Essay', esp. 240, 246–8, 255, 261–74; *Memoirs*, 392–9, 408–10; also *Tanks in the Great War*, 302–5, 313–15.

[57] *Naval Review*, 10 (1922), 73–104; *Memoirs*, 393–4; *The Reformation of War*, 136–48, 176–9; *On Future Warfare* (London, 1928), 215–18; *Towards Armageddon* (London, 1937), 133–5, 196–208.

what had been happening in civil life? a mechanical evolution, so rapid that no revolution in the whole world's history can compare to it. Every day brought to birth some new invention, every hour civilisation gathered greater speed; epochs crumbled away, epochs sprang up in the night, science was sweeping brute force off the face of the earth, and was replacing muscle by mechanical energy.[58]

Communications were one aspect of this rapid transformation. As Fuller would later suggest, the First Industrial Revolution, motivated by steam power, was followed by a second, powered by oil and electricity.[59] In the first wave, 'the locomotive, the railway, and the steamship, the great mechanical movers of civil life', made possible the assembly, transportation, and supply of armies of millions. Then, the invention of the internal-combustion engine and the lorry made it possible to 'mechanically link up the strategic base of operation, which consists of a network of railways, with the battlefield itself'. At the end of this highly advanced system there remained, however, the old foot armies—supported by riding and pack animals—of the pre-mechanized epoch. Is it any wonder that, despite all their efforts and sacrifices during the First World War, these armies proved so pathetically immobile and ineffective? The remedy lay with the proliferation of the internal-combustion engine. 'The next link to forge is a mechanical tactical striking force.'[60]

This wide historical perspective within which the mechanization of war was to be understood is now fairly well recognized. But so is any interpretive perspective once it has been formulated and absorbed into people's way of thinking. At the time, Fuller's ideas were eye-opening. It should be remembered that people were in real difficulty as to what to make of the tank. It did not fit into any previously known category. It was variously regarded during and after the war as a historical freak, a specialized mechanical instrument designed to overcome trenches and barbed wire, or, at best, a useful auxiliary arm to infantry or a substitute for cavalry in reconnaissance and pursuit. Fuller's interpretation proved so powerful because it offered a broad context within which the emergence and future development of the tank were understood as an integral, and in a way inevitable, aspect of the evolution of modern industrial society as a whole.[61] Heinz Guderian's later summary of the

[58] 'The Introduction of Mechanical Warfare on Land', *Royal Engineers Journal* (Jan. 1921), repr. in Fuller, *On Future Warfare*, 114–15.

[59] *Grant*, pp. viii, 26.

[60] 'The Introduction of Mechanical Warfare on Land', 115–22.

[61] Cf. Fuller, *Memoirs*, 452–3.

influence Fuller and his friends had on him testifies to precisely that sort of effect: 'They envisaged it [the tank] in relationship to the growing motorization of our age, and thus they became the pioneers of a new type of warfare.'[62]

Machine Age Armies and Machine Age Societies

Indeed, Fuller's main interest shifted increasingly from his attempt to develop a positivist science of war to an effort to put forward a positivist interpretation of military history. His mind and work were dominated throughout the interwar period by two closely related themes. First, he strove to lay out the main features of the new mechanical epoch. Next, he struggled to develop more deeply, both by means of *Kulturkritik* and in historical–positivist terms, how the new epoch fitted into the general evolution of modern society and, further, into the course of universal history. This he called 'the natural history of war'. Nominally, he wrote more than forty books during his lifetime, some of them—after he had left the army—for commercial reasons. But programmatically, he was now to write only two works, corresponding to the themes mentioned above and repeatedly reworked in sequences of conceptually similar books. First was *The Reformation of War* (1923), whose vision of machine warfare was reproduced with little variation in *On Future Warfare* (1928), and again in *Lectures on FSR III* (1932). Second was the cultural critique of *The Dragon Teeth: A Study of War and Peace* (1932), repeated in *The First of the League Wars* (1936) and again echoed in *Towards Armageddon* (1937). This category was also developed in a more historical form in *War and Western Civilization, 1832–1932: A Study of War as a Political Instrument and the Expression of Mass Democracy* (1932), later to be refurbished (and politically somewhat redressed) as *The Conduct of War, 1789–1961: A Study of the Impact of the French, Industrial and Russian Revolutions on War and Its Conduct* (1961). Fuller's other books amplified the same themes. By the 1930s his ideas and historical senses considerably widened and gained in depth, as he strove to develop the notions he had gradually evolved since his youth.

Dominated by science and by a revolution in communications, the new epoch, according to Fuller, would be moral, intelligent, mobile, and

62 H. Guderian, *Panzer Leader* (London, 1952), 20. More fully on this contentious subject, see my *British Armour Theory and the Rise of the Panzer Arm: Revising the Revisionists* (London, 2000).

élitist—in many ways the opposite of its predecessor—in war as in peace. As Condorcet had already foreseen in the 1790s, nineteenth-century mass armies were the product of the evolving mass society, or mass democracy—an era reflected in the writings of Clausewitz and Marx. Manual at first, like the agricultural epoch to which they belonged, these armies were later supported by the mass-production capabilities of the emerging industrial era. Thrown against one another, they relied on numbers and brute force. Their characteristic mode of operation was physical destruction of the enemy's armed forces. However, with the further expansion of scientific and industrial society, and as the laboratory was increasingly taking over the workshop at the forefront of civilization, both armies and the nature of war itself were being transformed. The armies of the new age would rely on highly advanced machines, especially cross-country armoured vehicles incorporating the old arms, supported by gas and by aircraft. Further into the future, as early as 1928 Fuller prophesied, lay automated, electric [electronic], 'robotic' warfare. Quality would be more important than numbers, and as sophisticated equipment was expensive, the old conscript armies would give way to smaller, professional, élite forces. Extremely mobile, these would seek to dislocate, paralyse, and cause the disintegration of their enemy by rapidity of movement and manoeuvre, rather than destroy him in a direct clash of forces and costly attrition.[63]

According to Fuller, this transformation of field warfare corresponded to a deeper change in the nature of war and of the international system in the industrial–commercial era. One of the earliest critics of the First World War, Fuller was quick to embrace Keynes's influential ideas in *The Economic Consequences of the Peace* (1920). As Keynes stressed, in the highly advanced, interdependent global economy that had emerged since the late nineteenth century, the enemy's

[63] See esp. Fuller, 'The Last Lap of the Physical Epoch' and 'The First Lap of the Moral Epoch', in *The Reformation of War*, 75–119, 229–55, and *passim*; *On Future Warfare*, pp. v-vii, 83–197 and *passim*; *Armoured Warfare* (London, 1943; originally *Lectures on FSR III*, 1932), 7–12, 32–42, and *passim*; *War and Western Civilization* (London, 1932), *The Dragon's Teeth: A Study of War and Peace* (London, 1932), 212–23, 229, 296–9 (robotics in the last two page references; also the TS 'Electrical Battles' (1928): Rutgers, II/12); *The First of the League Wars* (London, 1936), 99–106, 111–15, 125–8, 169–76 and *passim*; *Towards Armageddon*, 92, 132 (robotics); all repeated in later books during and after the Second World War. A similar conceptual framework has been recently advanced in A. and H. Toffler's *Third Wave* (New York, 1980) and *War and Anti-War* (New York, 1993); and, directly influenced by Fuller's work, R. Simpkin, *Race to the Swift: Thoughts on Twenty-First Century Warfare* (London, 1985).

ruin was no longer his problem alone, as it had been in agricultural, generally autarkic societies, but was seriously damaging to one's own economic prosperity and social well-being. War had to be cut short and made less destructive if it were not to become wholly counter-productive and lose its political rationale: the creation of a better peace.[64]

Of course, the logic of the economic argument had long led liberals to the conclusion that war was no longer an advantageous instrument of international relations and must therefore be abolished. Fuller was ambivalent about this prospect. As an anti-liberal and social-Darwinist he regarded war as biologically, socially, and metaphysically necessary and even beneficial, an antidote to degeneration and decadence—at least until humanity developed much further. He was particularly hostile toward the League of Nations. He criticized the League for attempting forcibly to freeze the global status quo to the advantage of the strong by pressing down on and papering over the dynamic currents and deep sources of discontent that lay at the roots of conflict. The treatment of the symptoms rather than the causes of the disease would never work. If the elimination of war was to be seriously attempted, its deeper sources had to be exposed and treated. In Fuller's opinion they sprang from the ills of modern society, and thus could only be approached in a wider context. In his view, the First World War was the product of the uncontrolled materialistic order of industrial civilization which set all against all. Fierce competition over global spaces for economic growth fuelled national anxieties in the international arena. Widening social gaps, poverty, and a loss of spiritual values bred social discontent, a fear of civilization, and a quest for moral transcendence. To remove these causes of strife and war, one had to abolish the old sick civilization for a new harmonious order. All forms of protectionism and tariff barriers had to be removed, to allow free trade and universal access to international resources and markets. European integration, federation, and unity, as well as the establishment of a just world state, based on genuine harmony rather than force, had to be pursued. Internally, chaotic and degenerating materialism must be replaced by a new spiritual revival and well-regulated order. For Fuller,

[64] Fuller, *The Reformation of War*, 75, 144, 187–8; Keynes is cited e.g. on p. 270, and repeatedly in Fuller's later works; *The Foundations of the Science of War*, 63, 76–7; *On Future Warfare*, 166–8, 212; *Armoured Warfare*, 41.

the instrument and expression of this comprehensive cultural transformation was fascism.[65]

Fuller's critique of mass democracy was scathing. In his official memorandum 'Tank Operations Decisive and Preparatory, 1918–1919', forwarded to the Chief of the General Staff, Field Marshal Henry Wilson, at the beginning of 1918, he wrote: 'Our destiny, as a great nation, lies in the hands of an ignorant and discontented proletariat, which is swayed by words.'[66] To be sure, similar views were not uncommon among the military (including C. G. S. Wilson himself) during the war, but intellectually and ideologically their significance in Fuller's case was much deeper. For him democracy was not the distasteful but inevitable trend of the future but, on the contrary, a doomed order belonging to a passing phase of civilization and collapsing on account of its ills and patent inadequacy for modern times. Democracy was predicated on quantity, whereas modern scientific society was based on quality. Truth and understanding were beyond the masses' reach. While still formally in the army, and even before the British Union of Fascists was created, Fuller wrote in a Nietzschean vein that Christianity, democracy, and socialism were the enemies of the forces of life and of true morality. Alien to knowledge and excellence, they represented the rule of ignorance and weakness. Sickly humanism and pacifism were among their more recent products. The growing standardization of life oppressed the individual, the ingenious, and the spiritual. Rampant materialism and false, barren rationalism bred nihilism, hedonism, and a return to bestial instincts. The new mass entertainment was passive and corrupting. The rise in the number of the poor degenerated the race. Demagoguery and emotionalism masqueraded as the will of the people. What the world needed was authority. The masses had to be controlled by the intelligent minority and by some mystical ideal.[67] It was no accident that Fuller joined the Fascists when the party was established.

[65] Fuller, *The Reformation of War*, 6–23, 211, 256–83; 'The Progress of War', *The Nineteenth Century and After*, 100 (1926), 483–94; *Grant*, pp. vii, 392–412; *The Dragon's Teeth*, 1–179; *War and Western Civilization, 1832–1932* (London, 1932), 7–9, 245–66; *Empire Unity and Defence* (London, 1934) 'The World at a Dead End', *Fighting Forces*, 10 (1934), 551–6; 'The Foundation of European Order', ibid. 11 (1934), 23–9; 'Fascism and War', *Fascist Quarterly*, 1 (1935), 140–55; *Memoirs*, 464–77; *The First of the League Wars*, pp. v–vii, 106–11, 123–4, 154–61.

[66] Quoted in Fuller, *Memoirs*, 237.

[67] Fuller, *War and Western Civilization*, 7–9, 224; *The Dragon's Teeth*, 7–13, 22–39, 58–9; *India in Revolt* (London, 1931), 134, 240, 244.

After joining the British Union of Fascists Fuller wrote that, whereas democracy had its origin in the agricultural and early industrial age, fascism was the expression of the new scientific epoch. While democracy was based on uncontrolled individual freedom which in practice led to exploitation, anarchy, and maldistribution of wealth by finance, fascism would rationally organize society for the common good and for a true, higher form of reasoned freedom. Admittedly, Continental fascist regimes of his time were still crude and experimental, but that was only their beginning. Against American capitalism and Soviet Bolshevism, both materialistic and Jewish-inspired, Europe was taking up fascism which promoted something beyond material needs—a unifying national and religious ideal. Virile, youthful, and full of energy and creativity, fascism would counter the forces of decadence, passivity, and corruption that had engulfed Western civilization. While peaceful and non-militaristic, it would infuse the military virtues of courage, honour, self-sacrifice, comradeship, and solidarity into civil life.[68]

These views, which Fuller had crystallized long before the creation of the British Union of Fascists, remarkably resembled the ideas of the man who founded the party, gave it its doctrines and public stature, was in effect the party—Sir Oswald Mosley (1896–1980). One of the most brilliant men in British politics, minister at the age of 33 and widely regarded as destined for greatness before he left the Labour Party in 1931, Mosley was a positivist and an evolutionist for whom fascism was the modern order, the new synthesis for the industrial–scientific age. Mosley espoused Keynesian economics and admired American efficiency and industrial methods. He wanted a well-regulated society and economy, ruled by a technocratic élite of managers, professionals, and technicians which would replace capitalist–democratic anarchy. Influenced by Goethe, Hegel, Nietzsche, Spengler, and Shaw, he called for Faustian vitality to counter decadence and decline. He was not particularly racist, and his anti-Semitism developed only in the 1930s, partly in response to Jewish hostility to his party. From the 1920s Mosley saw the balance of power system and commercial rivalry as the root cause of the First World War, and he wanted them, and war, eliminated. While initially supporting collective security and the League of Nations, he later blamed the League for perpetuating the Great War's

[68] Fuller, *The First of the League Wars*, 7–8, 88, 120–39, 148–54, 251–301; *Empire Unity and Defence*, 62, 82–3, 287, 294; *Towards Armageddon*, 236–7; 'Dictatorship and Generalship', *Army Quarterly*, 35 (1937), 57–8.

rivalry. Instead, he called for European political cooperation and economic union.[69]

Scholars agree that Mosley's, and Fuller's, advocacy of peace, of genuine European cooperation and conciliation, pre-dated not only their own formal fascist phase but also the rise of the National-Socialists to power in Germany. It became one of the BUF's main principles during the 1930s as 'the party of peace', not because of subservience to foreign interests. The BUF's leaders were unquestionably patriotic, and, while looking at the fascist regimes in Italy and Germany as welcome partners, maintained a British reserve towards all things foreign and certainly felt no inferiority towards them. Both Mosley and Fuller, who became a member of the BUF's Policy Committee in 1934 and Mosley's chief adviser on defence, advocated imperial unity and rearmament for strong defence. But once Germany and Italy were given their due in Europe, the BUF looked to close and peaceful cooperation with those countries in the interests of European civilization. Both believed that Hitler did not want war, and that German autarky was merely an expediency forced upon him by conflict.[70]

As international tensions mounted, Fuller, like Mosley, wanted Britain to stay out of Continental conflicts and leave Germany hegemonious in Europe and a bulwark against Russian communism. Otherwise, Fuller feared the coming of a new comprehensive world war of a quasi-religious nature, a new Armageddon, whose winner would impose its rule on Western civilization. For Fuller, the winner would either be fascism, the expression of the new scientific age, or communism, the culmination of the era of industrial democracy, 'the early coal and steam age'—both in violent forms, due to an unnecessary and ruinous war—but not parliamentary liberal-democracy, whose time had passed.[71] If war came, it would assume the character of 'totalitarian warfare', which was not Ludendorff's total war of endurance but a lightning one,

[69] C. Cross, *The Fascists in Britain* (London, 1961); R. Benewick, *The Fascist Movement in Britain* (London, 1972); R. Skidelsky, *Oswald Mosley* (London, 1981); K. Lunn and R. Thurlow (eds.), *British Fascism* (London, 1980); O. Mosley, *My Life* (London, 1968). Leslie Susser's regrettably unpublished Oxford dissertation, 'Fascist and Anti-Fascist Attitudes in Britain between the Wars' (1988), importantly expands on the cultural background of British fascism.

[70] Cf. Mosley, *My Life*, 382–8; Fuller, *Empire Unity and Defence*; *The First of the League Wars*, 145–7, 183–5; *Towards Armageddon*, 43–4.

[71] Fuller, *The First of the League Wars*, 159–65; *Towards Armageddon*, 236–8; 'The Soviet-Spanish War to September 1938', *Army Quarterly*, 37 (1939), 312–21.

launched by surprise, using high-quality mobile machine armies to paralyse and disarm the enemy.[72]

Positivist, evolutionary, and dialectical interpretations of history found expression not only in linear views of progress but also in cyclical and spiral conceptions. For Fuller, old forms and values, like spirituality or social cohesion, seemingly lost during the evolution of civilization, reappeared in new guises and higher syntheses to fulfil crucial functions. In the military field Fuller suggested that European history had seen two grand cycles of warfare: the Classical and the Christian. These divided respectively into three tactical cycles: cavalry, infantry, and artillery, which he later redesignated 'shock', 'shock and missiles', and 'missiles'. Roughly, both grand cycles reflected the transformation from rural to urbanized and industrialized civilization. Equally, they were motivated by an 'evolutionary pendulum of weapon power, slowly or rapidly swinging from the offensive to the protective and back again in harmony with the speed of civil progress'. Every measure enjoys a period of success following its introduction, but thereby provokes countermeasures to redress the balance. Fuller called this 'the constant tactical factor' which lay at the root of the 'law of military evolution'.[73] As his biographer points out, Fuller again drew extensively on the ideas and vocabulary of Spencer, Darwin, James, and Pearson in formulating his evolutionary scheme of military development and in explaining the psychological tension between aggressiveness and fear, impulse and inhibition, that fuelled it. Later on he found support for his views before in the works of Oswald Spengler and Arnold Toynbee.[74] Fuller suggested that the artillery, or projectile, cycle of the Christian era, which had started with the Industrial Revolution and which stretched from the middle of the nineteenth century to the First World War, was subsiding. The tank heralded a new (cavalry or shock) tactical cycle, thus implicitly opening a new grand cycle of civilization to supersede the Christian. In

[72] *The First of the League Wars*, 51–89, 165–225; *Towards Armageddon*, 48–54.

[73] Fuller, 'The Influence of Tanks on Cavalry Tactics', *Cavalry Journal*, 10 (1920); 'Science and War', *The Nineteenth Century and After*, 103 (1928), 88–96; *The Dragon's Teeth*, 212–49, quotation from p. 213.

[74] Although at times Fuller expressed scepticism about the rich and complex conceptions incorporated in Spengler's *Decline of the West* (London, 1926), he shared the latter's pessimistic *Kulturkritik* of Western civilization and the notion of its decline, prevalent among right-wing intellectuals before and after the First World War. For his scepticism, see Fuller, *India in Revolt*, 33; both Spengler and Toynbee are extensively cited e.g. in *Thunderbolts* (London, 1946); James is quoted in e.g. *Empire Unity and Defence*, 107; see the perceptive discussion in Reid, *Fuller*, 134–40.

one variant on the theme of élite modern society, Fuller speculated that armour might bring about a new, quasi-feudal regime run by a new mechanized aristocracy.[75] All the same, aware of the dialectical development of weapon power, by the late 1920s he wrote that the tank would soon have to contend with anti-tank devices such as the gun and the mine, which (in a new 'shock and projectile' cycle) would limit its rule and constantly vie with it for supremacy.[76]

Conclusion

This summary—perhaps any summary—of Fuller's ideas can never substitute for the original, levelling as it does the dazzling heights and embarrassing lows of his content and style. It cannot do justice to the wealth of tantalizing ideas, brilliant insights, original flashes of inspiration, and extremely suggestive historical interpretations which flow incessantly from Fuller's untamed, self-taught, and amateurish but ingeniously creative mind. At second hand they all lose much and pale somewhat, though gaining perhaps in coherence and readability. Stylistically, Fuller's works were always breathtaking, provocative, and engaging, but often obscure, mystifying, or mystical, at times deliberately so, as he thought wisdom was not intended for the masses. It was his friend, junior partner, and rival, Liddell Hart, who communicated many of his ideas to a wider public in a simplified and marketable form—and free from fascist overtones—taking much of the credit in the process.

Confining ourselves to the strictly military aspect, Fuller's ideas have attracted considerable criticism. In his remarkable critique *The 'Mechanization' of War* (1927) Victor Germains foreshadowed the opinion formed at the British War Office during the 1930 and anticipated virtually every point raised by later historians. Serialized and abstracted at the time by the Germans and Russians, his book has been undeservedly forgotten today. While expressing support for the tank and for mechanization, Germains claimed that Fuller and his disciples had been guilty of exaggeration, distortion, and oversimplification. He argued that mechanization did not economize on the overall number of people engaged—as the history of industrialization had

[75] *Thunderbolts*, 132.

[76] Fuller, 'One Hundred Problems of Mechanization', *Army Quarterly*, 19 (1929), 256–7; *The Dragon's Teeth*, 289–90; *Armoured Warfare* 20, 27, 85–94; 'The Problem of Tank and Anti-Tank Weapons', *Fighting Forces*, 14 (1937), 42–5; *Towards Armageddon*, 140–1.

shown—but merely redirected their contribution. In addition, he dismissed the claim that mechanized armies would be cheaper than their predecessors, or that civil industry and civil vehicles could be easily converted to military use. Thus he held that in the foreseeable future large-scale and necessarily unmechanized armies would be essential for supporting the mobile forces, in both offence and defence, in what was bound to be a protracted war. Mobile war did not necessarily promise quick decision. Modern industrial nations possessed vast resources and great endurance, and they would not succumb to rapid manœuvre alone. Further, Germains preceded and perhaps influenced Fuller in claiming that the development of the anti-tank gun and mine would considerably limit the tank's mobility. He also held that the naval analogy was false and misleading. Mobile forces would never be capable of travelling freely in any direction. Because of cost/effectiveness the railway would retain its primacy as a means of communication on land, followed by the lorry, and only lastly by the tractor. Roads were essential for land mobility, and much preferable even for cross-country vehicles. Unavoidably, they would face heavy pressure. Logistics, practically ignored by the mechanization enthusiasts, would remain a major restriction on manœuvre. Finally, in many non-European theatres and for policing the empire, unmechanized forces would be best.[77]

In any case, it is not our purpose here to evaluate Fuller's ideas but to bring out the intellectual thread running though his work. His anti-materialism and hostility towards bourgeois/mass society placed him within the ranks of the revived turn-of-the-century European right. His evolutionism and positivism indicated that he belonged to its radical and future-oriented, rather than conservative and nostalgic wing. He was a typical recruit to the modernist brand of proto-fascism and fascism, particularly powerful within the springs of Italian fascism, but noticeable everywhere in Europe, and later characteristic of Oswald Mosley's movement. He believed that the train of history was rapidly advancing towards a new qualitative scientific–technological–industrial age which would require a new, efficient, and highly organized form of social and economic regime, ruled by a professional–technocratic–meritocratic élite. Correspondingly, moral revival, new dynamism, and vitalism would replace democratic decadence. This wider trend of civilization development also provided the framework within which

[77] V. W. Germains, *The 'Mechanization' of War* (London, 1927), 43–4, 74–89, 94–5, 129–41, 166, 168–217, 225, 229, 244, and *passim*.

the future shape of armed forces was to be understood. They would be designed, organized, and run by scientific methods. They would become fully mechanized, making use of the latest products of industry and the laboratory, while reducing in numbers to become élite forces. Rapidity of movement, sophisticated control, and a highly discriminate mode of operations would make the moral dislocation and physical paralysis of the enemy their aim. Fuller was not the only one to hold these views. Throughout the West proto-fascists and fascists thought along similar lines.

3

Futurism, Proto-Fascist Italian Culture, and the Sources of Douhetism

The positivist vision of a modern, highly organized, and efficient society that we have seen most strikingly expressed in Fuller's (and Mosley's) brand of fascist modernism was matched by yet another strand, derived mainly from artistic sources, which aestheticized and celebrated the machine and the attributes of futurist society as a mighty force for moral liberation and human elevation. It is this strand of fascist modernism that we shall now examine more closely. Nowhere did it flourish more powerfully than in proto-fascist Italian culture; and in its arsenal of dynamic machines nothing equalled the symbolic potency of the aeroplane.

D'Annunzio, Marinetti, and the Air

It is widely recognized that one of the main sources of post-First World War Italian Fascism was pre-war Italian avant-garde culture. A forerunner of both was Italy's most famous poet, novelist, and playwright, the flamboyant and charismatic Gabriele d'Annunzio (1864–1938), whose international artistic celebrity was matched by the publicity raised by his extravagant love life and tempestuous politics. A parliamentary deputy for the conservatives from 1897, he swung to the left in 1900 to become a socialist deputy. In fact, no more a socialist than an ordinary conservative, he (as a considerable number of intellectuals would do in the following decade) was searching for a new form of politics and a new spiritual synthesis, to be discovered somewhere between extreme right and extreme left. Anti-democratic, influenced by Wagner and Nietzsche, and a Darwinist, d'Annunzio closely identified himself by the mid-1880s with the fashionable apprehensive literature then coming out regarding the psychology of the masses. He called for the defence of aristocratic values and high culture against the 'barbarians'.[1] Yet with the coming of the twentieth century d'Annunzio's contempt for the masses blended with a new attitude. At the same time as political theorists like Vifredo Pareto, Gaetano Mosca, and Robert Michels were developing their élite theories, d'Annunzio came to the conclusion that the masses could be mobilized, controlled, and harnessed by the élite for the achievement of great spiritual, nationalist, and imperialistic aims. This was the notion that he would perfect with the techniques of charismatic leadership and perpetual public liturgy characterizing his ominous nationalist-revolutionary rule in Fiume in 1919–21, techniques which were to be closely learnt and imitated by Mussolini.[2]

This political shift was also evident in d'Annunzio's art. During the 1880s and 1890s he had won international renown in the style of *fin-de-siècle* 'Decadence' and 'aestheticism'. His attitude towards the modern had been at best ambivalent. By the closing years of the century, however, he embraced modernity with enthusiasm. His elevated language and rich classical imagery were now blended with an exaltation of the power generated by industrial society and by the machine. In 1900 he wrote characteristically in an envious article on Germany:

> All of . . . its cities have become glowing refineries, centres of magnificent industries; the men of . . . its countryside have been attracted to the precise and shining machines; the smokestacks of the factories are myriad in . . . its skies . . . Upon the old Prussian military tradition the novelty of the industrial age has been miraculously grafted.

In the same vein d'Annunzio now celebrated the train, the street-car, the warship, and the torpedo boat:

> Ship of steel, flashing ahead straight and swift
> and beautiful as an unsheathed weapon,
> living and pulsing
> as though the metal enclosed a terrible heart.

By the first decade of the twentieth century, however, it was the dynamism and heroic individualism promised by the fast car and then by the aeroplane that most captivated d'Annunzio. For enthusiasts

[1] J. M. Becker, *Nationalism and Culture: Gabriele D'Annunzio and Italy after the Risorgimento* (New York, 1994) is particularly instructive here.

[2] G. Mosse, 'The Poet and the Exercise of Political Power: Gabriele d'Annunzio', in his *Masses and Man: Nationalist and Fascist Perception of Reality* (Detroit, 1987), 87–103; M. Ledeen, *The First Duce: D'Annunzio at Fiume* (Baltimore, 1977).

at the beginning of the century these were not merely machines but the engines of a new age of boundless revolutionary potential, moral and civilization-transforming forces. Much like Wells, d'Annunzio now believed that a new élite of technocrats and virile technological knights would replace the old élite at the head of modern society.[3]

These were the attitudes that d'Annunzio shared with the young avant-garde artists who launched a crusade against the bastions of established culture in Italy in the decade before the First World War, and whose relation to him mixed the conflicting sentiments of imitation, rejection, and envy. In Florence the group around the writers Giovanni Papini (1881–1956) and Giuseppe Prezzolini (1882–1983), the painter and critic Ardengo Soffici (1879–1964), and their journals *Leonardo* and *La Voce*, rebelled against the preoccupation of Italian culture with its past heritage, denounced decadence, and called for a virile spiritual, artistic, and moral regeneration. They proclaimed that the age of democracy had come to an end and that a new aristocratic age was beginning. The young socialist Benito Mussolini (1883–1945), already deeply influenced by Nietzsche, Sorel, and Pareto, corresponded with the leaders of the group, reading and contributing to its journals. However, the Florentine group was largely overshadowed by, and from 1913 began to cooperate with, another avant-garde group—which had been gaining international fame—Marinetti's Milanese Futurism.[4]

The poet Filippo Tommaso Marinetti (1876–1944) launched Futurism in a great public relations gesture that would become characteristic of his movement's mode of operation. His 'Manifesto of Futurism' was published on 20 February 1909 on the front page of one the most respected newspapers of Europe's cultural capital, *Le Figaro* of Paris. In the coming months it was echoed by other newspapers throughout Europe. It read as follows:

1. We intend to sing the love of danger, the habit of energy and fearlessness.
2. Courage, audacity, and revolt will be essential elements of our poetry.

. . .

4. We say that the world's magnificence has been enriched by a new beauty: the beauty of speed. A racing car whose hood is adorned with great pipes, like

[3] Becker, *D'Annunzio*, 183–202, is again especially good here; quotations from 184, 185, the latter from 'Naval Odes' (1892).

[4] W. Adamson, *Avant-Garde Florence: From Modernism to Fascism* (Cambridge, Mass., 1993); 'The Language of Opposition in Early Twentieth-Century Italy: Rhetorical Continuities between Prewar Florentine Avant-Gardism and Mussolini's Fascism', *Journal of Modern History*, 64 (1992), 22–51.

serpents of explosive breath—a roaring car that seems to run on grapeshot—is more beautiful than the *Victory of Samothrace*.

5. We want to hymn the man of the wheel, who hurls the lance of his spirit across the Earth, along the circle of its orbit.

. . .

8. We stand on the last promontory of the centuries! . . . Why should we look back? . . . We already live in the absolute, because we have created eternal, omnipresent speed.

9. We will glorify war—the world's only hygiene—militarism, patriotism, the destructive gesture of freedom-bringers, beautiful ideas worth dying for, and scorn for woman.

10. We will destroy the museums, libraries, academies of every kind, will fight moralism, feminism, every opportunistic or utilitarian cowardice.

11. We will sing the great crowds excited by work, by pleasure, and by riot; we will sing of the multicolored, polyphonic tides of revolution in the modern capitals; we will sing of the vibrant nightly fervour of arsenals and shipyards blazing with violent electric moons; greedy railway stations that devour smoke-plumed serpents; factories hung on clouds by the crooked lines of their smoke; bridges that stride the rivers like giant gymnasts, flashing in the sun with a glitter of knives; adventurous steamers that sniff the horizon; deep chested locomotives whose wheels paw the tracks like the hooves of enormous steel horses bridled by tubing; and the sleek flight of planes whose propellers chatter in the wind like banners and seem to cheer like an enthusiastic crowd.[5]

Unlike many of the widely diverging artistic styles coming under the title 'Modernism', the nature and programme of Futurism claimed to reflect the lexical meaning of the concept. Rather than apprehend and shrink from the products of modernity, from industrialization, urbanity, and their attendant social forms (an attitude that was widespread among Western cultural élites), Futurism embraced them with enthusiasm. Perhaps, as was suggested to Marinetti by the painter, writer, and would-be fascist Wyndham Lewis (1884–1957) who together with his friends founded Vorticism in Britain under Futurist influence, Futurism's modernistic enthusiasm was due to Italy's industrial backwardness when compared to Britain, France, or Germany.[6] This backwardness shamed her élite and made it eager to catch up. Futurist poets, painters, sculptors, and architects celebrated the rhythm and glitter of the 'electrified' metropolis, the functional beauty and radiating

[5] F. T. Marinetti, *Selected Writings* (New York, 1972), 39–44.

[6] Cited by D. Edgerton, *England and the Aeroplane: An Essay on a Militant and Technological Nation* (London, 1991), 13; more generally, F. Jameson, *Fables of Aggression: Wyndham Lewis, the Modernist as Fascist* (Berkeley, Calif., 1979), 5 and *passim*.

power of the industrial plant, the exhilarating, Dionysian speed of the car, and the boundless new horizons opened by the aeroplane. Rejecting democracy, parliamentarism, and mediocrity, Marinetti believed that the future belonged to a new vigorous élite, composed of artists, inventors, and technicians, that would engage in creative struggle—and war. In the often-cited words of the art critic and left-wing social theorist Walter Benjamin, Marinetti's work most strikingly reveals the nature of fascism as the aesthetization of politics and war.[7] In *War: The World's Only Hygiene* (1911–15) Marinetti depicted almost biological hybrids of man and machine and, as one essay was titled, a futurist 'Electrical War'. Having described a world dominated by science and technology, the essay went on:

> Intelligence finally reigns everywhere. Muscular work ceases to be servile, now having only three goals: hygiene, pleasure, and struggle . . . Twenty five great powers govern the world, fighting over the markets of a superabundant industrial production. And this is why we finally arrive at the first electric war. No more of those old explosives! Then we will know what to do with the rebellion of imprisoned gases that throb angrily beneath the atmosphere's heavy knees. Steel elephants, bristling with shining trunks pointed to the enemy, advance from two directions on the border between the two peoples—enormous pneumatic machines rolling down their tracks. . . . These slip away soon afterwards, to right and left along their tracks, making way for locomotives armed with electric batteries. . . . Twenty electric explosions in the sky, now a measureless glass chamber pneumatically emptied, have echoed the brave torments of two rival peoples with the fullness and splendor of their frightful interplanetary electric volleys.[8]

Marinetti and the Futurists reserved their most emotive imagery for the aeroplane. Recent studies have comprehensively described the decisive role the aeroplane and flight played in Western consciousness during the first decades of the twentieth century, which is similar to the later fascination with the exploration of space. The aeroplane promised the conquering of time and space, the vast extension of man's rule over nature and of the white man's domination over the world. It would usher in a new age of immense potential. The work of the Wright brothers after their first historic flight in 1903 initially attracted little attention. But in late summer 1908 Wilbur Wright came to France for a series of public flights that demonstrated the unrivalled performance of

[7] W. Benjamin, 'The Work of Art in the Age of Mechanical Reproduction', in his *Illuminations* (New York, 1968), 243–4.

[8] Marinetti, *Writings*, 106–7.

the Wright machine and awoke the vivid interest and enthusiasm of the Europeans. Royalty, aristocracy, artists, and literati came to Le Mans, Issy-les-Moulineaux, near Paris, and other sites to watch the fabulous machine in flight, have their photo taken with Wilbur Wright, and sometimes, for those who dared, join him in the air. In July 1909 Louis Blériot's flight across the Channel aroused excited public response. International air meetings now followed one another, attracting similar attention. In September 1909 one of the first such meetings was opened in Brescia, near Milan. Celebrities of all sorts attended, including d'Annunzio. He managed to persuade Glenn Curtiss and Mario Calderara to take him for a flight. He had been writing his first novel in ten years, *Forse che sì forse che no* (Perhaps Yes, Perhaps No), published in February 1910. Its heroes were flight pioneers whose supreme experience and daring were celebrated in d'Annunzio's elevated, heavily ornamented style. Like Wells, the German air novelist Rudolf Martin, and the French Émile Driant, d'Annunzio proclaimed that flying would change civilization, create a new ruling aristocracy of aviators, and revolutionize war.[9]

Marinetti was flying in the same direction. As d'Annunzio had done in *Alcyone* (1904), where he had portrayed himself as Icarus, Marinetti had been using images of flying in his poetry even before publishing his 'Manifesto of Futurism' in Paris in the wake of Wilbur Wright's flights. As he explained, the intention of the 'Manifesto' was 'to replace in people's imagination the silhouette of Don Juan with that of Napoleon, Andrée [a Swedish balloonist], and Wilbur Wright'. His 1909 play *Poupées électriques* (Electric Puppets) was dedicated to Wright. From the start the aeroplane was for Marinetti at once a leverage for human liberation and elevation from earthly confines and an engine of war. In 'Let's Murder the Moonlight' (1909) the aeroplane performs as the hero's mythological vehicle of war, where flesh and metal amalgamate. Taken for a flight for the first time in September 1910, over Milan, Marinetti sang the praises of the new epoch; he was an 'aeropoet', bestowing 'aeropoetical praise'. The flight over Milan opened his 'Technical Manifesto of Futurist Literature' (1912), calling for the transformation of language to suit the new mechanical age. His disciples, poets such as Mario Bètuda and Paolo Buzzi, followed in

[9] F. P. Ingold, *Literatur und Aviatik: Europäische Flugdichtung, 1909–1927* (Basle, 1978), 26–49; R. Wohl, *A Passion for Wings: Aviation and Western Imagination, 1908–1918* (New Haven, Conn., 1994), 115–22.

his footsteps in writing 'winged verses'.[10] The aeroplane figured prominently in Futurist painting, and even in Futurist cookery. Yet neither Marinetti nor d'Annunzio was content with words and images alone. They celebrated war, and they meant it.

In 1911–12 Italy waged war on Turkey for the conquest of Libya. The war was highly controversial, and Marinetti defended it from its critics on the left and in the Catholic establishment. In his political poem *Le Monoplan du pape* (The Pope's Monoplane) he flew over Italy singing the glory of war as the way to greatness through creative destruction. In real life he went to Libya and then to Turkey to watch the fighting and the first use of the aeroplane in war. Covering the war for European newspapers, he was filled with lyrical adulation of the Italian aviators who participated in the war and whose names were becoming nationally famous. His modernist poem *Zang tumb tumb* (1914) sought to convey the sounds and sights of war viewed from an aeroplane flying above the battlefield around Adrianople in 1912.[11] In his 'Electrical War' he again celebrated the monoplane and 'man having become airborne'.[12] The book which contained that essay, *War: The World's Only Hygiene*, comprising his works from the years 1911 to 1915, was intended as a propaganda weapon in the noisy campaign of agitation that radical nationalists were waging for Italy's entry into the First World War. As the title of the book implied, they believed that the war was a crucial cleansing process for decadent Italian society, politics, and culture—a heroic enterprise in which Italy could discover its mission and forge a renewed greatness. D'Annunzio and Mussolini agitated for the same cause, the latter departing from the Socialist Party on that account. When Italy finally entered the war, they all enthusiastically rushed to enlist.

While Marinetti—39 in 1915—and his Milanese group served together in the trenches on the Alpine front, as did Mussolini, d'Annunzio carved for himself a role of an entirely different order of glamour. Determined to live up to his reputation as a daredevil, the poet—52 in 1915—became Italy's most decorated war hero. He switched between the élite and technically most advanced units of the Italian armed forces, participating in the most extraordinary missions. At the outbreak of the war he was commissioned as a lieutenant in the

[10] Marinetti, *Writings*, 53, 84, 253; Inglold, *Literatur and Aviatik*, 59–80, 278–99, 342–5; Wohl, *A Passion for Wings*, 2, 138–44, 264–7.

[11] Ingold, *Literatur und Aviatik*, 238–47; Wohl, *A Passion for Wings*, 140–2, 264.

[12] *Writings*, 106.

cavalry, but being the national institution that he was he went where he pleased. As early as July–August 1915 he twice flew over Trieste, dropping leaflets and carrying out reconnaissance. He also joined a submarine on an active combat mission. The Adriatic coast and the air would remain his main theatre of operations, but on occasions he would leave to join land offensives, always striving to be at the forefront of danger. In the autumn of 1915 he fought on the ground at San Michele. He raided Trento from the air in September and Aisonizza in October, flew in support of the land war at the turn of the year, and again raided Trieste in January 1916. The next month he was seriously wounded in a forced landing, losing one eye and becoming incapacitated for six months. He bombed Parenzo in September 1916 and fought on the ground at Veliki in October. Between January and May 1917 he fought on the ground on the rivers Isonzo and Timavo. In August 1917 he led the three squadrons that bombed Pola, and in October led the aerial raid on Cattaro. In February 1918 he participated in a night raid by three high-speed torpedo boats on Austrian warships lying in a defended anchorage in the Adriatic. That year he was appointed commander of the 'First Naval Squadron of Torpedo-Carrying Airplanes'. In July 1918 he bombed Pola, and in August, after earlier failed attempts, he led an audacious air raid on Vienna, dropping leaflets. A major from 1917, he was raised to lieutenant-colonel in 1919.[13]

The air raids on Austrian cities, especially the long-range ones, required more than mere audacity and bravado. One had to have the machines. Together with Russia, Italy was the most industrially backward of all the great powers involved in the war. Yet tellingly, together with Russia, where futurist enthusiasm for the air matched Italy's, Italy pioneered the development of the heavy bomber. In the years preceding the war, the Russian Igor Sikorsky and Turin manufacturer Giovanni Battista Caproni had been separately working on the development of the world's only heavy-load, long-range, multi-engine aeroplanes. Sikorsky's giant four-engine plane entered active service with the Russian army in late 1914, and by the summer of 1915 the Caproni trimotor went into action with the Italian air service. If Russia was slightly ahead in terms of time and size, it was no match for Italy in numbers. Some

[13] D'Annunzio's wartime reports and letters are printed in G. Po (ed.), *Gabriele d'Annunzio: combattente al servizio della regia marina* (Rome, 1931); *Gabriele d'Annunzio: scritti, messaggi, discorsi e rapporti militari* (Rome, 1939). Mostly from the literary perspective is A. Bonadeo, *D'Annunzio and the Great War* (Madison, Wis., 1995).

800 Capronis, roughly equally divided between twin-motors and trimotors, were built by 1918, as compared with only 73 Sikorskys. The other great powers developed their heavy bombers considerably later. The famous German Gotha, ordered in 1915, entered service in 1916, and went into action over Britain in the spring and summer of 1917, after the failed Zeppelin offensive. But it was a twin-motor. The giant multi-engine R planes (*Riesenflugzeuge*), also participating in the raids on Britain, had the same career dates, but only 55–65 were built. The British equivalents to the Gotha, the twin-motor Handley-Page 100 and DH9, were also developed over the same years. Multi-engine British giants only went into service in 1918. From their total backwardness of only a few years earlier, the Italian aeronautical and engine industries made great strides, and kept abreast of technological developments during the war, winning lucrative contracts from their *Entente* allies up to the end of the war. The 1913 version of Caproni's trimotor was still powered by Gnome 80 hp rotaries. But by 1914 it switched to Fiat 100 hp engines, and by 1915 to Isotta-Fraschini 150 hp units, upgraded to 200 hp in 1916. In 1916–18 250 and 300 hp engines were developed and mass produced by Fiat, simultaneously with the German, British, and French designs. Units of 500 hp were developed by all Italian engine manufacturers by the end of the war.[14]

It was on the heavy Caproni trimotors that d'Annunzio based a scheme for the future of air operations. In May 1917 he drew up a memorandum to General Luigi Cadorna, chief of the Italian army's general staff. The air force, he suggested, would support the other arms through reconnaissance and bombing; but primarily it had the potential for an even more promising line of action. The giant planes were capable of striking at the centres of the enemy's industrial production. They would destroy and disorganize the armament and munitions plants and irreparably disrupt the work process. D'Annunzio calculated the carrying loads and distances for great air raids from France on Essen, which would deliver more than 100 tons of bombs. Closer to

[14] J. Morrow, *The Great War in the Air* (Washington, 1993) is particularly rich here; see also G. H. Haddow and P. Grosz, *The German Giants: The Story of the R Planes, 1914–1919* (London, 1969); P. Vergano, *Origins of Aviation in Italy, 1783–1918* (Genoa, 1964); A. D. Harvey, *Collision of Empires: Britain in Three World Wars, 1793–1945* (London, 1992), 394. For Russian Futurist enthusiasm for the aeroplane and air pioneering, see Ingold, *Literatur und Aviatik*, 133–89 and p. 114 below.

home he specified the Adriatic main port of Pola, and Vienna, as prize targets.[15]

To be sure, 'strategic' bombing on targets deep in the enemy's rear had been taking place since the beginning of the war. The French, under the influence of Commandant Barès, pioneered the idea as early as 1914, but doubts about the efficacy of the bombing and production difficulties rapidly lowered French interest in such efforts. The Zeppelin raids on Britain were conceived in 1914 and carried out in earnest from the spring of 1915. The Gotha and R plane raids on London began in the spring and summer of 1917, at the time d'Annunzio submitted his memorandum to Cadorna. Following these raids, the British moved to create an independent strategic bombing force within their newly constituted independent air force. This bomber force began its raids on Germany in the autumn of 1917 and intensified them from the summer of 1918.[16] Still, d'Annunzio's memorandum derived from the plans and and memoranda of Colonel Giulio Douhet, a friend of Caproni and d'Annunzio, who had encouraged the industrialist to take up the production of his heavy bombers in the first place, well before the Great War.[17] For, again, in order to have the heavy bomber, one had first to conceive the idea of it.

Douhet: Science, Poetry, Fascism, and Mechanized War

It was against the background of the intense modernist fascination with the latest advances of science and technology—with the automobile, with electricity, with gas, and finally with the aeroplane—prevalent in prewar Italian proto-fascist avant-garde culture that Giulio Douhet (1869–1930) evolved his visions of future mechanized and air warfare. Although widely known as the most extreme and most famous of the air theorists, and as closely associated with the idea of air warfare as Fuller is with that of mechanized land warfare, Douhet has received little

[15] The memorandum, dated 11 May 1917, is reprinted in Po, *D'Annunzio: scritti militari*, 75–88.

[16] See esp. Morrow, *The Great War in the Air*; L. Kennett, *The First Air War, 1914–1918* (New York, 1991); M. Cooper, *The Birth of Independent Air Power* (London, 1986). Still useful are H. A. Jones, *The War in the Air*, v and vii (Oxford, 1935 and 1937), 1–159 and 101–74 respectively; J. Cueno, *The Air Weapon, 1914–1916* (Harrisburg, Penn., 1947), 351–77.

[17] Some correspondence between d'Annunzio and Douhet is printed in A. Monti (ed.), *Giulio Douhet: scritti inediti* (Gennaio, 1951), 230–4. Also see for their cooperation n. 40 below and related text.

serious study.[18] Famous for his works during the 1920s, he had in fact developed the kernel of his later ideas and emerged as a military theorist of the first order well before the First World War. Himself an amateur novelist, poet, painter, and playwright—as well as a professional soldier—he was closely attuned to the dominant themes of his intellectual milieu, which he expressed in his own field in the more precise and practical language of technical, organizational, and operational schemes. His ardent Fascism, which he espoused from the movement's very inception in 1919, was the natural extension of the opinions and sentiments he had expressed long before the war.

Douhet came from a Piedmontese family of strong military and patriotic tradition. In 1888 he graduated from the artillery academy of the Italian army first in his class, and later entered Turin polytechnic, from which he again graduated with distinction. From the start he acquired a reputation of brilliance, and in 1900 was posted to the army's general staff. As with d'Annunzio and Marinetti, his first enthusiasm prior to the advent of the aeroplane was for electricity, chemistry, and the automobile, the exciting new products of the unfolding 'Second Industrial Revolution'. While Italian avant-garde artists marvelled at the power and glitter of electricity, Douhet studied it scientifically. His final paper at the polytechnic, 'The Calculation of Rotating Field Engines', was published, as was his 'Summary of the Current State of Electric Technology'.[19] In a scientific conference at the Sorbonne in Paris he read a paper, 'Separation of Oxygen and Hydrogen from Air by Means of a Fractional Distillation of Liquid Air' (1905).[20]

However, by the first years of the new century Douhet was preoccupied with the automobile and its military applications. By European, not only Italian, standards, he had been a leading advocate

[18] Most summaries of Douhet's life have appeared in Italian as introductions to the various collections of his writings. In English the sole accessible summary is E. Warner, 'Douhet, Mitchell, Seversky: Theories of Air Warfare', in E. M. Earle (ed.), *Makers of Modern Strategy from Machiavelli to the Second World War* (Princeton, NJ, 1943), 487–97, and the only comprehensive one is F. Cappelluti, 'The Life and Thought of Giulio Douhet' (doctoral dissertation, Rutgers University, 1967), which regrettably has not been published. See also Claudio Sergè, 'Douhet in Italy: Prophet without Honor?', *Aerospace Historian*, June 1979, 69–80; 'Giulio Douhet: Strategist, Theorist, Prophet?', *Journal of Strategic Studies*, 15 (1992), 351–66.

[19] For the first study, see Cappelluti, 'Douhet', 4, and for the second, G. Douhet, *Cenno sommario sullo stato attuale dell'elettrotecnica* (Turin, 1905; date of composition 1903); one chapter is devoted to the electric automobile.

[20] C. Ranieri, 'General Giulio Douhet', introduction to Douhet, *The Command of the Air* (Rome, 1958), p. ix.

of the mechanization of armies well before turning his attention to the air. In a series of lectures and pamphlets delivered and published from 1901 onward, when the automobile was barely beginning to develop from infancy into a commercial product, the then Captain Douhet envisaged the mechanization of whole armies. In *Mechanization, from the Military Point of View: A Scheme of Mechanization for Military Use* (1902) he wrote that every new invention had implications for the conduct of war. The essence of mechanization was the substitution of mechanical energy and mechanical work for animal-powered transportation. Mechanical energy could be extracted from a variety of sources: chemical (coal and petrol), electric, or dynamic (compressed gas), each potentially capable of powering automobiles. Comprehensively comparing their respective qualities on the basis of mathematical and physical computation, Douhet unequivocally supported the electric engine, his old favourite. This was not as misguided as it may appear in view of the ensuing development of the car, for at the turn of the century petroleum and electric engines still ran neck and neck as the preferred power for automobiles. Leading car pioneers such as Ferdinand Porsche, whose electric car was the sensation of the Paris Salon de l'Automobile of 1900, initially regarded the electric engine as more promising. In any case, Douhet's thoughts were on the largest scale from the outset. His pamphlet consisted of detailed schemes for the mechanization of complete army corps, elaborately working out payloads and speeds. The armies of the future would undoubtedly be mechanized, though Douhet thought in terms of mechanical mobility into the battlefield rather than for the fighting itself. He did not envisage the tank.[21] In the following years he became one of the foremost advocates of mechanization in the Italian general staff,[22] and was appointed first commander of a newly constituted élite mechanized Bersaglieri battalion. All this, it will be remembered, had begun more than a decade before the First World War. At least in *ideas* Italians were ahead of anyone else. Then, during the great years of breakthrough for aviation, 1908–9, Douhet

[21] G. Douhet, *L'Automobilismo, sotto il punto di vista militare: schema di un sistema automobilistico per uso militare* (Turin, 1902); *A proposito dell'articolo: gli automobili e la loro applicazione nell'arte della guerra* (Rome, 1902); *Automobilismo militare e pesante* (Genoa, 1904). For the electric car at the turn of the nineteenth century, see S. Bayley, 'Dead as a Flat Battery', *Times Literary Supplement*, 18 Aug. 1995, 25.

[22] See L. Ceva and A. Curami, *La Meccanizzazione dell'esercito italiano dalle origini al 1943* (Rome, 1989), 21–3.

too, like d'Annunzio and Marinetti, was taken by the prospects opened up in the air.

Douhet's 'The Problems of Air Navigation' was written in 1909 and published in the service journal *La Preparazione*, as well as in pamphlet form, in 1910. It was more or less contemporaneous with the works of the air novelists all over Europe and no different in its general messages. His work, however, was not a novel but a military tract, albeit of a visionary nature. The title of the work might be misleading: far from dealing with navigation in the strictly technical sense, it was an outline of future war in and from the air. As in any other new field, Douhet stated, at first the idea of flight required fantasy to realize its potential. And as with the mechanization of armies, he thought big from the outset. After surveying the history of flying, emphasizing the achievements of the Wright brothers and Blériot, Douhet predicted that air fleets would become a dominant feature of future war. He rejected the dirigible as too vulnerable to be used for military purposes, and for years would fight in the Italian army against any investment in it as sheer waste of money. But he viewed the aeroplane as having a tremendous potential for bombing over land and sea, as well as possessing great reconnaissance capability for all branches of the armed forces. He also claimed that the aeroplane was relatively cheap: 3,000 could be bought for the price of one battleship. Great air fleets would be deployed in the future, operating much as in sea warfare. Industrial preparation at home during peacetime would be required to produce the necessary equipment for the air force and keep it supplied.[23] In general this was a fair forecast of things to come. Unlike Douhet's later ideas, it did not assume the complete dominance of air power to the practical exclusion of armies and navies, nor did it prescribe 'strategic' bombing of the enemy's production centres and population as the only appropriate mission for air power. All the same, Douhet was later justified in proudly citing his early work as evidence that his main ideas went back to 1909–10, well before the First World War.

The work of 1909–10 was only the beginning, for Douhet now converted to the air. He was posted to the aviation battalion of the Italian army, created in Turin in 1912, and in the same year became its second commander. On the request of the war ministry he submitted a

[23] Maj. G. Douhet, *I Problemi dell'aereonavigazione* (Rome, 1910); a reprint can be found in the most significant collection of his works, the posthumous *Le Profezie di Cassandra* (Genoa, 1931), 61–87.

report detailing an organizational scheme for the air units. In this official report his tone was again relatively modest. He did not yet advocate an independent air force. He also held that it was too early to determine exactly how the aeroplane would be used in war, whether for reconnaissance, bombing, or air battle. For this reason he suggested the development for the time being of an 'all-purpose' aircraft, an idea to which he would return in the 1920s. He again emphasized close industrial cooperation as the most essential prerequisite for the development of a strong air force.[24] Douhet was a man who backed words with deeds. During his tenure of command in Turin he befriended Caproni, who became a close associate for life. It was under his urging and promise of support that Caproni took up the development of his heavy bomber. At the end of 1914 Douhet was removed from his post and made chief of staff to an infantry division for ordering Caproni's aircraft without authorization from his superiors or from the war ministry.[25]

But it was not engineering alone that gave wings to Douhet's imagination, nor was the dry prose of official reports his only language. In a lecture at the Turin polytechnic in 1913, following the war in Libya, he sang the glory of future air warfare, and 'sang' is the appropriate word here. Echoing d'Annunzio and Marinetti, Douhet waxed poetic in words worth quoting at some length:

> All of a sudden Italy was stricken by a new shudder meandering all over her, all the brows bent for so long were risen, its hearts pulsed more excitedly; a new unknown strength infused everyone: War!
>
> . . .
>
> Any doubt was silenced, any wavering disappeared in this emergency; spreading their wings the adventurous airway researchers flew toward the unknown.
>
> . . . The bent wings
of men are passing, Daedalus's
large devices, the field machines
made of stretched hemp-close and light
wood, which will carry man and his
dreadful thunderbolt on fragile supports.
>
> The delicate machines were reset on the new homeland of Italy, leaving the light trail of their talons on the wet sand of our seas; like new human eagles they rose against the enemy, the very first ones in the world, amazing all.

[24] Cappelluti, 'Douhet', 46–54.

[25] For the Douhet–Caproni relationship, based on archival material, see ibid. 56–61.

Uncertain machines struggling in the wind, guided by steady hands, as if made of bronze, and hearts steadier than bronze. Man and his machine with one strong pulsation in one single heart; a single tangle of nerves and steel shrouds in the large clever birds . . .

All the new Italian land, so much hoped for, was discovered before it became Italian, by their eyes which were burnt by both wind and sun, over the propeller's whirling star; and they discovered ambushes and traps, unexpected help for their brothers fighting on earth and sea, and they brought their message of peace and their message of death.

Moizo, Gavotti from your light glacis,
bowed in the danger of the winds
over the enemy who ignores the new assault!
. . .

A new weapon arose: an air weapon; a new battlefield opened: the sky; so very present everywhere that a new event took place in the history of war: the principles of war in the air.[26]

Douhet quoted air poetry again in a chapter dedicated to air warfare in his book *The Art of War* (1915), comprising a series of lectures he had given earlier at the Popular University of Turin.[27]

Indeed, although Douhet, like most self-styled prophets, failed to cite anybody who may have stimulated his inspiration, he none the less left a clear enough trail. For example, in September 1914, shortly after the outbreak of the First World War, he published an article entitled 'Futurism', in which he applied the message of the celebrated artistic movement to his own field, the art of war. He rejected both bourgeois values and the reliance on the past. Again, lengthy quotations are called for:

We love the Futurists. This advanced movement of unconventional youngsters who intend breaking every tradition and rejecting every old rubbish is likable, and it is likable even when it goes to extreme in order to 'épater le bourgeois', that poor bourgeois, secluded in dog's bed, with a tail stump between his trembling legs, begging for mercy, forgetful of all his past strength, and who has become the laughing stock of today's strong spirits.

Yes, we love those impetuous forerunners of tomorrow, because, in them, one finds something true. We often forget that we are living in the present, that the door of the past is closed while that of the future is wide open in front of us, and

[26] 'Prolusione al corso preparatorio di aviazione' (29 Jan. 1913), in *Profezie di Cassandra*, 88–101, quotations from 90–2. I am most grateful to Signor Renato Orsini, who made these artistic translations for me.

[27] Lt.-Col. Douhet, *L'Arte della guerra* (Turin, 1915), 127.

we are inexorably pushed towards it by a continuous power pressing behind our shoulders. . . .

History for example, which was called the teacher of life, it is a chain instead, to which life is tied and carried backwards. . . .

Never again will we find ourselves in the conditions of the battle of Salamis, Canne, Austerlitz and Sedan; let us leave once and for all those poor dead in peace . . . Hannibal is dead, Napoleon is dead, Moltke is dead; tomorrow we shall be dead too; let us respect the past, but let us create the future. . . .

The present war cannot be compared to the wars of the past . . . Judging it with old-fashioned methods is a mistake, the same as it would be mistaken to try and measure an electric potential with a double decimeter; it was absurd to prepare it with a backward look, the same as it would be absurd to try and build an induction coil with a string. . . .

All true geniuses of war . . . broke all past traditions, revolutionizing the present, anticipating the future. . . .

There is room for everybody. Archaeology to scholars, the present and the limits of the future, to men of action.[28]

The unanswered question of 'Futurism' regarding the direction of the future was answered two weeks later with the publication in the same journal of Douhet's 'Man and the Machine'. Modern war, he wrote, was machine war, everywhere replacing muscular labour with the latest products of science and technology—the rapid-firing gun, the machine-gun, the enhanced chemical energy of modern explosives, the railway, the armoured car, and the aeroplane—all exponentially increasing human power. The whole nation becomes a great factory of war. While Douhet's article was coached in a realistic military language as opposed to the sham-mythological science fiction of Marinetti's 'Electrical War' written about the same time, the parallels between the two visions are striking. It ought to be borne in mind that both pre-dated the growing mechanization of warfare that would take place during the later course of the First World War.[29]

Direct evidence linking Douhet to Marinetti also exists. Marinetti's literary remains, in the possession of the Beinecke Library at Yale, include two books by Douhet. One is *How Did the Great War End?* (1919), itself an insignificant history written in November 1918, immediately after the Central Powers' collapse, but personally dedicated to

[28] 'Futurismo', *Gazzetta del Popolo*, 24 Sept. 1914, repr. in *Profezie di Cassandra*, 189–92. Cf. e.g. Marinetti's 'Futurist Manifesto' above.

[29] Douhet, 'L'Uomo e le macchine', *Gazzetta del Popolo*, 7 Oct. 1914, repr. in *Profezie di Cassandra*, 207–11.

Marinetti by the author. The other book is fictional, *The Honourable Who Could No Longer Lie: A Story from Pre-War Times* (1921).[30]

It may be that the *personal* connection between Douhet and the aeropoets began or crystallized during the agitation to bring Italy into the war in 1914–15. In his journalistic articles Douhet, although a regular soldier, barely masked his desire to see Italy join the war, evoking the famous '*sacro egoismo*'.[31] Even before 1914, and after, he repeatedly urged the need for total national and industrial mobilization of all spiritual and physical resources for the purpose of war. Modern war, he emphasized time and again, was national and total.[32] Like other nationalist critics of parliamentary Italy, he castigated the widespread corruption of his country and complained that 'Italy is ruled by mediocrity'.[33] His highly critical stance towards the incompetence of the authorities only intensified after Italy entered the war.

Carefully following the strategic development of the war, analysing its features, and continuously drawing up schemes for action in a stream of private notes and memoranda to his superiors, Douhet sought a way around the stalemate of the trenches. As Fuller would do, he claimed that the belligerents were anachronistically trying to repeat 1870–1. Very early in the war he became convinced that the murderous offensives on the enemy's fortified lines were futile and had to be stopped. The army ought to assume the defensive until the necessary *matériel* was made available. On 3 July 1915, barely a month after Italy had declared war, he suggested that the air represented the most promising strategy for victory. Modern technology, he wrote, had made possible heavy multi-engine aircraft with a carrying capacity of up to 1,000–1,500 kg. These were able to strike hundreds of kilometres behind the front lines and against the enemy's vital industrial centres, upon which the strength of nations in modern war depended. The secret of success lay in the massive concentration of all available resources at the decisive point for a grand air offensive against the Central Powers. A great armada of 500 aircraft, each carrying some 500 kg. of explosives to a range of between 300 to 500 km., should be assembled. It would be sent

30 Col. G. Douhet, *Come finì la Grande Guerra* (Rome, 1919); id. *L'Onorevole che non potè più mentire. Racconto dei tempi ante-guerra* (Rome, 1921).

31 See e.g. 'Il sacro egoismo', *Gazzetta del popolo*, 20 Oct. 1914, repr. in *Le Profezie di Cassandra*, 212–16.

32 *L'Arte della guerra*, 1–4; 'La Preparazione industriale', 12 Nov. 1914, also 28 Aug. 1914, repr. in *Profezie di Cassandra*, 149–54, 227–30.

33 See e.g. 9 Nov. 1914, repr. in Monti, *Douhet: Scritti inediti*, 7.

to attack arsenals, ports, magazines, industrial plants, military centres, banks, and government ministries, inflicting immense, irreparable, and decisive damage on the enemy. In Douhet's calculation the whole proposition was relatively inexpensive, costing no more that 50 million Italian lire. (Optimistic claims that mechanization actually *saved* money were common among its pioneers.) The required type of machine was available in the shape of the Caproni 300. All that was needed was a strategic decision and the allocation of resources for its mass production.[34]

Douhet's scheme for an all-out air offensive was only the first in a series of plans. In January 1916 he submitted a memorandum to Generals Brusati and Cadorna. As before, he showed a firm grasp of the industrial and technological character of modern war. The memorandum began with the same broad historical reasoning that Fuller espoused later on: 'war follows the evolution of industry in the application of the machine. In the same way that the machine multiplies production, its introduction into the modern army multiplies destruction.' 'The modern army derives its strength from the machines it possesses. . . . Neither the genius of the commanders nor the valour of the soldiers can substitute for mechanical means.' Military power now rested on industrial and commercial might.[35] Again surveying the deadlock on land, Douhet returned to his proposal for a grand air offensive against the Central Powers:

> Modern armies represent the armoured shield behind which the nations at war work to prepare the means appropriate to feed the war; the powerful aeroplane is able to pass over such armour and strike at the nation itself in its centres of production and along the lines of supply running from the country to the army. Thus it is the best weapon to strike a fatal blow. . . the new weapon attacks not only the fist but the heart, and cuts the nerves and veins of the arm.[36]

An air fleet of 1,000 aircraft was capable of dropping 500 tons of explosives in one flight. It could destroy the Austrian navy in Pola, and completely cut off Austrian communications through the Tirol. More systematically, the priorities of the air offensive should be as follows: (*a*) to destroy the means of production of the enemy's nation, its wealth, resources, and morale; (*b*) to cut off the communications of

[34] 3 July 1915, in *Diario critico di guerra* (2 vols., Rome, 1921–2), i. 65–9; in an exception to his general rule, Douhet cites Wells's ideas.

[35] Jan. 1916, ibid. ii. 14, 17.

[36] Ibid. 16, 19–21; quoted in Harvey's excellent *Collision of Empires*, 393–4.

the enemy's army, isolating it from supplies and reinforcements; (*c*) to devastate its rear areas; and (*d*) to attack its front line. Industry should be organized to mass-produce aeroplanes in the same way as Fiat mass-produced trucks.[37]

During these years Douhet was kept away from any position related to the air. In his repeated criticism of the army's unpreparedness and strategy, his requests for resources for the air, and his demands for total mobilization of the nation's industry and morale, he made himself a nuisance in the eyes of his superiors. Far from restricting his criticism to army channels, he secretly briefed parliamentary deputies. On one such occasion he left behind in a railway carriage a confidential document criticizing the army. After it had been found and turned over to the authorities he was arrested, and sentenced by court martial in October 1916 to one year's imprisonment, which he duly served.[38] All the same, in June 1917, while still in prison and a month after d'Annunzio had submitted his own memorandum to Cadorna, Douhet again put forward a revised scheme for a grand Allied aerial offensive against the Central Powers. His recommended order of priorities was now, first, to win air superiority by bombing the enemy's aircraft, aeronautical installations, and plants for aeroplane production. Then, the enemy's rear and front could be attacked and his morale broken. A huge aerial armada, including 1,000 Italian aircraft, 3,000 French, 4,000 British, and 12,000 American, was capable of hurling 1,000 ton of bombs on Hamburg, Essen, Berlin, and Vienna, in one drop. In the not too distant future air power would dominate war.[39] A few days later, on 3 July 1917, in a memorandum co-signed by Douhet, d'Annunzio, and Caproni and submitted to the Chief of the Army's General Staff, General Carlo Porro, the three called for the creation of an independent air force.[40] In January 1918 Douhet was appointed Director of Technical Services in the Aeronautical Bureau, but in June he resigned from the post on the grounds that it lacked any power. Shortly afterwards he left the army. He was promoted to general in 1921.

Douhet incorporated the ideas he had developed during the war in

[37] Ibid. 21–2; see also Douhet, 'Proposte al generale Cadorna sull'impiego dell'aviazione', 19 Feb. 1916, in Monti, *Douhet: scritti inediti*, 14 ff.

[38] In addition to the Diary, see relevant material in *Le Profezie di Cassandra*, 299–350.

[39] Douhet, 'La Grande Offensiva aerea', 23 June 1917, in Monti *Douhet scritti inediti*, 114–31.

[40] This unpublished document, contained in Douhet's file in the ministry of war, is cited by Cappelluti, 'Douhet', 151.

his programmatic book *The Command of the Air* (1921). Since the book is known well enough and adds little to what we have already described, it can be briefly summarized. Air power is the offensive weapon *par excellence*. Whereas civilian population had traditionally been protected by the army, air power now made it vulnerable to attack. The modern nation's centres of industry, transportation, and government could be obliterated swiftly and with relative ease, perhaps within days or even hours, by bomber fleets of medium speed and heavy-load carrying capacity. There is practically no effective defence against such an attack, because the attacker is always free to choose the time and place of the raid. Pre-emptive strike to gain air superiority by destroying the enemy's air force on the ground is the only defence. Although Douhet still left a subsidiary role for auxiliary aviation to support the army and navy, he held that the role of these services was quickly diminishing, and that they should be progressively reduced and the air force expanded. The latter should be constituted as an independent service, with its own ministry responsible for the development of the country's aeronautical infrastructure and civil aviation.[41]

But writing on strategic and air matters was only one aspect of Douhet's activity in the immediate aftermath of the war. He painted, wrote literature, and established a nationalist weekly, *Il Dovere* (Duty), which he edited between 1919 and 1921. He also participated in the activity of the *Arditi*, the élite Italian storm troops of the war that became the nucleus of the extra-parliamentary opposition to the post-war liberal government and soon joined hands with Mussolini. In 1922 Douhet took part in the 'March on Rome', and after the Fascists seized power he was sent to d'Annunzio by Mussolini, together with two other army generals, carrying a letter of invitation that called upon the national poet to join the new regime.[42] Douhet's fortunes and that of his ideas seemed to have changed radically. As he wrote in the introduction to the second edition of *Command of the Air* (1926), conditions had become much more favourable to his ideas. Indeed, in the new political and intellectual climate he radicalized his rhetoric even further.[43] For, like the avant-garde artists with whom he associated and by whom he was influenced, Mussolini had been an enthusiast for the aeroplane from its beginning. He exalted its wider futurist and

[41] *Il Dominio dell'aria* (Rome, 1921), trans. as *The Command of the Air* (London, 1943), 1–79.

[42] Cappelluti, 'Douhet', 153, 159.

[43] *The Command of the Air*, introduction to 2nd edn. (1926), 5, 80.

spiritual significance, and was eager to identify it with the Fascist movement. The aeroplane and flight were among the Fascists' most potent symbols.

Mussolini, Balbo, and the Fascist Cult of Flying

In the mid-1930s Guido Mattioli lauded Mussolini's relationship to the aeroplane and flying in his book *Mussolini aviatore*, which the Italian authorities took care to translate into German and English. While obviously propagandistic, the work is doubly significant, as it remarkably testifies to the sort of image the Fascists sought to project as well as documenting the very real nature of Mussolini's interest in the aeroplane. The introduction to the book stated that, unlike the great leaders of the *Risorgimento*, the Duce did not merely send people to action but personally led them himself. He was a man of action and irresistible will, qualities for which flying provided a singular showcase. The book strove to demonstrate that Mussolini had not only, as it stated, realized General Douhet's theories by building one of the world's strongest air forces but was himself an aviator, personally leading the daring conquest of the skies. Numerous photographs of the Duce in full flying gear cleverly drove this point home. Mussolini was taken up in the air for the first time in 1918 and learnt to fly the year after. He established an 'aeronautical parliamentary group' in the Italian Chamber of Deputies when first elected, and made extensive use of the aeroplane for travelling during his campaign for power and after becoming the dictator of Italy. Moreover, he had been writing about the aeroplane since 1909. The record in Mattioli's book, to be sure partly coloured for effect but none the less resting on documentary evidence, has been summarized as follows by Robert Wohl:

> in July 1909, Mussolini wrote an article for a regional Italian newspaper in which he expounded on the meaning of the Channel flights. Exploits like that, the young Mussolini insisted, could not be understood simply in terms of sport. They were an expression of the deepest tendencies of the new century. Our age was heroic, perhaps even more so than the Ancient World. The word that summed up the new century was movement. 'Movement towards the icy solitude of the poles and toward the virgin peaks of the mountains, movement toward the stars and toward the depths of the seas . . . Movement everywhere and acceleration in the rhythm of our lives.' And when Blériot succeeded in flying the Channel, Mussolini saluted him as one of the first champions of a new race of Nietzschean *dominatori*, one of those restless figures who give meaning

to life through the pursuit of an ideal. The war, which Mussolini experienced from the immobility of the trenches, only increased his reverence for aviators. . . . Even before the war ended, Mussolini had begun to seek out the company of military pilots and aces. Several would be at his side when he came to power in October, 1922. . . . The ace Mario Stoppiani, who took Mussolini up for one of his first flights, remembered him as being in a state of 'enthusiastic delirium'. . . . Driving away from the airfield with a group of aviators, it occurred to Mussolini that these men represented 'the new Italian race of producers, builders, and creators'. They were the Italians of the future who would conquer the land, the sea, and the sky.[44]

'Aviation must remain the privilege of the spiritual aristocracy,' Mussolini wrote in 1909. 'Not every Italian can or should fly,' he said in a speech at the Aero Club of Italy in November 1923. 'But all Italians should envy those who do and should follow with profound feelings the development of Italian wings.'[45]

That this was the language of d'Annunzio and Marinetti which Mussolini borrowed and integrated in his political rhetoric is well recognized. The three men, all prima donnas with megalomaniac political ambitions—and increasingly playing on similar political grounds—had always paid the closest attention to one another. Their relationships were characterized by competition, envy, and tentative cooperation. Both Marinetti and Mussolini came to visit d'Annunzio in his hour of glory, after he had established his revolutionary regime in Fiume, where they were able to see, apart from everything else, his use of aeroplanes as a central element of his perpetual political carnival. They loathed the fact that he had caught the nation's attention, whereas he wanted no partners to share the glory with. In turn, d'Annunzio, who was himself entertaining plans for a march on Rome, was pre-empted by Mussolini.[46] For all that, Mussolini made him the cultural hero of Fascist Italy, a position he held for the duration of his life, and that of the regime.

Things were even more complex between Marinetti and Mussolini. Mussolini was quick to pick up the messages and learn from the public-relations techniques of Futurism. In addition, as he later wrote,

[44] Wohl, *A Passion for Wings*, 287–8; the evidence is derived from G. Mattioli, *Mussolini Aviator, and His Work for Aviation* (Rome, 1939), esp. pp. vii, 5, 8–10, 16–18, 41–4, 71–85. See also Mussolini's speech in the Italian senate on 30 Mar. 1938, in which he gave tribute to 'Douhet's vision' as the precursor of the Italian doctrine of air warfare: cited by Cappelluti, 'Douhet', 238, from Mussolini, *Opera omnia* (Florence, 1963), xxix. 81.

[45] Cited by Mosse, 'Fascism and the Avant Garde', in his *Masses and Man*, 230–1; Wohl, *A Passion for Wings*, 288.

[46] Ledeen, *The First Duce*.

Marinetti 'gave me the feeling of the ocean and the machine'. The agitation for war brought them together, and the two cooperated most closely in 1915–19. In 1918 Marinetti founded a political party, *Italia Futurista*, but Mussolini's Fascist Party founded a year later proved more successful. Marinetti was presented as the second candidate, after Mussolini, on the Fascist list for parliament in the elections of 1919. From then on their relations cooled. Marinetti strongly objected to Mussolini's compromises with the monarchy, the church, and the magnates of industry in order to win power, and the two broke with one another. Only in 1924 did Marinetti return to the ranks of the victorious Fascists. Although Mussolini discarded the radical edge of Futurism, and of his own youth, and increasingly preferred d'Annunzio and neo-classicism to artistic avant-garde, Marinetti joined his *Accademia d'Italia*, became secretary of the Union of Fascist Writers, rushed to volunteer for the war in Ethiopia at the age of 60, and remained loyal to the regime to the very end.[47]

Douhet too believed his time had come when the Fascists came to power, and he also would be at least partly disappointed. The new regime, which he had helped build and in which he held a place of honour, stood for vigour, efficiency, modernization, mobilization of the national effort, and the air—all of which he had preached for years. Mussolini made him commissioner of aviation and considered making him secretary of state for the newly constituted air ministry in 1923—the second to be created anywhere. But he decided against it in the end, and Douhet resigned from office after a few months.[48] Maintaining close relations with the regime, he returned to writing on defence matters and propagating the air gospel. As with other right-wingers all over Europe, the First World War only strengthened his conviction that modern war was a total national and industrial affair, requiring concerted effort in peacetime for thoroughly preparing the nation's material infrastructure and cultivating moral cohesion. He now urged

[47] For Marinetti's politics and fascism, see J. Joll, 'F. T. Marinetti: Futurism and Fascism', in his *Three Intellectuals in Politics* (New York, 1965), 133–78; C. Tisdall and A. Bozzolla, *Futurism*, 200–9; J. Davis, 'The Futures Market: Marinetti and the Fascists of Milan', in E. Timms and P. Collier (eds.), *Visions and Blueprints: Avant-Garde Culture and Radical Politics in Early Twentieth-Century Europe* (Manchester, 1988), 82–97; W. Adamson, 'Modernism and Fascism: The Politics of Culture in Italy, 1903–1922', *American Historical Review*, 95 (1990), 359–90; 'Fascism and Culture: Avant-Garde and Secular Religion in the Italian Case', *Journal of Contemporary History*, 24 (1989), 411–35.

[48] Douhet, *La Guerra integrale* (Rome, 1936), p. xv; some correspondence with Mussolini is printed in Monti, *Douhet: scritti inediti*, 238–45; also Cappelluti, 'Douhet', 160.

the creation of a combined ministry of defence to coordinate this effort. Furthermore, he held that modern war was technological and scientific. Very much as Fuller had done, Douhet developed his historical interpretation of the growth of mechanical warfare to be understood in terms of the overall industrialization of Western society. Production had been mechanized and rationalized, and could turn out commodities in mass volume. The railway had transformed military communications. The machine-gun and other mechanical machines of death had been rapidly propagating during the First World War, increasingly taking the place of the traditional arms, cavalry and infantry. The latest advances of science—electricity, gas, and the aeroplane—would soon achieve dominance. War had become the industry and science of destruction, and air power was the weapon of 'integral destruction'. In order to prepare for the future, armed forces had to reduce their personnel while increasing the lethality of weapons, cut down the army and navy, and invest in air and chemical warfare.[49]

It was the publication of the second edition of *The Command of the Air* in 1926 (to which a second part was added, basically repeating the same ideas) that really brought Douhet's vision of air warfare to the forefront of the strategic debate in Italy and won him increasing international celebrity. His *War of the Future* (1928), *The War of 19—* (1930), and many articles in which he answered his critics depicted a future war that was conducted and quickly decided almost entirely from the air by means of strategic bombing.[50] As with Fuller in respect to mechanized land warfare, it was Douhet's radicalism and sweeping vision that captured universal attention and stamped his name on the idea of air warfare, making 'Douhetism' a generic concept. At the same time, this inherent radicalism also often appeared, and later proved to be, fanciful and unrealistic.

It should be noted, for example, that, although Douhet was becoming a national monument and from 1926 was again officially employed by the air ministry to advance the cause of the air in public, his vision of air warfare was far from being fully accepted even by the independent Italian air force. During the late 1920s his writings were often criticized in the service journal *Rivista Aeronautica*, and Douhet, for his part, took

[49] G. Douhet, *La Difesa nazionale* (Rome, 1925).

[50] *Probabili aspetti della guerra futura* (Palermo, 1928); his articles during the last years of his life are reprinted in *Le Profezie di Cassandra* and *La Guerra integrale*; also in the British edn. of *The Command of the Air*.

on his critics with relish.[51] The Regia Aeronautica naturally upheld its independence and favoured the role of strategic bombing, but it did not share Douhet's rejection of fighter aircraft and his dismissal of the role of tactical air support for the army and navy. Under-Secretary and later Secretary of State for the Air, Italo Balbo—who had been maintaining close, warm, and respectful relations with Douhet, whom he treated as the grand old master of air warfare—fought vigorously to increase the allocation for the air force at the expense of the army and navy. He thought, for example, that investment in battleships and aircraft carriers was a waste of money because their roles could be better filled by land-based aircraft. At the same time, however, he held that both the strategic and tactical aspects of air power must have their share in the building of the air force: 'Neither of these theories can be altogether discarded. . . . I think there is virtue in both.' In an article to the *Enciclopedia italiana*, 'Air Warfare', published in 1938 after he had left office, Balbo maintained that, though Douhet was the 'precursor' of a 'new' and 'purely Italian' concept of 'total aerial warfare', whose ideas were discussed worldwide, 'not all of the Italian general's deductions are to be taken literally'. Douhet's theory applied mainly to wars between two industrial powers but not to other sorts of conflicts, such as the Ethiopian War, the Spanish Civil War, or the Sino-Japanese War.[52]

Italo Balbo himself (1896–1940) was an outstanding example of the fascist as airman syndrome. Coming to Milan from his native Ferrara to attend high school, he edited a literary journal just before the war. Like the other young rebels in literary circles, he considered d'Annunzio, who would later become his friend, to be decadent; was fascinated by the aeroplane and by the remarkable feats of the flight pioneers; and took to the streets to agitate for Italy's entry into the First World War. During the later part of the war he served as a storm platoon commander on the Alpine front, becoming involved after the war in nationalist activities both as a journalist and on the streets. He joined the Fascists in 1921, excelled as a blackshirt leader, and after the Fascist seizure of power, he was made governor of Ferrara. In 1926 he was appointed under-secretary for the air, becoming secretary in 1929, a position he held until 1933. Learning to fly in 1927, he personally led the daring

[51] Monti, *Douhet: scritti inediti*, 255 ff.; Douhet, *La Guerra integrale*, 3–70; Cappelluti, 'Douhet', 200–29; Sergè, 'Douhet in Italy'; L. Kennett, *A History of Strategic Bombing* (New York, 1982), 40, 56, 82.

[52] I. Balbo, 'Guerra aerea', in *Enciclopedia italiana*, xviii (Rome, 1938), 92–3; C. Sergè, *Italo Balbo: A Fascist Life* (Berkeley, Calif., 1987), 154–5, 189.

mass flights that earned Italian aviation worldwide renown and made Balbo himself—dashing, charming, and lovable—an international celebrity. His bearded face in flying headgear became a regular feature on the front pages of journals and magazines. In 1928 his group of sixty-one aeroplanes cruised the western Mediterranean. The next year he led thirty-five aeroplanes to the eastern Mediterranean, all the way to Odessa. In 1931 he went much further, crossing the Atlantic to Rio de Janeiro at the head of twelve aircraft. Two years later he led twenty-five aircraft in a double crossing of the Atlantic, to Chicago and back. (Like many Fascists, he was fascinated by American dynamic modernism.)

These flights had a double purpose. They were propaganda feats, intended to foster Fascism's image as an advanced, dynamic, and virile movement; and they were also designed to test the doctrine of strategic bombing. In August 1931 Balbo supervised a week-long, large-scale air manœuvre in which two aerial armies, totalling 860 aeroplanes, were pitted against each other. Mass day and night raids on La Spezia, Ancona, Genoa, Florence, Bologna, and Terni were carried out. The manœuvre was declared a complete success by the air ministry, but the supreme general staff under Marshal Pietro Badoglio was far less enthusiastic, and in the following year's manœuvres the Regia Aeronautica cooperated with the army.[53]

By the early 1930 Balbo wanted to take over Badoglio's position, and it is the platform on which he ran that is of interest to us. He wanted to see the Italian armed forces thoroughly mechanized. In the words of his biographer, 'Balbo was the leading candidate of the "modernists" within the Italian high command, who thought Badoglio, who was not a Fascist, to be 'both militarily and politically too conservative to remain at the head of a revitalized "fascist" military machine'. In a meeting with Mussolini in the summer of 1933, Balbo

> favored reorganizing the armed forces into a series of highly flexible and mobile forces. The army was to be reduced in size to twenty divisions, of which five would be Alpine, five armored, and ten motorized. Balbo viewed the new army as an ensemble of 'expeditionary forces' ready to embark at a moment's notice, primarily by rail or by sea, for Italy's four shores. These units would be well equipped, armed with the latest weapons, and trained in amphibious warfare. The Aeronautica's budget would be quadrupled. . . .[54]

[53] We now have a biography of Balbo in English: Sergè, *Balbo*, esp. 16, 148–9, 182. A contemporary biography which is in itself a document of the fascist mood is R. Italiaander, *Italo Balbo* (Munich, 1942).

[54] Sergè, *Balbo*, 279–80.

Nothing came of Balbo's plans for a military machine based on aircraft and armoured and mechanized formations, if only because it was Balbo, rather than Badoglio, that was replaced by Mussolini. Concerned that Balbo's great popularity might overshadow his own and position Balbo as the Duce's successor (an ambition that was not foreign to Balbo), Mussolini kicked him upward to the post of governor of Libya. Douhet's widow was among those who protested to Mussolini, but to no avail.[55] Later during the 1930s Balbo would wholly oppose Italy's alliance with Germany, adoption of racial policies, and involvement in the Second World War. In 1940 he was mistakenly shot down and killed by Italian gunners when landing in his aircraft in Tobruk.

Balbo's removal from the Regia Aeronautica illustrates the limitations of the Fascist modernist and Futurist rhetoric and the weakening of the movement's revolutionary stance which began once it assumed power. On the symbolic and propagandist level the Fascist affinity with the air was intensely cultivated. The regime financed and boasted of a series of major Italian triumphs in international air races that heightened the country's prestige during the second half of the 1920s. Flying aces like Francesco de Pinedo, Arturo Ferrarin, and Mario de Bernardi set international records for speed and distance flying and won numerous trophies, the Schneider Cup of 1926 being the most prestigious. Between 1927 and 1939 Italians set 110 flight records, and even at the latter date Italians kept thirty-six of the eighty-four records established by the International Aeronautical Federation. The Regia Aeronautica held a special place among the armed forces as the 'Fascist service', and during the first years of his regime Mussolini not only made the air force independent but also increased its budget sevenfold from its insignificant postwar amount. All the same, in budgetary terms the air force remained a poor third, far behind the army and navy. In this respect it was in no better and perhaps even in a slightly worse position than the French and British air forces, claiming only some 15 per cent of the total defence budget. Apart from everything else, Mussolini did not want to alienate the army and navy whose support for his regime was crucial. Only in the late 1930s, as in the other European powers, did appropriations for the Regia Aeronautica grow sharply, overtaking those of the navy in budget share. None the less, Italy's economic and industrial base had all along been much smaller than that of the other great powers. The achievements of pioneering

[55] Ibid. 283.

theorists and innovative designers that had given her a place of honour in the world of aviation could not be sustained for long once the other great powers began to rearm in earnest.[56]

Influence, Echoes, and Parallels

It is not the aim of this study to chart Douhet's 'influence' abroad, which was as ambivalent as it was at home. The fact remains, however, that from the late 1920s in France, Germany, and the Soviet Union—and in the United States even before then—his name and work increasingly came to symbolize the idea of a war-winning 'strategic' air force—whether this idea was accepted, rejected, or somewhere in between, as was most often the case. Translation dates of his books are misleading in this respect. For example, although Douhet's *The Command of the Air* was only translated into German in 1935, by the late 1920s future air warfare had become the hottest stuff on the pages of *Militär-Wochenblatt*, the German army's semi-official journal. It was regularly and intensely discussed, and Douhet's name and ideas were often cited. Prohibited from possessing aeroplanes, the Reichswehr eagerly watched developments abroad. In the mid-1930s the new and independent Luftwaffe was attracted to strategic bombing (albeit as one among several roles) and was paying considerable attention to Douhet's ideas. It was chiefly supply shortages, problems with the production of powerful engines, and the political drive for speedy production of a large number of aircraft that gradually swayed the Luftwaffe away from the heavy bomber.[57]

Things were even more intriguing in respect to the United States. In the spring and summer of 1917, as it entered the war in Europe, the world's most advanced industrial power, in which flight had been pioneered, was seriously looking for the machines and theory of air warfare not only to the *Entente*'s hitherto strongest industrial powers, Britain and France, but also to its least developed partner, Italy. To be sure, from the outset the United States embarked on a huge industrial mobilization that was ultimately planned to supply not only its own air force but also that of her allies. Yet, as the historian of American ideas of air warfare makes clear, 'on 6 April 1917, the American Army did not

[56] Sergè, *Balbo*, esp. 149, 157–66, 182–5.

[57] See E. Homze, *Arming the Luftwaffe* (Lincoln, Nebr., 1976), 34, 51–4, 121–5, 264; R. Overy, 'From Uralbomber to Amerikabomber: The Luftwaffe and Strategic Bombing', *Journal of Strategic Studies*, 1 (1978), 154–78; W. Murray, *Luftwaffe* (Baltimore, 1985), 4–15.

possess a single modern combat aircraft'. Furthermore, before producing aircraft one had to decide what aircraft ought to be produced and for what purposes.

To determine such questions a special Aeronautical Commission, headed by Maj. Raynal C. Bolling, was sent to Europe in June 1917. There its members worked in close cooperation with Lt.-Col. William ('Billy') Mitchell, who had arrived in France in May as an observer to the Allies' air forces and who had assumed the post of chief of the air service, American Expeditionary Forces, in June. Both the Bolling Commission in its report of 15 August and Mitchell's 'General Principles Underlying the Use of the Air Service', issued in the autumn of 1917, saw the air force as playing a double role, both in the tactical zone of operation in direct support of the ground forces and deeper, in 'strategic' bombing. On the whole this conception was modelled on British thoughts and practice at that stage of the war; the Bolling Commission was in touch with the British Air Board, and Mitchell spent a few days visiting the headquarters of Maj.-Gen. Hugh Trenchard, the Royal Air Force Commander in France. Yet the radical edge of the American concept came from contact with the Italians:

As a result of a visit to Italy, the Bolling Commission was evidently favorably impressed with Italian bombing raids against Austria, and the commission recommended that the United States should purchase Caproni biplanes and the license to manufacture Caproni triplanes. . . . Major Edgar S. Gorrell . . . was detailed in charge of the Air Service Technical Section in Paris . . . his studies led him to believe that the United States should purchase or build a sufficiently large number of night bombers to carry out a 'systematic bombardment' of Germany. What the influence of Count Caproni had been on the original Bolling mission report may only be speculative, but in October 1917 both Bolling and Gorrell were in active correspondence with the Italian aircraft manufacturer. Sometime during October, Caproni collaborated with his friend Captain Giulio Douhet in the preparation of a 'Memorandum on the "Air War" for the U.S. Air Service' which urged that mass attacks made at night by long-range Allied bombers against industrial targets deep within Germany and Austria could definitely overwhelm the enemy by substantially reducing his war production at the same time that Allied production was increasing. That same month, Caproni gave Gorrell a little book signed by Nino Salveneschi and entitled *Let Us Kill the War; Let Us Aim At the Heart of the Enemy.* Evidently written by a journalist to represent Caproni's views, this small English-text book was a further exposition of the concept of strategic bombardment. In November 1917, Bolling personally advised Howard Coffin, the Chairman of the Aircraft Production Board in Washington, that the United States ought to give a higher priority to the production and procurement of bomber aircraft than to observation and fighter aircraft . . . the United States initially undertook to manufacture Caproni bombers, but it was also decided to produce British-designed Handley-Page bombers.

By the end of the war, however, very little had come of this strategic plan.[58]

A World War hero, chief of the training and operations group at the headquarters of the postwar United States Army Air Service, and assistant chief of the Service, Billy Mitchell, leading a group of radicals within the Service, became the United States's foremost theorist of air warfare. He won national acclaim for his outspoken public crusade for the air force after the war and eventual trial for violation of military discipline, which resulted in his dismissal from the army. However, while his career so remarkably parallelled that of Douhet, historians and his biographer agree that he developed late as an air theorist, and that the evolution of his thought was crucially influenced (and thoroughly radicalized) by the ideas of Douhet and the Italians.[59]

While the Bolling Commission envisaged an independent status and an independent role for the air force as early as the summer of 1917, Mitchell arrived at that position only from 1919 on, partly under the pressure of the postwar cuts in the armed forces which practically eliminated the air service. During the war neither he nor his fellow American airmen in France ever thought that the air force should become anything other than an auxiliary arm of the army. By the end of the war, Mitchell's only original idea had been for a large-scale paratroop assault beyond the German lines, to be carried out in conjunction with a large tank offensive to end the war.[60] Even as he developed further, Mitchell's views in the immediate postwar period regarding the roles and capabilities of the aircraft initially remained admirably discriminating. He saw that air flight was going to transform

[58] R. F. Futrell, *Ideas, Concepts, Doctrine: A History of Basic Thinking in the United States Air Force, 1907–1964* (Maxwell Air Force, Ala., 1971), 10–14. This is based on the archival research of J. L. Atkinson, 'Italian Influence on the Origins of the American Concept of Strategic Bombardment', *Airpower Historian*, 4 (1957), 141–9. (I have been unable to obtain: Key, 'Some Papers of Count Caproni di Taliedo: Controversy in the Making?', Supplement to *Pegasus* (1955), 7–11.)

[59] A. Hurley, *Billy Mitchell: Crusader for Air Power* (New York, 1964); R. Flugel, 'United States Air Power Doctrine: A Study of the Influence of William Mitchell and Giulio Douhet at the Air Corps Tactical School, 1921–1935' (doctoral dissertation, University of Oklahoma, 1965).

[60] W. Mitchell, *Memoirs of World War I* (New York, 1960), 268–9.

both civil communications and war. He believed that a huge civil and military aeronautical infrastructure would have to be built and co-ordinated. He thought the air force must become an independent service and either have its own independent ministry to advance and protect its interests or work under a unified defence department incorporating all three armed services. He maintained that command of the air would be essential for the operation of the other services and be the first task of the air force. He believed air warfare was going to transform land and sea warfare. Yet he did not view the air force as being able to replace the army and navy. On the ground in particular, army targets were too numerous, diffuse, and capable of concealment for the air force to decide anything by itself. On the sea, large armoured warships had become too vulnerable to aircraft operating from aircraft carriers or from land bases, and their days were over. Much like Richmond and Fuller in Britain, and like eminent American admirals such as William Fullam, William E. Sims, and Bradely Fiske, Mitchell believed that the navy of the future would be composed of aircraft carriers and submarines. The air force itself would consist mostly of pursuit aircraft to protect the American continent and the land and sea theatres of war abroad. The remainder of the force would be divided between observation aircraft belonging directly to the army and navy, attack aircraft, and bombers. This mixture of types and missions was pretty much along the lines common during the later stage of the First World War in Europe. The bombers would constitute only a small part of the air force, although Mitchell believed that mostly night raids on the civil rear would cause massive destruction of cities and would become an integral aspect of future war, a threat to which the United States would not be immune. These were the ideas he developed and propagated, in collaboration with his friends, in a stream of memoranda, testimonies before Congress, and newspaper articles between 1919 and 1921, and incorporated in his book *Our Air Force* (1921).[61] Inevitably, he too had his share of errors and exaggerations, but on the whole his was an impressive forecast of the shape of things to come. Apparently, by this time he had not come into contact with Douhet or the Italians in any significant way, although this was soon to change.

In the winter of 1921/2 Mitchell was sent to Europe at the head of an

[61] *Our Air Force* (New York, 1921); see I. D. Levine *Mitchell: Pioneer of Air Power* (New York 1943), 83, and esp. Hurley, *Mitchell*, 1, 17, 39–55, 58, for his late development; Futrell's excellent *Ideas, Concepts, Doctrine*, 13–21, is particularly good on the opinions in the Air Service around Mitchell.

inspection group on air matters. In his report he described France as the strongest air force and Italy as the weakest. Nevertheless, he singled out the latter as possessing special excellence:

Mitchell knew Caproni and probably saw him again during this visit, but ten years passed before Mitchell ever mentioned having had 'frequent conversations' with Douhet. Mitchell was probably referring to Caproni and Douhet when he reported meeting 'more exceptional ability in Italy than we did in any other country'. . . . If he had heard nothing about *The Command of the Air* while he was in Italy, he nevertheless became aware of its main points a few months later. Lieutenant Colonel A. Guidoni, the Italian Air Attaché in Washington, sent an Italian aviation journal's summary of the book to Air Service Headquarters and to Lester Gardner, the editor of *Aviation* magazine. Gardner discussed the piece with Mitchell, called attention to it in his journal, and planned to publish a translation of the entire book. In a letter to Douhet, Guidoni quoted Gardner as saying that Mitchell was greatly impressed by the ideas of Douhet.[62]

Mitchell's contacts with Douhet and his work must have had a significant share in the transformation and radicalization of his views during the 1920s, which in the end became barely distinguishable from Douhet's. Thus, while Mitchell's *Winged Defence* (1925) mainly repeated the ideas of his *Our Air Force*, it incorporated some new thoughts and contained much more radical overtones. In the preface to the book Mitchell predicted, as Douhet had done, that the battle of attrition on land and at sea would diminish in importance because the air force would mount a direct strategic attack on the enemy's sources of power. He now claimed that air power would prevent and replace the transportation of troops by sea. Like the Italians, he no longer even believed in the aircraft carrier, claiming that it stood little chance against land-based aircraft.[63] In the introduction to his war memoirs, which he prepared for publication in 1926, Mitchell advanced similar views, misleadingly creating the impression that he had held them during the war. Here too he claimed that the struggle of attrition and

[62] Hurley, *Mitchell*, 75, also 76, 81–2; Guidoni's letter to Douhet is printed in Monti, *Douhet: scritti inediti*, 236–7. The translation promised by Gardner never appeared. However, a 5-page extract of *The Command of the Air* was prepared by the War Department Military Intelligence Division on 23 Mar. 1922 and found its way into the files of the Air Service Plans Division. A typescript translation of the first 100 pages of the book was received by the Air Service Field Officers' School on 3 May 1923; see Futrell, *Ideas, Concepts, Doctrine*, 21–2; the case for Douhet's influence on the air force from the late 1920s is made by Flugel, 'United States Air Power Doctrine'.

[63] *Winged Defence* (New York, 1925), esp. pp. xvi, 5–6, 99–138.

total destruction which had characterized the World War would be replaced by a direct, swift, inexpensive, and decisive air strike against the enemy's industrial centres, making extensive use of gas. By the mid-1920s Mitchell, too, had adopted an exclusive vision of air warfare.[64] In 1927, after his dismissal from the army, Mitchell again went on a tour of inspection of European aeronautics. He found all doors open to him, and in Italy his host was Italo Balbo. As in his earlier tour, he reported that the French had the strongest air power in Europe, but 'Italian aviation was in his view even more progressive'.[65] Mitchell repeated his forecast of future war in his *Skyways* (1930).[66] In his journalistic articles during the 1930s he consistently argued that a strategic air offensive from Midway and Alaska was the only effective course open to the United States in a war with Japan. He thought the navy's only contribution would be submarines, and regarded the aircraft carrier as a waste of money.[67]

Britain did not need Douhet or the Italians to adopt the idea of an independent, 'strategic', and even war-winning air force. In the wake of the German raids on London and following the recommendations of a board headed by Jan Christian Smuts, a separate air ministry was created in December 1917, and the world's first independent air force, the RAF, was established in April 1918. From the summer of 1917 the British air force in France under Trenchard was bombing strategic targets in the German rear. Air Minister William Weir and the RAF's Chief of Staff, Frederick Sykes, wanted this to become its principal mission, and Trenchard, Chief of the Air Staff in 1919–29, soon converted to this view and during the interwar period advocated strategic bombing as Britain's most promising strategy. In his *Reformation of War* (1923) Fuller made the aerial bombing of cities, especially with gas, one of the principal features of future warfare, and Liddell Hart copied his ideas for his *Paris* (1925). Later Liddell Hart rightly claimed that he had never heard Douhet's name until he saw his book in French translation in the mid-1930s, and that British thoughts on the use of air power had developed

[64] *Memoirs of World War I*, 4–5. His unjustified claim for hindsight wisdom has not escaped his biographer: Hurley, *Mitchell*, 117. Although based on Hurley, D. MacIsaac's brief reference to Mitchell in 'Voices from the Central Blue: The Air Power Theorists', in P. Paret (ed.), *Makers of Modern Strategy from Machiavelli to the Nuclear Age* (Princeton, NJ, 1986), 631, underestimates Mitchell's transformation during the 1920s.

[65] Hurley, *Mitchell*, 114, citing Mitchell's manuscripts.

[66] (Philadelphia, 1930), 253–70.

[67] Hurley, *Mitchell*, 122–3.

independently.[68] All the same, as some historians have noted, active public enthusiasm for the air in interwar Britain was disproportionately associated with the radical right.

Thus the seemingly mysterious 'second career' of T. E. Lawrence, 'Lawrence of Arabia', who in the 1920s first joined the Tank Corps and then the RAF under the pseudonyms 'Aircraftman Ross' and 'Private Shaw', is incomprehensible when separated from the intellectual outlook which brought it about. Lawrence stood on the fringes of and had a special status in radical British right-wing culture. Like the Italian Futurists, not only did he see the aeroplane, the fast motorcycle (on which he eventually died in a road accident), and the fast motor-boat (which he tested for the RAF) as exhilarating instruments of speed and a source of emotional elation; for him they, and especially the aeroplane, opened new frontiers and new horizons. The few who were engaged with the aeroplane were the heroic pioneers of a new age. As he told a friend, the air was 'the only first-class thing that our generation has to do. So everyone should either take to the air themselves or help it forward.' He joined where he believed the great drama of the future was unfolding.[69] As David Edgerton has written in his interesting study *England and the Aeroplane*: 'It is important to note the aristocratic basis of these ideas . . . "reactionary modernist" feeling was very widespread in the interwar years.'[70]

Edgerton's survey of some of the radical right-wing enthusiasts for the air runs as follows:

> Rear-Admiral Murray Sueter, a leading wartime naval aviator, was elected to Parliament as a candidate of Lord Rothermere's Anti-Waste League and Horatio Bottomley's Independent Parliamentary Group in 1921. He remained in the House as a Conservative until 1945, being knighted in 1934. His name crops up in all the main pro-air and pro-German organizations of the late 1930s. . . . Colonel the Master of Sempill was a senior member of the Air League, the Anglo-German Fellowship and the Link. He entered the House of Lords in the 1930s as Baron Sempill, and in 1939 was one of the hard core of German enthusiasts who urged publicly for peace with Germany from the Lords. But

[68] Fuller, *The Reformation of War*, 136–51; B. H. Liddell Hart, *Paris* (London, 1925), 41–62; for the interwar period, see mainly R. Higham, *The Military Intellectuals in Britain: 1918–1939* (New Brunswick, NJ, 1966), 119–259; H. Montgomery Hyde, *British Air Policy between the Wars* (London, 1976); M. Smith, *British Air Strategy between the Wars* (Oxford, 1984), esp. 64–6.

[69] Edgerton, *England and the Aeroplane*, 46; Wohl, *A Passion for Wings*, 1; and for Lawrence and the radical right, Susser, 'Fascist and Anti-Fascist Attitudes in Britain', 145–57.

[70] Edgerton, *England and the Aeroplane*, 46.

the most politically important pro-German peer after 1935 was Lord Londonderry, Secretary of State for Air, 1931–1935. He was a member of the Anglo-German Fellowship, but while still friendly to Germany was not a member of the Link. . . . Lord Rothermere was a particularly enthusiastic promoter of aviation in the interwar years . . . he had been Britain's first Secretary of State for Air, though he did not stay in the job long. . . . He called for an 'Air Dictator' to take control of aircraft production. . . . In 1935 Rothermere created a National League of Airmen, which was active in the General Elections of that year, though it was supposedly non-political. It was headed by Norman Macmillan, Fairey's test pilot, and had among its supporters the Duke of Westminster, Major-General Fuller and Admirals Sir Murray Sueter and Mark Kerr. . . . Rothermere's air campaign was part of a larger imperialist programme which was deeply hostile to the League of Nations. In the early 1930s he briefly supported Oswald Mosley and his British Union of Fascists, and his abandoning of Mosley did not make him any less a figure of the hard Right. It was not just ultra-right politics which they had in common. Mosley had flown for the RFC in the war, and saw in aircraft that combination of modern science and the Faustian, heroic spirit which was so central to his idea of the 'Modern Movement'. Mosley formed Fascist flying clubs in 1934. Several historians have noted that aviators formed a disproportionate element in the membership of the British Union of Fascists. . . . The connection between fascist politics and aviation in the interwar years may be considered at the level of lesser personalities too. A. V. Roe was a prominent financial and moral supporter of Mosley. Lady Houston, the wealthy widow of a Liverpool shipowner and Tory MP, was very well known as a pro-Italian fascist through her *Saturday Review*. . . . She did not at first like the Nazis but changed her mind in 1936. . . . Lady Houston is still remembered as the generous benefactress of the famous 1931 Schneider Trophy Race. This was not her only benefaction: she offered to give almost £200,000 to the British Union of Fascists and attempted to give equally large sums to the nation for the air defence of London.[71]

Richard Griffiths, also emphasizing the Fascists' special connection with aviation, adds other names to the list: 'the Secretary-General and the Secretary of the Air League, Air Commodore J. A. Chamier and Colonel Norman Thwaites, were members of the [fascist] January Club, the latter (who was editor of the journal *Air*) becoming its chairman in late 1934.' From the pages of *Aeroplane* which he edited from 1911 to 1939, C. G. Grey eulogized Nazi Germany, hailed her re-armament and the creation of the Luftwaffe, believed she defended Europe against communism, and called Britain to ally with her and

[71] Ibid. 47–9.

abandon France, 'essentially a feminine nation'.[72] On the whole, according to Edgerton, Winston Churchill's position, enthusiastically supporting air armament but opposing the 'active pro-German, pro-aviation Right' was 'a lonely one'. By the late 1930s even someone like Bertrand Russell, who had not hovered into or close to the fascist orbit, echoed Wells, d'Annunzio, Marinetti, Fuller, and Lawrence:

> We seem now, through the aeroplane, to be returning to the need for forces composed of comparatively few highly trained men. It is to be expected, therefore, that the form of government, in every country exposed to serious war, will be such as airmen will like, which is not likely to be democracy.[73]

It is this conclusion that we he have encountered again and again all over Europe. Those who expected a new fascist age were also the most enthusiastic for the aeroplane and for flying. Antoine de Saint-Exupéry, France's most famous airman-novelist during the interwar period, escaped this syndrome, even though he shared much of the spiritual yearning that led many of his friends to fascism. It has been charged that his 'code of hardship, duty, discipline, and sacrifice made him susceptible to the ideal of Airman-as-Fascist'. However, his conception of the flying machine was essentially developed in a 'Christian, pacifist, humane' direction. By contrast, his good friend and fellow pilot, Jean Mermoz, became vice-president of the fascist *Croix de Feu*.[74] In the late 1920s and early 1930s, like many others, the most prominent pioneer of modernist architecture in Europe, Le Corbusier (1887–1965), was moving from syndicalism towards semi-fascism and fascism in the *Redressement Français* and *planisme*, editing the journals of this vein *Plans* and *Prélude*. Like those movements, he was inspired by the French Utopian Socialists and impressed by Taylorism. He held that the modern technological republic of producers, interconnected in complex economic and urban systems, could only be hierarchic and rationally run by a paternalistic, authoritarian, technocratic élite, for which Le Corbusier planned grandiose skyscrapers, centred in his designed modernist metropolises. He believed a harmonious Second Machine Age was coming, replacing the First, which had been divisive and fuelled by greed and which had collapsed with the Great Depression. Increasingly anti-democratic, Le Corbusier dedicated his book *La Ville radieuse* (1935) 'To Authority'. During the Second World War he

[72] R. Griffiths, *Fellow Travellers of the Right* (London, 1980), 137–40.

[73] Edgerton, *England and the Aeroplane*, 46, 49.

[74] L. Goldstein, *The Flying Machine and Modern Literature* (London, 1986), 139–44.

looked in vain to Vichy to realize his modernist urban plans. In his introduction to his photo album *Aircraft* (1935) he described the aeroplane as 'the advance guard of the conquering armies of the New Age', the age of the 'machine' or 'mechanical civilization', of which the automobile was another symbol. He, too, traced his first encounter with the aeroplane to Paris in 1909.[75] As we shall see, the war hero, famous writer, and modernist right-wing radical Ernst Jünger wrote in the same vein in Germany. Finally, although Nazi Germany was a latecomer to aviation and far more ambiguous in its attitude to modernity than Italian Fascism, the Nazi mystique of the air and the role of the Luftwaffe in the regime's political liturgy were as prominent as they were in Fascist Italy, and with far more powerful industrial muscle to back them.

[75] See esp. R. Fishman, *Urban Utopias in the Twentieth Century: Ebenezer Howard, Frank Lloyd Wright, and Le Corbusier* (New York, 1977), 213–52; Le Corbusier, *Aircraft* (New York, 1988, original 1935), 5–13.

4

German Right-Wing Radicalism, Strategic Adventurism, and Mechanized Warfare

Any discussion of German fascism is inevitably dominated by Nazism, whose long shadow falls across modern German, Western, and world history. Yet the National Socialist Party and its fanatical leader, Adolf Hitler, only became a significant political force in Germany at the outset of the 1930s, when complex and somewhat conjunctural circumstances brought them into power and gave them the means to play out on such a grand scale their gruesome part in history. To be sure the party expressed and throve on deep and powerful currents within German national and political culture; but that precisely also meant that it had begun as only one element within a much wider phenomenon. Drawing on even earlier national traditions, German right-wing radicalism had been taking shape from the late nineteenth century, with the advent of mass society in the wake of Germany's industrialization.

The growth of the popular radical right in Germany before the First World War as a cultural and political force mixing nostalgic, *völkisch*, and pessimistic sentiments with modernist and vitalist notions, is fairly recognized and needs no elaboration here. Within the armed services, officers like Colamr von der Goltz, Friedrich von Bernhardi, August Keim, Erich Ludendorff, and Alfred Tirpitz spoke and acted for those among their civilian and military peers who sought ways of overcoming and exploiting the modern condition, which the traditional ruling and official classes had long viewed with alarm and despair. Skilfully using such modern devices as the media and mass popular movements, they wished to bridge class divisions and mobilize the masses behind the state in a new popular and nationalist unity. While the First World War brought about, under Ludendorff's orchestration, an unprecedented degree of social and industrial mobilization, it was widely believed in right-wing circles that Germany had ultimately lost the war because that degree had not been high enough. As with the Prussian reformers a century earlier, who had faced similar conditions of defeat and national humiliation, the need to create a modern *Volksgemeinschaft* (which might be imperfectly translated as 'popular national community') was widely regarded in these circles by officers and civilians alike as essential for Germany's military and political regeneration. It was also viewed as necessary for the survival and rejuvenation of her traditional élite's ethos, self-identity, and hold over the state under modern conditions.

Within the Reichswehr the generation that had been born during the last two decades of the nineteenth century, served as junior and middle-rank officers in the First World War, and was now rising into higher positions was generally inclined towards this view.[1] The more radical element of this generation aspired to a new, modern, totalitarian regime that would maximize the nation's cohesion, boost its morale and harness its resources for power politics and war. It was mostly these people that were particularly susceptible to, and active in implementing, radical visions of mechanized warfare. Not for the first time in her history, modernization was urged on Germany by the need to meet the demands of war. The Reichswehr as a whole, like all parts of the Reich's traditional élite, lent its more or less qualified support to Hitler's rise to power in the hope that he would bring the support of the masses, rejuvenate the nation, and undo Versailles. But within the Reichswehr the radicals were his most enthusiastic supporters.

Jünger: Machine Warfare and Machine Societies

Before turning to serving regular officers of the Reichswehr and Wehrmacht, one might start with one of their peers who had left the army after the First World War as a war hero to become a best-selling author and one of Germany's most distinguished writers of the twentieth century. From his youth Ernst Jünger (b. 1895) rebelled against his bourgeois background, searching for adventure, action, and purpose. At 17 he ran away from home to join the French Foreign Legion, only to be returned from North Africa on his parents' request. Fortunately for him, the war came soon after. He enlisted, underwent basic training, and served at the front for one month before being sent for officer training. Returning to the front in 1916, he was wounded seventeen times, four times critically, and was awarded the *Pour le Mérite*,

[1] See most notably M. Geyer, *Aufrüstung oder Sicherheit: Die Reichswehr in der Krise der Machtpolitik, 1924–1936* (Wiesbaden, 1980).

Germany's highest decoration. During the last year of the war he trained and commanded a platoon and a company of élite storm troops, participating in some of the fiercest battles of that year. He was among the few selected to remain in the small Reichswehr after the war, and contributed to the infantry sections of the German post-war field-service manual, *Führung und Gefecht der verbundenen Waffen*. His *In Stahlgewittern*, *Storm of Steel* (1920), based on his war diaries and describing his front-line experience, immediately made him famous, running through several editions during the 1920s. In 1923 Jünger left the army to start a career as a radical right-wing writer.[2]

Like Erich Maria Remarque, Robert Graves, Siegfried Sassoon, and other late-1920s authors in the war literature genre, Jünger described the trench warfare experience in a factual, quasi-realistic style. But the similarity ends here. Theirs would fundamentally be a liberal–pacifist attitude, evoking fear, exhaustion, horror, misery, brutalization, degradation, mutilation, disgust, and purposelessness. But for Jünger war was an exhilarating experience approached with relish, an opportunity to master fear and transcend bodily limits, the ultimate virile sport, a supreme fulfilment of one's self.[3] His unquestioned personal heroism aside, Jünger's attitude, like theirs, only acquires its meaning when seen in terms of his wider world-view, which he set out to develop in his later books.

In his extended essay *The Battle as Inner Experience* (1922), Jünger analysed the psychological qualities and emotions involved in battle. He also presented war as 'the father of all things', a force of crucial moral, historical, and social significance.[4] Three years later came his third war book, *Copse 125*. This he also based on his war memoirs, this time from a small section of the Western Front facing the British from the end of June to mid-July 1918. The memoirs, however, were intertwined with his reflections on the war, on war in general, and on what it stood for. Mostly, these reflections were of the all too familiar stuff of the German idealist and nationalist tradition, mixed with the influence of Nietzsche and Spengler, and they can be briefly summarized. War was the ultimate

[2] On Jünger, see esp. J. P. Stern, *Ernst Jünger* (New Haven, Conn., 1953); H.-P. Schwarz, *Der konservative Anarchist: Politik und Zeitkritik Ernst Jüngers* (Freiburg, 1962); G. Loose, *Ernst Jünger* (New York, 1974); J. Herf, *Reactionary Modernism* (Cambridge, 1984), 70–108.

[3] *In Stahlgewittern* (1920), reprinted in his *Sämtliche Werke*, i (1978); trans. as *Storm of Steel: From the Diary of a German Storm-Troop Officer on the Western Front* (New York, 1929).

[4] *Der Kampf als inneres Erlebnis*, reprinted in *Sämtliche Werke*, vii (1980).

moral and spiritual test for the greatness of a nation and for the ideas it represented. It was nature's way of selection, and the cleanser of internal weakness, corruption, and decadence for which economic or cultural competition could never substitute:

> We have never stopped it and never shall, because war is not the law of one age or civilization, but of eternal nature itself, out of which every civilization proceeds, and into which it must sink again if it is not hard enough to withstand the iron ordeal. For this reason those who seek to abolish war . . . a belated rearguard of an enlightenment . . . are the real pest of civilization though they have it always on their lips. . . . May they ever be a laughing-stock to the youth of our land . . . let us be hard and merciless on ourselves and on others.

According to Jünger, the First World War should have been fought until the end, rejecting any compromise. The defeat was only a breathing-space before the next struggle.[5]

But what form would the next war take and, hence how to prepare for it? Here Jünger had novel things to say. In the first place it would be machine war. *In Stahlgewittern* had already conveyed the notion that man was now operating under a 'storm of steel', within an overpowering *Materialschlacht*, in a new machine war epoch. In this world natural and artificial were mixed.[6] This notion was radically developed in 'The Technique of Future Battle', an article which Jünger published in October 1921 in *Militär-Wochenblatt*, the army's semi-official journal, and incorporated—further developed and expanded—in *Copse 125*.[7] He wrote that the spring of 1918 saw the fully fledged appearance of mechanized warfare. From then on,

> the theory of mobile war was gaining the upper hand and soon to be seen in action. With this arises the question of the further development of war. . . . What this war emphasizes again and again as the new and decisive factor is the entry of the machine into battle and the corresponding retirement of purely manual work. Of our three main arms, to which aviation was added as a fourth, two, infantry and cavalry . . . were wholly occupied in what I call manual work in distinction from machine work. Of these two, the cavalry will soon disappear altogether from the field of battle . . . The infantry will, perhaps, hold out

[5] *Copse 125: A Chronicle from the Trench Warfare of 1918* (London, 1930), 56–7, and similarly pp. viii–xii, 128, 181–4; the German original, *Das Wäldchen 125* (1925), is reprinted in *Werke*, i.

[6] See interestingly B. Hüppauf, 'The Birth of Fascist Man from the Spirit of the Front', in J. Milford (ed.), *The Attraction of Fascism: Social Psychology and Aesthetics of the 'Triumph of the Right'* (New York, 1990), 45–76.

[7] 'Die Technik der Zukunftsschlacht', *Militär-Wochenblatt* [*M–W*], 1 Oct. 1921, 287–90.

longer; but it, too, is threatened by a process of disintegration that has begun already. . . . As mobility increases, the exaggerated importance of artillery will fall away.[8]

As Jünger stated: 'The machine is more powerful than muscle':[9]

we shall have to break away from the idea of a massed attack in its old form . . . It is a question no longer of launching men in mass but machines . . . The solid earth, in default of roads, and with its changing contours, presents greater difficulties to the passage of machines than do the air and the sea, where the machine has finally established itself in the picture of war. But the peace-time invention of the motor-plough and the war-time one of the tank have made the first steps in overcoming these difficulties.[10]

Sea warfare 'where the mechanical problem came long ago and decisively to the front', serves as the best guide to the future of land war, though the latter will probably favour smaller machines.[11]

the tank is the most important invention of a war rich in contrivances, though it will not perhaps in this war reach by a long way its final stage. . . . Mobility, fire and cover are combined in it . . . For this reason and other too, in its further development it is bound to be the decisive engine of the battle of to-morrow with all other arms as its mere accompaniment.

Jünger went on to speculate that the development of the tank might be followed in the future by the development of flying tanks.[12] Scientific and technological innovation was moving fast, and now counted the most:

It is scarcely to be expected that European nations whose civilization proceeds from one mighty source will encounter one another with radically different methods of war, as in the case for example of the Spaniards and the Aztecs. But there will, all the same, be ideas in the air, such as the automatic steering of aeroplanes or wireless telephony, that one side will develop more quickly than the other. And it can never be foreseen what surprises of deadly nature may be expected. . . . It is precisely in a short war that such surprises are the more dangerous.[13]

Partly for that reason, the technological age will make armies not only mechanical but smaller, placing the emphasis on the most modern advancements of science and the most sophisticated and agile forms of organization:

[8] Copse 125, 4, 128–9, 133. [9] Ibid. 131. [10] Ibid. 130.
[11] Ibid. 130–1. [12] Ibid. 132–3. [13] Ibid. 136–7.

sheer mass, whether of men or material, will have little influence on the outcome of a war such as we are considering. . . . We see every day in all branches of industry how a new miracle of mind, fused into steel, abolishes at a stroke all that has gone before. . . . Why should it be otherwise in war? No, an army, too, in its entirety, is more than ever before a machine in which cog grips cog and every ounce of energy is transmitted to the driving belt of the attack. . . . For this an instrument is required so highly polished and fraught with spirit that the notion of mass is utterly foreign to it.[14]

These ideas, concepts, and general outlook, indeed the phrases themselves, ring all too familiar. In this author's opinion, their near one-to-one similarity to Fuller's is no coincidence. By 1921, when Jünger wrote the original article on the technique of future battle, he may have read Fuller's *Tanks in the Great War* (1920), either in English or in a German translation made at an unknown date during the 1920s and circulated in the Reichswehr in typescript for internal use. He also may have read Fuller's Gold Medal essay, published in the RUSI journal the year before. From 1924, as Jünger further developed the theme of mechanized warfare for *Copse 125*, Fuller's ideas, mainly through his disciple Liddell Hart, were prominently reviewed in *Militär-Wochenblatt*. Thus, like Liddell Hart, Jünger may have owed his conversion from an infantry specialist to a proponent of mechanized war to Fuller's influence.[15] In any event, already a right-wing radical himself, Jünger now worked out independently the wider social implications of machine warfare and, like Fuller, was soon to expand from the military field to consider the character of the machine epoch as a whole. In *Copse 125* he wrote:

[14] Ibid. 134.

[15] For translated copies of Fuller's *Tanks in the Great War*, see Bundesarchiv-Militärarchiv, Freiburg im Breisgau [BA-MA Freiburg], 8/v. 1745 and 1939. Liddell Hart's article 'The Next Great War' was abstracted as the opening piece of *M–W*, 25 July 1924, 713–15, after having been briefly reviewed on 5 May, ibid. 578. His 'The Development of a "New Model" Army' was briefly reviewed in *M–W*, 11 Nov. 1924, 501, and recommended for translation. On 18 Dec. 1924 another opening piece in *M–W*, 649–51, described the new thoughts in Britain of replacing the muscle armies by machine ones, leading to an all-armoured army and a reduction of 60% in manpower. Fuller was cited in the journal here and there, e.g. 15 Apr. 1924, 531. Jünger contributed an article on infantry tactics on 10 Aug. 1923, 51. Kurt Hesse wrote about him on 15 Mar. 1924, 451. Jünger's books were prominently advertised in the journal. His only divergence from Fuller's views in respect to future mechanized warfare was his belief that gas would lose its importance: *Copse 125*, 133–4. See also my *British Armour Theory and the Rise of the Panzer Arm: Revising the Revisionists* (London, 2000).

I hate democracy as I do the plague—besides, the democratic ideal of an army would be one consisting entirely, not of Fahnenjunker, but of officers with lax discipline and great personal liberty. For my taste on the contrary, and for that of young Germans in general to-day, an army could not be too iron, too dictatorial, and too absolute—but if it is to be so, then there must be a system of promotion that is not sheltered behind any sort of privilege but opened up to the keenest competition.

In addition, old barriers must come down so that officers could get in touch with their men in order to feel their pulse, inspire them, and enhance solidarity.[16] The intention was clear: old-fashioned conservative Prussianism would not do either, for it, too, had become obsolete and out of step with the needs of the modern age:

We young Germans would be the last to reject Prussianism so far as its moral side goes. We know well that the inspired and practical founders of it had an unsurpassed wisdom in setting men to a job. They built up a machine that worked economically, exactly, and reliably, and one that could inspire enthusiasm in spite of bleak outlines, because its aim was not self but the greatness of the country . . . generation after generation was reinforced by this will of steel. . . . But it is no longer in tune with our time nor with an army composed as ours is, nor with the resources that decide a battle of to-day.[17]

What was needed in the machine age was the fusion of men and machines into an integrated whole—modern, machine-like animated military and social bodies. Like Marinetti and the Futurists, Jünger did not hold that this fusion devaluated man. On the contrary, he glorified it as a new and enhanced opportunity for man to thrive, spiritually, morally, and aesthetically. It was towards this point of view that he strove to stir the German nationalist right, within which conservatism and a general fear of modernity had always been prominent elements:

where does the common man come in in all this? Is not all this a soulless and crushing business? A cold exalting of mechanical forces, an array of formulae in physics, chemistry, and the higher mathematics? Is this to be the test of life? Is it not giving the intellect and big business the mastery of the earth? . . . This is the question put now and then by the cultured German who prizes Weimar above Essen, and by the soldier too when he sees the instincts of the hero subdued to the technique of war. . . . But what do we, the coming generation, care for all this? . . . Every civilization has been great in creations that can be set

[16] *Copse 125*, 83.

[17] Ibid. 158–60; also 'Die Technik der Zukunftsschlacht' (1921), 289–90.

beside our own, but the machine is what we ourselves have created and we have a right to be proud of it . . . is it not we ourselves who stand behind it? Is it not our life and our blood that provide its impulse? . . . Good equipment is prized only by people whose virile nerve is still vigorous.[18]

Experience proves that the best warriors are produced by the most advanced industrial nations—the French, the British, and, above all, the Germans:

it is the man of Central Europe by whom the best machines are made, that also stand up for them best when they are in operation. The hardiest sons of the war, the men who led the storm-troops, and manipulate the tank, the aeroplane and the submarine are pre-eminent in technical accomplishment . . . accustomed to serve the machine and yet its superior at the same time.[19]

Modern power stemmed from society as a whole. If the army was to become 'a machine in which cog grips cog and every ounce of energy is transmitted to the driving belt', if it was 'to weld the pick of human and mechanical energy into one whole of such tempered force',[20] then so must society as a whole. A new machine-age society was in the making. How would it look like? *Copse 125* offered only glimpses. Like the army, it would be authoritarian, disciplined, meritocratic, and highly co-ordinated and cohesive. Like the army, it would be psychologically manipulated:

It is an important task of modern psychology to study these spheres of activity that invisibly and yet powerfully permeate the mass and magnetize it into changing formations like a heap of iron filings. There are laws here whose workings must be explored. . . . [It is] a very simple resource that must be put at the disposal of the leader as part of his equipment. For we must learn to practice a kind of demagogy from above . . .[21]

These again were the ideas of mass psychology that so fascinated anti-liberal radicals throughout the West, including Jünger's friend, the military writer Kurt Hesse. In any event, like Fuller, Jünger now turned to analyse the historical growth and central features of the coming machine age—in war and, increasingly, in society as a whole.

In his article 'Fire and Movement' (1930) Jünger traced the development of warfare in the fast-changing mechanical era since the nineteenth century. The growth of fire-power had been progressively paralysing armies, a process already apparent in the wars in South

[18] Ibid. 138–9. [19] Ibid. 48. [20] Ibid. 134. [21] Ibid. 173–4.

Africa and Manchuria and reaching its zenith on the Western Front during the First World War. Aircraft and, more importantly for land battle, the tank then revived movement on the battlefield, heralding a new machine age.[22] In another article written in the same year, 'Total Mobilization', Jünger traced the development of national war mobilization from the French Revolution to its logical conclusion in modern society. The production programmes of the latter part of the First World War, most impressively the massive American cooperation between army and industry, and, further still, the Soviet Five-Year Plan, showed the way towards a new centralized and planned economy. In disciplined societies and electrified cities of millions, transport systems, plants, engines, and aeroplanes were now intertwined with men into one complex which was working towards one goal. Following the wars of the knights, kings, and citizens successively, the twentieth century ushered in the war of the workers (*Arbeiter*), a special concept denoting functionaries and technocrats at all levels of a hierarchic organism, the human cogs of the new machine society.[23]

Jünger outlined the features of the new society in his next book, *The Worker* (*Der Arbeiter*, 1932). He claimed that humanity was about to enter a new age. The era of the bourgeois Third Estate would soon be superseded by that of the worker, as liberal democracy developed and evolved into the working state (*Arbeitsstaat*). The former had only the appearance of mastery and control which in reality hid internal divisions, lack of purpose, petty individualism, and moral weakness. By contrast, the latter would embody integral and cohesive power, replacing both the amorphous masses and the individualistic bourgeoisie. In the worker a new human type and a new social ethics would come into being—sturdy, 'post-critical', unreflectively dedicated to its mission—expressing the new *Arbeitsstaat*, in which everything was mobilized in peace and in war within a comprehensive working programme. Military mobilization, born in the age of the bourgeoisie, would now grow into total labour mobilization. Again, the Soviet Five-Year Plan showed the way to the future, though Jünger was not a Marxist internationalist.[24]

[22] 'Feuer und Bewegung' (1930), repr. in Jünger, *Werke*, vii. 107–17.

[23] Jünger, 'Die Totale Mobilmachung' (1930), repr. ibid. 121–42; see esp. 127–9. It was in reference to Jünger's work that Walter Benjamin first developed his interpretation of fascism as the aestheticization of politics, war, and technology—each becoming its own end—which he later applied to Marinetti: 'Theorien des deutschen Faschismus', in *Walter Benjamin: Gesammelte Schriften*, iii (Frankfurt, 1977), 238–50; trans. in *New German Critique*, 6 (1979), 120–8.

[24] *Der Arbeiter* (1932) is reprinted as vol. viii of his *Werke* (1981).

Jünger's literary career was matched by his intense public involvement in radical right-wing organizations. He participated in *Freikorps* activities during the early 1920. After his release from the army he exalted the nationalist saboteurs operating against the French occupation of the Ruhr: 'the men who are in love with dynamite'.[25] He became involved with the *Stahlhelm*, the largest ex-servicemen right-wing, anti-republic, anti-democratic, and anti-communist organization, to whose paper, *Die Standarte*, he regularly contributed agitating pieces. When the paper was closed down by the government, he helped to establish another right-wing paper, *Arminius*. At first, Jünger praised Hitler's nascent movement and sent him dedicated copies of his war books. Hitler reciprocated with a copy of *Mein Kampf* and in 1927 offered Jünger a National Socialist seat in the Reichstag, which he declined. Like the Italian Futurists in respect to Fascism, Jünger deplored any compromise with the existing order, disapproved of Hitler's decision to adopt legal methods, and feared that he was following in Mussolini's footsteps. In the way it had developed, Jünger now regarded Italian Fascism as no more than 'a late form of liberalism . . . Fascism is little suited to Germany as Bolshevism'. By the early 1930s Jünger became associated with a small group known as the 'National Bolsheviks'. This group sought to synthesize nationalism and planned centralized economy and society in a sort of 'Prussian socialism', and supported the cooperation with the Soviet Union against the West which was then reaching its zenith.[26] When the Nazis came to power, he remained aloof from politics—as the Futurists in Italy had initially done—regarding National Socialist rule as vulgar and plebeian, a caricature of his vision of a vigorous and cohesive modern machine society. Unlike the Italian Futurists, he retained his aloofness up to the end of the National Socialist regime. However, other right-wing radicals took a different attitude.

Indeed, this is one reason why Jünger merits our attention at such length. Although a writer of national reputation, he had little practical influence either inside or outside the army. Nevertheless, in his work the historian of ideas can find, developed in literary form, *all* the dominant themes also espoused by others, who wrote less but who were more strategically positioned and more closely involved with the practical affairs of army and state. General Werner von Blomberg

[25] Quoted in Stern, *Jünger*, 10.

[26] Schwarz, *Jünger*, 97–130; A. Hamilton, *The Appeal of Fascism* (London, 1971), 122–4.

(1878–1946) and Colonel Walter von Reichenau (1884–1942)—both future field marshals—accepted by Hitler in 1933 as war minister and chief of the ministerial office respectively, are the most prominent examples.

The Army Modernists and the Nazis

In discussing the army's attitude towards the National Socialist rise to power and regime, historians have emphasized the difference between Blomberg and Reichenau, on the one hand, and the rest of the army's high command, in particular Generals Fritsch and Beck, the army's commander-in-chief and chief of the General Staff, on the other.[27] What was this difference? After all, as mentioned earlier, the wide consensus in the Reichswehr welcomed the new regime. On the whole the Reichswehr's leadership was anti-democratic and anti-republican, and it stood for the reinstatement of Germany as a great power. Its members hoped Hitler would be able to begin rearmament and foster the desired *Volksgemeinschaft*. Still, historians agree, the army's high command was mostly composed of conservative-nationalists, heirs to the old Prussian tradition, however modified, whereas Blomberg and Reichenau represented something new and radical. Though also belonging to the right side of the political spectrum, theirs was the sort of right that conservatives found suspect. This difference predated the National Socialist rise to power. It consistently found expression in attitudes towards the army's role in the new National Socialist state, operational planning for war, and mechanized warfare.

Chief of the Reichswehr's disguised general staff (*Truppenamt*) in 1927–9, Blomberg had always been somewhat suspect to the majority of his peers. As the later Field Marshal Gerd von Rundstedt, a quintessential representative of the old army, would testify in Nurenberg: 'Blomberg was always somewhat strange to us; he hovered in other spheres. He adhered to Steiner's way, somewhat theosophic and so on. No one really liked him.'[28] But Blomberg, a cultured man of many interests with a lively mind, was suspect not only for his attraction to

[27] The standard books on the subject are J. Wheeler-Bennett, *The Nemesis of Power: The German Army in Politics, 1918–1945* (New York, 1967); R. O'Neill, *The German Army and the Nazi Party, 1933–1939* (London, 1966); K.-J. Müller, *Das Heer und Hitler: Armee und nationalsozialistisches Regime, 1933–1940* (Stuttgart, 1969); M. Messerschmidt, *Die Wehrmacht im NS-Staat: Zeit der Indoktrination* (Hamburg, 1969).

[28] Quoted in Müller, *Das Heer und Hitler*, 51.

the spiritual. Ever since the 1920s he had been searching for unorthodox ways of breaking out of the post-war mould which perpetuated Germany's military and political submission. As a leading historian of the Reichswehr in the 1920s has shown, in 1924–5, following the French occupation of the Ruhr, the then Head of the Operations Branch (T1) of the general staff, Colonel Joachim von Stülpnagel, advanced schemes for a war of national liberation, based on a sweeping popular uprising against the invaders. It would intensify the campaign of sabotage and civil resistance already taking place into a wide-scale, semi-regular, and guerrilla war of total patriotic commitment, which would engulf the whole nation. This concept was wholly at odds with that of the army's commander-in-chief (*Chef der Heeresleitung*), the conservative Hans von Seeckt. Like the schemes of the radical, modernizing Prussian reformers after Jena for popular insurrection against French rule, Stülpnagel's plan went beyond the regular army and regular warfare and presupposed total social mobilization. As in Napoleon's time, it promised to be ruinous for the country and possessed dubious prospects of success. In any event, Stülpnagel's ideas were shared by Blomberg, then head of the training branch (T4), later head of the operations branch, and, finally, chief of the General Staff. In the late 1920s, in case of war against a French–Polish coalition, Blomberg devised a two-tiered idea, based on total popular resistance and swift mobile operations. War games and manœuvres held in 1928–9 to test the plan demonstrated that it had little chance of success. War Minister Wilhelm Gröner, working for a *rapprochement* with the republic, declared it hopeless. But Blomberg continued to advocate radical operational schemes. In 1935, with the German army only at the very beginning of its expansion, he initiated a study in the war ministry on the possibility of a swift war of movement to overwhelm Czechoslovakia before France or the Soviet Union could come to her support. The initiative was blocked by Chief of the General Staff Beck, who protested strongly against the encroachment on his professional domain, arguing at the same time that the idea was strategically impractical. None the less, the ministry returned to raise similar ideas in 1937.[29]

Blomberg's radical operational schemes went hand in hand with

[29] M. Geyer, *Aufrüstung oder Sicherheit*. For the Czechoslovakian issue in 1935 and 1937, see also K.-J. Müller, *General Ludwig Beck: Studien und Dokumente* (Boppard a.m., 1980), 226–31, 240–5, 440–4.

radicalism in two attendant fields: the socio-political and the technological. Starting with the former, if popular national war was to be waged, absolute cohesion and patriotic dedication on the part of the people, a true *Volksgemeinschaft*, had to be achieved. To be sure, many in the army wanted that, but not everybody was prepared to go to the same length or to pay the price for it. Most members of the army's high command also wanted to preserve as much as possible of the Prussian conservative tradition, the status of the old élites, and their own self-identity. By contrast, Blomberg—and Reichenau—rejected a great deal of this as anachronistic, and were willing to look for wholly new and modern forms of social order to achieve the goal of national cohesion, efficiency, and power.[30] During the 1920s the techniques of either Bolshevism or fascism seemed capable of achieving these ends, with the mighty energies of *Amerikanismus* also casting a strong, albeit ambivalent, spell. In 1928, at the height of Soviet–German military cooperation, Blomberg, in his capacity as chief of the General Staff, travelled to the Soviet Union for an extensive tour. He wrote a long report on what he had seen, analysing both the Red Army's considerable advances and its lingering backwardness. However, above all he was deeply impressed by the degree of social mobilization, discipline, and energy he had found in the Soviet Union. This was a model of how a modern nation could be totally harnessed to produce immense power for peace or for war. As he would later confess only half-jokingly, Blomberg returned from the Soviet Union almost a Bolshevik. He wanted a military alliance with the Soviet Union. More significantly, he asked himself who in Germany could bring about a similar reorientation of society?[31] By the early 1930s he believed that Hitler and his movement had the potential to bring this about. In 1932 Reichenau, his chief of staff in the East Prussia military district (Wehrkreis I), of which Blomberg was given command after his tenure as chief of the General Staff, communicated with Hitler in order to learn about his intentions.[32]

In 1930 Blomberg led a German military delegation on a two-month

[30] K.-J. Müller, *The Army, Politics and Society in Germany, 1933–45* (Manchester, 1987), esp. 31–4, makes this point very well.

[31] J. Erickson, *The Soviet High Command* (London, 1962), 263–8, 307; Wheeler-Bennett, *Nemesis of Power*, 295–7; F. Carsten, *The Reichswehr in Politics 1918* to *1933* (Oxford, 1966), 281–2, 289–90; Geyer, *Aufrüstung*, 320–1. I have not been given access to Blomberg's MS autobiography in BA-MA N 52.

[32] T. Vogelsang, 'Hitlers Brief an Reichenau vom 4. Dezember 1932', *Vierteljahrshefte für Zeitgeschichte*, 7 (1959), 429–37.

tour to the United States, as official guests of the US Army. The delegation was taken across the country and shown all parts of American military establishment. Both Blomberg and Colonel Külental, head of the intelligence branch (T3) of the General Staff, who also participated in the tour, wrote a detailed report on what they saw. In his report Blomberg emphasized the war potential of the American system of Reserve, National Guard, and industry. 'The mission of the army today', he wrote, 'is to train commanders and weapon experts in large numbers, as well as to prepare for industrial mobilization'. 'The army, National Guard, organized reserves, and the preparation of war industry are cut out for the creation of an army of millions.'[33] The might of American industry had been particularly impressive for the Germans both on account of their First World War experience and in view of the United States' dominating economic power during the 1920s, on which the Locarno *détente* was based. On the one hand, American Mammonism, mass popular culture, and racial diversity had always been viewed with repugnance and alarm by the European élites, in Germany more than anywhere else. During the 1920s, as American popular culture in the shape of Hollywood and (black) jazz music was making strong headway, these impressions grew even stronger. On the other hand, German awe and admiration for the modernity, efficiency, and dynamism of American industry, symbolized by Detroit, was boundless. American scientific production and scientific management techniques were avidly studied by German industrialists: 'Taylorismus + Fordismus = Amerikanismus'.[34] In 1930 Captain Walter Warlimont was the first foreign officer to participate in the course of the US Army Industrial College.[35] Yet by that year the United States had been thrown deep into the Great Depression, and the mystique of her power was greatly diminished. As he had in the Soviet Union, Blomberg saw in the United States what he was looking for:

> The National Guard and the organized reserves are the bearers of a country's healthy, future-assured militarism . . . in the face of powerful, pulsating economic forces, there lives in the youth the feeling of commitment to military

[33] Reports in BA-MA RH 2/1825.

[34] See extensively in C. Maier, 'Between Taylorism and Technocracy: European Ideologies and the Vision of Industrial Productivity in the 1920s', *Journal of Contemporary History*, 5(2) (1970), 27–61; T. Hughes, *American Genesis: A Century of Invention and Technological Enthusiasm, 1870–1970* (New York, 1989), 284–94.

[35] Geyer, *Aufrüstung*, 162.

preparedness, to the defence of the country and, unexpressed but instinctive, an imperialistic will for the growth of American world position.[36]

All the same, the masses of the unemployed that Blomberg had seen and commented upon in his official report help explain why it was after all the totalitarian and cohesive Soviet Union, with its gigantic Five-Year Plan, that had left the greater impression on him.

For Reichenau, Blomberg's new chief of staff, a visit to the United States in 1913 with the German Olympic committee was a formative experience. Different in character from his chief, Reichenau nevertheless held a similar political outlook. While Blomberg's intellectual ability was not matched by a strong will and political astuteness, Reichenau was cold-minded, calculating, and possessed a clearer sense of where he was going. He too, was disliked and distrusted by many of his peers in the army. He, too, had been unorthodox in his attitudes towards tradition and modernity. From his visit to the United States Reichenau returned particulary impressed by the vitalism, sense of the future, realism, industrial might, informal manner, and sporting pursuits which permeated American culture. Some of these he conspicuously imported to Germany. In contrast to the Prussian tradition, he introduced a more open, face-to-face contact with the rank and file under his command. To the dismay of his fellow officers, he initiated and personally participated in field runs and games with his troops.[37] (The traditional school may have had a point: Reichenau would die in the field at the age of 58 of heart failure.) These almost trivial examples serve to demonstrate a point: Reichenau thought Prussian traditions old-fashioned, and modernization essential. But, like his chief, while he was egalitarian, it was not liberal-democratic values that he brought over from the United States.

It was probably their sympathetic attitude to the prospect of National Socialist rule that facilitated the nomination of Blomberg and Reichenau to the war ministry by agreement between Hindenburg and Hitler when the National Socialists came to power in 1933. In the ministry they were instrumental in bringing the army more closely under the new regime. Whereas the army's high command sought to preserve its traditional autonomy within the state, Blomberg and Reichenau worked to integrate it with the state. In a series of directives that effectively

[36] Ibid.

[37] W. Görlitz, 'Reichenau', in C. Barnett (ed.), *Hitler's Generals* (London, 1989), 209–10; Wheeler-Bennett, *Nemesis of Power*, 298.

extended the Reich's *Gleichschaltung* to the armed forces, they introduced Nazi insignia, Nazi political indoctrination, Nazi racial legislation, and the personal oath of allegiance to Adolf Hitler.[38] Neither of them had been or would ever become a confirmed Nazi. 'Fellow travellers' of National Socialism, they regarded it as an answer to the needs of a modern nation competing for power in the international arena. To be sure, in time both would find Hitler's strategic planning too risky even for their own tastes, and in consequence they lost favour in his eyes. At the famous conference in November 1937, recorded by Hossbach, where Hitler outlined his far-reaching plans for European expansion to high-ranking officers and officials, Blomberg was among those who expressed reservations about the risks of provoking a general European war. Shortly afterwards he was forced to resign after it became known that his new second wife possessed a dubious sexual past. During the winter of 1939/40 Reichenau, commanding the 6th Army, joined the universal resistance in the army's high command—which became conspiratorial—to Hitler's demand for a general offensive in the West, whose prospects of success the generals judged to be slim. In consequence, Hitler, who on earlier occasions had been keen to have Reichenau nominated as chief of the army's general staff, would now rule him out as a successor to Halder.

In any event, the same quest for a revival of Germany's status as a great power that had led Blomberg and Reichenau to seek unorthodox solutions in radical military schemes and radical modernist totalitarian politics also made them from very early on interested in, and enthusiastic for, the potential of modern mechanized forces. In May 1926 in a memorandum he wrote as head of the operations branch in the General Staff, Blomberg was among the first high-ranking German officers to emphasize the significance of the revolutionary advances in mechanization and armoured doctrine made in Britain at that time.[39] In 1928, during his tenure as chief of the General Staff, while Blomberg outlined his plans for a war of popular resistance and swift movement, the army took the decision to convert its motorized transportation units into combat units.[40]

[38] See esp. Messerschmidt, *Die Wehrmacht im NS-Staat*, 1–209.

[39] 29 May 1926, in RH 2/2195; the memorandum was abstracted in *M-W*, 4 Aug. 1926, 146.

[40] M. Geyer, 'German Strategy in the Age of Machine Warfare, 1914–1945', in P. Paret (ed.), *Makers of Modern Strategy from Machiavelli to the Nuclear Age* (Princeton, NJ, 1986), 559; W. Nehring, *Die Geschichte der deutschen Panzerwaffe, 1916 bis 1945* (Berlin, 1969), 54–6.

A year later, Blomberg drafted plans and asked for the resources needed for the creation of an independent tank regiment and motorized infantry unit, a step which was eventually intended to lead—when political conditions became favourable—to the creation of 'independent tank formations'.[41]

Thus it is not surprising that while leading the German delegation to the 1932 Geneva Disarmament Conference, Blomberg asked to meet Liddell Hart, who covered the conference for the *Daily Telegraph*, and told him of his admiration for his work.[42] Later that year Reichenau wrote to Liddell Hart to inform him that he was translating *Foch*, a book that was 'not following obsolete theories, but setting new rules'.[43] Fuller was a frequent official guest in Germany during the 1930s, invited both as a fellow fascist and as the leading expert on modern mechanized warfare, and extensively meeting with the country's political and military leadership. Col. Sir Andrew Thorne, the British military attaché in Berlin from 1932 to 1935, recalled after the war:

> during that time there I could not fail to be impressed by the extent to which both Liddell Hart's and 'Boney' Fuller's books were being studied by officers of all ranks and arms in the German Army. I knew both Blomberg (Minister of War) and Reichenau (Chief of the Defence Staff) very well, and they were both engaged in translating books by these two authors for use for non-English speaking German officers.[44]

As Guderian, who played a leading role in the creation of the Panzer force during the 1930s, was to testify, the promotion of Blomberg and Reichenau following Hitler's rise to power had 'an immediate effect on my work. Both these generals favoured modern ideas, and so I now found considerable sympathy for the ideas of the armoured force, at least at the highest levels of the Wehrmacht.' In 1938 Reichenau assumed command over Group Command 4, the army incorporating all the then existing armoured and mechanized corps of the German army.[45] Blomberg not only was very favourable towards the armoured forces but also lent his unqualified support to the nascent Luftwaffe, to

[41] T4 (signed Blomberg), 1 Sept. 1929, in BA-MA Freiburg RH 39/115; see also Geyer, 'German Strategy', 559.

[42] B. H. Liddell Hart, *Memoirs* (2 vols., London, 1969), i. 171–2; his records at the time: 7 and 8 Mar. 1932, in the Liddell Hart Centre of Military Archives, King's College, London [King's], 11/1932/1 and 11/1932/9.

[43] Reichenau to LH, 28 Nov. 1932, 9/24/87/R.

[44] Thorne to Hankey, 22 Mar. 1946, King's, 13/45.

[45] H. Guderian, *Panzer Leader* (London, 1952), 29, 37, 48.

which he made sure that élite army officers would be transferred.[46] In his testimony after the war before Allied interrogators in Nuremberg, Blomberg himself tied together the various aspects of his differences with the army conservatives during the National Socialist era (understandably failing to mention his radical war plans):

> The unification of the Higher Command of the Wehrmacht, the characteristic features of the 'Volksarmee' as compared with an isolated professional army (Reichswehr), the question of the mechanization of the army, the unaccustomed competition of the new 'Luftwaffe', these were, according to my impression, the facts that many Generals could not easily assimilate.[47]

The respective roles of British influence, Guderian, and the German general staff in the creation of the Panzer arm have all become contentious subjects in recent years, to which I have dedicated a separate special study. Here I shall only touch upon the themes relevant to our subject, referring interested readers to that study.[48] Chief of the army's General Staff Beck, accused in Guderian's memoirs of being a constant obstacle to his radical plans,[49] has been shown by recent scholarship to have played a crucial role in the creation of the Panzer force, including that of the first three armoured divisions in 1935. However, the fact remains that Beck came to the subject late, much under the stimulus of others, and moving cautiously, dispersed a large part of the tank force for cavalry-type and infantry support missions. The army's commander in chief, Fritsch, was favourably mentioned in Guderian's memoirs as a supporter of armour; and, indeed, as early as 1927, as chief of the operations branch in the general staff in succession to Blomberg, Fritsch had emphasized the independent use of armour as an operationally decisive weapon.[50] All the same, being the 'old Prussian gentleman' that he was, he could not help but accept 'reluctantly what he is said to have called "all those damnable innovations, cars, tanks, etc." '. As the historian who has done the most to make Beck's case in respect to armour concludes: the difference between Blomberg and Reichenau at the war ministry, on the one hand, and Fritsch and Beck at the army's high command, on the other, reflected a 'different attitude to the

[46] L. W. Murray, *Luftwaffe* (Baltmore, 1985), 7.

[47] 'Niederschrift Blomberg über seine Einstellung zu Adolf Hitler und dem Nationalsozialismus': Nov. 1945, BA-MA N 52/7, p. 2.

[48] Gat, *British Armour Theory and the Rise of the Panzer Arm*.

[49] Guderian, *Panzer Leader*, 32–3.

[50] Ibid. 31–2; Geyer, 'German Strategy', 559.

modern world. General von Fritsch represented more a stance rooted in pre-industrial feudalism. . . . The armed forces command, on the other hand, was of the opinion that the world had changed.'[51] Blomberg and Reichenau were modernists and in general favourably disposed towards the machine. They were also looking for any revolutionary means that might make it possible for Germany to break the ring around her and tilt the European balance of power in her favour. It is again significant that Guderian named the radical General Joachim von Stülpnagel, who had originated the idea of a popular war of national liberation and who retired from the army in 1931, as particularly favourable to the nascent mechanized force.[52]

Michael Geyer has suggested a distinction between the 'idealist' school and the 'technicians' in the German high command both before and during the Second World War. In this distinction the former was represented by Beck and his colleagues and continued the tradition of the old general staff. Allegedly, this school was accustomed to considering strategy within an overall perspective of the European and international balance of power, and duly assessed by the late 1930s that Hitler was leading Germany into a general European and world war which it had no chance of winning. By contrast, according to this view, the 'technicians'—mostly, like Guderian, of a younger generation—were totally preoccupied with technologies and techniques of warfare, losing sight of the overall strategic picture. Less constrained in this manner, they were more eager for war, and in general abdicated its overall strategic direction to Hitler.[53]

While partly helpful, this distinction seems to me to be somewhat off the mark and potentially misleading as to the more substantial nature of the difference between the two groups, which essentially lay in the degree of their political radicalism. The same mistake was for a long time made in regard to Schliefen of the old school. He also was dubbed a 'military technician' in comparison to the elder Moltke, notwithstanding the (misconceived) German political agenda at the turn of the nineteenth century for European hegemony and a status of world power that underlay his (misguided) military plan for total victory in a two-front war.[54]

[51] K.-J. Müller, *Army, Politics and Society*, 34. [52] Guderian, *Panzer Leader*, 25.

[53] Geyer, *Aufrüstung*, 79, but also 93; id., 'German Strategy', in Paret (ed.), *Makers of Modern Strategy*, 572, 584–6—much, in my opinion, against the general drift of his argument.

[54] Book II above, 364–7.

The younger generation in the Reichswehr and Wehrmacht was on the whole simply more radical than the older, convinced as it was that the goal of Germany's revival would necessitate more forceful means, more extreme measures, and more risky initiatives. 'Beck', as Guderian revealingly wrote even in his post-war memoirs, 'was above all a procrastinator in military *as in political matters*.'[55] It was because of their political radicalism, not only for the career opportunities he opened to them, that most members of the younger generation in the army supported Hitler and enthusiastically followed his plans of expansion and war. Only the onset of defeat made them more critical of his direction of the war, if mostly not of his overall aims. From the 1890s onward foreign policy and, correspondingly, also domestic attitudes in Germany underwent further radicalization with every successive generation.

It was within this broader perspective that the fiercely nationalistic Guderian, working to advance his radical conception of armoured warfare, immediately recognized Hitler as an ally. The setting of their first meetings, stressed by Guderian, are noteworthy:

> I saw and heard Hitler for the first time at the opening of the Berlin Automobile Exhibition, at the beginning of February [1933]. It was unusual for the Chancellor himself to open the exhibition. And what he had to say was in striking contrast to the customary speeches of Ministers and Chancellors on such occasions. He announced the abolition of the tax on cars and spoke of the new national roads that were to be built and of the *Volkswagen*, the cheap 'People's Car', that was to be mass produced.[56]

According to Guderian, in addition to Blomberg and Reichenau, 'it soon became apparent that Hitler himself was interested in the problem of motorisation and armour'. At the army's demonstration ground for weapon development at Kummersdorf—which, as Guderian stressed, Hitler was the first chancellor to attend in fifty years—Guderian gave Hitler a half-hour demonstration of his troops. He elicited from him the famous enthusiastic and repeated response: 'That's what I need! That's what I want to have!' As Guderian wrote in his memoirs: 'As a result of this demonstration I was convinced that the head of the government would approve my proposals for the organization of an up-to-date *Wehrmacht*, if only I could manage to lay my views before him.' Guderian went on to complain that the rigidity of

[55] Guderian, *Panzer Leader*, 32; my emphasis. [56] Ibid. 29.

military procedure, especially as things stood in the 1930s, made it difficult for him to appeal directly to Blomberg and Hitler.[57] None the less, it is widely agreed that Hitler's known interest in the mechanized forces and in radical operational doctrines proved a major spur to their development in Germany, as well as providing a personal safety net for Guderian's career.

The Nazi Nostalgic Mechanized Utopia

In general, the attitude of the Nazis and Hitler towards the modern was ambivalent.[58] Of all the fascist movements Nazism was probably the least modernist, even though it operated in Europe's most advanced industrial, technological, and scientific nation. Its strong *völkisch*, nostalgic, and mystical bent cast its futurist utopia in a mythological agrarian and pastoral past.[59] Like Mussolini, Hitler turned to suppress the most radical and avant-garde elements in his movement after coming to power. At a rally of the National Socialist Motor Corps in the summer of 1933, Guderian heard Hitler talking of the need for every revolution to become evolution at a certain point.[60] While a *Gleichschaltung* of the Reich was carried out, the SA was decimated and the social

[57] Guderian, 29–30.

[58] The debate here does not seem to be ebbing; see esp. R. Dahrendorf, *Society and Democracy in Germany* (London, 1968); D. Schenbaum, *Hitler's Social Revolution* (New York, 1966); K. D. Bracher, 'Tradition und Revolution im Nationalsozialismus', in *Zeitgeschichtliche Kontroversen* (Munich, 1976), 62–78; H. Mommsen, 'Nationalsozialismus als vorgetäuschte Modernisierung', in *Der Nationalsozialismus und die deutsche Gesellschaft* (Hamburg, 1991), 405–27; M. Rauch, 'Anti-Modernismus im Nationalsozialistischen Staat', *Historisches Jahrbuch*, 107 (1987), 94–121; N. Frei, 'Wie modern war der Nationalsozialismus?', *Geschichte und Gesellschaft*, 19 (1993), 367–87; A. Schildt, 'NS-Regime, Modernisierung und Moderne', *Tel Aviver Jahrbuch für deutsche Geschichte*, 23 (1994), 3–22; M. Prinz and R. Zitelmann (eds.), *Nationalsozialismus und Modernisierung* (Darmstadt, 1995); M. Roseman, 'National Socialism and Modernisation', in R. Bessel (ed.), *Fascist Italy and Nazi Germany: Comparisons and Contrasts* (Cambridge, 1996), 197–229.

[59] For the following, the best overall discussion is provided by G. Mosse, 'Fascism and the Avant Garde', in *Masses and Man: Nationalist and Fascist Perception of Reality* (Detroit, 1987), 230–4; also his 'Introduction' to Mosse (ed.), *International Fascism* (London, 1979), 7, 24–5; M. Eksteins, *Rites of Spring: The Great War and the Birth of the Modern Age* (New York, 1990), 322–8. For more specialized studies, see M. Renneberg and M. Walker (eds.), *Science, Technology and National Socialism* (Cambridge, 1994); A. D. Beyerchen, *Scientists under Hitler* (New Haven Conn., 1977); S. Wollgast, ' "Technikphilosophie" während der Herrschaft des deutschen Faschismus', in Wollgast and G. Kovács (eds.), *Technikphilosophie in Vergangenheit und Gegenwart* (Berlin, 1984), 115–35; J. Shand, 'The Reichsautobahn: Symbol for the Third Reich', *Journal of Contemporary History*, 19 (1984), 189–200; A. Rabinbach, 'The Aesthetics of Production in the Third Reich', in Mosse (ed.), *International Fascism*, 189–222.

[60] Guderian, *Panzer Leader*, 30.

radicals Ernst Röhm and Otto Strasser were eliminated. Whereas Futurism remained the semi-official artistic style of Fascist Italy—grudgingly sharing that status with Roman neo-classicism—Hitler's parochial and petty-bourgeois sensibilities were directed against artistic modernism. A brief flirtation with Expressionism, which the poet Gottfried Benn (1886–1956)—who, unlike most of his friends, supported National Socialism—hoped to make the official style of the new regime, was interrupted in 1934.[61] Realistic neo-classicism would henceforth occupy that rank. Despite efforts of the Bauhaus's director Mies van der Rohe and the support of Nazi intellectuals around Joseph Goebbels in Berlin, much the same happened regarding modernist architecture. Still, 'But for Hitler's interest in architecture, Albert Speer believed, modernism—as promulgated by the Weidemann–NS Students Association faction—would have developed as the 'official' style of National Socialism.'[62]

On the other hand, Hitler and National Socialism exalted the most spectacular and dynamic products of modern technology. Like Mussolini and the Italian Fascists, they associated themselves with and made extensive use of the aircraft and the fast car. The *Autobahn*, top-of-the-range Mercedes, and the popular Volkswagen symbolized their modernist programme. Radio and film played a similar role, as well as being one of the regime's most effective means of propaganda and political mobilization. While Nazi ideology had always contained an element of hostility towards industry and science, the regime inevitably acknowledged their necessity for the building of German national power. They were promoted, while harnessed to further the regime's ends and made to conform to its ideological principles, some of which, like racism and anti-Semitism, entailed considerable scientific penalties. Above all, science and industry were to produce the modern equipment for the revived armed forces, with an emphasis on revolutionary means which would intimidate Germany's neighbours and, in case of war, make it possible for her to escape the prospect of stalemate and attrition. As early as 28 February 1934, addressing army and SA leaders at the Reichswehr ministry, Hitler predicted that in order to gain living space in the east for the German people in the teeth of international opposition, 'short, decisive blows to the West and then to the East could be

[61] Hamilton, *The Appeal of Fascism*, 135, 149–52, 158–9.

[62] E. Hochman, *Architects of Fortune: Mies van der Rohe and the Third Reich* (New York, 1989), 311.

necessary'.[63] Only recently have scholars begun to realize that the famous 'Blitzkrieg' was not developed before the war in any formal or orderly manner, indeed, was not even a German term but one created by foreign media.[64] None the less, the notion that revolutionary means would assist Germany to prevail against a superior coalition was imprinted in the minds of Hitler, Blomberg, and many of the younger generation in the army. In *Mein Kampf* (1925) Hitler had written about 'the universal motorization of the world, which in the next war will be overwhelmingly decisive in the struggle'.[65] From very early on the mechanized forces in the army were among the beneficiaries of this notion, although by far the principal benefactor was, of course, the Luftwaffe.

Modernist enthusiasm and mystique went hand in hand with strategic considerations in the cultivation of the Luftwaffe. As everywhere else, the aeroplane was regarded in Germany, particularly by fascists, as the most potent symbol of the new age. Like the Italian Futurists, like Wells, and like Lawrence, Ernst Jünger celebrated the flyer as 'the new man, the man of the twentieth century.' Flyers, he wrote, would constitute the new aristocracy of the future. Flying was a vitalistic and dynamic force which countered decadence. It also had the potential to impose world power and order on barbarism. Here too Germany must break the Versailles restrictions and conquer the air.[66] Much as Mussolini had done during and after his struggle for power, Hitler flew 30,000 miles during the election campaign of 1932. Going from town to town under the slogan 'Hitler over Germany', he attended 200 meetings. He was the first German politician to use the aeroplane in this manner, and the propaganda value of this campaigning technique was as important as its efficiency. After coming to power, 'Hitler wanted the largest air force in the World and the best pilots. War in the air would be viewed as a Germanic form of battle.' Like Italo Balbo in Italy, Herman Goering, the First World War ace, second in the Nazi hierarchy and commander-in-chief of the Luftwaffe, held a special status in the

[63] R. O'Neill, *The German Army and the Nazi Party, 1933–1939*, (London, 1966) 127.

[64] Gat, *British Armour Theory and the Rise of the Panzer Arm*, 82–86.

[65] Cited by E. Bennett, *German Rearmament and the West, 1932–1933* (Princeton, NJ, 1979), 319.

[66] 'Der Flieger', *Der Tag*, 15 (1928); 'Nation und Luftfahrt', *Vormarsch*, 1 (1927–8), 314–17; cited in Herf, *Reactionary Modernism*, 85. Similarly in Jünger's introduction to the book he edited in the late 1920s, *Luftfahrt ist Not!* A fascinating study is P. Fritzsche, *A Nation of Fliers: German Aviation and the Popular Imagination* (Cambridge, Mass., 1992); Jünger is cited throughout and the Nazis are extensively covered.

regime, and the service he headed possessed a special aura.[67] Similar to the Regia Aeronautica in Mussolini's regime, the Luftwaffe was the Nazi service *par excellence*, unlike the Prussian army and Wilhelmine navy, with which Hitler jibed that he had to deal.

To conclude, irrespective of Nazism, the German armed forces sought to break the Versailles restrictions, expand, and modernize. Yet Nazi political support and the orientation of right-wing radicals within the armed forces were a significant factor in directing German rearmament—particularly the emphasis on the Luftwaffe but also the development of the Panzer arm—towards modern means of war, revolutionary doctrines, and radical operational schemes.[68]

[68] See also my 'Ideology, National Policy, Technology and Strategic Doctrine between the World Wars', *Journal of Strategic Studies*, 24:3 (2001), 1–18.

5

Comparisons and Contrasts (I): American Progressivism and Technological Modernism

Every picture gains in clarity when set against comparisons and contrasts. Having covered much of the proto-fascist and fascist spectrum, we might, finally, try to gain further insight into the connection between fascist modernism and visions of machine warfare by turning to examine two other pronouncedly modernist ideologies: American Progressivism and Marxism.

The Nazi's enthusiastic embrace of Charles A. Lindbergh (1902–74) was one expression of the fascists' effort to identify themselves with the images of youth, vigour, potency, advanced technology, and the conquest of the air, for which Lindbergh had become the greatest living symbol. With his upright character and sharp mind he slipped almost naturally into the role of the international superhero into which he had been launched by his trans-Atlantic flight in 1927. Everywhere he went he was showered with honours and acclaim, and much to his peril he found himself ever the focus of attention for the world's media. Everybody who was anybody, from royalty down, was eager to meet and talk with him. Governments, air forces, and industrialists sought his cooperation, advice, or simply the aura of his association. Civilian and military establishments alike in all countries were open to him, as they were for nobody else. So his value for Nazi propaganda is clear. His own part in the relationship is less clear, however. This chapter seeks to suggest a more general explanation for the Lindbergh affair, broadening our perspective to the United States and to some features of American Populism, Pragmatism, Progressivism, and Mid-West modernism.

It is widely held that fully fledged fascism never took root in America in any significant way, remaining confined to marginal immigrant associations such as the German–American Bund.[1] Yet scholars have

[1] See M. Schonback, *Native American Fascism During the 1930s and 1940s* (New York, 1985); also C. Sokol, *The German–American Bund as a Model of American Fascism: 1924–1940* (Ann Arbor, Mich., 1979).

discerned some family resemblance between fascism and aspects of American Populism and 'nativism', movements which grew in force and assumed political forms from the late nineteenth century in response to the pressures of modernity. Particularly strong among the agricultural communities of the Mid-West which found the new environment of international markets economically inhospitable, intellectually incomprehensible, and culturally alien, Populism and American nativism responded to the encroaching forces of the outside world with resentment, distrust, and anxiety. They exhibited the rising xenophobia and offended religious sensibilities that are all too characteristic of the reactions of small, parochial communities to the challenge of modernity. The arch-enemy in their eyes was international finance, whose greedy tentacles stretched around the world—sucking its wealth—from its centres in the City of London and Wall Street. Somewhere behind the conspiracy stood the demonic figure of the international Jew. More generally, there was animosity towards West Coast politicians, intellectuals, and urban megalopolises, swamped by alien immigrants.

However, side by side with these sentiments and their political manifestations, and not far removed demographically and geographically, there also arose from the turn of the century the Progressive movement, whose campaign against political corruption and rampant big-business capitalism and whose cult of modernism and efficiency had a profound effect on American public life. Here too the Mid-West was one of the main strongholds of the movement. And if engineers, lawyers, and other professionals were more prominent among the ranks of Progressivism than among those of Populism, then it is a telling fact that these professionals had mainly grown up in the farms of rural America, and affectionately carried with them both its memory and much of its ethics and ideals. Finally—and this fact perhaps has not been sufficiently recognized—it was in the rural communities of these very same provinces of the Mid-West that the mythological heroes of American technological modernism grew up, all cherishing for life this formative experience. Thomas Alva Edison was born in a Ohio village and grew up in a small Michigan community; Henry Ford was born and raised on a Michigan farm; the Wright brothers came from Dayton, Ohio; Frank Lloyd Wright was born and raised on his grandfather's farm in Wisconsin; Billy Mitchell was the son of a Wisconsin senator, and grandson of a railroad and banking magnate; and Charles A. Lindbergh was the son of a Progressive Congressman from Minnesota.

These American technological pioneers not only had similar roots, but some of them shared political ideals and even collaborated with one another in their political work.

Henry Ford is surely the most famous of the lot for his public and political activities. Having built his fabulous manufacturing empire in the decade before the Great War—transforming the automobile industry, becoming the guru of modern industry with his techniques of mass production and management, and turning into a symbol of modernity world-wide—he increasingly styled himself the authentic voice of popular America and the representative of true American values. Poorly educated and intellectually simple but also reflective, idealistic, and thoroughly convinced of his mission, he was able to use his fame and vast fortune for amplifying the mood, ideals, and prejudices of his native region and times. He first ventured into the public arena during the drive to keep the United States out of the First World War, a campaign in which Mid-West pacifists and isolationists (like the elder Lindbergh) were particulary active. He financed and led the 'Peace Ship' whose planned cruise of anti-war activists ended in failure.[2] It was, however, mainly after the war that Ford offered himself through the media to large audiences as a popular philosopher with the answers to the great challenges of modernity, and even considered running for the presidency. He preached a Jeffersonian popular democracy, in which a new, decentralized industrial society would be synthesized with—without fundamentally altering—the traditional values and life-style of rural America. The engine of his programme was of course the automobile which, as his life ambition had been, should come to every household in America, making it possible to spread industry to the small communities throughout the nation rather than concentrate it, and the people, in monstrous cities of millions. Ford attacked high finance, and became an extreme anti-Semite.

During the 1920s Ford published and distributed *The Protocols of the Elders of Zion*, a fake composed by the Czarist secret police and alleging a Jewish conspiracy to win control over the world. His newspaper, the *Dearborn Independence*, read mainly in the Mid-West, was thoroughly anti-Semite. In addition, by 1920 his reputation for benevolence toward his workers was tainted by his hard-line anti-unionist stance. Finally,

[2] See B. Kraft, *The Peace Ship: Henry Ford's Pacifist Adventure in the First World War* (New York, 1978); and, for Lindbergh the elder, B. Larsen, *Lindbergh of Minnesota* (New York, 1973).

during the 1920s and 1930s he strengthened his relations with quasi-fascists and fascists both at home and abroad. Heinz Spanknoeble, organizer of the Teutonia Society, Fritz Kuhn, would-be leader of the German–American Bund, and others of similar views worked for the Ford Company in Detroit, apparently not by coincidence. Ford himself was sympathetic to Fascist Italy and had particularly good relations with Nazi Germany, where he had long been admired and by which he was decorated. After the outbreak of the Second World War in Europe he again became one of the leading members of America First, the isolationist association that campaigned to keep America out of the war. All the same, during the war his factories poured automobiles, aircraft, ships, and other armaments for the war effort in the mass volume that had made Ford synonymous with American industrial–military might.[3]

So what does all this show? Ford himself was never a fascist and neither were any of the other figures that will be discussed here. Yet in the distinctively Mid-West American blend of agrarian nostalgia, nativist Populism, Progressivism, and celebration of technology there were many elements that resonated with fascist sentiments and ideas. These made Ford and people of similar outlook at least attentive and responsive, if not sympathetic, to the fascist regimes abroad. What would be the character of the emerging advanced industrialized society? How could its pains be alleviated by social planning, and how could it be reconciled with traditional communal values? These questions were at the root of the fascist mood, and it was much the same questions that preoccupied Ford and other Mid-West pundits of modernism and technology with whom he cooperated.

One of the people Ford admired deeply, befriended, and cooperated with was Thomas Edison. The two had much in common. Both were self-made men who came from small Michigan communities, received little formal education, but were endowed with technological genius that brought them to world fame. Both also shared the same basic outlook. Like Ford, Edison detested Wall Street, the banks, and high finance. He was anti-Semitic, and was ascetic in character and conduct.[4] Another man with whom Ford cooperated was the leading American

[3] See esp. Schonbach, *Native American Fascism*, 47, 68, 123; Kraft, *The Peace Ship*, 278–83; R. Wik, *Henry Ford and Grass Roots America* (Ann Arbor, Mich., 1972); D. Nye, *Henry Ford: 'Ignorant Idealist'* (New York, 1979); and R. Lacey, *Ford: The Men and the Machine* (Boston, 1986), 132–236.

[4] M. Josephson, *Edison* (London, 1961), 435–7, 463, 465–6.

figure of architectural Modernism, Frank Lloyd Wright. As Wright made his great comeback in the 1930s, after almost two decades of professional and public retreat, he came armed with a social philosophy which he preached and practised. Always evoking his childhood in his grandfather's farm in Wisconsin—'born in the prairie', as he liked to describe himself—he made this the cornerstone of his ideal for modern America. Like Ford, he wanted a decentralized Jeffersonian democracy and a revival of the disappearing qualities of rural life. His third wife, the power behind his return to architecture and public life, was a follower of the fashionable mystical thinkers and occultists Gurdjieff and his disciple Ouspensky, who preached a return to the harmonies of nature. While rejecting their mysticism, Wright was influenced by their social philosophy. He and his wife established a quasi-monastic institution, the Taliesin Fellows, in the wilderness of Wisconsin. Teaching holistic and organic architecture, the institution became a magnet for young and aspiring architects who came to live and work there as apprentices, and for many other guests, like the novelist and popular philosopher of Nietzschean individuality, Ayn Rand. Under the impact of the Great Depression Wright prophesied the demise of the metropolis and of the North-East model of anonymous, alienated, mass urban and industrial society. The cities were to remain as economic centres and work places, but they were not fit for human habitation. Like Ford, Wright developed his grand vision of life in America, a new 'integration', the so-called Broadacre scheme. People would move to the suburbs and to small towns spread out in the countryside, where the qualities of agrarian America and closeness with nature would be revived. A network of highways would link all parts of the nation together. The car, aeroplane, and radio had made it possible to combine dispersion with modern civilization. Retreat from excessive industrialism would also involve the forsaking of colonialism and trade conflicts. The United States ought to resume a pacifist and isolationist stance. In collaboration with Ford, Wright campaigned against American involvement in the Second World War.[5]

Wright was a democrat, who stood for individual freedom and rejected both forms of 'central European' totalitarianism—as he regarded them—fascism and Bolshevism. But he was also an anti-

[5] See esp. R. Fishman, *Urban Utopias in the Twentieth Century: Ebenezer Howard, Frank Lloyd Wright, and Le Corbusier* (New York, 1977), 97–150; Donald Leslie Johnson, *Frank Lloyd Wright versus America: The 1930s* (Cambridge, Mass., 1990).

capitalist communitarian. The first two tenets in his 'American' programme read: 'No private ownership of public needs. No landlord or tenant.' Another of his lists began: '1. No very rich nor very poor to build for—no gold. 2. No idle land except for common landscape—no real estate exploiters. . . . In short no speculation in money, land, or ideas.'[6] Most technological modernists in the United States who took a critical stand towards capitalism—especially during the 1930s—remained within the democratic camp, yet aspects of their teachings were congruent with fascist ideas and appealed to fascists, as was true in the opposite direction. The self-taught popular social thinker and antifascist Lewis Mumford, for example, inclined toward communitarism, environmentalism, and social planning. His brilliant *Technics and Civilization* (1934) greatly impressed Fuller, coinciding as it did with his own approach to the tracing of the 'natural history of war', taken up in his books from 1932 on.[7] Scepticism regarding the rationality of capitalism and suspicions of its wastefulness had been harboured in America long before the Depression and the New Deal. Before the First World War such sentiments were expressed by the exponents of American Pragmatism and rational social science. These included philosophers, sociologists, popular writers, politicians, and industrialists like Lester Frank Ward, Thorstein Weblen, Charles Sanders Pierce, John Dewey, George Herbert Mead, William James, Theodore Roosevelt, Frederick Taylor, Herbert Hoover, Graham Wallace, and Walter Lippman.[8] While they mostly remained within the democratic and sometimes even liberal sphere, it has long been recognized that their ideas of scientific management, social engineering, efficiency, planning, control, and social order contained Comtean-Positivist, non-liberal, and non-democratic elements. It has been hyperbolically remarked that the most radical schemes for the building of modern cities were initiated by Stalin, Mussolini, Hitler, and General Motors.[9]

We have already seen how Billy Mitchell was impressed and influenced by Italian ideas and by Douhetism after his visits to Europe and Italy in 1921–2 and again in 1927. On his second visit his host was Italo Balbo and he was granted an audience by Mussolini. According to

[6] Ibid. 115, 295.

[7] L. Mumford, *Technics and Civilization* (London, 1934); *The Culture of Cities* (London, 1934); T. Hughes and A. Hughes (eds.), *Lewis Mumford* (Oxford, 1990); J. F. C. Fuller, *The First of the League Wars* (London, 1936), p. viii.

[8] J. M. Jordan, *Machine-Age Ideology: Social Engineering and American Liberalism, 1911–1939* (Chapel Hill, NC, 1994).

[9] Fishman, *Urban Utopias*, p. xiii.

Mitchell's biographer, relying on his manuscripts of the time: 'The Fascist movement also caught Mitchell's attention. He came away from an interview with Benito Mussolini believing that the dictator "stands as one of the greatest constructive powers for good government that exists in the world today".'[10] Favourable opinion of Fascist Italy was much too widespread in the West during the 1920s to indicate any deep affinity with fascism, and the evidence in the matter is too slim anyhow. Yet Mitchell's emphasis on 'good government' is symptomatic of the concerns of American Progressivists and of 'efficiency movements' throughout the West. After his dismissal from the army, Mitchell, like Fuller, continuously advanced schemes for the reorganization not only of the defence establishment but of the whole machinery of federal government.[11]

The man who succeeded Mitchell as America's most popular aviator was Charles A. Lindbergh. And if sympathy for Fascist Italy in the 1920 was too widespread to be indicative of much, admiration for Nazi Germany in the 1930s was a different matter. Unlike Henry Ford, with whom he worked closely in America First, Lindbergh was a refined person who felt at ease in the best of companies. He too, however, looked back with affection on his 'boyhood on the upper Mississippi', as one of his biographies is called, and he bore the mark of the ideas with which he had grown up in his father's house. Progressive Congressman Lindbergh had been a champion of the American farmer, an enemy of the Money Trust, and an active member of the opposition to the United States' entry into the First World War.

After the sensational murder of his elder son in 1931, Charles Lindbergh and his family moved to Europe to escape the press, living in France and Britain. In 1936 Lindbergh was asked by the American military attaché in Berlin to go to Germany to assess the strength and capability of the Luftwaffe. By 1939 he had visited Germany five times, was accepted with state honours and great clamour, and was decorated by Goering. His reports and journals, as well as the writings of his wife, the novelist Anne Morrow Lindbergh, who shared his views, are a remarkable testimony to the sort of ambivalent fascination people like the Lindberghs felt towards fascism.

The Lindberghs were decent and well-meaning people—humanitarian, idealistic, sensitive, caring, pacifistic, and on the whole

[10] A. Hurley, *Billy Mitchell: Crusader for Air Power* (New York, 1964) 115.
[11] Ibid. 122.

driven by the best of motives. Like their peers of the enlightened post-First World War generation in the West, they felt that another world war was too horrific to contemplate, would bring about the end of Western civilization, and was wholly unacceptable. Yet Charles Lindbergh's belief in the need of the white race to keep its unity in order to defend itself against the Asian and Mongol hordes and against 'the infiltration of inferior blood', though also common enough among his generation, revealed another streak in his mind. While living in Britain, for which the Lindberghs felt deep affection and respect, Charles Lindbergh found the British depressingly inefficient, slow, indulgent, and increasingly slipping behind the modern world. Moulded during the age of the ship, their national character was in his opinion inadequate for the speed and precision of the new air age. In France, of which the Lindberghs were as fond as they were of Britain, Charles Lindbergh was equally troubled by the country's profound political divisions, general sense of aimlessness, and loss of spirit. Of the Soviet Union, where he was again lavishly entertained, Lindbergh had the worst opinion. He believed it was backward and inherently mediocre, and prophesied the imminent collapse of the communist system. By contrast, the Lindberghs were impressed by German efficiency, drive, unity, collective spirit, purposefulness, and modernist enthusiasm for science and technology. Charles Lindbergh reasonably assessed in 1937–8 that the Luftwaffe was the strongest air force in the world; and the air was in the 1930s the 'high-tech' field by which the level of advancement of any modern nation was measured. According to Lindbergh, Nazi Germany was a 'virile' nation that escaped the general 'softness' and decadence of the democracies.

The Lindberghs were well aware of the brutality of the Nazi regime. They were sincerely dismayed by it, and never 'liked' Nazi Germany. All the same, contemplating Nazi Germany, the Lindbeghs asked if their scruples were not merely the indulging of a passing age, the one that had proved itself bankrupt with the Great Depression. And, further, were not Nazi brutalities merely the labour pains of a new age, surface expression of the inevitable currents of history, of the forces that were fundamental to, and would inherit, the modern world? As Lindbergh wrote:

> Modern Germany does not permit a superficial judgment. She challenges our most fundamental concepts. . . . What measures the rights of men and of a nation? . . . Are we deluding ourselves when we attempt to run our governments

by counting the number of heads, without a thought of what lies within them? Are our standards true? . . . Is it possible to perpetuate a government, or a League of Governments, unless representation is clearly proportional to the strength which is available to support it?[12]

Anne Morrow Lindbergh recorded similar thoughts in her diaries.[13] She developed them further in her book *The Wave of the Future* (1940), a title that speaks for itself:

In recent years, my generation has seen the beliefs, the formulas, and the creeds, that we were brought up to trust implicitly, one by one thrown in danger, if not actually discarded: the sacredness of property, the infallibility of the democratic way of life, the efficiency of the capitalist system . . . innocent people are being punished, and peaceful nations overrun by force of aggression, which we were taught to believe were outmoded forms of action in our stage of civilization.[14]

How were these upheavals to be interpreted? According to Anne Morrow Lindbergh, in international relations they were largely the sour grapes of the unjust treatment on the part of the 'have' powers: the United States, Britain, and France, towards the 'have-not' powers: Germany, Japan, and Italy. And the same line of thought extended further, to the Western democracies' domestic order:

A world in which there were widespread depressions, millions of unemployed, and drifting populations was not going to continue indefinitely. A world in which young people, willing to work, could not afford a home and family, in which the race declined in hardiness, in which one found on every side dissatisfaction, maladjustment and moral decay—that world was ripe for change.

Something, one feels, is pushing up through the crust of custom. One does not know what—some new conception of humanity and its place on the earth. I believe that it is, in its essence, good; but because we are blind we cannot see it, and because we are slow to change, it must force its way through the heavy crust violently—in eruptions. Some of these eruptions take terrible forms, unrecog-

[12] *The War Time Journals of Charles A. Lindbergh* (New York, 1970), 11, 22–3, 172, 450, and *passim*; anecdotal perhaps, but typical of the generation's search for direction, is the account that Lindbergh too read Ouspensky's *A New Model of the Universe*: ibid. 490; E. Lindbergh, *Autobiography of Value* (New York, 1978), 145–62, and *passim*; W. Cole, *Charles A. Lindbergh and the Battle against American Intervention in World War II* (New York, 1974), 26–31, 35 (citation), 38, 80–1, and *passim*; L. Goldstein, *The Flying Machine and Modern Literature* (London, 1986), 107–9.

[13] *The Flower and the Nettle: Diaries and Letters, 1936–1939* (New York, 1976), esp. 100–1; *War Within and Without: Diaries and Letters, 1939–1944* (New York, 1980), esp. 80–1.

[14] *The Wave of the Future: A Confession of Faith* (New York, 1940), 7–8.

nizable and evil forms. 'Great ideas enter into reality with evil associates and with disgusting alliances. But the greatness remains, nerving the race in its slow ascent.'[15]

The struggle of the past against the future, she wrote, called to mind the old European élites' shocked reaction and opposition to the French Revolution and Terror. New social and economic forces were at work. 'There is no fighting the wave of the future . . . All you could do was to dive into it or leap with it. Otherwise, it would surely overwhelm you and pound you to the sand.' Rather than fight abroad, Anne Morrow Lindbergh urged the United States to revolutionize itself domestically. It must come up with a distinctive American solution to the challenges of the future, which would address the same fundamental problems that had given rise to fascism and communism abroad, while avoiding their brutality and excesses.[16]

To sum up our discussion, American social history has been widely regarded as unique and distinct in many ways from that of European societies—more so than the national uniqueness, and distinctiveness that have distinguished these societies from one another. There was very little native fascism in the United States, as well as very little organized socialism. However, if fascism, as developed in Europe, never really took root in the United States, many of the ideas, concerns, and sentiments it expressed had American equivalents. Interestingly, some of them came together in Mid-West Populism, Progressivism, and technological modernism. None of the great American heroes of technology examined here, who figured as potent symbols of modernity world-wide, was fascist. Yet it so happened that Mid-West enterprise, pragmatism, and industrial opportunity dominated American technological inventiveness; at the same time and often expressing themselves through the same people, Mid-West Populism and American nativism responded to the onset of modernity with an ambivalence and anxiety that sought ways of integrating the great advances of technological society with traditional communal and rural values. The Great Depression awoke in many Mid-West pundits of technological modernism long-held doubts regarding the efficiency, morality, and unity of capitalist and liberal-democratic society and its general adequacy to cope with the world of tomorrow. It is not surprising that some of them looked at the fascist regimes abroad with interest and even sympathy, and that the fascists, for their part, embraced them with enthusiasm.

[15] Ibid. 12–15, 17, 22.

[16] Ibid. 18–19, 34–5, and *passim*.

6

Comparisons and Contrasts (II): Marxist Modernism and the Doctrine of the 'Deep Battle'

Whereas fascism was ambivalent and 'Janus-faced' in respect to modernity—some of its strands more than others—Marxism was the modernist ideology *par excellence*, wholly directed towards the future and regarding itself as the ultimate conclusion of the era of the machine and industrial society. Indeed, many if not most of Europe's fascist leaders (Mussolini and Mosley being the best-known examples) had arrived at their new creed from the ranks of the left, particularly from French and Italian revolutionary syndicalism, and had often developed out of Marxist assumptions and a Marxist interpretation of history. As we have seen, many in fact remained on the fence between the two movements, hesitant or seeing no need to choose, some even claimed by both. Georges Sorel, a post-Marxist revolutionary syndicalist and author of *Reflection on Violence* (1908), inspired and was honoured by both Lenin and Mussolini. Marinetti hailed the Bolshevik Revolution in Russia, although he ultimately rejected its class-based character. He, too, was favourably regarded by Lenin and by the founder and theorist of the Italian Communist Party, Antonio Gramsci. His dynamic, anti-bourgeois, machine-dominated Futurism was viewed by the Soviets, before its alliance with Fascism became complete, as a potential artistic ally.[1] The Russian Futurists, like the poet Vladimir Mayakovsky, the poet and aviator Vasily Kamensky, and the painter Kazimir Malevich, celebrated the aeroplane every bit as much as Marinetti and his Italian circle. Lenin himself had taken great interest in the aeroplane ever since his stay in Paris, from December 1908, where he lived through the first

[1] C. Tisdall and A. Bozzolla, *Futurism* (London, 1977), 200–1, 205–6; J. Davies, 'The Futures Market: Marinetti and the Fascists of Milan', in E. Timms and P. Collier (eds.), *Visions and Blueprints: Avant-Garde Culture and Radical Politics in Early Twentieth-Century Europe* (Manchester, 1988), 82.

memorable years of enthusiasm for aviation.[2] On his road to fascism from his syndicalist position in France of the late 1920s, Le Corbusier looked favourably on Bolshevism as the creator of a new, centralized, authoritarian, meritocratic regime, suitable for the modern age. He was courted by the Soviets, honoured by the Soviet modernist architects—Konstantin Melnikov, the Vesnin brothers (Alexander, Victor, and Leonid), Moses Ginsburg, and N. A. Miliutin—and commissioned to build large projects in the Soviet Union.[3] It was not without reason that his American rival Frank Lloyd Wright denounced Le Corbusier's centralized, gigantic, and crushing urban utopias as being appropriate to fascist, Nazi, or communist authoritarianism, long before this charge was adopted by post-modernist architects. Wright too, however, was courted by the Soviets and by the Soviet modernist architects.[4] Ironically, like Hitler and, less severely, Mussolini—and as if to validate the 'totalitarian model'—by the mid-1930s Stalin had suppressed architectural and artistic modernism in favour of monumental classicism and 'socialist realism'. In Germany, Jünger was reproached by his friend Oswald Spengler for not being able to free himself from Marxist analysis in his portrayal in *Der Arbeiter* (1932) of a future machine-dominated society.[5] Like Blomberg, Jünger saw the Soviet Union as a model for his modernist right-wing designs. During the 1920s Lenin's and Soviet enthusiasm for American Taylorism and Fordism dwarfed even that of the Germans. In Lenin's slogan: 'Electrification + Soviet Rule = Socialism'.[6] In 1946, admittedly after horrendous trials, Stalin, like Fuller, proclaimed that Clausewitz had belonged to the 'hand-tool period of warfare', whereas it was now the machine age.[7] Fascist and Soviet modernism had much in common.

If Marxism as an ideology was so thoroughly modernist, even less

[2] F. P. Ingold, *Literatur und Aviatik: Europäische Flugdichtung, 1909–1927* (Basel, 1978), 52–9, 133–89; R. Wohl, *A Passion for Wings: Aviation and Western Imagination, 1908–1918* (New Haven, Conn., 1994), 145–53, 157–78. A detailed general study is V. Markov, *Russian Futurism: A History* (Berkeley, Calif., 1968).

[3] B. B. Taylor, *Le Corbusier: The City of Refuge, Paris 1929/33* (Chicago, 1987), 9.

[4] D. L. Johnson, *Frank Lloyd Wright versus America: The 1930s* (Cambridge, Mass., 1990), 176, 179–230, 244.

[5] A. Hamilton, *The Appeal of Fascism* (London, 1971), 124.

[6] C. Maier, 'Between Taylorism and Technocracy: European Ideologies and the Vision of Industrial Productivity in the 1920s', *Journal of Contemporary History*, 5(2) (1970), and extensively in T. Hughes, *American Genesis: A Century of Invention and Technological Enthusiasm, 1870–1970* (New York, 1989), 249–84.

[7] Book II above, 512.

ambivalently than fascism, then why were the pioneering visionaries of machine warfare before, during, and immediately after the First World War mostly associated with proto-fascism and fascism rather than with Marxism? It might be claimed that fascism was simply overtly militaristic whereas socialism was ideologically humanitarian and pacifist; but Marxist and socialist thinkers had been considering the issue of war since the nineteenth century, if only for the transition period when socialist revolutions would have to be carried out and defended. A more significant reason for the difference in question would be that, from Engels to Jaures (for all the former's brilliant analysis of the evolution of technology, society, and war)[8] the thinkers of the Second International and socialist movements had been heavily committed to militias and mass popular armies on the model of the French Revolution, and opposed regular élite forces. An unceasing debate along these lines between the left and the right had been going on in France since 1871 (if not 1815). It provided the political background for the way the idea of a small, élite, professional, armoured force was received when proposed (unoriginally) in 1934 by Charles de Gaulle, himself a dubious republican. In Russia, learning by experience during the Civil War, War Commissar Trotsky created a centralized regular Red Army much against party mood, and defended it against advocates of local militias and partisan warfare. However, once the war was over, it was Trotsky himself who requested that the army be converted into a locally based militia, winning the debates against the 'red commanders', Frunze, Gusev, and Tukhachevsky, in successive party congresses during the early 1920, though ultimately losing the political power struggle itself.[9]

From 1923 to 1924 a group of officers largely influenced by Mikhail Tukhachevsky began to synthesize the lessons of modern war—the First World War, the Civil War, and the Russian–Polish War—into a systematic strategic and operational doctrine. But it was only from around 1928–9 that radical modern ideas of mechanized warfare were gradually absorbed, progressively turning the old concept of war on broad fronts into the advanced and innovative conception of 'deep battle' and 'deep operations'. Several studies of these developments are currently under way in the newly opened Soviet archives, which should much extend our knowledge of them. But to anyone familiar

[8] Above, 501–2.

[9] J. Erickson, *The Soviet High Command* (London, 1962), 113–43.

with the evolution of mechanized doctrine from a comparative perspective throughout the developed world during the 1920s, it is not difficult to discern where at least the initial stimulus for the Soviets' newly awakened interest in radical conceptions of mechanized warfare came from at that particular moment. It originated with the path-breaking manœuvres of the British Experimental Mechanized Force in 1927–8, which made use of the world's first operational fast and long-range tank, the Vickers Medium, and were perceived in conjunction with the revolutionary theories and propagandist writings of Fuller and his disciples, chief among them Liddell Hart. All armies of the industrial world closely studied these manœuvres, translated the British writers, and established experimental armoured formations of their own. In 1928, on the instruction of Secretary of State for War D. Davis, who had witnessed the British 1927 manœuvres, the US army formed and tried out for the first time its own experimental armoured brigade. The French were quickening the mechanization of their cavalry. The Italians, too, were closely studying and much influenced by the British manœuvres.[10] The first Soviet mechanized regiments intended for independent use were created in 1929–30. The Red Army's Field Service Regulations of 1929 stipulated that, in addition to their traditional role of direct infantry support, tanks would be incorporated into independent groups (DD) to be used for penetration into tactical depths against the enemy's artillery. This was the first step in the development of the concept of mechanized 'deep battle'.[11]

Fuller's *Tanks in the Great War* had already been translated into Russian in 1923. His seminal *The Reformation of War* was translated in 1931, edited and prefaced by Tukhachevsky, who quoted liberally from the range of Fuller's writings. Apparently Fuller's *Lectures on FSR III* or *On Future Warfare*, or both, were also translated during the 1930s. *The Remaking of Modern Armies* (1927) by Liddell Hart, regarded at first as Fuller's disciple, was translated in 1930. Martel saw many translated copies of his own book *In the Wake of the Tank* (1931) during his visit to the Soviet Union in 1936. As was the case in

[10] R. Ogorkiewicz, *Armoured Forces* (London, 1970), 17–18, 87; J. Hendrix, 'The Interwar Army and Mechanization: The American Approach', *Journal of Strategic Studies*, 16 (1993), 77–81; L. Ceva and A. Curami, *La Meccanizzazione dell'esercito italiano dalle origini al 1943* (Rome, 1989), 113–32; and for the Germans again, see extensively my *British Armour Theory and the Rise of the Panzer Arm: Revising the Revisionists* (London, 2000).

[11] Erickson, *The Soviet High Command*, 316.

Germany, regular periodical translations were as, if not more, important. 'Each issue of *Voina i revolyutsiya* contained a highly technical commentary on the tactics and technology of "foreign armies", e.g. French military organizations, Polish military regulations, *British writings on tank warfare.*' In 1932 Karl Radek, the editor of *Izvestiya* and an expert on military affairs in his own right, told Fuller and Liddell Hart in Geneva that they were the best-known foreign military experts in the Soviet Union, and that Fuller's book (unclear which) sold there more than 100,000 copies. According to Liddell Hart, Radek told him that the Red Army was then creating its first armoured corps, and invited him to come to the Soviet Union as an official adviser.[12]

From 1928 Tukhachevsky began to develop the concept of large-scale mechanized battle. His fellow theorist Viktor K. Triandafillov's admirable book *The Nature of the Operations of Modern Armies* (1929), which summarized the Soviet theorists' early work on successive large-scale operations ('operational art') and provided a seminal formulation of the concept of deep battle, only began to acknowledge the operational potential of the new fast, long-range tank and to evolve towards a more radical conception of mechanized warfare. But at that time Triandafillov was already making great progress, and by the time of his death in an air crash in 1931 he was rewriting his book in that direction.[13] All the same, if British theory and practice provided an initial and crucial stimulus for Soviet development, their reception was by no means slavish, but dialectic and innovative. Both Tukhachevky and Triandafillov advanced similar and striking critiques of Fuller's conception of the nature of modern mechanized warfare. Both were extremely capable, and Tukhachevsky in particular was a man of broad intellectual interests. Familiar as they were with Victor Germains's book, both echoed his principal points.

[12] All existing studies more or less recognize the British precedent and influence: Erickson, *The Soviet High Command*, 270, 308; id. 'The Soviet Union', in E. May (ed.), *Knowing One's Enemies: Intelligence Assessment before the Two World Wars* (Princeton, NJ, 1984), 395 (quotation; my emphasis); R. Simpkin, *Deep Battle: The Brainchild of Marshal Tukhachevsky* (London, 1987), 46; and Tukhachevsky on Liddell Hart and Martel, ibid. 126, 130, 132; D. Glantz, *Soviet Military Operational Art: In Pursuit of Deep Battle* (London, 1991), 19. See also B. H. Liddell Hart, *Memoirs* (2 vols., London, 1965), i. 196–8, reproducing his notes at the time, Liddel Hart Centre for Military Archives, King's College, London, 19 Feb. 1932, in 11/1932/6; 26 Feb. 1932, in 11/1932/1; A. J. Trythall, *'Boney' Fuller: The Intellectual General* (London, 1977), 175, 210.

[13] V. K. Triandafillov, *The Nature of the Operations of Modern Armies*, with foreword by J. Kipp and Introduction by J. Schneider (Ilford, Essex, 1994), esp. 20–2, 91, 110; Simpkin, *Deep Battle*, 38. See also *The Evolution of Soviet Operational Art*, i: *1927–1964* (London, 1995), trans. H. S. Orenstein, foreword and introd. by D. Glantz.

To be sure, a hostile, xenophobic, and polemic style was the mandatory norm of Soviet commentary on foreign, non-socialist works. Without such commentary a book simply could not appear in the Soviet Union, the very fact that it did indicating that it was regarded as useful.[14] No capitalist-bourgeois writer could expect better, and Fuller was not merely that but a fascist, a fact that Tukhachevsky saw clearly in 1931 three years before Fuller joined the BUF when it was founded in 1934, from a book published eight years earlier than that.[15] All the same, none of this should be taken as diminishing the sincerity of Triandafillov and Tukhachevsky in criticizing Fuller's ideas. Both their strategic and Marxist viewpoints converged in their critique.

Small, élite, fully mechanized, high-technology armies, wrote Triandafillov and Tukhachevsky, might perhaps be suitable for Britain's needs, both on account of her insular position and because of the shortcomings of capitalist societies in mobilizing the masses (also evident in Seeckt's ideas in Germany). But such armies would not do for large-scale continental wars, nor express the strength of a socialist state. This was the mistake of A. I. Verkhovskii, who advocated them, in Fuller's footsteps, in the Soviet Union. From the wider historical–economic perspective Tukhachevsky, like Germains, questioned Fuller's analysis of modern developments, claiming that wherever mechanization had taken place it had not reduced manpower but only redirected its employment while vastly increasing productivity. The same would hold true for armies. Machine armies would be big, not small, with a larger part of the manpower absorbed in a much-expanded and essential services and maintenance sector. Strategically, Triandafillov and Tukhachevsky argued that Fuller's great merit had been that he had raised the idea of deep penetration by armour, giving Britain the lead in respect to future warfare. Such penetration, however, could not alone decide the outcome of battle, or of war as a whole. Small armoured forces risked isolation and destruction. The massive human and industrial resources possessed by modern states promised protracted struggle and staggering attrition rates. For these reasons the largest armoured forces possible (together with aircraft and air-mobile forces, which Tukhachevsky, like Liddell Hart, criticized Fuller for neglecting) would have to work side by side and in inter-arms cooperation with masses of foot infantry and

[14] Simpkin in *Deep Battle*, 82, perceives this clearly.

[15] Tukhachevsky's preface to Fuller's *The Reformation of War*, printed in Simpkin, *Deep Battle*, 125–6.

conventional artillery within armies of millions.[16] It was the scheme for such cooperation that the authors of 'deep battle' and 'deep operations' masterfully developed during the 1930s until Stalin's purges of 1937–8 broke them.

The doctrine of 'deep battle' had its weaknesses. In particular, its missions definition for armour was highly differentiated. Three specialized armour group types were envisaged, destined respectively for close and long-range infantry support and long-distance penetration. More crucially, there were to be specialized tank types for each mission. Thus, as in the French and British armies, the Soviet fast, long-range tanks were unable to cooperate effectively with the slow, infantry-support models. After learning this to their cost in the opening campaigns of the Second World War, the Soviets (faster than the British) abandoned the old categories for good, adopting the main battle tank (medium and heavy) for all mission types. Indeed, this was exactly the point that the creators of the Panzer arm during the 1930s had criticized in Soviet armour, which they otherwise held in esteem. Walter Nehring concluded that the Soviet permanent functional splitting of armour was schematic and inflexible. Guderian wrote that while 'there is something to be said' for it, it 'demands a whole inventory of specialized tanks, with all the attendant disadvantages'.[17] On the other hand, whereas Guderian and the creators of the Panzer arm concentrated primarily on their armoured divisions, while Beck strove for a more comprehensive approach but was not as radical and advanced as the Soviets, 'deep battle' was from the beginning both comprehensive and advanced. It was the only fully developed doctrine of mobile warfare consciously and systematically devised from above before the Second World War for the use of a modern mass army which was only partly mechanized. The Germans only confronted the problems entailed by a partly mechanized army when they actually encountered

[16] Triandafillov, *Modern Armies*, 26–9; Tukhachevsky's preface to Fuller, *The Reformation of War*, in Simpkin, *Deep Battle*, 127–33; Tukhachersky, 'New Questions of War' (1931–2), in Simpkin, *Deep Battle*, 135–58, echoing Fuller in many ways; see also ibid. 159–60.

[17] W. Nehring, *Kampfwagen an die Front!* (Leipzig, 1934), 26; H. Guderian, *Achtung Panzer* (London, 1992; German original 1937), 153; 'Schnelle Truppen einst und jetzt', *Militärwissenschaftliche Rundschau*, 4 (1939), 237–8. The German criticism in the 1930s of the Soviet armour doctrine has been well noted by H. Senff, *Die Entwicklung der Panzerwaffe im deutschen Heer zwischen den beiden Weltkriegen* (Frankfurt a.M., 1969), 22. See also my *British Armour Theory and the Rise of the Panzer Arm*, 74–76.

these problems in 1940–1, during their campaigns in the West and against the Soviet Union.

To be sure, during the 1930s the Germans, too, wanted as big an army as possible and total mobilization. But for Hitler, Blomberg, or Guderian the desire to escape a full-scale war of attrition, which German resources could not sustain, by gambling on swift, short, and unconventional coups was overwhelming. Soviet Russia, on the other hand, was not similarly constrained. Russia's traditional reliance on mass and space remained good, in a modern form, for the Soviet Union.[18] In addition, Soviet strategic ideas were largely shaped by socialist precepts. Taken together, these factors constituted the foundations upon which the doctrine of 'deep battle' and 'deep operations' was built. Ever attacked for their fascination with mechanization by the army conservatives around Defence Commissar Klementi Voroshilov, the authors of 'deep battle' advocated, not futuristic élite machine armies on the model of Fuller or Douhet, but modern machines *cum* the masses.

[18] See also my 'Ideology, National Policy, Technology and Strategic Doctrine between the World Wars', *Journal of Strategic Studies*, 24:3 (2001), 1–18.

7

Conclusion

Fascism is primarily associated with Mussolini's regime in Italy and with that of Hitler in Germany, the two major Western countries where it reached power, with explosive effect. Yet this study deals only marginally with the actual practices of these regimes, or with the debated question of their 'modernizing' nature and impact, or with their part in perpetrating the Second World War. Its main concern is with fascism as an idea and a cultural mood which attracted intellectuals well before the First World War and before fascism was transformed into mass political movements. Among early twentieth-century intellectuals proto-fascism and fascism enjoyed widespread appeal. To be sure, fascism inclined towards nationalism. In countries like Italy and Germany, which felt themselves deprived in the international arena, it also possessed a strong revisionist foreign policy element and a militaristic tendency, which constituted an important part of its appeal and helped it into power. On the whole, however, fascism was perhaps even more about domestic affairs. First and foremost, it was a cultural and political response to the rise of mass society, urbanization, and secularization which took place during the closing decades of the nineteenth century. While not all those born in the last quarter of the nineteenth century were fascists, practically all fascists were born during that period (d'Annunzio, born in 1863, was an exception and in this respect, too, is rightly regarded as a forerunner). The fascists were looking for a 'Third Way' to modernity that would preserve 'civilization' and élite culture from the threat of democratic and socialist plebeianism, that would encompass the masses without being dominated by them, and that would counter the 'disenchantment of life' associated with modern rationalism. As such, fascist varieties mixed varying degrees of pre-industrial nostalgia and agrarian mythology with the most strident modernist and futurist visions. It is this latter streak of fascist modernism, in its intimate relation to visions of modern machine warfare, that has concerned us here.

The fact that most if not all of the radical visionaries of machine warfare were associated with fascism does not indicate that it was more modernist than liberalism (the Marxist–socialist comparison has already been discussed); it was simply more enthusiastically so. By nature fascist modernism was avant-gardist, utopian, futuristic, and inclined to deploy sweeping rhetoric and flamboyant imagery. This is exactly the stuff of which visions are made and with which headlines are captured. By the same token, however, these qualities do not necessarily translate all that well into reality. For vision—and the word has been deliberately chosen—is different, has in it both more and less than doctrine. It is a prophetic and inspiring picture, strikingly sketched with compelling rhetorical devices, but with little systematic elaboration of detail. As such, visions are often partly or wholly far-fetched, poorly grounded in experience, and divorced from existing conditions, and they ignore the complexity of circumstances, sometimes deliberately. They may prove a sound bridge to the future, or they may not.

To be sure, whatever precedent fascists could claim in developing radical conceptions of machine warfare, such ideas were also adopted, for good or for ill, by others. What is more, when we move from the domain of abstract ideas to reality, the deployment of mechanized armies in a large-scale great-power war depended on industrial weight, and here Britain and the Soviet Union were each roughly equal to Germany, while the United States was far superior to all, and Italy did not count. Furthermore, in the ultimate test of war production the fascist regimes did not prove to be the model of efficiency that fascist modernists had envisaged they would be and that others, too, at the time believed they were. War production was far more systematically and efficiently organized by their enemies.

As it happened, contrary to Fuller's prediction and that of other radical modernists, it was neither fascism nor communism that emerged victorious from the Armageddon of the twentieth century but—as of today—the outdated and expected loser, liberal democracy. This was so perhaps because liberal democracy was after all more in tune with the nature of modernity than its rivals; or alternatively, maybe because the liberal democratic United States was simply so much more powerful than the other great powers that it decided in favour of the coalitions it joined all three great power conflicts of the twentieth century. Either way, as the twentieth century progressed, the world's greatest concentration of power, and the world's technologically most advanced societies, were increasingly to be found in the liberal democratic camp—in the West and among those who emulated its model. It remained for Fuller's disciple, Liddell Hart—who, unlike his mentor, had become a staunch liberal—to develop a strategic blueprint designed to fit the aims, capabilities, and limitations of a liberal West moving at the forefront of modernity.

Part II

Liddell Hart, Modern, and 'Post-Modern' Strategy

I

Introduction

Basil Henry Liddell Hart (1895–1970) is perhaps the most famous strategic theorist of the twentieth century. Yet since his death (which coincided with the opening of the British archives of the interwar period), his ideas have come under searching scholarly criticism, and his reputation has suffered heavy blows. The influential doctrines he advocated in the 1930s—such as the 'British Way in Warfare', Limited Liability, and the superiority of defence—have been criticized as historically dubious, politically unrealistic, and strategically harmful.[1] His (and Fuller's) reformist rhetoric, which blamed mostly conservatism and vested organizational interests for the British army's failure to adopt the British-pioneered doctrine of armoured warfare, has been qualified and revised.[2] The predominant role that he claimed in the development of that doctrine has been judged to be overstated.[3] Furthermore, strong evidence has been produced that Liddell Hart considerably exaggerated his influence on the creators of the German Panzer arm.[4] Indeed, most damaging of all, in these and other cases he has been found guilty of a recurring tendency to manipulate evidence, and people, in order to protect and enhance his reputation. The

[1] See esp. C. Barnett, *Britain and Her Army, 1509–1970* (London 1970); *The Collapse of British Power* (London, 1972), 497–503, 581; M. Howard, 'Liddell Hart' (1970) ['LH'] and 'The British Way in Warfare: A Reappraisal' (1974), reprinted in *The Causes of War* (London, 1984), 237–47, 189–207; P. Kennedy, *The Rise and Fall of British Naval Mastery* (London, 1976); B. Bond, *Liddell Hart: A Study of His Military Thought* (London, 1977) [*LH*], 65–118; *British Military Policy between the Two World Wars* (Oxford, 1980); J. Mearsheimer, *Liddell Hart and the Weight of History* [*LH*] (London, 1988); D. French, *The British Way in Warfare, 1688–2000* (London, 1990); H. Strachan, 'The British Way in Warfare', in D. Chandler (ed.), *The Oxford Illustrated History of the British Army* (Oxford, 1994), 417–34.

[2] M. Howard, *The Continental Commitment* (London, 1972); H. Winton, *To Change an Army: General Sir John Burnett-Stuart and British Armoured Doctrine, 1927–1938* (Lawrence, KS, 1988); Bond, *Military Policy.*

[3] Winton, *To Change an Army*; K. Macksey, *The Tank Pioneers* (London, 1981); Mearsheimer, *LH*, 42–4; J. P. Harris, *Men, Ideas and Tanks: British Military Thought and Armoured Forces, 1903–1939* (Manchester, 1995).

[4] K. Macksey, *Guderian: Panzer General* (London, 1975), 40–1; *The Tank Pioneers*, 118, 216; picked up and developed by Mearsheimer, *LH*, 160–7, 184–201.

unattractive side of Liddell Hart's character, his long-observed vanity and obsession with fame, was harshly exposed in the most recent full-scale study of his work, John Mearsheimer's *Liddell Hart and the Weight of History* (1988), overshadowing his more praiseworthy qualities and casting a sinister light on his entire career.

There has now developed heightened awareness of Liddell Hart's knack for self-advertisement and genius for cultivating contacts and personal relationships, all the more surprising in such a self-conscious, highly strung, and socially awkward man. This genius is testified to by the nearly 1,000 individuals whose files of correspondence with Liddell Hart, preserved in his huge archive, read like an international *Who's Who* of military, political, and academic personae. In his large country house Liddell Hart entertained a constant march of guests from all over the world, including most of the rising generation of young military historians. Although highly egocentric, he took genuine interest in their work, encouraged them, and invested enormous effort in helping them. In the process, however, they were chained to him by the 'hoops of steel' of friendship, respect, and gratitude, disarming them as potential critics, at least during his lifetime.[5] Since Liddell Hart, as Churchill jested about himself, decisively shaped scholarly and popular perceptions by writing so much of the history of his times and of his own deeds himself, the process of critical reassessment has been natural and more than necessary.

In my research I have discovered a great deal of new and unflattering information about Liddell Hart. Yet I have also found that the most serious charges levelled against him are factually erroneous and based on almost incredible historiographical slips on the part of his chief critic, John Mearsheimer. Most of this relates to Liddell Hart's theory of armoured warfare and his influence on the creators of the German Panzer arm, to which I have dedicated separate studies.[6] Therefore, in view of the distortions introduced both by Liddell Hart himself and by his critics, which cast doubt on all that supposedly was known about him, no less than a full-scale reconstruction of his work and influence has become necessary. Nothing could be taken for granted as accepted fact. However, while putting the record straight was an indispensable

[5] In addition to Mearsheimer, see the superb commentary in Howard, 'LH' (the quotation is from p. 238); and Bond, *LH*, 1–10.

[6] Compiled in my *British Armour Theory and the Rise of the Panzer Arm: Revising the Revisionists* (London, 2000).

preliminary condition for the present study, it is not in itself its purpose. The critical wave against Liddell Hart has been so sweeping that the idea that he holds a pivotal place in the development of twentieth-century strategic theory might appear strange and wholly outdated to many in the scholarly community. Yet this is precisely what this study sets out to establish. It will be argued here that Liddell Hart's life-work, whose full development remains largely unrecognized, was far weightier than it is commonly considered today. Moreover, it will be claimed that it reflected and foreshadowed, in the field of strategic theory, the conditions and outlook of a society and an age: the evolving Western liberal democracy, whose expanding orbit would increasingly dominate the twentieth century, and seems likely to extend further into the future. The strategic paradigm of an epoch is offered here through the intellectual biography of a man.

Our starting-point is the Great War, which during the past decades has been snatched from the hands of military historians by cultural historians, who have turned it into a growth industry. While not the beginning of modernity, the war is now widely regarded as a towering landmark in the growth of modern consciousness.[7] As John Mueller has argued in his *Retreat from Doomsday: The Obsolescence of Major Wars* (1989), the war signalled a profound change of attitude to the phenomenon of war and its conduct. However, in contrast to Mueller, it will be claimed here that it was predominantly liberal opinion that was strongly affected by this change for reasons that are inherent in the development of modern liberal societies.[8] Our location is thus the first, and historically the most deeply rooted, mass liberal-democratic great powers of the West, and in particular Britain. It was then and there that the problem of war for modern liberal societies first imposed itself in all its starkness, and that a distinctive strategic response began to evolve.

[7] See below, but also, for an important qualification stressing the continuity of traditional values and images, J. Winter, *Sites of Memory, Sites of Mourning: The Great War in European Cultural History* (Cambridge, 1995).

[8] J. Mueller, *Retreat from Doomsday: The Obsolescence of Major War* (New York, 1989). For criticisms somewhat like my own, see C. Kaysen, 'Is War Obsolete? A Review Essay', *International Security*, 14 (1990), 42–63; R. Schweller, 'Domestic Structure and Preventive War: Are Democracies More Pacific?', *World Politics*, 44 (1992), 235–69.

2

Background: The First World War in Western Consciousness

Historical

The First World War was a landmark in Western consciousness, yet its significance for the various nations involved differed greatly. A formal and vague consensus in favour of international reconciliation and co-operation and against the use of force in international relations, which appeared to have crystallized from the mid-1920s, proved fragile and short-lived. With the collapse of the international economic system, it was shaken off by those countries to whom the postwar order gave the least reason to be satisfied with the Locarno territorial status quo, and whose deep-seated national traditions made them less receptive to the so-called Locarno spirit. It proved more durable, however, in the countries which emerged on the winning side of the war, whose interests were less directly or obviously under threat, and in which internationalist and liberal notions were a far more important part of the national make-up. Indeed, rather than generating anything fundamentally new, the war effectively accentuated and polarized long-standing differences in national attitudes. Crudely put, one was moving along an attitude spectrum as one was travelling west, mentally as well as geographically. And it is with the westernmost parts of the West that this study is concerned. As early as the First World War, President Wilson's internationalist and liberal crusade had forced evasive tactics and clever rhetoric on the other, more cynical participants in the war and in the peace-making, thus producing a tension which led the United States to isolationism. But in Britain, too, the new attitudes came to the fore during the Locarno era, increasingly underlying public, political, and even official perceptions and reactions for most of the interwar period.[1] While hard-core pacifism, though stronger and

[1] For 'idealists' versus 'pragmatists' in British officialdom, see in P. Towle, 'British Security and Disarmament Policy in Europe in the 1920s', in R. Ahmann, A. M. Birke, and M. Howard (eds.), *The Quest for Stability: Problems of West European Security, 1918–1957* (Oxford, 1993), 127–53.

more vocal than before, remained a marginal phenomenon, there was a much wider loss of faith in the use of force in international relations, which, it was believed, was to be discarded and replaced by growing cooperation and by collective security. This change of outlook was bound up with a strong reaction against those features of the prewar political and value system which were held responsible for the war. Correspondingly came also a change of attitude towards the war itself.

By the beginning of the twentieth century the heightened international rivalries—brought about by the imperialist contest and made all the more inflammable by rapid social change—had given rise to nationalist forces and social-Darwinist notions throughout the West. Edwardian Britain (as well as Theodore Roosevelt's America) was no exception to this rule. Underlined by nationalist and racialist rhetoric and supported by political, journalistic, and academic propaganda, the Naval League, National Service League, Movement for Imperial Federation, and Movement for National Efficiency, while rarely equalling their German counterparts in chauvinist ferocity or in the extent of their official and popular support, were none the less prominent features of British public life in the prewar period.[2] When war came in 1914, these notions and forces moved closer to centre stage in all the belligerent countries.

As everywhere else in Europe, the declaration of war was greeted in Britain with widespread manifestations of popular enthusiasm. War was regarded in all countries as a defensive necessity, and after a decade of rising international tensions and repeated crises there was a common feeling, even a sense of relief, that things had to be settled once and for all, even by war. More deeply, historians have pointed out that in all countries workers seemed to have found in the war an exhilarating experience and an escape from a dull routine, and that the educated classes responded in essentially the same way. The intellectuals welcomed the war as the supreme test of nations' vitality and as a purifying and elevating experience for a mechanistic, materialistic, and decadent

[2] See G. R. Searle, *The Quest for National Efficiency* (Oxford, 1971); P. Kennedy and A. Nicholls (eds.), *Nationalist and Racialist Movements in Britain and Germany before 1914* (London, 1981); J. Gooch, 'Attitude to War in Late Victorian and Edwardian England', in *The Prospect of War: Studies in British Defence Policy, 1847–1942* (London, 1981), 35–51; A. J. A. Morris, *The Scaremongers: The Advocacy of War and Rearmament, 1896–1914* (London, 1984); M. Howard, 'Empire, Race and War in pre-1914 Britain', in *The Lessons of History* (Oxford, 1991), 63–80; P. Crook, *Darwinism, War and History* (Cambridge, 1994). Obsolete but still useful for its wealth of source material is C. E. Playne, *The Pre-war Mind in Britain* (London, 1928).

mass/bourgeois society, the product of modernity.[3] In all countries the educated young, of whom society expected the most, were particularly moved by these sentiments. In Britain, the public-school ethos and response to the war can be regarded as merely a local variant of a cross-European phenomenon. While not in itself militaristic, the public-school ethos, rooted and codified in the nineteenth century, cultivated the qualities of leadership, honour, sportsmanship, chivalry, Christian masculinity, and patriotism which proved so important in 1914 and after. During late 1914 student societies all over Britain, moved by the surge in patriotic sentiments, were passing resolutions exalting the noble qualities of war.[4]

The subsequent trauma of the war and of the so-called 'lost generation', especially in its British manifestation, is a widely familiar subject. Still, a brief summary of this complex experience is in order.[5] From the point of view of its impact on national consciousness and morale, the experience was seen mainly through the eyes of the educated classes, who arguably reacted the most traumatically or, in any case, were able to make their voice heard more prominently, and who constituted the British political, social, and cultural élite. Within these classes most attention has focused on the young who enlisted and bore the brunt of the war, the 'generation of 1914', particularly the graduates of the élite public schools.

From August 1914, public-school graduates streamed in their thousands to enlist, supplying the cadre of officers for Britain's New Armies throughout the war. Their romantic enthusiasm lasted long and, artistically, came to be symbolized for generations of schoolboys by the sublime and heroic war sonnets of Rupert Brooke, who died on his way to Gallipoli in April 1915. Only gradually, with the routine of trench warfare and the climactic bloodletting of Ypres, Neuve Chapelle, Loos, and the Somme, did a new note creep in. The more sensitive

[3] See esp. R. Stromberg, *Redemption by War: The Intellectuals and 1914* (Lawrence, KS, 1982), 1–24 and *passim*; also R. Wohl, *The Generation of 1914* (Cambridge, Mass., 1979); E. J. Leed, *No Man's Land: Combat and Identity in World War I* (Cambridge, 1979); M. Adams, *The Great Adventure: Male Desire and the Coming of World War I* (Bloomington, Ind., 1990); F. Fields, *British and French Writers of the First World War* (Cambridge, 1991).

[4] See P. Parker, *The Old Lie: The Great War and the Public-School Ethos* (London, 1987); for the resolutions, pp. 61–2; for the 'code' and its role in British culture, see L. Susser, 'Facist and Anti-Fascist Attitudes in Britain between the Wars' (doctoral dissertation, Oxford University, 1988).

[5] See esp. P. Fussell, *The Great War and Modern Memory* (Oxford, 1975) and, even more, S. Hynes, *A War Imagined: The First World War and English Culture* (London, 1990).

psyches, like the front-line poets Siegfried Sassoon, Wilfred Owen, and Robert Graves, assumed a distinctively realistic tone, depicting the horror and destruction of the war, blood and mud, fear, agony, exhaustion, death and mutilation. Front-line soldiers, of British as well as of other nationalities, consistently reported a failure of communication with the civilian rear. To the soldiers' surprise, people in the rear not only continued to live their life much the same as before (in Britain much more than in the blockaded Central Powers) but also, fed on the newspapers' rosy reports from the front line, failed to comprehend the nature of life there and identify with the combatants' experience.[6] These feelings were of existential rather than ideological or political nature. Only in about late 1916, after the Battle of the Somme, were a very few dissenting voices heard among front-line officers, blaming the 'Old Men' in government for prolonging the war by rejecting a negotiated peace on the basis of the *status quo ante*.[7] Even fewer, like the war hero Siegfried Sassoon, were those who made their opinions public and became conscientious objectors, to the disdain of their front-line fellows.

On the whole, however—and this cannot be emphasized too strongly—dissent in the British armed forces was a very marginal phenomenon. While the French army, which admittedly had undergone even harsher trials than the British, suffered from widespread mutinies in the summer of 1917, and the Italian, Russian, Austro-Hungarian, and German armies, each in turn, experienced collapses of morale by the end of the war, the British army never lost its fighting spirit. (Arguably, the 5th Army came close to it in the spring of 1918.)[8] High idealism and youthful enthusiasm may have gone, but they were superseded by dogged resilience. At home, where the government used unprecedented measures to mobilize the country's resources for war, suppress opposition to it, and censor information, there was relatively little dissent and only some 16,000 conscientious objectors.[9] While people hoped that the war would end wars, they also voted in their masses in the first peacetime elections for a peace that would make Germany pay the cost of the

[6] R. Graves, *Goodbye to All That* (London, 1929), 187–8; S. Sassoon, *Memoirs of an Infantry Officer* (London, 1930), 126–44, 243–71; Erich Maria Remarque, *All Quiet on the Western Front* (London, 1929), 183–6; Hynes, *A War Imagined*, 119.

[7] Sassoon, *Memoirs*, 273–334; Graves, *Goodbye to All That*, 307–8, 318–25.

[8] A recent study on this aspect is J. G. Fuller, *Troop Morale and Popular Culture in the British and Dominion Armies, 1914–1918* (Oxford, 1990).

[9] M. Ceadel, *Pacifism in Britain, 1914–1945* (Oxford, 1980), 38–41; A. J. P. Taylor, *British History, 1914–1945* (London, 1975), 87–8.

war. The army was proud of its victory, and soldiers would deny that they were in any way disillusioned or angry at the end of the war.[10] 'Disillusionment' came much later, was particularly noticeable and potent in the victorious Western powers, and can only be understood in reference to the overall political and cultural features of those powers.

Two stages have been discerned in the interwar reaction to the war in Britain. From the coming of peace to the mid-1920s there was growing disappointment with the outcome of the war. In Britain almost as strongly as on the Continent, the upper and middle classes in particular felt disoriented in a world that appeared to have changed radically. There was a nostalgic sense of loss focusing on the old European civilization and its supposed qualities of social order, well-being, and security, which the war was believed to have destroyed. Naturally, much of this was a reaction by the old élites to a society which had been changing irrespective of the war, which was becoming more pluralistic, and in which aristocratic rule was giving way to a more bureaucratic form of government.[11] All the same, the economic depression of the early 1920s was real enough, and so was the endemic problem of the German reparations and of Germany's status in the international political and economic system. Keynes's highly influential book *The Economic Consequences of the Peace* (1920) was increasingly shaping the way educated people viewed the aftermath of the war in the United States and Britain. The book denounced the 'Carthaginian peace' imposed on Germany, demonstrating not only that the reparation sums were utterly beyond her means but that in an age of economic interdependence her ruin also hindered the economic recovery of her former enemies, who were also her past, present, and future trade partners.

The Locarno era, based on the gradual settlement of the reparation problem and the reconstruction of the European economy, and heralding a new era of political reconciliation and cooperation, completed the change of attitude to the war. It was now increasingly regarded as a senseless massacre, a disaster which European civilization had barely survived and could certainly not repeat. Reflecting and in turn shaping this change of mood were the literary memories of front-line veterans, now erupting in a remarkably dense sequence. Best-sellers such as

[10] See e.g. H. Essame, *The Battle for Europe, 1918* (London, 1972), 2; also Hynes, *A War Imagined*, 450.

[11] Wohl, *Generation of 1914*, 121.

Edmund Blunden's *Undertones of War* (1928), Richard Aldington's *Death of a Hero* (1929), Robert Graves's *Goodbye to All That* (1929), Erich Maria Remarque's *All Quiet in the Western Front* (1929), Ernest Hemingway's *A Farewell to Arms* (1929), and Siegfried Sassoon's *Memoirs of an Infantry Officer* (1930), all appearing almost simultaneously a decade after the war's end, were some of the most famous works that came to represent the reaction against the experience of the war. In seemingly detached, absurd, and sometime macabre tone they depicted a picture of barbarity, degradation, and day-to-day misery in trench warfare life. Overshadowing all was the sense of a terrible and senseless sacrifice, of life, youth and innocence, associated with the notion of the 'lost generation'.

To be sure, many objected to the new attitude towards the war. T. E. Lawrence, 'Lawrence of Arabia', for one, argued that the experience of the war had been much less horrible for the participants than it had been made to appear in hindsight. Indeed, it has been shown that the war authors of the late 1920s treated the war retrospectively far more negatively than they had done during the war itself. Furthermore, even at the time the 'war literature' was coming out it is doubtful if its avant-garde spirit was in any proportional sense 'representative' of the veterans' attitudes. Thus, many scholars have been critical of the shape taken by historical memory and the popular image of the war.[12] They have found it necessary to remind people that the war was not a senseless affair, that the stakes were real and high, and that a German victory and German domination of Europe would have mattered a great deal both to Britain and to the course of world history. In respect to the so-called 'lost generation', it has been pointed out that the number of Britons killed in the war amounted to no more than 12 per cent of those who had enlisted. It was smaller in absolute—and even more in proportional—terms than the number of those killed in the other belligerent powers: some 750,000, to France's 1,300,000 and to Germany's two million. None the less, it has been admitted that the more than 37,000 officers killed came unproportionally from the élite public schools and university colleges, leaving appalling gaps in their ranks. Of the 5,588 Old Etonians who served in the war, 1,159 were killed and 1,469 were wounded. In other public schools proportions were similar and even

[12] See e.g. Essame, *The Battle for Europe, 1918*, 2; Hynes, *A War Imagined*, 450–5; Wohl, *Generation of 1914*, 120; Howard, 'Liddell Hart', in *The Causes of War*, 239, and repeatedly elsewhere; B. Bond (ed.), *The First World War and British Military History* (Oxford, 1991), 1–2.

worse. Among Oxford and Cambridge students the death toll of about one-quarter was double the national rate. Of Liddell Hart's matriculation year in Corpus Christi, Cambridge, (1913) 27 per cent were killed in the war.[13]

Establishing facts and dispelling myths are crucial for historical understanding, but it is just as essential to recognize that facts only get their meaning within comprehensive outlooks—integrating values, sensibilities, beliefs, attitudes, interests, and expectations. These are fundamentally subjective, vary between people, societies, and cultures, and change over time. Three-quarters of a million dead are *in themselves* neither a great many nor a few; nor were the overall losses and cost of the war unprecedented in the annals of European history.[14] Whether casualties on such scale are 'acceptable' or 'unacceptable' to any given society depends on cultural attitudes and historical circumstances.[15] In Germany, which, in relation to population, had suffered twice as many casualties as Britain, there was certainly much war-weariness and a widespread loss of enthusiasm for war. The most internationally famous anti-war author, Remarque, was a German liberal and pacifist, and many other German war authors wrote in a similar vein.[16] Furthermore, it was widely realized even by right-wingers that in case of a war a superior coalition would most likely again be created against Germany, a realization that served as a strong deterrent from war. For all that, Germany was defeated, humiliated, and eager to revise the peace settlement. Nationalism, militarism, and anti-liberalism were powerful elements within its political, social, and cultural fabric. Nostalgic memories of trench camaraderie thus played an important social and political role in the aftermath of the war, as they did in Italy. Ernst Jünger's books, glorifying his experience in the trenches and exalting the qualities of war, competed with Remarque's for popularity (at least in Germany) and were personally and artistically neither less nor more

[13] For a thorough study of the statistics, see J. M. Winter, *The Great War and the British People* (London, 1986), 65–75, 85–99, concluding that there was justification to the notion of the 'lost generation'; also Wohl, *Generation of 1914*, 113–15, 120–1; Parker, *Public-School Ethos*, 16–17, 279; Hynes, *A War Imagined*, 385–6; D. French, *British Strategy and War Aims* (London, 1916), 244–7; H. Strachan, 'Liddell Hart, Cruttwell, and Falls', in Bond, *The First World War*, 42.

[14] For the latter point see also J. Mueller, *Retreat from Doomsday: The Obsolescence of Major War* (New York, 1989), 7–8, 55.

[15] This point is well made in E. Cobley, *Representing War: Form and Ideology in First World War Narratives* (Toronto, 1993), 3, 14–15, 29–70, and *passim*.

[16] See Franz Karl Stanzel and Martin Löschnig (ed.), *Intimate Enemies: English and German Literary Reactions to the Great War* (Heidelberg, 1993).

'authentic' or 'objective'.[17] If, from the late 1920s on, people in Britain increasingly came to regard the price of the war as too terrible to bear, it is because by that time they increasingly came to regard the war itself and war in general as fundamentally senseless and unnecessary. Most of them would probably not have denied that, as things turned out, Britain had defended her vital interests in the First World War. Yet, more deeply, they came to feel that under modern conditions all-out wars between great powers were in *nobody's* interest in the first place, and that the whole process that had brought the war into being, and kept it going, was the result of outdated values and misguided goals, ruinously followed by both governments and peoples.

These, of course, were old liberal notions, and indeed it was predominantly with liberal opinion that the trauma of the war was thus expressed. Those societies where liberal values were the strongest reacted the most. It was in this factor, rather then in the actual losses sustained, that the clearest correlation of the reaction against the war is to be traced. The two most extreme cases for demonstrating this argument are the United States and Serbia. The mightiest power in the world was not traumatized by heavy losses and crippling economic costs, as were the European belligerents. She suffered relatively very light casualties in her brief involvement in the war and gained tremendously from it materially, replacing Britain as the world's leading banker, creditor, and insurer. Nevertheless, it was in the United States that the disgust with and regret about participating in the war were the most rapid and sweeping. By comparison, the small and backward Serbia suffered, relative to population, the heaviest casualties of all the warring nations and was totally ravaged by the war and occupation. Nevertheless, it hardly experienced the famous 'trauma' of and 'disillusion' with the war. A modern, industrialized and liberal society was a prerequisite for these sentiments.

While Liberalism, as a movement and an ideology, may have been a minority view in Britain, liberalism, in its broadest sense, was not. It would thus be a mistake to regard the change of outlook in respect to the war as confined to a particular avant-garde group or a minority. While it was mainly among parts of the educated élite that this change first became noticeable by the late 1920s, by the 1930s, as international

[17] As mentioned before, the significant differences that existed here between liberal and non-liberal countries is not sufficiently recognized in Mueller's *Retreat from Doomsday*, esp. 53–68.

tensions were again rising, a wide consensus prevailed among the British public against involvement in another large-scale war. As mentioned before, within this consensus only a small minority were hardcore pacifists.[18] The famous Oxford Union vote of 1933 against fighting for 'King and Country' was above all a gesture, reflecting how the attitudes of youth had changed by comparison with 1914. As the 'Peace Ballot' of early 1935 revealed, the majority of the British public at least nominally seems to have believed in international cooperation to deter would-be aggressors. In any case, the public mood was unmistakable; and in the more fully democratized Britain, where universal voting rights had been introduced after the war, popular opinion made or broke governments. By 1935 collective security had become the official policy of all the major parties in Britain. Indeed, rather than merely responding to their electorate, the majority of the political class itself genuinely felt as the 1930s unfolded that a repetition of anything like the First World War was simply too horrible to contemplate.

A change in public perceptions of the military conduct of the war developed hand in hand with the change of attitude to the war itself. Winston Churchill's criticism of the war of attrition in the West and the way it was directed, already harsh in the second volume (1923) of his widely read, brilliant, and controversial *World Crisis*, became even more sweeping in the third volume (1927). Lloyd George's *War Memoirs*, published during the mid-1930s, was another major indictment of the generals. Beyond the haggling, reproaches, and recriminations among politicians and generals over the heavy toll of the war, there lay the same fundamental problem that preoccupied interwar Britain: the mass killing and economic devastation of the Great War increasingly came to be regarded as wholly out of step with the needs and sensibilities of the modern world; in case of a conflict, were there any strategic alternatives?

Crucially influenced by Fuller, Liddell Hart developed during the 1920s into a critic of the First World War. In contrast to Fuller, however, he became a staunch liberal, and was thus better positioned to articulate the political and strategic dilemma which the First World War starkly imposed on the consciousness of modern liberal-democratic societies. Aged 19 when the war started, Liddell Hart was a typical representative of the 'generation of 1914'. His intellectual development mirrored the development of that generation almost theme by theme.

[18] M. Ceadel, *Pacifism in Britain, 1914–1945* (Oxford, 1980).

Biographical

Basil Hart (he would add his mother's maiden name, Liddell, to his surname only in the early 1920s) was born in 1895. His father was a Wesleyan minister, and Basil had a typical upper-middle-class upbringing. He went to St Paul's and from there to Corpus Christi College, Cambridge, to read history. As a boy he was sensitive, a little awkward, and dreamy. His lifelong bent could already be seen in his youthful enthusiasm for games, aviation, and military history, on which he wrote both fiction and journalistic pieces with the passionate absorption and vivid imagination which would characterize his entire career. The war which broke out before the beginning of his second year in Cambridge interrupted his formal education, which he would never complete. Against his parents' wishes and with an enthusiasm his later autobiography does not fully betray, he joined the volunteers to Kitchener's New Armies. He received a temporary commission, trained with the University's OTC, and became a second lieutenant in the King's Own Yorkshire Light Infantry. As his early letters and notes reveal, he found training and army life most exciting, a feeling he never lost throughout the war.

His enthusiasm has been fully documented by his biographers. In a note of an almost archetypal nature, dated 28 November 1914, he wrote:

> Before the war I, Basil Hart, was a Socialist, a Pacifist, an anti-conscriptionist and an anti-disciplinist, disapproving of all state checks on the liberty of the individual and one who hoped for internationalization. I held thinkers in greater admiration than warriors.
>
> Now having studied the principles of warfare and undergone military training and seen the effects of it on my companions the following are my opinions:
>
> 1. I *believe* (i) in the supremacy of the aristocracy of race (and birth) (ii) in the supremacy of the individual.
>
> 2. In compulsory military service because it is the only possible life for a *man* and brings out all the finest qualities of manhood.
>
> 3. I have acquired rather a contempt for mere thinkers and men of books who have not come to full realisation of what true manhood means. . . .
>
> 4. I exalt the great general into the highest position in the roll of great men and consider it requires higher mental qualities than any other line of life.
>
> 5. I consider the Slavs, by which I indicate a greater Russia, will rule both Europe and Asia and will have world domination, being the finest and most virile civilisation and having the finest qualities of all races, and that the day of conquest and expansion is not yet over.
>
> 6. Socialism and its forms are an impossibility unless human nature radically alters.
>
> . . .

> 8. Many of the German militarist ideas are sound, but I oppose the Germans because I do not consider that the German type of mind is the one to carry out their ideas.
>
> I prefer brilliance to mechanical and methodical mediocracy. . . . I certainly believe that absolute peace is detrimental to true manhood, but 20th Century war is too frightful. If you could have war without its *explosive* horrors it would be a good thing. . . . My belief in the necessary inferiority of women is more profound than ever.[19]

Rather than a biographical curiosity, this highly revealing document deserves to be included in any anthology of the 'generation of 1914'. Here was a typical statement of a turn-of-the-century outlook which with obvious modifications could have been attributed to either of the Moltkes. However, in the background was a no less typical credo of nineteenth-century liberalism, swept aside in the enthusiasm of war but destined to return when this enthusiasm would fade away.

This was not to occur during the war. Liddell Hart arrived in France in late summer 1915 but was shortly after disabled by illness. Having pressed to return to the front, he was soon concussed by a German shell and sent home to convalesce. He returned to France in time to participate in the Somme offensive, was gassed in its third week, and was disabled again, this time for good. His writings at the time reveal not only exhilaration at his front-line experience but also naïve admiration for everything related to the British military performance, an uncritical adulation of the qualities of the British staff work, and a virtual worship of the British commanding generals.[20]

Later to become one of the most famous detractors of the experience of the First World War and the scourge of the British high command, Liddell Hart wrote before the Somme offensive: 'In the first half of the war our leadership was flawless, and it may be noted that our generalship, alone of all the nations engaged, was perfect.'[21] The ensuing battle caused no change in his opinion. Convalescing in England in September 1916, he wrote a little book entitled *Impressions of the*

[19] Liddell Hart Centre for Military Archives, King's College, London [King's], 7/1917/10; B. Bond, *Liddell Hart: A Study of His Military Thought* (London, 1977) [*LH*], 15–16.

[20] Hero-worship was prevalent among the 'generation of 1914'; for Wilfred Owen, see Parker, *Public-School Ethos*, 194.

[21] King's, 7/1916/21; the following has been fully documented in Bond, *LH*, 17–18; J. Mearsheimer, *Liddell Hart and the Weight of History* (London, 1988) [*LH*] 22–5; also, briefly, B. H. Liddell Hart, *The Memoirs of Captain Liddell Hart* (2 vols., London, 1965), i. 26.

Great British Offensive on the Somme. 'Wonderful' was probably the most recurring adjective in this enthusiastic book. In praising the preparations for the would-be notorious first day of the offensive, he wrote about 'the amazing perfection of our organization, which in generalship and work were super-German'. He maintained that 'the British G.H.Q. . . . under Haig's regime comprises the most brilliant collection of brains in the world . . . 90 percent of our general staff officers are really brilliant men, with quite a large number of men amongst them who have a genius for war'.[22] In summary he wrote:

> War, at least modern war, as waged in the Western Front, is horrible and ghastly beyond all imagination of the civilian. Nevertheless it has an awe-inspiring grandeur of its own, and it ennobles and brings out the highest in a man's character such as no other thing could. Could one but remove the horrible suffering and mutilation it would be the finest purifier of nations ever known.[23]

In an early 1917 article for the *Saturday Review* Liddell Hart called civilian writers who had criticized the High Command 'armchair strategists', and argued that they failed to comprehend the nature of modern warfare.[24]

Medically unfit to return to front-line service, Liddell Hart was posted to a couple of clerical jobs before being assigned to train Volunteers, who at the decision of the War Office were being upgraded to take up the function of home defence from the Territorials, who had left for France. He performed this humble duty for the last year and a half of the war, and unwittingly it proved to be the springboard of his career. After 1916 the platoon replaced the company as the smallest independent combat unit, and there was much demand for clear directions and instructions for its drill.[25] Revealing a knack for devising, systematizing, and simplifying drill, Liddell Hart produced a number of

[22] King's, 7/1916/22, pp. 1, 76–85, 96. Liddell Hart's unreserved admiration for the high command can also be seen in his talk with John Buchan, who belonged to Haig's personal staff: King's, 7/1916/36.

[23] Ibid. 93. For reasons of field security the book was not authorized for publication, but Liddell Hart condensed its main arguments in an article entitled 'Great Generals of the War', published in the *Daily Express* on 21 Dec. 1916: King's, 7/1916/35.

[24] Note, King's, 7/1916/37; Liddell Hart, 'The Somme and Its Sequel': King's, 7/1917/5.

[25] See the testimony of the battle-experienced Graves, training regulars for France: *Goodbye to All That*, 304–5.

little manuals and booklets for the use of his men, which soon met with wider demand in other Volunteer units.[26]

This led to further developments after the war. In 1920, as he was struggling to stay in the army despite bad health, Liddell Hart won the patronage of General Sir Ivor Maxse, who had been inspector-general of training to the British armies in France during the later stage of the war and who was now the commander-in-chief, Northern Command. Maxse and his subordinate, Brigadier-General Winston Dugan, who had been appointed to compile the postwar infantry training manual, were favourably impressed by his work. They soon assigned him to work on the new manual which was to replace the obsolete prewar book. While getting rid of much outdated material and updating the manual in the light of the latest tactical developments of the war, Liddell Hart conceived his first contributions to infantry tactics (rather than to battle drill and methods of training). In the summer of 1920 he came up with some improvements to 'soft spots' tactics which the Allies had developed in 1918 in imitation of the famous German 'infiltration' tactics.[27] He called his improved methods of attack and defence in depth the 'expanding torrent' and 'contracting funnel' respectively.[28] Maxse and Dugan, both men of great experience in the subject who had been responsible for the training of the British armies in 'soft spots' tactics in the summer and autumn of 1918, examined his ideas and endorsed them as genuine improvements.[29] The ideas were incorporated in the new infantry training manual issued in 1921, which established Liddell Hart as an expert on infantry tactics.[30]

[26] Liddell Hart's numerous manuals and battle drills (King's, 7/1917; 7/1918) were compiled in his *Outline of the New Infantry Training*, later expanded and published as *New Method in Infantry Training* (Cambridge, 1918): King's, 7/1918/7; see also Liddell Hart, *Memoirs*, i. 28–33.

[27] See M. Samuels, *Doctrine and Dogma: German and British Infantry Tactics in the First World War* (New York, 1992), 7–110; P. Griffith, *Battle Tactics of the Western Front: The British Army's Art of Attack, 1916–18* (New Haven, Conn., 1994), 93–100.

[28] War Office, *Infantry Training* (1921), in King's, 7/1920; Liddell Hart, 'Memoranda of New Method and Developments of Method in Post-War Doctrine of the Army (as Embodied in 'Infantry Training') which originated with the present writer—B. H. Liddell Hart': King's, 7/1920/163; 'Autobiography' (1920–1), 17: King's, 7/1920/38; *Memoirs*, i. 43–5.

[29] Bond, *LH*, 26 and n. 29, is much closer here to the truth than Mearsheimer, *LH*, 31–2; Liddell Hart did not merely plagiarize 'infiltration' or 'soft spot' tactics, which had already been commonly known and used in the British army since 1918.

[30] Liddell Hart's lectures to the Royal United Service Institution were published as *The Framework of a Science of Infantry Tactics* (London, 1922; expanded and reissued 1923, 1926). His articles on infantry tactics appeared in British, American, Canadian, and Belgian military journals. His review of the French postwar *Réglement d'infanterie* was

But infantry tactics was only one direction in which Liddell Hart's ideas were developing. His preoccupation with training and battle drill led him to reflect upon the principles which supposedly underlay all combat activity. Stimulated by reading Foch and Colin, 'this course of thought led me to the conclusion that, on all levels, success depended on achieving a compound of "fixing, manœuvre and exploitation".'[31] This conception, which Liddell Hart termed the 'Man-in-the-Dark theory of war', is not to be confused with his infantry doctrines *per se*. Rather, it was his first, crude attempt to formulate a general theory of war.[32] At exactly that stage he made the acquaintance of Fuller, 'the greatest intellectual power I have ever come across, a titan among minnows',[33] whose influence upon Liddell Hart was overwhelming.

Liddell Hart initiated the relationship in late May or early June 1920, and it was not in connection with Fuller's expertise in the employment of tanks. This aspect of the relationship only came later. Having become aware of Fuller's lectures and articles on the principles of war, Liddell Hart sent him his *National Review* article on the 'Man-in-the-Dark' theory of war. Little impressed by what he read, Fuller reciprocated by sending a copy of his own work on the principles of war. Liddell Hart was deeply impressed. He described Fuller's work as the 'dawn of a new era in military thought'. His own rudimentary interests were stimulated and lifted to new heights by the comparatively awesome sophistication of Fuller's ideas on the science of war. On Liddell Hart's initiative, they soon met.[34]

All this helps to explain later and otherwise obscure traits of Liddell Hart's work. In the early 1920s, apart from his preoccupation first with infantry and later with armoured tactics, he was absorbed in the attempt to formulate a comprehensive theory or science of war, mostly based on

published in the *Revue Militaire Générale*. In Maxse's name he composed the greater part of the article on infantry for the *Encyclopaedia Britannica*. All in King's, 7/1919/12.

[31] *Memoirs*, i. 37–8; cf. Liddell Hart to Scammell, 1 June 1921: King's, 1/622; Liddell Hart to Fuller, 16 June 1922: King's, 1/302; 'Autobiography' (1920–1), 18: King's, 7/1928/38.

[32] See esp. 'The "Man-In-The-Dark" Theory of War: The Essential Principles of Fighting Simplified and Crystallized into a Definite Formula', *National Review* (June 1920), 473–84. The concept was integrated into other articles he wrote that year. See also 'Autobiography' (King's, 7/1928/38), 18.

[33] Liddell Hart to Scammell, 22 Feb. 1922: King's, 1/622.

[34] Fuller to LH, 7, 10 June 1920; LH to Fuller, 14 June 1920: King's, 1/302; also 7/1920/35.

Fuller's principles.[35] Partly for this reason he hailed Fuller's *The Reformation of War* as 'the book of the century',[36] and had a high regard for Fuller's much-criticized and often-ridiculed *The Foundations of the Science of War.* At that stage Liddell Hart still held Foch, whose principles had provided the initial inspiration for both Fuller and himself, in great esteem as a scientific soldier.[37] Liddell Hart outgrew his preoccupation with the principles of war in the mid-1920, and when he returned to them later it would be in a different, lighter and more sophisticated spirit.[38] But his rhetoric about the science of war, familiar to readers of his later works, remained, and so did his strong belief in a 'scientific' study of war which, as commentators have observed, characterized his 'social scientist' approach to history.[39]

There was another legacy of this phase of Liddell Hart's life. While he had entertained youthful dreams of grandeur, his innovations in infantry tactics and especially his preoccupation with the theory of war convinced him, in a way not uncommon for self-taught men discovering and walking the heights of abstract thought, that he was destined to become a great man. He was now filled with enormous pride and sense of superiority. From now on he would always have 'one eye on the future historian'.[40] In 1920–1 he wrote 13,000 words of

[35] This was the main subject of his extensive exchange of letters with his two major correspondents at the time, Fuller and Capt. J. M. Scammell of the American army, a student of Spenser Wilkinson, the Chichele Professor of Military History at Oxford: King's, 7/1921/69; Liddell Hart to Scammell, 1 June 1921: 1/622. In 1921 LH began working on a book-length MS, 'A Framework of War Founded on Man', which proved, however, beyond his capabilities at the time. See also L. V. Bond, 'The Tactical Theories of Captain Liddell Hart (A Criticism)', *Royal Engineers Journal* (Sept. 1922), 153–63; Liddell Hart, 'Colonel Bond's Criticism: A Reply', ibid. (Nov. 1922), 297–309.

[36] Liddell Hart to Scammell, 22 Feb. 1923: King's, 1/622.

[37] LH to Fuller, 16 Jan. 1922: King's, 1/302; 'Bardell' [Liddell Hart], 'Study and Reflection vs. Practical Experience', *Army Quarterly* (1923), 327; Scammell to Liddell Hart, 13 Jan. 1923: 1/622. Here also lay the root of his lifelong admiration for de Saxe. It did not stem only from the latter's renunciation of the need for battle but, echoing Fuller, was due to de Saxe's famous plea for a theory of war; J. F. C. Fuller, *The Reformation of War* (London, 1923), 24, 76; *The Foundations of the Science of War* (London, 1926), 24–5. Liddell Hart's article on de Saxe in *Blackwood's Magazine* (Aug. 1924), 143–60, was later incorporated in *Great Captains Unveiled* (London, 1927), 35–74, and, only slightly altered, in *The Ghost of Napoleon* (New Haven, Conn., 1934), 32–49.

[38] Liddell Hart, 'The Essence of War', *RUSI Journal* (Aug. 1930), incorporated in the subsequent editions of *Strategy of the Indirect Approach.*

[39] Mearsheimer, *LH*, 10. None the less, when hard-core scientism in the shape of American social sciences and game theory entered the field of strategic studies in the nuclear age, Liddell Hart found the new techniques and jargon baffling: Bond, *LH*, 211–12; L. Freedman, *The Evolution of Nuclear Strategy* (London, 1981), 307–8.

[40] King's, 7/1920/32.

'Notes for an Autobiography', outlining his background and development and detailing his achievements: his new tactical theory, new systems of infantry attack and defence, new battle drill, and 76 [*sic*] lesser new ideas incorporated in the infantry training manual.[41] Henceforth and for the rest of his life the record was stringently maintained in diary notes, memoranda, and periodical summaries of achievements on round dates, testifying to his amazing sense of superiority and craving for greatness.[42]

In the early 1920s Fuller influenced Liddell Hart decisively in respect to two subjects even more important than the principles and science of war. These were mechanization and the rejection of total war and the strategy of destruction, which will be discussed below. Correspondingly, under Fuller's direct influence and reflecting the growing doubts among the British public as a whole, came a change in Liddell Hart's attitude to the Great War and the generals who had conducted it. In 1920 or 1921 he had already noted 'How my hero-worship of 'generals' waned and disillusionment began, through close contact with the *best* of them—and finding their lack of fresh ideas—how they depended on a novice like me to show them the lessons of the war'.[43] In 1922, in a private memorandum composed in the wake of a public debate concerning Haig, Liddell Hart wrote that the fact that Haig had been an exponent of attrition in itself disqualified him from the list of great captains, whose distinctive mark was the use of surprise. He cited Fuller's 'Plan 1919' as an example of an alternative, imaginative way to have won the war.[44] By 1924 his change of attitude to the war had taken its familiar shape: 'A victory which has left us so crippled as a nation can hardly be regarded with complete satisfaction and is at least an incentive to inquire whether victory could have been hastened.'[45]

[41] King's, 7/1920/38, esp. p. 17; see also 'The Ideas Which I Invented during 1920, and Which I Wrote in Infantry Training 1920': 7/1920/164; 12/1920/165; 7/1921/68; 7/1922/21. Cf. Bond, *LH*, 31–2.

[42] See Liddell Hart's papers, sect. 11, including two autobiographies: King's, 11/1930/41, 11/1931/27.

[43] Cited without reference in Bond, *LH*, 20.

[44] Liddell Hart, 'Surprise v. Attrition', King's, 7/1922/26.

[45] Liddell Hart, *Army Quarterly* (Apr. 1924), 8.

3

Theory: Limited War, Moderate Peace, and the Strategy of Indirect Approach

Turning Military Theory Upside Down; Redrawing the Map of the Past

In 1923 Fuller published his first great book, *The Reformation of War*, in which he propounded the ideas which would become central to his entire thought. Echoing Keynes, he argued that the Great War

> was based on a gigantic misconception of the true purpose of war, which is to enforce the policy of a nation *at the least cost to itself and to the enemy* and, consequently, to the world, for so intricately are the resources of civilized states interwoven that to destroy any one country is simultaneously to wound all other nations.[1]

Militarily, he wrote,

> Ever since 1866 and 1870, the eyes of the General Staffs of Europe had been blinded by the brilliance of von Moltke's strategy. Soldiers had gazed on the bayonet points of Sadowa and Sedan until they were hypnotized by these great battles, and . . . dreamt of the next war as an immense 1870 operation involving unlimited slaughter. Their doctrine was founded on two tremendous fallacies. First, that policy is best enforced by destruction; secondly, that military perfection is based on numbers of soldiers.[2]

Both notions had been fallacious, claimed Fuller, because they had been rooted in a misapprehension of the nature of modern war. In the age of the internal-combustion engine, human masses had become insignificant in comparison with technological advance and technical perfection. The physical epoch had come to an end; the moral epoch was dawning. There was no longer a need literally to destroy the enemy's armies in the field, as the Allies had tried to do during the war. Aircraft using gas would disable, demoralize, and paralyse unarmoured troops,

[1] *The Reformation of War* (London, 1923), 75; italics in the original. Keynes's notion of a 'Carthaginian Peace' would from now on be constantly cited by Fuller.

[2] Ibid.

surface ships, and civilian populations and infrastructures alike. Armoured forces would paralyse, demoralize, and cause the disintegration of armies by striking at their rear communications and command system in the manner Fuller had suggested by the end of the Great War in his so-called 'Plan 1919'.[3] Politically, with slaughter and destruction reduced, war would become both more humane and more rational: 'To destroy a nation is to destroy the very objective of peace; consequently, the less destruction the more complete to the winner is the victory.' 'In the future, wars will be looked upon as a means of creating a better peace and not as a means of bruising a worn-out one.'[4]

The brilliant and prophetic as well as the fanciful aspects of these ideas are obvious, and are not our concern here. The point is that they are generally associated more with Liddell Hart than with Fuller. *The Reformation of War*, 'the book of the century' in Liddell Hart's words, was the most important influence on Liddell Hart's intellectual development, determining and shaping his view of war for life. So profoundly impressed was he with the book that he simply plagiarized it almost lock, stock, and barrel in his own first important book, *Paris, or the Future of War* (1925).

This little book represents a quantum leap in Liddell Hart's writing, incomparable both in content and style with his earlier work. In a nutshell it contains all the leading ideas and historical themes that he would develop in the following years in a succession of books: *Scipio* (1926), *The Remaking of Modern Armies* (1927), *Sherman* (1929), *The Decisive Wars of History* (1929) (later *Strategy: The Indirect Approach*), *Foch* (1931), and *The Ghost of Napoleon* (1933). The writing reveals all the stylistic traits which would become his trade mark; having previously been tepid and rather undistinguished in tone, it now all of a sudden becomes brisk, compelling, supremely confident, highly provocative, and iconoclastic—all to an even larger degree than in his more mature works. There were two main reasons for this change. Liddell Hart had been invalided out of the army in 1924 and was beginning his career as a journalist, first on an occasional basis in the *Morning Post* and then, from 1925 on, as the military correspondent of the *Daily Telegraph*. Thus he was now free from military authority and from the judgement of the editors of the military periodicals, and was addressing and catering to the taste of the wider general public. Simultaneously, he

[3] Ibid. 102–88. [4] Ibid. 107–8, 144, 188, and *passim*.

had been making great strides in his self-education in military history and theory. In the first half of the 1920s he developed from a humble infantry tactician entertaining dreams of glory to a dazzling, soon to be world-famous strategic thinker. There were four main influences on the development of his outlook, all of which he failed to acknowledge, with the result that they have remained undetected by historians. As mentioned, Fuller's was the primary one, and Liddell Hart's development and characteristic ideas are simply unimaginable without it. One is almost tempted to say that he sprang fully armed from Fuller's brow.

Fuller's irreverent, sweeping, and dazzling style undoubtedly set the model which the young Liddell Hart strove to emulate, though in a simplified, more popular, and more accessible form. He was also influenced decisively by Fuller's scathing criticism of the British high command and of the conduct of the First World War. By 1925 this criticism corresponded to the growing change of perspective in viewing the war and its outcome among educated public opinion in general. 'The Great War', wrote Liddell Hart,

> caused the direct sacrifice of eight million lives, to which the British Isles alone contributed three-quarters of a million. So ineffectual was the treatment prescribed by the military practitioners who were called in that the illness took over four years to run its course, during which the financial temperature mounted daily, until for this country alone it reached a cost of £8,000,000 a day. Our total war expenditure was nearly ten thousand million pounds; our National Debt has been increased tenfold. Moreover, these long years of strain and want so impaired the physical health of the peoples that they fell an easy prey to epidemic diseases, and the influenza scourge of 1918 and 1919 cost, among the civilian population of the world, more than twice as many lives as were lost in battle. It is surely clear that any further wars conducted on similar methods must mean the breakdown of Western civilization . . . in these post-war years of disillusionment . . . we are justified, standing amid the *débris*, in questioning the strategic aim and direction of the war . . . it was the destruction of the enemy's armed forces in the main theatre of war.[5]

Both Fuller and Liddell Hart rejected pacifism and did not believe in the power of formal agreements to eliminate war. In a brilliant anthropological–metaphysical tract in *The Reformation of War*, Fuller, the social Darwinist, explained how war was rooted in human nature and was an inherent and indispensable part of human evolution.[6] The young

[5] *Paris, or the Future of War* (London, 1925), 9–10, 12.
[6] *The Reformation of War*, pp. xi, 6–23, 56–74, 256–83.

Liddell Hart, whose interests and passionate preoccupation were still almost strictly military, dismissed the whole question with little speculation.[7] His conclusion was Fullerite:

> Should a millennium of Universal Peace fail to arrive, and nations still continue to settle by an appeal to force questions which vitally affect their policy, it may be that they will learn to wage war in a manner less injurious to the interwoven fabric of modern civilization, and incidentally to their own prosperity and ultimate security, than proved the case in the Great War of 1914–1918.[8]

The national objective in war must 'ensure a resumption and progressive continuance of what may be termed the peace time policy, with the shortest and least costly interruption of the normal life of the country'.[9] 'A statue of General Sherman in Washington bears this inscription: "the legitimate object of war is a more perfect peace."' Truer still, 'a more perfect peace is the only *rational* object of war.'[10]

The conduct of war itself should aim at the 'moral objective' [Fuller's] and undermine rather than literally destroy the enemy. Liddell Hart's portrayal of future warfare, in the air, on land, and at sea, was Fullerite through and through. Air power using the humane and non-destructive gas would dominate war, overwhelming in a very short period the enemy's civilian rear as well as immobilizing the obsolete mass armies. Concentrated armoured forces would travel the countryside, operating against the enemy's command and communications, his 'nerve system', in the manner Fuller had suggested in 1918. In the naval arena it would seem that, at least in closed seas, the aircraft and the submarine would displace the battleship.[11]

This was Fuller almost to the letter, yet only a couple of historians have noted this briefly. As one of them has written: 'the similarity in the approach, content and style of Fuller's *The Reformation of War* and Liddell Hart's *Paris* is striking though rarely remarked upon.'[12] To remove any doubt, this was not a case of ideas developed conjointly; nor do we have here two lines of thought running parallel, as Liddell Hart would sometimes claim in later years.[13] A comparative examination

[7] *Paris*, 7–9. [8] Ibid. 22. [9] Ibid. 25. [10] Ibid. 91–2.

[11] Ibid. 41–89; the reference to 'Plan 1919' (pp. 82–3) is the only direct citation from Fuller. More fully on Fuller's influence and Liddell Hart's subsequent development in respect to armour doctrine see my *British Armour Theory and the Rise of the Panzer Arm*, 1–42.

[12] B. H. Reid, *J. F. C. Fuller: Military Thinker* (London, 1987), 225; also M. Carver, *The Apostles of Mobility* (London, 1979), 43–4.

[13] See e.g. his briefing of John Wheldon, *Machine Age Armies* (London, 1968), 33–8.

of the development of Fuller and Liddell Hart respectively clearly reveals that the ideas which Fuller had developed by the early 1920s—not only regarding armoured warfare but in many other respects, including his fundamental approach to the questions of the conduct and aim of war in view of the subsequent peace—came as a revelation to the young and impressionable Liddell Hart, who made them his own. As we shall have the occasion to see, this was a pattern that would recur for years to come. Innumerable ideas used by Liddell Hart had originated in Fuller's works. Yet, although Liddell Hart's writings from the early and mid-1920 abound in references to Fuller's genius, he never acknowledged his heavy debts. Furthermore, from the late 1920s, with his own abilities and fame growing, he no longer assumed in public or in private a subordinate role to Fuller, as he had done earlier, and his attitude towards Fuller even assumed an aspect of Freudian patricide. Bearing this in mind, notwithstanding the well-documented frictions between them, Fuller behaved in an almost saintly manner. It has been pointed out that, in contrast to Liddell Hart, he showed little active preoccupation with his own reputation.[14] To know what he really thought, however, one should adopt the effective method of paying attention to his wife, the infamous Sonia, who in an angry exchange with Mrs Liddell Hart accused Liddell Hart of building his fame on her husband's ideas.[15]

Yet there were other major influences and major themes which, on the basis of Fuller's fundamental approach, went to shape Liddell Hart's evolving outlook in *Paris* and ever after. Following up on Fuller's criticism of the prewar faith in total war of destruction, Liddell Hart went beyond the Prussian model of 1866 and 1871. In this he was able to build upon three important contributions to modern military thought, which he adopted, synthesized, radicalized even beyond their originally radical thrust, expanded, and applied to reverse completely both the military theory and the picture of the past of the nineteenth century. Of these contributions, two had been well recognized but were somewhat out of the main-stream, while the third was new and sensational but fairly obscure. The first was the prominent French neo-Napoleonic school of the late nineteenth and early twentieth centuries, with its learned unravelling of the origins and nature of Napoleonic

[14] J. Mearsheimer, *Liddell Hart and the Weight of History* (London, 1988) [*LH*], 212.

[15] Liddell Hart to Fuller, 11 Mar. 1928, Liddell Hart Centre for Military Archives, King's College, London [King's], 1/302.

strategy and its comprehensive criticism of Clausewitz's interpretation of that strategy. The other two were Julian Corbett's rejection in the early twentieth century of the strategy of annihilation and its emphasis on the decisive battle, which Liddell Hart adapted from sea to land; and T. E. Lawrence's remarkably similar theorizing, which Liddell Hart expanded beyond its original desert guerrilla setting.

The French neo-Napoleonic school, though only hazily familiar to historians, has usually received a very mixed press.[16] Attitudes are always context-related, and, not wholly deservedly, the school's image has been associated with the growth of the disastrous doctrine of the *offensive à outrance* which almost ruined the French army, and France, in the opening phase of the First World War. Of French military studies of the period, only Jean Colin's scholarly researches on the origins of French revolutionary and Napoleonic warfare are widely recognized and held in esteem by modern historians. But Colin was merely taking part in, and building upon, the achievements of a much wider enterprise which had been central to French military thought since the mid-1880s. Stimulated by German military theory and relying on Napoleon's huge correspondence and on much other archival material, both unavailable to earlier commentators, L. Maillard, Édouard Pierron, Auguste Grouard and, especially, Henri Bonnal and Hubert Camon laid the foundations for a much deeper and fuller understanding of Napoleon's generalship and system of operations than had been offered by Jomini's seminal and penetrating analysis during the emperor's own time.[17] The few modern studies of the Napoleonic art of operations rely heavily on the work of the French school, most notably on Camon's illuminating analytical schemes.[18]

Liddell Hart's own familiarity with the authors and works of the pre-war French military school was fairly superficial even by the time he wrote *Foch* (1931). It is doubtful if he ever really read even the works of Henri Bonnal, the leading French military theorist of the period.[19] He

[16] The following derives from Book II above, 390–96.

[17] Cf. J. Colin's assessment, *Les Transformations de la guerre* (Paris, 1916), 253.

[18] See esp. H. Camon, *La Guerre napoléonienne* (5 vols., Paris, 1907–11), and *Le Systéme de guerre de Napolèon* (Paris, 1923); cf. D. Chandler, *The Campaigns of Napoleon* (London, 1966).

[19] The relevant sections from *Foch* were reproduced as 'French Military Ideas before the First World War', in M. Gilbert (ed.), *A Century of Conflict, 1850–1950* (London, 1966), 135–48. They were based mainly on the devastating revelations during the 1920s of Émile Mayer, with whom Liddell Hart corresponded. It should be noted, however, that

was well acquainted, however, with Camon's works, at least by the late 1920s.[20] More importantly, during the early 1920s he repeatedly referred to Colin's books, which were his chief guides to modern military history and theory. In them he could find a scholarly summary of the findings and conclusions of the French neo-Napoleonic school.

Dissecting Napoleon's campaigns, Maillard and after him Bonnal laid bare the features and qualities of the emperor's strategy.[21] They emphasized his clear determination of the decisive point and line of advance, resolute and carefully coordinated marches, and rapid concentration of all forces to overwhelm the enemy. Equally, however, they highlighted the flexibility of his operational formation, the so-called *bataillon carré*, loosely dispersed until the last moment, and maintaining its freedom of action to operate and strike in all directions. Colin, developing Pierron's earlier study, showed how this mode of operation, suggested in the middle of the eighteenth century by Pierre de Bourcet, one of the authorities who had shaped the young Bonaparte's military education, had helped to leave the enemy in the dark, and guessing, regarding Napoleon's intentions and ultimate line of attack; the pattern, he stressed, had been dispersion and only then concentration, with each of Napoleon's operational plans having 'many branches', or alternative options.[22] Bonnal, more than anyone else before him, brought to light the imaginative qualities of Napoleon's genius: his mastery of decep-

much earlier he had already been aware, for example, of the distinction which has been lost in many later history books: 'the division in France in pre-war days lay between the school of Foch, Bonnal and Langlois and the modern school of Grandmaison which was adopted by the French General Staff to their cost': Liddell Hart to Scammell, 22 Feb. 1923, King's, 1/622.

[20] Both Wilkinson and Scammell detected the influence of Colin and the French school on Liddell Hart's Strategy: Wilkinson to Liddell Hart 28 Dec. 1928, King's, 1/748; Scammell to Liddell Hart, 11 Feb. 1930, 1/622. Liddell Hart admitted the similarity of his ideas to Camon's: *Army Quarterly* (Jan. 1928), 401; also Liddell Hart to Scammell, 4 Apr. 1933, King's, 1/622.

[21] The following is based on my *The Development of Military Thought: The Nineteenth Century*, 126–7. See L. Maillard, *Éléments de la guerre* (Paris, 1891), pp. x–xv, 3; H. Bonnal, *De Rosbach à Ulm* (Paris, 1903), *La Manœuvre d'Iéna 1806* (Paris, 1904), *La Manœuvre de Landshut, 1808–1809* (Paris, 1905), *La Manœuvre de Vilna, 1811–1812* (Paris, 1905).

[22] É. Pierron, *Comment s'est formé le génie militaire de Napoléon Ier?* (Paris, 1889); Liddell Hart was familiar with the work: *The Ghost of Napoleon* (New Haven, Conn., 1934), 191; J. Colin, *L'Éducation militaire de Napoléon* (Paris, 1900), 93–6; *Transformations de la guerre*, 206 ff., 221–2, English trans. *The Transformation of War* (London, 1912), 241–50, 259–60. Colin was digested by S. Wilkinson, *The French Army before Napoleon* (Oxford, 1915), 37–8, 144–51; also see *The Defence of Piedmont, 1742–1748* (Oxford, 1927), 158, 176; *The Rise of General Bonaparte* (Oxford, 1930).

tion, feints, and diversions to create surprise, disorientation, and miscalculation on the enemy's part.

Thus, it is hardly surprising that Bonnal and his friends found Clausewitz's perception of Napoleonic strategy curiously crude and, in some respects, totally inadequate. Present-day historians, expressing uncritical reverence for Clausewitz, have tended to dismiss this affront to the great philosopher of war as nothing more than an expression of French chauvinism and wounded national pride. But although there is certainly a great deal of patriotic zeal in much of the French writings, this is totally beside the point. The French perceived very accurately that in viewing Napoleon's strategy from distant and defeated Prussia, Clausewitz had been primarily impressed by its immense energy, boldness, and decisiveness. Fiercely reacting against the old 'strategy of manœuvre', he had portrayed Napoleonic strategy as extremely direct and vigorously simple, and had missed a great deal of its subtlety of conception and manœuvre. They pointed out that, while it was true that Napoleon had always sought the great battle, he had never been as direct in going about it as Clausewitz had imagined. They were astonished by Clausewitz's assertion that 'Napoleon never engaged in strategic envelopment',[23] citing the many instances of Napoleon's *manœuvre sur les derrières*, the manœuvre against the enemy's rear, one of the most fundamental patterns of Napoleonic strategy. This had been the pattern which had underpinned the Marengo, Ulm, and Jena campaigns, to name only some of the most famous examples.[24]

It was these important ideas that Liddell Hart popularized, in both senses of the word, and forged into a weapon against nineteenth-century, Prussian-dominated military theory.[25] All-out war of destruction and the obsession with numbers, he argued, may have originated with Napoleon. But the main culprit had been his great and influential codifier, Clausewitz, whose interpretation of Napoleon had highlighted

[23] *Principles of War* (Harrisburg, Penn., 1942), 49.

[24] L. Rousset (ed.), *Les Maîtres de la guerre Frédérick II, Napoléon, Moltke, d'après des travaux inédits de M le général Bonnal* (Paris, 1899), 226–7; H. Bonnal, *De la méthode dans les hautes études militaires en Allemagne et en France* (Paris, 1902), 10–11; H. Camon, *Clausewitz* (Paris, 1911); and, echoing them, Colin, *The Transformation of War*, 298–300.

[25] The first three, virtually identical formulations are 'The Napoleonic Fallacy', *Empire Review* (May 1925), 510–22, King's, 7/1924/2–5; *Paris, or the Future of War* (London, 1925), 13–22; *The Remaking of Modern Armies* (London, 1927), 88–112; and repeatedly thereafter.

only crude concentration of mass and the direct, brute, and bloody clash of forces, to the neglect of all other elements of Napoleonic warfare. Clausewitz had been 'the Mahdi of mass and mutual massacre'; 'the generals of this last half century [had become] intoxicated with the blood-red wine of Clausewitzian growth'.[26] Indeed, in the same way as Clausewitz, the disciple, had been more to blame then Napoleon, his master, Clausewitz's own disciples, such as Foch, whom Liddell Hart took as typifying pre-First World War military theory, had become 'an amplifier for Clausewitz's more extreme notes'.[27] Unable to follow his complex logic and manner of speculation, they had caught only his bellicose catch-phrases and had missed his more subtle qualifying statements.[28]

The lever which enabled Liddell Hart to turn the French criticism of Clausewitz's interpretation of Napoleon into a much more sweeping and radical attack on the tenets of nineteenth-century military theory came, however, from a different source. This was T. E. Lawrence's chapters in his post-war *Seven Pillars of Wisdom* on the evolution of his military thought before and during his Arabian campaign. In this remarkable work one reads:

> In military theory I was tolerably read, my Oxford curiosity having taken me past Napoleon to Clausewitz and his school, to Caemmerer and Moltke, and the recent Frenchmen. They had all seemed to be one-sided; and after looking at Jomini and Willisen, I had found broader principles in Saxe and Guibert and the eighteenth century. . . . I began to drum out the aim in war. The books gave it pat—the destruction of the armed forces of the enemy by the one process—battle. Victory could be purchased only by blood.

This, realized Lawrence, would not do for the Arab irregulars fighting the stronger Turks:

> [I] was left . . . to find an alternative end and means of war. Ours seemed unlike the ritual of which Foch was priest. . . . In his modern war—absolute war he called it—two nations professing incompatible philosophies put them to the test of force. Philosophically it was idiotic . . . It sounded like a twentieth-century restatement of the wars of religion, whose logical end was utter destruction of one creed . . . This might do for France and Germany, but would not represent the British attitude. . . . [Moreover] such war depended on levy in mass, and

[26] *The Ghost of Napoleon* 120, 21. [27] Ibid. 133.

[28] Paris, 17–18; *The Ghost of Napoleon*, 123–6; *Strategy: The Indirect Approach* (London, 1954), 352–7. But perhaps the best statement of the argument is in *The British Way in Warfare* (London, 1931), 17–25.

> was impossible with professional armies; while the old army was still the British ideal. . . . [In addition] Battles in Arabia were a mistake . . . Napoleon had said it was rare to find generals willing to fight battles; but the curse of this war was that so few would do anything else. Saxe had told us that irrational battles were the refuges of fools. . . .
>
> In character our operations of development for the final stroke should be like naval war, in mobility, ubiquity, independence of bases and communications, ignoring of ground features, of strategic areas, of fixed directions, of fixed points. . . . Our tactics should be tip and run: not pushes but strokes. We should never try to improve an advantage. We should use the smallest force in the quickest time at the farthest place.[29]

Anyone who has ever read Liddell Hart would not fail to recognize these ideas, but they have never been traced to Lawrence and his writings. The story of the connection here requires some detective work, and (as is usually the case) Liddell Hart's own archive provides the most significant clues.

Lawrence's *Seven Pillars of Wisdom* was printed in early 1922 at the Oxford University Press, but only a handful of copies for private distribution were produced. A limited subscribers' edition appeared in 1926 but, because of Lawrence's whims, the book was not offered to the general public until 1935, after his death. Only a concise adaptation, entitled *Revolt in the Desert*, was published in 1927. However, invited to contribute an article, 'The Evolution of a Revolt', to the first issue of the *Army Quarterly* (Oct. 1920), Lawrence stitched together the two chapters from the manuscript of *Seven Pillars* dealing with his military ideas.[30] It was this article that the young Liddell Hart read when it appeared and, indeed, wrote to Lawrence about.[31] Coming as it did in conjunction with Fuller's influence and with Liddell Hart's studies of Colin's works, Lawrence's article inspired Liddell Hart's reversal of attitude to eighteenth- and nineteenth-century military thought. For, as Lawrence would later write to him: 'To provoke the

[29] *The Seven Pillars of Wisdom* (New York, 1936), 188–90, 196, 337.

[30] For the previously cited passages, see with some variations, T. E. Lawrence, 'The Evolution of A Revolt', *Army Quarterly*, 1 (Oct. 1920), 57–9, 64, 68. The same issue printed Fuller's 'The Foundations of the Science of War'.

[31] This first brief exchange of letters is mentioned but not included both in the printed edition of Lawrence's letters to Liddell Hart, which the latter edited, *T. E. Lawrence to his Biographer Liddell Hart* (London, 1939), 1, and in B. H. Liddell Hart, *Memoirs* (2 vols., London, 1965), i. 84. Nor is Liddell Hart's first letter to be found in his archive. However, Lawrence's reply does exist in the archive (7 July 1921, King's, 9/13/20), indicating that Liddell Hart had sent him for comment the work on principles of war with which he had then been preoccupied.

soldiers to battle on my own ground I kept on limiting what I said to irregular warfare.' But, 'for 'irregular war' you could write 'War of movement' in nearly every place, and find the argument fitted as well or ill as it did.'[32]

When in 1927 Liddell Hart, then military editor of the *Encyclopaedia Britannica*, again made contact with Lawrence to request an article on guerrilla warfare, he himself, assuming correctly that Lawrence would be reluctant to write one, raised the possibility that an adaptation of Lawrence's 1920 *Army Quarterly* article might be used. Lawrence accepted the suggestion, informing Liddell Hart that the article was in fact based on two chapters from *Seven Pillars* and advising him from whom that rare book could be obtained.[33] This was the beginning of a close friendship which lasted until Lawrence's death.

Liddell Hart cherished this friendship deeply, and not only for its snob appeal—Lawrence was a living legend, Britain's only post-war superhero. He admired Lawrence unreservedly and became his biographer, showering acclaim on his genius as a man of action and thought. However, not unlike his behaviour in Fuller's case, he pretended it was a mere coincidence that his ideas resembled so closely what Lawrence had written before.[34] Apart from the texts themselves, only Liddell Hart's voluntary references in 1921 and 1927 to Lawrence's 1920 article betray the true story. Other people, unfamiliar with Lawrence's *Seven Pillars*, were unlikely to notice; interestingly enough, not even Lawrence realized the actual sequence of events. Unlike Liddell Hart he did not keep a record of their correspondence over the years; indeed, he did not even possess a copy of *Seven Pillars* or of his 1920 article![35] As he repeatedly confessed, he had left his military interests, and his past, behind him as he moved on to new preoccupations. Thus, by 1932, after reading Liddell Hart's essay on the theory of strategy, he innocently wrote to the author: 'I may overestimate the goodness and value of your book because it hits my tender spot. In the Seven Pillars I wrote a chapter on theory, which was an expression in terms of Arabia, of very much of what you argue about the aim of war.'[36] Similarly, having read

[32] Lawrence to Liddell Hart, 17 Oct. 1928, in *Lawrence to Liddell Hart*, 3–4.

[33] Apart from the texts themselves, see Lawrence to Liddell Hart, 25 Oct. 1927, ibid. 1–3.

[34] *'T. E. Lawrence': In Arabia and After* (London, 1934), 164–75, 438–40.

[35] Lawrence to Liddell Hart, 25 Oct. 1927, in *Lawrence to Liddell Hart*, 2.

[36] Lawrence to Liddell Hart, 30 Aug. 1932, ibid. 49; the essay, 'Strategy Reframed', in *The British Way in Warfare*, was previously published in *The Decisive Wars of History* (London, 1929) later *Strategy: The Indirect Approach* (London, 1941).

The Ghost of Napoleon, he wrote to Liddell Hart: 'It has been a queer experience—like going back, in memory, to school—for by myself (though with far less knowledge, and hesitatingly) I had trodden all this road before the war.'[37] Liddell Hart officially dedicated the book 'To "T. E." who trod this road before 1914', but never hinted he had been following Lawrence's headlights.[38]

In some crucial respects Lawrence's ideas paralleled another, much greater, strategic theoretical edifice which also challenged the sacred tenet prescribing as the sole legitimate aim of war the destruction of the enemy's main armed forces in a major battle. This was Julian Corbett's thoroughgoing revision of strategic theory, culminating in his *Some Principles of Maritime Strategy* (1911). As with Lawrence's guerrilla doctrines, this book, notwithstanding its special subject, took much of its inspiration from military theory, claimed at least partial validity for all branches of war, and could thus be applied back from sea to land.

Historians have noted similarities, affinities, *and* differences between some of Corbett's ideas and Liddell Hart's conception of 'The British Way in Warfare'.[39] But since, to the best of my knowledge, Liddell Hart never cited Corbett's name or work, it has not been detected how directly and decisively he was influenced by Corbett, and in much more than the doctrine mentioned above, about which Liddell Hart diverged from as much as concurred with Corbett's argument. Corbett died in 1922 as Britain's most distinguished naval theorist and amid a controversy surrounding the publication of the official British naval history of the First World War which he had written. One may assume that Liddell Hart became acquainted with his work at that time, so crucial in his development, and it fitted in brilliantly with the influences of Fuller, Colin, and Lawrence. No 'smoking gun' for the Corbett–Liddell Hart connection can be produced. But from 1924–5 on Liddell Hart's work betrays the unmistakable and distinctive mark of Corbett's ideas. (See note 40).

Again, although generally treated with respect, Corbett's work has

37 Lawrence to Liddell Hart, in 1933, *Lawrence to Liddell Hart*, 132. Understandably, therefore, while noting the similarity of ideas between Lawrence and Liddell Hart, Brian Holden Reid missed its source: 'T. E. Lawrence and Liddell Hart', *History*, 70 (1985), 218–31; also 'T. E. Lawrence and his Biographers', in B. Bond (ed.), *The First World War and British Military History* (Oxford, 1991), 227–59.

38 Lawrence to Liddell Hart, 30 July 1933, ibid. 138–9; *The Ghost of Napoleon*, 5.

39 M. Howard, 'The British Way in Warfare' (1974), repr. in *The Causes of War* (London, 1984), 193–8; followed by B. Bond, *Liddell Hart: A Study of His Military Thought* (London, 1977) [*LH*], 69, 71, 75–6.

attracted less scholarly attention than it deserves. Only recently has its stock begun to rise.[40] Its main thrust amounted to a comprehensive attack on the dominance of the parallel Nelsonian–Napoleonic models over the strategic theory of his time, as exhibited in the all-powerful and, in this respect, also parallel Mahanite–Prussian theories. 'Our teachers', wrote Corbett, 'incline to insist that there is now only one way of making war, and that is Napoleon's way. Ignoring the fact that he failed in the end, they brand as heresy the bare suggestion that there may be other ways.'[41] He questioned the doctrines of unlimited war and concentration of all forces for the decisive battle even on land,[42] and claimed they were even less universally applicable at sea. The view he propounded was, as he put it,

> a direct negation of the current doctrine that in war there can be but one legitimate object, the overthrow of the enemy's means of resistance, and that the primary objective must always be his armed forces. It raises in fact the whole question as to whether it is not sometimes legitimate and even correct to aim at the ulterior object of the war.[43]

Corbett warned of the fallacy 'that war consists entirely of battles between armies and fleets'. This fallacy, he maintained, 'ignores the fundamental fact that battles are only the means of enabling you to do that which really brings wars to an end—that is to exert pressure on the citizens and their collective life'.[44] If battle were only a means to an end, he argued, then other means such as blockades, the destruction of commerce, and combined operations in selected theatres might sometimes prove no less effective.

We shall return to some of Corbett's other leading ideas later on, but first back to Liddell Hart. In *Paris*, when dealing with naval warfare, he reproduced Corbett's characteristic argument, directed against pre-First World War navalist thought, regarding the limitations of sea power. He then proceeded as follows:

[40] For example, the two standard textbooks, Earle's and Paret's editions of *Makers of Modern Strategy*, do not deal with Corbett (the latter does not even mention him); but see D. M. Schurman's excellent contributions in *The Education of A Navy: The Development of British Naval Strategic Thought, 1867–1914* (London, 1965), 147–84, and *Julian S. Corbett, 1854–1922* (London, 1981); E. J. Grove's Introduction to J. Corbett's *Some Principles of Maritime Strategy* (Annapolis, Md., 1988); and Book II above, 480–93, on which the following is based. Since I originally wrote the above, Alest Danchev, *Alchemist of War: The life of Basil Liddell Hart* (London, 1998), 175, 309 n. 56, has located the 'smoking gun' in the form of LH's markings on and reference to Corbett's *England in the Seven Years War*.

[41] *Some Principles of Maritime Strategy*, 20. [42] Ibid. 19–27, 74–5.

[43] Ibid. 74. [44] Ibid. 97.

As with land warfare, the destruction of the enemy's main fleet is often spoken of as the objective, whereas in reality this act is but a means towards it—by the destruction of the enemy's shield the way is opened for a more effective blockade or for the landing of an army.[45]

Liddell Hart's main use for Corbett was, however, far wider than the naval sphere. In Corbett's ideas he found an additional weapon against the nineteenth century's all-pervasive 'Napoleonic fallacy', which had prescribed 'that there was only one true objective in war—"the *destruction* of the enemy's main forces on the battlefield"'.[46] In truth, he argued, echoing Corbett,

the *destruction* of the enemy's armed forces is but a means—and not necessarily an inevitable or infallible one—to the attainment of our goal. It is clearly not, despite the assertion of military pundits, the sole true objective in war. . . . All *acts*, such as defeat in the field, propaganda, blockade, diplomacy, or attack on the centres of government and population, are seen to be but means to that end.[47]

To find a wider conception of strategy than the nineteenth-century one emphasizing the total overthrow of the enemy and the decisive battle, one had to go beyond its limited experience to the wider horizons of 'universal history' and especially to the pre-revolutionary, pre-Napoleonic era which had inaugurated total war. In particular, the relatively limited warfare of the eighteenth century, which had been anathema to Clausewitz and the men of the nineteenth century, was now to be rehabilitated.[48] The inspiration for this historical revision came clearly from Lawrence, who 'had found broader principles in Saxe and Guibert and the eighteenth century',[49] but Liddell Hart's other sources were also helpful in this regard. Before the First World War there had been two major, deeply historical, independent but remarkably parallel efforts to rehabilitate eighteenth-century warfare, each carrying clear implications for strategic theory in general. The first had been made by the great historian and publicist Hans Delbrück, leading to a famous and protracted controversy with German military opinion.[50] Liddell Hart, however, read no German and was unfamiliar with the whole affair when developing his ideas. All the same, what Delbrück had performed for land warfare Corbett in his more diplomatic but no

[45] Liddell Hart, *Paris*, 62–3. [46] Ibid. 14. [47] Ibid. 26; also 33–43.
[48] Ibid. 14, 18–19. [49] *Seven Pillars of Wisdom*, 188.
[50] See Book II above, 371–7, and the authorities cited there.

less sweeping manner had attempted to do for war at sea. Challenging nineteenth-century navalist opinion, he had defended the historical and strategic logic of eighteenth-century *guerre de course*, relatively cautious tactics, and more limited use of battle in deciding the issue of war.[51] The suggestive nature of his argument for land warfare was all too clear. Furthermore, although Colin, Liddell Hart's other major source of inspiration, had never gone as far as rehabilitating eighteenth-century warfare, his historical studies had not only shed favourable light on the dynamics of military ideas in that period but had also explained its military practices in the context of the conditions prevailing at the time. The materials for a revision of accepted opinion were all there, and Liddell Hart's treatment of the eighteenth century in his monograph *The Ghost of Napoleon* (1933) cast Colin's historical survey into Lawrence's new perspective. For Liddell Hart, eighteenth-century warfare was not only made legitimate by reference to the historical conditions of the time but provided a shining alternative model for contemporary strategic thought. It had been a period in which states had wisely adapted their military efforts to their means and political aims, and in which war had not engulfed, and spelled ruin for, the societies which had waged it.[52]

Liddell Hart's brilliant *The Decisive Wars of History* (1929; the title was given by the publishers and would be replaced in later editions by Liddell Hart's original choice, *The Strategy of Indirect Approach* or *Strategy: The Indirect Approach*) developed and consolidated the ideas first raised in *Paris*. In a *tour de force* sweep through history, Liddell Hart strove to show that the achievements of the great captains of all ages had rarely been brought about by the direct clash of forces but had usually involved the prior psychological and physical dislocation of the enemy. This historical survey was followed by a no less sweeping attempt 'to construct on the fresh foundation a new dwelling-house for strategic thought'.[53]

Liddell Hart aptly took as his starting-point Clausewitz's view of strategy, defined in *On War* as 'the art of the employment of battles as a means to gain the object of war'. He rightly pointed out (for this in general had indeed been Clausewitz's intention) that this definition 'narrows the meaning of "strategy" to the pure utilization of battle,

[51] Ibid. 213–22.

[52] See esp. *The Revolution in Warfare* (London, 1946), 40–5.

[53] Liddell Hart, *Strategy*, 333. The historical survey had been foreshadowed in *Paris*, 29–33.

thus conveying the idea that battle is the only means to the strategical end'.[54] A more valid definition, he suggested, would be 'the art of distributing military means to fulfil the ends of policy', which takes into account the many alternative and complementary means other than battle which strategy possesses.[55] Clausewitz's own logic would lead to its contradiction: 'even if the decisive battle be the goal, the aim of strategy must be to bring about this battle under the most advantageous circumstances. . . . The perfection of strategy would be, therefore, to produce a decision without any serious fighting.'[56] As Lawrence had put it, the object was 'to follow the direction of de Saxe and reach victory without battle, by pressing our advantages mathematical and psychological'.[57]

Strategy is based on movement and surprise. Physically, it should take the line of least resistance, while psychologically following that of least expectation. As Bourcet–Napoleon–Colin prescribed, it must have alternative objectives or, as Sherman described it, put the enemy on the horns of a dilemma.[58] The primary principle of concentration is in need of a major revision, as suggested by Colin, Lawrence, and Corbett alike:

> [it] needs to be amplified as the 'concentration of strength against weakness'. And for any real value it needs to be explained that the concentration of strength against weakness depends on the dispersion of your opponent's strength, which in turn is produced by a distribution of your own that gives the appearance, and partial effect of dispersion. . . . True concentration is the fruit of calculated dispersion.[59]

[54] The citation is from Clausewitz, *On War*, bk. iii. ch. 1, but the definition and the idea behind it can be found throughout Bks. ii–iv. Liddell Hart, *Strategy*, 333.

[55] Ibid. 335.

[56] Ibid. 338; also 339. Cf. Fuller: 'even in the past not a few battles have been won by surprise rather than by force of arms, and if battle can be won without suffering loss, surely this is the most economical, if not the most traditional, way of gaining the strategical object': 'Weekly Tank Notes', 31 May and 7 June, 1919, reprinted in *On Future Warfare* (London, 1928), published the year before Liddell Hart's book.

[57] *Revolt in the Desert* (New York, 1927), 66.

[58] Liddell Hart, *Strategy*, 337, 341, 343–4, 348.

[59] Ibid. 347, also 343; and *The British Way in Warfare*, 19–20. For Lawrence see *Revolt in the Desert*, 66: 'Our aim was to seek the enemy's weakest material link'; with the Arabs 'dispersal was strength. Consequently we must extend our front to the maximum.' For Corbett see *Principles of Maritime Strategy*, 'Concentration and Dispersion', 128–52; concentration, he wrote (p. 134), had become 'a kind of shibboleth'; 'victories have not only to be won, but worked for. They must be worked for by bold strategic combinations, which as a rule entail at least apparent dispersal.'

Above the operational level, or military strategy, there is, however, a higher sphere, touching upon policy, to be termed 'grand strategy'. Here the non-military means of waging war come into effect, as well as a longer view encompassing not only the object of the war but also the peace which follows it. In both respects Clausewitz's ideas are found deficient:

> fighting power is but one of the instruments of grand strategy—which should take account of and apply the power of financial pressure, and, not least of ethical pressure, to weaken the opponent's will. . . . Furthermore, while the horizon of strategy is bounded by the war, grand strategy looks beyond the war to the subsequent peace. It should not only combine the various instruments, but so regulate their use as to avoid damage to the future state of peace—for its security and prosperity.[60]

Before these ideas are assessed, their underlying significance ought to be highlighted. Against a background of a sweeping reversal of attitudes in Britain towards the First World War and the phenomenon of war in general, Liddell Hart undertook a wholesale revision of the accepted precepts of military theory. Any transformation of outlook and attitude in turn involves a reinterpretation and re-creation of history. Synthesizing Fuller, Colin, Lawrence, and Corbett, Liddell Hart thus projected a mirror image of nineteenth-century military theory and view of the past, which had been formulated on the Continent in the age of nationalism. Eighteenth-century warfare, discredited and despised by the men of the nineteenth century, became an example to be emulated and revived. The Napoleonic model became the Napoleonic fallacy. Clausewitz, previously revered as the intellectual inspiration behind the Prussian triumphs, became the false prophet whose teachings had been responsible for the disastrous world war. Total war was to be replaced by limited war; and the effort to gain victory by crushing the enemy's power substituted by a calculated action, mindful of the subsequent peace. The nation-in-arms was to be replaced by a small army of professionals; the decisive clash of forces in a major battle by indirect means; concentration by calculated dispersion.

While Liddell Hart may have borrowed all of these themes, none of his sources had weaved them into such a sweeping counter-theory and

[60] Liddell Hart, *Strategy*, 336. Cf. the similar formulation in Fuller, *Grant*, 7, written simultaneously and also published in 1929; it is difficult to establish, though perhaps less difficult to guess, who borrowed here from whom without acknowledgement; Fuller had already used the concept in his *The Foundations of the Science of War* (London, 1926), 105.

counter-history of war *and* possessed his tenacity in hammering them out and his gifts for simplification and marketing. Coming as it did in the wake of a crisis in the old patterns of war, it is no wonder people all over the world accepted this reversal of strategic values with interest and awe, and found it thought-provoking and stimulating.[61]

Assessment and Criticisms

Criticisms of Liddell Hart's ideas can be treated in reference to two main and related themes—how serious, historically sound, and strategically valid these ideas were—which in turn hinges largely on the evaluation of Liddell Hart's treatment of Clausewitz, the focus of his criticism in his counter-theory and counter-history of war. Scepticism is all the more necessary in view of Liddell Hart's status as a popular writer, reaching out for, and aiming to influence and educate, a large uninformed and semi-informed readership. First enchanted and overwhelmed by the force and brilliance of his arguments, people often started to doubt their validity and suspect they had been tricked by the rhetoric of an extremely clever man and master of exposition. He used strong medicines to get his message across, was anything but impartial, and had little use for balance and restraint. By the standards of scholarly discussion these, of course, are dubious and unacceptable credentials. But then, Liddell Hart was playing a somewhat different game, and in a different league. He was out to reverse strategic outlook and influence public attitudes, and while in some crucial respects this may have made him a poor objective historian, it also turned him into a figure of historical significance in his own right. As an eminent historian of ideas has written, revolutionary thinkers tend

> to overstate their central theses. Such exaggeration is neither unusual nor necessarily to be deplored. Those who have discovered (or think they have discovered) new and important truths are liable to see the world in their light . . . Many original thinkers exaggerate greatly. . . . Nor is it likely that their ideas would have broken through the resistance of received opinion or been accorded the attention that they deserved, if they had not.[62]

As critics have argued, Liddell Hart's definition of the 'indirect approach' was loose, and he stretched it even further, to explain by it

[61] See e.g. André Beaufre's recollections in M. Howard (ed.), *The Theory and Practice of War* (London, 1965), 138–9.

[62] I. Berlin, *Vico and Herder* (London, 1980), p. xxiv.

almost any military success. However, the core of his argument was not ambiguous at all. It amounted to the idea, advanced against nineteenth-century notions, that the enemy's psychological and physical dislocation was more crucial to its defeat than the brute clash of forces. If anything, this idea was partial and one-sided, rather than circular or tautological. The expression 'indirect approach' itself seemed lopsided to a man like Fuller, on whose ideas it had been largely based. He wrote to Liddell Hart: 'The object is to defeat the enemy and if this can be done by a direct approach so much the better.'[63] Yet the expression was largely used for provocation and effect. As T. E. Lawrence, another one of Liddell Hart's major sources who had himself found nineteenth-century military theory 'one-sided',[64] wrote to Liddell Hart:

> A surfeit of the 'hit' school brings on an attack of the 'run' method: and then the pendulum swings back. You, at present, are trying . . . to put the balance straight after the orgy of the late war. When you succeed (about 1945) your sheep will pass your bounds of discretion, and have to by chivvied back by some later strategist. Back and forward we go.[65]

If Liddell Hart had been too enthusiastic and naïve to have consciously realized this himself, he certainly acknowledged the point when Lawrence made it, for he seized and repeatedly cited it in his writings.[66]

In his treatment of history, Liddell Hart's one-sidedness and partiality were compounded by other, no less significant flaws. His search for trans-historical features and instruction, problematic though perhaps not illegitimate in itself, was marred by his unhistorical and naïve disregard for the particular conditions—social, economic and political—which had shaped each period's way of doing things.[67] Admittedly, over time he improved considerably in this respect. In his still immature article on de Saxe (1924), which he would unwisely incorporate unchanged in later works, his didactic approach to his subject was ludicrously unhistorical throughout. To cite only a couple of examples, one of his praises for de Saxe was that he had 'foreshadowed the four-company system—which was only adopted in the British Army on the

[63] Fuller to Liddell Hart, 19 June 1929, King's, 1/302.

[64] *Seven Pillars of Wisdom*, 188.

[65] 17 Oct. 1928, in *Lawrence to Liddell Hart*, 4; see also 31 Mar. 1929 and Whit Monday 1933, ibid. 6, 132.

[66] 'A Re-definition of Strategy', *United Services Institution of India Journal* (Apr. 1929), 117, 128 (incorporated in *The Decisive Wars of History*, London, 1929); *Thoughts on War* (London, 1944), 230; *Strategy*, 363; *Memoirs*, i. 85.

[67] Bond, *LH*, 57; Mearsheimer, *LH*, 48–9.

eve of 1914!' Similarly, he regarded Saxe's recommendation of body armour as having been vindicated by the appearance of the tank.[68] The other historical articles which he had originally published in 1924 and later compiled as *Great Captains Unveiled* (1927) were equally crude. However, as he wrote *Scipio* (1926), his barely disguised allusions to the present were offered with wit and lightness of touch. And whereas *Scipio* was still a lively sketch rather than a scholarly history, Liddell Hart's *Sherman* (1929), *Foch* (1931), and history of the First World War (1930; originally entitled *The Real War*) marked his growth into an accomplished historian, relying on a fairly extensive study of the available printed sources.

To be sure, these works, too, were written for a purpose and were not without their didactic biases, intrinsic in Liddell Hart's sweeping counter-history of war. Projecting a mirror image of the nineteenth-century picture of history, he also repeated in reverse the unhistorical attitude towards other epochs and styles of warfare of which he accused it.[69] After all, the era of total war had not been just a historical aberration but had grown out of the most fundamental developments shaping Western civilization in the modern period. In contrast to Liddell Hart, Fuller, deeply conscious of historical development, related the emergence of total war to the rise of mass society and the process of industrialization. Correspondingly, from the start he argued that the demise of total war would be brought about by the emergence of a new, technological era. More than 'wrong mental attitude' was involved.

Typically, Napoleon's rise and decline were attributed by Liddell Hart in his most famous work on the subject to purely operational reasons: while 'General Bonaparte' had achieved his great victories by his masterly use of manoeuvre, surprise, and deception, the 'Emperor Napoleon' had increasingly earned diminishing strategic returns because he had impatiently misused the vast resources at his disposal in progressively more massive, head-on assaults, supported by heavy artillery concentrations.[70] It barely seems to have occurred to Liddell Hart that the reason for Napoleon's growing difficulties, and changing methods, from 1807 onward had been rooted in deeper changes in objective conditions. Not only had Napoleon's adversaries become accustomed to his methods, but the extension of French hegemony

[68] Cited from *The Ghost of Napoleon*, 41 and 39; *Great Captains Unveiled* (London, 1927), 54, 47–9.

[69] *The Ghost of Napoleon*, 20.

[70] Ibid. 101–4; also *Strategy*, 127–8, 138–41.

over the Continent had been virtually forcing them to throw greater resources into the struggle, adopt French revolutionary military innovations, and ultimately also become more united and better coordinated. Brilliant operations, relying on improvised, self-contained logistics, could no longer do the trick for Napoleon.

Liddell Hart's *Sherman* is another case in point. For Liddell Hart, Sherman's mobile operations and march through the Confederacy to the sea presented a stark contrast to the direct and bloody clash of forces in the main, eastern theatre of the Civil War, indeed a stark contrast to the reality of the Western Front in the First World War. In his opinion Sherman's model indirect approach, which cut the Confederacy in two and separated it from its bread basket, proved to be the decisive act of the war. With Fuller, who was writing *Grant* (1929) at the same time as Liddell Hart wrote *Sherman* (1929), he became involved in a bitter exchange over the relative merits and importance of their heros, in which both protagonists made some very good points.[71] Yet, as Fuller emphasized brilliantly in *Grant* and in his later *Grant and Lee* (1933), and as other critics have pointed out, the American Civil War has often been regarded as the first modern war because it had involved, and had been ultimately decided by, industrial and mass human mobilization, resulting in a protracted process of attrition. As two one-time Oxford professors of military history, Spenser Wilkinson and Michael Howard, argued independently half a century apart, the operations of Grant and Sherman must be seen as complementary efforts in this process of attrition. In Howard's vivid image, they had related to each other like two blades of a scissors.[72] Sherman's campaign could not have been carried out before the North had developed its overall material superiority over the South, and had Grant at the head of the main Union's armies not been hammering at, and pinning down, the Confederacy's main forces before Richmond.

Liddell Hart's moralizing disregard for the complexity of conditions and considerations shaping historical causation and situations was intimately linked to his strong belief in the influence of individuals, or 'great men', abstract ideas, and accidents in history. This way of looking at things, which has been related to the British historiographical tradi-

[71] See their correspondence between Dec. 1928 and July 1929: King's, 1/302. Apart from Liddell Hart, *Sherman* (London, 1929), see his *Strategy*, 148–53. For Fuller, see B. H. Reid, *J. F. C. Fuller: Military Thinker* (London, 1987), 112–23.

[72] Wilkinson to Liddell Hart, 28 Dec. 1928: King's, 1/748; Howard in *The Listener*, 28 Dec. 1972, 894.

tion known as the 'Whig interpretation of history',[73] often led Liddell Hart to naïve and caricaturist propositions. For example, in his polemic tracing of the manner Britain moved towards military involvement in the Continent in the decade before the First World War, Liddell Hart practically ignored the intricate political constraints and strategic considerations which had influenced British decision making.[74] Instead, one may learn from him that the whole matter resulted from the friendship forged between Foch and Henry Wilson, director of military operations at the British War Office in the years preceding the war. 'There is no exaggeration in saying that this friendship diverted the course of English history,' he wrote; it was the case of 'the influence of a French governess and a cup of tea'. The personal link was reinforced by the change of intellectual fashion as Clausewitz's influence and continental military ideas reached Britain.[75] To be sure, the scale of this latter influence, both before and during the First World War—over British military education, in the new general staff, and specifically over Haig—has been well documented by recent scholarship.[76] None the less, George Orwell's appraisal of Liddell Hart's historical analysis could probably represent the balance of scholarly opinion: 'There is something unsatisfactory in tracing an historical change to an individual theorist, because a theory does not gain ground unless material conditions favour it.'[77]

The issue at the root of all this was the traumatic First World War and its lessons for the future. Fuller and Liddell Hart contributed significantly to the interwar debate, sparked by Churchill and Lloyd George, over the conduct of the war and the performance of the British

[73] See Mearsheimer, *LH*, 48–9; Liddell Hart, *The Ghost of Napoleon*, 11–13; *Thoughts on War* (London, 1944), 9.

[74] See W. S. Churchill, *The World Crisis, 1911–1918* (London, 1960), 42–53; M. Hankey, *The Supreme Command* (2 vols., London, 1961), i. 69–70, 78–82; S. Williamson, *The Politics of Grand Strategy: Britain and France Prepare for War* (Cambridge, Mass., 1969); M. Howard, *The Continental Commitment* (London, 1972), 31–52; J. Gooch, *The Plans of War: The General Staff and British Military Strategy, c.1900–1916* (London, 1974), 278–98; D. French, *British Economic and Strategic Planning, 1905–1915* (London, 1982), esp. 22–38.

[75] Liddell Hart, *The Ghost of Napoleon*, 138; 'Foch and the Fate of Britain: The Influence of a French Governess and a Cup of Tea', *Reveille*, 1 Aug. 1933; also *Foch* (London, 1931), 55–62; *The British Way in Warfare*, 16–17.

[76] T. Travers, *The Killing Ground: The British Army, the Western Front and the Emergence of Modern Warfare, 1900–1918* (London, 1987), esp. 37–61, 86, 92, 96, and *passim*.

[77] George Orwell's review of *The British Way in Warfare*, *New Statesman*, 21 Nov. 1942: King's, 1/557.

high command. Both sides of this debate have since been taken up by historians, and the argument shows no signs of coming to a conclusion—nor, perhaps, can it. Here again, facts are inseparable from attitudes. At the centre of the debate stands the murderous war of attrition on the Western Front, culminating for the British in the 'carnage' of the Somme and Passchendaele. On the personal level the debate has largely focused on the generalship of the British commander-in-chief in France, Field Marshal Sir Douglas Haig.

Something like a backlash against the interwar radicals and their followers in the anti-establishment 1960s has been slowly gathering momentum among scholars. They have pointed out the predicament of the World War generals who faced very difficult objective conditions, involving a tactical and operational impasse and leaving them with very narrow strategic options other than the grinding attrition campaign on the Western Front. Historians have stressed the achievement of the British high command which, lacking the experience of its continental counterparts and virtually from scratch, succeeded in the space of a few years in creating, equipping, training, and leading into battle new mass armies which played a decisive role in containing and defeating Germany. Critics have argued that despite his indignant rhetoric Liddell Hart never really came up with a satisfactory alternative solution as to the way the war should have been conducted.[78] He took up the accusations of the tank pioneers such as Ernest Swinton, Fuller, and Churchill that the British high command had used the new machines in an unimaginative manner, thus forfeiting surprise and diminishing their effectiveness. Yet the fact remains that it had been largely owing to the generally positive response of the high command that the British had pioneered the tank, had surmounted considerable teething problems of all sorts, had produced the machine in large numbers, and had led the way throughout the war in its use. As to 'Plan 1919' with which Fuller and Liddell Hart ushered in their 1920s polemics, it had been an

[78] See esp. C. Falls, *The First World War* (London, 1960), continuing the line of Edmonds's official history of the war without its worst biases; J. Terrain, *Douglas Haig: The Educated General* (London, 1963); *To Win a War: 1918* (London, 1978); H. Essame, *The Battle for Europe, 1918* (London, 1972); Howard, *The Continental Commitment*, 53–61; P. Kennedy, *The Rise and Fall of British Naval Mastery* (London, 1976), 239–65; B. Bond, *British Military Policy between the Two World Wars* (Oxford, 1980), 2–6; D. French, *British Strategy and War Aims, 1914–1916* (London, 1986), p. xi and *passim*; *The Strategy of the Lloyd George Coalition, 1916–1918* (Oxford, 1995); Mearsheimer, *Liddell Hart*, 61–71; J. M. Bourne, *Britain and the Great War* (London, 1989); Bond, *The First World War*, *passim*, esp. H. Strachan, '"The Real War": Liddell Hart, Cruttwell, and Falls', 43–53.

imaginative, futuristic vision, based on machines which did not yet exist in 1918. First World War tanks had been too slow and unreliable and possessed too short a range for such enterprises.[79]

After the war Winston Churchill advanced the argument, which Liddell Hart came to support, that during the years 1916–18 the Allies should have refrained from large-scale offensives on the Western Front. Churchill claimed that these offensives had cost the Allies three casualties to every two they inflicted on the Germans, and sometimes only two to one. He suggested that a strategy of dynamic defence and limited local offensives would have sufficed to pin down the Germans while the effects of the blockade slowly took effect.[80] In a drawn-out controversy, critics and the British official history of the war rejected Churchill's figures, claiming that Allied and German casualties were roughly equal and that, given Germany's narrower manpower base, her attrition rate was considerably greater and, indeed, won the war for the Allies. Furthermore, it has been pointed out that Germany would have taken advantage of a defensive posture on the part of Western allies to concentrate even greater forces against Russia, in which case the Western powers would have been obliged to do their utmost to relieve the pressure on their ally.

All the same, still newer literature, more meticulously researched than ever before, appears to be swinging the pendulum in the other direction once again and confirming at least some of the radicals' claims. For example, two comprehensive assessments of the evidence conclude that Churchill was after all right and his many adversaries were wrong regarding the relative casualty figures of the Allies and the Germans on the Western Front.[81] Liddell Hart's relentless struggle against the distortions of the British official history of the war, flaring up with every resurfacing of 'the old lies', as he called them, is thereby vindicated.[82]

[79] Fuller, still restrained in *Tanks in the Great War* (London, 1920), is categorical in his *Memoirs of an Unconventional Soldier* (London, 1936), 88–350; W. Churchill, *The World Crisis, 1911–1918*, 343–59, 747, 826–9 (citing Fuller); E. Swinton, *Eyewitness* (London, 1932), esp. 294–9. For the counter-arguments, see V. Germains, *The 'Mechanization' of War* (London, 1927), 43–54; Falls, *The First World War*, 175; Terrain, *Haig*, 218–28; Reid, *Fuller*, 48–55; and even the radicals themselves: G. Martel, *An Unspoken Soldier* (London, 1949), 17–18; Liddell Hart, *The Tanks* (2 vols., London, 1959), i. 216–17.

[80] *The World Crisis, 1911–1918*, 618–39. For Liddell Hart, see e.g. 12 June 1936, King's, 11/1936/68.

[81] R. Prior, *Churchill's 'World Crisis' as History* (London, 1983), 221–30; D. Winter, *Haig's Command: A Reassessment* (London, 1991), 48, 111–13.

[82] See Liddell Hart's letters to the press in King's, 6/1946 (following the publication of the 'Passchendaele' volume of Edmonds's official history); 6/1957 and 6/1959 (debate with John Terrain); 6/1967/1.

Admittedly, the new studies reaffirm that despite Germany's considerably lower casualty rates, the attrition she suffered probably did facilitate her collapse. But was the terrible cost to the British, who shouldered much of the burden in the last phase of the war, really 'unavoidable'? On this point, too, recent studies are damning, above all in respect to Haig.

It has been convincingly shown that Haig did prolong the murderous Third Battle of Ypres (Passchendaele) long after it became bogged down in the mud. Against the advice of his subordinates, who wanted a more limited offensive, he planed it as a war-winning effort and would not give up his ambition. In addition, it has been demonstrated in great detail that the British high command was indeed slow to adapt to new technologies and new tactics even in the later phase of the war, and that Haig in particular was practically incapable of grasping them. He failed to prepare the British army for modern defence in depth before Ludendorff's 1918 spring offensive. In the Allies' successful final offensives of that year, in which the British played a leading part, the strategic inspiration and planning came mainly from Foch, while tactical execution was left to the subordinate army and corps commanders, such as Rawlinson and Monash. Even Haig's supposedly stronger 'managerial' qualities, as an organizer, staff officer, and trainer, have come in for scathing criticism.[83] The dialectic progress of the debate is unlikely to end here, but Liddell Hart's critique of the British conduct on the Western Front looks much better today that it did a few years ago.

Moving to possible strategic alternatives to the deadlock on the Western Front, Liddell Hart (but not Fuller) sympathized and on occasions identified himself with the so-called Eastern school.[84] This is another controversy which never appears to die out, with most recent

[83] Winter, *Haig's Command*; T. Travers, *How the War Was Won: Command and Technology in the British Army on the Western Front, 1917–1918* (London, 1992) are in these respects practically unanimous in their conclusions. See also R. Prior and T. Wilson, *Command on the Western Front: The Military Career of Sir Henry Rawlinson, 1914–18* (Oxford, 1992); D. Graham and S. Bidwell, *Coalitions, Politicians and Generals: Some Aspects of Command in Two World Wars* (London, 1993), 92–125; M. Samuels, *Doctrine and Dogma: German and British Infantry Tactics in the First World War* (New York, 1992), 113–68; and, earlier, C. Barnett, *The Swordbearers: Studies in Supreme Command in the First World War* (London, 1963), 295–301. P. Griffith, *Battle Tactics of the Western Front: The British Army's Art of Attack, 1916–18* (New Haven, Conn., 1994) is more tepid. The books by Terrain and Winter (despite the latter's obvious paranoia) are the two indispensable representatives of both sides of the Haig debate; for a historiographical survey, see K. Simpson, 'The Reputation of Sir Douglas Haig', in Bond, *The First World War*, 141–62.

[84] See esp. *The British Way in Warfare*, 38–41.

historians again taking a sceptical view.[85] Little more about it will be said in the next chapter. At any rate, the Dardanelles operation, promising on paper, foundered on execution and lapsed into a debate over Churchill's responsibility for the failure.[86] As to the Salonika landing, its proponents, headed by Lloyd George, argued that if it had been carried out in early 1915 it could have created a Balkan league encompassing Serbia, Greece, Romania, and Bulgaria.[87] Critics, however, have stressed the unlikelihood of bringing together these bitterly antagonistic nations.[88] They have also pointed out that for reasons of logistics and geography it is very doubtful if the Allies would have achieved more success in the Balkans than on the Western Front, let alone bring about the collapse of Austro-Hungary. None the less, there may have been something in the argument of Lloyd George and Liddell Hart (rarely noted by their critics) that if Germany had been prevented from overrunning Romania and taking possession of her rich and vital supply of corn and oil, she could not have continued the war as long as she did.

In conclusion, it ought to be remembered that Liddell Hart wrote his most popular and best-known works when he was still relatively young, between the ages of 30 and 40, and that over time, though he would always remain above all the committed publicist, his historical senses would mature considerably and gain in depth. Thus a decade after he wrote *Scipio*, Liddell Hart no longer regarded it as a legitimate scholarly exercise.[89] Similarly, from the 1930s onwards, the more he involved himself in questions of policy and grand strategy, the more he presented Napoleon's fall as the outcome of his unrestrained and self-destructive pursuit of European hegemony rather than of operational military reasons.[90] Finally, in his *Revolution in Warfare* (1946), influenced by

[85] See n. 78 above.

[86] For a historiographical survey, see E. Spiers, 'Gallipoli', in Bond *The First World War*, 165–88; more recently, T. Ben-Moshe, *Churchill: Strategy and History* (Boulder, Colo., 1992), 29–69; J. Charmley, *Churchill: The End of Glory* (London, 1993), 105–25; M. Howard, 'Churchill and the First World War', in R. Black and W. R. Louis (eds.), *Churchill* (Oxford, 1993), 129–45.

[87] D. Lloyd George, *War Memoirs* (London, 1936), 1998–2002; Liddell Hart, *The British Way in Warfare*, 38–41. Liddell Hart assisted Lloyd George in the writing of his book, and it has been rightly pointed out that each reinforced the other's bias against the generals.

[88] See Lloyd George's arch-rival, W. Robertson, *Soldiers and Statesmen, 1914–1918* (London, 1926), ii. 87–8, also 175–7. D. R. Woodward, *Lloyd George and the Generals* (London, 1983), 27–47, offers a good assessment of the evidence and prospects, leaving the question open.

[89] Liddell Hart to Scammell, 31 May 1937, King's, 1/622; also *Memoirs*, i. 168.

[90] Barely hinted at in *Strategy*, 127; but see *The British Way in Warfare*, 18; *The Revolution in Warfare* (London, 1946), 43 ff.

Fuller's histories of the evolution of war, Liddell Hart produced a much more sophisticated historical survey than he had done before of the changing intensity and brutality of war from the Middle Ages to the Second World War, putting his discussion of Clausewitz's influence in a better historical perspective.[91]

Liddell Hart's treatment of Clausewitz's theories is central to his entire work and crucial to its assessment. Scholars have found much to criticize here, but to a large degree their criticisms are a reflection on the confused state of the interpretation of Clausewitz's own work. Perplexed by the contradictory ideas they have found in *On War* and failing to follow Clausewitz's tortuous intellectual development which left all these ideas mixed in his work, commentators could never really make up their minds what exactly Clausewitz meant to say. Naturally, this has made them extremely cautious. They seemed to have been able to find at least a qualifying, if not an opposite, phrase for any idea, and the ensemble of these conflicting ideas has generally been presumed to reflect Clausewitz's profundity. This has also made Clausewitz a man for all seasons, as each period has highlighted the ideas which suited its tastes and strategic requirements while explaining away those which have not.[92]

Spenser Wilkinson, the first professor of military history at Oxford and an unrivalled scholar among the occupants of the rare university posts specified for military history in Britain before the Second World War, was one of the earliest critics of Liddell Hart's attitude to Clausewitz. In the first place he claimed that Clausewitz's work was a philosophical study of the nature of war *rather than* a source of operational doctrines. This, however, was a misleading distinction which unfortunately was later to gain much currency. Although rejecting formal systems and principles, Clausewitz believed that the nature of war prescribed clear guidance for action, which he identified with fighting and the search for a major battle respectively; indeed, he felt deeply that military theory was utterly useless if it was not able to offer such guidance and merely confined itself to 'empty abstractions'. Wilkinson also tried to qualify Liddell Hart's correct assertion that Clausewitz had regarded the overthrow of the enemy's main armies as the sole legitimate means in war. At the same time, however, Wilkinson maintained, as he always had, that during the First World

[91] *The Revolution in Warfare*, 34–75.

[92] See Book I above, 192–265.

War there had been no alternative to the concentration of all forces against Germany on the Western Front.[93] No matter how justified he may have been on this point, it should serve as a reminder that Wilkinson was far from being the detached scholar passing sagacious judgement on Liddell Hart's propagandist endeavour. Rather, he himself was a distinguished and deeply committed exponent of the nineteenth-century military school, with a long and eminent career of journalistic and public campaigning over questions of national strategy and defence organization behind him.[94]

In a stream of books and articles written in the decades preceding the Great War, Wilkinson had championed a number of related causes: he had been the leading advocate of the creation of modern staff systems on the Prussian model for the British army and navy; he had striven to turn Britain into a real nation-in-arms which could match the continental powers; he had been a staunch Mahanite and the inspiration behind the creation of the British Navy League in 1894. As he put it: 'There is only one theory of war—that which is set forth, with some differences of expression and of detail, by Clausewitz, by Jomini, by Mahan.'[95] Liddell Hart's ideas were nothing new to him. Before the Great War he had already been one the most venomous critics of Julian Corbett's theories, which had challenged the navalist faith in the destruction of the enemy's navy in a major battle as the sole legitimate aim and means in war and which had suggested the desirability of limited wars and limited strategic efforts.[96] During the war Wilkinson wrote in a highly characteristic manner: 'The war that aims at striking down the enemy by the destruction of his forces is that of a successful State; the war that tries to limit its aims, and therefore its exertions, is that of the defeated.'[97] In 1911, years before he met Liddell Hart, he had argued against Norman Engell and those who had shared similar opinions that 'Peace cannot rationally be the object of policy'.[98] Finally,

[93] S. Wilkinson, 'Killing No Murder: An Examination of Some New Theories of War', *Army Quarterly* (Oct. 1927), 14–21.

[94] For Wilkinson, see J. Luvaas, *The Education of an Army* (London, 1965), 253–90.

[95] Scammell, 'Spenser Wilkinson and the Defence of Britain', *Journal of the American Military Institute*, 4 (1940), 141–2; cited by Luvaas, *The Education of an Army*, 280; for a learned account of nineteenth-century military thought, and Clausewitz, see S. Wilkinson, *War and Policy* (London, 1900), 150–4.

[96] Book II above, 490–1.

[97] Cited by Luvaas, *The Education of an Army*, 283–4.

[98] *Government and the War* (London, 1918), 64; cited by J. Gooch, *The Prospect of War: Sudies in British Defence Policy, 1847–1942* (London, 1981), 49.

in reaction to Liddell Hart's work he wrote that the financial and economic aspects of war ought to be treated separately from the military and naval sides, to which Liddell Hart replied that, on the contrary, they had been kept in separate, watertight compartments for far too long.[99]

Interpretations of Clausewitz changed with the advent of the nuclear age. It was now becoming the fashion sharply to contrast a 'good' Clausewitz with his 'bad' successors in the nineteenth-century Prussian-German tradition. In 1956 Michael Howard started to lecture on Clausewitz at King's College, London, reflecting the new 'Clausewitz renaissance' which was gathering momentum throughout the West. Diplomatically he wrote to Liddell Hart, his close friend, that he had always taken his criticism of Clausewitz's theories as having been directed against Clausewitz's disciples rather than against Clausewitz himself. But Liddell Hart held his ground, replying that he had gone over Clausewitz's work again and could not see how everything in *On War* could be explained away on the grounds of faulty interpretation. The intention in too many passages was unequivocally clear. Howard sensibly withdrew, proclaiming that a better familiarity with German philosophy of the time would be required to decide the issue.[100] However, two decades later he was to produce an excellent balanced assessment of the question in his introduction to a new translation of Clausewitz's *On War* (1976), acknowledging most of the features which Liddell Hart had criticized in Clausewitz's work. 'But the final picture Liddell Hart painted of Clausewitz's teaching', he concluded, 'was distorted, inaccurate, and unfair.[101]

So indeed it was. It was certainly inaccurate, if only because of the fact that, despite some inklings to the contrary, like most readers of Clausewitz, Liddell Hart tended to regard *On War* as an integrated whole rather than an unfinished draft whose author had completely changed his mind half-way through the work; then, in the latest parts of the work, which he had written before he died, rather than discard his old ideas, Clausewitz had striven to resolve his difficulties by trans-

[99] Wilkinson to Liddell Hart, 28 Dec. 1928; Liddell Hart to Wilkinson, 31 Dec. 1928: King's, 1/748.

[100] Howard commented on the passages on Clausewitz in Liddell Hart's, 'Armed Forces and the Art of War: Armies', written for *The New Cambridge Modern History*, 10 (1960), 302–30; Howard to Liddell Hart, 13 Dec. 1958; Liddell Hart to Howard, 3 Feb. 1959; Howard to Liddell Hart, 5 Feb. 1959: King's, 1/384.

[101] 'The Influence of Clausewitz', in Clausewitz, *On War* (Princeton, NJ, 1976), 39–41.

planting them into his new ones. This complex genealogy has resulted in an understandable confusion among Clausewitz's readers. Liddell Hart's picture of Clausewitz was also distorted and one-sided, though fundamentally no different from that of those commentators who in the nuclear age have subordinated one phase in Clausewitz's development to the other; although Liddell Hart cannot be recommended as a balanced authority for a study of Clausewitz, he is no worse in this regard than most of the more recent literature. Certainly, Liddell Hart was unfair to Clausewitz. Yet fairness was hardly to be expected. Liddell Hart was waging war against a highly influential conception of war and military theory which had dominated an age, and Clausewitz was an authority and a symbol which had to be dethroned.

Historians who participated in the 'Clausewitz renaissance' have lost sight of the fact that throughout his life, both in his theories and practical policy recommendations, Clausewitz was the most fervent exponent of all-out war and the strategy of destruction. Nobody in his generation formulated the Napoleonic experience in such extreme terms, not even his fellow reformers in Prussia who, like him, had been deeply shaken by their nation's disastrous defeat in 1806 and subsequent subjugation, and whose mood and opinions he generally expressed. Indeed, for all their obvious differences of character and style, a striking similarity in reverse exists between the respective historical positions and ideas of Clausewitz and Liddell Hart, something which in a sense supports the latter's allusive suggestions that he was the Prussian's equal. Both thinkers reacted to cataclysmic and epoch-making wars which had resulted in a national trauma and profound intellectual transformation. In both, their experiences produced a violent reaction against past military theory and practice, held to be responsible for the disaster; it is scarcely noted that the picture Clausewitz had painted of his predecessors was as inaccurate, distorted, and unfair as Liddell Hart's. Both advanced a new model of military theory, which they held to be universally valid and which involved an unhistorical approach to the special conditions which had determined the patterns of the past. Both were not just 'idly theorizing' but developed and preached their ideas out of consuming commitment to their countries' future. The difference between them, of course, was only that the one had stood at the dawn of total war and called on his country for an all-out national effort and on her army for a vigorous direct action, whereas a century later the other witnessed the peaking of total war and preached restraint and a return to manœuvre.

It is true that in 1827 Clausewitz's thought came to a crisis, after which, until his death, in what was above all a reaction against his own lifelong and strongly held opinions, he began to revise his theories, painfully recognizing the legitimacy of limited war and explaining it largely by the influence of policy which restrained war to suit its aims. It was these ideas that in the late nineteenth and early twentieth centuries, independent of each other, both Delbrück and Corbett developed and directed against the dominating theory of all-out war and the strategy of destruction. Thus Corbett based on Clausewitz's later theories the same ideas which Liddell Hart, Corbett's disciple, would direct against Clausewitz. This apparent paradox is rooted in the Janus face of Clausewitz's development and influence. More specifically, it ought to be noted that Clausewitz's revision of his early ideas had never gone so far as expressly to rehabilitate eighteenth-century warfare or fully to endorse alternative methods of warfare other than fighting. Both Delbrück and Corbett developed his ideas further, knowing his limitations and recognizing that he himself had never reached that far.

All the same, as critics have suggested, were not Liddell Hart's ideas regarding the subordination of war to policy and his concept of limited war in fact merely echoing Clausewitz (via Corbett)?[102] Undoubtedly, to a large degree they were. Yet they also went further, and added meaningful new dimensions to Clausewitz's line of reasoning. In Fuller's footsteps Liddell Hart developed an entire philosophy of politics, war, and peace: not only was the conduct of war to be bridled in accordance with the political aim of the war, but this aim itself had to be kept coolly in check with the view of adjusting it, beyond the inflamed emotions of an ongoing conflict, to the eventual desired state of peace. In time Liddell Hart would begin to doubt if a victorious war had ever really proved beneficial even to the victor in recent modern history. 'Victory' itself would thus appear to be a dubious aim not only in the military but also in the political sense. It is mainly in the light of these ideas that one should view Liddell Hart's assertion, in Fuller's spirit, that 'Clausewitz looked only to the end of war, not beyond war to the subsequent peace'.[103]

This was more than an abstract change of emphasis. Both Clausewitz and Liddell Hart were expressing a political ethos. Both were making

[102] Wilkinson, 'Killing No Murder', 20–1; Howard, 'The Influence of Clausewitz', 39–40; C. Bassford, *Clausewitz in English: The Reception of Clausewitz in Britain and America, 1815–1945* (Oxford, 1994), 133, 142.

[103] *The Ghost of Napoleon*, 121.

political statements. Both were exponents of powerful ideologies dominating their respective times, countries, and cultural circles. Although Clausewitz's work has often been naïvely proclaimed 'value-free', he in fact expressed the new attitudes in Germany of the Romantic period which in a sweeping reaction against Enlightenment ideas presented war as necessary and even beneficial.[104] These were the notions that during the nineteenth century grew to dominate German political ethos, shaped as it was by Germany's difficult course to unity and by her later struggle to win what she regarded as her proper place in the European and global order. By contrast, from the 1930s on, as the Nazi and Soviet threats presented in turn unparalleled challenges to the existing world order, Liddell Hart was to develop a fully conscious view of war which aimed to suit the needs of the liberal and politically satisfied Britain and, later, of the liberal and politically satisfied West. In the process, while building on his earlier, popular theories, Liddell Hart greatly developed and amended them. It is there, in his more mature but less-known ideas, that his main contribution to strategic theory lay, as well as the true measure of his originality and sophistication.

104 Book I above, 238–52.

4

Policy: Defence of the West (I): Containment in the 1930s

By the beginning of the 1930s, having written his history of the First World War, Liddell Hart set out to define more closely what fundamentally had 'gone wrong' with the war. He approached the question from a general point of view, reviewing Britain's historical war policy, from which he claimed she had diverged without real justification and with disastrous results in her massive continental involvement during the Great War.

He presented his interpretation of 'The British Way in Warfare' in a lecture delivered before the Royal United Services Institution in January 1931.[1] He argued that from the sixteenth century on Britain had owed much of her global pre-eminence and commanding influence in Europe to her unique strategic policy. Shielded as she had been from invasion by her insular position and naval preponderance, Britain had avoided large-scale military involvements in the great wars that had racked the Continent. Against major continental rivals, such as the Spain of Philip II and France from Louis XIV to Napoleon, she had employed a variety of other means. She had subsidized and supplied the armies of Continental allies to keep her great adversaries busy on land. While she had sent only relatively small armies to the main theatres of operations to support these allies and sustain them in the war, her amphibious expeditions and seaborne raids had distracted and tied down a great number of enemy troops. Most importantly, while Britain's naval blockade had destroyed her enemy's commerce, her overseas forces had captured his colonies, thus making Britain ever richer and all the more able to wage successfully her maritime and economic style of warfare. Finally, Britain had always known how to limit her wars to what had been politically feasible and economically

[1] 'Economic Pressure or Continental Victories', *Journal of the RUSI*, 76 (1931), 486–510; incorporated as 'The Historic Strategy of Britain', in *The British Way in Warfare*, (London 1932), 13–41, and *When Britain Goes to War* (London, 1935), 17–46.

profitable, and never engaged in a futile and costly effort to completely crush her enemies.

Unfortunately, argued Liddell Hart, under the influence of Clausewitz and Continental military ideas Britain had gone for an all-out war from 1914 on, building a huge army and throwing it against Germany's main forces on the Western Front. In the end she won 'victory', but the effort bankrupted her. In his speculative replay of the war, Liddell Hart suggested that once the initial German onslaught in the West had been checked, the British involvement in France should have been restricted to the stiffening of the French defence. The British forces should have been employed more profitably in more exposed theatres, exploiting the mobility and surprise offered by the Royal Navy. A more carefully planned and better coordinated Dardanelles operation could have opened communications with Russia and facilitated the formation of a Balkan league on the Entente's side. Britain certainly had had to expand her armies considerably, but should never have introduced conscription and created mass armies on the Continental model. Instead, being still by far the mightiest manufacturing and financial power in the Entente, she should have concentrated on the production of armaments and ammunition for her allies, particularly Russia. To win the war on the strength of Russia's seemingly inexhaustible reservoir of manpower had actually been the strategy of the governments and general staffs of the Western allies during the early stage of the war. Their failure to supply Russia with the resources she needed to continue the war had been regarded by Lloyd George both during and after the war as their main strategic blunder.[2] According to Liddell Hart, if Russia had not defected and if the Central Powers, subjected as they had been to the British naval blockade, had been denied the foodstuffs and raw materials of South-eastern Europe which fell into their hands in 1915–17, Germany and her allies would not have been able to continue the war for long. A satisfactory negotiated peace could then have been reached, at a much lower human and economic cost to Britain, as well as to the other belligerents.

Nothing in this historical interpretation of British strategic policy was new. As historians have pointed out, in propounding 'the British way in warfare' Liddell Hart merely restated the arguments of the so-called 'maritime school' in British history. This school, which had

[2] D. Lloyd George, *War Memoirs* (London, 1936), 240–88, 1998; K. Neilson, *Strategy and Supply: The Anglo-Russian Alliance, 1914–1917* (London, 1984).

figured prominently in the strategic debate in Britain since Elizabethan times, resurfaced in the late nineteenth century and, increasingly, towards and during the First World War.[3] Its principal ideas, formulated and popularized by the famous naval authors Alfred Mahan and Philip Colomb, held sway in naval circles and largely dominated official outlook as well. Although in the decade before 1914 the British government accepted the commitment of the small British regular army to France at the outset of a war against Germany, this represented no real divergence from a fundamentally maritime approach. Well into the summer of 1915 the majority of the cabinet ministers expected to leave most of the burden of land warfare to Britain's allies, and supported the search for seaborne initiatives in which it was hoped that British naval power would assist in bringing about more effective and profitable results than the campaign in France. Only later in the war did the Allies' failures in the Dardanelles and Salonika, the mounting German pressure on Russia and the drain on France's resources drive Britain to accept an increasingly significant role in the Allies' land offensives in the west. Even then, when Britain's resources and manpower were being fully committed to the land war, Lloyd George and his colleagues, in conflict with the generals, were looking for alternatives to the costly offensives on the Western Front.[4]

Churchill's *World Crisis* reactivated the debate after the war, and Liddell Hart's conception of 'the British way in warfare' was probably also influenced by the writings of Admiral Sir Herbert Richmond, the naval intellectual maverick and first commandant of the new Imperial Defence College in 1926–9. Richmond was in close touch with Liddell Hart from 1930, the two acting in alliance on a whole range of defence issues.[5] Richmond, however, held moderate, revised navalist views, influenced both by the lessons of the First World War and by the ideas

[3] M. Howard, 'The British Way in Warfare', in *The Causes of War* (London, 1984), 192–3.

[4] M. Howard, *The Continental Commitment* (London, 1972), 53–9; P. Kennedy, *Strategy and Diplomacy, 1870–1945* (London, 1983), 63–6; *The Rise and Fall of British Naval Mastery*, 255–9; D. French, *British Economic and Strategic Planning, 1905–1915* (London, 1982); *British Strategy and War Aims, 1914–1916* (London, 1986); *The Strategy of the Lloyd George Coalition, 1916–1918* (Oxford, 1995).

[5] Richmond is the only authority cited in Liddell Hart's RUSI lecture, which he attended and with whose thesis he generally expressed agreement in the debate that followed the lecture: Liddell Hart, *The British Way in Warfare*, 28; *Memoirs* (2 vols., London, 1965), i. 58, 284; their correspondence is in i. 598. See also B. Bond, *Liddell Hart: A Study of His Military Thought* (London, 1977) [*LH*], 75–7.

advanced even before the war by Julian Corbett.[6] None of the qualifying and more subtle notions in the work of Corbett and Richmond were embodied in Liddell Hart's tract. As we have seen before, Corbett's ideas regarding limited war and the special propensity of Britain's maritime strategy for that type of war—as opposed to the Continental total war—decisively influenced Liddell Hart's development and became central to his entire thought. However, Corbett had also been an acute critic of maritime strategy, and had emphasized its inherent limitations at least as much as its purported advantages.

To be sure, Corbett endorsed and articulated the navy's 'blue water' view, according to which the navy alone was to be entrusted with the defence of the British Isles against enemy invasion. This view was accepted in general by the Invasion Sub-Committee of the Committee of Imperial Defence which was set up to study the problem in 1907–8.[7] Corbett also advised the Admiralty committees which in 1906 and 1908 drew up the navy's proposals for a maritime strategy in a war against Germany. In the Committee of Imperial Defence which examined this problem in 1908 and again in 1911, the Admiralty objected in vain to the army's plans for the dispatch of a British expeditionary force to France on the outbreak of hostilities.[8] It is very doubtful, however, that Corbett shared the Admiralty's view on that particular point.[9] In open divergence from accepted navalist faith, one of the main themes of his voluminous scholarly study of British naval history from Drake to Nelson and of his *Some Principles of Maritime Strategy* was that British naval pressure alone had not been able to hurt a great Continental

[6] For Richmond's views in the relevant period, see his *National Policy and Naval Strength* (London, 1928), 27–73; *Sea Power in the Modern World* (London, 1934), esp. 75–6, 108. See also A. Marder, *Portrait of an Admiral: The Life and Papers of Sir Herbert Richmond* (Cambridge, Mass., 1952); D. Schurman, *The Education of a Navy* (London, 1965), 110–46; R. Higham, *The Military Intellectuals in Britain, 1918–1939* (New Brunswick, NJ, 1966), 31–5, 51–61.

[7] M. Hankey, *The Supreme Command* (2 vols., London, 1961), i. 66–8.

[8] Ibid. 39–40, 69–70, 78–82.

[9] Howard, 'The British Way in Warfare', 196–7, may be too definite on this point. The most that can be said is that Admiral Slade drew heavily on Corbett's material in outlining the Admiralty's proposals for economic pressure against Germany, about the immediate efficacy of which the Admiralty itself had its doubts. The objection to the dispatch of an expeditionary force to France came mainly from Fisher: Hankey, *The Supreme Command*, i. 66–8. Howard also implies that Corbett argued that a maritime power was able to apply limited power even to the attainment of the unlimited objective of total victory, whereas Corbett in fact held that this could be done only 'in concert with continental allies': Howard, 'The British Way in Warfare' 194–5; J. Corbett, *Some Principles of Maritime Strategy* (Annapolis, Md., 1988), 78.

power decisively. In opposition to navalist critics, he justified the dispatch of British armies to the Continent from Elizabethan times on. In 1907, commenting on the proposals of the Admiralty Committee, he pointed out that the capture of German colonies would have no effect on the object of the war. Two years before the outbreak of the First World War, he denied that he had ever maintained that his concept of limited maritime warfare applied to a war against Germany. During the war itself, he was sceptical of most of the schemes for amphibious and combined operations against the Central Powers.[10]

Developing the notions first advanced by Corbett, by the army's General Staff, and by Richmond, historians have left few remains of Liddell Hart's 'British way in warfare'.[11] They have argued convincingly that the dispatch of British armies to the main theatres of operations in Europe in support of Britain's allies had always been a central and essential component of her strategy. It was no smaller in fact, in terms of the manpower and money invested, than Britain's maritime and overseas efforts, or, indeed, relative to her population, than her allies' military contributions. If she was to prevent a hegemonic Continental power from establishing its supremacy over Europe, and thus control Britain's main markets and ultimately threaten her naval predominance as well, Britain simply could not risk her allies collapsing or defecting for lack of support, and of the most direct kind. Amphibious operations and raids provided no real substitute for such direct involvement, not least because their inherent complexity made them prone to fail, as their historical record clearly demonstrates. Britain employed a 'purely' maritime strategy only out of necessity, when her Continental allies were geographically remote and isolated, as Frederick the Great was in the Seven Years War; or after they had been crushed, as against Napoleon in 1807–12; or when she did not have any in the first place, as during the American War of Independence. In all these cases Britain's position was very precarious indeed.

Furthermore, in the industrial age strategic conditions changed considerably from what they had been during the early modern period. In

[10] 'War Plans: Secret: General Remarks on a War with Germany', Corbett Papers, Box 6; marginal note on 'Great Britain, Germany and Limited War', *Edinburgh Review*, Apr. 1912, Corbett Papers, Box 5; both cited by E. Groves, Introduction, to Corbett, *Maritime Strategy*, p. xlii.

[11] See the authorities cited in n. 1 of the Introduction to Part II (above). For Richmond's excellent analysis of most of the following points, see the references to his works in n. 6 above.

the first place, for all the clamour of the imperialist contest, the value of overseas gains for national wealth, and consequently their significance in war, decreased sharply. Secondly, while in the new global market of raw materials and goods the blockade had in fact become a far more effective instrument of war than it had been before, this was only true if the hegemonic Continental power was prevented from overrunning and occupying great stretches of the European land mass, thus making itself much less vulnerable to economic pressure. In addition, Britain herself had become even more vulnerable than her Continental rivals to a naval blockade. Thus it had become her vital interest to prevent the harbours of Western Europe from being occupied and turned into bases for enemy submarines. Finally, for the first time in history the advent of the railroad had made land transportation in the European theatre of war at least as quick and economical as sea transportation, and far more flexible. Seaborne operations on the peripheries of the Continent had thus become that much less promising and more dangerous. The advent of the aeroplane reinforced this trend, and also exposed the British Isles themselves to attack from the Continent, making Britain all the more interested in what was happening beyond her shores.

All these are perfectly valid points. The only thing is that Liddell Hart actually raised most, if not all, of them *himself*, though, admittedly, not in his well-known but superficial 1931 RUSI lecture. As it has been shrewdly put, 'it would be doing Liddell Hart an injustice' to regard that lecture as 'anything more than a brilliant piece of political pamphleteering'.[12] Indeed, even more, it would be to underestimate him considerably. There is no question that Liddell Hart was totally sincere and committed in his biases. But his 1931 lecture, although certainly programmatic in nature and directed to the future as much as to the past, was merely an abstract sketch. There was still no sign of any disturbance to peace, not even a definite enemy in view, in Europe or even in East Asia, at the beginning of the 1930s. Shortly afterwards, however, the Japanese invasion of Manchuria, Hitler's rise to power in Germany, and the subsequent actions by Germany, Italy, and Japan against the international status quo initiated a period of profound crises and once more made a great war a likely possibility. And after the tension exploded in a new world war there came yet another period of endemic crisis, with the Cold War between the communist world and the West.

[12] Howard, 'The British Way in Warfare', 192.

Thus, while before the mid-1930s circumstances had not really offered Liddell Hart the occasion to address any specific political situation or concrete strategic problem, from that time on questions of foreign and strategic policy were becoming his main field of concern. He was now required to adapt his hitherto abstract ideas and sweeping generalizations—including 'the British way in warfare'—to formulate much more carefully reasoned and precise policy recommendations, taking into account the particular conditions of the time and the place.[13] This he did, though not without some mistakes and the occasional blunder, with remarkable acuteness and foresight, much greater than he has been generally credited with by historians.

This, perhaps, becomes more apparent with the passage of time and the changing of historical perspectives; the opening of the British archives, for example, has altered our understanding of the 1930s, while the end of the Cold War makes possible a longer view of the fifty-year crisis. The policies which Liddell Hart advocated in relation to Nazi Germany and the Axis powers before and during the Second World War, and which he barely changed when the Soviet Union took Germany's place as the main threat to the West's interests and way of life, have become the stock-in-trade of modern strategic outlook. None the less, Liddell Hart has not been given sufficient credit as their pioneer. For all his talents for self-publicity, he himself never fully presented his case for the judgement of posterity, first, because it involved painful personal memories and second, because at the time he published his *Memoirs* in the mid-1960s events were too close to allow a wider assessment of his significance in the history of strategic thought, by himself as well as by others.

It is not the aim of this study to replay the momentous events and major decisions of the 1930s, 1940s, and 1950 and make the case for or against Liddell Hart's positions. Although discussion of available alternatives, in order to illuminate the decisions and courses of action actually taken at the time, is an essential part of historical understanding, hypothetical cases are impossible to prove or disprove and ought not be pursued too seriously. Neither is it my aim here to present Liddell Hart's role in British decision-making in any detail. By the late 1920s and early 1930s he had already become internationally famous as a military critic, theorist, and historian, and as a leading

[13] Cf. M. Howard, 'Liddell Hart' (1970), repr. in *The Causes of War*, 241; also J. Mearsheimer, *Liddell Hart and the Weight of History* (London, 1988) [*LH*], 99, 107.

proponent of armoured warfare. His position as the only regular military correspondent in a British newspaper and his many connections in the defence establishment and army earned him considerable influence. In the second half of the 1930s, as he moved to *The Times*, became the unofficial adviser to the War Secretary, Hore-Belisha, and regularly briefed senior politicians of all parties, his influence reached its peak. All the same, his main significance remains in the history of strategic ideas, and it is from this angle—in connection with the wider trends characterizing Western strategic thought in the twentieth century—that his policy recommendations will concern us here. For in response to the challenges facing Britain and the West from the mid-1930s on, Liddell Hart's thought expanded and assumed new dimensions. He now integrated the ideas and doctrines he had propounded in the 1920s within a fully conscious political and philosophical creed. Developing a blueprint for a strategic policy that would suit the needs of liberal and 'satisfied' nations who could no longer perceive themselves voluntarily embroiled in major great-power wars, he advanced the notions of containment and cold war, and outlined the means by which they could be implemented.

I. Collective Security

In early 1935 Liddell Hart transferred from the *Daily Telegraph* to take up the newly created post of defence correspondent of *The Times*. This new peak in his career coincided with the ending of Britain's postwar defence policy. Following the work of the Defence Requirements Committee in 1933–4 the British cabinet decided on a limited programme of rearmament to face the growing potential threats from Germany and Japan. Before assuming his new post with *The Times*, Liddell Hart conducted a comprehensive preparatory assessment of the strategic position of Britain and the Empire, whose conclusions he laid out in his first article in *The Times*. The only solution he saw for Britain's defence problems was collective security:

> there could be little promise of security, so far as one can see, in adopting a policy of isolation. The most 'forceful' argument for pursuing the method of collective security is the strategic . . . the development of a collective security is not only a moral ideal but a British interest.

In emphasizing the strategic dimension of collective security, Liddell Hart reflected a wider change in British political attitudes. Collective security had previously been regarded either as an empty, if not dangerous, slogan or as a substitute for and moral alternative to rearmament. By 1935, however, in the wake of the 'peace ballot' which overwhelmingly supported collective security and military means to enforce it, the strategic aspect of this policy was taken up by the Baldwin adminstration. It was particularly identified with Eden, foreign secretary from the end of that year. Soon it would be adopted both by the Labour and Liberal parties.[14] Even Churchill, who had long treated the concept with contempt, would embrace it in the late 1930s as a disguise for the old principle of the balance of power for the purpose of blocking Germany. Liddell Hart came to advocate collective security for the same reasons as the government. While supportive of the new rearmament measures, he suggested, echoing the assessments of the responsible defence authorities, that in view of the prospective threats facing Britain, even the most extensive and expensive rearmament programme, had it been possible, would fail to achieve for Britain the kind of security she had enjoyed in the nineteenth century. Admitting that previously he had been predisposed toward isolationism, he now maintained that it was out of the question. Britain's only hope for security lay in conjunction with her allies, with whom she must work in a concerted effort to maintain the status quo. His programmatic article, overlooked by historians, was at least as important as 'The British Way in Warfare' in determining his strategic attitude during the second half of the 1930s.[15]

His position during the coming years of crises may best be clarified in reference to Britain's official policy, as it would be shaped and steered in widely divergent courses under the successive powerful personal stamp of two dominating prime ministers, Neville Chamberlain and Winston Churchill. In each case Liddell Hart supported some aspects of their respective policy lines while bitterly opposing other aspects. In his

[14] See esp. K. Middlemas, *Diplomacy of Illusion: The British Government and Germany, 1937–39* (London, 1972), 26–35, 144–7, 157, and *passim*; R. A. C. Parker, *Chamberlain and Appeasement: British Policy and the Coming of the Second World War* (London, 1993), 45–7.

[15] *The Times*, 14 Mar. 1935; also 'Defence of the Realm', *Listener*, 11 Mar. 1936; 'Military and Strategic Advantages of Collective Security in Europe', *New Commonwealth Quarterly*, 9 (1938) 144–55; to Barrington-Ward, 29 Mar. 1938, Liddell Hart Centre for Military Archives, King's college, London [King's], 3/108; *The Defence of Britain* (London, 1939), 45; letter to the *New Statesman*, published on 19 Dec. 1942, in reply to George Orwell's review of the new edition of *When Britain Goes to War*; here LH specifically points out that in 1935 he revised his original concept of 'the British Way in Warfare'; *Memoirs*, i. 285–6; ii, 146. The article in *The Times* and its significance are only referred to (albeit partially) by Mearsheimer, *LH*, 106, 130.

opinion, in their opposite ways both ultimately failed to square Britain's resources and aims. Indeed, as the opening of the British archives broke the monopoly of the Churchillian version of the 1930s, this view is now widely shared by historians, who have come to a better appreciation of the intricacies of the security dilemma facing Britain at that time. As one historian has put it, neither Chamberlain's policies nor Churchill's '"solved' Britain's strategic and economic dilemmas . . . both appeasement and anti-appeasement brought disadvantages; they were only a choice of evils'.[16]

Like most politically minded Britons in the second half of the 1930s, with the exception of a small minority of isolationists and extreme appeasers, Liddell Hart regarded Germany as Britain's main security problem and thought that the prevention of a German hegemony over the Continent was a vital British interest which had to be defended even by force. Equally, however, he believed, like the overwhelming majority of official and public opinion, that another total war against Germany would be a disaster, and perceived, like Chamberlain and many others in the British establishment, that it would result in the subservience of Britain to the United States and in the end of the Empire. In line with his entire philosophy of war the problem, as he saw it, was how to apply force, if necessary, to stop the revisionist powers, Germany in particular, without falling into a mutually ruinous, counterproductive, and futile total war. In his view, it was in this difficult balancing act between the two equally disastrous political opposites of appeasement and total war that the test of British policy lay.

The international situation in Europe (and the Far East) deteriorated in stages, and it was only in hindsight that events would be viewed as a single, one-way process. The Japanese invasion of Manchuria in 1931 outraged Western and British public opinion. Yet the British political and defence establishment assessed that League sanctions against Japan might be answered by her with war, which nobody wanted and for which the British armed forces, which were supposed to carry most of the burden in case of a League action, were ill-prepared. Hitler's rise to power in Germany and the first steps of German rearmament alarmed the other powers but raised no serious thoughts of armed intervention. The Versailles Treaty and the 'denial of equality' to Germany had long been regarded in Britain as a historic mistake which was better

[16] P. Kennedy, *The Rise and Fall of the Great Powers* (London, 1989), 413; *Strategy and Diplomacy*, 100–6.

corrected as smoothly as possible. Between 1935 and 1938 the Italian invasion of Abyssinia, the German unilateral entry into the Rhineland demilitarized zone, and the Axis Powers' intervention in Spain each made some sort of action by the other European great powers a distinct possibility. By contrast, nobody considered that anything practical could be done about the German Anschluss with Austria in March 1938. The rapid German action created a *fait accompli* which could not be reversed short of total war, and the enforced treaty separation of the two German-speaking countries was anyhow something about which the Western powers had a bad conscience. It was only from the spring of 1938, with the coming of the Czechoslovakian crisis, that European (and British) politics became dominated by the prospect of a major war.

Liddell Hart's reaction to the crises of the 1930s underwent similar development. Although he would later denounce the inaction of Britain and the League of Nations over the Japanese invasion of Manchuria as the first step of appeasement and of the collapse of collective security, he does not seem to have been troubled by the matter at the time in any noticeable way.[17] In the following years, like other Britons, he was concerned about German rearmament, though when Germany reintroduced conscription, something which went against one of his most cherished doctrines, he raised the question whether the German army was not going to lose in quality what it was gaining in quantity.[18] He, too, did not suggest that anything practical could or should be done to stop German rearmament, and like many felt that Germany was justified in repudiating the discriminatory stipulations of Versailles. After the German army had marched into the Rhineland demilitarized zone in March 1936, Liddell Hart wrote privately that Germany was doing the right thing in the wrong way. She was justified in her claim for equality and in rejecting the dictated Treaty of Versailles, but she had signed the Locarno Treaty of her own free will and therefore her unilateral action could not be justified. Could she be trusted in the future? These sentiments were common in Britain, where again practically nobody recommended armed action to eject the Germans.[19]

If the last-mentioned crises could be regarded as internal German affairs, the crises over Abyssinia, Spain, and Czechoslovakia were not. As we have seen, in early 1935 Liddell Hart came to the conclusion that

[17] Cf. Mearsheimer, *LH*, 132. [18] *The Times*, 18 Mar. 1935.

[19] 7 Mar. 1936, King's, 11/1936/45; N. Gibbs, *Grand Strategy: History of the Second World War*, i (London, 1976), 227–54; B. Bond, *British Military Policy between the Two World Wars* (Oxford, 1980) 225–7.

collective security was the only conceivable method for safeguarding British security and was, therefore, a British interest. Henceforth he held firm to that doctrine, growing more persistent and vocal as each successive crisis presented an ever greater threat to British security. The strategic policy he advocated in each case was similar.

Liddell Hart's record on the Abyssinian crisis is scant but far from non-existent. As the crisis escalated over the summer and autumn of 1935, he denounced the British inaction in his private papers as short-sighted. He argued that the case was clear-cut, and reflected that it shed light on the true character of one's friends: who among them held that keeping promises was unimportant?[20] However, while commenting widely on the military operations of the war in *The Times*, he is not on record on the strategic policy he thought Britain ought to follow. This may be due to the fact that *The Times*, while strongly condemning Italy, did not support full sanctions against her. In later letters to the editor and to the assistant editor of *The Times*, the would-be ardent appeasers Geoffrey Dawson and Robin Barrington-Ward, who were arguably in a position to know whether or not what he said was true, Liddell Hart claimed that the cleavage between his opinions and their own had begun over the Abyssinian crisis when he had demanded a firm British line. He wrote that he had advocated the supply of arms to Abyssinia and supported the imposition of an oil embargo on Italy, which had been widely regarded as the only effective method of bringing her to her knees short of a war.[21] Since Britain controlled both entrances to the Mediterranean and the Italian sea route to Abyssinia, there was plenty of scope for indirect action to coerce Italy into withdrawing. Despite the scarcity of British forces in Egypt and the vulnerability of the Mediterranean route to the Italian air force and submarines, the British chiefs of staff were not very impressed by the Italian ability for effective counter-action. The reasons for the lack of determined action against Italy were mainly political: the British government saw no direct threat to British interests from the Italian occupation of Abyssinia; the British, and especially the French, were

[20] 30 June, 2 and 25 Sept. 1935: 11/1935/13, 28, 35.

[21] To Barrington-Ward, 30 Apr. 1937, King's, 3/107; to Dawson, 9 May 1938, 3/109; *Memoirs*, i. 287, 289. Mearsheimer, *LH*, 133–4, does not cite the references in this and the previous note. For the positions of *The Times*, Dawson, and Barrington-Ward, see M. Cowling, *The Impact of Hitler: British Politics and British Policy, 1933–1940* (Cambridge, 1975), 128–33.

reluctant to push Mussolini into Hitler's arms; and Britain was determined not to act without full French cooperation.[22]

Containment: Spain

It is obvious, however, that Liddell Hart did not feel about the Abyssinian crisis as strongly as he felt about the subsequent crises over Spain and Czechoslovakia, which strained his relations with *The Times* to the limit. From the outset, British attitudes towards the Spanish Civil War were marked by conflicting sympathies between left and right towards the warring parties, and by an even deeper official indifference. The British government believed that the outcome of the war mattered little to Britain, who would be able to maintain friendly relations with whoever won. It was in Britain's interest, however, agreed upon by all political parties, that all foreign intervention in the Spanish Civil War should be excluded. Yet by October 1936 it had become apparent that the non-intervention agreement, signed by the great powers at the end of August 1936, was almost openly disregarded by Italy and Germany, followed by the Soviet Union. In consequence, the Labour party swung against non-intervention, which remained the British and French policy up to the end of the war. Throughout 1937 Foreign Minister Eden was advocating stronger measures, including active naval surveillance, to prevent the violation of the non-intervention treaty. He was opposed, however, by his predecessor, now First Lord of the Admiralty, Sir Samuel Hoare, and by his other cabinet colleagues.[23]

Liddell Hart was similarly concerned by the course the war was taking. From November 1936 he disputed *The Times*'s editorial policy in respect to Spain and Eastern Europe, becoming ever more insistent and categorical. He protested that *The Times* was censoring information about Nationalist atrocities in order to create a false balance with Republican atrocities in this sad human and moral tale which had important public opinion implications.[24] At the beginning of April 1937 he still suggested that, as the stalemate in the Spanish Civil War went on, the Republicans' chances of holding on were improving,

[22] Gibbs, *Grand Strategy*, 189–222; also Bond, *British Military Policy*, 218–19; G. Post Jr., *Dilemmas of Appeasement: British Deterrence and Defence, 1934–1937* (London, 1993), 81–104.

[23] See J. Edwards, *The British Government and the Spanish Civil War, 1936–1939* (London, 1979); Parker, *Chamberlain and Appeasement*, 84–6.

[24] To Barrington-Ward, 4 Nov. 1936, and subsequent letter exchange: King's, 3/106; 19, 21 and 28 May 1937; memorandum, 'Conclusions from the Balance of Evidence', 21 May 1937; 25 Feb. 1938: all in 3/106–8; *Memoirs*, ii. 128–9.

provided that increased foreign intervention did not tip the scales against them. But from the end of that month, judging that Italian and German intervention was heavily influencing the course of the war, he is on record as opposing the British policy of non-intervention.[25] From early 1938 it was becoming clear that the Nationalists were finally winning the Civil War, a prospect which Liddell Hart viewed with the greatest anxiety. Precisely for that reason, however, he was no longer asked by *The Times* to contribute editorial leaders on Spain, and his commentaries on the war were not published. In March his article 'The Western Mediterranean', which he had originally written as a memorandum for the Secretary of State for War, Hore-Belisha, was refused publication on the grounds that it was wholly political and that its conclusions were unacceptable to the editor. From then on until the end of the Spanish Civil War in March 1939, Liddell Hart's writings on the war were regularly turned down by *The Times*.[26] Only in his articles in periodical journals was he able to express his opinions publicly.

What was he so concerned about? He was worried that if the Nationalists won the Civil War with the assistance of Italy and Germany, Spain might become a base for Axis air forces and naval light crafts and submarines. In a general European war these would close the western Mediterranean to Britain and France, and would constitute a serious threat to their naval routes around Africa and across the Atlantic. Liddell Hart argued emphatically that the gravity of this security risk was such that Britain simply could not responsibly ignore it in the hope that it would not materialize. From 1937 onward he discussed his views of the crisis with leaders of all three political parties. On two occasions he spoke with Eden, and in March and May 1938 Hore-Belisha, briefed by Liddell Hart, raised the subject of intervention in Spain in the cabinet.[27] To Liddell Hart's surprise, when discussing the question of Spain in June 1937 with the CIGS, Field Marshal Deverell, he got the impression that the latter had been entirely unaware of the strategic problem. French and British naval authorities had been aware

[25] 'Spain: Attack or Defence', *The Times*, 3 Apr. 1937; cf. *Europe in Arms* (London, 1937), 321; *Memoirs*, i. 372; to Barrington-Ward, 30 Apr. 1937, quoted ibid. ii. 132–3 (and out of context by Mearsheimer, *LH*, 136 n. 17); to Dawson, 1 Oct. 1937, quoted in *Memoirs*, ii. 135: letters in King's, 1/107.

[26] To Barrington-Ward, 25 Feb., 26 Mar., 10 Aug., 8 Nov. 1938; Barrington-Ward to Liddell Hart, 28, 29, 30 Mar., 1 Apr., and 2 Nov. 1938: all in King's, 3/108; much of this correspondence is printed in *Memoirs*, ii. 142–8.

[27] Talks with Eden, 23 Nov. 1937 and 1 June 1938: *Memoirs*, i. 136–7; King's, 11/1938/62; Cowling, *The Impact of Hitler*, 330.

of the potential danger since the beginning of the war in 1936; by late 1937 intelligence sources were reporting on Italian requests for bases in Spain. Nevertheless, it was only in March 1939 that the British chiefs of staff stressed the danger from a hostile Spain, in exactly the same terms as Liddell Hart and with equal gravity.[28]

What then did Liddell Hart suggest Britain and France should do? In his opinion, there was no need to get directly entangled in the fighting against the Italians and Germans on Spanish soil. Britain and France simply had to lift their embargo and provide the Republican forces with the arms and supplies they required. He believed that this was very likely sufficient to redress the balance and create a stalemate; in the past Spain had proved her immense capacity for absorbing foreign armies for years on end. It would then be left to the Italians and Germans to decide whether they wanted to settle the conflict at the negotiating table, or escalate it to their disadvantage:

> If Germany and Italy were to reply by a large increase in the quantities of material they have already sent, France and Britain are in better strategic position than they are for such competition—since the former powers would be locking up military resources in a potentially isolated theatre. If they dared to press their objections to the point of war, we should fight with all the advantages of the defensive and under more favourable circumstances of strategic geography than we could hope for once Spain has been conquered.[29]

With France controlling the land routes to Spain and the British and French navies the sea lanes, the odds were most favourable to the Western allies. Writing his *Memoirs* in the early 1960s, Liddell Hart likened this situation to the one prevailing during the Cuban crisis in 1962. Had he lived longer, he might also have cited Vietnam and

[28] A talk with Deverell, 29 June 1937, King's, 11/1937/56; *Memoirs*, ii. 140; J. Edwards, *The British Government and the Spanish Civil War, 1936–1939* (London, 1979), 23, 164, 212–14; G. Stone, 'The European Great Powers and the Spanish Civil War, 1936–1939', in R. Boyce and E. Robertson (eds.), *Paths to War: New Essays on the Origins of the Second World War* (London, 1989), 220–1; Gibbs, *Grand Strategy*, i. 727.

[29] Note, 13 Mar. 1938, King's, 11/1938/30, cited in *The Defence of Britain* (London, 1937), 64, and in *Memoirs*, ii. 142. More in 'The Strategic Future of the Mediterranean', *Yale Review* (Dec. 1936), 232–45, reprinted in *Europe in Arms* (London, 1937), 100–15; 'Strategy and Commitments', *Fortnightly* (June 1938), 642–5; 'Military and Strategic Advantages of Collective Security in Europe', *New Commonwealth Quarterly* (Sept. 1938), 147 ff.; 'Britain's Military Situation', *Yale Review* (Jan. 1939), 240; 'The Defence of Western Civilization', *New Commonwealth Review* (Jan. 1939), 25; 'What Spain Means to Britain', *Picture Post*, 4 Feb. 1939; extracts from Liddell Hart's memos and writings are printed in *The Defence of Britain*, 22, 24, 39, 64, 67–70, 81–2, 90, 138, 141–2, 285; *Memoirs*, ii. 128–30, 143–4.

Afghanistan. Interestingly, a study of Germany's intentions supports his view that Hitler was careful not to get deeply involved in the Spanish Civil War and certainly did not want to see it escalate into a general war.[30]

In the Abyssinian crisis, the limited and indirect course of action which was considered against Italy and which Liddell Hart supported may have succeeded had it been applied; but the strategic issue at stake, as opposed to the wider political and moral implications of the crisis, was insignificant. In the Spanish crisis the potential strategic threat to the Western allies, emphasized by Liddell Hart, was serious, and the limited and indirect course of action he advocated again appears plausible; yet, despite the Nationalists' victory, the threat did not materialize. The British government (and the editors of *The Times*) believed all along that Britain had enough economic leverage on Franco to prevent a Nationalist Spain from becoming hostile.[31] Indeed, in the event Spain would remain neutral during the Second World War, though, contrary to earlier beliefs, recent research has revealed Franco's eagerness to enter the war on the Axis side after Hitler's initial triumphs. If he did not, it was principally because Hitler was unwilling to accept his excessive colonial demands, mainly at the expense of Vichy France.[32] With the coming of the Czechoslovakian crisis, Liddell Hart viewed the potential threat as critical, and the methods he advocated were similar to those he had been advancing before. Czechoslovakia and Spain were engraved on his standard during 1938. Again he was in conflict with *The Times*, and after Munich he was in open public opposition to the British government's policy.

Containment: Czechoslovakia

Czechoslovakia was, after all, in Chamberlain's memorable phrase, 'a faraway country', inhabited by 'people of whom we know nothing'. In herself she was of practically no interest to Britain. Furthermore, whereas in the Abyssinian and Spanish crises the Western allies held the geo-strategic cards in their hands, being able to isolate the respective theatres of operations, it was Germany who held the cards in the Czechoslovakian crisis. Czechoslovakia was geographically isolated from the Western allies and, as the British chiefs of staff made clear and

30 Ibid. 130; G. Stone, 'The European Great Powers and the Spanish Civil War', in Boyce and Robertson (eds.), *Paths to War*, 220–1.

31 Dawson to Liddell Hart, 30 Oct. 1937; Barrington-Ward to Liddell Hart, 29 Mar. 1938: King's, 3/107–8.

32 P. Preston, *Franco* (London, 1993), 343–425.

Liddell Hart himself repeatedly stressed, there was virtually nothing Britain and France could do to directly assist in her defence. Why then did Liddell Hart regard Czechoslovakia as so critical to Britain's security as to justify war to defend it, and what course of action did he propose Britain should follow?

In Liddell Hart's opinion, rather than being an embarrassing liability, Czechoslovakia was one of the most vital elements of Britain's security system. His logic, explicitly traced to his study in 1935 of Britain's defence problems, was far more comprehensive than the critics of his 'British Way of Warfare' have given him credit for. He repeatedly stressed that the development of air power and the submarine had made British security interlinked with France's security against Germany: 'If France fell under hostile domination, and her ports and air bases were available for an enemy's use, the flow of our life blood could easily be stopped. Hence her risks are our risks.'[33] In turn, French security depended on the existence of a second front against Germany in Eastern Europe. The function of France's East European alliances, with Czechoslovakia in particular, consisted of more than their potential value for offsetting Germany's military superiority, dividing her strength, and relieving some of her pressure on France. The point, in Liddell Hart's view, was that the Western allies were simply too weak to hope they would be able to defeat Germany on the battlefield in any given time-scale. Their sole potent weapon of deterrence and coercion against Germany was the blockade which, despite her efforts to achieve autarky and develop ersatz goods, her highly industrialized economy could not withstand for very long. Over 66 per cent of Germany's ores for steel production came from abroad, as did 25 per cent of her zinc, 50 per cent of her lead, 70 per cent of her copper, 90 per cent of her tin, 95 per cent of her nickel, 99 per cent of her bauxite, 66 per cent of her oil, 80 per cent of her rubber, and 10–20 per cent of her foodstuffs.[34] As Liddell Hart noted, in the age of mechanized warfare Germany's shortages in certain key raw materials such as oil and metals for the aircraft industry actually made her even more vulnerable to the blockade than she had been during the First World War.[35] However, as he clearly saw, the blockade would be effective only if its implementation

[33] Quotation from *The Defence of Britain*, 136.

[34] Kennedy, *Strategy and Diplomacy*, 75; *British Naval Mastery*, 307; also W. N. Medlicott, *The Economic Blockade* (2 vols., London, 1978), i. 32. Cf. Liddell Hart, *The Defence of Britain*, 40–2; also *The Second World War* (London, 1970), 23–4.

[35] *The Defence of Britain*, 41.

by Britain on the sea was not circumvented by land, as Germany had partially succeeded in doing during the First World War. As Herbert Richmond had written in 1928:

It was only owing to the fact that the land frontiers of the enemies were sealed by the armies, and that every nation of importance was either actively assisting with her navies at sea, or passively by withholding trade, that the eventual degree of isolation was procured which contributed to victory.[36]

Liddell Hart viewed the situation in the same light: 'against a Continental state, sea power can only be a serious handicap, unless its land frontiers can also be closed. In that case, unless completely self-supporting, it may be gradually starved into submission.'[37] It followed that, with France and perhaps also the Low Countries on Britain's side, Germany had to be prevented from overrunning south-eastern Europe, and the Soviet Union's political, strategic, and economic cooperation had to be secured and denied to Germany. Hence Liddell Hart's staunch opposition to the Munich settlement, opposition based entirely on strategic grounds. The great question confounding British decision making in the late 1930s, what Hitler's and Germany's future intentions might be, did not matter to him at all in weighing the issue. As he saw it, Germany could not be effectively stopped, not even by a disastrous total war, once it broke loose of its restricted territorial base.[38] The sacrifice of the Czechoslovakian bastion would bring all the countries of the Danube basin with their agricultural and mineral wealth within German reach, and give Germany the ability to sustain a prolonged war. Like the breach of a dam, concessions to Germany in south-eastern Europe implied on Britain's part the forfeiting of its only potent weapon and the total collapse of any chance of stopping Germany by limited means and limited action, or indeed *by any means at all*. Great firmness and limited effort were thus the two interdependent sides of Liddell Hart's strategic equation.[39]

[36] *National Policy and Naval Strength* (London, 1928), 142; see also p. 71; cited with approval by Kennedy, *Strategy and Diplomacy*, 62, also 75; *British Naval Mastery*, 254–5.

[37] *The Defence of Britain*, 144.

[38] LH's conclusions bear a striking resemblance to those of the only two rigorous studies of the question from the strategic and economic point of view: W. Murray, *The Change in the European Balance of Power, 1938–1939* (Princeton, NJ, 1984), 27, 64–7, 160, 256–63, 362–3, and *passim*; D. E. Kaiser, *The Economic Diplomacy and the Origins of the Second World War: Germany, Britain, France, and Eastern Europe, 1930–1939* (Princeton, NJ, 1980), pp. xii, 218, 262, 283, 313, 315, and *passim*.

[39] Notes, 13 Mar. 1938, King's, 11/1938/30; *The Times*, 17 June 1938; 'Strategy and Commitments', 648–9; 'Military and Strategic Advantages of Collective Security in Europe', *New Commonwealth Quarterly* (Sept. 1938), 147–52; Notes, 9, 28 Sept. 1938, 11/1938/92

However Liddell Hart's analysis might be disputed, it serves to highlight how curiously incomplete was the strategic advice given during the crisis to the British government by the chiefs of staff. The chiefs of staff were duly pessimistic about the situation, fearing that Japan and Italy might take advantage of Britain's entanglement with Germany, stressing that the Western allies were unprepared for war and could do nothing to directly assist Czechoslovakia in her defence, and judging that Czechoslovakia would not be able to resist a German attack.[40] However, even though they made it very clear that Britain's strategy against Germany rested principally on the blockade, nowhere did the chiefs of staff discuss or even mention the implications for the feasibility of that weapon of the possible loss of south-eastern Europe that might follow the abandonment of Czechoslovakia. Such an assessment had in fact been called for by Oliver Stanley, representing those in the cabinet who doubted the wisdom of Chamberlain's policy. It was blocked, however, by General Ismay, the secretary of the Committee of Imperial Defence. Thus, strange as this may appear, the problem did not figure in the political, strategic, and public debate in Britain before Munich, even though the prospect of a German-dominated *Mitteleuropa* was recognized.[41] Nor has the problem been sufficiently recognized by historians until recently.

After Munich both Romania and Yugoslavia had no choice but to concede to a series of economic treaties which gave Germany priority in exploiting their highly important oil, mineral, and food resources. By occupying the rest of Czechoslovakia in March 1939, Germany considerably expanded her economic base and enriched her meagre reserves of foreign currency and raw materials, whose condition in

and 103; 'Britain's Military Situation', *Yale Review* (Dec. 1938), 230–45; 'The Defence of Western Civilization', *New Commonwealth Review* (Jan. 1939), 21–30; extracts are printed in *The Defence of Britain*, 22–4, 38–42, 63, 86–7, and *Memoirs*, ii. 130–1, 140–2, 145–6, 158–64.

[40] Howard, *Continental Commitment*, 119, 122; Gibbs, *Grand Strategy*, 642–3, 646–7; Murray, *European Balance of Power*, 157–62, 209–10.

[41] W. K. Wark, *The Ultimate Enemy: Britain Intelligence and Nazi Germany, 1933–1939* (London, 1985), 207–8. The question occurred to Ismay himself, who may have been influenced in this respect by Liddell Hart without accepting his conclusions (he also mentioned the advantage of the defensive in war): see the citation (22 Sept. 1938) in Howard, *Continental Commitment*, 123. See also R. Macleod and D. Kelly (eds.), *The Ironside Diaries, 1937–1940* (London, 1962), 62, 64.

1938 was extremely serious.[42] Germany incorporated the thriving Czechoslovakian arms industry, of which the Skoda and Zbrojovka factories in particular were among the world's best, making Czechoslovakia the fourth largest exporter of arms. The military equipment captured in Czechoslovakia in vast quantities was judged first-rate by the Germans, and found sufficient to equip twenty new German divisions, including three Panzer (divisions 6–8), armed with the Czechoslovakian T35 and T38. During the 1940 campaign in the West some 40 per cent of the German medium (gun-mounted) tanks were Czech models.[43]

Indeed, the *direct* loss that the abandonment of Czechoslovakia entailed has always been recognized by historians. Czechoslovakia was a significant military power, and, as all studies of her strength emphasize, her ability to resist Germany remains an open question.[44] Her army was strong, modern, and highly motivated. It numbered 1,250,000 soldiers, organized in fifteen corps (34–5 divisions) and in additional fortress troops. It possessed around 1,200 aircrafts, more than half of which of the first line, 700 tanks, 2,200 field-guns, and 2,500 anti-tank guns. The country's mountainous frontiers with Germany were heavily fortified. On the other side, the German army of 1938 was still in the midst of its expansion. Not only the Western allies but also the chiefs of the German armed forces felt totally unprepared for a general war. The Germans planned to deploy no more than thirty-seven divisions against

[42] For the significance of Germany's economic incorporation of Czechoslovakia and south-eastern Europe, see H.-E. Volkmann's contribution to Militärgeschichtliches Forschungsamt [MF] (ed.), *Germany and the Second World War*, i (Oxford, 1990), 332–49, 451; Murray, *European Balance of Power*, esp. 256–63, 291–2; Kaiser, *Economic Diplomacy*, 264–7 and *passim*. The point is fully conceded even by the otherwise revisionist R. Overy, 'Hitler's War Plans and the German Economy', in Boyce and Robertson, *Paths to War*, 111–12, 115–16. In Kaiser's summary: 'In 1938 the Munich agreement, which removed the last effective barrier to German military expansion eastward, also laid the region's economic resources at Hitler's feet. This peaceful triumph enabled Hitler to begin war one year later and to defeat the western powers in 1940' (p. xii). For Liddell Hart, see *The Defence of Britain*, 23–4, 38–9, 87.

[43] For the impressive products of the Czechoslovakian armour industry, see W. Spielberger, *Die Panzer-Kampfwagen 35(t) and 38(t)* (Stuttgart, 1980); also W. Oswald, *Kraftfahrzeuge und Panzer der Reichswehr, Wehrmacht und Bundeswehr* (Stuttgart, 1982), 356–7. Some 4500 T38 and derivative models were built for the Wehrmacht during the war.

[44] There are several excellent studies of the strategic balance: D. Vital, *The Survival of Small States* (Oxford, 1971), 26–34; M. Hauner, 'Czechoslovakia as a Military Factor in British Considerations of 1938', *Journal of Strategic Studies*, 1 (1978), 194–222; Murray, *European Balance of Power*, 119–21, 217–63; T. Taylor, *Munich: The Price of Peace* (New York, 1979), esp. 398–9, 681–731; also see W. Murray, 'German Air Power and the Munich Crisis', in B. Bond and I. Roy (eds.), *War and Society Yearbook*, 2 (1977), 114–15; MF, *Germany and the Second World War*, i. 334.

Czechoslovakia, leaving only five, together with four reserve and fourteen Landwehr divisions, against France. Three divisions were left to defend East Prussia. Contrary to the Allies' assessments at the time, the capacity of the German army for further expansion after the outbreak of hostilities was seriously limited by lack of equipment. The German Panzer force was still inexperienced and ill-equipped. Although numbering 2,100 tanks, it possessed only light, gunless models and still practically none of the new Marks III and IV medium tanks. Germany's greatest superiority was in the air, but the Luftwaffe, too, was still experiencing severe problems in the summer of 1938, arising from the transfer to a new generation of aircraft. Only little more then 50 per cent of the machines and air crews were operationally ready.[45] Here as well, the Germans planned to throw most of their weight against Czechoslovakia.

The Germans rated Czechoslovakia's strength very highly both before the crisis and when they examined what they saw after occupying the country. All the same, they planned to conquer it in a three-week campaign. The conservative and anti-war Chief of the General Staff Beck thought it would take longer.[46] Liddell Hart believed that the Czechs might well be capable of resisting indefinitely. He echoed, perhaps knowingly, the Czechoslovakian army's plan to withdraw into the depth of the country once its frontier lines were breached and to establish new defensive lines in the Moravian hills.[47] Admittedly, as we shall see, he vastly overrated the strength of defence. However, it ought to be noted that a year later he correctly judged that the Polish army stood no chance against the Germans.

Among the conditions Liddell Hart specified for the success of Czechoslovakia's resistance were that Poland and Hungary would not intervene against her, and the support of strong air reinforcements from the Soviet Union. He was fully aware of the difficulties the Soviet Union would encounter if she wished to support Czechoslovakia. The two countries had no common frontier. The Poles were unlikely to grant the Red Army free passage through their territory. Even if the Romanians were to allow such passage, communications through the Ruthenian corridor were narrow and poor.[48] So the Soviet Union's

[45] W. Murray, *Luftwaffe* (Baltimore, 1985), 18.

[46] See K.-J. Müller, *Gerneral Ludwig Beck: Studien und Dokumente* (Boppard a, R., 1980), 268–311, 502 ff.

[47] See Liddell Hart's memos reprinted in *The Defence of Britain*, 56–7, 61, 74–6; cf. Hauner, 'Czechoslovakia as a Military Factor', 199–200.

[48] It was thought at the time and is believed by historians that the Romanians would not have resisted a Russian land movement through their territory and would almost

ability to support Czechoslovakia in strength on the ground was at best limited. Liddell Hart suggested that some help could come through diversion by way of a Russian attack on East Prussia, assuming again that objections from the Baltic states to the Russians crossing their territory would not constitute an obstacle. But then again, the Soviet Union's military might had just been severely weakened by the liquidation of the better half of its officer corps in the great purges of 1937–8. On balance, we may assume today that Russian air reinforcements to Czechoslovakia would have been wiped out by the Luftwaffe.[49] It is equally clear, however, that in the long run Soviet cooperation was the most important condition for a successful war against Germany.

Like the Conservative, Labour, and Liberal opposition to Munich, Liddell Hart valued Soviet cooperation highly and feared the consequences on the Soviet Union's position if Czechoslovakia was abandoned.[50] He had been regularly meeting and exchanging sympathetic views with the Soviet ambassador in London, Ivan Maisky, who during the 1938 crisis was keeping in close touch with a group of senior public figures which included Winston Churchill, Harold Nicolson, Robert Boothby, Archibald Sinclair, Hugh Dalton, Arthur Greenwood, and David Lloyd George. Maisky was urging upon everybody, and was striving to convince the Foreign Office, that the Soviet Union desired to cooperate.[51] As early as March 1935 Liddell Hart, in a conversation with the Director of Military Operations and Intelligence, General John Dill, had objected to the popular idea of diverting Germany eastward (i.e. against the Soviet Union), thus 'feeding the tiger that might turn on you; we were the ultimate obstacle to Germany's ambition, as in the past'.[52] For Liddell Hart, as for Churchill and the rest of the opposition to Munich, this was not a matter of ideology but simply a question of the balance of power. Chamberlain, however, ruled out cooperation with

certainly have turned a blind eye to aerial traffic; they expected encouragement which did not come from Britain and France. The most detailed scholarly study is J. Haslam, *The Soviet Union and the Struggle for Collective Security in Europe* (London, 1984), 169–70, 179–80; also J. Hochman, *The Soviet Union and the Failure of Collective Security, 1934–1938* (London, 1984), 157–8.

[49] Cf. Murray, *European Balance of Power*, 124–7, 238.

[50] See most of the references in n. 39 above, and specifically regarding the latter point Liddell Hart, 'Strategy and Commitments', 649.

[51] The Maisky file: King's, 1/486, faithfully referred to in *Memoirs*, ii. 167, 195; also see S. Aster, 'Ivan Maisky and Parliamentary Anti-Appeasement, 1938–39', in A. J. P. Taylor (ed.), *Lloyd George: Twelve Essays* (London, 1971), 317–57.

[52] 27 Mar. 1935, King's, 11/1935/69; quoted in *Memoirs*, i. 291.

the Soviet Union, which he distrusted and detested even more than he did Germany.

The opening of the Soviet archives may soon provide a better insight into the development of Soviet foreign policy in the 1930s than has been possible until now. In the meantime, most historians of the subject assess that the Soviet Union's paramount fear of isolation *vis-à-vis* Germany made it anxious to cooperate with the West in the mid-1930s, a goal expressed in the double policy of 'collective security' and 'popular fronts'. It is agreed that by 1938 disappointments over Abyssinia and Spain had substantially cooled Soviet attitude. During the Czechoslovakian crisis the Soviet Union's posture was reserved and its actions ambivalent. Most historians believe, however, that this was due to the correct Soviet assessment that the British government had no serious intention of cooperating.[53] Indeed, working within the 'terms of reference' laid down by the prime minister, the British chiefs of staff, in their successive assessments of the situation after the German Anschluss of Austria in March 1938 and during the September crisis, did not even discuss the possibility of cooperation with the Soviet Union, let alone insist that it was vital for a war against Germany.[54]

Chamberlain was equally reluctant to rely on support from the United States in his dealing with the Axis powers. Not without reason, following repeated disappointments during the 1930s, he did not believe that this isolationist power could be counted upon for anything but words. Aware of the United States' wish to dismantle and inherit the British Empire, he regarded a European settlement and *détente* as Britain's best option by far.[55] This made good sense, if only this option had not have proved impossible. Thus Chamberlain rejected the only major alternative to appeasement—'collective security' or a 'Grand Alliance' of Britain, France, and the Soviet Union, with the economic backing of the United States, a slogan first mooted by Churchill in Parliament in March 1938.

[53] A. B. Ulam, *Expansion and Coexistence: The History of Soviet Foreign Policy, 1917–67* (London, 1968), 234–80; Haslam, *The Soviet Union and the Struggle for Collective Security*; G. Roberts, *The Unholy Alliance: Stalin's Pact with Hitler* (London, 1989); a minority position, distrusting Soviet seriousness, is expressed by G. L. Weinberg, *Germany and the Soviet Union, 1939–1941* (London, 1954); Hochman, *The Soviet Union and the Failure of Collective Security*.

[54] Murray, *European Balance of Power*, 157–62, 287; Kaiser, *Economic Diplomacy*, 227–8; Gibbs, *Grand Strategy*, 642–3, 646–7; Hauner, 'Czechoslovakia as a Military Factor', 196–8; Bond, *British Military Policy*, 282.

[55] A good summary of attitudes can be found in C. A. MacDonald, *The United States, Britain and Appeasement, 1936–1939* (London, 1981), 19–25.

Indeed the fear of a general coalition war against Germany following a German attack on Czechoslovakia was the nightmare of the German General Staff. Beck resigned on 21 August, after having failed in his hectic efforts during the spring and summer to reverse the course of German policy. He judged that the Allies would not launch major land offensives against Germany, but insisted that in the long run they were bound to strangle her economically. Similar views were widely held by senior German officers. Beck's successor, Franz Halder, and his allies in the German army and officialdom conspired to depose the regime if the order to attack were given. They made contact with the British government through various channels, but Munich put an end to the conspiracy. The apologetic nature of the German generals' postwar testimonies, their own nationalist political views, and doubts regarding the prospects of any successful attempt against the Nazi regime made historians sceptical in their attitude towards the German opposition to Hitler. All, however, agree that the pre-Munich activity—before Hitler's bloodless victory proved him smarter than anyone—was the most serious internal threat to his leadership.[56]

Finally, German air superiority and the fear of air attacks on the British and French cities were perhaps the single most important strategic factor influencing the Western allies' decision-making before Munich. Although since the early 1930s Liddell Hart had thought the threat of air attacks on cities overrated, he was very concerned about the state of the British air defences in 1938.[57] Nevertheless, he did not think that this should affect the decision to support Czechoslovakia. In retrospect it is clear that both the effect of city bombing and the German capabilities and intent for carrying it out were vastly exaggerated.[58]

Anti-appeasement

Liddell Hart tried to convince the editors of *The Times* of the vital importance of Czechoslovakia throughout the crisis. After the summer

[56] J. Wheeler-Bennett, *The Nemesis of Power* (London, 1961), 396–424; R. O'Neill, *The German Army and the Nazi Party, 1933–1938* (London, 1966), 151–69; K.-J. Müller, 'The German Military Opposition before the Second World War', in W. Mommsen and L. Kettenacker (eds.), *The Fascist Challenge and the Policy of Appeasement* (London, 1983), 61–75; and the documents in Müller, *Beck*, 268–311, 502 ff.; G. Weinberg, 'The German Generals and the Outbreak of the War, 1938–1939', in A. Preston (ed.), *General Staffs and Diplomacy before the Second World War* (London, 1978), 24–40; K. von Klemperer, *German Resistance against Hitler: The Search for Allies Abroad, 1938–1945* (Oxford, 1992), 105–12.

[57] See e.g. *The Defence of Britain*, 153–7; also U. Bialer, *The Shadow of the Bomber: The Fear of Air Attacks and British Politics, 1932–1939* (London, 1980).

[58] See esp. Murray, 'German Air Power and the Munich Crisis', 107–18.

of 1938, publication of his articles on the subject was often withheld, and he twice indicated that he might wish to terminate his employment with the newspaper. At the height of the September crisis he protested strongly against the famous *Times* leader which had suggested that the Sudleten were better handed over to Germany.[59] In the summer of 1938 he wrote: 'It would be a folly to buy momentary relief from the danger of war at the price of ultimate downfall . . . Nothing has proved more upsetting to peace-seeking calculations than the temptation of buying peace.'[60] As with other anti-appeasers, the Munich settlement was for him a turning-point which drove him into open public opposition to government policy. During and after the crisis he was often consulted by Eden, and assisted in drafting the strategic points in the latter's speeches. He was in regular contact with Churchill and spoke before 'Focus', the discussion support group Churchill created at the time of Munich. Liddell Hart was also consulted by Hugh Dalton and the leadership of the Labour party, as well as by Sir Archibald Sinclair and Lloyd George of the Liberals. He spoke about the dangers of the government's policy in various public meetings, and was even invited to stand for Parliament against the government's candidates, once as a Progressive with joint Liberal and Labour backing in the Rye Division, and again as an Independent with three-party support in the by-election for the Abbey Division of Westminster.[61]

For all that, John Mearsheimer has challenged Liddell Hart's image as a staunch anti-appeaser on two main grounds. In the first place, he has argued that Liddell Hart was not seriously aroused by any of the international crises of the 1930s until and except those of Spain and Czechoslovakia as late as 1938.[62] In this Mearsheimer is generally correct, but for the small fact that *nobody* was. As mentioned before, things looked differently, and were made to look differently, in hindsight, and not only by Liddell Hart. For example, Churchill's memoirs must be read between the lines and compared with his record at the time. In the 1931–2 crisis over Manchuria Churchill was almost overtly

[59] To Barrington-Ward, 4 Nov. 1936, King's, 3/16; correspondence with Barrington-Ward and Dawson in Mar. 1938 and 29 July 1938; to Dawson, 10 Aug.; to Barrington-Ward, 20 Sept.; to Dawson, 5 Oct.; to Barrington-Ward, 1, 8 Nov.; from Barrington-Ward, 2 Nov. 1938: all in 3/108. Much of this is reprinted in *Memoirs*, ii. 130–1, 145–6, 159–60, 165–6, 172, 178–81.

[60] 'Strategy and Commitments', 649; cf. *Through the Fog of War* (London, 1938), 353.

[61] Eden file, King's, 1/258; Churchill file, 1/171; personal notes in 11/1938; political offers, 13/43; cf. *Memoirs*, ii. 160–5, 167–70, 174–5, 186, 195–6, 206–12.

[62] Mearsheimer, *LH*, 131–43.

sympathetic to Japan, Britain's former ally. In 1937 he was concerned by her invasion of China but only because of her connection with Germany. In any case, he did not think Britain should get involved. During the Abyssinian crisis he was at first equivocal and then opposed the sanctions which might push Italy into Germany's arms. In the Spanish crisis he stood all along for strict non-interference by Britain and France, and had little sympathy for the Republicans. He expressed concern about the approaching Nationalist victory only in early 1939. His real preoccupation was Germany: he sounded the alarm about German rearmament and called for massive rearmament on Britain's part. However, contrary to what he would later imply, he did not suggest military action against the German occupation of the Rhineland. Nor did he think there was anything practical to be done after the German Anschluss with Austria, and, like Liddell Hart, only warned of the danger to Czechoslovakia. Things really came to a head only with the Czechoslovakian crisis.

As to the other notable 'anti-appeasers', Eden resigned from the cabinet in February 1938 over the Anglo-Italian Agreement. But, as historians have shown, he differed from Chamberlain not so much on the policy of appeasement itself: the need for a 'general European settlement' involving the dismantling of Versailles and major concessions to Germany and Italy; his main objection was to Chamberlain's wish to steer unilaterally ahead in implementing such a settlement rather than cement coalitions in order to negotiate with Germany and Italy from strength and bind them to their words. Duff Cooper resigned from the cabinet after Munich. The Labour party abandoned its hostility to rearmament only with the Spanish Civil War. In 1936–7 Lloyd George was still impressed by Hitler as 'a seeker of peace and social reformer'.[63] So by what standard is Liddell Hart's anti-appeasement to be measured? The reality of the international crises of the 1930s, as opposed to the retrospective rhetoric of anti-appeasement, was that the challenges to the Western powers grew more threatening in stages, and things looked disturbing and worrying before they appeared really critical.

[63] See the relevant places in W. S. Churchill, *The Second World War*, i (London, 1955); and in M. Gilbert, *Winston S. Churchill*, v (London, 1976); N. Tompson, *The Anti-Appeasers: Conservative Opposition to Appeasement in the 1930s* (Oxford 1971) A. J. P. Taylor's letter to K. Martin, printed in *London Review of Books*, 10 May 1990, 13; Cowling, *The Impact of Hitler*, 143–176; G. Schmidt, *The Politics and Economics of Appeasement* (New York, 1986), 9–10; D. C. Watt, *Personalities and Appeasement* (Austin, Tex., 1991), 17–18; N. Rose, *Churchill* (London, 1994), 236–40; Parker, *Chamberlain and Appeasement*, 93–123; Gibbs, *Grand Strategy*, 806–7.

Mearsheimer's second main argument against Liddell Hart's image as an anti-appeaser is that even over Spain and Czechoslovakia Liddell Hart never recommended the use of force by Britain and France or proposed policies that carried a serious risk of war; that he pointed out the dangers but never proposed any solutions.[64] Now, whatever the gaps in Liddell Hart's reasoning, this is a very misleading presentation of his positions. With a remarkable lack of intellectual sensitivity to its subject, it ignores the most salient features of Liddell Hart's approach to war in general and to the political and strategic threats of the late 1930s in particular. True, Liddell Hart looked for courses of action which would prevent as far as possible the prospect of total war and which by their deterrent effect would lessen the risk of war. This was one of the pillars of his thought and surely not unreasonable as such. The other pillar, however, was that warlike action might become necessary to safeguard national interests.

As we have seen, Liddell Hart strove to apply both principles to the crises of the late 1930s. After all, there was nothing improper in coercing Italy to withdraw from Abyssinia by sanctions, oil embargo, the provision of arms to the Ethiopians, and the blocking of the Suez Canal to Italian transportation to the army in Abyssinia, while strengthening British defences in case *Italy* chose to escalate in a 'mad dog' act. Similarly, it was all the better if the Nationalists and the Axis powers could be prevented from winning in Spain simply by a massive supply of arms and provisions to the Republicans, as perhaps it could. If necessary, the Western allies' command of the sea could be used to isolate the country, and would have proved decisive if the Axis powers decided, unprudently, to escalate. True, Liddell Hart became genuinely alarmed about the situation in Spain only at the beginning of 1938, as it became clearer that the Nationalists were winning the Civil War. But then again, as long as the Republicans were able to fight back and generally hold their own, as they had been doing for a year and a half, there may have been cause for concern but what cause for alarm? Finally, ringing Germany with a two-front coalition and strangling her with an economic blockade if she chose war over Czechoslovakia was a concrete enough plan for confronting her. One may doubt its efficacy but not dismiss it or, worse, fail to give an honest idea of its content.

Mearsheimer rightly points out that, starting from his 1935 study of Britain's defence problems, Liddell Hart came to a better appreciation

[64] Mearsheimer, *LH*, 131–43.

of the limits of sea power and of the difficulties facing the blockade, especially under modern conditions. Liddell Hart stressed the new vulnerability of British naval power to the aeroplane, the high-speed light craft, and the submarine, and argued that in itself, without the help of Continental allies, the blockade might not prove sufficient or effective enough to contend with Germany. However, within this system of alliances Liddell Hart (and the British defence establishment as a whole) still regarded the blockade as Britain's trump card. Mearsheimer cites the following passage as evidence of Liddell Hart's scepticism concerning the blockade during the Czechoslovakian crisis: 'We must realize that we cannot win a war against Germany except by economic pressure—and it is becoming doubtful whether this weapon will remain effective enough to produce victory.' He fails, however, to mention that this assessment was written not during, but immediately *after*, the crisis, on 12 October 1938, when Liddell Hart worked out the disastrous implications of the Munich settlement and of the expected German domination over south-eastern Europe for the blockade and hence for the Western allies' ability to defeat Germany—the very danger he had been warning against throughout the crisis.[65]

So Liddell Hart opposed appeasement as strongly as anybody and supported concrete actions to check the Axis powers. But was not his insistence on limited action and limited means an unrealistic obsession which ultimately could not provide the answer to Germany's unlimited drive? Indeed, was it not the kind of policy which made possible Hitler's initial triumphs? For, whereas Liddell Hart opposed Chamberlain and *The Times* over appeasement, he was their closest ally in respect to the strategic policy known as 'limited liability', toward which the British government was moving in the years 1934–8. This strategic policy laid down that Britain's contribution in case of war in Europe would be limited to naval and air power and almost entirely exclude ground forces. The resources allocated to the army in Britain's rearmament were therefore kept below what was required to prepare it either for backing Britain's diplomatic positions in the crises of 1938–9 or for fighting a war when it came in 1939–40. Most military historians have tended to judge this policy mistaken and harmful and have pointed out Liddell Hart's share in the blame. However, most of them have also been aware of major considerations which qualified this judgement, and

[65] The citation is from King's, 11/1938/114; cf. Mearsheimer, *LH*, 141; also 93, 106–7, 138.

of the difficulties of pointing out a viable alternative strategic policy to the one actually pursued.[66] Moreover, no sooner had military historians issued their verdict than economic historians began to undermine it. The complexity of the strategic problems and economic constraints facing Britain's decision-makers in the 1930s was baffling, and circumstances changed considerably from year to year before 1939, altering the strategic picture more than it has been acknowledged from a teleological postwar perspective.

II. Limited Liability

The advocates of limited liability were motivated by a mixture of psychological, strategic, and economic considerations. Psychologically, the revulsion against the carnage of trench warfare on the Western Front and the reluctance to repeat that experience were something which many politicians and soldiers shared with the public at large. Strategically, Britain was overburdened by conflicting pressures and liabilities, emanating from her multi-faceted position as an island state, off the shore of Europe, and a worldwide empire whose various possessions were scattered around the globe. With relatively decreasing economic power Britain faced a growing number of simultaneous challenges. She was not prepared to let Europe fall under German domination, but she was equally committed to the defence of her empire, especially against the Japanese threat in the Far East. In addition, the security of Britain's sea communications was vital to her existence. To add to her difficulties, from 1935 on Britain had to divert some of her scant forces to the defence of her Mediterranean communications and possessions against a previously friendly Italy. Of course, as historians have stressed, Britain's various commitments were complementary as much as they were conflicting, and the maintenance of the balance of power in Europe was essential for all the rest; in the long run, if Germany would have been allowed to rule Europe Britain's naval predominance and empire would have become untenable. Still, what was the balanced solution to the intricate strategic equation with which Britain's decision-makers were grappling, if indeed there was any? As the British political and strategic establishment recognized and Liddell

[66] For limited liability, see esp. C. Barnett, *The Collapse of British Power* (London, 1972), 237–577; Howard, *Continental Commitment*, 96–120; P. Dennis, *Decision by Default: Peacetime Conscription and British Defence, 1915–1923* (London, 1972); Gibbs, *Grand Strategy*, 93–131, 275–322, 441–529; Bond, *British Military Policy*, 191–286.

Hart indicated in his seminal article of 1935, and as historians have clearly shown, Britain's resources were simply too small to contend by herself with the various threats to her global position, caused since the late nineteenth century by the changes in the distribution of power in the world and aggravated by the emergence of new technologies. In Liddell Hart's own expressions, 'the British Empire is on the rack, suffering a two-way stretch'; it was becoming the greatest example of strategic overextension in history.[67]

It is therefore not surprising that when from 1934 Britain began to rearm, it was mainly the chancellor of the exchequer, Neville Chamberlain, who insisted, against the recommendations of the defence requirements committee, that definite priorities had to be set for the process, and who advanced the policy of limited liability. Being the leading figure in Baldwin's cabinet and prime minister himself from 1937, he was increasingly able to carry his position through. Home and imperial defence were placed at the top of Britain's defence priorities. A Continental role for the army in support of Britain's allies was never entirely discarded, but it was progressively downgraded. Between 1934 and 1938 the army's share among the services in Britain's defence expenditure fell from second to third place, though in fact never very far behind that of the air force and the navy. Even the regular army of five to six divisions, let alone the territorial army of twelve divisions, were not allocated the resources they needed to prepare them for participation in a European war. Special priority was given to the air force, whose share in Britain's defence expenditure leaped from a distant third to first place between 1934 and 1938. The air force was intended to defend the British Isles against the rapidly expanding Luftwaffe, first by deterring attack with the threat of counter-attack by the British bombers on the German rear and later, from 1937 on, increasingly by fighter squadrons, working within the world's first integrated air defence system. In addition, the air force was viewed as a 'cleaner' and more versatile substitute for the army for intervening in the Continent, both directly from Britain and from bases in the Low Countries and France, in support of Britain's allies.

Liddell Hart became an ardent advocate of limited liability in late 1935, though he had already argued in that direction in June 1934, after

[67] The first expression is from 'The Defence of the Empire', *Fortnightly Review* (Dec. 1937), repr. in *The Defence of Britain*, 59; the second is cited without reference by Kennedy, *Strategy and Diplomacy*, 18.

Chamberlain had first made his case in cabinet. Among the reasons for his objection to a major Continental role for the army he stressed the army's total unpreparedness for war and its reluctance to reform. This, however, was at best only a contributory reason for his position.[68] After all, he championed limited liability largely as an adaptation of his own concept of 'the British way in warfare' which he had voiced on principled lines as early as 1931. Interestingly, there was no direct, one-way influence here between Liddell Hart and Chamberlain. There is no sign that Chamberlain was familiar with Liddell Hart's original essay. The aversion to the idea of another entanglement in the Continent was a sentiment shared by many Britons in the 1930s. In the army General Sir Burnett-Stuart in particular championed an imperial rather than a Continental role for the army, and Chamberlain's strategic ideas were initially influenced mainly by Trenchard.[69] Liddell Hart, well-informed about the deliberations in the cabinet and the army and closely in touch with both Burnett-Stuart and Trenchard, echoed all these sources in his writings.

In 1935–8, in newspaper and magazine articles, books, conversations with officials and soldiers, and as an adviser to the secretary of state for war, actively influencing the shaping and implementation of policy, Liddell Hart persistently argued, with little variation, that Britain could not be strong everywhere; that home and imperial defence had to come first; that air defence and the navy had to take priority over the army; that an expeditionary force to the Continent was not necessary, might anyway fail to arrive in time to participate in the defence of Western Europe, and might be subjected to paralysing air attacks on its land and sea communications; that air contingents would be Britain's most effective contribution to her allies.[70] As mentioned before, many of these ideas had been previously voiced by Chamberlain. In turn, Liddell Hart's active support strengthened the opinions of Chamberlain and those who held similar views, like the government's chief industrial

[68] *Europe in Arms*, 78, 129–30; *Memoirs*, i. 294–5, 379–81, 385–6; ii. 21–3.

[69] See G. C. Peden, *British Rearmament and the Treasury, 1932–1939* (Edinburgh, 1979), 123–5; and for Burnett-Stuart, Liddell Hart, *Memoirs*, i. 292–4; since 1930 Liddell Hart had been cooperating with Trenchard on a whole range of defence issues; the Trenchard file: King's, 1/699.

[70] *Daily Telegraph*, 25 June 1934; *The Times*, 25 Nov. 1935, 10 Feb., 6 and 23 Mar., 30 Oct., 3 and 11 Nov. 1936, 5 Mar., 29 July 1937, 17 June 1938; conversations with Duff Cooper and Halifax, 18 and 21 Jan. 1936 respectively; cited in Dennis, *Decision by Default*, 62; also Peden, *British Rearmament*, 124–5; Liddell Hart, 'The Defence of the Empire', *Fortnightly Review* (Jan. 1938), 19–30; *Europe in Arms*, 59–60, 78–19, 116–19, 124, 130–3, 138–40; *The Defence of Britain*, 59, 209–11, 265–9, 278–9, 286–93; *Memoirs*, i. 292–9, 379–83, 385–7; ii. 2–3, 51–4, 97–9, 118.

adviser, Lord Weir. When Chamberlain became prime minister and moved to make limited liability official policy, he was happy to use such a popular and authoritative strategic writer as Liddell Hart as an ally. He recommended the chapter on 'The Role of the Army' in Liddell Hart's *Europe in Arms* (1937)—which Liddell Hart had sent him—to Hore-Belisha, whom he had newly appointed to the war office to carry out his policy. And in the cabinet discussions in 1937 Liddell Hart's writings in *The Times* and memoranda to Hore-Belisha were discussed and relied upon.[71] Two opinionated amateurs, Chamberlain and Liddell Hart, found in each other an ally in their effort to effect a radical reorientation of British strategic policy.

Of course, different reasons carried different weight in the respective motives of Chamberlain and Liddell Hart for espousing limited liability. With Chamberlain the economic considerations were more prominent, whereas, 'inescapably, Liddell Hart's thought was shaped by the First World War.'[72] While recognizing new developments which were affecting war, Liddell Hart basically considered the possibility of a new war in the light of the lessons he had been attempting to draw from the First World War, with the problem of which he had been grappling both in his own histories of the war and in his work on Lloyd George's memoirs. Strongly opposing the creation of British mass armies and their commitment to the Western Front during that war, he suggested that Britain 'might have raised Kitchener's "First Hundred Thousand", but certainly not his "Last" '.[73] As the debate over the direction of Britain's rearmament dragged on, Liddell Hart became deeply suspicious that the army did not acquiesce to the government's decision to limit the commitment of British land forces to the Continent. He believed that the army was still hoping to make that commitment the basis not only for the dispatch of the whole regular and territorial armies (eighteen divisions in all) to the Continent but ultimately also for the creation of a large British 'national army' which would fundamentally replay the First World War: 'commitment, entanglement, illimitable expansion, mass conscription, futile sacrifice, and material exhaustion, leading not only to prolonged impoverishment but immediately to the weakening of our influence over

[71] Liddell Hart's articles in *The Times* in Nov. 1935 were filed by Weir: Peden, *British Rearmament*, 124–5, 137; see also Liddell Hart's Chamberlain file, King's, 1/159; 11/HB 1937/68; R. J. Minney, *The Private Papers of Hore-Belisha* (London, 1960), 54; Liddell Hart, *Memoirs*, ii. 38–9; Bond, *British Military Policy*, 246–7; *LH*, 105–9.

[72] Howard, 'LH', 239.

[73] *The British Way in Warfare*, 39; *When Britain Goes to War*, 43.

the restoration of peace.'[74] It would be a mistake, however, to dismiss Liddell Hart's position merely as a backward-looking, unrealistic reaction to a trauma. The policy of limited liability and Liddell Hart's understanding of it deserve serious reconsideration.

Air Force, Navy, Army, the Economy

It can hardly be disputed that the investment in the air force was the most vital element in Britain's rearmament in the 1930s. Yet it has rarely been appreciated that in this respect the order of priorities set by the British government was far sounder than the inter-service compromises proposed by the defence requirements committee, whose respective reports of 1934 and 1935 were to ensure that the air force's share in the defence budget was to remain a distant third behind that of the other two services.[75] Even with the top priority given to it, Britain's air armament, still totally inadequate at the time of the Munich crisis and lagging behind even at the outbreak of the war, was only just ready to match the Germans in 1940. It might of course be argued that if the army had been given higher priority, the Battle of France might not have been lost, and consequently there would have been no need for the Battle of Britain. Yet even if the army had been strengthened more than it was, it still could only have played a secondary role at the start of a European war, and Britain might have faced the danger of a larger Dunkirk with a weaker air defence system than the one which ultimately saved her.[76] Air force first was the logical choice of an island empire like Britain, indeed perhaps of any first-class power in the second half of the 1930s, a point about which Churchill, for example, was practically in agreement with the Baldwin and Chamberlain administrations. The RAF might also have contributed much more than it did to the Battle of France had it taken more seriously the role of close tactical support to the land forces—as both the army chiefs and Liddell Hart wanted—rather than concentrating almost solely on strategic bombing. On the other side, as claimed by John Slessor, the head of the plans branch of the Air Staff in the years preceding the war, who

[74] *The Times*, 26 Oct. 1937; also *Europe in Arms*, 219–21; and esp. his talk with Deverell and the Director of Military Operations, Maj.-Gen. Haining, in 12 Nov. 1936: King's, 11/1936/99; *Memoirs*, i. 382–3.

[75] The exception is the authoritative official economic history of the war: M. M. Postan, *British War Production: History of the Second World War—Civil Series* (London, 1952), 14, 29; the figures can be found in Peden, *British Rearmament*, 205.

[76] Cf. e.g. the CIGS's assessment after the fall of France: Macleod and Kelly, *The Ironside Diaries*, 370.

had always wanted a versatile air force: the RAF's concentration on strategic bombing was itself at least partly caused by the policy of limited liability which envisaged no substantial British land involvement in the Continent.[77]

As with the Air Force, it is clear that the preparedness of the Royal Navy was vital to Britain, and it, too, was still severely deficient when war came, especially the navy's air arm, and escort and anti-submarine vessels. Incidently, here also, following Fuller and Richmond, Liddell Hart held that the navy ought to invest less in battleships and more in air defence, aircraft carriers, and flotilla craft.[78]

So the question is more about the absolute size of Britain's defence budget than about the army's relative share in it. In historians' criticism of the policy of limited liability, the dominating impression has been that the army was starved of resources before 1939. In reality, while the annual expenditure on the air force, which had lagged far behind the other two services in 1934, increased eightfold by 1938, that on the army also increased more than threefold in the same period, more than the increase in the expenditure on the navy; and even in 1937–8 the annual expenditure on the three services was of roughly the same order. Similarly, the army's investment in new equipment rose sixfold between 1934 and 1938, and its share among the services rose from 19 to 25.5 per cent. (Admittedly, some of this increase was intended for the purchase of anti-aircraft guns—in 1938 about half as much as the expenditure on new equipment for the field army.[79]) Thus the only reasonable query is whether Britain should not have increased her *overall* expenditure on rearmament *even more*, so as to bring the army to a state of readiness for a Continental role. However, as economic historians have shown, even if Britain could have done more, it would probably not have been that much more.

[77] See e.g. ibid., 394 and *passim*; Bond, *British Military Policy*, 207, 274–5, 339; Murray, *European Balance of Power*, 82–3; C. Webster and N. Frankland, *The Strategic Air Offensive against Germany, 1939–1945* (4 vols., London, 1961), i. 65–81, 94–101, 104–5; M. Smith, *British Air Strategy between the Wars* (Oxford, 1984); J. Slessor, *Air Power and Armies* (Oxford, 1936), *The Central Blue* (London, 1956), 183; A. D. Harvey, *Collision of Empires: Britain in Three World Wars, 1793–1945* (London, 1992), 644–8.

[78] See esp. *The Times*, 10 Feb. 1936; *Europe in Arms*, 92–9; Richmond, who had been the chief proponent of these ideas throughout the interwar period, is cited on pp. 94–5. Cf. S. Roskill, *Naval Policy between the Wars* (2 vols., London, 1968, 1976), i. 115–16, 224, 315, 444; ii. 56, 260. Fuller, too, repeated his earlier views along these lines: *Towards Armageddon* (London, 1937), 133–5, 196–208. See also Kennedy, *British Naval Mastery*, 282, 293, 303; Murray, *European Balance of Power*, 74–7.

[79] Again, the only historian to make these cardinal points is Postan, *British War Production*, 28, 30–1. For the expenditure on AA guns, see Harvey, *Collision of Empires*, 557.

TABLE 1. *British Defence Expenditure (£)*

	Army	Navy	Air force	% of Govt. expenditure
1934	39,691,603	56,610,010	17,607,893	14
1935	44,654,483	64,887,613	27,515,185	15
1936	55,015,395	80,976,124	49,995,697	21
1937	72,675,520	101,892,397	81,799,260	26
1938	121,542,932	132,437,403	143,499,642	38
1939	242,438,217	181,770,565	294,833,921	48

Source: R. P. Shay, *British Rearmament in the Thirties* (Princeton, NJ, 1977), 297; see also G. C. Peden, *British Rearmament and the Treasury, 1932–1939*, (Edinburgh, 1979), 205; N. Gibbs, *Grand Strategy: History of the Second World War*, i (London, 1976) 532.

TABLE 2. *The army's investment in equipment*

	Expenditure (£ m.)	% of total armed forces expenditure
1934	6.9	19
1935	8.5	20
1936	12.5	20
1937	21.4	21
1938	44.3	25.5
1939	67.6	26

Source: M. M. Postan, *British War Production: History of the Second World War—Civil Services* (London, 1952) 12, 28.

The problem here was both industrial and fiscal.[80] Run down as it had been in the lean years of the Ten Years Rule, the British arms industry lacked both the equipment and skilled labour for rapid expansion and was unable to respond to the demands of rearmament in the desired scope and speed. The bottlenecks and delays in the production of aircrafts and anti-aircraft guns in particular were the cause of repeated public outcries and parliamentary debates in 1937–38. Even when a Continental role for the regular army and the territorials was still

[80] For the following, see Postan, *British War Production*, 10–13; Shay, *British Rearmament*; Peden, *British Rearmament*; 'A Matter of Timing: The Economic Background to British Foreign Policy, 1937–1939', *History*, 69 (1984), 15–28; Gibbs, *Grand Strategy*, 275–322; also Howard, *Continental Commitment*, 134–6; Kennedy, *Strategy and Diplomacy*, 27, 100–2; *Great Powers*, 412–13.

envisaged, it was made clear that because of limited production capacity equipment for the latter could not be made available until well into the 1940s.[81] So the argument between those who favoured and those who objected to limited liability was in reality largely academic. Financially, the treasury's officials stressed that Britain, which was slowly but steadily recovering from the Great Depression, would simply not be able to sustain the arms race for long if rearmament were not kept within strict budgetary constraints. Otherwise, they calculated, by 1941 the economy would overheat, Britain would face a balance-of-payments crisis, and inflation would rise out of control. Since Britain's planned a protracted war against Germany, this was a major strategic consideration.

In the 1950s, 1960s, and 1970s historians were able to brandish Keynes's theories against orthodox treasury economics. But apart from the fact that those who lived through the 1980s are bound to be more sceptical about the ability to sustain large-scale 'uneconomic' expenditure on defence, economic historians have reminded us that the British government did in fact resort to large scale borrowing in 1937–8. Special defence loans financed about a quarter of the defence expenditure in 1937 and a third in 1938. There were no differences of opinion between Keynes and the treasury in this respect.[82] In 1939–40, when all financial constraints were finally dropped, Britain's defence expenditure was raised even further, so that it more or less equalled Germany's, and even surpassed it in percentage of GNP.[83] But, as the economists had predicted, Britain was bankrupt by the beginning of 1941 and could not have continued the war if it had not been for the United States' massive aid. 'The amount of cash that was needed to rebuild a two-ocean navy, to provide the RAF with both its fighter defences and its long-range bombers, and to equip the army for a European field role . . . was well beyond the industrial and financial capacity of the country.'[84] 'Experience showed', wrote Liddell Hart,

[81] Bond, *British Military Policy*, 199, 214, 222, 237–41.

[82] See R. A. C. Parker, 'British Rearmament 1936–9: Treasury, Trade Unions and Skilled Labour', *English Historical Review*, 96 (1981), 306–18; G. C. Peden, 'Keynes, the Economics of Rearmament and Appeasement', in Mommsen and Kettenacker, *The Fascist Challenge*, 142–56.

[83] B. A. Carroll, *Design for Total War* (The Hague, 1968), 184, 264–5; R. J. Overy, 'Hitler's War and the German Economy: A Reinterpretation', *Economic History Review*, 35 (1982), 286.

[84] Kennedy, *Strategy and Diplomacy*, 100; this verdict is an almost verbatim repetition of Chamberlain's own assessment on 25 Oct. 1936, cited and practically endorsed by Howard, *Continental Commitment*, 135.

'that to seek predominance both on land and sea overstrained the Power which attempted it. How much more probable is such a consequence when the effort has to be spread over land, sea, and air.'[85]

But if so, how could Germany, whose economy was only marginally larger than that of Britain and whose armaments industry had also been completely run down and took time to rebuild, conduct the race at such a swift pace and keep it up? In the years 1934–8 Germany spent nearly three times as much as Britain on her armed services, and even in 1938 Britain's annual defence expenditure was less than half that of Germany.[86] However, as historians have shown, apart from the fact that Germany's rearmament began earlier, which gave her a crucial head start, the answer is that she could not.[87] Assessments of the developments in Britain long suffered from the lack of a comparative perspective and from mythical popular images of German rearmament. Unlike the Conservative government in Britain, the German state intervened massively in the economy to enhance arms production. But, as in Britain, German economists were in despair about the ability of the German economy to sustain the quick pace of rearmament. It is now believed that the expenditure on armaments was only marginally significant in helping the German economy recover from the depression; and as this expenditure rose sharply after 1936, it overheated the economy and could not be kept up for long after 1939. Germany exceeded her limits in respect to raw materials, the balance of payments, and the work force. The crucial difference between Britain and Germany (and indeed Japan) was that Germany was bent on a policy of territorial expansion in Europe that would also progressively expand her economic base. As some historians have suggested, Germany's actions in 1938–9 were at least partly prompted by the economic problem, as her rearmament effort ran out of steam.[88] Finally, it might be mentioned that Germany, too, had to decide on strict priorities between the three armed services. In her case, the army and air force

[85] *Europe in Arms*, 221; see also *The Defence of Britain*, 46.

[86] Figures in Carroll, *Design for Total War*, 184, 264–5; Overy, 'War and the German Economy', 286; Murray, *European Balance of Power*, 20–1; MF, *Germany and the Second World War*, i. 237; Kennedy, *Great Powers*, 382.

[87] See esp. the respective contributions by Volkmann and Deist to MF, *Germany and the Second World War*, i. 157–540; Murray, *European Balance of Power*, 4–27, 48–9, and *passim*; Overy, 'War and the German Economy'; *The Nazi Economic Recovery, 1932–1938* (London, 1982); Kennedy, *Great Powers*, 394–400.

[88] See 'Debate: Germany, "Domestic Crisis" and War in 1939', *Past and Present*, 122 (1989), 200–40, for the argument between T. Mason, R. Overy, and D. Kaiser.

were allocated most of the money in 1933–9, with the navy left behind as a far third and totally unprepared for war.[89]

Britain's Allies

If Britain could not produce arms and expand her armed forces much more quickly than she actually did without undermining her economy and unbalancing her entire strategic position, what were the alternatives? Obviously they were not brilliant. The answer to the many threats and constraints with which Britain's policymakers were grappling had to be at least partly political. Chamberlain and Liddell Hart agreed that limited liability was possible only if and as long as it was backed by a complementary foreign policy, but they differed on the nature of that policy. Whereas the British government under Chamberlain combined limited liability with a diplomatic effort to meet Germany's grievances in the hope of integrating her within a stable European power system and avert conflict, Liddell Hart from 1935 on combined limited liability with strong support for collective security. Only in alliance with the powers of Western and Eastern Europe, he maintained, could Britain hope to check Germany's drive without over-exerting herself. Only if Britain was strategically able to respond to limited challenges to the status quo with less than total national mobilization and total war would she be willing to respond at all, thereby also making her deterrence posture more credible.[90]

Chamberlain's policy failed because Hitler's aims were much more far-reaching than he had assumed or was willing to accept. But were the policies advocated by Liddell Hart any more realistic? If allies in the west and east of the Continent were vital for Britain's defence, could they be expected to stand firm against Germany without the guaranteed support of a substantial British land army? In Western Europe Britain was after all the most powerful member of the alliance against Germany, and was obliged to act as a leader and show resolve if she wanted the others to follow suit. A system of collective security had its price and called for great responsibility, especially on the part of its most powerful members. Britain's non-committed attitude during and after the Rhineland crisis was one of the main reasons for Belgium's return to a policy of neutrality in 1936. That act not only made the defence of Germany much easier and that of France much harder; it also affected what was

[89] Figures in R. J. Overy, *War and Economy in the Third Reich* (Oxford, 1994), 203.
[90] See e.g. *The Defence of Britain*, 45–6, 49, 267.

considered a direct and vital British interest, namely, that Belgium's air fields and ports, just across the Channel, would not fall into Germany's hands.

It is, however, not at all clear that Britain's allies would not have been satisfied with anything less than a large British land army. They surely wanted an unequivocal British political and strategic commitment to their security and to the common cause of stopping Germany, a commitment which the British government was consistently reluctant to give. But the record shows that the Belgians, in the person of Prime Minister Paul van Zeeland, having learnt of Britain's political and strategic position and being most anxious for her cooperation, were willing to settle for no more than informal staff talks on air, naval, and industrial cooperation. Even that, however, the British government declined.[91] Similarly, both in late 1937, when the implications of the policy of limited liability were made clear to the French by Hore-Belisha, and in the Anglo-French talks in April 1938, at the beginning of the Czechoslovakian crisis, Premier Édouard Daladier and Chief of Staff Gamelin, though naturally not enthusiasticaly, were willing to recognize Britain's special strategic position and global obligations. They were willing to accept the two divisions offered by Britain rather than a large land army as a token of her European commitment. Obviously, they hoped for stronger forces later on. As the official British historian has written: 'The interesting feature of the French views was that they showed no shock at the limits on the size of Britain's contribution on land.'[92] Indeed, the veteran secretary of the committee of imperial defence, Maurice Hankey, who had earlier been working for the creation of a British expeditionary force to the Continent, changed his mind in 1937 on the grounds that the French themselves had ceased to demand such a force.[93] It should be borne in mind that until the Munich settlement and the dismemberment of Czechoslovakia, it was reasonable to suppose that France did not need a large British land force in her support or, at least, that that was not the Allies' first strategic priority.

This point underpinned Liddell Hart's strategic logic and was upper-

[91] See D. O. Kieft, *Belgium's Return to Neutrality* (Oxford, 1972), esp. 76–7, and 20–4, 70–2, 75–7, 80–2, 156–7, 161–6, 170–2, 187–8; also Gibbs, *Grand Strategy*, 111–14; Bond, *British Military Policy*, 228–33.

[92] Gibbs, *Grand Strategy*, 471–2, 637; also Dennis, *Decision by Default*, 132; Bond, *British Military Policy*, 275–6, 289.

[93] S. Roskill, *Hankey, Man of Secrets* (3 vols., London, 1970–4), iii. 285.

most in his mind throughout 1938. From 1936 he had insisted that Britain should not build a large army and send it across the Channel. As he perceived during the Czechoslovakian crisis, the integrity of Czechoslovakia and Soviet cooperation were essential for that policy and for the hope of stopping Germany while limiting the scale of Britain's commitments. After the abandonment of Czechoslovakia he very painfully but clearly recognized that there was no longer any question that France now needed the support of a British expeditionary force in a war against Germany.

Finally, it should be asked whether the commitment of a large British army to the Continent would have been militarily effective. Here, too, an affirmative answer is doubtful. As observers in Britain, France, and Germany pointed out at the time, the British regular and Territorial forces were composed of traditional, barely mechanized, infantry divisions, of the sort Britain's allies possessed in abundance and which could be of very limited value in a war against Germany. After all, in 1939–40 the British army *was* sent to the Continent and reinforced up to ten divisions by the time of the Battle of France, but was able to do very little to alter the outcome of the campaign.[94] One alternative was for Britain to create a fully mechanized force which could have contributed significantly in a war against Germany. That in fact was the line which the French themselves repeatedly urged the British to adopt. Both in late 1937 and in the staff talks in April 1938 the French premier Daladier, while saying that he understood that Britain's resources were not unlimited, asked that the two divisions Britain planned to send to France should at least be motorized. Similarly, in March 1938 Churchill was told by Daladier's would-be successor, Paul Reynaud, who had been championing de Gaulle's ideas in the French Chamber of Deputies and with the French public: 'We quite understand that England will never have conscription. Why do you not therefore go in for a mechanized army? If you had six armoured divisions you would indeed be an effective Continental force.' In July both Reynaud and the French military attaché in London, General Lelong, urged the dispatch of a small British mechanized force to France.[95] These pieces of evidence square with the findings of the archival research of French prewar strategic planning. It has been revealed that in the late 1930s Gamelin

[94] Again cf. CIGS Ironside's assessment after the fall of France that more British forces would have made no difference: Macleod and Kelly, *The Ironside Diaries*, 370.

[95] See n. 92 above; Churchill, *The Second World War*, i. 252–3; Liddell Hart, *Memoirs*, ii. 193.

was positively *not* interested in British unmechanized troops (he had enough of his own). He specifically and consistently wanted an armoured British contribution to strengthen the French mobile forces against the expected penetrations of the German Panzer divisions.[96] Needless to say, the creation of a small mechanized army as the most effective possible British contribution for war in Europe had been the line pursued by the armour enthusiasts in Britain—including Liddell Hart—throughout the interwar period.[97]

Mechanization or Imperial Policing

However, as the army chiefs and the defence requirements committee concluded in 1933–4 and as historians have later emphasized, one of the main roles of the British army was to police the Empire. This role could be most satisfactorily fulfilled by traditional troops on foot and horseback, or, at best, by lightly mechanized units, rather than by a fully mechanized and heavily armoured field force, or 'robot army'. Indeed, here too, in the late 1930s, as Liddell Hart began to adapt his older ideas into specific policy programmes, he addressed the problem much more seriously, comprehensively, and in greater detail than he had done before. Being one of the main champions of the policy of home and imperial defence, coupled with limited liability in the Continent, he was obliged to come to terms with the argument against the mechanization of the British army. As an adviser to Hore-Belisha, he devised interesting schemes for the redistribution of the British forces and the creation of an imperial reserve against any contingency. In addition to the infantry for imperial police and other duties, he recommended the creation of four regular armoured divisions: two to be stationed in Britain, one in Egypt, and one in India. He also advocated the conversion to armour of four out of the twelve territorial divisions.[98] Repeatedly writing in favour of limited liability, he argued that if British forces were to be sent to the Continent at all, Britain's best aid to her allies on land could be made in the form of two or more armoured divisions. As he pointed out, these would represent a major addition to

[96] M. Alexander, *The Republic in Danger: General Maurice Gamelin and the Politics of French Defence, 1933–1940* (Cambridge, 1992), 202, 254–78. For more on this, see n. 198 below and related text.

[97] Cf. H. Guderian, *Achtung Panzer!* (London, 1992), 140, echoing the British armour pioneers.

[98] See esp. *The Defence of Britain*, 275–8, 326–8; a selection of Liddell Hart's memoranda to Hore-Belisha on these matters in King's, 11/HB 1937–8 is reprinted ibid. 273–93.

France's armoured divisions (66 per cent in 1939) and would be most useful for counter-offensives against German penetrations.[99] Indeed, if Britain could have done more than she actually did in her rearmament effort, this might have been the most effective field for doing it.

In the event, however, the army chiefs complained to Liddell Hart that his objection to a major continental role for the army was relied upon by the government in its decision to keep down the expenditure on the army. Among other things, this was hindering and seriously delaying the process of mechanization and the creation of the single mobile division the army was planning (later reorganized into two smaller ones, in addition to the one created in Egypt, both as Liddell Hart had been urging). The first mobile division was not yet fully operational even by the time of the Battle of France in May 1940. Furthermore, precious time and resources were wasted on the design and manufacture of light tanks for imperial defence, the role upon which the army was called upon to concentrate. Indeed, there can be no doubt that the strategic confusion regarding the role of the British army was one of the main reasons for its unpreparedness for armoured warfare, which it never fully overcame during the Second World War.[100] For his part, Liddell Hart argued that the army should have altered its priorities and invested the limited funds allocated to it in armour rather than expanding, re-equipping and motorizing its infantry divisions.[101]

Collective Security, Limited Liability, Containment

In any case, the purpose of our discussion is not to prove Liddell Hart right or wrong on one point or another, but rather to bring out the

[99] He had been arguing along these lines since early 1936 and not, as Bond, *LH*, 102–3, and Mearsheimer, *LH*, 143–4, mistakenly believe (respectively), only from June or Jan. 1938. See e.g. *The Times*, 10 Feb., 30 Oct., 2 Nov. 1936; 5 Mar. 1937; 17 June 1938; 'The Defence of the Empire', *Fortnightly Review* (Jan. 1938), 19–30; *The Defence of Britain*, 209–11, 265–9, 287, 293 (the last 3 from 1937, of which the last 2 are memoranda to Hore-Belisha for use in the Cabinet in Nov.); cf. Peden, *British Rearmament*, 175. Alexander, *Gamelin*, 263–4, 273, mistakenly assumes that Liddell Hart objected to Gamelin's desire for a mechanized force from Britain; the two were in fact of the same mind; see also n. 198 below.

[100] Conversation with Deverell, 29 June 1937, King's, 11/1937/56; *Memoirs*, i. 382; see also Gibbs, *Grand Strategy*, 524; Bond, *LH*, 108–9, 114–15; *British Military Policy*, 256, 337–8; H. Winton, *To Change an Army* (Lawrence, Kan., 1988); Mearsheimer, *LH*, 173.

[101] See *Europe in Arms*, 227–8; talk before the Compatriots Club in the House of Commons, 3 Mar. 1939, King's, 11/1939/18; *Memoirs*, i. 382, 385. Peden, *British Rearmament*, 175, relying on the documents of the Treasury and the War Office, lends support to his view; see also Murray, *European Balance of Power*, 90.

edifice of his logic in approaching the overall political and strategic problem facing Britain in the late 1930s. It will not be argued that this logic was flawless or that it was entirely consistent, for, as A. J. P. Taylor wisely concluded, 'No one was consistent in the Thirties.'[102] The problems and constraints of all sorts were too complex. But repeatedly complaining about the failure in Britain to think through the defence problem in a clear and comprehensive manner, Liddell Hart made a consistent effort to devise a comprehensive and coherent grand strategy, tailored to Britain's special political requirements and strategic dilemmas. An analysis of the problem from the perspective of time may suggest that he was not very wide of the mark.

In his verdict on Liddell Hart's advocacy of limited war and limited liability, Michael Howard has written that he 'sought to escape the dilemma of his generation by what was, in the context of his time, little more than a nostalgic wishful thinking'.[103] Perhaps he did. He certainly sought a way out of the dilemma of his age, and, indeed, perhaps there was no way out. But it would be a mistake to think that his thought was rooted in the past, as his essay on 'The British Way inWarfare' of 1931 may suggest. His ideas were remarkably modern, and directed to the present and future. Although he had no particular inclination towards economic issues, he grasped very clearly in 1935, when he undertook his comprehensive study of Britain's defence problem, the basic fact recently pointed out by a distinguished historian of the period: 'Already in 1937, Britain, like France, was spending more of its GNP upon defence than either of those countries had done in the crisis years prior to 1914, but without any significant improvement in security—simply because of far higher arms spending of the manically driven, overheated German state.'[104] Britain's problem was that, while being a liberal-capitalist status quo state, she was called upon to stop predator powers—no weaker than herself and undergoing staggering rearmament, geared for expansion—without undermining her economic and, therefore, strategic position in the process.

In the remedy prescribed by Liddell Hart there were no doubt inherent tensions between collective security and limited liability. But it was predicated on the notion that all the powers of the status quo would cooperate in standing firm against Germany, so as to create a

[102] Taylor to K. Martin, printed in *London Review of Books*, 10 May 1990, 13.
[103] Howard, 'LH', 245.
[104] Kennedy, *Great Powers*, 412; also 400–1 for the following sentence.

force large enough to prevent her from breaking out of her limited power base, and strangle her if she tried, without overstretching the resources not only of Britain (as the critics of limited liability have often claimed) but in effect of *any* of the allies.[105]

From that point of view, everything depended on the strength of the coalition assembled against Germany and on its readiness to act before she secured the resources of Eastern Europe. Here Churchill, Eden, and Liddell Hart were basically at one. In 1938 the prospects were still good. As historians now recognize, Germany's later exploits, which would bring the wealth of the entire Continent under her domination, have blurred the fact that her fundamental weakness was economic. If Germany could be contained in the west, blockaded on the sea from the rest of the world, and denied the resources of south-eastern Europe and still more of the Soviet Union, her war economy, desperately short of raw materials, could not have survived for long. Munich, however, marked a watershed. Unlike many of his contemporaries, and many historians later on, who argued that Munich at least earned Britain and her allies time to prepare for war, Liddell Hart did not doubt that the balance of power had changed drastically for the worse.[106] Germany's power base expanded, and her ability to wage a long war increased; the Soviet Union was given the cold shoulder by Britain and the West; France could no longer be expected to hold her own against Germany without the support of British land forces.

III. From Containment to Cold War

The problem of the dispatch of British ground forces to France in case of a war against Germany was the first to arise after Munich. Initially

[105] Liddell Hart, *The Times*, 27 Oct. 1937; *The Defence of Britain*, 45, 50. Studies of the Soviet Union's role make an interesting point here; as one of them claims: 'In Soviet eyes Munich was the last opportunity to halt Hitler's advance short of all-out war. The accretion of German power resulting from the annexation of Austria and the subjugation of Czechoslovakia signified to Moscow that the threat of war would no longer be enough to deter Hitler. To that extent Munich marked the final failure of collective security's original objective . . . ' : Roberts, *Stalin's Pact with Hitler*, 92. The Soviet preference for a coordinated *limited* action during the Czechoslovakian crisis is also suggested by Taylor, *Munich*, 447–56.

[106] See esp. 'Britain's Military Situation', *Yale Review* (Dec. 1939), 230–45; also published in *Contemporary Review* (Jan. 1939), 26–36; 'British Freedom', *World Review*, (Dec. 1938), 21–7; 'The Defence of Western Civilization', *New Commonwealth Review* (Jan. 1939), 21–30; *The Defence of Britain*, 22–4, 39, 46; *The Second World War*, 23–4. Cf. again Murray, *European Balance of Power*; and Kaiser, *Economic Diplomacy*.

the British government saw no reason to change its policy of sending only the smallest army contingent to the Continent, while concentrating Britain's effort in the air and at sea. But the French government and army now insisted that Britain had to make up for the loss of the Czechoslovakian army. While still expressing preference for mechanized forces, they made it clear that nothing except the dispatch of a large British army to France right from the start of a war would reassure them and satisfy French public opinion. The British government thus came to realize that a change of policy could not be avoided if France were not to be pushed into seeking her own deal with Germany. Intelligence scares in January 1939 regarding German invasions of Holland and Switzerland forced a decision. In February 1939 it was decided to allocate the money necessary for the equipment of the whole Regular army and of four Territorial divisions for a European war, and for allowing the rest of the Territorials to train. On 8 March 1939, in presenting the army estimates in Parliament, Hore-Belisha suggested that in the longer run the entire British Regular and Territorial armies would be able to participate in a war in Europe. Because of the limits of industrial capacity, however, it was to take years before this plan was to be realized.[107]

By now the money allocated to the army as well as the total defence budget was nearly doubled in comparison to 1938, and the treasury warned and the government was aware that the new levels of expenditure could not be sustained for long. But after Munich there was really no other choice for, as one historian has put it, 'it was of little use to husband resources to sustain a long war if the enemy was able to defeat you in a short one'.[108]

As we have seen before, in contrast to the British government Liddell Hart had clearly and apprehensively foreseen during 1938 that France would not be able to do without the support of a British field force if Czechoslovakia were abandoned; and in the wake of Munich he was obliged to accept that there was now no other way but to send an army to the Continent. He continued to insist, however, that the British contribution on land should take the form of an armoured-mechanized

[107] Dennis, *Decision by Default*, 151–62, 169, 177; Howard, *Continental Commitment*, 125–8; Gibbs, *Grand Strategy*, i. 491–514; Shay, *British Rearmament*, 235–8; Bond, *British Strategic Policy*, 287–304; Murray, *European Balance of Power*, 274–8, 296.

[108] Howard, *Continental Commitment*, 136. For the economics, see G. C. Peden, 'A Matter of Timing: The Economic Background to British Foreign Policy, 1937–1939', *History*, 69 (1984), 15–28.

force. In comparison to a larger, old-style infantry army, he claimed, such a force would be far more effective, especially in the counterattack role against German penetrations of the Western Front, and much less likely to become entangled in a First World War style of warfare. Following Hore-Belisha's speech on 8 March, while expressing regret that the intended expansion of the field force would lessen the level of motorization previously planned for the army and divert resources from the tank force, Liddell Hart none the less did not object to the new plans. He admitted that, while the army had been too big for its previous imperial role, it was now too small for its new Continental one.[109] However, a week after Hore-Belisha's speech, on 15 March, Germany invaded and dismembered the rest of Czechoslovakia, and British policy took a new and far more radical turn.

The blatant German violation of the Munich agreement was a cruel blow to Western hopes regarding Hitler's intentions and the prospects of reaching accommodation with him. The British government never gave up its hope of achieving *détente* with Germany, but public opinion was transformed after 'Prague', and there was mounting pressure in Parliament and within the Conservative Party for strong measures to prevent further German aggression. Consequently, in the weeks following Prague the government drifted into accepting two major decisions, both hastily and haphazardly arrived at, without prior consultation with the responsible professional bodies: one decision was the massive expansion of the army, first by announcing the doubling the Territorial army and three weeks later by introducing conscription; the other was the unilateral guarantee to Poland, later extended also to Romania and Greece. While both decisions had their critics at the time, most people and the majority of the immediate postwar historians accepted them with relief as signalling the end of appeasement and retreat. Liddell Hart, however, regarded both as major errors, and since the opening of the British archives historians have almost unanimously come around to his view.

[109] Talk before Churchill's 'Focus', 30 Nov. 1939; talk with Eden, 30 Jan. 1939, King's, 11/1939/6; to Barrington-Ward, 2 Feb. 1939, 3/109; talk before the Compatriots Club in the House of Commons, 3 Mar. 1939, 11/1939/18; *The Defence of Britain*, 116, 209–10, 317–19; the series 'An Army Across the Channel?' in *The Times*, 7, 8 Feb. 1939, still emphasizing the arguments against the dispatch of ground forces to the Continent, had been written in early Dec. 1938 and was held back by *The Times* for 2 months; according to Liddell Hart, it was intended to lead in a roundabout manner, and against the editorial line at the time to the conclusion that the dispatch of ground forces was now necessary; *Memoirs*, ii. 193, 196–8, 211, 223.

Conscription

After Munich the British government had been able to resist the pressure developing both from within the Conservative Party and from the French to introduce conscription in Britain. But after Prague the pressure from both directions and especially from France rose sharply. In an effort to release the pressure and avoid conscription Chamberlain on 28 March accepted Hore-Belisha's idea, raised virtually on the spur of the moment, to take advantage of the flow of volunteers to the Territorial army and double the Territorials from thirteen to twenty-six divisions. Together with the Regulars, this would give the army the paper strength of thirty-two divisions. The decision was announced in Parliament the day after without the chiefs of staff being consulted. John Slessor summarized the reaction of the bewildered military:

> it was a political decision—just like that; well meaning no doubt but actually quite meaningless; there was not the remotest chance of actually getting an effective Field Force of thirty two divisions for years to come and its only immediate effect was . . . a weakening of the existing force by the inevitable dilution involved.[110]

There were simply none of the facilities, instructors, and above all the equipment necessary to make the new scheme a reality. In any case, the scheme did not succeed in alleviating the pressures on the government to introduce conscription, and French officials urged that it was absolutely vital even as a gesture for reassuring French public opinion. The integrity of the French alliance was, of course, vital, as was the government's parliamentary support. So in late April conscription was accepted, again on political grounds and without seeking the advice of the chiefs of staff. 'Very few men were actually called before the war broke out, in large part because Britain lacked the industrial capacity to equip them. In all, the decision to conscript brought a great deal more trouble than good.'[111]

Ever since the 1920s, when he had assimilated Fuller's conception of war, Liddell Hart had objected to conscription which lay at the root of mass armies. He wanted a small army of professionals which could be wholly mechanized and take full advantage of modern technology, and

[110] *The Central Blue*, 183–4.

[111] For the problems of conscription, see: Dennis, *Decision by Default*, 146, 148, 154–7, 163–5, 174, 178–81, 191–200, 206–25; Howard, *Continental Commitment*, 129–30; Gibbs, *Grand Strategy*, i. 516–21; Shay, *British Rearmament*, 272–3 (citation from 273); Bond, *British Military Policy*, 304–6, 308–10, 326–7; Murray, *European Balance of Power*, 297.

which was unlikely to repeat the First World War style of warfare. This army could be backed by a militia-type volunteers army (the Territorials). The rest of the country's population would be left in peace, and would be more profitably employed in producing the hardware essential for modern war. Liddell Hart was not impressed by the calculations of the Committee of Imperial Defence and the army, put to him by CIGS Deverell and DMO Haining in November 1936, that even after the demands of the air force, the navy, and industry for manpower were fully met, some five million men would still be left available for use by the army. He replied that the question was whether they could be *effectively* employed by the army, apart from the fact that the aftermath of the war and the avoidance of exhaustion ought also be considered. He suggested that in the technological age quality was more important than numbers.[112]

After Munich and Prague, when conscription was increasingly on the cards, Liddell Hart fought tenaciously against it in articles, lectures, and public meetings. He was supported by the authority of Sir Auckland Geddes, the director of recruiting in 1916–19. Once more in conflict with *The Times*'s editorial policy which had faithfully followed the government's turnabout on conscription, Liddell Hart again suggested to the editor that his association with the newspaper might better be discontinued. For him, conscription stood for all the bad things he had striven to avoid. By now he anchored his objection to conscription within his newly formed philosophical conception of what 'England' and the West were all about, which will be discussed later on. But his strategic arguments in themselves were formidable. By 1939 and for a long time to come the army had all the volunteers it wanted, and there was simply no equipment for the mass army projected after Prague. Furthermore, Liddell Hart anticipated that conscription would be positively harmful for the development of the army, in the first place because it would divert industrial resources from mechanization.[113]

Indeed, although after the outbreak of the war the British government, with the First World War in mind, planned the expansion of the army to fifty-five divisions, of which thirty-two would be British and the rest from the Dominions and India, it was soon realized that these

[112] Talk with Deverell and Haining, 13 Nov. 1936, King's, 11/1936/94; *Memoirs*, i. 382.

[113] 'British Freedom', *World Review* (Dec. 1938), 23; *The Times*, 8 Feb. and 24 Mar. 1939; to G. Dawson, 9 May 1938; talk before the Compatriots Club in the House of Commons, and throughout Liddell Hart's private notes during 1939, in King's, 11/1939; talks before the Cambridge and Oxford Unions respectively: 12/1939/39 and 44; *The Defence of Britain*, 84–5; *Memoirs*, ii. 228–37.

numbers were simply unachievable. Despite the total mobilization of manpower and industry and despite the massive American aid in war materials and equipment, the number of men and women under arms during the war in *all* of the three services never reached five million, and that of the army remained below three million. In 1944–5, despite all the efforts, the British army had no more than twenty-four divisions.[114] As Liddell Hart suggested, if the army had concentrated in 1939–40 on gradually bringing up to strength, equipping, and training the existing nineteen divisions of the Regulars and Territorials it could have possessed all the strength it needed for a very long time. In addition, it might have avoided some of the muddle created by the raising of new formations from scratch, which so unfortunately characterized its entry into both world wars.[115]

The Polish Guarantee

The decision to give Poland a guarantee that if she were attacked by Germany Britain would enter the war on her side was announced by Chamberlain on 31 March 1939, a week after Germany occupied Memel from Lithuania. Again the decision was taken by the British government in great haste and with total disregard for military advice.[116] In Parliament Lloyd George, briefed by Liddell Hart, severely criticized the decision, and although the majority of the House from all parties supported it, it is interesting to note that Churchill, for example, who welcomed the decision, was well aware of its problematic nature.[117] The main problem was the guarantee's unilateral and unconditioned nature, about which the chiefs of staff and Liddell Hart

[114] LH, *Memoirs*, ii 198–9; J. R. M. Butler, *Grand Strategy*, ii (London, 1957), 32–3, 255–6; W. K. Hancock and M. M. Gowing, *British War Economy: History of the Second World War—Civil Series* (London, 1949), 78; Postan, *British War Production*, 73–5, 129, 243; Macleod and Kelly, *The Ironside Diaries*, 103–6, 134, 136–7; also cf. J. Mearsheimer, *Conventional Deterrence* (Ithaca, NY, 1983), 92; Mearsheimer's strategic assessments in this book are almost antithetical to those in his later diatribe against Liddell Hart.

[115] For a defence of Kitchener's policy in the First World War, see P. Simpkin, *Kitchener's Army* (Manchester, 1988), esp. 40–6.

[116] For the following, see esp. S. Newman, *March 1939: The British Guarantee to Poland* (Oxford, 1976); A. Prazmowska, *Britain, Poland and the Eastern Front, 1939* (Cambridge, 1987); Gibbs, *Grand Strategy*, i. 689–707, 719–60, 804–6; Murray, *European Balance of Power*, 293–4, 297–305, 366–7; also Howard, *Continental Commitment*, 131–2; Dennis, *Decision by Default*, 200–5; Bond, *British Military Policy*, 306–8, 310–15, 317–19.

[117] *The Second World War*, i. 347, 375, and ch. 20; T. Ben-Moshe, *Churchill: Strategy and History* (Boulder, Colo., 1992), 110.

expressed similar concern.[118] Britain surrendered her freedom of decision on whether to go to war or not to 'the most romantic and least realistic people in Europe', in Liddell Hart's words, giving up any leverage she had on the Polish government before trying to make sure that the essential preconditions for the successful fulfilment of the guarantee were accepted by the Poles.

It was of secondary importance that the British government failed even to secure that the guarantee would be mutual—the Poles refused to give Romania a similar guarantee. The main point, stressed both by the chiefs of staff and by Liddell Hart, was that the Western Allies could not assist Poland directly, and the very little they could do to assist her indirectly could not prevent her being overrun by Germany within a short period of time. The chiefs of staff and Liddell Hart had very little faith in Poland's ability to resist, given its geography and the relative backwardness of her armed forces. Reversing their previous attitude, though still wavering in their successive assessments of the Soviet Union's strength and significance, the chiefs of staff now maintained, as Liddell Hart had done all along, that if Poland and the whole of Eastern Europe were to be defended from Germany, Soviet cooperation was vital. The French, too, regarded the guarantee to Poland as unwise, and preferred cooperation with the Soviet Union. For the problem was that the Poles would not hear of the Red Army entering their territory. They overestimated their own strength and underestimated that of Germany. Deceived by France and Britain into expecting Allied land and air offensive efforts in the West which would lessen the German concentration against them, they were confident of their ability to withstand attack. And having given the Polish government an unconditional guarantee, the Western Allies lost whatever leverage they had had for putting pressure on it to cooperate with the Russians.

Furthermore, their unconditional commitment to go to war over Poland lost the Western Allies most of their diplomatic leverage on the Soviet Union as well. The driving motive behind Soviet diplomacy in 1935–9 had been the fear that the Western powers would reach an accommodation with Hitler, leaving the USSR isolated and dangerously exposed. The British unilateral guarantee to Poland was therefore much to the Soviets' advantage. Being now increasingly satisfied that

[118] For Liddell Hart, see his summary notes of 27 Aug. and 10 Sept. 1939, in King's, 3/109; and 11/1939, esp. 29, 31; *The Defence of Britain*, 39, 80, 95–9; *The Current of War* (London, 1941), 142–7; *Memoirs*, ii. 214–22, 241, 249–50, 253, 255.

Germany and the Western Allies were bound for war if Poland was attacked, Stalin was in effect given a free hand to opt for neutrality at the highest price and with maximum security. The Soviet Union rather than Britain now held the European balance of power. The opinion of one historian of Soviet foreign policy is illuminating: 'There was one and only one argument that could have swayed Stalin to accept an alliance with Britain and France. This would have been a declaration that the West would *not* defend Poland *unless* the USSR joined in her defense.'[119]

Chamberlain, however, did not want a Soviet alliance anyhow. He gave the guarantee to Poland not so much with the possibility of war in mind but, first, in order to leave Hitler in no doubt that Britain meant business and thus deter him from war and bring him back to the negotiating table; and, second, because the Foreign Office suddenly became anxious that Poland might make a deal with Hitler if she could not be reassured of the Western Allies' backing. Indeed, unlike his aim in respect to Czechoslovakia in the previous year, Hitler's initial intention was to bring Poland into his camp, provided the Polish government did not object to the incorporation of the Free City of Danzig in the Reich and granted Germany extraterritorial routes to East Prussia through the Polish corridor. The winter negotiations quickly taught Hitler that there was scant chance that the Poles were going to concede to his demands. But only after the British guarantee had been given did Hitler on 3 April 1939 order his armed forces to plan a campaign for the conquest of Poland. Whether this mattered or not, there can be little doubt that, as Liddell Hart was warning, Hitler was provoked into, rather than deterred from, war by the British guarantee to Poland and possibly also by the British introduction of conscription. The Poles themselves were unenthusiastic about the British guarantee for the same reason. All the same, the important point was that if Europe was heading for war, the Soviet Union's cooperation was essential for the Western Allies; so even Chamberlain and Halifax could not for long withstand the three-party pressure in Parliament to open negotiations with her.

The Soviet–German Pact and Its Consequences

That Chamberlain and Halifax opened those negotiations reluctantly and half-heartedly is well known. Unlike their position before Munich,

[119] See Ulam, *Expansion and Coexistence*, esp. 266–75.

the Soviets now insisted on a full political and military Triple Alliance with Britain and France and on a guarantee to all the parties involved. The British government, which wanted no more than a Soviet participation in the guarantee to Poland, was finally forced to accept the idea of a treaty under pressure at home. Yet the slow pace of the negotiations during the spring and summer of 1939 and the story of the Anglo-French military delegation's trip to the Soviet Union in August, taking the slow sea route, composed of relatively junior representatives, and given little authority to decide on anything, did not impress the Russians that the Western Allies meant business. A week before the German occupation of Prague, Ambassador Maisky had told Liddell Hart, as he had been telling everybody who was prepared to listen and the Foreign Office, that after the Munich rebuff Stalin might turn away from the policy of cooperation with the West and into isolation.[120] On 3 May the Soviet foreign secretary, Litvinov, a Jew and the main proponent of collective security, was replaced by Molotov, an act which probably signalled Stalin's wish to widen his field of manœuvre. Secret negotiations between the USSR and Germany began seriously in late July. But only after the middle of August 1939, when the Soviets had become convinced that there was going to be no military alliance with the Western Allies, certain that Hitler intended to attack Poland very shortly, and had concluded that against his expectations this was most likely to involve Germany in war with the Western powers, did they concede to a treaty. On 22 August it was announced in Moscow, to the complete surprise of the Western powers, that the German foreign secretary, Joachim von Ribbentrop was flying to Moscow for the signing of a non-aggression pact between Germany and the USSR. The signing itself took place two days later.[121]

The Soviet–German pact changed everything, in Liddell Hart's view. As long as the West had been negotiating with the Soviet Union for military cooperation against Germany, he had not been too alarmed. Now, however, he fell into despair. At once, and more clearly than

[120] Liddell Hart, *Memoirs*, ii. 222; S. Aster, 'Maisky and Parliamentary Anti-Appeasement', in Taylor *Lloyd George*, 336–7.

[121] See Roberts, *The Unholy Alliance*; Haslam, *The Soviet Union and the Struggle for Collective Security*, 195–229; also J. Erickson, *The Soviet High Command* (London, 1962), 514–30. That these were indeed the Soviet calculations seems to be confirmed by the recent revelation from the Soviet archives of Stalin's speech before the Politburo on 19 Aug. 1939.

anybody, he saw the strategic implications of the new situation.[122] In the first place, nothing could now prevent Poland from being overrun by Germany; on this he was in agreement with professional opinion in the West. However, Anglo-French planning was now predicated on the assumption that in the longer run the Western powers, by fully mobilizing the resources of their empires backed by the economic resources of the United States, and by the use of economic blockade, would be able to defeat Germany; and for this assumption Liddell Hart saw no reason. He agreed that the allies' formula of 'economic and moral pressure' for the first stage of the war was their only practical strategy, but maintained that they were unlikely to assemble superior strength to defeat Germany in any time-range and argued that, as Germany now dominated Eastern Europe, the effect of the blockade might prove limited, especially if the Soviet Union were to supply Germany with the raw materials she needed.[123] Relying on the experience of both world wars, most historians now express similar assessments.[124]

But Liddell Hart's logic did not stop there. As he saw it, the political consequences of the new strategic situation were far-reaching and inescapable. During the tense week between the announcement of the Soviet–German pact and the outbreak of the war, he sent his views to Dawson as well as to a small circle of politicians with whom he had been in close touch: Eden, Cecil, Dalton, Sinclair, and Lloyd George. He claimed that there was no point in defending a hopeless cause in a war which one could not win. One had to know when and where to retreat. The Western powers had to recognize that, as the Soviet Union had changed sides, Poland could no longer be defended, or rescued from Germany. The Western powers, too, were therefore obliged to change their course, which was inevitably leading to war, while trying to get the best possible deal over Poland and for Poland. Liddell Hart argued that Hitler's demands regarding Danzig and the Corridor were not unreasonable nor unjustified. Both for the good of Poland itself—which

[122] For the following, see Liddell Hart's diary notes for 27 Aug. and 1 Sept. 1939; 'Summary of the Situation', 27 Aug.; 'A Personal Conclusion', 10 Sept. 1939: all in King's, 3/109 and 11/1939; *The Current of War*, 142–7, 160–1; *Memoirs*, ii. 252–5, 259.

[123] The latter point had been made by the chiefs of staff in urging cooperation with the Soviet Union in the spring, and had been also raised in the cabinet; now, however, it was optimistically underrated: Gibbs, *Grand Strategy*, i. 723–4; Butler, *Grand Strategy*, ii. 71–4; Murray, *The European Balance of Power*, 303.

[124] See e.g. Mearsheimer, *Conventional Deterrence*, 91–4, 98, which again stands in stark contrast to his *LH*. The latter completely fails to mention the Soviet–German pact as the reason for Liddell Hart's change of attitude over Poland.

might otherwise suffer heavily to no avail—and from the point of view of the West's interests, there was no alternative to meeting those demands.

However, as Liddell Hart discovered, even if most of his correspondents found his strategic assessment of the situation hard to resist, the majority of them recoiled from his political conclusions. Lloyd George was in agreement with him, but Hugh Dalton, a previous ally in the anti-appeasement campaign, was more typical of the reactions Liddell Hart received, in raising the question what would be next: what would stop Hitler after Poland? It was much better, Dalton insisted, to go to war with Poland on Britain's side than to face Germany without her help later on. 'It is ironical', he wrote, 'that now, when *The Times*, in my view, is shaping very much better, you should have become an appeaser!'[125] Indeed what was the difference between Poland at the end of August 1939 and Munich in 1938? As Liddell Hart saw it, the difference was not in the principle and at the level of political slogans but in the harsh strategic reality: before Munich Czechoslovakia could offer stiff resistance and the Soviet Union sought cooperation with the West, so Hitler's Germany could be deterred or contained and choked; by contrast, after the Soviet–German pact Poland could not be defended and Germany could not be coerced into submission or defeated. The West was obliged to face realities and wait for better days or for a change of circumstances.

The gravity of the strategic realities was not, however, something of which British public opinion was fully cognizant. Ever since Prague, in the week leading to the outbreak of the Second World War, and even after the rapid fall of Poland, Liddell Hart had noted a complete change of mood in British public opinion and politics. He recorded with dismay what he regarded as evidence of jingoism and delusionary optimism, clearly an expression of relief from the frustrations and disappointments of the previous years. The announcement of the Soviet–German pact was not followed by an Anglo-French backdown, as Hitler expected and Liddell Hart desired, as the only rational course of action open to the Western Allies, but, to the contrary, by revival of the British bulldog spirit. On 25 August Britain signed an official treaty of mutual defence with Poland. There were now public expectations (not shared by the defence establishment) of an early Allied victory over Germany and political expressions of commitment to the

[125] To LH, 31 Aug. 1939, King's, 11/1939/85.

destruction of Hitlerism, both of which Liddell Hart judged to be beyond the capability of Britain and France. As he saw it, this was a swing between poles from appeasement to a bellicose pursuit of victory—both of which equally unrealistic and equally disastrous.[126] Since the signing of the Soviet–German pact his world had broken down. The worst he had striven to avert was now happening: Britain and Europe were sliding into total war, entailing total destruction and exhaustion, with no feasible aim in sight.

In June Liddell Hart had experienced a heart attack and now, in the fourth week of August, he collapsed and was incapacitated for several months. In consequence he was discharged by *The Times*, which wanted a fully active military correspondent to cover the war. Although his discharge was against his wishes—he tried hard to convince the editors that the war was not going to end soon anyhow—it did not necessarily entail an economic loss for him. He had long been tempted to write as a freelance for the popular press, which offered him much greater sums of money than *The Times*.[127] However, for several months after the outbreak of the war, though bombarded with requests for articles, he turned them down because he expected that people would not be willing to listen to what he had to say. Judging by the experience of the First World War, he had long anticipated that in times of war the newspapers would refrain from printing unpleasant material. Indeed, when he did try to offer his views on the situation to the press, the newspapers' editors declined to publish them for being too depressing for the public.[128]

But what in fact did Liddell Hart propose that the Western Allies should do at that point of time? In order fully to understand this, it is

[126] See in King's, 11/1939; *Memoirs*, ii. 219–20, 252–3, 257–8, 261, 276–7.

[127] In his *Memoirs*, ii. 251–2, 258–9, Liddell Hart has tried to put on a brave face over his dismissal, implying that it was largely done on his own initiative and on matters of principle. The truth is somewhat different. He had three times threatened to resign when publication of his writings were withheld: over Spain, over the state of Britain's air defence during the Czechoslovakian crisis, and over the introduction of conscription. In none of these cases had he carried out his threat, but at the end of 1938 he had succeeded in securing the right to contribute to other newspapers. In this he had long been interested for material reasons as well, using the generous offers he had been receiving from the popular press as a lever for improving his conditions with *The Times*. However, having achieved the best of all worlds, he definitely did not want to resign when the war broke out, and was practically forced to do so, mainly on account of his health. See King's, 3/108–9, and esp. his letter exchange with Dawson between 28 Aug. and 7 Sept. 1939.

[128] See in King's, 11/1939; *Memoirs*, ii. 251–2, 257–8, 275.

time to examine the wider philosophical outlook he had developed in the late 1930s regarding the essence and aims of the West.

Defence of the West: Ideology and Strategy

Notwithstanding his youthful declaration of faith written in 1914,[129] Liddell Hart was not ideologically and politically aligned until the 1930s. During the 1920s he hardly ever transgressed from the strategic realm into politics. It is a mere curiosity, reflecting widespread attitudes in the West during the late 1920s, that he returned in 1928 from a tour of Italy and the Italian armed forces full of enthusiasm for the achievements of the Fascist regime.[130] By the 1930s, however, with the crisis of the democracies and the seemingly irresistible march of Nazism, fascism, and communism, politics polarized, ideology came to the forefront of public consciousness, and thinking individuals everywhere were struggling for define to themselves where they stood. Liddell Hart was no exception to this rule. While Fuller formally embraced fascism, Liddell Hart became a staunch partisan of liberal democracy.

From the mid-1930s Liddell Hart's private papers are full of statements of creed. While lamenting the mediocrity in the British army and government, he held that in the dictatorships things were far worse. His main objection to both fascism and communism was their oppressive nature. Quoting Lord Acton's famous dictum, he went on to express the following classical liberal positions, which rang far better half a century before or after than in the 1930s:

> Government at the best is a necessary evil. In the light of experience, autocratic government may produce an immediate increase of efficiency, but progressively undermine the foundations of ultimate efficiency. The virtue of Parliamentary government does not lie in its government, but in its available checks on governmental abuses. . . . Full freedom may be unattainable, but the minimum condition necessary for the development of the mind is that you should be free to be true in speech to what you think.[131]

[129] See pp. 657–8.

[130] The titles of his articles speak for themselves: 'Fascist Italy:—New-Born Efficiency, Traditional Courtesy', 'Pursuit of an Ideal', 'The Future: Training the Youth', 'A Patriotic Autocrat', 'The New Romulus and the New Rome': *Daily Telegraph*, 10, 11, 12, 16 Jan. 1928; *Atlantic Monthly* (July 1928); also *Yale Review*, June 1930, 665.

[131] See in King's, 11/1934; 4 Aug. 1936, 11/1936; quotation from 'Power and Freedom', 9 May 1937, 11/1937/40.

A week later, in a letter to Fuller responding to the latter's fascist writings, Liddell Hart denounced all forms of authoritarianism and the suppression of truth.[132] With their relationship already deteriorating (Liddell Hart is not even mentioned in Fuller's *Memoirs*, 1936), the breach between the two men was final. Their correspondence ceased, and they did not see each other again until 1942. The significance of this break was more than biographical, for it was now left to Liddell Hart to develop the notions he had absorbed from Fuller in the early 1920s into a strategic blueprint for a liberal-democratic West. Liddell Hart's strategic theory and political and philosophical creed became closely interconnected.

Liddell Hart defined the challenge facing Britain in the late 1930s in the opening essay of *Europe in Arms* (1937), 'The Defence of Freedom':

> This island, if now less than an island strategically . . . is more than ever an island politically. . . . Will England stand rocklike amid the totalitarian tide until that tide ebbs? Our constitution for several centuries has had its roots in the growing idea of individual liberty. . . . For a time, in the last century, our example had an ever-widening influence. . . . The war of 1914–18 interrupted this liberal expansion. . . . Alike to Communism and Fascism, uniformity is an ideal, and nonconformity a crime. . . . [In Britain itself] toleration has never been so widespread, nor violence so widely disfavoured. The decline of the Liberal party . . . has helped the spread of liberal ideas through all parties. . . . The only serious danger to-day lies outside our borders. . . . It threatens not only our national existence but all that makes existence worth while.

How was the danger to be faced? If need be, inescapably, by force of arms, but with a view to the desired aim. 'Patriots' and 'pacifists' must recognize each other's point: defence was essential, but only in the cause of freedom. Freedom must become an animating ideal at home and a shining example abroad.[133]

After Munich, when for the first time in his life the alarmed Liddell Hart actively enlisted in the public political campaign in meetings, lectures, debates, and pamphlets, he amplified these ideas. Against the peace movements he argued that peace was worth having only for the purpose of maintaining justice, freedom, free speech, and the conditions conducive to the life and growth of the individual. In the same way, fiercely campaigning against conscription, he declared repeatedly that totalitarianism must not be fought by totalitarian means. Individual rights were superior to state rights, and the end could never

[132] To Fuller, 16 May 1937, King's, 1/302.

[133] *Europe in Arms*, 1–7.

justify the means. Britain must safeguard and cultivate freedom, which is humanity's greatest achievement and the underlying direction of its development.[134]

Ideals, of course, are not an independent sphere but form part of a wider reality. As Liddell Hart grasped, a fundamental fact about Britain's political position in the 1930s was that, while already being a satisfied imperial power, she had progressively become a consumerist, liberal-democratic society with no interest in major wars unless the status quo was seriously threatened. In this, as in so many other aspects of the development of 'modernity', Britain and the strategic problems she faced might be seen as paradigmatically foreshadowing the condition of the 'West' as a whole later on. As already mentioned, Liddell Hart was the first to try to work out the theoretical framework of a grand strategy suited for this new or emerging model.

In his important 'Attack or Defence' series in *The Times* in late 1937 Liddell Hart put forward the outline of this grand strategy. He argued that Clausewitz's claim that, while being stronger than attack, defence was unable to produce a decision was true only 'so far as the positive overthrow of the enemy was necessary for the fulfilment of the purpose in war'. That object, however, was no longer necessary for the purpose of a non-aggressive Britain and her friends:[135]

> Military action should be ruled by its head: the national object. We may be drawn into war to defend our interests and ensure, in face of an aggressor, the continuance of liberal civilization, those larger ideas which we epitomize when we speak of 'England'. To attain that object, need not imply on our part a war *à outrance*. For the aggressor, aiming at conquest, the complete overthrow of the opposing forces and the occupation of the opponent's territory may be necessary to his success. But not for ours. Our object is fulfilled if we can convince the enemy that he cannot conquer.[136]

Searching for apt historical models for the new political and strategic requirements, Liddell Hart came up with one which had been held in

[134] See e.g. ibid. 219–21; 'Democratic Service', *Student Forum*, 30 Nov. 1938; 'British Freedom', *World Review*, Dec. 1938, 21–7; *The Defence of Britain*, 86; and the extensive documentation throughout King's, 11/1939; *Memoirs*, ii. 206–7, 210.

[135] Clausewitz himself had become increasingly aware of this; see Book I above, 215, 262; and my 'Clausewitz on Defence and Attack', *Journal of Strategic Studies*, 10 (1988), 20–6. Liddell Hart, *The Times*, 26 Oct. 1937, repr. in *The Defence of Britain*, 106–7.

[136] The Times, 27 Oct. 1937; repr. in *The Defence of Britain*, 42–3. Originally in a memorandum for the record: 23 Sept. 1937, King's, 11/1937/75.

contempt by the men of the nineteenth century who had exalted national vigour and decisive victories. This was the Byzantine tradition of imperial defence which, as Liddell Hart claimed, safeguarded Byzantium for more than 1,000 years—a feat unequalled in history—and must be judged a tremendous success in terms of adjusting means and ends:

> This new–old and strength conserving strategy of imperial defence does not imply a purely passive resistance. Its aim is to convince the enemy that it has nothing to gain and much to lose by pursuing a war. Its guiding principle is to eschew the vain pursuit of a decision by the offensive on our part. Its method is not merely to parry, but to make the enemy pay as heavily as possible for his offensive efforts. This implies in the military sphere an active and mobile defence, in which the effect of direct resistance is extended by *ripostes* both strategic and tactical as well as by continual harassing action. In this offensive–defensive strategy there is a part for mobile land forces as well as for the sea and air forces. And economic pressure in turn will be used to extend the wearing down process in the military sphere.[137]

These ideas formed the basis for a new chapter, 'Grand Strategy', which together with another new chapter—on Byzantine wars—was to be incorporated in the second edition of Liddell Hart's major theoretical work *The Strategy of Indirect Approach* (1941).

If Britain is viewed as 'the first modern nation', paradigmatically reflecting, as it were, 'the way of the future', the United States, the other English-speaking, oceanic, liberal-democratic, and capitalist-consumerist great power, is equally famously cast in a similar position. To demonstrate the idea of this study regarding the historical background and significance of Liddell Hart's work, one might turn to the United States for obvious parallels. Here was another nation whose experience of the First World War—though much briefer and less agonizing than Britain's, and economically far more rewarding—had resulted in a traumatic backlash. This had led to the ascendence of isolationism, which owing to more fortunate geopolitical conditions would be sustained longer than in Britain. Then, in the late 1930s, when the international crises across both the Pacific and Atlantic oceans posed challenges of a high order, what were the political and strategic notions which Roosevelt and the American adminstration began to toy with, no matter for the moment how seriously? Starting from Japan's invasion of China in the summer of 1937 and the signing of the tripartite Anti-Comintern Pact in November of that year (which was perceived in

[137] The Times, 27 Oct. 1937; repr. in *The Defence of Britain*, 120–2.

Washington as a global military alliance against the status quo powers), the notions of a coordinated policy of sanctions and containment against the aggressors were increasingly aired by the president. The idea was first embodied in his famous 'quarantine speech' on 5 December 1937. As Roosevelt told both his cabinet and the British ambassador in mid-December: 'We want to develop a technique which will not lead to war. We want to be smart as Japan and Italy. We want to do it in a modern way.' He argued that the Axis powers were pursuing a policy of 'undeclared war' which ought to be answered in kind. During the Czechoslovakian crisis Roosevelt called for a 'siege' of Germany. He suggested that the Allies ought to close their borders with Germany, even without declaring war, and stand on the defence, relying on the economic blockade to do the job. The United States would back them economically (everything except 'troops and loans'). Offensive actions would only result in 'terrific casualties' and, in view of German military power, would prove futile. Finally, after Munich and during 1939 Roosevelt stressed the importance of Soviet cooperation.[138]

Obviously, these notions were very hazily defined, took the form of presidential speculations rather than of official policy, lacked the support of Congress and of the majority of Americans, and therefore inspired little faith abroad. For example, without an American guarantee (which was not forthcoming) that the United States would join the war if Britain were attacked by Japan following a policy of sanctions, Chamberlain had no intention of risking such a policy in 1937–9 (as indeed in 1931 and 1934). It was finally implemented against Japan by the United States only in the summer of 1941.[139] All the same, it is Roosevelt's general trend of thought which is of interest to us. Liddell Hart was barely concerned about the Far East, and there was probably little if any consequential link between his own ideas and those being entertained across the Atlantic. Only the historical circumstances of and the strategic challenges facing Britain and the United States revealed an underlying similarity, and the same was true of the respective proposed solutions.

[138] See D. Reynolds, *The Creation of the Anglo-American Alliance, 1937–1941* (London, 1981), 17, 30–31 (quotation), 35, and *passim*; R. Dallek, *Franklin D. Roosevelt and American Foreign Policy, 1932–1945* (New York, 1979), 163–4, and *passim*; C. Macdonald, 'Deterrence Diplomacy: Roosevelt and the Containment of Germany, 1938–1940', in Boyce and Robertson *Paths to War*, 297–329; D. C. Watt, *Succeeding John Bull: America in Britain's Place, 1900–1975* (Cambridge, 1984), 82–3.

[139] That this amounted to a strategy of containment is again noted by J. Mueller, *Retreat from Doomsday: The Obsolescence of Major War* (New York, 1989), 75–7.

The grand strategy which Liddell Hart developed in the late 1930s for 'England' and the West was devised as an antidote to what he labelled 'camouflage war' or 'war by points', which he maintained had already been taking place for several years around the world against the interests of the Western powers.[140] This grand strategy was defensive in aim and, as we have seen in reviewing Liddell Hart's positions in respect to the successive international crises, it was based on containment and deterrence, economic coercion, peripheral war by proxy, blockade, and limited war, in that order. It was defensive because Liddell Hart assessed that Britain and her allies (the fully committed, not including the United States) were simply not strong enough to crush a major rival like Nazi Germany; and that any attempt to do so, even assuming this goal could be achieved, would bankrupt them in every respect, while being strictly unnecessary for the attainment of their fundamental aims. Defensive also because Liddell Hart grew to believe that the very concept of 'victory' was a mirage and a boomerang which more often than not created resentment in the defeated side, gave rise to new rivals, and sowed the seeds of the next round of conflict. By 1935 Liddell Hart wrote privately that he had lost faith in solutions by force.[141] This was typical of the way large sections of the British élite during the interwar period came to interpret modern and recent historical experience. Soundly or not, they were contrasting the heritage and durability of the victories and settlements of 1807, 1871, and 1919 on the one hand with those of 1815 and 1866 on the other. According to Liddell Hart, the West had to check the hostile forces but not embark on a crusade to crush them, which would 'only lead to mutual suicide, and the collapse of civilization'.[142]

Cold War

In Liddell Hart's view, all these considerations only grew in force after the outbreak of the war and Germany's overrunning of Poland in September 1939. As mentioned earlier, with the fall of Czechoslovakia and Germany's increasing domination of south-eastern Europe, Germany had become much less susceptible to economic coercion. The Soviet–German pact had made her even less susceptible, as well as practically nullifying the prospects of defeating her by force. Liddell

[140] For these concepts, see e.g. *The Defence of Britain*, 26; Note, 15 Mar. 1938, King's, 11/1938/32.

[141] 26 Dec. 1935, King's, 11/1935/55.

[142] *The Defence of Britain*, 19, also 20–1, 26, 35–8, 43; diary notes of 4 Aug. 1939, printed in *The Current of War*, 140–1.

Hart had been against going to war under these circumstances in the first place, and now he thought, like Lloyd George and Beaverbrook, that Britain and France ought not to reject Hitler's peace offers but to strive for a negotiated settlement.[143] Victory may be desirable in abstract in view of the nature of the Nazi regime, but it was simply unattainable. The alternative presented to the British people between either total victory or total defeat was unhistorical and irrational.[144] In the meantime Liddell Hart proposed that Britain and France should publicly declare that they were renouncing the offensive in the defence of Western civilization and the struggle against aggression. This would give the Allies the moral advantage, and provide less provocation for Germany to attack in the West.[145]

What does all this amount to? Having lost their ability to contain Germany within her old frontiers, choke her economically if she attempted to break out of them, and indeed win a war against her, the Allies' only desirable option, as Liddell Hart saw it, was in effect armed coexistence alongside her. Central and south-eastern Europe could not be rescued from Germany's domination (though Liddell Hart did not spell this out), at least until Germany fell out with the Soviet Union.[146] What the Western Allies ought to concentrate upon in terms of grand strategy was the security of the Western bloc or Western civilization. Until a satisfactory peace with Germany could be negotiated, there was to be no more than a continuation of the 'Twilight' or 'Phoney War' which was already prevailing on the Western Front—in effect, 'cold war'.

To that end, no provocative offensive action was to be attempted by the West, for no promising course of action could be envisaged anyhow and any Western offensive initiative would only drive Germany into action and lead to escalation. Here also the interesting point is that Liddell Hart's grand design was matched by very acute specific strategic

[143] After the fall of Poland, Lloyd George and Liddell Hart were practically unanimous about the war. Regarding the possibility of peace, Lloyd George thought in terms of an 'ethnic Poland', stripped of her German, Belorussian, and Ukrainian provinces and populations: P. Addington, 'Lloyd George and Compromise Peace in the Second World War', in Taylor *Lloyd George*, 361–84, esp. 367–71.

[144] Memorandum, 7 Nov. 1939, King's, 11/1939/128; other notes, memoranda, and articles are printed in *The Current of War*, 161–2, 185–92.

[145] 8 Sept. 1939, King's, 11/1939/100; published after a long delay as 'Is There a New Way to Fight This Strange War?', *Sunday Express*, 10 Dec. 1939, and reworked in many subsequent articles; the original memo was reprinted in *The Current of War*, 151–7, also 162–3; cf. *Memoirs*, ii. 275, which makes no mention of the actual content of the article.

[146] See ibid. 260, 276.

analyses. As the French and British high commands were agreed, the Allies would not be able to carry out for years to come a land offensive in the West. The bombing of the Ruhr and of German cities was clearly not in the Allies' interest, for they, and especially France, were more vulnerable than Germany to such attacks and because the Luftwaffe held the advantage in the air.[147] When in the winter of 1939–40 the idea of Anglo-French expeditions to Scandinavia captured the imagination of Allied public opinion, Liddell Hart rejected it outright. There was much enthusiasm for armed intervention in defence of the heroic Finns against the Soviet Union, and Hore-Belisha, for example, was not untypical when talking about the prospects of occupying Leningrad and smashing the Soviet Union, as an indirect move against Germany. Liddell Hart, however, saw very clearly that the Red Army's initial defeats created a false impression as to its real strength, and that in the end it was bound to conquer. He argued that the Soviet Union's demand for the removal of its border with Finland from the gates of Leningrad was strategically understandable and that its offer of a territorial exchange with Finland was reasonable. Finally, and most importantly, he stressed that to add the Soviet Union to the West's enemies and push it further into Germany's arms was total madness. On these grounds he also rejected the plans for bombing the Black Sea oil shipping to Germany and the Soviet Union's Caucasian oilfields from the Allies' Mediterranean air bases. These ideas were seriously considered, especially by the French, and widely publicized by the press. Only the collapse of Finland's resistance put an end to these schemes.[148]

The Allies' planned expedition to Finland was largely conceived as an excuse for cutting off the transport of the Swedish iron ores destined for Germany via neutral Norwegian waters. Liddell Hart totally opposed this idea, which had been championed in Cabinet by Churchill since the beginning of the war. Critics have remarked that in this he appears to have gone against his own major doctrines of the indirect approach and the British way in warfare. In a sudden about-turn he equated the proposed Norwegian scheme with the Salonika operation in

[147] See e.g. Liddell Hart, 'Will the Cities Be Bombed?', *Sunday Express*, 11 Feb. 1940; repr. in *The Current of War*, 195–201. The British official history of the war in the air still blamed the French for their lack of courage: C. Webster and N. Frankland, *The Strategic Air Offensive against Germany, 1939–1945* (4 vols., London, 1961), i. 137–43; but see Butler, *Grand Strategy*, ii. 166–71.

[148] To HB, 25 Feb. 1940, King's, 11/HB 1940/28; *Evening Standard*, 10 Feb. 1940, repr. in *The Current of War*, 220–6, also 216, 227–35; on the Soviet oilfields: *Evening Standard*, 2 March 1940, repr. *The Current of War*, 236–43; *Memoirs*, ii. 275–6.

the First World War, which he now presented as a failure. However, apart from the fact that Liddell Hart obviously never claimed that *any* indirect operation was necessarily good, the point is, of course, that he viewed the proposed Norwegian operation as undesirable in terms of the overall grand strategy he advocated, *as well as* being, specifically, strategically unsound. The Swedish ores were sufficiently important for Germany to provoke her into action, whereas the Allies were not strong enough to prevent her from overrunning Norway. When the alarmed Germans responded to the Royal Navy's action in Norwegian territorial waters by a pre-emptive invasion of Denmark and Norway, Liddell Hart, while urging that speed was now the most essential requirement of the Allies' response, regarded the ensuing events as a deserved punishment for a reckless folly.[149]

So we are back again to square one. The war against Germany could not be 'won', for she could not be either strangled or crushed by Britain and France. The Allies' only viable option was to continue the low-intensity 'phoney war' which would lessen the provocation for Germany to escalate the war against them and which, by demonstration to her that she also could not win and had much to lose from the continuation of the war, would pave the way for a negotiated settlement. This recurring theme in Liddell Hart's writings from 1937, emphasized in *The Defence of Britain* published on the eve of the war, appears to have been echoed virtually verbatim by Chamberlain, who after the outbreak of the war wrote to Roosevelt (and to his sisters) that Britain would not win the war 'by a spectacular and complete victory, but by convincing the Germans that they cannot win'. 'Hold out tight, keep up the economic pressure, push on with munition production and military preparations with the utmost energy', but 'take no offensive unless Hitler's begins it.'[150]

Interestingly enough, on the other side of the hill as well attitudes after the Polish campaign remarkably corresponded to Liddell Hart's trend of thought. The German high command, led by the army's commander-in-chief and by the chief of the army's General Staff, Generals Brauchitsch and Halder, who were supported by all three

[149] Liddell Hart's articles at the time are reprinted in *The Current of War*, 248–96; Bond, *LH*, 130.

[150] For these often-quoted extracts, see R. J. Overy, *The Origins of the Second World War* (London, 1987), 77; J. Charmley, *Chamberlain and the Lost Peace* (London, 1989), 210; Chamberlain may have also been intentionally responding to Roosevelt's ideas cited above. See also Mueller, *Retreat from Doomsday*, 70.

army group commanders, was almost unanimously against launching any offensive in the West. Most high-ranking German generals did not believe Germany was capable of decisively defeating the Allies, and feared such an offensive would develop into a high-intensity war of attrition which could only be to Germany's disadvantage. They thought that Germany ought to sit quietly and concentrate on absorbing the wealth of Eastern Europe. In the words of General Alfred Jodl of the OKW: 'There was, particularly in the army, a widespread opinion that the war would die a natural death if we only kept quiet in the West.' It was Hitler who forced the reluctant army into planning and executing an offensive in the West. His pressure gave rise to another round of conspiracy to overthrow him, involving most of the army's high command, including Reichenau, hitherto the regime's strongest supporter within the army. The conspiracy came to an end when Brauchitsch collapsed in an audience with Hitler. Hitler wanted to attack in the West because he did not trust the Allies not to move into the Low Countries and thus seriously threaten the Ruhr; because he wanted to pre-empt the build-up and arrival in France of large British forces; because he did not trust the Soviet Union and feared an American intervention; and because he had long thought that the final settling of accounts with France was necessary for the establishment of his new European order.[151] Liddell Hart argued later that if it were not for the Allies' provocative actions Hitler would not have taken the offensive in the West.[152]

To bring things into focus, what Liddell Hart was advocating was containment and something approaching cold war prior to the advent of nuclear weapons. Yet, in the absence of that Great Deterrent, what was there to prevent total war? In the first place, there was the general fear of rapid and mutual destruction from the air which was perceived by the men of the 1930s in terms quite similar to those by which the nuclear threat would be perceived later on. Secondly, there was the general trend of major wars between the great powers, as demonstrated in the First World War, to become ever more costly in all respects as well as increasingly more alien to the values and interests of modern

[151] H. Deutsch, *The Conspiracy against Hitler in the Twilight War* (Minneapolis, 1968); W. Warlimont, *Inside Hitler's Headquarters, 1939–1945* (New York, 1964), 36, 59; Wheeler-Bennett, *The Nemesis of Power*, 466–72; Müler, *Beck*, 190–206; B. Stegmann's and H. Umbreit's contributions to MF, *Germany and the Second World War*, ii. 9, 232–8; Mearsheimer, *Conventional Deterrence*, 101–12, quotation from 102.

[152] *The Current of War*, 210.

societies. The latter argument at least may have held force for the West, but was hardly compatible, for instance, with Hitler's world-view and vision of the future and of the 'modern'. But then, Liddell Hart was also advocating a calculated policy which would renounce all offensive action on the Allies' part in order to decrease the chances of a German pre-emption and of escalation. In addition, he was seeking any other element to strengthen deterrence and underline the futility of war. It was against this background that he made the greatest blunder of his career, preaching the growing strength and complete superiority of tactical and operational defence over attack. This time his grand strategic design seriously biased his judgement of practical strategy, though even here he demonstrated dazzling foresight in some crucial respects.

IV. Defence versus 'Blitzkrieg'

Mearsheimer has rightly pointed out that Liddell Hart's new emphasis on the superiority of defence was intimately related to his pre-occupation in the 1930s with policy and grand strategy.[153] In 1931–2, consulted by the British government regarding the position to be adopted in the coming disarmament conference in Geneva, Liddell Hart adopted and developed the scheme of 'qualitative disarmament', as opposed to the 'quantitative' approach around whose implementation the contentions between France and Germany in particular revolved. He thought that the best way to bypass the differences in the national points of view and deter aggression was to abolish 'offensive weapons', such as the heavy tank (above 5, 8, or 10 tons) and heavy gun (above 4-inch calibre), which had been developed as 'tin-openers' to overcome defensive lines and military stalemate. The temptation of a quick victory would thus be reduced. The new development in his thought was not easy for Liddell Hart because, as he admitted, it went against all that he had struggled for during the 1920s: precisely to overcome defensive lines and military stalemate, chiefly by the use of the tank. However, as he pointed out, this had to be sacrificed for the 'wider view' of deterring aggression. 'There is a higher point of view than the general's—that of a statesman', he replied to Fuller's scathing criticism; 'Prevention is better than cure—and once war has begun, any cure is a highly uncertain one.' Furthermore, Liddell Hart's reflections on the 'British way in warfare' the year before had already taught him that Britain in

[153] *LH*, 109–16.

particular, with her 'preservative policy, insular position, limited resources, and inherent slowness in preparing for war', had little to gain from lightning land campaigns.[154]

The problem of defining certain weapon systems as either defensive or offensive is not our concern here. Winston Churchill anticipated the arguments against that distinction when he said in Parliament, after the idea had become official British policy, that it was a 'silly expedient', since the character of weapons was determined by the way they were used and by the politics they served rather than by their inherent qualities. Liddell Hart made the opposite case no less ably in his response in the the *Daily Telegraph*.[155] It might be noted that 'qualitative disarmament', aimed at enhancing deterrence, was to become a guiding principle in the nuclear age, but then, nuclear weapons have made the rationale much clearer, at least in principle.

Other factors contributed to Liddell Hart's new trend of thought. By 1931 he had completed *Foch*, in which he had delved into the problematic development of military ideas between 1871 and 1914. Having in addition dealt with the American Civil War in *Sherman*, he became very conscious that the face of future war had all too often been reflected in earlier wars, but had been radically misinterpreted because of wishful thinking and lack of intellectual courage to face reality.[156] Now, with even greater attentiveness than before, he would always keep one eye on the First World War.

At first, in 1933–5, Liddell Hart argued that since the armies of the great powers retained their traditional character, being composed predominantly of infantry masses, the stalemate of trench warfare was most likely to recur in case of a war. Under these conditions air power would only add to the paralysis of movement on the battlefield, unless really strong air forces were created. Armoured forces, operating deep in the enemy's rear—as Liddell Hart had been advocating—have the best chances of success, but they barely existed at the time. By contrast, motorized (lorry-mounted) formations, beginning to appear in all armies, would again only strengthen the defender by enabling him to rush machine-gun troops to threatened sectors of his front and block enemy advances. The best use of these forces in the offensive would be

[154] 'Would the Scrapping of Heavy Guns and Tanks Cripple the Aggressor's Power?', *Daily Telegraph*, 1 Feb. 1932; 'Aggression and the Problem of Weapons', *English Review*, July 1932, 71–8 (a reply to Fuller), quotation from 71–2; *Memoirs*, i. 183–93, 207–10, quotation from 186.

[155] *Memoirs*, i. 207–8. See also *Europe in Arms*, 143–4.

[156] See e.g. ibid. 339–56; *The Defence of Britain*, 118–20.

in combining the threatening strategic attack, or leap forward, with the tactical defence when the enemy is obliged to move out to check the advance. This was to be Sherman's 'baited offensive' revived. In sum, however, Liddell Hart claimed that the defence retained, if not increased, its superiority, leaving little prospect for successful aggression.[157]

From 1935 on, as rearmament began in earnest and armoured divisions were increasingly being formed in all the major European armies, a new stage began. Would these new divisions break the stalemate, as Fuller, Liddell Hart, and the other armour enthusiasts had believed in the 1920s? By the second half of the 1930s both Fuller and Liddell Hart had grown sceptical about it, and as always it had been Fuller who had led the way. From the late 1920s he had been developing his concept of the dialectic and spiralling evolution of the offensive and defensive means of war, which in his view had always inaugurated new eras in military history. He had been giving ever-growing weight to the anti-tank gun and mine as the tank's equals. They would be used within a new system of defence in depth, in which the tank itself, concentrated in reserve for the counter-offensive, would play a major role.[158] Liddell Hart, always highly attentive to whatever Fuller was saying, picked up and elaborated on these ideas. In late 1935, discussing the British army's decision to create the Mobile Division which he desired so deeply, he wrote:

> It is setting expectations high to count on the programme of modernization to bridge the gulf that now separates armies from their desire for successful attack. My own view is that these potential developments in offensive power are far exceeded by the actual growth, largely unrecognized, of defensive power . . . Not only fire, but the means of obstruction and of demolition, may now be moved more swiftly to any threatened spot to thwart a hostile concentration of force.[159]

Liddell Hart now increasingly used the very same arguments against overly optimistic expectations of tanks and of tank forces which he had rejected in the 1920s. It was as if he were paraphrasing Victor

[157] Ibid.; *Spectator*, 17 Nov. 1933, 738–40; *New York Times Magazine*, 2 Dec. 1934, 3, 18; *The Times*, 17 Aug., 19 Sept., 27 Nov. 1935, 21 Aug. 1936.

[158] Fuller, 'One Hundred Problems of Mechanization', pt. ii, *Army Quarterly*, 19 (1929), 256–8. For a balanced assessment from the second half of the 1930s, see Fuller, 'The Problem of Tank and Anti-Tank Weapons', *Fighting Forces*, 14 (1937), 42–5.

[159] *The Times*, 26 Nov. 1935, repr. in *Europe in Arms*, 83; see also *The Times*, 23 Mar. 1936.

Germains; indeed he probably was. Only a couple of examples will be quoted here:

> It should not be forgotten that the extraordinary successes gained in the World War by British and French tanks at Cambrai, Soissons, and Amiens, were nothing else but surprises under conditions that would not occur again. They were gained (and they could only be gained) against a defence practically non-existent, impoverished with the most primitive of means, and completely inexperienced; and they could be expanded into decisive action only because the tank (at that time) was shrouded in the veil of the 'tank terror'.
>
> It is true that tanks have been improved and increased, but anti-tank weapons have made still more rapid progress—and, being cheaper, can be multiplied faster.[160]

In his generally acute analyses of the strategic lessons of the Spanish Civil War, Liddell Hart highlighted evidence which supported his view that 'the defence is paramount at present' and most likely to create stalemate. It is true that while the performance of mechanized troops in Spain was widely regarded at the time as falling short of the radical expectations pinned upon them, he at first pointed out correctly that these troops were mainly no more than motorized infantry which did not possess offensive tactical capability. He called attention to the fact that the tanks used were early light models which all armies were in the process of replacing with heavier ones, and that in many cases these tanks were employed in small numbers and over unsuitable ground.[161] However, in time he also began to stress that the Spanish Civil War demonstrated that large-scale tank breakthroughs were already a thing of the past.[162]

[160] LH, *The Times*, 21 May 1937; 'Military and Strategic Advantages of Collective Security in Europe', *New Commonwealth Quarterly* (Sept. 1938), 144, repr. in *Europe in Arms*, 54. For the same ideas, see also: *The Times*, 30 Oct., 2 Nov. 1936, repr. in *Europe in Arms*, 118; ibid. 125–9, 138–9; *The Defence of Britain*, 120–1. None of these passages was marked by Liddell Hart for inclusion in the list of his successful forecasts (13/3), which he carefully compiled for the writing of his *Memoirs*. Cf. V. Germains, *The 'Mechanization' of War* (London, 1927), 47–54, 74–89.

[161] 'Spain: Attack or Defence', *The Times*, 3 Apr. 1937; repr. in *Europe in Arms*, 323–32.

[162] *The Times*, 21 May 1937. The growth of anti-tank defence was recognized at the time even by the armour enthusiasts; cf. Tukhachevsky, citing the evidence from Spain and extensively quoting from Liddell Hart: 'In modern war the strength of the defence is steadily growing'; 'The Red Army Field Service Regulations', *Red Star*, 6 May 1937, in Richard Simpkin, *Deep Battle: The Brainchild of Marshal Tukhachevskii* (London, 1987), 161–2. None the less, Tukhachevsky, like Guderian, continued to hold that by virtue of its superior mobility it would be possible decisively to concentrate the tank in selected sectors of the front.

As mentioned before, this development in Liddell Hart's views was influenced by, and subordinated to, his 'wider view' concerning Britain's and the West's favoured policy and grand strategy. Pronouncing the superiority of defence was one of his chief means for alleviating the tension between the doctrines he championed of collective security and limited liability (together making containment), and for enhancing deterrence, particularly against war assuming a total form. In late 1937, as British strategic policy was being decided upon, Liddell Hart wrote in his programmatic 'Defence or Attack' articles:

> So great is the power of the defensive nowadays that a small reinforcement may suffice to establish a deadlock . . . comparatively slight provisions of up-to-date material—such as aircraft, anti-aircraft, artillery, and machine-guns—would have sufficed to make permanent and general the temporary and local stalemates which the aggressor repeatedly suffered. That provision would have made but a small drain on the resources of the Powers which had supported the principle of collective security, thereby removing the fear that they might be appreciably weakened in meeting other contingencies. . . .
>
> These reflections lead to speculation on the future of war. Will the effect of a spreading recognition of its indecisive trend, combined with the present mutual fear of air reprisals, lead to its full operation only against states which lack the means to resist on land or retaliate in the air; and to a self-imposed limitation if great powers become engaged? In other words, even though such powers may be drawn into war against each other through some clash of interests, will they perhaps in self-preservation confine themselves to strokes against out-lying forces on the remote parts of each other's territory, rather than risk a mutual holocaust of their great cities and a vain employment of their armies?[163]

Here was the outline of the strategic policy which Liddell Hart would advocate in the following years. The more he crystallized containment, limited liability, and deterrence into a comprehensive security programme against Germany, the more extreme he became in advocating the superiority of defence, with which he cemented together the whole concept.[164] The idea that Germany, or the Allies, might launch a successful attack could have ruined any of the pillars of this concept, which Liddell Hart put together as the only way of achieving security reasonably, without mutual devastation. Therefore, everything had to be done in order to eradicate that idea. Liddell Hart's motivated bias

[163] 'The Futility of Aggression', *The Times*, 27 Oct. 1937; repr. in *Europe in Arms*, 49–50.

[164] The connection is well made by Mearsheimer, *LH*, 110–11, 115–16.

regarding the strength of tactical defence was getting ever stronger during the crisis years before the war.

As the British army was resuming more serious training for war, Liddell Hart was publicly criticizing any trace of training for the offensive. He claimed that the offensive was deeply rooted in military tradition and in the soldier's creed, and suspected that the army was in effect preparing itself for an offensive Continental strategy in opposition to government policy.[165] The CIGS, Deverell, and the director of military operations and intelligence, Haining, tried to convince him that he was exaggerating about this. 'Haining also suggested that in my view of the superiority of the defence, I was relying too much on the experience of the last war. He remarked—"History never repeats itself"'—a view which Liddell Hart rejected.[166] When in late 1937 Deverell returned deeply impressed from the German army's manœuvres, in which Panzer forces were employed for the first time on a large scale, his fate was sealed. It did not help that the Germans had in fact been emulating the British model and closely studying Liddell Hart's writings.[167] 'He had come back from the German manœuvres with the report that the French could not stand against them, that the Maginot line would not hold, and that the offensive would succeed.'[168] The stupidity of the man became so obviously dangerous in the eyes of Liddell Hart and Hore-Belisha that they decided to get rid of him. After a careful preparation of the political ground they acted swiftly. On 30 November the Cabinet authorized the removal of Deverell and of his deputy, Knox, as well as a thorough purge of the army council. Gort, Hore-Belisha's military secretary who was on friendly relations with Liddell Hart, was pushed upwards to become the new CIGS. In December the memorandum 'On the Role of the Army' which Liddell Hart had prepared for Hore-Belisha was approved by the Cabinet.[169] Limited liability became official policy. The revolution was complete.

[165] See e.g. *The Times*, 14 Aug., 10 Sept. 1937; the latter repr. in *The Defence of Britain*, 374–5.

[166] Meetings between Liddell Hart and Deverell, 12 Nov. 1936, King's, 11/1936/99 (Haining attending); 29 June 1937, 11/1937/56; 18 Nov. 1937, 11/1937/94; cf. Liddell Hart, *Memoirs*, i. 382–3, in which Haining's remark is not cited.

[167] A. Gat, *British Armour Theory and the Rise of the Panzer Arm: Revising the Revisionists* (London, 2000).

[168] Talk with Hore-Belisha, 15 Oct. 1937, King's, 11/HB 1937/56; not cited in *Memoirs*. See also Wark, *The Ultimate Enemy*, 95–6.

[169] Liddell Hart's paramount role as the spirit behind Hore-Belisha and as kingmaker is amazingly revealed in his files: King's, 11/1937/96 ff., 11/HB 1937–8; partly printed in *Memoirs*, ii. 62–74.

To use an analogy which Liddell Hart would have appreciated, it was a repetition in reverse of the famous 1911 Michel affair within the French high command: the head of the army, who foresaw the outline of the German attack in the approaching war, was removed by the civilian minister of war, supported by the 'Young Turks' in the army who had little faith in their chief. While in France this affair had been largely caused by, and had led to the victory of, the spirit of the *offensive à outrance*, in Britain it was prompted by what one of his contemporaries aptly dabbed Liddell Hart's doctrine of the *défense à outrance*.[170]

Défense à outrance

The supremacy of the defence and its relation to the doctrines of collective security and limited liability were vital to Liddell Hart's approach to the security of France and of her East European allies. The ideas that Britain need not send an expeditionary force to the Continent (or send at most a small mechanized force); that France could hold her own against Germany, but that no major offensive against Germany in the West was possible even if France were reinforced by the British; and that, given Soviet support, Czechoslovakia could resist the Germans for a very long time—were all closely interdependent and largely based upon the power of the defence.[171]

Hence Liddell Hart's strategic position throughout the Czechoslovakian crisis of 1938. It was a strategy similar to the one Churchill had proposed in his *World Crisis* for the First World War. The Western Allies should remain in defence, refrain from large-scale, murderous, 'Passchendaele' offensives in the West, and confine themselves to limited selective attacks. This would suffice to pin down large German forces and ease the pressure on the Western powers' East European allies. Germany would be defeated in the long run by the strength of economic blockade.[172] As with Churchill's original proposal, scholars have pointed out, the trouble with this strategic scheme was that Germany was not going to be distracted from her target in the East by limited, mainly demonstrative Allied offensives in the West. Germany planned an overwhelming concentration against Czechoslovakia,

[170] Cited by Mearsheimer, *LH*, 118.

[171] See most strikingly in Liddell Hart's paper on 'The Military Situation in Europe', given at the Staff College in Dec. 1937; printed in *The Defence of Britain*, esp. 55, 57, 59–60.

[172] *The Times*, 17 June 1938; 'Military and Strategic Advantages of Collective Security in Europe', *New Commonwealth Quarterly* (Sept. 1938), 147–52; Notes 9 and 28, Sept. 1938: King's, 11/1938/92, 103; *The Defence of Britain*, 74–6, 86–7.

leaving only a small fraction of her forces on the French frontier. Especially if one believed, as Liddell Hart did, that Czechoslovakia was able to hold out for a very long time, thus allowing the Western Allies (France in particular) time to mobilize, it was inescapable that the Allies should have launched large-scale offensives against Germany in the West in order to divert her from her prey in the East and keep her forces divided. Given the German forces' weakness in the West in 1938, these attacks were in fact not without prospects of success. A pure double-defensive strategy against an enemy like Germany, who was expected to utilize very aggressively the interior lines in order to gain overwhelming concentrations on one front at a time and defeat each of its enemies separately, was an unpractical notion for the Allies.[173]

While being much less hopeful over the defence of Poland, Liddell Hart's basic strategic scheme during the Polish crisis changed only slightly from the one he had espoused during the Czechoslovakian crisis. He recognized very well that Poland could not hold her own in the defence against Germany, but continued to object to more than limited Allied offensives against the Siegfried Line.[174] Now, if the Soviet Union were to participate in the war against Germany, as Liddell Hart expected as a *sine qua non* until the signing of the Soviet–German pact in late August 1939, this was again an impractical strategy for the Allies, and for the same reasons. But if the Soviet Union could not be counted as an ally, as became clear after the signing of the Soviet–German pact, there was probably no other strategy for the West. In the first place, both the German army as a whole and the German forces on the French border (Army Group C) had practically doubled since 1938. Secondly, Germany was likely to overrun Poland much too quickly for the Western Allies to be allowed the time to mobilize and carry out large-scale offensives before German forces could be brought back westward.

During these years the fear that the French might take the offensive and drag the British along with them and into a massive Continental commitment was paramount in Liddell Hart's mind.[175] As the war approached, he grew increasingly alarmed about this, insisting that only the offensive could lose the war for the Allies. After the defection

[173] See e.g. Liddell Hart, *The Defence of Britain*, 78–9; for Mearsheimer's just criticism, see *LH*, 139–41.

[174] 'Gamelin', *Life Magazine*, 20 Feb. 1939, 63; *The Defence of Britain*, 209.

[175] See e.g. 'The Defence of the Empire', *Fortnightly Review* (Jan. 1938), 27–9; *The Times*, 17 Sept. 1938; *The Defence of Britain*, 209–10.

of the Soviet Union, the Allies were indeed incapable of attacking in the West; and their high commands recognized this very well and acted accordingly during the period known as the 'Phoney War'. But every rumour from general headquarters inflamed Liddell Hart's suspicions that offensive schemes were being entertained.[176]

In May–June 1940, within six weeks, the Low Countries and France fell before a lightning German campaign. Liddell Hart was as surprised as anybody. As his biographers have already revealed and contrary to what he himself claimed, he had not foreseen even the possibility of a German victory. Quite the reverse: for years he had been insisting that France was virtually secure from a German attack. Two of the major doctrines he had been advocating now appeared in a disastrous light. First, his insistent claim that the strength of modern defence was paramount and was continuing to grow was revealed to be fallacious. As Mearsheimer has shown, in later years Liddell Hart would do his utmost to eradicate this central and unhappy idea of his from historical memory, often by unscrupulous means.[177] His *Memoirs* barely mention it. Secondly, limited liability, of which Liddell Hart had been one of the chief exponents, now appeared to have been totally misguided and irresponsible. More than a decade before the fall of France, Germains had articulated ideas common among many army officers:

> 'A National Force, maintained at a high standard of efficiency, can only be produced by the works of years' . . . if we do not [take this to heart], and whether we have mechanized armies or not . . . we shall be very lucky indeed if the next war produces only Sommes and Paschendaeles, and not a swift and overwhelming defeat.[178]

Similarly, in January 1936 Colonel Henry Pownell of the secretariat of the Committee of Imperial Defence wrote in his diary against the advocates of limited liability:

[176] 'The Need for a New Technique', repr. in *The Current of War*, 152; cf. Roosevelt's phrase, n. 138 above and related text. Liddell Hart repeatedly wrote about Gamelin in very favourable terms: 'Gamelin', 56–63; *Sunday Express*, 29 Oct. 1939 and 18 Feb. 1940; *The Current of War*, 205, 209; Mearsheimer, *LH*, 124. His unfavourable testimony in *Memoirs*, ii. 18, tilts the original record. It might be noted, however, that before the war Gamelin was highly regarded by both the British and the Germans.

[177] *LH*, esp. 179–81, 216–17.

[178] *The 'Mechanization' of War*, 249–50. Cf. Montgomery-Massingberd's bitter charges against Liddell Hart shortly before Germany attacked in the West: 29 Apr. 1940, King's, 6/1940/5, 11/1940/29.

if war with Germany comes again (whether by Collective Security, Locarno or any other way) we shall again be fighting for our lives. Our effort must be the maximum, by land, sea and air. We cannot say our contribution would be 'so and so' and no more, because we cannot lose the war without extinction of the Empire. The idea of the 'half hearted' war is the most pernicious and dangerous in the world. It will be 100 per cent—and even then we may lose it.[179]

The nightmare of the 'Westerners' in the British strategic debate during the era of the two world wars, which had almost been realized during Ludendorff's spring offensives in 1918, came true. The security of France and of the Low Countries was simply too vital for Britain to risk on 'a too fine calculation'. Liddell Hart could reasonably claim that building a strong army for Europe had in any case been beyond Britain's economic capability, and that everything had changed and containment had broken down with Munich and with the rejection of Soviet cooperation. All the same, as with the even more promising Japanese case the year after, the policy of containment, economic coercion, and cold war floundered when the enemy did the unthinkable and in a highly successful lightning campaign broke down the walls built up against him. In his meeting with Daladier on 28–29 April 1938, Chamberlain justified limited liability by claiming that the power of the defensive in warfare had increased with modern methods and modern weapons: forms of attack previously thought of as irresistible, he argued, could now be met with a sufficiently organized defence. The official British historian who cites this wonders where Chamberlain found the inspiration for these views. But the answer to this, given the wording as well as the content of Chamberlain's argument, should not be too difficult to find.[180] Responsibility for the collapse of France could at least partly be laid at Liddell Hart's door. Consequently, his prestige suffered heavily, and justly. Apart from anything else, he was made to look silly.[181]

It must have been an awful feeling for Liddell Hart, and his first apologetic efforts in his early wartime books to explain France 1940—and the later Blitzkrieg victories—often read rather patheti-

[179] B. Bond (ed.), *Chief of Staff: The Diaries of Lieutenant-General Sir Henry Pownell* (London, 1972), 99.

[180] Gibbs, *Grand Strategy*, i. 637. Similarly, at the beginning of the war Chamberlain maintained that it was necessary to remain firm until the Germans saw the obvious—that in modern war the defensive side had the advantage; cited by Charmley, *Chamberlain*, 210.

[181] His painstaking efforts to save face are documented in sect. 6 of his papers; a selection can be found in Mearsheimer, *LH*, 152–4.

cally.[182] He argued, for example, that he had been obliged to conceal his real views about the Allies' weakness in order not to assist the enemy, and that he had developed his preference for the defensive before the war because he had known that the Allies possessed no real offensive weapon in the form of large mechanized forces. In truth, however, Liddell Hart favoured a defensive posture for the West predominantly because of what he regarded to be its ultimate political aims, and in order to deter and limit war; only then did he increasingly convince himself that the defensive was tactically and operationally becoming ever stronger. Also, while he did claim (justly) that Britain lacked armoured forces suited for the offensive, this was mainly a contributing factor to his argument.[183] He did not believe the offensive would work for the Germans either.

Despite his continued criticism of many aspects of the mechanization of the British army, Liddell Hart in fact was generally much encouraged by the process finally set in motion in the British and French armies as they rearmed in the late 1930s[184] He found reassurance in the growth in the number of French mobile formations and in the quality of the French newest tank models; and this was partly, but not wholly, due to his desire to create a favourable impression of the French ability to confront the Germans without the support of a substantial British army. He was fully informed of the British intelligence reports which throughout the period portrayed a fairly good picture of the strength, structure, and doctrine of the tank formations of the main antagonists. Before the war he accurately informed his readers that while the Germans possessed more armoured divisions than the French, the French had more and heavier tanks with their infantry.[185] The belief that by the 1940 campaign the Germans had managed to achieve overwhelming numerical superiority in tanks over the Allies was widely held just before and immediately after the German victory, and Liddell Hart

[182] For his 'apologia', see mainly his *Dynamic Defence* (London, 1940), 12–41, 57–64; *The Current of War*, 15–125, 193–4, 208–9, 214, 316, 320–2, 328–9, 337–8; *The Revolution in Warfare* (London, 1946), 15–16, 28–9; *The Defence of the West* (London, 1950), 3–11; *Memoirs*, ii. 28, 242–4, 280–1.

[183] *Europe in Arms*, 116–40; *The Times*, 25 Oct. 1937; also 2 Nov. 1936.

[184] In view of that development, he did not even strongly object to the mechanization of the cavalry, adopted in both Britain and France (and Germany) alongside the expansion of the armour corps. More surprisingly, during that period he also did not take a stand against the design and acquisition of special 'infantry tanks' by both the French and British armies; *Europe in Arms*, 122–3, 228.

[185] *The Times*, 23 Dec. 1935, 19 July 1938; *Fortnightly Review* (Jan. 1938), 26–7; *Life*, 20 Feb. 1939, 62; *Europe in Arms*, 43–4, 49–51; also Mearsheimer, *LH*, 122–3.

used it to excuse himself in his wartime writings. But by the end of the war it became clear that the earlier estimates had been all too accurate, and that it was in fact the Allies who held the superiority in tank numbers in May 1940, as well as enjoying rough parity in tank quality.[186]

So we turn to armoured doctrine. After 1940 Liddell Hart stressed that the Germans had applied the doctrine of armoured warfare which Fuller, himself, and the other British armour pioneers had evolved. Contrary to misconceptions which have recently gained the ascendancy in Anglo-American historiography, this was quite true.[187] However, was not this fact much depreciated by Liddell Hart's loss of faith in the late 1930s in sweeping armoured offensives? Here too the answer is much more intriguing than recent critics of Liddell Hart have allowed.

Mechanized Defence in Depth

It ought to be made clear that Liddell Hart's advocacy of the strength of defence by no means involved a withdrawal from the idea of armoured warfare. The battlefield and the sort of defence he foresaw before the war was markedly modern. It was dominated by mobile mechanized forces working closely with aircraft, but also by the anti-tank gun and other anti-tank measures which would be engaged in a constant struggle for supremacy with the tank.[188] So long as they survived, traditional foot and horse-drawn troops would be relegated to a secondary and subsidiary role, except on special ground. The defence itself would take the form of mobile defence in depth, in which armoured and mechanized divisions, stationed in the defender's rear, would counter-strike to check and destroy large-scale penetrations by the enemy's mechanized formations.

A prevailing impression regarding the German 'Blitzkrieg method' is that it came as an almost total surprise to the Allies. This was not at all the case. Throughout the late 1930s the Allies' intelligence services and high commands had possessed a good picture not only of the strength and composition of the Panzer troops but also of their doctrine and intended method of employment. The old French fear of a German *attaque brusquée*, now to be carried out with armoured and mechanized

[186] In Mar. 1940, while correctly assessing the number of German mobile divisions, Allied intelligence estimated the German tank force at 5,800–7,500, two to three times the actual number: F. H. Hinsley, *British Intelligence in the Second World War*, i (London, 1979), 134. But see e.g. Guderian to LH, 14 Dec. 1948: King's, 9/24/62.

[187] Gat, *British Armour Theory and the Rise of the Panzer Arm.*

[188] See e.g. Liddell Hart, *The Times*, 21 May 1937.

divisions which, without prior warning, would overrun the French defensive lines, penetrate deep into the country, and disrupt the French mobilization, was paramount in the Allies' strategic considerations and was widely discussed.[189] Gort's comment to Liddell Hart was prophetic but not entirely uncommon:

> May it not be possible for Panzer divisions and concentrated air forces to effect a breach and this attack can take place with little previous warning? If by rapidity, deception and surprise it is possible to make a bridgehead then the war will pass into open country once more. I feel novelty lies in some such direction as this as Belgium is hackneyed.[190]

To this, and to Deverell's similar suggestion in a conversation with Liddell Hart, the latter replied that the chances for such breakthroughs were doubtful and that modern and mobile defence, integrating armoured forces for counter-offensives, was likely to prove more effective.[191]

In the years 1935–7 Liddell Hart further developed his doctrine of large-scale armoured breakthroughs, which remarkably anticipated the outline of future 'Blitzkrieg' and which, indeed, profoundly influenced the creators of the Panzer arm.[192] However, while foreseeing amazingly accurately the prospects of such offensives, he also foresaw their limitations. Time and again during those years he concluded his scheme of how deep armoured breakthroughs might be achieved with the following qualifying remarks:

> it would be necessary to follow up the strokes [of the armoured forces] with reinforcements and occupying forces. Here would lie the invader's hardest problem . . . It is conceivable that an attacker by extraordinary foresight, by gauging the trend of developments exactly, and by perfectly calculated measures to diminish his own vulnerability while maintaining his strength, might succeed in producing the internal collapse of his adversary without courting his own—but such foresight has never been shown by any makers of war.[193]

[189] See e.g. Liddell Hart, *Europe in Arms*, 27–8, 48; *The Defence of Britain*, 101. For the British picture of German armour, see Wark, *The Ultimate Enemy*, 93–101. For the French, see R. Young, 'French Military Intelligence and Nazi Germany, 1938–1939', in E. R. May (ed.), *Knowing One's Enemies: Intelligence Assessment before the Two World Wars* (Princeton, NJ, 1984), 288–9.

[190] Gort's comments on LH's 'Defence or Attack', 6 Nov. 1937, King's, 11/1937/73.

[191] Conversation with Deverell, 29 June 1937, King's, 11/1937/56; Macleod and Kelly *The Ironside Diaries*, 38.

[192] See my *British Armour Theory and the Rise of the Panzer Arm*, 1–18, esp. 12, and *passim*.

[193] 'The Next Big War', *Listener*, 15 Mar. 1936.

> There is little doubt that the new mechanized divisions which the European armies now possess will be used in the first hours of war with the aim of penetrating the enemy's frontier and opening the way for the subsequent general advance . . . But there is reason to doubt whether this mechanized spearhead will produce the decisive advantage which is sought. The chances are against this, unless the enemy is not only taken unaware but is himself unmechanized.

The main problem would be deliberate obstruction and counterattacks by mechanized forces brought forward against the threat.[194] Finally,

> The general deduction that the defensive has a great and growing superiority does not, of course, imply that the offensive can never succeed. It is likely to succeed, as already noted, in a campaign where the defender has no effective counter-weapons to nullify such offensive instruments such as aircraft and tanks. It may possibly succeed against an opponent of similar equipment if the attacker displays a great superiority of art, and thereby produces a great local superiority of fire and psychological threat.[195]

Anyone familiar with the theme of 'the rise and fall of Blitzkrieg' during the Second World War cannot fail to be impressed by these insights. For Liddell Hart France 1940 was an accident, albeit a terrible and fateful one. During the second half of the 1930s he consistently emphasized the role of armoured formations which would be kept in the rear for counterattacks against enemy armoured penetrations within a modern system of mobile defence in depth.[196] For Liddell Hart this was the story of the 'expanding torrent' versus the 'contracting funnel' of the later stage and immediate aftermath of the First World War all over again, only by means of mechanized rather than infantry forces and, consequently, on a wider scale and at a much quicker pace. While valuing the Maginot Line, he pointed out that it was intended mainly as

[194] *Atlantic Monthly* (Dec. 1936), 693; similar ideas in 'Future Warfare', *English Review* (May 1937), 529–43, and 'The Defence of the Empire', *Fortnightly Review* (Jan. 1938), 19–30.

[195] *The Times*, 25 Oct. 1937; this extract is repr. in *The Defence of Britain*, 105. None of the above passages is cited by Mearsheimer; after conceding that, defensively employed, the tank 'can thwart a blitzkrieg', he writes that in Liddell Hart's 'pieces on the strength of the defense, especially those written in the late 1930s, he failed to discuss the significant offensive potential of the tank when a defender does not understand how to employ tanks on the battlefield (i.e. he fails to emphasize that a blitzkrieg was possible under certain circumstances)': Mearsheimer, *LH*, 113–14.

[196] The Soviets developed the same idea far more systematically in their 1936 Field Service Regulations, and it was also well recognized by the Germans; see Simpkin, *Deep Battle*, 47–8, 172–3; Ritter von Leeb, *Defence* (Harrisburg, Penn., 1943; originally in *Militärwissenschaftliche Rundschau, 1936–7*), 109–10.

a covering and delaying line against a sudden German attack and would require strong mobile reserves behind it. This was precisely the role he persistently advocated for the British armoured formations in conjunction with the French mobile divisions.[197]

France and Belgium

Indeed, as recent research has shown, this was also the role the French themselves envisaged in the second half of the 1930s for their new heavy armoured divisions (DCR: *Division Cuirassée de Réserve*), which were to be reinforced by a British armoured contribution and further supported by the French cavalry-type armoured divisions (DLM: *Division Légère Mécanique*) and motorized infantry divisions. Serious attention was given in France during those years to operational planning for mobile defence in depth. To be sure, French tank production was lagging, and the British armoured contribution failed to be ready in time for the Battle of France. Nevertheless, by the time of that battle, the French had been hastily creating their third and beginning to create their fourth DCR, which, as their title indicates, were specifically intended for the counter-offensive role against the Panzer divisions and destined for deployment as a strong mobile reserve in the area of Laon, Rheims, and Châlons-sur-Marne, at the centre of the French line. While these heavy formations were still inexperienced and suffered from many deficiencies, the three DLMs, although also inferior to the all-round combat concept of the German Panzer divisions, were well trained and incorporated the new and excellent SOMUA medium tanks. Finally, the seven French motorized divisions in fact slightly outnumbered their German counterparts.[198] Although the doctrine of the French army during the interwar period negated the idea of a mobile battle of manœuvre, the chances of these mobile formations to check German armoured penetrations were not altogether unfavourable, had not things turned out so badly for the Allies.

For the Allies' collapse in the West in 1940 was not predestined, but

[197] *The Times*, 30 Oct. 1936; 'The Defence of the Empire', *Fortnightly Review*, Jan. 1938, 24–9; *Europe in Arms*, 27–8, 47–8; *The Defence of Britain*, 55, 60, 104–5, 210, 307, 376–81.

[198] See H. Dutailly, *Les Problèmes de l'armée de terre française (1935–1939)* (Paris, 1980), 141–59, 314–37; M. Alexander, *The Republic in Danger: General Maurice Gamelin and the Politics of French Defence, 1933–1940* (Cambridge, 1992), 201–2; R. A. Doughty, *The Seeds of Disaster: The Development of French Army Doctrine, 1919–1939* (Hamden, Conn. 1985), 161–77. Liddell Hart was well informed about these developments at the time: *Europe in Arms*, 43–4.

involved a strong element of chance. Until the beginning of 1940 the Germans had planned a fairly conventional and limited advance into Holland and Belgium, spearheaded by their armoured and mechanized divisions. To this the Allies intended to respond by an advance into Belgium, led by their own mobile troops, either to the line of the River Scheldt (Plan E) or, more ambitiously, to the line of the River Dyle (Plan D). Both Liddell Hart and Fuller pointed out at the time that a campaign in the West would be an entirely different ball game from that experienced by the Germans in Poland. Belgian and Dutch territory was cut by rivers and water channels, posing great difficulty for mechanized forces, and in addition the Germans would face adversaries with modern equipment.[199] Senior German officers held the same view. In Halder's opinion: 'Techniques of Polish campaign no recipe for the West. No good against a well-knit army.' According to General Leeb, also rejecting the Polish comparison, 'the high value of the French army and its leadership must not be underrated and the equipment with armoured units and anti-tank weapons of the French and English armies must not be forgotten'.[200]

It was only during February–April 1940 that both sides changed their plans. The Germans adopted Manstein's plan, which switched their main offensive trust, including most of their mobile divisions, southwards to the Ardennes region. Almost simultaneously the Allies, still expecting the main offensive to come from the north, adopted an even more ambitious version of the Dale plan, incorporating the so-called Breda extension. The plan envisaged a rapid deep advance into Holland by the Allies' extreme left, diverting the cream of the French mobile divisions (and the semi-mobile British Expeditionary Force) westward. Only after that advance had been completed were these divisions planned to be withdrawn once more to the role of strategic reserve.[201] In view of the new German plans, the Allies' order of battle was thrown disastrously out of balance. Not only were the Allies' best troops deployed in the wrong direction, but their mobile strategic reserve was left dangerously weak. Despite desperate efforts, this situation

[199] For Fuller, see his 'Tanks Won't Do Much', *War Weekly*, 19 Nov. 1939, King's, 11/1939/146; for Liddell Hart, see e.g. *The Defence of Britain*, 55–60, and 11 May 1940, repr. in *The Current of War*, 301.

[200] Quoted by Mearsheimer, *Conventional Deterrence*, 102, 108.

[201] The best analysis of the Allies' strategic considerations is J. A. Gunsburg, *Divided and Conquered: The French High Command and the Defeat of the West, 1940* (London, 1979).

proved impossible to remedy when the full significance of the German breakthrough in the Ardennes became clear. Consequently, the German mechanized forces were only haphazardly and sporadically opposed during their breakthrough and race to the Channel. The conditions which Liddell Hart had specified for the complete success of a lightening mechanized campaign, and had regarded as exceptional, were disastrously realized.

Thus in his efforts to excuse himself after 1940 Liddell Hart argued that the fall of France had not been inevitable but had been caused by extraordinary strategic blunders on the part of the Allies' high command. In the immediate aftermath of the defeat, he himself wavered on the exact line the Allies should have taken.[202] But on the main issue, the French total neglect of the Ardennes, which had been traditionally regarded as unsuitable for the operations of large formations,[203] Liddell Hart possessed a good personal record upon which to base his criticism. For after travelling through the Ardennes in 1928 he came to the conclusion that, contrary to Allied perceptions in 1918, this region was not unsuitable for the movement of large formations, a point he repeated in the following decade in his successive books on the First World War.[204] In May 1936, after the German occupation of the Rhine demilitarized zone and more than a year before Gort would suggest to him the possibility of a German armoured breakthrough in a sector different from the traditional Belgian route, Liddell Hart had a talk (which he recorded at the time) with Ronald Adam and Col. Bernard Paget:

> I remarked that there was still a danger interval before the new Belgian defence were completed, or those of the French along the German frontier. I suggested that we ought not overlook the possibility that if the French took the offensive, the Germans while meeting them defensively, would launch a

[202] See initially, LH, *The Defence of Britain*, 216–19; then, *Dynamic Defence* (London, 1940), 18; *The Current of War*, 209, 316, 337; finally, 'Could the 1940 Collapse in the West Have Been Averted?', *Sunday Pictorial*, 28 Sept. 1947; repr. in *The Defence of the West*, 3–19; and as an Introduction to A. Goutard, *1940: The Battle of France* (London, 1958).

[203] Although recent research has done much to show logic behind the Allies' plans, it reaffirms that they (and Gamelin in particular) totally blundered regarding the Ardennes: R. J. Young, *In Command of France: French Foreign Policy and Military Planning, 1933–1940* (Cambridge, Mass., 1978), 169; Umbreit's contribution to MF *Germany in the Second World War*, ii. 271; C. Paillat, *Le Désastre de 1940*, i (Paris, 1983), 191–6; Alexander, *Gamelin*, 199–200.

[204] *The Decisive Wars of History* (London, 1929), 225; similarly, see *The Real War* (London, 1930), 461; *Foch* (London, 1931), 383; *A History of the First World War* (London, 1934), 577.

flank counter-stroke through Belgian Luxembourg with their 3 Mechanized divisions [*then in existence*].

Paget said that the chances were that the Belgians would have sufficient time to man their fortifications, but Liddell Hart replied that the Germans might attack by surprise.[205]

These various observations, made in different contexts, do not imply that Liddell Hart in any way 'predicted' the route the Germans would choose in 1940. He did not. No one, including the Germans, did or could have. They simply demonstrate that Liddell Hart had been clearly and more than most aware of the passibility of the Ardennes for large formations, including modern mechanized ones; and it was largely on this awareness that the campaign in the West in 1940 hinged, and was lost. In 1939 Liddell Hart's comprehensive and carefully weighed survey of the various strategic options open to the antagonists on the Western Front was on the whole optimistic about the prospects of the defence in the Ardennes sector, assuming the right measures would be adopted. The region, he wrote,

> might prove a strategic trap for an invader if he fails to cross the Meuse. . . . For the Belgians, the obvious plan of defence is to make sure of holding the Meuse moat, together with the Liège bridge-head beyond it, while utilizing the Ardennes as a spring-buffer to absorb the shock of any hostile advance which come through that way. The Ardennes offer such a series of fine defensive positions that it would be desirable to employ here sufficient forces to develop the full delaying power of this vast obstacle. It is difficult, however, for the Belgians to do so from their own resources without jeopardizing their main position on the Meuse. Moreover, they have to reckon with the possibility of having to meet danger from a new direction, where they are more vulnerable—on their Dutch flank. . . . The full development of the potentialities of the Ardennes as an obstacle thus depends on whether, and how soon, the limited Belgian forces here can be reinforced by those of a guarantor Power. During a recent tour . . . it was revealing to find how immensely strong by nature were the series of positions—the gorge of the Semois, the heights north of Sedan, and the Meuse—upon which the French might have stood [in 1914], yet which in the event they so swiftly abandoned.[206]

The concept in itself was impeccable, and in step with the ideas Liddell Hart had been developing in the second half of the 1930s regarding flexible defence in depth. Lacking the benefit of hindsight,

[205] 15 May 1936: King's, 11/1936/64; cited by Bond, *LH*, 101, 232–3, but not by Mearsheimer, *LH*, 182–3.

[206] *The Defence of Britain*, 217–19.

it kept all the options open. Given the uncertainty regarding the direction of the German main offensive effort, and especially the possibility of a German turning movement through Dutch territory, Liddell Hart saw the Ardennes as a scene of a delaying manœuvre on the Allies' part. Relying on the topographical features of that region, field fortifications, field forces, and wide-scale obstruction should be used to delay enemy columns long enough for the Allies to take up their main fortified line of defence along the heights overlooking the Meuse and deploy their mechanized reserves behind it. The attacking spearheads would then find themselves in an awkward position, experiencing logistic problems and having limited room for deployment and mutual support.

This assessment of the situation, made the year before the war, underpinned Liddell Hart's reactions when the German offensive in the West was launched on 10 May 1940. On the 11th he noted that the German advance through Holland, upon which all eyes in the Western camp were fixed, had been expected, but also pointed out that it might be a diversion. Two days later, before the German thrust through the Ardennes became publicly known and the centre of attention, his overall survey of the front again mentioned the Ardennes as a scene for delaying action. On the 15th, as the Ardennes offensive and the German crossing of the Meuse became known, Liddell Hart wrote that the attack had been expected, but that now that the Germans had reached Sedan the situation had become serious. He maintained, however, that French armour was designed specifically to meet such a German breakthrough, and even on the 19th, when all was lost, argued that the danger must not be exaggerated, for the German armoured penetration would hopefully lose its momentum. At the beginning of June he was still hoping for Allied counter-offensives which would stop the Germans as in 1918, and only on the 6th he finally resigned himself to the idea that the armour required for counter-attacking was simply not in place.[207]

Wholly concentrating on the Dutch and Flanders routes, the Allied high command left the Ardennes covered by only thirteen, mostly second- and third-class divisions. These forces were not designed to push strong delaying forces into the Ardennes, and were incapable of it. When the German Army Group A, totalling forty-four divisions, including seven Panzer and three motorized, and massively supported by the Luftwaffe, rolled into the Ardennes, the French were only able to

[207] Repr. in *The Current of War*, 299–300, 304, 309–10, 315–17, 338–44.

push in one horse cavalry division and several infantry battalions. Thus, even though the Belgian delaying forces performed quite effectively, especially on 10 May, the German mechanized spearheads encountered little opposition and no wide-scale obstruction. By the end of 13 May the Germans had begun to cross the Meuse, which the weak French forces in the area again proved incapable of holding. Since the French high command was slow to realize what was happening, the battle by then was practically lost.[208]

The Fall of 'Blitzkrieg'

So what does all this prove, first, in respect to Liddell Hart's ideas on defence? There is no doubt that his overriding concern during the 1930s to prevent the eruption of a new total war and lay down the ground rules for a limited strategic response to the Nazi challenge biased his judgement, most notably regarding the superiority of the defensive. He was all too eager to seize on new developments which were only beginning to take shape, such as the Allies' acquisition of tanks and anti-tank guns and creation of mobile formations, as if they were already a reality, rather than an incomplete and greatly deficient process. In addition, although the battlefield he foresaw was dominated by modern mobile forces rather than by the traditional arms of the First World War, he portrayed it all too frequently, if not as static, then at least as frozen in the operational sense as the battlefields of the Western Front in the previous war. On this he probably exaggerated, even in the long run. Nevertheless, viewed from a more distant perspective, was he on the whole that wrong, or mainly over-hasty?

As Liddell Hart would repeatedly point out for the rest of his life, by the second half of the Second World War all armies had learnt how to contend with armoured breakthroughs and had developed the techniques and the means for blunting them. These, he would claim, were the techniques of mobile defence in depth which he had advanced in the second half of the 1930s. By 1942, both in Russia and in North Africa, such techniques put an end to the spectacular spate of 'Blitzkrieg' successes. Thereafter, in Italy, Western Europe and the Eastern Front

[208] On the whole operation, see R. A. Doughty, *The Breaking Point: Sedan and the Fall of France, 1940* (Hamden, Conn., 1990). For the Belgian and French reading of German intentions regarding the Ardennes, see Bond, *France and Belgium, 1939–1940* (London, 1975), 60–1, 64–5, 76–7, 78–80; F. H. Hinsley, *British Intelligence in the Second World War*, i. (London, 1979) 129–36; Paillat, *1940*, ii (Paris, 1984), 299–354; Doughty, *The Breaking Point*, 73–7.

the war again became a gigantic struggle of attrition. Offensive operational success was now only achieved under conditions of overwhelming superiority in *matériel*, the very conditions Liddell Hart in his prewar writings had insisted would be required. More remarkably, he did not make this argument of self-justification retrospectively but in fact advanced it well before the event. In late 1940, after the dramatic fall of France and *prior* to the occurrence of even one instance of a successful defence in depth against mechanized forces, Liddell Hart wrote in *Dynamic Defence*, referring of course to himself:

> the knowledge gained in developing the new offensive technique led to the discovery of an effective counter-technique. But it had taken fully ten years to gain official acceptance for the former, and even then in a half-hearted way. So it was perhaps too much to expect that the antidote could have been approved and prepared in time, unless the war had been postponed until 1945!

He repeated his forecasts from the preceding years:

> While it is axiomatic that the attacker enjoys the advantage of the initiative, it may not carry him far save where he is met by slow-moving forces. The advantage is likely to be short-lived if the defender disposes of adequate mechanized forces. The advance of the attacker's armoured units through the defence, if they are in depth, is likely to be slower than the bringing up of the defender's armoured units along unobtrusive roads, or across country that they know. On arrival they can strike the attacker's armoured force at the moment when it is likely to be somewhat disorganized by its fighting advance.

This would be 'a reversed form of "soft spot" tactics', supplementing 'gradually contracting funnels' of defensive dispositions, in which 'the lanes would now be hedged with anti-tanks guns'.[209]

So if one were to take a very favourable view of the development of Liddell Hart's ideas, one could suggest that, rather than being—like the proverbial generals—always ready for the last war, he was consistently one war ahead in his thought: in the 1920s he anticipated the sweeping mechanized offensives of 1939–42; in the second half of the 1930s he was looking ahead to the curbing of 'Blitzkrieg' in 1942–5; and from the late 1930s he was calling for a strategy and policy of containment and cold war. But then, even if we were to present Liddell Hart's views in

[209] *Dynamic Defence*, 26, 52–4; see also his opinions *at the time* regarding the Soviet Union's prospects of defence in June 1941 and regarding the Western Desert, where he was interestedly following Rommel's use of anti-tank guns and defensive tactics within an offensive strategy: *This Expanding War* (London, 1942), 72–3, 138–40; *The Revolution in Warfare*, 15–23, 29; *The Rommel Papers* (London, 1953), 451–60; *Memoirs*, ii. 281.

this very favourable manner, how practical were these subsequent sets of ideas *in and for their times*? Was the vision of wide-ranging armoured warfare, developed in the 1920s, readily applicable? In many crucial respects—strategic, economic, and technological—it was not; yet it was meant as a programme for future development. Could 'Blitzkrieg' have been checked in the early stage of the Second World War? In France and the Low Countries in 1940 it was not, but perhaps it might have been, had Allied preparations been somewhat better focused or had their strategic conduct been less unfortunate. Finally, and most intriguingly, could containment have worked in the late 1930s, and cold war in the early 1940s? Some of the arguments relevant to these questions have been widely discussed by historians in different contexts, and speculation here is best cut as short as possible.

Containment in the 1930s: Conclusion

In hindsight it is clear that a diplomatic and strategic Great Power coalition against Germany was, as it were, the order of the day in the late 1930s if Germany were to be stopped. Whether under the mantle of 'collective security' or more soundly in accordance with the older principle of the 'balance of power', this was simply a vital interest of Britain, France, and the Soviet Union, backed by a favourably neutral United States. Whether the Western powers and the Soviet Union could really cooperate with one another on a sustained basis is an open question. A policy of 'Grand Alliance', no less than the alternative one of appeasement was full of uncertainties, risks, and pitfalls. Assuming that the West would have been willing to cooperate, Stalin's USSR was a notoriously difficult client. On the other hand, it feared being isolated *vis-à-vis* Hitler's Germany more than anything and anyone. A Grand Alliance, had it existed, would in the first place have had a great deterrence value, either for Hitler himself or for other power brokers in Germany who might have stopped him at an early stage and even short of war. This was the outlook Liddell Hart shared with more prominent public figures, such as Eden, Lloyd George, and Churchill. The opinion of one historian of the period, dwelling on the same problem in no relation to Liddell Hart, is interesting: 'The Eden–Baldwin policy, if it had been continued after 1936, might have advanced through deterrence the sort of stalemate created since the 1950s by nuclear stockpiles.'[210] Within a grand strategy

[210] Middlemas, *Diplomacy of Illusion*, 454.

of containment against the Axis powers, there was then much scope for the means Liddell Hart was striving to develop: economic pressure, supply of arms to small allies, war by proxy, naval isolation of outlying theatres of war, and limited war.

If deterrence against major war had failed, a coalition of West and East would have been even more necessary for stopping Germany. This coalition could not, however, have worked strictly on the basis of a pure 'double-defensive' strategy, a defence on both fronts, as Liddell Hart advocated. Active cooperation between the Allies in the East and West would have been essential both politically and strategically if Germany were not to defeat its enemies separately. On this point Liddell Hart's First World War trauma and ideas regarding the superiority of the defence led him seriously astray. However, assuming that Germany was contained in her 1938 or even 1939 frontiers, which would have left her ecenomically choked. Could the war then have been significantly limited and destruction and self-exhaustion decreased by burden-sharing between the Allies, and by the pursuit of a fundamentally defensive policy on their part which would have restricted their war aim to the termination of hostilities on the basis of the *status quo ante*, with or preferably without Hitler? On the face of it this is not inconceivable. But there is really no point in pursuing the 'ifs' any further.

The problems become all the more involved when considering Liddell Hart's position in favour of a cold war against Germany once the Soviet–German pact had abolished, at least for a time, the idea of a Grand Alliance and had made the Allies' prospects in a war against Germany strategically dubious. After the fall of France, this again was the option Liddell Hart was to advocate for Britain. During the Second World War he would be relegated to the wilderness as far as his official and public standing was concerned, not only because he was largely discredited by the fall of France but mainly because he would pose as an out-and-out opponent of Churchill's policy of total war against Germany.

5

Policy: Defence of the West (II): Cold War–Hot War

I. The Second World War

Liddell Hart's opposition to Britain's war policy during the Second World War relegated him to the wilderness. He still had many connections in the army, and a few high-ranking officers like Tim Pile and Percy Hobart (themselves unpopular) remained loyal to their old friendship. He still travelled extensively to visit army units and manœuvres. But the war office and the general staff, now largely occupied by his contemporaries and former friends, were closed to him, as was Whitehall. His collaboration with Churchill during the Munich crisis was over. Most of his previous political connections had been serving in Churchill's government and following his direction of the war. Eden was now politely acknowledging receipt of Liddell Hart's memoranda but nothing more. Their relationship ended for good. Hugh Dalton was minister of economic warfare and Archibald Sinclair was secretary of state for the air, both supervising policies which Liddell Hart criticized sharply. The only man in the cabinet who gave him any attention at all, and it too was not excessive, was the former isolationist Beaverbrook. Outside government during 1940 Lloyd George was preparing his return to the premiership to save the nation once Churchill's war policy had failed. When this did not happen, Lloyd George's star was rapidly eclipsed.

Thus Liddell Hart, who only shortly before had been well connected in government, adviser to all political parties, 'kingmaker' in the war office, and Britain's most popular and influential strategic publicist, was cut off from any involvement in the shaping of policy and strategy during his country's greatest and most desperate war. Showing considerable moral courage and psychological strength, he expressed views which were deeply unpopular with the large majority of the British people. He now crossed the line between the status of an unconventional iconoclast and that of an 'unsafe' fringe figure. The consequences for his career would be long-term. Thereafter, during the formative years of the Cold War, although he was consulted once or twice by the Labour secretary of state for war, Emanuel Shinwell, and remained in good terms with Field Marshal Montgomery, the government and defence establishment remained closed to him. Only with the coming of a younger generation of politicians and soldiers and during the anti-establishment 1960s did his popularity rise again. This time, however, he was cast as a vintage sage. Liddell Hart's practical involvement in, and influence upon, the shaping of policy were over by 1940. This is one of the reasons why our treatment of his views in this chapter can be cut shorter than before. Another reason is that he had crystallized practically all his ideas regarding Britain's and the West's desired defence policy by 1937–41, and would not change them from then on.

After the fall of France British policy was personified by the new prime minister, Winston Churchill. Liddell Hart's feelings toward him were mixed. During the 1920s Churchill had everything which qualified him to rank very highly in Liddell Hart's esteem. Churchill's criticism of the British high command's conduct in the First World War, his Easternism, and his views regarding the need for a limited and mostly defensive strategy on the Western Front were picked up and echoed by Liddell Hart. Churchill was a radical, a promoter of reform in the navy, one of the creators of the tank, a champion of air force, and an admirer of Lawrence. The only problem was that Churchill did not return Liddell Hart's love. His rudeness to friend and foe alike is famous. Liddell Hart was stung by his scornful dismissal of the idea of 'qualitative disarmament', and by his arrogance at several meetings in which both of them participated during the early 1930s. So his attitude cooled. Lloyd George's ambivalence towards his former ally, lieutenant, and rival reinforced this change in the mid-1930s. Churchill, in any case, was by now no longer regarded as a radical but as an anachronism, and was universally believed to be politically finished.[1] For all that, Liddell Hart's relationship to Churchill was ultimately determined by their respective positions on policy and strategy. On this ground they co-operated during the Munich crisis, and departed thereafter. With the outbreak of the war Churchill became the main force in the cabinet

[1] See very positively: Liddell Hart in the *Daily Telegraph*, 4 Mar. 1927; *The Remaking of Modern Armies* (London, 1927), 175, 281–91; *A History of the World War, 1914–1918* (London, 1934), 112–13; *'T. E. Lawrence': In Arabia and After* (London, 1934), 46–7; 'The New British Doctrine of Mechanized War', *English Review* (1929), 688–9; in the 1920s Liddell Hart was sending Churchill his books; for a cooler attitude, see King's, 11/1936/28, 40; *Memoirs*, i. 301–6; ii. 74–5; the Churchill file: 1/171.

pressing for the utmost effort and offensive ventures. He was the driving force behind the Norwegian project. After the fall of France it was he who would chart the course of British policy.

Despite sharp differences in basic attitudes and rhetoric, there is little real disagreement among most historians regarding Churchill's strengths and weaknesses as a war leader.[2] In his crusade against Churchill both during and after the Second World War, Liddell Hart pointed out most, if not all, of the weaknesses that would later be brought to the fore by revisionist historians. During the interwar period Churchill lost touch with the development of the tank which he had helped to pioneer and, against his earlier views, accepted the Admiralty's underrating of the potential of the aircraft in sea warfare and of the submarine. He was full of combative spirit and overflowed with brilliant but amateurish operational schemes which he pursued enthusiastically, with a mixture of eloquence and bullying, against professional opposition, without first ensuring that the means to realize them were in place. Hence the series of disasters and débâcles, from the Dardanelles on, with which his career had always been and would continue to be associated well into the Second World War. Above all there was the fundamental question of Churchill's overall direction of the war—the goals he set, the policies and strategies he advocated and implemented, and the postwar world his actions helped to shape. This was the main battleground for Liddell Hart, as well as for Churchill's later critics and defenders.

Can Britain 'Win' by Herself?

Churchill's crucial decision, by which he stamped his mark on history, was to keep Britain in the war after the fall of France and to continue the fight with total commitment of all resources until Nazi Germany was overthrown and 'victory' achieved. He succeeded in rallying the British people to that cause, inspiring them with hope and impressing the rest of the world (especially the USA) with Britain's determination. In government and in the defence establishment this 'act of faith' was

[2] See esp. J. R. M. Butler, *Grand Strategy: History of the Second World War*, ii (London, 1957), 562; J. M. A. Gwyer, *Grand Strategy*, iii (London, 1964), 432–3; M. Howard, *The Mediterranean Strategy in the Second World War* (London, 1968); 'Churchill and the First World War' and the other contributions to R. Black and W. P. Louis (eds.), *Churchill* (Oxford, 1993); T. Ben-Moshe, *Churchill: Strategy and History* (Boulder, Colo., 1992); J. Charmley, *Churchill: The End of Glory* (London, 1993); and for a summary of Liddell Hart's decades-long crusade, see his 'The Military Strategist', in A. J. P. Taylor *et al.* (eds.), *Churchill: Four Faces and the Man* (London, 1969), 155–202.

expressed in and sustained by the more rational and systematic language of professional political and strategic assessment. From the spring of 1940 an overall strategy was devised by which it was believed that Britain would not only survive but defeat Germany. This strategy guided Britain's war effort so long as she remained alone in the war against Germany and Italy, and even later. In hindsight historians agree that this strategy as a whole, as well as each of its component parts, was based on unsustainable and naïvely optimistic assumptions which had no prospect of materializing. Liddell Hart, however, assessed all that *at the time*.[3] He had no quarrel with Churchill's decision to continue the war, maintain Britain's independence, and resist Germany's domination of Continental Europe. He, too, believed deeply that Britain had to be the core around which Western civilization would be rebuilt. However, he assessed that Britain had no chance of defeating Germany militarily.

Devised by the chiefs of staff in May 1940 to take account of the expected fall of France and reaffirmed in September at the height of the Battle of Britain, British strategy held that Britain would never be able to create a land force strong enough to invade the Continent and defeat the German army head on. It was assumed, however, that German power, now spreading over the whole of Continental Europe, could be weakened by the application of combined pressures which ultimately, and relatively quickly, might lead to its collapse. The effort was to consist of three principal means—the blockade, strategic bombing, and subversion in the occupied countries—leading to armed insurrections against the Germans, supported by small, amphibious British expeditionary forces. This strategic conception was, of course, the 'Maritime', 'indirect', 'British Way in Warfare' which Liddell Hart had espoused. Churchill and the generation that now occupied Whitehall and the General Staff shared the same experiences and strategic notions which had shaped Liddell Hart's own thought. From 1935, however, Liddell Hart had considerably amended, qualified, and partly withdrawn from the simplistic sketch he had drawn in 1931. Like the responsible defence authorities, he, too, repeatedly stressed that Britain's only viable strategy after the fall of France was maritime and

[3] See esp. Butler, *Grand Strategy*, ii. 209–17, 343–4, and *passim*; D. Reynolds, 'Churchill and the British "Decision" to Fight On in 1940: Right Policy, Wrong Reasons', in R. Langhorne (ed.), *Diplomacy and Intelligence during the Second World War* (Cambridge, 1985), 147–67. LH's wartime books, in which he did not hesitate to include journalistic articles and private memoranda of a necessarily transitory nature, are often remarkable documents; from the beginning of 1941 he was covering the war for the *Daily Mail*.

indirect.[4] But like Corbett he maintained that this strategy would never be able to bring down a great power like Germany that ruled most of the Continent.

Despite Germany's occupation of Western Europe, domination over central and south-eastern Europe, and economic access to the Soviet Union—all of which were recognized by the British chiefs of staff—the latter none the less continually expressed their belief that Germany was critically dependent on raw materials, food, and especially oil from overseas. The chiefs of staff thus maintained that a British blockade would bring Germany's war economy to a halt within several months and create widespread famine. It was widely believed that the foundations of the Nazi regime were shaky, that morale of the German home front was very low, and that both might collapse at any moment. Although Germany's unexpected collapse in 1918 was in people's minds, it seems incredible today that professional opinion, which should have been well aware of the preconditions that had led to that collapse, could subscribe to such wishful thinking. But it universally did. Only in June 1941 (before the German invasion of the Soviet Union) was it realized that earlier expectations had been unrealistic, although it was still believed that the German war economy would collapse within two years.[5] Liddell Hart, however, had assessed after Munich, and especially after the signing of the Soviet–German pact in August 1939, that the economic blockade could no longer be regarded as a decisive weapon. It might have serious disruptive value, but it was no longer able to strangle the German war economy and win the war. Obviously, he did not change his mind after the fall of Western Europe.

With varying emphases, the authors of British strategy evaluated the efficacy of the blockade in conjunction with the effects of a strategic bombing campaign, targeted at the German war economy. In September 1940, after the first salvos of city bombing, Churchill went further than his military advisers, suggesting that Germany's control of Europe limited the potential of the blockade and claiming that the main hope for winning the war lay with Bomber Command.[6] The strategic bomb-

[4] *Dynamic Defence* (London, 1940), 43, 53; *The Current of War* (London, 1941), 402–3 (7 Jan. 1941); *This Expanding War* (London, 1942), 41–3 (3 May 1941).

[5] W. N. Medlicott, *The Economic Blockade* (2 vols., London, 1978); Butler, *Grand Strategy*, ii. 212–13, 215–16, 343–4; Gwyer, *Grand Strategy* iii. 21–3; F. H. Hinsley, *British Intelligence in the Second World War*, i. (London, 1979), 223–48, 305–11.

[6] Medlicott, *The Economic Blockade*, i. 420–1; Butler, *Grand Strategy*, ii. 234, 403.

ing campaign which had been evolving for some time was now unleashed with ever greater effort and ferocity.

Although highly charged, the facts about how city bombing began and escalated during the Second World War are in little real dispute among historians. In the mid-1930s there was great enthusiam for strategic bombing in all the major air forces. However, by the second half of the decade the Great Powers' leaderships were increasingly considering the desirability of keeping the civilian populations out of the air war, a goal which Chamberlain took up more actively on the eve of the war. Hitler, too, repeatedly proposed that air bombing should be restricted to the zone of military operations. In September 1939 both Britain and Germany declared their agreement with President Roosevelt's proposal not to bomb civilians and unfortified cities. To be sure, the Germans appalled Western public opinion with their devastating air attacks on Guernica in 1937, Warsaw in 1939, and Rotterdam in 1940. However, all these cities were defended military strongholds within the combat zone and were attacked as such, even if the so-called 'collateral damage' and terror effect were hardly discouraged. By the outbreak of the war the Luftwaffe was mainly geared for cooperation with the army, though it never relinquished its aspirations towards a truly 'strategic' role. In any case, at least in the West, terror bombing of civilians was positively *not* desired by Hitler. By an order issued on 1 April 1940, he specifically instructed that the air war in the coming campaign should not be allowed to escalate into city bombing. Hitler cannot, of course, be suspected of any humanitarian scruples. But against opponents who were able to retaliate, he was very sensitive to the safety of the German civilian rear. For similar reasons, he did resort to the use of poison gas during the Second World War. The RAF, for its part, wanted to bomb the Ruhr from the beginning of the war but was restrained partly by the British government, partly by the French. On 15 May 1940, following the German bombing of Rotterdam and after Churchill became prime minister, permission to bomb industrial targets east of the Rhine was given. The air raids did negligible damage, but British bombing became a link in a series of mutual irritations that were to push both sides to escalate.

During the Battle of Britain the Luftwaffe was under strict orders not to bomb civilian targets. Only Hitler could authorize such attacks. On 24 August, however, residential areas in London were bombed by mistake, and the next night the RAF retaliated by bombing Berlin. This was a major cause for the German decision to begin raids on

London on 7 September. Nevertheless, the attacks were still aimed at strategic targets in the capital. Hitler rejected requests from the Luftwaffe to bomb residential areas, which he wanted to reserve as a last resort to deter the British from bombing German cities. On 19 September Bomber Command was ordered to start a full-scale bombing offensive against Germany. Once the Germans, like the British before them, were forced to switch to night bombing, any discrimination between civilian and strategic targets became almost impossible, even if the belligerents so desired, which they increasingly did not. Churchill, who had always objected to restrictions on the bombing of civilians, pushed for all-out bombing of Germany's cities from September 1940. It was the air staff that objected, still hoping to pinpoint Germany's economic vitals, especially the oil industry. As the British bombing campaign began in earnest in 1941, restrictions on the deliberate bombing of civilians were quickly dropped—in retaliation for the Blitz and for operational reasons, when targets could not be located. During the year it gradually became clear that Bomber Command was not even remotely hitting its targets. By the end of 1941 it was therefore decided to concentrate on the bombing of cities—the only targets big enough to be located and hit—with the view of breaking the German morale. This policy was to be ruthlessly pursued by the new chief of Bomber Command, Air Marshal Sir Arthur Harris.[7]

Liddell Hart viewed these developments with alarm and despair. By the mid-1930 he no longer believed in out-and-out air attacks on the enemy civilian rear, as he had, in Fuller's footsteps, in *Paris*. In 1939 he supported the elimination of such attacks by agreement (though on the outbreak of the war he apparently took no chance, for he moved out of London). During the 'Phoney War' he objected to attacks on the German civilian rear for reasons mentioned in the previous chapter. During the summer and autumn of 1940 he anxiously recorded what he

[7] See U. Bialer, '"Humanization" of Air Warfare in British Foreign Policy on the Eve of the Second World War', *Journal of Contemporary History*, 13 (1978), 79–96; G. Best, *Humanity in Warfare* (New York, 1980), 273; R. J. Overy, *The Air War, 1939–1945* (London, 1980), 24, 104; C. Webster and N. Frankland, *The Strategic Air Offensive against Germany, 1939–1945* (4 vols., London, 1961), i. 134, 144–53; Butler, *Grand Strategy*, ii. 410–12, 567–70; the contributions by K. A. Maier and H. Rohde to Militärgeschtliches Forschungsamt [MF] (ed.), *Germany and the Second World War* (Oxford, 1990–), ii. 33–43, 121, 338, 386–91; the contributions by O. Groehler, M. Messerschmidt, and H. Boog to Boog and MF (eds.), *The Conduct of the Air War in the Second World War* (New York, 1992), 279–97, 298–309, 373–404; Overy, *The Air War*, 104; L. Kennett, *A History of Strategic Bombing* (New York, 1982), 105–41; and most recently J. W. Legro, *Cooperation Under Fire: Anglo-German Restraint During World War II* (London, 1995).

recognized at the time as steps in a slide into bombing of civilian population, claiming that German air doctrine did not prescribe city bombing. As early as January 1941 he already assessed, and repeated thereafter, that a bombing match between England and Germany was unlikely to be decisive, and that its only result would be vast, indiscriminate devastation and exhaustion. In April he accused Churchill of repeating Passchendaele in the air.[8]

The bombing campaign was to prove one of the biggest strategic disappointments of the Second World War. Yet, as historians have argued, strategic bombing was untried, and after Britain had been thrown out of the Continent it became her only means of striking at Germany. The point Liddell Hart was making was, however, more subtle and compelling. Not only did he regard the bombing of the enemy's civilian rear as barbaric, judging at the time that it would bring a great deal of misery but no decision; he also argued that in a bombing match between Germany and Britain, Germany, possessing air bases in France and the Low Countries, in close proximity to Britain, was bound to inflict on her much heavier punishment. It was a contest under wholly unequal terms, as the bombing campaign during the winter of 1941 demonstrated. The German invasion of the Soviet Union in June 1941 was to distract the Luftwaffe from Britain for the rest of the war; but the attack on the Soviet Union was not known when the British bomber offensive was launched, could have failed to take place, or might have ended differently. Under the circumstances prevailing at the time, Liddell Hart maintained that initiating or escalating a bombing campaign against Germany's civilian rear was a wholly irrational strategy for Britain. He believed that every effort should be made to de-escalate the air war, and held that Churchill's warlike nature and instinctive aggressiveness were pushing him again into a disastrous venture whose prospects for success and probable outcome had not been fully thought out.[9]

[8] 'War in the Air', *Helios* (1934), 235–41; also in *New York Times Magazine*, 28 Jan. 1934; *Europe in Arms* (London, 1937), 319–42; *The Defence of Britain* (London, 1939), 147–62, 188–94; July–Oct. 1940, King's, 11/1940/76–8, 92, 117–22; to the Bishop of Chichester, George Bell, 2 Nov. 1940, also 25 June 1943, 11/1943/37; *The Current of War*, 404 (7 Jan. 1941), and *This Expanding War*, 43 (3 May 1941), 258–63 (6 Aug. 1941); 17 Feb. 1941, 11/1941/3; 12 Apr. 1941, 11/1941/21. See also *The Revolution in Warfare* (London, 1946), 70, 72, 86.

[9] *The Current of War*, 404 (7 Jan. 1941), and *This Expanding War*, 43 (3 May 1941). The only historian to mention this crucial point is Best, *Humanity in Warfare*, 276; it has been picked up and made the centre of discussion in Legro, *Cooperation under Fire*. In the spring of 1941 a parliamentary group proposed a de-escalation of city bombing, but their initiative was rejected by the government: Kennett, *Strategic Bombing*, 132–3.

Britain's third strategy for the defeat of Germany after the fall of France was subversion, backed by amphibious sallies or even landings. Here too, however, once again anticipating the arguments against his own earlier theories, Liddell Hart saw no prospect for significant success. In November 1940 he poured cold water on Hore-Belisha's enthusiasm, writing to him that he had checked and found out that the overwhelming majority of amphibious operations carried out in the previous three centuries had been failures. While he agreed that action against Italy—especially in Africa—was the most promising strategy for Britain, he wrote that if Italy were ever to be brought to the point of collapse, German troops would overrun her with ease. British expeditionary forces would stand no chance against the strong, modern German army, and landing attempts would only lead to new Dunkirks.[10]

The Greek campaign was a case in point. Churchill sought to consolidate a Balkan front against the Axis from the beginning of the war, and British diplomatic activity in the capitals of this region was intensive throughout 1940. Yet the British military authorities claimed that Britain had no forces to spare and that whatever she sent would be swept away by the Germans. The Italian invasion of Greece at the end of October raised the question again. The chiefs of staff still thought that no aid to Greece could be spared or would be of any practical use, but Churchill succeeded in pressuring the reluctant secretary of state for war, Eden, and the commander-in-chief in the Middle East, Wavell (who was then husbanding resources for his planned counter-offensive against the invading Italian army in Egypt), to send scarce equipment to Greece. In the meanwhile, the Greeks succeeded in defeating the invaders by themselves and pursued them into Albania. The British then began to toy with the idea of gaining a foothold on the Continent, especially air bases from which the Romanian oilfields could be attacked. This, however, was precisely the sort of British involvement the Greeks did not want. They sought to avoid, not provoke, a German invasion. Indeed Hitler, who decided at the end of 1940 to attack the Soviet Union rather than pursue a Mediterranean strategy, was anxious to avoid any distractions. However, alarmed by the British activity and the potential threat to the Romanian oilfields, he felt that an invasion of Greece might become unavoidable.

[10] To Hore-Belisha, 21 Nov. 1940, King's, 11/HB 1940/47; also *The Current of War*, 403 (7 Jan. 1941).

In view of the German army's concentrations in Romania and entry into Bulgaria, and following the Italian defeat in Libya and the fall of Benghazi, Churchill renewed his pressure to have British forces sent to Greece. As the Greeks themselves were changing their minds, Eden, now foreign secretary, became supportive of the operation and the British high command was finally giving in. By then, however, Churchill himself was beginning to have doubts. He left the decision on the whole operation to Eden and the CIGS, Dill, both sent to confer with Wavell in the Middle East. Weary of months of harassment and bullying by the prime minister, Wavell reversed his earlier position and came to support the initiative. The renewal of the offensive in North Africa was postponed, and British forces began to disembark in Piraeus in the beginning of March. By that time Hitler decided that the occupation of Greece had indeed become unavoidable. By the end of the month, as Yugoslavia was coerced into joining the tripartite pact (but not to allow Axis troops through her territory), a pro-British coup took place in Belgrade. It led to a swift German invasion which occupied both Yugoslavia and Greece in less than a month. British prestige again suffered a severe blow, as the British expeditionary force had to be evacuated, leaving most of its equipment and 11,000 men behind. A month later the humiliation was completed with the fall of Crete. Whereas after the war it was believed that the Balkan campaign may have delayed Hitler's invasion of the Soviet Union and thus contributed to its failure, later studies have shown that its effect was almost negligible.[11]

Liddell Hart did not take any strong position in his commentaries during the Greek crisis. He was oblivious both of Hitler's overall strategic intentions and of the behind-the-scenes activity on the British side. Before the campaign he anticipated a possible new Dunkirk in case of a British involvement, but did not come out against it. He also pointed out that the completion of the British offensive in North Africa

[11] Butler, *Grand Strategy*, ii. 365–88, 439–59, 554; J. S. Koliopoulos, *Greece and the British Connection, 1935–1941* (Oxford, 1977); S. Lawlor, *Churchill and the Politics of War, 1940–1941* (Cambridge, 1994), 115–256; Ben-Moshe, *Churchill*, 132–63; G. Craig, 'The Political Leader as Strategist', in P. Paret (ed.), *Makers of Modern Strategy from Machiavelli to the Nuclear Age* (Princeton, NJ, 1986), 500. The German generals testified to Liddell Hart that the spring mud and river overflow had prevented an earlier invasion of the Soviet Union: *The Other Side of the Hill* (London, 1948), 249–55; M. van Creveld, *Hitler's Strategy, 1940–1941: The Balkan Clue* (Cambridge, 1973), 151–76, has shown that the German army needed the extra time to complete its preparations; he does mention, however, that the 12th Army was subtracted from the invasion of the Ukraine (p. 135).

would have to be postponed. As the defeat in Greece became clear, he returned to his more principled line, claiming that a Balkan strategy had been beyond Britain's capabilities. As Lloyd George, who was continuously in touch with Liddell Hart, said in Parliament, any idea of invading Europe was 'fatuous'. Liddell Hart maintained that British decisionmakers continued to ignore realities and, failing to think through the consequences, had encouraged the governments of Yugoslavia and Greece 'to over-estimate the chances of successful resistance'. As one historian has written: 'Churchill was convinced that it was the right or even the duty of great powers to sacrifice small neutrals for the sake of victory over Nazism.' Liddell Hart, however, charged that the sacrifices were made to no avail. In September 1941 he concluded that Churchill had dragged one small neutral after another into the war and Nazi occupation by means of foolish provocations that merely alarmed the Germans into action. After the war he argued that the Greek diversion had prolonged the war in North Africa for two years, because it allowed Rommel time to arrive and launch his counter-offensive in March and April 1941.[12]

Cold War

So Liddell Hart perceptively assessed that the strategy devised in Britain after the fall of France for the purpose of defeating Germany was based on illusions, and that the means it deployed were often counter-productive and recklessly dangerous. But what did he propose Britain should do instead? He had already crystallized his views on this matter during the Phoney War, when he assessed that even in alliance with France it was difficult to see how Britain could positively win the war against Germany. With Britain alone in the war, he initially thought, as did Lloyd George and the majority in the cabinet, that Britain should first try to strengthen her hand after the disaster in the Low Countries and France by repulsing Hitler's offensive and proving that she could not be defeated. Hitler might then agree to a more favourable peace than he had been willing to conclude in the summer of 1940.[13] However, once

[12] *This Expanding War*, 16–17 (18 Mar. 1941), 24 (6 Apr.), 38 (26 Apr.); P. Addison, 'Lloyd George and Compromise Peace', in A. J. P. Taylor (ed.), *Lloyd George: Twelve Essays* (London, 1971), 361; for the neutrals: van Creveld, *Hitler's Strategy*, 141; Liddell Hart, 6 Sept. 1941, 11/1941/62; but see also Lawlor, *Churchill*, 250; Liddell Hart, *Defence of the West*, 12–19.

[13] 3 and 14 Sept., and 12 Oct. 1940, King's, 11/1940/81, 87, 90, 91. For Lloyd George and Churchill's cabinet after the fall of France, see Addison, 'Lloyd George and Compromise Peace', 362, 375–83; D. Reynolds, 'Churchill and the British "Decision" to Fight On'.

the critical stage of the Battle of Britain was over, Liddell Hart no longer mentioned a negotiated peace with Germany. Instead he proposed a comprehensive programme for what was effectively a policy of cold war against her.

Liddell Hart maintained that historically the concept of 'victory' proved to be a ruinous but persistent delusion. In any case, Britain was unable to liberate occupied Europe by force. Thus, rather than exhaust herself in futile offensive efforts which would only bring American and Soviet domination of the world, Britain ought to adopt a long-term view of the conflict. The bombing campaign should, as much as possible, be de-escalated and then brought to an end. The blockade, which could only bring misery to the inhabitants of occupied Europe but no decision, should be adjusted and applied with discrimination. The mass army still planned should be scaled down, and resources invested in a smaller and highly mechanized force, as well as diverted from the military altogether. Britain's defences should be made impregnable, but all offensive efforts should be renounced. Britain should try to return to a state of normality and in collaboration with the United States resume economic growth and foster prosperity. Her best weapon would be the building up of a free and just society at home which would serve as a shining model and as an attractive alternative to the German 'New Order' in Europe. This model would be constantly subversive to German rule, until in time it might lead to its disintegration from within. For that purpose all the 'totalitarian' measures and restrictions on free speech adopted in wartime Britain should be withdrawn. About these measures, which in his view included conscription, Liddell Hart felt most deeply, and he tirelessly enlisted in every public campaign against them.[14]

Liddell Hart formulated this new strategic outlook into the language of theory in a new chapter on grand strategy which he added to the second edition of his *The Strategy of Indirect Approach* (1941). He repeated the distinction he had made in his 1937 *Times* article between 'acquisitive' and 'conservative' states, the latter being 'primarily concerned with the preservation of its security and the

[14] The argument was gradually perfected: 3 Sept. 1940, King's, 11/1940/81; *Dynamic Defence*, 53–6; *The Current of War*, 403–6 (7 Jan. 1941); 17 Mar. 1941, 11/1941/18; 12 Apr. 1941, 11/1941/21; *This Expanding War*, 43–5 (3 May 1941). For the propaganda, restrictions on speech, and repressive measures in wartime Britain, see C. Ponting, *1940: Myth and Reality* (London, 1990), 152–6. See also B. Bond, *Liddell Hart: A Study of his Military Thought* [*LH*] (London, 1977), 126–8.

maintenance of its way of life'. What would be the best strategy for this type of state?

> It is a folly to imagine that the aggressive types . . . can be bought off—or, in modern language, 'appeased' . . . But they can be curbed. Their very belief in force makes them more susceptible to the deterrent effect of a formidable opposing force. This forms an adequate check except against pure fanaticism . . . While it is hard to make a real peace with the predatory types, it is easier to induce them to accept a state of truce—and far less exhausting than an attempt to crush them . . . The experience of history brings ample evidence that the downfall of civilized States tends to come not from direct assaults of foes but from internal decay, combined with the consequences of exhaustion in war.

The policy of armed truce and deterrence has its difficulties, not least the psychological:

> A state of suspense is trying—it has often led nations as well as individuals to commit suicide because they were unable to bear it. . . . [furthermore] Peaceful nations are apt . . . to court unnecessary danger because, when once aroused, they are more inclined to proceed to extremes than predatory nations.[15]

Here were the leading ideas which, developed and discussed, would gain universal currency in the late 1940s and during the 1950s, with the Cold War. In retrospect they appear extremely interesting and intriguing. Yet two questions immediately suggest themselves. First, was not Liddell Hart unduly pessimistic after all? Was not British strategy, Churchill's in particular, based on the assumption that the United States would join the war, tip the scales against Germany, and make possible her defeat? Secondly, could the Nazi and Soviet cases be compared at all? And were not nuclear weapons anyhow essential for a cold war regime? We shall deal with the first question here and defer treatment of the second.

The American and Soviet Alliances

Although British strategy after the fall of France presupposed only American *economic* assistance, Churchill believed, and assured his cabinet colleagues and the defence establishment, that the United States would enter the war before long. This was an important psychological factor in the British decision to fight on. In turn, Britain's resolve greatly impressed the United States. American economic aid was indeed

[15] *The Strategy of Indirect Approach* (London, 1941), 205, 210–11; from the 1954 edn. on: pp. 368, 372.

forthcoming in great volume with Land-Lease from the beginning of 1941, though at a cost. It was given only after the US made sure that Britain had no more money to pay and had liquidated all her disposable foreign assets; and it included strict stipulations which secured American domination of world trade at Britain's expense. American entry into the war remained, however, a dubious matter. In the summer of 1940 Churchill believed that the US would enter the war after the presidential elections in November. This did not happen. By late spring 1941, as disillusionment with the efficacy of both the blockade and strategic bombing was growing in Britain, and following the defeats in Greece and North Africa, the British high command concluded, revising its earlier views, that full American participation in the war would be necessary for defeating Germany. However, with a declaration of war by the US not yet in sight and with Roosevelt apparently telling different people different things according to what they wanted to hear, waves of gloom began to spread through the British government and defence establishment. It was widely felt, and resented, that it was now the US who was employing Britain's traditional strategy and, taking advantage of American geographical isolation and economic might, was holding the world balance without risking herself in the fray. 'We are their Hessians,' was a common feeling in British official circles during the summer and autumn of 1941.[16]

We shall interrupt our treatment of the United States' position for a moment to take account of Hitler's invasion of the Soviet Union. As in Germany, American and British official assessments after the invasion held that the Soviet Union would be defeated in a matter of weeks or a few months. Soviet resistance was considered mainly as a valuable distraction for Germany from offensive action in the West in 1941. Churchill publicly expressed total support for the Soviet Union's struggle but, in contrast to Eden's more forthcoming response, did not intend to offer more than rhetoric and token material aid.[17] Liddell Hart, however, writing two days after the German invasion, immediately realized that the face of the war had changed completely. There was now a chance of positively defeating Germany, although, if Hitler's gamble paid off, he would be able to turn all his forces against Britain

[16] D. Reynolds, *The Creation of the Anglo-American Alliance, 1937–1941* (London, 1981); Gwyer, *Grand Strategy*, iii. 16–23.

[17] Butler, *Grand Strategy*, ii. 543–5; Gwyer, *Grand Strategy*, iii. 90; S. Lawlor, 'Britain and the Russian Entry into the War', in Langhorne (ed.), *Diplomacy and Intelligence*, 168–83.

with the resources of the Soviet Union at his disposal. Liddell Hart fully comprehended the enormity of Hitler's gamble. Explicitly going against Western professional opinion and the apparent implications of the Finnish war, he gave a remarkably accurate and balanced picture of the Red Army's enormous strengths, as well as weaknesses. He pointed out the great strides it had made in mechanized and modern techniques of war, as well as the traditional toughness of its rank and file. He judged that the Soviet Union's survival would depend on her ability to absorb the thrusts of the German mechanized forces by using her vast space for elastic defence and mechanized counter-offensives. He even suggested that Hitler's aim might be the Baltic, the Ukraine, and the Caucasus oil. Liddell Hart's commentary throughout the summer campaign remained very perceptive, and always cautiously optimistic. He noted that because of the stubbornness of the Soviet resistance and the enormity of their space, the Blitzkrieg—aiming at a speedy paralysis rather than physical annihilation of the enemy—was encountering serious difficulties.[18]

Still, even though Liddell Hart accurately judged in June 1941 that the Soviet Union stood a good chance of withstanding the German onslaught and that there now existed a possibility of victory over Germany, the realization of that possibility rested largely with the United States; and the prospects for her entry into the war remained foggy. During the summer of 1941 the US extended Land-Lease to the Soviet Union, took over the battle against the German submarines in the western half of the Atlantic, and garrisoned Iceland. In August Roosevelt and Churchill signed the Atlantic Charter, a declaration regarding the face of the post-war world. It was, however, clear to the British that American entry into the war was not to be expected in the near future. The majority of Americans and members of Congress still objected to the war, and Roosevelt's own intentions are unclear. He was surely not going to allow Britain to fall, and probably would have used the United States' growing weight to steadily increase American influence on the course of the war. But was he waiting for more progress to be made in US rearmament, and using the time to prepare American public opinion for its eventual participation in the war? Or was he quite satisfied with the existing situation, in which Britain and the Soviet Union were doing the fighting with massive American political and

[18] *This Expanding War*, 70–3 (24 June 1941), also 254 (6 Aug. 1941); 88–91 (31 July 1941); the campaign is followed on pp. 67–123.

economic support but without full American participation? This question remains in dispute and can probably never be decided. It is doubtful if Roosevelt himself knew. It was only Japan's surprise attack and the subsequent German declaration of war on the United States that finally decided the issue—as the German invasion of the Soviet Union had done for the USSR. Both of Britain's mighty allies in the coalition against Germany entered the war against their will.[19]

Whether Hitler's ultimate aims and the pressures of the war and of the war economy would anyhow have driven Germany into war with both the Soviet Union and the United States is difficult to tell. History is not preordained. It should be noted, however, that in the same way as Soviet participation did not necessarily mean victory over Germany until the United States joined in, American participation still left the path to victory very unclear had not the Soviet Union been brought into the war and survived to engage the lion's share of the German land forces. The participation in the war of both powers was necessary. Only the development of the atomic bomb can be cited as a sure way to victory for the West in the absence of Soviet participation.[20] All the same, what one historian has written regarding Lloyd George's peace policy may also be cited in respect to Liddell Hart's proposal for a cold war against Germany: 'Churchill won his great war and thus his great victory, but some alternative line would have to have been devised in the absence of the Russian and American alliances, or in the event of the rapid defeat of Russia in 1941 and continued benevolent neutrality of the United States.'[21] One might further add that Liddell Hart's proposed policy of cold war so long as Britain remained alone in the war left room for possible future escalation to active warfare once conditions had changed. It was to Churchill's attempt actively to win the war on

[19] Gwyer, *Grand Strategy*, iii. 111–24; R. Dallek, *Franklin D. Roosevelt and American Foreign Policy, 1932–1945* (New York, 1979), 285; in recent years historians have become increasingly sceptical regarding American intentions of joining the war: Reynolds, *The Anglo-American Alliance*, esp. 214–19; Charmley, *Churchill*, 332; *Churchill's Grand Alliance* (London, 1995), 16–17, 38–44, 356; J. Keegan, 'Churchill's Strategy', in Blake and Louis (eds.), *Churchill*, 338–9; N. Rose, *Churchill* (London, 1994), 276, 288; G. L. Weinberg, *A World at Arms: A Global History of World War II* (Cambridge, 1994), 238–45 (citing recently discovered documentation).

[20] Interestingly enough, here too—though, of course, he was not privy to the development of the atom bomb—Liddell Hart took care to leave a loophole in his analysis by repeatedly mentioning 'the possible discovery of some revolutionary new weapons of paralysing effect' as one way of breaking the German hold over occupied Europe: *The Current of War*, 403–4 (7 Jan. 1941); *This Expanding War*, 257–8 (6 Aug. 1941).

[21] Addison, 'Lloyd George and Compromise Peace', 383.

Britain's own strength, and to the means employed for that purpose, rather than to his decision to leave Britain in the war, that Liddell Hart objected before the Grand Alliance came into being. After Pearl Harbor his advocacy of a cold war against Germany, which spanned the years 1939–41, was over.

Unconditional Surrender

Liddell Hart's views and proposals during the remainder of the Second World War will be reviewed here only briefly. In principle they represent little that is new beyond the ideas he had been developing since the 1920s; and seen from the transitory point in time in which this book is written, they appear less important. Although the grounds shifted considerably after the Grand Alliance took shape, Liddell Hart only intensified his opposition to the British and Western Allies' war policy. While the military defeat of Germany had now become a very real possibility, he concluded that a victory achieved at the end of a protracted total war would completely bankrupt Britain and cause her to lose her empire. As he wrote: 'Spain, Sweden, Holland, France and Austria all exhausted themselves through overstraining themselves in offensive war-efforts that were beyond their capability.' Furthermore, echoing Corbett, Liddell Hart pointed out that, relative to her Continental rivals, Britain had always been a small nation which had never been able, nor had attempted, to crush her enemies completely.[22] He endlessly reiterated that history had proved the concept of 'victory' to be illusory and called for a cool view forward, free from the passions of war, into the ensuing state of peace. He judged that the pursuit of victory would lead to American and Soviet domination of the world and only saw the seeds of the next conflict. Liddell Hart thus returned to advocate a negotiated settlement to the war. He believed that once the odds had changed against Germany, a new German leadership might arise which, provided that German independence and national integrity were maintained, would seek peace on terms that could be acceptable to the West. This would help to restore the European and global balance of power and keep the Soviet Union in check. In October 1943 Liddell Hart predicted that the war would leave the Soviet Union in control of eastern and central Europe, including part of Germany, with the West in control of the other part. Thus, in contrast to some present-day revisionist critics of Churchill, Liddell Hart advocated peace with

[22] 29 July 1942, King's, 11/1942/59; repeated in May and 4 July 1943, 11/1943/26.

Germany, not when German power was at its apogee, but from 1942, when it could be checked again. On one occasion he even wrote to Robert Graves that Britain had always known how to get out of wars in which her former allies continued to fight (presumably implying departing from the Soviet Union rather than the United States).

All this focused from the summer of 1943 into out-and-out opposition to the demand made by Roosevelt and Churchill in Casablanca for 'unconditional surrender' by the Axis powers. Liddell Hart hastily sent the British government a memorandum arguing against that demand. In his view, unconditional surrender, which closed the door to a negotiated end to the war, would leave no way out for the German people and opposition, thus playing into Hitler's hands. These were the themes he reiterated in his books at the end of the war and ever after. In the general jubilation of VE day he grimly concluded that his predictions had come true: Europe lay ruined and divided, communism was rampant, and Britain was exhausted and rendered economically dependent. As the Cold War broke out, Liddell Hart wrote that the only possible response to the Soviet threat was to retract the Western Allies' mistake and rearm the Germans as quickly as possible—a measure which would be taken after the Korean War.[23] Indeed, with the coming of the Cold War, criticism of the policy of unconditional surrender and of the Western Allies' alleged failure to consider the Soviet threat during the Second World War became widespread. Even Churchill in his memoirs misleadingly attempted to play down his involvement in the proclamation of unconditional surrender. He and others similarly created the enduring legend that well before the defeat of Nazi Germany he had been gravely concerned about the future Soviet threat and had tried to direct Western strategy accordingly. In truth, it has been shown that Churchill refused to consider the shape of the post-war world until Nazi Germany had been defeated, and began to contemplate the Soviet threat only in the very last months of the war. 'First catch your hare' was his slogan.[24]

[23] 3 Sept. 1942, King's, 11/1942/70; 24 Jan. 1943, 11/1943/3; 17 Apr. 1943, 11/1943/26; 31 July 1943, 11/1943/47; 11 Aug. 1943, 11/1943/49; 1 Oct. 1943, 11/1943/62; 1 Dec. 1943, 11/1943/75; to Graves, 3 Oct. 1942, 1/327; some of this already in the 1941 ed. of *The Strategy of Indirect Approach*, 203, 208–10; *Why Don't We Learn from History?* (London, 1944) 7 May 1945, 11/1945/5; Liddell Hart to George Bell, 19 Feb. 1948.

[24] Howard, *The Mediterranean Strategy*, pp. ix–x, 56, 63–5; *Grand Strategy: History of the Second World War*, iv (London, 1972), 281–5; Charmley, *Churchill*, 464–74, 521; Ben-Moshe, *Churchill*, 225–44, 277–324; D. Reynolds, 'Great Britain and the Security "Lessons" of the Second World War', in R. Ahmann, A. M. Birke, and M. Howard (eds.), *The Quest for Stability: Problems of West European Security, 1918–1957* (Oxford, 1993), 301–4.

In June 1942, after five years of separation, Liddell Hart again met Fuller, and the two outcasts, each for different reasons, made up. They were both campaigning against total war and the bombing offensive—ideas which Liddell Hart had adopted from Fuller twenty years earlier. Liddell Hart was also in touch with other leading critics of total war and air bombing such as George Bell, the Bishop of Chichester. With Soviet participation closing the holes in the blockade and the American Eight Air Force joining British Bomber Command, Liddell Hart no longer claimed that the air offensive and the blockade were not harming the German war effort significantly. Rather, he emphasized their barbaric and wasteful nature, which only escalated the war and would lead to exhaustion through attrition. In 1941 he had already suggested that Hitler's Blitzkrieg was more humane than Britain's air offensive and blockade. He now insisted that the blockade had always been used by Britain in limited wars for limited aims, whereas its employment in a war to the finish was wholly barbaric. Again reversing his older ideas, he took up his critics' arguments of the 1920s, denouncing the Allies' Sherman- and Mongol-like warfare against civilians. By the end of the war he was able to reaffirm that the strategic air offensive had failed to achieve its goals.[25]

As the US Air Force strategic bombing surveys would show, although Germany's cities were destroyed, German civilian morale did not collapse, and German military output actually rocketed in 1943–4, during the height of the bombing offensive. Admittedly, that offensive diverted the Luftwaffe from the Eastern Front to the defence of Germany, and diverted German industry from the production of bombers to fighters. Industrial resources, raw materials, and (mainly second-grade) manpower were also diverted to air defence and reconstruction. Furthermore, if it had not been for the bombing, German military production would probably have risen even more than it actually did. Yet, as the bombing offensive probably absorbed more than a third of the Western Allies' war production, the question of cost-effectiveness and possible alternative usage of resources is bound to arise. Although the Allies' (namely, American) resources were huge, they were not boundless. For example, tactical air cooperation with the army was inadequate until 1943–4, and Western tank models never

[25] 17 Mar. 1941, King's, 11/1941/18, and *This Expanding War*, 260 (6 Aug. 1941); 12 Jan. 1943, 11/1943/26; 3 July 1943, 11/1943/40; *Why Don't We Learn from History?*, 87; *The Revolution in Warfare*, 24–5, 74–5.

caught up with those of Germany (and the Soviet Union). The supply of landing craft proved to be another crucial bottleneck for Allied strategy. Critics have also suggested the possibility of more accurate, versatile, and discriminating alternatives within the strategic air offensive option to the high-altitude 'carpet' bombing by heavy four-engine aircraft.[26]

The arguments against Liddell Hart's views on these contentious issues are as strong as, or even stronger than, his own. Indeed, they question his entire system of thought. While thinking Hitler and the Nazi regime tyrannical, brutal, and despicable, he clearly did not grasp the scope and intensity of their murderous racial vision, the lengths to which they would go in implementing their policies, and their success in winning the support of the German people. For him, they were not the first and probably not the last of their kind that Britain and the West had faced and would still have to face. He would not accept that the Second World War was fundamentally different from earlier wars. He soberly pointed out that it was a common psychological phenomenon, arising from the passions of war and the needs of propaganda, to regard the current enemy—Louis XIV, Napoleon, Kaiser Wilhelm—as different, more barbaric and more menacing than earlier ones.[27] A. J. P. Taylor has remarked that in the First World War German atrocities were universally believed in but were in fact rare, whereas in the Second World War atrocity stories were generally discounted even though they were in fact all too true.[28] However, Liddell Hart did not change his position much even after the war, when the horrendous reality became known. His bias was clearly motivated. It was crucial to his critique of the Allies' aims and conduct of the war. He would never concede that 'victory' in the Second World War mattered or that the

[26] D. MacIsaac (ed.), *The United States Strategic Bombing Survey* (10 vols., New York, 1976) Webster and Frankland, *The Strategic Air Offensive*, ii and iii, Butler, *Grand Strategy*, ii. 527–33; Overy, *The Air War*, 122–5; M. Smith, 'The Allied Air Offensive', in J. Gooch, *Decisive Campaigns of the Second World War* (London, 1990), 67–83; MF *Deutschland und der zweite Weltkrieg*, vi (Stuttgart, 1990), 560–5; A. D. Harvey, *Collision of Empires: Britain in Three World Wars, 1793–1945* (London, 1992), 644–8, 703–6. The bombing effort is improbably estimated by Webster and Frankland, *The Strategic Air Offensive*, i. 92, at 10% of British war production; A. J. P. Taylor estimates it at more than a third: *The Second World War* (London, 1975), 129, accepted by M. Hastings, *Bomber Command* (New York, 1979), 107, and Kennett, *Strategic Bombing*, 181; Overy places the air war investment of all the warring powers at 40–50% of which the bombers took the lion's share on the Allies' side: 'Air Power in the Second World War', in H. Boog and MF (eds.), *The Conduct of the Air War in the Second World War* (New York, 1992), 12, also 18.

[27] *Why Don't We Learn from History?*, 51.

[28] Cited in Bond, *LH*, 168.

Soviet Union—tyrannical and brutal as she was—posed a less sinister threat to the West and to humanity than Nazi Germany.

Unconditional surrender may not have been the most subtle diplomacy. Many in both the American and British administrations thought so at the time, including Foreign Secretaries Hull and Eden. But it was extremely effective for the aims set by its initiators. As Louis Namier would write to Liddell Hart, negotiations with Germany would have rapidly strengthened her hand by allowing her to play the partners of the Grand Alliance—who were deeply suspicious of each other—against one another, as Talleyrand had done in 1815.[29] The bombing offensive, too, terrible and strategically blunt as it was, was largely a political tool. From late 1941 Churchill no longer believed that it would win the war. But it was one of the very few things the Western Allies were able to offer the Soviet Union in 1942–4 as a substitute for a Second Front, and it drove the war and defeat home to the German people.

Both Roosevelt and Churchill thought it necessary to completely eradicate Nazism, leave the Germans in no doubt that they had been totally defeated, and prevent the repetition of the post-1918 survival of the German nationalist tradition. It is very doubtful whether during the middle phase of the war, and until it became too late to matter, any alternative German government would have been able to come to power or accept peace on terms acceptable to the West. No alternative government was also likely to be other than conservative-nationalist. Roosevelt in particular, who in the late 1930s had been entertaining ideas similar to Liddell Hart's regarding the need for developing a 'new technique' of waging war, based on containment and cold war, now wanted complete victory in order to shape a new world order in which Germany and Japan would be democratized and collective security enforced by the victors.[30] The outcome of the war may have divided Europe, but it created a Western bloc which encompassed the world's most advanced industrial societies, except the Soviet Union. For this purpose it may have been necessary to destroy Germany and Japan first and then build them up again—futile as this may be made to sound by critics. The

[29] Namier to Liddell Hart, 24 Mar. 1951, King's, 1/539; A. J. P. Taylor, from whom Liddell Hart expected more sympathy, argued the same thing: see their letters of 2 and 27 Mar., 9 and 12 Apr. 1961, 1/676.

[30] Dallek, *Roosevelt and American Foreign Policy*, 359, 373–8; Reynolds, *The Anglo-American Alliance*, 251–66; J. L. Gaddis, *Strategies of Containment: A Critical Appraisal of Postwar American National Security Policy* (New York, 1982), 10.

West was not merely preserved by the war—the goal Liddell Hart had desired—but widely expanded. Contrary to the views of Liddell Hart and modern, enlightened opinion in interwar Britain, this time at least military victory in war decisively shaped history, as that nineteenth-century man, Winston Churchill, had always believed it had.

Cold War against Nazi Germany: Conclusion

Many of these arguments may also apply to Liddell Hart's advocacy of a policy of cold war against Germany during the period when Britain stood alone. Liddell Hart was remarkably perceptive in most of his strategic judgements, and correct in assessing that by herself Britain stood no chance of defeating Germany. But was a policy of cold war any more viable? Can the later successful implementation of that policy against the Soviet Union be taken as a comparable model? Some of the differences are obvious. The Western bloc that would face the communists would include the world's most advanced industrial societies, and even then the security and psychological burden would be felt by them to be almost too heavy. By contrast, in 1940–1 Britain stood alone, with only the United States behind her. As for the opponent, the Soviet leadership would always be much more conservative and cautious in its policies than Hitler. It is not only that he corresponded more to the category of 'fanatics', which Liddell Hart suggested were difficult to contain; Germany was also driven to adventurist and aggressive policies by her lack of economic self-sufficiency, whereas the Soviet Union was largely autarkic. It is doubtful that Hitler would have agreed to settle into a state of indefinite cold war with Britain and the US, especially if the blockade was to continue, albeit in a modified form. In any case, the US would have probably been able to prevent Britain from falling. But it is difficult to see how Britain could have relaxed her defence effort sufficiently to return to a state of normality and resume economic growth and prosperity, as Liddell Hart wished and as the West would be able to do during the Cold War. As to the end of the Cold War, the Soviet collapse would be caused primarily by economic failure, whereas there is no reason to suppose that a German economic circle would have become similarly inefficient. While German terror was rivalled by the Soviet, it was genocidal towards the Jews, gypsies, and other special groups, and semi-genocidal towards the Slavs. Repression, however, neither brought about by itself nor allowed the disintegration of the Soviet bloc, and can scarcely be expected to have done so in the case of Germany's New Order, even if some mellowing of the regime might have occurred after Hitler was gone. Britain emerged exhausted from the war, but a policy of cold war was unlikely to have conserved her forces any better. It was her good fortune that Hitler's Germany became embroiled in war with both the Soviet Union and the United States.

Finally, there is the question of the viability of a Cold War regime before the advent of nuclear weapons. There is no question that that 'great deterrent' concentrated the minds of the Cold War antagonists wonderfully and created that type of powerful inhibition to war that Liddell Hart had sought in vain in preaching the doctrine of the superiority of defence. Nuclear weapons thus made a Cold War regime much more stable and endurable than it could ever have been before. It would be a mistake, however, to think that it was solely the nuclear factor that brought that regime into being.[31] As a leading historian of the Cold War has pointed out, it is all too often forgotten that when the policy of containment and the Cold War regime against the Soviet Union were being evolved after the Second World War, the US had a monopoly on nuclear weapons and theoretically had every reason to pre-empt and force her way without fear of retaliation.[32] Had the Soviet Union or Nazi Germany, rather than the United States, possessed a nuclear monopoly, there can be little doubt that they would have pressed for the massive production of nuclear weapons and carried out a worldwide policy of conquest and coercion. The notions of containment and cold war, already discernible before the Second World War in both Britain and the United States, pre-dated the Bomb and the Cold War, and their roots went deeper into the modern 'Western condition'.

II. The Nuclear Age

The advent of the atom bomb made very little change in Liddell Hart's thought. He immediately recognized it to be not 'just another new weapon'—as many military experts who were struggling to digest its significance held—but a revolutionary one, for which no satisfactory defence existed or could be envisaged in the foreseeable future. At the

[31] I here stand between the two poles represented by Mueller, *Retreat from Doomsday: The Obsolescence of Major War* (New York, 1989), and 'The Essential Irrelevance of Nuclear Weapons: Stability in the Postwar World', *International Security*, 13 (2) (1988), 55–79, and M. van Creveld, *The Transformation of War* (New York, 1991).

[32] J. L. Gaddis, 'The Origins of Self-Deterrence: The United States and the Non-use of Nuclear Weapons, 1945–1958', in his *The Long Peace: Inquiries Into the History of the Cold War* (New York, 1987), 104–46.

same time, however, Liddell Hart viewed nuclear weapons as only the last step in a long process which had been increasing the cost and destructiveness of war so as to threaten the very existence of civilization and render total war irrational. Since he continued to believe, again in contrast to another prevailing view of the Bomb, that armed conflict and war would continue until international society underwent fundamental transformation—limiting sovereignty, curbing nationalism, and strengthening forms of European and World Federation and world order—the problem for him remained unchanged: how to limit war effectively, while making the most of its still considerable strategic potential. The means he foresaw for this dual purpose also remained as before: qualitative disarmament and control of nuclear weapons; deterrence, mutual restraint, and collective security; subatomic conventional warfare, to be carried out by small, fully mechanized armies relying on mobility and calculated dispersion, as well as by airborne forces for the role of imperial strategic reserve; indirect approach, 'camouflage war', peripheral war, infiltration, subversion, and guerrilla and non-violent techniques.

Liddell Hart advanced this remarkable blueprint for the nuclear age in the very first months after Hiroshima and Nagasaki, and had no trouble in incorporating it as a postscript to his *The Revolution in Warfare* (1946), which he wrote before the conclusion of the Second World War and the introduction of the Bomb, but which contained fundamentally the same ideas.[33] Although in time the book would be recognized as pioneering, the scope and perceptiveness of its vision are becoming all the more apparent as the Cold War era can be viewed in perspective and, one dares venture, as the outline of the post-Cold War world is emerging. During the formative years of the nuclear age Liddell Hart had no access to classified technological and strategic information, nor did he have to deal with the practical, day-to-day problems and constraints with which politicians and soldiers were

[33] See already in Liddell Hart to Hobart, 21 Aug. 1945, King's, 1/376; *The Revolution in Warfare*, 83–93; also 'War, Limited', *Harper's Magazine* (Mar. 1946), 193–202. The pros and cons of the balance of power, unification, or federation are first discussed in the 1941 edn. of *The Strategy of Indirect Approach*, 203–4. See also M. Howard, 'The Classical Strategists', in his *Studies in War and Peace* (London, 1970), 159, and 'Liddell Hart', in his *The Causes of War*, 246; L. Freedman, *The Evolution of Nuclear Strategy* (London, 1981), 97–100. Bond, *LH*, 164–214, provides the sole extensive summary of Liddell Hart's work in the nuclear age. The only new idea in *The Revolution in Warfare* was the automatization of warfare, which was in fact borrowed unacknowledged from Fuller's much earlier works: cf. p. 552 above.

grappling. For these same reasons, however, he was again free to take the longest view.

Liddell Hart's view regarding the policy to be adopted in respect to the Soviet Union was also similar to the one he had developed against the German threat in 1937–41: 'The military policy of a peaceful minded nation, aiming at self-preservation but not at expansion, should . . . concentrate . . . *primarily on defence*.'[34]

> The more one weighs all the factors, the more probable it appears that there could be no victory in a war between the Western Powers and the Soviet Union, but only a common loss. . . . There is a school of thought—more common in triumphant America that in war-weary Britain—which regarding war with Russia as bound to come, is inclined to force the issue. It talks of the importance of being ready 'to strike first' regardless of the basic fact that America's comparative remoteness entails delay in exerting her weight, and of the risk that war might be needlessly precipitated in the attempt. It ignores the likelihood of initial Russian success, the long road to recovery in consequence, and the irreparable damage that civilization would suffer in the process. It underrates the difficulties of gaining so-called 'victory' over Russia when the balance of strength has turned.[35]

For all that, Liddell Hart's pioneering formulation of the doctrines of containment and cold war has not been recognized. Partly this was because he lost public stature and was himself deeply scarred by his wartime isolation. He no longer developed his views as effectively as he had done in 1937–41, and the popular illustrated magazines to which he occasionally contributed in the second half of the 1940s, for handsome sums of money, were no substitute for the wide and influential readership of *The Times*. In addition, the hub of world power which during the interwar period, owing to Germany's collapse and the partial retreat of the United States and the Soviet Union from the international scene, had at least appeared to reside in Britain—giving the ideas of Fuller and Liddell Hart extra resonance—moved away, to the United States. And, as is always the case, the centre of strategic thought was moving in the same direction. Global policies and strategies were now decided in Washington, and it was there that intellectuals were coming forth to stimulate, articulate, and criticize them. It was left to a younger and fresher voice than Liddell Hart to stamp his name on the doctrine of

[34] 'War, Limited', 201; similarly *The Revolution in Warfare*, 87.

[35] 'What War with Russia Would Mean', *John Bull*, 30 Nov. 1946, 7, 9; repr. in *The Defence of the West* (London, 1950), 149–50.

Containment. This was George Kennan (b. 1904), probably the greatest of the Cold War intellectuals. The political and strategic programme for the West which he advanced in the early post-war years bears a stunning resemblance to that which Liddell Hart had developed during the struggle against Germany.

Kennan and Containment

During the Second World War, as a career diplomat who was serving in central and eastern Europe and was in contact with the German opposition, Kennan did not believe in any sort of compromise solution to the war with Germany. He felt that Nazi Germany had to be completely crushed, and the country repartitioned into small states. In retrospect he would come to look at this with astonishment, believing that the Western Allies missed opportunities for dealing with the German conservatives and army leaders. He also expressed the opinion that over time Hitler's empire would have collapsed of its own repressive nature and corruption, but that the damage that it would have done would have been too heavy to bear. All the same, when in 1945–7 Kennan developed the notion of the containment of the Soviet Union, he stressed that, threatening to the West as it was, the Soviet Union was different from Nazi Germany in possessing more time and in being more cautious.[36] It was this and not the nuclear factor that made the difference for him. As he would specifically point out, the idea of containment was formed in a fundamentally non-nuclear set of mind and derived from pre-1945 experiences.[37] The atom bomb is not even mentioned in either his 'Long Telegram' from Moscow of February 1946 or his famous 'X' article of 1947. It should be remembered that it was universally believed until the Soviet surprise of 1949 that it would take the Soviet Union much longer to develop nuclear weapons. Moreover, Kennan insisted throughout the second half of the 1940s that the US must refrain from using nuclear weapons as an active instrument of diplomacy and war, and he would have liked to see them abolished by agreement.

[36] Kennan's 'Long Telegram' from Moscow, 22 Feb. 1946, printed in *Memoirs* (2 vols.; Boston, 1967, 1972), i. 557–8, also 116–19, 239; his 'X' article in *Foreign Affairs*, 25 (1947), repr. in *American Diplomacy* (New York, 1985 (1951)), 118–21, also 87–8. In Kennan's unpublished lectures, some of which are confidential, given at various official and unofficial forums and now deposited at the Seeley G. Mudd Manuscript Library, Princeton [Mudd], see 8 Jan. 1948, King's, 17/1; 17 Sept. 1948, 17/11.

[37] *American Diplomacy*, pp. vi–vii.

Kennan had always been a 'realist', believing in a firm and dispassionate line towards the Soviet Union. He gradually developed the notion of her containment from the end of the Second World War. However, he would remember his period as one of the deputy commanders at the newly established National War College, from September 1946 to May 1947, as 'enormously stimulating and interesting' for him. 'It was at that time—in the background reading, in the attendance at lectures by distinguished outsiders, in the agonizing over my own lectures—that some of the ideas were conceived that have been basic to my views on American policy ever since':

we had, as it turned out, virtually nothing in the way of an established or traditional American doctrine which we could take as a point of departure for our thinking and teaching. . . . We found ourselves thrown back, perforce, on the European thinkers of other ages and generations: on Machiavelli, Clausewitz, Gallieni—even Lawrence of Arabia. We had the admirable compilation *Makers of Modern Strategy*, edited by E. M. Earle to draw on . . . But it was obvious that in no instance was the thinking of these earlier figures fully relevant or remotely adequate to the needs of a great American democracy in the Atomic age. . . .

The precedents of our Civil War, of the War with Spain, and of our participation in the two world wars of this century, had created . . . an unspoken assumption that the normal objective of warfare was the total destruction of the enemy's ability and will to resist and his unconditional capitulation. . . .

The most significant of the appreciations to which I came during that year at the War College was that this approach to the cultivation and use by our country of armed forces would no longer work. I doubted that it had been a sound one even in the pre-atomic age. It seemed to me that in each of the two world wars, the application of it, while successful in the immediate military sense, had complicated—very gravely indeed—the problems of the peace. . . .

This meant, it seemed to me, a need for return to much earlier concepts. The doctrine of total war had been a doctrine of the nineteenth and twentieth centuries. We would now have to revert to the concepts of limited warfare prevalent in the eighteenth century. The aims of warfare, accordingly, would have to become limited. If weapons were to be used at all, they would have to be employed to temper the ambitions of an adversary, or to make good limited objectives against his will—not to destroy his power, or his government, or to disarm him entirely. . . .

From these two appreciations . . . I went ahead to develop a concept of the peacetime requirements of our armed force establishment which laid emphasis on the maintenance of small, compact, alert forces, capable of delivering at short notice effective blows on limited theaters of operation far from our own shores.[38]

From the mid-1950s these ideas would become commonplace among strategic theorists, but they were not so in 1946–7. Although it is the argument of this study that it was the West's overall political and strategic conditions that produced the strategy of containment, the question whether Kennan was in any way influenced by Liddell Hart's strikingly similar ideas arises, and is one for which the present author has no definite answer. Liddell Hart's name is conspicuously not among the authorities cited by Kennan, either in the passage quoted above or in his lectures at the time, now held at the Seeley G. Mudd Manuscript Library at Princeton. After the war Liddell Hart was in eclipse, and an unwise choice as an ally. The chapter devoted to him in Earle's *Makers of Modern Strategy*, the book Kennan cites, was very critical. However, Liddell Hart's 'War, Limited' appeared in the March 1946 issue of the popular American intellectual journal *Harper's Magazine*, and his *The Revolution in Warfare*, which contained exactly the same strategic ideas and historical interpretation as would be espoused by Kennan, came out in Britain in 1946 and was published in America by Yale University Press in 1947. It seems unlikely that a book by such a well-known writer, relating to the new strategic challenges of the era and issued by a prestigious American publishing house, was unknown to those at the new War College who exactly at that time were struggling to form their minds in respect to US defence policy. Indeed the book, and Liddell Hart's earlier works that express similar ideas—the 1941 edition of *The Strategy of Indirect Approach*, reissued in 1946, *The Current of War* (1941), *This Expanding War* (1942), *Thoughts on War* (1944), and *Why Don't We Learn from History?* (1944)—all exist in the original editions in the library of the National Defence University to which the War College now belongs.[39]

Either way, Kennan's notion of containment against the Soviet Union took shape in early 1947, and was offered to the public in an article signed 'X' in the July issue of *Foreign Affairs*. When it was revealed that

[38] *Memoirs*, i. 308–11; these recollections, published in 1967, mention the nuclear factor far more prominently than Kennan's writings at the time. This is also pointed out by Gaddis, *The Long Peace*, 112–13.

[39] My attempts to raise the question in letters to Mr Kennan himself have been unsuccessful, his secretary replying that owing to his many commitments and advanced age he was not responding to any queries: T. Bramley to the author, 27 Oct. 1994 and 24 Apr. 1995.

the author was the nominated head of the newly established Policy Planning Staff at the State Department, it immediately gained great publicity. Coming as it did in close proximity to the announcement of the Truman Doctrine and the Marshall Plan, it was generally taken as an almost official expression of policy. In the article Kennan argued that the Soviet Union was fundamentally hostile to the capitalist world and ideologically committed to its destruction. There was no prospect for it being drawn into peaceful coexistence and cooperation with the West. In contrast to Napoleon or Hitler, however,

> it is more sensitive to contrary force . . . and thus more rational in the logic and rhetoric of power. On the other hand it cannot be easily defeated or discouraged by a single victory on the part of its opponents. . . . In these circumstances it is clear that the main element of any United States policy towards the Soviet Union must be that of a long-term, patient but firm and vigilant containment of Russian expansive tendencies. It is important to note, however, that such a policy has nothing to do with outward histrionics: with threats or blustering or superfluous gestures of outward 'toughness'. . . . Like almost any other government, [the Kremlin] can be placed by tactless and threatening gestures in a position where it cannot afford to yield even though this might be dictated by its sense of realism.[40]

Kennan suggested that the Soviet Union suffered from many problems and internal tensions: her success was achieved at the price of tremendous economic and human toll; her people were war-weary and disillusioned; the occupied nationalities of her empire were ever a source of unrest; and she was overall weaker than the West. For her part, the US must strive to solve her internal problems and project to the rest of the world an attractive model and a vital and confident vision. It must never adopt the methods of its enemy. Rejecting both options of retreat and pre-emptive war, the United States ought to work together with local allies, particularly in Western Europe, so as to create a strong enough coalition against the Soviet Union and share the burden of containment against her, a burden which the United States could not carry alone. In this way,

> the United States has it in its power to increase enormously the strains under which Soviet policy must operate, to force upon the Kremlin a far greater degree of moderation and circumspection than it has had to observe in recent years, and in this way to promote tendencies which must eventually find their

[40] 'The Sources of Soviet Conduct', *Foreign Affairs*, 25 (1947), repr. in *American Diplomacy*, 118–19.

outlet in either the break-up or the gradual mellowing of Soviet power. For no mystical, Messianic movement . . . can face frustration indefinitely . . .[41]

Once again the similarity between Kennan's ideas and those which Liddell Hart had developed in respect to Nazi Germany is striking, though a circumstantial explanation for their likeness cannot be ruled out: many of the notions which both men expressed were derived from the Allies' planning during the Second World War; some were 'in the air', as the perceived Soviet threat increasingly dominated American consciousness. In addition, Kennan's knowledge of Soviet and European affairs was infinitely superior to Liddell Hart's. Kennan held strong views on foreign affairs, and his powers of observation, deduction, and articulation were tremendous.

Be that as it may, given the similarity of their respective positions, it is not surprising that Kennan's image developed in a way similar to Liddell Hart's. During the immediate post-war period (like Liddell Hart in respect to Germany during the Munich crisis) Kennan was perceived as a hard-liner for mistrusting the Soviet Union and advocating her containment. In his capacity as head of the Policy Planning Staff at the State Department, a position he held until January 1950, he played a leading role in shaping American policy during the formative stage of the Cold War. However, by the end of his tenure and thereafter, as the Cold War was becoming dominated by the threat of nuclear war and as the United States became entangled in messy local conflicts, especially in east Asia, Kennan thought that American policy was veering in the other direction and he became progressively more critical of it. Consequently, he was now viewed as 'soft' and 'unsafe', and found himself increasingly isolated from official circles.[42] He believed all along that the Soviet threat, and hence containment itself, was mainly political rather than military, and that the Russians had no practical intention of invading Western Europe.[43] For his War College students he developed

[41] Ibid. 120–1, 126–7. On more specific points, see also Kennan's 'long telegram' of Feb. 1946, ibid. 559; 6 Nov. 1947, in A. K. Nelson (ed.), *The State Department Policy Staff Papers, 1947–1949* (3 vols., New York, 1983), i. 130 and *passim*; 26 June 1950, King's, 17/18.

[42] See esp. *Memoirs*, ii. 249–61.

[43] Kennan's position in this respect at the time, unclear to readers of Mr X and only revealed in his *Memoirs*, i. 358–9, is fully confirmed by the archival evidence. See e.g. 22 Oct. 1946, Mudd, 16/17; 10 Apr., 9 May, 28 July, and Dec. 1947, 16/29, 32, 33, 39 and 40; 8 Jan. 1948, 17/1. See also T. H. Etzold and J. L. Gaddis (eds.), *Containment: Documents on American Policy and Strategy, 1945–1950* (New York, 1978), 64–81, 90–7, 154, 173–211; Nelson *Policy Staff Papers*, i. 129; ii. 281–92, 490–6. Finally see Kennan, *Realities of*

a catalogue of 'Measures Short of War' which were the most suitable in the struggle to contain the Soviet threat.[44] He rejected the common view that the victory of the communists in China and the conflicts in Korea and Vietnam were Moscow-inspired and represented a world-wide, coordinated communist bid for power. As he saw it, these were predominantly indigenous conflicts, involving local forces which were very likely to fall out with the Kremlin, did not constitute a significant threat to the United States, and called for as little as possible high-handed American meddling in the affairs of desperately poor and help-less peoples.[45]

Kennan supported the initial American intervention to reinstate the status quo in Korea, but was deeply concerned that the conflict would escalate into total war:

> The thought of a war with Russia . . . was particularly alarming and abhorrent to me because of my acute awareness . . . that in a war of this nature the American side would have no realistic, limited aims. Falling back on the patterns of the past and seized by wartime emotionalism, we would assuredly attempt once again to achieve the familiar goals of total enemy defeat, total destruction of the enemy's armed forces, his unconditional surrender, the complete occupation of his territory, the removal of the existing government and its replacement by a regime that would respond to our concept of 'democratization'. . . . I had tried to bring home to my War College students, that in a war between the United States and the Soviet Union, there could be no complete military victory. Neither country was occupiable by the forces of the other. Both were simply too large, too different—linguistically, culturally, and in every other way.[46]

Kennan always held that the horrible and suicidal nature of nuclear weapons made them sterile and impractical as instruments of Western strategic policy. Within the adminstration, he was against the develop-

American Foreign Policy (Princeton, NJ, 1954), 64–5; *Russia, the Atom and the West* (New York, 1958), 16–19 and *passim*.

[44] 16 Sept. 1946, Mudd, 16/12.

[45] Etzold and Gaddis, *Containment*, 226–8; Nelson, *Policy Staff Papers*, ii. 121–3, 412–51; Kennan, 'America and the Russian Future', *Foreign Affairs*, 29 (1951), repr. in *American Diplomacy*, 152; beautifully stated in *Realities of American Foreign Policy*, 96–99; and *Russia, the Atom and the West*, 66–82; also *Memoirs* ii. 23–60.

[46] This is the wording of *Memoirs*, ii. 94–5; see similarly: 'America and the Russian Future', in *American Diplomacy*, 129–30; ibid., 101–2; *Realities of American Foreign Policy*, 79–81. Similarly in the classified material of the late 1940s: 26 June 1950, Mudd, 17/18; Etzold and Gaddis, *Containment*, 173–211, 344–64; Nelson, *Policy Staff Papers*, ii. 372–411: 'United States Objectives with Respect to Russia' in peace and war, Aug. 1948.

ment of thermonuclear weapons by the United States and called for an agreement with the Soviet Union to prohibit their deployment.[47] Later, he rejected both the notion of 'massive retaliation' and the reliance on tactical nuclear weapons for the defence of Europe. He maintained that there should never be a 'first use' of nuclear weapons by the West, and that at most they should be reserved for deterrence against similar weapons. He argued that if war was to come it had to be kept limited and conventional. He believed that a Soviet attack on Western Europe, the sceptre which dominated Western strategic policy, was unlikely, and suggested once that even if it came, Europe would be better off relying on guerrilla resistance by paramilitary militias and on civil disobedience rather than on rigid forward defence by armies.[48] While he repeatedly pointed out the ethnic diversity of the Soviet empire as a source of endemic trouble and weakness, he ruled out any attempt by the West to encourage the occupied nationalities to revolt, or to lead a crusade for their liberation. He believed that this would only push the Soviet Union to extreme actions, make war imminent, and court disaster for the entire world.[49] He believed that Western defence policy must be defensive. The West's most potent offensive weapon was the long-term alternative it presented to the Soviet system. The West must have patience, and do its utmost to demonstrate to the peoples of the communist world that it is not their enemy. Historical evolution was bound to change the Soviet Union from within. No regime based on evil and terror was durable. 'If . . . anything were ever to occur to disrupt the unity and efficacy of the Party as a political instrument, Soviet Russia might be changed overnight from one of the strongest to one of the weakest and most pitiable of national societies.'[50]

Increasingly critical of Western policy, Kennan began to argue that much of the responsibility for the escalation and militarization of the Cold War rested with the West, whose hard-line measures, resulting from misconceptions of Soviet intentions and actions, alarmed the Soviets into stronger and largely protective measures of their own.

[47] See e.g. 23 Jan. 1947, Mudd, 16/21; memorandum to Dean Acheson, 20 Jan. 1950, in Etzold and Gaddis, *Containment*, 373–81.

[48] *Realities of American Foreign Policy*, 84–5; *Russia, the Atom and the West* (New York, 1958), 52–65; *Memoirs*, ii. 246–9.

[49] 'America and the Russian Future', in *American Diplomacy*, 140–2; *Realities of American Foreign Policy*, 76–81; *Memoirs*, ii. 97–102.

[50] 'The Sources of Soviet Conduct', in *American Diplomacy*, 125; see also 'America and the Russian Future', in *American Diplomacy*, 148–53; *Realities of American Foreign Policy*, 79, 92–3.

Kennan believed that the exhausted and cautious Soviet Union, while never forsaking its hostile designs against the West, never realistically intended to invade Western Europe. Both by ideology and in view of the political and strategic realities, the Soviets' favoured methods were subversion, infiltration, propaganda, and political influence. The Soviet Union therefore interpreted the unilateral reconstruction and militarization of West Germany and Japan by the West, the creation of Nato as a *military* alliance, and the Western reliance on nuclear weapons (all of which Kennan criticized) as offensive actions against her.[51] In this line of argument Kennan foreshadowed much of the revisionist analysis of the origins of the Cold War. Needless to say, he also again strikingly paralleled many of the arguments Liddell Hart had advanced regarding British and Allied policy towards Germany and was in fact advancing in respect to Western policy towards the Soviet Union.

Interestingly, the two men first made personal contact when Kennan held a visiting fellowship at Oxford during the academic year 1957–8 and delivered his BBC Reith Lectures on Russia, the West, and the nuclear threat. Commenting on Liddell Hart's paper 'Basic Problems of European Defence' which Liddell Hart had sent him, Kennan wrote: 'I read it with utter amazement, and much gratification, at the fact that our minds should have run so closely together . . . had I read your paper at an earliest date I should have suspected myself of subconscious plagiarism.'[52]

Liddell Hart: Deterrence and Defence

Indeed, Liddell Hart and Kennan held remarkably similar views. While Liddell Hart supported the resurrection and rearmament of Germany within some sort of a European federation and combined European defence system,[53] he too maintained that, despite the Soviets' aggressive appearance, they were war-weary, mostly concerned about their own security, and conscious of the realities of the global balance of

[51] Etzold and Gaddis, *Containment*, 101, 135–44, 153–8; *Memoirs*, i. 397–448; ii. 137–8, and Kennan's masterful dispatch from Moscow of 8 Sept. 1952, ibid. 327–51; *Russia, the Atom and the West*; Gaddis, *The Long Peace*, 63–71.

[52] To Liddell Hart, 29 Oct. 1957, King's, 1/415. While they met during the year on official and academic occasions and corresponded extensively—as usual, on Liddell Hart's urging—Kennan evaded any personal relationship, politely declining Liddell Hart's persistent invitations to come to his nearby Buckinghamshire house.

[53] The 'European idea' already mooted in the 1941 edition of *The Strategy of Indirect Approach*, 203–4, is regarded as essential in the *Sunday Pictorial*, 24 Aug. 1947, and repeatedly in the following years.

power. Their most promising strategy was subversion and 'camouflaged' or 'cold' war. He predicted that, for the West, 'the best chance might lie in an internal split, starting near the top—since it is almost impossible to overthrow a totalitarian regime from below, by popular revolt'. The Soviet explosion of a nuclear device in 1949 strengthened Liddell Hart in his view that the West could not rely on nuclear weapons for anything other than deterring a nuclear attack. In view of their horrific nature, nuclear weapons provided neither credible deterrence nor defence against either a Soviet invasion of Western Europe or any other sort of non-nuclear threat around the globe. The West's only rational option was non-nuclear and limited. It should be noted that Liddell Hart wrote all this in the late 1940s, before Korea and before the idea of limited war and the opposition to 'massive retaliation' was taken on by Western defence intellectuals. Furthermore, Liddell Hart who had pioneered the idea of limited war during the 1920s, had become increasingly cautious and circumspect about the circumstances of its implementation long before Vietnam would cool the defence intellectuals' enthusiam for it.[54]

Liddell Hart maintained that for the defence of Western Europe conventional forces must be created. He continued to reject mass conscript armies of the old type, which would be slow to mobilize and unable to respond quickly enough to a surprise Soviet attack. Instead, he restated his previous advocacy for two types of force. One, always kept in a state of high alert, was to be an élite, high-tech, professional striking force, composed of some twenty wholly armoured and fully mechanized divisions, a number of airborne divisions, and a powerful air force. The other was to comprise militias on the pattern of the British Territorials, locally resisting and obstructing the enemy's advance. Civil disobedience, for all its problems against a ruthless adversary, should also be considered. Civil defence and the protection of industry must be seriously taken up.[55]

In the second half of the 1950s a fast-growing community of defence intellectuals and strategic analysts was forming in the United States and

[54] Similarly, Liddell Hart amended his views regarding guerrilla warfare, now underlining its destructive effect and long-term harmful legacy to those who practised it: Liddell Hart, *Defence of the West*, 53–7, expanded and incorporated into the 1967 edn. of *Strategy: The Indirect Approach*.

[55] Liddell Hart's articles from the second half of the 1940s were collected in *Defence of the West*; see esp. 57, 88, 94–5, 97–8, 125–6, 129–30, 132, 136–40, 144–5, 148–50, 188–90, 216–42, 328–38, 366–80; quotation from p. 132. Also see *Deterrent or Defence* (London, 1960), 5, 16 and *passim*.

Britain. In 1954 Liddell Hart took part in the creation of the Military Commentators Circle, which in 1958 would develop into the Institute for Strategic Studies. The new strategic community held almost unanimously, as Liddell Hart and Kennan had done all along, that with the Soviet Union possessing nuclear and thermonuclear capability, a Western defence policy based on a massive nuclear attack lacked credibility in response to anything but a massive Soviet nuclear attack.[56] A wave of literature espousing the idea of limited war rose in the second half of the 1950s, naming, however, Clausewitz's later ideas as its classical source of inspiration. Where the defence intellectuals were mostly divided was over the desirability of relying on tactical nuclear weapons which had been developed and had begun to enter service toward the mid-1950s. Liddell Hart had rejected their use well before the argument started, pointing out that the devastation to Europe would be unlimited. Like Kennan, he continued to insist that conventional forces were the only viable option for Western defence policy.[57]

The argument over the West's reliance on nuclear weapons for the defence of Europe was to continue with new twists and turns until the collapse of the Soviet empire. Liddell Hart, however, retired in 1960 from participation in current strategic debates. He dedicated the last decade of his life to completing his *Memoirs* and *History of the Second World War*, while also maintaining extensive contacts with, and offering help and much encouragement to, young scholars from all over the world. Knighted in 1965, he died in 1970.

Assessment

Again, weighty arguments could be, and have been, advanced against Liddell Hart's (and Kennan's) philosophy of war, as applied to the Cold War. These are the sort of arguments that will probably always be contested in the debate between 'hawks' and 'doves' over the Cold

[56] For Liddell Hart's immediate rejection of the American 'New Look' and of the similar British defence thinking represented by the chief of the Air Staff, Sir John Slessor, see *Daily Mail*, May 1954, 26–7; *World*, 1 June 1954; Preface to the 1954 edn. of *Strategy: The Indirect Approach*, 14–15; *Deterrent or Defence*, 17–26. Reviewing the latter book for the *Saturday Review*, 3 Sept. 1960, 17–18, presidential candidate Senator John F. Kennedy made it a vehicle for outlining his critique of the outgoing adminstration's defence policy. Interestingly, Liddell Hart was a well-known figure to him: Kennedy's remarkably mature and comprehensive Harvard dissertation, which turned into a national bestseller, *Why Britain Slept* (New York, 1940), had cited him widely. The Liddell Hart–Kennedy correspondence file: King's, 1/418.

[57] *Picture Post*, 19 Feb. 1953; *Deterrent or Defence*, 24, 58–62, 74–81. For Kennan, see *Russia, the Atom and the West*, 56–65.

War; while information about the conflict will certainly become more abundant and accurate over time, historical alternatives can never be tested, and differences of perspective, temperament, and values among commentators are inherent in the intellectual construction which is 'historical judgement'.

Thus, it may be claimed that conditions of nuclear abundance, achieved only in the 1960s, had to be reached before the nonsensical, suicidal nature of a full-scale nuclear war between the superpowers was fully realized. Even then, and certainly before, however irrational the Western threat to *initiate* the use of nuclear weapons may have been, the risk that the threat would be carried out was horrifying enough to deter a Soviet attack on Western Europe, if indeed the Soviets ever seriously contemplated such an attack. The nuclear race was thus a stabilizing as well as a destabilizing force in the Cold War. Because of their economic, social, and political priorities, the conventional defence option proved beyond the reach of the countries of Western Europe. Only their reliance on the American nuclear force gave the Europeans a measure of protection, and psychological reassurance. This may have been an irresponsible defence policy, and it certainly appeared so at the time, but in the event it contributed to Western Europe's remarkable political and economic recovery. Indeed, it was the protracted and wasteful arms race—both nuclear and conventional—that proved too heavy a burden for the Soviet Union and contributed to its collapse. How crucial a contribution was it to an economy that was failing for other, more fundamental reasons is still to be assessed.

Going deeper, one may argue that war, even when 'cold', involves risks, anxieties, and passions which it would be simply unrealistic to rule out, even in the name of the most realistic and sober calculations. In a conflict involving animosity, fear, gaps in information, and suspicion, there is a mutual quest for wider margins of safety, occasional scares over imagined or real dangers, a great deal of waste, and much non-linear logic. From this point of view, Liddell Hart's approach—and Kennan's—may appear too 'sensible' and sensitive, too detached and rational for a phenomenon like war. Even assuming that their vision of cold war proved in the end more comprehensive and far-sighted than others, did they not shrink from the passions and violence of conflict and war that had to be endured on the way? Did they not have too clinical a view of the role of mass psychology and of the necessity of mobilizing and keeping attuned to public opinion, especially in democracies?

Whatever position one may take on these points, the argument of this study is that Liddell Hart, followed by Kennan, expressed and pioneeringly codified a new and emerging view of war which is in some fundamental way typical of advanced Western and 'Westernized' liberal-democratic societies. The ideas of containment, cold war, and limited war—their core ideas—reflected a growing aversion in these societies to the phenomenon of war in general. War was becoming increasingly in conflict with their domestic values and practices. It was more and more out of place and debilitating within the system of global trade in raw materials, manufactured goods, finance, services, and information, upon which their economic prosperity was increasingly based. It was progressively at odds with the social and economic expectations of the people, whose volatility Liddell Hart and, more deeply, Kennan, distrusted, but who with the decline of authority and relaxation of social control increasingly refused to shoulder its burden. Among Western élites there was now growing awareness of the limitations of military force, especially under modern conditions, and of the complexity of exchanging military victories into political gains; a growing tendency to try to understand and take account of the other's point of view; and a growing demand to curb the passions to which conflict and war gave rise.

Under these conditions, 'defence', that is, the maintenance of a political, economic, and international order that was working in accordance with Western interests, came to be regarded as the only sensible and legitimate strategic policy for the West. It was thus the political and strategic techniques that promised maximum defence at minimum cost and with minimum bloodshed, and made use of the West's strongest assets—its economic power and technological supremacy—that came to the fore in the shape of containment, cold war, economic coercion, and limited war. Nuclear weapons tremendously strengthened this trend, but only as one of a much wider set of factors underlying Western strategic policy. The new strategic attitudes were in the ascent before the advent and proliferation of nuclear weapons, and, with some differences, they also largely characterize the Western approach towards non-nuclear antagonists.

The new strategic paradigm and the trends that had brought it into being have widened and deepened momentously during the twentieth century. They have long been implicit in the philosophy and realities of economic and political liberalism that since the eighteenth century has been increasingly manifest in Western Europe and North America. And it is no coincidence that it was among 'enlightened' public opinion, in the leading liberal-democratic powers, Britain and the United States, in the wake of the First World War and the Versailles settlement, that such factors became a potent political force. As economic and political liberalism expanded rapidly all over the developed world after the Second World War, so did the attitudes towards war that grew out of it. To some extent these attitudes have always expressed themselves in pacifism, isolationism, and support for unilateral disarmament. But in a world in which conflict and the threat of war remained a possibility, they have also led to an ongoing search for defence policies that would be the least in conflict with the new political, economic, social, and cultural modes.

Kennan himself—another early twentieth-century Mid-Westerner, born and raised in Milwaukee, Wisconsin, and deeply nostalgic for the America of the small community and 'whitewashed fences'—has been a lifelong critic of the ills of modernity, as he saw them: uninformed and volatile democracy; self-indulgent and permissive society; rampant consumerism; vulgar and corrupting media; overdevelopment, urban decay, and destruction of the environment; and the decline of communal values. In the 1930s he devised a scheme for a new form of élite, meritocratic, and hierarchic political system to replace mass democracy, and he would express similar views even in 1947. At the same time, however, he cherished above all the classical liberal rights and civic freedoms of the Anglo-American and Western tradition.[58] His memorandum to Secretary of State Dean Acheson, in which he expressed in a remarkably similar language the same ideas which Liddell Hart had formulated more than a decade earlier, is in this respect most revealing:

> Whether or not war on a grand scale can achieve positive aims for an aggressive totalitarian power, it is my belief that it cannot achieve such aims for a democracy. It would be useful, in my opinion, if we could recognize that the real purposes of the democratic society cannot be achieved by large-scale violence and destruction; that even in the most favorable circumstances war between great powers spells a dismal deterioration of world conditions from the standpoint of the liberal-democratic tradition; and that the only positive function it can fulfil for us—a function, the necessity and legitimacy of which I do not

[58] 18 June 1947, King's, 16/34; *Memoirs*; also the 3 biographies: B. Gellman, *Contending with Kennan* (New York, 1984), 83–105, and *passim*; A. Stephanson's hostile *Kennan and the Art of Foreign Policy* (Cambridge, Mass., 1989), 211, 216–21, 232–8, and *passim*; D. Mayers, *George Kennan and the Dilemmas of US Foreign Policy* (New York, 1988).

dispute—is to assure that we survive physically as an independent nation . . . For such positive purposes as we wish to pursue, we must look to other things than war: above all to bearing, to example, to persuasion, and to the judicious exploitation of our strength as a deterrent to world conflict.[59]

It is a telling fact that Liddell Hart, the man who first translated the new conditions and sensibilities of the modern world into the language of strategic theory, did so while increasingly identifying himself with the liberal creed. As we have seen, by the second half of the 1930s his newly developed views regarding Britain's desired defence policy of containment and cold war went hand in hand with what he perceived and strongly affirmed as her liberal political culture, institutions, and values (though also her worldwide imperial interests). At that time Liddell Hart sought to maintain his position as an 'impartial' strategic adviser to all parties. But by 1945 he had lost this position anyhow, and had become more committed than ever. From being a conscientious liberal, he now came out openly as a Liberal. He enlisted in the party's electoral campaigns in both 1945 and 1950, speaking in public meetings on its behalf and serving on the Liberal campaign fund national committee.[60] Since he was a man of his times, his liberalism was of the 'New Liberalism' mould of the late nineteenth and early twentieth centuries. Like Kennan, he advocated social reform as well as individual rights, was more liberal then democratic, and thought men and women fundamentally unequal. Like Kennan he also rejected the Messianic and crusading brand of Wilsonian liberalism.

The Liberal Party which Liddell Hart joined was reaching the nadir of its long decline. However, as he wrote in 1937, the decline of the Liberal Party came with the adoption of liberal values by all parties and the incorporation of these values throughout the fabric of British society. To be sure, even the most 'Western' regions of the 'West' have never been solely or perhaps even principally dominated by liberalism—politically, socially, economically, or philosophically. Yet liberalism, in all these aspects, has been for centuries the agent and expression of these regions' development of modernity, and it is as such that it has won its status as the West's 'defining' characteristic. In this sense, like John Locke or John Stuart Mill, although representing no

[59] Memorandum from Kennan to Acheson, 20 Jan. 1950, in Etzold and Gaddis, *Containment*, 378–9.

[60] His file of correspondence and activities connected with the Liberal Party is King's, 5/21; for his speeches in meetings, see also 12/1945/1, 12/1950/3, 4, 7.

more than one school of thought or even a minority opinion, Liddell Hart was a quintessentially 'English' thinker. At the same time, however, to the extent that the liberal-democratic model would come to dominate the developed world in the course of the twentieth century, he developed in the language of theory the strategic paradigm of the future.

6

Conclusion: 'The Western Way in Warfare', Past and Future

This study suggests that Liddell Hart's contribution to strategic theory goes much further, and is more serious, than the popular doctrines, such as the 'indirect approach' or the 'British way in warfare', which won him fame in his youth.[1] This contribution, and Liddell Hart's more substantial claim for originality, should be understood in their historical context. New and significant intellectual constructions usually emerge at times of fundamental change or paradigmatic shifts, when prevailing ways of interpreting and coping with reality no longer seem adequate. Rather than being alone in their views, the thinkers who generate them usually make their names by early sensing, conceptualizing, and turning into philosophical and political programmes the feelings and notions which are beginning to emerge, more or less hazily, around them. From the perspective of time, the reaction against the First World War—particularly noticeable among the West's most liberal and increasingly democratic societies, Britain and the United States—can be seen as marking such a paradigmatic 'break'. For leading sectors of public opinion and of the political élite in those societies the idea of a major war, involving massive loss of life and wealth, was simply becoming unacceptable. Liberal-democratic, status quo powers, whose wealth was based on manufacturing and vast global trade, called for a wholly different set of strategic ideas from those required by etatist-nationalist, still largely agrarian, politically expansionist, or disunited, or revisionist, and economically less secure powers, whose wars had provided the model for nineteenth-century strategic theory.

It had fallen mainly to Clausewitz personally to experience, internalize, and formulate in the language of strategic theory the marrying of etatism and surging nationalism which had made its debut on the

[1] Cf. M. Howard in 'Liddell Holmes', *Listener*, 28 Dec. 1972, 896. For his contribution to armoured doctrine, again see my *British Armour Theory and the Rise of the Panzer Arm: Revising the Revisionists* (London, 2000).

European scene with the French Revolution. While still representing only a minority view in Prussia and pushed to the political fringes with the post-1815 European order, Clausewitz was riding the wave of the future in nineteenth-century Europe. True, during the last years of his life he came to recognize, against his own strongly held views throughout his career, that limited war and indecisive strategy—associated with the discredited eighteenth-century type of warfare—was a 'legitimate' option for belligerents whose circumstances and policy so dictated. Nevertheless, the implications and practical strategies for that type of war were left to be worked out by later societies, for which limiting war was again becoming not just a *theoretical* option. For these societies, military 'victory' increasingly appeared, while not disconnected from, more and more difficult to identify with a successful peace and an overall gain—a notion still alien to Clausewitz. A major reformulation of strategic theory was thus required, was first attempted, even before the First World War, by Julian Corbett—another Edwardian liberal—and was then developed during the inter-war period by Liddell Hart.

The sort of ideas that Keynes articulated in his *The Economic Consequences of the Peace* were to become widespread among Western élites by the 'Locarno era', and a general abhorrence of war would gain massive popular hold in the West by the 1930s. It was in this context that Liddell Hart crystallized his early doctrines in the 1920s, developing them further in his more mature, less known, and largely discredited writings of the second half of the 1930. The doctrines he now advanced for the West were those of strategic, economic, and ideological containment and cold war. Liddell Hart was not alone in thinking along these lines. No longer able to embrace isolationism, both the British and American adminstrations attempted policies which veered between political accommodation and economic reward on the one hand ('appeasement') and containment and economic coercion on the other (e.g. Roosevelt's notions of 'quarantine' and 'a modern technique').[2] Neither Britain nor the United States embarked on all-out war until forced into doing so by the surprising collapse of their defences in May–June 1940 in Western Europe and in December 1941 in the Pacific. Indeed, this political and strategic order of priorities, along a

[2] For the origins of this posture in that 'first "reasonable" nation', Britain of the second half of the nineteenth century, see P. Kennedy, *Strategy and Diplomacy, 1870–1945* (London, 1983), 15–39.

scale stretching from isolationism to appeasement, containment and cold war, limited war, and only reluctantly fully fledged war, became the pattern for the West.[3]

While the experience of Hitler and the Second World War was to stiffen attitudes again for a while, the same aversion to and loss of faith in war were soon to return on a much wider scale and with ever-increasing force throughout the West and among those affected by its model. These attitudes now manifested themselves not only in those fortunate countries which historically had been sheltered by sea from invasion and large-scale land warfare and had experienced relatively little serious border or nationalist problems; they have, for example, become strongly evident in that quintessential 'Continental' country, the democratized and liberalized West Germany, and increasingly potent within the formerly heavily mobilized Israeli society from the 1980s on. Aware of the still major defence problems facing their countries, many observers in the West were much concerned about their societies' 'loss of belligerency' which seemed to border on an irresponsible flight from reality. By and large, however, the West's record does not look too bad, either by luck or, more probably, because, belligerent or not, Western societies have enjoyed supremacy in resources and technology over their rivals.

Scholars' attitude to Liddell Hart is likely to remain ambivalent, and not only because of the unflattering revelations about him. Too much of what he wrote is considered dogmatic, superficial, or unhistorical. These, indeed, are the very same charges that have been levelled since the eighteenth century against the liberal doctrine and liberal thinkers by their sometimes more sophisticated critics. None the less, whatever its philosophical and practical shortcomings, an amazing part of the liberal programme came to be realized simply because it proved to be almost inseparably intertwined with the West's course into modernity. And much the same may apply to Liddell Hart's ideas as well. More balanced minds than his have criticized, qualified, or rejected them. Yet, viewed from a longer perspective, his dogmatism appears to have had a Gordian knot-cutting greatness about it, cutting through genuine complexity, to be sure, but riding the most powerful currents of the age, anticipating the course of things to come. Thus, for example, Liddell

[3] For a concentrated elaboration of this thesis, see my 'Isolationism, Appeasement, Containment, Limited War: Western Strategic Policy from the Modern to the "Post-Modern" Era'. in A. Gat and Z. Maoz (eds.), *War in A Changing World* (Ann Arbour, 2001), 77–91.

Hart's theories have often been dismissed wryly on the grounds that he advocated wars without the spilling of blood. Yet the profound reaction in the West to the casualty list of the First World War signalled a new and ultimately much enhanced unwillingness on the part of individuals and society as a whole to accept the sacrifice of life in war. Indeed at the turn of the twenty-first century this has become an overwhelming social imperative and a reality which no government in any advanced society can ignore.

Partly for that reason and because of a decreasing willingness by civil society to enlist at all, partly because of worldwide commitments, and partly because of the growing sophistication and cost of modern weapon systems—as mechanization was followed by another revolutionary wave of electronics, affecting armies as it had air forces and navies—professionals, as opposed to conscripts, are increasingly in vogue in the developed world. Even in a country like Israel, the most extreme case to be sure, where traditionally all available manpower has been mobilized for war and where preparations for large-scale land warfare continue to be made, a change is increasingly noticeable, and was under way even before the collapse of the Soviet Union and the great advances in the peace process. The nation in arms is still there in Israel and is likely to remain, for military as well as symbolic reasons, but both for the capital-intensive, high-tech battlefield and for the lowly 'policing' of hostile populations smaller forces of professionals are increasingly preferred to the masses of reservists.

As the West at present no longer confronts a technologically advanced Second World, either Axis or Soviet, the strategic challenges it faces are obviously considerably altered and lightened. Yet much of what became the pattern of international relations during the interwar period—when the modern global industrial and trading system which had been emerging since the end of the nineteenth century took shape—seems to be enduring, deepening, or even returning. War appears increasingly removed from any obvious or immediate interest of Western societies. However, local conflicts and 'aggressive' actions by local powers, either close by or further away around the globe, pose disturbing problems. Some of these conflicts affect Western interests and spheres of influence in ways not very different from how similar conflicts affected the formal empires of the interwar period. Some, however, appear wholly irrelevant to these interests and, as then, only arouse concern either in public opinion for humanitarian reasons or as an undesirable example for others. The economy, ecology, demography, communications, cultural transfers, and nuclear proliferation are making the world increasingly interdependent. Yet the ability of advanced societies to isolate themselves from problems beyond their borders is still considerable; and their willingness to pay the price of intervention—armed or not—or ability to achieve much by it are very limited. Furthermore, as before, the West is far from being a monolith, and it is difficult to unite its members for concerted action, or prevent them from 'defecting' or from pursuing 'selfish' national interests. Under these conditions there are inherent and frustrating tensions—first experienced during the interwar period—between isolationism, a search for some sort of world order and collective security regimes, and traditional *Realpolitik* or balance-of-power considerations.

When force is applied, it is usually along the lines first mooted during the 1930s and championed by Liddell Hart. The favoured techniques include economic sanctions; the provision of money and hardware to cement coalitions and strengthen local forces against adversaries; blockade; naval and aerial actions, in which advanced countries possess a clear superiority; and limited, 'surgical' operations by highly mobile and technologically superior striking forces. Direct large-scale warfare, especially on land where casualties might be high, would tend to be avoided. Heightened awareness of the elusiveness of victory and of the intricacy of military and political causes and effects—as well as self-imposed restrictions on ruthlessness and, increasingly, nuclear proliferation—result in half-way measures, stop/go strategies, and a general indecisiveness.

These methods have had a mixed and often disappointing record, from the 1930s onward. They are politically and strategically difficult to apply, often ineffective, and they bring their own sort of psychological strains for those who practise them. Still, given the nature of modern Western societies, of their foreign affairs, strategic requirements, and cultural sensibilities, this way of war-making appears to be their norm, as much as all-out war was for their predecessors.

SELECT BIBLIOGRAPHY
I
FROM THE ENLIGHTENMENT TO CLAUSEWITZ

Works Composed before 1837

BERENHORST, GEORG HEINRICH VON, *Betrachtungen über die Kriegskunst, über ihre Fortschritte, ihre Widersprüche und ihre Zuverlässigkeit* (3rd edn.; Leipzig, 1827), including *Randglossen* and *Aphorismen.*

—— *Aus dem Nachlasse*, ed. E. von Bülow (2 vols.; Dessau, 1845, 1847).

BINZER, J. L. J., *Über die militärischen Werke des Herrn von Bülow* (Kiel, 1803).

BRENCKENHOFF, L. S. VON, *Paradoxa, gröstentheils militärischen Inhalts* (n.p., 1783).

BÜLOW, A. H . D. VON, *The Spirit of the Modern System of War* (London, 1806).

—— *Der Feldzug von 1800, miliärisch-politisch betrachtet* (Berlin, 1801).

—— *Neue Taktik der Neuern, wie Sie seyn sollte* (Leipzig, 1805).

—— *Lehrsätze des neuern Krieges, oder reine und angewandte Strategie aus dem Geist des neuern Kriegssystems* (Berlin, 1805).

—— *Der Feldzug von 1805, militärisch-politisch betrachtet*, (n.p., 1806).

—— *Militärische und vermischte Schriften*, ed. E. Bülow and W. Rüstow (Leipzig, 1853).

—— *Pacatus Orbis* (London, 1867).

CARL VON OESTERREICH [Archduke Charles], *Ausgewählte Schriften*, ed. F. X. Malcher. (6 vols.; Vienna and Leipzig, 1893–4).

CLAUSEWITZ, CARL VON, *Hinterlassene Werke* (10 vols.; Berlin, 1832–7).

—— *On War*, ed. and trans. M. Howard and P. Paret, introductory essays by P. Paret, M. Howard, and B. Brodie, with a commentary by B. Brodie (Princeton, 1976).

—— *Vom Kriege*, ed. W. Hahlweg (16th edn.; Bonn, 1952).

—— *Verstreute klein Schriften*, ed. W. Hahlweg (Osnabrück, 1979).

—— *Carl von Clausewitz. Politische Schriften und Briefe*, ed. H. Rothfels (Munich, 1922).

—— *Clausewitz, Geist und Tat*, ed. W. M. Schering (Stuttgart, 1941).

—— *Strategie aus dem Jahr 1804 mit Zusätzen von 1808 und 1809*, ed. E. Kessel (Hamburg, 1937).

—— *Principles of War* (Harrisburg, 1942).

—— *Karl und Marie von Clausewitz. Ein Lebensbild in Briefen und Tagebuchblättern*, ed. K. Linnebach (Berlin, 1916).

—— 'Über das Leben und den Charakter von Scharnhorst', in L. von Ranke (ed.), *Historisch-politische Zeitschrift*, I (1832).

CLAUSEWITZ, CARL VON, 'Über das Fortschreiten und den Stillstand der Kriegerischen Begebenheiten', *Zeitschrift für preussische Geschichte und Landeskunde*, XV (1878), 233–40.

—— *Historische Briefe über die grossen Kriegsereignisse im Oktober 1806*, ed. J. Niemeyer (Bonn, 1977).

—— *Carl von Clausewitz, Schriften, Aufsätze, Studien, Briefe*, ed. W. Hahlweg, i. (Göttingen, 1966).

—— *The Campaign of 1812 in Russia* (London, 1843).

—— *Two Letters on Strategy*, ed. and trans. by P. Paret and D. Moran (Carlisle, 1984).

DIDEROT AND D'ALEMBERT, *Encyclopédie* (Paris and Amsterdam, 1751–80).

DUMAS, MATHIEU, *Précis des événemens militaires, ou essais historiques sur les campagnes de 1799 à 1814* (19 vols.; Paris, 1817–26).

FEUQUIÈRES, A. P. MARQUIS DE, *Memoirs Historical and Military* (2 vols.; London, 1736).

FOLARD, JEAN CHARLES DE, *Histoire de Polybe* (Amsterdam, 1774), including Folard's related military works.

FREDERICK THE GREAT, *Œuvres*, ed. J. D. E. Preuss, vols. 28–30 (Berlin, 1856).

—— *Werke*, ed. G. B. Volz (Berlin, 1913), vol. vi.

—— *Posthumous Works*, trans. T. Holcroft (13 vols.; London, 1789).

GROTIUS, HUGO, *The Rights of War and Peace* (London, 1738).

GUIBERT, JACQUES ANTOINE HIPPOLYTE DE, *A General Essay on Tactics* (2 vols.; London, 1781).

—— *Œuvres militaires* (5 vols.; Paris, 1803).

—— *Observations on the Military Establishment and Discipline of the King of Prussia* (London, 1780).

—— *Journal d'un voyage en Allemagne 1773* (2 vols.; Paris, 1803).

HEGEL, G. W. F., *The Philosophy of Right* (Oxford, 1942).

HERDER, G. J., *Outlines of a Philosophy of the History of Man* (London, 1800).

JOMINI, ANTOINE HENRI, *Treatise on Grand Military Operations* (2 vols.; New York, 1865).

—— *Summary of the Art of War* (New York, 1854; another edn. Philadelphia, 1862).

—— *Histoire critique et militaire des guerres de la révolution* (Paris, 1820–4).

—— *Introduction à l'étude des grandes combinaisons de la stratégie et de la tactique* (Paris, 1829).

JOMINI, ANTOINE HENRI, *Tableau analytique des principales combinaisons de la guerre et de leur rapports avec la politique des états* (Paris, 1830).

—— *Life of Napoleon* (4 vols.; New York, 1864).

KANT, IMMANUEL, *The Critique of Judgment* (Oxford, 1961).

LESPINASSE, MLLE J. DE, *Letters*, trans. K. P. Wormeley (London, 1902; a fuller edn. London, 1929).

LINDENAU, KARL FRIEDRICH VON, *Über die höhere preussische Taktik* (Leipzig, 1790).

LIPSIUS, JUSTUS, *Sixe Bookes of Politickes or Civil Doctrine* (London, 1594).

—— *De militia Romana* (Antwerp, 1596).

LLOYD, HENRY HUMPHREY EVANS, *The History of the Late War in Germany between the King of Prussia and the Empress of Germany and her Allies* (2 vols.; London, 1781, 1784).

—— *An Essay on the English Constitution* (London, 1770).

—— *An Essay on the Theory of Money* (London, 1771).

—— *A Rhapsody of the Present System of French Politics, of the Projected Invasion and the Means to Defeat It* (London, 1779).

—— *A Political and Military Rhapsody on the Invasion and Defence of Great Britain and Ireland* (London, 1798; a later edn. of the former entry).

LOSSAU, F. K. VON, *Der Krieg* (Leipzig, 1815).

—— *Ideale der Kriegführung* (3 vols.; Berlin, 1836).

MACHIAVELLI, NICCOLÒ, *The Chief Works and Others*, ed. Allan Gilbert (Durham, 1965).

MAIZEROY, PAUL GIDEON JOLY DE, *Cours de tactique, théoretique, pratique et historique* (4 vols.; Paris, 1766, 1785).

—— *A System of Tactics* (2 vols.; London, 1781).

—— *Théorie de la guerre* (Nancy, 1777).

MILLER, FRANZ, *Reine Taktik* (2 vols.; Stuttgart, 1787–8).

MONTECUCCOLI, RAIMONDO, *Ausgewählte Schriften des Raimund Fursten Montecuccoli*, ed. A. Veltzé (4 vols.; Vienna and Leipzig, 1899–90).

MONTESQUIEU, C. L. DE SECONDAT, *The Spirit of the Laws*, trans. T. Nugent (New York, 1949).

NAPOLEON, 'Military Maxims', in *Roots of Strategy* (Harrisburg, 1940).

—— *Mémoires pour servir à l'histoire de France sous Napoléon, écrits à Sainte Hélène*, ed. C. J. F. T. Montholon (Paris, 1823).

—— *Talks of Napoleon at St. Helena*, ed. G. Gourgaud (6 vols.; London, 1904).

—— *Notes inédites de l'Empereur Napoléon Ier sur les mémoires militaires du général Lloyd* (Bordeaux, 1901).

NICOLAI, FERDINAND FRIEDRICH VON, *Versuch eines Grundrisses zur Bildung des Offiziers* (Ulm, 1775).

—— *Essai d'architecture militaire* (n.p., 1755).

NOCKHERN VON SCHORN, FRANÇOIS, *Versuch über ein allgemeines System aller militairischen Kenntnisse* (Nuremberg, 1785).

PUYSÉGUR, J. F. C. MARQUIS DE, *Art de la guerre par principes et par règles* (2 vols.; Paris, 1748).

RÜHLE VON LILIENSTERN, J. J. A., *Handbuch für den Offizier, zur Belehrung im Frieden und zum Gebrauch im Felde* (Berlin, 1817).

—— *Rühle von Lilienstern et son apologie de la guerre*, ed. and trans., Louis Sauzin (Paris, 1937).

SANTA CRUZ DE MARZENADO, N. O., *Reflections, Military and Political* (London, 1737).

SAXE, MAURICE DE, *Mes rêveries* (2 vols.; Amsterdam and Leipzig, 1757).

—— *Reveries*, T. Phillips (ed.), *Roots of Strategy* (Harrisburg, 1940).

—— *Esprit des lois de la tactique* (2 vols.; La Haye, 1762).

SCHARNHORST, GERHARD VON (ed.), *Militair Bibliothek* (Hanover, 1782–4).

—— (ed.), *Bibliothek für Offiziere* (4 issues; Göttingen, 1785).

—— *Handbuch für Offiziere in den angewandten Theilen der Krieges Wissenschaften* (3 vols.; Hanover, 1787–90).

—— *Militairisches Taschenbuch zum Gebrauch im Felde* (3rd edn.; Hanover, 1794).

—— *Militärische Schriften von Scharnhorst*, ed. C. von der Goltz (Berlin, 1881).

—— *Ausgewählte Schriften*, ed. U. von Gersdorff (Osnabrück, 1983).

—— *Scharhorsts Briefe*, ed. K. Linnebach (Munich and Leipzig, 1914).

SCHLEIERMACHER, F. D. E., *On Religion* (London, 1893).

STAËL, MME LA BARONNE DE, *Œuvres complètes* (Paris, 1821), ed. by her son.

TEMPELHOFF, G. F. VON, *History of the Seven Years War* (2 vols.; concise edn: London, 1793).

TURPIN DE CRISSE, L. DE, *The Art of the War* (2 vols.; London, 1761).

VAUBAN, SÉBASTIEN LE PRESTRE DE, *Traité de l'attaque et de la défense des places* (2 vols.; La Hare, 1737).

VENTURINI, JOHANN GEORG JULIUS, *Lehrbuch der angewandten Taktik, oder eigentlichen Kriegswissenschaft* (2 vols.; Schleswig, 1800).

VOLTAIRE, 'Tactics', in *Works*, trans. T. Smollett (London, 1799–81), misc. i. 126–30.

WAGNER, A., *Grundzüge der reinen Strategie* (Amsterdam, 1809).

ZANTHIER, FRIEDRICH WILHELM VON, *Versuch über die Kunst den Krieg zu studiren* (n.p., 1775).

—— *Versuch über die Märsche der Armeen, die Läger, Schlachten und den Operations Plan* (Dresden, 1778).

Works Composed after 1837

ADAMS, F. D., *The Birth and Development of the Geological Sciences* (London, 1938).

AESCH, A. G. VON, *Natural Science in German Romanticism* (New York, 1941).

ALEXANDER, W. M., *Johann Georg Hamann, Philosophy and Faith* (The Hague, 1966).

ALGER, J. I. *Antoine Henri Jomini: A Bibliographical Survey* (West Point, 1975).

ANDRÉ, LOUIS, *Michel le Tellier et Louvois* (Paris, 1943).

ANGELI, M. E. VON, *Erzherzog Carl von Oesterreich als Feldherr und Heersorganisator* (Vienna and Leipzig, 1896).

ARIS, REINHOLD, *History of Political Thought in Germany from 1789 to 1815* (London, 1965).

ARON, RAYMOND, *Clausewitz, den Krieg denken* (Frankfurt am Main, 1980).

—— *Peace and War, A Theory of International Relations* (New York, 1967).

—— 'What is a Theory of International Relations?', *Journal of International Affairs*, XXI (1967), 185–206.

BAHN, RUDOLF, *Georg Heinrich von Berenhorst* (doctoral diss. Halle, 1910).

BARKER, THOMAS M., *The Military Intellectual and Battle: Montecuccoli and the Thirty Years War* (New York, 1975).

BAYLEY, C. C., *War and Society in Renaissance Florence* (Toronto, 1961).

BECK, L. W., *Early German Philosophy, Kant and his Predecessors* (Cambridge Mass., 1969).

BECKER, CARL, L., *The Heavenly City of the Eighteenth Century Philosophers* (New Haven, 1932).

BEHRENS, C. B. A., 'Which Side was Clausewitz On?', in *The New York Review of Books*, 14 Oct. 1976.

BERLIN, ISAIAH, *Against the Current: Essays in the History of Ideas* (Oxford, 1981).

—— *Vico and Herder* (London, 1976).

BLANNING, T. C. W., *Reform and Revolution in Mainz 1743–1803* (Cambridge, 1974).

BLOCK, WILLIBALD, 'Die Condottieri: Studien über die sogenannten "unblutigen Schlachten"', *Historische Studien*, CX (1913).

BLOMFIELD, R., *Sébastien Le Prestre de Vauban* (London, 1938).

BORGERHOFF, E. B. O., *The Freedom of the French Classicism* (Princeton, 1950).

BRODIE, BERNARD, *War and Politics* (New York, 1973).

BRUMFITT, J. H., *Voltaire—Historian*, (Oxford, 1958).

BRUNSCHWIG, HENRI, *Enlightenment and Romanticism in Eighteenth Century Prussia* (Chicago, 1974).

BURKE, PETER, *The Renaissance Sense of the Past* (London, 1969).

—— *Montaigne* (Oxford, 1981).

BURY, J. B., *The Idea of Progress* (New York, 1932).
BUTTERFIELD H., *The Statecraft of Machiavelli* (London, 1955).
CAEMMERER, R. VON, *The Development of Strategical Science during the 19th Century* (London, 1905).
—— *Clausewitz* (Berlin, 1910).
CAMON, H., *La Guerre Napoléonienne* (5 vols.; Paris, 1907).
—— *Le Système de guerre de Napoléon* (Paris, 1923).
—— *Clausewitz* (Paris, 1911).
CAMPORI, CESARE, *Raimondo Montecuccoli, la sua famiglia e i suoi tempi* (Florence, 1876).
CARRIAS, E., *La Pensée militaire allemande* (Paris, 1948).
—— *La Pensée militaire français* (Paris, 1960).
CASSIRER, ERNST, *The Philosophy of the Enlightenment* (Princeton, 1951).
CHANDLER, DAVID, *The Campaigns of Napoleon* (New York, 1966).
—— *The Art of Warfare in the Age of Marlborough* (London, 1976).
CHICHESTER, H. MANNERS, 'Lloyd', in *Dictionary of National Biography* (London, 1909), xi. 1301–2.
COHEN, HERMANN, *Von Kants Einfluss auf die deutsche Kultur* (Berlin, 1883).
COLIN, J., *L'Éducation militaire de Napoléon* (Paris, 1901).
—— *L'Infanterie au XVIIIe siècle* (Paris, 1907).
—— *La Tactique et la discipline dans les armées de la Révolution* (Paris, 1902).
—— *Les Campagnes du Maréchal de Saxe* (3 vols.; Paris, 1901–6).
COURVILLE, XAVIER DE, *Jomini ou le devin de Napoléon* (Paris, 1935).
CREUZINGER, PAUL, *Hegels Einfluss auf Clausewitz* (Berlin, 1911).
CREVELD, MARTIN VAN, *Supplying War* (Cambridge, 1977).
CRISTE, O., *Erzherzog Carl von Oesterreich* (Vienna and Leipzig, 1912).
D'ALDÉGUIER, F., *Discours sur la vie et les écrits de Guibert* (Paris, 1855).
DEBUS, A. G., *The Chemical Philosophy, Paracelsian Science and Medicine in the Sixteenth and Seventeenth Centuries* (2 vols.; New York, 1977).
DELBRÜCK, HANS, *History of the Art of War within the Framework of Political History*, vols. 1–4 (London, 1975–85).
DUFFY, CHRISTOPHER, *The Army of Frederick the Great* (London, 1974).
—— *Fire and Stone. The Science of Fortress Warfare 1660–1860* (London, 1975).
—— *Siege Warfare: The Fortress in the Early Modern World 1494–1660* (London, 1979).
—— *The Fortress in the Age of Vauban and Frederick the Great 1660–1789* (London, 1985).
EARLE, E. M. (ed.), *Makers of Modern Strategy, Military Thought from Machiavelli to Hitler* (Princeton, 1943).
EASLEA, BRIAN, *Witch-hunting, Magic and the New Philosophy* (Sussex, 1980).

ELKAN, A., 'Die Entdeckung Machiavellis in Deutschland zu Beginn des 19. Jahrhunderts', *Historische Zeitschrift*, CXIX (1919), 427–58.

ENGELL, JAMES, *The Creative Imagination, Enlightenment to Romanticism* (Cambridge Mass., 1981).

EPSTEIN, KLAUS, *The Genesis of German Conservatism* (Princeton, 1966).

EVANS, R. J. W., *Rudolf II and his World, a Study in Intellectual History 1576–1612* (Oxford, 1973).

—— *The Making of the Habsburg Monarchy 1550–1700* (Oxford, 1979).

FULLER, J. F. C., *The Foundations of the Science of War* (London, 1925).

GALLIE, W. B., *Philosophers of Peace and War, Kant, Clausewitz, Marx, Engels and Tolstoy* (Cambridge, 1978).

GAT, AZAR, 'Clausewitz on Defence and Attack', *Journal of Strategic Studies*, X, (March, 1988).

GAY, PETER, *The Enlightenment; an Interpretation* (2 vols.; London, 1967–9).

—— *Voltaire's Politics* (Princeton, 1959).

Le Général Antoine Henri Jomini 1779–1869, Bibliothèque Historique Vaudoise, 41 (Lausanne, 1969).

GIBSON, R. W., *Bacon: A Bibliography of his Works and Baconiana to the Year 1750* (Oxford, 1950).

GILBERT, FELIX, *Machiavelli and Guicciardini* (Princeton, 1965).

GILMORE, M. P., 'The Renaissance Conception of the Lessons of History', in his *Humanists and Jurists* (Cambridge Mass., 1963).

GUY, BASIL, 'The French Image of China before and after Voltaire', *Studies on Voltaire and the Eighteenth Century*, XXI, (1963).

HAGEMANN, ERNST, *Die deutsche Lehre vom Kriege, von Berenhorst zu Clausewitz* (Berlin, 1940).

HAHLWEG, WERNER, *Clausewitz. Soldat, Politiker, Denker* (Göttingen, 1957).

—— 'Philosophie und Theorie bei Clausewitz', in Clausewitz Gesellschaft (ed.), *Freiheit ohne Krieg* (Bohn, 1980), 325–32.

—— *Die Heersreform der Oranier und die Antike* (Berlin, 1941).

—— (ed.), *Klassiker der Kriegskunst* (Darmstadt, 1960).

HALE, J. R., *Renaissance War Studies* (London, 1983).

—— *War and Society in Renaissance Europe 1450–1620* (Leicester, 1985).

—— The military chapters in the *New Cambridge Modern History* (vols i–iii; 1957–8).

HANDEL, MICHAEL (ed.), *Clausewitz and Modern Strategy* (London, 1986).

HARRASCHIK-EHL, C., *Scharnhorsts Lehrer: Graf Wilhelm von Schaumburg-Lippe in Portugal* (Osnabrück, 1974).

HAUSER, ARNOLD, *The Social History of Art* (London, 1951), ii.

HAY, DENYS, *Annalists and Historians* (London, 1977).

HAZARD, PAUL, *The European Mind 1680–1715* (London, 1953).

—— *European Thought in the Eighteenth Century* (London, 1954).

HILLGARTH, J. N., *Raymon Lull and Lullism* (Oxford, 1971).
HOBOHM, WALTER, *Machiavellis Renaissance der Kriegskunst* (Berlin, 1913).
HÖHN, REINHARD, *Revolution, Heer, Kriegsbild* (Darmstadt, 1944).
—— *Scharnhorsts Vermächtnis* (Bonn, 1952).
HOWARD, MICHAEL ELIOT (ed.), *The Theory and Practice of War* (London, 1965).
—— *Clausewitz* (Oxford, 1983).
—— *War in European History* (London, 1976).
HUGHES, G. L. T., *Romantic German Literature* (London, 1979).
IGGERS, G. G., *The German Conception of History, the German Tradition of Historical Thought from Herder to the Present* (Middletonn Conn., 1968).
JÄHNS, MAX, *Geschichte der Kriegswissenschaften* (3 vols.; Munich and Leipzig, 1889–91).
JANY, KURT, *Geschichte der Königlich Preussischen Armee* (4 vols.; Berlin, 1928–37).
KAUFMANN, HANS, 'Raimondo Graf Montecuccoli, 1609–1680' (doct. diss.; Berlin, 1972).
KESSEL, EBERHARD, 'Georg Heinrich von Berenhorst', *Sachsen und Anhalt*, IX (1933), 161–98.
—— 'Zur Entstehungsgeschichte von Clausewitz Werk "Vom Kriege"', *Historische Zeitschrift*, CLII (1935), 97–100.
—— 'Carl von Clausewitz: Herkunft und Persönlichkeit', *Wissen und Wehr* XVIII (1937).
—— 'Zur Genesis der modernen Kriegslehre', *Wehrwissenschaftliche Rundschau*, III/9 (1953).
—— 'Die doppelte Art des Krieges', *Wehrwissenschaftliche Rundschau*, IV/9 (1954), 298–310.
KIERNAN, COLIN, 'Science and the Enlightenment in Eighteenth Century France', in T. Besterman (ed.), *Studies on Voltaire and the Eighteenth Century*, LIX (1968).
KLIPPEL, G. H., *Das Leben des Generals von Scharnhorst* (3 vols.; Leipzig, 1869–71).
KNUDSEN, JONATHAN, B., *Justus Möser and the German Enlightenment* (Cambridge, 1986).
KRIEGER, LEONARD, *The German Idea of Freedom, History of a Political Tradition* (Boston, 1957).
LATREILLE, A., *L'Armée et la nation à la fin de l'ancien régime* (Paris, 1914).
LAZARD, P. E., *Vauban* (Paris, 1934).
LECOMTE, FERDINAND, *Le Général Jomini, sa vie et ses écrits* (Paris and Lausanne, 1860).
LEHMANN, MAX, *Scharnhorst* (2 vols.; Leipzig, 1886–7).

LENIN, V. I., 'The Collapse of the Second International', *Collected Works* (Moscow, 1964), vol. 21.

LÉONARD, E. G., *L'Armée et ses problèmes au XVIIIe siècle* (Paris, 1958).

LIDDELL HART, B. H., *The Ghost of Napoleon* (New Haven, 1934).

—— *Strategy, the Indirect Approach* (London, 1954).

LLOYD, HANNIBAL EVANS, *Memoir of General Lloyd* (London, 1842).

LORENZ, REINHOLD, 'Erzherzog Carl als Denker', in August Faust (ed.), *Das Bild des Krieges im deutschen Denken* (Stuttgart and Berlin, 1941), 235–76.

LOVEJOY, ARTHUR, 'Herder and the Enlightenment Philosophy of History', in his *Essays in the History of Ideas* (Baltimore, 1948) 166–82.

LUDENDORFF, ERICH, *The Total War* (London, n.d.).

LYNN, JOHN A., *The Bayonets of the Republic* (Chicago, 1984).

MCCLELLAND, CHARLES, E., *State, Society and University in Germany, 1700–1914* (Cambridge, 1980).

MALLETT, MICHAEL, *Mercenaries and Their Masters: Warfare in Renaissance Italy* (London, 1974).

MARTIN, KINGSLEY, *French Liberal Thought in the Eighteenth Century* (2nd rev. edn., London, 1954).

MARWEDEL, ULRICH, *Carl von Clausewitz, Persönlichkeit und Wirkungsgeschichte seines Werkes bis 1918* (Boppard am Rhein, 1978).

MEINECKE, R. L. F., *Cosmopolitanism and the National State* (Princeton, 1970).

—— *Machiavellism, the Doctrine of Raison d'Etat and its Place in Modern History* (London, 1957).

—— *Historicism, the Rise of a New Historical Outlook*, (London, 1972).

MILLER, R. D., *Schiller and the Ideal of Freedom, A Study of Schiller's Philosophical Works with Chapters on Kant* (Oxford, 1970).

NISBET, H. B., *Herder and the Philosophy and History of Science* (Cambridge, 1970).

NOHN, ERNST AUGUST, 'Der unzeitgemässe Clausewitz', *Wehrwissenschaftliche Rundschau*, V (1956).

OESTREICH, GERHARD, *Neostoicism and the Early Modern State* (Cambridge, 1982).

OLDRIDGE, O. A., 'Ancients and Moderns in the Eighteenth Century', in P. Wiener (ed.), *Dictionary of the History of Ideas, Studies of Selective Pivotal Ideas* (New York, 1968), i. 76–87.

OMAN, CHARLES, *The Art of War in the Middle Ages* (2 vols.; London, 1924).

—— *The Art of War in the Sixteenth Century* (London, 1937).

OMMEN, HEINRICH, 'Die Kriegsführung des Erzherzogs Carl', *Historische Studien*, XVI (Berlin, 1900).

PAGEL, WALTER, *Joan Baptista van Helmont* (Cambridge, 1982).

PARET, PETER, *Clausewitz and the State* (Oxford, 1976).

PARET, PETER, *Yorck and the Era of the Prussian Reform* (Princeton, 1966).

—— 'Education, Politics and War in the Life of Clausewitz', *Journal of the History of Ideas*, XXIX (1968), 394–408.

—— 'Die politischen Ansichten von Clausewitz', in Clausewitz Gesellschaft (ed.), *Freiheit ohne Krieg*, 332–48.

—— (ed.), *Makers of Modern Strategy from Machiavelli to the Nuclear Age* (Princeton, 1986).

PARKER, GEOFFREY, 'The "Military Revolution 1560–1660"—a Myth?' *Journal of Modern History*, XXXXVIII (1976), 195–214.

PARKINSON, ROGER, *Clausewitz* (London, 1970).

PASCAL, ROY, *The German Sturm und Drang* (London, 1953).

PEBALL, KURT, 'Zum Kriegsbild der österreichischen Armee und seiner geschichtlichen Bedeutung in den Kriegen gegen die Französische Revolution und Napoleon I', in Groote, W. V., and Müller, K. J. (eds), *Napoleon I und das Militärwesen seiner Zeit* (Freiburg, 1968), 129–82.

PERIÉS, G., 'Army Provisioning, Logistics and Strategy in the Second Half of the 17th century', *Acta Historica Hungaricae* XVI 1–2 (1970), 1–51.

PICHAT, HENRY, *La Campagne du Maréchal de Saxe 1745–6* (Paris, 1909).

PIERI, PIERO, 'La formazione dottrinale di Raimondo Montecuccoli', *Revue internationale d'histoire militaire*, III (1951), 92–125.

PINSON, K. S., *Pietism as a Factor in the Rise of German Nationalism* (New York, 1968).

PÖHLER, J., *Bibliotheca historico-militaris* (4 vols.; Leipzig, 1887–97).

POIRIER, LUCIEN, *Les Voix de la stratégie—Guibert* (Paris, 1977).

POTEN, K. G. H. B. VON, *Geschichte des militär-Erziehungs und Bildungswesens in den Landen deutscher Zunge*, vols. 10, 11, 15, 17, 18 of C. Kehrbach (ed.), *Monumenta Germaniae Pedagogica* (Berlin, 1889–97).

PRIESDORFF, KURT VON, *Soldatisches Führertum* (10 vols.; Hamburg, 1936–42).

QUIMBY, ROBERT, *The Background of Napoleonic Warfare, the Theory of Military Tactics in Eighteenth Century France* (New York, 1957).

RANDALL Jun., J. H., *The Career of Philosophy from the Middle Ages to the Enlightenment* (New York, 1962).

REIL, PETER HANNS, *The German Enlightenment and the Rise of Historicism* (Berkeley, 1975).

RITTER, GERHARD, *The Sword and the Scepter* (Miami, 1969).

ROBERTS, MICHAEL, *Gustavus Adolphus* (2 vols.; London, 1958).

—— 'The Military Revolution 1560–1660' in his *Essays in Swedish History* (London, 1967).

ROSINSKI, HERBERT, 'Die Entwicklung von Clausewitz Werk "Vom Kriege" im Licht seiner "Vorreden" und "Nachrichten"', *Historische Zeitschrift*, CLI (1935), 278–93.

ROTHENBERG, G. E., *Napoleon's Great Adversaries, The Archduke Charles and the Austrian Army, 1792–1814* (London, 1982).

—— KIRÁLY, B. K. AND SUGAR, P. F. (eds), *East Central European Society and War in the Pre-Revolutionary Eighteenth Century*, vol. ii of *War and Society in East-Central Europe* (New York, 1982).

ROTHFELS, HANS, *Carl von Clausewitz, Politik und Krieg* (Berlin, 1920).

SAINTE-BEUVE, C. A., *Le Général Jomini, étude* (Paris, 1869).

SANDONNINI, TOMMASO, *Il Generale Raimondo Montecuccoli e la sua famiglia* (Modena, 1914).

SAUNDERS, J. L., *Justus Lipsius, the Philosophy of Renaissance Stoicism* (New York, 1955).

SCHENK, H. G., *The Mind of the European Romantics* (London, 1966).

SCHERING, WALTER MALMSTEN, *Die Kriegsphilosophie von Clausewitz* (Hamburg, 1935).

—— *Wehrphilosophie* (Leipzig, 1939).

SCHOTTEN, COL. J. VON, *Was muss ein Offizier wissen?* (Dessau and Leipzig, 1782).

SCHRAMM, WILHELM VON, *Clausewitz, Leben und Werk* (Munich, 1976).

SCHWARTZ, KARL, *Leben des Generals Carl von Clausewitz und der Frau Marie von Clausewitz* (2 vols.; Berlin, 1878).

SHANAHAN, WILLIAM, *Prussian Military Reforms 1786–1813* (New York, 1945).

SHARPE, LESLEY, *Schiller and the Historical Character* (Oxford, 1962).

SIMON, W. M., *Friedrich Schiller: the Poet as Historian* (Keele, 1966).

SKINNER, QUENTIN, *The Foundations of Modern Political Thought* (Cambridge, 1978).

STADELMANN, RUDOLF, *Scharnhorst. Schicksal und geistige Welt, ein Fragment*, (Wiesbaden, 1952).

STERN, J. P., *Lichtenberg, a Doctrine of Scattered Occasions* (Indiana, 1959).

STRAUSZ-HUPÉ, ROBERT, *Geopolitics: The Struggle for Space and Power* (New York, 1942).

TAYLOR, F. L., *The Art of War in Italy 1494–1529* (Cambridge, 1921).

THORNDIKE, LYNN, *A History of Magic and Experimental Science* (New York, 1923–58) vols. vi–viii.

TOOLEY, R. V. AND BRICKER, C., *A History of Cartography* (London, 1968).

TROELTSCH, ERNST, 'The Idea of Natural Law and Humanity in World Politics', Appendix to O. Gierke, *Natural Law and the Theory of Society 1500–1800* (Cambridge, 1934), 201–22.

TYMMS, RALPH, *German Romantic Literature* (London, 1955).

USCZECK, HANSJÜRGEN, *Scharnhorst. Theoretiker, Reformer, Patriot*, (East Berlin, 1979).

VAGTS, ALFRED, *A History of Militarism* (London, 1959).

VEHSE, E., *Memoirs of the Court and Aristocracy of Austria* (2 vols.; London, 1856).

VENTURI, FRANCO, 'Le avventure del generale Henry Lloyd', *Rivista Storia Italiana* [RSI], XCI (1979), 369–433.

WADE, IRA O., *The Structure and Form of the French Enlightenment* (2 vols.; Princeton, 1977).

—— *The Intellectual Origins of the Enlightenment* (Princeton, 1971).

WAGNER, GEORGE, *Das Türkenjahr 1664, Raimund Montecuccoli, die Schlacht von St. Gotthard-Mogarsdorf*, issue 48 (1964) of *Burgenländische Forschungen*.

WAGNER, WILHELM, *Die preussischen Reformer und die zeitgenössische Philosophie* (Cologne, 1956).

WALKER, D. P., *Spiritual and Demonic Magic from Ficino to Campanella* (London, 1958).

WALLACH, JEHUDA L., *Das Dogma der Vernichtungsschlacht* (Frankfurt am Main, 1967).

—— *Kriegstheorien, ihre Entwicklung im 19. und 20. Jahrhundert* (Frankfurt am Main, 1972).

WARD, ALBERT, *Book Production, Fiction and the German Reading Public, 1740–1800* (Oxford, 1974).

WELLEK, RENE, *A History of Modern Criticism* (London, 1955), vol. i.

WELLS, G. A., *Herder and After* (Gravenhage, 1959).

—— *Goethe and the Development of Science* (The Netherlands, 1978).

—— 'Herder's Two Philosophies of History', *Journal of the History of Ideas*, XXI (1960), 527–37.

WENIGER, ERICH, 'Philosophie und Bildung im Denken von Clausewitz', in W. Hubatsch (ed.), *Schicksalswege Deutscher Vergangenheit* (Düsseldorf, 1950), 123–43.

WILKINSON, SPENSER, *The French Army before Napoleon* (Oxford, 1915).

WILLISEN, WILHELM VON, *Theorie des grossen Krieges* (Berlin, 1840).

WRIGHT, C. H. C., *French Classicism* (Cambridge Mass., 1920).

YATES, F. A., *Giordano Bruno and the Hermetic Tradition* (London, 1964).

—— *The Art of Memory* (London, 1966).

—— *Theatre of the World* (London, 1969).

—— *The Occult Philosophy in the Elizabethan Age* (London, 1979).

YORK VON WARTENBURG, *Napoleon as a General* (2 vols.; London, 1902).

ZEISSBERG, H. R. VON, *Erzherzog Carl von Oesterreich* (Vienna and Leipzig, 1895).

II
THE NINETEENTH CENTURY

Primary Sources

American State Papers, Military Affairs, i (Washington, DC, 1832).

Ardant du Picq, C. J. J. J., *Études sur le combat* (Paris, 1880); 2nd edn. ed. Ernst Judet, Paris, 1903; trans, as *Battle Studies* (Harrisburg, Pa., 1947).

Balck, Wilhelm, *Modern German Tactics* (London, 1899). First publ. German 1892.

Berenhorst, Georg Heinrich von, *Betrachtungen über die Kriegskunst* (3rd edn.; Leipzig, 1827).

Bernhardi, Friedrich von, *Delbrück, Friedrich der Große und Clausewitz* (Berlin, 1892).

—— *On War of To-Day* (2 vols; London, 1912).

—— *Britain as Germany's Vassal* (London, 1914; trans. of *Unsere Zukunft*).

—— *Germany and the Next War* (New York, 1914).

—— *Vom Kriege der Zukunft* (Berlin, 1920).

—— *Denkwürdigkeiten aus meinem Leben* (Berlin, 1927).

Berthaut, J. A., *Principes de stratégie, étude sur la conduite des armées* (Paris, 1881).

Bigge, Wilhelm, *Feldmarschall Graf Moltke* (Munich, 1901).

Bismark, Friedrich Wilhelm von, *Lectures on the Tactics of Cavalry* (London, 1827, 2nd edn. 1855).

Bleibtreu, Carl, *Napoleon'sche und Moltke'sche Strategie* (Vienna, 1901).

Bloch, Jean, *La Guerre future* (6 vols.; Paris, 1898).

—— *Is War Now Impossible?* (London, 1899).

Blume, Wilhelm von, *Strategie: Eine Studie* (Berlin, 1882).

—— *Moltke* (Berlin, 1907).

Boguslawski, Albrecht von, *Die Nothwendigkeit der Zweijährigen Dienstzeit* (Berlin, 1891).

—— *Der Krieg in seiner wahren Bedeutung für Staat und Volk* (Berlin, 1892).

—— *Die Parteien und die Heeresreform* (Berlin, 1892).

—— *Volkskampf—nicht Scheinkampf: Ein Wort zur politischen Lage im Innern* (Berlin, 1895).

—— *Betrachtungen über Heerwesen und Kriegführung* (Berlin, 1897).

BONNAL, HENRI, *Les Maîtres de la guerre: Frédéric II, Napoléon, Moltke, d'après des travaux inédits de M. le général Bonnal*, ed. Léonce Rousset (Paris, 1899).
—— *De la méthode dans les hautes études militaires en Allemagne et en France* (Paris, 1902).
—— *La Récente Guerre sud-africaine* (Paris, 1903).
—— *De Rosbach à Ulm* (Paris, 1903).
—— *L'Art nouveau en tactique* (Paris, 1904).
—— *La Manœuvre d'Iéna 1806* (Paris, 1904).
—— *La Manœuvre de Saint–Privat* (3 vols.; Paris, 1904–12).
—— *La Manœuvre de Landshut 1808–1809* (Paris, 1905).
—— *La Manœuvre de Vilna 1811–1812* (Paris, 1905).
—— *Sadowa: A Study* (London, 1907).
BOUCHER, ARTHUR, *L'Offensive contre l'Allemagne* (Paris, 1911).
—— *La Belgique à jamais indépedante* (Paris, 1913).
BOURDE DE VILLEHUET, JACQUES, *Le Manœuvrier, ou essai sur la théorie et la pratique des mouvements du navire et des évolutions navales* (Paris, 1765). (Eng. trans. publ. 1788).
BRUCE, H. A. (ed.), *Life of General Sir William Napier* (London, 1864), written anonymously by Patrick MacDougall.
BYELY, B., FYODOROV, G., KULAKOV V. (eds.), *Marxism-Leninism on War and Army* (Moscow, 1972).
CAEMMERER, R. VON, *The Development of Strategical Science during the 19th Century* (London, 1905).
CAMON, HUBERT, *Clausewitz* (Paris, 1911).
CARDOT, LUCIEN [writing as Loukiane Carlovich], *Éducation et instruction des troupes* (3 vols.; Paris, 1896–7).
—— *Hérésies et apostasies militaires de notre temps* (Paris, 1908).
CHARMES, GABRIEL, *Naval Reform* (London, 1887).
CHERFILS, MAXIME, *Cavalerie en campagne* (2nd. edn.; Paris, 1893).
CHURCHILL, WINSTON, S., *The World Crisis* (6 vols.; London, 1923–31).
CLAUSEWITZ, CARL VON, *Politische Schriften und Briefe*, ed. Hans Rothfels (Munich, 1922).
—— *Principles of War* (Harrisburg, Pa., 1942).
—— *On War*, trans. Michael E. Howard and Peter Paret (Princeton, NJ, 1976), (2nd edn. 1984).
—— *Verstreute kleine Schriften*, ed. W. Hahlweg (Osnabrück, 1979).
COLIN, JEAN, *L'Éducation militaire de Napoléon* (Paris, 1900).
—— *The Transformation of War* (London, 1912).
COLOMB, JOHN, *The Protection of Our Commerce and Distribution of Our Naval Forces Considered* (London, 1867).
—— *Imperial Defence* (London, 1871).
—— *Colonial Defence (London, 1877).*
—— *The Defence of Great and Greater Britain* (London, 1880).

—— *Naval Intelligence and Protection of Commerce in War* (London 1881).
—— *Imperial Federation: Naval and Military* (London, 1886).
COLOMB, PHILIP, *Naval Warfare, Its Ruling Principles and Practice, Historically Treated* (London, 1891).
—— *Essays on Naval Defence* (London, 1893).
CONRAD VON HÖTZENDORF, FRANZ VON, *Aus meiner Dienstzeit, 1906–1918* (5 vols.; Berlin, 1921–5).
CORBETT, JULIAN S., The Corbett Papers, The National Maritime Museum, Greenwich.
—— *Drake and the Tudor Navy* (2 vols.; London, 1898).
—— *The Successors of Drake* (London, 1900).
—— *England in the Mediterranean, 1603–1713* (2 vols.; London, 1904).
—— (ed.), *Fighting Instructions, 1530–1816* (London, 1905).
—— *England in the Seven Years War: A Study in Combined Strategy* (2 vols.; London, 1907).
—— (ed)., *Signals and Instructions, 1776–1794* (London, 1908).
—— *The Campaign of Trafalgar* (London, 1910).
—— *Some Principles of Maritime Strategy* (Annapolis, Md., 1988).
CULMANN, FRÉDÉRIC, *Deux tactiques en présence* (Paris, 1904).
—— *Tactique d'artillerie: Le Canon de tir rapide dans la bataille* (Paris, 1906).
DAHN, FELIX, *Moltke als Erzieher* (Breslau, 1892).
DANY, JEAN, 'La Littérature militaire d'aujourd'hui', *La Revue de Paris* (Mar.–Apr. 1912), 611–24.
DARRIEUS, GABRIEL, *La Guerre sur mer: Stratégie et tactique* (Paris, 1907).
DAVELEY, RENÉ, *L'Esprit de la guerre navale* (3 vols.; Paris, 1909–10).
DEBENEY, MARIE-EUGÈNE, *La Guerre et les hommes* (Paris, 1937).
DECKER, CARL VON, *Ansichten über die Kriegführung im Geist der Zeit* (Berlin, 1817).
—— *Grundzüge der praktischen Strategie* (2nd. edn.; Berlin, 1841).
—— *Der kleine Krieg* (Berlin, 1822).
DELBRÜCK, HANS, *Historische und politische Aufsätze* (Berlin, 1886).
—— *Die Strategie des Perikles erläutert durch die Strategie Friedrichs des Großen* (Berlin, 1890).
—— *Erinnerungen, Aufsätze und Reden* (Berlin, 1902).
—— *Numbers in History* (London, 1914).
—— *Krieg und Politik* (3 vols; Berlin, 1918–19).
—— *Ludendorff, Tirpitz, Falkenhayn* (Berlin, 1920).
—— *Ludendorffs Selbstporträt* (Berlin, 1922).
—— *Government and the Will of the People* (New York, 1923). First publ. in German 1914.
—— *Vor und nach dem Weltkrieg, politische und historische Aufsätze, 1902–1925* (Berlin, 1926).

DELBRÜCK, HANS, *History of the Art of War within the Framework of Political History* (4 vols; London, 1975–85). First publ. in German 1920.

DERRÉCAGAIX, V. D., *Modern War* (Washington, DC, 1888).

—— *la Guerre et l'armée* (Paris, 1901).

DILKE, CHARLES W., 'The French Armies', *The Fortnightly Review*, 1 Nov. 1891.

DOUGLAS, HOWARD, *Naval Evolutions: A Memoir* (London, 1832).

DRAGOMIROV, M. I., *Manuel pour la préparation des troupes au combat* (3 vols.; Paris, 1886–8).

—— *Principes essentiels pour la conduite de la guerre: Clausewitz interprété par le Général Dragomiroff* (Paris, 1889).

ELDIN, JOHN CLERK OF, *An Essay on Naval Tactics, Systematical and Historical* (2nd. edn.; Edinburgh, 1804).

ELLIOT, GEORGE, *A Treatise on Future Naval Battles and How to Fight Them* (London, 1885).

ENGELS, FRIEDRICH, *Selected Correspondence, Karl Marx and Friedrich Engels* (London, 1934).

—— *Ausgewählte militärische Schriften* (2 vols.; Berlin, 1958, 1964).

—— *Engels as a Military Critic: Articles by Friedrich Engels Reprinted from the Volunteer Journal and the Manchester Guardian of the 1860s*, ed. H. Chaloner and W. O. Henderson (Manchester, 1959).

—— *On America and the Civil War* (New York, 1972).

—— and MARX, KARL, *Collected Works* (1975–).

—— *Herr Eugen Dühring's Revolution in Science* (London, n.d.).

—— *Marx-Engels Gesamtausgabe* (Berlin, 1975–).

FISHER, JOHN, *Fear God and Dread Nought: The Correspondence of Admiral of the Fleet Lord Fisher of Kilverstone*, ed. A. Marder (3 vols.; London, 1956).

FOCH, FERDINAND, *De la conduite de la guerre* (2nd edn., Paris, 1909).

—— *The Principles of War* (London, 1920). First publ. in French (1903).

—— *Foch Talks*, ed. C. Bugnet (London, 1929).

—— *Marshal Foch: His own Words on Many Things*, ed. Raymond Recouly (London, 1929).

—— *The Memoirs of Marshal Foch* (New York, 1931).

FREDERICK, CROWN PRINCE OF PRUSSIA, *The War Diary of the Emperor Frederick III, 1870–1871* (London, 1927).

FREYTAG-LORINGHOVEN, HUGO BARON VON, *Die Heerführng Napoleons und Moltkes* (Berlin, 1897).

—— *Der Infanterie-Angriff in den neuesten Kriegen: Ein Beitrag zur klärung der Angriffsfrage* (Berlin, 1905).

—— *Die Macht der Persönlichkeit im Kriege: Studien nach Clausewitz* (Berlin, 1905).

—— *Krieg und Politik in der Neuzeit* (Berlin, 1911).

—— *Deductions from the World War* (London, 1918).
—— *A Nation Trained in Arms or a Militia* (London, 1918).
—— *Generalfeldmarschall Graf von Schlieffen* (Leipzig, 1920).
GALLIÉNI, GAËTAN, *Les Carnets de Galliéni* (Paris, 1932).
GAREEV, M. A., *Frunze, Military Theorist* (Suffolk, 1988).
GAY DE VERNON, S. F., *A Treatise on the Science of War and Fortifications* (2 vols.; New York, 1817).
The General Staff, War Office (ed.), *The Operations of Large Formations* (London, 1914).
GILBERT, GEORGES, *Essais de critique militaire* (2nd edn.; Paris, 1890).
—— *Sept études militaires* (Paris, 1892).
—— *Lois et institutions militaires* (Paris, 1895).
—— *La Guerre sud-africaine* (Paris, 1902).
GOLTZ, COLMAR VON DER, *The Conduct of War* (London, 1899). First publ. in German 1895.
—— *The Nation in Arms* (London, 1906).
—— *Von Rosbach bis Jena* (Berlin, 1906). Earlier version *Rosbach und Jena*, 1883.
—— *Kriegsgeschichte Deutschlands im Neunzehnten Jahrhundert* (Berlin, 1910), i.
—— *Jena to Eylau* (London, 1913).
—— *Denkwürdigkeiten* (Berlin, 1929).
GOLTZ, FRITZ VON DER, *Moltke* (Berlin, 1903).
—— *Die gelbe Gefahr im Licht der Geschichte* (Leipzig, 1907).
GRANDMAISON, F. J. L. L. DE, *Dressage de l'infanterie en vue du combat offensif* (Paris, 1906).
—— *Deux conférences faites aux officiers de l'état-major de l'armée (février, 1911); La Notion de sûreté et l'engagement des grandes unités* (Paris, 1911).
GRENIER, J. R. DE, *L'Art de la guerre sur mer, ou tactique navale* (Paris, 1787).
GROUARD, A., *La Perte des états et les camps retranchés; Réplique au général Brialmont* (Paris, 1889).
—— *Fallait-il quitter Metz en 1870?* (Paris, 1893).
—— *Stratégie: objet, enseignement, éléments* (Paris, 1895).
—— *La Campagne d'automne de 1813 et les lignes intérieures* (Paris, 1897).
—— *Maximes de guerre de Napoléon I*[er] (Paris, 1898).
—— *Comment quitter Metz en 1870? Avec une note sur le ròle de la fortification* (Paris, 1901).
—— *La Critique de la campagne de 1815* (Paris, 1904).
—— *France et Allemagne; La Guerre éventuelle* (Paris, 1913; periodical publ. from 1911).

GUILLON, E., *Nos écrivains militaires* (2 vols.; Paris, 1898).

HALLECK, HENRY W., *Elements of Military Art and Science, or Course of Instruction in Strategy, Fortification, Tactics of Battles etc.* (New York, 1846).

HAMILTON, ALEXANDER, *The Works of Alexander Hamilton*, ed., H. C. Lodge (New York, 1886).

HAMLEY, EDWARD BRUCE, *The Operations of War* (London, 1866).

HOSTE, PAUL, *L'Art des armées navales* (Lyon, 1697). Eng. trans. 1762, 1834.

IDEVILLE, H. D', *Memoirs of Marshal Bugeaud. From his Private Correspondence and Original Documents* (2 vols.; London, 1884).

JÄHNS, MAX, *Feldmarschall Moltke* (3 vols.; Berlin, 1894–1900).

JAURÈS, JEAN, *L'Armée nouvelle* (Paris, 1913).

JOFFRE, JOSEPH, *The Memoirs of Marshal Joffre* (2 vols.; London, 1932).

JOMINI, ANTOINE HENRI, LLOYD, H. E., TEMPELHOFF, G. F., *The History of the Seven Years War* (London, n.d. [1808?]).

—— *Histoire critique et militaire des guerres de la révolution* (15 vols.; Paris, 1820–4).

—— *An Exposition of the First Principles of Grand Military Combinations and Movements, Compiled from the Treatise upon Great Military Operations*, ed. J. A. Gilbert (London, 1825).

—— *Summary of the Art of War* (New York, 1854; another edn. Philadelphia, 1862).

—— *Treatise on Grand Military Operations*, trans. Colonel S. B. Holabird (2 vols.; New York, 1865).

—— *Life of Napoleon*, trans. Major-General H. W. Halleck (4 vols.; New York, 1864).

JUNG, THÉODORE, *La Guerre et la société* (Paris, 1889).

—— *Stratégie, tactique et politique* (Paris, 1890).

—— *La République et l'armée* (Paris, 1892).

KEIM, AUGUST, *Graf Schlieffen* (Berlin, 1921).

KRAFT ZU HOHENLOHE-INGELFINGEN, *Letters on Artillery* (Woolwich, 1887).

—— *Letters on Cavalry* (London, 1889).

—— *Letters on Infantry* (London, 1889).

—— *Letters on Strategy* (London, 1898). First publ. in German 1887.

KRAUSS, ALFRED, *Moltke, Benedek und Napoleon* (Vienna, 1901).

LANGLOIS, HIPPOLYTE, *L'Artillerie de campagne en liason avec les autres armes (2 vols.; Paris, 1892).*

—— *Questions de défense nationale* (Paris, 1906).

—— *Lessons From Two Recent Wars, The Russo-Turkish and South African War* (London, 1909).

—— *The British Army in a European War* (London, 1910).

LAUGHTON, JOHN K., *Essays on Naval Tactics* (London, 1874).
—— 'The Scientific Study of History', *Journal of the Royal United Services Institution*, 18 (1875), 508–27.
—— *Studies in Naval History* (London, 1887).
LEER, H. A., *Vorträge über Strategie* (Vienna, 1868).
—— *Positive Strategie* (Vienna, 1871).
LEHAUTCOURT, PIERRE, 'Le Colonel Ardant du Picq', *La Revue de Paris* (May–June 1904), 347–66.
LENIN, V. I., *Collected Works* (London, 1960–70).
—— *Les Fondements théoriques de la guerre et de la paix en U.R.S.S.—suivi du Cahier de Lénine sur Clausewitz*, ed. B. C. Friedl (Paris, 1945).
LEWAL, J. L., *La Réforme de l'armée* (Paris, 1871).
—— *Le Maréchal de Moltke, organisateur et stratège* (Paris, 1891).
—— *Introduction à la partie positive de la stratégie* (Paris, 1892).
—— *Stratégie de marche* (Paris, 1893).
—— *Stratégie de combat* (2 vols.; Paris, 1895–6).
LINCOLN, ABRAHAM, *The Collected Works of Abraham Lincoln*, ed. Roy P. Basler (New Brunswick, 1953).
LUCE, STEPHEN B., 'War Schools', *United States Naval Institute Proceedings*, (1883), pp. 633–57.
—— 'Naval Administration III', *United States Naval Institute Proceedings* (Dec. 1903).
—— *The Writings of Stephen B. Luce*, ed. J. D. Hayes and J. B. Hattendorff (Newport, RI, 1975).
LUNDENDORFF, ERICH, *My War Memories, 1914–1918*, (London, 1919).
—— *Kriegführung und Politik* (Berlin, 1922).
—— *Der totale Krieg* (Munich, 1935).
MACDOUGALL, PATRICK, *The Theory of War, Illustrated by Numerous Examples from Military History* (London, 1856).
—— (publ. anonymously), *Life of General Sir William Napier*, ed. H. A. Bruce (London, 1864).
MACKINDER, HALFORD J., 'The Geographical Pivot of History', *Geographical Journal*, 23 (1904), 421–37.
MAHAN, ALFRED THAYER, *The Influence of Sea Power upon History, 1660–1783* (London, 1890), cited in the text as 'Influence I'.
—— *The Influence of Sea Power upon the French Revolution and Empire* (2 vols.; London, 1892), cited in the text as 'Influence II'.
—— *The Navy in the Civil War: The Gulf and the Inland Waters* (London, 1898).
—— *Lessons of the War with Spain and Other Articles* (Boston, 1899).
—— *The Life of Nelson: The Embodiment of the Sea Power of Great Britain* (London, 1899).
—— *The Problem of Asia and Its Effects upon International Policies* (London, 1900).

Mahan, Alfred Thayer, *Retrospect and Prospect: Studies in International Relations, Naval and Political* (London, 1902).
—— *Sea Power in Its Relation to the War of 1812* (2 vols.; London, 1905).
—— *Types of Naval Officers Drawn from the History of the British Navy* (London, 1902).
—— 'Reflections, Historic and Other, Suggested by the Battle of the Japan Sea', *United States Naval Institute Proceedings* (1906), 447–71.
—— *From Sail to Steam: Recollections of Naval Life* (London and New York, 1907).
—— *Some Neglected Aspects of War* (London, 1907).
—— *Naval Administration and Warfare* (Boston, 1908).
—— *The Interest of America in International Conditions* (London, 1910).
—— *Naval Strategy, Compared and Contrasted with the Principles and Practice of Military Operations on Land* (London, 1911).
—— *Armaments and Arbitration, or the Place of Force in the International Relations of States* (London, 1912).
—— *The Major Operations of the Navies in the War of American Independence* (London, 1913).
—— *Letters and Papers of Alfred Thayer Mahan*, ed. Robert Seager II and Doris D. Maguire (3 vols.; Annapolis, Md., 1975).
—— *Admiral Farragut* (New York and London, 1920).
—— *A Bibliography of the Works of Alfred Thayer Mahan*, ed. John B. Hattendorf and Lynn C. Hattendorf (Newport, RI, 1986).
Mahan, Denis Hart, *An Elementary Treatise on Advanced Guard, Out-Posts and Detachment Service of Troops . . . with a Historical Sketch on the Rise and Progress of Tactics* (New York, 1847).
Maillard, L., *Éléments de la guerre* (Paris, 1891).
Marchand, A., *Plans de concentrations de 1871 à 1914* (Paris, 1926).
Marmont, A. F. L. V. de, *De l'esprit des institutions militaires* (Paris, 1846).
Mayer, Émile, *Nos institutions militaires* (Paris, 1901).
—— *Comment on pouvait prévoir l'immobilisation des fronts dans la guerre moderne* (Paris, 1916).
—— *Autour de la guerre actuelle* (Paris, 1917).
—— *La Psychologie du commandement, avec plusieurs lettres inédites du Maréchal Foch* (Paris, 1924).
—— *Trois maréchaux: Joffre, Galliéni, Foch* (Paris, 1928).
Messimy, Adolphe-Marie, *Mes souvenirs* (Paris, 1937).
Milovidov, A. S. (ed.), *The Philosophical Heritage of V. I. Lenin and the Problems of Contemporary War* (Moscow, 1972).
Mitchell, John, *Thoughts on Tactics and Military Organization* (London, 1838).
—— *The Fall of Napoleon* (3 vols.; London, 1845).

—— *Biographies of Eminent Soldiers of the Last Four Centuries* (London, 1865).

MOLTKE, HELMUTH, C. B.. VON, *Gesammelte Schriften und Denkwürdigkeiten* (8 vols.; Berlin 1891–3); trans, as:

—— *Letters of Field-Marshal Count von Moltke to his Mother and Brothers* (New York, 1892).

—— *Moltke, His Life and Character, Sketched in Journals, Memoirs, a Novel and Autobiographical Notes* (New York, 1892).

—— *Essays, Speeches and Memoirs of Field-Marshal Count Helmuth von Moltke* (2 vols.; New York, 1893).

—— *Field-Marshal Count Helmuth von Moltke as a Correspondent* (New York, 1893).

—— *Militärische Werke* (17 vols.; Berlin, 1892–1912).

MOLTKE (the younger), HELMUTH VON, *Betrachtungen und Erinnerungen* (Hamburg, 1914).

MOROGUES, S. F. V. B. DE, *Tactique navale* (Paris, 1763). Eng. trans. 1767.

NAPIER, WILLIAM, 'Traité des grandes opérations militaires', *The Edinburgh Review*, 35 (1821), 377–409.

—— *History of the War in the Peninsula and in the South of France from the Year 1808 to the Year 1814* (6 vols.; London, 1828–40).

—— *Six Letters in Vindication of the British Army, Exposing the Calumnies of the Liverpool Financial Reform Association* (London, 1849).

NAPOLEON, *Mémoires pour servir à l'histoire de France sous Napoléon, écrits à Sainte Hélène*, ed. C. G. F. T. Montholon (Paris, 1823).

NÉGRIER, FRANÇOIS DE, *Lessons of the Russo-Japanese War* (London, 1906). First publ. in the *Revue des deux mondes*, 15 Jan, 1906.

PERCIN, ALEXANDRE, *1914: Les Erreurs du haut commandement* (Paris, 1920).

—— *Le Massacre de notre infanterie, 1914–1918* (Paris, 1921).

PIERRON, ÉDOUARD, *Stratégie et grande tactique, d'après l'expérience des dernières guerres* (Paris, 1887).

—— *Comment s'est formé le génie militaire de Napoléon Ier?* (Paris, 1889).

—— *La Stratégie et la tactique allemandes au début du XXe siècle* (Paris, 1900).

Reichsarchiv, *Der Weltkrieg, 1914–1918; Kriegsrüstung und Kriegswirtschaft* (Berlin, 1930).

ROGNIAT, A. DE, *Considérations sur l'art de la guerre* (Paris, 1816).

—— *Réponse aux notes critiques de Napoléon* (Paris, 1823).

RÜSTOW, WILHELM, *Der deutsche Militärstaat, vor und während der Revolution* (Osnabrück, 1971).

—— *Der Krieg und seine Mittel* (Leipzig, 1856).

RÜSTOW, WILHELM, *Die Feldherrkunst des neunzehnten Jahrhunderts* (2 vols.; Zurich, 1857).
—— *Geschichte der Infanterie* (Gotha, 1857).
—— *Der Krieg von 1805 in Deutschland und Italien, als Anteilung zu kriegshistorischen Studien* (Zurich, 1859).
—— *The War for the Rhine Frontier 1870* (3 vol.; London, 1871).
—— *Strategie und Taktik der neuesten Zeit* (3 vols.; Zurich, 1872–4).
SAINT-CYR, GOUVION, *Mémoires pour servir à l'histoire militaire sous le directoire, le consulat et l'empire* (4 vols.; Paris, 1831).
SAVKIN, YE., *The Basic Principles of Operational Art* (Moscow, 1972).
SCHÄFER, DIETRICH, *Zu Moltkes Gedächtnis. Rede* (Jena, 1901).
SCHERFF, VON, *The New Tactics of Infantry* (London, 1873).
—— *Von der Kriegführung* (Berlin, 1883).
—— *Die Lehre vom Kriege* (Berlin, 1897).
SCHLICHTING, S. W. L. VON, *Taktische und strategische Grundsätze der Gegenwart* (3 vols; Berlin, 1897–9).
—— *Moltkes Vermächtniß* (Munich, 1901).
—— *Moltke und Benedek* (Berlin, 1909).
SCHLIEFFEN, ALFRED VON, *Gesammelte Schriften* (4 vols; Berlin, 1913).
—— *Briefe*, ed. E. Kessel (Göttingen, 1958).
SCHMERFELD, FERDINAND VON (ed.), *Die deutschen Aufmarschpläne, 1871–1890* (Berlin, 1929).
SIMS, W. S., 'The Inherent Tactical Qualities of the All-Big-Gun, One Caliber Battleship of High Speed, Large Displacement and Gun Power', *The United States Naval Institute Proceedings* (1906), 1337–66.
SORB, *La Doctrine de défense nationale* (Paris, 1912).
SPROUT, HAROLD and MARGARET, *The Rise of American Naval Power, 1776–1918* (2nd edn.; Princeton, NJ, 1966).
SYDENHAM OF COMB, CLARKE GEORGE, LORD, 'Sea Heresies', *The Naval Review*, (May 1931).
—— BACON, R., BIRD, W. D., OMAN, C., *The World Crisis by Winston Churchill: A Criticism* (London, 1927).
THEOBALD, J. VON, *Die Kunst der großen Kriegsoperationen nach den besten Quellen frey bearbeitet* (Stuttgart, 1820).
THOUMAS, *Les Transformations de l'armée française* (2 vols.; Paris, 1887).
TIRPITZ, ALFRED VON, *My Memoirs* (2 vols.; London, 1919).
TREITSCHKE, HEINRICH VON, *Politics* (2 vols; London, 1916).
TROCHU, LOUIS, *L'Armée française en 1867* (20th edn.; Paris, 1870).
TROTSKY, LEON, *Military Writings* (New York, 1969).
VALENTINI, GEORG WILHELM VON, *Die Lehre vom Krieg* (2nd edn.; Berlin, 1833).
VERDY DU VERNOIS, *Studien über den Krieg* (4 vols.; Berlin, 1891–1909).

WALDERSEE, ALFRED VON, *Denkwürdigkeiten*, ed. H. O. Meisner (3 vols.; Berlin 1923).
WILKINSON, SPENSER, *The Early Life of Moltke* (Oxford, 1913).
WILLISEN, KARL WILHELM VON, *Theorie des großen Krieges* (Berlin, 1840).
—— *Der italienische Feldzug des Jahres 1848* (Berlin, 1849).
YATES, EDWARD, *Elementary Treatise on Strategy* (London, 1852).
—— *Elementary Treatise on Tactics* (London, 1853).
COMMANDANT Z . . ., Montéchant, H., *Les Guerres navales de demain* (Paris, 1891).

Secondary Sources

ADAM, JULIETTE, *Le Capitaine Georges Gilbert* (Paris, 1924).
AMBROSE, STEPHEN E., *Halleck: Lincoln's Chief of Staff* (Baton Rouge, La, 1962).
ARNOLD, JOSEPH, 'French Tactical Doctrine 1870–1914', *Military Affairs*, 42 (1978), 61–7.
ARON, RAYMOND, *Clausewitz, Philosopher of War* (London, 1986).
ASTON, GEORGE, *The Biography of the Late Marshal Foch* (London, 1929).
BAMFORD, PAUL WALDEN, *Forests and French Sea Power, 1660–1789* (Toronto, 1956).
BAUER, REINHARD, 'Hans Delbrück', in B. Schmitt (ed.), *Some Historians of Modern Europe* (Chicago, 1941).
BÉDARIDA, FRANÇOIS, 'L'Armée et la république: Les Opinions des officiers français en 1876–78', *Revue historique* (1964), 119–64.
BERGER, MARTIN, *Engels, Armies, and Revolution: The Revolutionary Tactics of Classical Marxism* (Hamden, Conn., 1977).
BERGHAHN, VOLKER, *Der Tirpitz-Plan* (Düsseldorf, 1971).
BEST, GEOFFREY, *War and Society in Revolutionary Europe* (Leicester, 1982).
BOND, BRIAN, *The Victorian Army and the Staff College, 1854–1914* (London, 1972).
—— *War and Society in Europe, 1870–1970* (London, 1984).
BOWDITCH, JOHN, 'The Concept of Élan Vital: A Rationalization of Weakness', in E. M. Earle (ed.), *Modern France* (Princeton, NJ, 1951).
BRODIE, BERNARD, *Sea Power in the Machine Age* (Princeton, NJ, 1941).
BUCHOLTZ, ARDEN, *Hans Delbrück and the German Military Establishment: War Images in Conflict* (Iowa, 1985).
CALLEO, DAVID, *The German Problem Reconsidered* (New York, 1978).
CARRIAS, E. *La Pensée militaire française* (Paris, 1960).
—— *La Pensée militaire allemande* (Paris, 1948).

CASE, LYNN M., *French Opinion on War and Diplomacy during the Second Empire* (Philadelphia, 1954).

CHALMIN, PIERRE, *L'Officier français de 1815 à 1870* (Paris, 1957).

CHARLTON, D. G., *Positivist Thought in France during the Second Empire, 1852–1870* (Oxford, 1959).

CHICKERING, ROGER, *Imperial Germany and a World without War: The Peace Movement and German Society, 1892–1914* (Princeton, NJ, 1975).

—— *We Men Who Feel Most German: A Cultural Study of the Pan-German League* (Boston, 1984).

COCHENHAUSEN, F. VON (ed.), *Von Scharnhorst zu Schlieffen, 1806–1906: Hundert Jahre preußisch-deutscher Generalstab* (Berlin, 1933).

COLE, RONALD, H., ' "Forward with the Bayonet! ": The French Army Prepares for Offensive Warfare, 1911–1914' (unpub. diss., University of Maryland, 1975).

CONTAMINE, HENRI, *La Revanche* (Paris, 1957).

COOLIDGE, LOUIS A., *Ulysses S. Grant* (Boston, 1922).

CRACKEL, THEODORE J., 'The Founding of West Point: Jefferson and the Politics of Security', *Armed Forces and Society*, 7 (1981), 529–43.

CRAIG, GORDON, *The Politics of the Prussian Army* (Oxford, 1955).

—— *The Battle of Königgrätz* (London, 1964).

—— *Germany, 1866–1945* (Oxford, 1978).

CRESWELL, JOHN, *British Admirals of the Eighteenth Century* (London, 1972).

CUNLIFFE, MARCUS, *Soldiers and Civilians: The Martial Spirit in America, 1775–1865* (London, 1969).

DANIELS, EMILE, 'Delbrück als Politiker', in id. (ed.), *Am Webstuhl der Zeit* (Berlin, 1928).

DEIST, WILHELM, 'Die Armee in Staat und Gesellschaft, 1890–1914', in M. Stürmer (ed.), *Das kaiserliche Deutschland: Politik und Gesellschaft, 1870–1918* (Düsseldorf, 1970), 312–39.

—— *Flottenpolitik und Flottenpropaganda, 1897–1914* (Stuttgart, 1976).

—— 'Zur Geschichte des preußischen Offizierkorps, 1888–1918', in H. H. Hofmann (ed.), *Das deutsche Offizierkorps, 1860–1960* (Boppard am Rhein, 1980).

DEMETER, KARL, *The German Officer-Corps in Society and State, 1650–1945* (London, 1965).

DEMIRHAN, PERTEV, *General-Feldmarschall Colmar von der Goltz* (Göttingen, 1960).

DEWEY, JOHN, *German Philosophy and Politics* (New York, 1915).

DEXTER, BYRON, 'Clausewitz and Soviet Strategy', *Foreign Affairs*, 29 (1950), 41–55.

DONALD, DAVID, 'Refighting the Civil War', in id., *Lincoln Reconsidered* (New York, 1956).

—— (ed.), *Why the North Won the Civil War* (Baton Rouge, La., 1960).

Dronberger, Ilse, *The Political Thought of Max Weber* (New York, 1971).

Dülffer, Jost, *Regeln gegen den Krieg? Die Haager Friedenskonferenzen von 1899 und 1907* (Frankfurt a. M., 1981).

——, and Holl, Karl (eds.), *Bereit zum Kreig: Kriegsmentalität im wilhelminischen Deutschland, 1890–1914* (Göttingen, 1986).

Dupuy, R. E., *The Story of West Point, 1802–1943* (Washington, DC, 1943).

Earle, E. M. (ed.), *Makers of Modern Strategy from Machiavelli to Hitler* (Princeton, NJ 1943).

Egville, Howard d', *Imperial Defence and Closer Union: A Short Record of the Life Work of Sir John Colomb and of the Movement Toward Imperial Organization* (London, 1913).

Elting, John R., 'Jomini: Disciple of Napoleon', *Military Affairs*, 28 (1964), 17–26.

État-Major de l'Armée, *Les Armées françaises dans la grande guerre* (Paris, 1936).

Farrar, L. L., *The Short-War Illusion* (Oxford, 1973).

—— *Arrogance and Anxiety: The Ambivalence of German Power, 1848–1914* (Iowa City, 1981).

Fischer, Fritz, *Germany's Aims in the First World War* (New York, 1967). First publ. in German 1961.

—— *War of Illusions* (London, 1975).

Foerster, Wolfgang, *Graf Schlieffen und der Weltkrieg* (2nd ed.; Berlin, 1925).

—— *Aus der Gedankenwerkstatt des deutschen Generalstabs* (Berlin, 1931).

Forman, Sidney, *West Point* (New York, 1950).

Förster, Stig, *Der doppelte Militarismus: Die deutsche Heeresrüstungspolitik zwischen Status-quo-Sicherung und Aggression, 1890–1913* (Stuttgart, 1985).

Fortescue, John W., *Historical and Military Essays* (London, 1928).

—— *A History of the British Army* (London, 1930), vols. xi–xiii.

Fossati, W. J., 'Educational Influences in the Career of Marshal Ferdinand Foch of France' (unpub. doc. diss., University of Kansas, 1976).

Freeman, Douglas S., *R. E. Lee* (4 vols.; New York, 1934).

Friedberg, Aaron L., *The Weary Titan: Britain and the Experience of Relative Decline, 1895–1905* (Princeton, NJ, 1988).

Gallie, W. B., *Philosophers of Peace and War: Kant, Clausewitz, Marx, Engels and Tolstoy* (Cambridge, 1978).

Gamelin, M., *Manœuvre et victoire de la Marne* (Paris, 1954).

Garthoff, Raymond, *Soviet Military Doctrine* (London, 1953).

GAT, AZAR, 'Clausewitz on Defence and Attack', *Journal of Strategic Studies*, 10 (1988), 20–6.

—— *The Origins of Military Thought from the Enlightenment to Clausewitz* (Oxford, 1989).

GAULLE, CHARLES DE, *France and Her Army* (London, 1945).

GAYL, FREIHERR VON, *General von Schlichting* (Berlin, 1913).

GIRARDET, RAOUL, *La Société militaire dans la France contemporaine, 1815–1939* (Paris, 1953).

GLEAVES, ALBERT, *Life and Letters of Rear Admiral Stephen B. Luce, U. S. Navy, Founder of the Naval War College* (New York, 1925).

GODWIN-AUSTIN, A. R., *The Staff and the Staff College* (London, 1927).

GOERLITZ, WALTER, *The German General Staff* (London, 1953).

GORCE, PAUL-MARIE DE LA, *The French Army: A Military-Political History* (London, 1963).

GRAHAM, GERALD S., *The Politics of Naval Supremacy: Studies in British Maritime Ascendancy* (Cambridge, 1965).

GRIFFITH, P. G., *Military Thought in the French Army, 1815–1851* (Manchester, 1989).

GROENER, WILHELM, *Das Testament des Grafen Schlieffen* (Berlin, 1927).

—— *Der Feldherr wider Willen* (Berlin, 1930).

GUILMARTIN JUN., JOHN FRANCIS, *Gunpowder and Galleys: Changing Technology and Mediterranean Warfare at Sea in the Sixteenth Century* (Cambridge, 1974).

HAHLWEG, WERNER, 'Lenin und Clausewitz', *Archiv für Kulturgeschichte*, 36 (1954), 30–59, 357–87.

—— 'Clausewitz, Lenin and Communist Military Attitudes Today', *Journal of the Royal United Services Institute*, 105 (1960), 221–5.

HANSON, VICTOR D., *The Western Way of Warfare: Infantry Tactics in Classical Greece* (Oxford, 1990).

HARRIES-JENKINS, GWYN, *The Army in Victorian Society* (London, 1977).

HARSH, JOSEPH L., 'Battlesword and Rapier: Clausewitz, Jomini and the American Civil War', *Military Affairs*, 38 (1974), 133–8.

HERTZ, FREDERICK, *The German Public Mind in the Nineteenth Century* (London, 1975).

HERWEGH, MARCEL, *Guillaume Rustow: Un grand soldat, un grand caractère* (Paris, 1935).

HERZFELD, HANS, *Die deutsche Rüstungpolitik vor dem Weltkrieg* (Bonn, 1923).

HILLGRUBER, ANDREAS, *Germany and the Two World Wars* (London, 1981). First publ. in German 1967.

—— 'Hans Delbrück', in H.-U. Wehler (ed.), *Deutsche Historiker* (Göttingen, 1972).

HINTZE, OTTO, 'Delbrück, Clausewitz und die Strategie Friedrichs des

Großen', *Forschungen zur Brandenburgischen und preußischen Geschichte*, 33 (1920), 131–77.
—— *The Historical Essays of Otto Hintze*, ed. Felix Gilbert (New York, 1975).
Höhn, Reinhard, *Sozialismus und Heer* (Berlin, 1959).
Holmes, T. R. E., *Four Famous Soldiers* (London, 1889).
House, Jonathan, 'The Decisive Attack, A New Look at French Infantry Tactics on the Eve of World War I', *Military Affairs*, 40 (1976), 164–9.
Howard, Michael E., *The Franco-Prussian War* (London, 1961).
—— (ed.), *The Theory and Practice of War* (London, 1965).
—— 'Wellington and the British Army', in id. *Studies in War and Peace* (London, 1970).
—— *War in European History* (London, 1976).
Hughes, H. Stuart, *Consciousness and Society: The Reorientation of European Social Thought, 1890–1930* (London, 1959).
Hull, Isabel, *The Entourage of Kaiser Wilhelm II* (Cambridge, 1982).
Iggers, Georg, *The German Conception of History* (Middletown, Conn., 1968).
Irvine, Dallas, 'The French and Prussian Staff Systems before 1870', *Journal of the American Military Institute* 2 (1938), 192–203.
—— 'The French Discovery of Clausewitz and Napoleon', *Journal of the American Military Institute*, 4 (1942), 143–61.
Jacobs, Walter D., *Frunze: The Soviet Clausewitz, 1885–1925* (The Hague, 1969).
Jany, Kurt, *Die königlich-preußische Armee und das deutsche Reichsheer, 1807 bis 1914* (Berlin, 1933).
Jauffret, Jean-Charles, 'L'Organisation de la réserve à l'époque de la revanche, 1871–1914', *Revue historique des armées* (1989), 27–37.
John, Hartmut, *Das Reserveoffizierkorps im deutschen Kaiserreich, 1890–1914* (Frankfurt a. M., 1981).
Jones, Archer, 'Jomini and the Strategy of the American Civil War: A Reinterpretation', *Military Affairs*, 34 (1970), 127–31.
—— Connolly, Thomas L., *The Politics of Command; Factions and Ideas in Confederate Strategy* (Baton Rouge, La., 1973).
—— Hattaway, Herman, *How the North Won* (London, 1983).
Karsten, Peter, *The Naval Aristocracy: The Golden Age of Annapolis and the Emergence of Modern American Navalism* (New York, 1972).
Kehr, Eckart, *Schlachtflottenbau und Parteipolitik, 1894–1901* (Berlin, 1930).
—— *Economic Interest, Militarism and Foreign Policy: Essays*, ed. G. Craig, (Berkeley, Calif., 1977).
Kelley, Alfred, *The Descent of Darwin: The Popularization of Darwinism in Germany, 1860–1914* (Chapel Hill, NC, 1981).

KENNEDY, PAUL, *The Rise of the Anglo-German Antagonism, 1860–1914* (London, 1914).
—— *The Rise and Fall of British Naval Mastery* (London, 1976).
—— (ed.), *The War Plans of the Great Powers, 1880–1914* (London, 1979).
—— *The Rise and Fall of the Great Powers* (London, 1988).
KESSEL, EBERHARD, *Moltke* (Stuttgart, 1957).
—— *Militärgeschichte und Kriegstheorie in neuerer Zeit*, ed. Johannes Kunisch (Berlin, 1987).
KITCHEN, MARTIN, *The German Officer Corps, 1890–1914* (Oxford, 1968).
KLOSTER, WALTER, *Der deutsche Generalstab und der Präventivkrieg-Gedanke* (Stuttgart, 1932).
KRAUSE, MICHAEL D., 'Anglo-French Military Planning before the First World War (1905–1914): A Study in "Military Diplomacy" ' (unpubl. diss., Georgetown University, 1968).
KRUMEICH, GERD, *Armament and Politics in France on the Eve of the First World War: The Introduction of the Three Years Conscription* (London, 1984).
KUHL, H. VON, *Der deutsche Generalstab in Vorbereitung und Durchführung des Weltkrieges* (Berlin, 1920).
LANGER, WILLIAM L., *The Diplomacy of Imperialism* (New York, 1951).
LIDDELL HART, B. H., *Foch, The Man of Orleans* (London, 1931).
—— 'French Military Ideas before the First World War', in M. Gilbert (ed.), *A Century of Conflict 1850–1950* (London, 1966), 135–48.
LIDER, JULIAN, *The Political and Military Laws of War: An Analysis of Marxist-Leninist Concepts* (Guildford, 1979).
LIVEZEY, WILLIAM E., *Mahan on Sea Power* (Norman, Okla., 1947).
LOTTMAN, HERBERT R., *Pétain: Hero or Traitor?* (New York, 1985).
LUVAAS, JAY, *The Education of an Army: British Military Thought, 1815–1940* (London, 1965).
MACKAY, R. F., *Fisher of Kilverstone* (Oxford, 1973).
MARDER, ARTHUR, *The Anatomy of British Sea Power* (London, 1940).
—— *From the Dreadnought to Scapa Flow* (5 vols.; London, 1961–9).
MATTINGLY, G., *The Defeat of the Spanish Armada* (London, 1959).
MAY, ERNEST R. (ed.), *Knowing One's Enemies: Intelligence Assessment before the Two World Wars* (Princeton, NJ, 1984).
MICHON, GEORGES, *La Préparation à la guerre: La Loi de trois ans (1910–1914)* (Paris, 1935).
Militärgeschichtliches Forschungsamt (ed.), *Handbuch zur deutschen Militärgeschichte, 1648–1939* (4 vols.; Munich, 1979).
MILLER, STEVEN E. (ed.), *Military Strategy and the Origins of the First World War* (Princeton, NJ, 1985).

MITCHELL, ALLAN, *Victors and Vanquished: The German Influence on Army and Church in France after 1870* (London, 1984).

MOMMSEN, WOLFGANG J., *Max Weber and German Politics, 1890–1920* (London, 1984).

MONTEILHET, J., *Les Institutions militaires de la France (1814–1924)* (Paris, 1926).

MOSSE, GEORGE L., *The Crisis of German Ideology* (London, 1966).

—— *Toward the Final Solution: A History of European Racism* (London, 1978).

NA'AMAN, SHLOMO, *Lassalle* (Hanover, 1970).

NICHOLS, J. ALDEN, *Germany after Bismarck: The Caprivi Era* (Cambridge, Mass., 1958).

PARET, PETER, *Clausewitz and the State* (Oxford, 1976).

—— (ed.), *Makers of Modern Strategy from Machiavelli to the Nuclear Age* (Princeton, NJ, 1986).

PELGER, H. (ed.), *Friedrich Engels, 1820–1970* (Hanover, 1971).

PETTER, WOLFGANG, ' "Enemies" and "Reich Enemies": An Analysis of Threat Perceptions and Political Strategy in Imperial Germany, 1871–1914', in Wilhelm Deist (ed.), *The German Military in the Age of Total War* (Worcester, 1985), 22–39.

POLIAKOV, LÉON, *The Aryan Myth: A History of Racist and Nationalist Ideas in Europe* (London, 1974).

PORCH, DOUGLAS, *Army and Revolution: France 1815–1848* (London, 1974).

—— *The March to the Marne: The French Army, 1871–1914* (Cambridge, 1981).

—— 'Clausewitz and the French, 1871–1914', in M. Handel (ed.), *Clausewitz and Modern Strategy* (London, 1986).

PRITCHARD, JAMES, *Louis XV's Navy, 1748–1762: A Study of Organization and Administration* (Montreal, 1987).

PULESTON, WILLIAN D., *Mahan: The Life and Work of Captain Alfred Thayer Mahan* (New Haven, Conn., 1939).

RALSTON, DAVID, *The Army of the Republic: The Place of the Military in the Political Evolution of France, 1871–1914* (Cambridge, Mass., 1967).

REVOL, J., *Histoire de l'armée française* (Paris, 1929).

RICHMOND, HERBERT, *Statesmen and Sea Power* (Oxford, 1947).

RINGER, FRITZ K., *The Decline of the German Mandarins: The German Academic Community, 1890–1933* (Cambridge, Mass., 1969).

RITTER, GERHARD, *The Schlieffen Plan* (London, 1958). First publ. in German 1956.

—— *The German Problem* (Columbus, Oh., 1965).

—— *The Sword and the Scepter* (4 vols.; Miami, Fla., 1969), German original 1954.

RÖHL, JOHN, SOMBART, NICOLAUS (eds.), *Kaiser Wilhelm II: New Interpretations* (Cambridge, 1982).

ROPP, THEODORE, *The Development of a Modern Navy: French Naval Policy, 1871–1904* (Annapolis, Md., 1987).

ROSINSKI, HERBERT, *The German Army* (London, 1939).

—— *The Development of Naval Thought*, ed. B. M. Simpson (Newport, RI, 1977).

ROSKILL, S. W., *The Strategy of Sea Power* (London, 1962).

RÜDT VON COLLENBERG, LUDWIG, *Die deutsche Armee von 1871 bis 1914* (Berlin, 1922).

RYAN, STEPHEN, *Pétain the Soldier* (London, 1969).

SCHMIDT, F. J., MOLINSKI, K., METTE, S., *Hans Delbrück. Der Historiker und Politiker* (Berlin, 1928).

SCHULTE, BERND-FELIX, *Die deutsche Armee, 1900–1914: Zwischen Beharren und Verändern* (Düsseldorf, 1977).

SCHURMAN, D. M., *The Education of a Navy: The Development of British Naval Strategic Thought, 1867–1914* (London, 1965).

—— *Julian S. Corbett, 1854–1922* (London, 1981).

SEAGER II, ROBERT, *Alfred Thayer Mahan: The Man and His Letters* (Annapolis, Md., 1977).

SEDGWICK, ALEXANDER, *The Third French Republic, 1870–1914* (New York, 1968).

SEMMEL, BERNARD, (ed.), *Marxism and the Science of War* (Oxford, 1981).

—— *Liberalism and Naval Strategy: Ideology, Interest and Sea Power during the Pax Britannica* (London, 1986).

SERMAN, WILLIAM, *Les Origines des officiers française, 1848–1870* (Paris, 1979).

SETZEN, JOEL A., 'The Doctrine of the Offensive in the French Army on the Eve of World War I' (unpub, diss., University of Chicago, 1972).

SHAND, ALEXANDER I., *The Life of General Sir Edward Bruce Hamley* (2 vols.; London, 1895).

SHOWALTER, DENNIS, *Railroads and Rifles: Soldiers, Technology and the Unification of Germany* (Hamden, Conn., 1975).

SIMON, W. M., *European Positivism in the Nineteenth Century* (New York, 1963).

SNYDER, JACK, *The Ideology of the Offensive* (Ithaca, NY, 1984).

SPECTOR, RONALD, *Professors of War: The Naval War College and the Development of the Naval Profession* (Newport, RI, 1977).

SPIERS, EDWARD M., *The Army and Society, 1815–1914* (London, 1980).

STADELMANN, RUDOLF, *Moltke und der Staat* (Krefeld, 1950).

STAMFORD, PETER M., 'The Work of Sir Julian Corbett in the Dreadnought Era', *United States Naval Institute Proceedings*, 77 (1951), 61–71.

STEINBERG, JONATHAN, *Yesterday's Deterrent: Tirpitz and the Birth of the German Battle Fleet* (London, 1965).

STERN, FRITZ, *The Politics of Cultural Despair* (Berkeley, Calif., 1961).

STONE, NORMAN, *The Eastern Front, 1914–1917* (London, 1975).

STRACHAN, HEW, *European Armies and the Conduct of Wars* (London, 1983).

—— *Wellington's Legacy: The Reform of the British Army* (Manchester, 1984).

—— *From Waterloo to Balaclava: Tactics, Technology and the British Army, 1815–1854* (Cambridge, 1985).

STROMBERG, RONALD, *Redemption by War: The Intellectuals and 1914* (Lawrence, Kan., 1982).

STUART, REGINALD C., *The Half-Way Pacifist: Thomas Jefferson's View of War* (Toronto, 1978).

—— *War and American Thought from the Revolution to the Monroe Doctrine* (Kent, Oh., 1982).

SULLIVAN, A. T., *Thomas-Robert Bugeaud* (Hamden, Conn., 1983).

SWIFT, EBEN, 'The Military Education of Robert E. Lee', *Virginia Magazine of History and Biography*, 35 (1927), 97–108.

SYMPOX, GEOFFREY, *The Crisis of French Sea Power, 1688–1697, From the* guerre d'escadre *to the* guerre de course (The Hague, 1974).

TANENBAUM, JAN KARL, *General Maurice Sarrail, 1856–1929* (Chapel Hill, NC, 1974).

TAYLOR, A. J. P., *The Struggle for Mastery in Europe* (Oxford, 1954).

TAYLOR, CHARLES C., *The Life of Admiral Mahan* (New York, 1920).

TESKE, HERMANN, *Colmar Freiherr von der Goltz* (Göttingen, 1957).

THIMME, ANNELISE, *Hans Delbrück als Kritiker der Wilhelminischen Epoche* (Düsseldorf, 1955).

THOMAS, WILLIAM, *The Philosophic Radicals* (Oxford, 1979).

THRALL, MIRIAM, *Rebellious Frazer's: No. 1 Yorke's Magazine in the Days of Maginn, Thackeray and Carlyle* (New York, 1934).

TRAVERS, T. H. E., 'Technology, Tactics and Morale: Jean de Bloch, the Boer War, and British Military Theory, 1900–1914', *Journal of Modern History*, 51 (1979), 264–86.

TROELTSCH, ERNST, 'The Idea of Natural Law and Humanity in World History', app. to O. Gierke, *Natural Law and the Theory of Society, 1500–1800* (Cambridge, 1934).

TUCHMAN, BARBARA, *The Guns of August* (New York, 1962).

VAGTS, ALFRED, *A History of Militarism* (London, 1959).

WALLACH, JEHUDA L., *Das Dogma der Vernichtungsschlacht* (Frankfurt a. M., 1967).

—— *Die Kriegslehre von Friedrich Engels* (Frankfurt, a.M., 1968).

WALSER, JOHN RAYMOND, 'France's Search for a Battlefleet: French Naval Policy, 1898–1914', (unpub. doc. diss., University of North California, 1976).

WEBER, EUGEN, *The Nationalist Revival in France, 1905–1914* (Berkeley, Calif., 1959).

WEBER, MAX, *Economy and Society* (New York, 1968).

WEHLER, HANS-ULRICH, *The German Empire* (Leamington Spa, 1985). First publ. in German 1973.

WEIGLEY, RUSSEL F., *History of the United States Army* (Bloomington, Ind., 1967).

—— *The American Way of War: A History of United States Military Strategy and Policy* (London, 1973).

WERNHAM, R. B., 'Elizabethan War Aims and Strategy', in S. T. Bindoff, J. Hurstfield, and C. H. Williams (eds.), *Elizabethan Government and Society* (London, 1961).

WHITTON, F. E., *Moltke* (London, 1921).

WILLIAMS, T. HARRY, 'The Return to Jomini: Some Thoughts on Recent Civil War Writing', *Military Affairs*, 39 (1975), 204–6.

WILLIAMSON, SAMUEL, *The Politics of Grand Strategy: Britain and France Prepare for War, 1904–1914* (Cambridge, Mass., 1969).

WOHL, ROBERT, *The Generation of 1914* (Cambridge, Mass., 1979).

ZANIEWICKI, WITOLD, 'L'Impact de 1870 sur la pensée militaire française', *Revue de Défense Nationale*, 26 (1970), 1331–41.

ZIRKE, GERHARD, *Der General: Friedrich Engels, der erste Militärtheoretiker der Arbeiterklassen* (Leipzig, 1957).

III
FASCIST AND LIBERAL VISIONS OF WAR

ARCHIVES

Bundesarchiv-Militärarchiv, Freiburg im Breisgau.

J. F. C. Fuller's Papers, Rutgers University, New Brunswick, NJ.

George Kennan's Papers, Seeley G. Mudd Manuscript Library, Princeton University.

Liddell Hart Centre for Military Archives, King's College, London.

BOOKS AND ARTICLES

ADAMS, M., *The Great Adventure: Male Desire and the Coming of World War I* (Bloomington, Ind., 1990).

ADAMSON, W., 'Fascism and Culture: Avant-Garde and Secular Religion in the Italian Case', *Journal of Contemporary History*, 24 (1989), 411–35.

—— 'Modernism and Fascism: The Politics of Culture in Italy, 1903–1922', *American Historical Review*, 95 (1990), 359–90.

—— 'The Language of Opposition in Early Twentieth-Century Italy: Rhetorical Continuities between Prewar Florentine Avant-Gardism and Mussolini's Fascism', *Journal of Modern History*, 64 (1992), 22–51.

—— *Avant-Garde Florence: From Modernism to Fascism* (Cambridge, Mass., 1993).

ALEXANDER, M., *The Republic in Danger: General Maurice Gamelin and the Politics of French Defence, 1933–1940* (Cambridge, 1992).

ATKINSON, J. L., 'Italian Influence on the Origins of the American Concept of Strategic Bombardment', *Airpower Historian*, 4 (1957), 141–9.

BALBO, I., 'Guerra aerea', in *Enciclopedia italiana*, xviii (Rome, 1938), 92–3.

BARNETT, C., *The Swordbearers: Studies in Supreme Command in the First World War* (London, 1963).

—— *Britain and Her Army, 1509–1970* (London 1970).

—— *The Collapse of British Power* (London, 1972).

—— (ed.), *Hitler's Generals* (London, 1989).

BASSFORD, C., *Clausewitz in English: The Reception of Clausewitz in Britain and America, 1815–1945* (Oxford, 1994).

BAYLEY, S., 'Dead as a Flat Battery', *Times Literary Supplement*, 18 Aug. 1995, 25.

BECKER, J. M., *Nationalism and Culture: Gabriele d'Annunzio and Italy after the Risorgimento* (New York, 1994).
BENEWICK, R., *The Fascist Movement in Britain* (London, 1972).
BENJAMIN, W., 'The Work of Art in the Age of Mechanical Reproduction', in *Illuminations* (New York, 1968), 243–4.
—— 'Theorien des deutschen Faschismus', in *Walter Benjamin: Gesammelte Schriften*, iii (Frankfurt, 1977), 238–50; trans. in *New German Critique*, 6 (1979), 120–8.
BEN-MOSHE, T., *Churchill: Strategy and History* (Boulder, Colo., 1992).
BENNETT, E., *German Rearmament and the West, 1932–1933* (Princeton, NJ, 1979).
BERLIN, I., *Vico and Herder* (London, 1980).
BEST, G., *Humanity in Warfare* (New York, 1980).
BEYERCHEN, A. D., *Scientists under Hitler* (New Haven, Conn., 1977).
BIALER, U., '"Humanization" of Air Warfare in British Foreign Policy on the Eve of the Second World War', *Journal of Contemporary History*, 13 (1978), 79–96.
—— *The Shadow of the Bomber: The Fear of Air Attacks and British Politics, 1932–1939* (London, 1980).
BILLIG, M., *Fascists* (New York, 1978).
BLACK, R., and Louis, W. R. (eds.), *Churchill* (Oxford, 1993).
BONADEO, Al., *D'Annunzio and the Great War* (Madison, Wis., 1995).
BOND, B. (ed.), *Chief of Staff: The Diaries of Lieutenant-General Sir Henry Pownell* (London, 1972).
—— *France and Belgium, 1939–1940* (London, 1975).
—— *Liddell Hart: A Study of His Military Thought* (London, 1977).
—— *British Military Policy between the Two World Wars* (Oxford, 1980).
—— (ed.), *The First World War and British Military History* (Oxford, 1991).
BONNAL, H., *Les Maîtres de la guerre Frédérick II, Napoléon, Moltke, d'après des travaux inédits de M le général Bonnal*, ed. L. Rousset (Paris, 1899).
—— *De la méthode dans les hautes études militaires en Allemagne et en France* (Paris, 1902).
—— *De Rosbach à Ulm* (Paris, 1903).
—— *La Manoeuvre d'Iéna 1806* (Paris, 1904).
—— *La Manoeuvre de Landshut, 1808–1809* (Paris, 1905).
—— *La Manoeuvre de Vilna, 1811–1812* (Paris, 1905).
BOOG, H., and Militärgeschichtliches Forschungsamt (eds.), *The Conduct of the Air War in the Second World War* (New York, 1992).
BOURNE, J. M., *Britain and the Great War* (London, 1989).
BOYCE, R., and ROBERTSON, E. (eds.), *Paths to War: New Essays on the Origins of the Second World War* (London, 1989).
BRACHER, K. D., 'Tradition und Revolution im Nationalsozialismus', in *Zeitgeschichtliche Kontroversen* (Munich, 1976), 62–78.

BUTLER: see *Grand Strategy*

CAMON, H., *La Guerre napoléonienne* (5 vols., Paris, 1907–11).

—— *Clausewitz* (Paris, 1911).

—— *Le Système de guerre de Napoléon* (Paris, 1923).

CAPPELLUTI, F., 'The Life and Thought of Giulio Douhet' (dissertation, Rutgers University, 1967).

CARROL, D., *French Literary Fascism* (Princeton, NJ, 1995).

CARROLL, B. A., *Design for Total War* (The Hague, 1968).

CARSTEN, F., *The Reichswehr in Politics, 1918 to 1933* (Oxford, 1966).

CARVER, M., *The Apostles of Mobility* (London, 1979).

CAVENDISH, R., *A History of Magic* (London, 1977).

—— *The Magical Arts* (London, 1984).

CEADEL, M., *Pacifism in Britain, 1914–1945* (Oxford, 1980).

CEVA, L., and CURAMI, A., *La Meccanizzazione dell'esercito italiano dalle origini al 1943* (Rome, 1989).

CHACE, W., *The Political Identities of Ezra Pound and T. S. Eliot* (Stanford, Calif., 1973).

CHANDLER, D., *The Campaigns of Napoleon* (London, 1966).

CHARMLEY, J., *Chamberlain and the Lost Peace* (London, 1989).

—— *Churchill: The End of Glory* (London, 1993).

—— *Churchill's Grand Alliance* (London, 1995).

CHESNEAUX, J., *The Political and Social Ideas of Jules Verne* (London, 1972).

CHURCHILL, W., *The World Crisis, 1911–1918* (London, 1960).

—— *The Second World War* (6 vols., London, 1948–55).

CLAUSEWITZ, C. VON, *Principles of War* (Harrisburg, Penn., 1942).

—— *On War* (Princeton, NJ, 1976).

COBLEY, E., *Representing War: Form and Ideology in First World War Narratives* (Toronto, 1993).

COLE, W., *Charles A. Lindbergh and the Battle against American Intervention in World War II* (New York, 1974).

COLIN, J., *L'Éducation militaire de Napoléon* (Paris, 1900).

—— *Les Transformations de la guerre* (Paris, 1911); trans. as *The Transformation of War* (London, 1912).

COOPER, M., *The Birth of Independent Air Power* (London, 1986).

CORBETT, J., *Some Principles of Maritime Strategy* with introd. by E. Grove (Annapolis, Md., 1988).

COWLING, M., *The Impact of Hitler: British Politics and British Policy, 1933–1940* (Cambridge, 1975).

CROOK, P., *Darwinism, War and History* (Cambridge, 1994).

CROSS, C., *The Fascists in Britain* (London, 1961).

CUENO, J., *The Air Weapon, 1914–1916* (Harrisburg, Penn., 1947).

DAHRENDORF, R., *Society and Democracy in Germany* (London, 1968).

DALLEK, R., *Franklin D. Roosevelt and American Foreign Policy, 1932–1945* (New York, 1979).

D'ANNUNZIO, G., *Gabriele d'Annunzio: combattente al servizio della regia marina*, ed. G. Po (Rome, 1931).

—— *Gabriele d'Annunzio: scritti, messaggi, discorsi e rapporti militari*, ed. G. Po (Rome, 1939).

De FELICE, R., *Fascism* (New Brunswick, NJ, 1977).

DENNIS, P., *Decision by Default: Peacetime Conscription and British Defence, 1915–1923* (London, 1972).

DEUTSCH, H., *The Conspiracy against Hitler in the Twilight War* (Minneapolis, Minn., 1968).

DOUGHTY, R. A., *The Seeds of Disaster: The Development of French Army Doctrine, 1919–1939* (Hamden, Conn., 1985).

—— *The Breaking Point: Sedan and the Fall of France, 1940* (Hamden, Conn., 1990).

DOUHET, G., *L'Automobilismo, sotto il punto di vista militare: schema di un sistema automobilistico per uso militare* (Turin, 1902).

—— *A proposito dell'articolo: gli automobili e la loro applicazione nell'arte della guerra* (Rome, 1902).

—— *Automobilismo militare e pesante* (Genoa, 1904).

—— *Cenno sommario sullo stato attuale dell'elettrotecnica* (Turin, 1905; date of composition 1903).

—— *I Problemi dell'aereonavigazione* (Rome, 1910).

—— *L'Arte della guerra* (Turin, 1915).

—— *Come finì la Grande Guerra* (Rome, 1919).

—— *L'Onorevole che non potè più mentire: racconto dei tempi ante-guerra* (Rome, 1921).

—— *Diario critico di guerra* (2 vols., Rome, 1921–2).

—— *Il Dominio dell'aria* (Rome, 1921; second enlarged edn. 1926), trans. as *The Command of the Air* (London, 1943).

—— *La Difesa nazionale* (Rome, 1925).

—— *Probabili aspetti della guerra futura* (Palermo, 1928).

—— *Le Profezie di Cassandra* (Genoa, 1931).

—— *La Guerra integrale* (Rome, 1936).

—— *Giulio Douhet: scritti inediti*, ed. A. Monti (Gennaio, 1951).

DUTAILLY, H., *Les Problèmes de l'armée de terre française (1935–1939)* (Paris, 1980).

EARLE, E. M. (ed.), *Makers of Modern Strategy from Machiavelli to the Second World War* (Princeton, NJ, 1943).

EDGERTON, D., *England and the Aeroplane: An Essay on a Militant and Technological Nation* (London, 1991).

EDWARDS, J., *The British Government and the Spanish Civil War, 1936–1939* (London, 1979).

EKSTEINS, M., *Rites of Spring: The Great War and the Birth of the Modern Age* (New York, 1990).

ERICKSON, J., *The Soviet High Command* (London, 1962).

ESSAME, H., *The Battle for Europe, 1918* (London, 1972).

ETZOLD, T. H., and Gaddis, J. L. (eds.), *Containment: Documents on American Policy and Strategy, 1945–1950* (New York, 1978).

Evolution of Soviet Operational Art, The, i: 1927–1964, trans. H. S. Orenstein, foreword and introd. by D. Glantz (London, 1995).

FALLS, C., *The First World War* (London, 1960).

FIELDS, F., *British and French Writers of the First World War* (Cambridge, 1991).

FISHMAN, R., *Urban Utopias in the Twentieth Century: Ebenezer Howard, Frank Lloyd Wright, and Le Corbusier* (New York, 1977).

FLUGEL, R., 'United States Air Power Doctrine: A Study of the Influence of William Mitchell and Giulio Douhet at the Air Corps Tactical School, 1921–1935' (dissertation, University of Oklahoma, 1965).

FREEDMAN, L., *The Evolution of Nuclear Strategy* (London, 1981).

FREI, N., 'Wie modern war der Nationalsozialismus?', *Geschichte und Gesellschaft*, 19 (1993), 367–87.

FRENCH, D., *British Economic and Strategic Planning, 1905–1915* (London, 1982).

—— *British Strategy and War Aims, 1914–1916* (London, 1986).

—— *The British Way in Warfare, 1688–2000* (London, 1990).

—— *The Strategy of the Lloyd George Coalition, 1916–1918* (Oxford, 1995).

FRITZSCHE, P., *A Nation of Fliers: German Aviation and the Popular Imagination* (Cambridge Mass., 1992).

FULLER, J. F. C. [books only; a full bibiliography of articles in journals can be found in Reid, *J. F. C. Fuller*, 261–4]:

—— *The Star in the West: A Critical Essay upon the Works of Aleister Crowley* (London, 1907).

—— *Hints on Training Territorial Infantry* (London, 1913).

—— *Training Soldiers for War* (London, 1914).

—— *Tanks in the Great War, 1914–1918* (London, 1920).

—— *The Reformation of War* (London, 1923).

—— *Sir John Moore's System of Training* (London, 1924).

—— *British Light Infantry in the Eighteenth Century* (London, 1925).

—— *On Future Warfare* (London, 1928).

—— *The Generalship of Ulysses S. Grant*, (London, 1929).

—— *Yoga: A Study of the Mystical Philosophy of the Brahmins and Buddhists* (London, 1925; 2nd edn. 1933).

—— *The Foundations of the Science of War* (London, 1926).

—— *Grant* (London, 1929).

—— *India in Revolt* (London, 1931).

—— *Armoured Warfare* (London, 1943; originally *Lectures on FSR III*, 1932).

FULLER, J. F. C. *War and Western Civilization, 1832–1932: A Study of War as a Political Instrument and the Expression of Mass Democracy* (London, 1932).
—— *The Dragon's Teeth: A Study of War and Peace* (London, 1932).
—— *Grant and Lee* (London, 1933).
—— *The Secret Wisdom of the Qabalah: A Study of Jewish Mystical Thought* (London, 1936).
—— *The First of the League Wars* (London, 1936).
—— *Memoirs of an Unconventional Soldier* (London, 1936).
—— *Towards Armageddon* (London, 1937).
—— *Thunderbolts* (London, 1946).
—— *Armament and History* (London, 1946).
—— *The Conduct of War, 1789–1961: A Study of the Impact of the French, Industrial and Russian Revolutions on War and its Conduct* (London, 1961).
FULLER, J. G., *Troop Morale and Popular Culture in the British and Dominion Armies, 1914–1918* (Oxford, 1990).
FUSSELL, P., *The Great War and Modern Memory* (Oxford, 1975).
FUTRELL, R. F., *Ideas, Concepts, Doctrine: A History of Basic Thinking in the United States Air Force, 1907–1964* (Maxwell Air Force, Alabama, 1971).
GADDIS, J. L., *Strategies of Containment: A Critical Appraisal of Postwar American National Security Policy* (New York, 1982).
—— 'The Origins of Self-Deterrence: The United States and the Non-use of Nuclear Weapons, 1945–1958', in his *The Long Peace: Inquiries Into the History of the Cold War* (New York, 1987), 104–46.
GAT, A., 'Clausewitz on Defence and Attack', *Journal of Strategic Studies*, 10 (1988), 20–6.
—— *British Armour Theory and the Rise of the Panzer Arm: Revising the Revisionists* (London, 2000), incorporating:
—— 'Liddell Hart's Theory of Armoured Warfare: Revising the Revisionists', *Journal of Strategic Studies*, 19 (1996), 1–30.
—— 'British Influence and the Evolution of the Panzer Arm: Myth or Reality?', *War in History*, 4(2) (1997), 150–73; 4(3) (1997), 316–38.
—— 'Ideology, National Policy, Technology and Strategic Doctrine between the World Wars', Journal of Strategic Studies, 24:3 (2001), 1–18.
—— 'Isolationism, Appeasement, Containment, Limited War: Western Strategic Policy from the Modern to the "Post-Modern" Era', in A. Gat and Z. Maoz (eds.), *War in a Changing World* (Ann Arbor, 2001), 77–91.
GELLMAN, B., *Contending with Kennan* (New York, 1984).
GERMAINS, V. W., *The 'Mechanization' of War* (London, 1927).
GEYER, M., *Aufrüstung oder Sicherheit: Die Reichswehr in der Krise der Machtpolitik, 1924–1936* (Wiesbaden, 1980).
GIBBS: see *Grand Strategy*
GILBERT, M., *Winston S. Churchill*, v (London, 1976).

GLANTZ, D., *Soviet Military Operational Art: In Pursuit of Deep Battle* (London, 1991).

GOLDSTEIN, L., *The Flying Machine and Modern Literature* (London, 1986).

GOOCH, J., *The Plans of War: The General Staff and British Military Strategy, c.1900–1916* (London, 1974).

—— 'Attitude to War in Late Victorian and Edwardian England', in *The Prospect of War: Studies in British Defence Policy, 1847–1942* (London, 1981), 35–51.

GOODRICK-CLARKE, N., *The Occult Roots of Nazism* (New York, 1985).

GOUTARD, A., *1940: The Battle of France* (London 1958).

GRAHAM, D., and BIDWELL, S., *Coalitions, Politicians and Generals: Some Aspects of Command in Two World Wars* (London, 1993).

Grand Strategy: History of the Second World War, vol. i. by N. Gibbs (London, 1976); ii, by J. R. M. Butler (London, 1957); iii, by J. M. A. Gwyer (London, 1964); iv, by M. Howard (London, 1972).

GRAVES, R., *Goodbye to All That* (London, 1929).

GREGOR, A. J., *The Ideology of Fascism* (New York, 1969).

—— 'Fascism and Modernization', *World Politics*, 26 (1974), 370–84.

—— 'Fascism and the "Countermodernization of Consciousness"', *Comparative Political Studies*, 10 (1977), 239–58.

GREIL, A., 'The Modernization of Consciousness and the Appeal of Fascism', *Comparative Political Studies*, 10 (1977), 213–38.

GRIFFIN, R., *The Nature of Fascism* (London, 1991).

GRIFFITH, P., *Battle Tactics of the Western Front: The British Army's Art of Attack, 1916–18* (New Haven, Conn., 1994).

GRIFFITHS, R., *Fellow Travellers of the Right* (London, 1980).

GUDERIAN, H., *Achtung Panzer!* (London, 1992; German original 1937).

—— 'Schnelle Truppen einst und jetzt', *Militärwissenschaftliche Rundschau*, 4 (1939), 237–8.

—— *Panzer Leader* (London, 1952).

GUNSBURG, J. A., *Divided and Conquered: The French High Command and the Defeat of the West, 1940* (London, 1979).

GWYER: see *Grand Strategy*

HADDOW, G. H., and GROSZ, P., *The German Giants: The Story of the R Planes, 1914–1919* (London, 1969).

HAMILTON, A., *The Appeal of Fascism* (London, 1971).

HANCOCK, W. K., and GOWING, M. M., *British War Economy: History of the Second World War—Civil Series* (London, 1949).

HANKEY, M., *The Supreme Command* (2 vols., London, 1961).

HARPER, G. M. (ed.), *Yeats and the Occult* (Canada, 1975).

HARRIS, J. P., *Men, Ideas and Tanks: British Military Thought and Armoured Forces, 1903–1939* (Manchester, 1995).

HARVEY, A. D., *Collision of Empires: Britain in Three World Wars, 1793–1945* (London, 1992).

HASLAM, J., *The Soviet Union and the Struggle for Collective Security in Europe* (London, 1984).

HASTINGS, M., *Bomber Command* (New York, 1979).

HAUNER, M., 'Czechoslovakia as a Military Factor in British Considerations of 1938', *Journal of Strategic Studies*, 1 (1978), 194–222.

HENDRIX, J., 'The Interwar Army and Mechanization: The American Approach', *Journal of Strategic Studies*, 16 (1993), 77–81.

HERF, J., *Reactionary Modernism* (Cambridge, 1984).

HEWITT, A., *Fascist Modernism: Aesthetics, Politics, and the Avant-Garde* (Stanford, Calif., 1993).

HIGHAM, R., *The Military Intellectuals in Britain, 1918–1939* (New Brunswick, NJ, 1966).

HINSLEY, F. H., *British Intelligence in the Second World War*, i (London, 1979).

HOCHMAN, E., *Architects of Fortune: Mies van der Rohe and the Third Reich* (New York, 1989).

HOCHMAN, J., *The Soviet Union and the Failure of Collective Security, 1934–1938* (London, 1984).

HOMZE, E., *Arming the Luftwaffe* (Lincoln, Nebr., 1976).

HOUGH, G., *The Mystery Religion of W. B. Yeats* (Brighton, Sussex, 1984).

HOWARD, M. (ed.), *The Theory and Practice of War* (London, 1965).

—— *The Mediterranean Strategy in the Second World War* (London, 1968).

—— 'The Classical Strategists', in *Studies in War and Peace* (London, 1970).

—— *The Continental Commitment* (London, 1972).

—— 'Liddell Hart' (1970) and 'The British Way in Warfare: A Reappraisal' (1974), repr. in *The Causes of War* (London, 1984), 189–207, 237–47.

—— 'Empire, Race and War in pre-1914 Britain', in his *The Lessons of History* (Oxford, 1991), 63–80.

—— See also *Grand Strategy.*

HOWE, E., *The Magicians of the Golden Dawn: A Documentary History of a Magical Order, 1887–1923* (London, 1972).

—— *Astrology and the Third Reich* (Wellingborough, Northants, 1984).

HUGHES, T., *American Genesis: A Century of Invention and Technological Enthusiasm, 1870–1970* (New York, 1989).

HUGHES, T., and HUGHES, A. (eds.), *Lewis Mumford* (Oxford, 1990).

HURLEY, A., *Billy Mitchell: Crusader for Air Power* (New York, 1964).

HYDE, H. M., *British Air Policy Between the Wars* (London, 1976).

HYNES, S., *A War Imagined: The First World War and English Culture* (London, 1990).

INGOLD, F. P., *Literatur und Aviatik: Europäische Flugdichtung, 1909–1927* (Basel, 1978), 26–49.

ITALIAANDER, R., *Italo Balbo* (Munich, 1942).

JAMESON, F., *Fables of Aggression: Wyndham Lewis, the Modernist as Fascist* (Berkeley, Calif., 1979).

JOES, A. J., 'On the Modernity of Fascism', *Comparative Political Studies*, 10 (1977), 259–68.

JOHNSON, D. L., *Frank Lloyd Wright versus America: The 1930s* (Cambridge, Mass., 1990).

JOLL, J., 'F. T. Marinetti: Futurism and Fascism', in his *Three Intellectuals in Politics* (New York, 1965), 133–78.

JONES, H. A., *The War in the Air*, v and vi (Oxford, 1935 and 1937).

JORDAN, M., *Machine-Age Ideology: Social Engineering and American Liberalism, 1911–1939* (Chapel Hill, NC, 1994).

JOSEPHSON, M., *Edison* (London, 1961).

JÜNGER, E., *Sämtliche Werke*, i (Stuttgart, 1978), vii (1980), viii (1981).

—— 'Die Technik der Zukunftsschlacht', *Militär-Wochenblatt*, 1 Oct. 1921, 287–90.

—— *Storm of Steel: From the Diary of a German Storm-Troop Officer on the Western Front* (New York, 1929).

—— *Copse 125: A Chronicle from the Trench Warfare of 1918* (London, 1930).

KAISER, D. E., *Economic Diplomacy and the Origins of the Second World War: Germany, Britain, France, and Eastern Europe, 1930–1939* (Princeton, NJ, 1980).

KAYSEN, C., 'Is War Obsolete? A Review Essay', *International Security*, 14 (1990), 42–63.

KENNAN, G. F., *American Diplomacy* (New York, 1985).

—— *Realities of American Foreign Policy* (Princeton, NJ, 1954).

—— *Russia, the Atom and the West* (New York, 1958).

—— *Memoirs* (2 vols., Boston, 1967, 1972).

KENNEDY, J. F., *Why Britain Slept?* (New York, 1940).

KENNEDY, P., *The Rise and Fall of British Naval Mastery* (London, 1976).

—— and NICHOLLS, A. (eds.), *Nationalist and Racialist Movements in Britain and Germany before 1914* (London, 1981).

—— *Strategy and Diplomacy, 1870–1945* (London, 1983).

—— *The Rise and Fall of the Great Powers* (London, 1989).

KENNETT, L., *A History of Strategic Bombing* (New York, 1982).

—— *The First Air War, 1914–1918* (New York, 1991).

KEYNES, J. M., *The Economic Consequences of the Peace* (London, 1920).

KIEFT, D. O., *Belgium's Return to Neutrality* (Oxford, 1972).

KLEMPERER, K. VON, *German Resistance against Hitler: The Search for Allies Abroad, 1938–1945* (Oxford, 1992).

KOLIOPOULOS, J. S., *Greece and the British Connection, 1935–1941* (Oxford, 1977).

KRAFT, B., *The Peace Ship: Henry Ford's Pacifist Adventure in the First World War* (New York, 1978).

LACEY, R., *Ford: The Men and the Machine* (Boston, 1986).
LARSEN, B., *Lindbergh of Minnesota* (New York, 1973).
LARSEN, S. T., HAGTVET, B., and MYKLEBUST, J. P. (eds.), *Who Were the Fascists?* (Bergen, 1980).
LAWLOR, S., *Churchill and the Politics of War, 1940–1941* (Cambridge, 1994).
LAWRENCE, T. E., 'The Evolution of A Revolt', *Army Quarterly*, 1 (Oct. 1920).
—— *Revolt in the Desert* (New York, 1927).
—— *The Seven Pillars of Wisdom* (New York, 1936).
—— *T. E. Lawrence to his Biographer Liddell Hart*, ed. B. H. Liddell Hart (London, 1939).
LE BON, G., *The Crowd: A Study of the Popular Mind* (London, 1896).
—— *The Psychology of Peoples* (London, 1899).
LE CORBUSIER, *Aircraft* (New York, 1988, original 1935).
LEDEEN, M., *The First Duce: D'Annunzio at Fiume* (Baltimore, 1977).
LEEB, RITTER VON, *Defence* (Harrisburg, Penn., 1943; originally in *Militärwissenschaftliche Rundschau*, 1936–7).
LEED, E. J., *No Man's Land: Combat and Identity in World War I* (Cambridge, 1979).
LEGRO, J. W., *Cooperation Under Fire: Anglo-German Restraint during World War II* (London, 1995).
LEVINE, I. D., *Mitchell: Pioneer of Air Power* (New York, 1943).
LIDDELL HART, B. H. [books only]:
—— *New Methods in Infantry Training* (Cambridge, 1918).
—— *The Framework of a Science of Infantry Tactics* (London, 1922; expanded and reissued 1923, 1926).
—— *Paris, or the Future of War* (London, 1925).
—— *A Greater than Napoleon: Scipio* (London, 1926).
—— *Great Captains Unveiled* (London, 1927).
—— *The Remaking of Modern Armies* (London, 1927).
—— *Sherman* (London, 1929).
—— *The Decisive Wars of History* (London, 1929); later *Strategy: The Indirect Approach*, rev. and enlarged edns.: 1941, 1946, 1954, 1967.
—— *The Real War* (London, 1930); enlarged as *A History of the World War, 1914–1918* (London, 1934).
—— *Foch* (London, 1931).
—— *The British Way in Warfare* (London, 1932).
—— *The Ghost of Napoleon* (New Haven, Conn., 1934).
—— *'T. E. Lawrence': In Arabia and After* (London, 1934).
—— *When Britain Goes to War* (London, 1935).
—— *Europe in Arms* (London, 1937).
—— *Through the Fog of War* (London, 1938).
—— *The Defence of Britain* (London, 1939).
—— *Dynamic Defence* (London, 1940).

—— *The Current of War* (London, 1941).
—— *This Expanding War* (London, 1942).
—— *Thoughts on War* (London, 1944).
—— *Why Don't We Learn from History?* (London, 1944).
—— *The Revolution in Warfare* (London, 1946).
—— *The Other Side of the Hill* (London, 1948).
—— *The Defence of the West* (London, 1950).
—— (ed.), *The Rommel Papers* (London, 1953).
—— *The Tanks* (2 vols., London, 1959).
—— *Deterrent or Defence* (London, 1960).
—— *Memoirs* (2 vols., London, 1965).
—— *The Second World War* (London, 1970).
'Liddell Hart: The Captain Who Taught Generals', *Listener*, 28 Dec. 1972.
LINDBERGH, A. M., *The Wave of the Future: A Confession of Faith* (New York, 1940).
—— *The Flower and the Nettle: Diaries and Letters, 1936–1939* (New York, 1976).
—— *War Within and Without: Diaries and Letters, 1939–1944* (New York, 1980).
LINDBERGH, C., *The War Time Journals of Charles A. Lindbergh* (New York, 1970).
—— *Autobiography of Value* (New York, 1978).
LLOYD GEORGE, D., *War Memoirs* (London, 1936).
LOOSE, G., *Ernst Jünger* (New York, 1974).
LUNN, K., and THURLOW, R. (eds.), *British Fascism* (London, 1980).
LUVAAS, J., *The Education of an Army* (London, 1965).
MACDONALD, C. A., *The United States, Britain and Appeasement, 1936–1939* (London, 1981).
MACISAAC, D. (ed.), *The United States Strategic Bombing Survey* (10 vols., New York, 1976).
MACKSEY, K., *Guderian: Panzer General* (London, 1975).
—— *The Tank Pioneers* (London, 1981).
MACLEOD, R., and KELLY, D. (eds.), *The Ironside Diaries, 1937–1940* (London, 1962).
MAIER, C., 'Between Taylorism and Technocracy: European Ideologies and the Vision of Industrial Productivity in the 1920s', *Journal of Contemporary History*, 5(2) (1970), 27–61.
MAILLARD, L., *Éléments de la guerre* (Paris, 1891).
MARDER, A., *Portrait of an Admiral: The Life and Papers of Sir Herbert Richmond* (Cambridge, Mass., 1952).
MARINETTI, F. T., *Selected Writings* (New York, 1972).
MARKOV, V., *Russian Futurism: A History* (Berkeley, Calif., 1968).
MARTEL, G. Le Q., *In the Wake of the Tank* (London, 1931).
—— *An Outspoken Soldier* (London, 1949).

MARTIN, A., *The Mask of the Prophet: The Extraordinary Fictions of Jules Verne* (Oxford, 1990).

MASON, T., OVERY, R. and KAISER, D., 'Debate: Germany, "Domestic Crisis" and War in 1939', *Past and Present*, 122 (1989), 200–40.

MATTIOLI, G., *Mussolini Aviator, and His Work for Aviation* (Rome, 1939).

MAY, E. R. (ed.), *Knowing One's Enemies: Intelligence Assessment before the Two World Wars* (Princeton, NJ, 1984).

MAYERS, D., *George Kennan and the Dilemmas of US Foreign Policy* (New York, 1988).

MEARSHEIMER, J., *Conventional Deterrence* (Ithaca, NY, 1983).

—— *Liddell Hart and the Weight of History* (London, 1988).

MEDLICOTT, W. N., *The Economic Blockade* (2 vols., London, 1978).

MESSERSCHMIDT, M., *Die Wehrmacht im NS-Staat: Zeit der Indoktrination* (Hamburg, 1969).

MIDDLEMAS, K., *Diplomacy of Illusion: The British Government and Germany, 1937–39* (London, 1972).

MILFORD, J. (ed.), *The Attraction of Fascism: Social Psychology and Aesthetics of the 'Triumph of the Right'* (New York, 1990).

Militärgeschitliches Forschungsamt (ed.), *Germany and the Second World War* (Oxford, 1990–); German original: *Das deutsche Reich und der zweite Weltkrieg* (10 vols., Stuttgart, 1979–).

MINNEY, R. J., *The Private Papers of Hore-Belisha* (London, 1960).

MITCHELL, W., *Our Air Force* (New York, 1921).

—— *Winged Defence* (New York, 1925).

—— *Skyways* (Philadelphia, 1930).

—— *Memoirs of World War I* (New York, 1960).

MOMMSEN, H., 'Nationalsozialismus als vorgetäuschte Modernisierung', in *Der Nationalsozialismus und die deutsche Gesellschaft* (Hamburg, 1991), 405–27.

MOMMSEN, W., and KETTENACKER, L. (eds.), *The Fascist Challenge and the Policy of Appeasement* (London, 1983).

MORRIS, A. J. A., *The Scaremongers: The Advocacy of War and Rearmament, 1896–1914* (London, 1984).

MORROW, J., *The Great War in the Air* (Washington, DC, 1993).

MOSLEY, O., *My Life* (London, 1968).

MOSSE, G., *The Crisis of German Ideology* (New York, 1964).

—— *The Nationalization of the Masses* (New York, 1975).

—— *Nazism* (Oxford, 1978).

—— (ed.), *International Fascism* (London, 1979).

—— *Masses and Man: Nationalist and Fascist Perception of Reality* (Detroit, 1987).

MUELLER, J., 'The Essential Irrelevance of Nuclear Weapons: Stability in the Postwar World', *International Security*, 13 (2) (1988), 55–79.

—— *Retreat from Doomsday: The Obsolescence of Major War* (New York, 1989).

MÜLLER, K.-J., *Das Heer und Hitler: Armee und nationalsozialistisches Regime, 1933–1940* (Stuttgart, 1969).
—— *General Ludwig Beck: Studien und Dokumente* (Boppard a.R., 1980).
—— *The Army, Politics and Society in Germany, 1933–45* (Manchester, 1987).
MUMFORD, L., *Technics and Civilization* (London, 1934).
—— *The Culture of Cities* (London, 1938).
MURRAY, W., 'German Air Power and the Munich Crisis', in B. Bond and I. Roy (eds.), *War and Society Yearbook*, 2 (1977), 114–15.
—— *The Change in the European Balance of Power, 1938–1939* (Princeton, NJ, 1984).
—— *Luftwaffe* (Baltimore, 1985).
NEHRING, W., *Kampfwagen an die Front!* (Leipzig, 1934).
—— *Die Geschichte der deutschen Panzerwaffe, 1916 bis 1945* (Berlin, 1969).
NEILSON, K., *Strategy and Supply: The Anglo-Russian Alliance, 1914–1917* (London, 1984).
NELSON, A. K. (ed.), *The State Department Policy Staff Papers, 1947–1949* (3 vols., New York, 1983).
NEWMAN, S., *March 1939: The British Guarantee to Poland* (Oxford, 1976).
NOIRAY, J., *Le Romancier et la machine: l'image de la machine dans le roman français (1850–1900)*, ii (Paris, 1982).
NOLTE, E., *Three Faces of Fascism* (New York, 1969).
NYE, D., *Henry Ford: 'Ignorant Idealist'* (New York, 1979).
NYE, R. A., *The Origins of Crowd Psychology: Gustave Le Bon and the Crisis of Mass Democracy in the Third Republic* (London, 1975).
OGORKIEWICZ, R., *Armoured Forces* (London, 1970).
O'NEILL, R., *The German Army and the Nazi Party, 1933–1939* (London, 1966).
OSWALD, W., *Kraftfahrzeuge und Panzer des Reichswehr, Wehrmacht und Bundeswehr* (Stuttgart, 1982).
OVERY, R. J., 'From Uralbomber to Amerikabomber: The Luftwaffe and Strategic Bombing', *Journal of Strategic Studies*, 1 (1978), 154–78.
—— *The Air War, 1939–1945* (London, 1980).
—— *The Nazi Economic Recovery, 1932–1938* (London, 1982).
—— 'Hitler's War and the German Economy: A Reinterpretation', *Economic History Review*, 35 (1982).
—— *The Origins of the Second World War* (London, 1987).
—— *War and Economy in the Third Reich* (Oxford, 1994).
PAILLAT, C., *Le Désastre de 1940* (2 vols., Paris, 1983, 1984).
PARET, P. (ed.), *Makers of Modern Strategy from Machiavelli to the Nuclear Age* (Princeton, NJ, 1986).
PARKER, P., *The Old Lie: The Great War and the Public-School Ethos* (London, 1987).
PARKER, R. A. C., 'British Rearmament, 1936–9: Treasury, Trade Unions and Skilled Labour', *English Historical Review*, 96 (1981), 306–18.

PARKER, R. A. C., *Chamberlain and Appeasement: British Policy and the Coming of the Second World War* (London, 1993).
PAYNE, S., *Fascism: Comparison and Definition* (Madison, Wis., 1980).
—— *A History of Fascism, 1914–1945* (Madison, Wis., 1995).
PEDEN, G. C., *British Rearmament and the Treasury, 1932–1939* (Edinburgh, 1979).
—— 'A Matter of Timing: The Economic Background to British Foreign Policy, 1937–1939', *History*, 69 (1984), 15–28.
PIERRON, É., *Comment s'est formé le génie militaire de Napoléon Ier?* (Paris, 1889).
PLAYNE, C. E., *The Pre-War Mind in Britain* (London, 1928).
PONTING, C., *1940: Myth and Reality* (London, 1990).
POST, G. Jr., *Dilemmas of Appeasement: British Deterrence and Defence, 1934–1937* (London, 1993).
POSTAN, M. M., *British War Production: History of the Second World War—Civil Series* (London, 1952).
PRAZMOWSKA, A., *Britain, Poland and the Eastern Front, 1939* (Cambridge, 1987).
PRESTON, A. (ed.), *General Staffs and Diplomacy before the Second World War* (London, 1978).
PRESTON, P., *Franco* (London, 1993).
PRINZ, M., and ZITELMANN, R. (eds.), *Nationalsozialismus und Modernisierung* (Darmstadt, 1995).
PRIOR, R., *Churchill's 'World Crisis' as History* (London, 1983).
—— and WILSON, T. '*Command on the Western Front: The Military Career of Sir Henry Rawlinson*', *1914–18* (Oxford, 1992).
RAUCH, M., 'Anti-Modernismus im Nationalsozialistischen Staat', *Historisches Jahrbuch*, 107 (1987), 94–121.
REID, B. H., 'T. E. Lawrence and Liddell Hart', *History*, 70 (1985), 218–31.
—— *J. F. C. Fuller: Military Thinkers* (London, 1987).
REMARQUE, E. M., *All Quiet on the Western Front* (London, 1929).
RENNEBERG, M., and WALKER, M. (eds.), *Science, Technology and National Socialism* (Cambridge, 1994).
REYNOLDS, D., *The Creation of the Anglo-American Alliance, 1937–1941* (London, 1981).
—— 'Churchill and the British "Decision" to Fight On in 1940: Right Policy, Wrong Reasons', in R. Langhorne (ed.), *Diplomacy and Intelligence during the Second World War* (Cambridge, 1985).
—— 'Great Britain and the Security "Lessons" of the Second World War', in R. Ahmann, A. M. Birke, and M. Howard (eds.), *The Quest for Stability: Problems of West European Security, 1918–1957* (Oxford, 1993), 301–4.
RICHMOND, H., *National Policy and Naval Strength* (London, 1928).
—— *Sea Power in the Modern World* (London, 1934).
ROBERTS, G., *The Unholy Alliance: Stalin's Pact with Hitler* (London, 1989).
ROBERTSON, W., *Soldiers and Statesmen, 1914–1918* (London, 1926).

ROSE, N., *Churchill* (London, 1994).

ROSEMAN, M., 'National Socialism and Modernisation', in R. Bessel (ed.), *Fascist Italy and Nazi Germany: Comparisons and Contrasts* (Cambridge, 1996), 197–229.

ROSKILL, S., *Naval Policy between the Wars* (2 vols., London, 1968, 1976).

—— *Hankey, Man of Secrets* (3 vols., London, 1970, 1974).

SAMUELS, M., *Doctrine and Dogma: German and British Infantry Tactics in the First World War* (New York, 1992).

SASSOON, S., *Memoirs of an Infantry Officer* (London, 1930).

SCHENBAUM, D., *Hitler's Social Revolution* (New York, 1966).

SCHILDT, A., 'NS-Regime, Modernisierung und Moderne', *Tel Aviver Jahrbuch für deutsche Geschichte*, 23 (1994), 3–22.

SCHMIDT, G., *The Politics and Economics of Appeasement* (New York, 1986).

SCHONBACK, M., *Native American Fascism during the 1930s and 1940s* (New York, 1985).

SCHURMAN, D. M., *The Education of a Navy: The Development of British Naval Strategic Thought, 1867–1914* (London, 1965).

—— *Julian S. Corbett, 1854–1922* (London, 1981).

SCHWARZ, H.-P., *Der konservative Anarchist: Politik und Zeitkritik Ernst Jüngers* (Freiburg, 1962).

SCHWELLER, R., 'Domestic Structure and Preventive War: Are Democracies More Pacific?', *World Politics*, 44 (1992), 235–69.

SEARLE, G. R., *The Quest for National Efficiency* (Oxford, 1971).

SENFF, H., *Die Entwicklung der Panzerwaffe im deutschen Heer zwischen den beiden Weltkriegen* (Frankfurt a.M., 1969).

SERGÈ, C., *Italo Balbo: A Fascist Life* (Berkeley, Calif., 1987).

—— 'Douhet in Italy: Prophet without Honor?', *Aerospace Historian*, June 1979, 69–80.

—— 'Giulio Douhet: Strategist, Theorist, Prophet?', *Journal of Strategic Studies*, 15 (1992), 351–66.

SHAND, J., 'The Reichsautobahn: Symbol for the Third Reich', *Journal of Contemporary History*, 19 (1984), 189–200.

SHAY, R. P., *British Rearmament in the Thirties* (Princeton, NJ, 1977).

SIMPKIN, P., *Kitchener's Army* (Manchester, 1988).

SIMPKIN, R., *Race to the Swift: Thoughts on Twenty-First Century Warfare* (London, 1985).

—— *Deep Battle: The Brainchild of Marshal Tukhachevsky* (London, 1987).

SKIDELSKY, R., *Oswald Mosley* (London, 1981).

SLESSOR, J., *Air Power and Armies* (Oxford, 1936).

—— *The Central Blue* (London, 1956).

SMITH, M., *British Air Strategy Between the Wars* (Oxford, 1984).

—— 'The Allied Air Offensive', in J. Gooch (ed.), *Decisive Campaigns of the Second World War* (London, 1990), 67–83.

SOKOL, C., *The German–American Bund as a Model of American Fascism, 1924–1940* (Ann Arbor, Mich., 1979).

SPENGLER, O., *Decline of the West* (London, 1926).

SPIELBERGER, W., *Die Panzer-Kampfwagen 35(t) and 38(t)* (Stuttgart, 1980).

STANZEL, F. K., and Martin Löschnig (eds.), *Intimate Enemies: English and German Literary Reactions to the Great War* (Heidelberg, 1993).

STEPHANSON, A., *Kennan and the Art of Foreign Policy* (Cambridge, Mass., 1989).

STERN, J. P., *Ernst Jünger* (New Haven, Conn., 1953).

STERNHELL, Z., *Neither Right nor Left* (Berkeley, Calif., 1986).

STRACHAN, H., 'The British Way in Warfare', in D. Chandler (ed.), *The Oxford Illustrated History of the British Army* (Oxford, 1994), 417–34.

STROMBERG, R., *Redemption by War: The Intellectuals and 1914* (Lawrence, Kan., 1982).

SURETTE, L., *The Birth of Modernism: Ezra Pound, T. S. Eliot, W. B. Yeats, and the Occult* (London, 1993).

SUSSER, L., 'Fascist and Anti-Fascist Attitudes in Britain between the Wars' (dissertation, University of Oxford, 1988).

SWINTON, E., *Eyewitness* (London, 1932).

SYMONDS, J., *The Great Beast: The Life and Magic of Aleister Crowley* (London, 1971).

TAYLOR, A. J. P. *et al.* (eds.), *Churchill: Four Faces and the Man* (London, 1969)

—— (ed.), *Lloyd George: Twelve Essays* (London, 1971).

—— *British History, 1914–1945* (London, 1975).

—— *The Second World War* (London, 1975).

—— Letter to Kingsley Martin, printed in *London Review of Books*, 10 May 1990, 13.

TAYLOR, B. B., *Le Corbusier: The City of Refuge, Paris 1929/33* (Chicago, 1987).

TAYLOR, T., *Munich: The Price of Peace* (New York, 1979).

TERRAIN, J., *Douglas Haig: The Educated General* (London, 1963).

—— *To Win a War, 1918* (London, 1978).

TIMMS, E., and COLLIER, P. (eds.), *Visions and Blueprints: Avant-Garde Culture and Radical Politics in Early Twentieth-Century Europe* (Manchester, 1988).

TISDALL, C., and BOZZOLLA, A., *Futurism* (London, 1977).

TOFFLER, A. and TOFFLER, H., *The Third Wave* (New York, 1980).

—— *War and Anti-War* (New York, 1993).

TOMPSON, N., *The Anti-Appeasers: Conservative Opposition to Appeasement in the 1930s* (Oxford 1971).

TOWLE, P., 'British Security and Disarmament Policy in Europe in the 1920s', in R. Ahmann, A. M. Birke, and M. Howard (eds.), *The Quest for Stability: Problems of West European Security, 1918–1957* (Oxford, 1993), 127–53.

TRAVERS, T., 'Future Warfare: H. G. Wells and British Military Theory, 1895–1916', in Brian Bond and I. Roy (eds.), *War and Society* (London, n.d.), 67–87.

—— *The Killing Ground: The British Army, the Western Front and the Emergence of Modern Warfare, 1900–1918* (London, 1987).

—— *How the War Was Won: Command and Technology in the British Army on the Western Front, 1917–1918* (London, 1992).

TRIANDAFILLOV, V. K., *The Nature of the Operations of Modern Armies*, with foreword by J. Kipp and introd. by J. Schneider (Ilford, Essex, 1994).

TRYTHALL, A. J., *'Boney' Fuller: The Intellectual General* (London, 1977).

TURNER, H. Jr. (ed.), *Reappraisals of Fascism* (New York, 1975).

ULAM, A. B., *Expansion and Coexistence: The History of Soviet Foreign Policy, 1917–67* (London, 1968).

VAN CREVELD, M., *Hitler's Strategy, 1940–1941: The Balkan Clue* (Cambridge, 1973).

—— *The Transformation of War* (New York, 1991).

VERGANO, P., *Origins of Aviation in Italy, 1783–1918* (Genoa, 1964).

VERNE, J. J., *Jules Verne* (New York, 1976).

VITAL, D., *The Survival of Small States* (Oxford, 1971).

VOGELSANG, T., 'Hitlers Brief an Reichenau vom 4. Dezember 1932', *Vierteljahrshefte für Zeitgeschichte*, 7 (1959), 429–37.

WAGAR, W., *H. G. Wells and the World State* (New York, 1961).

WARK, W. K., *The Ultimate Enemy: British Intelligence and Nazi Germany, 1933–1939* (London, 1985).

WARLIMONT, W., *Inside Hitler's Headquarters, 1939–1945* (New York, 1964).

WATT, D. C., *Succeeding John Bull: America in Britain's Place, 1900–1975* (Cambridge, 1984).

—— *Personalities and Appeasement* (Austin, Tex., 1991).

WEBB, J., *The Occult Establishment* (La Salle, Ill., 1976).

WEBER, E., *Varieties of Fascism* (Princeton, NJ, 1964).

WEBSTER, C., and FRANKLAND, N., *The Strategic Air Offensive against Germany, 1939–1945* (4 vols., London, 1961).

WEINBERG, G. L., *Germany and the Soviet Union, 1939–1941* (London, 1954).

—— *A World at Arms: A Global History of World War II* (Cambridge, 1994).

WEISS, J., *The Fascist Tradition* (New York, 1967).

WELLS, H. G., *Anticipation of the Reaction of Mechanical and Scientific Progress upon Human Life and Thought* (London, 1902).

—— *The War in the Air* (1908).

—— *The World Set Free* (1914).

—— *Italy, France and Britain at War* (New York, 1917).

—— *The Outline of History* (London, 1920).

—— *The World Set Free* (London, 1927).

—— *The Shape of Things to Come* (1933).

—— *Experiment in Autobiography* (New York, 1934).

WHEELER-BENNETT, J., *The Nemesis of Power: The German Army in Politics, 1918–1945* (New York, 1967).

WHELDON, J., *Machine Age Armies* (London, 1968).

WIK, R., *Henry Ford and Grass Roots America* (Ann Arbor, Mich., 1972).

WILKINSON, S., *War and Policy* (London, 1900), 150–4.

—— *The French Army Before Napoleon* (Oxford, 1915).

—— *Government and the War* (London, 1918).

—— *The Defence of Piedmont, 1742–1748* (Oxford, 1927).

—— 'Killing No Murder: An Examination of Some New Theories of War', *Army Quarterly* (Oct. 1927), 14–21.

—— *The Rise of General Bonaparte* (Oxford, 1930).

WILLIAMSON, S., *The Politics of Grand Strategy: Britain and France Prepare for War* (Cambridge, Mass., 1969).

WINTER, D., *Haig's Command: A Reassessment* (London, 1991).

WINTER, J., *The Great War and the British People* (London, 1986).

—— *Sites of Memory, Sites of Mourning: The Great War in European Cultural History* (Cambridge, 1995).

WINTON, H., *To Change an Army: General Sir John Burnett-Stuart and British Armoured Doctrine, 1927–1938* (Lawrence, Kan., 1988).

WOHL, R., *The Generation of 1914* (Cambridge, Mass., 1979).

—— *A Passion for Wings: Aviation and Western Imagination, 1908–1918* (New Haven, 1994).

WOLLGAST, S., '"Technikphilosophie" während der Herrschaft des deutschen Faschismus', in his and G. Kovács (eds.), *Technikphilosophie in Vergangenheit und Gegenwart* (Berlin, 1984).

WOODWARD, D. R., *Lloyd George and the Generals* (London, 1983).

WOOLF, S. J. (ed.), *European Fascism* (New York, 1969).

YOUNG, R. J., *In Command of France: French Foreign Policy and Military Planning, 1933–1940* (Cambridge, Mass., 1978).

INDEX